THE WESTMINSTER DICTIONARY OF

New Testament
and
Early Christian Literature
and Rhetoric

To

Karl Erik

Kris & Heidi

Kurt, Lynette & Luke

Karen & Ben

with love and gratitude

THE WESTMINSTER DICTIONARY OF

New Testament and Early Christian Literature and Rhetoric

David E. Aune

Westminster John Knox Press
LOUISVILLE • LONDON

Cover design by Jennifer K. Cox

First edition
Published by Westminster John Knox Press
Louisville, Kentucky

This book is printed on acid-free paper that meets the American National Standards Institute Z39.48 standard. ♾

PRINTED IN THE UNITED STATES OF AMERICA

03 04 05 06 07 08 09 10 11 12 — 10 9 8 7 6 5 4 3 2 1

Library of Congress Cataloging-in-Publication Data

Aune, David Edward.
The Westminster dictionary of New Testament and early Christian literature and rhetoric / David Aune.
p. cm.
Includes bibliographical references.
ISBN 0-664-21917-9
1. Bible. N.T.—Dictionaries. 2. Christian literature, Early—Dictionaries. I. Title.

BS2312.A86 2003
270.1'03—dc21

2003050176

Abbreviations

AAWG	Abhandlungen der Akademie der Wissenschaft in Göttingen
ABRL	Anchor Bible Reference Library
ACW	Ancient Christian Writers, 1946–
ADB	*Anchor Dictionary of the Bible*. Edited by D. N. Freedman. 6 vols. New York: Doubleday, 1992.
AGJU	Arbeiten zur Geschichte des antiken Judentums und des Urchristentums
AJP	*American Journal of Philology*
ALGHJ	Arbeiten zur Literatur und Geschichte des hellenistischen Judentums
ANRW	*Aufstieg und Niedergang der römischen Welt.* Edited by H. Temporini and W. Haase. Berlin: Walter deGruyter, 1972–.
ANTC	Abingdon New Testament Commentaries
ARW	*Archiv für Religionswissenschaft*
ATANT	Abhandlungen zur Theologie des Alten und Neuen Testaments
BA	*Biblical Archaeologist*
BAK	Beiträge zur Altertumskunde
BBB	Bonner biblische Beiträge
BCNH,ST	Bibliothèque Copte de Nag Hammadi, Section "Textes." Québec: Université Laval; Louvain and Paris: Peeters, 1977–.
BDF	Friedrich Blass, Albert Debrunner, and R. W. Funk. *A Greek Grammar of the New Testament and Other Early Chrisitan Literature.* Chicago: University of Chicago, 1961.
BDR	Friedrich Blass, Albert Debrunner, and Friedrich Rehkopf, *Grammatik des neutestamentlichen Griechisch.* 16th ed. Göttingen: Vandenhoeck & Ruprecht, 1984.
BETL	Bibliotheca ephemeridum theologicarum lovaniensium
BETS	*Bulletin of the Evangelical Theological Society*
BFCT	Beiträge zur Förderung christlicher Theologie
BHT	Beiträge zur historischen Theologie
Bib	*Biblica*
BibOr	Biblica et orientalia
BIS	Biblical Interpretation Series
BJRL	*Bulletin of the John Rylands Library*
BJS	Brown Judaic Studies
BKA	Bibliothek der klassischen Altertumswissenschaften
BNTC	Black's New Testament Commentaries
BR	*Biblical Research*
BSac	*Bibliotheca sacra*
BTB	*Biblical Theology Bulletin*

BVC	*Bible et vie chrétienne*
BWANT	Beiträge zur Wissenschaft vom Alten und Neuen Testament
BWAT	Beiträge zur Wissenschaft vom Alten Testament
BZ	*Biblische Zeitschrift*
BZAW	Beihefte zur Zeitschrift für die alttestamentliche Wissenschaft
BZNW	Beihefte zur Zeitschrift für die neutestamentliche Wissenschaft
CA	*Classical Antiquity*
CBQ	*Catholic Biblical Quarterly*
CBQMS	Catholic Biblical Quarterly Monograph Series
CCSA	Corpus Christianorum, Series Apocryphorum
CIL	*Corpus inscriptionum latinarum*
CJ	*Classical Journal*
ConBNT	Coniectanea biblica: New Testament Series
CP	*Classical Philology*
CQ	*Classical Quarterly*
CRINT	Compendia rerum iudaicarum ad Novum Testamentum
CSCO	Corpus scriptorum christianorum orientalium. Edited by I. B. Chabot et al. Louvain: Peeters, 1903–.
CurBS	*Currents in Research: Biblical Studies*
DBSup	*Dictionnaire de la Bible: Supplément.* Paris: Librairie Letuzey, 1934–.
DCH	*Dictionary of Classical Hebrew.* Edited by D. J. A. Clines. Sheffield: Sheffield Academic Press, 1993–.
DJD	Discoveries in the Judean Desert
DKP	*Der Kleine Pauly: Lexikon der Antike in fünf Bänden.* Edited by Konrat Ziegler, Walther Sontheimer, and Hans Gärtner. 5 vols. Stuttgart: A. Druckenmüller, 1964–75.
DNP	*Der Neue Pauly: Enzyklopädie der Antike.* Edited by Hubert Cancik and Helmuth Schneider. Stuttgart and Weimar: Verlag J. B. Metzler, 1996–.
DSD	*Dead Sea Discoveries*
ECDSS	Eerdmans Commentaries on the Dead Sea Scrolls
EDB	*Eerdmans Dictionary of the Bible.* Edited by David Noel Freedman. Grand Rapids: Eerdmans, 2000.
EDNT	*Exegetical Dictionary of the New Testament.* Edited by Horst Balz and Gerhard Schneider. 3 vols. Grand Rapids: Eerdmans, 1991.
EEC	*Encyclopedia of the Early Church.* Edited by A. Di Berardino. Translated by A. Walford. 2 vols. New York: Oxford University Press, 1992.
EKKNT	Evangelisch-katholischer Kommentar zum Neuen Testament
EPRO	Études préliminaires aux religions orientales dans l'empire romain
EstB	*Estudios biblicos*
ETL	*Ephemerides theologicae lovanienses*
ETR	*Études théologiques et religieuses*
EvQ	*Evangelical Quarterly*
EvT	*Evangelische Theologie*
ExpTim	*Expository Times*

FC	The Fathers of the Church
FGH	*Die Fragmente der griechischen Historiker.* Edited by F. Jacoby. Berlin: Weidmann, 1923–58; Leiden: Brill, 1993–.
FOTL	Forms of the Old Testament Literature
FRLANT	Forschungen zur Religion und Literatur des Alten und Neuen Testaments
FTS	Frankfurter theologische Studien
FVS	*Fragmente der Vorsokratiker.* Ed. H. Diels and W. Kranz. 3 vols. 6th ed. Zurich and Hildesheim: Weidmann, 1951.
GCS	Die griechischen christlichen Schriftsteller
GR	*Greece and Rome*
GRBS	*Greek, Roman, and Byzantine Studies*
GTA	Göttinger theologischer Arbeiten
HDR	Harvard Dissertations in Religion
HNT	Handbuch zum Neuen Testament
HR	*History of Religions*
HSCP	*Harvard Studies in Classical Philology*
HSM	Harvard Semitic Monographs
HTKNT	Herders theologischer Kommentar zum Neuen Testament
HTR	*Harvard Theological Review*
HTS	Harvard Theological Studies
HUCA	*Hebrew Union College Annual*
HUT	Hermeneutische Untersuchungen zur Theologie
IDBSup	*The Interpreter's Dictionary of the Bible: Supplementary Volume.* Edited by K. Crim. Nashville: Abingdon, 1976.
ITQ	*Irish Theological Quarterly*
JAAR	*Journal of the American Academy of Religion*
JAF	*Journal of American Folklore*
JAOS	*Journal of the American Oriental Society*
JBL	*Journal of Biblical Literature*
JBR	*Journal of the Bible and Religion*
JCPS	Jewish and Christian Perspectives Series
JECS	*Journal of Early Christian Studies*
JEH	*Journal of Ecclesiastical History*
JETS	*Journal of the Evangelical Theological Society*
JHC	*Journal of Higher Criticism*
JHP	*Journal of the History of Philosophy*
JHS	*Journal of Hellenic Studies*
JJS	*Journal of Jewish Studies*
JPOS	*Journal of the Palestine Oriental Society*
JQR	*Jewish Quarterly Review*
JR	*Journal of Religion*
JRH	*Journal of Religious History*
JRS	*Journal of Roman Studies*
JSJ	*Journal for the Study of Judaism*
JSNT	*Journal for the Study of the New Testament*

JSNTSup	Journal for the Study of the New Testament Supplement Series
JSOT	*Journal for the Study of the Old Testament*
JSP	*Journal for the Study of the Pseudepigrapha*
JSPSup	Journal for the Study of the Pseudepigrapha Supplement Series
JTS	*Journal of Theological Studies*
KEK	Kritisch-exegetischer Kommentar
LCL	Loeb Classical Library
LCT	Literature, Culture, Theory
LTQ	*Lexington Theological Quarterly*
Neot	*Neotestamentica*
NHC	Nag Hammadi Codices
NHMS	Nag Hammadi and Manichaean Studies (formerly NHS)
NHS	Nag Hammadi Studies
NICNT	New International Commentary on the New Testament
NIGTC	New International Greek Testament Commentary
NovT	*Novum Testamentum*
NovTSup	*Novum Testamentum* Supplements
NRT	*Nouvelle revue théologique*
NTA	*New Testament Apocrypha*. Edited by W. Schneemelcher. Translated by R. McL. Wilson. 2 vols. Cambridge: James Clark; Louisville, Ky.: Westminster/John Knox, 1991–92.
NTAbh	Neutestamentliche Abhandlungen
NTG	New Testament Guides
NTOA	Novum Testamentum et Orbis Antiquus
NTS	*New Testament Studies*
NTT	*Norsk Teologisk Tidsskrift*
NTTS	New Testament Tools and Studies
OBO	Orbis biblicus et orientalis
OCD	*The Oxford Classical Dictionary*. Edited by S. Hornblower and A. Spawforth. 3d ed. Oxford and New York: Oxford University Press, 1996.
OEANE	*The Oxford Encyclopedia of Archaeology in the Near East*. Edited by E. Meyers. 5 vols. New York and Oxford: Oxford University Press, 1997.
OLD	*Oxford Latin Dictionary*
OTP	*Old Testament Pseudepigrapha*. Edited by J. H. Charlesworth. 2 vols. Garden City: Doubleday, 1983.
PA	Philosophia antiqua
PEQ	*Palestine Exploration Quarterly*
PGM	*Papyri graecae magicae: Die griechische Zauberpapyri*. Edited by K. Preisendanz and A. Henrichs. Stuttgart: Teubner, 1973–74.
PNTC	Pelican New Testament Commentaries
PR	*Philosophy and Rhetoric*
PTS	Patristische Texte und Studien
PVTG	Pseudepigrapha Veteris Testamenti Graece
PW	Pauly, A. F. and G. Wissowa. *Paulys Realencyclopädie der classischen Altertumswissenschaft*. 24 vols. Stuttgart: J. B. Metzler, 1894–1963.

QJS	*Quarterly Journal of Speech*
RAC	*Reallexikon für Antike und Christentum*
RB	*Revue biblique*
RE	*Realencyklopädie für protestantische Theologie und Kirche*
REA	*Revue des études anciennes*
REJ	*Revue des études juives*
RevQ	*Revue de Qumran*
RevScRel	*Revue des sciences religieuses*
RNT	Regensburger Neues Testament
RQ	*Restoration Quarterly*
RSR	*Recherches de science religeuse*
RTAM	*Recherches de théologie ancienne et médiévale*
SAC	Studies in Antiquity and Christianity
SANT	Studien zum Alten und Neuen Testaments
SB	Subsidia biblica
SBA	Studies in Biblical Archaeology
SBB	Stuttgarter biblische Beiträge
SBLDS	Society of Biblical Literature Dissertation Series
SBLMS	Society of Biblical Literature Monograph Series
SBLRBS	Society of Biblical Literature Resources for Biblical Study
SBLSBS	Society of Biblical Literature Sources for Biblical Study
SBLSCS	Society of Biblical Literature Septuagint and Cognate Studies
SBLSP	*Society of Biblical Literature: Seminar Papers*
SBLWAW	Society of Biblical Literature Writings from the Ancient World
SBS	Sources for Biblical Study
SBT	Studies in Biblical Theology
SC	Sources chrétiennes
SCHNT	Studia ad corpus hellenisticum Novi Testamenti
SCSS	Septuagint and Cognate Studies Series
SEÅ	*Svensk exegetisk årsbok*
SecCent	*Second Century*
SEG	Supplementum epigraphicum graecum
SGU	Studia Graeca Upsaliensia
SJLA	Studies in Judaism in Late Antiquity
SJT	*Scottish Journal of Theology*
SNT	Studien zum Neuen Testament
SNTSMS	Studiorum Novi Testamenti Societas Monograph Series
SO	*Symbolae osloenses*
SPap	*Studia papyrologica*
SPhilo	*Studia philonica*
ST	*Studia theologica*
STDJ	Studies on the Texts of the Desert of Judah
SVF	*Stoicorum veterum fragmenta.* H. von Arnim. 4 vols. Leipzig: Teubner, 1903–24.
SVTP	Studia in Veteris Testamenti pseudepigrapha
SwJT	*Southwestern Journal of Theology*

TAPA	*Transactions of the American Philological Association*
Teubner	Bibliotheca scriptorum graecorum et romanorum teubneriana
TF	Theologische Forschung
TJT	*Toronto Journal of Theology*
TLZ	*Theologische Literaturzeitung*
TS	*Theological Studies*
TSAJ	Texte und Studien zum antiken Judentum
TU	Texte und Untersuchungen
TynBul	*Tyndale Bulletin*
TZ	*Theologische Zeitschrift*
UALG	Untersuchungen zur antiken Literatur und Geschichte
VC	*Vigiliae christianae*
VT	*Vetus Testamentum*
VTSup	Supplements to Vetus Testamentum
WBC	Word Biblical Commentary
WJT	*Westminster Journal of Theology*
WMANT	Wissenschaftliche Monographien zum Alten und Neuen Testament
WUNT	Wissenschaftliche Untersuchungen zum Neuen Testament
ZAW	*Zeitschrift für die alttestamentliche Wissenschaft*
ZBK	Zürcher Bibelkommentare
ZKG	*Zeitschrift für Kirchengeschichte*
ZNW	*Zeitschrift für die neutestamentliche Wissenschaft*
ZPE	*Zeitschrift für Papyrusforschung und Epigraphik*
ZST	*Zeitschrift für systematische Theologie*
ZTK	*Zeitschrift für Theologie und Kirche*

Introduction

This dictionary, in preparation for ten years, is designed to fill a gap in existing reference works that treat the New Testament and early Christianity. The primary focus is on the literary and rhetorical dimensions of early Christian literature from its beginnings, about 50 C.E., through the mid-second century C.E. Since early Christian literary activity cannot be adequately understood in isolation from the literary and cultural traditions of its day, entries are included on various aspects of other important bodies of literature that were part of early Christianity's historical and cultural setting, including Gnostic, Jewish, Greek, and Roman Literature. The contextual historical framework for this enterprise is that of the Hellenistic and Roman periods, about 300 B.C.E. to about 200 C.E. In entries that treat subjects not directly related to the New Testament and early Christian literature, I have attempted to address that issue directly toward the end of the entry.

During the 1970s and 1980s, New Testament scholars were increasingly influenced by the kinds of literary methods used by scholars of Western literature (particularly English and French). During that same period, the relevance of Greco-Roman society and culture for interpreting the early Christian literature was increasingly evident in the study of the New Testament. As part of this renewed discovery of the Greco-Roman world, ancient Greek and Roman rhetoric also came to play an increasingly important role in understanding the arguments used by early Christian authors, particularly in early Christian letters. The number of ancient texts that have been edited or reedited in the last decade is enormous, and the secondary literature on many aspects of ancient literature and rhetoric has grown exponentially. The central purpose of this dictionary, therefore, is to synthesize and present the specific ways in which ancient and modern comparative literature, literary criticism, and rhetoric have been and could be applied to the literature of the New Testament. However, since there are several excellent dictionaries and handbooks of modern literary criticism and rhetoric available, the emphasis here is on ancient literature and rhetoric and ancient literary criticism. There is no convincing reason that ancient literary and rhetorical conceptions and methods should not be supplemented with modern perspectives, and for that reason this dictionary does not draw a hard and fast line between ancient and modern literary and rhetorical methods. In an earlier book, *The New Testament in Its Literary Environment* (Louisville, Ky.: Westminster/John Knox Press, 1987), I mapped out some of the ways in which comparative ancient literature provides insights into the meaning and interpretation of New Testament and early Christian literature. This dictionary continues that program in a more ambitious way, using an alphabetical format to provide easier access to material relevant for the reader.

An explanation of some of the features of this dictionary is necessary. Words or phrases that are asterisked indicate that separate entries can be found for those words or phrases. At the end of each entry is a list of related entries found elsewhere in the dictionary. There is a hierarchical relationship among some of these cross-references in that some direct the reader to more general or more specific aspects of the same topic; other cross-references point to related topics. Most articles have a bibliography with abbreviated entries consisting of the surnames of authors and the dates of publications. These bibliographies will help the reader to find more complete and detailed information than can be included in a dictionary entry. Complete bibliographical information for each short entry can be found in the bibliography at the end of the volume. Throughout the dictionary are a number of tables designed to help the reader to navigate a great deal of information quickly.

The author is responsible for the vast majority of the entries in this dictionary, which means that there is a general consistency and uniformity in approach and critical perspective neither typical nor possible for edited works. The limitations of this approach, however, are obvious: no one person can command the enormous bibliography of works related to the entries found in this dictionary.

Eight current or former students, all good scholars, have contributed a total of twenty-one articles to this dictionary, and I want to express my gratitude and appreciation to them:

Leslie Baynes (*Adam and Eve, Lives of*; Papyrus; Philo of Alexandria [with D. E. Aune])
Jon Bergsma (Codex; Genealogy; Irenaeus; Quotations; Testimonia; Testimony Book Hypothesis)
John Fotopoulos (Apuleius of Madauros; Graffiti)
Brian Gregg (Mark, Gospel of [with D. E. Aune])
Paul J. Kim (John, First Letter of [with D. E. Aune]; John, Second Letter of [with D. E. Aune]; John, Letters of; John, Third Letter of [with D. E. Aune])
Brant Pitre (Rewritten Bible)
Steven Schweitzer (Jude, Letter of; Peter, Second Letter of)
Eric Stewart (Cebes, *Tabula*; Philostratus)

The final draft of this dictionary was completed during the early fall of 2002 at the W. F. Albright Institute of Archaeological Research in Jerusalem, where I held the appointment of Annual Professor for 2002–2003 (a fellowship sponsored by the American Schools of Oriental Research). I therefore want to acknowledge the generous support of the W. F. Albright Institute of Archaeological Research (AIAR), as well as the Educational and Cultural Affairs (ECA) division of the U.S. Department of State, and the Horace Goldsmith Foundation. I am grateful as well to the École Biblique et Archéologique Français in Jersualem for the privilege of using their magnificent library and to the librarian, Fr. Kevin McCaffrey, OP. I am also grateful to the American Council of Learned Societies for a generous grant, and to the University of Notre Dame for providing supplementary funding enabling me to spend this year in Jerusalem. I also want to thank the Institute for Scholarship in the Liberal Arts at the University of Notre Dame for providing financial support for a graduate research assistant to work on this project during the summer of 2000. Finally, Westminster John Knox has been a very patient publisher, and I especially want to thank the academic and reference editor, Dr. Donald K. McKim, for his longsuffering and good humor and the project editor, Dan Braden, for helping to transform this ponderous manuscript into a book.

David E. Aune
December 2002

Abbreviations are standard forms of shortened words to save time in writing and space on valuable writing materials. Abbreviations are common in Greek inscriptions, papyri, and manuscripts, and the compilation by Oikonomides (1974) is indispensable for understanding these abbrevations. There are several types of abbreviation. The most common type is to abbreviate by suspension, i.e., to write the first one or two letters of a word and omit the rest, often with some kind of mark indicating the omission. The *nomina sacra* (see below) abbreviate by using a contracted form of the word, usually the first and last letters of the word (in its inflected form), with a superlinear stroke over the word to indicate abbreviation. In ordinary Greek abbreviation, there is usually no standard system for abbreviation discernible.

One early Christian form of shorthand was the use of *nomina sacra*, a phrase coined by Traube (1907) to describe the abbreviations by contraction, in Greek and Latin manuscripts, of certain "sacred names" from the 4th cent. C.E. on. The *nomina sacra* are now attested for the 2d cent. C.E., and it seems reasonable to suppose that they originated in the 1st cent. C.E. While the Greek words for "Jesus," "Christ," "Lord," and "God" are the earliest examples of such abbreviations, other terms with religious associations were also abbreviated, such as "Spirit," "Man," and "Cross." Examples of the most common abbreviations, which have a superlinear line over them, are KC (κύριος, "Lord"), IC XC (Ἰησοῦς Χριστός, "Jesus Christ"), CHP (Σωτήρ, "Savior"), ΔΑΔ (Δαυίδ, "David"). The *nomina sacra* abbreviations appear to be a distinguishing characteristic of early Christianity (C. H. Roberts 1979, 26–48), for there are no manuscripts of certain Jewish origin that contain *nomina sacra*. It appears that the *nomina sacra* were used not for the purposes of abbreviation, but to express religious reverence (Hurtado 1998).

*Contractions *Shorthand

Blanchard 1974; S. Brown 1970; Hurtado 1998; McNamee 1981; Millard 1994; Oikonomides 1974; Traube 1907

Acclamation, a shout of approval (expressing sentiments such as joy, praise, welcome, good wishes) or disapproval (including condemnation), expressed in unison by a group of people and addressed to a king, emperor, high magistrate, or other prominent person at public appearances (such as accessions and arrivals) and by extension to deities. A distinction can be made between formulaic ritual acclamations and spontaneous acclamations (though "spontaneous" acclamations are normally confined to expected forms). A typical ceremonial acclamation, addressed to a deity, is found in Acts 19:28, 34: "Great is Artemis of the Ephesians!" here uttered as an anti-Christian protest. A spontaneous acclamation of approval is found in Acts 12:22, where the crowd addressed by Herod Agrippa responds, "The voice of a god, not a man!" (cf. Luke 7:16; Acts 8:10). The cry "Crucify him! Crucify him!" shouted by the crowd at the trial of Jesus exemplifies a spontaneous acclamation of disapproval (Luke 23:21; John 19:6, 15; Mark 15:13; Matt. 27:22; cf. *Mart. Pol.* 12:3). Such acclamations occur in crowd scenes in Greek novels (Heliodorus, *Ethiopika* 8.9), where they add excitement to the narrative (Peterson 1926, 199). In the *Acts of Paul,* the women in Iconium, gathered in the arena, cry, "One is God, who delivered Thecla!" (§38). Analogous acclamations occur in Bel 18 (Theod.): "You are great, Bel!" (LXX: "Great is Bel!"), and Bel 41 (Theod.): "You are great, Lord, God of Daniel!" (LXX: "Great is the Lord God!"); on the distinction between second-person and third-person address, see *Du-Stil, *Er-Stil. See Aristides, *Or.* 1.467, 471: "Great is Asklepius!"

*Liturgical formulas

Berger 1984, 231–36; Haenchen 1971, 573; *DKP* 1: 30–31; *OCD* 4; Peterson 1926, 196–215

Achilles Tatius (or Achilles Statius) The author of a Greek novel in eight books, *The Adventures of Leukippe and Kleitophon*; an excellent idiomatic English translation by Winkler is found in Reardon 1989, 170–284 (text of Vilborg 1955–62). Written in a basically Atticistic style (*Atticism), and reflecting a sophistic background (the characters frequently make speeches), *Leukippe and Kleitophon* was probably written ca. 150 C.E. (POxy 3836, a fragment of that work, dates to the late 2d cent.).

Analysis. The only Greek novel written in the form of a first-person autobiographical narrative (*autobiography), the story begins with an **ekphrasis*, or description of a picture, of Europa riding a bull led by Eros in Sidon, which sets the theme of the power of Eros or sexual love (the first *ekphrasis* of several; cf. 3.6–8; 5.3–5). Like all Greek novels, Achilles Tatius centers on the theme of romantic love, the love of Kleitophon (a Phoenician from Tyre) for his cousin Leukippe (daughter of his uncle, a Byzantine general). The story is encapsulated by Kleitophon toward the end (8.5). But unlike most novels, it largely lacks the emphasis on chastity, for Kleitophon plots to perform "the rites of Aphrodite [τὰ τῆς Ἀφροδίτης ὀργία]" with Leukippe, i.e., seduce her (1.16–19; 2.10). While viewing the picture, the author meets Kleitophon, who tells him his story. Typically structured as romance-separation-reunion, after Kleitophon's unsuccessful seduction of Leukippe, they elope on a ship headed for Alexandria. The ship is wrecked in a storm, but the lovers float to safety on part of the prow (3.1–5). They were captured by bandits (3.9–12), but rescued by Egyptian soldiers (3.13). Meanwhile, Kleitophon thinks he sees Leukippe being slaughtered as a sacrifice by bandits, but the incident is actually an elaborate trick by friends to help her escape (3.15–22). Charmides, the Egyptian general, falls for Leukippe. Leukippe, drugged by another admirer, an Egyptian soldier named Gorgias (now deceased), goes mad for ten days until Kleitophon is told what has happened and is given an antidote (4.9–19). After arriving in Alexandria, Leukippe is kidnaped by pirates (paid by Chaireas the Egyptian general). When pursued by Kleitophon, they apparently behead her and toss her body in the sea (5.7), though they really behead a slave girl dressed like Leukippe (8.16). Melite, a wealthy widow, wants to seduce Kleitophon, who agrees to consummate their marriage only when they are back in Ephesus (5.11–13), but miraculously her husband Thersandros, supposedly lost at sea, shows up alive after all (5.23). Kleitophon, who now knows that Leukippe is alive, goes to bed with the love-crazed Melite for "therapeutic reasons" (5.26–27). Thersandros, thinking that Melite and Kleitophon were lovers, falls in love with Leukippe who has survived and been sold as a slave to the household of Melite (6.4). Kleitophon, jailed in Ephesus, is made to think that Leukippe has been murdered (7.3–4). The couple is reunited in Ephesus, after Leukippe is able to play the syrinx of Pan in the temple of Artemis, a chastity test.

*Novels, Greek

Bartsch 1989; Durham 1938; Hägg 1971; Plepelits 1980; Reardon 1989, 1991; Vilborg 1955–62

Acta, a Latin term meaning "what has been done," refers to the records compiled by officials on their activities, the proceedings at which they presided, and binding declarations made before them by private individuals (testimonies and donations).

A. Berger 1953, 340; *DKP* 1:54–56; *OCD* 10

Acts, Apocryphal The Apocryphal Acts are fictional narratives loosely framed by chronological accounts of the fictional travels and adventures of apostles, usually culminating in martyrdom. Since the literary focus is on the individual episode, some of which function as *novellas, the loose structure of these works made it relatively easy to break off sections for separate circulation (e.g., the *Acts of Paul and Thecla* and the *Martyrdom of Paul*; the *Acts of Philip* and the *Martyrdom of Philip*). Individual episodes often focus on miraculous healings or resurrections, and there is a tendency to prolong the tension and emphasize the *pathos of narratives dealing with human suffering and grief (e.g., *Acts of John* 19–25, 30–37; *Acts of Andrew* 9–15). Though the authors use the third person, occasionally the first-person plural is found (*Acts of John* 19, 60–62, 72–73).

The problem of genre. The generic links between the Apocryphal Acts and the Greek *novel have been examined in detail by Söder (1932), who chose five essential novelistic features that occur in various combinations in ancient narrative fiction: (1) demonstrations of supernatural power by the hero (the aretalogical element), (2) the travel theme, (3) religious or philosophical propaganda, (4) the love theme, and (5) interest in the exotic and unfamiliar (the teratological element). While aretalogical and teratological elements appear frequently in the Apocryphal Acts, they are absent from Greek novels. The erotic element, on the other hand, which is prominent in the Greek novels, is absent from the Apocryphal Acts. The generic links between the ancient novel and the Apocryphal Acts, therefore, is only indirect. The Apocryphal Acts have closer ties with a literary genre that has not been widely preserved: popular narratives centering on the adventures, wonders, and romances of fictional heroes.

While the love theme is central to the Greek novel, it plays an entirely different role in the Apocryphal Acts. While the Greek novel emphasizes the involuntary *temporary* separation and then ultimate reunion of lovers; the Apocryphal Acts emphasize the *permanent* separation of lovers (virgins from fiancés, wives from husbands). Yet while the temporary separation of lovers moves the plot in Greek novels (functioning as the exciting force), the motif of permanent separation in the Apocryphal Acts provides dramatic tension only for individual episodes. In many episodes in the Apocryphal Acts, tension is generated by the desire for sexual abstinence on the part of converted women and the desire of unconverted lovers or husbands for normal sexual or conjugal relations. The apostles, depicted as holy men, act as agents of the supernatural world in facilitating this religious motivated "alienation of affection." The Apocryphal Acts, in contrast to Greek novels, exhibit a negative view of the world, reflecting the outlook of those Christian communities in which they were produced.

The travel theme functions in different ways in the two types of literature. In most Greek novels, travel to distant places prolongs the tension of the plot, which is moved by the separation of two lovers whose love and faithfulness are severely tested. Travel accounts also provide entertainment for readers by describing exotic features of faraway places and peoples. Yet the travel theme is not indispensable to the Greek novel, for it is missing in Longus's *Daphnis and Chloe*. It is insignificant in the *Acts of Peter*, and even in the *Acts of Thomas* it is part of the narrative in just three brief passages (3–4, 16–17, 68–71). Even in the Apocryphal Acts that emphasize travel to a great extent (*Acts of Paul*, *Acts of John*, *Acts of Andrew*), itineraries loosely connect particular dramatic episodes, while the compositions as a whole typically lack dramatic unity.

Apocryphal Acts and lives of philosophers. The Apocryphal Acts are not biographies, for they exhibit little concern with the lives of the apostles before Jesus' death and resurrection. The figure of the apostle is of interest chiefly as a messenger of God who both exemplifies and proclaims the Christian message. There are therefore numerous similarities between apostles depicted in the Apocryphal Acts and contemporary biographies of philosophers (e.g., Philostratus, *Life of Apollonius*; Iamblichus, *Life of Pythagoras*; Porphyry, *Life of Pythagoras*). Particularly striking are the parallels between the *Acts of Thomas* and Philostratus, *Life of Apollonius*: (1) Both Thomas and Apollonius travel to the exotic land of India; (2) both have dealings with nobility (Thomas visits the Indian king Gundaphorus); (3) both preach, perform miracles, and experience persecution and suffering; (4) both are models of chastity.

Apocryphal Acts and canonical acts. The titles of the Apocryphal Acts imitated the title Πράξεις ("Acts"), which was affixed to the canonical Acts of the Apostles probably before 150 C.E. (del Cerro 1993, 208). The generic links between the canonical Acts and Apocryphal Acts go beyond just the replication of a title, for it is likely that the former inspired the production of the latter (del Cerro 1993), but they also have some distinctive features. There are important similarities and differences between canonical Acts and the Apocryphal Acts: (1) The author of Acts presents his work as *history* (i.e., with a referent to the real world, whether or not he got it right), while the authors of the Apocryphal Acts were intentionally writing *fiction. (2) While the apostles are depicted as stereotypical holy men in the Apocryphal Acts, this imagery is only marginal in canonical Acts (e.g., the healing qualities of Peter's shadow, Acts 5:15; Paul's miraculous handkerchiefs, 19:12). (3) While the literary focus of the Apocryphal Acts is the individual episode, canonical Acts, while lacking a "plot" in the conventional sense, nevertheless has chronological movement toward a goal, the proclamation of the gospel in Rome. Yet despite these superficial differences, it seems clear that the canonical Acts provides a literary paradigm for the Apocryphal Acts.

**Acts of Andrew, *Acts of John, *Acts of Paul and Thecla, *Acts of Peter, *Acts of Philip, *Acts of Thomas*

Bovon 1988; Bovon, Brock, and Matthews (eds.) 1999; Bovon and Geoltrain 1997; Bremmer 1995, 1996, 1998, 2000; S. L. Davies 1980; Dobschütz 1902; Klijn 1962; Lalleman 1998; Lipsius and Bonnet 1891–1903; MacDonald 1990; Pervo 1987; Praeder 1981; Schierling and Schierling 1978; Söder 1932; Stoops 1997

Acts of Andrew, the least well preserved, though probably originally the longest, of all the Apocryphal Acts, is first mentioned by Eusebius (*Hist. eccl.* 3.25.6). The *Acts of Andrew* consists of two major sections, the journey and the martyrdom. The journey, as reconstructed from an epitome preserved by Gregory of Tours (in which only the basic travel framework appears reliable), involves a trip by the apostle Andrew from Pontus to Achaea, during which he performed many miracles, and that brought him to the cities of Amasea, Sinope, Nicaea, Nocomedia, Byzantium, Perinthus on the Thracian coast to Philippi and Thessalonica in Macedonia, and finally to Patrae in Achaea.

Content. One certain section of the *Acts of Andrew,* preserved by P. Copt. Utrecht I (*NTA* 2. 123–28), narrates the story of how Andrew met a young soldier named Varianus who was possessed with a demon, who said, "O Varianus, what have I done to you that you should send me to this god-fearing man?" The story is then told of the ascetic virgin sister of Varianus. A young magician desperately wanted her and sent demons to knock at her door to tempt her, apparently in the guise of her brother, whom she sent to Andrew for healing. Andrew cast out the demon, and then the young man took off his uniform in exchange for "the garment of the immortal King of the Ages," which he had hitherto rejected.

The next extensive section, preserved in Codex Vaticanus 808, begins with the end of a sermon by Andrew exhibiting some features of Asianic antithesis (e.g., "We belong to the better; therefore we flee the worse. We belong to the noble, through whom we drive away the mean; to the righteous, through whom we cast away unrighteousness"). After this sermon, Andrew sends the brothers away, and Maximilla, Iphidamia, and others stay with Andrew in prison (§2). Andrew's chief opponent is Aegeates, a city official and judge, who unsuccessfully tries to win back his wife Maximilla, whose affections have been alienated by the apostle Andrew (§§3–4). Maximilla (with Iphidamia) then visits Andrew in prison and reports to him Aegeates' demands. Andrew encourages her to resist the allurement of sexual intercourse and then compares her to Eve, who disobeyed, while she, Maximilla, obeys, and himself with Adam, whose imperfection Andrew has perfected by taking refuge with God (§5). Andrew continues to speak to Maximilla using the Gorgianic figure of *epanaphora §6):

> *Well done,* O nature, you who are saved despite your weakness and though you did not hide yourself. *Well done,* O soul, you who have cried aloud what you have suffered and are returning to yourself. *Well done,* O man, you who are learning what is not yours and desiring what is yours [a Stoic sentiment]. *Well done,* you who hear what is being said.

Andrew then repeats the Adam and Eve comparison, again urging Maximilla to remain chaste (§7), and tells her that the Lord appeared to him in a vision saying, "Andrew, Aegeates' father, the devil, will release you from prison" (§8), and he again urges her to remain steadfast (§9). Turning to Stratocles, one of the brothers, he uses a string of rhetorical questions to comfort him as he weeps (§§10–11). Stratocles responds that he is concerned only for Andrew and knows what will happen to him and says that he needs Andrew's constant help and support (§12). Andrew then tells Stratocles that tomorrow Aegeates will hand him over to be crucified (§13). Meanwhile, Maximilla has gone to the pretorium and told Aegeates that she will not have sex with him. He in response has begun plotting Andrew's death. "But Maximilla, the Lord going before her in the form of Andrew, went with Iphidamia to the prison" (§14). In prison, Andrew gives a farewell address to those assembled, encouraging them to stand fast in the faith (§§15–16), and not to be troubled by his impending death at the hands of an evil man (§§17–18).

The last segment is the reconstructed text of the martyrdom of Andrew (*NTA* 2.135–51), in which Andrew is crucified by Aegeates and is bound rather than nailed to increase his torment. Andrew dialogues with his followers including Stratocles (the brother of Aegeates), when Aegeates resolves to free Andrew lest the crowd turn on him. Approaching Andrew, he is rebuked by the apostle, who then dies. Maximilla buries the body of Andrew and continues to live a chaste life, living apart from Aegeates, who commits suicide by throwing himself off a building. Stratocles refuses to claim any of the property of the unfortunate Aegeates, and when the crowd sees that Aegeates is dead, they cease their uproar.

*Acts, Apocryphal, *Apocrypha, New Testament, *Novel

Bremmer 2000; *NTA* 2.101–151 (intro. and English trans.); MacDonald 1990, 1994a; Prieur 1989, 1995. Schneemelcher (ed.) 1991–92, 2.118–51 (intro. and English trans.)

Acts of the Apostles (see *Luke-Acts)

Acts of the Christian Martyrs, or *acta martyrum*, is a relatively extensive body of literature dating from the second through the fourth centuries C.E. (and beyond), narrating the trials and executions of Christians. The brief narrative of the martyrdom of Stephen in Acts 6:8–7:60 is important because it is a relatively lengthy account of the first Christian martyr, and because Stephen's death is in part modeled on that of Jesus in Luke's first volume. The account consists primarily of a lengthy defense speech before the high priest, emphasizing the Jewish disregard of the Law of Moses and hence calculated to enrage his audience. As in many subsequent martyr acts, a heavenly vision is experienced by Stephen just before his death, and on the point of death he prays that this sin will not be held against his murderers (cf. Jesus in Luke 23:34). Stephen's murder is not narrated as the carrying out of a legal procedure (though see Acts 7:58), since a formal verdict is never pronounced by the high priest, nor is permission received from the Roman governor, but rather his murder is an example of lynch law. The *acta martyrum* constitute a large portion of those Christian texts which are called Hagiography (the term 'αγιόγραφος, meaning "written by inspiration," was used of Scripture in general and then of certain groups of books of the Old Testament; more recently it has been applied to the corpus of saints' lives and to the scientific historical study of those lives (see Aigrain 2000, 7; a review of hagiographical research is found in Aigrain 2000, 291–388, through ca. 1953). The term "Acts" (see *Acta) is used of those compositions which resemble "protocols," or official accounts of the hearings and trials scenes at which Roman authorities sentenced Christians to death (e.g., *Acts of St. Cyprian, Acts of Maximilian*). More common, however, is the term "Martyrdom" (Grk. μαρτύριον) used in the titles of most Greek compositions about martyrs (e.g., Martyrdom of Polycarp, Martyrdom of Perpetua and Filicitas), while "Passion" (Latin *passio*, "suffering, passion") is used in the titles of most Latin compositions about martyrs (e.g., Passion of the Scillitan Martyrs, Passion of Saints Perpetua and Felicitas).

Four martyr acts originated in the 2nd cent. C.E.: (1) The *Martyrdom of Polycarp* (ca. 155–56 C.E.), written on the basis of the eyewitness testimony of one Marcianus; (2) the *Acts of Justin* (ca. 163–67 C.E.) and his companions Chariton, Charito, Euelpiste, Hierax, Paeon, and Liberien before the prefect Rusticus. This work, ostensibly based on court records, has undergone three recensions revealing progressive editing; (3) the *Letter of the Churches of Lyons and Vienne* (177 C.E.), a circular letters perhaps redacted by Irenaeus and preserved in Eusebius, *Hist. eccl.* 5.1–3 (Frend 1965, 1–30); and (4) the *Acts of the Scillitan Martyrs* (180 C.E.).

Third cent. C.E. martyr acts include (1) the *Martyrdom of Saints Perpetua and Felicitas* (203 C.E.), an important work which combines features of an apocalypse with those of act of the martyr (Aune 1986, 73–74), and incorporates the diary of Felicitas and an account of a vision of Saturus, which he apparently wrote himself (*Martyrdom of Saints Perpetua and Felicitas* 11–13; see 11:1: "But the blessed Saturus has also made known his own vision and he has written it out with his own hand"); (2) the *Acts of Cyprian* (258 C.E.); (3) the *Martyrdom of Fructuosus and Companions* (259 C.E.); and (4) the *Martyrdom of Marian and James* in North Africa (259 C.E.).

Delahaye (1955, 101–18) distinguished six types of acts of the martyrs: (1) those that are based on official court records and legal procedures, such as the *Acts of Justin, Acts of Cyprian*, and the *Acts of the Scillitan Martyrs*; (2) those based on the accounts of eyewitnesses or even of the martyrs themselves (*Martyrdom of Polycarp*); (3) those texts which are based on a written document, i.e., one or both of those mentioned above, either official court records or eyewitness reports; (4) those which are not based on written sources but are essentially historical romances, i.e., historical novels which are based on a historical core; (5) those texts which are purely fictional compositions ("romans d'imagination"); and (6) those texts which are forgeries, i.e., written with the intention of fooling the reader. This typology of martyr acts is based on a variety of criteria including types of sources and authorial intentions, though few formal features are drawn into the discussion. Earlier, Delehaye (1921) had distinguished four main genres of martyr acts: (1) historical martyrdoms, (2) panegyrics (i.e., eulogistic homilies on the life of the martyr delivered on his or her feast day), (3) epic martyrdoms, and (4) secondary genres and mixed genres. This is a complex area of study which requires a great deal of further scholarly work. For other discussions of the genre of the *acta martyrum*, see Aigrain (2000, 206–72).

Musurillo, who recognizes the wide variation in form and content found in the *acta martyrum*, nevertheless suggests some common features, including the tense dramatic movement toward the execution of the martyrs, in which there will be no quarter given by the authorities and also great courage shown by the martyrs who experience various forms of gruesome torture and humiliation (1972, liii). Claiming to build on Delehaye's typology, Musurillo (1972, lii) has a quite different approach, by listing a variety of the motifs found in the *acta martyrum*: (1) Documents or sections based on the court-record style (*Acts of the Scillitan Martyrs, Acts of Cyprian*): (a) witty judges, (b) recorded retorts from bystanders, (c) the martyr's expression of faith, and (d) the martyr urges the judge to do his duty; (2) scenes from the martyrs' imprisonment or execution (*Martyrs of Lyons and Vienne, Polycarp, Cyprian, Perpetua,* and *Felicitas*): (a) special cruelty of soldiers or executioners (*Polycarp*), (b) special prayer of the martyr before death (*Polycarp*), (c) martyr's comments under torture, (d) retorts of crowds and bystanders, (e) use of first-person narrative technique (*Polycarp, Martyrs of Lyons and Vienne*); (3) tales of visions or miracles: (a) visions of the martyrs (*Perpetua* and *Felicitas*; *Marian and James*), (b) apparitions of the martyrs after death (*Fructuosus, Cyprian*); (4) apologetic speeches (*Justin*); and (5) anti-semitism (*Polycarp*).

*Martyrdom of Polycarp

Aigrain 2000 (originally published 1953); Delehaye 1921, 1955; Frend 1965; Musurillo 1972.

Acts of John, an incomplete apocryphal work, the title of which, Πράξεις Ἰωάννου, first occurs in Eusebius, *Hist. eccl.* 3.26.6. The work was probably written between 150 and 200 C.E. (Junod and Kaestli 1983, 694–95). Based on the number of *stichoi* attributed to the Acts of John in the Stichometry of Nicephoros (2,500 lines), about 70 percent of the text has survived, with the main lacunae before chapter 18, between chapters 36 and 37, and between chapters 55 and 58 (Lalleman 1998, 23; on the complex history and character of the text, see Lalleman 1998, 5–24). The text of the *Acts of John* has in fact been pieced together from several manuscripts. The reason for its fragmentary survival is probably due to orthodox censorship of a text that has clear docetic and gnostic features, at a time when the orthodox Christian faith was being defined by a series of synods and councils (4th and 5th cents. C.E.). Junod and Kaestli (1983, 581–632) argue that the *Acts of John* was originally a non-gnostic work into which a gnostic section has been added (*Acts of John* 94–102, 109).

The *Acts of John* contains stories of John's travels from Miletus to Ephesus (where he took up residence), then to Smyrna and Laodicea, then back to Ephesus. The critical Greek text of the *Acts of John* is found in Lipsius and Bonnet (1897–1903, II.1.151–216), and English translations are available, with critical introductions, in *NTA* 2.152–212.

Literary character. The *Acts of John*, like the other Apocryphal Acts (see *Acts, Apocryhal) is an extended work of narrative fiction in the form of a *novel. It is a long, rambling work filled with episodes abounding in *pathos and miracles. The characters are all flat and two-dimensional, and the plots of the episodes very melodramatic. Unlike most characters in the Apocryphal Acts, the apostle John does not suffer martyrdom at the end. The longest sustained story is a series of episodes related to Drusiana, the wife of Andronicus: the unwelcome pursuit of Callimachus, who had designs to become her lover; her death; and a frustrated attempt of Callimachus to have sex with her corpse in a sepulchre (§§63–86). The *Acts of John* also contains a lengthy revelation discourse delivered by John (§§88–102), which contains a hymn (§§94–96) that Jesus sings with his disciples holding hands in a large circle and dancing.

Literary analysis and précis. The beginning of the *Acts of John*, consisting of chapters 1–17, is lost but probably narrated John's departure from Jerusalem for Miletus, or alternatively, his trial and banishment to Patmos. In §18 as John travels to Ephesus from Miletus in response to a vision with several companions (Demonicus, Aristodemus, and Cleobius), he hears the heavenly voice of Jesus about the success he will have in Ephesus.

John's first stay in Ephesus (narrated in §§19–55) begins with a first-person plural narration (which disappears after §19), telling the story of the healing of Cleopatra and the resurrection of her husband Lycomedes (§§19–25). As John approaches Ephesus, Lycomedes, the praetor of Ephesus, comes running to John asking healing for his paralyzed wife, since he was told in a dream that a man named John was being sent to heal her (§19). At the house of Lycomedes, John finds his paralyzed wife Cleopatra. An emotional Lycomedes says his wife is the victim of the evil eye and in an impassioned speech threatens to end his own life (§20). John rebukes Lycomedes, who apparently drops dead, and then weeps because he fears that the citizens will not let him leave the house alive (§21). The people of Ephesus gather at the house of Lycomedes, thinking him dead. John prays and then tells Cleopatra, "Arise in the name of Jesus Christ" (§22). Cleopatra arises and the Ephesians are amazed. She asks about her husband, and John promises that he will be raised through God's power (§23). Finding her husband dead in the bedroom, Cleopatra goes to pieces but calms down and attends to John. John leads Cleopatra to her dead husband and has her command him to rise from the dead. She does so, and Lycomedes arises, then prostrates himself to kiss John's feet (§24). The couple urgently beg John and his companions to stay with them a while, which they do (§25).

The allegory of the portrait of John (§§26–29): Lycomes arranges for an artist to secretly paint John's portrait while he teaches in his home (§26). When the picture is finished, he makes it the center of a shrine in his bedroom. John rebukes him for his paganism, but Lycomedes responds that "he is my God who raised me from death" (§27). John thinks the portrait too good looking, but Lycomedes gives him a mirror to show how accurate it is (§28). John urges Lycomedes to be a good painter, using the colors of faith in God, knowledge, reverence, kindness, fellowship, mildness, goodness, and so forth, and to present that picture to the Lord Jesus Christ (§29).

The healing of the old women (§§30–37): John orders Verus to bring all the old women of Ephesus out so that he can care for them. Verus reports that almost all over the age of 60 are ill, and expressing indignation that so many are sick, John orders him to bring them to the theater of the city (§30). Lycomedes tells the crowd that gathers at his home to assemble the next day in the theater to see the power of God, since the praetor Adronicus has spread the rumor that John will perform the impossible (§31). When John has all the sick old women brought into the theater (§32), he addresses the crowd, telling them that he has come on a mission from Jesus Christ and will heal all the ill old women (§33). He tells them not to rejoice in wealth, or try to defraud people (§34), nor to be proud of good looks, delight in adultery, indulge in anger, or be slaved to filthy desire (§35). Evildoers, including murderers, sorcerers, robbers, swindlers, and sodomites, will experience eternal torment (§36). Ending his speech, he heals all the sick old women (§37).

There is then a long missing section, which Lipsius and Bonnet fill in with §§38–86, which probably belongs after §105 and which we will summarize below. The narrative picks up with a scene in which John attempts to explain how Christ appeared to his disciples, as he had to Drusiana, in many forms, and concludes by narrating how Jesus danced a circle dance with his disciples while singing a hymn replete with riddles and antitheses (§§87–105), a lengthy section that is framed by references to Drusiana in §87 and §105. Drusiana claims that the Lord appeared to her in the tomb in the form of John and a young man (§87). John then attempts to describe the various ways in which the Lord appears. When the Lord chose Peter, Andrew, James, and John, he asked John who the child is on the shore who was calling them, though John saw only a handsome man (§88). When they beached their boat, Jesus helped them, looking like a bald man with a long beard to John, but James saw him as a young man. John observes how he seems to change in appearance (§89). Relating the episode of the transfiguration of the Lord, John describes the transformation of Jesus and how Jesus grabbed him by the beard, which caused him pain for thirty days (§90). Peter and James took John aside and asked who Jesus was speaking with. John considered "his unity within many faces" and told them to ask him themselves (§91). Once in a house in Gennesaret, John pretended to sleep and saw another one like Jesus come down and tell Jesus that his chosen ones did not believe him (§92). Sometimes when John touched Jesus, he touched a material body, but at other times Jesus was immaterial. When Jesus and his disciples dined out, each was given a loaf of bread, but Jesus broke his own loaf, which was miraculously enough for all. Sometimes John watched the ground where Jesus walked but found that he left no footprints (§93).

Before Jesus was arrested by the Jews, he told the disciples to form a circle holding each other's hands, and Jesus stood in the middle, singing a song and asking the disciples to respond "amen" (retrospectively called a dance in §97). The song included many "I will" antithetical predictions, including "I will be wounded, and I will wound—Amen," "I will eat and I will be eaten—Amen," "I will flee, and I will remain—Amen," "I have no house, and I have houses—Amen" (§§94–96).

Following the circle dance, Jesus was crucified and at the same time gave a revelation of the meaning of the cross to John, who had fled and was hiding in a cave on the Mount of Olives. The revelation contains many paradoxical and antithetical sayings analogous to the kind of sayings found in the hymn sung in §§94–96, e.g., "You hear that I suffered, yet I suffered not; and that I suffered not, yet I did suffer." John then saw Jesus taken up, though the crowd did not see this (§§97–102). John concludes by telling his listeners that Jesus is with them in all the difficult experiences of life and that he has called them to worship an unchangeable and invincible God (§§103–5).

Miracles in Ephesus (§§37–53): Urged by his companions from Miletus to go to Smyrna, John first wishes to visit the temple of Artemis (§37). Two days later, when the temple is being dedicated and all the worshipers are wearing white, John wears black and consequently is attacked. Climbing on a high platform, he addresses the crowd (§37). Rebuking them for being corrupted by their ancient rituals and ignoring the many miracles he has performed, he challenges them to pray to Artemis for his death; but if they are unsuccessful, he will pray for their deaths (§39). Knowing what John can do, they beg him not to kill them. John gives them no alternative: either they must be converted or he must be slain by the goddess (§40). John then prays to God, who has been rejected by the Ephesians, that he will drive out all the demons from the temple (§41). As he prays, the altar and seven images of Artemis fall to pieces, and the temple collapse kills the priest instantly; the crowd immediately fall to their knees and are converted, giving glory to God (§42). John then urges the people to rise and asks them to acknowledge God, emphasizing the impotence of Artemis to protect herself (§43). The crowd then throws down the rest of the temple, and begs John to help them and teach them (§44). Even though John is anxious to leave for Smyrna to make converts there, he agrees that he will not leave them "until I have weaned you like children from the nurse's milk and set you upon a solid rock" (§45). While John receives the crowd at the home of Andronicus, a relative of the dead priest of Artemis brings his corpse and leaves it outside the house. John, knowing the thoughts of the relative, tells the crowd what he has done. The relative is terrified and throws himself at John's feet, and the apostle promises to raise the priest from the dead (§46). He tells the youth to take the priest by the hand and say, "John, the servant of God, says to you, arise!" John tells the risen man that he will not really be alive unless he believes in the name of Jesus, which he does and begins to keep company with John (§47). John dreams that he has walked three miles outside Ephesus and upon awaking leaves the city. He finds a man who has kicked his father to death because he forbade him to have sex with the wife of his friend (§48). John sees the young man running away with a sickle, intending to kill his paramour, her husband, and himself (§49). John promises to raise his father to life, if the young man will steer clear of the woman in the future, and the young man agrees (§50). Returning to the place where the dead father lies, John prays that he may be able to resurrect the man (§51). John raises the man and tells him that if he really wants to live, he must believe in the Lord, which he does (§52). When the young man sees his father rise, he castrates himself with the sickle and runs and throws his testicles down before the feet of his paramour, telling her that God has shown her his power (§53). John tells him that he should not have castrated himself, since it is not the genitals that are evil but rather the hidden springs that stir up shameful emotions. The young man repents and accompanies John (§54).

John, as a preacher of God, is invited by the people of Smyrna to visit their city (§55). A pagan priest comes to John and sees him watching a partridge bathe in the dust, and is offended at the sight of an old man enjoying such a sight. John, knowing his thoughts, rebukes him, saying that it is better to watch a partridge bathing in dust than to be dirtied by pagan practices, for the partridge is a symbol of one's own soul (§56). The priest immediately prostrates himself and repents, recognizing that God dwells in John (§57).

John now decides to return to Ephesus, and when his brothers grieve at the prospect, he tells them that Christ is always with them (§58). He leaves them money for distribution and takes with him several companions originally from Ephesus, including Andronicus and Drusiana, the household of Lycomedes and Cleobius, and others (§59). When they stop overnight at an inn, John's companions put their garments on a bed for him to lie in. When the bedbugs bother him, he tells them to keep their distance from the servants of God for one night (§60). In the morning, they see a pile of bugs at the door. When they tell John what they have seen, he tells the bugs that they can go back to their bed, which they promptly do. The moral is that these bugs listened to a human voice and obeyed, but people hear the voice of God and disobey (§61). When John and company arrive in Ephesus at the house of Andronicus, many of the brothers come to greet him, and those who touch his clothes are healed (§63). Things are going great, when a man named Callimachus, inspired by Satan, falls in love with Drusiana, the wife of Andronicus. People tell him that since Drusiana has been shut in a tomb by Andronicus because she will not have sex with him, and ask, will she commit adultery with Callimachus? (§63). Callimachus tells Drusiana of his intentions, and she is so depressed that she dies (§64). Andronicus mourns her greatly, but John tells him that she has gone to a better hope (§65). At the burial, Andronicus becomes aware that John grieves for her more than he does (§66). In his funeral speech, John gives several similes about finishing a task appropriately despite the obstacles (§67), comparing these similes with faith which, despite hindrances and temptations, can end one's life appropriately (§§68–69), and leave transitory things for things eternal. Callimachus, bribing the steward of Andronicus, opens the grave of Drusiana, intending to have sex with her corpse (§70). Once in the tomb, a serpent kills the steward, trips Callimachus, and then sits upon him (§71). The next day, John and Andronicus come to the tomb, but the keys are lost. This was appropriate, says John, because she is not there and the doors will open of themselves (§72). Approaching the tomb of Drusiana, they find a beautiful young man, an angel, who says he came for the sake of Drusiana who was almost dishonored by the man who lies dead near her tomb. He then ascends to heaven (§73). Andronicus, seeing the two dead men by the tomb, recalls that Callimachus has threatened to violate her when she is dead. He asks John to raise Callimachus so that he can confess to what happened (§74). John prays and Callimachus arises but is senseless for an hour (§75). When he is fully conscious, John interrogates him. He tells how he uncovered Drusiana, but found a handsome young man covering her with his cloak, who told Callimachus that he must die in order to live. He then promises John to be faithful and godfearing henceforth (§76). John then gives thanks that God shows mercy to those who are completely undeserving (§77), and he then kisses Callimachus, rejoicing that he has been rescued from madness and summoned to a renewal of life (§78). Andronicus then begs John to raise up Drusiana also, which he promptly does, since the young man who threatened her has had a change of heart and life (§79). Drusiana is then raised by John and learns what has happened (§80). Drusiana, seeing Fortunatus the steward lying dead, asks that he too be raised to life; Callimachus objects, but John cautions him since all are unworthy. Since Callimachus does not want me to raise Fortunatus, says John, Drusiana must do it (§81). Drusiana then prays a long prayer narrating her experiences and asking that God raise up Fortunatus (§82). Taking his hand, she says, "Rise up, Fortunatus, in the name of our Lord Jesus Christ." He arises, but on seeing John, Andronicus, and Drusiana, says that he would rather be dead than see them, and flees away (§83). John marvels at Fortunatus's lack of repentance and prays that he be removed from the Lord (§85). John then takes bread and brings it into the tomb to break it and offer a prayer of thanksgiving (§85). After praying, he distributes the Eucharist and tells Andronicus that his spirit predicts that the bite of the snake will yet kill Fortunatus and he will turn black. One of the young men runs out and finds Fortunatus dead, as John has predicted (§86).

The last days of John are narrated in §§106–15. In his final speech, John reminds the brothers of the miracles that God performed through him and urges them to be true, avoiding distress, insult, disloyalty, and injury to God (§106). Let God rejoice, he continues, at our honorable and pure lives. He gives them this charge because he is nearing the end of his life (§107). He then prays for the protection of the brothers (§108), and asking for bread, offers a prayer (§109), and then breaks the bread and offers them the Eucharist (§110). He then orders Verus to take some men with two baskets and shovels and follow him. Arriving at the tomb of a brother, he urges them to dig. When they have dug deep enough, he lays his garments in the bottom and begins to pray (§111), mentioning many of his experiences with the Lord Jesus (§112), including how he has mercifully been kept from marrying and so remained a virgin, and how he has fulfilled the charge given him by the Lord (§113–14). He seals himself all over, and then gives up his spirit (§115).

*Acts, Apocryphal, *Apocrypha, New Testament, *Novel

Bonnet (text) 1898; Bremmer (ed.) 1995; Junod and Kaestli (eds.) 1983; Lalleman 1998; Logon 1991; Schäferdiek 1992; Zahn 1880

Acts of the Pagan Martyrs (Acta Alexandrinorum) consists of eleven anonymous fragmentary texts (plus ten dubious fragments), most extant in single papyrus copies found in Egypt and dating from the 1st to the 3d cent. C.E. Exceptions are the *Acta Isidori* (three recensions) and the *Acta Appiani* (two overlapping fragments). These *Acta* resemble legal "protocols," i.e., documents recording legal proceedings, and they center on the dialogue between various Alexandrian leaders and Roman emperors from Augustus to Commodus, before whom they are on trial. The *Acta* are in fact anti-Roman literary propaganda produced by Alexandrian nationalists, which also exhibit some anti-Semitic features. Despite previous speculation, it appears that the *Acta* have not exerted any traceable literary influence on the *Acts of the Christian Martyrs.

*Acts of the Christian Martyrs

Musurillo 1954, 1961

Acts of Paul, probably the earliest of the Apocryphal Acts, includes the *Acts of Paul and Thecla* (Rordorf 1993c, 378–87), **3 Corinthians* (Havhanessian 2000), and the *Martyrdom of Paul*; segments of the whole work (parts of all these works are found in Papyrus Heidelberg, a Coptic MS of the 5th or 6th cent. C.E.) were detached and circulated independently. The style and vocabulary of the *Acts of Paul* and the *Acts of Thecla* indicates that they were the product of a single author and were composed together. The *Acts of Thecla* were separated from the *Acts of Paul* to serve the needs of the Thecla cult, which flourished from the 4th cent. C.E. on in Asia Minor. Tertullian regarded the *Acts of Paul* as a forgery (*De baptismo* 17.5):

> But if certain Acts of Paul [*Acta Pauli*], which are falsely so named, claim the example of Thecla for allowing women to teach and to baptize, let me know that in Asia the presbyter who compiled that document, thinking to add of his own to Paul's reputation, was found out, and though he professed he had done it for love of Paul, was deposed from his position.

These comments of Tertullian, who wrote *De baptismo* between 198 and 206 C.E., indicate that he knew the *Acts of Paul and Thecla* (though Tertullian's words do not fit the work precisely, since Thecla never baptizes anyone in it) as a separately circulated composition, and perhaps that he knew the *Acts of Paul* as a whole. The *Acts of Paul* were therefore written before the end of the 2d cent. C.E., perhaps ca. 175 C.E., for though it originated in Asia Minor (probably southwest Asia Minor; Bremmer 1996b, 56), it was already circulating in North Africa ca. 200 C.E. Though S. L. Davies (1986) argues that Tertullian was not referring to the *Acts of Paul*, this has been refuted by Rordorf (1993c, 475–84). Later, Origen quotes from the *Acts of Paul* twice (*Princ.* 1.2.3; *Comm. Jo.* 20.12), indicating that the work was held in high regard.

Texts and translations. There are a number of Greek manuscripts of the *Acts of Paul*, including 11 papyrus pages from the 3d or 4th cent. P. Hamburg, as well as several other 4th-cent. Greek fragments including P. Michigan 1317; P. Michigan 3788 and P. Berlin 13893. A 5th-cent. Coptic MS (P. Heidelberg) contains the whole of the *Acts of Paul*. For a list of the editions of Greek, Latin, Coptic, Syriac, Ethiopic, Arabic, Armenian, and Slavonic MSS, see J. K. Elliott (1993, 357–62).

Intertextual issues. The *Acts of Paul* seems to be dependent on the canonical Acts of the Apostles (see *Luke-Acts), though its relationship to the apocryphal *Acts of Peter* and the *Acts of John* is more problematic (MacDonald 1997). While the complete independence of the *Acts of Paul* from the canonical Acts has been argued (Rordorf 1993b), most scholars accept the literary dependence of the *Acts of Paul* on the Acts of the Apostles (C. Schmidt 1905, 215; Hills 1994, 1997; Herczeg 1996, 144–45). A major issue emerging from the assumption of literary dependency is whether the *Acts of Paul* was intended as a sequel to Acts (Bauckham 1993, 1997) or a replacement of Acts (Pervo 1995). While the *Acts of Paul* and canonical Acts share the theme of Paul as an itinerant missionary in the same geographical theater and with a similar title (Πράξεις, "Acts"), there are several differences: a different itinerary, different characters, a more hagiographical treatment of Paul, and a different message (Bauckham 1993, 107–11).

Content and literary analysis. The textual history of the *Acts of Paul* is complex, and the following summary represents the reconstruction found in *NTA* 2.237–65. One feature of the narrative strategy of the author is the principle of gradual disclosure. The facts about persons and events are first narrated generally, and details are filled in as the narrative moves on. Examples: Thamyris is introduced as the fiancé of Thecla in §8, but we only later learn that he is "the first man of the city" (§11); much later we learn that Thecla is also "one of the first of Iconium" (§26); we learn that Paul is fasting at the beginning of §23, but not until the end of that section do we learn that he has been fasting for six days.

Act 1: After Paul's conversion outside Damascus, he entered Damascus and gave a sermon. He then traveled to Jericho, where the baptism of the lion occurred. Act 2: In Antioch, the son of Anchares and Phila had died. Paul came to help but was repulsed by Phila. Anchares fasted and prayed until the crowd came to take out his son, when Paul appeared and raised the boy.

Act 3: The longest section of the *Acts of Paul* circulated separately as the *Acts of Paul and Thecla* but was originally part of the whole work. Fleeing from Antioch, Paul went to Iconium with Demas and Hermogenes, both false friends, though Paul loved them (§1). Hearing that Paul had come to Iconium, Onesiphorus [2 Tim. 1:16; 4:19] went to meet Paul, though he knew him only by the description of Titus (§2). Onesiphorus looked for Paul on the road. A famous description then follows: "And when he saw Paul coming, a man small of stature, with a bald head and crooked legs, in a good state of body with eyebrows meeting and nose somewhat hooked, full of friendliness; for now he appeared like a man, and now he had the face of an angel" (§3).

Onesiphorus greeted Paul and invited him to stay at his house, and Demas and Hermogenes became jealous (§4). When Paul entered the house, he pronounced a series of 13 beatitudes (using a figure of speech called *epanaphora, each line beginning with the same word), many emphasizing chastity (§§5–6). Thecla, a woman betrothed to Thamyris, was immobilized for three days and nights in a window, listening to Paul's gospel of the virgin life (§7). Her mother sent for Thamyris and told him about Thecla's strange behavior (§8), complaining that Paul was upsetting Iconium with his message of "fear one single God only, and live chastely" (§9). Thamyris and Theocleia both asked Thecla why she was so distracted, Thamyris mourning the loss of a wife, Theocleia the loss of a daughter (§10). Thamyris, claiming to be the first man of the city, went down to the street and offered to pay Demas and Hermogenes to tell him about the false teacher (§11–12). The two went home with Thamyris and enjoyed a sumptuous banquet with him and then he asked about Paul's teaching (§13). They suggested that Paul be arraigned before Castellius and then executed to get Thecla back. They offered to tell Thamyris that the resurrection that Paul claims is a future event which has already happened (§14). Leading an angry mob to the house of Onesiphorus, Thamyris charged Paul with sedition and hauled him before Castellius (§15). Standing at the judgment seat, Thamyris accused Paul of not allowing maidens to marry, while Demas and Hermogenes advised him to accuse Paul of being a Christian. The proconsul asked Paul who he was and what he taught (§16). Paul replied that he was sent by the living God, to preach and teach that in God's Son people have hope—is that so wrong? The proconsul then had Paul jailed until another hearing (§17). Thecla bribed the guards to let her see Paul, who proclaimed to her the mighty acts of God while she kissed his chains (§18). Meanwhile Thamyris and Thecla's people found out where she had gone and reported it to the governor (§19). The governor had Paul and Thecla brought to the judgment seat and heard Paul speak of Christ. Summoning Thecla, he asked her why she did not marry Thamyris, while her mother demanded that Paul be burned (§20). He had Paul beaten and expelled from the city, but sentenced Thecla to be burned. Looking around the theater, she saw the Lord sitting in the guise of Paul, and took courage (§21). Thecla was placed on a burning pyre, which was suddenly extinguished by rain and hail sent by God (§22). After Paul, accompanied by Onesiphorus and his family, had been fasting, the son of Onesiphorus was sent to buy some food and met Thecla, who was seeking Paul (§23). Thecla was brought to Paul and they engaged in a sort of prayer dialogue; Paul, unaware of her presence, was praying for her deliverance; she thanked God for delivering her; Paul responded in thanksgiving that God had already answered his prayer (§24). Thecla wanted to cut off her hair and follow Paul and receive the seal, but he put her off (§25). Paul then sent Onesiphorus and family back to Iconium, while he and Thecla headed for Antioch. Arriving at Antioch, Alexander, "one of the first of the Antiochenes," fell immediately in love with Thecla. He embraced her right there on the street, but she rejected his advances and tore his cloak in the process (§26). With mixed feelings he brought her to the governor; when she confessed what she had done, he condemned her to the beasts, but all the women of Antioch protested. A rich woman whose daughter had died, Tryphaena, gave Thecla her protection (§27). Thecla was bound to the back of a lioness walking in a procession followed by Tryphaena, who had been told in a dream by her dead daughter to adopt Thecla (§28). After the procession, Tryphaena took charge of Thecla until the games the next day (§29). The next day, Alexander came to fetch Thecla, but Tryphaena resisted and prayed that God would deliver Thecla (§30). When soldiers came for Thecla, Tryphaena relented and reluctantly decided to bring Thecla to the games herself (§31). The crowd was yelling for Thecla to be brought out (§32), and she was forcibly taken from Tryphaena, stripped, given a girdle and thrown into the stadium. A lioness protected Thecla by killing a bear, but the lioness died fighting against Alexander's lion, which also died. All the women in the stadium mourned (§33). When many more beasts were sent in, Thecla prayed and then baptized herself in a pit of water filled with ferocious seals, saying "In the name of Jesus Christ I baptize myself on the last day!" But all the seals died, and Thecla was surrounded by a cloud of fire to conceal her nudity and repel the beasts (§34). When more animals were released, the women in the crowd threw petals and spices into the arena, and the animals were drugged by the perfume. Thecla was then tied by the feet to two bulls with hot irons on their bellies, but the flames burned the ropes and she was released (§35). Tryphaena fainted, and the crowd thought she had died. Alexander then asked the governor to set Thecla free, since Tryphaena was a relative of Caesar, who would destroy the city if he heard about what had happened (§36). Thecla, summoned and questioned by the governor, called herself a handmaid of the living God, and claimed that she had been protected because she had believed in God's Son (§37). He then had garments brought for her, and issued a decree freeing Thecla. The women in the arena all cried, "One is God, who has delivered Thecla" (§38). Tryphaena had meanwhile revived and taken Thecla to her home where Thecla instructed her and her household in the word of God (§39). Thecla then wanted to find Paul; hearing that he was in Myra, she put on male clothes and went to find him. When she found him, she told him of her baptism (§40). In the house of Hermias, Thecla told Paul all that had happened, and then resolved to teach the word of God in Iconium (§41). Returning to Iconium, to the house of Onesiphorus, she fell on the spot where Paul taught the oracles of God and prayed a *doxology (§42). Thamyris had died, but her mother was still living, and she exhorted her to believe in the Lord. After bearing witness in Iconium, she went to teach the word of God in Seleucia, where she died (§43).

Act 4: Paul in Myra (P. Heid. 28–35). In Myra, Paul met and healed Hermocrates, who had the dropsy. His son Hermippus was angry with Paul because he wanted his father to die so he could inherit his property. Dion, his younger brother, listened to Paul eagerly but accidentally fell and died. Paul raised Dion from the dead, though that part of the text is missing. Hermippus and a gang of hooligans came to kill Paul, but he was blinded and repented and was healed by Paul.

Act 5: Paul in Sidon (P. Heid. 35–39; very fragmentary; see *NTA* 2.249–50). Paul left Myra for Sidon, accompanied by some brothers, including Thrasymachus and Cleon. On the way he met an old man at a pagan altar who gave examples of how the gods punish those who abandon them. Paul was shut up in the temple of Apollo, and after he fasted and prayed, the temple collapsed. Paul and his companions were then led out to the theater, where he apparently made a speech that won the crowd over.

Act 6: Paul in Tyre (P. Heid. 40) is too fragmentary to reconstruct. Act 7: Paul in Ephesus (P. Hamb. 1–5). Paul traveled from Smyrna to Ephesus, where he stayed with Aquila and Priscilla. He gave a sermon mentioning his conversion and the baptism of the lion. Paul was then brought before Hieronymus the proconsul, where Paul defended himself. The proconsul found him blameless, but the crowd demanded that he be thrown to the wild animals, among whom a ferocious lion is conspicuous. Meanwhile the conversion of Artemilla, the wife of Hieronymus, is narrated. After speaking with Paul she desired baptism, which occurred with the help of Christ himself. After celebrating the Eucharist, Artemilla returned home. The next day, Paul was put into the arena with a lion, the one he had baptized. When the lion failed to harm Paul other animals were released, but a hail storm interrupted the games. The lion went back to the mountains, while Paul joined the crowd fleeing from the fall of a city and boarded a ship for Macedonia.

Act 8: Paul in Philippi (P. Heid. 45–50, 41, 42, 44). The Corinthians, distressed over the false teaching of Simon and Cleobius, who said there was no resurrection of the flesh but only of the spirit, wrote a letter to Paul in Philippi. The letter to Paul, drafted by Stephanus and several presbyters, described the teachings of Simon and Cleobius (*NTA* 2.254): "We must not, they say, appeal to the prophets, and that God is not almighty, and that there is no resurrection of the flesh, and that the creation of man is not God's (work), and that the Lord is not come in the flesh, nor was he born of Mary, and that the world is not of God, but of the angels." Threptus and Eutychus, Corinthian deacons, brought the letter to Paul in prison at Philippi, who was distraught at what was happening in the Corinthian congregation. He then wrote a letter in which he emphasizes that the opposite of what Simon and Cleobius teach is true, taking up the issues raised in the Corinthian letter and answering them point by point.

Act 9: Paul in Corinth (P. Hamb. 6–7; P. Heid. 44, 43, 51, 52). Paul traveled from Philippi to Corinth and stayed with Epiphanius and recounted his sufferings in Philippi to the brothers assembled there. He then preached repentance for forty days, continually praising God and Christ Jesus. Paul referred to his coming death, which was confirmed by Cleobius, who is filled with the Spirit. Myrta was then inspired by the Spirit and told the brothers that Paul would save many in Rome. After sharing the Eucharist, Paul prepared for his departure to Corinth.

Act 10: Paul boarded a ship for Rome whose captain was Artemon, who had been baptized by Peter. Paul fell asleep and had a vision of the Lord walking on the sea and saying to him, "Paul, I am about to be crucified afresh." When they arrived, Claudius greeted Paul and with Artemon took his things to his house. Paul then addressed the people there, summarizing biblical stories of how God was able to deliver people from the lawless. He then mentioned how Jesus was able to do wonderful works, including raising people from the dead. [The speech then breaks off.]

Act 10: The Martyrdom of the Holy Apostle Paul. Luke and Titus were waiting for Paul at Rome, where he proclaimed the gospel and made many converts. Patroclus, Caesar's cupbearer, came late and because of the crowd sat in a high window to hear Paul. Because of the envy of the devil, he fell down and died. Paul was aware of what happened, and Patroclus was raised from the dead and sent to Caesar's house. Nero heard that Patroclus had died, but then he returned alive and told Nero that Christ Jesus the king of the ages had given him life [cf. the story of Eutychus in Acts 20:7–12]. When others around Nero admitted to being Christians, he threw them in prison, tortured them, and commanded that all Christians should be rounded up and killed. Paul was one of those arrested; before Nero he admitted to recruiting "soldiers" from the whole world. Paul appealed to Nero to believe, for the world would eventually be destroyed by fire. Nero commanded the prisoners to be burned, but Paul to be beheaded. Appearing before Nero again, Paul promised that if he were beheaded, he would arise and appear to Nero in proof that he is not dead but alive to the Lord Christ Jesus. Escorted by Longus and Cestus, Paul was taken out and beheaded, and milk squirted on the soldier's clothing. The soldiers reported to Nero what had happened, and at the ninth hour Paul appeared alive before Caesar and then departed. Longus and Cestus went to Paul's tomb as he had told them to do, and they saw two men (Titus and Luke) praying with Paul between them. Longus and Cestus believed and were baptized, and Titus and Luke glorified God.

*Acts, Apocryphal, *Apocrypha, New Testament, *Novel

Bauckham 1993, 1997; Bremmer (ed.) 1996a, 1996b; Brock 1994; P. Dunn 1996; J. K. Elliott 1993, 350–89; Herczeg 1996; Hilhorst 1996; Hills 1994, 1997; Klijn 1963; MacDonald 1992, 1993a; Rordorf 1993b; C. Schmidt 1905, 1936; Testuz 1959

Acts of Peter, a fictional narrative focusing on the adventures of Peter, a prominent disciple of Jesus, is part of an extensive cycle of pseudepigraphical Petrine literature including the canonical letters of 1 Peter and 2 Peter, the *Gospel of Peter*, the *Preaching of Peter*, the *Apocalypse of Peter*, the Clementine Homilies and Recognitions, the *Kerygmata Petrou,* and the Coptic-gnostic treatises entitled *The Acts of Peter and the Twelve Apostles* (NHC 6.1), and *The Apocalypse of Peter* (NHC 7.3).

Texts and Translations. The Greek text of the *Acts of Peter* is available in Lipsius and Bonnet (1891–1903, 1.45–103). The *Actus Vercellenses*, dating to the 6th or 7th cent. C.E., is the earliest and most important MS witness to the *Acts of Peter*, though it appears to preserve only about two-thirds of the original text. The *Actus Vercellenses* is a Latin translation of a Greek exemplar which was probably made not later than the 3d or 4th cent. C.E. The martyrdom of Peter (§§30–42) was separated at a relatively early date from the main text and has a wide independent circulation, surviving in Arabic, Armenian, Coptic, Ethiopic, Slavonic, and Syriac translations.

Early Attestation and Date. The earliest attestation for the existence of the *Acts of Peter* is found in Eusebius (*Hist. eccl.* 3.3.2), who knows a work entitled Πράξεις Πέτρου (the "Acts of Peter"). Origen (according to Eusebius (*Hist. eccl.* 3.1.2) related that Peter was in Rome and when condemned to die requested that he be crucified upside down, a tradition which is also found in the *Acts of Peter* 37–38. While the **Acts of Paul* can be dated confidently before the end of the 2d cent. (see Tertullian *De baptismo* 17.5), the dating of the *Acts of Peter* is problematic. If it is dependent on the *Acts of Paul*, then it can be dated to the 3d cent. C.E, but if the *Acts of Paul* is dependent on the *Acts of Peter*, then the latter can be dated as early as 150 C.E. C. Schmidt (1903, 82–86) argued that the *Acts of Peter* were dependent on the *Acts of Paul*, and that the former was written ca. 200–10 C.E. After the discovery of the Hamburg Papyrus, Schmidt changed his mind and argued instead that the *Acts of Paul* were dependent on the *Acts of Peter*, and that the latter were compiled ca. 180–90 C.E. (C. Schmidt 1930; 1936, 127–30).

Composition History. The *Acts of Peter* has been regarded as a compilation of several sources or as a work revised by a redactor for particular reasons (*NTA* 2.281). Poupon (1988) has argued that chapters 1–3, 30, and 41 are interpolations added to the *Acts of Peter* sometime after its composition (Harnack [1901] and Vouaux [1922, 27–33] argued earlier that chapters 1–3 and 41 were interpolations), and chapters 4, 6, and 10 have been revised. Poupon sees the direct influence of the *Acts of Paul* on chapter 41. In chapters 1–3, Peter and Marcellus are not mentioned, and the other characters mentioned, with the exception of the priest Narcissus, do not appear in the rest of the narrative. The interpolator was trying to link reminiscences from Acts 28:30 and Rom. 15:24 with the Roman legend of the death of Paul.

Analysis of Content. While the beginning of the *Acts of Peter* has not survived, the Berlin Coptic Papyrus 8502 contains a story of how Peter healed his paralyzed virgin daughter, and then made her paralyzed again. Peter explained that the girl's beauty had caused a certain Ptolemaeus to take her and have sex with her. As a result, the girl was paralyzed, and Ptolemaeus went blind but was miraculously converted before he died. A few other episodes may have appeared in the first part of the *Acts of Peter*, including Peter's prayer for a gardener's daughter that God would give her what was appropriate for her soul. She immediately dropped dead. The gardener begged Peter to resurrect his daughter, which he did. Eventually a stranger passed through and seduced the girl and took her away. They were never heard from again.

In general, the version of the *Acts of Paul* preserved in the *Actus Vercellenses* is a relatively unified composition when compared with other apocryphal acts. Apart from a few episodes, the overall plot consists of the continuation of an earlier conflict between Peter and Simon the Magician, this time set in Rome. The usual emphasis on the gospel of sexual purity is largely missing from the *Acts of Peter*, with the exception of several chapters in the Martyrdom of Peter (§§33–34), which therefore stand out as having a different origin than the rest of the document. In the Martyrdom, in fact, angry husbands holding high offices are the chief reason for the execution of Peter (§34).

Act 1 of the *Actus Vercellenses* begins with Paul in Rome, where he receives a vision from the Lord commissioning him to go to Spain to proclaim the gospel; when his friends try to prevent him, the Lord speaks from heaven confirming Paul's mission and the fact that "he will be perfected before your eyes" by the hand of Nero, an obvious allusion to Paul's death (§1). During a final celebration of the Eucharist, a woman named Rufina begged to receive the Eucharist from Paul. Paul denounced her as an adulteress and she immediately fell down paralyzed on the left side from head to toe. Paul used this terrifying occurrence to preach a sermon on Christian morals, concluding with a set of three antitheses (trans. *NTA* 2.289):

> I was once a blasphemer,
> but now I am blasphemed;
> I was once a persecutor,
> but now I suffer persecution from others;
> once an enemy of Christ,
> but now I pray to be his friend.

A large crowd of Paul's friends and followers escorted Paul to the harbor and saw him off on his journey (§3).

The plot of the *Acts of Peter* centers on the conflict between two main characters, Peter and Simon Magus, both of whom are depicted as rather flat, two-dimensional characters. Act 2 focuses on the arrival of Simon the Magician in Rome, followed by the arrival there of Peter, thus setting the stage for the conflict between these two central characters (§§4–6). Simon performed many miracles and called himself "the great power of God" [an allusion to Acts 8:10], and announced that he would fly over the city gate on the next day. Simon did precisely that and attracted a large following from among the believers in Rome, leaving only seven who remained faithful and who lamented the absence of Paul (§4). Meanwhile, the Lord appeared in a vision to Peter in Jerusalem, telling him that Simon (whom he had expelled from Jerusalem) must be thwarted in Rome as well. Peter boarded a ship in Caesarea bound for Rome, and during the journey converted and baptized Theon, the captain (§5). Arriving in Puteoli, the port of Rome, Theon brought Peter to stay with Ariston, a Christian with whom Theon often stayed. Ariston then related to Peter how nearly all the believers in Rome have been alienated by Simon since the departure of Paul. Since the Lord had predicted Peter's coming, Ariston had come to Puteoli from Rome to await his arrival. When Peter learned about these things from Ariston, he insisted on leaving immediately for Rome, where he stayed at the house of the presbyter Narcissus, one of the few believers to have remained faithful (§6).

Acts 3 and 4 center on Peter's preaching in Rome and his restoration of the Church there (§§7–11). Peter appeals to a large gathering of renegade believers to return to the faith, using the example of how he himself was subverted by Satan into denying the Lord three times (§7). They all repent, ask Peter's help in overthrowing Simon, and then tell Peter how Simon now resides with senator Marcellus, once a model believer, but now a blasphemer. Peter responds with a long reproach addressed to the devil (§8). Peter, accompanied by a throng of believers, then marches off to the house of Marcellus to confront Simon. The doorkeeper, however, says that Simon anticipated Peter's arrival and instructed the doorkeeper to say that he was not at home. Peter then commands a dog to go in and tell Simon to come out in public, which he does, with the result that Simon is dumbfounded by the talking dog (§9). Marcellus reacts by prostrating himself before Peter and repenting, and Peter gives thanks to God for reassembling his flock (§10). A young man possessed with a demon told Peter about a contest inside between Simon and the dog. Peter exorcises the demon, who tips over and knocks to pieces a statue of Caesar on his way out; Marcellus is stunned for this is a great crime. Peter tells Marcellus to sprinkle water over the pieces of the statue, which is immediately restored, to the joy of both Peter and Marcellus (§11).

Act 5 begins with Simon in the house of Marcellus telling the dog to tell Peter that he is not at home. The dog, however, rebukes Simon at some length, and then returns to Peter and in a brief speech encapsulates the rest of the story (§12; trans. *NTA* 2.298):

> Messenger and apostle of the true God, Peter, you shall have a great contest with Simon, the enemy of Christ, and with his servants; and you shall convert many to the faith that were deceived by him. Therefore you shall receive from God a reward for your work.

As a sign convincing his audience to believe, Peter took a smoked fish and threw it into a pond, where it became alive and began to swim. Many believed in the Lord because of this sign (§13). Meanwhile Marcellus returned to his house and had his servants kick Simon out; Simon then goes to the house where Peter is staying and challenges him (§14).

In Act 6, Peter sent a woman who was breast feeding a seven-month-old child to confront Simon; the baby denounced Simon and commanded through Christ that he be struck dumb, which happened immediately. In the evening Peter had a vision of Jesus, who told him about his coming trial of faith and about the number of Gentiles and Jews that would be converted (§16). Peter then related this vision to the brethren along with a story of how Simon, after being expelled from Jerusalem, had stayed with Eubula, a rich woman. Using a magic spell, Simon and two accomplices took all the woman's money, but Eubula blamed the theft on her household slaves. Peter then had a vision in which he learned how Eubula had been robbed, and a trap is set for the two accomplices who plan to fence some of the stolen gold objects. Eubula told the story to Pompeius the magistrate, who had Simon's two accomplices tortured until they confessed. When Simon saw the two in chains, he fled Judaea. Eubula then gave all her wealth and property for the care of the poor (§17). Peter closes his story with an exhortation to fast and pray that the Lord will expose the messenger of Satan (§18).

Act 7 begins with Marcellus informing Peter that he had ritually sprinkled his home to cleanse it of the defiling presence of Simon, and inviting him to his house (§19). When Peter arrives, he finds that the gospel is being read (apparently the story of the transfiguration from Mark 9 or one of its parallels). After rolling up the book, Peter explains the meaning of the story of the transfiguration in which he uses his own role as an example of how the Lord shows mercy. He concludes with a series of twelve asianic-style antitheses applied to Jesus (§20; trans. *NTA* 2.304):

> This (God) who is both great and little,
> beautiful and ugly,
> young and old,
> appearing in time and yet in eternity wholly invisible;
> whom no flesh has seen, yet now he is seen;
> whom no hearing has found, yet now he is known as the word that is heard;
> whom no suffering can reach, yet now is (chastened) as we are;
> Who was never chastened, yet now is chastened;

who is before the world,
yet now is comprehended in time;
the beginning greater than all princedom, yet
now delivered to the princes
beauteous, yet appearing among us as poor
and ugly.

Several old blind widows spoke up when the hour for prayer arrived and asked that Peter restore their sight. After a short meditation on the greater value of inner compared with outer sight, Peter prays for their healing. A great bright light floods the room, and the sight of the widows is miraculously restored. On being asked by Peter what they saw, one said she saw an old man, others a growing lad, and others a boy who gently touched their eyes (§21). Marcellus, after attending to the virgins of the Lord, told Peter of a dream he had of an old hag in filthy rags who was dancing. In the dream, Peter told Marcellus to behead the demonic figure, but he could not; Peter then beheaded and dismembered the demonic figure (§22).

Act 8 centers on the contest between Peter and Simon in the Forum (§§23–29). After the believers and the Romans had assembled in the Forum, Peter addressed them all, including Simon, providing a thumbnail sketch of his previous dealings with Simon in Jerusalem and Judaea, and how he had beguiled Eubula. He also recounts the event that occurred in Acts 8:18–24, when Simon had offered to pay Peter and Paul for the ability to heal people. Peter claims because he believes in the living God, that he will be able to destroy Simon's prophecies. Simon then provides a short rebuttal including such rhetorical questions as: "You men of Rome, is God born? Is he crucified?" The Romans were pleased with these statements (§23). Peter responds with a litany of OT prophetic passages which predict the events of the life of Jesus, and challenges him to perform a deceitful miracle (§24). The prefect (whom we later learn is named Agrippa) asks Simon to kill one of his servants and asks Peter to restore him to life. Meanwhile, one of the Christian widows appeals to Peter to resurrect her son who has died (§25). Peter has Agrippa take his dead servant by the right hand, and when he does so the servant is immediately restored to life (§26). Meanwhile the widow's son is carried in on a stretcher, and Peter restores him to life, promising that he will hold the office of deacon and bishop (§27). The mother of a recently deceased senator then appealed to Peter to restore her son to life. The woman had her servants bring the body of her son into the Forum. Peter then issues a challenge to Simon to restore the senator to life, and this challenge was accepted by all those present. Simon makes the dead man appear to move, and the crowd is ready to burn Peter. Peter tells the Romans that they are blind, and that the man has not really been restored to life. Agrippa runs over to check, and finds that the man is still dead, and the enraged crowd threatens to burn Simon rather than Peter. Peter then restored the son (whom we finally learn is named Nicostratus) to life (§28). After these events had concluded, the people treated Peter like a god. The widow of the resurrected senator then brought two thousand gold pieces to Peter to be distributed to the virgins of Christ (§29).

The ninth and final act narrates the martyrdom of Peter (§§30–41). One day when Peter was preaching on the Lord's day, a woman named Chryse gave him ten thousand pieces of gold, claiming that she had been commanded to do so in a dream. Those around Peter told him that he shouldn't accept her money because she was a fornicator. Peter paid no attention, maintaining that the woman was a debtor to Christ providing for the servants of Christ (§30). Peter healed many people from their diseases and many believed in the name of Jesus Christ. Simon continued to perform false miracles, though no one believed in him. Finally, he promised that on the next day he, "the Standing One," would fly up to God (§31). The following day, before a large crowd, Simon entered into Rome and, standing on a high place, flew around the city of Rome. Peter prayed and Simon fell from a great height, breaking his leg in three places. Shortly after, he died during an operation (§32). After this Peter proclaimed the message of sexual purity to the four concubines of Agrippa the prefect. When they would not have sex with Agrippa he threatened to kill them and burn Peter alive (§33). Many other women, including Xathippe the wife of Albinus the friend of Caesar, accepted the message of sexual abstinence and separated from their husbands. Albinus and Agrippa made plans to kill Peter (§34). On being warned of the plot to kill him, Peter left Rome and met the Lord entering Rome. In this famous *quo vadis* (where are you going?) scene, Peter asks him, "Lord, where are you going [*quo vadis*]?" to which he replied "I am coming to Rome to be crucified," a reference to the crucifixion of Peter (§35). Peter then returned to Rome and was arrested and brought to the place of execution (§36). After a brief soliloquy to the cross, Peter insisted on being crucified head down (§37). Hanging upside down, Peter addressed a sermon to those who were standing by (§§38–39). After Peter's death, Marcellus took him down from the cross and embalmed his body. That night Peter appeared to Marcellus (§40). When Nero found that Agrippa had executed Peter without his knowledge, he was angry because he had wanted to torture Peter. However, as the result of a threatening dream, after the death of Peter he no longer persecuted Christians (§41).

*Acts, Apocryphal

Harnack 1901; MacDonald 1992; Poupon 1988; Rordorf 1998; C. Schmidt 1903, 1930; Vouaux 1922

Acts of Philip, compiled toward the end of the 4th cent. C.E. at the earliest (Zahn 1900, 18; Amsler, Bovon, and Bouvier 1996, 80), though others suggest a slightly earlier date in the 4th cent., i.e., between 300 and 330 (Erbetta 1966, 453; Moraldi 1971, 1625), perhaps by a monk with an encratite orientation, since the *Acts of Philip* contains polemics against the Great Church, Jews, and pagans (Amsler, Bovon, and Bouvier 1996, 30; Amsler 1999, 13–16, 429–31; cf. 469–520 on "Asiatic Encratism of the 4th and 5th cents. C.E."). The *Acts of Philip,* one of the latest of the Apocryphal Acts (see *Acts, Apocryphal), sometimes makes use of earlier Apocryphal Acts and for that reason has often been held in low esteem. The earliest date for the various sections of *Acts of Philip* is the composition of the five main Apocryphal Acts (all of which date no later than the early 3d cent. C.E.): the *Acts of Peter*, the *Acts of John*, and probably also the *Acts of Paul*, the *Acts of Andrew,* and the *Acts of Thomas*, on which the *Acts of Philip* is dependent (Amsler 1999, 437). The *Acts of Philip* is a complex compilation of four independent texts written in the mid-4th to the late 5th cent. (Amsler 1999, 438): Act 1 (end of 4th cent. or beginning of 5th cent.); Act 2 (second half of 5th cent.); Acts 3 to 7 (end of the 4th cent.); Acts 8 to Martyrdom (middle of the 4th cent.).

Text and translations. The *Acts of Philip* exists in two recensions. The longer recension, represented only by the 14th-cent. MS *Xenophontos 32* (discovered in 1974 at Mount Athos by Bovon and Bouvier), contains all 15 acts and the martyrdom, and serves as the basis for the new critical text in Bovon, Bouvier, and Amsler (1999, xiii–xx), and the French translation in Amsler, Bovon, and Bouvier (1996) and in Bovon, Bouvier, and Amsler (1999). No English translation that includes *Xenophontos 32* is currently available (a précis of the text is available in Matthews 2002, 198–215). A commentary by Amsler (1999) focuses primarily on issues related to the composition and structure of the *Acts of Philip*.

The shorter recension is represented by *Vaticanus graecus 824*, an 11th-cent. MS, containing only Acts 1–9 and a longer version of the martyrdom than *Xenophontos 32* (Bovon, Bouvier, and Amsler 1999, xx–xxi; Amsler, Bovon, and Bouvier 1996, 23). Sixteen other MSS contain various segments of the *Acts of Philip* (Erbetta 1966, 454), such as longer versions of the martyrdom, and Act 2 (described in Bovon, Bouvier, and Amsler 1999, xx–xxx). A helpful chart showing the contents of the extant seven MSS is found in Amsler, Bovon, and Bouvier 1996, 88. The parts of the *Acts of Philip* that are lost include the beginning of Act 11, the whole of Act 10, and parts of Acts 14 and 15. Ancient translations of parts of the *Acts of Philip* are extant in Latin, Coptic, Arabic, Ethiopic, Syriac, Armenian, Georgian, Old Slavonic, and Irish (Herbert and McNamara 1989, 106–8).

Composition history. The composition of the *Acts of Philip* was a complex process (following Amsler 1999, 431–34; cf. Matthews 2002, 162–66). Act 2 is an independent composition that was compiled after Act 6 and the Martyrdom (Act 2 and the Martyrdom circulated independently). Acts 3 to 7 (which contains no allusions to Act 8–Martyrdom) and Acts 8–Martyrdom (which contains no allusions to Acts 3–7) originated as two independent cycles that were in existence when Act 2 was redacted. Matthews (2002, 164–65) suggests that Acts 5–7 always formed a unit and perhaps circulated separately, and the same is suggested for Acts 1–4, though this appears doubtful. Act 2 is a revision of Act 6 (Matthews 2002, 182–89). Acts 8–Martyrdom is probably the earliest cycle, because of the early date of the traditions associated with Philip at Hierapolis. Act 1 is an isolated episode that contains no allusions to any of the other Acts.

Sources. The *Acts of Philip* reflects dependence on the other five major Apocryphal Acts. Schneemelcher argued that the *Acts of Philip* exhibits dependence on the *Acts of Peter* (Schneemelcher in *NTA*, 2.276–77), though this is disputed in a labored and unconvincing way by Matthews 2002, 180–96, who argues that "A judgment of 'literary dependence' obscures our recognition of an ancient writer's pursuit and valuation of practiced imitation as a legitimate compositional technique" (181).

The Hymn of Christ (*Acts of John* 94–96) is reused in *Acts of Philip* 11 as a eucharistic prayer. Philip's crucifixion upside down is obviously modeled after the similar fate of Peter narrated in *Acts of Peter* 38. *Acts of Philip* 3 relies on place names and motifs found in Acts of the Apostles 8 (though Matthews 2002, 168–69, seems to suggest dependence on independent tradition, reflecting a confusion of Philip the evangelist with Philip the apostle).

The *Acts of Philip* contains some Christian traditions that may reach back to the 2d cent. C.E., including Jesus traditions that may be based on much older collections of sayings. One example cited by Bovon (1989, 30) is from *Acts of Philip, Martyrdom* 29:

> At that moment, the Savior appeared and said to Philip: "Who is the one that puts his hand to the plow [Luke 9:62], then looks back and makes his row straight? Or who is the one who gives his lamp to others, and then himself remains sitting in the darkness? . . . Or which athlete runs with ardor in a stadium and does not receive the prize, O Philip? Here, the wedding chamber is ready, blessed is the guest of the spouse, for rich is the harvest of the fields and blessed is the worker who is able.

Another example is the beatitude spoken by Philip in Act 1.3, related to Luke 6:22–23=Matt. 5:11–12: "Blessed are you when people speak every lie against you. Rejoice and be glad, for your reward is great in heaven."

Content. The *Acts of Philip*, in its most complete form, consists of 15 acts, each separately labeled. The structure of *Acts of Philip* falls into two main parts (Amsler 1999, 429–31), reflecting the boundaries of separately written and circulated collections. Acts 1–7 focuses on Philip as the main character and contains a fanciful itinerary, with travels in Galilee (Act 1), "Hellas of Athens" to Parthia (Act 2), Parthia and the region of the Candacians to Azotus (Acts 3–4), and then to Nicatera, apparently an imaginary city in Greece (Acts 5–7). Act 8 narrates the adventures of Philip and others (his sister Mariamne and Bartholomew and the apostle John, as well as a leopard and a goat) on a journey to Ophiorymos (representing Hierapolis) that culminates with Philip's martyrdom. Because of the unavailability of an English translation, a synopsis of the longer text is given below (based on Bovon, Bouvier, and Amsler 1999).

In Act 1, entitled "Act 1 of the holy apostle Philip, when he raised the dead after leaving Galilee," Philip the apostle comes from Galilee and resurrects a dead child, the only son of a widow, by praying over the corpse (perhaps dependent on the story of Jesus' raising of the dead son of the widow of Nain in Luke 7:11–17). The young man, with an interpreting angel (Michael), narrates the terrifying scenes of torment that he has seen in the underworld. The young man and his mother are instrumental in converting many others who are then baptized.

Act 2, entitled "Act 2 of the holy apostle Philip in Hellas of Athens," narrates Philip's arrival in Athens, where 300 philosophers want to hear some new thing [cf. Acts 17] (§§1–2). Philip tells them about Jesus, who came into the world and chose twelve men to preach the good news (§3–4). Wanting three days to discuss the name of Jesus, the philosophers send a letter to Ananias, the high priest in Jerusalem (§§5–7). Ananias, inspired by Mansemat (Satan) goes to Athens with 500 men to kill Philip (§8). Before the assembly, Ananias calls Philip a sorcerer and magician whose master was an imposter (§9). After giving a negative version of the beginnings of Christianity (Jesus was crucified to thwart his teaching and his followers stole his body, but were then driven out of Jerusalem) (§10), Ananias attacks Philip, but his hand withers, and he and his 500 henchmen are blinded (§§11–13). When Ananias still refuses to believe, Jesus miraculously descends from heaven in glory, then ascends again; a great earthquake splits the earth (§§14–16). Ananias still refuses to believe, and after Philip prays, "Zarbarthan, sabathabat, bramaouch [see *Magical Papyri] come quickly!" the stubborn Ananias is swallowed up by the earth slowly and painfully (§§17–23a). Philip then raises a young man from the dead, the 500 henchmen repent and are baptized, and Philip stays in Athens for two years to establish the faith, then leaves for Parthia (§23b–24)

In Act 3, entitled "Act 3 of the holy apostle Philip in Parthia," Philip meets Peter and John and other disciples and is told about the missions of Andrew, Thomas, and Matthew (§§1–2). Philip prepares for his own mission and is given a vision of Christ in the form of a cruciform eagle on a great tree (§§3–6). Jesus then speaks to Philip through the eagle, promising to empower his mission (§§7–9). The ship on which he travels to Azotus is attacked by locusts, who are killed by a cross of light that miraculously appears (§§10–12). After a lengthy prayer (§13) those on the ship witness another miraculous vision (§14). The crew is converted, and when they arrive at Azotus, they announce Philip's arrival (§15). Philip speaks before the city gate, telling how continence, abasement, and pity have beneficial effects on the soul, and urges his audience to forsake the world (§§16–18). Immediately many sick are healed and are baptized.

Act 4, entitled "Act 4 of the holy apostle Philip in Azotos, when he healed Charitine the daughter of Nicocleides," narrates how Philip's fame as a miracle worker and exorcist spreads in Azotus, though some think he is a magician (§§1–2). After miraculously finding a place to stay, he expresses his satisfaction with spiritual rather than physical nourishment (§3). He then heals the right eye of Charitine, the daughter of Nicocleides (§4–6).

Act 5, entitled "Act 5 of the holy apostle Philip in the city of Nikatera," narrates the arrival of Philip and many disciples in Nikatera, where the inhabitants fear that the whole city will follow him (§§1–2). The citizens try to prevent Philip from staying, since he wants husbands and wives to separate (§§3–5). The Jews also oppose Philip, but one of them, named Ireus, counsels moderation, while Philip counsels Ireus to leave his wife (§§6–7). At home, his wife Nercella argues with Ireus about Philip (§§9–11). Philip then visits them at home, knowing about the quarrel, and after Christ appears to Nereus, his wife and daughter also believe, embrace the new celibate lifestyle, and exchange their expensive clothes for more humble attire (§§12–21). Philip is encircled by a great light, the entire household fears him (§§22–23), and he then teaches them humility through beatitudes (§24). Ireus gives Philip and his disciples bread and vegetables to eat, but Philip does not partake (§25). The crowd gathered at Ireus's house believes, and miracles of healing and exorcisms occur (§26).

In "Act 6 of the apostle Philip at Nikatera," Jews and pagans in the city call Philip a magician and are angry that Ireus and his family have believed in Christ (§1). Representatives from the city and their spokesman Onesimus confront Ireus, who is now humbly dressed (§§2–3). Onesimus urges Ireus not to be led astray by teaching that separates married couples, requires chastity, and maintains the resurrection of the dead (§4). The Jews want Philip expelled from the house, but he urges Ireus not to fear (§5). Philip leaves with 300 slaves of Ireus, but the crowd seizes him nonetheless and intends to beat him (§6). Ireus rescues him and demands to know why he deserves a beating (§7). Aristarchus, a prominent citizen and a Jew, wants to have Philip stoned, but before he can act, his hand withers, he becomes deaf, and his right eye is blinded (§§8–11). Aristarchus is healed, and thereafter he and Philip have a short debate (§§12–13), and the crowd acquits Philip (§§14–15). A dead boy named Theophilus is carried in, and Philip challenges Aristarchus to raise him from the dead, but he is unable (§§16–18). Philip then resurrects the boy, with the result that 3,000 people believe (§§19–22).

In "Act 7 of the holy apostle Philip in the city of Nikatera, where Nercella found faith," Ireus and Nereus, the father of the resurrected Theophilus, spend a great deal of money building a synagogue (§§1–2), which the Jews oppose (§3). Philip, entering the new building, urges those present to live in purity (§§4–5). Those present are very sad that Philip must leave and accompany him for some way on his journey (§§6–7). Though the crowd sees no boat, Philip sends them back to the city, and thereupon the audible voice of Jesus tells him that a boat awaits him in the upper harbor (§8).

In "Act 8 of the holy apostle Philip, where the goat and the leopard find faith in the wilderness," Jesus assigns various apostles to different mission regions, but Philip is dissatisfied with his assignment to Hellas (§§1–2a). Mariamne, his sister, intervenes on his behalf, and the Savior orders her and Bartholomew and eventually John to accompany Philip, because he cannot be trusted alone (§§2b–3). Mariamne is ordered to dress like a man and accompany Philip to Opheorymos, where people worship the mother of serpents (§§4–5). The Savior tells them that he will accompany them everywhere and give them protection (§§6–7). Philip is afraid that he will revenge himself on those who persecute him (§8), so the Savior gives him various lessons from nature intended to bolster his resolve to act appropriately (§§9–15). Philip then encounters a leopard who speaks with a human voice and tells Philip that he was about to eat a goat, when the goat urged the leopard to be mild, since the apostles were in the area (§§16–17). The leopard spared the goat, and takes Philip to see it, alive and well (§§18–19). The leopard and the goat then praise God for transforming their wild nature, and Philip lets them accompany their party (§§20–21).

In the very short "Act 9 about the vanquished dragon," Philip, Mariamne, Bartholomew, the leopard, and the goat, after traveling five days, meet a terrifying dragon (§1). After praying and purifying the air with a cup, Bartholomew and Mariamne sprinkle the air with its contents, and the dragon and its offspring are immediately destroyed (§§2–5).

Act 10 and the beginning of Act 11 are lost, including their titles. Act 11 (attested by a single

MS, *Xenophontos 32*) picks up the narrative when Bartholomew and Mariamne are about to celebrate the Eucharist when an earthquake occurs, revealing 50 demons sharing one nature that dwell there (§§1–2). The dragon among them is compelled by Philip to tell his story, beginning with Eden, and Philip then prays that the form of the demons will be revealed (§3–4). The demons depart the broken rocks in the form of 50 snakes, and then after a great earthquake a great dragon appears, questioning Philip's authority. The dragon asks why Philip wants to destroy them and asks to be sent to the mountains of the labyrinth (§§5–6). He offers to build a church, and with the help of the 50 demons he finishes it in six days, transporting 50 huge pillars through the air (perhaps symbolizing the restoration of paradise and alluding to the creation of the world in six days; see Amsler 1999, 347), and more than 3,000 people gather there for worship (§7–8a). Philip then prays and shares the Eucharist with Mariamne and Bartholomew (§8b–10).

In "Act 11 of the holy Philip, when the leopard and the goat request the Eucharist," the leopard and the goat weep because they cannot partake of the Eucharist (§1). The leopard tells the apostle why they are weeping and gives an elaborate argument why they should be given the Eucharist (§§2–5). Philip, recognizing that these animals have spoken the word of God, prays that they will appear in human form (§§6–7). When he sprinkles them with the cup, they immediately take human form and glorify God for what has happened (§8).

"Act 13 of the holy apostle Philip on his arrival in Hierapolis" is a brief episode in which Philip, Bartholomew, and Mariamne see Hierapolis from a mountain, but as they approach it, they encounter seven men with snakes used to distinguish friends from enemies; they bite only the latter (§1). The serpents bow their heads and bite their own tongues, indicating to the seven men that the apostles are not enemies (§2). As Philip's band enters the city gates, the two dragons guarding the city roar at each other and die when Philip looks at them (§3). They take over an abandoned surgery and make it into a center for healing (§4), after which Philip offers an extended prayer (§5).

"Act 14 of the holy apostle Philip on Stachys the blind man" narrates the story of how Stachys and rich man who had been blind 40 years, after hearing Philip's prayer, sought healing from him (§1a). He tells how he had persecuted strangers and excelled in worshiping the viper [ἔχιδνα] and the snakes, but was blinded when he applied some juice from snake eggs to his eyes (§§1b–3). He also relates a dream in which a voice promises that he will regain his sight if he goes to the city gate. When he arrives there, he finds a man with three faces, a youth, a woman, and an old man (§4). Philip prays (§5), and then, using Mariamne's saliva, heals Stachys, who prepares a great dinner for them (§§6–7). The people of the city hear about this and are convinced that the power of God is with these people (§8). Many are healed and exorcised, and Philip baptizes the men, while Mariamne baptizes the women; all are amazed when the leopard and the goat say, "Amen" (§9).

"Act 15 of the holy Apostle Philip concerning Nikanora the wife of the governor" deals with Nikanora, the Syrian wife of the governor, who was bit by one of the snakes when she first came to the city. When she hears of the healing of Stachys, she asks her servants to take her to the apostles (§1). Philip is delivering a sermon to Stachys on the necessity of self-denial, asceticism, and continence and tells him that the house will become a house of prayer (§§2–3). Philip prays that his staff will bud as a sign and means of healing; the staff becomes a laurel and all are amazed (§4). After three jars of food are distributed to the poor (§5), Nikanora forgets her illness in her joy at hearing the word of God, though her servants warn her about how angry her husband will be if he discovers that she was brought to the house of Stachys (§6). At home, Nikanora prays for physical and spiritual healing, and her husband threatens to punish the apostles (§7). This episode is then followed by the story of the martyrdom of Philip, which circulated in several versions.

*Acts, Apocryphal, *Apocrypha, New Testament, *Novel

Amsler, Bovon, and Bouvier 1996; Bovon, Bouvier, and Amsler 1999; Lipsius and Bonnet 1891–1903, 2.vii–98 (text); Matthews 2002; W. Wright 1871, 2.69–92 (Syriac text and trans.); Zahn 1900, 18–24

Acts of Thecla (see *Acts of Paul*)

Acts of Thomas, a work of prose fiction narrating the adventures of Judas Thomas, the twin brother of Jesus (§39), written ca. 200–225, the period of the heyday of the Apocryphal Acts (see *Acts, Apocryphal). The *Acts of Thomas* is part of a Syrian-Christian tradition that includes the *Gospel of Thomas* and emphasizes the role of the apostle Thomas, like the central figures in the other Apocryphal Acts, as a surrogate for Jesus. The *Gospel of Thomas* takes this a step further, since it presents Judas Thomas as the twin brother of Jesus (the term "Thomas" means twin since the Greek form Θωμᾶς is a transliteration of the Aramaic word *t'ôma'*). As the narrative unfolds, Jesus is sometimes seen by people (sometimes invisible to those around) as a look-alike of Thomas (§54). Both the *Gospel of Thomas* and the *Acts of Thomas* seem to have arisen in Syria and were part of an extensive interest in the figure of Thomas that some have described as a "School of Thomas" or "the Thomas authority" (Crossan 1991, 427). Another Thomas work is the Coptic-gnostic *Book of Thomas the Contender*.

Text and translations. Unlike the rest of the Apocryphal Acts, the *Gospel of Thomas* is preserved in its entirety in a 7th-cent. Syriac MS and an 11th-cent. Greek MS, as well as in many fragments. The Syriac text was edited and translated by W. Wright (1871), but is considered less reliable than the Greek text. The Greek text, edited by Lipsius and Bonnet (1891–1903, II.2.99–288), is based on 21 Greek MSS, of which the most important are the Codex Vallicellian B 35, at Rome and a Paris codex from the 11th or 12th cent. That the Greek text is a translation from the Syriac is the general view of scholarship (see the review in Attridge 1990b). English translations are available in *NTA* 2.339–411 and J. K. Elliott 1996, 447–511.

Literary character. The *Gospel of Thomas* is a fictional work whose only two historical figures are "Judas Thomas," one of the traditional disciples of Jesus, and King Gundaphorus (attested by coins to have ruled in India during the 1st cent. C.E.). Though the bulk of the *Acts of Thomas* is set in India, there is a striking lack of local color, none of the cities visited are named, and apart from king Gundaphorus, none of the names are even remotely Indian. The characters are generally relatively flat (see *character) with two exceptions. In Act 1 Judas Thomas acts in an unpredictable and surprising way by refusing the commission to evangelize India, even when he is asked to do so directly by Jesus in a supernatural appearance. However, this behavior is typical of the motif of the reluctant emissary (see examples below). The only truly "round" character in the work is Charisius, whose wife Mygdonia has been alienated from him when she embraced the gospel of celibacy proclaimed by Thomas. Though a pagan, the author depicts Charisius as a three-dimensional, complex character who has both good and bad characteristics, though the good is dominant (analogous to Hector in the *Iliad*). Charisius's emotional appeals to his beloved wife, Mygdonia, pleading with her to behave toward him as she did formerly, are extremely well depicted, and the reader responds with empathy to his plight (see *pathos).

The story emphasizes miracles, including a surrogate resurrection (§§53–54; Thomas tells the young man what to say to the girl he killed to raise her from the dead) and exorcisms (§§20, 75). Like the tours of hell in the *Apocalypses* of Paul and Peter, the *Acts of Thomas* narrates the story of a woman who returns from the dead and relates a terrifying tour of hell (§§55–58). Among the wonders narrated are a talking serpent (§31) and talking asses (§§74, 78–79). Though the work is often labeled "Gnostic," that designation primarily fits the Hymn of the Pearl (§§109–13) and does not accurately reflect the character of the rest of the *Acts of Thomas*, which appears rather to reflect a popular type of Christianity that was probably widespread in the eastern Mediterranean area.

Literary analysis and précis. The *Acts of Thomas* consists of thirteen acts narrating the fictional adventures of Judas Thomas, the twin brother of Jesus (*Acts of Thomas* 39). Act 1, "How the Lord sold him to the merchant Abban, that he might go down and convert India," contains two linked episodes. The first features the motif of the reluctant emissary (cf. Moses in Exod. 3:7–4:17; Gideon in Judg. 6:11–24; Saul in 1 Sam. 9:15–21; Jeremiah in Jer. 1:4–7; Philip in *Acts of Philip* 8) and begins with the apostles dividing up the regions of the world for missionary work (with a close parallel in *Acts of Philip* 8). Judas Thomas gets India, but refuses to go, even though the Savior appears to him and encourages him to go. Jesus then sells Thomas to Abban, an Indian merchant sent by King Gundaphorus, for his skills as a carpenter and stonemason. In the second episode (centering on a punitive miracle that reveals Thomas to be a holy man), they arrive in India and participate in a feast, but Thomas neither eats nor drinks, saying that "For something greater than food or drink am I come hither and that I may accomplish the king's will" (§5). A Hebrew flute girl approaches him (only she can understand his Hebrew), and he is slapped by a cupbearer, whose hand he predicts will be dragged away by dogs. He then sings a beautiful wedding hymn in Hebrew about "the daughter of light" (§§6–7; see

Marcovich 1988), and thereafter the Hebrew flute girl has eyes only for him. The cupbearer, attempting to draw water from a well, is killed by a lion and torn to pieces, and a black dog takes his mangled right hand into the feast (§8). The flute girl, realizing that Thomas's prediction has come true, smashes her flute and sits at the feet of Thomas, telling everyone that what he had prophesied in Hebrew has been fulfilled. In the third episode (focusing on Philip's message of celibacy), the king asks Thomas to pray for his daughter, who was about to be married, but must take Thomas forcibly (§9). Thomas then prays for the couple (§10). Jesus then appears in the bridal chamber to the king and the couple in the likeness of Thomas (the first in a series of such appearances) and urges them to abandon filthy intercourse, since physical children often turn out badly, while spiritual children befit a true marriage (§§11–12). Both the bride and the bridegroom choose to remain celebate (§§13–15). The king, angry, gives orders that the sorcerer be arrested, but Thomas has already left. He finds the flute girl, who also claims to find rest, and continues to teach in "the cities of India" (§16).

Act 2, "Concerning his coming to King Gundaphorus," which begins with the resumptive mention of "the cities of India," is a single episode, an elaborate dramatization of the sentiment found in Matt. 6:19–20: Do not lay up treasure on earth, but treasure in heaven (confirmed by allusions to Matt. 6 in §28). Thomas is presented to King Gundaphorus, who interviews him about his trade, and Thomas agrees to build the king a palace (§17). The king shows Thomas the site; he refuses to start building immediately but traces out a plan on the ground that greatly pleases the king, who leaves him with building funds (§18). Thomas, rather than building, distributes the money to the poor. When the king asks about the project, Thomas tells him that only the roof remains to be finished. The king sends yet more money, and Thomas continues to distribute it to the poor (§19). When the king arrives, his friends tell him that no palace has been built but that Thomas has given the money to the poor, taught them about a new God, and driven out demons. The king is shocked (§20) and sends for the merchant and Thomas to inquire about his palace. Thomas replies that he has built it but that the king cannot see it until the next life. The king imprisons both and, encouraged by his dying brother, Gad, intends to flay them alive and burn them (§21). Now Gad dies and in heaven was shown the palace that Thomas has built for the king. He asks to return to earth to try to buy it from his brother (§22). Gad revives on earth, to the amazement of the king, and asks to buy his heavenly palace (§23). The king refuses but suggests that Gad have Thomas build him one as well. The king, summoning the merchant and Thomas from prison, begs their forgiveness (§24). Thomas then offers a long prayer of thanksgiving and asks for the protection of the king and his brother (§25). Gundaphorus and Gad then follow Thomas, accept his teaching, and beg him to give them the seal (§26). Thomas anoints them with oil and recites a nine-line invocation, each line beginning with "Come!" (see *Epanaphora). The scene ends with the vision of a young man with a blazing torch symbolizing the fact that the Lord is their light (§27). Thomas then preaches a threefold message of abstinence from fornication, greed, and gluttony, alluding to Matt. 6:34; 6:26; 6:30 (§28). Thomas, told by the Lord in a dream to leave the city, celebrates the Eucharist with those with him (§29).

Act 3, "Concerning the serpent," focuses on a single episode in which a serpent, an embodiment of evil in the universe, is conquered in a transparently allegorical story (see *Allegory). Thomas leaves the town and discovers the body of a young man near the road (§30). A large serpent comes out of a hole and claims to have killed the youth and explains why. One day he had seen the youth have sex with a girl on the Lord's Day and killed him that evening for what he had done. Thomas asks who he is (§31), and the snake replies with a series of "I am" predications (see *Epanaphora) revealing a series of incarnations in which he was the snake in the garden of Eden, the one who hardened Pharaoh's heart, the one who led the Israelites astray in the wilderness, and so on (§32). Thomas then commands the snake to suck the poison out of the youth, who then revives. The snake, however, bloated with venom, explodes and dies and is swallowed up by a great chasm (§33). The youth reveals how he had seen two people, Thomas and someone else telling Thomas to resurrect the youth (i.e., Jesus, the twin of Thomas). The youth then gives a long monologue about how he has been freed from sin and evil and begs to see the Son of Truth again (§34). Thomas encourages him to persevere in his resolve (§35), and taking him by the hand goes to the city, all the while teaching him about the life of temperance and abstinence, using several allusions to the

Gospels, including Matt. 19:23; 11:8; Luke 21:34; Matt. 6:25 (§36). A crowd joins the youth, and Thomas urges them to abandon their former materialistic life and embrace a new abstemious one by believing in the Lord Jesus Christ (§37). The crowd, speaking with one voice, agrees to follow God if he will forgive them, and Thomas replies that he is always ready to forgive transgressions committed ignorantly (§38).

Act 4, "Concerning the colt," resumes with Thomas before the crowd mentioned in §38, also referring to the Eucharist with which Act 5 concludes. When a young man who had committed a wicked deed takes the Eucharist, both hands wither. Thomas tells the youth that the Lord's Eucharist, often a source of healing, has convicted him of an evil deed. The youth falls at the apostle's feet and tells him that he and a certain woman are in love. After believing Thomas's message and receiving the seal, he tries to persuade his girlfriend to live in chastity. When she refuses, he kills her with a sword (§51). After a brief righteous tirade, Thomas calls for a basin of water and tells the man to wash. His hands are immediately restored, and he professes to believe that the Lord Jesus is able to do all things (§52). Thomas has the man take him to the inn where the body of the woman lies. After she is placed on a bed, Thomas lays his hands on her and prays that she be raised to life, since Jesus has said "Ask, and it shall be given to you, seek and ye shall find, knock and it shall be opened unto you" [Matt. 7:7] (§53). Thomas tells the man to take her by the hand and say, "I with my hands killed you with iron, and with my hands by faith in Jesus I raise you up." Immediately she comes to life, and asks Thomas where that other person is who delivered her to Thomas requesting that she be made perfect (§54), another reference to Jesus appearing as Thomas's twin. Thomas asks her where she has been, and she relates a frightening visit to hell, escorted by a black dirty figure, where she saw people tormented for various sins (§§55–56). Her escort did not leave her there because he was ordered to deliver her to Thomas's twin. She then begs Thomas not to let her go to the places of punishment that she visited (§57). Thomas tells those assembled that there are even worse punishments for those who do not forsake all evil practices and appeals to them to "put off the old man and put on the new" [Col. 3:19] (§58). All the people believe and bring money for the relief of widows, which he distributes through his deacons. Thomas does not cease teaching and preaching Jesus the Christ whom the Scriptures have proclaimed and explains, "beginning from the prophets, the things concerning Christ, that he must come and that in him all that been prophesied concerning him must be fulfilled" [Luke 24:27], and many are healed (§59). Thomas then offers a lengthy prayer of praise to Christ (§§60–61).

Act 7: "Concerning the captain," though containing no formal links with what has preceded, begins a series of interlinked episodes that continue through Act 13. Act 7 is specifically linked to the following two episodes in Acts 8 and 9, by the character of the captain, whom we later learn is named Siphor. This episode begins when Thomas is approached by a captain of King Misdaeus. A wealthy man with a wife and daughter, he sends them to a wedding put on by close friends, though they don't want to go (§62). In the evening, he sends an escort to fetch them, but finds that a tragedy has occurred, for he learns that a man and a boy [demons] have attacked the two women, who flee them but fall to the ground writhing. Finding them prostrate in the marketplace, the captain brings them home, where they are revived (§63). The captain asks them what has happened, and the wife relates how she and her daughter saw a black, filthy man and his son on the way to the wedding but managed to avoid them. On the way back, the ugly pair struck them down. As soon as she had said this, the demons attacked them again. Consequently he has had to keep them confined for the last three years (§64). Thomas encourages the captain to commit himself to Jesus, who will be able to heal the women, which he does. Thomas then has Xenophon the deacon assemble the people (§65), and Thomas delivers a farewell address (§66), after which he prays that the Lord will be with Xenophon's flock. Laying his hands on them, Thomas says, "The peace of the Lord be upon you and go with us" (§67).

In Act 8: "Concerning the wild asses," Thomas, who is seated on a wagon, is about to depart when the captain begs the driver for the privilege of driving Thomas's wagon (§68). After a while, Thomas asks the captain to sit with him, but as they continue, the asses become overheated and stop, and Thomas promises the distressed captain a miracle. On seeing a herd of wild asses, Thomas tells the captain that, if he believes in Jesus, he should tell the asses that "Judas Thomas, the apostle of Christ the new God, says to you, Let four of you come, of whom we have need" (§69). The apprehensive captain does as he is told; the whole herd comes and wants to be yoked to the wagon, but Thomas takes the four strongest and dismisses the rest (§70). Arriving at the captain's house where the whole city is assembled (§71), Thomas disembarks and offers a prayer to Jesus (§72). The crowd gathers to see Thomas, who tells one of the wild asses to call the demons forth from the city, which it does in a short speech (§§73–74). When the women emerge from their house, Thomas addresses the demons, "In the name of Jesus, depart from them and stand by their side." The women immediately fall down dead, and one of the demons addresses Thomas in a sneering tone (§75) and relates how inversely similar their missions are (§76). Thomas commands the demons to depart and never enter into humans again. After a futile objection, the demons disappear, leaving the women lying in the ground as if dead (§77). The wild ass whom Thomas sent to address the demons then addresses Thomas and exhorts him to perform mighty works (§78), and enjoins the crowd to believe in the apostle of Jesus Christ and provides a short summary of Thomas's message (§79). Thomas, claiming no power to declare who Jesus is, gives a brief review of who he is and what he has done (§80) and then prays over the prostrate women, who arise and are led into the captain's house. After this Thomas leads the wild asses safely out of town and returns to the captain's house (§81).

In Act 9, "Concerning the wife of Charisius," Mygdonia, the wife of Charisius, a close relative of the king, wants to see Thomas; finding it difficult, she gets a larger contingent of servants from her husband to help push people out of the way and is rebuked for these tactics by Thomas (§82). Turning to her bearers, he tells them that they are unjustly burdened (§83) and urges them to abstain from all evils, including sexual intercourse, "the mother-city of all evils" (§84), but to walk in holiness and meekness (§85–86). Mygdonia springs from her chariot and prostrates herself before Thomas, begging him that the compassion of God will come upon her and she may be sealed and become a holy temple (§87). Thomas addresses Mygdonia, telling her that physical beauty and adornment is worthless before God, and then dismisses her, telling her that Jesus will be present with her (§88). Meanwhile, Charisius comes home for dinner and asks about his wife. Being told that she is ill, he goes to her and asks her to dine with him, but she refuses either to eat with him or to have sex with him (§89–90). Charisius then relates a dream to his wife: he and king Misdaeus were eating together when an eagle snatched the two partridges they were eating; though the king tried to kill the eagle when he returned, it was unharmed (§91). After dressing, Charisius asks Mygdonia the meaning of the dream, but she gives him a vague answer (§92). Mygdonia then visits Thomas, who is telling the captain and the crowd about her situation, but also that her husband will not be able to harm her if she remains faithful to the Lord (§93). Mygdonia, addressing Thomas, promises to remain faithful; Thomas then pronounces a series of eleven beatitudes, confirming Mygdonia in the faith (§94). Meanwhile, when Charisius comes home, his wife is gone. A servant tells him that she went to visit the stranger, but when Mygdonia arrives and Charisius asks where she has been, she replies, "To the doctor." "Is the stranger a doctor?" he retorts. "Yes," she says, "a physician of souls." When Charisius dines, his wife refuses to join him (§95). Charisius then confronts Mygdonia, suspicious that she will not eat or have sex with him, and blames Thomas, who is accused of sorcery (§96). Charisius goes to dinner without Mygdonia, who remains in her room praying that she will not have to have sex with Charisius (§97). After dinner, Charisius comes to her room, tells her he is through with her, but attempts to have sex with her anyway; but she cries out in prayer to Jesus for protection and then flees from him naked (§98). In despair, Charisius soliloquizes about his problems, mourning the loss of his wife and intending to ask the king to deal with the problem (§§99–100). The next day, Charisius dresses shabbily and goes to tell the king about his problem. He accuses Thomas of teaching that eternal life is possible only for those who rid themselves of their wives or husbands and asks that he be killed (§101). King Misdaeus promises to take care of Thomas and get Charisius's wife back, but learns that both Siphor, the captain of the guard, and Mygdonia are sitting at the feet of Thomas. In response to messengers from the king, Siphor returns to Misdaeus (§102). Thomas then speaks with Mygdonia and finds out that Charisius is angry because she refused to have sex with him; Thomas responds that Jesus will work out all her problems (§103). Meanwhile, Siphor is being interrogated by the king about Thomas and is given a positive account of his teachings (§105). The king then sends soldiers to Siphor's house, but they are afraid to act because of the crowd. Charisius then goes himself and finds Thomas, but Mygdonia has already left for home (§106). Charisius arrests Thomas after denouncing him as a magician (§107). Thomas is led to prison, rejoicing that he has been called a sorcerer and magician for the sake of Jesus (§108). In prison he recites the 105-line Hymn of the Pearl (§109–13). Charisius goes home thinking that everything will be as it was but finds his wife with her hair shorn and her garments torn, and promises her that Thomas will be dealt with (§114). Mygdonia responds with lamentation, and Charisius declares his undying love for her and cannot understand why everything has changed between them; he laments that Thomas has taken his real riches, his wife Mygdonia, from him (§§115–16). Mygdonia then professes her great love for her heavenly Lord and declares that all wealth and beauty are transient. In response, Charisius promises that if things return to the way they were before, he will have Thomas released from prison and sent to another country (§117). Mygdonia goes to bribe the guards to let her see Thomas but meets him on the way, proceeded by a great light, but takes him for one of the rulers, and goes off and hides herself in the city (§118).

Act 10, "How Mygdonia receives baptism," continues the narrative from Act 9 without interruption. Thomas appears standing over Mygdonia, exhorting her not to be afraid, for Jesus will not desert her. Mygdonia is amazed that Thomas is out of prison (§119). She requests the seal of Jesus Christ and takes Thomas to visit her nurse Marcia, from whom she requests a loaf of bread, wine mixed with water, and oil (§120). Thomas then baptizes Mygdonia in a spring of water nearby, and they offer her the Eucharist and give her the seal (§121). Returning to prison, Thomas finds the doors open but the guards still sleeping; when they awake, they see the open doors and wonder if the prisoners are still inside (§122). At dawn, Charisius goes to Mygdonia and overhears her invoking God to turn the anger of Charisius away. He tells her again that Thomas is a sorcerer who will do her no good (§123), and Mygdonia tells him that earthly marriage passes away but heavenly marriage, with Jesus as bridegroom, lasts forever (§124). Charisius then goes to the king, who commands that Thomas be brought to him for execution (§125), but when Thomas arrives the king interrogates him, objecting to his teaching that people must maintain purity for God. Thomas replies that servants of the king must be holy, pure, and free from all grief and care for children, etc. (§126). Impressed with this answer, Misdaeus releases Thomas and demands that he bring concord to the marriage of Mygdonia and Charisius (§127). Charisius then approaches Thomas and offers him anything if he will restore his relationship to his wife; if not, he promises to kill Thomas and commit suicide (§128). Arriving at Charisius's house, they find Mygdonia wishing for death so that she may go "where there is neither day nor night, nor light and darkness, nor good and evil, nor poor and rich, male and female, no free and slave, no proud that subdues the humble" (§129). Thomas then commands Mygdonia to obey Charisius, but she refuses, and he threatens to chain her up (§130). Thomas returns to the house of Siphor, who expresses the desire of his family to live in holiness and purity (§131). After giving a short homily on baptism, Thomas anoints them with oil, and baptizes them with water from a basin (§132), followed by the Eucharist (§133).

In Act 11, "Concerning the wife of Misdaeus," when Misdaeus frees Thomas, he goes home to tell his wife Tertia about the misfortune that has befallen Charisius, how his wife has been alienated by the sorcerer. He suggests that she try to persuade Mygdonia to be reconciled to her husband (§134). Tertia immediately goes to visit Mygdonia, finds her praying in sackcloth and ashes on the floor, and begs her to become reconciled for the sake of honor to Charisius. Mygdonia relates to her the difference between transient materialistic values and eternal values (§135). Tertia begs Mygdonia to take her to Thomas so that she may hear him and worship his God. Mygdonia sends Tertia to the house of Siphor, where she meets Thomas and asks to become a partaker of life, and he tells her that God freely gives of his riches (§136). Tertia returns home and tells her husband about the teaching of the apostle of God. Misdaeus is angry with himself and Charisius, whom he blames for his wife's disaffection (§137). Misdaeus goes out and finds Charisius in the market, where he chews him out because Thomas has bewitched Tertia. They both go to the house of Siphor, where they find Thomas. Misdaeus hits him with a chair and has his soldiers drag him off to the place of judgment (§138).

In Act 12, "Concerning Vazan, the son of Misdaeus," Vazan tries to reason with Thomas and tells him the influence he has with his father. Thomas responds that Misdaeus is king for a season, but Jesus Christ is an eternal king. Thomas contrasts their two lifestyles: he boasts in poverty, humility, fasting, and prayer, while Vazan boasts in possessions, slaves, robes, and impure sexual relations (§139).

Vazan is persuaded and tries to release Thomas, but Misdaeus arrives and has Thomas brought before him bound, and begins to interrogate him. The king is annoyed and orders iron plates heated to put on the bare feet of Thomas. When they put the plates on his feet, water gushes from the ground, swallowing up the plates (§140). Afraid, the king asks Thomas to pray to God to save him from the flood. Thomas prays and immediately the water is consumed. Misdaeus then has Thomas taken back to prison (§141). Thomas is accompanied to the prison by Vazan and Siphor and the women to hear the word of life. Thomas gives a farewell address, knowing that he will soon die (§142–43). He then stands and recites the Lord's Prayer as an introduction to a longer prayer (§144–49).

In Act 13, "How Vazan receives baptism with the others," Vazan then appeals to Thomas to come home with him, with the guards' permission, so that he may receive the seal. Though he has been married seven years, Vazan claims that he and his wife have lived chastely and will continue to do so (§150). Meanwhile, Tertia, Mygdonia, and Marcia arrive and bribe the guard to be let in to see Thomas (§152). Tertia relates how the king believed that she had not yet been bewitched by the oil, water, and bread of Thomas, but when she said that he had power over her body but not her soul, he shut her up in a room, and Charisius shut Mygdonia up with her. However, "Thomas" (i.e., Jesus) let them out and brought them here. She then requests the seal to thwart Misdaeus (§152). While Thomas praises Jesus for appearing in his form, the guard appears and tells them to extinguish all lights, since the king is coming. In the dark, Thomas prays for enlightenment and immediately the prison is illuminated (§153). Vazan leads the others out of the prison, since the doors are miraculously open, and when he is out, he meets his wife Mnesara, who claims that a young man is leading her by the right hand to visit the stranger (§154). When they all arrive at Vazan's house, Mnesara recognizes Thomas as the man who has led her to the prison (§155). Thomas then prays, giving a brief narrative of the salvific work of Christ, specifically for Vazan, Tertia, and Mnesara (§156). Thomas then pours oil on the heads of Vazan, Tertia, and Mnesara, saying, "In thy name, Jesus Christ, let it be to these souls for remission of sins, and for the turning back of the adversary, and for salvation of their souls." He then baptizes them in water in the name of the Father and of the Son and of the Holy Spirit (§157). Following their baptism he offers them the Eucharist (§158).

The final section of the *Acts of Thomas* is "The martyrdom of the holy and esteemed apostle Thomas," which may have circulated separately. Continuing the narrative from Act 13, Thomas, accompanied by Tertia, Mygdonia, and Marcia, goes to the prison, where he gives them another brief farewell address. (§160–61). He is then taken into the dark house in the prison, leaving the grieving women (§162). The guards complain to the king that even though they lock the doors, they find them open, with all of the friends of Thomas able to visit him. The king inspects the locks and accuses the guards of lying (§162). Thomas is hauled before Misdaeus, who again interrogates him, and Thomas tells him that his master is Lord of heaven and earth. Misdaeus tells Thomas that he will destroy his sorcery with him (§163). Misdaeus has four armed soldiers escort Thomas out of the city, intending to kill him with spears on the mountain (§164). Upon reaching the place of execution (§165), Thomas appeals to his captors to believe in God and thereby to become truly free men (§166). The guards, persuaded by Vazan, allow Thomas to go off and pray (§167), after which he bids the soldiers to do their duty. They immediately spear him to death (§168). Siphor and Vazan remain on the mountain overnight, where Thomas appears to them saying, "I am not here. Why do you sit here and watch over me? For I have gone up and received what was hoped for" (§169). Some time later, one of Misdaeus's sons is possessed by a demon, and his father thinks that if the bones of Thomas are put on him, he may be healed. Thomas appears to him asking why, if he did not believe in the living, he could believe in the dead. Misdaeus cannot find the bones, however, for the brothers took them away to the west. However, Misdaeus takes dust from the tomb, and when he applies it to his son, he is healed. When this happens, Misdaeus comes to Siphor and the brothers and prays for mercy from Jesus Christ.

*Acts, Apocryphal, *Apocrypha, New Testament, *Novel, *Thomas, Gospel of

---

Attridge 1990b; J, K. Elliott, 1996, 447–511; *NTA* 2.322–4.11; Klijn 1962; Marcovich 1988

Adam, Apocalypse of (see *Nag Hammadi literature)

Adam and Eve, Lives of The biblical account of Adam and Eve in Gen. 2–4 evoked a large body of commentary and interpretation in early Jewish and Christian literature (treated up to Milton by J. M. Evans 1968), of which the most important items are the Greek and Latin *Lives of Adam and Eve*. The Greek version was incorrectly designated the "Apocalypse of Moses" by Tischendorf (1866 reprinted in 1966), because of its introductory line (trans. M. Johnson 1983–85, 2.259): "The narrative and life of Adam and Eve the first-made, revealed by God to Moses his servant when he received the tablets of the law of the covenant from the hand of the Lord, after he had been taught by the archangel Michael." However, since Moses is not mentioned elsewhere in this work, and it is not an *apocalypse, a more appropriate title is the Greek *Life of Adam and Eve* (*GLAE*). The Latin version, "Vita Adam et Evae," will be referred to as the Latin *Life of Adam and Eve* (*LLAE*). Among the complex issues surrounding the books of Adam and Eve are date, provenance, and the relationship of the many manuscripts and translations to one another. There is general consensus that a shorter form of the *GLAE* constituted the earliest form of the work, vaguely dated between 100 and 600 C.E. The Latin version is related to the Armenian and Georgian, which may have a common ancestor in the longer Greek version (de Jonge and Tromp 1997, 35–40). It is clear that an early form of the work underwent a long and complicated process of evolution, addition, and compression.

All of the manuscripts of the *Life of Adam and Eve* (*LAE*) were preserved by Christians, but this has little bearing on the question of whether the work has a Christian origin. For much of the 20th cent. scholars held that the extant manuscripts of the *LAE* were recensions of a Hebrew or Aramaic version (M. Johnson 1983–85, 2.251) and therefore of Jewish origin, but that view began to be disputed (Stone 1992, 58–61). Following Stone, many commentators on the *LAE* believe that it was originally written in Greek. The issue of Jewish or Christian authorship is still problematic. Although almost all versions of the *LAE* contain references to Christ or specifically Christian themes, this does not negate the possibility that Christians redacted an earlier Jewish work. On the other hand, the fact that the earliest form of the work, the shorter Greek manuscript, does not contain any Christian references does not necessarily prove it to be a Jewish work. While the Greek and Latin versions of the *LAE* have much material in common, there are also significant differences between the two. These similarities and differences involve literary genre, constituent literary forms, and the special treatment of certain themes. Both the Greek and Latin lives can be categorized generically as forms of *Rewritten Bible, since they rework the narrative in Gen. 2–4. *LAE* begins after the expulsion of the first human couple from the garden par-

Comparision of the *GLAE* with the *LLAE*

	GLAE	*LLAE*
1. Adam and Eve search for food and repent by standing in the Jordan and Tigris rivers.	—	1–8
2. Satan, disguised as an angel, convinces Eve to curtail her penitence.	—	9–11
3. Satan explains his fall and consequent enmity toward Adam.	—	12–17
4. Eve escapes death and bears Cain by means of Adam's intercession.	—	18–22
5. Eve bears (Cain [*GLAE* 1:3]), Abel, Seth, etc.	1:1–5:1	23–24
6. Adam reveals to Seth his rapture to paradise to see God.	—	25–29
7. Adam, on his deathbed, sends Eve and Seth on an unsuccessful quest for the oil of mercy.	5:2–14:3	30–44
8. Eve exhorts her children to obey by recounting the temptation by Satan and expulsion from paradise.	15–30	—
9. Adam dies.	31–32	45
10. Adam is pardoned.	33–37	46
11. Adam is buried.	38:1–42:2	47–48
12. Eve commands her children to preserve her and Adam's life on tablets of stone and clay.	—	49:1–50:2
13. Eve dies and is buried.	42:3–43:4	50:3–51:3

adise (Gen. 3:24) gives an important role to Seth, the youngest named child of Adam and Eve (Gen. 4:25–26), whose death and burial is narrated. However, the *LLAE* contains a number of traditions not found in the *GLAE,* while the *GLAE* has a discourse delivered by Eve that is not found in the *LLAE.* Levison (1992) has produced a chart *(see p. 27)* illustrating many of the shared and unique sections of the Greek and Latin *Lives*.

Both Lives assume the "fall" of the first couple for eating the forbidden fruit, but only the *GLAE* relates the story of human disobedience in any detail. While the above chart notes Eve's long discourse about those events in the *GLAE* (No. 8), it does not mention Adam's much shorter discourse in *GLAE* 5–8 (parallel *LLAE* 30–34). These speeches are examples of the *farewell address or *testament, in which an ancient worthy delivers a deathbed address to his (or more rarely, her) assembled children, then dies and is buried. The typical testament consists of *paraenesis or moral exhortation, illustrated by events from the speaker's life. As de Jonge and Tromp observe (1997, 46), the use of the farewell discourse in the *GLAE* differs from other examples of the form in two respects: (1) it contains two farewell speeches, and (2) the second speech is delivered not by the dying Adam, but "vicariously" by Eve. Eve, however, does not deliver a farewell discourse before her own death. The fictional rationale for Eve's vicarious delivery of this discourse is due to Adam's weakened condition. Its underlying purpose is to stick Eve with the responsibility for giving in to temptation, which has resulted in pain and death for Adam and the rest of humankind. The discourse itself is a flashback to the garden of Eden, consisting of a reworking of the temptation story and its consequences, serving as warnings to their children.

One of the more interesting aspects of the *LAE* in both Greek and Latin is the treatment of the character of Eve. In the *GLAE* 32, Eve emphasizes her sin, crying out that she has sinned greatly before the Lord, and that all sin has come about through her. The *LLAE* exonerates Adam and denigrates Eve in a series of events that do not appear in the *GLAE*. Three examples: (1) Eve asks Adam to kill her, reasoning that if this happens the Lord will allow Adam to reenter paradise, but he rather rebukes her (3). (2) Satan in the form of an angel deceives Eve yet again while she performs her penance in the River Tigris (9–11), but Adam completes his penance (17). (3) Eve is unable to give birth to Cain until Adam intercedes for her (19–22). None of these events has a parallel in the *GLAE*. Levison (1989) argues that Eve's account of the primeval deception, transgression, and expulsion from paradise in *GLAE* 15–30 originated independently from chapters 1–14 and 31–43: (1) The exoneration of Eve in 15–30 contrasts with her denigration elsewhere. (2) Distinctive views of paradise in *GLAE* 15–30 differentiate that section from the rest of the work. (3) *GLAE* 15–30 has the features of an independent narrative that was later incorporated into *GLAE*.

Just as in their treatment of the character of Eve, *GLAE* and *LLAE* share similar overall themes but have different specific emphases. While both works are greatly concerned with illness, death, and the mercy of God, the *LLAE* emphasizes human penitence (1–8, 10, 27, 40), which receives little attention in the *GLAE*. The *GLAE* places some emphasis on resurrection, promised by God in 28:4 and 41:3, but the *LLAE* does not mention resurrection at all. Both versions, however, were attempted to address the fundamental problems and hopes of humanity represented by Adam and Eve.

*Pseudepigrapha, Jewish, *Rewritten Bible, *Testament

Anderson and Stone (eds.) 1999; Anderson, Stone, and Tromp 2000; De Jonge and Tromp 1997; J. M. Evans 1968; M. D. Johnson 1983–85; Knittel 2002; Levison 1988, 1989, 1992, 2000; Stone 1992; Tischendorf 1966 [1866], x–xii, 1–23 (Greek text)

LESLIE BAYNES

Ad Herennium (see **Herennium, Rhetorica ad*)

Admonition is a type of negative exhortation in which people are warned against taking a particular course of action or against behaving in a particular way (Gammie 1990, 58).

*Paraenesis

Gammie 1990

Agrapha, a transliteration of the plural form of the Greek adjective ἄγραφον, meaning "unwritten," refers to sayings of Jesus *not* found in the canonical gospels. The term is not wholly appropriate, however, for it gives the mistaken impression that such sayings are oral rather than written, whereas they have obviously been preserved in written form largely as fragmentary quotations in early Christian literature. Usually sayings attributed to the preexistent or resurrected Jesus are not considered *agrapha* because they are not presented as sayings of the historical Jesus (Hofius, 355–56; *NTA* 1.89). Toward the end of the 19th cent. Alfred Resch (1882) collected some 300 such *agrapha*, of which he considered only 36 to be genuine sayings of Jesus. A few years later, Ropes (1896) critically evaluated the work of Resch, concluding that he had been far too optimistic, and stated that only 14 agrapha that Resch had collected were probably authentic, while 13 were possibly authentic. Both scholars were primarily concerned with the question of authenticity, though that is but one of many issues. More recently, Jeremias reexamined the whole question of the *agrapha*, and concluded that while 21 sayings are compatible with the Synoptic tradition, only 11 are genuine sayings of Jesus (J. Jeremias 1964, 21–22). Finally, Stroker (1989) has assembled a collection of extracanonical sayings of Jesus, making use of Bultmann's form critical categories and including texts, translations, and parallel passages for 42 apophthegms, 17 parables, 60 prophetic and apocalyptic sayings, 39 wisdom sayings, 61 I-sayings, and 47 community rules, i.e., a total of 266 sayings of Jesus. No attempt has been made to judge their historical authenticity.

*Apocryphal NT, *Gospels, apocryphal, **Gospel of Thomas*

Jeremias 1964; Resch 1906; Ropes 1896; Stroker 1981, 1988, 1989

Alexander Romance, a Greek *novel written between 140 and 340 C.E. (perhaps ca. 300 C.E.; Reardon 1989, 650), falsely ascribed to Callisthenes, the court historian of Alexander the Great (hence the author is sometimes referred to as Ps.-Callisthenes). The work was enormously popular in antiquity and exists in about 80 versions in 24 languages. The manuscript history of the work is extremely complex, for scribes freely added and subtracted from the work as they transmitted it, making the reconstruction of the original text very difficult if not impossible. The work was compiled from three main sources (Merkelbach 1977): (a) a "biography" of Alexander (Hägg 1983, 115); (b) a fictional work that perhaps dates to the late 2d or early 1st cent. B.C.E., consisting of a "novel-in-letters" or epistolary novel consisting of an exchange of fictitious letters between Alexander and others; and (c) a number of longer letters from Alexander to Olympia (his mother) and Aristotle (his teacher).

Hägg 1983, 125–40; Merkelbach 1977; Reardon 1989, 650–735

Alexandrian canon Aristophanes of Byzantium (ca. 257–180 C.E.), a famous grammarian and librarian at the museum in Alexandria (ca. 195 B.C.E.), apparently drew up lists of "selected" or "approved" authors (the kind of literature now referred to as "classics"). The main evidence for this "canon" is found in Quintilian (1.4.3; 10.1.53–72). The term for choosing and recording the name of particular authors on a list was ἐγκρίνειν ("to select, admit"), hence those so selected were called ἐγκριθέντες ("those selected"). Since 1768 (Pfeiffer 1918, 1.207) classical scholars have used the term "Alexandrian canon" for this catalog of more than 80 classical authors, which included five epic poets, ten orators, nine lyric poets, five tragic poets, and so on. A list of the canon of nine lyric poets (see next page), which covers a 200-year period from 650 to 450 B.C.E., is preserved in *Anth. Pal.* 9.184, an anonymous epigram of uncertain date. The so-called "canon of ten Attic orators" (Quintilian 10.1.76; see *Orators, Attic) does not go back to the Alexandrian grammarians, but appears to have been first formulated by the 1st-cent. B.C.E. Augustan critic Caecilius of Kale Akte in Sicily, who wrote a treatise "On the Style of the Ten Orators" (Schmid and Stählin 1920–24, 2.28–29; esp. 29 n. 1; Worthington 1994, 254–59). The works on these lists were intended to serve as models of style and composition. The Alexandrian canon had both positive and negative effects on ancient literature. The works of "approved" authors were read in schools and by the educated; they were copied, recopied, and commented upon, and thus preserved for posterity. The works of "unapproved" authors, however, were neglected and eventually lost. Hellenistic literary culture regarded the works of approved authors as models worthy of emulation. An orator who wanted to describe a contemporary battle was expected to go to Herodotus, Thucydides, and Xenophon for their descriptions (Menander, *Rhetor.* 2.373). The following list (apart from the philosophers and the poetic pleiade) has been drawn from Sandys 1967, 1.131 (see below).

DNP 6.249–50; O'Sullivan 1997; Pfeiffer 1968, 1.204–9

The Alexandrian Canon (ἐγκριθέντες)

1. Epic Poets (5)	**2. Iambic Poets (3)**	**3. Lyric Poets (9)**	**4. Tragic Poets (5)**
Homer	Semonides	Alcman	Aeschylus
Hesiod	Archilochus	Alcaeus	Sophocles
Peisander	Hipponax	Sappho	Euripides
Panyasis		Stesichorus	Ion
Antimachus		Pindar	Achaeus
		Bacchylides	
		Ibycus	
		Anacreon	
		Simonides	
5. Comic Poets (14)	**6. Elegaic Poets (4)**	**7. Orators (10)**	**8. Historians (10)**
a. Old comedy	Callinus	Antiphon	Thucydides
Epicharmus	Mimnermus	Andocides	Herodotus
Cratinus	Philetas	Lysias	Xenophon
Eupolis	Callimachus	Isocrates	Philistus
Aristophanes		Isaeus	Theopompus
b. Middle comedy		Demosthenes	Ephorus
Antiphanes		Aeschines	Anaximines
Alexis		Hypereides	Callisthenes
c. New comedy		Lycurgus	Hellanicus
Menander		Dinarchus	Polybius
Philippides			
Diphilus			
Philemon			
Apollodorus			
9. Philosophers (5)	**10. Poetic Pleiade (7)**		
Plato	Apollonius Rhodius		
Xenophon	Aratus		
Aeschines	Philiscus		
Aristotle	Homer the Younger		
Theophrastus	Lycophron		
	Nicander		
	Theocritus		

Allegory, a transliteration of the Greek word ἀλληγορία meaning "figurative or metaphorical language." The corresponding Latin rhetorical term is the transliterated *allegoria* or *inversio* (Quintilian 8.6.44–59). The verb ἀλληγορεῖν means "to say something different from what one means," i.e., "to speak figuratively or metaphorically." Allegory is a rhetorical term with two distinct uses (Caird 1980, 167; R. Anderson 1999, 173): (1) to deliberately allegorize in speech or writing, a rhetorical strategy that uses brief comments framed in metaphorical language (*DNP* 1.518–23; R. D. Anderson 2000, 14–16); and (2) to interpret a text allegorically in a way not intended by the author, a hermeneutical move (*DNP* 1.523–25). Caird (1980, 167–71) distinguished among five types of allegorism: (1) rationalist allegorism (features in a "sacred" text are impossible to accept); (2) moralist allegorism (the quest for moral truth in veiled narrative form); (3) "atomic allegorism" (a phrase coined by Moore [1927–30, 1.248] for the allegorical rabbinical method that "interprets sentences, clauses, phrases and even single words, independently of the context or the historical occasion"); (4) exegetical allegorism (allegory attributed to the biblical writer, not applied by the interpreter); and (5) polemical allegorism (allegory used only because the opponents use it, e.g., Paul). In an earlier categorization of nonliteral rabbinic methods of biblical interpretation,

Wolfson (1957, 25–30) listed the legal, moral, prudential, credal, rationative, historically predictive, and eschatologically predictive. The distinctions of Caird and Wolfson, however, are not particularly helpful, since they are a mishmash of motives and content that reveal little about the hermeneutical method itself. Allegorical interpretation is an attempt to departicularize a text in the interest of universal applicability. The assumption of most allegorists in the ancient world is that the authors they are interpreting were fully conscious of the allegorical meaning of their narratives. According to D. A. Russell (1981, 97), "No one in antiquity seems to have had the idea that, instead of beginning with a message and embodying it in fiction one might begin with a story or subject and treat it as a symbol of happenings or truths which have some formal resemblance to it."

Homeric allegory. The allegorical reading of Homer began in the late 6th cent. B.C.E. Theagenes of Rhegium (ca. 525 B.C.E.), the supposed inventor of allegorical interpretation (Tatian, *Adv. Graecos* 31), proposed that the warring Olympian gods in Homer represented types of matter (hot, wet, dry, cold) or aspects of human psychology (Dowden 1992, 40–41). Some ancient sages, such as Xenophanes, complained that Homer and Hesiod ascribe to the gods what is shameful for people (Clement, *Strom.* 5.110). The offensive parts could be sterilized through excision (Plato, *Republic* 2.387b), or more commonly by allegorical interpretation. Socrates, as presented by Plato, refers ironically to the suggestion that the golden chain with which Zeus challenges the other Olympians to a tug of war is "nothing else but the sun" (Plato, *Theaet.* 153c). In the Greek world, the allegorical interpretation of Homer practiced by the Stoics (Long 1992) constitutes both an analogy and precedent for the early Christian use of allegory. In the Greek use of allegory as an interpretive method, the assumption is that λόγος ("reason, logic") can be extracted from μῦθος ("story, myth"). Scholars still disagree on the issue of whether Greek allegorical interpretation is a "positive" philosophical technique or a "defensive" tactic to protect the poets against philosophical attacks (Dawson 2000, 90). Several 1st- and 2d-cent. C.E. works survive that treat Homeric allegory, including Cornutus, *De natura deorum*, Heraclitus, *Quaestiones homericae* (both 1st cent. C.E.), and Ps.-Plutarch *De vita et poesi Homeri* (2d cent. C.E.). Heraclitus, who defines ἀλληγορία as saying one thing in order to indicate something else, emphasizes the importance of reading Homer allegorically (*Quaest. hom.* 1.1–3, 3.2):

> Great and grievous is the case brought from heaven against Homer for his irreverence towards the divine. If everything he wrote is not an allegory, everything is an impiety. Sacrilegious tales full of blasphemous folly run riot throughout both epics. If we are to believe that it is all said according to poetical tradition, with no philosophical basis and no concealed allegory, Homer is a Salmoneus or a Tantalus "with tongue unchastened, worse disease of all." . . . Should there be persons who do not recognize Homer's allegory and have not penetrated into the recesses of his wisdom, but have made rash judgments of truth without testing them, and seize on what appear to be mythical fictions because they do not understand the philosophical intention—well, let them go their way, while we, who have been made pure within the holy precincts, pursue the solemn truth of the poems in the proper manner.

These authors were convinced that Homer and Greek mythology contained a systematic account of Greek medicine, natural history, and philosophy, and they searched the text for allegorical interpretations. Few allegorical interpretations of entire texts (analogous to the task of *Philo) were attempted. While Heraclitus (*Quaest. hom.*) follows the general narrative sequence of the *Iliad* and *Odyssey*, he chooses only occasional episodes for interpretation. Only in Neoplatonic allegory (3d to 5th cents. C.E.) are there attempts to interpret entire texts, such as Homer or Plato's *Republic*. Neoplatonists interpreted the whole of the *Odyssey* as a spiritual journey through the neoplatonic universe (Long 1992, 45).

Allegory in early Judaism. The ancient "Song of the Well" quoted in Num. 21:18 refers to "the well that the leaders sank, that the nobles of the people dug," which is interpreted in CD 3:16 and 6:3–10 as a reference to seeking meaning in the Torah, clearly an allegorical reading of the text (Kister 1998, 109–10). Philo (*De somn.* 2.271) refers to the same text with a related allegorical meaning: "By the 'well' I mean knowledge [i.e., philosopical truth], which for long has been hidden, but in time is sought for and finally found, knowledge whose nature is so deep, knowledge which ever serves to water the fields of reason in the souls of those who desire to see." In Deut. 19:14, we read "You must not remove your neighbor's boundary marker, set up by former generations." Here "marker" is taken allegorically to refer to the commandments of Torah by CD (1.16), and by Philo (*De spec. leg.* 4.149–50).

Philo's allegory. The allegorical interpretation of the Pentateuch is particularly characteristic of *Philo of Alexandria, a Jewish interpreter of the Torah (Cazeaux 1973; Christiansen 1969; Leopold 1983; Nikiprowetzky 1977; Pépin 1966). Like the later Christian exegete Origen, Philo used the analogy of "body" and "soul" for the "text" and its "meaning." He maintained that the literal and allegorical interpretation of the Pentateuch are as inseparable as body and soul (*De migratione Abrahami* 93; LCL trans.): "Nay, we should look on all these outward observances as resembling the body, and their inner meanings as resembling the soul. It follows that, exactly as we have to take thought for the body, because it is the abode of the soul, so we must pay heed to the letter of the laws." Philo sometimes read the Torah as intentionally written allegorically with no valid literal meaning (*De opificio mundi* 157; LCL trans.): "Now these are no mythical fictions, such as poets and sophists delight in, but modes of making ideas visible, bidding us resort to allegorical interpretation guided in our renderings by what lies beneath the surface."

The literal meaning of the text was sometimes unacceptable to Philo. He thought it foolish to think that the world was created in six literal days (*Leg. alleg.* 1.2.2), or that God planted a garden (*Leg. alleg.* 1.14.43), or that Cain built a city (*Post.* 14.50). On the other hand, Philo opposed the extreme allegorists in Alexandria, when he argued that some commandments in the Torah should be literally understood and obeyed (*Migr.* 16.89–93). He also argued against the literalists (*Quaest. in Gen.* 1.8, 10, 18; *De fuga* 179–80; *Det.* 22; *De somn.* 1.39; 2.301; see Shroyer 1936). Philo referred to the philosophical teachings that lay under the surface of the text as ὑπόνοια ("underlying meaning"), and sometimes as ἀλληγορία ("allegory"), referring both to the text to be allegorically interpreted and the allegorical method of interpretation itself (Plutarch refers to these two interpretive methods negatively in *Moralia* 19e–f).

Allegory in the NT and ECL. The Pauline use of allegory is a debated issue, primarily because the allegorical method has often been regarded with suspicion and widely regarded as an illegitimate hermeneutical method in the ancient as well as the modern world. Ellis tries to distance Paul from allegorical interpretation by emphasizing that OT narratives refer to actual history (1957a, 52), and that even when Paul speaks explicitly about allegorizing in Gal. 4:24 (see below), his interpretive method has more in common with typology than allegory (Ellis 1957a, 53). Of course, both "typology" and "allegory" are figurative ways of interpreting texts that have much in common. Ellis concludes by wanting to maintain Paul's debt to Jewish exegesis but at the same time tries to distance Paul from allegory and from the influence of Alexandrian exegesis, i.e., Philo (Ellis 1957a, 54): "In all things but allegorical interpretation, Paul's Jewish methodology reflects a Palestinian milieu, and even in that the Alexandrian contact does not appear to be close or direct." Elsewhere, in dealing with Paul's allegory of the spiritual rock that followed the people of Israel in the wilderness and from which they drank (1 Cor. 10:1–5), Ellis again wants to regard this interpretation of Num. 21:17 as typological (Ellis 1957b). According to Caird (1980, 167–71), Paul used allegory only because his Jewish opponents used it, and he is therefore fighting fire with fire. The rhetorical use of ἀλληγορία is found in 1 Cor. 5:6 and Gal. 5:9, where Paul quotes the identical short proverb formulated with a clearly allegorical intention: "A little yeast leavens the whole batch of dough," which he does not interpret, since its meaning is clear in the context. In the context of Gal. 5:9, the retrograde practice of circumcision threatens to contaminate the entire religious life of the Galatian Christians. In the context of 1 Cor. 5:6, Paul appends to the proverb a transparent interpretation in which he combines the language of the allegory to make clear how he thinks it should be understood (v. 7): "Clean out the old yeast so that you may be a new batch, as you really are unleavened." Leaven refers to the immoral person mentioned in 1 Cor. 5:1–2, whom Paul thinks should be excommunicated.

More problematic is Paul's use of the verb ἀλληγορεῖν in a periphrastic participle in Gal. 4:24, where he says of the story of the sons born to Abraham by Sarah and Hagar (Gal. 4:21–27), "this is an allegory," and proceeds to interpret Hagar as representing bondage and the unnamed Sarah as representing freedom (i.e., the stunning and unexpected interpretation that Jews are spiritual descendants *not* of Sarah but rather of Hagar). Paul does not appear to assume that the story had two levels, a literal and an allegorical, but rather seems to mean that the story was expressly written as an allegory (R. D. Anderson 1999, 177–80). A shorter example of a law intended to be allegorical is found in 1 Cor. 9:9–10: "It is written in the law of Moses, 'You shall not muzzle an ox when it is treading out the grain.' Is it for oxen that God is concerned? Does he not speak entirely for our sake?"

Parables of Jesus and allegory. Before the work of Jülicher (1919), the parables of Jesus were routinely interpreted allegorically. Jülicher argued that the parables of Jesus make a single point, and since his work, parables and allegories have come to be sharply distinguished: parables contain only a single *tertium comparationis*, and they make only one point. By the late 20th cent. the pendulum had begun to swing the other way, and "allegory" was defined more acceptably by Boucher (1977, 20) as "an extended metaphor in narratory form." Reflecting this viewpoint and in light of modern literary criticism, a number of scholars argue (against Jülicher) that a fuzzy border separates parables from allegories (Drury 1985; Caird 1980, 160–67; Blomberg 1991). Not all features of the authentic cores of the parables of Jesus are realistic (Huffman 1978, 208–15), and this lack of realism, according to some, is also a characteristic of allegory (Blomberg 1991, 52). Modern interpreters of parables find it difficult consistently to avoid allegorical interpretation, at least in the tendency to suggest that main characters in the parable represent something or someone (Black 1960; Blomberg 1991, 52). Further, interpreters often identify a variety of different "single points" in the parable. An example is the parable of the Prodigal Son in Luke 15:11–32, in which the main point has been argued to be the generosity of the father's love, the opportunity for repentance for any prodigal, and the need to avoid the hard-hearted attitude of the elder brother (Blomberg 1991, 53). It is perhaps better to admit the polyvalent character of the parable. Based on a detailed study of more than 300 Tannaitic parables, Johnston (1978, 636–37) concludes that the distinction between parable and allegory is unusable.

*Midrash, *Typology

R. D. Anderson 1999, 172–80; 2000, 14–16; M. Black 1960; Blomberg 1991; Chadwick 1998; Christiansen 1969; Dawson 1992, 2000; Dowden 1992; Drury 1985; Ellis 1957a, 1957b; Huffman 1978; Kister 1998; Klauck 1978; Jülicher 1919; Lamberton 1986, 1992; Leopold 1983, 155–70; Long 1992; *RAC* 1.283–93; Runia 1984, 1987; Whitman 2000; Wolfson 1956, 24–72

Alliteration, the repetition of an initial letter or sound in a closely connected series of words, was used with some frequency by ancient writers. Among Greek authors, Gorgias was particularly fond of alliteration (B. Smith 1921; Schiappa 1999, 87–88), and alliteration occurs with some frequency in Greek proverbs, perhaps for the purpose of making them more memorable (Russo 1983). The author of Hebrews is fond of π-alliteration, which occurs five times in 1:1, five times in 11:28, four times in 12:11, and three times each in 2:2; 7:25; and 13:19. Hebrews 1:1 is particularly striking, where the initial letter "p" is repeated five times in a clause of twelve words in a way impossible to reproduce in English: ***p**olymeros kai **p**olytropos **p**alai ho theos lalesas tois **p**atrasin en tois **p**rofetais*, "God spoke fragmentarily and in many ways to the fathers by the prophets." In James 1:2, the second sentence of the letter, the author uses a phrase with three π-alliterations: *hotan peirasmois peripesete poikilois*, "when you experience varied testings." Luke uses π-words five times in the *preface Luke 1:1–4, just as Plutarch uses π-words seven times in the first sentence of the preface in *Septem sapientium convivium* 146C. Six π-words are found in the first quatrain of four beatitudes in Matt. 5:3–6 (C. Michaelis 1968), while the second quatrain of four beatitudes is framed by an alliteration of two δ-words in 5:6 and two in 5:10 (H. B. Green 2001, 39). Alliteration with "m" and "p" occurs in 1 Pet. 1:16–17; "p" and "l" in 1 Pet. 1:19–20. A slightly different form of alliteration is found in Gal. 4:14, where the first syllable is repeated: *ouk exouthenēsate oude exeptysata*, "you did not scorn or despise," where Paul consciously chose the unusual word *ekptyein* over the more common *apoptyein* (Lightfoot 1981, 175).

Denniston 1952, 126–29; C. Michaelis 1968; Russo 1983; B. Smith 1921

Allusions (see also *Quotations) are references to earlier works that are not as formal as quotations and are sometimes difficult to recognize. Hays (1989, 29–32) has suggested some criteria for determining whether allusions (particularly to the OT) are found in NT literature (he focused on the letters of Paul): (1) *Volume*: What was the volume or the degree of explicit repetitions of words or grammatical patterns? (2) *Recurrence*: How often does the same author refer to the same text elsewhere? (3) *Prominence*: How distinctive or prominent is the precursor text? How much rhetorical stress does the reference receive in the author's discourse? (4) *Dissimilarity*: Are the thoughts in question dissimilar to other influences like Greco-Roman thought or Jesus traditions? Can the passage be distinguished from other Scripture texts? (5) *History of interpretation*: Have others seen a reference to the particular text? (6) *Thematic coherence*: How well does the supposed primary text fit into the line of argument that the author develops? Does it illuminate the surrounding discourse?

———

Hays 1989; M. Thompson 1991

Amanuensis (see *Secretary)

Amen, a transliteration of the Hebrew term אמן, meaning "certainly, truly," often translated in the LXX by the optative verb γένοιτο ("may it be"), which is used in liturgical contexts as a responsory affirmation, as it still is in Jewish and Christian prayers and liturgies. Since the term "amen" is often used to conclude prayers in Judaism and in prayers and doxologies in early Christianity, pious scribes often inserted the term in the texts they were copying at points they thought appropriate.
*Liturgical Formulas

A minore ad maius (see *Lesser to greater argument)

Anacolouthon, a transliteration of the Greek word ἀνακολούθον (a neuter adjective formed with an alpha privative, ἀν-ακολούθον "not following," hence "inconsistent, anomalous"), referring to syntactical incoherence or inconsistency within a sentence, particularly a shift in an unfinished sentence from one construction to another. A clear example is found in Rev. 3:9: "I will make [διδῶ] those of the synagogue of Satan who say that they are Jews and are not, but lie—behold, I will make [ποιήσω] them come and bow down before at your feet." The author abandons the first main verb ("I will," translated here as "I will make"), whose object is the partitive genitive, and begins again with another verb ("I will force," translated here as "I will make"), this time completing the sentence with a pronominal object and a final or consecutive ἵνα-clause. A more extensive anacolouthon occurs in Eph. 3:1–14 (Norden 1956, 253 n. 1; Lincoln 1990, 167–68), in which v. 1 (which begins with τούτου χάριν, "for this reason") is interrupted by a *digression in vv. 2–13, with the syntax resumed in v. 14 (which begins again with τούτου χάριν).
*Style, *Parenthesis

———

BDF ¶466–70; Robertson 1934, 435–40

Anaphora (a transliteration of the Greek word ἀναφορά, a frequent synonym is ἐπαναφορά) is the repetition of the same word at the beginning of a series of successive statements (see *Rhetorica ad Herennium* 4.19). This stylistic figure is found in the OT (Ps. 29:1–2). In Heb. 11:3–31, the term πίστει ("by faith") is used to introduce eighteen *exempla* (Cosby 1988), one of the most extensive uses of anaphora in ancient literature. In Phil. 3:2: "*Look out* for the dogs, *look out* for the evil-workers, *look out* for those who mutilate the flesh" is another example of anaphora. In 1 Cor. 12:4–6, Paul introduces three statements with the word διαιρέσεις, "varieties."
*Epanaphora, *Repetition, *Sorites

———

R. D. Anderson 2000, 19; Denniston 1952, 84–98

Anecdote (see *Chreia)

Angelus interpres is a Latin phrase meaning "interpreting angel" and refers to the stock figure of the angelic guide found in Jewish apocalypses, who either escorts the visionary in his *ascent to heaven or mediates visions to him on earth, providing answers to questions asked by the visionary. The figure of the interpreting angel first appears in later prophetic books of the OT which exhibit some features characteristic of later Jewish apocalypses (Ezekiel and Zechariah). The figure of the interpreting angel is ubiquitous in Jewish apocalypses including Dan 7–12; 1 Enoch 17–36; 37–71; 4 Ezra; 2 Baruch and 3 Baruch.

Relevance for the NT and ECL. In the NT, the literary device of the *angelus interpres* is used only in Revelation. In the introduction to the book, the interpreting angel is singled out as the agent by which the exalted Christ reveals visions of the future to John (1:1). This same figure reappears in the conclusion of the book (22:6–16), where John's attempt to worship him is rebuffed (22:8–9). In the body of the work, however, the *angelus interpres* plays a negligible role. Only in Rev. 17 does this angelic figure play a role analogous with the stock apocalyptic figure of the *angelus interpres*, by explaining the meaning of the visions John has seen (17:6b–18). This interpreting angel introduces his explanations of the meaning of John's vision with these words (17:7): "I will tell you the mystery of the woman, and of the beast with seven heads and ten horns that carries her" (the lengthy explanation of the detailed features of the image follows). Apparently the same angelic figure appears again in Rev. 19:9–10 and 21:9–22:9, but in the latter passage, while the angel shows John various features of the New Jerusalem, he explains nothing to him. The interpreting angel is also a prominent literary device in the later Christian apocalypses, including the **Apocalypse of Paul* and **Third Baruch* (Himmelfarb 1983).

*Apocalypse, *Ekphrasis, *Revelatory dialogue

———

Reichelt 1994.

Anonymity refers to literary works in which the author is not explicitly identified. Despite the fact that many books of the OT and the NT are anonymous, a striking literary feature, the subject has been almost completely neglected. Many books in the Hebrew Bible lack explicit claims to authorship, including the books of the Pentateuch (Genesis, Exodus, Leviticus, Numbers, Deuteronomy), the Former Prophets (Joshua, Judges, Samuel, Kings), and some of the works categorized as Writings (1–2 Chronicles, Ezra, Esther, Job). The great majority of the Dead Sea Scrolls texts are also anonymous (e.g., CD, 1QS, 1QM, 1QH, the Pesharim, etc.; see Bernstein 1988). There are also many anonymous works in the NT, including the four Gospels (Matthew, Mark, Luke, John), Acts, Hebrews, and 1 John. Sometime during the 2d cent. C.E., the Gospels were attributed to earlier figures, some apostles (Matthew, John) and some not (Mark, Luke).

A phenomenon related to anonymity is the use of a self-designation other than a name in connection with a written text. In the OT, Ecclesiastes is attributed to "the Preacher" (Koheleth), a thinly veiled reference to Solomon (so that Ecclesiastes in fact is one of the Solomonic pseudepigrapha). In the Dead Sea Scrolls that were produced by the sectarians themselves, not a single individual who belonged to the community or their enemies is named. Code names such as the "Teacher of Righteousness" and the "Wicked Priest" are used, presumably of figures known to the community but not historically identified. In the NT, 2 John and 3 John claim to be written by "the Elder," just as the Gospel of John is apparently attributed to "the Beloved Disciple" (John 21:24).

Possible reasons for anonymity are these: (1) to conceal the name of the author from recrimination because of the controversial or politically dangerous character of the text (*pseudepigraphy may have a similar function); (2) because the recipients of the text are well aware of the identity of the author and to claim authorship would be both unnecessary and redundant; (3) because the idea of claiming individual authorship would be unthinkable, since the text represents traditions "owned" by the community in which the author writes, and in such communities originality is a thing to be avoided.

Anthological style, a designation for an implicit exegetical method that is a reflection or meditation on earlier texts and develops, enriches, and transposes the earlier message (Bloch, *DBSup* 5.1270–71, 1273, 1279; Robert, *DBSup* 5.411). Both Bloch and Robert regard the anthological style as midrash, since it exhibits the two basic features of the midrashic genre: "meditation on Scripture and actualization of Scripture for contemporary needs," though Wright disagrees with the equation of anthological style with midrash (Wright 1966, 443–44). The Benedictus (Luke 1:68–79), the Magnificat (Luke 1:46–55), and 1QM 12 are identified by Wright (1966: 444) as examples of the nonmidrashic anthological style. Wright (1966, 444–47) also finds examples of "midrashic anthological style" in CD 20.17–20 (a pastiche of allusions to Isa. 59:20; Mal. 3:16; Isa. 56:1; Mal. 3:18; Exod. 20:6; and Deut. 7:9); Bar. 2:20–25; 2:27–35; Dan. 9:1–19; Isa. 60–62; Prov. 1–9. Presumably the "anthological style" is what Tov (1995) refers to as "excerpted and abbreviated" biblical texts from Qumran, which he subdivides into three types: (1) liturgical collections; (2) exegetical-ideological anthologies (4QTest; 4Qapocr Joshua); (3) copies made for personal reading (4QDeut^{q}, with excerpts from Deut 32, and 4QCant$^{a\text{-}b}$, with parts of several chapters of the Song of Songs).

———

Tov 1995; Wright 1966, 443–50

Anthology (see *Anthological style)

Antilogic, a transliterated form of the Greek word ἀντιλογικός ("quarrelsome, disputatious"), refers to the opposition of one λόγος ("reason, argument") with another (Kerferd 1981, 63). Antilogic is a specific rhetorical technique using either contrariety or contradiction. Plato thought that "antilogic" was inferior to dialectic (Plato, *Republic* 454a; *Theatetus* 164c). Protagoras was credited with the view that there are two λόγοι ("arguments") about everything, and these are opposed to each other (Diogenes Laertius 9.51; Diels-Kranz 1952, 2.253 [80A1]), i.e., one can take any side of a question and debate it with equal success (Kerferd 1981, 84).

Kerferd 1981

Antithesis, a transliterated form of the Greek word ἀντίθετον, is the conjunction of contrasting ideas, particularly characteristic of Greek style using the paired contrasting correlative particles μέν and δέ ("on the one hand . . . but on the other"), and οὐ . . . ἀλλά ("not . . . but"). "Thus the basic feature of the two-part form is antithesis" (Lausberg 1998, §443). Antithesis is also a rhetorical figure in which two clauses are used in opposition to each other or two opposing phrases are joined by the same verb (Aristotle, *Rhetorica* 3.9.7–8). The Greek sophist Gorgias (ca. 485–380 B.C.E.) was particularly renowned for his elaborate use of antithesis (see *Gorgianic figures). A modern example is the famous saying of John Fitzgerald Kennedy: "Ask not what your country can do for you; ask what you can do for your country" (this is also an *enthymeme). A striking example of a series of antitheses, perhaps hymnic in origin, is found in Ign. *Eph.* 7:2: "There is one physician, who is both flesh and spirit, born and yet not born, who is God in man, true life in death, both of Mary and of God, first passible and then impassible, Jesus Christ our Lord." The cohesion of the partial text in 2 Cor 4:16–5:10 is indicated in part by the pervasive antithetical structure in this passage. Paul frequently uses antithetical *proverbs: "Knowledge puffs up, but love builds up" (1 Cor. 8:1b). "[God] has made us competent to be ministers of a new covenant, not of the letter but of spirit; for the letter kills, but the Spirit gives life" (2 Cor. 3:6). Paul often uses the οὐ . . . ἀλλά form in antitheses: "For the kingdom of God depends not on talk but in power" (1 Cor. 4:20); "For God is a God not of disorder but of peace (1 Cor. 14:33). Antithesis also occurs in the Johannine corpus, as in John 1:20: "He [John the Baptist] confessed, and did not deny it, but confessed" (Bauer 1925, 29, mentions two parallel uses of "confess" and "not deny": Aelian, *Nat. an.* 2.43; Josephus, *Ant.* 6.151: "Saul confessed that he was guilty and did not deny the sin"). Other instances of antithesis include John 1:3 ("All things came into being through him, and without him not one thing came into being"), and 1 John 2:21 ("I write to you, not because you do not know the truth, but because you know it").

R. D. Anderson 2000, 21–22; Denniston 1952, 70–77; Holloway 1998; Lanham 1991, 16–17; Lausberg 1998, §787–92; Schneider 1970

Antithetical parallelism (see *Parallelism)

Antithetical style (see *Antithesis)

Aphorism, a transliterated form of the Greek word ἀφορισμός ("pithy saying"), belonging to the same semantic field as the Greek terms χρεία (Latin *usus*) and γνώμη (Latin *sententia*), may be defined as the verbal expression of personal insight and vision attributed to particular individuals, from whom they receive their authority and validity (Williams 1981, 78–80; Crossan 1983, 18–25). In general, the Greeks used the term γνώμη to refer to unattributed aphorisms, and the term χρεία to refer to attributed sayings or actions (or a combination of the two). Aphorisms are concise attributed sayings that give pithy expression to an insight about life, the validity of which is generally recognized and approved. In the canonical gospels, Küchler (1979, 587–92) counts 108 aphorisms, while Carlston (1980, 91) counts 102. One of the more detailed studies of the aphorisms of Jesus is Crossan (1983), based on the analysis of 133 aphorisms in Mark and Q and the parallels in Matthew, Luke, and extracanonical Jesus literature. More recently, Crossan has produced a handbook called *Sayings Parallels* (1986), in which he presents 291 aphorisms of Jesus from canonical and extracanonical literature with all parallel versions, 77 of which are found only in extracanonical sources. The *Gospel of Thomas* alone contains 114 aphorisms of Jesus (according to the traditional enumeration). There is a strong tendency to collect individual aphorisms to form a genre called the gnomologium, and to assemble pronouncement stories or anecdotes into **chriae* collections; both Q and the *Gospel of Thomas* have combined these two generic tendencies to form what might be designated as "wisdom gospels." While relatively short collections of aphorisms are found in the canonical gospels (often, but not always, as part of the sayings source Q), both Q and the *Gospel of Thomas* are primarily collections of sayings of Jesus.

Aphorisms in the OT. The Hebrew term *mashal* is a broad term covering all types of figures of speech (Scott 1989, 8–19), including a wide variety of oral and literary forms including parables (2 Sam. 12:1–6), allegories (Ezek. 17:2–24), enigmatic oracles (Num. 23:7), taunts (Isa. 24:1), proverbs (1 Sam. 10:11–12; 24:13; Ezek. 12:22; 18:2; Jer. 31:29). In the LXX, the term παραβολή is regularly used to translate *mashal.* In the Synoptic Gospels, the term παραβολή is occasionally used of proverbs or aphorisms (Mark 7:17; Luke 4:23; 5:36; 6:39; 14:7). The term λόγος is also used for a proverb quoted in John 4:37, and in Matt. 19:11 λόγος refers to the aphorism used in Matt. 19:12. Form criticism of the OT distinguishes between the "proverb," a purely observational saying derived from experience, and the "wisdom saying" (*Weisheitsspruch*), a didactic saying based on experience or tradition that inculcates some value or lesson (Murphy 1981, 180, 184). The term *mashal,* however, is such a broad category (perhaps equivalent to the English term "trope") that it is of little practical use in distinguishing between various oral and literary forms of popular wisdom.

Characteristics of the aphorism. Aphorisms have a number of stable features:

1. Specific attribution to individuals. This feature is important because it is a necessary characteristic of the chreia (Theon, *Progym.* 202.4–5) and excludes the consideration of allusions to, for example, the sayings of Jesus that are not explicitly attributed to him. In most instances, aphorisms attributed to Jesus in earlier stages of transmission do not lose that attribution. On the other hand, sayings not initially attributed to Jesus can receive such an attribution. A clear example of this process is tracing the saying of unknown origin that Paul introduces in 1 Cor. 2:9 with the quotation formula καθὼς γέγραπται, "as it has been written,"

> What no eye has seen, nor ear heard,
> nor has the heart of man conceived

This saying is explicitly attributed to Jesus in *Gos. Thom.* 17:

> Jesus said, "I shall give you what no eye has seen and what no ear has heard and what no hand has touched and what never occurred to the human mind."

2. The aphorism, like the chreia, is subject to expansion and contraction (συστέλλειν) in a variety of ways.

3. Aphorisms appear in a variety of contexts in early Christian literature: (a) as dialogical elements within the framework of a narrative composition, e.g., as the culminating saying in a *pronouncement story or chreia; (b) as individual sayings or clusters of sayings attributed to Jesus within both canonical and extracanonical gospels, often arranged in the form of an argument; (c) as individual sayings or clusters of sayings as examples or proofs within early Christian discourse, often with a strong paraenetic emphasis (e.g., *1 Clem.* 13:2–3).

4. The basic function of the aphorism is didactic, a feature that is implicit in sentences and questions, and explicit in admonitions, which can be framed either positively or negatively.

5. There is a marked tendency to serialize aphorisms, and most such collections of maxims (gnomologia) or collections of *chreiai* are attributed by definition to specific authors as a means of guaranteeing the reliability and authority of the constituent sayings (R. O. P. Taylor 1946, 81; Kloppenborg 1987, 292–94).

6. Maxims were not uncommonly provided with narrative frameworks when they were decontextualized from oral speech and resituated in literary context with specific scenes and appropriate casts of characters. This transition from oral to written, accompanied by the addition of a narrative framework, is a process that folklorists have observed in the study of proverbs (Abrahams and Babcock 1977, 414–29). The fact that the culminating sayings of many apophthegmata or pronouncement stories can stand alone (and many very probably circulated in that form) led Bultmann to designate those apophthegmata in which the culminating saying is inseparable from the narrative framework as having an *einheitliche Konzeption,* "unified conception" (1967, 49).

Types and forms of aphorisms. 1. *Makarisms or beatitudes.* There are 15 aphoristic beatitudes in the canonical Gospels: (a) Matt. 5:3=Luke 6:20b; (b) Matt. 5:4=Luke 6:21b; (c) Matt. 5:5; (d) Matt. 5:6=Luke 6:21a; (e) Matt. 5:7; (f) Matt. 5:8; (g) Matt. 5:9; (h) Matt. 5:10; (i) Matt. 5:11–12=Luke 6:22–23; (j) Matt. 5:13, 15= Luke 10:23; (k) Luke 11:28; (l) Luke 12:37; (m) Luke 12:23, 29=*Gos. Thom.* 79c; (n) John 13:17=Jas. 1:25b; (o) John 20:29=*Apoc. Jas.* 3.5; 8.3. There are 13 aphoristic beatitudes in the *Gospel of Thomas,* six without parallel (7 [=*P. Oxy.* 654.7], 18, 19, 49, 58, 103), one with a parallel in Q (54=Matt. 5:3=Luke 6:20), and two groups of three each that have some connection with the Synoptic tradition: (a) a series of three aphoristic beatitudes occur in *Gos. Thom.* 68–69 (cf. Matt. 5:11=Luke 6:23; Matt. 5:10; 5:6=Luke 6:21), and (b) another series of three in *Gos. Thom.* 79 (Luke 11:27–28; 23:29; John 13:17=Jas. 1:25). Some extracanonical aphorisms of Jesus appear less developed than their parallel versions in the canonical gospels, and may therefore reflect an earlier stage in the oral transmission process. One such aphorism is *GThom* 31 (= P. Oxy. 1): "Jesus said, "No prophet is accepted in his own village; no physician heals those who know him."

2. *"Whoever" or "one who says" sayings.* These are introduced with a relative pronoun (ὅς ἄν or ὅστις ἄν) or a substantival participle (Crossan 1983, 67–75). These introductory forms occur frequently in the protases of legal formulations in the Hebrew Bible (Exod. 21:12; 35:2; Lev. 15:10, 19; Num. 31:19) and are also used in *meshalim* (Prov. 9:4, 16; 12:1; 20:1). Many aphorisms in this form occur in Sirach (3:3, 4, 5, 6, 16, 26, 31; 4:12, 13, 15). This form occurs frequently in the sayings of Jesus, e.g., Mark 3:35 (and its many parallels: Matt. 12:50; Luke 8:21; *Gos. Thom.* 99; *2 Clem.* 9:11; *Gos. Eb.* 5):

> Whoever [ὅστις γὰρ ἄν] does the will of
> God is my brother, and sister, and
> mother.

Another example is found in Mark 8:35 (and its many parallels: Matt. 16:25d; Luke 9:24; Matt. 19:39; Luke 17:33; John 12:25):

> For whoever [ὅς γὰρ ἐάν + subj.] would
> save his life will lose it;
> and whoever [ὃς δ' ἄν + subj.] loses his
> life for my sake and the Gospel's will
> save it.

Other examples of this form occur in Mark 8:38 (and par.); 9:42 (and par.), and *Gos. Thom.* 1, 44, 55, 56, 67, 80, 82, 94, 101, 105, 108, 110, 111b.

3. *Conditional sayings.* Sayings in which the condition or protasis is assumed as real or possible are introduced with the conditional particles εἰ or ἐάν, or the participial structure mentioned above with no change in meaning, i.e., what Crossan designated "performancial variations" (1983, 67–73). An example is found in Mark 3:24–25 (and par. Matt. 12:25 and Luke 11:17), in which the protasis is introduced with ἐάν with the subjunctive, while the apodosis has a verb in the indicative:

> If [ἐάν] a kingdom is divided against itself,
> that kingdom cannot stand.
> And if [ἐάν] a house is divided against
> itself, that house will not be able to
> stand.

A number of aphorisms in the *Gospel of Thomas* have a conditional protasis in which the condition is assumed to be real. These have several forms, either introduced with the conditional particles *ešje* or *ešope* ("if"), or the conditional conjugation, i.e., the Present II with the particle *-san-* (e.g., *Gos. Thom.* 3 [three conditional protases]). An example is found in *Gos. Thom.* 14a:

> Jesus said to them,
> If you fast [*etenšanrnēsteue*] you will beget
> sin for yourselves
> and if you pray [*etetnšašlel*] you will be condemned,
> and if you give [*etentnti*] alms, you will do
> evil in your spirits.

See also *Gos. Thom.* 19b, 27, 29, 34, 48, 50, 70, 95.

4. *Aphorisms in synonymous couplets.* An example is found in Matt. 10:24–25a:

> A disciple is not above the teacher, nor a
> slave above the master;
> it is enough for the disciple to be like his
> teacher and the slave like the master.

It appears that this aphorism is an expansion of a shorter version found in Luke 6:40:

> A disciple is not above the teacher,
> but everyone who is fully qualified will be
> like the teacher.

The independent character of this saying is confirmed by *Dial. Sav.* 53, "the disciple resembles his teacher." Matthew has effected this expansion by inserting a slave/master saying, similar to that found paired synonymously with a sender/emissary saying in John 13:16:

> Truly, truly, I say to you,
> a servant is not greater than his master;
> nor is he who is sent greater than he who sent
> him.

Thus the tendency to expand single-line aphorisms by pairing them with analogous sayings in synonymous parallelism suggests the literary character of the transformation. There are many other examples of aphorisms in the Jesus tradition that consist of synonymous couplets (Mark 2:21a, 22b and par.; Mark 3:24–25 and par.; Mark 4:22 and par.; Mark 3:24–25 and par. Luke 6:43=Matt. 7:17; Luke 6:44=Matt. 7:16; Luke 11:23=Matt. 12:30; Luke 12:23= Matt. 10:27; Matt. 10:41).

5. *Antithetical and paradoxical aphorisms* (Beardslee 1970, 66–68; Perdue 1986, 9–10). One characteristic type of *parallelismus mem-*

brorum is the antithetical couplet, a type found frequently when two types of existence or experience are contrasted, e.g., Prov. 10:1:

> A wise child makes a glad father,
> but a foolish child is a mother's grief.

An example of an aphorism that consists of a synonymous couplet in the NT is Mark 10:31 (and the many parallels: Matt. 19:30; 20:16; Luke 13:30; P. Oxy. 654.4.2; *Gos. Thom.* 4b):

> But many that are first will be last,
> and the last first.

An antithetical couplet is also found in, e.g., *Gos. Thom.* 82 (Davies 1983, 2): "Jesus said, 'He who is near me is near the fire, and he who is far from me is far from the kingdom.'"

6. *Wisdom admonition.* This form of aphorism focuses on exhortation and consists of a clause formulated with a verb in the imperative, typically followed by a supportive clause. Though second-personal singular imperatives are commonly found in admonitions in ancient proverbs literature, second-person plural forms occur frequently in admonitions attributed to Jesus (Zeller 1977, 142–85). Wisdom admonitions occur with some frequency in Q, the Sayings Source (Luke 6:27–31=Matt. 5:44–45; Luke 6:37–8=Matt. 7:1–2; Luke 11:9–10=Matt. 7:7–8; Luke 12:4=Matt. 10:28; Luke 12:22–23= Matt. 6:25; Luke 12:33b–34=Matt. 6:19–21; Luke 12:58–59=Matt. 5:25–26; Luke 12:23–24=Matt. 7:13–14). An interesting instance of how an aphoristic sentence could be transformed into a wisdom admonition is found in Luke 12:3=Matt. 10:27; Matt. 10:27 contains the following admonition:

> What I tell you in the dark utter in the light,
> and what you hear whispered, proclaim upon the housetops.

The parallel in Luke 12:3, however, is phrased as an aphoristic sentence:

> Whatever you have said in the dark shall be heard in the light,
> and what you have whispered in private rooms shall be proclaimed upon the housetops.

Here Luke appears to have preserved the earlier form of the Q saying with the two future passive verbs, while Matthew has transformed this aphoristic sentence into a wisdom admonition (Fitzmyer 1981–85, 956). Further, the more specific application of the aphorism in Matt. 10:27 appears to be based on the more general character of the aphorism in Luke 12:3 (Piper 1989, 57–58). Wisdom admonitions also occur without the supportive clause (Zeller 1977, 21–22), such as the admonition about non-retaliation (Luke 6:29–30=Matt. 5:39–42). Supporting or motive clauses seem to be omitted occasionally in transmission. The admonition in Luke 12:22–23=Matt. 6:25 has a motive clause that is eliminated in P. Oxy. 655.1–17 and *Gos. Thom.* 36 (assuming the dependence of both on either Luke or Matthew).

7. *Aphoristic Sentences.* These are general declarative statements in the indicative mood that encapsulate general insights. They usually consist of two lines or members in synonymous or antithetical parallelism, e.g., Prov. 17:27 (synonymous parallelism):

> He who restrains his words has knowledge,
> and he who has a cool spirit is a man of understanding.

The Synoptic tradition contains many aphorisms of Jesus in both synonymous parallelism (Matt. 10:24; Mark 4:22=Matt. 10:26; Matt. 10:41), and antithetical parallelism (Luke 9:58=Matt. 8:20; Luke 6:45=Matt. 12:35). There are many types of aphoristic sentences including the following: (a) *where/there aphorisms* (Luke 12:34=Matt. 16:21; Luke 17:37=Matt. 24:28; Matt. 18:20 [Goulder 1974, 78]); (b) *as/so correlatives* (Luke 17:26–30=Matt. 24:37–39; Luke 11:30=Matt. 12:40; Luke 17:24=Matt. 24:27); (c) *future reversal sayings* (Mark 8:35=Matt. 16:25= Luke 9:24; Mark 10:23b, 24=Matt. 19:23=Luke 18:24; Hermas *Sim.* 9.20.2b, 3b; Mark 10:25=Matt. 19:24=Luke 18:25; Mark 10:31=Matt. 19:30=Luke 13:30=Matt. 20:16= *P. Oxy.* 654=*Gos. Thom.* 4; Luke 14:11=Matt. 23:12; Luke 18:14b); (d) *better or comparison aphorisms* (*Tobsprüche*) occur frequently in the OT (Prov 15:16, 17; 16:8; 17:1; 19:22; 25:24; 27:5, 10), often in Sirach (11:3; 19:24; 20:2, 18, 25, 31; 25:16; 30:14–17; 41:15; 42:14; cf. Zimmerli 1933, 192–93; von Rad 1972, 29; Ogden 1977, 489–505). The *Tobspruch* involves a comparison using the formula "better/than," i.e., A is better than B, or A with B is better than C with D (Prov. 15:16–17; 16:32; 27:10; Eccl. 7:1–8; 9:4, 18; Wis. 4:1; Sir. 30:14; *m. Abot* 6.6; Diogenes Laertius 4.49). Proverbs 16:8 is a typical example:

> Better is a little with righteousness
> than great revenues with injustice.

Another example is found in Ps.-Phocylides, *Sententiae* 130: "Better [βέλτερος] is a wise man than a strong one." A distinctive form of the "better saying" is found in the collection of four aphorisms in Mark 9:42–48 using the formula "it is better . . . than" (καλόν ἐστιν). Parenthetically, since Hebrew and Aramaic have no special form for the comparative, καλόν used in the sense of "better" is widely considered a Semitism (Black 1967, 117; Blass, Debrunner, and Rehkopf 1984, §245.3). Mark 9:45 is one of the four aphorisms in Mark 9:42–48:

> And if your foot causes you to sin, cut it off;
> it is better [καλόν ἐστιν] for you to enter life lame
> than with two feet to be thrown into hell.

In this couplet, the first line is a condition consisting of a protasis and an apodosis containing an admonition with a second-person singular imperative, while the second line provides the basis for the recommended action. Another aphorism similar to the "better saying" is found in Mark 10:25 (and par.):

> It is easier for a camel to go through the eye of a needle
> than for a rich man to enter the kingdom of God.

The function of aphorisms. The aphorisms of Jesus have three possible settings: in the life of Jesus, in the life of the early church, and in the literary setting of texts in which they were preserved. In ancient societies, aphorisms typically functioned as vehicles for articulating and preserving traditional values and norms by expressing general and typical truths refracted through particular situations and occurrences (Williams 1981, 36, 40). The idea of a cosmic order linked to divine rule and justice is at the core of much of the proverbial wisdom of the Bible (Williams 1981, 17). The human problems that wisdom addresses include those of suffering and death, injustice in life, and the perils of adultery, strong drink, and the tongue (Crenshaw 1981, 18). The large number of aphorisms in the sayings of Jesus suggests the special functions these might have had in the ministry of Jesus himself, as well as in the lives of the early Christians who transmitted them in both oral and written form. While some of the aphorisms of Jesus served to validate those traditional norms and values that Jesus and early Christians shared with the societies in which they lived (i.e., that could be expressed in terms of popular wisdom), other aphorisms gave expression to the dissident views of reality maintained by Jesus and early Christians (i.e., aphorisms whose truth is considered self-evidently valid only within the Christian community). In recent years a number of scholars have focused on the radical features of the aphorisms of Jesus (e.g., Beardslee 1970, 61–73; Perrin 1976, 48–54). Ricoeur, with specific reference to the radical features of the parables of Jesus, has described this as the pattern of orientation, disorientation, and reorientation (1975, 122–28). Given the relative status and relationship between masters and slaves in the ancient world, for example, the aphorism in Luke 12:37 envisions a radically reversed relationship between the two: "Blessed are those slaves whom the master finds alert when he comes; truly I tell you, he will fasten his belt and have them sit down to eat, and he will come and serve them." Other radical sayings include the following: Luke 9:60=Matt. 8:22: "Leave the dead to bury their own dead"; Mark 8:35: "Whoever would save his life will lose it"; and Mark 10:31: "But many that are first will be last, and the last first" (Perrin 1976, 52). Williams (1981, 32–34), has described biblical wisdom in terms of two perspectives, order (Proverbs and Sirach) and counterorder (Ecclesiastes and Jesus). Yet the themes of order and counterorder do not necessarily describe characteristic features of the aphorisms of Jesus. Carlston (1980, 91–99) has discussed themes commonly found in ancient practical wisdom that are striking by their absence from the aphorisms of Jesus: (1) education, (2) personal character and habits, (3) friendship, (4) women and family relationships, (5) ethical issues, (6) politics, and (7) prudence. While these themes pervade ancient wisdom generally, they are largely missing from the aphorisms of Jesus.

Identifying aphorisms. Aphorisms are distinct from other types of discourse material found in Jesus literature. "Aphorism" is one of several English terms used to refer to popular wisdom sayings. Common synonyms include "proverb," "maxim," "gnome," and "adage." Each of these terms is used to refer to concise, autonomous sayings that give pithy expression to an insight about life, the validity of which is generally recognized and approved (Aristotle, *Rhetorica* 13984b; John 4:37). Proverbs can be distinguished from aphorisms, though both are just part of one end of the spectrum of figurative speech subsumed under the Hebrew term *meshalim.* "Proverb" (Greek γνώμη, Latin *sententia*; both etymologically mean "a way of thinking") is an unattributed saying that gives expression to collective wisdom and for that reason is accepted as true. The "aphorism" (Greek χρεία; Latin *usus* or *chria*), on the other hand, is an expression of personal insight and vision, attributed to particular individuals (from whom they derive their authority and validity) and often reflecing specific situations (Williams 1981, 78–80; Crossan 1983, 18–25). Attribution to named persons, however, does not guarantee authenticity. Carlson (1980, 89) observes that "proverbial sayings seem positively to engender false attributions."

Bultmann distinguished five types of *Herrenworte* or "dominical sayings" (1967, 73–113): logia (i.e., proverbs or aphorisms), prophetic and apocalyptic sayings, legal sayings and church rules, "I"-Sayings, and similitudes and similar forms (see *Form criticism). These distinctions are made partially on the basis of form, but largely on the basis of content, and are inherently problematic, because different kinds of criteria are mixed together in defining "form." Crossan followed a simpler taxonomy and distinguished only between parables and aphorisms, using the latter category somewhat indiscriminately for *all* nonnarrative sayings of Jesus (1983, 1986, 22–130).

The five categories of *Herrenworte* proposed by Bultmann have not been unanimously adopted by other form critics but have been designated by other terms such as *Paradigmata* or *Paränese* by Dibelius (1971, 34–66, 234–65), "sayings of Jesus" (Taylor 1935, 88–100), and "aphoristic meshalim" (Gerhardsson 1988, 341–42). Aphorisms can also be distinguished from parables or narrative meshalim (Gerhardsson 1988), which may be defined succinctly as very short stories with double meanings. Similitudes (*Gleichnisse*) tend to blend with figurative sayings (*Bildwörter*), many of which have the character of popular proverbs (Bultmann 1970, 179–89). Though Bultmann's detailed discussion of the various forms of practical wisdom on the continuum of metaphor to parable has not really been superseded so much as simply ignored, a number of important studies have made significant contributions to the study of the aphorisms of Jesus. Since there is a heavy concentration of practical wisdom traditions in Q, studies that have focused on the non-Markan parallel traditions in Matthew and Luke have also contributed to the study of the aphorisms of Jesus (Lührmann 1969; Hoffmann 1972; Edwards 1976; Kloppenborg 1987; Piper 1989).

Aune 1991; Beardslee 1967, 1970, 1972; Carlston 1980; Chadwick 1959; Crenshaw 1974, 1981; Crossan 1983; S. L. Davies 1983; Edwards 1976; Eissfeldt 1913; Gerhardsson 1988; Goulder 1974; Hills 1990; Hoffmann 1972; Kloppenborg 1987; Küchler 1979; Lührmann 1969; Murphy 1981; Ogden 1977; Perdue 1986; Perrin 1976; Piper 1989; von Rad 1972; Ricoeur 1975; Snyder 1996–97; R. O. P. Taylor 1946; Williams 1981; Zeller 1977; Zimmerli 1933

Apocalypse, literary genre of The term "apocalypse" is a transliterated form of the Greek term ἀποκάλυψις, which means "disclosure, revelation." The author of the Apocalypse or Revelation to John was the first Jewish or Christian author to use the term ἀποκάλυψις in describing the content of his work, which is essentially a narrative of a series of revelatory visions that disclose the events surrounding the imminent end of the present age: "[This is] the revelation [ἀποκάλυψις] of Jesus Christ, which God gave him to show to his servants what must soon take place" (Rev. 1:1). Following Rev. 1:1, the term "apocalypse" has been used as a generic term to describe documents with a content and structure similar to the Revelation to John since the early nineteenth century, when it was popularized by the German NT scholar Friedrich Lücke (1791–1854).

All extant Jewish apocalypses are pseudonymous, that is, written under the names of prominent ancient Israelite or Jewish figures such as Adam, Enoch, Moses, Daniel, Ezra, and Baruch. Only the earliest Christian apocalypses, the Revelation to John and the Shepherd of Hermas, were written under the names of the actual authors. The most likely reason for the phenomenon of apocalyptic pseudonymity is that it was a strategy to provide credentials and thereby assure the acceptance of these revelatory writings at a point in Israelite history when the reputation of prophets had sunk to an extremely low point.

"Apocalypticism" is a term used to describe the particular type of eschatological expectation characteristic of early Jewish and early Christian apocalypses. The Jewish religious compositions written between 200 B.C.E. and 200 C.E. that are generally regarded as apocalypses include Dan. 7–12 (the only OT apocalypse), the five documents that compose *1 Enoch* (1–36, the Book of Watchers; 37–71, the Similitudes of Enoch; 72–82, the Book of Heavenly Luminaries; 83–90, the Animal Apocalypse; 92–104, the Epistle of Enoch), *2 Enoch, 4 Ezra, 2 Baruch, 3 Baruch*, and the

Apocalypse of Abraham. Early Christian apocalypses include (in the early period) the Revelation to John (the only NT apocalypse) and the Shepherd of Hermas (late 1st through the mid-2d cent. C.E.), and the Apocalypses of Paul and Peter from the later period (late 2d to mid-3d cent. C.E.).

Defining the genre. One of the more widely accepted descriptions of the literary genre "apocalypse" is that of Collins (1979, 9): "'Apocalypse' is a genre of revelatory literature with a narrative framework, in which a revelation is mediated by an otherworldly being to a human recipient, disclosing a transcendent reality which is both temporal, insofar as it envisages eschatological salvation, and spatial insofar as it involves another, supernatural world."

Following the proposal of Hellholm (1986), it is useful to define the apocalypse genre further in terms of form, content, and function (Aune 1987, 230): In *form* an apocalypse is a first-person prose recital of revelatory visions or dreams, framed by a description of the circumstances of the revelatory experience, and structured to emphasize the central revelatory message. The *content* of apocalypses involves, in the broadest terms, the communication of a transcendent, often eschatological, perspective on human experience. Apocalypses exhibit a threefold *function*: (1) to legitimate the message (and/or the messenger) through an appeal to transcendent authorization, and (2) to create a literary surrogate of the revelatory experience for hearers or readers, (3) so that the recipients of the message will be motivated to modify their views and behaviors to conform to transcendent perspectives.

The setting of apocalypses. The fact that most apocalypses are pseudonymous (the Revelation of John and the *Shepherd of Hermas, both Christian apocalypses, are exceptions) has made it difficult to reconstruct the social situations within which they were written and to which they responded. There is nevertheless wide agreement that Jewish apocalypses were written or revised during times of social or political crisis, though such crises may run the spectrum from real to perceived. Focusing his attention on the period 400–200 B.C.E., Ploeger discerned a split in the postexilic Jewish community into two sharp divisions, the theocratic party (the ruling priestly aristocrats), which interpreted prophetic eschatology in terms of the Jewish state, and the eschatological party (forerunners of the apocalyptists), which awaited the fulfillment of the eschatological predictions of the prophets. More recently Hanson has argued that apocalypticism is a natural development of Israelite prophecy that originated in the intramural struggle between visionary prophets and hierocratic (Zadokite) priests that took place from the 6th through the 4th cent. B.C.E.

*Cosmology

Aune 1987; J. J. Collins 1979, 1982; Hanson 1979; Hellholm 1986

Apocalypse of John (see *Revelation to John)

Apocalypse of Paul, a pseudepigraphal apocalypse probably written between 395 and 416 C.E. (Piovanelli 1993, 45–59), in Greek in Egypt, reflects the general recognition of an interim afterlife and an otherworldly geography adapted to the new requirements of a triumphant church (Piovanelli 2000, 266). J. K. Elliott argues that the earliest form of the work was written in the mid-3d cent. C.E. The *Apocalypse of Paul* was originally written in Greek but has survived in an abbreviated form. The oldest and most complete form of the *Apocalypse of Paul* has been preserved in a Latin translation and a less complete form of that same version. There is also a Coptic version that, after the Latin version just mentioned, is the most important witness. It survives also in a Syriac translation; from Syriac it was translated into Armenian, in which it exists in four forms.

Genre. While the author of the *Apocalypse of Paul* consciously wrote within what he understood to be the apocalypse genre, there are some striking differences between his work and earlier Jewish and Christian apocalypses. First, the only eschatology that is really pertinent is that relating to the end of the life of the individual. The return of Christ and the final resurrection and judgment are referred to but only in a formal way. Second, the purpose of the *Apocalypse of Paul* is not to comfort the people of God in their experience of opposition and persecution in the world but rather to provide a strong sanction for moral living.

In the Greco-Roman world, tours of the other world are referred to occasionally, including Plato's Myth of Er (*Rep*. 10.13–16), the Dream of Scipio (Cicero, *Rep*. 6.9–26), the visions of Timarchus (Plutarch, *On the Genius of Socrates* 21–22), and the experiences of Thespesius (Plutarch, *On the Delays of Divine Justice* 22–31) and Menippus (Lucian, *Icaromenippus*). Most of these "apocalypses" consist of journeys in which the postmortem rewards of the righteous or the punishments of the wicked are seen and reported for the purpose of instilling fear and motivating correct behavior when these experiences are narrated (Diodorus 1.2.2; LCL trans.):

> For if it be true that the myths which are related about Hades, in spite of the fact that their subject-matter is fictitious, contribute greatly to fostering piety and justice among men, how much more must we assume that history, the prophetess of truth, she who is, as it were, the mother-city of philosophy as a whole, is still more potent to equip men's character for noble living!

This is clearly the purpose for which the *Apocalypse of Paul* was written, to scare the wits out of Christians, particularly those holding ecclesiastical offices, who were not living appropriately.

Texts and translations. A detailed bibliography of the editions of the various versions in which the *Apocalypse of Paul* survives is found in Silverstein and Hilhorst (1997, 47–58). There are just two Greek MSS of the work, a 13th-cent. MS in Munich and a 15th-cent. MS in Milan; both are summaries of the original. The longer Latin versions are more reliable, and recently Silverstein and Hilhorst (1997) have published seven Latin texts of the long version of the *Acts of Paul*, in three versions: L^1 (based on three MSS: Paris, St. Gall, and Escorial), L^2 (based on three MSS: Vienna, Graz, and Zürich), and L^3 (based on the MS Arnhem). These three versions are to be distinguished from several medieval Latin redactions that show significant alterations and tend to focus on the torments in Hell. A translation of the Latin MS Paris 1631 is given in J. K. Elliott 1993, 616–51.

Content. The work is introduced as "The revelation of the holy apostle Paul: the things which were revealed to him when he went up even to the third heaven and was caught up into Paradise and heard unspeakable words." This is a clear allusion to 2 Cor. 12:1–4, where Paul narrates his own experience of a heavenly ascent, where he "heard things that cannot be told, which man may not utter." The author of the *Apocalypse of Paul*, however, carefully distinguishes what Paul could tell from what he could not tell, thus defending the work (*Apoc. Paul* 21).

The miraculous discovery of the *Apocalypse of Paul* in the consulship of Theodosius the Younger and Flavius Constantius, i.e., 420 C.E. (388 C.E. is the more common date, but this is incorrect; see Silverstein and Hilhorst 1997, 11), is briefly narrated at the beginning of the work. A certain man who lived in Tarsus, in a house previously owned by Paul, was told by an angel in a dream to break up the foundations of the house and make public what he found. Prodded by a second dream he finally did so and found a marble box containing the *Apocalypse of Paul* along with a pair of Paul's sandals (§§1–2).

The work so discovered began with a speech of Paul (§§3–8) in which he began in imitation of OT prophetic models: "The word of the Lord came to me thus: Say to this people: 'How long will you transgress and add sin to sin and tempt the Lord who made you?'" The sun, the moon, and stars and the sea, he continued, have cried to God over the sins of the human race; God responded that he knew everything and would act in judgment. At sunset, Paul maintained, the angels go to worship God and report the deeds of people (§8), some reporting about those who had renounced the world; God promised to keep them through his beloved Son (§9), while other angels reported about those who did not live with pure and whole hearts; God encouraged the angels to guide them to repentance (§10).

At this point one of the angels near Paul caught him up in the Holy Spirit to the third heaven, serving as an **angelus interpres*, and promised to show him the place of the righteous dead and then the abyss where the souls of sinners dwell. Paul then saw pitiless angels who attend the wicked (§11) and shining angels, whom his angelic guide explains are angels of righteousness who attend the souls of the righteous (§12). When Paul explained that he wanted to see the souls of the righteous and sinners as they leave the world, the angels directed Paul's gaze down to the earth far below (§13). Paul saw a righteous man on his deathbed. When his soul left him, it was received by righteous angels, but there was a battle between these righteous angels and evil powers. The latter were powerless, however, because the soul had done the will of God on earth. The righteous angels then escorted the soul to the presence of God, who after positive angelic testimony entrusted the soul to Michael to lead into the paradise of joy until the day of resurrection (§14). Paul was then shown the death of an ungodly person, whose soul was immediately taken by the wicked angels (§15). The soul's guardian angel, who had reported to God daily about his evil conduct and hated his job, announced that he was abandoning the wicked soul. Yet because of the presence of God's image, the guardian angels insisted on taking the soul to God so God could make the decision. The guardian angel gave a negative report of the soul to God, who then consigned it to the angel of Tartarus (§16). Then Paul saw two angels leading a weeping soul who claimed to be righteous. The angel of the sinful soul was summoned by God and presented a document of all the sins committed by the soul. God swore by himself that if the soul had been righteous for the five years before the death of the body, he would have pardoned its sins (§17). God then summoned two souls as witnesses; the man had killed one a year earlier and fornicated with the other. God immediately consigned him to the torments of Tartarus (§18). The angelic guide then took Paul to the third heaven to show him the places of the righteous. There he saw on golden pillars two golden tablets on which the names of the righteous on earth were inscribed (§19). Entering the gates of paradise, Paul met first one, then another old man, whom the angel identified as Enoch and Elijah, who wept because most people did not accept the promises of God (§20). At this point the angels told Paul, "Whatever I now show you here and whatever you will hear, do not make it known to anyone on earth," but promised to show him what he could tell openly.

Paul was then led from the third heaven to the second heaven to the firmament and then to the gates of heaven. The angel opened a door through which Paul saw Ocean. Coming out of heaven he saw a bright land that is where Christ will reign for a thousand years (§21). Looking around, he saw a river flowing with milk and honey and astonishingly fruitful vines and trees, apparently an allegory of the abundance God gives to the righteous. The angel then showed Paul the rewards for the married who have lived chastely and the sevenfold rewards for virgins who afflict themselves for God. He was then shown Lake Acherusia, by which the city of Christ is located, and in which Michael baptizes righteous souls before leading them into the city (§22). The angels then took Paul on a boat to the golden city of Christ, surrounded by the four rivers of Gen. 2 (§23). On the way in, Paul saw people weeping who were not allowed into the city because, though they fasted day and night and practiced renunciation, they were really proud and self-centered (§24). Entering the city itself, he saw by the river of honey the major and minor prophets who did not do their own will (§25), and by the river of milk he saw the infants slain by Herod, as well as those who preserved their chastity and purity (§26). By the river of wine he saw Abraham, Isaac, and Jacob and other saints, where those who have given hospitality to strangers are taken by Michael (§27), and by the river of oil he saw those who dedicated themselves completely to God (§28). In the middle of the city he saw twelve golden thrones and between them other thrones for those who, though not knowing the Scriptures nor many Psalms, nevertheless obeyed the commands of God. Paul then saw a high altar next to which stood a shining figure saying, "Hallelujah!" identified by the angel as David, who must sing psalms at the time of the offering of the body and blood of Christ (§29). On asking what "Hallelujah" meant, Paul was told that it means "tecel. cat. marith. macha.," which means "Let us bless him all together" (see *Magical papyri). Those who are able but do not sing "Hallelujah" sin (§30).

The angelic guide then told Paul that he was taking him to the place of the godless and sinners. Passing the river Ocean that surrounds the earth, they passed into a region of darkness. Paul then saw a boiling fiery river, with men and women in it, some up to their knees, those who were neither righteous nor wicked; some up to their navels, those who received the Eucharist and then fornicated; some up to their lips and eyebrows, those who slandered each other in church and plotted evil against their neighbors (§31). Paul was shown another place of punishment where a river of fire poured over people who did not have faith in the Lord and were sinking in a bottomless abyss (§32). Though Paul wept at the sight, the angel responded that God knows what he is doing (§33). An old man being strangled by angels, Paul learned, was a fornicating presbyter (§34), and another old man tortured by four angels had been a bishop who did not execute his office properly and did not give justice to widows and orphans (§35). Another man, standing in fire up to his knees, with worms crawling out of his mouth, was identified as a deacon who fornicated; another man whose lips were being lacerated by a red-hot razor was said to be a lector who did not keep the commandments he read (§36). He was shown a multitude, identified as those who exacted interest, being devoured by worms and another multitude, who reviled the Word of God in church, chewing their tongues (§37). Below the pit where all the punishments are found were magicians, fornicators, and adulterers (§38). Girls wearing black and holding red-hot chains were virgins who defiled their virginity, and people with lacerated feet and who were naked in ice and snow were those who harmed orphans, widows, and the poor (§39). Blind men and women in bright clothing were pagans who gave alms but did not know God, while people on a fiery pyramid being torn to pieces by animals were those who did not pay attention when Scripture was read. After seeing yet more people in torment, Paul wept but was again reprimanded by the angel, since God does only what is just (§40). Paul was then taken to a fiery pit sealed with seven seals, which was opened for him. He was told that it was reserved for those who have not confessed that Christ came in the flesh and was born of the Virgin Mary and that the Eucharist is the body and blood of Christ (§41). He was guided to another place where he saw a two-headed worm and people gnashing their teeth; they are identified as those who say that Christ has not risen from the dead and that flesh does not rise again (§42). Michael then descended, and those tormented saw him and begged God for mercy. He told them that he had prayed for them continually and urged them to repent and weep on the chance that God would show them mercy (§43). Paul then saw heaven shake, and the tormented ones fell down before the throne of God and the 24 elders and the four beasts who were worshiping God. The Son of God then descended from heaven, and admonished them for not repenting earlier and promised them one day and one night of relief from their torments (§44).

Paul was then led by the angel to paradise, where Adam and Eve sinned, to meet the righteous. He saw a great tree from which the four rivers of paradise flowed and the tree of the knowledge of good and evil, as well as the tree of life (§45). He then saw a virgin coming toward him accompanied by 200 singing angels. The angel explained that this was the Virgin Mary. She greeted Paul and told him that she welcomed the righteous before they meet her beloved Son (§46). He then saw three handsome men, identified as Abraham, Isaac and Jacob, who greeted him, followed by the twelve patriarchs (§47). Another handsome man arrived, identified as Moses, who was weeping over the children of Israel who have not entered into the promises of God while pagans have (§49). Three others then arrived, identifying themselves as Isaiah, Jeremiah, and Ezekiel, each of whom described their martyr deaths. Paul then met and spoke to Lot, Job, Elijah and Elisha, Zechariah and John the Baptist, and Adam, each of whom tells Paul about their main concerns while on earth (§50). (It is probable that the *Apocalypse of Paul* concluded at this point.) Paul was then escorted to the Mount of Olives, where he met the apostles and Christ, who asked him if he was fully convinced of what he saw. Christ then continued:

> Amen, Amen, I tell you that whoever will take care of this apocalypse, and will write it and set it down as a testimony for the generations to come, to him I shall not show the underworld with its bitter weeping, until the second generation of his seed. And whoever reads it with faith, I shall bless him and his house. Whoever scoffs at the words of this apocalypse, I will punish him.

These sayings are obviously modeled after the integrity formula in Rev. 22:18–19.

*Apocalypse (literary genre)

Carozzi 1994; Charlesworth 1987, 289–94; J. K. Elliott 1993, 616–44; Silverstein and Hilhorst 1977; Himmelfarb 1983, 1993; Piovanelli 1993; 2000; Silverstein and Hilhorst 1997

Apocalypse of Peter is a *pseudepigraphal work composed before 150 C.E., not to be confused with the Coptic Gnostic *Apocalypse of Peter* (see *Nag Hammadi literature). Bauckham (1994, 8) argues that the *Apocalypse of Peter* originated during the Bar Kokhba war (132–35 C.E.). Clement of Alexandria (in Eusebius, *Hist. eccl.* 6.14.1) mentions the work. Eusebius (*Hist. eccl.* 3.25.3–4) puts the work "among the books which are not genuine [νόθοις] must be reckoned the Acts of Paul, the work entitled the Shepherd; the Apocalypse of Peter, and in addition to them the Letter called of Barnabas and the so-called Teachings of the Apostles [τῶν ἀποστόλων αἱ λεγόμεναι Διδαχαί].

Texts and translations. The *Apocalypse of Peter* is known from three Greek fragments, the largest from Akhmim is from the 8th or 9th cent. C.E., in the same MS containing part of the *Gospel of Peter* (see **Peter, Gospel of*) and part of *1 Enoch* in Greek. The *Apocalypse of Peter* is also preserved in an Ethiopic translation. The main debate is whether the Greek Akhmim fragment or the Ethiopic translation is a better representative or more original form of the text. The Ethiopic version is approximately the same length as the work mentioned in the Stichometry of Nicephorus (300 lines).

Content and literary analysis (Ethiopic version). The *Apocalypse of Peter* begins with Jesus seated on the Mount of Olives with his disciples, who ask him about the signs of his second coming and of the end of the world [cf. Mark 13:3–4 and parallels]. Then follows a series of allusions to the Olivet discourse in Mark 13 and parallels (§1). After telling the disciples the parable of the fig tree [Mark 13:28–29], Peter asks Jesus to explain its meaning. The fig tree is the house of Israel, explains Jesus, and then tells the parable of the Barren Fig Tree (Luke 13:6–9), and moves from there into a prediction of the coming of a false Christ or deceiver who will cause many martyrs. Enoch and Elijah will then appear to instruct people about the deceiver and his signs and wonders (§2). Jesus then shows Peter in the palm of his right hand a picture of what will happen on the last day, namely the reward and punishment of the righteous and sinners. Peter laments that it would be better had the sinners not been born but is rebuked by Jesus for resisting God, who said that he would show him their sinful deeds (§3). Jesus begins to tell Peter what sinners will experience on the day when God comes and hell, devouring animals, and the earth give back what is in them (§4). On the day of the judgment of sinners, cataracts of fire and darkness shall cover the world, and heaven and earth will be consumed by fire and destroyed. This involves the author in a contradiction (*NTA* 2.628):

> And as soon as the whole creation is dissolved, the men who are in the east shall flee to the west and those in the west to the east; those that are in the south shall flee to the north and those in the north to the south, and everywhere will the wrath of the fearful fire overtake them.

If the whole of creation is destroyed, how can be there any humans left on the earth to flee chaotically to other parts of the earth? The answer is simply that the author is probably using the figure of *proteron-hysteron* ("first-last"), in which the order of events is logically reversed.

Jesus then tells how he will return in glory, accompanied by angels, and be enthroned and crowned by God. The nations will see and weep and be consigned to the river of fire, while each individual will be recompensed in accordance with his or her own works. The elect will be protected, but the wicked will be punished with fire eternally (§6). Those who have blasphemed will be hung up by their tongues. Women who fornicated will be hung by the neck and cast into the pit of fire by their hair. The men who fornicated with them will be hung up by their thighs in that burning place. Murders will be cast into the flames, and the angel Ezrael will bring their victims to watch them in torment (§7). Women who aborted babies are in a deep, fiery pit filled with filth, while their children are in a place of delight crying out to God for what their parents did to them. The children will be given to the angel Temlakos, and those who killed them will be tormented forever (§8). Ezrael, the angel of wrath, brings men and women half burning and throws them into darkness; they are those who persecuted the righteous; slanderers chew their tongues and are tormented with red-hot irons. Those who relied on their wealth are cast down on a sharp fiery pillar (§9). Elsewhere, men and women stand in filth up to their knees; they lent money at exorbitant interest. Others, driven up and down a hill by demons are those who worshiped idols (§10). At another hill, people climb up and roll down in fire; they are those who did not honor their parents, while their children are brought by Ezrael to see them suffer. Young women clad in black have their flesh torn to bits; they are those who did not remain virgins until marriage (§11). Nearby, blind and dumb people with white raiment fall on coals of fire; they gave alms and thought themselves righteous before God but did not strive for righteousness (§12). Then Jesus says that angels will bring the righteous and clothe them in the garments of eternal life, and they will witness the punishment of those who hated them. The angel Tartarouchos will chasten those who did not repent while there is yet time; they will recognize the righteous judgment of God (§13). Christ continues: then I will give the righteous the baptism and salvation that they desire in the field of Acherusia or Elysium. I will cause the nations to enter into his eternal kingdom. Christ then commissions Peter to go to the special vineyard in the west and spread his gospel (§14). The Lord Jesus Christ then invites Peter and the disciples to his holy mountain, where they see two men who are indescribably brilliant (§15). Peter asks who they are, and Christ tells him they are Moses and Elijah. Peter offers to make three tabernacles but is rebuked by Christ for being obtuse. Looking up, the disciples see men who are greeting Jesus, Moses, and Elijah and goes with them to the second heaven. When the heavens shut, the disciples praise God who has written the names of the righteous in heaven in the book of life (§16).

*Apocalypse, literary genre of, *Apocalypse of Paul, *Revelation of John

Apocalyptic, a transliterated form of the Greek adjective ἀποκαλυπτικός based on the Greek verb ἀποκαλύπτειν, meaning "to disclose, reveal." The term "apocalyptic" is a modern designation widely used to refer to a worldview that characterized segments of early Judaism from ca. 200 B.C.E. to 200 C.E. and centered on the expectation of God's imminent intervention into human history in a decisive manner to save God's people and to punish their enemies by destroying the existing fallen cosmic order and by restoring or re-creating the cosmos in its original pristine perfection. Knowledge of cosmic secrets (one of the contributions of the wisdom tradition to apocalyptic) and the imminent eschatological plans of God were revealed to the apocalyptists through dreams and visions, and the apocalypses they wrote were primarily narratives of the visions they had received that were explained to them by an **angelus interpres* ("interpreting angel").

There are four aspects of apocalyptic that need to be distinguished: (1) "apocalyptic eschatology," a type of eschatology found in apocalypses which is similar to the eschatology of apocalypses, characterized by the tendency to view reality from the perspective of divine sovereignty (e.g., the eschatologies of the Qumran community, Jesus, and Paul); (2) "apocalypticism" or "millennialism," a form of collective behavior based on those beliefs (e.g., the movement led by John the Baptist and the revolts of Theudas reported in Acts 5:36 and Josephus, *Ant.* 20.97–98, and the unnamed Egyptian reported in Acts 21:38; Josephus, *Ant.* 20.169–72; *War* 2.261–63); (3) "apocalypse," a type of literature in which those beliefs occur in their most basic and complete form, centering on the revelation of cosmic lore and the end of the age; and (4) "apocalyptic imagery," the various constituent themes and motifs of apocalyptic eschatology used in various ways in early Jewish and early Christian literature. The focus in this article will be on Jewish apocalyptic eschatology and the ways in which Paul adapted some of the basic themes and structures of apocalyptic eschatology into his own theological thought.

A distinction has generally been made between eschatology and apocalypticism. Eschatology is a term that began to be used in the 19th cent. as a label for that aspect of systematic theology dealing with (a) topics relating to the future of the individual (death, resurrection, judgment, eternal life, heaven and hell), and (b) topics relating to the corporate or national future, i.e., the future of the Christian church or the Jewish people (e.g., the coming of the Messiah, the great tribulation, resurrection, judgment, the second coming of Christ, the temporary messianic kingdom, the re-creation of the universe). A distinction has often been made between prophetic eschatology and apocalyptic eschatology, which serves the useful function of emphasizing the continuities as well as the changes in Israelite-Jewish eschatological expectation. Following this model, prophetic eschatology, an optimistic perspective, anticipated that God would eventually restore the originally idyllic pristine conditions by acting through historical processes. The Israelite prophet proclaimed God's plans for Israel to both king and people in terms of actual historical and political events and processes and saw the future as arising out of the present. Apocalyptic eschatology, a pessimistic perspective, regards the future as breaking into the present.

The origins of apocalyptic. The origins of apocalypticism are disputed. Following Lücke, many scholars have viewed apocalypticism as a development of OT prophecy, perhaps as a result of the disillusionment of the postexilic period, which included subjection to foreign nations and tension within the Jewish community. Prophecy and apocalyptic exhibit elements of both continuity and discontinuity. The sharp contrasts often thought to exist between them are somewhat moderated by the recognition that prophecy itself underwent many changes and that there are numerous striking similarities between late prophecy and early apocalyptic (P. D. Hanson, 1979). Late prophetic books with tendencies that later emerged more fully developed in Jewish apocalyptic literature include the visions of Zech. 1–6 (with the presence of an angelic interpreter), Isa. 24–27, 56–66, Joel, and Zech. 9–14.

Others have argued that there was a fundamental break between prophecy and apocalypticism. Von Rad (1972), for example, rejected the view that the primary roots of apocalypticism were to be found in Israelite prophecy. He described apocalypticism as consisting in a clear-cut dualism, radical transcendence, esotericism, and gnosticism, and proposed that apocalypticism arose out of the Wisdom literature of the OT. Themes that are common to wisdom and apocalyptic literature and suggest the connection between the two types of literature include the following: (a) both sages and apocalyptists are referred to as "the wise," and preserved their teaching in written form, often emphasizing their special knowledge" and its antiquity; (2) both exhibit individualistic and universalistic tendencies; (3) both are concerned with the mysteries of nature from a celestial perspective; and (4) both reflect a deterministic view of history.

The suggestion that Israelite wisdom was the mother of Jewish apocalypticism has found little scholarly support in the form proposed by von Rad. The wisdom tradition in Israel was one of many influences upon the development of Jewish apocalypticism. There are some clear connections between wisdom and apocalyptic (Wis. 7:27; Sir. 24:33), both of which are scribal phenomena. Two types of wisdom should be distinguished, *proverbial wisdom* and *mantic wisdom*. The role of the "wise" in interpreting dreams is reflected in the biblical traditions concerning Joseph and Daniel, both of whom were able to explain the meaning of ambiguous revelatory dreams or visions through divine wisdom (Gen. 40:8; 41:25, 39; Dan. 2:19–23, 30, 45; 5:11–12). The figure of the **angelus interpres* ("interpreting angel") occurs frequently in Jewish apocalypses where he plays the analogous role of a supernatural revealer who is able to reveal the deeper significance of the dreams and visions experienced by the apocalyptist (Dan. 7–12; Zech. 1–6; 4 *Ezra*).

Other scholars proposed that many of the basic features of apocalypticism originated in Iran and had penetrated Jewish thought from outside during the Hellenistic period (ca. 400–200 B.C.E.) or more generally from the syncretistic tendencies during the Hellenistic period, when there was a blending of religious ideas from both west and east. This proposal has not proven persuasive.

Characteristics of apocalyptic. There are several widely acknowledged characteristics of apocalyptic: (1) the temporal dualism of the two ages; (2) the radical discontinuity between this age and the next, coupled with pessimism regarding the existing order and otherworldly hope directed toward the future order; (3) the division of history into segments (e.g., four, seven, twelve) reflecting a predetermined plan of history; (4) the expectation of the imminent arrival of the reign of God as an act of God spelling the doom of existing earthly conditions; (5) A cosmic perspective in which the primary location of an individual is no longer within a collective entity such as Israel or the people of God, and the impending crisis is not local but cosmic in scope; (6) the anticipation that a cataclysmic intervention of God will result in salvation for the righteous, conceived as the regaining of Edenic conditions; (7) angels and demons introduced to explain supernatural influence on historical events and eschatological events; (8) the introduction of a new mediator with royal functions. These characteristics are not exhaustive but serve the useful purpose of focusing on some of the distinctive features of the apocalyptic worldview.

One of the central characteristics of apocalypticism listed above is cosmological dualism, the conviction that the cosmos is divided into two opposing supernatural forces, God and Satan, who represent the moral qualities of good and evil. However, the Jewish conviction of God's absolute sovereignty implies that God is the originator of evil and that the resultant dualism of good and evil is limited, not eternal or absolute like the dualism of Iranian religion. This essentially limited cosmological dualism was understood in various different but related types of dualistic thought in early Jewish apocalypticism:

1. Temporal or eschatological dualism makes a sharp distinction between the present age and the age to come. The belief in two successive ages or worlds developed only gradually in Judaism. The earliest occurrence of the rabbinic phrase "the world to come" is found in *1 Enoch* 71:15 (ca. 200 B.C.E.). The doctrine of two ages is fully developed by ca. 90 C.E., for according to *4 Ezra* 7:50, "The Most High has not made one Age but two" (see 8:1). The day of judgment is considered the dividing point between the two ages (*4 Ezra* 7:113): the "day of judgment will be the end of this age and beginning of the immortal age to come."

2. Ethical dualism is based on a moral distinction between good and evil and sees humanity divided into two groups, the righteous and the wicked, in a way which corresponds to good and evil supernatural powers. Daniel 12:10 therefore distinguishes between the "wicked" and the "wise." *Jubilees* distinguishes between Israelites who are "the righteous nation" (24:29), "a righteous generation" (25:3), and the Gentiles who are sinners (23:24; 24:28). The Qumran War Scroll similarly distinguishes between the people of God and the Kittim (1QM 1.6; 18.2–3), and the *Testament of Asher* contrasts "good and single-faced people" (4.1) with "people of two faces" (3.1).

3. Psychological or microcosmic dualism is the internalization of the two-age schema that sees the forces of good and evil struggling for supremacy within each individual. In this type of dualism the antithetical supernatural cosmic powers, conceived of in the moral categories of good and evil, have an analogous correspondence to the struggle between good and evil experienced by individuals. In some strands of Jewish apocalyptic thought, notably the Qumran community and the circles that produced the *Testaments of the Twelve Patriarchs*, it was believed that God created two spirits, the spirit of truth and the spirit of error (i.e., the evil

spirit called Belial, 1QS 1.18–24; *T. Jud.* 20:1–5; see John 14:17; 15:26; 16:13; 1 John 4:6), and humans may live in accordance with one or the other; the Prince of Lights controls the lives of the children of righteousness, while the Angel of Darkness has dominion over the children of deceit (1QS 3.17–4.1; 4.2–11; 1QM 13.9–12). However, even the sins of the children of righteousness are ultimately caused by the spirit of error, for both spirits strive for supremacy within the heart of the individual (1QS 4.23–26; *T. Ash.* 1:3–5). The dominion of the spirit of error is temporally limited, however, for God will ultimately destroy it (1QS 4.18–19). The doctrine of the spirit of truth and the spirit of error that strive for supremacy in the heart of each person is similar to the rabbinic doctrine of the good and evil impulses.

Apocalyptic and messianic expectation. Messianism was not a necessary feature of Jewish apocalyptic. Two main types of Jewish messianism arose during the Second Temple period (513 B.C.E. to 70 C.E.), restorative and utopian messianism. *Restorative* messianism anticipated the restoration of the Davidic monarchy and centered on an expectation of the improvement and perfection of the present world through natural development (*Pss. Sol.* 17), modeled on an idealized historical period; i.e., the memory of the past is projected into the future. *Utopian* messianism anticipated a future era that would surpass everything previously known. Jewish messianism tended to focus, not on the restoration of a dynasty, but on a single messianic king sent by God to restore the fortunes of Israel. However, as a theocratic symbol, the Messiah is dispensable, since a messiah is not invariably part of all Jewish eschatological expectation. No such figure, for example plays a role in the eschatological scenarios of Joel, Isaiah 24–27, Daniel, Sirach, *Jubilees,* the *Assumption of Moses,* Tobit, 1 and 2 Maccabees, Wisdom, *1 Enoch* 1–36 [the Book of Watchers], 90–104 [the Epistle of Enoch], *2 Enoch.*

The eschatological antagonist. In Jewish apocalyptic literature there are two traditions of a wicked eschatological figure who functions as an agent of Satan or Beliar in misleading, opposing, and persecuting the people of God. Both traditions represent historicizations of the ancient combat myth. One tradition focuses on a godless, tyrannical ruler who will arise in the last generation to become the primary adversary of God or the Messiah. This satanic agent was expected to lead the forces of evil in the final battle between the forces of evil and the people of God (1QM 18.1; 1QS 4.18–18; *T. Dan* 5:10–11; *T. Mos.* 8). The historicization of the combat myth is already found in the OT, where the chaos monsters Rahab and Leviathan are sometimes used to symbolize foreign oppressors like Egypt (Pss. 74:14; 87:4; Isa. 30:7; Ezek. 29:3; 32:2–4). Several OT traditions provided the basis for the later apocalyptic conception of the Eschatological Antagonist, including the figure of Gog, the ruler of Magog in the Gog and Magog oracle in Ezek. 38–39 (see Rev. 20:8; *3 En.* 45:5); the references to a vague "enemy from the north" found in several OT prophecies (Ezek. 38:6, 15; 39:2; Jer. 1:13–15; 3:18; 4:6; 6:1, 22); and the depicting of Antiochus IV, the "little horn" in Dan. 7–8 as the oppressor of the people of God. The career of the Greco-Syrian king Antiochus IV Epiphanes (175–164 B.C.E.), whose actions against the Jewish people are described in 1 Macc. 1:20–61, and 2 Macc. 5:11–6:11, is presented as a mythologized apocalyptic figure in Dan. 11:36–39, who claims to be God or to be equal with God (Dan. 11:36–37; *Sib. Or.* 5.33–34; *Ascen. Isa.* 4:6; *2 Enoch* [Rec. J] 29:4). Later the characteristics of the Eschatological Antagonist were augmented and embellished by traditions based on the Roman emperors Caligula and Nero, both of whom had divine pretensions that their Roman contemporaries considered tacky and that outraged the Jews. The other tradition concerns the false prophet who performs signs and wonders to legitimate his false teaching (Deut. 13:2–6). Occasionally Satan and the Eschatological Antagonist are identified as the same person, as in *Sib. Or.* 3.63–74 and *Ascen. Isa.* 7:1–7, where Nero (=the Eschatological Antagonist) is regarded as Beliar (=Satan) incarnate.

The transformation of the cosmos. In Isa. 65:17 and 66:22 the creation of a new heaven and a new earth is predicted. The theme of the re-creation or renewal of creation was taken up into apocalyptic literature as the final eschatological act. Essentially the expectation of a new creation or a renewed creation is a particular application of the two-age schema in which the first creation is identified with the present evil age (or world) and the new or renewed creation is identified with the age (or world) to come. While there are many references to the new creation in Jewish apocalyptic literature, it is not always clear whether (a) the present order of creation is reduced to chaos before the act of re-creation (*1 En.* 72:1; 91:16; *Sib. Or.* 5.212; *Jub.* 1:29; 4:26; *L.A.B.* 3:10; *Apoc. El.* 5:38; 2 Pet. 3:13; Rev. 21:1, 5; see 2 Cor. 5:17; Gal.

6:15), or (b) the renewal or transformation of the existing world is in view (*1 En.* 45:4–5; *2 Apoc. Bar.* 32:6; 44:12; 49:3; 57:2; *L.A.B.* 32:17; *4 Ezra* 7:30–31, 75; see Rom. 8:21). In many of these passages the pattern for the new or transformed creation is based on the Edenic conditions thought to have existed on the earth before the fall of Adam and Eve.

*Cosmogony, *Cosmology, *Eschatology, *Protology

J. Collins 1984a, 1997, 1999; Collins and Charlesworth (eds.) 1991; P. D. Hanson 1976, 1979; Hellholm 1989; Koch 1970; Lambrecht (ed.) 1980; W. R. Millar 1976; Rowland 1982; Stone 1976, 1984a; VanderKam and Adler (eds.) 1996; D. S. Russell 1964; von Rad 1972

Apocalypticism (see *Apocalyptic)

Apocrypha, New Testament (NTA) is a general modern term for an extremely heterogenous corpus of about 100 pseudonymous and *anonymous early Christian writings, some of which were written in conscious imitation of the types of literature found in the NT, and thus includes the four primary NT genres, apocryphal gospels (see *Gospels, Apocryphal), acts (see *Acts, Apocryphal), *letters, and *apocalypses, written under the names of various men and women associated with the apostolic period (*NTA*, 1.50–61). The plural term "apocrypha" itself is a transliteration of the neuter plural form of the Greek word ἀπόκρυφος, meaning "hidden, concealed," and by extension, "obscure, hard to understand" (and then "false, spurious"). This designation was applied to particular types of early Christian literature on analogy with the notion of an OT Apocrypha (see *Apocrypha, OT). The phrase ἀπόκρυφα βιβλία ("secret books") was used by the late 2d cent. C.E. to refer to esoteric writings, whether pagan, heretical, or gnostic. The ἀπόκρυφαι καὶ νόθαι γραφαί ("secret and spurious writings") of the Marcosians are referred to by Irenaeus (*Adv. haer.* 1.20.2), and Epiphanius similarly refers to the ἀπόκρυφοι βίβλοι ("secret books") of the Archontics (*Pan.* 40.2). Toward the end of the 2d cent. the term "apocrypha" came to mean "spurious, false" (Irenaeus, *Adv. haer.* 1.20.1; Tertullian, *De pud.* 10.12). The term "apocryphal New Testament" was used for the first time by Fabricius (1719), as the title of a three-volume collection of early Christian writings entitled *Codex apocryphus Novi Testamenti.* Through the apocryphal gospels, along with apocryphal acts, epistles, and apocalypses, make up what has come to be known as the NTA, the designation is itself problematic, for it incorrectly suggests that these texts are in some sense always ancillary to the NT. The more neutral label "ancient Christian apocrypha" is preferable (Junod 1983). The NTA are often understood as early Christian writings not accepted into the Christian canon of Scripture, though that is inaccurate, since some of these documents were written before, during, and after the lengthy canonization process that resulted in the twenty-seven book NT common to most Eastern and Western branches of the Christian church.

Recent scholarship. Since the 1980s the long-neglected NTA have increasingly attracted the attention of scholars. The "Association pour la littérature apocryphe chrétienne" was founded in 1981, with a Swiss team of scholars under F. Bovon working on apocryphal acts of apostles, and a French team under P. Geoltrain and F. Schmidt working on apocryphal gospels and apocalypses (Bovon 1983). The *Series Apocryphorum* in the *Corpus Christianorum* was initiated that same year (DuBois 1984). Another factor in the increasing interest in the NTA is the result of the current reassessment of the historical and theological function and contents of the Christian canon of Scripture. For most Christians, the canonical status of the four NT Gospels means that they have a theologically normative status that extracanonical gospels lack. What Hedrick (1988, 1–8) has called "the tyranny of the Synoptic Gospels" in NT scholarship is not really difficult to understand. Past NT scholarship was largely confined to Christian institutions of higher learning with a heavy theological investment in interpreting biblical literature for Christian faith and life. More recently, the increasing presence of NT studies at secular universities has somewhat diverted the emphasis from theological concerns toward historical, social, religious, and literary issues. This shift has encouraged renewed interest in the NTA. The special theological status of the NT literature does not mean that it is superior to the NTA historically or literarily.

The formation of the NT canon was a long process that began in the 2d cent. C.E. and was largely completed by the end of the 4th cent. C.E. By the 3d cent., Origen noted that while the church had four gospels, the sects had many more, including gospels called *According to the Egyptians*, *According to the Twelve Apostles*, *According to Basilides*, *According to Thomas*, *According to Matthias*, and many more (*Hom. in Luc.* 1; cf. Jerome, *Comm. Matt.* 35).

*Clement of Alexandria (ca. 115–215 C.E.), on the other hand, regarded the *Preaching of Peter* as an actual work of Peter (*Strom.* 2.15.68; 6.5.39ff.) and accepted the *Apocalypse of Peter* as genuinely Petrine (Eusebius, *Hist. eccl.* 6.14.1). Even then, various sections of the great church did not restrict their collection of sacred Christian literature to the 27 documents recommended by Athanasius of Alexandria in his 37th Festal Letter (367 C.E.), in the East, or in the Acts of the Council of Hippo (393 C.E.) or the Third Council of Carthage (397 C.E.), in the West. Though this fact has long been recognized, the residual effects of the theological distinction between canonical and extracanonical early Christian literature has been to ignore the historical, literary, sociological, and theological value of the NTA. Yet they are intrinsically valuable and deserve to be studied intensively in and of themselves, and not simply for the light they might shed on the canonical Gospels or the contrasts that might be drawn between them and the canonical Gospels.

*Acts, Apocryphal, *Apocalypses, *Gospels, Apocryphal, *Letters, *Nag Hammadi literature, *Pseudepigrapha, NT

ABD 1:294–97; Bovon 1983; Charlesworth 1987; DuBois 1984; Erbetta 1966; James 1924; Junod 1983; Layton 1987; Moraldi 1971; Robinson (ed.) 1988; Schneemelcher 1991–92

Apocrypha, Old Testament is a designation for about a dozen books or parts of books that are not found in the Hebrew Bible or in the Protestant OT but are part of the deuterocanonical portion of the Roman Catholic OT and are (with some variations) part of the Bible of Eastern Orthodox churches. The term "apocrypha" was used by Jerome for books and parts of books found in the *Septuagint, but not in the Hebrew Bible. The books generally included in the OT Apocrypha are: (1) 1 Esdras, (2) 2 Esdras=4 Ezra (not included among the Roman Catholic deuterocanonical books), (3) Tobit, (4) Judith, (5) Wisdom of Solomon, (6) Ecclesiasticus, (7) Baruch, (8) Prayer of Manasseh (not included among the Roman Catholic deuterocanonical books), (9) 1 Maccabees, (10) 2 Maccabees. In addition, there are a number of books that exist in an expanded form in the Septuagint, when compared with the versions found in the Masoretic Text of the Hebrew Bible: (1) Additions to Esther (six separate additions, one beginning and one concluding the book, with the rest punctuating the text; the name of God is frequently mentioned in these additions but is absent from the Hebrew version of the book); (2) Additions to Daniel (including two separate stories: Susanna, Bel and the Dragon, and one hymn: the Song of the Three Children). Finally, the books of Jeremiah and Ezekiel exist in a shorter form in the Septuagint compared with the Masoretic Text; in both instances the shorter text reflects a more original version (see Tov 1986 on Ezekiel)—though the shortened form in neither text is normally considered part of the Apocryphal OT.

Goodspeed 1959

Apograph, a transliterated form of the Greek word ἀπόγραφον ("copy"), is a term used for an extant manuscript that is a direct copy of another extant manuscript and therefore of little or no use for establishing a critical text of the text in question. For example, *British Museum Loan Nr. 36*, dated 2 April 1541 (containing the three extant works of *Justin Martyr) is an apograph of *Codex Parisinus graecus* 450, dated 11 September 6872=1363 C.E. This can become quite complicated. And 2258, a 17th-cent. minuscule manuscript of Revelation, is an apograph of 2076 (16th cent.), and Rev. 11:18–22:21 is in turn an apograph of 2073 (14th cent.). In this case all three MSS were produced at the Iviron monastery on Mount Athos. The term "apograph" is also used by some for the original copy of a text made by the author (Diéz Merino 1994, 51).

Apollonius of Tyana (see *Philostratus)

Apologetic literature The term "apologetic" (the Greek word ἀπολογία means "defense") can refer to a formal legal defense of someone accused of breaking the law (e.g., the defense of Socrates in Plato's *Apology*, and the defense speeches of Paul in Acts 22:1–21; 24:10–21; 26:1–29, each of which is introduced with the noun ἀπολογία or the verb ἀπολογεῖσθαι). "Apologetic" has been defined as "the defense of a cause or party supposed to be of paramount importance to the speaker. It may include *apologia* in the sense of Plato's *Apology*, the defense of a single person, but is distinguished from polemic (which need not assume any previous attack by the opponent) and from merely epideictic or occasional orations" (Edwards, Goodman, Price and Rowland 1999, 1). Frequently the "cause" involves religious or philosophical traditions.

The specific phrase "apologetic literature" is sometimes understood in a broad sense as referring *both* to a reasoned defense against accusations or slander (in legal or nonlegal contexts) and to propagandistic attempts to persuade outsiders of the truth of a particular position or belief. This latter emphasis is more properly called *protreptic (Koester 1982, 2.138–40; Guerra 1995, 1–3). Conventional wisdom has assumed that apologetic literature is normally directed to the opposition (as the *First Apology* of *Justin Martyr clearly was, given the appended rescript from the *A libellis*), though it is probable that both apologetic and protreptic literature played an important internal role in providing self-definition for the group within which it arose. Apologetic literature often emerges from minority groups who have conflicting attitudes toward the dominant culture (Grant 1988, 9). An ἀπολογία is not an independent literary genre, but rather an argumentative oral or literary form, with direct speech as the primary discourse mode, belonging to the category of forensic rhetoric. While narrative plays a role in apologetic speeches, as in all forensic speeches, the speaker will always be there to explain the narrative (Alexander 1999, 24–25).

Greco-Roman apologetics. There are a number of literary works called "apologies" that defend an individual in a juridical setting, including Demosthenes *De corona*; Plato, *Apologia*; Xenophon, *Apologia* (two defenses of Socrates); and Apuleius, *Apologia* (a self-defense against the charge of magic). There are a number of other literary works in which the apologetic element is more general in nature, such as the apologetic historiography of Josephus (Sterling 1992; see *Historiography).

Hellenistic Jewish apologetics. The cultural challenge for both Judaism and Christianity was simply that in the Greco-Roman world, "Nothing could be new and true" (F. Young 1997, 52). Hellenistic Jewish apologetic literature arose in the setting of a large Jewish Diaspora population which had incurred enmity and misunderstanding on the part of their pagan neighbors by maintaining various degrees of social and cultural separation. Hellenistic Jewish apologetic was directed to two different fronts. The earliest opponents of Jewish apologists were educated pagans. Though most Hellenistic Jewish apologetic literature has not survived (Schürer 1973–87, 3.609–16), one important document has been preserved. *Josephus, at the beginning of the 2d cent. C.E., wrote *Contra Apionem*, a reply to critics of his *Antiquities of the Jews* as well as to anti-Semitism more generally. In this work he emphasizes the great antiquity of Moses and the dependence of Greeks and other cultures on the achievements of Moses (Droge 1989). Though the cultural dependence of the Greeks on Moses is a frequent theme of early Jewish apologetic literature (e.g., Aristobulus the Jewish philosopher, fl. ca. 160 B.C.E.), that theme was based on the Greeks' own tendency to trace the origins of their beliefs and philosophical systems back to the East (Bollansée 1999, 108–11) and is found in Hecataeus of Abdera (*FGH* 264 F 25 §69–98), and Hermippos of Smyrna, late 3d cent. B.C.E. (F 1 in Bollansée 1999, 14–15).

Later, Hellenistic Jews directed polemic against Christians. How long this latter debate lasted is disputed. While some scholars think that the debate between Judaism and Christianity ended when the latter emerged from the former, ca. 80 C.E. (Harnack 1930), others think that discussion continued on well into the 2d cent. C.E. (Stanton 1985), and Boyarin (1999) has recently argued provocatively that in fact there was a hazy line between early Judaism and early Christianity well into the 3d cent. Early Jewish polemic against Christians in the Jewish-Christian debate included such motifs as Jesus as a *deceiver* who had led Israel astray, a charge based on Deut. 13 (Matt. 27:63; John 7:12, 47; *T. Levi* 16:3; Justin, *Dial.* 69; 108; *Acts Thom.* 48, 96, 102; 106–7; *b. Sanh.* 43a; 107b; Martyn 1968, 72–81; Stanton 1985, 379–82), and the tandem charge that Jesus was a *magician* or *sorcerer* (*b. Sanh.* 43a; 107b). Christians are also accused of destroying the law (Luke 23:2; Justin, *Dial.* 17.1). Christians responded that it was the Jewish leaders who had led Israel astray, and that it was the Jews who misinterpreted Scripture.

Christian apologetics. While none of the books of the NT appears to have been specifically written for the purpose of convincing outsiders of the truth of Christianity or to rebut false charges made against Christians, *Luke–Acts has often been thought to have an apologetic purpose (survey in Alexander 1999, 15–44). This apologetic purpose has been construed along five different lines (Alexander 1999, 16–19): (1) as an inner-Christian apologetic (e.g., as antignostic; see Talbert 1966, 115); (2) as an apologetic directed toward Judaism; (3) as an apology directed to the Greeks (taking up the apologetic program developed in Hellenistic Judaism); (4) as a political apologetic defending the innocence of Paul and hence all Christians against Roman charges; and (5) as an apologetic aimed at forging group identity (Sterling 1992), to explain and justify Christianity to the members of his [Luke's] community" (Esler 1987, 222). Sterling (1992, 386), however, properly observes that "Josephos made his case *directly* to the Hellenistic world; Luke–Acts makes its case *indirectly* by offering examples and precedents to Christians so that they can make their own *apologia*." However, since apologies constitute a subgenre of forensic speech, they imply a particular audience and are dominated by direct discourse, which is absent from Luke–Acts. Luke–Acts is therefore not an apology in the accepted sense of the term. However, there are a number of dramatic scenes, particularly in Acts, in which various characters defend themselves in judicial contexts with apologetic speeches (Pervo 1987, 34–50). Five defense speeches (the third is truncated) are attributed to Paul (before a hostile crowd in the temple: Acts 22:1–21; before the Sanhedrin: 23:1–21; before Felix and Ananias: 24:10–21; before Festus: 25:6–12; before Festus and Agrippa: 26:1–32). Each, with the exception of the second, is described as an "apology" using either the verb ἀπολογεῖσθαι (24:10; 26:1, 2, 24) or the noun ἀπολογία (22:1; 25:16); see Alexander 1999, 36. However, Christianity was relatively diverse throughout the second half of the 1st cent., with the result that various groups of Christians found it necessary to define themselves over against what they regarded as dissident groups. In *Galatians, for example, Paul defends his version of Christianity against the alternate vision of those he called the "circumcision party" (Betz 1979). Christianity did not tend to think of itself as a new religious tradition, but rather emphasized a supercessionist relationship to Israel. Two critical boundary areas needed attention: (1) The relationship between followers of Christ and Judaism—complicated by the fact that Christianity emerged from Judaism only gradually and hesitatingly—was worked out in various ways during the first three centuries C.E., and beyond (A. L. Williams 1935). (2) The relationship between Christians and Greco-Roman paganism was equally complex, since for some, pagan "insights" could be incorporated into the Christian belief system (e.g., Acts 17:22–23), while others were convinced that Greco-Roman culture and religion had to be rejected lock, stock, and barrel (*Tatian, *Oratio ad Graecos*). During the 2d cent., Christians began to think of themselves as "the third race" in addition to Greeks and Romans.

Justin, Tatian, and Theophilus all emphasized the antiquity of Moses and his role as the source of Greek culture in their attempt to answer the charge of novelty (Droge 1989). While Justin offered literary parallels to prove that Plato had read Moses, Tatian constructed a chronological argument to prove that Moses was more ancient than all the Greek writers (*Oratio ad Graecos* 31). Phoenician and Egyptian sources, he argued, provide evidence to date Solomon and Moses. The latter, he maintained, lived four hundred years before the Trojan war (Droge 1989, 92–95). The Christian apologists had also appropriated the Hebrew Scriptures, widely regarded as "an ancient collection of barbarian texts" (F. Young 1997, 54), as the foundation documents of Christianity. This expropriation of the Jewish classical texts was inherently problematic, since Christians did not interpret them as the Jews did. *Justin's *Dialogue with Trypho* can be construed as a concentrated effort to showcase the propriety of the Christian interpretation of Scripture, which the Jew read in a completely wrong way. The reverse side of the argument is represented by the pagan philosopher Celsus's anti-Christian work, the *True Word*, quoted in lengthy sections in Origen's *Contra Celsum*.

The Jewish-Christian debate. Toward the end of the 2d cent. C.E., Celsus expressed the opinion that the running argument between Christians and Jews was foolish, since there wasn't a dime's worth of difference between them (Origen, *Contra Celsum* 3.1). Christians and Jews, of course, did not see it that way, since the things they held in common were the very things about which they disagreed the most (e.g., the Torah). However, the distinction between "Jewish" and "Christian" is largely anachronistic for the first century C.E., when hard and fast boundaries were not yet drawn between Judaism and Christianity (Pilch 1998, 3). The so-called "parting of the ways" between Judaism and Christianity, which many date to ca. 85 C.E., was not a single event but rather the result of a series of unconnected conflicts that unfolded over a relatively wide geographical area ca. 90–130 C.E. (Stanton 1985), and even beyond (Boyarin 1999).

*Aristides, *Josephus, *Justin Martyr, *Protreptic literature, *Quadratus

———

Monique Alexandre 1998; Aune 1991b, 1992; Belkin 1936; Buell 1999; Droge 1989; 1992; Edwards, Goodman, and Price 1999; Esler

1987; Feldman 1990; Friedländer 1903; Grant 1988a, 1988b; Guerra 1988, 1995; Hardwick 1996; Kinzig 1989; Koester 1982, 1.338–45; Kofsky 2000; Meiser 2000; Pilhofer 1990; Pouderon and Doré 1998; Schürer 1973–87; Stanton 1985; Sterling 1992; Swain 1996; Tcherikover 1956

Apologists, Christian, a group of Christian intellectuals who began to write exoteric defenses of the charges brought against Christians (ca. 125–200 C.E.), beginning with *Quadratus (ca. 125 C.E.), who wrote under Hadrian.

*Apologetic literature, *Athenagoras of Athens, *Irenaeus, *Justin Martyr, *Quadratus

---

Grant 1988

***Apology* of Aristides** (see *Aristides)

***Apology* of Quadratus** (see *Quadratus)

***Apophthegmata Patrum*,** a Latin title meaning "Sayings of the [Desert] Fathers," a designation for several sayings collections, some in Coptic and others in Greek, all attributed to Egyptian monks who flourished in the 4th through the 5th cents. C.E. (see *Chreia). Many of these sayings are attributed to Poeman, who died early in the 5th cent. It may have been Poeman's death which stimulated the process of collecting such sayings, which are organized alphabetically by the names of the monks to whom they are attributed.

*Chreia, *Pronouncement stories

Lilienfeld 1977; McVey 1998; Regnault 1974

Aporia (pl. aporiai or aporias), a transliterated Greek word meaning "difficulty, problem, question," is used in several literarily relevant ways: (1) Aporia is used as a *rhetorical question (introduced with "how" or "who") in introductory sections of ancient Greek hymns (Bundy 1972, 57–77), as in the *Homeric Hymn to Apollo* 19, 207: "How shall I sing of you, who are in all ways worthy of song?" See also *Iliad* 2.484–93; 11.218; 14.508; Callimachus, *Hym. Jov.* 91–92; Horace, *Carm.* 1.31.1–2). The incomparability of God in the Jewish tradition is emphasized by hymnic aporiai introduced by the phrase "who is like" (Exod. 15:11; Pss. 35:10; 113:5). One of the hymns in magical papyri, found in *PGM* XII.244–52 (written in hexameter), contains six occurrences of τίς ("who" or "what") in the first four lines (trans. Betz 1986, 163; cf. the commentary in Merkelbach and Totti 1990, 1.16–19):

> Who molded the forms of the beasts? Who formed their routes?
> Who was the begetter of fruits? Whose raises up the mountains?
> Who commanded the winds to hold to their annual tasks?
> What Aion nourishing an Aion rules the Aions?

In the NT this device occurs in Rev. 5:2, "Who is worthy to open the scroll and break its seals?" and Rev. 13:4, "Who is like the beast, and who can fight against it?"

(2) In rhetoric, and particularly in the *exordium of a speech, the speaker feigns to be at a loss as how to begin (Quintilian 9.2.19; Race 1982, 20–21).

(3) In the context of philosophical dialectic, aporiai are the problems or questions posed as the starting point for philosophic discussion, followed by reviews and critiques of previous opinions on the subject, and then concluded with a more satisfactory solution (εὐπορία, λύσις); see Aristotle, *De anima* 1.403; *Nichomachaean Ethics* 7.1145b.

(4) In modern source-critical analysis, the term "aporia" is used of literary inconsistencies, contradictions, interruptions, sudden turns, non sequiturs, and doublets (often collectively designated "seams") in texts that suggest the original order of the text has somehow been interrupted in the editorial process. The detection of aporiai is one method source-critical analysis used to separate tradition from redaction. Three examples: (a) Mark 10:46: "And they came to Jericho. And as he was leaving Jericho . . ." (b) 2 Cor. 2:13 seems to be continued in 2 Cor. 7:5, suggesting that the intervening text in 2:14–7:4 is a later insertion (Welborn 1996; see *Corinthians, Second Letter to the, and *Interpolation). (c) John 5 confuses the geographical continuity between John 4 and 6 (von Wahlde 1989, 17–20); see *John, Gospel of.

*Interpolation, *Source criticism, *Unity, literary

Nicol 1972, 27–30; Peters 1967, 22–23; von Wahlde 1989

Apostolic Fathers is a modern collective designation for an essentially arbitrary collection of Christian writings that originated from the late 1st cent. to the mid-2d cent. C.E. (ca. 96–150). The name was first applied by J. B. Cotelier in 1672 to a collection of writings including *Barnabas, 1 Clement,* the Shepherd of Hermas, the letters of Ignatius, and Polycarp, and the martyr acts of Clement, Ignatius and Polycarp. A. Gallandi expanded the collection in 1765 to include the letter to Diognetus and the fragments of Papias and *Quadratus. The *Didache*, discovered in 1873, was immediately added to the corpus. Even in the mid-20th cent. various editors tended to vary the contents of the Apostolic Fathers.

The works conventionally included in the Apostolic Fathers include fifteen authors or compositions: *1 *Clement, 2 *Clement,* the seven letters of *Ignatius of Antioch (also found in a larger collection of thirteen letters, including six from a later unknown author), the letter of *Polycarp to the Philippians, the **Martyrdom of Polycarp,* the letter of **Barnabas,* the **Didache,* the *Shepherd of Hermas and the fragments of *Papias. The Letter to **Diognetus* (which is an apologetic treatise, not a letter) has often been included in this collection, though it probably belongs to a slightly later period. Several of these works are preserved in Codex Hierosolymitanus (*1 Clement, 2 Clement, Letter of Barnabas*, and the longer recension of the Letters of Ignatius). Though all of these writings were excluded from the NT canon, many of them were sometimes included in biblical manuscripts (e.g., *1 Clement* and *2 Clement* in Codex Alexandrinus, *Barnabas* and *Hermas* in Codex Sinaiticus), suggesting that those who produced these manuscripts considered them canonical. All of these writings are concerned only with the internal situation and spiritual needs of various Christian communities. They also represent the earliest developments of Christian traditions found outside the canonical NT.

The adjective "apostolic" means disciples of apostles, while the term "fathers" means significant orthodox writers of the past (Grant 1964, v). The dates of these writings vary widely. *First Clement* was certainly written before the end of the first century C.E., and the letter of *Barnabas* and the *Didache* may have been. Similarly, the earliest part of the Shepherd of Hermas (Vis. 1–4) may date to the end of the 1st cent. and the remainder to the mid-2d cent.

Tools for studying the Apostolic Fathers. (1) *Text*: the basic Funk and Bihlmeyer (1956) text is now available in Lindemann and Paulsen (1992), with the Greek text and German translation on opposing pages. An earlier publication of the Greek text with an English translation is found in Lake (1912, 1). Geerard 1983 provides brief bibliographies and locations of the Greek texts and the versions for each of the Apostolic Fathers: Clement of Rome (5–6), Ignatius of Antioch (12–17), Polycarp (18–20), Papias (20–21), Barnabas (21–22), Hermas (22–23), Letter to Diognetus (55). (2) *Translations*: Glimm, Marique, and Walsh (1947), Staniforth (1968), Holmes (1989, 1992 [a revision of the Lightfoot and Harmer translation]). (3) *Concordances*: Goodspeed 1910 (individual words, broken down by inflected forms); H. Kraft 1963 (words placed in the context of a short lemma). (4) *Greek lexica*: Lampe (ed.) 1961; Bauer, Danker, Arndt, and Gingrich 2001.

**Barnabas, Letter of, *Clement, First Letter of, *Clement, Second Letter of, *Didache,* *Ignatius of Antioch, *Ignatius, letters of, *Shepherd of Hermas

---

Jefford 1996; Schoedel 1989; Staniforth 1968; Tugwell 1990

Apostolic parousia is the designation for an epistolary topos in the Pauline letters in which Paul speaks of an anticipated visit or "travelogue" in order to make his apostolic authority and power present in the churches to which he writes. The instances of the "apostolic parousia" in the Pauline letters include 1 Thess. 2:17–3:10; Rom. 1:8–13; 15:14–33; 1 Cor. 4:14–21; 16:1–11; 2 Cor. 8:16–23; 9:1–5; 12:14–13:13; Gal. 4:12–20; Phil. 2:19–24; Phlm. 22. Funk suggests a fivefold structure for these "travelogues" (1967, 252–53): (1) a statement of Paul's disposition or purpose in writing; (2) "the basis of Paul's apostolic relation to the recipients"; (3) "implementation of the apostolic *parousia*"; (4) "invocation of divine approval and support for the apostolic *parousia*," and (5) "benefit from the apostolic *parousia* accruing" with three subfeatures. The function of the "apostolic parousia" in 1 Thessalonians, however, does not emphasize the apostle's authority and power so much as express his love and concern for the Thessalonian Christians (Jervis 1991, 116).

*Epistolography, *Letters, literary genre of

Funk 1967; Jervis 1991, 110–31

Apostrophe, a transliteration of the Greek word ἀποστροφή ("a turning away") is a figure of speech in which a discourse is interrupted in order to address a person or personified thing (Lanham 1991, 20; cf. Quintilian 9.3.24). Two examples of apostrophe occur in Romans 2: 2:1–16: "Therefore you have no excuse, O man, whoever you are, when you judge another," etc. (directed to people generally), and 2:17–29: "But if you call yourself a Jew and rely upon the law," etc. (directed to the Jews); see R. D. Anderson 1999, 209.

———

R. D. Anderson 2000, 25

Apuleius of Madauros was a wealthy, well-educated orator and writer born in Madauros, North Africa, ca. 124 C.E. (Griffiths 1975). Although he is commonly referred to as Lucius Apuleius, the *praenomen* "Lucius" is uncertain, perhaps derived from the name of the protagonist in Apuleius's *Metamorphoses*, with whom Apuleius identifies himself at the end of the novel (*Metam.* 11.27.9). What is known about Apuleius is based largely on his own works and from the attacks against them by Augustine (Harrison 1996; Horsfall Scotti 1990). Although Apuleius probably knew Punic, a western form of Phoenician (Harrison 2000), his extant works were composed in Latin, exemplifying a Latin *Asianism marked by archaic words, poetry, rhythm, assonance, and the influence of Greek (Harrison 1996). His fluency in Greek, which Apuleius would have his audiences believe was equal to that of his Latin (*Apol.* 36–39; *De deo Socr.* 145), was frequently paraded before North African listeners who were not proficient in Greek in order to give him greater status. After having studied a variety of subjects in Carthage, Athens, and Rome, such as poetry, natural science, oratory, and philosophy in the 150s, Apuleius boasted that he was a *philosophus Platonicus* (*Apol.* 10.6), indicating his affinity for Platonic philosophy. During his time in Greece he was probably initiated into the mysteries of Demeter at Eleusis, Isis at Kenchreai, and possibly Dionysos (*Apol.* 55.8–11; *Metam.* 11.21–25). While in Athens, Apuleius became friends with a certain Pontianus, also a North African, who persuaded Apuleius to marry his wealthy widowed mother, Pudentilla, to protect Pontianus's inheritance. However, after the marriage Pudentilla's disgruntled relatives charged Apuleius in 158 or 159 with having seduced her by magic to obtain her wealth (Syme 1959; Griffiths 1975; Harrison 2000). This is the context for Apuleius's *Apologia* (or *Pro se de Magia*; Hijmans 1993), his earliest extant work, in which he launches a victorious self-defense against the legal charge of having practiced magic to seduce a wealthy widow—a crime punishable by death (Walsh 1994). Much of Apuleius's career in the 160s was spent in Carthage, where he lectured as an orator. The philosophical work *De deo Socratis*, likely composed after the *Apology*, reveals his Platonism and provides a significant ancient survey of *daemones*. Apuleius classifies *daemones* variously as intermediate powers subject to emotion, located between the gods and humans, whose function is to manage religious activity between heaven and earth, indispensable for the practice of divination. His work entitled *Florida* is an anthology of fragmentary *epideictic orations delivered at different times in Carthage displaying his considerable learning and oratorical abilities. Apuleius's most significant work, the *Metamorphoses*, referred to by Augustine as *asini aurei* (*Golden Ass*), seems to have been written later in Apuleius's career, ca. 170 C.E. (Griffiths 1975). Based in part on a lost Greek epitome entitled *Lucius or Ass* (H. J. Mason 1993), *Metamorphoses* has the distinction of being the only complete extant Latin novel (Harrison 1996). The narrative is marked by intercalated tales having comic, ideal, and religio-allegorical features (Sandy 1993). The central narrative describes the protagonist Lucius's attempt to change into an owl by means of a magic ointment to facilitate his travels for future amorous encounters. Fortuitously given the wrong ointment, Lucius is magically transformed into an ass and suffers many melodramatic misfortunes while wandering in search of the magic antidote, a single elusive rose. It is only after an epiphany of Isis and her tender intervention that Lucius is led to the antidotal rose during a procession for the *Navigium Isidis* in Kenchreai and is transformed into human form, subsequently being initiated into the goddess's mysteries. The central narrative and episodic tales convey that people evaluate others with asinine judgment, since humans are not what they appear (W. S. Smith 1993) and that all people are in need of Isis's salvation from cruel *Fortuna* and a transformation from asinine existence to genuine human dignity bestowed by the goddess. The *Metamorphoses* provides the only detailed literary account of initiation into a mystery cult and its meaning by an initiate, an account that assumes increased importance since Lucius's initiation occurs in Kenchreai, the location of an early Pauline assembly (cf. Rom. 16:1). Beyond 170 there is no reliable evidence for Apuleius's activities (Vallette 1960). In addition to the aforementioned extant works, known lost works of Apuleius are *De arboribus*, *Epitome histori-*

arum, *Eroticus*, orations partially represented within the *Florida*, *Hermagoras*, *Ludicra*, *De medicinalibus*, *Phaedo*, *De proverbiis*, *Quaestiones conviviales*, *De republica*, and works on various scientific subjects. There are also several disputed works of Apuleius, including *De Platone*, *De mundo*, and other works that are clearly spurious.

*Novel

Beaujeu 1973; Callebat 1993; Griffiths 1975; Harrison 1996, 2000; Hijmans 1987, 1993; Horsfall Scotti 1990; H. J. Mason 1993; Robertson 1971; Sandy 1993; W. S. Smith 1993; Syme 1959; Valette 1960; Walsh 1994

JOHN FOTOPOULOS

Aramaisms (see *Semitisms)

Archaism, literary and linguistic From the late 1st cent. through the 3d cent. C.E. and beyond, there was a widespread nostalgia for the past among both Greeks and Romans. This was a cultural challenge for both Judaism and Christianity, for, in a word, "Nothing could be new and true" (F. Young 1997, 52). This archaism took several forms. The imitation of the language and literary style of the Attic prose writers of the classical period (450–330 B.C.E.) is called linguistic *Atticism. The preference for literature written in Attic or Atticistic Greek contributed to the neglect and eventual loss of most Hellenistic literature originating from the late 4th cent. B.C.E. through the late 1st cent. C.E. Thematic archaism was also prevalent. Greek historians focused on the period of Alexander or earlier, neglecting the recent past. *Diogenes Laertius, writing on "Lives of the Philosophers," ca. 217 C.E., ended his account in the late 3d cent. B.C.E., suggesting that the golden age of philosophy was in the past (Brent 1999, 182). Orators declaimed on themes from the classical past, such as "Athens the greatest city" and "Alexander the greatest Greek." Archaism was both the cause and result of emphasizing literary models of the classical past. The value of antiquity is reflected in these words of advice of Pliny the Younger (using Cicero as a model; see Sherwin-White 1966, 477) to his friend Maximus, headed for mainland Greece for a governmental post (*Ep.* 8.24.2–3):

> Remember that you have been sent to the province of Achaia, to the pure and genuine Greece, where civilization, and literature, and agriculture, too, are believed to have originated. . . . Respect the gods, their founders, and the names they bear, respect their ancient glory and their very age, which in man commands our veneration, in cities our reverence. Pay regard to their antiquity, their heroic deeds, and the legends of their past.

*Alexandrian canon, *Asianism, *Atticism, *Orators, Attic

Architextuality, a neologism coined by Genette (1992), defined as "the entire set of general or transcendent categories—types of discourse, modes of enunciation, literary genres—from which emerges each singular text" (1997b, 1). Architext is a substitute for the term *genre and refers to those particular persistent and enduring modes (like narration and discourse), themes (like love and death), and formal features, when linked in a persistent and enduring way. Genette is a prominent French literary theorist who has developed an elaborate structuralist poetics (Allen 2000, 95–115). For Genette, "genre" is a literary category, while "mode" involves aspects of language itself and can be divided into "narration" (the recounting of facts or events without placing emphasis on the one recounting) and "discourse" (placing the focus on the person speaking and the situation in which he or she speaks). The relationship between a text and its architext is "architextuality" (Genette 1992, 83). Thus "architextuality" is a more comprehensive form of *intertextuality.

*Form, *Genre, *Mode

Allen 2000; Genette 1992, 1997a, 1997b

Aretalogy, a transliterated form of the Greek word ἀρεταλογία (extremely rare in antiquity), is a narrative centering on "a hero whom it celebrates, by reporting one or more of his marvellous deeds" (M. Smith 1971, 196). However, the assumption that this is a literary genre with fixed rules of style and content is mistaken (Winkler 1985, 236).

*Gospel, literary genre of, *Miracle stories

Hadas and Smith 1965; Kee 1973, 1975; J. Z. Smith 1975; M. Smith 1971; Tiede 1972; Winkler 1985

Aristeas, Letter of (see *Pseudepigrapha, OT)

Aristides, P. Aelius (November 26, 117–180 C.E.) was one of the more prominent rhetoricians in Roman Asia during the 2d cent. C.E. The family of Aristides were citizens of Smyrna and received Roman citizenship from Hadrian in 123 C.E. His father was a priest of the temple of Zeus Olympios. He studied with some of the greatest rhetoricians of the day in Smyrna (with Antonius Polemo and Alexander of Cotiaeum, later called to Rome to be the tutor of Marcus Aurelius), Pergamum (with Claudius Aristocles), and Athens (with Herodes Atticus). He began to declaim (see *Declamation) publicly in 141 C.E., fell ill while in Egypt in 142 C.E., and had serious respiratory problems for the rest of his life. He consulted the healing god Asklepios and incubated (a technical term for sleeping in the temple of a healing divinity for the purpose of receiving revelatory dreams that prescribed healing) at the Asklepeion in Pergamon for two years (145–47 C.E.). During this period, he received many dreams from Asklepios with prescriptions for various regimens (vomiting, bloodletting, ice-cold baths, etc.). He recorded about 130 of these dreams in a work which survives called the ἱεροὶ λόγοι, or "Sacred Tales," *Or.* 47–52 (Behr 1968). These unusual and remarkable autobiographical documents of a remarkable hypochondriac (Phillips 1952) are strikingly personal and candid and have been regarded without exaggeration as the most detailed firsthand account of personal religious experience in pagan antiquity (Festugière 1954); see *Autobiography. Between the autobiographical elements of the Pauline letters and the *Confessions* of Augustine, there is nothing quite like Aristides' narrative of his attempts to find religious healing. In 154 C.E. he resumed his career as an orator fulltime, with lecture tours in Greece and even Rome. One of his last major public appearances was a declamation before Marcus Aurelius and his court during their visit to Smyrna in 176 C.E.. Throughout his public career, Aristides was a confident representative of rhetoric in the centuries-old conflict between rhetoric and philosophy (Karadimas 1996). His defense of rhetoric is the focus of three orations: *To Plato: In Defense of Oratory* (*Or.* 2), *To Plato: In Defense of the Four* (*Or.* 3), and *To Capito* (*Or.* 4). Aristides maintained that the good speech of rhetoric is identical with speech that is both virtuous and morally right (Karadimas 1996, 3).

Aristides conformed to the highest standards of *Atticism (Boulander 395–412). Fifty-one authentic works survive, all entitled *Orationes*, though this does not fit the genre of all the material. Behr (1973, xv) has classified the *Orationes* of Aristides as follows: (1) treatises, the writings against Plato (*Or.* 2–4), and on the Nile (*Or.* 36); (2) panegyrics and symbouleutic speeches to cities or on public issues (*Or.* 1, 17–24, 26, 27, 29); (3) speeches on rhetoric (*Or.* 28, 33, 34); (4) speeches to individuals and funeral orations (*Or.* 30–32); (5) religious speeches and writings (*Or.* 5–16, 47–52), and (6) declamations (*Or.* 5–16)

Relevance to NT and ECL. The works of Aristides are an important source for the social, religious, and rhetorical history of the Roman world during the 2d cent. C.E. Rostovtzeff regarded *Or.* 26 (according to the Keil and Behr numbering) as the best description of the Roman Empire of the 2d cent. C.E. His devotion to Asklepios and the narration of his dream, vision, and healing experiences at various temples in Anatolia are particularly significant. His collection of autobiographical dream experiences contains valuable parallels to the form of the many dream and vision forms and narratives in the NT (see Aune 1983, 266–68). An extremely helpful study that explores the many parallels between the orations of Aristides and the NT, written by van der Horst (1980), is arranged in the order of the various NT texts from Matthew to Revelation, with the parallels cited in Greek. One interesting folktale (see *Folklore) motif found in both Aristides and the NT (omitted by van der Horst) is the account in *Or.* 49.45 (part of the Sacred Tales) in which the author recounts that he was ordered by Isis in a dream to sacrifice two geese to her. He sent men ahead into town to find the appropriate sacrificial animals. Only two geese in the entire town were for sale, but when the agents of Aristides sought to buy them, they were turned down. The owner had been commanded by Isis to save them for a certain Aristides. The obvious parallel to this story is found in Mark 11:1–6 and parallels, where Jesus is depicted as sending two disciples to fetch a colt for use later in the triumphal entry. Bultmann refers to this story (as he does to the parallel story about the upper room in Mark 14:12–16) as containing a *Märchenmotiv* ("folktale motif"). The story in Aristides is one of the closest folkloristic parallels to Mark 11:1–6, though it is cited by no commentator on Mark. Again, Aristides reports that in a dream he entreated Asklepios to save the life of his friend and companion Zosimus. Three times he entreated the god by grasping his head. Twice the god refused, but the third time he assented. The obvious parallel is Paul's account in 2 Cor. 12:8–9, regarding his threefold entreaty to the Lord to remove the thorn in his flesh, though without apparent success.

Behr 1968, 1973; Boulanger 1968; Karadimas 1996; Phillips 1952; van der Horst 1980

Aristobulus (see *Historiography)

Aristotle's *Rhetorica*, written after the middle of the 4th cent. B.C.E., is one of the earliest systematic discussions of rhetorical theory, as well as the most respected (Kennedy 1963, 81). It is, further, the only complete extant Greek rhetorical treatise surviving from the Hellenistic period through the late 1st cent. C.E. Aristotle (384–322 B.C.E.) draws on sophistic rhetoric but also on his own studies of logic, politics, and ethics. While it has frequently been argued that the *Rhetorica* is a defense against Plato's attacks, there are no explicit responses directed against the positions on rhetoric espoused by Socrates, Plato, or Isocrates, either in the *Rhetorica* or in the *Poetica*. Rather, the *Rhetorica* should be viewed positively as a "political inquiry designed to understand rhetoric as an art which can be a civic practice" (Garver 1994, 21). If rhetoric is a practical as well as a civic art, it cannot be a specialized one.

Composition. The parts of the *Rhetorica* were apparently written at different times, and perhaps thoroughly revised, late in Aristotle's career (Dionysius Hal., *1 Amm.* 6–9). Some scholars are impressed with the unity (Grimaldi 1980), others with the inconsistencies in the work. The number of inconsistencies in the *Rhetorica* suggest that even the final version was not prepared by Aristotle for *publication (Kennedy 1963, 82–83). Aristotle probably worked on the *Rhetorica* 340–335 B.C.E. toward the end of his twelve-year absence from Athens following the death of Plato in 348 B.C.E., before returning to Athens in 334 B.C.E. It is possible that, of the three books of the *Rhetorica*, books 1 and 2 constituted a separate work (Diogenes Laertius 5.24 lists Aristotle's *Rhetorica* as consisting of two books) to which Aristotle later added book 3 (Kennedy 1996, 418–21), parts of which may go back to the 350s (Burkert 1975). The book division is probably that of Aristotle himself, and each book is an appropriate size for a single *papyrus roll. The *Rhetorica* Quintilian knew consisted of three books (2.17.14). The earliest core of the *Rhetorica* was either 1.5–15 (Rist 1989, 85–86, 136–44) or 1.3–15 (Kennedy 1991, 299–305; 1996, 419). The *Rhetorica*, which is very difficult to understand, is one of the esoteric works Aristotle never arranged for publication (R. D. Anderson 1999, 42).

Analysis. Even though the *Rhetorica* has a history largely separate from the rest of the works of Aristotle, some insist on treating it as a *philosophical* treatise in the context of Aristotle's other philosophical writings (Garver 1994), while others argue that it be read in conscious isolation from other Aristotelian works (Wisse 1989, 12). While there are advantages to both approaches, it seems clear that Aristotle's conception of rhetoric was wedded to his political conception of the polis, and his innovative thesis that the genus of rhetoric had three species was formulated on analogy with his biological studies.

In its present form, the work is divided into three books, treating the three main tasks or functions of the orator (later called the *officia oratoris* or the *vis oratoris*): (1) εὕρεσις, the "invention" or "discovery" and arrangement of material (books 1–2), in which the arrangement of 1.3–2.26 (1354a–1403b) is structured around Aristotle's central conception of the ἐνθύμημα; see *Enthymeme, (2) λέξις, "style" (3.1–12; 1403b–1414a), and (3) τάξις, the "arrangement" of the parts of the speech (3.13–19; 1414a–1420a).

The work begins with an introduction and general definitions (1.1–2; 1354a), including a definition of rhetoric "as the faculty of discovering the possible means of persuasion in reference to any subject whatever" (1.2.1; 1355b). Aristotle distinguishes between ἔντεχνοι or "artificial proofs," i.e., those based on the art of the orator, and ἄτεχνοι or "inartificial proofs," e.g., witnesses and contracts (1.2.2; 1355b). These latter are of three kinds, the proofs furnished by the moral character of the speaker, by putting the hearer in a certain frame of mind, and by the argument of the speech itself insofar as it proves or seems to prove (1.2.3; 1355b–1356a). The first time that Aristotle mentions that ἦθος is a source of conviction or argument, he emphasizes the fact that it must be the ἦθος that comes from the speech itself, not from any preconceived idea of the speaker's character (1.2.4; 1356a). The largest section of the work, comprising books 1–2 (1.3–2.26; 1354a–1403b) revolves about Aristotle's conception of πίστεις, or the means of persuasion in public address, including ἐνθύμημα. In 1.2.20–21 (1358a) two kinds of *enthymemes are distinguished: those whose προτάσεις ("premises") are based on established views or facts and those based on

Aristotle's Logical, Dialectical, and Rhetorical Systems

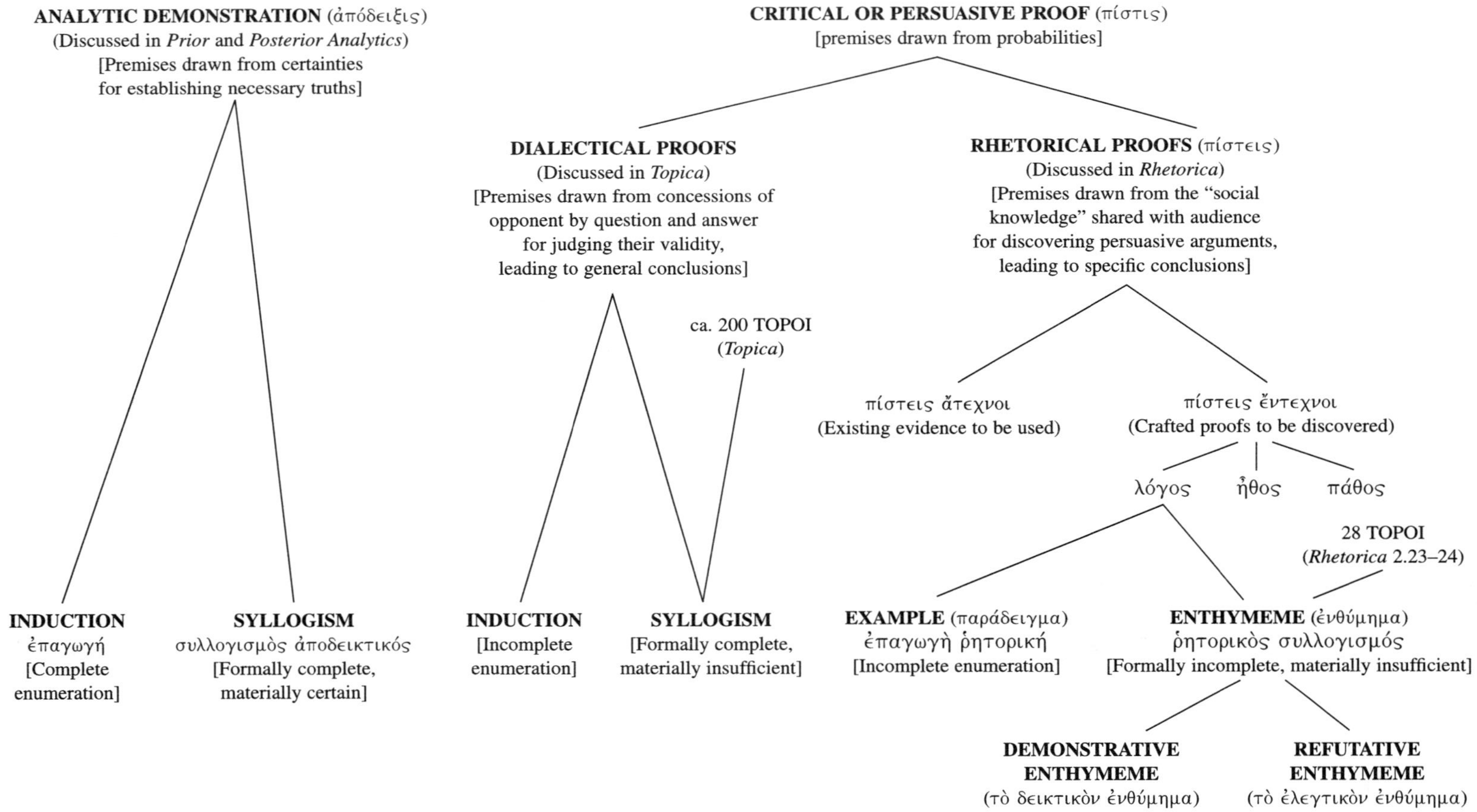

particular modes of argumentation or τόποι; only those based on the latter are true enthymemes. Enthymemes whose προτάσεις ("premises") are based on established views or facts are treated in 1.3–2.17 (1354a–1391b) under three headings: τὸ πρᾶγμα, those concerned with "the matter" itself; ἦθος, those concerned with the reliability of the speaker's character; and πάθος, those relating to the emotional manipulation of the audience. Arguments involving the matter itself are treated under the headings of the three kinds of rhetoric, or *tria genera causarum*, proposed in 1.3–15 (1354a–1377b), i.e., συμβουλευτικόν ("deliberative rhetoric"), ἐπιδεικτικόν ("epideictic rhetoric"), and δικανικόν ("judicial rhetoric"). They constitute one of the more original and influential features of his rhetorical theory (Solmsen 1941, 42; Quintilian 3.4.1). After this, there is a short discussion of the reliability of the speaker's ἦθος or character, which should have three evident qualities, φρόνησις ("prudence"), ἀρετή ("virtue") and εὔνοια ("good will" [2.1.5–7; 1378a]); it is striking that Aristotle treats ἦθος only in a very short passage (*Rhet.* 2.1.5–7; see Garver 1994, 14). Next comes a lengthy discussion of πάθος, i.e., the emotional manipulation of the audience (2.1.8–2.11.7; 1378a–1388b; see *Patros). This is followed by a digression on the characteristics (emotions, habits, and fortunes) of citizens in each of the three common divisions of the life span: youth, old age, and maturity (2.12–17; 1388b–1391b). In 2.18–26 (1391b–1403b), after separating out three κοινά, "necessary preconditions to all rhetorical discourse" (R. D. Anderson 1999, 44, following Grimaldi 1980, 349), Aristotle discusses λόγος or reason as a source of argument and treats rhetorical proofs properly so-called: παραδείγματα ("examples"), inductive proofs (2.20.2–9; 1393a–1394a), and ἐνθυμήματα, deductive proofs (2.21–25; 1394a–1403a). Aristotle has already discussed λόγος extensively in 1.4–14 (1359a–1375a). R. D. Anderson observes (1999, 45) that nothing is said in the first two books about "the *function* and *placement* of various arguments" (an issue very important to later rhetoricians). In book 3, following an introduction (3.1; 1403b–1404a), he discusses λέξις, "style" (3.2–12; 1404b–1414a), beginning with the ἀρετὴ λέξεως, "virtue of speech," i.e., clarity and propriety (3.2–4; 1404b–1407a), the ἀρχή of speech, and proper and clear use of language (3.5; 1407a–1407b), the ὄγδος ("expansiveness") of speech (3.6; 1407b–1408a), propriety (3.7; 1408a–1408b), and the σχῆμα (rhythmical) form of speech (3.8; 1408b–1409a). After a discussion of paratactic and periodic sentence structure (3.9; 1409a–1410b), he treats the source of popular and witty sayings, which is primarily the four types of metaphor (3.10–11; 1410b–1413b), and finally the contexts suitable for particular types of discourse (3.12; 1413b–1414a). The last section (3.13–19; 1414a–1420a) treats τάξις, "arrangement." While Aristotle maintains that speeches could consist of two parts, πρόθεσις ("statement") and πίστις ("proof"), he allowed as many as four parts (*Rhet.* 3.13 [1414a–b]): (1) προοίμιον ("introduction"), (2) πρόθεσις ("statement"), (3) πίστις ("proof"), and (4) ἐπίλογος ("epilogue"). However, it should be made clear that Aristotle makes an emphatic break with traditional methods of organizing material under the various heads of the "parts of a speech" (μόρια λόγου, or *partes orationis*). Aristotle rather organizes his presentation under the categories representing the essential qualities or functions of any speech: the orator must seek to prove his or her point, to elicit a particular emotional reaction in the audience, and convey an impression of his or her character (Solmsen 1974, 279–80).

History and influence. Aristotle's private *library including his own works, some unpublished (among which, very probably, were the *Rhetorica* and *Poetica*), was willed to his successor Theophrastus (the following account is detailed in Moraux 1951, 3–58). After Theophrastus (died 286 B.C.E.), the collection was willed to Neleus (the will of Theophrastus is preserved in Diogenes Laertius 5.51–57), who moved it to the town of Skepsis in the Troad, where it was kept in a cellar by Neleus and his heirs. Badly cared for and suffering damage, it was acquired by Appelikon of Teos, a rich book collector who lived in Athens. Sulla appropriated the library after the fall of Athens in 86 B.C.E., and sent it to Rome (Strabo 13.1.54; Plutarch, *Sulla* 26.1–2). The *Rhetorica* appears to have been one of Aristotle's works that was "lost" from Theophrastus (ca. 286 B.C.E.) to after 80 B.C.E., though the contents may have been known to early Peripatetics (Kennedy 1989, 190). In Rome, Tyrannion the grammarian arranged the works of Aristotle (ca. 46 B.C.E.), and sent copies to Andronikos of Rhodes (presumably working in Rome), who published them and drew up lists of Aristotle's works; Andronikos was probably active between 20 and 40 B.C.E. (Düring 1957, 421). Porphyry (*Vita Plotini* 24) observes that Andronikos "divided the works of Aristotle and Theophrastus into treatises [πραγματεῖαι], bringing together related discussions under a single head."

There are, in fact, three catalogues of the works of Aristotle, the one preserved by *Diogenes Laertius, the anonymous author of the *Vita Menagiana* (which consists of a list much like that in Diogenes with an addition) and that of an otherwise unknown Ptolemy (texts available in Düring 1957, 41–50, 83–89, 221–31). The lists in Diogenes and the Anonymous are striking by their omission of many major surviving works of Aristotle, but they also are ancient and may predate the removal of the library to Skepsis. C. Lord (1986, 141), in fact, proposes that these two old catalogues represent an inventory of the works of Aristotle sent to Skepsis (an inventory already reduced by the subtraction of many of the major Aristotelian works). Cicero, in his early work *De inventione* (1.7), knew that Aristotle had written on rhetoric and clearly had knowledge of Aristotle's *Rhetorica* when he wrote *De oratore* in 55 B.C.E. (Wisse 1989, 155–56; Kennedy 1996, 422). Dionysius of Halicarnasus, who lived in Rome during the last third of the 1st cent. B.C.E., knew the *Rhetorica*, perhaps the version revised by Tyrannio (*Ep. ad Ammaeum* 1), though his use of the *Rhetorica* is attenuated in mature works (Wooten 1994). Aristotle's works were reedited extensively in later antiquity, beginning with Alexander of Aphrodisias, ca. 200 C.E. (see Van Ophuijsen 2001), though little attention was paid to the *Rhetorica*.

The degree of influence exercised by the *Rhetorica* or the Aristotelian dialectical rhetorical tradition during the Hellenistic and Roman periods is a critically important issue. The preceding considerations suggest that the *Rhetorica* was not widely available or known in the late Hellenistic period. Cicero had probably read the *Rhetorica* by 55 B.C.E. (Wisse 1989, 105–89), but he makes this telling observation in *Topica* 1.3 (LCL trans.): "I am not indeed astonished in the slightest degree that the philosopher [Aristotle] was unknown to the teacher of oratory, for he is ignored by all except a few of the professed philosophers." Of course, rhetorical theory did not stand still after Aristotle, and a number of developments (e.g., the stasis theory propounded by Hermagoras in the 2d cent. B.C.E.) would have made the *Rhetorica* seem out of fashion, had it been available. Several further points need to be made (R. D. Anderson 1999, 46–49): (1) Hellenistic rhetoric neither appropriated nor fully understood Aristotle's view of the ἐνθύμημα (which had a focal emphasis in the *Rhetorica*), even though syllogistic reasoning was incorporated into discussions of the ἐπιχείρημα. (2) Later rhetorical theory typically did not follow Aristotle in distinguishing between ἔντεχνοι and ἄτεχνοι proofs (1.2.2; 1355b), a distinction made only by theorists influenced by philosophical tradition. (3) Aristotle's emphasis on the three types of proofs (πάθος, "emotion," ἦθος, "character," and τὸ πρᾶγμα, "the matter itself") is not reflected in later rhetorical traditions. (4) Aristotle's detachment of the three κοινά from other τόποι (2.18) is not picked up by later rhetorical theorists, and his use of κοινοὶ τόποι as abstract patterns of argument (*Rhetorica* 2.23) was only taken up in philosophical rhetorical treatises. (5) Aristotle's discussion of εὕρεσις (*inventio*), or "discovery," lacks two important components typically found in Hellenistic rhetorical treatises, namely a treatment of *stasis theory (which became important following the work of Hermagoras in the 2d cent. B.C.E.), and the treatment of the parts of a speech. Aristotle treated the arrangement of the parts of a speech under τάξις (*Rhetorica* 3.13–19), while Hellenistic and Roman school texts would treat them under εὕρεσις. (6) Aristotle's classification of a single ἀρετὴ λέξεως ("virtue of speech"), even though it has multiple characteristics, was eclipsed by the division of virtue into four types, proposed by Theophrastus. R. D. Anderson (1999, 49) concludes with a caveat: "Aristotle's treatise as a whole should be used with extreme caution, and is probably better left aside." Despite the fact that the *Rhetorica* is a classic, its influence has been marginal, even negligible (Garver 1994, 4). Yet it is appropriate to speak of an Aristotelian dialectical tradition in rhetoric (Solmsen 1974; Kennedy 1989, 190). Therefore when NT scholars argue for the utilization of Aristotelian rhetoric in NT compositions, as Diefenbach (1993, 47) does for the Gospel of Luke, such claims must be considered *cum grano salis*.

*Rhetorical handbooks, **Rhetorica ad Alexandrum*

Burkert 1975; Düring 1957; Forgenbaugh and Mirhady 1994; Garver 1994; Kennedy 1963, 81–114; 1989, 190–94; 1996; C. Lord 1986; Moraux 1951; Rist 1989; Wisse 1989; Wooten 1994

Arrangement (Greek τάξις, οἰκονομία [Dionysius Hal., *On Demosthenes* 51], σύστασις [Aristotle, *Poetica* 6.14; 50b]); Latin *dispositio*, *ordo*), refers to the task of composing, arranging, or structuring a literary text, and more importantly is used for one of the five tasks or functions of the orator (the *officia oratoris* or the *vis oratoris*), i.e., the composition of the parts of a speech (see also the other tasks of the orator: *invention, *style, delivery, memory). Those who composed oral and written speeches in the Greco-Roman world were taught in school to structure them to include as many as six parts, which they called the arrangement (Greek τάξις; Latin *dispositio*) of a speech: *Rhet. Her.* 1.3.4; Cicero, *Inv.* 1.14.19): **exordium*, **narratio*, *partitio confirmatio*, *refutatio*, with the sixth part, the *peroratio*, drawing together the parts of the argument.

Dispositio in the sense of "structure, arrangement" can also be used for the *analysis* of the train of thought for an entire argumentative text (whether a speech or a letter), not merely a general outline, but identifying major issues, phases of argumentation, conclusions and digressions from the main line of argumentation, and identifying the various rhetorical devices and figures of speech.

Four-part (and five-part) arrangements. Aristotle argued for two basic divisions of a speech, the πρόθεσις (the statement of the issue) and the πίστις ("proof," i.e., the arguments for and against the issue), both optionally framed by an emotional προοίμιον ("introduction") at the beginning and an emotional επίλογος ("epilogue") at the end (*Rhetoric* 3.13 [1414a–b]). In the synthetic presentation of ancient rhetoric by Lausberg (1998), the same four-part structure is maintained, with lavish references to rhetorical handbooks both early and late: (1) *exordium* (§§263–88), (2) *narratio* (§§289–347), (3) *argumentatio* (§§348–430), (4) *peroratio* (§§431–42). Aristotle's four-part arrangement is also briefly mentioned in Cicero, *Topica* 97–98 (in connection with the use of the appropriate topics in each section), and *Partitiones oratoriae* 4: (1) *principium*, (2) *narratio*, (3) *fides* (a literal translation of πίστις), or *confirmatio*, (4) *peroratio*. A five-part scheme is found in Anaximenes (*Rhet. Alex.* 1 [1422a]):

> The most complete and perfect argument, then, is that which is comprised of five parts: the Proposition [*propositio*], the Reason [*ratio*], the Proof of the Reason [*confirmatio*], the Embellishment [*exornatio*], and the Résumé [*conplexio*]. Through the Proposition we set forth summarily what we intend to prove. The Reason, by means of a brief explanation subjoined, sets forth the causal basis for the Proposition, establishing the truth of what we are urging. The Proof of the Reason corroborates, by means of additional arguments, the briefly presented Reason. Embellishment we use in order to adorn and enrich the argument, after the Proof has been established. The Résumé is a brief conclusion.

The six-part arrangement. In Greek rhetorical theory, sometime before Cicero, two more parts were added, making a total of six (Cicero, *De inventione* 1.14.19; *Rhetoric ad Herennium* 1.34): (a) *exordium* ("introduction"), (b) *narratio* ("narrative"), (c) *divisio* or *partitio* ("division" or "case"), (d) *confirmatio* ("proof"), (e) *confutatio* or *reprehensio* ("refutation"), and (f) *peroratio* or *conclusio* ("conclusion"). The standard six-part arrangement is first discussed in **Rhetorica ad Herennium* 1.3.4, a work written in the 80s B.C.E. in Rome, but ultimately dependent on a Greek source: (1) Introduction (Greek προοίμιον; Latin *exordium*) is designed to capture the interest and attention of the audience. The exordium can have several functions: (a) the speaker seeks to influence or manipulate the audience by seeking their goodwill; (b) the speaker acknowledges the situation; (c) the speaker establishes his *ethos or character. (2) Narration (Greek πρόθεσις; Latin *narratio*) functions primarily to set forth the facts, particularly useful and important in *judicial rhetoric, but often omitted in *deliberative rhetoric. The narration contains the proposition, involving the *stasis or issue being discussed. (3) Division or case (Latin *divisio*, *propositio*, or *partitio*) sets forth the points agreed on by both parties and the points to be contested. (4) Proof (Greek πίστις; Latin *confirmatio* or *probatio*) sets forth the arguments designed to confirm the case. In deliberative rhetoric the speaker often appeals to the honor and advantage (or self-interest) of the audience. The appeals to honor and advantage are often supported by two kinds of persuasion: (a) *ethos, an appeal to the good character of the audience (a development which first appears in Cicero); and (b) *pathos, an appeal to the emotions of the audience. (5) Refutation or rebuttal (Latin: *confutatio* or *reprehensio*) consists of the refutation of the arguments of the opponent. (6) Peroration or conclusion (Greek ἐπίλογος; Latin *conclusio* or *peroratio*) sums up the arguments and stirs the emotions of the audience: (a) the speaker seeks the goodwill of the audience; (b) the speaker recapitulates the

Synopsis of Greek and Latin Rhetorical Four-Part Arrangements (τάξεις or *dispositiones*)

	τάξις or *dispositio*	Aristotle, *Rhet.* 3.13	*Rhet. ad Alex.* 31, 36	Cicero, *Topica* 97–98	Cicero, *Part. or.* 4
1	προοίμιον or *principium*	[προοίμιον]	προοίμιον including	*principium*	*principium*
2	πρόθεσις or *narratio*	πρόθεσις	διήγησις	*narratio*	*narratio*
3a	πίστις or *fides*, or *confirmatio*	πίστις	βεβαίωσις or πίστις	*fides*	*confirmatio*
3b	προκατάληψις		προκατάληψις		
4	ἐπίλογος or *peroratio*	[ἐπίλογος]	κεφάλοιος	*peroratio*	*peroratio*

Synopsis of Greek and Latin Six-Part Rhetorical Arrangements (τάξεις or *dispositiones*)

	τάξις or dispositio	*Rhet. Her.* 1.3.4	Cicero, *Inv.* 1.14.19	Cicero, *De or.* 2.80	Quintilian 3.9.1
1	προοίμιον or *exordium* or *prooemium*	*exordium*	*exordium*	*exordium*	*prooemium*
1a	*principium*	*principium* (1.4.6)			*principium* (4.1.42)
1b	*insinuatio*	*insinuatio* or ἔφοδος (1.4.6)			*insinuatio* (4.1.42)
2	διήγησις or *narratio*	*narratio*	*narratio*	*narratio*	*narratio*
3	*divisio* or *partitio* or *propositio*	*divisio*	*partitio*	*propositio*	
4	*confirmatio* or *probatio*	*confirmatio*	*confirmatio*	*confirmatio*	*probatio*
5	*confutatio* or *reprehensio*	*confutatio*	*reprehensio*	*refutatio*	*refutatio*
				[*digressio*]	
6	ἐπίλογος or *conclusio* or *peroratio*	*conclusio*	*peroratio*	*peroratio*	*peroratio*

arguments; (c) the speaker makes an emotional appeal.

Aletti 1990, 1992; Lausberg 1998, 209–14; Wuellner 1997

Ascension (see *Ascent, heavenly)

Ascension of Isaiah in its present form is a Christian composition compiled about the late 2d cent. C.E. The work falls into two parts. The first half (1–5), called the "Martyrdom of Isaiah," is probably the oldest part. It is Jewish and contains the legendary tradition about Isaiah referred to in Heb. 11:37 (i.e., that Isaiah was killed by being sawn in two). The first part also contains a lengthy Christian interpolation (3:13–4:21) that predicts the descent of the Beloved from the seventh heaven, his crucifixion, resurrection, and subsequent return to the seventh heaven, followed by an apostasy (3:13–29). This eschatological scenario is continued in 4:1–21, in which the coming of Beliar as Antichrist is predicted, together with the final destruction of Beliar and his followers by the Beloved upon his return.

The second half (6–11) constitutes the vision or ascension of the prophet Isaiah. Isaiah is the center of a prophetic school of 40 prophets. While speaking through the Holy Spirit to Hezekiah, Isaiah suddenly became silent and had an out-of-body experience of ascending to the seventh heaven that he subsequently narrated in 7:1–11:43.

*Pseudepigrapha, OT

Translation: *NTA* 2:603–20. Bibliography: Acerbi 1989; Hall 1990

Ascent, heavenly functioned in two primary ways in the ancient world: (1) as an alternate to or consequence of death, either in Judaism as an indication of divine approval accorded to a righteous person (Enoch in Gen. 5:24; Elijah in 2 Kgs. 2) or in Greco-Roman traditions as an indication of the deification of a noteworthy person (Plutarch *Romulus* 27; cf. Luke 24; Acts 1); (2) as a mode of divine revelation reflected in Greco-Roman, early Jewish, and early Christian literary sources, in which particular individuals with prophetic or revelatory gifts are thought to have experienced a heavenly journey during which they learned cosmic and divine secrets. While there is evidence that such actual mystical experiences were sought after in the ancient world, most of the first-person accounts of such heavenly journeys are pseudonymous and based on literary conventions of mystical experiences. In Judaism, the conception that prophets could be present in the heavenly court and eavesdrop on the deliberations of the divine council (1 Kgs. 22:19–23; Mullen 1980, 209–26), provided a pattern for the development of ascent traditions. The earliest Jewish ascent text is found in *1 Enoch* 14 (Stone 1991, 193), which is dependent on Ezekiel's vision of the throne chariot in Ezek. 1. First-person accounts of heavenly ascents are narrated in several pseudonymous early Jewish and early Christian apocalypses, including *1 *Enoch* 14, *2 *Enoch*, *3 *Baruch*, the *Testament of *Levi*, and the *Testament of Abraham*. However only in 2 Cor. 12:2–4 and in the *Revelation to John are there narratives of the experiences of the authors.

*Apocalypses, *Cosmology, *Revelation to John

Bousset 1901; Culianu 1983; Dean-Otting 1984; Himmelfarb 1993; Lohfink 1984; Rowland 1982; Segal 1980; Tabor 1986

Asianism is a pejorative designation for a flowery and redundant literary style consisting of plays on words, metaphors, parallelism, and antithetical phrases attributed to practitioners of Asianic rhetoric. Asianic rhetoric apparently "began" in Pergamon in the late 4th and early 3d cent. B.C.E. Hegesias of Magnesia (3d cent. B.C.E.), whose works survive only in fragments (exhibiting "*Gorgianic figures" and rhythmic short cola), was regarded as the embodiment of all that was bad about Asianism, and he was disparaged by many subsequent critics (Cicero, *Brut.* 286; Dionysius Hal., *Comp.* 4.28; Longinus 3.2). Asianism had a significant impact on Roman rhetoric, since many of the Greek teachers of rhetoric who came to Rome beginning with the 2d cent. B.C.E. were Asiatic Greeks. The most important practitioner of Roman Asianism was Q. Hortensius Hortalus (d.50 B.C.E.). Cicero distinguished two types of Asianism (*Brutus* 325; LCL trans.):

> Of the Asiatic style there are two types, the one sententious and studied, less characterized by weight of thought than by the charm of balance and symmetry. Such was Timaeus the historian; in oratory Hierocles of Alabanda in my boyhood, and even more so his brother Menecles, both of whose speeches are masterpieces in this Asiatic style. The other type is not so notable for wealth of sententious phrase, as for swiftness and impetuosity—a general trait of Asia at the present time—combining with this rapid flow of speech a choice of words refined and ornate. This is the manner of which Aeschylus of Cnidus and my contemporary Aeschines of Miletus were representatives. Their oratory had a rush and movement which provoked admiration, but it lacked elaborate symmetry of phrase and sentence.

Hortentius, claims Cicero, was skilled in both types. The Asiatic style also preferred particular prose rhythms (Cicero, *Orator* 212; see *Prose rhythm), such as the ditrochaic (-˘-˘), a long vowel, followed by a short vowel, then again by a long and short vowel. Cicero also referred to the Asiatics as "slaves to rhythm" (*Orator* 230). During the second half of the 1st cent. B.C.E., the conflict between Asianists and *Atticists in Roman oratory became solidified. Influential Atticists include Marcus Brutus and C. Licinius Calvus (d. 47 B.C.E.). Cicero (*Brutus* 46, 51) gives a succinct summary of the characteristics of both traditions:

> Once eloquence set out from the Piraeus to travel all over the islands and all of Asia, it came into contact with other ways of life and lost the healthy sanity of Attic diction as well as the capacity of speaking well. Then came those Asiatic orators whose style lacks succinctness and is excessively redundant though its rapidity and abundance are not to be despised. The Rhodians, however, remained saner and more like Attic orators.

Asianic style is said to characterize the style of the Letters of *Ignatius and 4 Maccabees (Perler 1949; Riesenfeld 1961; Schoedel 1985, 7–8). "Asianism," however, was primarily a term of abuse used by Atticists of those who refused to emulate Attic style (Wilamowitz-Moellendorff 1900; Wooten 1975). Siegert (1993, 43) suggests that the social context in which Asianism was popular virtually required the orator to use language as different as possible from everyday speech; the orator was under pressure to impress his audience by any rhetorical means available.

A number of scholars have identified the style of 2 Peter as Asianic rhetoric (Bauckham 1983a, 137; Green 1968, 18, 41; Reicke 1968, 146–47). Thurén suggests that 2 Peter is the best example of Asian rhetoric in the Bible (1996, 340 n. 65). Watson (1988, 146), however, is less convinced: "2 Peter is not the best example of Asian style, but does possess several of its characteristics." Ignatius of Antioch has often been regarded as linked to the Asianic rhetorical tradition (Perler 1941; Riesenfeld 1961; Schoedel 1985, 7–8), and *Diog.* 11–12 is also an example of Asianism.

*Atticism, *Diognetus, Letter to, *Hiatus, *Peter, Second Letter of, *Style

---

Ø. Anderson 2002, 88–90; E. M. B. Green 1968; Norden 1909; Perler 1949; Reicke 1964; Riesenfeld 1961; Siegert 1993; Watson 1988, 146; Wilamowitz-Moellendorff 1900; Wooten 1975

Asides (see *Narrative asides)

Assumption (see *Ascent, heavenly)

Assumption of Moses* or *Testament of Moses (see *Pseudepigrapha, OT)

Asyndeton, from the Greek word ἀσύνδετον, meaning "unconnected, not bound together" (Latin *dissolutio*), refers to the intentional omission of connective particles or conjunctions between words, sentences, and paragraphs, sometimes for rhetorical effect (see also *Polysyndeton).

Asyndeton in rhetoric. The lack of the use of connecting particles was classified as one of the tropes or figures of speech, σχήματα λέξεως or *figurae*, discussed in *rhetorical handbooks (Demetrius, *On style* 4.192–94; Lausberg 1998, §§709–11). It can function to increase the tempo and emotion of the language used (Longinus 20.1–3; Lausberg 1998, §709). There are two types of asyndeton, one between words or clauses within a sentence and one between sentences (Denniston 1952, 99). Since the Greek language exhibits a particularly large variety of coordinating markers, the absence of coordination is striking. Earlier Greek authors tended to avoid asyndeton (Denniston 1960, 99). Asyndeton was also used in Latin, and Quintilian observes that it is useful "when we speak with particular vigor, for it impresses the details on the mind and makes them appear more numerous than they actually are" (*Inst. Or.* 3.3.50). While Aristotle thought that asyndeton was inappropriate for written texts, it could be used effectively orally (*Rhet.* 3.12.2 [1413b]), but Quintilian (9.4.19–21) thought that asyndeton was particularly appropriate in letters (*epistolography). A famous passage in Demosthenes (*Phil.* 3.27) is referred to or imitated by later orators (cf. Cicero, *Mil.* 87; *Rhet. Her.* 4.54, 68), as a particularly effective use of asyndeton (even in an English translation the use of asyndeton to produce a hurried, frantic effect comes through): "but he [Philip] is off to the Hellespont, just as before he hurried to Ambracia; in the Peloponnese he occupies the important city of Ellis; only the other day he intrigued against the Megarians. Neither the Greek nor the barbarian world is big enough for the fellow's ambitions."

Asyndeton in the NT and ECL. *John, in contrast to *Matthew, *Mark, and *Luke, is inclined to use asyndeton in narrative, as is Hermas (see *Shepherd of Hermas). By breaking up a series of words through the omission of conjunctions and other connective particles, asyndeton produces a hurried effect. Asyndeton occurs frequently in lists, such as *catalogues of vices and virtues, a striking example of which is Rom. 1:29–31: "They were filled with all manner of wickedness, evil, covetousness, malice. Full of envy, murder, strife, deceit, malignity, they are gossips, slanderers, haters of God, insolent, haughty, boastful, inventors of evil, disobedient to parents, foolish, faithless, heartless, ruthless." Other NT examples of asyndeta as a rhetorical device are Matt. 15:19; John 5:3; 1 Cor. 3:12; 7:27; 14:24; 15:1–2; Heb. 11:32–34; 1 Pet. 4:3.

In an important study of asyndeton in Paul, Güting and Mealand (1998, 10–23) synthesize Paul's epistolary use of asyndeton: (1) The prescript is separated by asyndeton from the thanksgiving period or body of the letter (Rom. 1:8; 1 Cor. 1:4; 2 Cor. 1:3; Gal. 1:6; Phil. 1:3; 1 Thess. 1:2; Phlm. 4). (2) While the theme of a letter and new subjects are introduced syndetically, the introduction is separated by asyndeton from the rest of the discussion (Rom. 4:10; 1 Cor. 1:13; 7:1, 27; 8:1; 12:1; 13:1; 1 Thess. 5:3; cf. Denniston 1952, 110). (3) A "solitary" μέν is placed toward the beginning of a letter to alleviate the harsh effect of the asyndeton required by convention (Rom. 1:8; Phil. 1:3; cf. Denniston 1934, 382; 1952, 111). (4) When not introduced by a verb of request, instruction is given asyndetically (Rom. 16:1 [*var. lect.*]; 1 Cor. 5:4; 16:15b; Gal. 1:9b; Phil. 4:2; Phlm. 10). (5) Asyndeton marks the concluding statement following the discussion of a subject (Rom. 7:24; 11:33; 1 Cor. 7:11b; Phil. 4:18b). (6) Salutations are expressed asyndetically (Rom. 16:3; 1 Cor. 16:19–20; 2 Cor. 13:12; Phil. 4:21–22; 1 Thess. 5:26–27; Phlm. 15). (7) Asyndeta mark the end of a letter (Rom. 16:20; 1 Cor. 16:21–24; 2 Cor. 13:13; Gal. 6:18; Phil. 4:23; 1 Thess. 5:28; Phlm. 15). Unmentioned by Güting and Mealand (1998) is the fact that when Paul inserts apologies (Rom. 3:5; 6:19; 1 Cor. 9:8; Gal. 3:15), they are always introduced asyndetically (Cranfield 1975–79, 1.325). For lists of asyndeta in Romans and 1 and 2 Corinthians, see Güting and Mealand 1998, 113–71.

There is a striking series of seventeen short antithetical clauses and sentences in *Diogn.* 5:5–15 (see *Diognetus, Letter to for a detailed analysis).

Aune 1975, 308–9; Denniston 1934, 1952, 99–123; Güting and Mealand 1998; Kühner and Gerth 1890–1904, 2.339–47; Lausberg 1998, §§709–11; Schwyzer 1950–71, 2.632–33; Smyth

Atbash or athbash alphabet, based on the sequence of four Hebrew letters, אתבש, which refers to the rabbinic exegetical method of substituting letters: א (the first letter) is written instead of ת (the last letter), ב (the second letter) is written instead of ש (the second from last letter), and so on (Lieberman 1950, 69, 73). Atbash is one of the hermeneutical rules of Haggadah.

Lieberman 1950

Athenagoras of Athens, a Christian apologist of the mid-2d cent. C.E., who addressed an apologetic work called *Supplicatio* to the emperors Marcus Aurelius and Commodus, between 176 and 180 C.E. The *Supplicatio* is preserved in the Arethas Codex (Parisinus Graecus 451). In the same MS, the *Supplicatio* is followed by the *De resurrectione*, with the title ΤΟΥ ΑΥΤΟΥ ΠΕΡΙ ΑΝΑΣΤΑΣΕΩΣ ΝΕΚΡΩΝ ("By the same [author], On the Resurrection of the Dead"), though it is likely that the archetype bore only the title ΠΕΡΙ ΑΝΑΣΤΑΣΕΩΣ ΝΕΚΡΩΝ (Barnard 1976, 5). The end of the MS has the *subscriptio* ΑΘΗΝΑΓΟΡΑΣ ΠΕΡΙ ΑΝΑΣΤΑΣΕΩΣ ("Athenagoras, On the Resurrection"). Doubts have been raised about the attribution of *De resurrectione* to Athenagoras (Grant 1954; Schoedel 1972, xxv–xxxii), but Barnard (1976) argues that the *Supplicatio* and the *De resurrectione* were written by the same author.

*Apologetic literature

Barnard 1976; Grant 1954; Schoedel 1972

Atticism, or classicism, an intellectual and literary reactionary movement that began in the mid-1st cent. C.E. in Rome. Gaius Lucinius Calvus (ca. 82–47 B.C.E.), along with Marcus Caelius Rufus, 82–48 C.E. (Cicero, *Brutus* 273), was part of a new rhetorical school in Rome to which Calvus gave the name "Atticism" (Cicero, *Brutus* 283–84). Cicero quotes the motto of the Roman Atticists (Cicero, *Brutus* 287): "*Atticorum similes esse volumus*" ("We want to be Attic"). Marcus Calidius, an older contemporary of Calvus, was perhaps the earliest member of this new rhetorical movement (he is praised by Cicero in *Brutus* 274–75). In reacting against Roman Atticism, Cicero argues that there is no single Attic style to imitate (*Orator* 28–29), but rather a multiplicity of styles (*Brutus* 285; LCL trans.):

> Who, for example, are more unlike than Demosthenes and Lysias? Than either of them and Hyperides, than all of these and Aeschines? Whom then are you going to imitate? If one only, do you mean that all the others did not speak pure Attic? If all, how can you imitate them when they are so unlike each other?

In Cicero's discussion of the three styles of rhetoric (see *Style), he regards the "plain" style as that characteristic of the Roman "Attic" orators (*Orator* 75).

Among Greek rhetoricians resident in Rome, Dionysius of Halicarnassus (the earliest extant

Atticistic author) and Caecilius of Kale Akte in Sicily (whose work is preserved only in fragments) founded literary atticism in 1st cent. B.C.E. Rome, a phenomenon that continued in the *Second Sophistic (ca. 60–230 C.E.); see Schwyzer 1953, 1. The rhetorical and historical views of Dionysius were closely related, and Atticism was reflected in both programs. Dionysius saw cultural history in three stages (*De antiquis oratoribus* 1–3): (1) the classical age to Alexander the Great (a period of cultural decline); (2) the post-Alexander period, which included a time of Asian supremacy; and (3) the Augustan classical revival ("Asian" values were anti-Roman). Imitation of classical models was the central emphasis of Atticism and the Second Sophistic and the basis for the formation of the various "canons" of authors and literary genres that were intended to serve as models for good prose and poetry (Reardon 1971, 3–11). Atticism primarily involved the imitation of the language and literary style of the Attic prose writers of the classical period (450–330 B.C.E.). This preference for literature written in Attic Greek contributed to the neglect and eventual loss of most Hellenistic literature which originated from the late 4th cent. B.C.E.. through the late 1st cent. C.E. Modern scholars, working with the traditional model of linguistic and cultural deterioration during the Hellenistic period, have sometimes regarded Atticism as a symptom of general cultural decline in which the emphasis on μίμησις was a way of disguising a widespread lack of linguistic and literary creativity, as well as a reaction to the Hellenistic period and the prevalence of Asianism (Michaelis 1923, 94). Atticism represents the further separation of a literary language from the language of everyday speech, compared to earlier periods (Frösén 1974). This split survives into modern Greek, in which Katharevsa is the term for the literary language, and Demotic for common speech. In *De antiquis oratoribus*, an introduction to his discussion of various Greek orators (Lysias, Isocrates, Isaeus, and Demosthenes; essays on Hyperides and Aeschines have not survived), Dionysius deplores the degeneration of the Greek language since the time of Alexander, referring indirectly to *Asianism. In his essay on Isocrates, Dionysius presents him as a paragon of literary and moral virtue: patriotism, justice, piety, and moderation (Gabba 1991, 33). The novel by *Achilles Tatius, "The Adventures of Leukippe and Kleitophon," was written ca. 150 C.E. in a basically Atticistic style and reflects a sophistic background (the characters frequently make sophisticated speeches). Josephus, who apparently greatly improved his Greek after arriving in Rome (Rajak 1984, 62), learned and wrote a good quality Koine with strong influences from Atticism (Pelletier 1962). Other important surviving representatives of Atticism include Dio Chrysostom, *Lucian of Samosata (Chabert 1897), Aelius *Aristides (Boulanger 1968, 395–412), and Aelian. Atticistic preferences included ττ instead of σσ, ρρ instead of ρσ, ἐς instead of εἰς, ξύν instead of σύν. While Moulton and Howard (1979, 5–6) regard 2 Peter as an example of an NT book influenced by Atticism, Thurén argues that 2 Peter is the best example of Asian rhetoric in the Bible (1996, 340 n. 65); see *Asianism. Atticism has been used as a criterion for determining the earlier form of the text of the NT, since scribes influenced by Atticism introduced changes into the texts they copied before 200 C.E. (Kilpatrick 1963). A short list of the proposed adoption of variants that are poorly attested but nevertheless reflect non-Atticistic language is given in Metzger (1968, 178). The figure of *litotes*, e.g. οὐκ ὀλίγος ("not a few"), is an example of a usage favored by Atticists and occurs eight times in Acts (12:18; 14:28; 15:2; 17:4, 12; 19:23, 24; 27:20); see Cadbury 1927, 120–21.

*Alexandrian canon, *Archaism, *Asianism, *Orators, Attic, *Style

---

Ø. Anderson 2002, 88–90; Frösén 1974; Gabba 1991, 24–34; Kilpatrick 1963; Pelletier 1962; W. Schmid 1887–96; Wilamowitz-Moellendorff 1900, 1912, 218–23; Wisse 1995

Autobiography, Autobiographical

The words *autobiography* and *autobiographical* are modern formations, which first appeared in English in the late 18th and early 19th centuries, and are used to refer to an author who tells his or her own history. The origins of autobiography, in an unabashedly self-laudatory form, can be traced to the ancient near east, and include tomb biographies written in the first-person of the deceased which recount his or her life and achievements, e.g., the Egyptian tomb biography of Ahmose of Nekheb, 18th dynasty, late 16th cent. B.C.E. (Hallow and Younger 2000, 5–7), as well as monumental inscriptions celebrating military victories, such as the extended first-person section of the Battle of Qadesh poem of Ramesses II, early 13th cent. B.C.E. (Hallow and Younger 2000, 32–38). Among Neo-Assyrian inscriptions are the Kurkh Monolith, ca. 853–52 B.C.E. (Hallow and Younger 2000, 261–64). Among the earlier autobiographical inscriptions in Greek are the inscriptions of Ptolemy I,

Euergetes (*OGIS* 54), and Antiochus I (*OGIS* 383). In Judaism, first-person accounts occur in the so-called Ezra Memoir (Ezra 7:27–9:15, with the possibility that 7:1–26 and Neh. 8–9:5 have been changed from the first to the third person by the Chronicler), and the Nehemiah Memoir (1:1–7:73a; 11:1–2; 12:31–43; 13:4–31). There are also autobiographical elements in the testaments. In Greco-Roman antiquity, no terminological distinction was made between "*biography" and "autobiography," though Cicero was aware of the difference, which turns on the widespread ancient aversion to self-praise or *boasting, for Cicero considered biography to be encomiastic, but a biography written about oneself must be marked less self-laudatory (*Ad familiares* 5.12.8; LCL trans.):

> [If Lucceius refuses to write a eulogistic biography of Cicero] I shall perhaps be driven to a course often censured by some, namely to write about myself—and yet I shall have many illustrious precedents. But I need not point out to you that this *genre* [*in hoc genere vitia*] has certain disadvantages. An autobiographer must needs write over modestly where praise is due and pass over anything that calls for censure. Moreover, his credit and authority are less, and many will blame him and say that heralds at athletic contests show more delicacy, in that after placing garlands on the heads of the winners and loudly proclaiming their names, they call in another herald when it is *their* turn to be crowned at the end of the games, in order to avoid announcing their own victory with their own lips. I am anxious to escape these drawbacks, as I shall, if you take my case. I beg you to do so.

Momigliano (1971, 18) proposes that "autobiography" be used of literary works in which the author narrates his or her own past, while "autobiographical" be used in the wider sense of any statement that an author makes of himself or herself (comparable to the German term *Selbstdarstellung*). Lewis (1993, 630 similarly distinguishes between "autobiography" and "autobiographic writing." If autobiography in the strict sense of the term necessitates a self-reflective, self-conscious individuality, then according to Weintraum (1978, 1), autobiography begins historically with Augustine's *Confessions,* and (one might add), Gregory of Nazianzus (*De vita sua,* and *De rebus suis,* both in *Carmen* 2.1.11 and 2.1.1)

In Greek culture, autobiographical passages occur in several different kinds of contexts (Gjörgemanns 1997, 349–50): (1) Rhetoric: In juridical speeches, particularly defense speeches, the speaker often used autobiographical elements to defend his life and character (Demosthenes *De corona*; Plato *Apologia*). (2) Letters often included autobiographical material, either for apologetic purposes or for purposes of moral exhortation (Plato *Ep.* 7). (3) Memoirs, particularly those written by political personalities (Nikolaos of Damascus; Flavius Josephus). (4) Authors sometimes presented themselves to the public (Lucian *Somnium*; Libanius *Or.* 1, 5). (5) The Stoic practice of self-examination was transformed into a literary form by Marcus Aurelius in his *Meditations.*

Roman autobiographical writing includes several types: (1) *Commentarii,* i.e., the records of magistrates and military commanders of their exploits (Caesar *Commentarii de bello Gallico*); see Lewis 1993, 633–52. (2) The memoirs of Agrippina the Younger (the mother of Nero), called *commentarii* by Tacitus, but in this case referring to a sort of autobiographic work extending from birth to the time of writing. This work survives only in fragments in the writings of Tacitus and Pliny (see Lewis 1993, 652–58). (3) Comprehensive autobiography, i.e., the coverage of a whole life to the time of writing (see Lewis 1993, 658–76), all of which have been lost, including the the autobiographies of Augustus, which covered the period to 25 B.C.E., M. Vipsanius Agrippa, *De vita sua,* Tiberius, and Hadrian.

There are however, a number of important ancient works that blur the distinction that Momigliano makes, including those by Isocrates, Demosthenes, Cicero, and Josephus. Aelius *Aristides, who flourished during the 2nd cent. C.E., wrote six books of "Sacred Tales" (*Or.* 47–52), which are important in that they provide the most detailed first-person report of the religious experience of a pagan author. In the strict sense of the term, autobiography is a *first-person narrative used in both ancient fiction (*Achilles Tatius is the author of the only Greek novel in autobiographical form) and non-fiction.

Gaventa (1986), points to the closer parallels between autobiographical passages in Paul (particularly Gal. 1:11–2:21), and autobiographical passages in other ancient letters. She uses some of the letters of Seneca and Pliny the Younger as examples of autobiographical passages written in the interest of moral exhortation and instruction. One pertinent example is from Pliny *Ep.* 4.24.4–7:

> My profession brought me advancement, then danger, then advancement again; I was helped by my friendship with honest men, then injured

by it, and now am helped again. If you add up the years it would not seem very long, but it would be a lifetime if you count the changes of fortune. This should be a warning never to lose heart and to be sure of nothing, when we see so many fluctuations of fortune following each other in rapid succession. It is a habit of mine to share my thoughts with you and to set out for your guidance the rules and examples which shaped my own conduct. That was the purpose of this letter.

Relevance for the NT and ECL. There are several autobiographical passages in the Pauline letters (1 Cor. 15:8–10; 2 Cor. 11:21b–33; Gal. 1:11–2:21; Phil. 3:4–16). While four of the five peristasis or hardship catalogues inserted by Paul in his letters are couched either in the third-person plural or in generalities (1 Cor. 4:9–13; 2 Cor. 4:8–9; 2 Cor. 6:4–10; 2 Cor. 12:10), the one with the most strikingly autobiographical features is found in 2 Cor. 11:23–28. An "autobiographical" section of a pseudepigraphal letter is found in 2 Pet. 1:16–18.

Rigaux (1962, 171–72) has devoted little more than a page to a classification of the autobiographical passages in the Pauline letters: (1) simple autobiography (1 Cor. 16:5–9; 2 Cor. 7:5; Rom. 1:11–14; Phil. 1:12–26), (2) apostolic autobiography, (a) expressions of his zeal: 1 Thess. 2:1–12, 18; 3:1–2, 6; 1 Cor. 1:12–14; 2 Cor. 1:18–6:10; Rom. 15:17–21; Col. 2:1–3; 3:7–9, (b) examples to imitate: 2 Thess. 3:7–9; 1 Cor. 3:9–13; 7:9; (c) essence of his mission: 1 Cor. 1:14–16; 2:1–5; 3:1–4, 10, 11, 23), (3) apologetic and polemical biography (1 Cor. 9:1–27; 15:9; 2 Cor. 10:1–12:21; Gal. 1:11–2:14), (4) mystical autobiography (2 Cor. 12:1–10; Eph. 3:1–13), (5) The first-person, frequently used in Paul, sometimes functions as an ideal type (Rom. 7:14–25). While this catalog includes all of the relevant autobiographical passages in Paul, some of them overlap and the categories used are not always that helpful (e.g., "mystical autobiography").

Gal. 1:11–2:14 has been one of the more discussed of the Pauline autobiographical passages, frequently because of its assumed historical value (questioned by J. T. Sanders 1966). The passage has frequently been thought to have an apologetic function, a view underlined by the rhetorical analysis of Betz (1979), which regards this passage as the *narratio* of a juridical (specifically apologetic) speech.

Berger (1984a, 276) suggests several functions for autobiographical reports in early Christian literature: (1) First-person reports are important for early Christianity as a religion of personal conversion. (2) Apologetic autobiography is a means of refuting slanders about a person's earlier life. (3) Autobiographical passages also have an exemplary function; the life and character of the teacher (or other figure of authority) is shown to embody the teachings of the group.

*Biography, *Ethos, *Galatians, Letter to the

Berger 1984a, 275–76; Gaventa 1986; Gjörgemanns 1997; Lewis 1993; Lyons 1985; Misch 1951; Momigliano 1971; Revell 1996; Rigaux 1962; J. T. Sanders 1966; Weintraub 1978

Autograph, epistolary, refers to the fact that, at the conclusion of ancient letters (many of which were dictated), authors who were literate (for illiteracy formulas, see Weima 1994, 50–51) often took the pen from the scribe or secretary and wrote the last part of the letter.

Ancient letters. There are numerous examples of epistolary autographs among the documentary papyri, evident only from the change of handwriting at the end or toward the end of the letter (Weima 1994, 45–47). By "autograph," however, is not meant the signing of the author's own name at the conclusion of the letter (unnecessary, since the Hellenistic letter form began with the name of the sender), but rather the fact that the author herself or himself has written the concluding portion of the letter. There are, however, very few extant instances in which an autograph formula similar to that used by Paul (see below) occurs (Weima 1994, 119).

NT letters. The closing sections of several of Paul's letters include an autograph (1 Cor. 16:21; Gal. 6:11; 2 Thess. 3:17; Phlm. 19; Col. 4:18a). The epistolary formula (Richards 1991, 173) τῇ ἐμῇ χειρί, "with my hand," occurs three times in the undisputed letters of Paul (1 Cor. 16:21; Gal. 6:11; Phlm. 19) and twice in the disputed letters (2 Thess. 3:17; Col. 4:18a). In each instance, the natural implication is that while a secretary had written the bulk of the letter, now Paul has taken the pen to conclude the letter.

*Epistolography, *Letters, literary genre of

Bahr 1968; Roller 1933, 70–78; Weima 1994, 45–50, 118–35; Ziemann 1912, 362–65

Autographon, a transliterated neuter form of the adjective αὐτόγραφος ("written in one's own hand"), a manuscription actually written by the author (cf. Dionysius of Halicarnasus 5.7.1). A brief account of the production of an autographon is narrated in Ovid, *Metamorphoses* 9.522–29 (LCL trans.):

> And she proceeds to set down with a trembling hand the words she has thought out. In her right hand she holds her pen, in her left an empty waxen tablet. She begins, then hesitates and stops; writes on and hates what she has written; writes and erases; changes, condemns, approves; by turns she lays her tablets down and takes them up again. What she would do she knows not; on the point of action, she decides against it.

Autographa of Greek works are known only from the Byzantine period, and Reinsch gives the examples of four authors, each working in different genres: Dioskoros (5th cent. C.E.; Dorandi 1991, 18–19), Eustathios of Thessalonike (12th cent.), Matthaios of Ephesos, and Kritobulos of Imbros (15th cent.). In addition there are about eighteen papyrus fragments dating from the 1st to the 7th cent. C.E. that may very well be autograph manuscripts (Dorandi 1993, 73).

*Dictation, *Publication

———

Dorandi 1993; Reinsch 1980

Authorship or "onymity" (Genette 1997, 39–42) is an apparently simple notion that in reality masks a rather complex conception. While Greek epic was intended to perpetuate the life of the hero (thus avoiding death), the notion of authorship in the epic virtually substituted the author for the hero, and death was conquered through the ensuing fame of the author as the creator of the literary product. Foucault (1979, 141) regards the notion of authorship as reflecting a significant step in individualization in the history of ideas. Viewing the issue from a poststructuralist perspective, Foucault (1979, 142) sees the "author" as "creating a space into which the writing subject constantly disappears."

*Anonymity, *Pseudepigraphy

———

Foucault 1979; Genette 1997

Barnabas, Letter of *Barnabas* follows the *Revelation to John in the 4th-cent. Codex Sinaiticus. Origen designated it as a "Catholic letter" (*Contra Celsum* 1.63), and Eusebius considered it among the antilegomena or disputed works (*Hist. eccl.* 3.25.4).

Text. Barnabas survives in two complete Greek manuscripts (the original language of composition), Codex Sinaiticus (4th cent.) and *Codex Hierosolymitanus* 54 (dated June 11, 1056, the manuscript also contains the *Didache*, *1 Clement*, *2 Clement*, and the long form of the letters of Ignatius of Antioch), and nine short Greek texts of chapters 5–21 that follow Polycarp's letter to the Philippians without a break. There is one Latin manuscript (Codex Coreiensis, 9th cent.) that consists of chaps. 1–17. The Latin translation appears to reflect an earlier stage of the Greek text than the extant Greek text itself. The Latin translation ends at chap. 17, thus excluding the Two Ways tradition in *Barn.* 18–20.

Wengst (1972), Kraft (1961), and Prigent (1961) maintain that: (1) *Barnabas* is not a unified composition but rather consists of at least two previously existing documents or clusters of traditional Christian material (*testimonia traditions and *two-ways traditions). (2) *Barnabas* is not a genuine letter, but rather an edifying, didactic treatise with some quasi-epistolary features artificially tacked on secondarily. (3) *Barnabas* is also artificial in the sense that it did not arise within a concrete rhetorical situation but was rather a sort of studied theological exercise dealing with certain theological and hermeneutical issues of interest to the author. (4) The anti-Jewish polemic in *Barnabas* is purely academic and theoretical. Judaism and Christianity had completely separated by the early 2d cent. C.E., and had long since ceased to confront each other publicly, in part because Christians thought Judaism was a dying religion that lacked vitality. While the first two positions are probably correct, the last two fail to recognize that *Barnabas* reflects a state of Christian-Jewish relations in which Judaism was still taken seriously.

Authorship. The unknown author of *Barnabas* appears to have been a Gentile Christian (14:5; 16:7) who had access to Jewish training in Greek, perhaps originally as a proselyte or God-fearer. The addressees were probably Gentile Christians as well. The author was a teacher, though little is known of this role. Zimmermann (1988, 50) argues that the term διδάσκαλος is actually ambiguous, since "it is often used in a negative way." However, it is preferable to say that the term διδάσκαλος is construed in a negative way only by the *context*, not by semantics, i.e., by the addition of adjectives such as "false," and does not itself contain a negative semantic range of meaning. (2) It is probable that the author understood himself as a "charismatic teacher." In phases of early Judaism (e.g., the Qumran community) and early Christianity (e.g., Paul), there was a general awareness, expressed in a variety of ways, that the special understanding of the OT shared by the community had somehow been divinely revealed to them. (3) One of the major esoteric functions of the Hellenistic philosophical school was the reading, discussion, and interpretation of earlier authoritative texts. This is precisely the kind of activity which is reflected in *Barnabas.*

Date. Scholars are in general agreement that 70 C.E. is the *terminus a quo* for the composition of *Barnabas,* because the author very explicitly and conveniently mentions the destruction of the Jerusalem temple that took place in that year (*Barn.* 16:15). There is, however, no specific scholarly consensus for the temporal placement of *Barnabas* during the decades following 70 C.E. Two texts in *Barnabas* are critical for determining the date of the composition, *Barn.* 4:3–6 and 16:3–4. *Barnabas* 16:3–4 reads as follows:

> 3 Further, he says again: "Behold, those that tore down this temple will build it up themselves." 4 This is taking place [γίνεται]. For because they went to war, it was torn down by their enemies; now the very servants of their enemies will build it up again.

The temple in view is a physical rather than a spiritual temple; of the two possibilities of physical temples—a third Jewish temple and the temple of Jupiter erected during the reign of Hadrian—the latter is probably in view, indicating that *Barnabas* was written ca. 130–32 C.E., just before the outbreak of the second Jewish revolt.

Provenance. Among those scholars who have discussed the problem of the provenance of *Barnabas*, a majority favor Egypt, more specifically Alexandria, as the place of origin. Other possible places of origin are Syria-Palestine and Asia Minor, but while *Barnabas* has affinities with traditions associated with these regions, the composition as a whole cannot be placed with certainty in any of these locations. Clement of Alexandria and Origen are the first to mention and quote *Barnabas*, weighty evidence suggesting an Alexandrian origin. Clement quotes *Barnabas* eight times (Origen quotes him three times), calls the author "the apostle Barnabas" (*Stromata* 2.116), and claims that he derived his key notion of γνῶσις from *Barnabas* (*Stromata* 5.10; quoted in Eusebius, *Praep.* 9.749]). Here we have to do with a Christian intellectual tradition that placed an emphasis on γνῶσις, certainly a Christian and Gnostic-Christian conception that was particularly at home in Alexandria. *Barnabas* 9:6 (where Ps.-Barnabas claims that every Syrian and Arab and all idol-worshiping priests are circumcised, and that even the Egyptians practice circumcision), is strong evidence for Egypt, for only in Egypt were priests circumcised, and there is convincing evidence that circumcision was common among Egyptian priests in the Hellenistic and Roman period. A number of ancient witnesses indicate that circumcision was practiced not only by Jews, but also by Egyptians, Colchians, Ethiopians, Phoenicians, and Syrians, i.e., by lay people as well as priests. In Roman times, particularly from the time of Hadrian on, circumcision in Egypt was limited to priests, who were exempt from the general imperial prohibition of circumcision.

Occasion and purpose. There is an explicit statement of purpose found in *Barn.* 1:5, where the author expresses the desire to supplement the faith of the addressees with perfect knowledge, i.e., "knowledge of the way of righteousness" (5:4), one of the "two ways," though the specific occasion for writing is not made explicit. In *Barn.* 2:9 and 3:6, however, the author warns his readers against becoming like Jews. In *Barn.* 4:6–7, where Ps.-Barnabas reacts against the view that "the covenant is both theirs [Jews] and ours [Christians]" by claiming that it is "ours" (Christians') alone, a unique single-covenant early Christian theology emerges. This reflects the possibility that Ps.-Barnabas regarded Judaism as a threat to the existence of Christian congregations, i.e., that Ps.-Barnabas knew Judaism not as a theoretical entity but (like Justin) as a living religion. The emphasis on fasting in *Barnabas* (a ritual rarely mentioned in the OT) is one strong indication of this. With regard to the strong ethical orientation of *Barnabas*, the author thought that he had to show that the Jewish understanding of the commandments of God was wrong, and that the Christians were concerned with obeying God's commands understood correctly.

Literary genre. In discussing the literary character of *Barnabas*, the homily and the letter are the two obvious options. While there are homiletic sections and traditions in *Barnabas*, the composition should be categorized as a genuine letter, and more specifically a *protreptic letter. The *logos protreptikos* or "speech of exhortation" is designed to win someone over to a particular way of life and therefore exhibits both epideictic and symbouleutic features.

Analysis. Hvalvik has proposed an outline of *Barnabas* with five sections: (1) introduction (1:1–2:3), (2) proofs (2:4–16:10), (3) transition

(17:1–18:1a), (4) the Two Ways (18:1b–20:2), and (5) conclusion (21:1–9). Jefford (1996, 28–29) proposes a different analysis:

- I. Greeting (1:1)
- II. Thanksgiving (1:2–3)
- III. Reason for writing (1:4–5)
- IV. The three doctrines (1:6–17:2)
  - A. Introduction (1:6–8)
  - B. The hope of life according to faith (2:1–4:5)
    1. On virtue (2:1–3)
    2. On that sacrifice which pleases God (2:4–10)
    3. On fasting (3:1–6)
    4. On the final trial (4:1–5)
  - C. Righteousness according to judgment (4:6–12:11)
    1. On Israel's lost covenant (4:6–8)
    2. On steadfast obedience to God's ways (4:9–14)
    3. On the reason for the cross (5:1–8:7)
    4. On Christ revealed in the law (9:1–10:12)
       - a. In truc circumcision (9:1–9)
       - b. In dietary laws (10:1–12)
    5. On Christ revealed in the Law and Prophets (11:1–12:11)
       - a. In baptismal imagery (11:1–11)
       - b. In crucifixion imagery (12:1–11)
  - D. Love of joy as witness to righteousness (13:1–16:10)
    1. On the true heirs of the covenant (13:1–14:9)
    2. On the Sabbath (15:1–9)
    3. On the temple (16:1–10)
  - E. Conclusion (17:1–2)
- V. The Two Ways (18:1–20:2)
  - A. Introduction (18:1–2)
  - B. The way of light (19:1–12)
  - C. The way of darkness (20:1–2)

Allegorical interpretation. The kind of allegory present in *Barnabas* is typical of Alexandria, and the exegetical methods are those of Hellenistic Judaism. There are some similarities between Philo and *Barnabas*, but more impressive similarities between *Barnabas* and the *Letter of Aristeas*. The *Letter of Aristeas* is clearly Alexandrian, and there are striking links between it and *Barnabas*. Both documents share an interpretation of the Torah that is both ethical and apologetic, a combination typical of Alexandria. With the exception of the Song of Songs, Palestinian-Babylonian Jewish exegesis was generally not allegorical.

Ps-Barnabas regarded the Scriptures as prophetic (though he tended to categorize Scripture as law and commandments), and the focus of its predictions is Christ. The work contains 99 OT quotations, interpreted by means of four types of interpretation: typology, allegory, spiritualization, and literal interpretation. Ps.-Barnabas does not maintain a theory of multiple meanings, but rather looks for the real meaning intended by God but misunderstood by the Jews. Ps.-Barnabas did not think that the laws of sacrifice, fasting, circumcision, and temple were once valid but were later annulled, but rather that God never demanded such things in the first place—they were, rather, misunderstood by the Jews. For Ps.-Barnabas all Jewish rites and institutions are made by mortals and hence idolatrous. All this suggests that the situation in which Ps.-Barnabas wrote was a struggle between Jews and Christians over the legitimate ownership of Scripture.

The Two-Ways tradition. Jews and Christians in *Barnabas* are frequently dichotomized as "they" and "us." The Two-Ways section (*Barn.* 18–20) incorporates traditional material but is carefully integrated into the theological scheme of *Barnabas.* When the Jews turned to idols at Sinai (the golden calf episode) and Moses broke the tables of the law, they forever forfeited their potential status as God's people. Christians got the place originally intended for the Jewish people (*Barnabas* never speaks about a new covenant, since for him there is only one). The covenant of Christ in *Barnabas* is forgiveness, which marks the difference between the two peoples. However, Christians must also fulfill God's commandments, and they become participants in the covenant through baptism.

*Allegory, *Apostolic Fathers *Two Ways Tradition

Carleton Paget 1994; Hvalvik 1996; Kraft 1961, 1965; Prigent 1961; Prigent and Kraft 1971; Wengst 1972, 1984; Windisch 1920

Baruch, Fourth (see *Pseudepigrapha, OT)

Baruch, Second, also called the *Syriac Apocalypse of Baruch,* written ca. 100–120 C.E., consists of two sections, the apocalypse proper (1–77) and an appended letter (78–87), though some have argued for the original unity of 1–87 (Bogaert 1969, 1:67–72). The text of the apocalypse is based on one Syriac manuscript, itself a translation from Greek (expressly claimed in the Syriac subtitle) of a Hebrew original written in Palestine. The detached *Epistle of Baruch*

(*2 Bar.* 78–87) was considered canonical in the Syriac Orthodox Church.

Second Baruch, like *4 *Ezra,* was written as a response to the destruction of the temple and Jerusalem by the Romans in 70 C.E. (Bogaert 1969, 1:270–85), which the author fictionally masked as the destruction of Jerusalem and the temple by the Babylonians in 587 B.C.E.), and is therefore dominated by the problem of theodicy. The author argues that an individual's future fate depends on his or her present obedience of the law, for a major theme of the work is a person's capacity to obey the law (A. L. Thompson 1977, 133). Adam's disobedience affected him alone, for each person is his or her own Adam (54:19).

Second Baruch, again like *4 Ezra,* consists of a series of dialogues between the seer and God (modeled on Job 32:1–48:6), with God frequently correcting the seer and arguing that God is both just and powerful. The narrative moves from expressions of distress by Baruch to the gradual consolation offered by God (Sayler 1984). *Second Baruch* is commonly divided into seven sections, though there is some disagreement on the extent of each section, since they are not as clearly indicated as are the seven parts of 4 Ezra (Bogaert 1969, 1.558–67; Collins 1984, 170; Murphy 1985, 11–29). The common elements of a prayer of Baruch, a dialogue between God and Baruch, and an address of Baruch to the people, occur in sections three, four, and six: (1) God's warning to Baruch of the imminent destruction of Jerusalem (1:1–8:5); (2) Baruch's lament and his dialogue with God on the merit of being righteous (9:1–20:6); (3) the prayer of Baruch; God's prediction of 12 calamities; Baruch's address to the people (21:1–34:1); (4) the vision of the forest and its interpretation by God; dialogue on the wicked and righteous Israelites; Baruch's testament to the people (35:1–47:1); (5) the prayer of Baruch; dialogue with God (47:2–52:7); (6) the vision of the clouds and waters (a lengthy historical review) and its interpretation by the angel Remuel; dialogue with God; address to the people (53:1–77:10); (7) the letter of Baruch, which can be construed as summarizing the main points of the entire work (77:11–87:1) and which Whitters (2002) has argued is in the form of a testament or *farewell address. The work includes just two visions: (1) the dream vision of the vine and the cedar (35:1–37:1), followed by an interpretation by God (38:1–40:4), and (2) the dream vision of the clouds (53:1–12), followed by an interpretation by the angel Ramael (55:1–74:4). What appears to be a vision of the open heaven is simply a formal way of introducing another dialogue between God and Baruch (22:1–30:5).

The figure of Baruch is modeled after Moses and frequently emphasizes the importance of obeying the law (44:3–7; 46:5; 51:3) and the consequences of disobedience (77:3–5), i.e., he stresses the continuing validity of the Deuteronomistic schema of covenant curses and blessings. The author also takes up the apocalyptic notion of the two ages (the full development of which is reflected in *2 Baruch* and *4 Ezra*; *NTA* 2:549–50), arguing that the future age is infinitely superior to the present age (44:8–15). Since the second temple belonged to the present age and, unlike the first, will not be rebuilt, it is eclipsed in importance by the heavenly Jerusalem and a heavenly temple. The author does not expect an earthly restoration of Israel but rather a heavenly one. There is a close relationship between *2 Baruch, 4 Ezra,* and the *Biblical Antiquities of Pseudo-Philo. Many have argued that *2 Baruch* is dependent on *4 Ezra,* but it is rarely maintained that *2 Baruch* was written before *4 Ezra* (Bogaert 1969, 1:284–88). It is more likely that they share common sources and traditions.

Relevance to NT and ECL. Second Baruch and *4 Ezra* are apocalypses that are contemporary with the *Revelation of John, and all share particular traditions of early Jewish apocalyptic eschatology (U. B. Müller 1972, 13; Bogaert 1980), though Bogaert rather improbably maintains that *Revelation knew *2 Baruch* and was used by *4 Ezra* (1980, 56). All three incorporated their own particular messianic perspective in their reading and utilization of Dan. 7 (*2 Baruch* 39–40; *4 Ezra* 11–12; Rev. 13). *Fourth Ezra* 7:26–27 and 10:25–28 refer to the eschatological revelation of the heavenly Jerusalem. In all three, "Babylon" is a cipher for Rome. All three share the notion that a fixed number of the righteous must be completed (*2 Baruch* 23:4–5; *4 Ezra* 4:36; Rev. 6:11). Though transmitted by Christians, *2 Baruch* shows no sign of Christian interpolation.

*Apocalypses, Jewish, *Pseudepigrapha, OT, *Farewell address

Translation: *OTP* I, 615–52. Bogaert 1969; Collins 1984, 170–80; Harnisch 1969; Klijn 1970, 1976, 1983; Murphy 1985; Sayler 1984; A. L. Thompson 1977; Whitters 2002

***Baruch, Third* (the *Greek Apocalypse of Baruch*)** is a pseudepigraphon written in the name of the 6th-cent. B.C.E. Jewish scribe

Baruch couched as a first-person narration of his ascent through five heavens, accompanied by an angelic guide named Phanuel (*3 Bar* 2–16), and his return to earth (*3 Bar* 17). Since Baruch ascends through only five heavens, rather than the usual seven, and since his ascent does not culminate in a vision of God (promised in 4:2 [Slavonic]; 6:12 [Greek]; 7:2; 11:2; 16:4 [Slavonic]), many have argued that the end of the work is missing (survey of research in Harlow 1996, 22–24). It has been pointed out that Origen, in *Princip.* 2.3.6, mentions a book of Baruch which enumerates seven heavens. Particularly the last part of the work, *3 Bar* 11–17, which narrates Baruch's ascent to the fifth heaven, is thought not only to represent an abridgment of an originally longer apocalypse, but also to reflect more obvious Christian redactional efforts. Like other Jewish apocalypses, a major issue is whether *3 Baruch* was composed as a Christian work or was originally Jewish and later adapted and revised for Christian use. The work, which survives in Slavonic and Greek, was probably written in the 2d cent. C.E., perhaps in the Jewish Diaspora.

*Apocalypses, Jewish, *Ascent, heavenly, *Pseudepigrapha, OT

Collins 1983, 232–36; Hage 1974; Harlow 1996; Picard 1967 (text)

Beatitude, a transliterated form of the Latin noun *beatitudo* ("happiness, bliss, blessedness"), formed from the Latin adjective *beatus* ("happy, fortunate, blessed") is a translation equivalent of the Greek noun μακαρισμός ("blessing, beatitude"), from which the transliterated form "makarism" is derived, and a cognate of the Greek adjective μακάριος ("happy, good"). The Greek work εὐλογητός ("blessed, praised") is often used in contexts similar to those in which μακάριος is found, with the important exception that εὐλογητός or "eulogy" (in Jewish and Christian sources) is used almost exclusively of God (e.g., Rom. 4:7; 9:5; 2 Cor. 1:3; Eph. 1:3; 1 Pet. 1:3), while μακάριος is used just as exclusively of people or things. The Greek word ὄλβιος ("happy, blessed") is a traditional Greek formula for μακαρισμός (N. J. Richardson 1974, 313), typically used as the initial predicate adjective in Greek beatitudes.

Distribution. Beatitudes are found in a variety of literary contexts throughout the cultures of the ancient world (Betz 1995, 92–93). Greek beatitudes, which typically begin with ὄλβιος used as a predicate adjective, are widely attested (Hesiod *Theog.* 954–55; *Homeric Hymn to Demeter* 480–83; Pindar frg. 121 in Bowra 1964, 90; Empedocles in *FVS* 1.365 [frag. B 135]; see Dirichlet 1914). The beatitude found in Pindar (trans. Bowra) is an example of one recurring emphasis: the happiness of those who have been initiated into a mystery cult (N. R. Richardson 1974, 313): "Blessed is he who, having seen these things, passes under the earth; he knows the end of life, and knows its god-given beginning." However, the view that the "original" context of the religious beatitude was liturgical (Betz 1985, 28; 1995, 93), is a speculative and ultimately irrelevant issue for the various contexts in which beatitudes were actually used. Beatitudes occur frequently in ancient Egyptian literary texts (Dupont 1966; Assmann 1979), which provide the most ancient evidence for the beatitude as a literary form. Beatitudes also occur frequently in the OT, including 26 times in the Psalms (e.g., Ps. 1; 31:1–2; 40:2–3; 64:5; 83:5–6, 12; 88:16–17; 111), 12 times in the OT wisdom literature, particularly Proverbs. A series of four beatitudes, each beginning with *ashre,* a Hebrew word for "blessed" is found in 4Q525 = 4QBeatitudes, a wisdom composition (quote just three; trans. García Martínez and Tigchelaar 1998: 12.1053): "Blessed are those who adhere to his laws, and do not adhere to perverted paths. Blessed are those who rejoice in her [wisdom], and do not burst out in insane paths. Blessed are those who search for her with pure hands, and do not pursue her with a treacherous heart." Each of these is a single declarative sentence focusing on wisdom.

There are fifteen beatitudes in the canonical Gospels, most of which occur in the Sermon on the Mount (Matt. 5:3–12) and the Sermon on the Plain (Luke 6:20–23): (a) Matt 5:3 = Luke 6:20b; (b) Matt 5:4 = Luke 6:21b; (c) Matt 5:5; (d) Matt 5:6 = Luke 6:21a; (e) Matt 5:7; (f) Matt 5:8; (g) Matt 5:9; (h) Matt 5:10; (i) Matt 5:11–12 = Luke 6:22–23; (j) Matt 5:13, 15 = Luke 10:23; (k) Luke 11:28; (l) Luke 12:37; (m) Luke 12:23, 29 = *Gos. Thom.* 79c; (n) John 13:17 = James 1:25b; 915) John 20:29 = *Apoc. Jas.* 3.5; 8.3.

There are thirteen beatitudes in the *Gospel of Thomas,* six without parallel (7 [= *P. Oxy.* 654.7], 18, 19, 49, 58, 103), one with a parallel in Q (54 = Matt 5:3 = Luke 6:20), and two groups of three each that have some connection with the Synoptic tradition: (a) a series of three beatitudes occur in *Gos. Thom.* 68–9 (cf. Matt

5:11 = Luke 6:23; Matt 5:10; 5:6 = Luke 6:21), and (b) another series of three in *Gos. Thom.* 79 (Luke 11:27–28; 23:29; John 13:17 = James 1:25). For examples of beatitudes in *Thomas* with no parallels in the Synoptic Gospels, I cite logia 7, 58, and 49. The first is an example of a beatitude combined with a curse: "Jesus said, 'Blessed is the lion which the man eats and the lion will become man; and cursed is the man whom the lion eats and the lion will become man.'" Logion 58 is a two-part beatitude: "Jesus said, 'Blessed is the man who has suffered, he has found life.'" Here the connective particle is missing but inferred (i.e., "for he has found life"), and both parts deal with present experience. Logion 49 is also a two part beatitude, but in this case it is likely that the first part concerns the present, while the second part describes the future: "Jesus said 'Blessed are the solitary and elect, for you shall find the kingdom; because you come from it, and you shall go there again.'" Here the pattern appears to combine the third-person character of the first line of the Matthaean parables with the second-person plural direct address of the Lukan parables.

Beatitudes also occur with some frequency in the *Apocryphal Acts, typically within the context of a literary fiction of a homily or evangelistic appeal by an apostle. In the *Acts of Paul,* the author presents Paul as pronouncing a series of 13 beatitudes, many emphasizing chastity (*Acts of Paul* §§5–6), as he proclaims the gospel of chastity to the inhabitants of the house; here are the first five (*NTA* 2.239):

> Blessed are the pure in heart, for they shall see God.
> Blessed are they who have kept the flesh pure,
> for they shall become a temple of God.
> Blessed are the continent,
> for in them God will speak.
> Blessed are they who have renounced this world,
> for they shall be well pleasing unto God.
> Blessed are they who have wives as if they had them not,
> for they shall be heirs to God.

Apart from the first beatitude, which is a quotation of Matt. 5:8, the rest focus on the present spirit of those who practice asceticism, reflecting the values that pervade the *Apocryphal Acts. In the *Acts of Philip,* Philip is encircled by a great light that causes an entire household to fear him (§§22–23); he then teaches them humility through beatitudes (§24). In the *Acts of Thomas,* Mygdonia, addressing Thomas, promises to remain faithful and Thomas then pronounces a series of eleven beatitudes, confirming Mygdonia in the faith (*Acts of Thomas* §94).

Form and content of beatitudes. A beatitude or a makarism in its most simple form is a short declarative statement consisting of a single clause pronouncing someone or something "blessed," "fortunate," or "happy." Most beatitudes have this form, though the single clause can sometimes be quite long. While beatitudes have been almost exclusively preserved in literary contexts, they are used in at least three ways: in the context of public acclamation, in liturgical contexts, and in didactic contexts.

Beatitudes sometimes function as an *acclamation (in literary settings that imitate public situations), as in the cry of the crowd during Jesus' triumphal entry: "Blessed (μακάριος) is he who comes in the name of the Lord!" (Mark 11:9; Matt. 21:9; John 12:13; cf. Luke 13:35), or (in the Lukan alternative), "Blessed is the King who comes in the name of the Lord! (Luke 19:38). For another example of such acclamations, see Luke 11:27. Mark includes two similar acclamations that Matthew and Luke, critical of Markan doublets, omitted (11:9): "Blessed is he who come in the name of the Lord! Blessed is the kingdom of our father David that is coming."

In exclusively literary contexts, beatitudes sometimes consist of two clauses, the first of which pronounces a certain person or thing blessed or fortunate (the protasis), while the second (often linked to the first clause by an inferential particle such as "for," or a causal particle such as "because") states the basis for the pronouncement, the apodasis. The beatitudes in the Sermon on the Mount in Matthew 5:3–12 (cf. Luke 6:20–23) have this familiar form, e.g., Matt. 5:3: "Blessed are the poor in spirit, for theirs is the kingdom of heaven." Beatitudes can refer to a single person (typically formulated in the third-person singular) or to a group of people (typically formulated in the third-person plural or in the second-person plural when direct address is involved). Most of the beatitudes in Matt. 5:3–12 and Luke 6:20–23 are formulated in the third-person plural with μακάριοι + plural substantive participle, so that a literal translation of the protasis of Matt. 5:3 reads: "Blessed are those who are poor in spirit." A beatitude with the protasis in the second-person plural is found in Matt. 5:11–12 (cf. Luke 6:22), "You are blessed (μακάριοί ἐστε) whenever . . ." (the reasons for pronouncing the beatitude then follow). The differences between beatitudes addressed to single persons and groups of people, however, are minimal. For example, Rev. 20:6 reads "Blessed and holy is he who shares in the first resurrection!" While it is unusual in that this beatitude begins with a double predicate, it is clear that all who share in the first resurrection are blessed and holy.

Beatitudes are used in literary contexts both singly and in collections. While beatitudes tend to occur singly in the OT, occasionally two occur together (Ps. 32:1–2; 84:5–6; 119:1–2; 137:8–9; 144:15; Sir. 14:1–2). A series of eight beatitudes occurs in Sir. 14:20–27, while a series of ten occurs in Sir. 25:7–10. A series of five beatitudes occurs in 4Q525 = 4QBéat frag. 2 ii 1–3. The five beatitudes in 4Q525 exhibit similarities to those of Matt. 5:3–12 and Luke 6:20–23 (Fitzmyer 1992). Series of beatitudes also occurs in the *Apocryphal NT (*Gospel of Thomas* 68–9, 79; *Acts of Paul* 5–6; *Acts of Thomas* 94; *Acts of Philip* 24). When a series of beatitudes each begins with the word μακάριος, that constitutes the figure of speech called *epanaphora.

Beatitudes in Matt. 5:3–12 and Luke 6:20–23. The nine beatitudes in Matt. 5:3–12 and the four beatitudes in Luke 6:20–23 are widely thought to be based on the *Q source (the reconstructed text of Q is found in Robinson, Hoffman and Kloppenborg [eds.] 2000, 44–53), though more probably the Sermon on the Mount was a pre-Matthaean source that the first evangelist redacted and integrated into the composition of the first Gospel (Betz 1985, 18). The first eight beatitudes in Matthew and the first three in Luke have the same brief third-person plural form in the first line: the word μακάριοι introduces the protasis, while the second line, the apodasis, is introduced by ὅτι ("for, because"), e.g., "Blessed (μακάριοι) are those who are poor in spirit, for (ὅτι) they shall be comforted" (Matt. 5:3). However, while the third-person singular format is retained in Matthew, it is cast in the second-person plural in Luke, e.g., "Blessed are the poor, for (ὅτι) yours is the kingdom of God" (Luke 6:20b). The last beatitude in Matt. 5:11–12 and Luke 6:20–23 has a strikingly different form, for it is in the second-person plural and is quite lengthy, and has a ὅτι-clause which is in turn supported by a γάρ-clause (Dodd 1968, 1–2). Dodd (1968, 2) regards this very different beatitude as not part of the original series expressed in stereotyped form, but rather a transition to the next part of the Sermon on the Mount or the Sermon on the Plain. Luke continues in vv. 24–26 with four "woes," obviously designed as an antithetical series resembling the three or four previous beatitudes in both form and content; he also couches them in the second-person plural, e.g., "But woe [οὐαί] to you who are rich, for (ὅτι) you have received your consolation" (Luke 6:24). The juxtaposition of beatitudes and woes are found in the OT and early Jewish literature (Isa. 3:10–11; Eccl. 8:12–12; 10:16–17; Tob. 13:12, 14; *b.*; *2 Enoch* 52:1–15; *Ber.* 61b). *2 Enoch* 52:1–5 is a particularly good example that juxtaposes seven beatitudes with seven curses; the second will serve as an example (trans. *OTP* 1.178): "Happy is he who opens his lips, both blessing and praising God. Cursed is [he who] opens his lips for cursing and blasphemy, before the face of the Lord all his days." The juxtaposition of blessedness and its opposite is also found in the oldest Greek beatitude known, formulated in the third person and directed to those who have been initiated in the Eleusinian mysteries in the *Homeric Hymn to Demeter* 480–83 (trans. Foley 1994, 26): "Blessed is the mortal on earth who has seen these rites, but the uninitiate who has no share in them never has the same lot once dead in the dreary darkness." These parallels indicate that the antithetical collection of four beatitudes and four woes in Luke 6:20–26 form a unified compositional unit (Dodd 1968, 4). These beatitudes and woes announce an eschatological reversal (J. M. Robinson 1962) in which those who are now poor, hungry, sorrowful, and outcast will possess the Kingdom of God, will have enough to eat, will be joyful, and will have a reward in heaven.

The collection of eight beatitudes in Matt. 5:3–10, part of the Sermon on the Mount, constitutes a unified poetic text (Burney 1925, 116ff., even though he has to fiddle with the wording to maintain a three-stress rhythm; see **parallelismus membrorum*, *poetry). The collection is marked off by an **inclusio* consisting of the phrase "for theirs is the kingdom of heaven," and the first four beatitudes (Matt. 5:3–6) exhibit six instances of π-*alliteration (C. Michaelis 1968). The second group of four beatitudes is framed by an alliteration of two δ-words in 5:6 and two δ-words in 5:10 (H. B. Green 2001:39). Unlike the Lukan collection of beatitudes and woes, the Matthaean beatitudes do not emphasize the eschatological reversal of roles, since those who are merciful will not obtain less mercy in the eschaton (Matt. 5:7), nor will those who are pure in heart be less pure when they see God (Matt. 5:8), nor will the role of the peacemakers be reversed in the future (Matt. 5:9); rather, these are all types of behavior of which God approves (Dodd 1968, 7). This ethical emphasis of the three beatitudes in Matt. 5:6–9 seems to provide a context for understanding the other beatitudes, and this is surely the case with the first Matthean beatitude that refers to those who are "poor in spirit" (5:3), since the phrase "in spirit" is absent from Luke 6:20b, and appears to have been part of the Matthaean redaction of traditional material (Dodd 1968, 7–8).

Beatitudes and Apocalyptic. Beatitudes occur only occasionally in an apocalyptic literary context, and not always with an apocalyptic significance.. The apocalyptic section of Daniel concludes with a beatitude: "Blessed is he who waits and comes to the thousand three hundred and thirty-five days" (Dan. 12:12). A series of nine beatitudes are found in *2 Enoch* 42:6–14, and a series of seven beatitudes paired with seven curses are found in *2 Enoch* 52:1–15. The first is "Happy is the person who reverences the name of the Lord, and who serves in front of his face always, and who organizes his gifts with fear, offerings of life, and who in this life lives and dies correctly!" All nine beatitudes are declarative statements that attribute happiness or blessedness to a person who fulfils certain ethical injunctions, and none of them reflect an apocalyptic worldview. The beatitudes in Matt. 5:3–12 and Luke 6:20–23 have a clear eschatological significance, since the first line (or protasis) of each beatitude concerns human behavior in the present, while the second line describes God's future eschatological response (J. M. Robinson 1962), described by Betz (1995, 94) as "anticipated eschatological verdicts." There are seven beatitudes that punctuate the text of Revelation (1:3; 14:13; 16:15; 19:9; 20:6; 22:7, 14). Five have an apocalyptic orientation (14:13; 16:15; 19:9; 20:6; 22:14), while two have a liturgical setting (1:3; 22:7). In view of the author's interest in the symbolic significance of the number seven (which he uses 53 times), his inclusion of seven beatitudes is clearly intentional.

*Benediction, *Epanaphora, *Poetry

Betz 1985, 1995; Bieder 1954; Broer 1986; Dirichlet 1914; Dodd 1968; Fitzmyer 1992; Gladigow 1967; H. B. Green 2001; Guelich 1982; Hamm 1990; McKenna 1999; Meier 1994:317–36; Puech 1993; N. J. Richardson 1974; J. M. Robinson 1962; Schweitzer 1972–73

Bible, a term derived from the Greek word βιβλία (from the singular form βιβλίον, a diminutive of the word βίβλος="papyrus roll") meaning "books." The term "Bible" is applied to the collection of writings held sacred by Christianity and, by extension, to Judaism or other religions.

*New Testament, *Old Testament, *Canon, biblical

Bicolon, a term synonymous with *distich, refers to a two-line poetic couplet.

*Poetry

Biobibliography (also called "pinakography"), a technical term for bibliographies that contain biographical information about the authors whose works are listed, a characteristic of almost all ancient and medieval bibliographies. The oldest and most important of the Greek biobibliographies was an extremely long work of *Callimachus called *Pinakes* ("lists"), consisting of lists of Greek authors by classes and according to literary forms or scholarly disciplines (Blum 1991, 150–60). The biobibliographical lists of Hesychios of Miletus (mid-6th cent. C.E.) have survived in quotations in the Suda.

Blum 1991; Pfeiffer 1968, 127–34

Biography, one of the more complex and varied literary forms of antiquity. Though the Greek biographical tradition had its roots in the 5th cent. B.C.E., the actual term "biography" (Greek βιογραφία) first appears in the late 5th cent. C.E. Earlier authors generally referred to such works as "lives" (Greek βίοι; Latin *vitae*). As a literary genre, biography has often been defined rather narrowly. The problem of defining the genre becomes acute when the hundreds of fragments of lost Greco-Roman works on aspects of the life of an individual are considered. Rather than craft a definition of the biographical genre that excludes numerous writings on the basis of formal criteria (particularly when such writings cannot easily fit into other generic categories), it seems appropriate to work with a broad and relatively simple definition, i.e., all literary works primarily concerned with the life of one or (in the case of collections) several people (Radicke 1999, x). This fits the more flexible conception of literary genre that has emerged in recent years (Conte 1994a; Marincola 1999; see *Genre criticism). If more formal criteria are applied, such as those that emerge from an analysis of Plutarch's *Lives* (for example), the number of writings that qualify as biographies is considerably reduced (Radicke 1999, x). If, for example, the whole life of a person must be treated, the two works entitled *Lives of the Sophists* by Philostratus and Eunapius would fall out of consideration. Again, if speeches are excluded, Marinus's *Life of Proclus* would not pass muster, nor would the various speeches steeped with biographical content in honor of various emperors (the fragments of nine *encomia and *panygyrics are collected in Radicke 1999, 280–353, F1085–93). Perhaps *Lives of Philosophers* by Diogenes Laertius should rather be considered a history of philosophy (the *Life of Pythagoras* by Porphyry was part of a similar work).

The genre of Greco-Roman biography is typically defined as an independent literary composition, usually focused on the character, achievements, and lasting significance of a memorable and exemplary individual from birth to death, with the emphasis on his public career. But, as we have seen, not always. Following this formal definition, biography as an independent literary form is rarely attested, and it developed only very late in Israelite and early Jewish literature (1st cent. C.E.), however, and under Hellenistic influence. Once biography is defined more broadly, a "biographical" interest in the lives of individuals can be seen in various guises throughout the OT and early Jewish literature. In the Greco-Roman world, most biographies were written, as one might expect, by scholars and antiquarians. During the imperial period (27 B.C.E. on), collections of biographies were more common than individual biographies (e.g., Suetonius's *Lives of the Caesars*, Plutarch's *Parallel Lives,* and Diogenes Laertius's *Lives and Opinions of Eminent Philosophers*). In addition to the antiquarian interest reflected in many biographies (which are often compilations of earlier material), there was also a strong philosophical tradition that focused exclusively on the lives of philosophers with a primarily philosophical purpose. There is a strong hagiographical element present in these lives, particularly evident in the presentation of the lives of Pythagoras (e.g., by Nicomachus of Gerasa [Radicke 1999, F1063], Apollonius of Tyana [Radicke 1999, F1064], and Apollonius of Tyana himself (e.g., Damis of Nineveh [Radicke 1999, F1065], and Maximus of Aegeae [Radicke 1999, F1066], and Philostratus).

Types of Hellenistic biography. The most influential modern study of ancient biography was by Leo (1901), who distinguished two major types of biography. Peripatetic biography (exemplified by Plutarch, *Lives*), and Alexandrian biography (exemplified by the Suetonius, *Lives of the Caesars*, and Diogenes Laertius, *Lives of the Philosophers*). Bakhtin (1981, 140–42) prefers the more descriptive designations "energetic biography" (e.g., Plutarch's biographies), in which a person's inner character is expressed through actions and statements, and "analytic biography" (e.g., Suetonius's biographies), in which a person's life is discussed in terms of defined categories such as social life, family life, and conduct in war. Both types originated with Aristotle and his Peripatetic school. Peripatetic biography is characterized by a chronological arrangement with literary pretensions. This type was suitable for presenting the lives of politicians, generals, and philosophers, with the dominating conception that a person's character was revealed through his actions. Alexandrian biography, on the other hand, reportedly originated with the grammarians at the Museum at Alexandria (see *biobibliography, *Diogenes Laertius, *libraries), who were also under the influence of Aristotle. This type of biography is characterized by topical and systematic arrangement, had no real literary pretensions, and was particularly suited to presenting the lives of famous artists and authors. These biographies were often designed to serve as introductions to commentaries on the works of famous artists and literary figures. The two types of biography described by Leo were also recognized by *Quintilian (3.7.17; LCL trans.):

> Praise awarded to character is always just, but may be given in various ways. It has sometimes proved the more effective course to trace a man's life and deeds in the due chronological order, praising his natural gifts as a child, then his progress at school, and finally the whole course of his life, including words as well as deeds. At times, on the other hand, it is well to divide our praises, dealing separately with the various virtues, fortitude, justice, self-control and the rest of them and to assign to each virtue the deeds performed under its influence.

Ancient writers not infrequently combined the chronological and topical approaches in the presentation of the life of a famous person. Xenophon's encomium *Aegesilaus* begins with a chrological narrative of the deeds of Aegesilaus (1–2), yet is dominated by a topical exposition of his virtues (3–11). The chronological tendency exhibited in Peripatetic biography probably originated in Hellenistic historiography with its largely chronological presentation of political and military matters within the framework of the war monograph (e.g., Herodotus, Thucydides) or the more comprehensive framework of the universal history (e.g., Polybios). Alexandrian biography, on the other hand, owes much to the systematic discussions of antiquarians (e.g., Dionysius of Halicarnassus, Suetonius). The chronological and topical tendencies in ancient biography, however, are frequently combined.

Since Leo's twofold ideal typology of Greco-Roman biography makes no accommodations for biographies in which features from both types are present, others have proposed modifications and amplifications of Leo's scheme. Wehrli (1973) proposed a related typology consisting of three types of ancient biography with many mixed forms: (1) biographies of philosophers and poets (Leo's Peripatetic type); (2) encomiastic-rhetorical biographies of statesmen and generals; (3) short biograpical sketches, particularly of famous authors. Berger (1984, 1231–43), building on both Leo and Wehrli, has proposed a fourfold biographical typology: (1) the encomium type (Isocrates, *Evagoras*; Xenophon, *Aegesilaus*; Philo, *Vita Mosis*; Tacitus, *Agricola*; Lucian, *In Praise of Demosthenes*); (2) the Peripatetic type, a chronological narrative of moral character exemplified by deeds (Plutarch, *Lives*); (3) the popular, novelistic type (Xenophon, *Cyropaedia*; the anonymous *Vita Secundi,* see *Secundus, life of); and (4) the Alexandrian type, systematically organized (Suetonius). The typologies of both Wehrli and Berger, however, are unsatisfactory, since constitutent categories are based on inconsistent generic criteria. Wehrli's appeal to "mixed types" reveals the difficulty of any such typology. Talbert (1977, 92–93) has proposed a typology based exclusively on five possible *functions* of biography: (1) to provide a pattern for emulation, (2) to replace a false image with a true image of the teacher worthy of emulation, (3) to discredit a teacher, (4) to indicate where authentic tradition is to be found, and (5) to validate or provide an interpretive key to a teacher's doctrine. Yet this proposal is not fully satisfactory, since it focuses on the *function* of biography to the exclusion of other salient generic features. The development of a more satisfactory typology of Greco-Roman biography can only be achieved when many examples of the biographical literary form have been subject to rigorous literary analysis, a task yet to be achieved. Burridge (1992) proposes a model of four generic features of biography: (1) opening features (e.g., title, prologue, preface); (2) subject; (3) external features (e.g., size, sequence, scale); and (4) internal features (e.g., setting, motifs, style, attitude, quality of characterization). He examines five early and five late Greco-Roman biographies to establish his case.

Major features of Greco-Roman biography. Greco-Roman biography, in contrast to its modern counterpart, was primarily focused on famous people as representative *types* (i.e., as illustrations of group values), rather than as unique individuals (Malina 1981, 51–70). In philosophical lives, the philosophy is presented as an embodiment of his teachings and of the philosophical way of life in general (Radicke 1999, xi). The primary identity of ancient people was anchored in kinship groups (γένος, "family"; φρατρία, "clan"; φυλή, "tribe"), as well as in larger social and political units (οἶκος or οἰκία, "household"; ἔρανος or θίασος, "social club"; δῆμος, "commune"; πόλις, "city"). Individual personalities were assumed to be as fixed and unchanging as the kinship groups and the social and political units within which they were enmeshed. Greco-Roman biographies, therefore, are more *idealistic* than *realistic*. Consequently the subjects of most ancient biographies are depicted as static personalities who function as paradigms of traditional virtues (and more rarely, vices). Several features of ancient biography can be correlated with this emphasis on the typical and the ideal. First, the subjects thought most suitable for biographical description were those prominent in public life (i.e., those active in the assembly, the marketplace, the gymnasium, the theater, the battlefield, and the law courts), whose lives appropriately reflected the norms and values of the state (e.g., statesmen, generals, politicians, kings, philosophers, poets, orators [see *Orators, Attic]). The public function of these figures meant that males, who alone led "public" lives, were thought to be appropriate subjects of biography. Second, the chronological framework used in ancient biography was the means of organizing the external facts of the subject's life, not for tracing the development of his personality (which was assumed to be static). Third, the idealistic approach to biographical writing combined with the rhetorical purpose of portraying the subject as a model of virtue inevitably led to distortion and the inclusion of fictional elements. Greco-Roman biography is an *inclusive* literary form that provides a framework for a variety of short forms, including anecdotes or χρεῖαι (see *chreia), *maxims (γνῶμαι), and reminiscences (ἀπομημονεύματα). Chreiai are essentially sayings or actions (or a combination of the two) set in a brief narrative framework (e.g., the question-and-answer section of the *Vita Secundi* (see **Secundus, Life of*). γνῶμαι are proverbial sayings lacking both attribution and a narrative framework, and ἀπομημονεύματα are expanded χρεῖαι transmitted by memory. Examples of longer literary forms that can be included in biographies are *novellas, *speeches, and *dialogues.

In ancient biographical traditions, there is a deeply rooted assumption that the actions and words of a person sum up his or her character more adequately than any comments by an observer. Hellenistic biography was an extremely flexible and varied literary type that continued to change and develop throughout antiquity. As a literary genre, biography is primarily determined by its content: the literary presentation of the life of a public person, optionally introduced by an account of his or her birth and youth and concluded by his or her death and lasting significance. While it is certainly useful to group together biographies that appear to have closer affinities to each other than to other biographies, in no single biographical subgenre are all the possible formal features present. A great deal of cross-fertilization occurred between various types of biography. That means that it is methodologically incorrect to try to link the Gospels rigidly only with that specific type of ancient biography with which they appear to have the closest affinities. The canonical Gospels then constitute a subtype of Hellenistic biography, one that exhibits the syncretistic insertion of a Judaeo-Christian message in a Hellenistic envelope.

*Autobiography, *Gospels, literary genre of

Aune 1982; Bollansée 1999; Burridge 1992; Chance 1991; Dundes 1977; Gundry 1974; Hadas and Smith 1965; Koester 1990; Lefkowitz 1981; Misch 1951; Momigliano 1981, 1993; Radicke 1999; Stanton 1974, 1989; Talbert 1977, 1996

Boasting, or self-praise, was an issue more important in ancient popular philosophical ethics than in rhetorical theory. Self-praise or boasting about one's person or achievements was a social taboo throughout the ancient world. On the Israelite side there is Prov. 27:2: "Let another praise you, and not your own mouth; a stranger, and not your own lips." From the perspective of late Greek philosophical ethics, Epictetus (*Encheiridion* 33.14) recommends:

> In parties of conversation, avoid a frequent and excessive [ἀμέτριος] mention of your own actions and dangers. For however agreeable it may be to yourself to mention the risks you have run, it is not equally agreeable to others to hear your adventures.

In Israelite and Jewish culture, self-praise was thought inappropriate because it implicitly diminished the majesty and power of God (Ps. 75:4–7). In Greek culture, there was the analogous conception that excessive pride would provoke the jealousy and wrath of the gods (a conception encoded in myths such as those about Bellerophon and Arachne in which the principal characters are punished for their hubris).

Terminology for Self-Praise. The Greeks had a large ethical vocabulary of words belonging to the semantic domain of pride and arrogance, including ἀλαζονεία ("boastfulness"), καυχᾶσθαι ("to boast"), κενοδξία ("vanity, conceit"), οἴησις ("self-conceit"), περιαυτολογία ("speaking about oneself"), τῦφος ("vanity, arrogance"), ὑπεροψία ("contempt, disdain"), φιλαυτία ("self-love"), and φυσᾶσθαι ("to be puffed up"). The terms that are formed with the καυχ-stem, including the verb καυχᾶσθαι ("to boast") and the nouns καύχημα (what is said, i.e., "boast") and καυ´χησις (the act of "boasting"), are as pejorative in Greek as they are in English. In his essay *De laude ipsius,* Plutarch frequently uses the reflexive expression αὐτὸν ἐπαινεῖν, "to praise onself" (540C). Plutarch also uses the term περιαυτολογία ("speaking about oneself"), which is a comparatively soft expression with either positive or negative connotations, depending on the context. περιαυτολογία is not found in Demosthenes' *De corona* 4, 321 (as claimed by De Lacey and Einarson 1958, 110), where the phrase λέγειν περὶ ἐμαυτοῦ is used, and it is not a technical rhetorical term (another claim made by De Lacey and Einarson 1958, 110, 119, n. a), for περιαυτολογία is conspicuously absent from the indices of Lausberg 1998 and R. D. Anderson 2000).

Self-Praise in Rhetoric. Self-praise or boasting as a rhetorical device (absent from Aristotle's *Rhetorica*) is discussed in only a cursory manner in a few Greco-Roman rhetorical handbooks (*Rhetorica ad Herennium* 1.5.8; Cicero *De inventione* 1.16.22; Quintilian 11.1.15–28), and famously in an ethical context reflecting some rhetorical influence in Plutarch *De laude ipsius, Moralia* 539A-547F. In both the *Rhetorica ad Herennium* and *Cicero's *De* *inventione* (which share common material widely thought to go back to a Greek rhetorical treatise), self-praise is used as a device to achieve the goodwill (*benevolentia*) of the audience in the context of the *exordium* of a forensic speech (note that it is inappropriate to use these passages out of context as if they dealt with the issue of self-praise generally, as does Sampley 1988).

Both Quintilian and Plutarch refer to the oration *De corona* by Demosthenes in which the famous Athenian orator defends his right to be awarded a crown for public service in response to the negative charges made by Aeschines. The issue of self-praise found in this oration by one of the greatest of all Greek orators made *De corona* a textbook example of how to deal with the problem rhetorically, as well as ethically. The nature of the charge made it necessary for Demosthenes to argue his worth to the Athenian court. Toward the beginning of his speech, Demosthenes explicitly mentions a major disadvantage under which he labors (*De corona* 4; LCL trans.), namely "the natural disposition of mankind to listen readily to obloquy and invective and to resent self-laudation [τοῖς ἐπαινοῦσι δ' αὑτούς]."

Cicero's discussion of how to gain the good will of the audience in the context of an *exordium* involves the careful utilization of self-praise (*De inventione* 1.16.22; LCL trans.):

> We shall win goodwill from our own person if we refer to our own acts and services without arrogance; if we weaken the effect of charges that have been preferred, or of some suspicion of less honourable dealing which has been cast upon us; if we dilate on the misfortunes which have befallen us or the difficulties which still beset us; if we use prayers and entreaties with a humble and submissive spirit.

The parallel in *Rhetorica ad Herennium* 1.5.8 (LCL trans.) contains only a few differences:

> From the discussion of our own person we shall secure goodwill by praising our services without arrogance and revealing also our past conduct toward the republic, or toward our parents, friends, or the audience, and by making some reference to [lacunae] . . . provided that all such references are pertinent to the matter in question; likewise by setting forth our disabilities, need, loneliness, and misfortune, and pleading for our hearers' aid, and at the same time showing that we have been unwilling to place our hope in anyone else.

Plutarch on Self-Praise. Plutarch, who treats the subject primarily from an ethical rather than rhetorical perspective (though some rhetorical influence is evident), suggests that self-praise is generally considered offensive and irritates the hearer. Further, self-praise is ultimately self-defeating, since it typically offends the listener, engendering a negative attitude toward the speaker. He gives three major reasons why it should be avoided (*De laude ipsius* 539D–E): (1) If decent people are expected to be embarrassed when praised by others, the person who praises himself must be completely lacking in decency (cf. Demosthenes *De corona* 128; Quintilian 11.1.22). (2) Since praise can only be expressed properly by others, those who praise themselves are unfairly usurping the rights of others. (3) If the listener remains silent when listening to someone indulge in self-praise he or she experiences such bad feelings as envy that destroy the relationship with the speaker. On the other hand, if the listener joins in, he becomes a flatterer, which is an inappropriate way of praising someone. A fourth reason is added by Betz (1978, 376) from *De laude ipsius* 574D: self-praise impresses the audience negatively and frustrates the persuasiveness of the speech. Along this line, Quintilian (11.1.15–17) suggests that self-praise usually proves disgusting to an audience since people react negatively to those who are superior to them, though positively to those who are inferior to them.

Yet the purpose of Plutarch's essay is to propose ways in which self-praise can be achieved without giving offense. Plutarch suggests several circumstances in which this can be used appropriately (4–14; 540C–544D): (1) Self-praise is appropriate when the speaker is defending himself in response to slander. (2) Self-praise is appropriate when the speaker has experienced misfortune and hardship and uses self-praise to move from a lowly humble state to convey an attitude of triumph and pride. (3) Self-praise is appropriate when the speaker has experienced an injustice and uses freedom of speech and boldness as a means of self-defense (cf. Quintilian 11.1.18). (4) One can admit to a charge but argue that the opposite of what one has been accused of would have been shameful. (5) One can praise others whose aims and acts are the same as one's own and thus effectively praise onself indirectly. (6) One can attribute one's achievements partly to oneself and partly to the gods. (7) "With the fair-minded it is not amiss to use another device, that of amending the praise: when praised as eloquent, rich, or powerful, to request the other not to mention such points but rather to consider whether one is of worthy character, commits no injuries, and leads a useful life" (*De laude ipsius* 12.543A–B). (8) It is also effective to moderate one's excellent reputation by mentioning a few shortcomings to deflect the displeasure or disapproval of the audience.

Plutarch then mentions a few situations in which a person can inadvertently be tempted to indulge in self-praise (18–21; 546C-547C): (1) Reacting in jealousy at the praise of others. (2) To be so pleased with oneself regarding an enterprise that went well so that we drift into self-praise. (3) To magnify ourselves when we censure others. (4) To allow flattery to elicit in us a desire to ask for yet more praise.

Relevance for the NT & ECL. Several studies of the rhetorical functions of self-praise or boasting have illumined a number of passages in the NT and early Christian literature (Betz 1978, 377–82), particularly 2 Cor. 10–13 where there is a concentrated emphasis on "boasting" (Betz 1972; Forbes 1986; Danker 1991; DiCicco 1995; Sampley 1988; Travis 1973; Watson 2002). In 2 Cor. 10–13, self-praise or boasting (10:8, 13, 17–18; 11:10, 16–18, 21b–30; 12:1–10) and invective (10:7–18; 11:13–15, 20) are combined in Paul's spirited defense of his apostleship (10:13–18; 11:5–15) and his ministry (2 Cor. 12:19). There are a number of striking features in this lengthy passage: (1) The general view that Paul is ill-at-ease in boasting is correct (based on 2 Cor. 10:8, 13, 15; 11:16, 18, 30; 12:1, 5, 6), but should not be considered an unwitting revelation of his troubled conscience but rather a calculated attempt to make his audience feel that he has been forced into self-praise. (2) Paul's frequent use of words for "boast" based on the Greek καυχ-stem have a strongly negative connotation, and are generally not found in rhetorical or ethical discussions of self-praise, where ἐπαινεῖν αὐτὸν is generally used negatively, while other less intrinsically negative locutions are used such as λέγειν περὶ ἐμαυτοῦ ("to speak about myself") or περιαυτολογία ("speaking about myself"). Paul's opponents indulged in boasting themselves (11:12, 18, 21; cf. 5:12). (3) Some have inappropriately associated the boasting motif of 2 Cor. 10–13 with Paul's use of the phrase συνιστάνειν ἑαυτόν, "to recommend oneself" in 2 Cor. 3:1; 5:12; 10:12, 18 (Hafemann 1990, 69–74), used positively in 3:1 and 5:12, but negatively in 10:12, 18. These negative uses, however, have nothing to do with impropriety of self-commendation, which is in fact a social institution (P. Marshall 1987, 124–9, 259–77). (4) Paul is aware that there is a line between appropriate and inappropriate boasting, and claims that he has not crossed it (2 Cor. 10:13, 15: "we will not boast excessively [ἀμέτριος]"). He is well aware of the biblical injunction "Let him who boasts, boast of the Lord" (10:17; 1 Cor. 1:31; allusions to the LXX version of Jer. 9:24 and 1 Sam. 2:10; cf. Ps. 20:7; 34:2), and if he seems to violate it, the reason is probably that he understands his boasting to be ultimately "in the Lord." (5) Paul makes an issue of being "comparable" to his detractors using the technique of σύγκρισις, "comparison" (10:7), and since they are "fools" (11:19), Paul plays the part of a "fool" himself (11:16, 17, 21; 12:6, 11), and the so-called "fools speech" in 2 Cor. 11:21b-12:10 is a rhetorical *prosopopoiia,* a "speech in character," in which Paul adopts the procedure of his rivals and boasts of his own credentials. (6) Paul's "admission" in 11:6 ("Even if I am unskilled in speaking, I am not in knowledge") is simply a widely-used rhetorical ploy to gain the good will of the audience. See Dio Chrysostom *Or.* 32.39: "I am quite ordinary and prosaic in my public speaking, though not ordinary in my theme" (see also Dio Chrysostom *Or.* 57.4–5). (7) Paul paradoxically claims that he wants to boast about his weaknesses (12:5–10), which takes away the opprobium from the act of boasting itself.

Paul's use of boasting does not conflict at any point with the recommendations made by Plutarch on how to use self-praise inoffensively, and in several respects, according to Betz (1972, 75–9), he follows Plutarch's advice quite closely. Yet others (John Dillon and Thomas Conley in Betz 1975, 17–23) find the links between the Greco-Roman tradition of praising oneself inoffensively and Paul's use of boasting in 2 Cor. 10–13 as unconscious and coincidental. Paul's boasting in 2 Cor. 10–13 functions in four ways (P. Marshall 1987, 354–5): (1) Paul boasts only because he finds it necessary to defend himself (11:30; 12:1, 11). (2) Further, he boasts of his interest and care for the Corinthians (11:2, 10–11, 28, 29; 12:14–15). (3) His boasting is intended to counter the different gospel proclaimed by his opponents, and remind them of the gospel that Paul proclaimed to them (11:1–4). (4) He uses boasting to refute and shame his opponents (11:12, 18, 20) as well as humble the Corinthians (11:14–18).

John Chrysostom (349–407 C.E.) was concerned about the rhetorical and ethical problem of Paul's self-praise. Because of the similar use of topoi relating to boasting in both Plutarch's essay *De laude ipsius* and Chrysostom's defense of Paul's self-praise, some have argued that Chrysostom was dependent on Plutarch (Mitchell 2002, 341). Particularly in *De laudibus sancti Pauli* 5.15, part of a series of homilies on 2 Corinthians, Mitchell (2002, 343; her trans.) has called attention to Chrysostom's enumeration of five different ways in which Paul's boasting basically functioned as φιλανθρωπία ("affection for people"), since it was done for the instruction, correction, and salvation of his addressees:

> Do you see how many means he employed to instruct his hearer not to boast frivolously? First, by showing that he did this from necessity. Second, by calling himself a fool, and repeatedly begging off from engaging in it. Third, but not telling everything, but hiding his greater deeds—and this was when there *was* a necessity. Fourth, by assuming another persona and saying "I know a man" [2 Cor. 12:2]. Fifth, by not publicizing every other virtue, but only that portion for which the present time has special need.

Each of these five points is discussed in detail by Mitchell (2002, 344–52).

*Autobiography

Berger 1984b, 1271–74; Betz 1972, 1978; Danker 1991; Fitzgerald 1988; Forbes 1986; Hafemann 1990; Judge 1968; P. Marshall 1987; Mitchell 2002; Sampley 1988; Watson 2002

Books and book divisions The English term "book" is derived from the Greek word βίβλος (derived from βύβλος); the equivalent Latin term is *volumen*. βίβλος could refer to a single roll of papyrus (Herodotus 2.100), or to the number of rolls or books into which a literary work was divided (Diodorus Siculus 1.4.6–7; Lucian, *Herodotus* 1.1), or to a literary work as a whole (Acts 19:19). In Jewish and Christian usage, βίβλος in the singular could be used of the Scripture of the Jews, though it existed in several individual rolls (Aristeas 3.16; Josephus, *Ant.* 12.113, 256), or to part of a single section of Scripture, such as "the book of Moses" (Mark 12:26), or "the book of Psalms" (Acts 1:20), or "the book of the prophets" (Acts 7:42). The Homeric epics, the oldest Greek literature, are each divided into 24 books, divisions that are probably not original (How and Wells 1912, 1.224, referring to Herodotus 2.116), though some argue that they are (Stanley 1993, 279–93). The 24 divisions of the *Odyssey* were probably patterned after the *Iliad*. The only ancient writer to discuss the book divisions of Homer attributes them to Aristarchus the Alexandrian librarian (Ps.-Plutarch, *Life of Homer* 2.4), though this is probably incorrect. Modern scholars have used aesthetic criteria to understand Homeric book divisions (e.g., the internal structure of each book; whether passages on each side of book divisions indicate natural breaks, etc.). Heiden (1998) argues that books in the *Iliad* end with "low-consequence" scenes and begin with "high-consequence" scenes; i.e., the latter have an effect on the upcoming events in the story (e.g., the description of Achilles' shield that concludes *Iliad* 18.478–617), while the former have no immediate consequences in the story (i.e., book endings that tend to lack the closure modern critics expect). The term ῥαψωδία, meaning a Homeric "book," indicates that the traditional segmentation of the Homeric epics was thought to be based on rhapsodic performances. Diodorus Siculus speaks of the divisions of his history as αἱ βίβλοι (1.4.6–7), and Lucian similarly refers to the nine divisions of Herodotus's history as βίβλοι (*Herodotus* 1.1).

Transitions between books. *Quintilian uses the beginning of book 3 of the *Instituto Oratoria* to summarize the contents of book 2 and provide a brief overview of book 3 (LCL trans.: "In the second book the subject of inquiry was the nature and the end of rhetoric, and I proved to the best of my ability that it was an art, that it was useful, that it was a virtue and that its material was all and every subject that might come up for treatment. I shall now discuss its origin, its component parts, and the method to be adopted in handing and forming our conception of each" (3.1.1). Of the 12 books of the *Instituto*, most begin with a brief account of the content of the book (the exception is book 2). *Josephus divided his work *Contra Apionem* into two books, apparently because the size of the work required two papyrus rolls (*Contra Apionem* 1.320). Book 2 begins with a recapitulation of the contents of book 1 (*Contra Apionem* 2.1), just as Acts 1:1 recapitulates the content of Luke.

*Chapter, *Titles

Heiden 1998

Book titles (see *Titles of books)

Callimachus (ca. 305–240 B.C.E.) was born in Cyrene but spent most of his adult life in the court of Ptolemy II Philadelphus (308–246

B.C.E.) in Alexandria as a poet and scholar who was a member of the Museion. His most important work, in 120 books, was the *Pinakes*, "Lists" (Blumer 1991, 150–60), which has not survived. Most of the biographical information about him is preserved in this notice in Suidas (Adler 1928–38, 3.19–20; trans. Blumer 1991, 124):

> Kallimachos, son of Battos and Mesatma, from Kyrene, grammarian, pupil of the grammarian Herokrates of Iasos, married the daughter of Euphrates of Syracuse. His sister's son was the younger Kallimachos who wrote about islands in verse. He was so zealous that he wrote poems in every meter and many books in prose. And he wrote more than eight hundred books. He lived in the time of Ptolemaios Philadelphos. Before he was introduced to the king, he was a teacher in an elementary school in Eleusis, a suburb of Alexandria. And he lived until the time of Ptolemaios Euergetes, the 127th Olympiad, in the second year of which Ptolemaios Euergetes began his reign. . . . Among his books are the following: . . . *Lists of Those who Distinguished Themselves in All Branches of Learning*, in 120 books.

It is not known whether or not Callimachus became director of the Museion library (the issues are spelled out in Blumer 1991, 127–28). Though the *Pinakes* has not survived, on the basis of fragments the following observations can be made about the character of the work (Blumer 1991, 153): (1) C. divided authors into classes and, if necessary, into subclasses. (2) C. arranged the names of the authors alphabetically (by first letter only). (3) He added biographical data to the name of each author. (4) Under an author's name he listed the titles of his works, combining similar works into groups. (5) C. cited the opening words of each work. (6) He cited the extent of each work in terms of the number of *stichoi or lines.

*Bibliography, *Library

Blumer 1991; Pfeiffer 1968; F. Schmidt 1922

Call narratives are conventional literary narratives in which God selects a human emissary for a divine mission.

OT prophetic call narratives. The literary form of NT call narratives (e.g., Gal. 1:11–17; Rev. 1:9–20; 10:8–11) was often modeled after prophetic call narratives in the OT. The prophetic call narrative includes both speech and narrative elements and involves a procedure similar to that used in the commissioning of a messenger (e.g., Gen. 24:34–48). The focal point of the call narrative is the prophet's commissioning by God, and for this reason the narrative could easily be designated "the installation of the prophet" (Baltzer 1968, 569). Although these narratives appear autobiographical, the formal features they share have suggested that they are not reflections of actual experience but proclamations serving to legitimate the prophets' vocation (Habel 1965, 17). The fact that call narratives tend to be placed at the beginning of oracle collections indicates that they function to validate the prophet as a legitimate spokesman for Yahweh. Since formal patterns are not antithetical to experiences that are naively thought of as spontaneous and unstructured, prophetic call narratives might well reflect a restructuring of actual experience and provide a vehicle for legitimating the prophetic vocation. There are a number of call narratives in the OT (Moses in Exod. 3:1–12; Gideon in Judg. 6:11–17; Isaiah in Isa. 6:1–13; Jeremiah in Jer. 1:4–10; Ezekiel in Ezek. 1:1–3:11; Deutero-Isaiah in Isa. 40:1–11). Jeremiah 1:4–10 reflects the typical literary prophetic call form used in the OT, and is also interesting because it is alluded to in Paul's own narrative of his apostolic commission in Gal. 1:11–17. The structure of Jer. 1:4–10, with its main structural features indicated by the descriptions on the left is indicated in the table on the following page.

This call narrative, as well as several of the others, features the motif of the reluctant emissary (cf. Moses in Exod. 3:7–4:17; Gideon in Judg. 6:11–24; Saul in 1 Sam. 9:15–21); i.e., the one called expresses hesitation and needs to be convinced. The same motif occurs in the call of Thomas to India narrated in *Acts of Thomas* 1–3 and the call of Philip in *Acts of Philip* 8.1–3).

Zimmerli (1979, 97–100) has distinguished between two main types of prophetic calls: the narrative type, which includes a dialogue with Yahweh (Exod. 3:7–4:17; Judg. 6:11–24; Jer. 1:4–10), and the throne-theophany type, which prefaces the prophetic commission with a vision of the heavenly throne of Yahweh (1 Kgs. 19:11–21; Isa. 6:1–13; Ezek. 1:1–3:11).

Baltzer 1968; Droge 1983; Habel 1965; Lindblom 1962; Skarsaune 1976

Canon, Alexandrian (see *Alexandrian canon)

Canon, biblical The term "canon" comes from the Greek word κανών, a "Mediter-

Jeremiah's Prophetic Call

Structure	Jer. 1:4–10
1. Divine confrontation (v. 4)	Now the word of the LORD came to me saying
2. Introductory word (v. 5a)	"Before I formed you in the womb I knew you, and before you were born I consecrated you;
3. Commission (v. 5b)	I appointed you a prophet to the nations."
4. Objection (v. 6)	Then I said, "Ah, Lord GOD: Behold, I do not know how to speak, for I am only a youth."
5. Reassurance (vv. 7–8)	But the LORD said to me, "Do not say, 'I am only a youth'; for to all to whom I sent you you shall go, and whatever I command you you shall speak. Be not afraid of them, for I am with you to deliver you, says the LORD."
6. Sign (vv. 9–10)	Then the LORD put forth his hand and touched my mouth; and the LORD said to me, "Behold, I have put my words in your mouth. See, I have set you this day over nations and over kingdoms, to pluck up and to break down, to destroy and to overthrow, to build and to plant."

ranean" word found in several of the languages of peoples around the Mediterranean. The Hebrew word *qaneh*, for example, means "reed, stalk" (1 Kgs. 4:15; Isa. 19:6) and by extension "measuring rod" (Ezek. 40:3, 5). The Latin word *canna* means "small reed" and "pan pipe" (*OLD*, 266), while the related word *canon* means "the sound-board of a water-organ" and "model, standard" (*OLD*, 266). The Greek word κάννα or κάννη (closely related to the Hebrew word קנה, means "reed" or "reed mat," while κανών means "bar," "straight rod," "ruler," "straight edge," and by extension "model," "rule," and "standard." It is worth noting that "canon" was never used by the Greeks to mean an authoritative list or selection of works. The word was first used with this meaning in 1768 by David Ruhnken for lists of classical authors (Pfeiffer 1968, 1.207), though Ruhnken may have been dependent on the use of the term in Christian circles, not for a list of writers but for a list of books (see Eusebius, *Hist. eccl.* 6.25.3, referring to Origen). The concept of a canon of sacred writings is significant for students of ancient literature because it means that such writings were read within a certain religious or theological framework, and not as ordinary literature.

Old Testament. The phrase "Old Testament" is a Christian designation for the Hebrew Bible that implies that it is both subordinate to and fulfilled in the "New Testament." Jewish terms for the Old Testament included "Scripture" (הכתוב), "Mikra" (המקרא, "what is read"), and Tanak, an acrostic for the three divisions of the Hebrew Bible, Torah (תורה, "law, instruction"), Nebiim (נביים, "prophets"), and Ketubim (כתבים, "writings"). At the end of a long process of the production and liturgical use of books that would be included in the Hebrew Bible, the canon of 22 books emerged by the end of the 1st cent. C.E. (Josephus, *Contra Apionem* 1.37–41; *4 Ezra* 14:45). In 180 B.C.E., in the preface of the Wisdom of Sirach, the grandson of the author refers to "the law, the prophets and the other writings," indicating that the first two divisions of the Hebrew Bible were already fixed by the beginning of the 2d cent. B.C.E. Similarly, 4QMMT (4Q397 14–21 10 and 4Q398 14–17 2–3), refers to "the book of Moses and the books of the prophets and David." This is very similar to Luke 24:44: "everything written about me in the law of Moses and the prophets and the psalms must be fulfilled." Though *4 Ezra* 14:45 refers to 24 books (the standard number) the number 22 (important because there are 22 letters in the Hebrew alphabet) was maintained by some by appending Ruth to Joshua and Lamentations to Jeremiah. No fixed canon of texts is evident in the manuscripts from Qumran, and it is clear that the notion of a fixed text did not exist. While the books of the Hebrew Bible were canonized, there is no evidence that the *text* of the Hebrew Bible was canonized (Orlinsky 1989, 557–62; Ulrich 1999).

The three divisions of the Hebrew Bible are often thought to have originated in a three-stage process of canonization, in which the Torah was canonized by 400 B.C.E. (Nehemiah 8), the Prophets by 200 C.E. (Prologue to Ecclesiasticus), and the Writings by 90 C.E. at Yavneh (Ryle 1909; Beckwith 1988, 51–58).

The Alexandrian canon hypothesis. On the basis of the content of manuscripts containing the *Septuagint (Codex Sinaiticus and Codex Vaticanus, both 4th cent. C.E.; Codex Alexandrinus, 5th cent C.E.), it has been widely held that the OT canon was larger in Hellenistic Judaism than it was in Palestinian Judaism, containing books called *Apocrypha by Protestants and Deuterocanonical by Roman Catholics. Many thought that Hellenistic Jews had a laxer view of the boundaries of the canon than did Palestinian Jews and, unlike Palestinian Jews, did not subscribe to the notion of the cessation of prophecy, so important in the closing of the canon of the Hebrew Bible. It is, of course, true that the collections of Jewish writings included in the Septuagint did have a profound effect on the OT canon of the Christian Church. The OT canons of the Roman Catholic Church and the Greek Orthodox Church include a number of books not found in the Hebrew Bible; these works were mediated through the Latin Vulgate (which included many books found in the Septuagint but not found in the Hebrew Bible) or the Septuagint, which Greek Orthodoxy considers their OT.

The Alexandrian canon hypothesis, however, has some fatal weaknesses (Sundberg 1964; Beckwith 1988, 81–84): (1) The extant Septuagint manuscripts were copied by Christians, not by Jews. (2) Hellenistic Jews were not disconnected from Palestinian Judaism, as was often supposed, and often exhibited even more conservative tendencies than their Palestinian confrères. (3) Many of the Jewish works preserved in the great Septuagint manuscripts were not originally written in Greek, but were originally composed in Hebrew or Aramaic in Palestine (e.g., Wisdom, Tobit). (4) There is no evidence that any of the apocryphal or deuterocanonical books ever had a place in the threefold division of the Jewish Bible. (5) Philo, an Alexandrian Jew, never quotes from any of the books of the Apocrypha, which would be peculiar, had they been part of the Jewish Alexandrian canon of Scripture.

New Testament. The canonization of the New Testament was a long sorting process that began in the second century and reached a "conclusion" (the term is used advisedly; when does it become obvious that such a process has reached completion?) in the great church in the West at the end of the 4th cent. at the Council of Hippo (387 C.E.), and the Third Council of Carthage (393 C.E.) and in the East was signaled by the 37th Festal Letter of Athanasius of Alexandria (367 C.E.). This canonical process was rooted in the perception that the teachings of certain past authorities continued to be valid (e.g., Jesus, Paul, and the apostles). New Testament writings that originally *described* a variety of early Christian religious systems gradually came to be regarded as normative documents which *prescribed* the standards and beliefs appropriate for Christian faith and life. In actual practice, however, the shared beliefs of the interpreter's community functioned as the hermeneutical presupposition for using harmonistic and figurative interpretive strategies that legitimated those

Torah (Law)	**Nebiim (Prophets)**	**Ketubim (Writings)**
Genesis	**Former Prophets**	Psalms
Exodus	Joshua	Job
Leviticus	Judges	Proverbs
Numbers	Samuel	Ruth
Deuteronomy	Kings	Song of Songs
	Latter Prophets	Ecclesiastes
	Isaiah	Lamentations
	Jeremiah	Esther
	Ezekiel	Daniel
	The Twelve	Ezra-Nehemiah
		Chronicles

beliefs by finding them reflected in the New Testament. For Origen, for example, historical discrepancies in the Gospels point to spiritual truth (Origen, *Joh. Comm.* 10.5.19; SC 157, 395; see also Laeuchli 1952). The theological unity of the New Testament was an external criterion imposed on the New Testament rather than elicited from it.

While much of the process whereby the 27 documents of most Christian New Testaments became sacred is unknown, it is clear that the process was a gradual one. The two basic elements of the NT are the Gospel and the Apostle. The "Apostle" is a designation for the ten letters of Paul that were collected within a generation of his death and circulated together. The earliest date for this collection is ca. 90 C.E. (such a collection was unknown to the author of Acts, which was written ca. 90 C.E.). The "Gospel" refers to the *Fourfold Gospel (see *Four Gospels), collected within a generation of the composition of the Gospel of John (i.e., 90 C.E.), the last Gospel to be included in the NT canon. The earliest date for this collection is ca. 125 C.E.

In the summary comments of Eusebius of Caesarea (d. 340 C.E.) on the sacred status of early Christian literature in his day, we find a threefold categorization of writings that were thought to be Scripture, using language used earlier by Origen: (1) τὰ ὁμολογούμενα, "acknowledged, accepted, received [books]," (2) τὰ ἀντιλεγόμενα, "disputed [books]," and (3) νόθοι, "spurious [books]" (*Hist. eccl.* 3.25.1–4; LCL trans.):

> At this point it seems reasonable to summarize the writings of the New Testament which have been quoted. In the first place should be put the holy tetrad of the Gospels. To them follows the writing of the Acts of the Apostles. After this should be reckoned the Epistles of Paul. Following them the Epistle of John called the first, and in the same way should be recognized the Epistle of Peter. In addition to these should be put, if it seem desirable, the Revelation of John, the arguments concerning which we will expound at the proper time. These belong to the Recognized Books [ὁμολογουμένοις]. Of the Disputed Books [ἀντιλεγομένων], which are, nevertheless, known to most are the Epistle called of James, that of Jude, the second Epistle of Peter; and the so-called second and third Epistles of John which may be the work of the evangelist or of some other with the same name. Among the books which are not genuine [νόθοις] must be reckoned the Acts of Paul, the work entitled the Shepherd; the Apocalypse of Peter, and in addition to them the Letter called of Barnabas and the so-called Teachings of the Apostles [τῶν ἀποστόλων αἱ λεγόμεναι Διδαχαί]. And in addition, as I said, the Revelation of John, if this view prevail. For, as I said, some reject it, but others count it among the Recognized Books [ὁμολογουμένοις].

Criteria for canonicity. From the late 2d cent. on, the criteria for canonicity most frequently mentioned were three: orthodoxy (i.e., conformity to the *regula fidei*, "rule of faith" or the *regula veritatis*, "rule of truth"); apostolicity (real or putative attribution to an apostle or close connections with an apostle); and consensus (acceptance by many churches over a long period of time). (1) The criterion of orthodoxy: interpretive strategies of 4th-cent. Christianity were flexible enough that the (or any) *regula fidei* or *regula veritatis* of orthodoxy could be imposed on the New Testament. (2) The criterion of apostolicity, from a historical perspective, is problematic because of the probable pseudepigraphical character of many NT letters (1–2 Timothy, Titus, 1–2 Peter, James, Jude), and the recognition that the four Gospels were not actually connected in a meaningful way with apostles (Matthew and John) or "apostolic associates" (Mark and Luke). Tertullian qualifies this by distinguishing between apostles (John and Matthew) and companions or friends of apostles (Luke and Mark); see *Adversus Marcionem* 4. (3) The argument from *consensus* did not apply to the edges of the NT, i.e., Hebrews and Revelation, except in a regional sense. In addition, several more criteria of lesser importance were sometimes invoked: (1) The criterion of *antiquity*: books for inclusion in the sacred collection had to be handed down by tradition from the apostolic age. (2) The criterion of *catholicity*: books suitable for inclusion in the canon had to be catholic, i.e., suitable for the church generally. According to Justin, *1 Apol.* 67, "the memoirs of the apostles [= the Gospels] and the writings of the prophets" are read in church.

Aune 1991; Beckwith 1985, 1988; F. F. Bruce 1988; Gamble 1985; Hahneman 1992; Laeuchli 1952; Leiman 1976; J. P. Lewis 1964; L. M. McDonald 1995; Metzger 1987

Canon criticism is a form of distinctively biblical criticism that focuses on the interpretation of the OT or the NT in its canonical context and in relationship to the community of faith. Canon criticism is in part an attempt to go beyond traditional historical criticism in order to focus on a text that has meaning for a community of faith. The impetus for canon criticism came from the work of OT scholars J. A. Sanders (1972, 1984), who has focused on the process of canonical formation, emphasizing how a text took shape historically and how such texts controlled the formation of other texts, and Childs (1979), who has focused on the final canonical form of the text, including the shape of the canon, how its parts reflect the interests of the canonical community of faith, and how these interests can guide interpretation. Childs has also extended this method to the NT (1984). Porter and Clarke (1997) purport to use canonical criticism to investigate the relationship between Colossians and Ephesians, but their procedure is a thinly veiled exercise in historical criticism manipulated to affirm Pauline authorship of both letters, an issue that is not the concern of canon criticism (Childs 1984, 322–28; Wall and Lemcio 1992, 285).

Childs 1979, 1984; Porter and Clarke 1997; J. A. Sanders 1972, 1984; D. E. Smith 2002; Wall and Lemcio 1992; Ulrich 1999

Captatio benevolentiae, a Latin phrase meaning "fishing for goodwill" (equivalent to *petitio veniae*), is often used for a certain type of *exordium* in a speech, though it is not a technical term found in the Latin *rhetorical handbooks (note its absence from the eclectic Lausberg 1998, §§263–88). The phrase was apparently first used by Boethius (d. 524 C.E.), in his commentary on Cicero, *Topica* (Boethius, *In Ciceronis Topica I*, p. 272, 4; Orelli). The purpose of the *exordium* is to make hearers *attentum*, *docilem*, and *benevolum*, "attentive, receptive and well-disposed" (*Ad Herennium* 1.4.6). An *exordium* that focuses on *benevolum* can be called a *captatio benevolentiae*. Winter (1991, 507–8) defines the role of the *captatio benevolentiae* in papyrus petitions as "to win the goodwill of the prefect by drawing his attention to an aspect of his own judicial and administrative competence which made him highly suited to hear a particular case, rather than have it referred to a subordinate official for a jury trial." Winter (1991, 514) quotes the *captatio benevolentiae* from P. Coll. Yutie 66C, lines 45–50: "Your celestial highmindedness, great commander, has extended its philanthropy over all your (inhabited) world and sent it out over every place, has led me too to the good hope of presenting a petition to your divine fortune, (a petition) related to both reason and lawfulness, and it is this."

A *captatio benevolentiae* is used to introduce two speeches in Acts 24. The orator Tertullus is mentioned in Acts 24:2–8 but is not given an extensive speech, apart from a brief *captatio benevolentiae* in vv. 2b–4, followed by a twofold accusation (vv. 5–8); see Winter 1991, 515–21. The *exordium* in vv. 2b–4 is very brief: "Since through you we enjoy much peace, and since by your foresight, most excellent Felix, reforms are introduced on behalf of this nation, in every way and everywhere we accept this with all gratitude." Paul's response in Acts 24:10–21 similarly begins with a *captatio benevolentiae* (v. 10b), continues with a brief *narratio* (v. 11) and a *propositio* (v. 12); see Winter 1991, 521–26. The *exordium* itself runs: "Realizing that for many years you have been judge over this nation, I cheerfully make my defense." After examining these two examples of an *exordium* in the form of a *captatio benevolentiae* in Acts 24, Winter (1991, 529–31) argues that the two speeches of which they are part should be regarded as sources used by Luke rather than as example of Luke's ability to compose rhetorically appropriate speeches.

The *thanksgiving period that frequently occurs in early Christian letters, particularly those of Paul, is typically designed to function as a *captatio benevolentiae*, securing the goodwill of the recipients (Berger 1974, 219–24). Analogously, Quintilian (10.1.48) tells us that in the opening or introductory lines of the *Iliad*, "He [Homer] secures the goodwill [*benevolum*] of the audience by invoking the goddesses believed to preside over poets, its attention [*intentum*] by his statement of the importance of his subject, and its readiness to learn [*docilem*] by his brief summary of the facts." This is, of course, an analysis of a Greek composition by means of the conventions of rhetorical handbooks.

**Exordium, *Preface, *Prooimoion*

Berger 1974; Winter 1991

Catalogues of vices and virtues Virtue (Greek ἀρετή; Latin *virtus*) and vice (Greek κακία; Latin *vitiositas*, *vitium*) catalogues occur frequently in Greco-Roman, Jewish, and Christian writings, in both literary and nonliterary sources. These catalogues reflect current standards of conventional morality, and they were used for a number of purposes, including characterization, description, exemplification, instruction, exhortation, apology, and polemic (Fitzgerald 1992, 857). Most scholars agree that the lists derive ultimately from Stoic ethical teaching. Following Plato, the Stoics articulated four cardinal virtues: wisdom (σοφία), temperance (σωφροσύνη), justice (δικαιοσύνη), and courage (ἀνδρεία). Corresponding to these four virtues are four vices: folly (ἀφροσύνη), profligacy (ἀκολασία), injustice (ἀδικία), and cowardice (δειλία) (*SVF* 3:63).

While individual elements of the Stoic lists occur in New Testament catalogues (i.e., δικαιοσύνη and δίκαιος in Eph. 5:9, Phil. 4:8), those elements nowhere appear in their traditional fourfold grouping in the NT. Some NT lists, however, contain elements that differ from those employed by pagan moralists, and by separating these uniquely Christian items from the "traditional" pagan elements, the reader may learn more about the historical situation that elicited the list (Karris 1973). NT catalogues may be composed of abstract virtues and vices, or they may list people who practice such virtues and vices. Romans 1:29–31 begins with a list of nine vices and continues with a list of twelve types of practitioners, combining both types: "They were filled with all manner of wickedness, evil, covetousness, malice. Full of envy, murder, strife, deceit, malignity, they are gossips, slanderers, haters of God, insolent, haughty, boastful, inventors of evil, disobedient to parents, foolish, faithless, heartless, ruthless."

In form, most Greco-Roman lists are asyndetic (i.e., Epict. 2.16.45: λύπη, φόβος, ἐπιθυμία, φθόνος, etc.). While many New Testament lists are asyndetic or without connective particles (see *asyndeton), as in Rom. 1:29–31, others are polysyndetic or with connective particles (see *polysyndeton), as in 1 Cor. 5:11. They may also be composed of elements scattered loosely throughout a more extended discourse, as in Jude 16–19. Analysis of NT lists demonstrates that they cannot be reduced to a single, coherent form (McEleney 1974).

Catalogues of virtues and vices in the NT function similarly to their Greco-Roman counterparts. Authors in the NT used catalogues of virtues and vices in description, or *ekphrasis* (e.g., Gal. 5:19–23), polemic (e.g., 2 Tim. 3:1–5; see Karris 1973), and *paraenesis (e.g., Titus 2:3–5). Their role in paraenesis and in protrepsis is particularly significant. In paraenesis, virtues and vices could be used in antithesis (i.e., Col. 3:5–17), in bringing to mind a former worse state of life (i.e., Col. 3:12–13), or they could simply appear by themselves (i.e., 2 Pet. 1:5–7). In protrepsis, vice lists served to describe the state of the soul that required salvation (i.e., Titus 3:1–7). In both pagan and Christian literature, virtue and vice lists delineate the qualities desired or reviled in one holding a position of authority (Dio Chrysostom 4.83–96; 1 Tim. 3:2–6, 8–13; see Malherbe 1986, 138–41; Kamlah 1964).

Many Greco-Roman authors employed virtue and vice lists, including Pseudo-Aristotle (*On Virtues and Vices*); Cicero (*Tusc. Disp.* 4.11–17); Dio Chrysostom (see Mussies 1972); Diogenes Laertius (e.g., 7.92–93, 110–12); Horace (e.g., *Ep.* 1.1.33–40; 6.12); Musonius Rufus (e.g., Fragment 16); Plutarch (e.g., *Mor.* 468B, 523D), and many more (Fitzgerald 857).

In early Jewish literature. While only a few virtue and vice catalogues appear in the Hebrew Bible (e.g., Jer. 7:9, Hos. 4:2), they proliferate in later Jewish literature, including, but not limited to, *Apoc. of Abraham* 24; *3 Baruch* 4:1; 8:5; 13:4; *1 Enoch* 10:20; 91:6–7; *Jubilees* 7:20–21; 21:21; 23:14. For lists in rabbinic literature, see Kamlah 1964, 150–60 and Vögtle 1936, 106–7, and in the Dead Sea Scrolls (1QS 4:3–14) see Kamlah 1964, 39–50; Wibbing 1959, 43–76. In Philo, *Sacr.* 32 appears to contain the longest vice list in ancient literature.

In the NT. Catalogues of virtues and vices are found with some frequency in the Pauline letters (Dunn 1998, 662–65). Vice lists are more common than virtue lists (Rom. 1:29–31; 13:13; 1 Cor. 5:10–11; 2 Cor. 12:20; Gal. 5:19–21; Col. 3:5, 8), and the virtue lists tend to be shorter (2 Cor. 6:6; Gal. 5:22–23; Phil. 4:8; Col. 3:12). The diversity of Pauline lists suggests that Paul was not simply recycling existing lists as he found them, which indicates that he may have designed lists for the particular audience he was addressing. Here is a comprehensive list of NT vice and virtue lists: (1) virtue lists: 2 Cor. 6:6–7a; Gal. 5:22–23; Eph. 4:2–3, 4:32–5:2; 5:9; Phil. 4:8; Col. 3:12; 1 Tim. 3:2–4, 8–10, 11–12; 4:12; 6:11, 18; 2 Tim. 2:22–25; 3:10; Titus 1:8; 2:2–10; Heb. 7:26; 1 Pet. 3:8; 2 Pet. 1:5–7; (2) vice lists: Matt. 15:19; Mark 7:21–22; Rom. 1:29–31; 13:13; 1 Cor. 5:10–11; 6:9–10; 2 Cor. 12:20–21; Gal. 5:19–21; Eph. 4:31; 5:3–5; Col. 3:5–8; 1 Tim. 1:9–10; 6:4–5; 2 Tim. 3:2–4; Titus 1:7; 3:3; 1 Pet. 2:1; 4:3, 15; Rev. 9:21; 21:8; 22:15 (Mussies 1972, 67, 172).

In ECL. Much less attention has been devoted to virtue and vice lists in Christian literature outside the NT. Such lists occur frequently in writings such as *Barn.* 2:2–3; 18–20; *1 Clem* 3:2; 30:1, 3, 8; *Did.* 2:1–5:2; Justin, *Apol.* 2.2; 5; *Acts Andr.* 8; 10; *Acts John* 29; 35–36 (Fitzgerald 858).

*Asyndeton, *Epideictic rhetoric, *Lists, *Paraenesis, *Protreptic literature

---

Berger 1984: 1088–92; J. D. Charles 1997; Dunn 1998, 662–65; Easton 1932; Fitzgerald, *ABD* 6:857–59; Kamlah 1964; Karris 1973; McEleney 1974; Malherbe 1986, 138–41; Mussies 1972; Quinn 1990; Schweizer 1979; Vögtle 1936; Wibbing 1959

Catchword is a term used for a composition technique based on the use of similar terms. The collocation of compositional units based on "catchword bonds" (*Stichwortverbindungen*) is found in the *Gospel of Thomas* (see *Thomas, Gospel of), such as the theme of "the elect" in logia 49 and 50. For a list of "potential" catchwords in the *Gospel of Thomas*, see Patterson 1993, 100–102. *Gospel of Thomas* logia 18 and 19 both end with the phrase "will not experience death" (Coptic: *fnadji tipe anmmou*); logia 28 and 29 both focus on "flesh"; logia 50 and 51 are linked by the term "rest"; logia 83 and 84 are linked by the common use of "image." In Rom. 15:9–12 four quotations from the OT are strung together (Ps. 17:50; Deut 32:43 [LXX]; Ps. 116:1; Isa. 11:1, 10), united by the term "heathen" or "nation" (Fitzmyer 1974c, 66). The three verses composing Luke 16:10–12 (concluding the parable of the Dishonest Manager in Luke 16:1–13) are tied together by the adjective πιστός ("faithful"), which occurs four times.

Catholic Epistles (see *General Epistles)

Cebes, Tabula is a work of Hellenistic philosophy that teaches its readers the difference between true and false *paideia*. It is written in the Koine Greek that was common in the Hellenistic period (Joly 1963, 13–21). While there is no consensus on a precise date for the work (Fitzgerald and White 1983, 1–4), a date from the 1st cent. B.C.E. to the 1st cent. C.E. seems likely. As with many philosophical works of the period, it is an eclectic philosophical mix combining elements of Stoicism, Cynicism, Pythagoreanism, Platonism, and Socratic philosophy (Fitzgerald and White 1983, 20–27; Joly 1963, 25–42). The work itself is an example of *ekphrasis, that is, a description of a painting that the narrator and his companions have come upon in a temple of Cronus (1.1). The document is structured around the various scenes in the painting, which an old man describes to the narrator before going on to make general moral points about each scene depicted therein. The old man warns the hearers of a danger that comes with the explanation he will provide (3.1–4). Those who understand the explanation will be wise and happy, whereas those who do not understand are condemned to be without wisdom, unhappy, miserable, and without learning. The old man then explains that the fable represented in the painting is an allegory for life, in which those who enter are instructed by a *daimon* as to which road they should take in life (4.2–3; see *Two Ways). Upon entering life, each person is forced by Deceit to drink Error and Ignorance (5.1–3). The goal of life, consistent with the philosophical bent of the tract, is ultimately to arrive at true *paideia* (15.1–4) by means of Perserverance and Self-Control (16.2).

*Ekphrasis

Fitzgerald and White 1983; Joly 1963

ERIC STEWART

Chapter, from the Latin term *capitulum*, literally "little head," in late Latin comes to mean "division of a book." Eusebius of Caesarea introduced a system of "chapters" into the Greek manuscripts of the Gospels, 355 in Matthew, 233 in Mark, 342 in Luke, and 232 in John. Each "chapter" either contains material found in all four Gospels, or when a passage contains material not found in all four Gospels, a new "chapter" is begun. Eusebius prepared ten lists, called "canons," consisting of the numbers of sections where (1) all four Gospels are in agreement; (2) Matthew, Mark, and Luke are in agreement; (3) Matthew, Luke, and John agree; (4) Matthew, Mark, and John agree; (5) only Matthew and Luke agree; (6) Matthew and Mark agree; (7) Matthew and John agree; (8) Luke and Mark agree; (9) Luke and John agree; and (10) there is no parallel in another Gospel.

Modern chapter divisions in the Bible were first made in 1204 or 1205 by Stephen Langton, the archbishop of Canterbury (d. 1228).

Character, characterization Along with *plot, character is an essential element in a narrative. Characters can be dynamic (when they change and grow) or static (when they do not). Forster (1955, 46–54) introduced the distinction between "round" ("three-dimensional") and "flat" ("two-dimensional") characters, which has been picked up by subsequent literary critics (e.g., Harvey 1965, 192; Chatman 1978, 131–34; Galef 1993). "Round" characters exhibit a variety of qualities, creating the impression that they are real people, while "flat" characters have few traits and are predictable in their behavior. They are "types" and "caricatures" that are constructed around a single trait or idea (Forster 1955, 46–47). According to Forster (1955, 54), "The test of a round character is whether it is capable of surprising in a convincing way. If it never surprises, it does not convince, it is flat pretending to be round." Kingsbury (1988) has applied Forster's typology to characterization in Matthew, and been critiqued by Black (2001, 23–46).

De Boer (2000) shows how John presents Pilate as a reluctant participant in the drama of the trial and crucifixion of Jesus (John 18:28–19:22) and thus as a round character. In John 19:1–22 Pilate repeatedly refers to Jesus as "the King of the Jews" (culminating in the titulus he has affixed to the cross), the spokesperson of an ironic truth he does not understand or believe, i.e., Pilate repeatedly affirms what the Jews of the narrative reject, namely, that Jesus is their king.

Black 2001, 23–46; Bloom 1998; De Boer 2000; Delft 1993; Forster 1955; Galef 1993; Gardiner 1987; Gruber 1994; L. L. Harris 1990; Hochman 1985; Lauther 1998; Lynch 1998; May 1988; Stein 1992; Steinrück 1992; Zanker 1994

Charismatic exegesis, a phrase coined by Ginsberg (Brownlee 1951, 61 n. 4), to describe the type of biblical interpretation practiced in the Qumran community by the author of the Habakkuk commentary (1QpHab). "Charismatic exegesis" is an umbrella term for a wide variety of methods of biblical interpretation that share several core features: (1) it is *commentary*; (2) it is *inspired*; (3) it has an *eschatological orientation*; and (4) it was a type of *prophecy* prevalent during the late Second Temple period (Aune 1993, 126–27). Whether or not exegesis is "inspired" or not is a subjective opinion that does not alter the methods exhibited in the text. "Charismatic exegesis," then, is an ideological homologue that corresponds to other forms of exegetical methods, whether the exegete recognizes it or not.

*Pesharim

Aune 1993; Brownlee 1951

Chariton of Aphrodisias (southwest Asia Minor) is the author of *Chaereas and Callirhoë* (1st cent. C.E.), which survives entire in a single Greek manuscript of the 13th cent. C.E. The text and an English translation are conveniently available in Goold 1995, and an English translation alone in Reardon 1989, 17–124. Rohde (1914, 521–22) dated Chariton to the 5th or 6th cents. C.E., but the discovery of papyrus fragments of Chariton dating to the 2d or 3d cent. C.E. suggests that it is one of the earliest novels, perhaps composed in the 1st cent. C.E. (Reardon 1989, 17). Some even date the novel as early as the 1st cent. B.C.E. (Papanikolaou 1973). Chariton has been regarded as a "pre-sophistic" or "non-sophistic" novel (Hägg 1983, 34–35; see *Second Sophistic), because the author does not atticize (Reardon 1989, 17). This reflects the early date of composition. Despite the fictional intentions of the author, the story is set in the real world, and some of the characters are historical figures. This pretense of reality and historicity is evident from the very beginning of the story (Chariton 1.1; trans. Reardon 1989, 21): "My name is Chariton, of Aphrodisias, and I am clerk to the attorney Athenagoras. I am going to tell you the story of a love affair that took place in Syracuse" (here an allusion to the opening lines of Herodotus and Thucydides is apparent; see Konstan 1998, 11).

Content. The work is a historical novel set in the 4th cent. B.C.E. in a cosmopolitan Mediterranean world with Syracuse, Miletus, Palestine, Egypt, and Babylon as the major theaters of action. The two central characters, Chaereas and Callirhoe, are introduced as incredibly beautiful young people whose fathers are the highest ranking citizens in Syracuse (1.1.1–3). Callirhoe's father, Hermocrates, was a historical Syracusan politician who was part of the successful resistance against the Athenian expedition against Sicily in 415–413 B.C.E. During a festival of Aphrodite, Chaereas and Callirhoe see each other by chance and fall in love instantly (1.1.4–6). They marry, but Chaereas becomes jealous, mistakenly thinking that Callirhoe is unfaithful. He kicks her, and when she falls unconscious, he thinks she is dead; she is quickly buried after an elaborate funeral. A band of pirates intent on robbing tombs, led by Theron, break into the tomb, find her alive, take her along with the booty, and in Ionia sell her to Dionysius as a slave. Chaereas, learning that Callirhoe is actually alive, pursues her and finds the pirate vessel, with all aboard dead except Theron. The pirate is brought into the assembly, tortured, questioned, and then crucified. The city sends a ship to rescue Callirhoe, with Chaereas accompanied by his friend Polycharmus. Crossing to Miletus, they meet Dionysius, who had bought Callirhoe for a talent. Though he loved her, he did not touch her; but when Callirhoe discovered that she was pregnant by Chaereas, she felt she had to marry Dionysius to preserve his honor. When the child was born, she pretended that it was the son of Dionysius.

When Chaereas lands at Miletus, he sees a gold statue of Callirhoe in a temple of Aphrodite (erected by Dionysius), but then a band of Phrygian robbers attacks them and burns the ship, slaughtering the crew but selling Chaereas and Polycharmus as slaves in Caria to a slave of Mithridates, governor of Caria. Some members of the chain gang murder their guard, and Mithridates orders the rest, including Chaereas and Polycharmus, to be crucified. When Mithridates learns that Chaereas was one of those being crucified, he rescues him and has him write a letter to Callirhoe, which Dionysius intercepts. He does not believe that Chaereas is really alive, but that Mithridates himself has designs on Callirhoe, and accuses Mithridates to the Persian king. The case is heard in Babylon. Dionysius brings Callirhoe, and Mithridates brings Chaereas. After pleading their cases, the king acquits Mithridates and announces his attention to arbitrate between Chaereas and Dionysius for the hand of Callirhoe. He delays, however, because he himself is smitten with Callirhoe. At that point there is a rebellion in Egypt and Callirhoe's guardian, Queen Statira, to protect her, sends her away. Chaereas hears a false report that the king has given Callirhoe to Dionysius, so he joins the Egyptian rebels to get revenge on the king. He captures Tyre, wins a sea battle against the king, and captures Aradus, where the king has left the queen and his wealth in safety. Chaereas sets up the Egyptian king as master of all Asia, though shortly after he is killed in battle. Chaereas regains the friendship of the king by sending him his wife and by sending the families of his nobles back to them. With Callirhoe, Chaereas returns to Syracuse with 300 Greek troops and a contingent of Egyptians as well. The crowd who meets him wants to learn about their adventures ("Begin at the beginning, we beg you—tell us the whole story, don't leave anything out!" [8.7]), they assemble in the theater, and Chaereas provides a summary of his adventures that also functions as a summary of the novel (8.7.1–8.8.11; Hock 1988, 135).

Relevance for the NT and ECL. A collection of parallels between Chariton and the NT, collected by Van der Horst (1990), includes some interesting stylistic features. Ascough (1996) compares crowd scenes in Chariton with those in Luke-Acts, convinced that the similarities suggest that Luke was using the narrative technique of a novelist (1996, 73, 81). He compares four narrative functions of crowd scenes (1996, 72–80): (1) crowds as an audience (Chariton 3.4; 8.6; 8.7; Luke 4:42–43; 8:42, 45, 47; 9:10–17, 37–43); (2) crowds as an indication of popularity (Chariton 1.1; 2.3; 3.2; 5.3; 5.5; Luke 5:1, 15; 6:19; 8:19; Acts 14:11; Josephus, *War* 2.1); (3) crowds that prevent hostile action (Chariton 1.1; Luke 19:47–48; 20:19; 22:2; 23:48); (4) crowd involvement in disturbances (Chariton 1.5; Luke 23:18–23; Acts 17:8, 13; 21:27–30); (5) crowds as part of the narrative flow, i.e., they move the plot of the story along (Chariton 1.1; 1.3; 3.3; 3.4; Luke 19:37; 11:14, 29; 12:1, 13, 54; 13:14; 14:25 [all in the context of the travel narrative in Luke 9:51–19:27]; Josephus, *War* 2.80, 342–43, 402, 608–10). The main problem with Ascough's conclusions is that the use of "the crowd" as a character is Greco-Roman narratives is naturally not limited to Luke-Acts and the Greek novel, but also occurs in historical works. The references to Josephus included above demonstrate this. Crowds function analogously in historical as well as biographical literature (see the crowd scenes in Josephus), which suggest that "narrative technique" is not an infallible indicator of "generic designation."

*Fiction, *Novel

Ascough 1996; Goold 1995; Konstan 1998; Papanikolaou 1973; Rohde 1914; Van der Horst 1990

Chiasmus (a transliterated form of the Greek word χιασμός, which is postclassical in origin; see Lausberg 1998, §723 n. 3) is a term derived from the Greek letter χ (*chi*, which resembles the English letter "X") and refers to a form of inverted parallelism. The Greek rhetorical term ἀντιμεταβολή ("transposition"), found in Quintilian 9.3.85 and corresponding to the Latin term *commutatio* (Lausberg 1998, §800), "consists in the opposition of an idea and its converse by means of the repetition of the two word stems, with reciprocal exchange of the syntactic function of both stems in the repetition." An example of *commutatio* is found in *Rhetorica ad Herennium* 4.28.39: "You must eat to live, not live to eat" (*edere oportet ut vivas, non vivere ut edas*).

There are several forms of chiasmus. Dahood (1976) distinguished between micro-chiasmus and macro-chiasmus. Micro-chiasmus involves relatively simple chiasms of four lines, while macro-chiasmus involves larger segments of text, even entire books. In NT studies, this distinction has been picked up by Luter and Lee (1995), Thomson (1995), and Porter and Reed (1998). The term "chiastic" is rejected by P. S. Cameron (1990) in favor of "palinstrophe," a term he borrows from McEvenue (1971, 29), by which he means an arrangement of larger units that does not "frame" a unit but whose essential feature is return.

While chiasm (at least micro-chiasmus) is certainly an observable rhetorical feature of ancient texts (Stock 1984), it is a feature neither conceptualized nor discussed by rhetorical theorists (Kennedy 1984, 28–29), until the 4th cent. C.E., when it is mentioned by Ps.-Hermogenes (*De inventione* 4.3.2; see Thomson 1995, 14–15). Porter and Reed (1998, 217) thus regard "chiasmus" as a problematic etic category (my language) unknown to ancient speakers and writers:

> In other words, if chiasm is identified in ancient documents, apart possibly from instances of reverse parallelism in four-clause sentences, a modern category is being utilized, one probably unknown and unrecognized by the ancients. At most, the ancients would have had a vague idea of inverted parallelism, although certainly no clear formulation of how it was constructed and what defined its elements, and certainly not that it was a category that could be applied to entire literary works.

With some exaggeration, they label chiasm as "a modern scholarly construct" (Porter and Reed 1998, 219). Further, macro-chiastic structures, should they exist, do not constitute a "genre" (contra Porter and Reed 1998, 226), but rather a formal surface structure of texts.

One of the central assumptions of most chiastic analysis is the discovery of the focal text around which the author has arranged paired statements in concentric symmetry (Lund 1942, 7; Breck 1986; Thomson 1995, 27 [who claims that this is "often" the case]). W. Harrington, for example, argues that Mark arranged the conflict stories in Mark 2:1–3:6 and the debate over Jesus' source of power in Mark 3:20–35 according to an A B C D C' B' A' pattern. Even within Mark 2:1–3:6, the author has made use of chiasmus on a lesser level (on chiasmus in this passage, see Dewey 1973, 1980, 132–36). Mark 2:15–16 refers first to "tax collectors and sinners" and then to "sinners and tax collectors." The recognition of the presence of chiastic structures in texts enables the interpreter to appreciate comparisons and contrasts, to apprehend the emphasis of the textual unit defined by the chiasmus, to understand the point being made, and to determine the point or purpose of a composition (Man 1984).

Methodological considerations. In response to Dewey (1973), D. J. Clark (1975) attempted to extract criteria for identifying macro-chiasmus. He proposed five criteria: (1) content (though highly abstract, there should be significant similarity between units); (2) form or structure (relatively quantifiable and applies when forms in different units are regarded as similar or identical); (3) language (primarily catchwords, words with similar roots, grammatical forms); (4) setting (a focused type of content dealing with place and time, usually found at the beginning of a textual unit); (5) theology (extremely vague).

Blomberg (1989), aware of Clark (1975), has proposed nine criteria for identifying an extended chiasmus (see the critique of Blomberg in Porter and Reed 1998, 219–21): (1) There must be a problem in conventional approaches to outlining the structure of a given text. (2) There must be clear examples of parallelism between the corresponding halves of the chiasmus. (3) Verbal or grammatical as well as conceptual or structural parallelism should characterize most of the corresponding items. (4) Verbal parallelism should involve significant imagery or terminology. (5) Both verbal and conceptual parallelism should involve words and ideas not readily found elsewhere in the chiastic structure. (6) Multiple sets of correspondences between the members of the chiasmus are desirable. (7) The chiastic outline should divide the text at natural breaks in the text that are generally recognized. (8) The center of the chiasmus should be a text worthy of that position, either theologically or ethically. (9) Ruptures in the outline should be avoided if possible.

Chiasm in the Pauline letters. Lambrecht (2001, 310) proposed a macro-chiastic arrangement of 2 Cor. 10–13 with the following pattern:

A Exhortation (10:1)
  B Authority (10:2–18)
    C Denial of inferiority (11:5–12)
      D The fool's speech (11:22–12:10)
    C′ Denial of inferiority (12:11b–18)

B′ Authority (13:1–10)
A′ Exhortation (13:1)

However, Lambrecht admits that the structure of 1 Cor. 10–13 should not be exaggerated, and he does not think that the D core (the fool's speech) is surrounded by "neatly delineated" A B C and C′ B′ A′ sections, for there is no evidence that Paul intended a rigidly formal ring structure; these are three unequal rings that loosely surround the discourse, each with its own thematic emphasis (2001, 320).

In his argument that 2 Cor. 6:14–7:1 is an interpolation, Walker (2001, 202) proposed the coherence of 2 Cor. 6:11–13 and 7:2–3 based on a chiasmus:

A Assurance of affection (6:11): "Our mouth is open to you, Corinthians, our heart is wide."
B Disclaimer of responsibility for alienation (6:12): "You are not restricted by us, but you are restricted in your own affections."
C Appeal for affection (6:13): "In return—I speak as to children—widen your hearts also."
C′ Appeal for affection (7:2a): "Open your hearts to us."
B′ Disclaimer of responsibility for alientation (7:2b–3a): "We have wronged no one, we have corrupted no one, we have taken advantage of no one."
A′ Assurance of affection (7:3b): "I do not say this to condemn you, for I said before that you are in our hearts, to die together and to live together."

Several scholars, including Lund (1942, 219), Welch ([ed.] 1981, 225–26), and Heil (2001) have proposed chiastic arrangements of Philemon. Welch identifies 20 units of text chiastically arranged with J (v. 14) and J′ (v. 15) as a pair of units (which Welch calls "central comments") located at the center of this complex chiasm (or macro-chiasm). Heil proposes a macro-chiastic structure of Philemon that not only indicates a balanced formal structure but also reveals "more precisely the purpose and meaning of this shortest and subtlest of Paul's letters" (Heil 2001, 178). For Heil, chiasm is a hermeneutical key to unlock the meaning of texts that otherwise seem obscure. He argues that there are nine identifiable units in Philemon forming an A B C D E D′ C′ B′ A′ pattern: A (vv. 1–3); B (vv. 4–7); C (vv. 8–10); D (vv. 11–13); E (v. 14); D′ (vv. 15–17); C′ (vv. 18–19); B′ (vv. 20–22); A′ (vv. 23–25). Heil regards v. 14 as the "central and pivotal point" of the chiastic structure (a phrase he repeats several times; Heil 2001, 188, 198, 205): "but I preferred to do nothing without your [Philemon's] consent in order that your goodness might not be by compulsion but of your own free will." This passage, claims Heil (2001, 198) refers to all the preceding units (A through D), and also contains key parallels to other units, though some of these parallels seem trivial, e.g., ἵνα-clauses in v. 14 (E) as well as in v. 13 (D) and v. 15 (D′). It is striking that Welch (1981, 225–26) identified vv. 14–15 as the center of the chiasm in an analysis very similar to that of Heil.

Other early Christian literature. Chiasmus occurs with some frequency in the Gospels. For micro-chiasmus in the form of inverted parallelism, see Luke 6:43: "For no good tree bears bad fruit, nor again does a bad tree bear good fruit." Similarly the floating saying on reversed status found in Matt. 20:16 and Luke 13:30: "So the last will be first, and the first last," or in reverse order in Mark 10:31 and Matt. 19:30: "But many that are first will be last, and the last first." Another example of micro-chiasmus is found in John 16:28:

A I came from the Father
B and have come into the world;
B′ again, I am leaving the world
A′ and going to the Father.

One of many examples of the use of micro-chiasmus in the *Gospel of Thomas* is found in logion 112:

A Jesus said: Woe to the flesh
B which depends on the soul;
B′ Woe to the soul
A′ which depends on the flesh.

Another example is found in *Gos. Thom.* 92:

A Yet what you asked me about in former times
B and which I did not tell you then,
B′ now I do desire to tell,
A′ but you do not inquire after it.

See also *Gos. Thom.* 43b.

There are, in addition, a number of chiastic analyses of the Gospels as whole that can be briefly mentioned. Macro-chiastic analyses of Matthew, for example, have been proposed by Lohr (1961), Combrink (1982), and H. B. Green (1968).

Schüssler-Fiorenza (1977, 56–66; 1985, 175–76) proposes a sevenfold macro-chiastic structure of Revelation:

A 1:1–8
B 1:9–3:22
C 4:1–9:21; 11:15–19
D 10:1–15:4
C′ 15:1, 5–19:10
B′ 19:11–22:9
A′ 22:10–22:21

Problematic issues. There are several obvious problems with chiastic analysis. (1) When chiastic arrangements are exceedingly complex (as in the proposal of Welch 1981 and that of Heil 2001, which is only slightly less complex), it seems difficult to suppose that such intricate macro-chiastic patterns could easily be picked up by ancient readers, even though chiasm is a surface structure. For this reason Thomson (1995) is skeptical of the category, and Porter and Reed (1998) essentially reject it. (2) Advocates of chiastic analysis frequently assume or argue the hermeneutical significance of the central feature of chiasms, though in fact (if they are not an imposition on the text) they may be simply a formal design with no particular interpretive significance; some chiastic structures may have hermeneutical significance, while others are simply formal, geometric literary designs. (3) Macro-chiastic schemes should use argued criteria for defining textual units and should not use supposedly formal chiastic patterns to override the existing texture of the text. (4) The presence of *inclusio* or of ring composition should not be taken to indicate that more complex antithetical or parallel pairs of nested clauses or paragraphs exist. (5) The presence of macro-chiastic structures are sometimes enlisted to "prove" the unity of a text whose integrity has been placed in doubt by critical scholarship (e.g., Luter and Lee 1995 for *Philippians). However, the precarious nature of macro-chiastic analysis, which includes the temptation to manipulate and massage individual textual units to make them fit into a larger structural pattern, makes this enterprise suspect (see the comments of Porter and Reed 1998, 228–31).

*Antithesis, **Inclusio*, *Ring composition, *Symmetrical structure

---

R. D. Anderson 2000, 22; Blomberg 1989; Breck 1987; Brouwer 2000; Combrink 1982; Dahood 1976; Denniston 1952, 74–77; Dewey 1973, 1980; H. B. Green 1968; Harvey 1998; Heil 2001; Jeremias 1958; Lambrecht 2001; Lohr 1961; Lund 1942, 1992; Luter and Lee 1995; Man 1984; Porter and Reed 1998; Schüssler Fiorenza 1977, 1985; Stock 1984; Thomson 1995; Welch 1981a, 1981b; Welch and McKinlay 1999

Chreia (see also *Pronouncement stories) is a transliteration of the Greek word χρεία, or "anecdote" (the basic meaning of χρεία is "use, advantage," so that χρείαι are considered useful for life). χρεία is a relatively comprehensive term used by the Greeks and Romans (*chreia* is a Greek loanword in Latin) used for those types of discourse that New Testament scholars variously label aphorisms, pronouncement stories, and apophthegmata (Dibelius 1971, 149–64). Chreiai are indigenous to Hellenistic culture and are relatively rare in Near Eastern wisdom traditions (Kloppenborg 1987, 263). In most cases the chreiai found in the Synoptic Gospels reflect the way in which Jesus traditions were transformed in a Hellenistic environment, rather than the original form of the traditions themselves (Dibelius 1971, 162–63). A chreia can be defined as "a saying or action that is expressed concisely, attributed to a character, and regarded as useful for living" (Hock and O'Neill 1986, 26). The *progymnasmata often divide chreiai into three categories: (1) sayings chreiai, (2) action chreiai, and (3) mixed chreiai (Theon, *Progym.* 202.19–206.8 [Walz]; Hermogenes, *Progym.* 6.7–14 [Rabe] (Hock and O'Neill 1986, 27; Robbins 1988, 4–14). Maxims (γνῶμαι or *sententiae*) on the other hand, are always sayings, never actions. Unlike chreiai, they are never attributed to a character (Theon, *Progym.* 202.3–11; Hermogenes, *Progym.* 7.4–6). A reminiscence (ἀπομνημόνευμα), on the other hand, is an expanded chreia (Hock and O'Neill 1986, 109–10).

*Aphorism, *Biography

Hock and O'Neill 1986, 2002; Wehrli 1973

Church Order (genre), an amorphous literary form whose primary purpose is to provide doctrinal, liturgical, and ethical direction and regulation for Christian churches. The Church Order has the following characteristic features (Hills 1991, 371–72): (1) declaration of authority or credentials, emphasizing tradition; (2) affectionate address, e.g., "child," "my children"; (3) communal discipline; (4) warning against heresy and/or insistence on orthodoxy; (5) ethical exhortation in gnomic form; (6)

teaching about eschatology; (7) lists of responsibilities directed to specific groups in the community; (8) qualifications for or tests of vocation or ministry; (9) instructions concerning liturgy and sacraments; (10) other testamentary features (e.g., farewell). Representatives of this genre in early Christianity include 1 Timothy, the *Didache*, the *Apostolic Tradition*, the *Didascalia Apostolorum*, and the *Apostolic Constitutions*.

*Didache, **Didascalia Apostolorum*, **Elchasai, Book of*, *Hippolytus, *Apostolic Tradition*, *Timothy, First Letter to

———

Berger 1984, 135–41; Bradshaw 1982, 80–110; Hills 1991; Schöllgen 1996; Steimer 1992.

Cicero, Marcus Tullius (106–43 B.C.E.), was a famous Roman lawyer, orator, politician, and philosopher. He studied with the philosopher Antiochus (of the Old Academy) in Athens as well as with the Greek rhetorician Demetrius, and did a kind of oratorical internship for two years in Asia Minor under the supervision of several rhetoricians, including Menippus of Stratonicea (Cicero, *Brutus* 315–16); he was fluent in Greek as well as Latin (Cicero, *Brutus* 310). He wrote approximately 106 speeches, of which 58 survive in whole or in part, and several major works on rhetoric. He referred to five of his books that constitute a corpus of works on rhetoric comparable to the works of Aristotle and Theophrastus (*De divinatione* 2.4), i.e., *De oratore* (3 books), the *Brutus*, and the *Orator*. A corpus of some 900 literary letters, 800 by Cicero and 100 to him by others, provides incomparable insight into Roman history and culture during the mid-1st cent. B.C.E.

*Ethos, *Pathos

———

Janson 1964, 40–45; Kennedy 1972; May (ed.) 2002

Cicero, *Brutus* is a literary *dialogue in which the two interlocutors of Cicero are Atticus and Brutus. The work is preserved in a single manuscript, the Codex Laudensis, which was discovered in 1421, copied several times, and then disappeared in 1425. Codex Laudensis contained five rhetorical works, *De inventione*, *Rhetorica ad Herennium*, *De oratore*, *Brutus*, and *Orator*. *Brutus* was written during the first part of 46 B.C.E. with the purpose of defending the author's approach to oratory by reviewing the entire history of Roman oratory, based on the historical research found in the *Liber Annalis* (a chronological table of Roman history) of T. Pomponius Atticus, 109–32 B.C.E. (Cicero, *Brutus* 13–15, 19). Marcus Junius Brutus (85–42 B.C.E.) had written a letter of *consolation to Cicero following the death of his contemporary Hortentius (Quintus Hortensius Hortalus), 114–50 B.C.E., providing a formal reason for composing the work.

Contents. The work begins with a *prooemium* (1–9) referring to the death of Hortensius, Cicero's long association with him, and the contemporaneous collapse of the republic and the muffling of oratory. Then follows the setting of the dialogue and the introduction of the interlocutors, Atticus and Brutus (10–24). The main section on "the praise of eloquence" (*laudare eloquentiam*) occupies 25–330, beginning with a brief section on the origins of Greek oratory (25–52). In the long section on Roman oratory, he distinguishes between Stoic oratory and old Roman oratory (116). The work concludes with an epilogue (331–33).

Cicero, *De inventione*, the oldest prose work by Cicero, is a *rhetorical handbook compiled in the 1st cent. B.C.E., with close similarities to the only other contemporary Latin handbook, **Rhetorica ad Herennium*. Both of these works are dependent on a lost Greek rhetorical handbook. The *terminus post quem* for the work is 91 B.C.E., while the *terminus ante quem* is about 85 B.C.E., since Cicero claims that he wrote it when very young (*De oratore* 1.2.5). The preface to *De inventione* has an apologetic character, since in early 1st-cent. Rome, literary activity was thought an inappropriate occupation for a Roman aristocrat, added to the fact that the Romans had a generally negative attitude toward the Greeks. The social situation reflected in the *De inventione* is very similar to that of the *Rhetorica ad Herennium* (Janson 1964, 32–33).

Cicero divides the argument into two parts in the *De inventione*: induction and deduction. He further divides deduction into five parts: (1) *propositio* ("proposition," the major premise of a syllogism); (2) *propositionis approbatio* ("proof of proposition"); (3) *assumptio* ("assumption," i.e., the minor premise of a syllogism); (4) *assumptionis approbatio* ("proof of assumption"); (5) *complexio* ("summation," i.e., the conclusion of the syllogism). This scheme probably derives from *Hermagoras, a renowned Stoic rhetorician, who apparently was ignorant of the Aristotelian enthymeme and developed in its place the logical syllogistic form called an *epicheireme*. Stoics were primarily interested in dialectic but had little interest in plausible argumentation and so avoided the rhetorical tradition of τοπική, "topics" (Cicero, *Topics* 6).

The most important part of *De inventione* is arguably the section on the doctrine of *constitutio causae*, or "determination of the issue," which is derived, with modifications, from Hermagoras of Temnos (Hubbell 1949, xiii). Hermagoras's most influential work was on "invention" or "discovery" (εὕρεσις), which primarily included his stasis theory (Kennedy 1963, 313). Following Hermagoras, Cicero identified four issues, i.e., στάσις or *status* (Jolivet 1997, 311–12; *De inventione* 1.10–16): (1) The conjectural issue or the issue of fact (*coniectura*; στοχασμός) dealt with whether a person committed a particular act and was supported by conjectures and inferences. (2) The definitional issue (*definitiva*; ὅρος) involved the precise definition of an act—should a homicide be regarded as murder or manslaughter? (3) The qualitative issue (*generalis*; ποιότης) involved, in the case of homicide, whether there were extenuating circumstances such as self-defense or temporary insanity. (4) The translative issue (*translativa*; μετάληψις) involved procedural objections such as motions of dismissal because the wrong person was bringing the charge or the wrong penalty was sought for a particular time.

**Rhetorica ad Herennium*, *Rhetorical handbooks

Bittner 1999; Janson 1964; Loutsch 1994; May (ed.) 2002; Ruch 1958

Cicero, *De optimo genere oratorum* ("On the Best Kind of Orator") is a short rhetorical treatise written by Cicero in 46 B.C.E. for the purpose of introducing a pair of orations translated from Greek into Latin, Demosthenes, *De corona,* and Aeschines, *Against Ctesiphon*. There is no evidence, however, that these translations were ever made.

Cicero, *De oratore* This is a work written by Cicero in 55 B.C.E. in three books, each with a preface (Ruch 1958, 105–8, 185–202), dedicated to his brother Quintus. In the preface to book 1 (the most important one of the entire work), Cicero begins by commenting on which way of life should be considered particularly happy. This introduces the first main section of the preface (1.1.1–3), which deals with the situation of the author. He then relates a request from Quintus and claims that he will fulfill it (1.1.4). After mentioning eloquence as the subject on which Quintus has asked him to write (1.2.4–5), he turns to the subject of rhetoric itself (1.2.6–1.6.21). Though he confines himself to rhetoric as defined by the Greeks (1.6.22), he contrasts himself with the Greeks and their abstract theories, preferring to show how Roman practice gives substance to Greek theory (1.6.23; see Janson 1964, 37). The similarities to the preface of the **Rhetorica ad Herennium* are clear, but literary dependence is out of the question. Rather, both prefaces share a common scheme or outline (Janson 1964, 38), the dedicatee is directly addressed, and there is some discussion of the author's relationship to the dedicatee, the subject, and his predecessors.

The subtext of the *De oratore* is the rapprochement between philosophy and rhetoric, which had been seen since the time of Plato as antithetical disciplines, because philosophy sought for the truth, while rhetoric sought to persuade. In the *De oratore*, Cicero combines the roles of philosopher and rhetorician. He maintains that Demosthenes was a student of Plato and continues (*Orator* 16; LCL trans.): "Surely without philosophical training we cannot distinguish the genus and species of anything, nor define it nor divide it into subordinate parts, nor separate truth from falsehood, nor recognize 'consequents,' distinguish 'contradictories' or analyse 'ambiguities.'" Philosophy provides training in thought, while rhetoric provides training in expression (*Orator* 17).

Bittner 1999; Janson 1964; Loutsch 1994; May (ed.) 2002; Narducci 2001; Ruch 1958

Cicero, *Orator,* composed in 46 B.C.E., is the last of Cicero's five rhetorical writings, and focuses on a description of the ideal orator that is actually an apology for Cicero's own career as an orator, written in response to the criticisms of the Atticists, of which Brutus was one (see *Atticism). The treatise is written in the form of a letter to Marcus Junius Brutus, one of the interlocutors in Cicero's *Brutus*, in which Cicero responds to a request of Brutus to sketch a portrait of the perfect orator. Most of the treatise focuses on *elocutio* or style, and it contains the longest and most detailed extant treatment of *prose rhythm available in ancient literature (149–203). Under the heading of *collocatio* ("arrangement"), one of the five duties of the orator, there are three subtopics (201): *compositio* ("arrangement"), *concinnitas* ("skillful composition"), and *numerus* ("rhythm").

Cicero, *Topica*, a treatise on rhetoric composed in 44 B.C.E. while the author was traveling to Rhegium (Cicero, *Ad familiares* 7.19). The *Topica* was written at the request of a friend, C. Trebatius Testa, as an explanation of Aristotle's *Topica,* which Trebatius had found in Cicero's library in Tusculum but found difficult to understand (Cicero, *Topica* 1–3). The problem is that since the *Topica* has little in common with Aristotle's *Topica*, it seems likely that Cicero is dependent on a late Hellenistic treatise on *Topica* that he had somehow confused with the Aristotelian treatise. Speculative suggestions for the author of the treatise Cicero used include two of his Greek teachers, Antiochus of Ascalon and Diodotus.

Cicero divides the art of rhetorical discovery into two main parts, intrinsic (*intrinsecus*; Greek ἔντεχνοι) topics (arguments inherent in the nature of the subject) and extrinsic (*extrinsecus*; Greek ἄτεχνοι) topics (arguments that are separate from the subject, e.g., human evidence, such as the testimony of witnesses and the evidence of documents, and divine evidence, such as oracles). Cicero then treats intrinsic topics with a brief example of each (9–23), followed by a fuller analysis of each topic (26–71). The extrinsic topics are introduced briefly (24) and then discussed in greater detail (73–78). Elsewhere he defines *loci* as "places in which arguments are stored" (*Partitiones oratoriae* 5). A virtually identical list of topics is found in Cicero, *De oratore* 2.162–72 (see also Cicero *Partitiones oratoriae* 7).

*Cicero, *Brutus*; *Cicero, *De inventione*; *Cicero, *De optimo genere oratorum*; *Cicero, *De oratore*; *Cicero, *Orator*; *Rhetorical handbooks; *Topos

---

May (ed.) 2002

Citations (see *Quotations)

Clausula, a term used of the end of a sentence in Greek or Latin and the patterns of prose rhythm used there.

*Prose rhythm

Clement, First Letter of, is a letter sent from the church of Rome to the Christian church at Corinth, ca. 93–96 C.E. (Lindemann 1992, 12; for the uncertainties involved, see Erlemann 1998), for the purpose of recommending concord to a divided community. The language of unity and sedition found throughout *1 Clement* is based on the traditional political language of civic concord and discord in the Hellenistic world (explored in detail by Bakke 2001).

Text and translations. First Clement is preserved in two Greek MSS, *Codex Hierosolymitanus* 54 (completed on June 11, 1056), which contains the longest and most important

Cicero's Topics (Loci)

	Topic	Reference in *Topica*	Reference in *De oratore*
1.	Definition	*Topica* 9, 26–29	*De oratore* 2.164
2.	Partition	*Topica* 10, 30–34	*De oratore* 2.165
3.	Etymology	*Topica* 10, 35–37	*De oratore* 2.165
4.	Conjugates	*Topica* 11–12, 38	*De oratore* 2.167a
5.	Genus	*Topica* 13, 38–39	*De oratore* 2.167b
6.	Species	*Topica* 14, 38–40	*De oratore* 2.168a
7.	Similarity	*Topica* 15, 41–45	*De oratore* 2.168b
8.	Difference	*Topica* 16, 46	*De oratore* 2.169a
9.	Contraries	*Topica* 17, 47–49	*De oratore* 2.169b
10.	Adjuncts	*Topica* 18, 50–52	*De oratore* 2.170
11.	Consequents	*Topica* 19, 53–57	*De oratore* 2.170a
12.	Antecedents	*Topica* 20, 53–57	*De oratore* 2.171b
13.	Contradictions	*Topica* 21, 53–57	*De oratore* 2.171b
14.	Causes	*Topica* 22, 58–66	*De oratore* 2.171a
15.	Effects	*Topica* 23, 67	*De oratore* 2.171b
16.	Comparison of things greater, less, and equal	*Topica* 23, 68–71	*De oratore* 2.172

text (it also contains the *Didache*, the *Epistle of Barnabas*, *2 Clement*, and the long form of the letters of Ignatius of Antioch). The second and earliest witness is Codex Alexandrinus (5th cent. C.E.), which contains a text lacking 57:7–63:4. In addition, it is preserved in Latin, in a Coptic papyrus codex (5th cent. C.E.), and in a Syriac translation surviving in one MS dated 1169 C.E., Cambridge University, MS add. 1700 (Kennett 1899). The Greek text is available in the edition of Lindemann and Paulsen (1992), which contains the Funk-Bihlmeyer text (Bihlmeyer 1956) with a facing German translation. The Greek text with an English translation is available in Lake (1912, 1.3–121), while an English translation is available in Glimm, Marique, and Walsh (1947) and a more recent translation in Holmes (1989; 1992), a revision of Lightfoot and Harmer. Commentaries are available in Lindemann 1992; Grant and Graham 1964.

First Clement is the longest of all the early Christian letters. It begins with a Pauline epistolary prescript, consisting of a superscription, adscription, and salutation, and concludes with several epistolary closing formulas, including a concluding prayer (64), instructions for the messengers (65:1), and a *doxology (65:2). The epistolary prescript is followed by a **captatio benevolentiae* (1:2–3:1). The theme of the letter is introduced in 3:2 with the catchwords "jealousy and strife," followed by a string of examples of the perils of both (3:3–6:4). The purpose of the letter is therefore an attempt on the part of the leadership of the Roman church to establish order and peace in the Corinthian church, which has experienced internal conflict and dissension. *First Clement* 7:1–8:5 deals with the theme of repentance, while 9:1 introduces a transition to the theme of obedience, followed by biblical examples of those who obeyed God (9:2). The letter is summarized in *1 Clem* 62. It is a letter sent from one community to another, similar to the **Martyrdom of Polycarp* and *2 Maccabees.

Literary genre. *First Clement* is a deliberative speech framed as a letter, in which the author advises the divisive and discordant Corinthian congregation to attain peace and concord (van Unnik 1970; Aune 1987, 203; Bakke 2001).

The title "The Letter of the Romans to the Corinthians," found only as a subscription in the Coptic version, is probably original. The letter is introduced by an epistolary prescript that contains the typical superscription (sender), adscription (addressee), and the salutation:

Superscription:	The church of God which dwells in Rome
Adscription:	to the church of God which dwells in Corinth, to those who are called and sanctified by the will of God through our Lord Jesus Christ.
Salutation:	Grace and peace from God almighty be multiplied to you through Jesus Christ.

The letter closing (64:1–65:2) includes a doxology (64:1), a request that the Roman messengers, Claudius Ephebus, Valerius Vito, and Fortunatus, be sent back very soon (65:1), a grace benediction (65:2), and a concluding "Amen" (65:2).

The deliberative character of the body of the letter is mentioned explicitly in 58:2 (Aune 1987, 203), where the Corinthians are urged to "receive our counsel [συμβουλή]," the Greek term for deliberative or "symbouletic" rhetoric. A deliberative speech (Greek γένος συμβουλευτικόν: Latin *genus deliberativum*) is derived from political speeches delivered in a public assembly in which a speaker advises for or against a future action (Lausberg 1998, 97 [§224]). The word pair εἰρήνη ("peace") and ὁμόνοια ("concord") found in *1 Clement* was a common formula in Greek speeches and writings that were opposed to στάσις ("civic disturbance"); van Unnik 1970, 129–204; Bowe 1988, 58–73. On this basis both van Unnik and Bowe argued that *1 Clement* was a deliberative letter. Bakke (2001) has taken this much farther and examined the numerous *topoi* in *1 Clement* that deal with the political problem of factionalism. Deliberative rhetoric consists of arguments that advise an audience to pursue or avoid a particular form of action in the future (Aristotle, *Rhetorica* 1.3.4; Quintilian 3.4.7). An analogous deliberative speech urging the Nicomedians to seek concord with the Nicaeans is found in Dio Chrysostom, *Or*. 38, one of many parallels to the theme of ὁμόνοια vs. στάσις, which was a major political problem that plagued many Greek cities in the Hellenistic period.

A rhetorical analysis of *1 Clement* can be found in Bakke (2001, 205–79) presented here with some minor modifications:

Epistolary prescript (*praef.*)
I. *Exordium* (1:1–2:8)
II. *Narratio* (3:1–4)
III. *Probatio* (4:1–61:3)
  A. *Quaestio infinita* (4:1–39:9)
  B. *Quaestio finita* (40:1–61:3)
IV. *Peroratio* (62:1–64:1)
Epistolary postscript (65:1–2).

In this analysis, the *narratio* functions as a very generic statement of the facts as this quotation from *1 Clem.* 3:1–4 indicates:

> All glory and enlargement was given to you, and that which was written was fulfilled, "My Beloved ate and drank, and he was enlarged and waxed fat and kicked" [Deut. 32:5]. [2]From this arose jealousy and envy, strife and sedition, persecution and disorder, war and captivity. [3]Thus "the worthless" rose up "against those who were in honor" [Isa. 3:5], those of no reputation against the renowned, the foolish against the prudent, the "young against the elders" [Isa. 3:5]. [4]For this cause righteousness and peace are far removed, while each deserts the fear of God and the eye of faith in him has grown dim, and men walk neither in the ordinances of his commandments nor use their citizenship worthily of Christ, but each goes according to the lusts of the wicked heart, and has revived the unrighteous and impious envy, by which also "death came into the world" [Wis. 2:24].

In the first part of the probatio or argument, 4:1–39:9, the author concentrates on virtues and behavior that promote concord and vices and behaviors that provoke discord, and this section is appropriately described by Bakke (2001, 278) as "a treatise on the principles of concord for a Christian community." In the second part of the argument, 40:1–61:3, the author applies the general principles of the first part of the argument to the specific situation of the Corinthian church.

Content outline. First Clement can be outlined as follows (Jefford 1996, 114):

- I. Greeting to church at Corinth (Preface)
- II. Situation at Corinth (1:1–3:4)
  - A. Reason for writing (1:1)
  - B. Distinguished history of Corinth (1:2–2:8)
  - C. Current problems (3:1–4)
- III. Concerning the Christian life (4:1–39:9)
  - A. On jealousy (4:1–6:4)
  - B. On the need to repent (7:1–8:5)
  - C. On obedience, faith, piety (9:1–12:8)
  - D. On humility and peace (13:1–20:12)
  - E. On the virtuous life (21:1–23:5)
  - F. Promises of the future in God (24:1–28:4)
  - G. On holiness (29:1–36:1)
    - 1. Call to holiness (29:1–30:8)
    - 2. The ways of a holy life (31:1–36:6)
  - H. Summary and conclusion
- IV. Solving the Corinthian problem (40:1–61:3)
  - A. The divine origin of church order (40:1–44:6)
  - B. The contentious nature of the wicked (45:1–46:9)
  - C. Call for love in the community (47:1–50:7)
  - D. Call for repentance and obedience (51:1–58:2)
  - E. Prayer for God's help (59:1–61:3)
- V. Concluding summary and blessing (62:1–65:2)

*Apostolic Fathers, *Diatribe, *Homily, *Letters

Bakke 2000; Barnard 1967a; Bowe 1988; Erlemann 1998; Grant and Graham 1964; Hagner 1973; Jeffers 1991; Jefford 1996, 98–116; Kennett 1899; Lightfoot 1900; Lindemann 1992; Lindemann and Paulsen 1992; Norris 1976; van Unnik 1970; Wilhelm-Hooijbergh, 1975; Wong 1977

Clement, Second Letter of

Texts and Translations. There exist just three manuscripts of *2 Clement*: (1) Codex Alexandrinus (5th cent.), which contains 1:1–12:5a; (2) *Codex Hierosolymitanus* 54 (it was completed June 11, 1056 C.E. by a scribe named Leo and also contains the *Didache*, the *Epistle of Barnabas*, *1 Clement*, and the long form of the letters of Ignatius of Antioch); and (3) a Syriac translation preserved between the Catholic Letters and the Corpus Paulinum in a manuscript copied in 1070. Translations: Holmes 1989, 68–78.

Authorship and date. Harnack has argued that *2 Clement* was the lost letter from Bishop Soter of Rome (ca. 165–75 C.E.) to the Christian congregation in Corinth mentioned by Eusebius in *Hist. eccl.* 4.23.9–11 (1958, 238–50), a view accepted by Goodspeed (1950, 83). There is, however, no convincing evidence to indicate the identity of the author. While very little specific evidence within *2 Clement* suggests a date within relatively narrow boundaries, it may be as early as 98–100 C.E. (Frend 1984, 121, 146; Donfried 1974, 1–15). Donfried based his early dating on its close relationship to *1 Clement.* This early dating is supported in part by the fact that *2 Clement* is dependent on oral rather than written Gospel traditions (Donfried 1974, 56–82). Koester (1984, 2.233–36) argues that *2 Clement* is an antignostic sermon from Egypt written before the middle of the 2d cent. C.E.

Literary genre. Second Clement was first called a "letter" (ἐπιστολή) by Eusebius (*Hist. eccl.* 3.38.4), and it is given the same designation (along with *1 Clement*) in the table of contents of Codex Alexandrinus (5th cent. C.E.). However, the absence of any of the main formal epistolary features from the text of *2 Clement* argues against the letter genre. *Second Clement* is neither a letter nor a *homily in the form of a letter (Donfried 1974, 24), but simply a homily (Donfried 1974, 25–34) in the form of a hortatory address (1974, 34–48).

Structure. Donfried (1974, 42–48) argues for a threefold pattern: (1) a theological section (1:1–2:7); (2) an ethical section (3:1–14:5); and (3) an eschatological section (15:1–18:2).

*Apostolic Fathers, *Homily

Baarda 1982; Donfried 1974; Harnack 1905, 1958, 438–50; Lindemann 1992; Wengst 1984

Climax, a transliteration of the Greek term κλίμαξ, "ladder" (Latin *gradatio*), is a figure of speech formed by a rigid interlocking of words in which each phrase picks up the last word of the previous phrase and builds on it *Ad Herennium* 4.25; Quintilian 9.3.54–57). A clear instance is Demosthenes, *De corona* 179 (an example cited by Quintilian): "My speech was universally applauded, and there was no opposition. I did not speak without moving, nor move without serving as ambassador, nor serve without convincing the Thebans" (see also *Iliad* 2.101–8). An equally clear NT example is found in Rom. 8:29–30 (which combines climax with *anaphora): "For those whom he foreknew he also predestined . . . and those whom he predestined he also called; and those whom he called he also justified; and those whom he justified he also glorified." The presence of climax often goes unrecognized by commentators (e.g., Cranfield 1975–79, 1.432–33, who speaks of a "five-fold chain"; Dunn 1988, 1.482–86; Fitzmyer 1992, 524–26, who speaks of "five steps"). See also Rom. 5:3–5 (Kennedy 1984, 155; R. D. Anderson 1999, 224); 10:13–15 (Cranfield 1975–79, 1.261); 10:14–15 (a κλίμαξ constructed of four *rhetorical questions); 10:17.

*Catalogues, *Priamel, *Sorites

Lanham 1991, 36; Race 1982, 24.

Coauthors Several passages in the Pauline letters attribute authorship to other figures in addition to Paul; these include Sosthenes (1 Cor. 1:1), Timothy (2 Cor. 1:1; Phil. 1:1; Phlm. 1; cf. Col. 1:1); "all the brothers with me," Gal 1:2; Silvanus (Silas) and Timothy (1 Thess. 1:1; 2 Thess. 1:1). Further, the use of first-person plural verbs and pronouns are sometimes, but not always, indicators of joint authorship. Uses of the first-person plural which suggest coauthorship occurs infrequently (see Gal. 1:8–9; 2:4–5, 9–10; 2 Cor. *passim*). For other uses see *First-person plural. In Philippians, though Timothy is mentioned as a coauthor (1:1), the first-person-singular dominates the letter, though first-person plurals which associate Paul with the recipients also occur (3:3, 15–16, 20–21; 4:20).

*Co-senders, *First-person plural

Byrskog 1996

Codex is the Latin term for a "book" of wooden tablets, later made of papyrus or vellum, the forerunner of the modern book. A codex consisted of one or more quires, each quire being a stack of papyrus or vellum sheets folded down the middle and stitched at the seam. A sheet, when folded, had two leaves, and each leaf had two sides or pages (Robinson 1979, 13). Because codices allowed both sides of the writing material to be inscribed, they were more compact, portable, and economical than rolls (Skeat 1982). Julius Caesar may have antedated the common use of the codex by using a codex notebook for letters to the Roman senate (Suetonius 1.56.6). First appearing in the late 1st cent. C.E. (Kenyon 1951, 100), by the 4th cent. they had displaced scrolls as the preferred medium of publication (Kenyon 1951, 96–97, 111–12).

Christian use of the codex. The Christian community in particular was remarkably quick to adopt the codex form. Some have suggested that Christians invented it (Roberts 1954; Roberts and Skeat 1983; Skeat 1982; Gamble 1995, 49–66), though this seems unlikely (van Haelst 1989). Over 90 percent of recovered Christian biblical manuscripts or manuscript fragments from the first four centuries C.E. are codices. Of the few extant scrolls, most are of the Old Testament. Rare papyrus fragments in roll form include *P.Oxy.* 1075 (a text of Revelation on the back of a roll of Exodus); *P.Oxy.* 1228 (a text from John on the back of a blank roll; *P.Oxy.* 657 (a text from Hebrews on the back of a nonbiblical work (Roberts and Skeat 1987, 39). Similarly, P^{12}, P^{13}, P^{18}, and P^{22} are all *opisthographs (Epp 1995, 5). No text of any part of the NT is known to be written on the recto (front) of a scroll (Roberts and Skeat

1987, 40). Although codices were easier to consult for references and had all the advantages over scrolls mentioned above, these factors alone do not seem sufficient to explain their overwhelming popularity with Christians. Therefore, some have suggested that one or more of the Gospels (Roberts 1954, 187–90; Skeat 1969, 55–79) or the Pauline Epistles (Gamble 1995, 58–65) were first published as codices, and this form quickly acquired a sentimental, symbolic, even iconic value for the Christian community (L. Alexander 1998, 77; Roberts and Skeat 1987, 54–61). The fact that so many early Christian texts share the codex format, a similar style of script, and the use of *nomina sacra* (uniquely Christian abbreviations of divine names; see *Abbreviations) seems to indicate an impressive degree of communication, organization, and uniformity among the Christian communities throughout the Mediterranean (Roberts and Skeat 1987, 57). This has implications for the reconstruction of the social history of the early church, and for hypotheses concerning the intended readership of various NT writings, e.g., the Gospels (L. Alexander 1998, 99–105).

Codex and canonization. The widespread use of the codex may also have implications for the process of canonization. Unlike scrolls, which could contain at most one of the longer Gospels, codices could easily have contained the four canonical Gospels and Acts, or the entire Pauline corpus. Though some have argued that these two collections may already have been circulating as books by the end of the 2d cent. (Kenyon 1951, 101; Skeat 1997, 1–34), it is doubtful that any 2d-cent. codex contained more than one Gospel (D. C. Parker 1997, 19). From early in the 3d cent., ca. 200 C.E., a single papyrus book containing all four Gospels survives, in three separate fragments, P^1, P^{64}, and P^{67} (Skeat 1997). The codex made the collection of several books into one volume possible and prompted the question of which writings should be included, and in which order. However, the codex format was only one among several factors—including intra-Christian theological debate and controversies with heterodox sects—that led to the establishment of the Christian canon of Scripture (see *Canon, biblical).

*Minuscule, *Palimpsest, *Papyrus, *Uncial

L. Alexander 1998; Epp 1995; Finegan 1956; Gamble 1995; Haelst 1989; Kenyon 1951; McCown 1941; Quinn 1974; Roberts 1954, 1970, 1974; Roberts and Skeat 1983; J. M. Robinson 1979; Skeat 1969, 1982, 1997; Turner 1977, 1980

JON BERGSMA

Colon, a transliterated form of the Greek word κῶλον (the Latin equivalent is *clausula*), means a "member" or "clause" of a periodic sentence (Ps.-Demetrius, *On Style* 1). In poetic contexts, a colon is a single metrical phrase of not more than ca. 12 syllables, and consists of four to six metrical feet. For Ps.-Demetrius, the colon is the basic unit of prose style (*On Style* 16–17). The standard colon was about the length of a dactylic hexameter, generally consisting of two groups of words that created a caesura between them. According to Ps.-Demetrius (1.3), the opening sentence of the *Anabasis* of Xenophon consisted of two cola:

> Δαρείου καὶ Παρυσάτιδος γίγνονται παῖδες δύο
> Darius and Parysatis had two children,
> πρεσβύτερος μὲν Ἀρταξέρξης, νεώτερος δὲ Κῦρος.
> the elder was Artaxerxes, and the younger Cyrus.

These two colons constitute a single period, and each is the approximate length of a hexameter line. The caesura in the first colon follows the name Παρυσάτις, while the caesura in the second line follows the name Ἀρταξέρξης.

M. L. West 1982

Colophon, transliterated from the Greek word κολοφών (meaning "summit, top, finishing"), first used in the 18th cent. as a designation for information placed at the end of a manuscript, particularly including the total number of *stichoi and a personal remark by a scribe (Pfeiffer 1968, 127). Sometimes colophons contain curses (L. S. Thompson 1952; Metzger 1992, 19–21). The term "colophon" is also used less accurately for other information at the conclusion of a manuscript, including such things as the title, the name of the author, the name of the copyist, and the place and date of copying.

Gevaryahu 1975; Metzger 1968, 17–21; Thompson 1952.

Colossians, Paul's Letter to the Colossians is one of the four "prison letters" attributed to Paul (Col. 1:24; 4:3, 10, 18; see also *Philippians, *Philemon, *Ephesians), but its authenticity is disputed. The problem of dating Colossians is linked to the question of authenticity, and for that reason Best (1998, 35) dates the letter very generally from 60 to 90 C.E. The church at Colossae was not founded by Paul (like the Christian congregations in Rome), but by Epaphras (1:7–8; 4:12–13); many members of this congregation had never actually seen Paul before (2:1). Colossae itself was a small town in western Anatolia in the vicinity of Laodicea and Hierapolis, and the congregation appears to have been primarily Gentile. The town was severely damaged by an earthquake in 61 C.E., suggesting that Colossians was either written somewhat earlier than that (ca. 60 C.E.) or quite a bit later by someone other than Paul (ca. 80–90 C.E.).

Authorship and date. While Paul's name occurs three times in the letter (1:1, 23; 4:18), and all three emphasize Paul as author of the letter, Timothy is mentioned as the *co-sender (1:1), as he frequently is in other Pauline letters (2 Cor. 1:1; Phil. 1:1; 1 Thess. 1:1). There is a great debate over the issue of the authorship of Colossians. While many have supported the traditional view of Pauline authorship, others have argued that the letter was written by someone other than Paul (Bujard 1973; Gnilka 1980, 19–26; Schweizer 1982; M. Y. MacDonald 2000, 6–9), yet others are cautiously unsure (Lohse 1971, 177–83). During the latter half of the 2nd cent. C.E., the opinion was of course unanimous that Paul was the author of Colossians (Irenaeus, *Adv. haer.* 3.14.1 [citing Col. 4:14]; 5.2.2 [citing Col. 1:14]; Tertullian, *De praescr. haer.* 7; Clement of Alex, *Strom.* 1.11 [citing Col. 2:4, 6, 8]; Origen, *Contra Celsum* 5.8). Dunn (1996) has suggested that while Colossians is substantially different than the undisputed Pauline letters, it is nevertheless a type of "bridge" document between the genuine Pauline letters and the later deutero-Pauline letters. Specifically, Colossians was probably written about the same time as Philemon, but actually written by Timothy (the co-sender, according to 1:1), while Paul was in prison, and that Paul himself only added a few personal touches at the end, in 4:7–18 (Dunn 1996, 35–39, 269). Best (1998, 35) argues that Colossians was written between 60 and 90 C.E., because even though he leans toward non-Pauline authorship, he keeps the options open.

Identification of opponents. In general the opponents whom Paul is combating appear to belong to the Christian congregation at Colossae, but profiling them has proved difficult. The opponents have frequently been identified as Gnostics, though the character of Gnosticism during the mid-first century is problematic, i.e., little is really known about the movement. There is widespread agreement that the opponents worshiped angels (2:18). Here the phrase "θρησκεία τῶν ἀγγέλων," has been construed to mean either "the worship of angels" (objective genitive), or "the angelic worship [of God]" (subjective genitive). The phrase "στοιχεία τοῦ κόσμου" or "elementary spirits of the universe" is a key phrase which has been understood as referring to angels, the four primal elements, the Jewish law, or religious regulations.

Colossians and Ephesians. A close comparative reading of Colossians and Ephesians suggests that there is some kind of literary relationship between the two letters: (1) the prescript, thanksgiving, and intercessory prayer, (2) the emphasis on alienation and reconciliation, (3) the discussion of Paul's suffering as an apostle and minister of the mystery of God, (4) head and body relations, (5) contrast between the old and new man, (6) the household code, (7) the exhortation to prayer, (8) the commendation of Tychicus, (9) the benediction. With regard to vocabulary, 34 percent of the words found in Colossians are also found in Ephesians, while 26.5 percent of the words in Ephesians are found in Colossians.

While most critical scholars hold the view that Ephesians is dependent on Colossians (Mitton 1951), there are also some who argue that Colossians is dependent on Ephesians. The view that Ephesians is literarily dependent on Colossians is an argument for the authenticity of Colossians. Best (1998, 20–36) has reviewed the evidence for the various positions on the literary relationship between Colossians and Ephesians, and concluded that even though there is a relationship between the two letters, it cannot be proven that Ephesians is dependent on Colossians (Best 1998, 35). Best also considers it likely that Colossians and Ephesians were written by two different people (Best 1998, 36). For a chart on verbal similarities between Colossians and Ephesians, see *Ephesians, Paul's Letter to the. The older view of Holtzmann, that Colossians is a genuine letter of Paul which has been heavily edited by the author of Ephesians, has been represented in a more cogent form by E. P. Sanders (1966), who argues that the non-Pauline elements in Colossians, and hence the section that appears most similar to Ephesians, is located in the first two chapters.

Epistolary structure and content. Colossians is in the form of a *letter written for exhortation and encouragement (Bujard 1973, 129, 229). The letter opening consists of a prescript consisting of a superscription mentioning the senders, Paul and Timothy (1:1); an adscription mentioning the recipients, "the faithful brethren in Christ at Colossae" (1:2a); and a grace benediction (2b), followed by a thanksgiving period, a single lengthy sentence (1:3–8). The body of the letter consists of three sections: (1) affirmations of the apostolic gospel (1:9–2:7), (2) warnings about false teachers (2:8–23), and (3) exhortations to lead a Christian life (3:1–4:6), including a section of household rules (3:18–4:1). The general structure of the letter therefore conforms to the Pauline tendency to begin with a doctrinal section and conclude with a paraenetic section. The closing epistolary formulas (4:7–18) consists of a commendation of Paul's emissaries Tychicus and Onesimus (4:7–9), secondary and personal greetings (4:10–17), the autograph formula (4:18a), and the grace benediction (4:18b).

Rhetorical analysis. The rhetorical analysis of Colossians has been largely neglected (see the meager bibliography in Watson and Hauser 1994, 199). Van der Watt (1986) argued that Col. 1:3–12 is an *exordium* using the conventional prescriptions found in the *rhetorical handbooks. Wolter (1993) proposed an initial analysis of the epistolary structure of Colossians: (1) prescript (1:1–2), (2) proömium (1:3–23), (3) self-conception of the apostle (1:24–2:5), (4) body of the letter (2:6–4:6), (5) epistolary conclusion (4:7–18). Wolter then focuses on a rhetorical analysis of the body of the letter (2:6–4:6): (1) *partitio* (2:6–8); (2) *argumentatio* (2:9–23), consisting of (a) *probatio* (2:9–15), and (b) *refutatio* (2:16–23); (3) *peroratio* (3:1–4); and (4) *exhortatio* (3:5–4:6). This is a relatively artificial and arbitrary way of applying rhetorical categories to Colossians. The division between 2:8 and 2:9 is particularly problematic, for those two verses must be taken as part of a single textual unit (Hübner 1997, 22). Hübner (1997, 22–23), though receptive to the rhetorical analysis of Galatians proposed by Betz, is nevertheless skeptical of the viability of rhetorical analyses of Colossians (or Ephesians, for that matter), in part because they are deutero-Pauline compositions which are partly dependent on genuine Pauline epistolary models, but they are being written in a very different situation.

Use of preformed traditions. Colossians contains two important textual units widely thought to reflect the use of earlier, preformed traditions, the hymn in 1:15–20 and the Hausfafen in 3:18–4:1.

1. *The Colossian hymn.* Col. 1:12–20 was first identified as a preexisting hymn which Paul, or the pseudonymous author, has inserted into the letter by Norden (1956 [originally published in 1913], 250–54), who divided the whole into three strophes (vv. 12–14, 15–18a, 18b–20). Subsequently the extent of the hymn has been delimited to vv. 15–20, though structural analyses have exhibited considerable variation (for a succinct history of earlier research see Stettler 2000, 1–35). Typically, the text has been divided into two sections or strophes, one focusing on creation (vv. 15–18a), the second on redemption (vv. 18b–20). Berger regards Col. 1:15–20 as an encomium in the "er-Stil," or the third-person singular style (1984a, 345–46). Analyses of the hymn or poem in Col. 1:15–20 typically omit or bracket phrases that appear to be redactional additions by the author of Colossians (Käsemann 1964). An argument for the integrity of the received text is found in Wright 1990, who notes that if portions were added, portions could also have been omitted, making the reconstruction of the hypothetical original impossible (this is hardly a cogent argument). The use of the first-person plural in Col. 1:12–14 is switched to the third-person singular in vv. 15–20, and then in vv. 21–22, the author addresses the recipients in the second-person plural. The conclusion that this section is pre-Pauline is supported by a dozen non-Pauline expressions and several ideas that are not found elsewhere in the Pauline letters. There is also evidence, however, that the hymn has been adapted to its present context. Several ways of understanding the structure of this hymn have been proposed. Schweizer (1976, 50–74) argues that the basic structure of the hymn is revealed by the parallel phrases in vv. 15 and 18b (ὅς ἐστιν . . . πρωτότοκος, "who is . . . the firstborn"), indicating a division into two strophes (the bracketed phrases are those added by the author of Colossians):

15 He is the image of the invisible God,
the firstborn over all creation.
16 For by him all things were created:
things in heaven and on earth, visible and invisible
[whether thrones or powers or rulers or authorities];
All things were created by him and for him.
17 He is before all things, And in him all things hold together.
18 And he is the head of the body (the church);

18b he is the beginning and the firstborn from among the dead,
[so that in everything he might have the supremacy.]
19 For God was pleased to have all his fullness dwell in him,
20 and through him to reconcile to himself all things whether things on earth or things in heaven, by making peace [through his blood, shed on the cross].

There are more parallels between words and phrases than Schweizer mentions, and Wright (1990) displays them graphically:

ὅς ἐστιν (15a) . . . πρωτότοκος (15c)
Who is . . . the firstborn
ὅτι ἐν ἀυτῷ (16a)
because in him
δἰ αὐτοῦ καὶ ἐις αὐτόν (16f)
through him and for him
καί αὐτός (17a)
and he
καὶ αὐτος (18a)
and he
ὅς ἐστιν (18c) . . . πρωτότοκος (18d)
Who is . . . the firstborn
ὅτι ἐν αὐτῷ (19)
because in him
δἰ αὐτοῦ καὶ εἰς αὐτόν (16f)
through him and for him

Wright (1990, 447) analyzes the poem as a chiasmus: A (vv. 15–16), B (v. 17), B′ (v. 18ab), A′ (vv. 18c-21).

Martin (1989, 113–24; 1991, 105–7) proposes a three-strophe structure, indicating Pauline modifications in brackets:

Strophe I
v. 15 (He) is the image of the invisible God,
The firstborn over all creation;
v. 16 For in him all things were created, both in heaven
and on earth
[Visible and invisible,
Whether thrones or dominions,
Or principalities or authorities]
All things were created through him and for him.

Strophe II
v. 17 He is before all things,
And in him all things cohere;
v. 18a And he is the head of the body [the church];

Strophe III
v. 18b (He) is the beginning,
The firstborn from the dead
[In order that he might be preeminent in all things]
v. 19 For in him all the fullness was pleased to reside,
v. 20 And through him, to reconcile all things to himself,
Whether things on earth or in heaven
[So effecting peace by the blood of his cross].

One of the more recent and detailed hymnic analyses of Col. 1:15–20 is Stettler (2000, 92), who returns to a two-strophic structure, though he places the division between v. 17 and v. 18, rather than between v. 18a and v. 18b:

I. [Blessed is Jesus Christ]
15a He is the image of the invisible God,
b The firstborn over all creation.
16a For by him all things were created
b things in heaven and on earth
c visible and invisible,
d whether thrones or powers or rulers or authorities;
f all things were created by him and for him.
17a He is before all things
b and in him all things hold together.
II. 18a And he is the head of the body, the church;
b He is the beginning and the firstborn from among the dead
c So that in everything he might have the supremacy.
19 For God was pleased to have all his fullness dwell in him.
20a And through him to reconcile to himself all things
b by making peace through his blood, shed on the cross,
c to himself, whether things on earth
d or things in heaven

2. *The household code.* The household code in 3:18–4:1 appears to be a self-contained textual unit which consists of a section of paraenesis or moral exhortation in which the type of behavior and reciprocal responsibilities appropriate for three paired roles, one dominant and the other submissive, in the ancient household (really an extended family including slaves),

such as wives and husbands, children and parents, slaves and masters. The fact that such household codes are found elsewhere in early Christian literature (Eph. 5:22–6:9; 1 Pet. 2:18–3:7; 1 Tim. 2:8–15; 3:4; 6:1–2; Titus 2:1–10; Ignatius, *Polyc.* 4:15:1; Polycarp, *Phil.* 4:2–6:1), has indicated that such codes are traditional material. If household codes are traditional formulations of conventional social ethics, one major issue is the extent to which they are formulated to fit the situations to which the letter into which they are inserted is addressed. In a study specifically focused on the household code of Colossians, Crouch (1972), arguing against the view that the household codes in early Christian literature were basically Stoic with a Christian veneer, maintained that they reflect Hellenistic Jewish moral codes (Philo, *Apol. Jud.* 7.14; Josephus, *Contra Apionem* 2.190–219). Since the hierarchical structure of the family is emphasized (within the hierarchical structure of the city and the empire), it now seems probably that household codes are an instance of the topos "concerning household management" (see Aristotle, *Politics* 1.1253bb 1–14; *Nichomachean Ethics* 8.1160a-1161a; Ps.-Aristotle *Magne moralia* 1.1194b; see Balch 1988 for a history research on Haustafeln, a translation of *Concerning Household Management and Politics*, by Arius Didymus, and an annotated bibliography). Balch (1981), who presents impressive evidence for regarding the Christian household codes as based on the Hellenistic household management topos, also argues that NT household codes have an apologetic function as a response to the criticisms of outsiders.

*Letters, Pauline, *Pseudepigrapha, NT

Balch 1981, 1988; Best 1998; Bujard 1973; Crouch 1973; DeMaris 1994; Dunn 1996; Hay 2000; Hübner 1997; Kiley 1986; Lincoln 2000; Lohse 1971; Martin 1989, 1991; Mitton 1951; Norden 1956; Porter and Clarke 1997; Sanders 1966; Schweizer 1982; Stettler 2000; Wolter 1993; Wright 1990

Comma, a Latin word literally meaning "a chip," is defined by Ps.-Demetrius, *On Style* 1.9 as a portion of a period less than a *colon, while according to Quintilian (9.4.22), "most writers regard it merely as a portion of a colon."

Commentary, a systematic series of explanations and interpretations of a written text. The term "commentary" is derived from the Latin word *commentarius*, which could refer to various types of written records used to assist the memory, including accounts, notes for speeches, legal notes, private notes, unpolished histories (e.g., Caesar, *Commentarii*; see *Autobiography), and commentaries on earlier works (e.g., Julius Hyginus, *Commentarii* on Vergil, late 1st-cent. B.C.E.). The very fact that commentaries are written to explain an earlier text indicates both that the earlier text is regarded as having some type of special status and that it is no longer clearly understood. There are two main types of commentaries, those in which the interpretation is somehow incorporated or merged into the text being interpreted (translations, *rewritten Bible), and those in which the text and the explanation are kept separate.

Greek and Latin commentaries. The plural form *commentarii* was a translation of the Greek plural form ὑπομνήματα, which was also used for the Homeric commentaries of Aristarchus (Scholion on *Iliad* 2.420). The earliest commentaries in the Mediterranean world are Greek commentaries on Homer. Pfeiffer (1968, 212–21) proposed that Aristarchus wrote *hypomnemata* based on Aristophanes' edition of Homer, and later produced his own διόρθωσις ("correction"), providing the basis for a new edition edited by his students (e.g., Ammonius). The term *"scholion," a transliteration of the Greek word σχόλιον, refers to annotations written in the margins or between the lines of a text, primarily of an exegetical or critical nature. Scholia can be random notes, or they can constitute a continuous commentary. One of the more common type of commentaries is the "lemmatic" type, in which a section of the original text is quoted followed by a transitional formula of some kind, which in turn is followed by the interpretation (e.g., *midrash, *pesharim). A second type of commentary deals with problems in a text (ἀπορίαι; see *Aporia), for the purpose of offering solutions (λύσεις).

Early Jewish commentaries. Among the earliest surviving Jewish commentaries on Scripture are those of *Philo of Alexandria. Philo's exegetical writings, or commentaries, are of three types: (1) the *Quaestiones in Genesim* and the *Quaestiones in Exodum* (6 treatises); (2) the Allegorial Commentary, based upon Gen. 2:1–41:24 (21 treatises); and (3) the Exposition of the Law (12 treatises). Philo's Allegorical Commentary and his Exposition of the Law exhibit the following form (Dillon 1983, 77–87): (1) The text is divided into short passages or *lemmata.* (2)

Each *lemma* is interpreted word by word or phrase by phrase, sometimes beginning with an overview of the meaning of the entire passage. (3) In individual sections of the commentary (κεφάλαιον), first literal, then ethical, then allegorical interpretations are given. (4) Toward the beginning of individual commentary sections, previous interpreters are mentioned and criticized and difficulties (ἀπορίαι) found in the text are solved. The six books that compose the *Quaestiones in Genesim* and the *Quaestiones in Exodum* have the form of questions and answers (ζητήματα καὶ λύσεις or *quaestiones et responsiones*), a form that goes back at least to Aristotle, in which the focus is on framing specific problems found in the text and then solving them.

The Qumran pesharim. The term "pesharim" is a designation for a type of biblical commentary found among the Dead Sea Scrolls. The term "pesher" (from the Hebrew term פשר), means "commentary, interpretation" (the plural form is "pesharim" (פשרים). Fragments of 18 pesharim have been found among the Dead Sea Scrolls, all in single copies. Continuous pesharim, like 1QpHab, exhibit a fixed literary structure quite different from the midrashim, consisting of a quotation of the biblical text to be interpreted, followed by the commentary, typically bridged by a "spacer" (the term of P. Alexander 1984a, 16 n. 4), introduced by various formulaic phrases such as: כשרו ("its interpretation [is]"), or אשר פשרו ("its interpretation [is] that"), or פשרו על ("its interpretation concerns"), פשר הדבר ("the phrase means"). The older pesharim (e.g., 4QpIsa^{c} and 4QpPs^{a}) are less rigid in their form, i.e., quotations from other books are used and parts of the focal book are neglected, phenomena that do not occur in late pesharim such as 4QpNah (Steudel 1992, 538).

Rabbinic midrashic commentaries. The basic form of rabbinic midrashic commentary is lemma (a brief quotation of a biblical text) plus commentary; the lemma can be drawn from a continuous text or a collection of biblical texts, and exhibits several formal features that distinguish it from *Mishnah and *Targum (P. Alexander 1984, 3–4; 1990, 104): (1) Verses of Scripture are quoted as proof texts, introduced by standard citation formulae. (2) The interpreter often strings scriptural verses together. (3) The interpreter quotes authorities by name (e.g., Rabbi Ishmael, Rabbi Akiva). (4) The *darshan* sometimes cites contrary interpretations typically introduced by the formula *davar aher* ("another interpretation"). (5) The interpreter commonly employs parables (*meshalim*) to solve interpretive issues.

Early Christian commentaries. Christian biblical interpretation has its beginnings in the very early post-Easter period, when the early followers of Jesus used their knowledge of the OT to interpret the meaning of Jesus. Since early Christians were initially all Jews, they were heirs of Jewish messianic exegetical traditions, which they applied to Jesus. The earliest extant Christian biblical interpreter is Paul, whose interpretive technique has similarities to midrash pesher, a form of Qumran biblical interpretation, found in concentrated form in Rom. 9–11 (Ellis 1957, 139–47), though this is disputed, for reasons that are not persuasive (Lim 1997). Among the Gospels, Matthew has the most complex and sophisticated messianic interpretation of the OT, which has also been compared favorably to midrash pesher (Stendahl 1967, 35, 183–202; Hay in *IDBSup* 443–44). A complex form of typological interpretation of the OT is found in Hebrews (Synge 1959; Kistemacher 1961; Sowers 1965; Schröger 1968) and the *Letter of Barnabas.*

The sayings of Jesus soon became texts for interpretation alongside those of the OT. Papias reportedly wrote a book on "Exegesis of the Oracles of the Lord" (Eusebius, *Hist. eccl.* 3.39.1; cf. Irenaeus, *Adv. haer.* 5.33.3), and the 114 sayings of Jesus preserved in the *Gospel of Thomas* (see **Thomas, Gospel of*) reflect a complex exegetical tradition in which the interpretation becomes part of the source through revision, addition, and deletion. While these represent interpretive strategies, they are not commentaries in the formal sense of the term.

No commentaries on Scripture are extant among early Christian literature of the 2d cent. C.E. (F. Young 1997, 82). Pantaenus, the teacher of Clement of Alexandria, is said to have written many commentaries on Scripture (Jerome, *De vir. inlustr.* 39); none have survived, though Bousset (1915, 162, 192) has proposed that fragments of his commentary on the Psalms survive in Clement Alex., *Eclog. proph.* 43–64 and *Strom.* 2.67–68). It is possible that the earliest Christian commentary was the *Antitheses* of Marcion, which was an interpretation of the Gospel of Luke and the Pauline letters (Tertullian, *Adv. Marc.* 4.1; von Harnack 1960, 256–313; Bardy 1934, 76–77). The first commentary or ὑπομνήματα on the Gospel of John was written by Heracleon (fl. 145–80 C.E.), a disciple of Valentinus (Clement Alex., *Eclog. proph.* 25; *Strom.* 4.9.71). The fragments of this work (which strangely includes commentary only on John 1–8) have been preserved only in the form of quotations in Origen's commentary on the Gospel of John (the fragments have been edited by Brooke 1967; see also de Faye 1925, 76–102; Pagels 1973; Wucherpfenning 2002). Heracleon is sometimes credited with the authorship of the *Nag Hammadi *Tripartite Tractate* (NHC I,2). Two of the most important early writers of biblical commentaries are Hippolytus of Rome in the West (works listed in Bardy 1934, 81–85) and Origen of Alexandria in the East (works listed in Bardy 1934, 85–94).

In early Christianity, commentaries on Scripture took one of four forms (Bardy 1932): (1) scholia (short notes on particular passages); (2) homilies (addresses to the faithful in which the interpretation of Scripture played a major role) (see Mitchell 2002); (3) commentaries; and (4) questions and answers (ζητήματα καί λύσεις or *quaestiones et responsiones*), a form that goes back at least to Aristotle and was used in Homeric commentaries, in Philo's *Questions and Answers in Genesis* and *Questions and Answers in Exodus*, and in Plutarch's *Platonic Questions*.

Modern Bible commentaries. What is a modern biblical commentary and what is its purpose? According to Krentz (1982, 373):

> Simply stated, the commentary clarifies for a reader a text that is unclear, incomprehensible, or even (given a change in culture, language, or politics) embarrassing or ambiguous.

During the 19th and 20th cents., there were two main generic forms of biblical commentary, both influenced by the historical-critical method. One type was intended for academics, and focused on a minute critical examination of the biblical text in its original language, word-by-word and phrase-by-phrase, with the focus on the historical and theological meaning of the text. The second type was developed for more popular consumption (for educated laity and pastors) and avoided biblical languages and detailed historical critical concerns and focused rather on the theological meaning of the text and its relevance for contemporary living. Both types share a common approach, however, which is the sequential exposition of all pericopae or sense units in the text.

During the last third of the 20th cent., biblical studies underwent a transformation when the historical-critical method was supplemented by the utilization of literary, rhetorical, and sociological approaches to the text. Reflected particularly on the impact of literary criticism on the conception of the commentary, Moore (1987, 29) observes:

> The genre of the biblical commentary is in the process of being creatively extended. It is being remodeled to accommodate new questions, methods, and emphases—so much so as to force us to ask what the minimal defining characteristics of a commentary are. The transformation is still an incipient one—a series of independent experiments in biblical commentary, inspired by nonbiblical literary criticism.

These methodologies have produced two specialized forms of commentary, the *narrative commentary (Moore 1987), the social-science commentary (Malina and Rohrbaugh 1992; Malina and Pilch 2000), and the socio-rhetorical commentary (Robbins 1998; Watson 2002; cf. Witherington 2001).

The social-science commentary is based on a particular form of historical criticism that recognizes the gap which exists between the agrarian, preindustrial world in which the New Testament was written and the modern world in which New Testament readers live. Though the distance between the world of the first cent. C.E. and our world is typically measured historically, it must also be measured socially. According to Malina and Rohrbaugh (1992, 2): "Such social distance includes radical differences in social structures, social roles, values, and general cultural features." The social-science commentary, then, focuses on reconstructing and using the social system assumed by the first cent. C.E. NT authors and their audiences. Typically, social-science commentaries are intended to supplement, not replace, the historical concerns typical of other biblical commentaries. The focus of social-scientific criticism is described by MacDonald (2000, 1):

> Social-scientific criticism of the NT is also very much concerned with context [like historical criticism], but context is generally understood much more broadly. Rather than concentrating on the unique circumstances underlying a particular document, social-scientific interpreters seek to understand the place of the document within the broader society and thus pay attention to the social mechanisms at work both within the particular group where the document was produced and in the interplay between the group and the wider social order.

In the commentaries by Malina and Rohrbaugh (1992), Malina (1998), and Malina and Pilch

(2000), there is an emphasis on "Reading Scenarios" in which social-science perspectives are brought to bear on a particular pericope, explicating aspects of the social science system encoded in the text.

The socio-rhetorical commentary is based on an interdisciplinary conception of biblical interpretation developed by Robbins (1996a, 1996b). Socio-rhetorical criticism interprets a text in terms of five "textures": inner texture (the relationship of linguistic and narrative patterns that produce argumentative and aesthetic patterns in texts), intertexture (the representation in the text of phenomena in the "outside" world, e.g., physical objects, historical events, customs, values, institutions, etc.), social and culture texture (the social and cultural language, voices, and location of texts), ideological texture (the system of beliefs and values reflecting the needs and interests of those producing the text), and sacred texture (the way the text speaks of the supernatural world and the relationship of people to that world); see Watson 2002, 129–30. The present form of biblical commentary cannot easily accommodate the program of socio-rhetorical criticism, necessitating a new of commentary format. A proposal for what shape such a commentary might take is proposed by Watson (2002) in a programmatic article.

*Edition *Midrashim, *Narrative commentary, *Pesharim, *Rewritten Bible, *Scholion

---

B. Anderson 1982; Bardy 1931, 1932, 1934; Bousset 1915; Brooke 1967; Ellis 1957; Hobbs 1978; Krentz 1982; Lohfink 1974; Malina 1998; Malina and Pilch 1992; Malina and Rohrbaugh 1992; Moore 1987; Pagels 1973; Pfeiffer 1968; Robbins 1996a, 1996b, 1998; Watson 2002; Witherington 1995, 1998, 2001; Wucherpfennig 2002.

Comparison (Greek: σύγρισις or παραβολή; Latin: *comparatio*) is used in rhetoric in two ways: (1) in the comparison of cases in the *peroratio* of a juridical speech, and (2) as a means of amplification (αὔησις) in an encomium in *epideictic rhetoric (Aristotle, *Rhetorica* 1368a). Zuntz (1953, 286) defines the latter use of σύγρισις as "a traditional device of encomiastic Greek and Latin rhetoric: the person, or object to be praised is placed beside outstanding specimens of a comparable kind and his, or its, superiority (ὑπεροχή) urged (type: 'Hercules overcame the lion, but you . . . .'" σύγρισις is discussed in several *rhetorical handbooks. Plutarch's *Parallel Lives,* in which prominent Greeks and Romans are compared, is an elaborate exercise in σύγρισις.

Paul uses comparison in 2 Cor. 10–13, especially in 11:21b–29 (Forbes 1986). A number of scholars have recognized the presence of σύγρισις in Hebrews (Zuntz 1953, 286; Attridge 1989, 104; Aune 1987, 213). Seid (1999) has recognized the frequency with which σύγρισις occurs in Hebrews and has proposed an outline which juxtaposes sections of σύγρισις with sections of paraenesis (1999, 326): (1) Heb. 1:1–2:18: Synkrisis of Son and Angels (1:1–14); Paraenesis (2:1–18). (2) Heb. 3:1–4:16: Synkrisis of Moses and Christ (3:1–6); Paraenesis (3:7–4:16). (3) Heb. 5:1–6:20: Synkrisis of Aaron and Christ (5:1–10); Paraenesis (5:11–6:20). (4) Heb. 7:1–8:3: Synkrisis of Melchizedek/Christ and Levitical Priesthood (7:1–25); Paraenesis (7:26–8:3). (5) Heb. 8:4–10:18: Synkrisis of First Covenant and New Covenant (8:4–10:18); Paraenesis (10:19–12:29). (6) Heb. 13:1–25: Epistolary Appendix. Seid (1999) discusses the σύγρισις in Heb. 7 in detail. There is an elaborate σύγρισις in *Diogn.* 6:1–10, in which the basic thesis, "What the soul is to the body, Christians are to the world" (6:1), is amplified in a series of comparative statements, though no use is made of the common comparative particle ὥ.

*Progymnasmata

Forbes 1986; Lausberg 1998, §1130; Seid 1999; Zuntz 1953

Composition criticism, an extension of *redaction criticism, focuses on the whole literary work, usually with an emphasis on the thought or theology of the work rather than an analysis of the narrative.

*Literary criticism, *Narrative criticism

Talbert 1982

Concordance, an alphabetical list of all the words in a book, listed with references to the passages where each word is found. There are concordances to the Greek text of the NT available, as well as concordances prepared for specific translations of the Bible in modern languages.

Contraction, an ancient form of *abbreviation in which the first and last letters of a word are retained as an abbreviation of the entire word. The divine name Alpha and Omega may be a contraction for the seven Greek vowels αεηιουω, widely thought in antiquity to refer to the name of God (Ps.-Demetrius, *On Style* 2.71; *PGM* III.661; XIII.39; XXI.11–12). For Eusebius (*Preparation for the Gospel* 519d), the seven vowels represented the Tetragrammaton or *yhwh,* the four-letter name of God: "[The Hebrews] say also that the combination of the seven vowels contains the enunciation of one forbidden name, which the Hebrews indicate by four letters and apply to the supreme power of God, having received the tradition from father to son that this is something unutterable and forbidden to the multitude."

*Abbreviation

Aune 2002a

Controversy stories (Streitgespräche), or "conflict stories" (Hultgren 1979, 52–58), frequently consist of a set scenario: an act of Jesus and/or his disciples leads to a question or challenge posed by various opponents. This challenge is met with a riposte from Jesus, who frequently does not argue with the challenge and its theological implications but simply overwhelms the opponents with a forceful declaration of authority, sometimes backed up by a display of miraculous power (Mark 2:9–10; 3:4–5). The story usually concludes without a response from the opponents.

Occurrences. Hultgren (1979, 26–27) has identified 18 controversy stories in the Synoptic Gospels:

1. Eleven in Mark, with parallels in Matthew and Luke:
   (a) Mark 2:1–12, the healing of the paralytic (Matt. 9:1–8 // Luke 5:17–26)
   (b) Mark 2:15–17, eating with tax collectors and sinners (Matt. 9:10–13 // Luke 5:29b–32)
   (c) Mark 2:18–22, the question about fasting (Matt. 9:14–15 // Luke 5:33–35)
   (d) Mark 2:23–28, plucking grain on the Sabbath (Matt. 12:1–8 // Luke 6:1–5)
   (e) Mark 3:1–5, healing on the Sabbath (Matt. 12:9–13 // Luke 6:6–10)
   (f) Mark 3:22–30, the Beelzebul controversy (Matt. 12:22–32 // Luke 11:14–23)
   (g) Mark 7:1–8, the Tradition of the Elders (Matt. 15:1–9)
   (h) Mark 10:2–9, on divorce (Matt. 19:3–9)
   (i) Mark 11:27–33, the question about authority (Matt. 21:23–27 // Luke 20:1–8)
   (j) Mark 12:13–17, paying taxes to Caesar (Matt. 22:15–22 // Luke 20:20–26)
   (k) Mark 12:18–27, on the resurrection (Matt. 22:23–33 // Luke 20:27–40)
2. One conflict story in Q (Luke 11:14–23 // Matt. 12:22–32).
3. Two conflict stories in special Lukan material.
   (a) Luke 13:10–17, healing the crippled woman on the Sabbath
   (b) Luke 14:1–6, healing the man with dropsy on the Sabbath
4. Three conflict stories in Matthew, based in part on Mark and Q.
   (a) Matt. 12:38–42, the refusal of a sign (partially based on Mark 8:11–12 and Q, Luke 11:29–32)
   (b) Matt. 22:34–40, the double commandment of love (partly from Mark 12:38–42 and Q, Luke 10:25–28)
   (c) Matt. 22:41–46, the question about David's son, partly from Mark 12:35–37)
5. One conflict story in Luke, partly based on Mark: Luke 7:36–50, the sinful woman at Simon's house (partly based on Mark 14:3–9)

There is a group of six controversy stories in Mark 2:1–3:6 on such issues as the forgiveness of sin (2:1–12), table fellowship (2:15–17), voluntary fasting (2:18–22), and the Sabbath (2:23–28 and 3:1–6). These stories reflect a pre-Markan collection that the author has incorporated into his work (H.-W. Kuhn 1971, 53–95). A second group of six controversy stories is found in Mark 11:27–12:37.

*Pronouncement stories, *Stories about Jesus

Albertz 1921; Bultmann 1963, 1967, 1971; Dewey 1980; Dibelius 1934, 37–69; Hultgren 1979; Kee 1977, 38–41; H.-W. Kuhn 1971; V. Taylor 1935, 63–87

Conversion stories are stereotypical descriptions of conversion to Christianity from Judaism or paganism. The basic motif in conversion stories is language that contrasts the former state with the latter state, typically using the metaphor of darkness vs. light, error vs. truth, worshiping idols vs. worshiping the living God.

Early Christian conversion stories. The most famous "conversion" story in the NT is that of Saul of Tarsus (Acts 9, 22, 26), though some have argued that these narratives are not "conversion stories" in the proper sense, but rather "[prophetic] commission stories." The issue, however, is not what the historical Paul experienced on the road to Damascus (alluded to several times in his letters, see Gal. 1:11–17; 1 Cor. 9:1; 15:8) but the literary dramatization of that experience presented by the author of Luke–Acts, which is almost certain presented in conversion language.

Another famous conversion story in early Christian literature is that of Justin Martyr. In the prologue to the *Dialogue* (the whole of which is a literary fiction; see van Winder 1971, 118), Justin recounts his journey to Christianity, the true philosophy (the conversion story is essentially literary convention; Droge 1989, 50–51). The issue is whether Justin's conversion happened in the manner he relates at all, or whether what happened has been overlayed by "literary devices and following the conventions of conversion stories" (Osborn 1973, 67).

The darkness and light contrast. Dualistic language is frequently used in retrospect to describe the experience of conversion, in both early Christian and early Jewish texts, language that explicitly or implicitly alludes to the cosmological language of Gen. 1:2–5. In Christian contexts the motif is used in baptismal homilies. One example is Acts 26:18, where the heavenly Jesus commissions Saul to go to the Gentiles, "to open their eyes, that they may turn from darkness to light and from the power of Satan to God, that they may receive forgiveness of sins and a place among those who are sanctified by faith in me." Here "from darkness to light" is parallel to "from the power of Satan to God." Since the last phrase reflects the basic form of moderate cosmic dualism frequently occurring in early Christian literature, the first phrase represents the impact this cosmic dualism has at the level of the salvation of the individual, who participates in the cosmic struggle between God and Satan when he or she is converted. Very similar conversion language occurs in Col. 1:12–13, where the cosmic force of evil is conquered by believers who are transferred to the sphere of light:

> . . . giving thanks to the Father, who has qualified us to share in the inheritance of the saints *in light*. He has delivered us from *the dominion of darkness* and transferred us to the kingdom of his beloved Son, in whom we have redemption, the forgiveness of sins.

The allusion to Gen. 1:2–5 is explicit in 2 Cor. 4:6:

> For it is the God who said, "Let light shine out of darkness," who has shone in our hearts to give the light of the knowledge of the glory of God in the face of Jesus Christ.

First Clement 59:2 speaks of God's beloved child Jesus Christ, "through whom he called us from darkness to light, from ignorance to the full knowledge of the glory of his name." Here "darkness to light" again symbolizes the move from "ignorance to full knowledge." According to Eph. 5:8, "[F]or once you were darkness, but now you are light in the Lord; walk as children of light," and again in 1 Pet. 2:9, the Christians addressed in this letter are God's own people who are encouraged to "declare the wonderful deeds of him who called you out of darkness into his marvelous light." An early Jewish text that uses the same conversion metaphor is *Joseph and Aseneth* 8:9, the opening lines of the prayer said on the occasion of Aseneth's conversion to Judaism: "Lord God of my father Israel, the Most High, the Powerful One of Jacob, who gave life to all (things) and called them from the darkness to the light, and from error to truth, and from death to life; you, Lord, bless this virgin." In *T. Gad* 5:7 (trans. Hollander and de Jonge), we find the darkness=ignorance and the light=knowledge equations: "For godly and true repentance destroys ignorance and drives away darkness, and it enlightens the eyes and gives knowledge to the soul, and it leads the disposition to salvation." See also *Joseph and Aseneth* 15.12; Philo, *De Abr.* 70.

Other types of dualistic conversion language. Another type of conversion language uses an expression such as turning to the true God from idols, sometimes correlated with the light-darkness, truth-lie language (1 Thess. 1:9; Col. 1:13–14, 21–23; 2:13; 3:7–8; Eph. 2:1–10; *Barn.* 16.8; Justin, *1 Apol* 14; 16.4; 25; 39; 49.1; *2 Apol.* 2.1–2). An example of conversion language from Justin, *1 Apol.* 14:

> We who once reveled in impurities,
> now cling to purity;
> We who devoted ourselves to the arts of magic,
> now consecrate ourselves to the good and unbegotten God.
> We who loved above all else the ways of acquiring riches and possessions,
> now hand over to a community fund what we possess, and share it with every needy person.
> We who hated and killed one another and would not share our hearth with those of another tribe because of their customs,

now, after the coming of Christ, live together with them, and pray for our enemies.

On the other hand, Justin describes his own conversion elsewhere as a move from false philosophy to true philosophy (*Dial.* 2–8).

*Call narratives, *Justin Martyr, *Protreptic literature

Bardy 1947; Guerra 1992; Nock 1933; Segal 1990; Skarsaune 1976

Corinthians, First Letter to the, one of two canonical letters written by Paul and addressed to the Christian house churches in Corinth (see also *Corinthians, Second Letter to the). The authenticity of 1 Corinthians is not disputed. The Christian congregation in Corinth was founded by Paul ca. 50 C.E. (1 Cor. 3:5–11; Acts 18:1–17), and 1 Corinthians was probably written in 56 or 57 C.E. from Ephesus (1 Cor. 16:8).

Unity. First Corinthians 5:9 refers to a "previous letter" that is either lost or, in the view of some, preserved in 2 Cor. 6:14–7:1. While most scholars regard 1 Corinthians as a compositional unity (for a carefully crafted essay on the unity of 1 Corinthians, see Hurd 1994), a number have argued for a partition theory, based on unevenness in the composition (Jewett 1978; Schenk 1969; Merklein 1984). Some have proposed that the letter is a complex combination of two letters (Schmithals 1971, 90–96, based on Weiss 1910, xl–xliii, followed by Jewett 1971, 23–25), or even three letters (Sellin 1991). Some propose a middle position, arguing that 1 Corinthians was written in response to *two* events, the arrival of "Chloe's people" from Corinth (1:11), with the news of factionalism that gave rise to 1 Cor. 1–4, and the arrival of a delegation of three Corinthian men, Stephanas, Fortunatus, and Achaicus (16:17), who probably delivered a letter from the Corinthian church (7:1) along with an oral message (11:18; 15:12), both of which gave rise to 1 Cor. 5–16 (de Boer 1994). The fact that several formal features of epistolary closing formulas are found in 1 Cor. 4:14–21 (Sellin 1991, 554; de Boer 1994, 234–40) supports this hypothesis.

Epistolary analysis. First Corinthians is an extremely long letter, framed by typical Pauline epistolary formulas. The epistolary prescript, 1 Cor. 1:1–3, consists of a superscription in v. 1 naming Paul and Sosthenes as cosenders of the letter and qualifying the mention of Paul's name with "called by the will of God to be an apostle of Christ Jesus." The prescript is followed by a thanksgiving period (1:4–9) which is generally understood to function as an *exordium* as well (Kremer 1997, 17). The letter ends with an epistolary closing (16:1–24).

An important formal marker for structuring 1 Corinthians is the recurring introductory phrase περὶ δέ ("now concerning"). There are six instances of this formula in 1 Cor. (7:1, 25; 8:1; 12:1; 16:1, 12). It has widely been assumed that each occurrence of the περὶ δέ formula introduces Paul's response to questions put to him in a letter or oral report from Corinth, for in 1 Cor. 7:1 he writes: "Now concerning [περὶ δέ] the matters about which you wrote." Two different Corinthian delegations either wrote or visited Paul (1 Cor. 1:11; 16:17). This communication is also made explicit by Paul's statement in 1 Cor. 5:1: "It is actually reported that there is immorality among you." This formula, which occurs widely in a variety of ancient genres, functions to introduce topics for discussion that are readily known to writer and reader (Mitchell 1989). It is also possible that

Synopsis of Rhetorical Analyses of 1 Corinthians

***Dispositio* (Divisions of a Speech)**	**Mitchell (1991); Betz & Mitchell (1992)**	**Witherington (1995)**	**R. F. Collins (1999)**
Epistolary prescript	1:1–3	1:1–3	1:1–3
Epistolary thanksgiving *Exordium*	1:4–9	1:4–9	1:4–9
Propositio or *prothesis*		1:10	1:10
Narratio	1:10–17	1:11–17	none
Probatio	1:18–15:57	1:18–16:12	1:10–15:58
Peroratio	15:58	16:13–18	15:57–58
Epistolary closing	16:1–24	16:19–24	16:1–24

the περὶ δέ formula was used in schools in disputations between students and teachers (Baasland 1988), for the formula introduces eschatological teaching (1 Thess. 4:1) as well as problems of living within the Christian community (1 Cor. 7:1, 25; 8:1; 12:1; 16:1, 12).

Rhetorical analysis. A number of attempts have been made to analyze the rhetorical structure of 1 Corinthians. In the view of many, 1 Corinthians is a deliberative letter (Kennedy 1984, 87; Schüssler Fiorenza 1987; Mitchell 1991, 20–64; Schrage 1991–2001, 1.80; R. F. Collins 1999, 19). Others suggest, less persuasively, that it is epideictic (Wuellner 1979; 1987, 460). Mitchell's compositional analysis of the letter is arranged as follows: (1) epistolary prescript (1:1–3); (2) epistolary thanksgiving functioning also as the rhetorical **exordium* or **prooimion* (1:4–9) (in this case the *prooimion* contains key terms that will be incorporated into the extensive argument for concord which follows); (3) epistolary body (1:10–15:58), including (a) the *prothesis* or "thesis statement" in 1:10 (Mitchell 1991, 198–200): "I appeal to you, brethren, by the name of our Lord Jesus Christ, that all of you agree and that there be no dissensions among you, but that you be united in the same mind and the same judgment"; (b) the statement of facts or διήγησις (1:11–17); (c) proofs or πίστεις (1:18–15:57); (d) conclusion of the argument or ἐπίλογος (15:58); (4) epistolary closing (16:1–24).

The analysis of Witherington (1995) closely follows that of Mitchell (1991) and Betz and Mitchell (1992), though he diverges from them, extending the *probatio* to 16:12 (which is problematic because 15:1–58 is certainly a rhetorical unit; see Eriksson 1998, 233), and defines the *peroratio* as consisting of 16:13–18, which is impossible, given the content of that section.

R. F. Collins (1999) seems to be following Mitchell (1991), except for the fact that he explicitly denies the existence of a *narratio* in the letter, then locates the *propositio* or *prothesis* in 1:10, but then makes 1:10 the beginning of the *probatio* (1:10–15:58). This is acceptable, however, since Quintilian (4.4.1) argues that the beginning of every *confirmatio* is a *propositio*. Similarly, though 15:58 ends the *probatio* section, he also regards it as the *peroratio*. He identifies six arguments in the body of the letter (1:10–15:58): (1) first rhetorical demonstration (1:18–4:21); (2) second rhetorical demonstration (5:1–7:40); (3) third rhetorical demonstration (8:1–11:1); (4) fourth rhetorical demonstration (11:2–34); (5) fifth rhetorical demonstration (12:1–14:40); (6) sixth rhetorical demonstration (15:1–58).

A number of scholars attempt to analyze rhetorically portions of 1 Corinthians as if they were complete speeches. Bünker (1984, 51–59) argues for the following rhetorical divisions in 1 Cor. 1:10–4:11: (1) first part: 1:10–17 (*exordium*); (2) second part: 1:18–3:23: (a) *narratio* (1:18–2:16), (b) *probatio* (3:1–17), (c) *peroratio* (3:18–23); (3) third part: 4:1–21: (a) *refutatio* (4:1–13), (b) *peroratio* (4:14–21).

Also 1 Cor. 12–14 has attracted a number of rhetorical analyses (Standaert 1983; Smit 1993). Smit (1993) regards 1 Cor. 12 and 1 Cor. 14 as deliberative but 1 Cor. 13 as demonstrative or epideictic (on the varied judgments of the possible genre of 1 Cor. 13, see Focant 1996, 212–13).

Bünker also provides a similar rhetorical analysis of 1 Cor. 15, which he regards as judicial rhetoric (1984, 59–72): (1) *Exordium* (15:1–2); (2) *Transitus* (15:3a); (3) *Narratio* (15:3b–11); (4) *Argumentatio* I (15:12–28); (5) *Peroratio* I (15:29–34); (6) *Argumentatio* II (15:35–49); (7) *Peroratio* II (15:50–58). Mack (1990, 56–59), who regards 1 Cor. 15 as an example of deliberative rather than judicial rhetoric, has what appears to be an analysis essentially similar to that of Bünker (1984). However, he argues that deliberative rhetoric was gradually transformed into a standard outline for thesis elaborations in declamations (Mack 1990, 42), and hence he breaks down the "argument" section (vv. 21–50) into five parts: (1) paradigms, (2) opposite, (3) examples, (4) analogies, (5) citation. Thiselton (2000), though generally avoiding rhetorical analysis throughout his commentary on 1 Corinthians, nevertheless largely adopts Eriksson's (1998) rhetorical analysis of 1 Cor. 15.

*Corinthians, Second Letter to the, *Letters, Pauline.

Aletti 1992; R. D. Anderson 1999; Baasland 1988; Barrett 1976; Bieringer 1996; Branick 1982; Bünker 1983; A. D. Clarke 1993; R. F. Collins 1996, 1999; de Boer 1994; Focant 1996; R. A. Horsley 1998; Hurd 1983; Jewett 1971, 1978; Kremer 1997; Litfin 1994; Marshall 1987; Merklein 1984; Mitchell 1989, 1991; Pogoloff 1992; Probst 1991; Schenk 1969; Schmithals 1969; Schrage 1991–2001; Schüssler Fiorenza 1987; Sellin 1991; Sigountos 1994; Smit 1991, 1993; Thiselton 2000; Watson 1989a; 1993b; J. Weiss 1910;

Synopsis of Rhetorical Analyses of 1 Corinthians 12–14

Dispositio	Standaert (1983)	Smit (1993)
Propositio	12:1–3	
Exordium	12:4–11	12:1–3
Narratio or *similitudo*	12:12–30	
Argumentatio		12:4–30
Partitio		12:4–6
Confirmatio		12:7–30
Digressio	12:31–13:13	12:31–13:13
Propositio		12:31
Amplificatio		13:1–12
Conclusio		13:13
Argumentatio	14:1–36	
Partitio		14:1–5
Confirmatio		14:6–33a
Peroratio	14:37–40	14:37–40

Synopsis of Rhetorical Analyses of 1 Corinthians 15

Dispositio	Bünker (1984)	Mack (1990)	Aletti (1992)	Watson (1993b)	Eriksson (1998)	Thiselton (2000)
Exordium	1–2	1–2	1–2	1–2	1–2	
Transitus	3a					
Narratio	3b–11	3–11	3–11	3–11	3–11	1–11
Argumentatio or *Probatio*	12–28	21–50	12–34	[12–28]	12–57	
Refutatio				12–19	12–19	12–19
Confirmatio				20–28	20–34	20–34
Peroratio	29–34		33–34	29–34		
Argumentatio or *Probatio*	35–49		35–58	[35–57]		
Refutatio				35–44a	35–49	35–49
Confirmatio				49b–57	50–57	50–57
Peroratio	50–58			58	58	58
Conclusio		51–58				

Welborn 1987a, 1987b; H. H. D. Williams 2001; Winter 2001; Witherington 1995

Corinthians, Second Letter to the

The Pauline authorship of 2 Corinthians is not seriously disputed (with the exception of 2 Cor. 6:14–7:1). It was written in 57 C.E. Paul's Greek style in 2 Corinthians comes close to that which contemporary literary criticism would regard as *Asianism (see 2 Cor. 11:21–23; Fairweather 1994, 229–30).

Unity. While some scholars still argue for the unity of 2 Corinthians (Bates 1965; Kümmel 1975, 287–93; P. Barnett 1997, 17–25; Amador 1999, 2000; Manzi 2002, 20–26), the composite character of the letter is widely accepted, though there is disagreement regarding the exact number and extent of the constituent letters or letter fragments. The most common way of partitioning the letter is to regard 2 Cor. 1–9 and 10–13 as originally separate letters which were combined in a later editorial process (Furnish 1984, 35–48; R. P. Martin 1986; de Silva 1993). Other critics find as many as six independent compositions in 2 Corinthians (Schmithals 1971, 96–101): (1)

1:1–2:13; 7:5–16, the letter of reconciliation (Weiss 1959, 1:349–53; Welborn 1996). (2) 2:14–6:13; 7:2–4. Frequently 2:14–7:4 has been construed as a *digression (Plummer 1915, 67). Part of the evidence for this are the close parallels in 2:12–13 and 7:5, verses which frame the "digression" (see Welborn 1996):

> 2 Corinthians 2:12–13
> When I came to Troas to preach the gospel of Christ, a door was opened for me in the Lord; but my mind could not rest because I did not find my brother Titus there. So I took leave of them and went on to Macedonia.
>
> 2 Corinthians 7:5
> For even when we came into Macedonia, our bodies had no rest, but we were afflicted at every turn—fighting without and fear within.

Yet 2 Cor. 7:5 can also be regarded as the continuation of 2 Cor. 2:12–13, indicating that the intervening material is a secondary insertion, for as Welborn maintains (1996): "A resumption, after a long digression, should have been handled differently." (3) 6:14–7:1, an interpolated fragment (Fitzmyer 1974b), perhaps referred to in 1 Cor. 5:9 but sometimes thought to be an anti-Pauline fragment (Betz 1973), though some prominent scholars regard it as possibly genuine (Dahl 1977, 62–69). (4) 8:1–24, a letter to Corinth concerning the collection for Jerusalem (Betz 1985). (5) 9:1–15, a circular letter to Achaia about the collection (Betz 1985). (6) 10:1–13:13, the so-called "sorrowful letter" referred to in 2:4 (Welborn 1995). Chapters 10–13 (see *boasting) which is primarily an appeal, is an example of a mixed letter type, for it also includes other elements, such as an ultimatum backed by a threat, an apology, a counteraccusation of Paul against his opponents, and an accusation and reproach directed to the Corinthians for allowing themselves to be taken in by Paul's opponents (Fitzgerald 1990).

Purpose and destination. Given the probability that 2 Corinthians consists of two or more letters, scholars have frequently sought to determine the purpose and destination of each of the original letters or letter fragments. Chapters 10–13, for example, were probably written by Paul to defend himself from the attacks of the "superlative apostles" (2 Cor. 11:5). Chapters 8–9, whether originally one or two letters, were intended to prepare for the collection in the Corinthian church. Kurz (1996), however, has asked about the intended audience or implied readers of the entire composite letter as well, and when, where, and why the composite letter was created. Similarly, Dahl (1977) had asked what new function the non-Pauline fragment 2 Cor. 6:14–7:1 played in its new epistolary context. The composite letter can no longer be directed to the original problems, situations, opponents, or audience to which the original parts were directed. The composite letter may not have been intended for Corinth at all. Secondary audiences must reapply and readapt the composite letter to their own circumstances. It is possible that Paul himself combined his letters into an "authorized" collection, which included Romans, 1–2 Corinthians, and Galatians (Trobisch 1994,

Synopsis of Rhetorical Analyses of 2 Corinthians

Dispositio	**Kennedy (1984, 87–91)**	**Witherington (1995)**	**Thompson 2001**	**Manzi (2002, 26–55)**
Epistolary prescript	—	1:1–2		1:1–2
Epistolary thanksgiving	—	1:3–7		1:3–11
Exordium	1:3–8		1:1–7	
Narratio	1:8–2:13	1:8–2:16	1:8–11	—
Propositio	2:14–17	2:17	1:12–14	1:12
Probatio	3:4–6:13	3:1–13:4	1:15–9:15	1:12–13:10 [3 *subpropositiones*: 1:12–7:16; 8:1–9:15; 10:1–13:10]
Peroratio	7:2–16	13:5–10	10:1–13:14	—
Epistolary closing	—	13:11–13		13:11–13

73–86), though most critics assume that a later editor combined several letters and letter fragments to produce 2 Corinthians Kurz asks (1996, 46), "Does the collection of fragments into a composite letter have the same effect on the interpretation of those fragments as did the Pauline letter collection on the interpretation of the individual letters?" He suggests that in the adscription in 2 Cor. 1:1b: "To the church of God which is at Corinth, with all the saints who are in the whole of Achaia," the last phrase was added in the redaction of 2 Corinthians to broaden the audience of the composite letter (Kurz 1996, 51).

Rhetorical analysis. Not often has 2 Corinthians been the subject of rhetorical analysis, perhaps because of the general conviction that it is a combination of several letters and/or letter fragments. Some have construed it as consisting primarily of judicial rhetoric, though 2 Cor. 8 and 9 have been considered deliberative (Kennedy 1984, 87). P. Barnett (1997, 18), identifies 1:1–11 with a classical *exordium,* which begins with thanksgiving and encouragement. The *narratio* begins within the *exordium* (1:8–11), and surfaces again periodically (2:3–13; 7:5–16; 8:1–6, 16–23; 9:2–5; 11:22–12:10). The proofs presumably are found in 1:12–12:10 (Barnett is vague on this point), and 2 Cor. 10–13 is a peroration.

Amador (1999, 2000) uses "a rhetorical theory of dynamic argumentation" to argue for the unity of 2 Corinthians. He begins by distinguishing six rhetorical units within the letter (1999, 414): (1) introductory unit (1:1–14); (2) unit 1: a ring composition which begins and ends with the *narratio* of past missionary activities (1:15–2:13); (3) unit 2: the purpose and experience of the ministry in the present (2:14–7:4); (4) unit 3: a two-part structure picking up the thread of the *narratio* in 7:5, 8:1–2, and 9:2; the first part, 2 Cor. 8, is an argument from consistency, and the second, 2 Cor. 9, ends with a promise of future abundance (7:5–9:15); (5) unit 4 (10:1–13:9); (6) concluding remarks (13:10–14). Amador then argues that a complex web of modal and deictic units links together the argumentative units into "coherency" (Amador 1999, 419). "Coherence" and "unity" are critical concepts for Amador's project, though he never defines precisely what he means by them. Amador thinks that the burden of proof has now shifted to those who maintain a multiple-source theory for 2 Corinthians: "Can such a theory be maintained without recourse to a model of communication which would reject the presence of complex communication performances?" (Amador 1999, 430).

The reconstructed "letter of reconciliation" (2 Cor. 1:1–2:13; 7:5–16; 13:11–13) has been rhetorically analyzed by Betz (1992): (1) epistolary prescript (1:1–2); (2) *exordium* (1:3–7); (3) *narratio* (1:8–11); (4) *probatio* (1:12–2:13; 7:5–16); (5) epistolary postscript (13:11–13).

Hughes (1997) argues that the letter fragment 2 Cor. 2.14–6:13 and 7:2–4 can be rhetorically analyzed as a fully integral and persuasive letter with the exception of the missing epistolary prescript.

Betz (1985, 35, 38–41, 132–33) has argued that 2 Cor. 8 was an originally separate letter that exhibits the following rhetorical structure: [Lost epistolary prescript], (1) *Exordium* (8:1–5), (2) *Narratio* (8:6), (3) *Propositio* (8:7–8), (4) *Probatio* (8:9–15), (5) Commendation of envoys (8:16–22), (6) their authorization (8:24), (7) *Peroratio* (8:24) [lost epistolary postscript].

Betz (1985, 88–90) similarly maintains that 2 Cor. 9 was originally a separate letter that exhibits a coherent rhetorical structure: (1) *Exordium* (9:1–2), (2) *Narratio* (9:3–5a), (3) *Propositio* (9:5bc), (4) *Probatio* (9:6–14), (5) *Peroratio* (9:15).

Second Corinthians 10–13. Second Corinthians 11:22–12:10 has been called the "Fool's Speech" (Lambrecht 2001), though some see this passage as the core of a larger section consisting of 11:1–12:13 (Heckel 1993, 22–23). Lambrecht (2001, 310) proposed a chiastic arrangement of 2 Cor. 10–13 with the following pattern:

A Exhortation (10:1)
- B Authority (10:2–18)
  - C Denial of inferiority (11:5–12)
    - D The fool's speech (11:22–12:10)
  - C′ Denial of inferiority (12:11b–18)
- B′ Authority (13:1–10)

A′ Exhortation (13:1)

*Letters, Pauline, *Corinthians, First Letter to the

Amador 1999, 2000; Barnett 1997; Bates 1965–66; Betz 1973, 1985a; Bieringer 1996; Bornkamm 1962a; Dahl 1977; Duff 1994; Fitzgerald 1990; Fitzmyer 1974b; Furnish 1984; Hafemann 1998; Hughes 1997; Kennedy 1984, 86–96; Lambrecht 2001; Manzi 2002; R. P. Martin 1986; Murphy-O'Connor 1991, 10–11; Rolland 1990; Stowers 1993; Thompson 2001; Thrall 1994; Welborn 1995, 1996; Winter 2001; Witherington 1995; Zmijewski 1978

Corinthians, Third Letter to the, is a pseudepigraphal pair of letters, one from the Corinthians (Stephanus and the presbyters with him) to Paul reporting the activity of two heretical teachers, Simon and Cleobius, and one attributed to Paul in which he answers their queries by rejecting the ideas of these teachers, frequently by referring to his earlier teaching in Corinth. This short exchange of letters, sometimes connected with a brief narrative mentioning that Paul received the Corinthian letter while a prisoner in Philippi, was originally part of the **Acts of Paul.* C. Schmidt (1905, 132, 144), thought that the Corinthian correspondence was separated from the *Acts of Paul* in the 4th cent. C.E. Others have argued that it was written by a different author from the rest of the *Acts of Paul* and had a separate existence (Testuz 1960, 221–22; J. K. Elliott 1993, 354). In the Armenian and Syriac churches, 3 Cor. was temporarily part of the NT canon (Metzger 1987, 219, 223). It was included in the edition of the Armenian Bible by Jean Zohrab that was published in Venice in 1805.

Content. The Corinthians, disturbed over the false teaching of Simon and Cleobius, who claimed there was only a resurrection of the spirit, not a resurrection of the flesh, wrote a letter to Paul in Philippi. The letter to Paul, drafted by Stephanus and several presbyters, described the teachings of Simon and Cleobius (*NTA* 2.254–56): "We must not, they say, appeal to the prophets, and that God is not almighty, and that there is no resurrection of the flesh, and that the creation of man is not God's (work), and that the Lord is not come in the flesh, nor was he born of Mary, and that the world is not of God, but of the angels." Threptus and Eutychus, Corinthian deacons, brought the letter to Paul in prison at Philippi. Distraught at what was happening in the Corinthian congregation, he then wrote a letter in which he emphasizes that the opposite of what Simon and Cleobius teach is true, taking up the issues raised in the Corinthian letter and answering them point by point.

Manuscript evidence. Originally 3 Corinthians was written in Greek, which survives only in P. Bodmer X. A single 3d-cent. Coptic MS survives. Various parts of 3 Corinthians are also extant in a Coptic translation, several Latin manuscripts, and a number of Armenian manuscripts.

*Acts of Paul

———

Havhanessian 2000; Klijn 1963; Luttikhuuizen 1996; Rordorf 1993; Testuz 1959, 1960

Cosenders are mentioned in the prescripts of all the genuine *Pauline letters except Romans and among the Deutero-Pauline letters only in Colossians (1:1) and 2 Thessalonians (1:1). While some have considered a cosender as a *secretary, there is little hard evidence to support this proposal (Tertius, who names himself the secretary Paul is using to write Romans in 16:22, is not a cosender of the letter). According to Byrskog (1996, 248–49), the mention of cosenders had two functions: (1) the mention of cosenders known to the recipients fostered good relations with them; (2) the mention of cosenders legitimated the letter in the collegiality of Paul's associates. There is no evidence to prove that cosenders functioned as *coauthors.

*Coauthors, *First-person plural

———

Byrskog 1996

Cosmogony, compounded from the Greek words κόσμος ("world order, universe") and γονεία ("generation, production"), means an account of the origin of the universe, in contrast to *cosmology, which focuses on a description of the universe after it has come into existence. Texts from the ancient Near East, including the OT, reveal the existence of a primeval cosmic battle pattern or protology (Oden 1992, 1164–65): (1) A divine warrior battles the monsters of chaos, variously named Sea, Tannin, Death, or Leviathan. (2) The world of nature joins in the fray, helping to defeat the forces of chaos. (3) The divine warrior is enthroned on a mountain surrounded by subordinate deities. (4) The divine warrior speaks, and nature brings forth the created world. This cosmic battle was celebrated annually through ritual reenactment. This myth is taken up in apocalyptic and projected into the future so that a cosmic battle becomes the decisive moment in an extensive *eschatology (Zech. 14).

*Cosmology

———

Oden 1992; Yarbro Collins 1976

Cosmology refers to a model for understanding the structure of the universe or the nature of reality, which in the ancient world was understood in both mythological and rational ways. A knowledge of ancient cosmologies is important for interpreting early Christian literature, because particular cosmologies are sometimes used to structure certain types of *revelatory literature, particularly *apocalypses, and are also presupposed in other literary works.

By the late 5th cent. B.C.E., through the influence of the Greek pre-Socratic philosophers, the term κόσμος became a technical term for the universe, which had previously been designated "the whole" or "the all." The pre-Socratics regarded the κόσμος as a living, intelligent being, a macrocosmos of which the individual person was a small-scale model, or microcosmos (Wright 1995, 56–74). However, two quite different naturalistic or scientific models of the universe arose from the 6th to the 4th cent. B.C.E. in Greece: the closed universe model and the infinite universe model (Furley 1987, 1–8; 1989, 223–35). The *closed universe* model had three main subtypes: (1) the world was created by a god (Plato, *Timaeus*); (2) the world had no beginning and will have no end (Aristotle); or (3) the world has a beginning and end as part of an endlessly repeated cycle of destruction and renewal (Stoicism). All forms of the closed universe model are characterized by these suppositions: (1) permanence (the kinds of things that exist in the world do not change); (2) teleology (the world is an organic structure moving to an end or goal; human beings are at the top of the hierarchy of living forms and the unique function of human beings is reason); and (3) the view that the world is an uninterrupted material continuum, spherical in shape, which fills everything. The more monolithic *infinite universe* theory, promulgated by atomists such as Democritus and incorporated into the physics of the Epicureans, also carried with it several suppositions: (1) impermanence, with everything in the cosmos, including the cosmos itself, subject to growth and decay; (2) a universe consisting of units of matter that do not change except to move and collide; and (3) a universe made up of invisible particles (atoms) that move in a void with no center and no boundaries.

In addition to these rational or naturalistic cosmologies, there were two major mythological cosmologies in the ancient world. The archaic cosmology conceived of the world in terms of a three-tiered cosmos consisting of the earth as a flat disc in the middle, surrounded by the river Ocean (the Greek version) or floating on water (the Israelite version), with heaven above and the underworld beneath; the underworld, called *sheol* by the Hebrews and *tartarus* or *hades* by the Greeks, was considered the dwelling place of the dead (Exod. 20:4; Pss. 33:6–8; 77:19; 115:15–17; Prov. 8:27–29). A mountain frequently served as a cosmic center (e.g., the Greek Mount Olympus, the Israelite Mount Sinai [Deut. 33:2–3] and Mount Zion or the Ugaritic Mount Zaphon), the meeting place of the divine assembly, and the point where earth and heaven were united (Clifford 1972). In this cosmology the divine world was close to earth, and God or the gods frequently intervened in human affairs. This three-storied universe is also presumed in a number of early Jewish apocalypses (the five apocalypses that compose *1 *Enoch*, the *Testament of Abraham*, and the *Apocalypse of Ezra*), as well as in the *Revelation to John in early Christianity (Rev. 5:3, 13).

During the Hellenistic period a geocentric model of the universe largely replaced the older three-tiered universe model, for Greek thinkers (such as Aristotle and Eratosthenes) proposed that the earth was a sphere suspended freely in space (Nilsson 1946, 1969, 96–103). According to this cosmological model, the earth was stationary at the lowest or innermost part of the cosmos and was surrounded by seven planetary spheres (arranged in the following order: Moon, Mercury, Venus, Sun, Mars, Jupiter, and Saturn). The seven planetary spheres were enclosed by an eighth sphere consisting of the fixed stars, most important of which were the twelve signs of the zodiac. God or the gods were thought to dwell in the highest heaven or sphere, i.e., the eighth. While several Jewish apocalypses presuppose a universe consisting of seven heavens (*Testament of *Levi* 2:7–9; *2 *Enoch* [recension A]; *3 Enoch* 17:1–3; 18:1–2; *Apocalypse of Zephaniah*; *Apocalypse of Abraham*; **Ascension of Isaiah* 6–11; b. Hagigah 12b); the **Apocalypse of Paul*), none of them correlates the seven heavens with the seven planets (Culianu 1983, 56). A cosmology of *three* heavens is reflected in Paul's visionary ascent to heaven in 2 Cor. 12:1–5 (Segal 1990, 34–71), the *Apocalypse of Moses* 37, and the *Apocalypse of Sedrach* 2:3–5. A cosmos of five heavens is depicted in the extant Greek and Slavonic manuscripts of *3 *Baruch*, though seven heavens may be presupposed and the text may also have been abridged (Harlow 1996, 41–50). Ten heavens are mentioned in the longer recension of *2 Enoch* (22:1) and in the Coptic-Gnostic *Apocalypse of Paul.*

*Ascent, heavenly, *Apocalypse (literary genre)

Furley 1987, 1989; Guthrie 1952; Knight 1985; Lloyd 1975; Oden 1992; Stadelmann 1970; Wright 1995; Yarbro Collins 1995

Crasis, a transliterated form of the Greek word κρᾶσις ("mixing, blending"), is the combination of the vowels of two syllables into one long vowel or diphthong (e.g., κἄν for καὶ ἄν, or to τοὔνομα for τὸ ὄνομα).

Creeds, creedal formulas The terms "creed" and "creedal" are based on the Latin word *credo*, meaning "I believe," and refer to declarative statements of varying length that are typically recited by groups in the setting of worship as a way of expressing common beliefs and values. Often called "confessions" by Protestants (e.g., the "Augsburg Confession" of Lutheranism and the "Westminster Confession" of Presbyterianism), the earliest creedal statements of Christianity are found in the NT and are extremely concise expressions of belief, such as "Jesus is the Christ" (John 20:31), "Jesus is the Son of God" (1 John 4:15), "Jesus is Lord" (Rom. 10:9; 1 Cor. 12:3), "Jesus Christ is Lord" (Phil. 2:11), and "Jesus Christ has come in the flesh" (1 John 4:2; Polycarp, *Phil.* 7:1; cf. Ignatius, *Smyrn.* 5:2). Romans 10:9–10 is particularly revealing: "If you confess with your lips that Jesus is Lord and believe in your heart that God raised him from the dead, you will be saved." The verb ὁμολογεῖν, "to confess" occurs in many of these contexts (Rom. 10:9; Phil. 2:11; 1 John 4:2, 15; Polycarp, *Phil.* 7:1), making it natural to label such statements "confessions."

*Hymns, *Form criticism

Beasley-Murray 1980; Murphy-O'Connor 1981; Wengst 1972a, 1972b

Critical edition (see *Edition)

Dead Sea Scrolls, a general term for a collection of more than 800 works and fragments of works, all dating between 200 B.C.E. and 70 C.E., discovered in eleven caves in the desert surrounding Khirbet Qumran near the northwest shore of the Dead Sea in the years following 1947. These texts belonged to a local sect of Essenes who hid the texts in nearby caves to protect them from the approaching Romans, ca. 68 C.E. The texts were written in Hebrew (including 50 texts in "cryptic" script, all in Hebrew; see Pfann 2000), Aramaic, and Greek.

Overview. These works date from the late 3d or early 2d cent. B.C.E., from the time when the Essene sect that wrote and collected them was founded, to the mid-1st cent. C.E., when Palestine was overrun by the Romans in consequence of the First Jewish Revolt (66–72 C.E.). Though often called a "library," that term does not mean that all of the works included in the Dead Sea Scrolls were written by scribes at Khirbet Qumran. On the contrary, it is important to distinguish among three categories of texts (Dimant 1995, 27–29): (1) biblical texts (Abegg, Flint, and Ulrich 1999; Ulrich 1999; Flint [ed.] 2001); (2) sectarian texts (those that seem to have been written by members of the Essene community, such as 1QS, 1QM, 1QH, 11QTemple, and the *pesharim); and (3) nonsectarian texts (those which were collected at Qumran from various places in Palestine, particularly Jerusalem), including such pseudepigraphal works as *1 Enoch*, *Jubilees*, and such apocryphal works as Tobit. Virtually all the fragments that can be pieced together and coherently understood have now been published in the Discoveries in the Judean Desert (DJD) series, and an enormous number of articles and monographs have been published about them.

Tools for studying the Dead Sea Scrolls. Those who are not specialists in the study of the scrolls can have access to them and various studies about them through the many study tools now available. Some of the more important tools are: (1) keys to abbreviations (García Martínez 1997, 467–519, and Vermes 1996, 601–19); (2) bibliographies (García Martínez and Perry 1996; Pinnick 2001); (3) introductions (VanderKam 1994; F. M. Cross 1995; García Martínez and Trebolle Barrera 1995); (4) dictionaries (Schiffman and VanderKam [eds.] 2000); (5) texts (DJD); (6) texts and translations (García Martínez and Tigchelaar [eds.] 1997–98; Charlesworth [ed.] 1994–); (7) translations (García Martínez 1996; Vermes 1997); (8) concordances (Charlesworth 1991).

The abbreviations of the texts belonging to the Dead Sea Scrolls have been standardized in recent years. Earlier abbreviations frequently had the form 1QpHab or 1QHabakkuk Pesher. The "1Q" refers first to the number of the cave in which the texts were found (there were eleven such caves), while the "Q" refers to "Qumran" (other texts have been found elsewhere in the Judaean desert that do not include the "Q" in their identification). The "p" refers to "pesharim," a type of biblical commentary, while "Hab" refers to the prophetic book of Habakkuk. The more recent abbreviations have assigned a number to each of the texts found in each of the caves, thus "1Q14" is now the preferred way of referring to 1QpMic or 1QMicah Pesher. A list of all Qumran texts according to the more recent numerical abbreviation system is found in García Martínez (1997, 467–519) and Vermes (1996, 601–19), though unfortunately a reverse list is included in neither catalogue. For example, if you find a reference to 4QJub^{e} or 4QJubilees^{e} (the superscript

[e] refers to one of the fragments of this text), there is no way of finding out that the alternate abbreviation is 4Q220 in García Martínez 1977 or Vermes 1996. However, García Martínez and Tigchelaar (eds.) 1997–98, 2.1313–60 contains both an index of manuscripts translated in the two volumes arranged by the newer numbering system (1313–25) and an index of titles with the equivalent number, e.g., 4Q 3 Tongues of Fire=4Q376 (1327–60).

Biblical interpretation. The pesharim are biblical commentaries in which a portion of the biblical text, called a lemma, is quoted, followed by the commentary, introduced by a limited number of formulaic phrases, such as: פשרו ("its interpretation [is]"), or פשרו אשר ("its interpretation [is] that"), or פשרו על ("its interpretation concerns"), פשר הדבר ("the phrase means"). A distinctive formal feature of the comment is the fact that it focuses on comparatively recent historical events that are presaged by the portion of Scripture cited in the lemma and that are assumed to have occurred at the end of the age. There are 18 texts from Qumran that can be categorized as continuous pesharim, and many were written after 72 B.C.E. (Steudel 1993, 241–42). All exist in single copies only, possibly *autographs. The pesharim are all commentaries on prophetic books with the addition of the Psalms. The best known pesher commentary is 1QHabakkuk Pesher=1QpHab (Elliger 1953; Brownlee 1979; Horgan 1979).

Community rules. Also called constitutional rules, this is a literary category that prescribes an ideal form of behavior (Dimant 1984, 490–503; Metso 1998–99). This category includes the Damascus Document (CD), the Community Rule (1QS), and the Rule of the Congregation (1QSb).

Eschatological works. Even though the Qumran Community has been called an apocalyptic sect, of the more than 200 documents that make up the corpus of literature produced at Qumran, not a single document identified as an apocalypse appears to have originated within the Qumran community (J. J. Collins 1997, 1998–99; Aune 1998–99, 626). Several texts either have a strong eschatological or apocalyptic orientation or have been called apocalypses by one or another scholar but do not appear to fully conform to this generic designation. For example, the War Scroll (1QM), even though it narrates the future eschatological war between the sons of light and the sons of darkness, is not in the form of an apocalypse, nor is 4Q246= 4QAramaic Apocalypse, edited by Puech.

Hymns and liturgical works (Newsom 1985; Nitzan 1994; Falk 1998; Falk, García Martínez, and Schuller 2000, 77–193; Davila 2000). Among the Dead Sea Scrolls are the Hodayot or Thanksgiving Psalms (1QH); the Songs of the Sabbath Sacrifice (4Q400–407, 11Q17), which describe the worship and sacrificial cult of angels in heaven before the throne of God; and 4QBerakhot (4Q286–90, 4Q280?), a version of the annual covenant renewal ceremony, similar to the ritual described in 1QS 1–2.

Rewritten Bible. The fragmentary *Genesis Apocryphon* is one of the more extensive examples of *rewritten Bible texts in the Dead Sea Scrolls (on the genre of the *Genesis Apocryphon,* see Fitzmyer [1971, 5–12], who regards it as a prototype of midrash). The work retells the stories of the patriarchs Lamech, Noah, Abraham, and others narrated in Genesis. It also includes some word-for-word translations like the *targums, as well as some imaginative embellishments like haggadic *midrash. However, since the *Genesis Apocryphon* does not distinguish text from commentary, it does not belong to the midrash genre (C. A. Evans 1988).

Wisdom literature (Falk, García Martínez, and Schuller 2000, 13–75; Harrington 1996; Kampen 1998–99). The biblical figures of Lady Wisdom and Dame Folly are treated in 4Q184 ("Wiles of the Wicked Woman") and 4Q185. Dame Folly, the wanton woman who leads people astray, is found in Prov. 2:16–19; 5:1–23; 6:23–26 and elsewhere, though in 4Q184 she takes on cosmic stature (Kampen 1998–99, 223). On the other hand, Lady Wisdom, familiar from Prov. 1–9 and Ben Sira, is found in 4Q185. Tobin (1990) argues that this texts goes beyond the imitation of biblical material. Other important wisdom texts include *Sapiential Work A* (1Q26, 4Q415–18, 4Q423), one of the more extensive wisdom compositions at Qumran. Harrington (1996, 41) argues that a cosmic and eschatological framework is present at the beginning of 4Q416 frg. 1:

> In heaven he shall pronounce judgement upon the work of wickedness, but all his faithful children will be accepted with favor by Him . . . and every spirit of flesh will be laid utterly bare but the sons of Heaven shall rejoice in the day when it (i.e. wickedness) is judged. And all iniquity shall come to an end until the epoch of destruction will be finished.

Other wisdom texts now available are 4QMysteries (1Q27, 4Q299, 4Q300), 4QWays of Righteousness (4Q420–21), and 4QWisdom

Text with Beatitudes (4Q525). The portions of five beatitudes exhibit similarities to those of Matt. 5:3–12 and Luke 6:20–23.

Relevance for the NT and ECL. The Dead Sea Scrolls are extremely important for the study of early Christian literature, since they are virtually the only Jewish literature in Hebrew, Aramaic, and some Greek that can be securely dated to the late Second Temple Period (ca. 250 B.C.E. to 65 C.E.), and thus are either antecedent to or contemporary with the literature that makes up the NT. In discussions of possible parallels and influences of the Dead Sea Scrolls on the NT, the focus is typically on particular historical figures, e.g., John the Baptist (Lichtenberger 1992) and Jesus of Nazareth (C. A. Evans 1998–99); on themes (eschatology, messianic, biblical interpretation); and on texts or groups of texts, such as the Fourth Gospel (Aune 2002b), the Pauline letters (H.-W. Kuhn 1992; Fitzmyer 1998–99), the Acts of the Apostles, and the Synoptic Gospels, while little attention is usually paid (for example) to the Revelation to John (Aune 1999).

*Apocalypses, *Rewritten Bible

Abegg, Flint, and Ulrich 1999; Aune 1998–99, 2002; Brownlee 1979; Charlesworth (ed.) 1994–; Charlesworth 1991; J. J. Collins 1997, 1998–99; F. M. Cross 1995; Dimant 1984, 1995; Elliger 1953; C. A. Evans 1998–99; Falk 1998; Falk, García Martínez, and Schuller 2000; Fitzmyer 1971, 1998–99; Flint (ed.) 2001; Harrington 1996; García Martínez 1997; García Martínez and Tigchelaar (eds.) 1997–98; Horgan 1979; H.-W. Kuhn 1992; Lichtenberger 1992; Metso 1998–99; Newsom 1985; Nitzan 1994; Pinnick 2001; Schiffman 1994; Steudel 1993; Tobin 1990; Ulrich 1999; VanderKam 1994; Vermes 1996

Declamation, from the Latin term *declamatio*, is a rhetorical exercise in which the speaker pretends to be someone else and composes and delivers an imaginary set speech in character. The prerequisite for declamation was the completion of a preliminary course of rhetorical exercises called *progymnasmata (Quintilian, *Inst.* 2.10.1; Theon, *Progym.* 2).

Roman declamation. Declamation was a playful, competitive, and oral performance designed to train Roman boys to develop the speaking ability necessary to function well as advocates and orators, and in so doing to produce a *vir bonus,* "good man," i.e., an ideal Roman who exhibits the virtues of Roman culture summed up in the term *Romanitas* (Imber 2001, 199). Roman teachers of rhetoric regularly scheduled recitals in which students declaimed before an audience of their fathers and important social and political contacts (Suetonius, *Gramm. et rhet.* 7, 10). The four major declamatory corpora that have been preserved are (1) the *Declamationes minores* (a teacher's manual); (2) the *Declamationes maiores* of Ps.-Quintilian, the only collection of complete declamations, nineteen in all (Häkanson 1982; Sussman 1987; Winterbottom 1984); (3) the *Controversiae* of Seneca the Elder (Winterbottom 1974), which consist largely of excerpts (though the *controversiae* are preserved in complete form); and (4) the *Declamationum excerpta* of Calpurnius Flaccus, in which the *controversiae* are also preserved in unexcerpted form (Sussman 1994). Imber (2001) argues that *controversiae* are problems designed to prompt oral performance and that the restricted number of basic story lines (with a limited number of stock characters and memorable actions) they contained were already familiar to audiences who then looked for the particular rhetorical features that the declaimer might introduce.

Each declamation contains two major units, the *controversia* (the title of the text and a statement narrating a brief history of a conflict between two parties that had ended up in a lawsuit or a hearing before a tribunal; it may or may not refer to laws related to the conflict), and the *declamatio* (the speech itself). In addition, school texts, such as those of Ps.-Quintilian, may contain *sermones* (comments explaining the particular rhetorical problem to the student and suggesting approaches for formulating a declamation). The themes of declamations are primarily concerned with conflict and competition, i.e., they are generally agonistic, such as the father burdened with both a dissolute and a sober son, the rivalry of a rich and a poor man, the mother who protects a son against a ruthless and tyrannical father (Imber 2001, 202–3). The issue of *Romanitas* is evident in the fact that most declamations center on conflicts of allegiance to two social roles played by a single person, e.g., a son's affection for his mother challenges loyalty to his father (Imber 2001, 208). Here is an example of the *controversia* of Ps.-Quintilian, *Declamationes minores* 276 (Winterbottom 1984):

> *Title*: A brave stepson has been drugged.
>
> *Facts*: When a war was about to commence, a man who had acted bravely drank a sleeping potion offered by his stepmother. Accused of

desertion he pled his case. Found innocent, he accuses the stepmother of poisoning.

*Rhetorical theory, *Education

Bonner 1949; Dominik (ed.) 1997; Häkanson 1982; Imber 2001; D. A. Russell 1983; Russell and Winterbottom 1972; Sussman 1987, 1994; Winterbottom 1974, 1980, 1984

Decrees (see *Edicts)

Dedications (of books) The dedication of a literary work to a friend or patron functioned as the symbolic presentation of the work to the person named. Dedications, which are often but not invariably placed in *prefaces, became a common feature of the prefaces of prose and poetic works beginning with the late 5th cent. B.C.E. Dedications were not typically included in epic or *historiography (*DKP* 5.1373–74; L. Alexander 1993, 27). The earliest extant dedication (*DKP* 5.1373; *OCD* 438) is found in a quotation in Athenaeus 15.669d–e (West 1971–72, 1.58–59) from an elegy by Dionysios Chalcos (ca. 450 B.C.E.; *DNP* 3.642): "Receive, O Theodoros (for that is your true name), this poem pledged as a toast from me. I sent it on its right course to thee first of our company, mixing in the cup of the Graces the graces of friendship." Another early example of a dedication is the *Ad Nicoclen* of Isocrates, and (somewhat later) the *Ad Demonicum* of Ps.-Isocrates. The first extant instance of a historical work with a dedication is C. Velleius Paterculus (b. ca. 20 B.C.E.), who wrote a summary of Roman history down to the year of composition, 30 C.E. This work lacks a preface (but the first part of the work is fragmentary), and following the author's name and the title of the work is the brief dedication: *Ad M. Vicinium Cos.* ("Dedicated to M. Vinicius, Consul"). This is an example of a bare-bones factual dedication that can be contrasted to more textually integrated dedication. An example is the next extant history (following Velleius Paterculus) that contains a dedication: Josephus, *Antiquitates*. While there is no explicit dedication in the preface, in *Ant.* 1.8, Josephus does single out one particular person: "However, there were certain persons curious about the history who urged me to pursue it, and above all Epaphroditus, a man devoted to every form of learning, but specially interested in the experiences of history." In *Vita* 430 (a work intended by Josephus as an appendix to *Antiquitates*; see *Ant.* 20.266) it becomes clear that the *Antiquitates* was dedicated to Epaphroditus: "Having now, most excellent [κράτιστε ἀνδρῶν] Epaphroditus, rendered you a complete account of our antiquities, I shall here for the present conclude my narrative." The honorific form of address (κράτιστε ἀνδρῶν) clearly indicates the perceived social superiority of Epaphroditus. The dedicatee was probably M. Mettius Ephaphroditus, a wealthy Greek grammarian who lived in Rome toward the end of the 1st cent. C.E. (Thackeray 1967, 53; *DNP* 3.1064–65). With a library of 30,000 volumes, Epaphroditus undoubtedly served as both a patron and literary resource for Josephus. The preface of Josephus's **Contra Apionem* (1.1) also contains a dedication to Ephaphroditus.

Dedications were relatively common in Latin prose and poetic works, though Genette (1997, 117, 129) is clearly wrong in claiming that the dedication originated with Latin literature. The frequent occurrence of dedication in Latin literature can be attributed to the importance of the patron-client relationship (Gold 1982), often masked by the ostensibly egalitarian language of *amicitia*, or "friendship" (P. White 1978). Lucretius (ca. 99–50 B.C.E.), dedicated *De rerum natura* to Memmius Gemellus (1.26, 42), to whom he refers in the third person in the context of an introduction addressed to Venus: "I crave as partner in writing the verses, which I essay to fashion touching the Nature of Things, for my good Memmius, whom thou, goddess, hast willed at all times to excel, endowed with all gifts" (1.24–27). Memmius is probably the patron of Lucretius (Gold 1982b, 8). Horace dedicated *Ars poetica*, which is framed as a letter, to the Pisones, and the *Georgics* to Maecenas. This last dedication has had lasting influence, since the French word for "patron" is "mécène" (as well as the name "Maecenas"), while "patronage" is "mécénat" (Genette 1997, 118 n. 1). This reflects the fact that Maecenas was the literary patron par excellence of poets during the early Augustan period (G. Williams 1982, 14–16), and his name was ubiquitous in literary dedications (Fraenkel 1957, 214–33). He was Augustus's right-hand man and lived a life of legendary luxury (Pliny, *Hist. nat.*). After 20 B.C.E., Augustus took over literary patronage from Maecenas (G. Williams 1968, 86–88), signaled by the disappearance of Maecenas from Horace's dedications after *Epistles* 1 (written ca. 19 C.E.). Horace dedicates book 1 of the *Satires* to Maecenas (1.1.1) and reminds the reader of this dedication in 1.6.1, a repetition that has few if any parallels (Fraenkel 1957, 101). However, Vitruvius dedicates *De architectura* to Augustus (designated with the title "imperator") in the *praefationes* of all five books.

In addition to reflecting the patronage of the dedicatee, dedications sometimes suggest that the work was written at the specific request of the dedicatee, a request which the author claims that he could not refuse. Thus in **Rhetorica ad Herennium* 1.1.1: "Yet your desire, Gaius Herennius, has spurred me to compose a work on the Theory of Public Speaking, lest you should suppose that in a matter which concerns you I either lacked the will or shirked the labor." A similar motif is found in Cicero's dedication of *De oratore* to his brother Quintus (1.1.4) and in his dedication of *Topica* to Trebatius (1.1–5). Authors also dedicated works to important people who they expected would help in publishing and distributing the work (Schubart 1962, 134–39).

NT and ECL. Luke–Acts is the only work in the NT with a dedication. In the context of a *preface in Luke 1:1–4, the author says in v. 3 that his purpose is "to write an orderly account for you, most excellent Theophilus [κράτιστε Θεόφιλε]." Theophilus, probably his literary patron, is addressed again in the vocative in Acts 1:1: ὦ Θεόφιλε. The honorific address "most excellent" is a clear indication that Theophilus is the social superior and very probably the patron of the author of Luke–Acts (cf. Acts 23:26; 24:3; 26:5; *Diogn.* 1:1; Dionysius Hal., *De orat. ant.* praef.). Since dedicatees of literary works were frequently expected to facilitate the publication and distribution of the work (Schubart 1962, 134–39), it likely that Luke expected that service from Theophilus (Vielhauer 1975, 368). The so-called *Letter to *Diognetus* is misnamed, for it is not in letter form but is rather an anonymous apologetic treatise dedicated to "most excellent Diognetus (κράτιστε Διόγνητε)." Origen claims to have written the *Contra Celsum* because "Ambrose" requested that he provide a written response to the accusations which Celsus made against Christians (*praef.* 1–6), but this falls short of a dedication. Epiphanius's *Panarion* is prefixed by a letter by Acacius and Paul, two monastic leaders, requesting that he write a book on heretics and their beliefs, while the preface of the work itself has the form of a letter of response to Acacius and Paul.

———

L. Alexander 1993, 27–29; *DKP* 5.1373–74; Genette 1997, 117–36; Gold 1982, *OCD* 438–39; Ruppert 1911; Wheatley 1968; White 1978; G. Williams 1968, 1982

Deliberative rhetoric (in Greek γένος συμβουλευτικόν, in Latin *genus deliberativum*) is one of the three main species of rhetoric (the others are *forensic and *epideictic rhetoric); see *rhetorical genres. For Aristotle, each speech comprises three parts: the speaker, the subject he discusses, and the person to whom it is addressed (*Rhet.* 1.3.1–3 [1358a–b]). Deliberative rhetoric is derived from political speeches made before a public assembly in which a speaker recommends or advises against an action belonging to the future (Lausberg 1998, 97 [§224]). Deliberative rhetoric consists of arguments which advise an audience to pursue or avoid a particular form of action in the future (Aristotle, *Rhet.* 1.3.4; Quintilian 3.4.7; Mitchell 1991, 24). Success in this type of rhetoric is based on establishing two primary motives for action, honor (*honestas*) and advantage (*utilitas*); see Aristotle, *Rhet.* 1.3.4–6; Cicero, *De inventione* 2.52–54; *De oratore* 2.82.334; *Rhet. ad Alex.* 3.2.3; Quintilian 3.8.1. The two types of advice can be called ὁ προτρέπων, "persuasion," or ὁ ἀποτρέπων, "dissuasion" (Aristotle, *Rhet.* 1.3.3; *Rhet. Alex.* 1.1421b; Quintilian, *Inst.* 3.8.6), and the special purpose or end of deliberative rhetoric "is the expedient or useful; for he who exhorts recommends a course of action as better, and he who dissuades advises against it as worse" (Aristotle, *Rhet.* 1.3.4 [1358b]). Mitchell proposes that deliberative argumentation was characterized by four features (1991, 23): (1) focus on future time as the subject of deliberation; (2) use of a particular set of appeals or ends, the most distinctive of which is that which is advantageous (τὸ συμφέρον); (3) proof by example (παράδειγμα); (4) appropriate subjects for deliberation (factionalism and concord are particularly common).

*Rhetorical genres

———

Kennedy 1972, 18–21; Lausberg 1998, 97–102 (§§224–38); Martin 1974, 167–76; Sloane 2001, 209–17

Demetrius, *On Style,* is an anonymous treatise incorrectly attributed to the Peripatetic Demetrius of Phaleron, ca. 360–280 B.C.E. More likely, it was written by another Demetrius, and later attributed to his more famous namesake. The unknown author is dependent on Aristotle and refers also to Theophrastus and other Peripatetics (Solmsen 1931). The treatise has been dated within broad limits: 3d cent. B.C.E. to 2d cent. C.E. (Chiron 1993, xiii–xv), some dating it as early as the mid-3d cent. B.C.E. (Kennedy 1963, 285–86) and others as late as the 1st cent. B.C.E. (Innes [1972, 172], or suggest the first part of the 1st cent. B.C.E., since the work is apparently unknown to Dionysius of Halicarnassus), it is more likely much later and belongs to the 1st cent. C.E. (Schenkeveld 1964, 135–48). The dating problem centers on the fact that the author was probably writing in the 1st cent. C.E. but apparently limiting himself to sources from the 2d and early 1st cent. B.C.E., without adopting theories current in his own time (Schenkeveld 1964, 147; cf. Schmid and Stählin 1920, 2/1.79, who opt for the 1st cent. C.E.). While some regard *On Style* as a work of literary and rhetorical criticism (Kennedy 1963, 286), the frequent occurrence of imperatives indicates that the work was intended to be a didactic treatise, i.e., a rhetorical treatise suggesting stylistic options to the future orator (Schenkeveld 1964, 51–52). The author's scheme of four styles (see below) was less common than the three-style schema: grand, plain, and middle (Cicero, *Orator* 75–121).

Outline. The treatise falls into two main parts: (1) 1.1–35, on the structure of rhythmical sentences, dealing with the nature of the colon, comma, and period with general rules for the use of these forms of arrangement (see Schenkeveld 1964, 23–50); and (2) 2.36–4.239, on the four styles. Each style is treated under three aspects (subject, diction, and arrangement of words): (a) χαρακτὴρ μεγαλοπρεπής: the grand or elevated style (2.38–113), whose opposite is the frigid [ψυχρότηs] style (2.114–27); (b) χαρακτὴρ γλαφυρός: the elegant style (3.128–85), whose opposite is the affected style (3.186–89); (c) χαρακτήρ ἰσχνός: the plain style (4.190–235), whose opposite is the arid (ξηρός) style (4.236–39); and (d) χαρακτὴρ δεινός: the forceful style (240–301), and its opposite, the unpleasant style (302–4).

*Style

Chiron 1993; Grube 1961, 1964; Innes 1972; Roberts 1927; Schenkeveld 1964; Solmsen 1931

Demosthenes (see *Orators, Attic)

Description (see *Ekphrasis)

Deuteropauline letters (see *Pauline Letters; *Pastoral Letters; *Ephesians; *Colossians; *Thessalonians, Second Letter to the)

Diairesis (διαίρεσις, "division") is a rhetorical term for two or more possibilities, of which only one can be correct (Aristotle, *Rhet.* 2.23.10; Cicero, *Topica* 10.33–34; *De oratorio* 2.165; **Rhetorica ad Herennium* 4.40–41; see R. D. Anderson 2000, 32–33). Christiansen (1969) argues that Paul is a thoroughgoing Platonist trained in using διαιρεσις as an analytical technique, but this position is problematic (Alexander 1999, 11). An example is Gal. 2:16: "[we] know that a person is not justified by works of the law but through faith in Jesus Christ, even we have believed in Christ Jesus, in order to be justified by faith in Christ, and not by works of the law, because by works of the law shall no one be justified" (R. D. Anderson 1999, 2000, 155; Alexander 1999; Christiansen 1969).

Dialogue, a transliteration of the Greek word διαλόγος, meaning "conversation," is used of a literary form perfected by Plato in an attempt to reproduce a kind of philosophical conversation patterned after Socrates. The philosophical dialogues of Plato and Aristotle (the latter are all lost) became literary models for subsequent dialogues, and the dialogue was one of the more popular literary genres of antiquity. According to Diogenes Laertius (3.48=*FVS* 29A10), Zeno of Elea was the first to write dialogues, though this is extremely doubtful (as are most Greek claims about who did what first). As the dialogue developed, the contributions by the main speaker increased in length, making the dialogue form appear increasing artificial, often simply an excuse for long monologues on various subjects. The dialogue form was revived in the 1st and 2d cents. C.E. by Plutarch and Lucian.

Peripatetic dialogues. The peripatetic dialogue or περίπατος is a literary account of a philosophical or religious discussion that takes place during a stroll. It is essentially an introductory setting for a literary dialogue. The περίπατος and the dialogue were first combined by Epicurus (Hirzel 1895, 1.364 n. 1). Diogenes Laertius refers to a certain Athenodoros as the author of a literary work entitled Περίπατοι (3.3; 5.36; 6.81; 9.42). In the Greco-Roman period, the term "peripatetic" was applied to Epicurean philosophers (Cicero, *Letters to Atticus* 7.1.1). By the 2d cent. C.E., when Plutarch and Lucian had revived the dialogue as a literary form suitable for ethical, religious, and philosophical discussion, the περίπατος had become, to judge by Plutarch's 14 surviving dialogues, a feature (Plutarch, *Amatorius* 771d; *De facie* 937c; *Non posse suav.* 1086d). In Pluarch's dialogues one frequently finds a seated conversation following a περίπατος (Hirzel 1895:2.187). Thus a περίπατος can provide the setting for part or all of a dialogue of Plutarch, or it may be regarded as having occurred prior to the beginning of the seated dialogue. Thus *De defectu oraculorum*, *De E apud Delphos*, *De Pythiae oraculis*, and *Septem sapientium convivium* all begin with a περίπατος and conclude with a seated dialogue. *De sera numinis* contains a dialogue that occurs during a περίπατος which lasts throughout the entire composition.

Temple dialogues. Another form of the Greco-Roman dialogue is designated by Hirzel (1895, 2.66) as the *Kirchen-* or *Tempeldialog* (church or temple dialogue), so named because either a religious sanctuary is the setting for the dialogue, or the dialogue is occasioned by religious questions concerning something observed or said in or near a sanctuary. The *De re rustica* of Varro is the earliest surviving example of a temple dialogue. It begins with Varro entering the temple of Tellus on the occasion of the festival of the Sementivae, where he meets those who will participate in the ensuing conversation (2.1). An imperfectly preserved temple dialogue is the *Vergilius orator an poeta* of Florus, which was set in a temple in Tarraco (Spain), and written ca. 122 C.E. (Hirzel 1895, 2.66). Other temple dialogues include one by Cebes of Thebes (1st cent. C.E.) and one by Numenius (late 2d cent. C.E.); see Hirzel 1895, 2.258, 359. Plutarch wrote two dialogues that can be designated temple dialogues, the *De defectu oraculorum* and the *De E apud Delphos*.

Oracular dialogues. One distinctive form of oracular response in Greco-Roman divination is the oracular dialogue. In revelatory literature of the Greco-Roman period, particularly in Jewish and Christian apocalypses, Gnostic dialogues, and the Hermetic literature, divine revelation is frequently elicited through a question-and-answer format (*erotapokrisis*). The questions are posed by a mortal, and the revelatory answers are provided by a supernatural being (in *apocalyptic literature, the supernatural being is often an *angelus interpres, or "interpreting angel"). The simplest form of an oracular dialogue consists of two successive questions to an oracular deity. Oracle questions often had two parts, e.g., "Shall I or shall I not do such and such?" (Thucydides 1.134.4; Xenophon, *Ways and Means* 6.2–3; *Anabasis* 3.1.5–7; Dionysius Hal., *Ant. Rom.* 1.23.4). Greco-Roman magical literature has many procedures for gaining control of various kinds of supernatural beings to obtain oracular responses to various questions. Once such a séance had started, a dialogue often followed. Here are two examples from a Demotic magical papyrus that instruct a magician how to initiate a revelatory dialogue (Griffith and Thompson 1974):

> You cause him (the boy medium) to say to Anubis: "The god who will inquire for me today, let him tell me his name." When he stands up and tells his name, you ask him concerning everything you wish.

> "The god who will ask for me, let him put forth his hand to me and let him tell me his name." When he tells you his name, you ask him as to that which you desire. When you have ceased asking him as to that which you desire, you send him away.

Lucian (*Alex.* 43) created an extensive satirical oracular dialogue, probably modeled after more conventional oracular dialogues:

Sacerdos: Tell me, Lord Glykon, who are you?
Glykon: I am the new Asklepios.
Sacerdos: Different than the former one? What do you mean?
Glykon: It is not lawful for you to hear that.
Sacerdos: How many years will you remain here giving oracles?
Glykon: One thousand and three.
Sacerdos: Where will you go then?
Glykon: To the region of Baktria, for it is necessary that the barbarians gain something from my presence.
Sacerdos: Do the other oracles in Didyma and Claros and Delpi have your father Apollo delivering oracles, or are the oracles now delivered there false?
Glykon: You must not desire to know this. It is not lawful.
Sacerdos: Who will I be after this present life?
Glykon: A camel, then a horse, then a wise man and prophet not less than Alexander.
Glykon: Do not trust Lepidus, for a dismal fate follows.

Revelatory dialogues. Acts 1:3 briefly mentions the 40-day period between the resurrection and ascension of Jesus, when he spoke to his disciples of the kingdom of God. This tradition provided a basis for the creation of post-resurrection fictional dialogues between the risen Jesus and his disciples. Later Jesus literature expanded this interim period to 550 days (*Ap. John* I, 2.19–20) or even to 11 years (*Pistis Sophia* 1.1). The form of the revelatory dialogue, based on the question-and-answer scheme from ancient school tradition (*erotapokrisis), was frequently used for these fictional postresurrection seminars chaired by Jesus. Postresurrection revelatory dialogues were particularly favored by gnostic Christians, who regarded the accounts about the apostles in the canonical Gospels as reflecting a period of their ignorance and incompetence before the enlightenment that occurred only after the resurrection, e.g., *Gospel of Mary* 7,1–9, 24 (Perkins 1980, 37–58; Luttikhuizen 1988). Revelatory dialogues were also current with other forms of Christianity as well (e.g., *Epistula Apostolorum* 10–51).

———

Perkins 1980; Plezia 1970

Diatessaron, a transliteration of the Greek phrase διὰ τεσσάρων, "through the four [Gospels]," the name given to a *Gospel harmony first mentioned by Eusebius (*Hist. eccl.* 4.29.6). The most famous Gospel harmony in the early church was the *Diatessaron* of Tatian (first mentioned by Eusebius, *Hist. eccl.* 4.29.6), compiled after the middle of the 2d cent. C.E. in Syria (ca. 170), by Tatian, a student of *Justin Martyr (for a comprehensive review of *Diatessaron* studies, see W. L. Petersen 1994). The *Diatessaron* was a conflation of the four Gospels (and perhaps a fifth) into one continuous composition, one type of Gospel harmony. The *Diatessaron*, called the "Gospel of the Mixed" in Syriac, was canonical in Syria until the 5th cent. C.E., when it was replaced by the "Gospel of the separated ones," i.e., the four separate Gospels. There is evidence that an earlier harmony or collection of some harmonized passages of the Synoptic Gospels (though not John) were used by Justin (Bellinzoni 1967, 139–42; Osborn 1973, 125–31), which was picked up by Tatian, who incorporated Justin's harmony into the *Diatessaron* (W. L. Petersen 1990, 1994, 346–48). W. L. Petersen has argued that Justin's harmony must be earlier than 160 C.E. and possibly earlier than 150 C.E. (1994, 348). Though the evidence is fragmentary, there appears to be evidence for other early Gospel harmonies as well. One likely candidate is the *Gospel of the Ebionites* (seven fragments quoted in Epiphanius, *Haer.* 30.13.2–8; 30.14.5; 30.16.4–5; 30.22.4; see Bertrand 1980). Several harmonies are mentioned but have not survived, such as that based on the four Gospels by Theophilus of Antioch (Jerome, *Ep.* 121.6.15).

*Four Gospels, *Harmonies (of the Gospels), *Synoptic Gospels

———

Osborne 1973; Petersen 1990, 1994

Diatribe, based on the Greek noun διατριβή, can mean "conversation," "discourse," "lecture," and even "school" (Aune 1999, 832; LSJ 416; Renehan 1975, 66–67). Diatribe is a modern literary term describing an informal rhetorical mode of argumentation principally characterized by a lively dialogical style including the use of imaginary discussion partners (often abruptly addressed), to whom are attributed hypothetical objections and false conclusions (Fuentes González 1998, 44–78).

Diatribe as a genre? Both Usener (1887, lxix) and Wendland (1895), dependent on Wilamovitz-Moellendorf's use of the term for the "preaching" of Teles the Cynic philosopher (see Fuentes González 1998), used "diatribe" as a generic term for an ancient type of conversational discourse used by philosophers and rhetoricians that included hypothetical questions and objections (*DNP* 3.530–31). After the work of Wendland (1895) and Bultmann (1910) during the late 19th and early 20th cent. (detailed reviews of the history of research are found in Stowers 1981, 7–48; 1988, 71–74; Schmeller 1987, 1–54), the diatribe was widely considered a literary genre reflecting the oral preaching style of wandering Cynic and Stoic philosophers.

διατριβή and διατριβαί as ancient generic terms? The terms διατριβή and διατριβαί (plural) are occasionally used in the titles of Hellenistic literary works, though most such works have perished. Gottschalk (1983, 91) argues that in the phrase ἐν τῷ κατὰ τῆς Πλάτωνος διατριβῆς found in Athenaeus 11.508c (which I would translate "In the [work] against the School of Plato"), διατριβή refers to a literary genre as part of the title of a work by Theopompus, and that this generic term is repeated in the context. What this excerpt from Theopompus actually says, however, is that Plato in his "dialogues" plagiarized material from the διατριβαί of Aristippus. This second use of διατριβαί means "lectures," and refers to a transcription of an originally oral philosophical lecture (Schmeller 1987, 10–11). Porter (1991, 658–59) points out that the term διατριβαί is used in the titles of works listed by *Diogenes Laertius of Aristippus, Zeno, Persaeus, Ariston, Cleanthes, Sphaerus, and other Stoics (2.83–85; 7.34, 36, 163, 174–75, 178). Porter proposes three arguments for regarding διατριβαί as a generic term: (1) works with διατριβαί in their titles are distinguished from terms for other literary forms or genres; (2) the term διατριβαί is sometimes modified by reference to its number, subject, or content; and (3) the ancients sometimes refer to the writing of (what Porter calls) "diatribes" (e.g., Diogenes Laertius 7.34). The problem with these arguments is that it is unnecessary to read anything more into the titular use of διατριβαί than a term for a transcribed philosophical lecture, which is the setting for certain types of discourse but not a generically determinative one. Further, all these works have in fact perished, making an analysis of their form and style impossible.

Diatribe as an oral-literary style. While the generic character of the diatribe continues to be maintained by some (Porter 1991, 665–70), this notion is problematic, since the diatribe exhibits no regular or typical structure (Jocelyn 1982, 1983; Stowers 1988, 75; Donfried 1991b, 112–19). More recently the diatribe has come to be regarded as a "style" (Stowers 1981, 49) or "mode" (Malherbe 1986, 129), or a lively informal style and the particular activity of preaching (Fuentes González 1998, 44–78). The diatribe style, which pervades Rom. 1–11 and also occurs in other NT letters (1 Cor. 15:29–41; Gal. 3:1–9; 3:19–22; James 2:1–3:12; 4:13–5:6), has often been considered a Christian adaptation of the style of public discourse typical of popular philosophers, perhaps mediated through the Hellenistic synagogue (Aune 1987, 200). Stowers (1981) has shown that diatribes did not originate as public lectures, but rather as records of oral classroom discussions and discourses of philosophical schools where the teacher used the Socratic methods of "censure" (ἐλεγτικός) and "persuasion" (προτρεπτικός). The distinguished features of the diatribe is its dialogical or conversational character, a pedagogical method based on the model of Socrates (Dio Chrysostom, *Or.* 13.14–29; Epictetus 2.12; against Fuentes González 1998, 56–61). The literary style of the diatribe (which is basically paratactic) is the result of transforming a conversational mode of communication to writing, which ranges stylistically from ὑπομνήματα, or "lecture notes in rough draft" (the *Discourses* of Epictetus originated as Arrian's lecture notes), or as ἀπομνημονεύματα, i.e., in rewritten and polished form (Musonius Rufus, Plutarch). Ancient authors who used this style include Bion and Teles (both 3d cent. B.C.E.), Musonius Rufus, Dio Chrysostom, Horace, Philo, Seneca, Plutarch, Epictetus, and the writer of the pseudepigraphical letters of Heraclitus. According to Stowers (1981, 76), "The diatribe is not the technical instruction in logic, physics, etc., but *discourses and discussions in the school where the teacher employed the "Socratic" method of censure and protreptic.* The goal of this part of the instruction was not simply to impart knowledge, but to transform the students, to point out error and to cure it." The attempt of Fuentes González (1998, 56–61) to distance the diatribe from Socratic dialectic is not successful.

Characteristic features of the diatribe. The dialogical style of diatribes makes frequent use of imaginary opponents, hypothetical objections, and false conclusions. The questions and objections of the imaginary opponent and the teacher's responses oscillate between censure and persuasion. Censure exposes contradiction, error, and ignorance. Persuasion overcomes these with a call to the philosophic life by describing and illustrating virtue. The imaginary opponent is not a real opponent against whom the author argues but represents a synthesis of possible objections voiced by the students whom he is trying to teach.

The imaginary opponent plays a central role in the diatribe: (1) He is abruptly addressed (Epictetus 2.6.16; Plutarch, *Moralia* 525c; Rom. 2:1, 17; 9:19). (2) He is frequently addressed in the vocative as an anonymous "man," or "fool" (Rom. 2:1, 3; 9:20), less commonly as a figure from history or myth representing a negative example or personification (Seneca, *Ep.* 24.14; Rom. 11:19). (3) The opponent is frequently addressed with a singular "you" (Rom. 2:4, 17; 11:19). (4) An imaginary representative of a group is singled out and indicted for inconsistency (Epicetus 2.9.17; 2.21.11–12; 3.2.8–10; Rom. 3:1). (5) The author responds to an opponent's objection (Epictetus 4.9.5–6; Seneca, *Ep.* 7.5). (6) The address to the opponent begins with indicting statements or rhetorical questions emphasizing his ignorance (Epictetus 1.12.24–26; Rom. 2:4); error, i.e., wrong behavior or wrong thinking (Epictetus 3.22.81–82; Rom. 2:3; 9:20–24), or inconsistency (Epictetus 2.1.28; Seneca, *Ep.*

77.18; Rom. 2:21–22). (7) Vice lists are used in the context of diatribes (Epictetus 4.9.5–6; Rom. 2:8, 21–23).

Dialogical objections and false conclusions also characterize the diatribe, where they are used primarily for the purpose of indictment: (1) Objections are frequently introduced by expressions like "What then?" (Rom. 3:1) or "Come now, you who say" (Jas. 4:13), or the objector is referred to in the third-person singular or plural: "But some one will ask" (1 Cor. 15:35) or "They say." (2) The adversative particle ἀλλά ("but") frequently introduces the opponent's objection (1 Cor. 15:35; Jas. 2:18). (3) False conclusions are framed as questions (Seneca, *Ep.* 14.15; Plutarch, *Moralia* 527a; Epictetus 1.29.9; Rom. 3:9; 6:1, 15; 7:7; 9:14). (4) Hypothetical objections are posed by the author (Dio Chrysostom, *Or.* 74.8, 23; Rom. 3:1) or attributed to an imaginary interlocutor ("You will say," Rom. 9:19; 11:19). (5) Objections and false conclusions are rejected with such expressions as "not at all!" or "by no means!" (Epictetus 4.8.26–28; Rom. 3:4; 6:2; 9:14; 11:1) and by citing examples (Abraham in Rom. 4:1). (6) Objections or false conclusions are placed at major turns in the argument (Rom. 3:1; 6:1; 7:7; 9:14) and are often restated in subsections (3:9; 6:15; 7:13; 9:19). (7) Ironic imperatives and hortatory subjunctives used ironically are frequent, e.g., "If the dead are not raised, 'Let us eat and drink, for tomorrow we die'" (1 Cor. 15:32).

Paul was a Christian teacher of both Jews and Gentiles. The diatribe is a teaching style that he used in dealing with various constituencies both orally and through letters. He used the diatribe style extensively in Romans since he knew less about the recipients' situation than he did about communities he himself had founded. His teaching in Romans was therefore not called forth specifically by the epistolary situation but by his past experience as a teacher of Jews and Gentiles. Diatribe style occurs only occasionally in 1 Corinthians and Galatians because Paul is more familiar with the local situation and tailors his advice more directly to the epistolary situation he creates. The presence of diatribe style in James coheres with the author's extensive use of general paraenetic material not specifically formulated to fit a specific epistolary situation.

Diatribe and midrash. Ulmer (1997), in a comparative study of the use of argumentation in the midrashim and the Greek diatribe, lists a number of rhetorical techniques and tropes found in both types of texts: asyndeton, anaphora, parataxis, similes, citations, anecdotes, exempla, sententia, prokatalepsis, questions, and counterquestions. Forms of argumentation found in both types of text include thesis and antithesis, syllogism, analogies, comparisons, and a fortiori.

Diatribe in the NT and ECL. Although the Cynic-Stoic diatribe as a popular form of moral exhortation and discourse is widely regarded as having had a decisive impact on the formal style of the Pauline letters, Hebrews, and James, its impact on their content (mutatis mutandis) has been less widely considered. The clearest and most concentrated use of the diatribe in the NT is in Romans and 1 Cor. 15:29–34, though vestiges of this popular oral-literary style are found in varying proportions throughout Christian epistolary literature. While the letters of Ignatius are still regarded as having been influenced by the Asianic rhetoric of the author's Hellenistic education, there are few features of his style that cannot be accounted for by hypothecating the influence of the characteristic style and rhetoric of the diatribe form. Stowers (1981, 85–115; 1984, 707–22) has argued that Romans exhibits the use of diatribe style in several passages (Rom. 2:1–5, 17–29; 3:1–9; 3:27–4:25; 6:1–16; 9:19–21; 11:17–24; 14:4–10).

**Clement, First Letter of,* *James, letter of *Romans, Paul's Letter to the

———

ADB 2.190–93; Aune 1975; 1987, 200–202; 1999; Blomquist 1997; Campbell 1994; *DNP* 3.530–33; Donfried 1991b; Fuentes González 1998; Gottschalk 1982, 1983; Jocelyn 1982, 1983; Malherbe 1989b; Porter 1990, 1991; Schmeller 1987; Stowers 1981, 1984, 1988, 1994; Ulmer 1997

Dicolon, synonymous with *bicolon, normally refers to a two-line poetic couplet. Dicolon can also refer to the pairing of two words with similar meaning, a popular rhetorical device in classical Latin, e.g. *lepida hilara* ("charming and gay"), *reppulit propulit* ("pushed back and forth"), *labitur liquitur* ("glides and flows"), *dant danunt* ("give and donate"), *vi violentia* ("by force and violence"), *servitutem servire* ("have the status of a slave"), *armis animisque* ("by arms and courage"). This trope is popular in many Western languages including English: "bound and determined," "flotsam and jetsam," "hither and yon."

Dictation, i.e., oral discourse for the primary purpose of immediate transcription, was a method of writing often preferred among ancient authors, such as the 2d-cent. C.E. physician Galen (A. E. Hanson 1998, 27). Dio Chrysostom preferred dictation to writing himself (*Or.* 18.18): "Writing, however, I do not advise you to engage in with your own hand, or only very rarely, but rather dictate to a secretary [ἐπιδιδόναι]." Cicero also gave several reasons for dictating his letters (*Ad Quint.* 2.2.1; 2.16.1; 3.1.19; 3.3.1). Quintilian discusses some of the disadvantages of dictation: unlike dictation, writing by hand is slower and gives us time to think; the presence of a stenographer has a negative effect on the dictation process; and a slow stenographer can be an hindrance (10.3.18–20). Skeat (1956) argued that some extant manuscripts, such as the 4th-cent. C.E. biblical manuscript Codex Sinaiticus, had been dictated. Evidence for this proposal is based on the numerous phonetic errors that occur in the manuscript. A brief description of an author's role in manuscript production is found in a description of the literary activity of Origen (Eusebius, *Hist. eccl.* 6.23.2; LCL trans.): "For as he [Origen] dictated there were ready at hand more than seven shorthand-writers [ταχυγράφοι], who relieved each other at fixed times, and as many copyists [βιβλιογράφοι], as well as girls skilled in penmanship [καλλιγράφειν]."

Dictation is indirectly related to the general practice of reading aloud, which was the normal way to read in antiquity (Balogh 1927). Balogh investigated the association, in Latin literature, of the adjective *tacitus* ("silent, silently") in the immediate context of the verb *legere* ("to read") and concluded that reading aloud was the norm, while reading silently (often with the lips moving) was exceptional.

DNP 1:34–39; Dorandi 1991, 1993; A. E. Hanson 1998; Petitmengin and Flusin 1984; Skeat 1956

Didache, a transliteration of the Greek word διδαχή ("teaching"), a shortened form of the title of the *Teaching of the Twelve Apostles*, is a short handbook of early Christian ethics and liturgy (on the title, see Audet [1958, 91–103]), who argues that the original title was Διδαχαὶ τῶν ἀποστόλων [1958, 102]. The short title in *Codex Hierosolymitanus* 54, which occupies a line separated from the text, is Διδαχὴ τῶν δώδεκα ἀποστόλων ("Teaching of the Twelve Apostles"), while the long title that begins the text is Διδαχὴ κυρίου διὰ τῶν δώδεκα ἀποστόλων τοῖς ἔθνεσιν ("Teaching of the Lord through the Twelve Apostles to the Nations"). Cyprian refers to it as the *Doctrinae apostolorum*, and Eusebius refers to "the so-called Teachings of the Apostles [τῶν ἀποστόλων αἱ λεγόμεναι Διδαχαί]," as belonging to the νόθοι, "spurious [books]" (*Hist. eccl.* 3.25.4), along with the *Acts of Paul,* the Shepherd of Hermas, the *Apocalypse of Peter,* the *Epistle of Barnabas,* and in the view of some, the Revelation to John. Somewhat later (367 C.E.), Athanasius (*Festal Letter* 39) referred to "the so-called teaching of the apostles [Διδαχὴ τῶν ἀποστόλων]," with other writings permitted for the instruction of catechumens, such as Tobit, the Wisdom of Solomon, Ecclesiasticus, Esther, and the Shepherd. There is general consensus that the *Didache* originated in a rural area in Syria-Palestine, which is unusual, since most early Christian literature arose in urban centers (Crossan 1998a, 372–73).

The dating of the *Didache* is a rather subjective issue, since there are no clear internal or external indications of date. While some date the composition of the *Didache* to ca. 50–70 C.E. (Audet 1958, 187–210; Rordorf and Tulilier 1978 date it to 70 or shortly thereafter), a date between 100 and 125 C.E. is more reasonable. There are also those who date the *Didache* to the second half of the 2d cent. C.E. (R. A. Kraft 1965, 76–77). However, dating is particularly problematic for a document that is almost certainly composite (see below), for each component could well have originated at a different time and place, and the final date would refer only to the last redaction of the text. Some of the main sources must have almost certainly originated before the end of the 1st cent. C.E. (Niederwimmer 1993, 78–80).

There are several primitive features, which suggest an earlier rather than a later date: (1) The section concerning how to deal with traveling apostles and prophets (*Did.* 11–15) seems to reflect a primitive situation in which itinerancy is common and local churches are less hierarchically structured and have relatively loose connections with other Christian communities. (2) The eucharistic prayers for the community meal in *Did.* 9–10 are striking because they contain no reference to the body and blood of Jesus, unlike the Pauline eucharistic prayers in 1 Cor. 11:23–26 (see Lietzmann 1979, 188–94). (3) These eucharistic prayers have parallels with the primitive christological titles of Jesus found also in prayers in Acts (4:30), in which Jesus is designated as παῖς [θεοῦ], "servant or child [of God]." Both features are evident in the eucharistic prayers in *Did.* 9:1–4 (trans. Cody in Jefford 1995, 5–8):

1 As for the Eucharist, give thanks this way.
2 First, with regard to the cup:
We thank you, our Father,
for the holy vine of David your servant
which you made known to us through
Jesus your servant [τοῦ παιδός σου].
To you be glory forever.
3 And with regard to the bread:
We thank you, our Father,
for the life and knowledge
which you made known to us
through Jesus your servant [τοῦ παιδός σου].
To you be glory forever.
4 As this bread lay scattered upon the mountains
and became a single loaf when it had been gathered,
may your church be gathered into your kingdom
from the ends of the earth.
For glory and power are yours,
through Jesus Christ, forever.

After the Eucharist, a concluding prayer is inserted (*Did.* 10:2–6):

> 2 We thank you, holy Father, for your holy name, which you have caused to dwell in our hearts, and for the knowledge and faith and immortality which you have made known to us through your son Jesus [τοῦ παιδός σου]; to you be the glory forever. 3 You, Almighty Master, created all things for the sake of your name, and give men food and drink to enjoy, that they might give thanks to you, but to us you give spiritual food and drink and eternal life through your son [τοῦ παιδός σου]. 4 Above all, we give thanks that you are powerful; to you be the glory forever. 5 Remember your congregation, Lord, to redeem it from all evil and perfect it in your love; and gather it together, the one that has been sanctified, from the four winds into your kingdom which you have prepared for it; for yours is the kingdom and the glory forever. 6 May grace come, and may this world pass away. Hosanna to the God of David! If anyone is holy let him come; if anyone is not, let him repent. Maranatha. Amen.

It is striking that the prayer over the cup in 9:1–4 precedes the prayer over the bread, unlike the order found in Paul (1 Cor. 11:23–26) and the Synoptic Gospels (Mark 14:22–24; Matt. 26:26–29; Luke 22:18–20).

Text. The text of the *Didache* is based on a single manuscript, Codex Briennios, completed on June 11, 1056, by a scribe named Leo, discovered in Constantinople in 1873, and published in 1883 by Philotheos Bryennios, then Metropolitan of Nicomedia, after whom it was named. The MS was moved to the library of the Greek Patriarchate in Jerusalem in 1887, and was renamed *Codex Hierosolymitanus* 54, where it remains (on this MS, see van de Sandt and Flusser 2002, 16–24; I have personally examined this manuscript in the Library of the Greek Patriarchate in Jerusalem). The Jerusalem Codex also contains the *Epistle of Barnabas*, *1 Clement*, *2 Clement*, and the long form of the letters of Ignatius of Antioch, and several other works). Two small Greek fragments of a single MS of the *Didache* were found at Oxyrhyncus (P. Oxy 1782) dating to the 4th cent. C.E. (containing 1:3c–4a and 2:7–3:2). In addition, fragments of a Coptic translation have also been found (P. Lond. Or. 9271), dating to the 3d or 4th cent. C.E. (containing 10:3b–12:2a), which some argue represents an earlier and shorter version of the *Didache* that ended with 12:2 (Patterson and Jefford 1989–90, a view refuted by Jones and Mirecki 1995, 82–83). Part of the *Didache* was incorporated into the *Didascalia* (2d to 3d cent.) and the *Liber Graduum* (3d to 4th cent.), and was included in its entirety in the *Apostolic Constitutions* (3d to 4th cent.). There is also a Latin translation of *Did.* 1–6 (Schlect 1901).

Content. The *Didache* consists of four sections: (1) a section focusing on Christian ethics (1–6); (2) a section focusing on instructions about liturgy (7–10); (3) a section focusing on the protocol for dealing with traveling apostles and prophets (11–15); and (3) a concluding eschatological scenario (16). The literary analysis of these sections suggests that the *Didache* is a composite document, combined by one or two editors (Neiderwimmer 1998, 42–52; Kloppenborg 2000, 134–35).

Literary genre. There is widespread agreement that the genre of the *Didache* is that of the *church order, for the text focuses on the topics of catechesis (*Did.* 1–6), liturgy (7–10, 14), church offices (11–13, 15), and eschatological paraenesis (16), and generally neglects doctrinal or theological issues (Niederwimmer 1993, 13; Schöllgen 1996). Yet the genre issue is problematic, since each of the major sections of the *Didache* belongs to a different literary genre (Niederwimmer 1993, 13; van de Sandt and Flusser 2002, 28). Catechesis, liturgy, and church offices with very detailed rules are the main focus of church orders, not dogmatic questions. Schöllgen (1996) argues that the *Didache* is not a comprehensive church order and that its intention is not to regulate the life of the community as a whole or even its most important areas. The *Didache* is concerned with external forms already existing in communities; it corrects abuses and addresses new rules to changed circumstances.

Sources and redactional elements. There is wide agreement among scholars that the *Didache* is not a homogenous text (van de Sandt and Flusser 2002, 28). One apparently redactional insertion is the short collection of sayings of Jesus (1:3b–2:1) between 1.1–3a and 2.2 (van de Sandt and Flusser 2002, 40–42). *Didache* 1:3b–2:1 does not occur in the *Doctrina XII apostolorum* (Schlecht 1901) or the *Canons of the Holy Apostles* (Schermann 1914). This section is found in the *Apostolic Constitutions* (7.2.2–6), which is therefore dependent on the *Didache* and not on an earlier Two Ways source.

There are convincing reasons for regarding as incomplete the ending of the *Didache,* which breaks off abruptly at 16:8 (Aldridge 1999). Aldridge (1999) argues convincingly that the original ending of the *Didache,* or at least one version of it, is preserved in *Apost. Const.* 7.32, which adds the following four-and-one-half verses to the ending:

> [8]Then the world will see the Lord coming upon the clouds of heaven with the angels of His power, in the throne of His kingdom, [9]to condemn the devil, the deceiver of the world, and to render to every one according to his deeds. [10]Then shall the wicked go away into everlasting punishment, but the righteous shall enter eternal life, [11]to inherit those things which eye hath not seen, nor ear heard, nor have entered into the heart of man, such things as God hath prepared for them that love Him. [12]And they shall rejoice in the kingdom of God, which is in Christ Jesus.

The Two Ways tradition. The most widely accepted written source for the *Didache* is the so-called Two Ways tradition, reflected in the close parallels between *Didache* 1–5 and *Barnabas* 18–20. The Two Ways section of *Barnabas* (18–20) is very similar to the 1QS 3.13–4.26. See *Two Ways tradition.

Outline of contents. The following outline focuses on the succession of issues with which the author-editors are dealing, without regard for the boundaries of the sources incorporated into the text. For a different, simpler outline, see Jefford 1996, 49–50.

- I. The Two Ways (1:1–6:2)
  - A. Introduction (1:1)
  - B. The way of life (1:2–4:14)
  - C. The way of death (5:1–2)
  - D. Conclusion to the Two Ways (6:1–2)
- II. Liturgical instructions (6:3–10:7)
  - A. On food (6:3)
  - B. On baptism (7:1–4)
  - C. On fasting (8:1)
  - D. On prayer (8:2–3)
  - E. Eucharistic prayers (9:1–10:7)
    - 1. Prayers of the cup and bread (9:1–5)
      - a. Introduction (9:1)
      - b. Over the cup (9:2)
      - c. Over the bread (9:3–4)
      - d. Requirement for participation (9:5)
    - 2. Concluding prayer (10:1–7)
- III. Dealing with itinerant ministers (11:1–14:7)
  - A. Teachers (11:1–2)
  - B. Apostles and prophets (11:3–12)
  - C. Other itinerant Christians (12:1–5)
  - D. Prophets who come to stay (13:1–7)
- IV. Moral requirements for weekly worship (14:1–3)
- V. Qualifications for bishops and deacons (15:1–2)
- VI. Concluding exhortations (15:3–4)
- VII. Eschatological sanctions for moral behavior (16:1–8)

The Didache and ECL. The *Didache* also contains a version of the Lord's Prayer (8:2), which is very close to the version found in Matt. 6:9–13. Schnelle (1998, 355) thinks that by "the gospel" (8:2; 11:3; 15:3, 4) the compiler means the Gospel of Matthew. Similarities with the sayings of Jesus in Matthew may suggest that Matthew and the *Didache* both stem from related communities in Syria-Palestine (Mack 1995, 241–42).

*Apostolic Fathers, *Church order, *Two Ways tradition

Aldridge 1999; Audet 1958; Connolly 1929; Court 1981; Dix 1937; Draper 1996a, 1996b; Jefford 1989, 1995; Kraft 1965; Niederwimmer 1998; Patterson and Jefford 1989–90; Rordorf and Tuilier 1978; Schöllgen 1991, 1996;

Tuckett 1996b; van de Sandt and Flusser 2002; Wengst 1984

Didactic literature refers to literature intended to be instructional or to inculcate certain sets of values in the reader. A number of narrative works in early Judaism have a predominantly didactic character: Tobit, Judith, the Letter of Aristeas, 3 Maccabees, and 4 Maccabees. Hellenistic education assumed that classical Greek poetic and prose works taught moral lessons. The NT and early Christian epistolary literature is primarily didactic in character.

P. R. Davies 2001

Didascalia apostolorum, or "Teaching of the Apostles," is a work which exists in complete form only in a Syriac translation and in partial form in a Latin translation of a Greek original composed in Syria during the first half of the 3d cent. C.E. (Vööbus 1979, 1 [402].23). The work is pseudepigraphical, since it reinterprets Acts 15 and presents itself as having been written jointly by the 12 apostles (*Didascalia* 24): "it seemed to us in one mind to write this catholic Didascalia for the confirmation of you all" (Vööbus 1979, 4 [408].214). The *Didascalia* forms the first six chapters of the *Apostolic Constitutions*. The fictitious setting of the work is that of the Apostolic Council in Acts 15, ignoring the Pauline letters (i.e., Gal. 2) completely (J. Taylor 1992). Generically, the *Didascalia* belongs to the *church order genre and also contains a great deal of *paraenesis. Though widely thought to have originated in Jewish-Christian circles, the *Didascalia* is typically read as a Christian text. Fonrobert (2001) argues that the *Didascalia*, written within a generation of the codification of the Mishnah, was framed as a "counter-Mishnah" for Christians.

R. H. Connolly 1929; Fonrobert 2001; Taylor 1992; Vööbus 1979

Digression, based on the Latin term *digressio* (related terms are *egressio, egressus, excessus*), a translation of the Greek rhetorical terms παράβασις, παρέκβασις, ἐκδρομή, or ἐκβολή (on the latter, Thucydides 1.97).

Rhetoric. Digressio, not mentioned by Aristotle in his *Rhetorica*, finds its classical expression in Cicero's *De oratore* in his discussion of **dispositio*, under the aspect of *conciliare*, i.e., the gaining the goodwill of the audience (2.307–32). As a rhetorical term, *digressio* refers to the insertion of a relatively long and independent segment into a text with which it is somehow thematically connected (Cicero, *De oratore* 3.53.203; Quintilian 4.3.12). Cicero suggests that a *digressio* can be effective in eliciting emotion, and therefore suggests that the most appropriate place for inserting one in a speech is in the introduction or conclusion (*De oratore* 2.77 [311]). Quintilian recommends several persuasive topics and functions for this figure: praise of persons and places, description of regions, records of particular historical or legendary events (4.3.12). Some digressions can simply be pleasant diversions, such as Cicero's digression on the history of Ceres and Proserpina on the island of Sicily in his case against Verres (*Verrine Orations* 2.4.48–49 [107–8]; cf. Volkmann 1885, 152). Cicero inserts a very lengthy and complex ethical digression in *Pro Milone* 72–91 in which he progresses from reasoned argument to arguments from character and emotion (May 1979). He defines παρέκβασις as "the handling of some theme, which must however have some bearing on the case, in a speech" (4.3.14; on the use of digressions in Cicero, see Canter 1931). Quintilian suggests that a *digressio* may sometimes, but not routinely, be placed after the *narratio* (4.3.4; cf. Cicero, *De oratore* 2.77 [312]). In *De inventione* 1.19 [27], Cicero mentions that a digression can be added to a *narratio* "for the purpose of attacking somebody, or of making a comparison, or of amusing the audience in a way not incongruous with the business in hand, or for amplification."

Greco-Roman literature. Digressions are also a literary phenomenon, defined as a temporary interruption of the flow of a narrative or exposition, in which the author treats a matter not directly related to the subject at hand. Literary and rhetorical digressions are obviously very closely related. Ancient authors were not (for example), trained to write history, but rather trained in rhetoric, which they applied to historiography. After particularly long digressions, authors frequently pick up the main threads of the narrative again with an apology to the reader (Dio Chrysostom, *Or.* 12.38). Thucydides, who normally excluded biographical details from his narrative, included several biographical digressions, such as those on Kylon (1.126.3–12), Pausanias (1.128–34), and Themistocles (1.138). Similarly Xenophon included biographical digressions in his *Anabasis*, including the one on Cyrus (1.9).

Digressions can function in several ways: (1) they can be the ancient equivalent of footnotes, appendices, and excursuses; (2) they may supply important background information necessary for understanding the narrative (e.g., geographical information, descriptions of institutions and customs, surveys of conditions); (3) they may have a didactic function, emphasizing the moral and political lessons to be drawn from the narrative (often in Polybius, e.g., 4.31; 4.74; see also 2 Macc. 6:12–17, an address to the reader); and (4) they can provide variety and enjoyment by relieving a long and tedious narrative (see Polybius 38.5–6; Diodorus 20.2.1) and by including entertaining stories (Polybius 38.6.2). Herodotus included more than 200 digressions in his history, including all of book 2, which is a digression on Egypt. Literature and rhetoric were closely related in the ancient world. So closely related, in fact, that many of our modern assumptions about ancient literature are misleading. The numerous (and entertaining) excursuses in the first six books of Herodotus's *History of the Persian Wars,* for example, appear to be there precisely because he wrote with the intention of public recitation. Digressions are often difficult to distinguish from later insertions or *interpolations, since they are often framed by an **inclusio*.

Graeco-Jewish literature. Josephus begins his *Contra Apionem* with a digression (1.6–56) that he specifically labels a παρέκβασις ("digression") in 1.57. This section is not really a digression, for it demolishes the assumption that everything worth saying about history was said by Greeks (Mason 1992, 77). In the same work, Josephus frames a long digression on the three philosophical traditions within Judaism by beginning with a reference to Jewish philosophizing (*Contra Apionem* 2.119) and using this same term when he concludes the digression in 2.166: "Such is what I have to say on the Jewish philosophical schools." He inserts a much shorter digression on the same subject in a later work, *Antiquities* 13.171–73, which concludes with a cross-reference to the earlier treatment in *Contra Apionem* 2.119–66: "Of these matters, however, I have given a more detailed account in the second book of the Jewish History."

NT and ECL. In the NT, 2 Cor. 6:14–7:1 is widely considered an interpolation or digression. It is preceded by 2 Cor. 6:13 ("In return—I speak as to children—widen your hearts also"), and followed by 2 Cor. 7:2 ("Open your hearts to us; we have wronged no one"). Digressions or excursuses have been identified in the Pauline letters: 1 Cor. 2:6–16; 6:1–11; 9:1–27; 10:1–13; 13:1–13 (J. Weiss 1910, xliii; Kümmel 1975, 278), and 2 Cor. 5:14–6:2 (Kümmel 1975, 281). C. Koester (2002, 117–19) identifies three digressions in Hebrews (5:11–6:20; 10:26–39; 12:25–27) and argues that they serve as transition between major argumentative sections of the text (2:10–5:10; 7:1–10:39) and between the final argumentative section (11:1–12:27) and the peroration.

**ekphrasis, *inclusio,* *interpolation

R. D. Anderson 2000, 85–86; Austin 1966; Barker 1976; Canter 1931; Chihocka 1975; Emmet 1981; Gaisser 1969; Härter 2000; C. Koester 2002; May 1979; Race 1978, 1980; Volkmann 1885, 164–67

Diogenes Laertius (DL) is the author of the Βίοι φιλόσοφων or *Vitae prophetarum,* "Lives of the Philosophers" (*VP*), written toward the beginning of the 3d cent. C.E. (ca. 217 C.E.; see Hope 1930, 6–7). Nothing is known of DL's life apart from disputed views that have been teased out of various opaque passages in his work (*DNP* 3:601). *VP* is the more important of three collections of biographies of persons from a single professional category that have survived from antiquity, the other two of which are *Philostratus, *Lives of the Sophists*, and Ps.-Plutarch, *Lives of the Ten Orators* (among fragmentary survivals are the two or three fragments of Seleucus of Alexandria's *Lives of Philosophers* (Radicke 1999, 1056, F1–3). The *VP* is a skewed source for Greek philosophy but is valuable to the extent that DL uses or cites valuable sources (Hope 1930, 96; on his use of sources, see Mejer 1978, 7–16, 29–46). DL tends to mention sources when treating philosopher's lives but not when presenting their teachings (Mejer 1978, 4), a characteristic that suggests where his real interests lie. Combining *biography (including many anecdotes or *chreiai) with *doxography and a bibliography of the subject's written works (an example of ancient *biobibliography), he treats 82 individuals, some of whom left no writings at all.

Purpose. DL writes within an existing historiographical διαδοχαί tradition that traced the internal relationships of schools of philosophical thought by means of persons rather than ideas. διαδοχή ("legitimate succession") is the process by which a particular philosopher is succeeded by another in a philosophical tradition and how a philosophical system itself grows (Brent 1999, 182). DL writes within a well-defined generic tradition of διαδοχαί, and refers to several earlier writers who also wrote works entitled Διαδοχαὶ τῶν φιλόσοφων or Διαδοχὴ φιλόσοφων, "Successions of the Philosophers" (or very similar titles), such as Sotion, fl. 200–170 B.C.E. (1.1, 7; 2.12, 74, 85; 5.86; 6.80; 8.86; 9.110, 112); Alexander Polyhistor, ca. 110–after 40 B.C.E., FGrH 273 (1.116; 2.19, 106; 3.4, 5; 4.62; 7.179; 8.24); Sosicrates (1.107; 2.84; 6.13, 80; 8.8); Antisthenes of Rhodes, *FGH* 508 (referred to 13 times including 2.39, 98; 6.77, 87; 7.168; 9.6, 27, 35). Since DL ends his work in the late 3d cent. B.C.E. with Epicurus (341–271 B.C.E.) and Chrysippus (282–206 B.C.E.), it is obvious that he regards the golden age of Greek philosophy as a thing of the past (Brent 1999, 182; see *archaism). The philosophical possibilities for him reached an end with the development of Platonism, Stoicism, Aristotelianism, and Epicureanism. For DL, there were two origins (ἀρχαί) of philosophy, one which got its start with Anaximander (a student of the sage Thales) and concluded with Cleitomachus, Chrysippus, and Theophrastus, with whom the school of Ionia came to an end (1.13–15). The other origin, the Italian school, began with Pythagoras (the student of the sage Pherecydes) and concluded with Epicurus (1.13–15). DL wrote with one dominant purpose, to demonstrate (in opposition to his predecessors who had written in the διαδοχαί genre) that philosophy was something specifically Greek (Mejer 1978, 51; Brent 1999, 183). DL is an unabashed Hellenocentrist: "These authors [his predecessors] forget that the achievements they attribute to the barbarians belong to the Greeks, with whom not merely philosophy but the human race itself began" (1.2). DL therefore regards his succession schema as confirming the coherence of the philosophical traditions of Hellenistic civilization (Brent 1999, 184).

Structure and contents. In the **prooimion* (especially 1.13–16), DL provides an overview of the subjects he will treat in his work. He arranges the individual philosophers in two unequal main geographical divisions, the Ionian or eastern philosophers (books 1–7) and the Italian or western philosophers (book 8), followed by a treatment of the σποράδην or "scattered" category of philosophers (8.91), i.e., those who did not found communities and who did not found successions, i.e., Heraclitus and Xenophanes, Parmenides, Melissus, Zeno of Elea, and Leucippus (book 9). He concludes with a treatment of Epicurus (book 10). Throughout, he organizes individual philosophers by school and chronologically, focusing on the principle of succession (even when completely fabricated, as in the case of the Cynics). DL uses a stereotypical pattern in his work (*DNP* 3.602): (1) the patronym and origins of the philosopher, (2) his teachers, (3) the period of adult activity, death, and the provisions of the will (if any), (4) a synopsis of his teaching, (5) anecdotes or chreiai from his life, (6) maxims, and (7) a list of other famous persons with the same name. The work consists of ten books, which treat the following subjects: Book 1: The Seven Wise Men (Thales, Solon, Chilon, Pittakos, Bias, Kleobulos, Periander, and several additions). Book 2: Ionian philosophers (including Anaximander, Anaximines, Anaxagaoras, and Archelaos), Socrates and the Socratics (Xenophon, Aeschines, Aristippos, Phaedo, Euclides, Stilpo, Krito, Simon, Glaukon, Simmias, Cebes, Menedemus). Book 3: Plato. Book 4: Plato's successors in the Academy from Speusippos to Kleitomachos. Book 5: Aristotle, Theophrastus, and their successors to Heraklides in the Lyceum. Book 6: Antisthenes, Diogenes, and later Cynics (Monimos, Onesikratos, Krates, Metrokles, Hipparchia, Menippos, and Menedemos). Book 7: the Stoics from Zeno to Chrysippos. Book 8: The Italian philosophers, beginning with Pythagoras and including Empedocles and Eudoxos. Book 9: A miscellaneous group including Heraklitos, Xenophanes, Parmenides, Demokritos, Protagoras, and Pyrrho the Sceptic. Book 10: Epicurus, concluding with his κύριοι δόξαι.

Relevance to NT and ECL. Based on the model of *VP*, Talbert (1974, 125–34) has argued that Luke–Acts is a *succession narrative*, a type of Greco-Roman biography. His argument is based on the judgment that the *VP* has three major components: (1) life of the founder (the founders of the Greek philosophical schools, e.g., Plato, Aristotle, Epicurus, were venerated as divine figures); (2) narratives about disciples and successors (the successors of the founder formed a type of religious community "created and sustained by the divine figure," a community which possessed "many of the characteristics of a church" [1974, 126]); (3) summaries of the doctrine of the philosophical schools, "sometimes in the words of the founder, sometimes in the words of his disciples and successors" (1974, 127). He further suggests that it is necessary to determine the function each of these three elements would have had independently of their combination in DL (1974, 128): (1) the life of a philosopher was designed to define the way of life of the school or group associated with him; (2) a succession list or narrative indicated where the true and living tradition of the school could be found; (3) the list of books and a summary of the master's teaching ensured an accurate rather than a skewed view of the tradition.

A number of scholars have found Talbert's proposal suggestive. L. Alexander found Talbert's thesis that Luke–Acts is a "biographical succession narrative" attractive, though ultimately inadequate. Taking a clue from Talbert, L. Alexander suggests that "The role of such biographical material within the school traditions should certainly be explored in any future investigation of the literary genre of Luke–Acts" (1993, 202–3). She finally concludes, however, that "the difficulties involved in treating the Gospel as a 'philosophical biography' suggest that we should be looking in a different direction" (L. Alexander 1993, 204).

While this intriguing proposal has the advantage of suggesting a generic analogy to the whole of Luke–Acts, it founders in several respects: (1) διαδοχαί literature, based on the analogy with dynastic succession, was limited to the histories of philosophical schools. Despite the cultic features of Hellenistic philosophical schools, the divinity of their founders (somewhat overemphasized by Talbert), and a superficial resemblance of early Christian groups to philosophical schools or "scholastic communities" (Judge 1960; see Malherbe 1983, 45–59) during the first century, Christian communities simply did not consider themselves philosophical schools (though this idea does appear before the mid-2d cent. C.E., particularly in Rome; see Brent 1999). (2) Talbert observes that, although the biographical schema in the *VP* is topical rather than chronological, other ancient biographies exhibit the same arrangement (1974, 128). True enough, but those biographical traditions he is referring to are Alexandrian and were designed for treating the lives of artists, authors, and philosophers. Luke–Acts, by contrast, is a chronological narrative with a plot and is far different from DL's treatment of the lives of philosophers. Though Talbert argues that VP "usually" consists of three elements (life+successors+teachings), only six of the 82 lives exhibit this pattern (Aristippos, Plato, Zeno, Pythagoras, Pyrrho, Epicurus). (2) Talbert's contention that the succession narrative reveals where authentic tradition is found is not confirmed in *VP*, where the concern is rather who studies with whom and who succeeds whom, not with the legitimacy of their views. (3) The phrase "succession *narrative*" is an inappropriate designation for brief *lists* of students or successors. Nevertheless, *VP* contains an invaluable collection of biographies shaped in the early 3d cent. C.E.

*Biography

———

L. Alexander 1993; Bickermann 1952; Brent 1999; Hope 1930; Judge 1960; Malherbe 1983; Mejer 1978; Talbert 1974

Diognetus, Letter to, an anonymous apologetic treatise, falsely attributed to Justin, has been associated with the mixed group of texts in the *Apostolic Fathers since 1765, though it would more appropriately be grouped with the early Christian *apologists.

Date. *Diognetus* has been dated as early as before 70 C.E., a view based on the fact that the existence of the Jewish sacrificial cult and of the temple (*Diogn.* 3:5) is apparently presupposed (Marrou 1962, 242–43), and the 13th- or 14th-cent. MS that solely attests the text of *Diognetus* is based on an exemplar not later than the 7th cent. C.E. (Harnack 1958, 513). Within these wide chronological boundaries, Harnack (1958, 514) suggests the narrower time frame of 110–310 C.E., probably toward the middle of that period. F. Overbeck (1965, 1–92) argued forcefully for a post-Constantinian date, suggesting the 4th or 5th cent. C.E. (1965, 74). However, the references to persecution (1:1; 2:6; 5:11–6:10; 7:7–9; 10:7–8) actually indicate that the Constantinian period is the *terminus ante quem* (Wengst 1984, 307). Overbeck was fully aware of these references (1965, 12–16, 55–56, 86–87) but regarded them as part of a literary fiction. Baumeister (1988), even more than Wengst (1984, 307), argues that the frequent references to persecution cannot possibly be fictional. He goes on to argue that technical Christian martyrological language (e.g., μάρτυς="martyr," ὁμολογεῖν, "confess," ὁμολογία, "confession") is not attested earlier than the *Martyrdom of Polycarp*, ca. 160 C.E. He concludes, after a brief survey of the appearance of martyological language in various areas of the Roman Empire, that *Diognetus* must have been written before the work of *Clement of Alexandria, probably in Alexandria (a locale for which he provides no supporting argumentation) and probably before 200 C.E. Baumeister should have based his case for the nonfictional references to persecution on the absence of the kind of technical martyrological language one might expect in a 3d- or 4th-cent.

context. The logic of his argument also suggests a date *before* the composition of the *Martyrdom of Polycarp*, ca. 155 C.E. Since the work has numerous similarities with 2d-cent. Christian *apologetic literature, a date of ca. 150 C.E. appears probable for many scholars (Bihlmeyer 1956, xlix; Meecham 1949, 62–63; Wengst 1984, 308).

Text. The text of *Diognetus,* along with four works attributed to *Justin Martyr, was preserved in a single manuscript (*Argentoratensis Graecus* 9) dating from the 13th or 14th cent. C.E. that was located in the Stadtbibliothek of Strassburg, but was was destroyed during the Prussian siege of the city on August 24, 1870 (Wengst 1984, 285–86). However, three copies of the MS were made in the 16th cent. *Diognetus* is not cited in any early Christian document.

Integrity. Despite arguments for the unity of *Diognetus* (Marrou 1965, 219–27), it is generally agreed that chapters 11–12 constitute a secondary addition by a different author (Harnack 1958, 515; Wengst 1984, 287–90). The main arguments for the secondary character of this section include: (1) *Diogn.* 11–12 exhibits *Asianic rhetoric, a style not found in *Diogn.* 1–10. (2) *Diogn.* 1–10 is directed to a pagan public, while *Diogn.* 11–12 is aimed at a Christian readership. (3) *Diogn.* 11–12 uses proof from OT prophecy, while this is missing from *Diogn.* 1–10. (4) In *Diogn.* 1–10 "Greeks" and "Jews" are played off against each other, but *Diogn.* 11–12 mentions neither.

Genre. Diognetus was incorrectly labeled a letter (by Henricus Stephanus in the editio princeps of 1552), but since it does not have an epistolary form (contra Bihlmeyer 1956, xlviii and Meecham 1949, 7–9), it is a treatise that should rather be titled *Ad Diognetum*, on analogy with other works such as Theophilus, *Ad Autolycum* and Tertullian, *Ad Scapulum* (Marrou 1965, 92 n. 2). Scholars are agreed that *Diognetus* has an apologetic and protreptic character (Marrou 1965, 92–93; Baumeister 1988, 110). The work is a λόγος προτρεπτικός, or "speech of exhortation" (see *Protreptic literature, and *Analysis* below), intended to win converts and introduce them to a new way of life (Aune 1991d, 105; *DNP* 3.607).

Style. Diognetus contains 698 words, of which ca. 95 percent are classical (i.e., in the Greek lexicon before 322 B.C.E.), while just 34 are postclassical (Meecham 1949, 9). According to Norden (1958, 2.513 n. 2) "the Letter of Diognetus, from all these perspectives [i.e., contents, arrangement, style, and language], belongs to the most splendid of works written by Christians in the Greek language." Chapters 5–6 exhibit a structural unity that consists of numerous parallels in thought between chapter 5 and chapter 6 (Lona 2000). One large segment of chapter 5 consists of a striking series of asyndetic clauses and sentences (5:5–17):

> [5]They live in their own homelands,
> but (ἀλλ') like aliens;
>
> They share everything like citizens,
> but (καί) endure everything like strangers.
>
> Every foreign country is their homeland,
> but (καί) every homeland is a foreign country.
>
> [6]They marry like everyone, they bear children,
> but (ἀλλ') do not expose their infants.
>
> [7]They furnish an open table,
> but (ἀλλ') not an open bed.
>
> [8]They live "in" the flesh,
> but (ἀλλ') they do not live "according to" the flesh.
>
> [9]They live on earth,
> but (ἀλλ') they are citizens of heaven.
>
> [10]They obey the established laws,
> yet (καί) in private behavior, they excel the laws.
>
> [11]They love everyone
> but (καί) are persecuted by everyone.
>
> [12]They are unknown,
> but (καί) they are condemned.
>
> They are put to death,
> but (καί) they are made alive.
>
> [13]They are poor,
> but (καί) they enrich many.
>
> They lack everything,
> but (καί) have everything in abundance.
>
> [14]They are dishonored,
> but (καί) they are glorified in their dishonor.
>
> They are maligned,
> but (καί) they are vindicated.
>
> [15]They are abused,
> but (καί) they are blessed.
>
> They are insulted,
> but (καί) they give respect.
>
> [16]When they do good, they are punished as evildoers,
> when they are punished they rejoice as those made alive.

[17]By the Jews they are attacked as aliens,
and (καί) by the Greeks they are persecuted,
and (καί) the reason for their hostility, those who despise them cannot explain.

This entire section is set apart from its context by the calculated omission of connective particles between the 17 short antithetical clauses and sentences in vv. 5–15 (the second antithetical clause is introduced either with ἀλλά or καί-*adversativus* (Blomqvist 1979). The passage changes style and tempo in v. 16 with a bicolon of synonymous *parallelism, and concludes with a tricolon underlining the irrationality of the general antagonism toward Christians. The use of *asyndeton here functions to increase the tempo and emotion of the language used (Longinus 20.1–3; Lausberg 1998, §709).

The elaborately crafted section in 5:5–17 is matched by a second extended series of largely asyndetic comparisons (see *asyndeton*) that amplify the theme stated in 6:1: "What the soul is to the body, Christians are to the world." Though others have found no real parallels to this theme in the ancient world, J. B. Bauer (1963), on the basis of a partial parallel in Aphrahat (ca. 345 C.E.), argues that the elaborate metaphor originated with early Judaism or Jewish Christianity, though his suggestion is far from persuasive. σύγκρισις (see *Comparison) is one of the topoi for αὔξησις according to Theon, *Progym.* (Spengel 1853–55, 2.108, 3–15), a *trope that the author of *D* uses simply by juxtaposing the ways in which Christians are to the world what the soul is to the body, avoiding the direct use of comparative particles. The series of asyndetic comparative bicola are found in 6:2–10:

[2]The soul permeates all the limbs of the body,
and (καί) *Christians* are throughout the cities of the world

[3]The soul (μέν) inhabits the body,
but (δέ) does not belong to the body,
and (καί) *Christians* inhabit the world,
but (δέ) do not belong to the world.

[4]The soul is invisible,
confined in a visible body,
and (καί) *Christians* are known since they are in the world,
but (δέ) their piety remains invisible.

[5]The flesh detests and opposes the soul,
Though in no way mistreated,
because it hinders it from enjoying pleasures,
the world hates also (καί) Christians,
though it has in no way mistreated them,
because they oppose its pleasures.

[6]The soul loves the flesh and limbs which despise it,
and (καί) *Christians* love those who hate them.

[7]The soul (μέν) has been enclosed in the body,
but (δέ) itself holds the body together,
and (καί) *Christians* are confined (μέν) in the world as in a prison,
but (δέ) they hold the world together.

[8]The soul immortal inhabits a mortal body,
and (καί) *Christians* live as aliens among corruptible things,
Expecting the incorruptible in heaven.

[9]The soul, deprived of food and drink, becomes better,
and (καί) *Christians*, when punished daily increase.

[10]God has appointed them to such an important position,
Which is not right for them to refuse.

The work concludes with twelve short cola that exhibit the concluding rhyme called *homoioteleuton, since 11 lines end with -ται (to show this I must cite the Greek as well as the English translation of *Diog.* 12:8b–9):

ὧν ὄφις οὐχ ἅπτεται
[God] whom the serpent does not touch

οὐδὲ πλάνη συλχρωτίζεται
nor error defile

οὐδὲ Εὔα φθείρεται
nor Eve corrupt

ἀλλὰ παρθένος πιστεύεται
but a virgin is trusted

καὶ σωτήριον δείκνυται
and salvation is revealed

καὶ ἀπόστολοι συνετίξονται
and the apostles are made to understand

καὶ τὸ κυρίου πάσχα προέρχεται
and the Easter festival of the Lord approaches

καὶ καιροὶ συνάγλονται
and the seasons are brought together

καὶ μετὰ κόσμου ἁμόξονται
and are harmonized with the world

καὶ διδάσκων ἁγιους ὁ λόγος εὐφραίνεται
and the Logos rejoices while teaching the saints

δἰ οὗ πατὴρ δοξάζεται
through whom the Father is glorified

ᾧ ἡ δόξα εἰς το ὺς αἰῶνας ἀμήν
to whom is the glory for ever. Amen.

Analysis. *Diognetus* is a λόγος προτρεπτικός or *protreptic discourse (Aune 1991d, 105), divided into twelve chapters (with chapters 1–10 constituting a unified composition and 11–12 a later addition). Like other λόγοι προτρεπτικόι, the treatise falls naturally into three main parts (Aune 1991d, 95–101), framed by a *preface and a later addition (chaps. 11–12) that was probably seen by the editor as a way of amplifying chapter 10, the original conclusion of the treatise. The work begins, then, with a *prooimion* or *preface, which consists of a single periodic sentence of 114 words (*Diogn*. 1) with several of the stereotypical features of such a literary form, including a dedication to the author's social superior Diognetus (otherwise unknown), complimentary remarks about the dedicatee (a **captatio benevolentiae*), and the implication that he has requested the following work. The questions that the author attributes to Diognetus in the preface provide (in roughly reverse order) an overview of the subjects the author discusses in the treatise (LCL trans.), a strategy recommended by Cicero, *De inv*. 1.16.23 (see **Exordium*): "Who is the God in whom they [Christians] believe [chaps. 7–8], and how they worship him, so that all disregard the world and despise death [chaps. 5–6], and do not reckon as God those who are considered to be so by the Greeks [chap. 2], nor keep the superstition of the Jews [chaps. 3–4], and what is the love which they have for one another, and why this new race or practice has come to life at this time and now formerly [chaps. 9–10]." The first part (*Diogn*. 2–4) consists of a section designed to dissuade (ἀποτρέπειν) and censure (ἐλέγχειν) the two major religious options apart from Christianity: pagan idolatry (*Diogn*. 2) and Jewish superstition (*Diogn*. 3–4). In chapter 2, the author fires away with a series of 19 indicting rhetorical questions, a style typical of the *diatribe (Stowers 1981, 87). The second main part, the προτρεπτικός proper, is primarily positive and consists of an attempt to persuade (προτρέπειν) the dedicatee by describing the positive moral character of Christians and summarizing the theological basis for Christian beliefs (*Diogn*. 5–9). The third main part (*Diogn*. 10) consists of an appeal to the dedicatee to become a convert to Christianity.

*Apologetic literature, *Apostolic Fathers, *Protreptic literature

---

Andriessen 1947; Barnard 1965; Baumeister 1988; Connolly 1935; Harnack 1958, 513–15; Lona 2000; Meecham 1949; Marrou 1965; F. Overbeck 1965; Riggi 1987; Rizzi 1989; Wansink 1986; Wengst 1984

Dionysius of Halicarnassus was a Greek scholar who came to Rome in the middle of the 187th olympiad (30 B.C.E.) from his native city of Halicarnassus (*Rom. Ant*. 1.7.2–4), where he lived and worked until ca. 10 B.C.E. He taught rhetoric but also focused on the production of his large work *Roman Antiquities*, which was 22 years in the making.

Bonner 1969; Gabba 1991; Pritchett 1975; Wooten 1994

Direct discourse, or direct speech, is the use of language that reproduces the content and the expressive or subjective features of the represented utterance and is generally translated within quotation marks (Banfield 1982, 4), though with the necessary changes in pronouns and verb forms. In the *Iliad* and *Odyssey*, speech is normally presented as direct discourse, though indirect discourse is used in certain marginal instances (de Jong 1987, 114–18). About 50 percent of the *Iliad* consists of direct discourse, with 677 examples of direct speech, 88 cases of indirect discourse, rarely longer than two lines, and 39 instances in which a speech act is mentioned but not reported (de Jong 1987, 115). In the Homeric *Hymn to Demeter*, which consists of 40 percent direct speech (191 out of 495 lines), direct discourse and indirect discourse occur in approximately equal proportions (Beck 2001, 54–55).

*Indirect discourse

Banfield 1982; Beck 2001; de Jong 1987

Dispositio (see *Arrangement)

Divine names The Israelite name for God, usually transliterated Yahweh, was regarded as extremely holy, and Jews were reluctant to pronounce this divine name. Consequently a series of divine names were substituted for Yahweh, e.g., "the Most High," "the Almighty," "Adonai=Lord," thereby enriching the Israelite and Jewish vocabulary of name for God. In later rabbinic literature, God is frequently referred by the circumlocution "the Holy One, blessed be

He." One consequence of these Jewish practices is the tendency for NT and early Christian authors with Jewish backgrounds and sensitivities to use various circumlocutions for the name of God, such as "the one who sits upon the throne" (Rev. 5:1) or "the throne" (Rev. 4:6), or "the kingdom of heaven" (frequent in Matthew), or what has been called "the passive of divine activity" in such phrases as "Jesus was raised from the dead" (Rom. 6:4; 8:34; 1 Cor. 15:4), meaning "God raised Jesus from the dead."

Doxography, from the Greek words δόξαι ("opinions") and γράφή ("writing"), is a systematic collection of the opinions of philosophers on various topics. The Latinized term *doxographus* is modern, coined either by Hermann Diels or Hermann Usener (Pfeiffer 1968, 84 n. 6). There are three main types of doxographies: (1) those in which opinions on particular philosophical themes are collected; (2) the systematic summary of a philosophical school (e.g., the Epicureans, the Stoics) or of a particular philosopher (the prime example of this type is *Diogenes Laertius, who wrote on the lives, succession, and doctrines of Greek philosophers and included doxographic sections in his work; (3) succession narratives (διαδοχαί).

*Diogenes Laertius

Diels 1879; *DNP* 3.803–6; Mejer 1978, 81–89

Doxology is a short *liturgical form that usually ascribes the attribute of glory (δόξα) to God and may be modified by the use of other attributes also. A doxology is formally distinct from a blessing (i.e., a benediction or *berakah*, which is normally introduced by the term "blessed" (Greek εὐλογητός); see Pss. 41:13; 72:18–19; 89:52; 106:48; Tob. 13:18; *1 Enoch* 81:1–4. In some instances the doxology and the benediction are mixed, as in *1 Enoch* 90:40: "I woke up and blessed the Lord of righteousness and ascribed glory to him." Although doxologies are rare in Judaism, they do occur frequently in early Christian texts (Deichgräber 1967, 40–43). If a doxology is defined strictly as a liturgical form that includes the term δόξα ("glory"), there are no synagogue prayers that can be properly designated doxologies (Baumstark 1958, 67).

Form. Doxologies normally consist of four stereotypical elements (Berger 1984, 237; Aune 1997–98, 1.43–45): (1) reference to God or (less frequently) Christ (usually in the dative case; sometimes the genitive), to whom one or more attributes are ascribed; (2) mention of the specific attributes, of which δόξα ("glory") is the most common (usually in the nominative case); (3) a formula describing the length of time during which the one praised will possess this attribute, usually "forever," or "for ever and ever," or "to all generations" (Eph. 3:21), or "from generation to generation" (*Mart. Polyc.* 21); (4) a concluding "amen." All four elements are found in most succinct form in Rom. 11:36: "(1) To him (2) be the glory (3) forever. (4) Amen." Doxologies can be addressed to God either in the third-person singular (*er-Stil) or the second-person singular (*du-Stil). Doxologies in the third-person singular frequently use the relative pronoun ᾧ or the intensive pronoun αὐτῷ, either in the dative of indirect object, the dative of advantage (*dativus commodi*), or the dative of possession. Doxologies in the second person singular are comparatively rare; none occur in the NT, and only seven are found in the *Apostolic Fathers. Some are introduced with σου ("of you [sing.]" or "your [sing.]"), a pronoun in the genitive of possession, e.g., *Did.* 8:2: "Yours (σου) is the power and glory for ever" (see also *Did.* 9:4; 10:5), while more commonly they are introduced with σοί ("to you [sing.]," a pronoun in the dative of advantage, e.g., *Did.* 9:2: "To you (σοί) is the glory for ever (see also *Did.* 9:3; 10:2, 4; *1 Clem.* 61:3).

Each of the four doxological elements outlined above (with the exception of the concluding "amen") can be expanded in a variety of ways: (1) by adding and qualifying various attributes (1 Tim. 1:17: "to the King of ages, immortal, invisible, the only God"); (2) by adding attributes (two attributes: 1 Tim. 1:17; 1 Pet. 4:11; *Did.* 8:2; 9:4; 10:5; *1 Clem.* 20:12; 61:3; 64:1; four attributes: Jude 24–25; *Mart. Pol.* 21; five attributes: *1 Clem.* 65:2) or qualifying phrases (Eph. 3:21); and (3) by the addition of various expressions for unending time (Eph. 3:21: "to all generations, for ever and ever"). Romans 16:25–27 is an even more extensive doxology in which the first part has an unparalleled expansion (in fact, vv. 25–26 are a digression), while the other parts remain typically brief (my translation):

> [25]To him who has power to make you stand firm, according to my gospel and the proclamation of Jesus Christ, according to the revelation of that divine secret kept in silence for long ages [26]but now disclosed, and by the eternal God's command made known to all nations through prophetic scriptures, to bring them to

faith and obedience—[27]to the only wise God through Jesus Christ be glory for endless ages! Amen.

The doxology is a liturgical form in the sense that its original setting is Christian worship. When doxologies are incorporated into written texts, they function in several ways: (1) They are included at appropriate junctures in written versions of oral liturgies (*Did.* 8:2; 9:2, 3, 4; 10:2, 4, 5). (2) They are imitative of their original worship setting (Rev. 4:9; 5:13–14; 7:12; 19:1). (3) The text into which they are inserted is often designed to be read in a setting of worship. Just as doxologies frequently mark the conclusion of a liturgical celebration, so they can be used to conclude religious texts (4 Macc. 18:24; 3 Macc. 7:23; *1 Clem.* 64:2; *2 Clem.* 20:5) or to conclude major sections of religious texts (Rom. 11:36; 1 Tim. 1:17; 1 Pet. 4:11; *1 Clem.* 20:12). This use of the doxology occurs with special frequency in *1 Clement* (20:12; 32:4; 38:4; 43:6; 45:7; 50:7; 58:2; 6:3). Doxologies may also have a special epistolary function either in the opening (Gal. 1:5; Rev. 1:6), or (more frequently) the closing parts of a letter (Rom. 16:25–27; Phil. 4:20; 1 Tim. 6:16; 2 Tim. 4:18; Heb. 13:21; 1 Pet. 5:11).

Berger 1984, 236–37; Deichgräber 1967, 40–43; Wainwright 1980

Du-Stil, or "thou style," refers to the second-person pronouns and verb forms used for addressing a deity directly.

**Er-Stil,* *Hymns

Norden 1956, 143–63

Echoes (see *Quotations).

Edicts, or *edicta,* are announcements a Roman magistrate or emperor made to a particular people in a particular region articulating orders or policies. Edicts did not have universal validity but were valid only for the region and people originally addressed and only during the lifetime of the emperor or magistrate who issued the edict. *Edicta* are one of four types of *constitutiones principium* ("imperial juridical decisions"). The other three types include (1) *decreta* ("decrees"), juridical decisions pronounced by the emperor in court; (2) *mandata* ("mandates"), directives from the emperor to officials in the imperial service (see the correspondence between Pliny the Younger and Trajan); and (3) *rescripta* ("rescripts"), imperial correspondence consisting of written replies of the emperor either in separate letters (*epistulae principium*) or in marginal notes on the original petition (Sherk 1969, 189–97).

There were three formal elements of the edict (see Benner 1975, 33–175). (1) The *praescriptio* ("introduction") contained the title(s) and name(s) of the emperor or magistrate issuing the edict, followed by a verb of declaration such as (Latin) *dicit,* or (Greek) λέγει ("he says"), or *dicunt* or λέγουσι ("they say"). (2) The central section of edicts consisted of four elements, not all of which were invariably present: (a) the *proemium* ("preface") proclaiming the benevolence of the author toward the addressees; (b) the *promulgatio* ("proclamation"), a publishing phrase such as "I make known that"; (c) the *narratio* ("narrative"), a concise acount of the state of the matter providing the facts leading up to the enactment; (d) the *dispositio* ("arrangement"), the focus of the edict, which contained the decisions of the magistrate or emperor. (3) The *sanctio* ("sanction") final clauses were intended to ensure obedience to the edict.

The seven proclamations of Rev. 2–3 do not exhibit the formal characteristics of ancient letters (see *epistolography) but rather bear close similarities to aspects of the form and content of royal or imperial edicts outlined above (Rudberg 1911; Aune 1990; 1997–98, 1.126–29). The seven proclamations share seven stereotypical features: (1) The *adscriptio* or address, with the typical form, "To the angel of the church in so-and-so." (2) The command to write (often taken together with the *adscriptio*) is expressed by the aorist imperative verb γράψον ("write"). (3) Each of the seven proclamations is introduced with the formula τάδε λέγει, an archaic expression that means "thus says," resembling a Greek translation of an OT prophetic formula τάδε λέγει ὁ κύριος ("thus says the Lord"), but was also used (often as simply λέγει, "says") to introduce pronouncement of Persian kings and edicts of Roman emperors. (4) The next feature is the christological predications, i.e., various phrases and epithets describing various attributes of the risen Jesus (largely drawn from the vision in Rev. 1:9–20). (5) The οἶδα-clause, which introduces the *narratio* of each proclamation and is extremely varied in content, provides a description of the situation of each community in the past and/or present that serves as the basis for the *dispositio,* or response, that immediately follows. The following sections function as *narrationes*: Rev. 2:1–4, 6; 2:9; 2:13–15;

2:19–20; 3:1b, 4; 3:8; 3:15. (6) The *dispositio* is the central section of the proclamations, i.e., the reason that each was written. It is closely connected to the *narratio*, which serves as the basis for assertions made in the *dispositio*. Unlike other fixed features of the proclamations, the *dispositio* is not marked with a stereotypical phrase used consistently throughout the proclamations. The following sections function as *dispositiones*: 2:5–6; 2:10; 2:16; 2:22–25; 3:4–6; 3:9–11; 3:16–20. (6) The proclamation formula (see Enroth 1990), i.e., "let the one who has ears hear," occurs at the end of each of seven proclamations (2:7, 11, 17, 29; 3:6, 13, 22), sometimes before and sometimes after the promise-of-victory formula, and is an aphoristic saying rooted in the Jesus tradition where it is closely associated with parables. (7) The promise-of-victory formula is located at the very end of three proclamations (2:7b, 11b, 17b) but just before the proclamation formula in the last four proclamations (2:26–27; 3:5, 12, 21). The author's adaptation of the edict form in Rev. 2–3 is part of his strategy to polarize God (and Jesus Christ) and the Roman emperor, who is a pale and diabolical imitation of the sovereignty and power of God.

Aune 1990, 1997–98, 1.126–29; Benner 1975; Enroth 1990; Millar 1977; Rudberg 1911; Sherk 1969

Edition is a transliterated form of the Latin word *editio* (literally "a bringing forth," hence a "publication"), similar in meaning to the Greek term ἔκδοσις, and to such modern language equivalents as German *Ausgabe* and Norwegian *utgave*, which refer to the mechanism whereby a private text is made available to the public. *Publication should be distinguished from the production of a "critical edition," a designation for the publication of an ancient text based on the scientific principles and standards that take the entire manuscript tradition, or a representative sample of that tradition, of a work into consideration. From the Hellenistic period until today, the editing of a text implies the virtual canonicity of a text, that is, the importance that such texts are thought to have in educational curricula. Since most Greek and Latin texts survive in relatively few manuscripts (many survive in a single manuscript copy, e.g., Tacitus's *Annals* 1–6, the *Letter to *Diognetus*, and *Justin, *1 Apology*), the modern editor has few manuscripts to contend with. Aristophanes' *Clouds* was produced in Athens in 423 B.C.E., but the text that has come down to us is not based on the original but is a revision made some years later. In the case of the New Testament, however, the hundreds of extant manuscripts, fragments of manuscripts, and evidence from quotations make the task of producing a critical edition extremely difficult and complex. Manuscript witnesses to a literary work can also vary widely in quality. A summary of one system of critical symbols used by ancient grammarians is found in *Diogenes Laertius 3.66 (in connection with editions of the works of Plato).

Alexandrian editions. A number of critical editions of Homer and other canonical Greek writers were produced at the Museion or *Library of Alexandria, led by a famous series of Alexandrian scholars including Zenodotus (the first head of the library at Alexandria, ca. 284 B.C.E.), Aristophanes of Byzantium (who became head ca. 194 B.C.E.), and Aristarchus (who became head of that library in ca. 153 B.C.E.). Zenodotus (Pfeiffer 1968, 105–19; Nikau 1977; Rengakos 1993, 12–14) produced critical editions of Homer, Hesiod's *Theogony*, Anacreon, and Pindar. He is thought by some to have been the first to divide the *Iliad* and *Odyssey* into 24 books, and he used the obelus to mark lines of doubtful authenticity. Aristarchus, who was a cautious editor, attempted to remove corrupt readings, conjectures, and interpolations in his production of critical editions (διορθώσεις) of Homer, Hesiod, Archilochus, Alcaeus, Anacreon, and Pindar. Montanari (1998) maintains that when the Alexandrian philologists produced an ἔκδοσις of a literary work, that task typically involved both the choice of textual variants when two or more manuscripts of a work were collated (that they did this is often denied by modern scholars), as well as conjectural emendation (the term διόρθωσις encompasses both tasks; see Pfeiffer 1968, 110). The real character of an Alexandrian ἔκδοσις continues to be debated. A grammarian such as Zenodotus could have produced an entire copy of a literary work containing his text, in the form he thought correct and appropriate, or he could have worked on an existing copy indicating preferred variants and critical emendations with sigla of some kind. The latter view is to be preferred (Pfeiffer 1968, 110; Thiel 1992, 1 n. 1; Montanari 1998, 6). Thiel (1997, 15–16) suggests four types of annotations which Zenodotus made on a selected copy of the *Iliad* or *Odyssey*: (1) variants of the tradition, (2) conjectures, (3) parallel passages, (4) snippets of commentary. While Thiel (1997, 14–15) thinks that parallels and commentary constituted the bulk of the grammarians' work, Montanari (1998, 6) dissents, proposing that the variants and conjectures composed the major portion of these marginal notes and that Zenodotus's heavily marked copy of the text, when made available (ἐκδοθεῖσα) to other scholars and students at the Museion in a way that identified Aristarchus's edition of Homer is also problematic. Pfeiffer (1968, 212–21) proposes that Aristarchus wrote *hypomnemata* based on Aristophanes' edition of Homer and later performed his own διόρθωσις providing the basis for a new edition edited by his students (e.g., Ammonius).

Galen. Galen made a close study of many Hippocratic treatises and was concerned about the state of their preservation. In *De diff. resp.* 3.2 (trans. A. E. Hanson 1998, 35) he observes that "Nothing prevents one in the case of [unclear passages] from adding what is omitted, or correcting what is wrong to produce the perfect and true discourse. Just as it is rash to change old readings, so also preserving what is written and solving the difficulties with some small addition or subtraction is the work of the good writers of commentaries."

*Publication, *Textual criticism

Apthorp 1980; Kenney 1974; Montanari 1998; Most (ed.) 1998; Nickau 1977; Rengakos 1993; Thiel 1992, 1997; Valk 1949; M. L. West 1973; S. West 1988.

Editorial seam (see **Inclusio*)

Editorial "We" (see *First-person plural)

Education Greek education had three different levels: *prodaideia, paideia,* and advanced studies. (1) *Prodaideia* ("preliminary education") occurred in the home and was given by mothers or female slaves. (2) Encyclical *paideia* involved sending boys to a local school and perhaps placing them under the oversight of a *paidagogos*, who would escort them to and from school and be in charge of discipline. The three emphases of this essentially primary level of education each involved a specialist teacher: (a) In γυμναστική, the παιδοτριβής dealt with sporting activities and physical education. (b) In μουσική, the κιθαριστής superintended training in music, and (c) in γραμματική, the γραμματιστής taught reading, writing, arithmetic, and the reading and memorization of great poets such as Homer and Hesiod (Plato, *Protagoras* 325d–326a). (3) Advanced studies concentrated on rhetoric and philosophy, both of which thrived on debate. This tertiary level of Greco-Roman education (where the student could "major" in either rhetoric or philosophy) required texts on rhetorical theory and practice, several of which have survived. While these rhetorical texts tended to focus on oratory, the structures and arguments they recommended were equally (and increasingly) applicable to literary composition as well. Ancient curricula did not include courses on biographical or historical writings; those trained in rhetoric simply extended their skills to cover such tasks. They were of course aided by the existence of literary models. A final caution needs to be expressed. There were no universal educational standards in antiquity. The three levels of education discussed above therefore represent an ideal conception which in fact varied widely from time to time and place to place in the Greco-Roman world.

*Progymnasmata

D. L. Clark 1957; M. L. Clarke 1996

Ekdosis (see *Publication)

Ekphrasis, a transliteration of the Greek word ἔκφρασις, "description" (plural ἐκφράσεις or *ekphraseis*), is a literary term (eventually) used for "the rhetorical description of a work of art" (*OCD* 377).

The ekphrasis *as a constituent literary form. Ekphraseis* were used in epic and prose narratives as *digressions. The *ekphraseis* found in the Homeric epics, the earliest Greek literature, include the relatively lengthy description of the shield of Achilles (*Iliad* 18.478–608; see A. S. Becker 1990) and the relatively brief description of the cup of Nestor (*Iliad* 11.632–32). Both became literary models for later authors. Most *ekphraseis*, like these two Homeric examples, are descriptions of works of art or handcraft, such as beautiful garments (the mantle of Jason in Apollonius Rhodius, *Argonautica* 1.721–67, the very lengthy description of the shield of Dionysus in Nonnus, *Dionysiaca* 25.380–567, and the shield of Euryplus in Quintus Smyrnaeus, *Posthomerica* 6.471–92. In addition to works of art, landscapes (W. Elliger 1957; Leach 1988), places, and buildings, including the palace and garden of Alkinoos (*Odyssey* 7.84–132), the palace of Aeëtes (Apollonius Rhodius, *Argonautica* 3.213–48), and the cave of the nymphs (Quintus Smyrnaeus *Posthomerica* 6.471–92) were also the subject of *ekphraseis*. By the 2d cent. C.E., descriptions of paintings were frequently used to introduce entire compositions or large sections of compositions (Mittelstadt 1967, 757 n. 1). A painting depicting the story of Europa and the bull (closely corresponding to similar scenes on coins from Sidon) is described at the beginning of Achilles Tatius, *Leucippe and Clitophon* 1.1–2, and later the author includes descriptions of the painting of Perseus and Andromeda (3.6–7) and Prometheus (3.8). The use of *ekphraseis* in Greek *novels has been comprehensively discussed by Bartsch (1989).

The ekphrasis *as a literary genre.* The *ekphrasis* was eventually transformed from a constituent literary form used as a digression in narrative passages to an independent literary form, evident in such literary works as the *Imagines* ("Paintings") of Philostratus Major, the *Imagines* of Philostratus Minor (the production of *imagines* was apparently a family business), *Cebes' *Tabula,* and Callistratus's *Descriptiones* (descriptions of 14 statues). During the Roman period *ekphraseis* became a very popular literary form. One work that became popular during the medieval period was the *Tabula* of Cebes (1st cent. C.E.), which consists of a lengthy discussion of the contents and significance of a picture on a votive tablet in a temple. The work is essentially a discussion of the major themes of popular morality. The *Tabula* is a dialogical *ekphrasis* in which a group of visitors to a temple sees a votive tablet with a picture on it that they cannot understand, i.e., they sense that the picture carries a hidden symbolic meaning. An old man offers to explain the meaning of the picture and provides a moralizing allegorical explanation for the various figures. The ensuing dialogue between the old man and the visitors is replete with questions, often varied forms of "What is this?" and "Who is this?" coupled with answers introduced with "This is" or "That is."

Ekphrasis *in the OT and Judaism.* Literary descriptions of impressive buildings and works of art are found throughout the ancient world and were not originally derived from Greek *ekphraseis.* Despite the fact that *ekphraseis* occur less frequently in the OT than in early or nearly contemporaneous Greek literature, the OT does contain detailed descriptions of the temple at Jerusalem (1 Kgs. 6:14–36; 7:15–50) and Solomon's palace (1 Kgs. 7:2–12). Josephus expanded and embellished both in *Ant.* 8.63–98; 8.133–40. *Ekphraseis* become relatively common only in Jewish apocalyptic literature, where the detailed description of metaphorical visions plays a significant role in the narrative (Downey 1959, 932).

Ekphrasis *in rhetoric.* The term *ekphrasis* (Latin *descriptio*) is not regularly used in rhetoric until the *Second Sophistic (2d cent. C.E.; see Lausberg 1998, §1133). The only two previous rhetorical uses of the term are found in Dionysius of Halicarnassus, *De imitatione* fr. 6.3.2 and *Ars rhetorica* 10.17 (Bartsch 1989, 8). The term *ekphrasis* frequently appears in the **Progymnasmata* (Hermogenes, *Prog.* 10; Aphtonius, *Prog.* 12; *Theon, *Prog.* 11; Nicolaus, *Prog.* 12). Theon defines *ekphrasis* as "a descriptive account bringing what is illustrated vividly before one's sight" (*Progymnasmata* 7; Spengel 1853–54, 3.491; trans. Bartsch 1989, 111). Thus the purpose of the *ekphrasis* is ἐναργεία ("vividness"). Nicolaus suggests that "ekphrasis undertakes to fashion spectators out of auditors" (*Prog.* 12; Spengel 1853–54, 3.49). Though *ekphrasis* is commonly defined as "the rhetorical description of a work of art" (*OCD* 377), this is somewhat restrictive, for the rhetorical handbooks listing the topics appropriate for *ekphrasis* include persons, circumstances, places, periods of time, customs, festivals, and assemblies, as well as statues and paintings (Bartsch 1989, 10–14). When people are the subject, the description should move from head to foot (Nicolaus, *Progym.* 12); cf. Rev. 10:1; 19:12; but violated in Rev. 1:13.

Allegorical interpretations of ekphraseis. There are two major approaches to the use of *ekphraseis* by the time of the Second Sophistic during the 2d cent. C.E. One approach centers on the importance of understanding and interpreting the work of art itself. The other focuses on the hidden meanings conveyed by the work of art, which are usually revealed through an *allegorical mode of interpretation (Bartsch 1989, 22–31). There are two subtypes of such allegorication descriptions. Those whose meaning is obvious (as in Lucian, *De mercede cond.* 42 [in which the *Tabula* of Cebes is specifically mentioned] and Lucian, *Calumniae* 4–5) and those whose meaning is not apparent and must be carefully explained by someone who is knowledgeable (Lucian, *Hercules*; Cebes, *Tabula*). In both Lucian's *Hercules* and Cebes' *Tabula*, the narrator is puzzled over the meaning of the representation.

Relevance for NT and ECL. While there are numerous descriptive passages in narratives, the one in the NT with the closest affinities to the Greek *ekphrasis* tradition is Rev. 17, which differs strikingly from the other vision reports in Revelation in that it has a static or tableau quality (i.e., no actions occur). Only here in Revelation does the *angelus interpres* play a significant role in explaining the meaning of visions to John the apocalyptist. The vision John sees is narrated in 17:3b–6:

> I saw a woman sitting on a scarlet beast which was full of blasphemous names, and it had seven heads and ten horns. [4]The woman was arrayed in purple and scarlet, and bedecked with gold and jewels and pearls, holding in her hand a golden cup full of abominations and the impurities of her fornication; [5]and on her forehead was written a name of mystery: "Babylon the great, mother of harlots, whores and of earth's abominations. [6]And I saw the woman, drunk with the blood of the saints and the blood of the martyrs of Jesus.

In the angelic interpretation that follows, the seven heads of the beast are identified as seven mountains on which the woman is seated (v. 9). Both the vision, and the angelic interpretation that follows (17:7–18), constitute an *ekphrasis* or description of a bas-relief depicting the goddess Dea Roma seated on the seven hills of Rome. While the bas-relief itself has not survived, a depiction of it is preserved on the reverse of a sesterius minted under the Emperor Vespasian, 69–79 C.E. (Aune 1997–98, 3.920–22; Vermeule 1974, 41).

Several scholars have proposed that the Shepherd of Hermas contains *ekphraseis* dependent on Cebes, particularly in Hermas, *Vis.* 3.8 and *Sim.* 6.2–4; 9.15 (C. Taylor 1901, 1903a, 1903b, 1910; Joly 1963; Hilhorst 1976, 47). Despite the motifs and thought world shared by Hermas and Cebes, *Tabula* (e.g., the moralizing allegory of female figures), it is not necessary to suppose that the former is literarily dependent on the latter (Brox 1991, 53–54; Osiek 1999, 25). The main issue, however, is whether Hermas adapted the *ekphrasis* genre by basing literary vision reports on allegorical interpretations of pictures or sculpture. That appears to be precisely what he has done. The static character of at least one of Hermas's visions (*Vis.* 4) suggests that this may well be an *ekphrasis* based on a unknown work of art. Another lengthy *ekphrasis* is found in *Apoc. Abr.* 21:7–29:21, written ca. 80–100 C.E. In this passage God explains the meaning of a picture of creation that remains static in 21:7–26:7.

*Allegory, *Cebes *Tabula,* *Progymnasmata *Revelation to John

---

R. D. Anderson 2000, 40; Bartsch 1989; A. S. Becker 1990, 1994; Davidson 1977; *DNP* 3.942–50; Downey 1959; E. C. Evans 1948; Fitzgerald and White 1983; Fowler 1991; Goldhill 1994; Joly 1963; Lausberg 1998, §1133; Leach 1988; Mittelstadt 1967; Palm 1965–66; C. Taylor 1901, 1903a, 1903b, 1910; Vermeule 1974

Elchasai, Book of, is mentioned by Hippolytus (*Ref.* 9.13–17; 10.29), Origen (Eusebius, *Hist. eccl.* 6.38) and Epiphanius (*Haer.* 19, 30), and exists only in fragments quoted by Hippolytus and Epiphanius (English translation in *NTA* 1992, 2.685–90). Elchasai began to proclaim his message in 101 C.E. (Hippolytus, *Ref.* 19.13.3–4) and was active during the rest of Trajan's reign (98–117 C.E.).

The problem of genre. The genre of the *Book of Elchasai* is disputed. It is frequently categorized as an *apocalypse (Luttikhuizen 1987) or a prophetic revelation (Hilgenfeld 1884, 434; Ferguson 1997, 369), because the first fragment describes a revelation made to Elchasai by an enormous angel (Hippolytus, *Ref.* 9.13.1–3). An unsuccessful attempt has also been made to identify it as a *church order (Jones 1996).

The Jewish-Christian sect reflected in the book taught that serious sins could be forgiven by a second baptism undergone while fully clothed (Hippolytus, *Ref.* 9.15.1–3), and required sabbath observance (Hippolytus, *Ref.* 9.16.2–4), prayer facing Jerusalem (Epiphanius, *Haer.* 19.3.5), and healing by repeated self-baptisms (Hippolytus, *Ref.* 9.15.4–16.1). Mani, the 3d-cent. founder of Manichaeism, was an Elkesaite, according to the Cologne Mani Codex (Cameron and Dewey 1979).

Cirillo 1984; Jones 1996; Luttikhuizen 1985, 1987; Schneemelcher 1992, 2.685–90

Elision, i.e., pronouncing two words by omitting either the concluding vowel of the first word (e.g., ἀλλ' δέ for ἀλλά δέ), or the initial vowel of the following word.

Elocutio (see *Style)

Encomium, a transliteration of the Latin form of the Greek word ἐγκώμιον ("praise"), one of the three main types of *epideictic rhetoric. The other two are the πανηγυρικὸς λόγος, or "festival speech," and the ἐπιτάφιος λόγος, or "funeral oration." According to Quintilian (3.7.6; Lausberg 1998, §243), the encomium, i.e., an epideictic speech of praise, can be directed to gods (Quintilian 3.7.6–9), human beings (e.g., a king or emperor;

Quintilian 3.7.10–18), animals and inanimate objects (e.g., a city, a country; Quintilian 3.7.26–28; example: Aelius Aristides, *Roman Oration* [*Or*. 26]; see Oliver 1953). There are four degrees of defensibility for an encomium (Menander, *Rhetor,* 3.346 [Russell and Wilson 1981, 30–33]; Lausberg 1998, §241): (1) praise of topics recognized as worthy of praise (e.g., God); (2) praise of serious evils (e.g., demons); (3) praise of topics that are in part worthy of praise and in part blameworthy; and (4) playful praise of topics that do not deserve praise (e.g., death, poverty). The latter are called παράδοξα ἐγκώμια ("paradoxical encomia"). In praising a person, the three basic divisions used are praise of the soul, praise of the body, and praise of external circumstances (*Rhetorica ad Herennium* 3.6.10). Quintilian (3.7.10–18) discusses encomia on individuals in three categories: (1) the time before they were born (e.g., country, parents, ancestors); (2) their lifetime (based on the three topics of mind, body, and external circumstances); and (3) the time subsequent to their death (honorary decrees, divine honors, statues erected at public expense). The outline of Theon's discussion of topics to be included in a biographical encomium have been helpfully summarized by Marrou (1956, 272–73):

I. Exterior excellences
   A. Noble birth
   B. Environment
      1. Native city
      2. Fellow citizens
      3. Excellence of the city's political regime
      4. Parents and family
   C. Personal advantages
      1. Education
      2. Friends
      3. Fame
      4. Public service
      5. Wealth
      6. Children, number of and beauty of
      7. Happy death
II. Bodily excellences
   A. Health
   B. Strength
   C. Beauty
   D. Vitality and capacity for deep feeling
III. Spiritual excellences
   A. Virtues
      1. Wisdom
      2. Temperance
      3. Courage
      4. Justice
      5. Piety
      6. Nobility
      7. Sense of greatness
   B. Resultant actions
      1. With regard to objectives
         a. Altruistic and disinterested
         b. Good, not utilitarian
         c. In the public interest
         d. Braving risks and dangers
      2. As to circumstances
         a. Timely
         b. Original
         c. Performed alone
         d. More than anyone else?
         e. Few to help him?
         f. Old head on young shoulders?
         g. Against all odds
         h. At great personal cost
         i. Prompt and efficient

Several scholars have proposed that Heb. 11 is an encomium of faith (Kennedy 1984, 156; Mack 1990, 73–76), and that 1 Cor. 13 is an encomium of love (Kennedy 1984, 18; Mack 1990, 64–66; Smit 1991; Sigountos 1994). It should be noted that Quintilian (3.7.1–3) refers to instances in which epideictic rhetoric is used as part of a speech belonging to a different genre, e.g., praising or discrediting a witness in a forensic speech. Wuellner (1990) regards 1 Thessalonians as an example of the παράδοξον ἐγκώμιον or "paradoxical encomium," based on what he regards as the oxymoron in 1 Thess. 1:6: "And you became imitators of us and of the Lord, for you received the word in much affliction, with the joy of the Holy Spirit." The oxymoron consists of regarding the experience of "tribulation as validating their services to the living God and to one another" (Wuellner 1990, 126–27). Wuellner bases his approach on the thesis of Plank (1987, 3–4) that Paul uses the language of affliction to create a textual world in which suffering and weakness are considered characteristic of human life in the world. This is a very clever move on Wuellner's part, but problematic in that this oxymoron (if that's what it is) does not pervade 1 Thessalonians. He must therefore supplement it with a second "oxymoron" that consists of the "empirical fullness of the spiritual life in the present while 'waiting' for yet fuller completion at the parousia" (Wuellner 1990, 127).

Shuler (1982) argues that the Gospel of Matthew is a type of Greco-Roman βίος or "biography," more specifically that it was written in praise of its subject, and that therefore it is epideictic oratory, more specifically, the encomium (Shuler 1982, 37) or the "laudatory biographical genre" (Shuler 1982, 45). Shuler argues that Matthew is a biographical encomium by rehearsing the topoi found in Matthew (family background and genealogy, miraculous birth, upright earthly father, escape from death as an infant, stories of the baptism and temptation, topoi surrounding the death of Jesus (the plot by opponents, supernatural events, emphasis on innocence, and resurrection). Shuler also discusses the techniques (the historicization of traditions, use of OT quotations, thematic organization of material, amplification, and comparison). However, none of these elements is distinctive of ancient encomia. Shuler is not successful in demonstrating that Matthew is an encomium or laudatory biography, because if that can be said of Matthew, it can also be said of virtually every other ancient biography that presents the human subject from an ideal perspective. Mitchell (2002) has provided convincing rhetorical analyses of seven homilies of John Chrysostom, collectively designated **In Praise of St. Paul,* and argues that they are a specific type of encomium called λαλία.

*Biography, *Epideictic, *Rhetorical theory, *Panegyric

Burgess 1902; Kennedy 1984; Mack 1990; Mitchell 2002; Oliver 1953; Pernot 1993; Russell and Wilson 1981; Shuler 1982; Sigountos 1994; Smit 1991

Enoch, First Book of (Ethiopic Enoch) is a compilation of five separate apocalypses pseudonymously united under the name of the enigmatical OT antediluvian figure Enoch (Charles 1912, xlvi–lvi; Nickelsburg 2001, 7–8). *Ethiopic Enoch* is part of the biblical canon of the Ethiopic Orthodox Church (Cowley 1974, 319–20). The seventh of ten antidiluvian patriarchs, Enoch reportedly lived 365 years (hinting at astronomical associations), and the cryptic narrative from the Priestly writer in Gen. 5:21–24 concludes by saying that he "walked with God" and was removed from the world by God (VanderKam 1984, 23–51). The Genesis account was probably modeled on Mesopotamian mythical traditions, specifically the cycle concerning the Sumerian king Enmeduranki, the seventh antediluvian king and diviner (VanderKam 1984, 33–51). These traditions further embellished the figure of Enoch, who became a paradigmatic prophet, sage, and mediator in Judaism (*Jub.* 4:6–25; Jansen 1939; Grelot 1958b).

Texts and translations. First Enoch is preserved in an Ethiopic translation (Charles 1906; Knibb 1978) of a Greek translation (Bonner 1937; Black 1970; Larson 2001) of an Aramaic original (Milik 1976). The Aramaic fragments of *1 Enoch* have been edited by Milik 1976 and are also included in Beyer 1984. The Greek texts have been edited most recently by Black 1970 (see the large number of addenda and corrigenda in Black 1985, 419–22), though some critics regard Black's edition as "completely unreliable" (Tigchelaar 1996, 146). The basic critical texts of the Ethiopic are those of Flemming 1902, Charles 1906, and Knibb 1978 (who bases his text on Ethiopic MS 23, part of a later group of revised texts designated Eth II, which most scholars regard as inferior). The translation of *1 Enoch* by Ephraim Isaac in Charlesworth (ed.) 1983–85, 1.5–89 is based on the oldest group of five Eth I manuscripts, a single Ethiopic manuscript, including Tana 9, or K-9, and EMML 2080 (see Tigchelaar 1996, 148–49), and pays no attention to the Greek and Aramaic fragments. A more eclectic translation is that by Black (1985), based on the Eth I texts and taking full account of the Greek and Aramaic witnesses and including many conjectures. The text of Uhlig 1984 is based on Eth I, emended on the basis of the Aramaic and Greek witnesses, and avoids conjecture.

The five booklets in 1 Enoch. The five constituent apocalypses include (Charles 1912, 1–3): (1) the Book of the Watchers (1–36), a term derived from the heading of Georgius Syncellus, Ἐκ τοῦ πρώτου βιβλίου Ἐνὼχ περὶ τῶν γρηγόρων; (2) the Similitudes of Enoch (37–71); (3) the Astronomical Book (72–82); (4) the Book of Dreams (83–90); and (5) the Epistle of Enoch (92–108). Though Milik regards this fivefold work as modeled after the Pentateuch (1976, 54–55), this has been generally rejected (Greenfield and Stone 1977).

Survey of the five booklets. The Book of the Watchers (1–36), written by the mid-3d cent. B.C.E., narrates the story (based on Gen. 6:1–4) of how angelic beings called "Watchers" descended to earth, sinned with mortal women by having sexual intercourse with them and thus corrupting humankind, were barred from heaven, and were then imprisoned awaiting final punishment. The work is compiled from various earlier sources (Martínez and Tigchelaar 1989, 136–37). *First Enoch* 1–5 is perhaps intended to serve as an introduction to

1 Enoch as a whole (Hartman 1979, 138–45). The work has five divisions (Charles 1912, xlvii–xlviii; Nickelsburg 1981, 48–55; VanderKam 1984, 110): (1) an eschatological admonition (1–5); (2) narrative about the Watcher's descent and sin (6–11); (3) Enoch and the Watchers' petition (12–16); (4) Enoch's western journey (17–19); (5) Enoch's journey around the world (20–36). *First Enoch* 1–5 was probably written as an introduction to 6–36 as well as *1 Enoch* as a whole (Hartman 1979, 8–9, 136–37). The introduction in 1:1–3a (which begins with the third person in 1:1–2a and then switches to the first person in 1:2b–3; cf. Rev. 1:1–3) alludes to the legendary seer Balaam in Num. 22–24 (Hartman 1979, 22–23; VanderKam 1984, 115–18); the author describes a *theophany in which it is predicted that God will come to judge sinners and reward the righteous (1:3b–9), alluding to Deut. 33:2. Nature's obedience to the rule of God is emphasized in 2:1–5:3, while 5:4–9 curses those who disobey God's rules, using the second person, and blesses the wise who obey God, using the third person (cf. Sir. 16:26–28; *T. Naph.* 3:2–5). In *1 Enoch* 6–11, two stories of how sin was introduced on earth are spliced together. One story relates how Semyaza, leading a band of 200 Watchers, descended to earth intent on marrying mortal women (6:1–8). They each chose wives and became unclean through intercourse with them. They taught them charms and spells and fathered children who were gigantic and violent and who, after devouring all available food, turned to cannibalism (7:1–6; these giants are later called "evil spirits" in 15:8–12). In the second story, Azazel taught various forbidden heavenly secrets to humans, such as how to make weapons, jewelry, dyes for luxurious clothing, and cosmetics, thus corrupting humankind (8:1–4). According to both versions, the cry for vengeance from oppressed humankind led to the binding or imprisonment of the offending angels until the day of judgment (9:1–10:14). This section ends with an anticipation of the flood that will destroy the wicked and save the righteous (10:14–11:2). While "Enoch" was absent from chapters 6–11, he reappears in chapters 12–16, which begins with an elaboration of the Enoch tradition in Gen. 5:24. Here Enoch functions as an emissary from God to reprove the fallen Watchers (chaps. 12–13). Chapters 12–16 center on a throne vision (14:8–25), based largely on allusions to 1 Kgs. 22:19–22, Isa. 6, and Ezek. 1. Enoch is lifted up to heaven by the winds (14:8) and is brought to the door of the divine throne room, where God sits in unapproachable majesty (14:14–24). Since even angels cannot stand before the presence of God (14:21), the implication is that Enoch has a status greater than angels. The Lord then dictates a message of judgment that Enoch is to relay to the Watchers (15:1–16:4). In *1 Enoch* 17–36, journeys to various parts of the earth are emphasized. Enoch sees various parts of the world in 17:1–18:13, and in 18:14–19:3 his angelic guide explains what he has seen. After the six (or seven) angels of the presence are named (20), Enoch sees the place where the seven stars (=angels) who disobeyed the commands of God are imprisoned until judgment (21). In chapters 21–36 Enoch begins to ask his angelic guide various questions about what he has seen. While some places are recognizable (i.e., Jerusalem in 26–27), the geographical descriptions are largely mythical, perhaps reflecting a late Babylonian *mappa mundi*, "map of the world" (Grelot 1958a). Sheol is divided up into three places for the righteous dead and one place for the sinners (22:1–13). Enoch's tour of the earth is punctuated by pauses to praise the creator (22:14; 25:7; 27:5; 36:4). The final judgment is emphasized in 21–36.

The Similitudes of Enoch (37–71). This should probably be entitled the "Second Vision of Enoch" (37:1; cf. Milik 1976, 89), assuming that *1 Enoch* 1–36 constituted the first vision (cf. *1 Enoch* 1:2; VanderKam 1995, 133) or the "Vision of Wisdom" (37:1; Suter 1981, 193). The present title is derived from 68:1, which uses the phrase "Book of Parables." This apocalypse is extant only in Ethiopic, and its date is uncertain, though it probably originated sometime between the 1st cent. B.C.E. to the mid-1st cent. C.E. (Knibb 1979; Black 1985, 188; Suter 1981, 29). The main theme throughout the work is that of the final judgment, when God will vindicate God's people and punish their oppressors (Nickelsburg 1981, 214). The work is divided into three *meshalim* or parables: (1) 38–44 (see 37:5 and 38:1); (2) 45–57 (see 45:1); (3) 58–69 (see 57:3; 58:1, and 69:29), with chapter 37 as an introduction and chapter 71 as a later appendix. The term *mashal* first occurs in *1 Enoch* 1:3, and can be understood to mean "a vision report" (Charles 1912, 64, 70), for in Num. 23–24 (cf. 23:7, 18) *mashal* refers to the oracles of Balaam and in Job 27–31 (cf. 27:1) is used of a lengthy wisdom speech by Job. Nevertheless, taking *mashal* as "comparison," it is clear that *1 Enoch* 37–71 focuses on a comparison between the fates of the righteous and the wicked (Suter 1981).

The Astronomical Book (72–82). Probably written before 200 B.C.E. (Milik 1976, 7–8, 273–74; VanderKam 1984, 79–88), this is a first-person account of Enoch revealing and writing down for his son Methuselah astronomical and geographical phenomena and laws (79:1–6; 82:1–2), which are shown to him by the angel Uriel (72:1; 74:2; 75:3–4; 78:10; 79:2, 6; 82:7). The only eschatological reference is to the "new creation" in 72:1. Since the content of chapters 80–81, however, is ethical rather than astronomical, with a strong eschatological emphasis, they appear to be later additions to the text. The contents of the originally independent composition also appear disordered; the original order likely consisted of chapters 72–78, 82:9–20, 79, 82:1–8 (VanderKam 1984, 76–79). The Astronomical Book exhibits several apocalyptic features: (1) it features an angelic mediator of revealed scientific knowledge; (2) it is pseudepigraphic; (3) it emphasizes the transmission of revelation in written form; (4) the fact that Uriel is repeatedly said to "show" Enoch the heavenly bodies and earthly geographical features, together with the repeated "I saw," suggests a vision, possibly in the context of an otherworldly journey; (5) it has a narrative framework.

The Book of Dreams (83–90), written before 125 B.C.E., contains a historical survey in the form of *vaticinia ex eventu* ("prophesies after the event") and was written about the 2d or 3d quarter of the 2d cent. B.C.E. (Milik 1976, 41). A few sentences of *1 Enoch* 86 and much of 88–89 are preserved in Aramaic. Assuming the narrative setting found in *1 Enoch* 81:5–82:2, this part of *1 Enoch* contains two apocalypses, a vision in 83:3–5 and the much larger Animal Apocalypse (85–90), which provides a historical survey of the past and predictions of the future. The switch from *vaticinia ex eventu* to authentic predictions occurs in 90:9–16, where the horned animal, probably Judas Maccabeus, is first mentioned (indicating that this was written before 161 B.C.E. when Judas died, perhaps ca. 164 B.C.E.), and 90:17 begins the authentic predictions (VanderKam 1984, 161–63). This apocalypse is presented as a vision in which people and nations are represented by animals (inspired by Jer. 25).

The Epistle of Enoch (91–108). This section dates to the end of the 2d or beginning of the 1st cent. B.C.E. and is designated an "epistle" in 100:6. The fact that Enoch is presented as addressing his sons suggests the literary form of testament (VanderKam 1984, 150). Chapters 106–7, probably additions, contain a historical survey in the form of *vaticinia ex eventu*. The major apocalypse in this section is the Apocalypse of Weeks (93:1–10; 91:11–17), written between 175 and 167 B.C.E. (VanderKam 1984, 149), perhaps composed by the author of the rest of 91–105 (Milik 1976, 255–56). A shorter Methuselah Apocalypse is found in 91:1–10. The literary structure of the Apocalypse of Weeks consists of a historical review that periodizes Israelite-Jewish history into seven "weeks" of years which lead to the writer's own time. Future events begin in 91:12–13 with the prediction of an eighth, ninth, and tenth week in which various states of the last judgment are narrated, culminating in the replacement of the old heaven and earth and the creation of a new heaven and earth (91:14–16), followed by "many weeks without number" (91:17). Though "Enoch" claims to have gotten his knowledge from heavenly visions and angels and heavenly tablets (93:2), the form of the Apocalypse of Weeks is that of a testament, with no direct mention of the mode of revelation. Throughout 91–107 a distinction is made between the "righteous" and the "sinners," which some have tried to link with the Pharisees and Sadducees respectively. *First Enoch* 108, not extant in either Greek or Aramaic, is probably an addition to the *Epistle of Enoch* (Nickelsburg 1981, 151).

Relevance for NT and ECL. While Jude 14–15 is the only explicit quotation from *1 Enoch* in the NT (Lawlor 1897), Nickelsburg argues that many passages about the Son of Man in the canonical Gospels are dependent on tradition found in *1 Enoch* 37–71 (2001, 83–86). Charles argued that the author of *Revelation was dependent on *1 Enoch* (1920, 1.lxxxii–lxxxiii): *1 Enoch* 9:4 (Rev. 17:14; 19:16); *1 Enoch* 14:15 (Rev. 4:1); *1 Enoch* 18:13 (Rev. 8:8); *1 Enoch* 46:1 (Rev. 14:14); *1 Enoch* 47:3–4 (Rev. 6:11); *1 Enoch* 48:9 (Rev. 14:10); *1 Enoch* 51:1 (Rev. 20:13); *1 Enoch* 62:3, 5 (Rev. 22:2); *1 Enoch* 86:1 (Rev. 9:1); *1 Enoch* 99:7 (Rev. 9:20). Yet in virtually every instance apocalyptic commonplaces are involved.

*Pseudepigrapha, OT, *Apocalypses

Black 1985; Cowley 1974; Larson 2001; Martínez and Tigchelaar 1989; Vanderkam 1984. *1 Enoch* 1–36: Hartman 1979; Newsom 1980; Nickelsburg 1977a, 2001; VanderKam 1984, 110–40. *1 Enoch* 37–71: Suter 1979, 1981. *1 Enoch* 72–82: VanderKam 1983, 1984, 76–109. *1 Enoch* 92–107: Dexinger 1977; Nickelsburg 1977b

Enthymeme, a transliteration of the Greek term ἐνθύμημα which means both "thought" and "consideration, argument," while the cognate verb ἐνθυμεῖσθαι means "to think about something; consider it." ἐνθύμημα is also transliterated into Latin as *enthymema*, or translated as *commentatio* ("argument," Quintilian 5.10.1), *commentum* ("argument," Quintilian 5.10.1; 9.2.106), and *contrarium* ("argument from contraries," Cicero, *Topica* 47–49; Quintilian 5.10.2). The **Rhetorica ad Herennium* refers to the enthymeme under the rubric *contrarium* (4.25–26), with several examples, including the following: "When they outnumbered us, they were no match for us; now that we outnumber them, do we fear that they will conquer us?"

Two lists of types of enthymemes. For Quintilian, the term ἐνθύμημα had five meanings, all of which he claimed were based on Greek works on rhetoric (5.10.1–3): (1) a thought, (2) a maxim supported by a reason (*sententia cum ratione*), (3) an inference from consequents (*ex consequentibus*) or contraries (*ex pugnantibus*), (4) a rhetorical "syllogism" (*oratorius syllogismus*), (5) and an incomplete "syllogism" (*imperfectus syllogismus*). Ps.-Demetrius (perhaps 1st cent. C.E.) has a list of four meanings of the enthymeme, all found in Quintilian's list (*De elocutione* 30–33): (1) a thought (διανόημα), (2) a thought derived from an incompatibility (ἐκ μαχῆς) or consequence (ἐν ἀκολουθίας σχήματι), (3) a kind of rhetorical syllogism (συλλογισμός τις ῥητορικός), and (4) an imperfect syllogism (συλλογισμός ἀτελής; Schenkeveld 1964, 48–50).

There are several interesting features in these two lists: (1) Demetrius lacks the second item on Quintilian's list (a maxim with a supporting reason). This is not a Latin rhetorical innovation but goes back to Aristotle, who illustrates the difference between an enthymeme and a maxim by citing the maxim "There is no man who is really free," and observes that it becomes an enthymeme with the addition of "for he is the slave either of wealth or of fortune" (*Rhet.* 2.21.2; 1394b; from Euripides, *Hecuba* 864–65). (2) The close similarities between the lists confirms Quintilian's claim of a Greek rhetorical origin (*Inst.* 5.10.1). (3) The lists indicate the ways in which the enthymeme was understood in both Greek and Latin rhetoric by the 1st cent. C.E. (4) The lists contain the first clear statements that the enthymeme is an imperfect syllogism, an argumentative form which probably originated in Stoic logic (Burnyeat 1994, 39–46). These varied conceptions of the enthymeme suggest that the following judgment by R. D. Anderson (2000, 47) is an exaggeration: "The standard definition of an ἐνθύμημα in rhetorical theory remained what it had already been before Aristotle, namely, a short argument or consideration based on contraries."

The enthymeme in modern rhetoric and logic. In traditional presentations of classical rhetoric for modern use, the "enthymeme" is typically defined as a "truncated syllogism" (Corbett 1990, 60):

> In modern times, the enthymeme has come to be regarded as an abbreviated syllogism—that is, an argumentative statement that contains a conclusion and one of the premises, the other premise being implied. A statement like this would be regarded as an enthymeme: "He must be a socialist because he favors a graduated income-tax." Here the conclusion (He is a socialist) has been deduced from an expressed premise (He favors a graduated income-tax) and an implied premise (either [a] Anyone who favors a graduated income tax is a socialist or [b] A socialist is anyone who favors a graduated income tax).

Similar definitions are also proposed by logicians, e.g., Hurley (1988, 256):

> An enthymeme is an argument that is expressible as a categorical syllogism but that is missing a premise or a conclusion. Examples:
>
> The corporate income tax should be abolished; it encourages waste and high prices.
>
> Animals that are loved by someone should not be sold to a medical laboratory, and lost pets are certainly loved by someone.
>
> The first enthymeme is missing the premise "Whatever encourages waste and high prices should be abolished," and the second is missing the conclusion "Lost pets should not be sold to a medical laboratory."

While lacking the characteristics of categorical syllogisms (i.e., when all three statements are categorical propositions beginning with "all," "no," or "some"), these "enthymemes" can be converted into categorical syllogisms. The second enthymeme, for example, can be converted into the following categorical syllogism (a typed called "Celarent," part of a medieval mnemonic poem designating the syllogistic form EAE: E=No S are P [a universal negative proposition]; A=All S are P [a universal affirmative proposition]:

Major premise:
No animals that are loved by someone should be sold to a medical laboratory.

Minor premise:
All lost pets are certainly loved by someone.

Conclusion:
No lost pets should be sold to a medical laboratory.

Aristotle's Enthymeme. Aristotle's *Ars Rhetorica* is an esoteric (or "in-house") work (no works prepared for "publication" by Aristotle have survived) completed ca. 335 B.C.E., probably after Anaximines' *Rhetorica ad Alexandrum*, composed ca. 340 B.C.E. (there is no evidence that that author had read the *Rhetorica*; see Mirhady 1994, 55–56), after Aristotle had returned to Athens (Grimaldi 1972, 53–82; Brandes 1989, 1–2). The *Rhetorica* has a complex compositional history, however, and was probably in process of revision for a relatively long period. It has been characterized as "a set of professor's notes" (Solmsen 1976, 175; Brandes 1989, 4–5), revised for publication long after the author's death in 322 B.C.E. (Kennedy 1963, 82–83). It is possible that of the three books of the *Rhetorica*, books 1 and 2 constituted a separate work (Diogenes Laertius 5.24 lists Aristotle's *Rhetorica* as consisting of two books), to which Aristotle later added book 3 (Kennedy 1996, 418–21), parts of which may go back to the 350s (Burkert 1975, 65–72).

Aristotle does not adequately define the enthymeme in the *Rhetorica* (or anywhere else), and scholars have found it difficult to arrive at a satisfactory inductive definition. According to Ross (1949, 499), "The enthymeme is discussed in many passages of the *Rhetoric*, and it is impossible to extract from them a completely consistent theory of its nature." Yet the enthymeme was crucially important for the rhetorical theory proposed by Aristotle in the *Rhetorica* (1.2.8 [1356b]; trans. Kennedy 1991):

> I call a rhetorical syllogism [ῥητορικὸν συλλογισμόν] an enthymeme, a rhetorical induction [ἐπαγωγὴν ῥητορικήν] a paradigm. And all [speakers] produce logical persuasion by means of paradigms or enthymemes and by nothing other than these. As a result, since it is always necessary to show something either by syllogizing or by inducing (and this is clear to us from the *Analytics*), it is necessary that each of these [i.e., the enthymeme and the example] be the same as each of the others [i.e., the syllogism and induction].

The conventional rendering of συλλογισμός as "syllogism" in Kennedy's translation is problematic, obscuring the important difference between deduction and syllogism, which has led to misunderstandings of Aristotle's logic; συλλογισμός in Aristotle regularly means "deduction" or "deductive argument," and almost *never* "syllogism" in the technical logical sense (Solmsen 1929, 41–43; Ross 1949, 291; Barnes 1981, 23; 1994, 83, 294; Burnyeat 1994, 9–11). By ῥητορικὸς συλλογισμός, Aristotle generally meant "rhetorical deduction" (W. R. Roberts' translation of the phrase in Barnes 1984, 2.2156), and when he refers to the enthymeme "as a kind of syllogism [συλλογισμός τις]," he does not mean "a kind of syllogism," but rather "a syllogism of a kind," i.e., a certain type of deductive argument (Burnyeat 1994, 17). All syllogisms are deductions, of course, but not all deductions are syllogisms.

Despite the disagreement on defining the Aristotelian enthymeme, Conley (1984, 168–68) has proposed six issues which have received wide support: (1) The enthymeme is a deductive argument. (2) The enthymeme should not be reduced to a formalistic conception, i.e., it is not just a truncated syllogism. (3) Enthymemes are sometimes expressed as truncated syllogisms for practical rather than formal reasons (e.g., the interest in brevity). (4) The premises of enthymemes are probabilities, not certainties, making them "rhetorical," though using scientific premises is not necessarily excluded. (5) If an enthymeme is expressed as an abbreviated syllogism, the audience must fill out the argument. (6) The premises of an enthymeme can involve matters of character (ἦθος) and emotion (πάθος) in addition to reason (λόγος).

The second and fourth points deal with important issues: whether the enthymeme is by definition an abbreviated syllogism and whether an abbreviated syllogism is one among several types of enthymemes. Following modern rhetoricians and logicians, NT scholars commonly understand the Aristotelian enthymeme as an incomplete syllogism. However, an impressive number of scholars are critical of this view. McBurney (1974, 31–32) argues that "There appears to be no place in Aristotle's writings where he defines the enthymeme as an elided syllogism, nor is there any satisfactory evidence that he so understood it." Several features of Aristotle's discussion of the enthymeme problematize its definition as a truncated syllogism: (1) In his discussion of the more than fifty τόποι in *Rhetorica* 2.23 that are sources for enthymemes, Aristotle *never* discusses syllogistic structure (Sprute 1975, 78). (2) Nowhere does Aristotle attempt to convert an enthymeme into a rhetorical syllogism (or the reverse), a method often used by modern scholars to verify the presence of an enthymeme and to understand its implied logic. (3) Nowhere does Aristotle define the enthymeme as a truncated syllogism.

The locus classicus for the definition of the enthymeme as an abbreviated syllogism is *Rhetorica* 1.2.13; 1357a (trans. Kennedy 1991): "Thus it is necessary for an enthymeme and a paradigm to be concerned with things which are for the most part capable of being other than they are—the paradigm inductively, the enthymeme syllogistically—and drawn from few premises and often less than those of the primary syllogism." This text is frequently read to suggest that "a missing or unexpressed proposition (either premise or conclusion) is a differentia of the enthymeme" (Lanigan 1974, 211), but Grimaldi rightly maintains that a close reading of the text excludes this view (Grimaldi 1980, 57–58).

C. S. Peirce (Hartshorne and Weiss 1960, 2.§449 n. 1) was a careful reader of Aristotle and had several important observations to make about the enthymeme:

> An *incomplete* argumentation is properly called an *enthymeme*, which is often carelessly defined as a syllogism with a suppressed premiss, as if a sorites, or complex argumentation, could not equally give an enthymeme. The ancient definition of an *enthymeme* was "a rhetorical argumentation," and this is generally set down as a second meaning of the word. But it comes to the same thing. By a rhetorical argumentation was meant one not depending upon logical necessity, but upon common knowledge as defining a sphere of possibility. Such an argument is rendered logical by adding as a premiss that which it assumes as a leading principle.

Bitzer (1974, 149) argues that "the definition of the enthymeme as an incomplete syllogism must be rejected, unless we use the term 'incomplete syllogism' in a special sense," i.e., "the speaker does not *lay down* his premises but lets his audience supply them out of its stock of opinion and knowledge" (1974, 150). Bitzer then proposes the following "tentative and exploratory" definition (1974, 151): "The enthymeme is a syllogism based on probabilities, signs, and examples, whose function is rhetorical persuasion. Its successful construction is accomplished through the joint efforts of speaker and audience, and this is its essential character." Specifically, the speaker argues A, therefore C; the audience supplies the suppressed minor premise B to make sense of the connection between A and C. The missing premise must be a common notion widely shared by the audience, or else the enthymeme will not make sense. Lanigan (1974, 212–13), critical of Bitzer, insists that the missing assumptions are suggested to, not asked of, the audience.

Ryan (1984, 31) argues that the Aristotelian enthymeme should not be defined as a truncated or abbreviated syllogism. If brevity alone distinguishes the enthymeme from other forms of syllogisms, he contends, one must ask whether an enthymeme is valid or invalid. But since the purpose of an enthymeme is persuasion, its formal validity is irrelevant. Formal completeness is unnecessary, and "because formal completeness has nothing to contribute to the aim of rhetoric, . . . the genuine enthymeme is not missing anything that needs to be added, or even that can be added without changing it. The genuine enthymeme is in its own way complete as it is, complete, that is, as a convincing argument" (1984, 44).

According to Ryan, Aristotle realized that uneducated people could be convinced by skillful speakers and attempted to discover why their arguments were convincing. He deduced common patterns (τόποι) underlying these arguments (or enthymemes), which had a plausibility they shared with the enthymemes derived from them (Ryan 1984, 48). While dialectical syllogisms are either valid or invalid, rhetorical syllogisms are either convincing or unconvincing (1984, 55, 69–77). While this violates the rule of the excluded middle (i.e., either a proposition or its negative must be true), an enthymeme is a unique class of argument that must be evaluated differently from other arguments (1984, 61). A sample enthymeme illustrates this (*Rhetorica* 1.6.19; 1362b23–24; trans. Kennedy 1991): "If it is especially advantageous to our enemies for us to be cowards, it is clear that courage is especially advantageous to our citizens." Here the protasis may be true but the apodasis false, so that the whole cannot be judged within the framework of validity or invalidity. Yet in a particular rhetorical setting it could be completely persuasive. Only by fiddling with this

ENTHYMEMIC CONTENT[1]

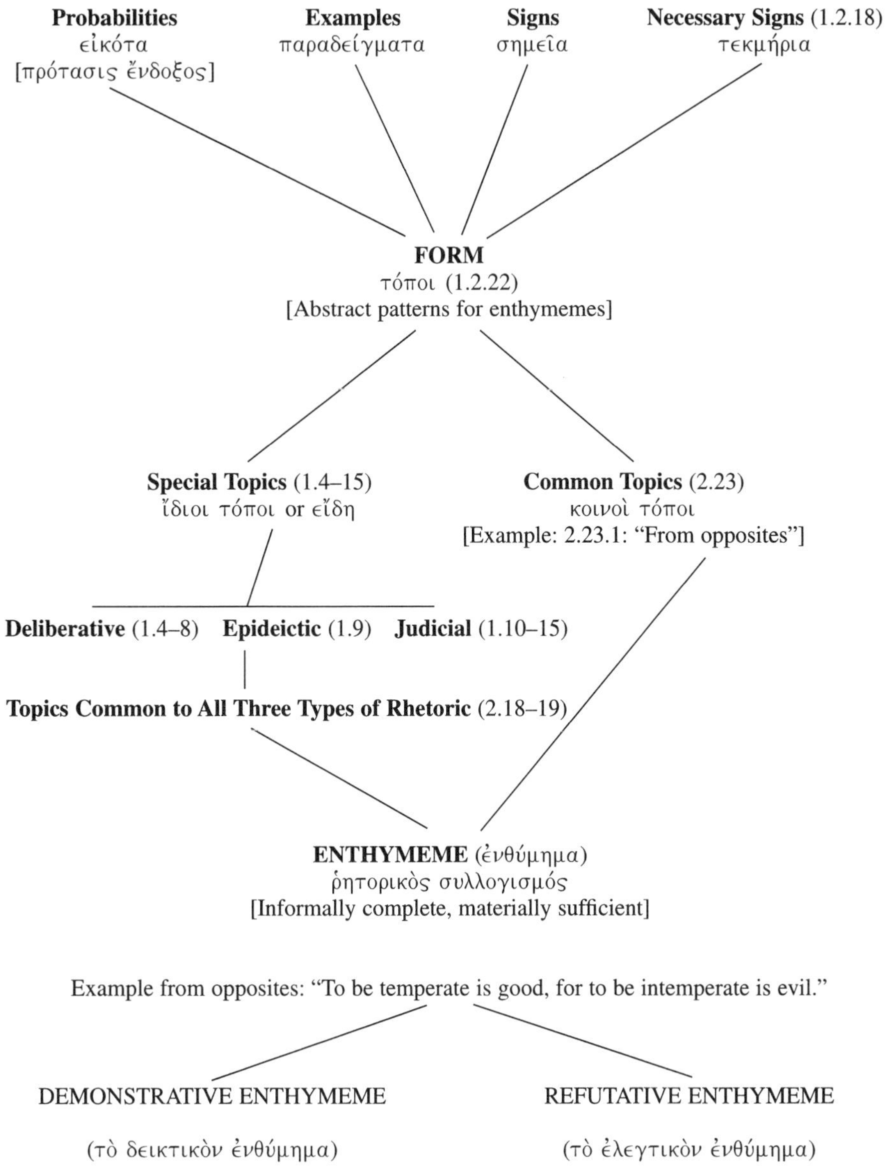

[1]*Rhetorica* 2.25.8; 1402b; *Analytica Priora* 2.27: "an enthymeme is a syllogism from probabilities or signs."

enthymeme by supplying a supposedly "missing premise" could it be turned into a valid or invalid argument.

Ryan's definition of Aristotle's enthymeme accommodates theoretical statements about the enthymeme in the *Rhetorica*, emerges from an analysis of each of the 28 τόποι in *Rhetorica* 2.23, and is confirmed by an analysis of many of the enthymemes cited by Aristotle (96):

> The enthymeme is a relatively brief argument, consisting of a statement enunciating some conviction with regard to human affairs (the conclusion), plus usually one reason why this conviction ought to be accepted (premise), with the reason being such that it is (1) a proposition that is generally accepted as true, and (2) related to the conviction in such a way that the conclusion will ordinarily be accepted, because it ought ordinarily to be accepted, by the hearer.

Two further issues require brief consideration: (1) If enthymemes are *brief* arguments, how do they fit the argumentative sections of deliberative, juridical, or epideictic speeches? (2) If the enthymeme is a complete argument, how did the view arise that the enthymeme is a truncated syllogism?

Aristotle suggests that enthymemes not be used in series (*Rhetorica* 3.17.6 [1418a]), that they be brief, and that they be expressed in periodic form. Rather than the rhetorical argument that constitutes a speech, it seems that by "enthymeme" Aristotle has in view "nicely turned sentences or questions raised at climactic points in the course of the speech" (Conley 1984, 171). Rather than constitute the entire argument, enthymemes are used to encapsulate arguments, i.e., they function as "sound bites," and this function of the enthymeme led to its categorization in Latin *rhetorical handbooks as a stylistic element.

The availability of Aristotle's Rhetorica *in antiquity*. The extent of the influence exercised by Aristotle's *Rhetorica*, as well as by the Peripatetic dialectical and rhetorical tradition during the Hellenistic and Roman periods, is a critically important issue for deciding the extent to which the use of Aristotelian rhetorical theory by early Christian authors was possible. Aristotle's private library including his own unpublished works (among which, very probably, were the *Rhetorica* and *Poetica*) was willed to his successor Theophrastus (Moraux 1951, 3–58). After Theophrastus (died 286 B.C.E.), the collection was bequested to Neleus (the will of Theophrastus is preserved in Diogenes Laertius 5.51–57), who moved it to the town of Skepsis in the Troad, where it was kept in a cellar by Neleus and his heirs. Badly cared for and suffering damage, it was acquired by Appelikon of Teos, a rich book collector who lived in Athens. Sulla appropriated the library after the fall of Athens in 86 B.C.E. and sent it to Rome (Strabo 13.1.54; Plutarch, *Sulla* 26.1–2). The *Rhetorica* appears to have been one of Aristotle's works that was "lost" from Theophrastus (died ca. 286 B.C.E.) to after 80 B.C.E. In Rome, Tyrannion the grammarian arranged the works of Aristotle (ca. 46 B.C.E.), and sent copies to Andronikos of Rhodes (presumably working in Rome 40–20 B.C.E.), who published them and drew up lists of Aristotle's works. Porphyry (*Vita Plotini* 24) observes that Andronikos "divided the works of Aristotle and Theophrastus into treatises [πραγματεῖαι], bringing together related discussions under a single head." There are, in fact, three catalogues of the works of Aristotle, the one preserved by Diogenes Laertius, the anonymous author of the *Vita Menagiana* (which consists of a list much like that in Diogenes, with an addition) and that of an otherwise unknown Ptolemy (texts available in Düring 1957, 41–50, 83–89, 221–31). The lists in Diogenes and the Anonymous are striking by their omission of many major surviving works of Aristotle, but they also are ancient and may predate the removal of the library to Skepsis. C. Lord (1986, 41), in fact, proposes that these two old catalogues represent an inventory of the works of Aristotle sent to Skepsis (an inventory already reduced by the subtraction of many of the major Aristotelian works). Cicero, in his early work *De inventione* (1.7), knew that Aristotle had written on rhetoric and clearly had knowledge of Aristotle's *Rhetorica* when he wrote *De oratione* in 55 B.C.E. (Wisse 1987, 155–56; Kennedy 1996, 422). However, he makes this telling observation in *Topica* 1.3 (LCL trans.): "I am not indeed astonished in the slightest degree that the philosopher [Aristotle] was unknown to the teacher of oratory, for he is ignored by all except a few of the professed philosophers." Dionysius of Halicarnassus, who lived in Rome during the last third of the 1st cent. B.C.E., knew the *Rhetorica*, perhaps the version revised by Tyrannion, and cites from it extensively in *Ep. ad Ammaeum* 1.6–9, arguing that it was a work of his later years. Dionysius's use of the *Rhetorica*, however, becomes more attenuated in his later, more mature works (Wooten 1996). Aristotle's works were reedited extensively in later antiquity, beginning with Alexander of Aphrodisias, ca. 200 C.E. (van Ophuijsen 2001), though little attention was paid to the *Rhetorica*. The 23-volume collection of *Commentaria in Aristotelem Graeca* (Berlin, 1882–96) contains no commentary on the *Rhetorica*, and the first Latin commentary was not written until the 12th cent. C.E. Aristotle's theory of the enthymeme had little observable effect on the subsequent history of the enthymeme, and his *Rhetorica* was used only to a limited extent by some Roman rhetoricians.

Rhetorical theory did not stand still after Aristotle, of course, and a number of developments (e.g., the stasis theory propounded by Hermagoras in the 2nd cent. B.C.E.) would have made the *Rhetorica* seem out of fashion, had it been available. Hellenistic rhetoric neither appropriated nor fully understood Aristotle's view of the ἐνθύμημα (which had a focal emphasis in the *Rhetorica*), even though syllogistic reasoning was incorporated into discussions of the ἐπιχείρημα. R. D. Anderson (1999, 49) concludes with a caveat: "Aristotle's treatise as a whole should be used with extreme caution, and is probably better left aside."

Aristotle's enthymeme and ECL. Using the Aristotelian enthymeme as a means for understanding the structure and persuasiveness of arguments in early Christian literature is a project beset by a series of difficulties: (1) The earliest and most extensive discussion of the enthymeme is found in the *Rhetorica* of Aristotle, a complex and sometimes contradictory work, not composed in finished form for publication and riddled with compositional interpretive difficulties, many of which involve the enthymeme. (2) The *Rhetorica* was apparently not available outside Peripatetic tradition (if indeed it was available there) until the mid-1st cent. C.E. in Rome, as made evident in Cicero, Dionysius of Hallicarnassus, and Quintilian. (3) Aristotle's *Rhetorica* was a text not widely known in antiquity, and indeed one with only a marginal influence on rhetoric until the 20th cent. (Garver 1994, 2), and the extent to which it was known outside Rome during the 1st and 2d cent. C.E. remains a matter of debate.

The presence of enthymemes in argumentative texts in the NT (some embedded in narratives) has been identified by NT scholars, particularly in Paul (Siegert 1985; Hellholm 1995; Moores 1995; Holloway 2001b; Debanné 2002), Deutero-Paul (Donelson 1986), and the Gospels and/or Acts (Kurz 1980a; Robbins 1998; Bloomquist 1999). Only a few examples of the analyses of enthymemes by these authors can be given (a basic knowledge of syllogistic logic is presumed).

Kurz (1980b) detects an enthymeme in Acts 17:2b–3, where Paul argues with the Jews "from the scriptures, explaining and proving that it was necessary for the Christ to suffer and to rise from the dead, and saying, 'This Jesus, whom I proclaim to you, is the Christ,' and some of them were persuaded, and joined Paul and Silas." Kurz converts this into an enthymeme by supplying the minor premise (1980a, 179):

Major premise:
The Christ must suffer and rise from the dead.

[*Minor premise:*
Jesus fulfilled the characteristics of the Christ, that is, death and resurrection from the dead.]

Conclusion:
This is the Christ, Jesus, whom I proclaim to you.

Kurz does not categorize this syllogism, but apparently regards it as categorical. The major and minor premises are materially invalid, however, since "suffer and rise from the dead" are not necessarily actions exclusive to the Christ, a notion which Kurz thinks is assumed (179). This is, at best, a deduction rather than a syllogism. All the examples of enthymemes suggested by Kurz (Acts 2:25–32, 36; Luke 24:26–27; 24:44–48) are similarly problematic.

Hellholm (1995) finds an enthymene in Rom. 6:4, which he converts into a mixed hypothetical syllogism in *modus ponens* (158):

Premise 1:
If Christ's resurrection implies a new life for the Christian [given; ὥσπερ . . . οὕτως . . .], and

Premise 2:
if Christ rose [given; ὥσπερ ἠγέρη Χριστός],

Conclusion:
then we live in a newness of life [given (!); οὕτως . . .].

Since in *modens ponens* it is essential that the antecedent of the first premise be repeated in the second, this syllogism is invalid, since "resurrection [of Christ]" is the antecedent of the first premise, while "Christ" is the antecedent of the second. Hellholm holds that Paul has included both the premises and the conclusion, but has not given the argument syllogistic form. Hellholm restates the syllogism, again in the form of *modens ponens* (1995, 159):

Premise 1:
If, if Christ's death is real, the death of the baptized is real

Premise 2:
then if Christ's resurrection is real,

Conclusion:
the new life of the baptized is also a reality.

Like the earlier version, this syllogism is also invalid, since the antecedent of the first premise ("death of Christ") is not the antecedent of the second premise ("the resurrection of Christ"), a rule characterizing the two valid types of mixed hypothetical syllogisms *modus ponens* ("mood that affirms") and *modus tollens* ("mood that denies").

Donelson devotes a chapter to "Forms of Argument" (1986, 67–113), with a major section on "The Enthymeme" (1986, 69–90). To understand the "ethical logic" of the Pastorals, he turns to Aristotle's *Rhetorica*, more useful than the more chronologically proximate works of Cicero and Quintilian (1986, 71–72). Thinking to follow Aristotle, he regards rhetorical proofs as formally incomplete syllogisms in which either of the premises or the conclusion can be missing (1986, 74). Donelson (1986) identifies 1 Tim. 1.15 as an enthymeme: "The saying is sure and worthy of full acceptance, that Christ Jesus came into the world to save sinners. And I am the foremost of sinners." He converts this "argument" into syllogistic form:

Major premise:
Jesus saves sinners

Minor premise:
I am a sinner

Conclusion:
Thus Jesus saved me

This is problematic for two reasons: (1) 1 Tim. 1:15 contains a single proposition, for the phrase "among whom I am the foremost" is a relative clause modifying "sinners." It is not an argument, but an assumption shared by author and audience. (2) The reconstructed syllogism is invalid, for it conforms to none of the basic syllogistic forms (categorical, hypothetical, or disjunctive), and the middle term ("sinners") is undistributed. It could be formulated as a categorical syllogism if it began "All sinners are saved by Jesus," but then the major premise would be materially false. Donelson has reconstructed a deduction rather than a syllogism. There is no compelling reason for regarding 1 Tim. 1:15 as an enthymeme, since it is not formulated as an argument.

Holloway (2001b, 335) describes the enthymeme of the late Hellenistic and early Roman periods, "as a brief and pointed argument drawn from contraries. Ideally, it was no longer than a single sentence. By the late Republic it had come to be viewed primarily as a figure of speech and was almost always expressed in the form of a question. For further effect, enthymemes were sometimes employed in series."

He identifies several enthymemes in the Pauline letters, all formulated as contraries expressed as rhetorical questions, from which I select some samples (2001b, 335–38): (1) "If you, though a Jew, live like a Gentile and not like a Jew, how can you compel the Gentiles to live like Jews?" (Gal. 2:14). (2) "Having begun in the Spirit, are you now ending with the flesh?" (Gal. 3:3). (3) "Shall I therefore take the members of Christ and make them members of a prostitute? Never!" (1 Cor. 6:15b). (4) "Are we to continue in sin that grace may abound?" (Rom. 6:1). (5) "How can we who died to sin still live in it?" (Rom 6:2). The strength of Holloway's analysis is that he has taken a conception of the enthymeme current in the 1st cent. C.E. and located valid examples in Paul.

A final example is from Debanné (2002), who finds 25 potential enthymemes in Phil. 1, which he whittles down to 19 actual enthymemes, three of which he converts to syllogisms and discusses in detail. I will mention only Phil. 1:3–6 (NRSV trans.): "[3]I thank my God every time I remember you, [4]constantly praying with joy in every one of my prayers for all of you, [5]because of [here Debanné substitutes "for"] your sharing in the gospel from the first day until now. [6]I am confident of this, that the one who began a good work among you will bring it to completion by the day of Jesus Christ." He converts this passage into the following categorical syllogism:

Major premise:
God brings to completion any good work that he begins among you [as believers],

[Minor premise:
Your sharing in the gospel from the first day until now is {clearly} a good work begun by God among you.] [Supplied]

Conclusion:
[God will bring to completion your sharing in the gospel from the first day until now.] I thank my God every time I remember you . . . because of [it].

In this cumbersome syllogism, the minor premise, "God," can be regarded as distributed in the first premise through the artifice of regarding it as the only member of a class, turning the whole into a quasi-syllogism. The middle term "good work" is distributed in the major premise because of the adjective "any," though this crucial term is supplied by Debanné without comment. The supplied minor premise consists of an exegetically questionable equation of "sharing in the gospel" with "a good work begun among you." This is an interpretive issue, of course, but it seems more appropriate to regard "the gospel" as the *means* whereby people's lives are changed, and "a good work" as the *effect* of believing in the gospel. Also problematic is the fact that the minor premise conforms to none of the four modes of categorical statements. Debanné's work is promising, but he errs in assuming that *all* enthymemes are truncated syllogisms (see Holloway 2001b, above for another approach to enthymeme) and that to understand their meaning they need to be converted into syllogisms (i.e., into logically valid forms). Further, his operating assumption, that all statements with supporting reasons are enthymemes, is too broad, since not all statements with supporting reasons are enthymemes (though any predication accompanied by a supporting predication can be converted into an enthymeme).

Summary evaluation. The discussion of Aristotle's theory of the enthymeme and the review of the reception-history of Aristotle's *Rhetorica* discussed above should make it clear that the conception of the enthymeme as a "truncated syllogism" is a development that postdates Aristotle (probably originating in Stoic logic; see Burnyeat 1994, 39–46), and that the *Rhetorica* was generally unknown outside Rome during the 1st cent. C.E. Not only was Aristotle's *Rhetorica* a text virtually unknown and unused in antiquity; it exerted only a very marginal influence on rhetoric before the 20th cent. (Garver 1994, 4). It is therefore extremely problematic to assume, with Kurz (1980a), Donelson (1986), and Hellholm (1995), that the Aristotelian enthymeme was a truncated syllogism and that Aristotle's rhetorical theory was widely known in the eastern Mediterranean during the 1st cent. C.E. It is even more problematic to define the enthymeme simplistically as a statement combined with a supporting reason (Robbins 1998; Debanné 2002).

Since the enthymeme was thought to function in at least four different ways by rhetoricians of the 1st cent. C.E., it is problematic to assume that one use is more important than all the rest, an assumption found in the work of those who appeal to Aristotle (Kurz 1980a, Donelson 1986, and Hellholm 1995) as well as those who do not (Moores 1995, Robbins 1998, Holloway 2001b, and Debanné 2002). For Moores (1995), Robbins (1998), and Debanné (2002), who are directly or indirectly in thrall to modern logic or rhetoric, the enthymeme is by definition a truncated syllogism. While not incorrect, this is just one of four possible functions of the enthymeme. Holloway (2001b) is the only scholar mentioned above who argues that an enthymeme is an argument based on contraries, a type of enthymeme known from Isocrates to late antiquity. However, he too assumes that this type of enthymeme is the only one known to Paul, though evidence is largely restricted to Latin rhetorical works of the 1st cent. B.C.E. and C.E., and the connection to Paul assumed rather than argued.

Perhaps the most striking characteristic of many of the works mentioned above, by those regarding the enthymeme as a truncated syllogism (except Hellholm 1995 and Debanné 2002), is that the syllogisms they reconstruct tend to be invalid in one or another respect, i.e., they are unfamiliar with the modes and figures of valid syllogistic forms. This is fatal for those convinced that the enthymeme is a truncated syllogism that requires conversion into syllogistic form to be fully understood.

*Syllogism, *Maxim, *Lesser to greater argument, *Topos

Alexandre 1999, 42–51; Bitzer 1959; Burnyeat 1994; Conley 1984; Corbett 1990, 59–68; Donelson 1986; Grimaldi 1972, 53–135; Hellholm 1995; Holloway 2001b; Kurz 1980a; McBurney 1974; Moores 1995; Robbins 1998; Siegert 1985; Solmsen 1974; Van Ophuijsen 2001; Vinson 1991; Wuellner 1991b

Envelope (see *Ring composition)

Epanadiplosis is a figure of speech involving the repetition of an important word for emphasis, as in Acts 19:34: "*Great* is Diana of the Ephesians. *Great* is Diana of the Ephesians."

*Epanaphora, *Gorgianic figures, *Paronomasia

Blass and Debrunner 1961, §493

Epanaphora, a rhetorical technique in which the same word is used at the beginning of a series of clauses or sentences (Quintilian, *Inst.* 9.3.30). Example: 1 Cor. 10:23: "'All things are lawful,' but not all things are helpful. 'All things are lawful,' but not all things build up." The use of Asianic rhetoric in speeches in the *Acts of Andrew* is common and includes a number of figures involving assonance, including epanaphora, as in *Acts of Andrew* 6 (*NTA* 2.130):

> *Well done*, O nature, you who are saved despite your weakness and though you did not hide yourself. *Well done*, O soul, you who have cried aloud what you have suffered and are returning to yourself. *Well done*, O man, you who are learning what is not yours and desiring what is yours [a Stoic sentiment]. *Well done*, you who hear what is being said.

Collections of beatitudes that begin with the predicate "Blessed" (μακάριος) are types of epanaphora (Sir. 14:20–27; Matt. 5:3–10; *Gospel of Thomas* 68–69, 79; *Acts of Paul* 5–6; *Acts of Thomas* 94; *Acts of Philip* 24).

*Epanadiplosis, *Paronomasia

Ephesians, Paul's Letter to the, one of four "prison letters" explicitly attributed to Paul (see also *Philippians, *Colossians, and *Philemon), but widely regarded as *pseudonymous (A. Lincoln 1990, lix–lxxxiii). The date of the letter, assuming its inauthenticity, is generally placed toward the end of the 1st cent. (i.e., 70–90 C.E.).

Genre. The epistolary prescript of Ephesians reads as follows: "Paul an apostle of Jesus Christ, by the will of God, to the saints who are in Ephesus and to the faithful in Christ Jesus" (Eph. 1:1). Critics have placed question marks against each of the main claims of this prescript, arguing that Paul is not the author, the church at Ephesus is not its destination, and it is not a letter (Bouttier 1991, 20–21). While Ephesians has the form of a letter, its destination lacks specificity (see below). Some have characterized Ephesians as a *homily (Gnilka 1971a, 33; A. Lincoln 1990, xxxix; Best 1998, 61–63), others as a theological treatise on the theme "Christ and the church," a testament, a meditation, a wisdom speech, or an introduction to Paul's letters. Not all these suggestions are mutually exclusive. Dahl has argued that Ephesians belongs to a type of Greek letter that substitutes a public speech for a private conversation; the epistolary purpose was to overcome separation and establish contact between the sender and the recipients (1977, 314; *IDBSup* 268), and constitutes a letter of congratulations.

Structure and content. Ephesians has the typical form of a Pauline letter with some distinctive features. It begins with a prescript consisting of superscription (sender), adscription (receiver) and salutation (1:1–2), though the adscription is distinctive because it lacks a specific destination, for the phrase "in Ephesus" was added to the text (Metzger 1994, 532) sometime during the 2d cent. C.E. This has been thought to imply either that Ephesians was a circular letter sent to several Christian communities in Asia Minor, that it was crafted to introduce a collection of seven Pauline letters, or even that Ephesians is actually the letter referred to in Col. 4:16 (Goulder 1991, referring to Tertullian, *Adv. Marc*. 5.17.1, where Marcion claims that Ephesians was really Laodiceans).

The prescript is followed by a lengthy eulogy or blessing (1:3–14; see O'Brien 1979), which Norden (1956, 253) referred to as a "monstrous conglomeration of clauses." Epistolary eulogies are also found in 2 Cor. 1:3–7 and 1 Pet. 1:3–12. The eulogy in turn is followed by a *thanksgiving (1:15–23), unusual only for its length. The body of the letter, found in 2:1–6:20, consists of two main sections. The first is a panegyric describing how God through Christ gave life to us who were dead, raised us up with Christ to sit in heavenly places (2:1–10), and abolished the difference between Jews and Gentiles through the death of Christ (2:11–22). (Eph. 2:1–7 violates Aristotle's warning against inserting too many intermediate clauses before completing the main thought [*Rhetorica* 3.5.2], something that occurs again in Eph. 3:1–7.) Paul's role is to reveal the mystery of how the Gentiles are part of the people of God (3:1–13), for which the author gives thanks and praise (3:14–21). The first half is rounded off with a doxology and an "amen" (3:20–21). The first three chapters in fact have the character of a long thanksgiving (J. T. Sanders 1962). The second section (4:1–6:20) consists almost entirely of exhortation, introduced thematically in Eph. 4.1: "I therefore . . . beg you to lead a life worthy of the calling to which you have been called." The author urges the recipients to maintain unity (4:1–16), to put off the old nature and put on the new one (4:17–24), and to avoid unrighteous practices (4:25–5:20). The final emphasis, on the standards of community living, includes an extensive household code (5:21–6:9). The epistolary closing in 6:21–24 consists of the commendation of Tychicus (6:21–22), the peace wish (6:23), and the grace benediction (6:24).

Rhetorical analysis. Dahl (1988, 1212) has proposed that "The rhetoric of Ephesians is a variant of the demonstrative (or epideictic) genre, which was used, for example, to praise the excellence of a god, an outstanding person, a virtue, or a city and its laws." A. Lincoln (1990, 46) and Mayer (2002, 20), the latter apparently unaware of the former, also classify Ephesians as *epideictic, a view rejected by Furnish (*ADB* 2.536). Mayer (2002, 20) admits that though Ephesians is an epideictic speech in letter form, it does not quite fit the schema found in the rhetorical handbooks. The letter in fact resists generic classification (A. Lincoln 1990, xxxvii–xxxviii; Furnish in *ADB* 2.536). Hübner (1997, 22–23) suggests that both Colossians and Ephesians might be considered deliberative, though he remains basically skeptical about the viability of rhetorically analyzing either letter.

A. Lincoln (1990, xliii–xliv) has proposed a rhetorical outline of Ephesians (which he regards as basically epideictic, though both epideictic and deliberative elements are present):

I. *Exordium* (1:1–23)
 A. Prescript (1:1–2)
 B. Eulogy (1:3–14)
 C. Thanksgiving and prayer (1:15–23)
II. *Narratio* of Grounds for Thanksgiving (2:1–3:21)
 A. Reminder of readers' salvation in Christ (2:1–10)
 B. Reminder of readers' privileges as Gentile participants in the new creation and new temple (2:11–22)
 C. *Digressio*: Reminder of readers' debt to Paul and his ministry (3:[1]2–13)
 D. *Transitus* of intercessory prayer and doxology (3:1, 14–22)
III. *Exhortatio* (4:1–6:9)
 A. Exhortation to maintenance of the church's unity (4:1–16)
 B. Exhortation to live as the new humanity (4:17–24)
 C. Seven specific exhortations about the old and new life (4:25–5:2)
 D. Exhortations about speech, sexual morality, and living as children of light (5:3–14)
 E. Exhortation to wise and Spirit-filled living in worship and in household relationships (5:15–6:9)
IV. *Peroratio* (6:10–24)
 A. Final exhortation to stand firm in the spiritual battle (6:10–20)
 B. Postscript (6:21–24)

This analysis is problematic for several reasons. First, the extended section labeled *exhortatio* does not correspond to the structure of normal epideictic (or deliberative) speeches. Second, the absence of a section in which arguments are amplified is also anomalous. This analysis, then, does little to advance our understanding of the composition. Mayer has also proposed a rhetorical analysis of Ephesians, which differs from A. Lincoln, whom she apparently has not read. Since Mayer does not argue in any detail for the epideictic structure of Ephesians but produces only a general outline, the similarities and differences between Lincoln and Mayer can be seen in the synopsis below. Mayer's distinction of the **captatio benevolentiae* from the **exordium* is peculiar, since a *captatio benevolentiae* is a type of *exordium*, even though the designation does not occur in the Latin rhetorical handbooks.

A chiastic structure for Ephesians has been proposed by P. S. Cameron (1990), though he rejects the term "chiastic" for "palinstrophe" (borrowed from McEvenue 1971, 29), by which he means an arrangement that does not "frame" a unit but whose essential feature is return. Cameron's palistrophic structure is based exclusively on lexical features, rather than content (P. S. Cameron 1990, 13):

A Eph. 1:1–2
B 1:3–14
 1:15–23
C 2:1–10
 2:11–22
D 3:1–7
 3:8–13
E 3:14–4:6
 4:7–16
EE 4:17–19
 4:20–24
DD 4:25–32
 5:1–20
CC 5:21–24 (and 6:1–3//6:4,
 5:25–33 6:5–8//6:9
BB 6:10–12
 6:13–17
AA 6:23–24

A very different formal analysis consisting of two chiastic sections has been proposed by Mayer (2002, 21), who suggests that the center of each chiastic section is emphasized by the structure:

I. Theological-instructive section (1:3–3:21)
 A. Eulogy (1:3–14)
 B. Thanksgiving and intercessory prayer (1:15–23)
 C. Reminder of salvation at baptism (2:1–10)

- D. Reminder of the unity of Jews and Gentiles in one church (2:11–22)
- C'. Reminder of the revelation of the mystery of Christ to Paul (3:1–13)
- B'. Intercessory prayer (3:14–19)
- A'. Doxology (3:20–21)

II. Paraenetic-admonitory section (4:1–6:9)
- A. Unity of the body of Christ (4:1–6, 7–16)
- B. The old and new person (4:17–24)
- C. Catalogue of individual admonitions (4:25–32)
- D. The Christian ethos: Imitation of God as modeled by Christ (5:1–2)
- C'. Catalogue of individual admonitions (5:3–14)
- B'. The old and the new person (5:15–20)
- A'. Household code: The family as a model of unity (5:21–6:9)

Use of the OT. There are two formal quotations of the OT in Ephesians: (1) Ps. 68:19 [MT 68:18] is introduced with the quotation formula "therefore it says" in Eph. 4:8 and represents a modification of the LXX text (though Best 1998, 77 does not regard this as a quotation of Scripture); see Lincoln 1982, 18–25. (2) The LXX version of Exod. 20:12 is broken into two parts and cited in Eph. 6:2–3, with the phrase "which is the first commandment with promise" inserted in the middle and serving as a formal indication of quotation (see Lincoln 1982, 37–40). The remaining possible allusions to the OT lack introductory formulas: (1) Pss. 110:1 and 8:6 in Eph. 1:20, 22 (see Lincoln 1982, 40–42); (2) Isa. 57:19 in Eph. 2:17 (see Lincoln 1982, 25–30); (3) the LXX version of Zech. 8:16 in Eph. 4:25; (4) MT and LXX agreement for an allusion to Ps. 4:5 in Eph. 4:26; (5) Prov. 23:31 in Eph. 5:18; (6) MT and LXX agreement in the allusion to Gen. 2:24 in Eph. 5:31–32 (Lincoln 1982, 30–36); (7) Isa. 11:4–5; 52:17; 59:17 in Eph. 6:14–17. The author of Ephesians does not favor the use of the OT in a promise-and-fulfilment manner, as Paul tends to do in Galatians and Romans, but rather adopts the perspective expressed in Eph. 3:4b–6 (a reworking of Col. 1:26–27): ". . . the mystery of Christ, which was not made known to the sons of men in other generations as it has now been revealed to his holy apostles and prophets by the Spirit; that is, how the Gentiles are fellow heirs, members of the same body, and partakers of the promise in Christ Jesus through the gospel." In the author's view, the OT prophets were ignorant of the true meaning of their prophecies. The absence of the promise-and-fulfillment mode of understanding the OT also characterizes the Gospel of Mark and the Revelation to John. Hübner (1997, 425–79) lists all possible quotations and allusions to the OT in Ephesians, no matter how slight, and comes up with about 94 quotations and allusions.

Relation to Colossians. At least nine common features of organization suggest a literary relationship between Ephesians and Colossians: (1) the prescript, thanksgiving, and intercessory prayer; (2) the message about alienation and reconciliation; (3) the discussion of Paul's suffering as an apostle and minister of the mystery; (4) head and body relations; (5) contrast between the old and new person; (6) the household code; (7) the exhortation to prayer; (8) the commendation of Tychicus; (9) the benediction. With regard to vocabulary, 34 percent of the words found in Colossians are also found in Ephesians, while 26.5 percent of the words in

Synopsis of Rhetorical Analyses of Ephesians

Dispositio	**A. Lincoln 1990, xliii–xliv** **Epideictic**	**Mayer 2002, 19–23** **Epideictic**
Epistolary prescript		1:1–2
Exordium	1:1–23	1:3–14
Captatio benevolentiae		1:15–23
Narratio	2:1–3:21	2:1–22
[*Propositio*]	—	[3:6]
Argumentatio	—	3:1–21
Exhortatio	4:1–6:9	4:1–6:9
Peroratio Epistolary postscript	6:10–24	6:10–20 —

Parallels between Colossians and Ephesians

Col. 4:7–8 (29 consecutive Greek words in agreement)	*Eph. 6:21–22* (29 consecutive Greek words in agreement)
	[21]Now that you also may know how I am and what I am doing,
[7]*Tychicus*	*Tychicus*
	the beloved brother and faithful minister in the Lord
will tell you all about my affairs; . . .	*will tell you everything*
[8]*I have sent him to you* *for this very purpose,* *that you may know how we are,* *and that he may encourage your hearts.*	[22]*I have sent him to you* *for this very purpose* *that you may know how we are,* *and that he may encourage your hearts.*
Col. 1:1–2 (7 consecutive Greek words in agreement) [1] *Paul, an apostle of Christ Jesus by the will of God,* and Timothy our brother. [2]*To the saints and faithful brethren in Christ* at Colossae: *Grace to you and peace from God our Father.*	*Ephesians 1:1–2* (7 consecutive Greek words in agreement) [1]*Paul, an apostle of Christ Jesus by the will of God,* [2]*To the saints who are also faithful in Christ* Jesus: *Grace to you and peace from God our Father.* and the Lord Jesus Christ.
Col. 1:25 (7 consecutive Greek words in agreement) of which I became a minister according to *the stewardship of God which was given to me for you,* to make the word of God fully known.	*Eph. 3:2* (7 consecutive Greek words in agreement) assuming that you have heard of *the stewardship of God*'s grace *which was given to me for you*
Col. 1:26 (7 consecutive Greek words in agreement) *the mystery hidden for ages* and generations but now made manifest to his saints	*Eph. 3:9* (7 consecutive Greek words in agreement) and to make all men see what is the plan of *the mystery hidden for ages* in God who created all things
Col. 1:14 (5 consecutive Greek words in agreement) *in whom we have redemption,* *the forgiveness* of sins	*Ephesians 1:7* (5 consecutive Greek words in agreement) *In whom we have redemption* through his blood, *the forgiveness* of our trespasses, according to the riches of his grace
Col. 2:19 (5 consecutive Greek words in agreement) and not holding fast to the Head, *from whom the whole body*, nourished and *knit together through* its *joints* and ligaments, grows with a growth that is from God	*Eph. 4:16* (5 consecutive Greek words in agreement) *from whom the whole body*, joined and *knit together through* every *joint* with which it is supplied, when each part is working properly, makes bodily growth and upbuilds itself in love

Ephesians are found in Colossians. Some argue that neither Ephesians nor Colossians is dependent on the other (Best 1998, 36–40), one variant of which is common authorship (i.e., held by those who regard both letters as authentically Pauline), while most scholars hold that Ephesians is dependent on Colossians (A. Lincoln 1990, xlvii–lviii).

*Colossians, *Epistolography, *Letters, Pauline

Best 1998; Bouttier 1991; P. S. Cameron 1990; Dahl 1988, 2000; Gnilka 1971a; Goulder 1991; Hendrix 1988; Hübner 1997; Kirby 1968; A. Lincoln 1990; Mayer 2002; Mouton 1996; O'Brien 1979; Porter and Clarke 1997; J. T. Sanders 1962

Epideictic rhetoric (Greek γένος ἐπιδεικτικόν; Latin *genus demonstrativum*), is the designation of the third main genre of Greek rhetoric. Aristotle discussed epideictic as the rhetoric of praise or blame. There are several types of epideictic speeches, including the ἐγκώμιον, "praise," πανηγυρικὸς λόγος, the festival speech, and ἐπιτάφιος λόγος, the funeral oration.

Epideictic is given a dominant role in rhetoric in the New Rhetoric of Perelman (1979) and Perelman and Olbrechts-Tyteca 1958, 47–57). Kennedy (1997a, 45) also supports a more prominent role for epideictic: "Epideictic is perhaps best regarded as including any discourse, oral or written, that does not aim at a specific action or decision but seeks to enhance knowledge, understanding, or belief, often through praise or blame, whether of persons, things, or values." While written versions or revisions of juridical and deliberative speeches simply become literature once they are taken from their original oratorical context, epideictic has permanent significance (Perelman 1979, 6): "[T]he epideictic genre is not only important but essential from an educational point of view, since it too has an effective and distinctive part to play—that, namely, of bringing about a consensus in the minds of the audience regarding the values that are celebrated in the speech." To some extent this expanded conception of epideictic is anticipated by Cicero, who also gives an extended description of some of the characteristic stylistic features of epideictic (*Orator* 37; LCL trans.):

> There are several kinds of speeches differing one from the other, and impossible to reduce to one type; so I shall not include at this time that class to which the Greeks give the name *epideictic* because they were produced as showpieces, as it were, for the pleasure they will give, a class comprising eulogies, descriptions, histories, and exhortations like the *Panegyric* of Isocrates, and similar orations by many of the Sophists, as they are called, and all other speeches unconnected with battles of public life. . . . This style increases one's vocabulary and allows the use of a somewhat greater freedom in rhythm and sentence structure. It likewise indulges in a neatness and symmetry of sentences, and is allowed to use well defined and rounded periods; the ornamentation is done of set purpose, with no attempt at concealment, but openly and avowedly, so that words correspond to words as if measured off in equal phrases, frequently things inconsistent are placed side by side, and things contrasted are paired; clauses are made to end in the same way and with similar sound.

*Rhetorical genres, *Rhetorical theory, *Encomium, *Panegyric

---

Buchheit 1960; Kennedy 1972, 21–23; Perelman 1979; Perelman and Olbrechts-Tyteca 1958

Epilogue, a transliteration of the Greek term *epilogos*, refers to the closing part of a speech, often the most emotional part.

See *Arrangement.

Epistolary handbooks (see *Epistolography)

Epistolary theorists (see *Epistolography)

Epistolography deals with the form, style, and content of letters, and has two main aspects: the first, ancient epistolary theory, provides prescriptions for how letters should be written; the second focuses on the deductive descriptive analysis of the form, style, and content of ancient letters, based on a comparative analysis of actual examples (this latter topic is dealt with primarily in the discussions of individual letters).

Epistolary theorists. One of the first *rhetorical handbooks to comment on epistolary style (ὁ ἐπιστολικὸς χαρακτήρ) is Ps.-Demetrius, *De elocutione* 223–35. While the date of this work is disputed (see *Demetrius, *On Style*), the work can probably be assigned to the 1st cent. C.E. The epistolary handbook of Ps.-

Demetrius (*Epistolary Forms*), contains 21 designations for different styles, along with short samples. A later epistolary handbook (which seems to have no literary relationship with Ps.-Demeterius) is Ps.-Libanius (*Epistolary Styles*), which contains 41 styles of letters, each of which is named and defined, and later in the treatise is given an example. In the following table, the letter types of Ps.-Demetrius have been alphabetized in the left-hand column (followed by the paragraph in *Epistolary Types* in which they are discussed). In the middle column, the English translation of the letter type is given. In the right-hand column, the categories of Ps.-Libanius are given. It is striking that just thirteen categories overlap.

Stowers (1986, 91–152) collapses many of these types into a typology of six epistolary types: (1) letters of friendship; (2) family letters; (3) letters of praise and blame; (4) hortatory letters (seven subtypes): (a) paraenetic letters, (b) protreptic letters, (c) letters of advice, (d) letters of admonition, (d) letters of rebuke, (e) letters of reproach, (f) letters of consolation; (5) letters of recommendation or mediation; (6) accusing and apologetic letters.

One of the greatest obstacles to the formal analysis of Hellenistic letters, including early Christian letters, is the fact that the body of such letters exhibit few formal features (J. L. White 1971b, 91 n. 2). According to Stowers (1986, 22): "Modern epistolary research has found very little to say about the body of the letter." Unlike the documentary letters with which the Pauline letters have frequently been compared, Paul's letters are more literary in character, a phenomenon that includes the mixture of letter types and the internal rhetorical design of the letters (Betz 1985, 130–31).

Exler (1923) distinguishes several types of documentary letters, each with its own opening phrases: (1) familiar letters, i.e., letters written to family and friends (1923, 24–36); (2) business letters, including contracts, leases, receipts, etc. (1923, 36–42); (3) petitions (1923, 42–50); (4) official letters (1923, 50–60).

Literary letters. Literary letters are those that were preserved and transmitted through literary channels and were valued either as epistolary models, as examples of literary artistry, or as vignettes into earlier lives and manners. They exhibit wide variety, including: (1) real letters written by an educated person with no thought of publication (e.g., many of the *epistulae commendaticidae*, or letters of recommendation, by Cicero, Pliny, and Fronto; (2) real letters written with a broader public in view (Cicero, Pliny, Libanius; see *Letter collections); (3) ideal letters using a "high" style and written with publication in view (Horace, Ovid, Seneca, Statius); (4) fictional letters using epistolary conventions to frame human interest stories or interesting anecdotes (Alciphron, Aelian, Philostratus); (5) fictional letters composed for insertion in historical and fictional narratives and those written as rhetorical exercises as though by some famous person (*Achilles Tatius, *Chariton); (6) letter-essays (Ps.-Demetrius, *On Style* 4.228), in which essays or treatises on various subjects are prefaced by an epistolary prescript (Plutarch, Fronto). The educated could write both public and private letters. Public letters were intentionally written to be read by those other than their original addressees (Cicero, *Ad fam.* 15.21.4).

Letters of recommendation played an increasingly important role in upper-class society from the end of the Roman republic to late antiquity. They are the Roman counterpart of the Greek letter of introduction mentioned in the *epistolary theorists (Ps.-Demetrius, *Epistolary Types* 2 [συστατικός]; Ps.-Libanius, *Epistolary Styles* 8, 55 [συστατική]). Many letters of this type are preserved in the epistolary collections of Cicero (106–43 B.C.E.), Pliny (ca. 61–112 C.E.), Fronto (100–166 C.E.), and Libanius (314–93 C.E.). The collection of Cicero's letters, made during the reign of Nero (ca. 60 C.E.), contains numerous letters of recommendation that served as models for later writers (see the ten letters of recommendation or *commendationes* to Acilius in *Ad fam.* 13.30–39). The Roman Empire was fundamentally a patronage system in which vertical bonds between people of different classes or orders took precedence over horizontal relationships between equals (thus effectively preventing an ancient "class consciousness"). The reciprocity ethic (i.e., favors bestowed incurred obligation) permeated all aspects of life, between people and their gods, within families, and among "friends." Influential patrons could recommend their clients for administrative positions under the control of those (like the emperor) who typically exercised personal discretion in such appointments. The patronage system meant that officials regularly used (and were expected to use) their positions to secure benefits for family and friends. Influential men like Cicero, Pliny, Fronto, and Libanius recommended their protégés on the basis of moral qualities (e.g., uprightness, soberness, intelligence, and diligence), rather than professional skills (Fronto, *To Marcus* 5.37; *To Friends* 1.1–5; *To Pius* 9). The Roman conception of friendship had an important utilitarian aspect, i.e., the

Types of Letters

	Ps.-Demetrius	Type of Letter	Ps.-Libanius
1	αἰτιολογικὸς τύπος (16)	Accounting	
2	ἀξιοματικός (12)	Supplicatory	
3	ἀλληγορικός (15)	Allegorical	
4	ἀπειλητικός (8)	Threatening	ἀπειλητική (13, 60)
5	ἀπευχαριστικός (21)	Thankful	εὐχαριστική (10, 57)
6	ἀπολογητικός (18)	Apologetic	
7	ἀποφαντικός (14)	Responding	ἀποφαντική (38, 85)
8	εἰρωνικός (20)	Ironic	εἰρωνική (9, 56)
9	ἐπαινετικός (10)	Praising	ἐπαινετική (30, 77)
10	ἐπιτιμητικός (6)	Censorious	ἐπιτιμητική (34, 81)
11	ἐρωτηματικός (13)	Inquiring	ἐρωτηματική (35, 82)
12	κατηγορικός (17)	Accusing	
13	μεμπτικός (3)	Blaming	μεμπτική (6, 53)
14	νουθητικός (7)	Admonishing	
15	ὀνειδιστικός (4)	Reproachful	ὀνειδιστική (17, 64)
16	παραμυθητικός (5)	Consoling	παραμυθητική (25, 72)
17	συγχαρητικός (19)	Congratulatory	συγχαρητική (20, 67)
18	συμβουλευτικός (11)	Advisory	
19	συστατικός (2)	Commending	συστατική (8, 55)
20	φιλικός (1)	Friendly	φιλική (11, 58)
21	ψεκτικός (9)	Vituperative	
22		Enigmatic	αἰνιγματική (41, 88)
23		Consulting	ἀναθετική (37, 84)
24		Counter-accusing	ἀντεγκληματική (22, 69)
25		Replying	ἀντεπισταλτική (23, 70)
26		Reporting	ἀπαγγελτική (27, 74)
27		Denying	ἀπαρνητική (13, 61)
28		Maligning	διαβλητική (33, 80)
29		Didactic	διδασκαλική (31, 78)
30		Reproving	ἐλεγκτική (32, 79)
31		Erotic	ἐρωτική (44, 91)
32		Praying	εὐκτική (12, 59)
33		Conciliatory	θεραπευτική (19, 66)
34		Grieving	λυπητική (43, 90)
35		Mocking	μετριαστική (40, 87)
36		Repenting	μεταμελητική (16,63)
37		Mixed	μικτή (45, 92)
38		Commanding	παραγγελματική (15, 62)
39		Encouraging	παραθαρρυντική (36, 83)
40		Paraenetic	παραινετική (5, 52)
41		Requesting	παρακλητική (7, 54)
42		Contemptuous	παραλογιστική (21, 68)
43		Provoking	παροξυντική (24, 71)
44		Diplomatic	πρεσβευτική (29, 76)
45		Mocking	σκωπτική (39, 86)
46		Sympathetic	συμπαθητική (18, 65)
47		Angry	σχελιαστική (28, 75)
48		Insulting	ὑβριστική (26, 73)
49		Suggestive	ὑπομνηστική (42, 89)

mutually beneficial exchange of various kinds of goods and services, since there were no impersonal institutional means for distribution. A letter of recommendation was in effect an act of friendship, addressed to one friend on behalf of another friend.

Letter-essays. Stirewalt (1991, 1993, 18–20), proposes the distinct literary form of the "letter-essay," though he recognizes that it was not considered a genre by ancient authors. Examples of letter-essays include *Dionysius of Halicarnassus, *Letter to Gnaeus Pompeius*; 2 Maccabees; **Martydom of Polycarp*. Letter-essays are treatises that make only a limited use of epistolary conventions, particularly in opening formulas. Epistolary *prefaces, for instance, appear for the first time in the scientific treatises of Archimedes (287–212 B.C.E.), which were addressed and dedicated to friends. Seneca was the first rhetorical writer to use epistolary prefaces; all his *Moral Epistles* have them. Quintilian introduces his *Institutes* with a double preface, one epistolary and the other rhetorical. Pliny the Elder's *Natural History* also has a prose epistolary preface. Philostratus, *Lives of the Sophists* (written after 202 C.E.), has a prefatory letter. The **Rhetorica ad Alexandrum*, a late 3d-cent. C.E. rhetorical handbook compiled by Anaximines of Lampsacus, is prefaced by a letter with the bogus prescript "Aristotle to Alexander, best wishes," and concludes with a simple "farewell." Among Plutarch's letter-essays, *On Tranquility* is a deliberative essay written in response to the addressee's request. Two other deliberative letter-essays are *Consolation to His Wife* (written when he learned, while away from home, of the death of their daughter) and *Conjugal Precepts* (advice to newlyweds). A fourth letter-essay is *On the Generation of the Soul* (a treatise on Plato's doctrine of the soul requested by the author's two sons). Plutarch always used εὐ πράττειν ("best wishes") as a salutation, a common formula in literary letters.

A special type of letter-essay is the philosophical letter. The 1st cent. C.E. was a period when moral philosophers increasingly made use of the letter form as a vehicle for instruction. The letters of Plato, Aristotle, and Epicurus were important models for this development (Plato's *Ep.* 7, for example, was very influential on later authors). Several of the letters of Epicurus survive, though the one to Pythocles is of doubtful authenticity. Three letters of Epicurus are preserved in Diogenes Laertius 10.34–83, one to Herodotus (epitomizing Epicurus's philosophy of nature), one to Pythocles (summarizing his meteorology, at the request of the addressee), and one to Menoeceus (summarizing Epicurean morality). The Letter to Menoeceus is a symbouleutic or protreptic letter urging the study of philosophy.

Many pseudepigraphical letters and letter collections made their debut in the 1st cent. C.E., including the lengthy collection attributed to Hippocrates (some of which exhibit the *diatribe style), and the pseudepigraphical collections of Cynic letters attributed to such philosophers as Socrates, Anacharsis, Crates, Diogenes, and Heraclitus (Attridge 1976; Malherbe 1977). These Cynic letters and Seneca transformed the diatribe into an epistolary form in the 1st cent. C.E.

Official letters. The form and style of official letters, written from governmental representatives to others in official capacities, are similar to private letters. The ancients were very familiar with such letters, since they were often published by posting or by inscribing them on stones placed in prominent places for public viewing. Publication meant that they were tools for influencing public opinion. Important discussions of official letters include Welles (1974; originally published in 1934) and Sherk (1969).

By the 2d cent. B.C.E., the Hellenistic monarchies in the Greek east had developed bureaucracies with royal chanceries whose staff drew up and preserved official governmental correspondence and kept archival copies of all royal edicts. Typically, a city's request was presented to the king by ambassadors. The request might involve the acceptance of honors voted to the monarch, for which various favors might be asked in return (e.g., arbitration of a dispute, settlement of a legal point). The king would then draft a reply that the chancery staff would put in finished form. The king added a concluding "farewell" himself. The heads of these royal chanceries gave a distinctive form and style to these letters. The prescripts reflected the conventions of the private letter: "X [nominative] to Y [dative], greetings [χαίρειν]," and concluded with ἔρρωσθε ("farewell"), written on the original document by the monarch himself. Rhetoric influenced chancery correspondence only very slowly. Welles (1974) distinguished between two basic structural features of official letters, one containing a statement or announcement alone (e.g., praise, a royal decision, a favor) and another containing a statement that is the basis for an order.

During the period of the Roman Republic, official Roman correspondence took the form of letters sent by the Roman Senate or magistrates to officials of foreign cities, outlining official policy in particular matters. During the Empire, diplomatic correspondence was very common. *Epistulae principium* ("imperial epistles") and *rescripta* (written responses by the emperor to the questions of officials) were the primary means for the emperor to create law and convey his will to provincial cities. *Epistulae principium* were issued only by the *Ab epistulis*, the imperial bureau (with both Greek and Latin departments) concerned with the emperor's private and official correspondence (A. Berger 1953, 338; F. Millar 1977, 556–66).

Official Roman letters of the late Republic and early Empire addressed to Greek cities followed Hellenistic models. Senatorial decrees and other official communications were translated into Greek (a measure taken for no other language group under Roman authority) and published as inscriptions. They usually began with a typical epistolary prescript: "X [nominative] to Y [dative], greetings [χαίρειν]." The adscript included the name of the city in the genitive and the name or names of city officials or governing bodies in the dative. After 150 B.C.E., official letters sometimes included the health formula after the greeting. Motives for writing, such as information or requests from Greek envoys, are then mentioned. Also included were the names of the Greek envoys, where they met the magistrate, and the information they brought. The body of such letters then included such matters as (1) the bestowal of various benefits, (2) the restoration of lands, (3) decisions and edicts, (4) arbitration, (5) the communication of *senatus consulta* ("resolutions of the senate"). Diplomatic letters concluded with a wish for the well-being of the addressee, usually ἔρρωσθε ("farewell"), in imitation of Hellenistic letters.

Documentary letters. Documentary or nonliterary private letters constituted the common-letter tradition of antiquity, a tradition that remained stable from the Ptolemaic period (3d cent. B.C.E., the date of the earliest papyrus letters) to the Roman period (3d cent. C.E. and later). The thousands of ancient papyrus letters preserved by the dry Egyptian climate provide the bulk of our knowledge of the ancient Greek common-letter tradition.

Such letters functioned in three basic ways: (1) to maintain contact with family and friends, (2) to communicate information, (3) to request information or favors. Private letters therefore include several types distinguished on the basis of function: (1) letters of request or petition, (2) letters of information, (3) letters of introduction (Kim 1972), (4) letters of recommendation (Keyes 1935), (5) letters of order and instruction, (6) family letters, and (7) business letters (contracts, leases, receipts, etc.). While some letters exhibit only one function, occasionally they combine several functions.

The body of the papyrus letter and of the Pauline letter can be divided into three components: (1) the introductory section introducing the reasons for writing, (2) the middle section carrying the relevant details or disclosing new information, (3) the concluding section both reiterating the primary occasion for writing and laying the groundwork for future communication (J. L. White 1971b, 45–46).

The prescript of the ancient letter typically contained three elements: the superscription (sender), the adscription (addressee), and the salutation: "X [nominative] to Y [dative], greetings [χαίρειν]." A more formal variant, used in petitions, complaints, and applications, was "To Y [dative] from X," usually omitting the salutation. These two patterns were found from the 3d cent. B.C.E. to the 3d cent. C.E. Many variations were also found. The basic pattern of Greek epistolary prescripts was subject to various forms of amplification and elaboration. The superscription and adscription could be expanded through the addition of epithets, titles, terms of relationship (e.g., "X to his sister Y") and endearment (e.g., "X to my dearest friend Y"), and geographical location. The salutation was also capable of expansion by using adjectives or adverbs emphasizing degree ("warmest greetings") or by adding a health wish ("greetings and health"). This capacity for amplification allowed the Christian letter to develop its own distinctive features.

The *formula valetudinis* or health wish (typically using the verb ὑγιαίνειν), also found at the close, often followed the prescript: "If you are well, it would be excellent. I too am well." Since there are several health formulas that exhibit some variation, the health wish might better be described as a *topos* or theme. The ἐρρῶσθαι wish (from the 3d cent. B.C.E. on) could occupy a separate position at the beginning of the main part of the letter separate from the prescript, or it could be joined syntactically to the salutation of the prescript: "greetings and best wishes [χαίρειν καὶ ἐρρῶσθαι]."

The *proskynema formula*, a prayer (often of thanksgiving; προσκύνημα means "act of worship"), frequently either followed or was blended with the formula of health. Compare Hunt and Edgar (1932–34), no. 97: "Isias to her brother Hephaestion, greeting. If you are well and other things are going right, it would accord with the prayer which I make continually to the gods." Another example is from Hunt and Edgar (1932–34), no. 120: "Antonius Longus to Nilous his mother, very many greetings. I pray always for your health; every day I make supplication for you before the Lord Serapis." This prayer report formula appeared in the 1st cent. C.E. and remained popular until the 4th cent.

The *closing formulas* most commonly used were ἔρρωσο or ἔρρωσθε ("farewell"), and also the verb [δι]ευτύχει ("farewell" or "best wishes"), frequently with the date. The closing formula could also be omitted. Formulas at the conclusion of the main part included "take care of yourself that you might be well" (from the 3d cent. B.C.E.). This was gradually replaced by the ἀσπάζεσθαι ("greeting") formula, from the 1st cent. B.C.E. on, in which the writer asked the recipient to greet acquaintances not directly addressed by the letter or conveyed the greetings of others. There was also the illiteracy formula: "X writes on behalf of Y," usually in business letters and official letters. Oath formulas occurred at the end of certain types of business letters, such as sworn declarations and various official statements.

Epistolary rhetoric. The vast majority of ancient letters were relatively short communications written for a specific occasion and discarded soon afterward. By the 1st cent. C.E., rhetoric had come to exert an indirect influence on the composition of letters, particularly among the educated. Their letters functioned not only as means of communication but also as sophisticated instruments of persuasion and vehicles for displaying their literary skills.

Earlier rhetorical handbooks, however, have little to say about the art of letter writing, and it is generally true to say that "letter-writing remained only on the fringes of formal rhetorical education throughout antiquity" (Stowers 1986, 34) and that "the letter-writing tradition was essentially independent of rhetoric" (Stowers 1986, 52). Suspicious of this argument from silence, Bakke (2001, 29) argues that one should not hastily draw the conclusion that letter writing was relatively uninfluenced by rhetoric and that the real proof can lie only in the analysis of actual letters.

Epistolography and rhetoric in NT letters. The widespread interest in the rhetorical analysis of the Pauline letters and other NT letters, following the stimulus of the rhetorical analyses of Betz (1974–75, 1976, 1979) is based largely on the assumption that the ancient letter was a substitute for speech and therefore an appropriate subject for rhetorical analysis. The application of rhetorical critical methods to letters has been subject to critical scrutiny in the last few years (Watson and Hauser 1994, 120 n. 103; Kern 1998; Weima 2000; Bakke 2001, 26–31; Sänger 2002). Interpreters have approached the NT letters from one of three perspectives (Watson and Hauser 1994, 120–21): (1) as letters, with epistolographical elements of primary importance and rhetorical elements of secondary importance; (2) as speeches in letter form capable of being analyzed in accordance with rhetorical theory; and (3) as combinations of epistolographical and rhetorical conventions, which should be given equal emphasis or even integrated (Byrskog 1997, 27). The use of rhetorical theory for epistolary analysis has been thought problematic for several reasons. First, rhetorical conventions do not pervade letters to the extent that many rhetoric critics assume (Reed 1993). Second, letters in the Greco-Roman world were not considered a customary avenue of expression for rhetorical genres, structures, and arguments (Porter 1997, 251–52). Third, those epistolary handbooks that do exist are late and very general and provide little purchase for analyzing literary letters such as those written by Paul. Fourth, Aristotle (*Rhet.* 3.12.2 [1413b]) recognized that there are different stylistic rules for oral speeches and written texts, an insight borne out of modern socio-linguistics.

One of the great letter writers of late antiquity was the Antiochean rhetorician Libanius, who wrote more than 1,600 letters (Seeck 1906; Liebeschuetz 1972). Libanius had an extensive network of personal connections, many relating to his role as patron, largely maintained by his voluminous correspondence. Many letters recommended former students for employment to provincial governors (e.g., *Ep.* 134, 161, 807). Others were letters of introduction requesting private hospitality for traveling students and friends (*Ep.* 268, 704). He also reported on students' progress by writing reassuring letters to parents (*Ep.* 141, 190, 324). For Libanius, letter writing was an art. Rigidly adhering to epistolary conventions, he limited letters to a single topic. News and information extraneous to the letter were left for oral communication by the bearer (*Ep.* 753, 1429). Most of his letters had three sections: (1) expressions of friendship to the recipient, (2) praise to the bearer, and (3) the main purpose of the letter. It was conventional to omit everything extraneous to the main purpose of the letter. This meant that it was theoretically easy to "type" letters, since they tended to have one primary function. Personal feelings (e.g., personal experiences, private ideas, and opinions) were not expressed in letters except through such conventional *topoi* as longing, friendship, jealousy at the preference of one friend for another, consolation for a bereavement. Not to write when someone was going to see one of a person's friends was taken as an insult (*Ep.* 212, 326, 410). It was also considered bad manners to write to a stranger, and the beginning of a new friendship demanded special justification (*Ep.* 95, 448, 645, 836), since such a relationship inevitably led to a demand for favors (given the patron-client social structure).

*Letter collections, *Novelistic letters *Rhetorical theory, *Letters, literary genre of

---

Attridge 1976b; Exler 1923; Hunt and Edgar 1932–34; Keyes 1935; Kim 1972; Koskenniemi 1956; Malherbe 1977b, 1988; Mullins 1962, 1964, 1973; Peter 1901; Probst 1991; Reed 1997; J. H. Roberts 1986; Rosenmeyer 2001; J. L. Sanders 1962; C. Schneider 1954, 2.15–20; Schnider and Stenger 1987; Stirewalt 1991, 1993, 2002; Stowers 1986; Sykutris 1924; Thraede 1970; Welles 1974; J. L. White 1971b, 1972a, 1972b, 1986, 1988

Epyllion, a transliterated form of the Greek word ἐπύλλιον ("versicle, bit of poetry"), a diminutive of ἔπος ("poetry"), which first appears in Athenaeus 2.65a with the meaning "miniature Homeric epic." During the first quarter of the 19th cent. (Most 1982), the term began to be used as a technical term for Alexandrian mini-epic in hexameter (e.g., Callimachus, *Hecale*). While some have argued that the term was not used for the mini-epic by the ancients and therefore should not be used today (W. Allen 1940). Merriam (2001) has argued convincingly that there was an unbroken tradition of narrative hexameter poems from Theocritus through Ovid that, considered together, constitute a *subgenre of narrative epic. The epyllion only rarely exceeds 400 lines, never more than 900 lines (Merriam 2001, 2), and is descended from the *Argonautica* of Apollonius Rhodius. The epyllion avoids the typical grand themes of epic (e.g., the battlefield, the sea voyage, the difficult journey by land, the centrality of the male hero) and fills the gaps in earlier epics by developing lesser themes (e.g., domestic scenes, the panels on Achilles' shield representing domestic life). Gutzwiller referred to these themes as a subversion or inversion of traditional epic ideals (1981). Crump (1931) defined the epyllion as a short narrative poem, not exceeding 500 lines, focusing on a little-known episode in the life of a hero or heroine, and with little or no emphasis on the role of the gods. Later Alexandrian and Latin epyllia tended to focus on love stories and the heroine. Unlike epic, the epyllion focuses on lesser characters who are marginal and unheroic, with a particular emphasis on female characters (Merriam 2001, 6). Examples include Theocritus, *Idyll* 24 (featuring Alcmena and the infant hero Heracles; see Merriam 2001, 21–49); Moschus, *Europa* (Merriam 2001, 51–73); and Catullus 64: Peleus and Thetis (Catullus contrasts Thetis with Ariadne; see Merriam 2001, 75–125). The Latin epyllia represent a final state in the development of the genre (Merriam 2001, 127–57). Merriam (2001, 160) argues that "The chief importance of the epyllion in literary history lies in its status as the ancient genre which focuses most exclusively upon women, their worlds and their works, from what might be considered a female perspective." In the epyllion, these women tell their own stories and become the centers of attention, while the traditional heroic figures of epic (fathers, husbands, lovers, and heroes) are used as stage decorations. For a list of Hellenistic epyllia, see *DNP* 4.31–32.

Relevance for NT and ECL. While there are no mini-epics written in Greek or Latin hexameter in early Christian literature, a number of scholars have proposed that ancient epics (particularly *Homer and Virgil) have influenced the structure of some works of NT or early Christian literature, particularly Mark (D. R. MacDonald 2000), Luke–Acts (R. MacDonald 1994b, 1999; Bonz 2000), and the *Acts of Andrew* (D. R. MacDonald 1990, 1994a). In addition, the countercultural focus on the role of the female in the epyllion is important in understanding the role of gender ideology in ancient literature and particularly in early Christian literature.

*Homer

Allen 1940; Crump 1931; *DNP* 4.31–33; Gutzwiller 1981; Jackson 1913; Merriam 2001; Most 1982

Eristic, a transliterated form of the Greek word ἐριστικός (from ἔρις, "strife"), is used in Plato to mean "seeking victory in argument" (Kerferd 1981, 62) and is used of several argumentative techniques. Plato is completely opposed to eristic, because it involves refuting whatever people say, whether it is true or false.

*Antilogic

Er-Stil, literally "he-style," refers to the use of third-person pronouns and verb forms in speaking about the deity, a grammatical form even used in hymns and prayers (see *du-Stil*). For the *er-Stil* in a prayer, see Aeschuylus, *Agamemnon* 146–51 (LCL trans.): "And I implore Paean, the healer, that she may not raise adverse gales with long delay to stay the Danaan fleet from putting forth by reason of her urgence of another sacrifice."

**Du-Stil*, *Hymn, *Prayer

Norden 1956, 163–66

Eschatocol, from the Greek word ἐσχατοκόλλιον (meaning the end of a papyrus roll), refers to a concluding clause or formula in a manuscript, and by extension (primarily in German) to the concluding formulas in a letter.

*Colophon

Etacism is a term referring to the pronunciation of the Greek letter η (eta), with a long ā, as in the English word "ale." This is a characteristic of the Erasmian pronunciation of Greek.

*Itacism

Ethos, a transliteration of the Greek word ἦθος, meaning "character," is a term used in philosophical discussions, such as those of Aristotle, for "character" in the narrow sense of the moral qualities of a person (Aristotle, *Ethica, Poetica*), but is expanded to include intellectual as well as moral qualities in the *Rhetorica* of Aristotle (Wisse 1989, 30–32). Quintilian (*Inst.* 6.2.8), observes that there is no Latin translation equivalent to ἦθος(May 1988, 4).

Greek Rhetoric and Aristotle. Plato argued that the person who wishes to be an honorable orator should not only possess a good character, but also be knowledgeable, alert, and able to adapt his argument to his audience (*Phaedrus* 261a, 270b, 271d). A similar emphasis on the character of the speaker, defined primarily in terms of reputation, is found in a speech by Isocrates, a contemporary of Aristotle (*Antidosis* 278; LCL trans. with modifications):

> The man who wishes to persuade people will not be negligent as to the matter of character [ἦθος]; no, on the contrary, he will apply himself above all to establish a most honorable name among his fellow-citizens; for who does not know that words carry greater conviction when spoken by men of good repute than when spoken by men who live under a cloud, and that the argument which is made by a man's life is of more weight than that which is furnished by words? Therefore the stronger a man's desire to persuade his hearers, the more zealously will he strive to be honorable and to have the esteem of his fellow-citizens.

It was Aristotle, however, who was the first to introduce ethos into rhetorical theory and to consider it a distinct form of proof (Garver 2000, 15; this is true despite the possibility that the *Rhetorica ad Alexandrum,* which contains a brief passage treating "character" in 14.8–9; 1431b, may predate Aristotle's *Rhetorica*). For him, ethos was a category of persuasion which, along with *pathos ("emotion") and logos ("*argument"), constituted the three basic types of artificial rhetorical proofs (πίστεις ἔντεχνοι) warranting the judgment of opinion (*Rhet.* 1.2.3–6; cf. Cicero *De oratore* 2.114). All three types of proof were together part of what later rhetoricians called *inventio,* the "discovery [of arguments]," one of three parts of Aristotle's *officia oratoris,* i.e., duties of an orator (*Rhet.* 3.1.1; 1403b). For Aristotle, the primary role of character in speech served to make the speaker appear to be a moral person and therefore trustworthy, ἀξιόπιστος (*Rhet* 1.2.4; trans. Kennedy 1991, 38):

> [There is persuasion] through character whenever the speech is spoken in such a way as to make the speaker worthy of credence; for we believe fair-minded people to a greater extent and more quickly [than we do others] on all subjects in general and completely so in cases where there is not exact knowledge but room for doubt. And this should result from the speech, not from a previous opinion that the speaker is a certain kind of person.

It is important to note that for Aristotle the speech itself was the vehicle for conveying the character of the speaker, not his reputation or social authority (Garver 1994, 93). Reputation and social authority are particularly important for Romans where personal relations were often decisive factors, while personal relations were of lesser importance in democratic Athens. Aristotle goes so far as to claim that "character is almost, so to speak, the controlling factor [κυριωτάτην] in persuasion" (*Rhet.* 1.2.4; trans. Kennedy 1991, 38). Though Aristotle discusses each of the three kinds of proof, ethos, pathos, and logos, there is some disagreement about where his discussion of ethos is found. While some locate the discussion of ethos in *Rhet.* 2.1.1–9 (Fortenbaugh 1988, 260; Vickers 1988, 20), Wisse (1989, 29–36) properly limits the discussion of ethos to the very short thirteen-line section found in *Rhet.* 2.1.5–7. Aristotle discusses a different application of the term ἦθος in *Rhet.* 2.12–17, where he treats the "characters" of different age groups (the young, the old, those in their prime), and social groups (those with noble birth, the wealthy, the powerful, and their opposites), but this use of "character" refers primarily to the audience, not the speaker (Wisse 1989, 36–43). Aristotle's discussion of the ethos of the speaker, which includes both moral and intellectual qualities (Wisse 1989, 30) is short enough to be quoted in entirety (*Rhet.* 2.1.5–7; trans. Kennedy 1991, 120–21):

> 5. There are three reasons why speakers themselves are persuasive; for there are three things we trust other than logical demonstrations. These are practical wisdom [φρόνησις] and virtue [ἀρετή] and good will [εὔνοια]; for speakers make mistakes in what they say or advise through failure to exhibit either all or one of these; 6. for either through lack of practical sense they do not form opinions rightly; or through forming opinions rightly they do not say what they think because of a bad character; or they are prudent and fair-minded but lack good will, so that it is possible for people not to give the best advice although they know [what] it [is]. These are the only possibilities. Therefore a person seeming to have all these qualities is necessarily persuasive to the hearers. 7. The means by which one might appear prudent and good are to be grasped from analysis of the virtues; for a person would present himself as being of a certain sort from the same sources that he would use to present another person; and good will and friendliness need to be described in a discussion of the emotions.

Aristotle's conception of ethos is essentially rational, since it is directed not at sympathy (as in Cicero), but at reliability and is therefore unrelated to the emotions (Wisse 1989, 241).

The use of ethos as a concept in Greek rhetoric after Aristotle is problematized by its absence. The **Rhetorica ad Alexandrum* (probably written before Aristotle's *Rhetoric,* though this is a moot issue) contains a brief discussion of the "ethos" of the rhetor, though the term ἦθος (itself is not used (14.8–9; 1431b; see Wisse 1989, 51–53). The three types of proof are also mentioned by Dionysius Hal. *Lysias* 19 (LCL trans.):

> I shall begin with what are called rhetorical proofs, dealing with each of the three kinds that are distinguished, the factual [πρᾶγμα], the emotional [πάθος] and the moral [ἦθος].

Dionysius then discusses Lysias' approach to ethos in more detail (*Lysias* 19; LCL trans.):

> He [Lysias] also seems to me to show very notable skill in constructing proofs from character. He often makes us believe in his client's good character by referring to the circumstances of his life and his parentage, and often again by describing his past actions and the principles governing them. And when the facts fail to provide him with such material, he created his own moral tone, making his characters seem by their speech to be trustworthy and honest. He credits them with civilised dispositions and attributed controlled feelings to them; he makes them voice appropriate sentiments, and introduces them as men whose thoughts befit their status in life, and who abhor both evil words and evil deeds.

Generally, however, ethos and pathos seem to have dropped out of rhetorical handbooks after Aristotle (Wisse 1989, 80–83), and certainly after Hermagoras of Temnos, fl. 150 B.C.E. (Solmsen 1974). In part this was due to Stoic influence, since the Stoics were very much interested in rhetoric, but rejected emotional and ethical appeals and therefore did not adopt Aristotle's scheme of the three proofs. The absence of ethos and pathos from rhetorical handbooks is attested in a conversation attributed to the Academic philosopher Charmadas ca. 102 B.C.E. in Cicero *De oratore* 1.87 (LCL trans.; italics added):

> For he [Charmadas] was of opinion that the main object of the orator was that he should both appear himself, and to those before whom he was pleading, to be such a man as he would desire to seem (*an end to be attained by a reputable mode of life, as to which those teachers of rhetoric had left no hint among their instructions*), and that the hearts of his hearers should be touched in such fashion as the orator would have them touched (another purpose only to be achieved by a speaker who had investigated all the ways wherein, and all the allurements and kind of diction whereby, the judgment of men might be inclined to this side or to that); *but according to him such knowledge lay thrust away and buried deep in the very heart of phi-*

losophy, and those rhetoricians had not so much as tasted it with the tip of the tongue.

In general, however, it is true to say that while ethos and pathos no longer existed as independent concepts under the task of *inventio,* ethos was primarily associated with the exordium of a speech and pathos with the epilogue (Cicero *De inventione* 1.98–109; *Rhetorica ad Herennium* 2.47).

Roman Rhetoric and Cicero. Roman oratory made more extensive use of ethos than did Attic oratory (Kennedy 1968, 436). Roman juridical rhetoric was fundamentally different from its Greek counterpart in that it was common in Rome for a litigant (in the role of client) to be represented by a patron playing the role of defender, while in Greek practice the litigant was usually required to speak for himself, even though he might memorize a ghost-written speech prepared by a professional (Kennedy 1968; Wisse 1989, 100–103). Further, Roman audiences were intolerant of slippage between a person's words and his actions, and for this reason the reputation of the rhetor (a factor that Aristotle sought to exclude from ethos as a rhetorical proof), his ethos or character, was extremely important. The earliest Latin rhetorical handbooks, Cicero's *De inventione* (written when he was seventeen) and the *Rhetorica ad Herennium* (both essentially Greek rhetorical works in Latin dress), do not treat ethos and pathos like Aristotle did as two of the three types of rhetorical proof under invention. When elements that might be associated with ethos and pathos are mentioned, they are found subordinated to rational argument, i.e., *inventio* consists almost exclusively in using topics to come up with the appropriate rational arguments (Wisse 1989, 93–103). Later, in *De oratore,* Cicero treats ethos, pathos, and logos in Aristotelian fashion as the three types of proof under invention (*De oratore* 2.99–306), focusing first on rational argumentation [2.114–177], then on ethos [2.182–4], and then on pathos [2.185–211a]); see Wisse 1989, 190–221. He summarizes the role of each in *De oratore* 2.128:

> Under my whole oratorical system . . . lie three principles [*rationes*], as I said before, first the winning of men's favour [ethos], secondly their enlightenment [logos], thirdly their excitement [pathos].

Later Latin rhetoricians, such as Quintilian, regarded logical proof as of lesser importance than *ethos and *pathos (*Inst.* 5.14.29–31). The political and legal speeches of Cicero have been used as examples of Cicero's oratorical use of ethos (May 1988). Cicero's discussion of ethos (though the term itself does not occur), is not particularly Aristotelian (Kennedy 1972, 222).

While some have understood Cicero's use of the verb *conciliare* ("to secure good will") as the Ciceronian equivalent to Aristotle's ἦθος (Fantham 1973; Fortenbaugh 1988), Wisse (1989, 235–6) argues that *conciliare* cannot be understood as a technical term and an equivalent to ἦθος. Enos and Schnakenberg (1994) have argued that Cicero's theoretical understanding of ethos involved three essential character traits: (1) *ingenium* (or *natura*), a natural talent for eloquence (*De oratore* 1.113–14, 146; 3.82–86), (2) *prudentia,* or a prudent character, i.e., the ability to adapt a discourse to any situation in the sense that a rhetor is able to "convey to an audience the moral issues at stake and the need to adhere to the cause he is championing" (Enos and Schnakenberg 1994, 199; see *De oratore* 2.184, 337), and (3) *diligentia,* or passion and commitment that is apparent to the audience (*De oratore* 2.182). All three of these character traits together constitute *dignitas,* i.e., the rhetor must meet the standards of his immediate audience as well as the social standards of Roman culture (*De oratore* 3.177–78), and "an audience's recognition and acceptance of such traits would, in turn, prompt them to view the rhetor as manifesting *dignitas*" (Enos and Schnakenberg 1994, 202). For Cicero, a lifelong manifestation of *dignitas* would earn the ascribed reputation of *auctoritas,* "reputation, authority" (*De senectute* 61–63), *honor,* "honor, dignity" (*De senectute* 61), and *gloria* "fame, renown" (*De republica* 6.20). Enos and Schnakenberg (1994, 205) conclude:

> There is no doubt that *ethos,* as created and transmitted in the act of discourse, extends beyond the immediate rhetorical situation and develops over time; that is, *ethos* is being continually created between the rhetor and the public. The sustained formation of this *ethos* is manifested in *auctoritas,* and with it come the benefits of a personal *honor* and a public *gloria* of communal recognition.

However, Enos and Schnakenberg have limited "ethos" in Cicero to the reputation of the speaker, but there are two other ways of describing ethos: in connection with the speech and in connection with the audience (Wisse 1989, 234). The verb *conciliare,* for example, is primarily concerned with the audience and with Cicero's "ethos of sympathy." Wisse

(1989, 240) provides a short description of ethos and pathos in Cicero:

> Ethos is the favourable presentation of the character of speaker and client (content), aimed at the hearers' sympathy (effect), pathos is aimed at arousing violent emotions in the hearers (effect). None of the two categories can be dispensed with: pathos, as a whole (in contrast with the individual emotions), has no specific content, so its description needs effect, whereas ethos cannot be described by effect only, since it is firmly tied to character-drawing.

Some (e.g., Solmsen 1974) have maintained that Cicero understood ethos to refer to the gentler, milder emotions, while pathos apparently refers to the stronger and more vehement emotions (*De oratore* 2.183–184, 212). However, Wisse argues that ethos in Cicero should not be equated with the *leniores affectus* ("gentler emotions"), and pathos with the stronger emotions, a view found in Quintilian.

Relevance to the NT & ECL. A number of scholars have explored the applicability of the rhetorical notion of ethos for understanding early Christian written texts. Two monographs that treat ethos-theory will be critiqued here. DiCicco (1995) approaches ethos-theory from the diachronic perspective of historical criticism, while Carey (1999) approaches classical ethos-theory and practice from the synchronic perspective of a postmodernist critic and as part of three strategies to explicate the narrative ethos of the Apocalypse.

DiCicco (1995) uses the three Aristotelian methods of proof, ethos, pathos, and logos, and their subsequent use in rhetorical theory and written speeches to analyze Paul's argumentation in 2 Cor. 10–13. DiCicco (1995, 77) finds that ethos "was a standard and studied technique in any persuasive discourse in classical antiquity," only by ignoring the peculiar absence of Aristotle's three types of rhetorical proof (ethos, pathos, and logos), as rhetorical concepts, in subsequent rhetorical handbooks. He also assumes that all uses of ἦθος in the *Rhetorica* are part of Aristotle's grand conception of ethos (following Cope 1867), but in this he and Cope are quite wrong. Further, he jumps from Aristotle to Cicero with no recognition of the very different understanding that Cicero had of ethos than did Aristotle, or of the fact that the ethos-pathos-logos distinction of Aristotle had fallen out of rhetorical theory until resurrected by Cicero. While there is no doubt that Paul was a victim of character assassination and had to defend himself in 2 Cor. 10–13, there is nothing distinctive in that defense which suggests that he was drawing on what he had learned about ethos in his putative rhetorical education (DiCicco 1995, 23–8). While DiCicco (1995, 78) claims that Paul "had to convey his ἦθος in a way that convinced his congregation that he was a man of φρόνησις, ἀρετή, and εὔνοια, the sources from which ἦθος arose," none of those terms are found in 2 Cor. 10–13, but rather constitute a rhetorical attempt to "push" Paul's language nearer the categories of ancient rhetoric, a tendency evident in his repeated use of the term ἦθος of Paul's person. Despite DiCicco's ahistorical use of the concept of ethos in rhetorical theory, he has nevertheless illuminated the rhetorical texture of 2 Cor. 10–13, though that illumination owes very little to *ancient* Greco-Roman rhetorical theory (despite DiCicco's explicit intention to demonstrate the historical influence that ancient rhetoric exerted on Paul; see DiCicco 1995, 13), as the cross-cultural study of rhetoric suggests (Kennedy 1998).

Carey (1999) uses the rhetorical conceptions of ethos as part of a complex strategy to understand the authority inscribed in the Apocalypse by its author. The author attempts to understand John's "narrative ethos" by approaching the subject using three perspectives (Carey 1999, 45–76): (1) classical rhetorical conceptions of ethos, (2) the function of narrators in literary criticism, and (3) narrative authority in colonial resistance literature, all in the interest of learning how "John constructs his ethos, his authority or credibility as a person to whom his audience should listen" (Carey 1999, 6). Unlike DiCicco, Carey does not use ancient ethos-theory as diachronic tool for understanding how John presented himself and his opponents in the text, but rather as one of several synchronic methods that attempts to construct a plausible reading of the Apocalypse from a postmodernist perspective (Carey 1999, 48, 184). He does not claim, for example, that his reading of the text conforms to the original author's intentions (Carey 1999, 94). Carey's review of ethos-theory in classical rhetoric is relatively nuanced, for he recognizes changes between Aristotle and Cicero, though he seems unaware of the general absence of ethos as a rhetorical concept in most rhetorical handbooks.

*Argument, *Aristotle, *Rhetorica,* *Autobiography, *Pathos, *Rhetorical Criticism, *Rhetorical Genres

---

Carey 1999; DiCicco 1995; Enos and Schnakenberg 1994; Fantham 1973;

Fortenbaugh 1988; Garver 1994, 2000; Gill 1984; Kennedy 1968; May 1988; North 1979; Sattler 1947; Süss 1910; Wisse 1989

Etymology, an interpretive technique that focuses on the meanings of individual words that are particularly difficult or particularly important. Etymologies are typically devoid of valid historical or linguistic perspectives. The etymology of Greek names begins, as one might expect, with Homer in Greek literature (*Odyssey* 12.85–86; 19.407–9). One of the more famous false biblical etymologies is the supposed meaning of "Eve" as "the mother of all living" because her name resembled the Hebrew term for "life." In the *Acts of Peter* §23, "Peter" is said to mean "prepared for all things."

*Commentary, *Scholion

Evangelist, an English transliteration of the Greek term εὐαγγελιστής for the author of a Gospel, first appears in Hippolytus (ca. 170–236 C.E.), and is regularly used by Origen (ca. 185–251 C.E.); see Lampe 1961, 559, under εὐαγγελιστής, 2.e. εὐαγγελιστής is used of Matthew (Hippolytus, *De consummatione mundi* 41); of Mark (*Const. Apost.* 7.46.5); of Luke (Marcellus in Epiphanius, *Haer.* 72.2); of John (Eusebius, *Praep. evang.* 11.18).

Example, a translation of the Greek word παράδειγμα ("precedent, example"), is a rhetorical term referring to examples used as inductive arguments (Aristotle, *Rhet.* 2.20; Anaximines, **Rhet. ad Alex.* 8); the Latin term is *exemplum*. For Aristotle, there are two kinds of examples of illustrative stories or anecdotes: (1) examples from real life or what could actually happen (παραβολαί) and (2) fictional examples, such as fables (Aristotle, *Rhet.* 2.20.2). The first-person section in Rom. 7:7–25 is a personal παράδειγμα, i.e., Paul is using his own experience to buttress his argument (R. D. Anderson 1999, 232). In 1 Cor. 9, Paul uses a "self-exemplary argument" demonstrating that he renounces apostolic rights, supporting his arguments against those Corinthians who have argued for their right to eat sacrificial food (Mitchell 1991, 243–50). In Rom. 4, Paul argues using the example that, since Abraham was justified by faith and not by works (4:2–9), the Gentiles also may be justified by faith and not by works (4:10–12, 22–24).

*Example stories, *Fable, *Fiction, *Parables, *Priamel

———

R. D. Anderson 2000, 87–88

Example stories, or "exemplary narratives" (German: *Beispielerzählungen*) is the widespread designation introduced by Jülicher (1919) for stories that present a specific case illustrating a general principle (Boucher 1981, 20). The example stories in the Synoptic Gospels (all of which occur in Luke) were identified on the basis of function rather than form (Baasland 1986). There are just four example stories in the canonical gospels, and all four are found in Luke: (1) parable of the Good Samaritan (10:25–37), (2) parable of the Rich Fool (12:16–21), (3) parable of the Rich Man and Lazarus (16:19–31), (4) the Pharisee and the tax collector (18:9–14). The one example story not found in Luke is the parallel to Luke 12:16–21 in *G.Thom.* 92 (though missing the supernatural element found in Luke 12:16–21). Crossan (1973, 56) argues that the four example stories of Luke were originally narrative parables and were transformed into examples by Luke.

*Parables

———

Baasland 1986; Boucher 1981; Hultgren 2000, 92–128; Jülicher 1919

Excerpting refers to the practice of ancient scholars of excerpting literary works by copying down passages of particular interest while reading (or being read to), a practice encouraged by the difficulty of finding passages in the papyrus-roll format. Xenophon refers to Socrates' penchant for collecting excerpts from the poets (*Memorabilia* 1.2.56; 1.6.14). Pliny provides this description of his uncle, the elder Pliny, who after eating would lie in the sun and make notes and extracts (*adnotabat excerpebatque*) while a book was read to him (*Ep.* 3.5.10–11). In fact, "There was nothing he read that he did not excerpt (*excerperet*) (3.5.10). Pliny claims that his uncle left him 160 notebooks of selected passages, written in a minute hand on both sides of the page (*Ep.* 3.5.17). There are several important implications that the tendency to produce excerpts has for understanding the work of ancient scholars (Mejer 1978, 18–19): (1) Excerpts are by definition out of context. (2) The use of an excerpt will often lead to the use of an excerpt from the same source, whether or not it fits the context or is on the same subject. (3) As an ancient scholar worked on a theme, the use of excerpts would follow a certain pattern; i.e., in reading a series of sources, he or she would excerpt less and less. (4) As a result of these practices, the tendency of modern scholars to identify the "main source" of an ancient author should be avoided. Mejer (1978, 19–29) finds abundant evidence in *Diogenes Laertius that he is using excerpts to write his work.

Mejer 1978:16–29; Skydsgaard 1968

Excursus (see *Digression)

Exegesis, a transliterated form of the Greek word ἐξήγησις (with two basic meanings: "narrative, description" and "explanation, interpretation"), is a technical term used in biblical studies for a detailed interpretation of a biblical text, and in historical studies as a synonym for "biblical interpretation." The term tends to be restricted to various perspectives from which biblical interpretation is undertaken, e.g., "Jewish exegesis," "patristic exegesis," "theological exegesis." Exegetical handbooks (Fee 2002; Hayes and Holladay 1987; Gorman 2001) emphasize the examination and interpretation of a passage of Scripture from as many perspectives as possible, including the text (the emphasis is on the original text and the significant textual variants that affect interpretation), translation of the text (often compared with several modern versions), the literary and historical contexts of the passage, the structure of the passage, the literary forms of the passage, grammatical issues and problems, lexical analysis or word studies, and (important from the standpoint of the professional training of pastors, priests, and rabbis) the application of the passage to the community of faith in the modern world.

Fee 2001, 2002; Gorman 2001; Hayes and Holladay 1987

Exegesis, Jewish biblical The sanctity of the Torah and the Prophets was a central and unifying feature of early Judaism. Yet the Bible, like all sacred foundational texts (whether oral or written), was subject to manipulation through interpretation. Various understandings of the same sacred texts served to legitimate the often conflicting views held by diverse groups.

While there were many formal and informal principles and procedures used to interpret Scripture in early Judaism, the written product of these methods was expressed in a variety of literary forms (Patte 1975). Some, though not all, were adopted by early Christians, who tended to see Scripture in terms of either eschatological prophecy (see *Pesharim) or typological anticipations of the Christian dispensation (see *Typology). This exegesis took several forms: (1) In *paraphrastic translation*, particular understandings of the text are folded into a translation, such as the Aramaic *Targumim (the earliest examples are 4QtgLev, 4QtgJob, and 11QtgJob) and the *Septuagint (Seeligmann 1948, 82). (2) In **rewritten Bible*, portions of the Hebrew Bible were understood in new or different ways through additions, deletions, and modifications (canonical example: 1 and 2 Chronicles; extracanonical examples: *Jubilees*; Ps.-Philo, *Liber Antiquitatem Biblicarum*; the Genesis Apocryphon, or 1QapGen; the Temple Scroll, or 11QTemple; Philo, *De vita Mosis*; Josephus, *Jewish Antiquities*). (3) In **anthological style*, the biblical text is not explicitly cited and commented upon but is rather woven into the style of the composition (1QH, the Jewish apocalypses). (4) In **commentaries*, the biblical text is quoted and interpreted (pesharim, *midrashim; many of the works of *Philo of Alexandria, including *Legum allegoriae*, *De cherubim*, etc.). This category can again be subdivided into verse-by-verse commentary and thematic commentary.

By the Second Temple period, the Jewish concern with the study of the Torah was increasingly expressed in terms of the necessity for receiving divine enlightenment to understand it. The theme is reiterated in Ps. 119 (vv. 12, 18–19, 27, 33–35, 73); Ps. 119:18 is typical: "Open my eyes, that I may behold wondrous things out of thy law." This motif is also reflected in the description of the vocation of the sage in Sir. 39.1–11, esp. vv. 6–7 (NRSV): "If the great Lord is willing, he will be filled with the spirit of understanding; he will pour forth words of wisdom of his own and give thanks to the Lord in prayer. The Lord will direct his counsel and knowledge, as he meditates on his mysteries."

*Charismatic exegesis, *Midrash, *Pesharim, *Quotation, *Testimony book hypothesis, *Typology

---

Aune 1993; Patte 1975; Seeligmann 1948

Exegesis, patristic biblical, refers to the methods of interpreting Scriptures found in Christian authors and Christian texts beginning with the *Apostolic Fathers of the late 1st to mid-2d cent. C.E. Early Christian exegetical methods and procedures were the product of several earlier exegetical traditions, both Jewish and Hellenistic. In Hellenistic schools, the focus of the curriculum was the reading and interpretation of classical texts from the past (see *Archaism, *Atticism, *Alexandrian Canon). One of the few sources that reveal the procedure in the elementary stages of Hellenistic education, after the student had learned to read and write, is Quintilian (1.4–9). This level of education emphasized the art of speaking correctly and the interpretation of the poets as well as all other types of literature (1.4.2). What a teacher did as he read the classics with his students was to analyze a verse into parts of speech and meter, to notice linguistic usage, focusing particularly on what is acceptable and unacceptable (including barbarisms and solecisms), to discuss the various meanings which words may have, to comment on unusual or foreign words, to explain the origins of names, to explain figures of speech and stylistic features (F. Young 1989, 184–85). When reading myths, the teacher would explain the various allusions, including identifying the gods, the heroes, and the various legends. The atomistic exegesis practiced in school, which focused on diction and style, also assumed that authors had theses to argue and that these needed to be recognized, though interpretation was always oriented toward how the reader understood the text, not what the author intended (F. Young 1989, 186). In a word, "ancient literary criticism had no true historical sense" (F. Young 199, 79). School exegesis therefore consisted of four elements (F. Young 1989, 187): (1) the establishing agreement about the correct and corrected text to be read (διόρθωσις); (2) the correct reading of the text (ἀνάγνωσις); (3) comments on the language and explanatory notes regarding historical references, i.e., places, dates, genealogies, characters, actions, etc., whether mythical or historical ἐξήγησις); and (4) the discerning of what is good, involving less aesthetic and critical issues than the search for virtue (κρίσις).

In early Christianity, at least from the 2d cent. on, "the unity of the Bible and its witness to Christ was the assumption underlying its 'reception' by readers and hearers in the 'public' assembly of the community" (F. Young 1997, 19). For Irenaeus, this unity of the Bible could be expressed as the Canon of Truth or the Rule of Faith (*regula fidei*), while Athanasius of Alexandria was concerned with discerning the unitive διανοία ("mind") of Scripture. According to F. Young (1997, 21):

> Neither the Rule of Faith nor the creed was in fact a summary of the whole biblical narrative. . . . They provided, rather, the proper reading of the beginning and the ending, the focus of the plot, and the relations of the principal characters, so enabling the "middle" to be heard in it as meaningful. They provided the "closure" which contemporary style prefers to leave open. They articulated the essential hermeneutical key without which texts and community would disintegrate in incoherence.

Thus, in early Christianity, as in Judaism, the canon of many books was functionally treated as a single book, so that the context for a particular verse was not only the immediate context or the particular writing, but the bounds of the entire canon. The priority of Christ over the OT had even been suggested by Ignatius (*Philad.* 8):

> Certain people declared in my hearing, "Unless I can find a thing in our ancient records [the OT], I refuse to believe it in the Gospel." When I assured them that it is indeed in the ancient Scriptures, they retorted, "That has got to be proved." But for my part, my records are Jesus Christ; for me the sacrosanct records are His cross and death and resurrection, and the faith that comes through him. And it is by these, and by the help of your prayers, that I am hoping to be justified.

This reflects the christological hermeneutic that permeated early Christian biblical interpretation.

*Allegory, *Barnabas, letter of, *Historical criticism, *Justin Martyr, *Typology

———

Bauer 1997; Bobertz and Brakke 2002; Chadwick 1998; Fiedrowicz 1998; Froehlich 1984; Grant and Tracy 1984; Hamman and Congourdeau 1997; Hammond Bammel 1995; Hanson 1959; Lauro 2001; Longenecker 1999; Simonetti 1994; Vogt 1999; F. Young 1989, 1990, 1997

Exemplum (see *Example)

Exordium is a Latin designation for the beginning or introduction of a speech. According to Quintilian (4.1.5): "The sole purpose of the exordium is to prepare our audience in such a way that they will be disposed to lend a ready ear to the rest of our speech." In relation to the other parts of a speech, the *exordium* is in the initial position, and its primary function is preparatory (Loutsch 1994, 22). Other designations include *prooemium* (Quintilian, *Inst.* 4.1.1) and *principium* (Quintilian, *Inst.* 4.1.1), the Greek term for which is προοίμιον,

(Aristotle, *Rhet.* 3.13 [1414a–b]; Quintilian *Inst.* 4.1.1). An *exordium* might function either as a *prooemium* or an *insinuatio*. The purpose of the *prooemium,* or "starting point," was to make the listener *benevolum* ("of goodwill"), *docilem* ("receptive"), and *attentum* ("attentive"), i.e., to gain the sympathy of the audience for the main arguments of the speech (Aristotle, *Rhet.* 3.14 [1414b–1416a]; *Rhet. Her.* 1.4.6; Quintilian, *Inst.* 4.1.5). The phrase **captatio benevolentiae* ("fishing for goodwill") is used to describe the *exordium* but is not itself an ancient Latin rhetorical term.

There were several possible starting points for a speech (Cicero, *De inv.* 1.16.22–23): (1) *Ab nostra* (from one's own person), i.e., the speaker could arouse sympathy for himself by discreetly commending himself (see *Boasting), suggest how he had experienced unwanted adversities (see *Peristasis Catalogues), or pretend to be unprepared or incapable of speaking (Quintilian 4.1.9). (2) *Ab adversariorum* (from the person of the opponents), i.e., the speaker could attempt to gain goodwill by denigrating his adversary. (3) *Ab iudicum persona* (from the persons of the jury), i.e., he could say very positive things about the jury. (4) *A causa* (from the case itself); in order to attract the interest and attention of the listeners, he could promise to speak about something new or important, to claim brevity, or to declare that what would be said would be particularly relevant for the listeners. To make the listener responsive it helped to enumerate the points that would be covered in the next part of the speech.

The second type of *exordium* was the *insinuatio,* which could be used in certain situations, such as when the audience had a negative attitude, was biased, or was tired. The strategy was to obtain the goodwill and attention of the audience through some surprising move and then gradually move into the real subject of the speech.

The directions for compositing an *exordium* found in rhetorical handbooks are of a very general nature, since they are intended to apply to a great variety of situations. Since *exordia* are almost infinitely flexible, it is often difficult to determine whether a particular rhetorician is following the "rules."

The orator Tertullus is mentioned in Acts 24:2–8 but is not given an extensive speech, apart from a brief *captatio benevolentiae* (i.e., an *exordium* aimed as securing goodwill by flattering the governor) in vv. 2b–4, followed by a twofold accusation (vv. 5–8). The *exordium* in vv. 2b–4 is very brief: "Since through you we enjoy much peace, and since by your provision, most excellent Felix, reforms are introduced on behalf of this nation, in every way and everywhere we accept this with all gratitude." Paul's response in Acts 24:10–21 similarly begins with a *captatio benevolentiae* (v. 10b), continues with a brief *narratio* (v. 11) and continues with a *propositio* (v. 12). The *exordium* itself runs: "Realizing that for many years you have been judge over this nation, I cheerfully make my defense." A further example is found in a literary context in *1 Clem* 1:2–3:1.

*Arrangement, **Captatio benevolentiae*, *Preface

Lausberg 1998, 121–36 (§§263–88); Loutsch 1994; Martin 1974, 60–75; Volkmann 1885, 127–48; Zweck 1989, 94–96

Exoterica, a Latin term referring to literary works intended for publication. Aristotle referred to his earlier writings as *exoterica* (*Poetica* 15.1454b), none of which have survived. All of his extant writings are **esoterica,* i.e., they were never revised in final form for publication.

*Aristotle, *Rhetorica,* *Enthymeme, *Esoterica, *Publication

Explanatory comments (see *Narrative asides).

Explicit, from the verb *explicare* ("to unfold, unroll"), perhaps from the phrase *explicitus ist liber* ("the book is unrolled"="here ends"), a statement placed at the end of a manuscript.

Ezekiel the Tragedian, a 2d-cent. B.C.E. author known only from the fragments of his only surviving work, a drama called the *Exagoge* (a Greek poetical work in iambic trimeter), based on the LXX story of Exod. 1–15, preserved in Eusebius, *Praep. evang.* 9.28–29 (seventeen excerpts from Polyhistor's lost *On the Jews*) and in Clement of Alexandria's *Stromata.* E. shows influence from great Greek playwrights before him, particularly Euripides and Aeschylus (Holladay, 1989, 303–4; van der Horst 1992). Much of the material consists of a simple retelling of Exodus. The plagues are related by God as future events rather than narrated as they happen, perhaps because it would not have been possible to perform such things on stage (van der Horst, 1992). A major divergence from the biblical text, however, appears in fragments six and seven. There, Moses has a vision of a celestial throne, whose occupant relinquishes the throne to Moses. Jethro interprets this dream to mean that Moses will judge and lead humanity.

Holladay 1989, 2:301–529; van der Horst 1992

Ezra, Fourth Book of (called "Second Esdras" in the KJV, the RSV, and the NRSV, and "Fourth Esdras" in the Latin Vulgate), is an apocalypse written about 95 C.E. (Myers 1974, 10; Stone 1984, 412; 1990, 9–10), a date based on the identification of the apocalyptic vision of three heads in *4 Ezra* 11 with the Flavian emperors, Vespasian, Titus, and Domitian (69–96 C.E.).

Language and unity. Fourth Ezra was probably written in Palestine in Hebrew (lost), secondarily translated into Greek (lost except for a papyrus fragment containing 15:57–59), and then translated into other ancient languages, including Latin, Syriac, Georgian, Ethiopic, and Coptic (Stone 1990, 1–9). The Ethiopic and Georgian preserve the best text (Stone 1984, 412). *Fourth Ezra* 7:36–105, a section often bracketed in English translations, is missing from the Vulgate (except for two manuscripts) but present in the Syriac, Ethiopic, Arabic, and Armenian versions.

Ezra literature. Ezra the scribe, the central figure in the OT books of Ezra and Nehemiah, is chiefly remembered as the one who reintroduced the Torah into the life of the returned exiles (Neh. 8), which constitutes the beginning of Judaism, with its emphasis on Torah as the central feature of life and worship. The work is found in the Vulgate and in the Protestant Apocrypha. Works attributed to Ezra/Esdras are easily confused; the table (*see below*) differentiates the various names (adapted from Attridge 1984, 157–58 n. 1). There are also other later apocalypses attributed to Ezra, including the *Apocalypse of Esdras,* the *Apocalypse of Sedrach,* and the *Vision of Ezra.*

Purpose. Like *2 *Baruch,* with which it has some literary connection, *4 Ezra* was written as a Jewish response to the destruction of Jerusalem and the temple in 70 C.E. by the Romans, fictionally masked as the destruction of Jerusalem and the temple by the Babylonians in 587 B.C.E.. The theodicy issue dominates the first three visions, all in the form of dialogues (3:1–9:25), the largest section of the work. Eschatological issues dominate visions four through six (9:26–13:58), while the function of the restored sacred books as a means of warning those who come after Ezra is the emphasis in the seventh vision (14:1–48).

Literary structure. The main part of *4 Ezra* is a series of seven revelations in which the *dialogue form is prominent. The first three are dialogues between Ezra and Uriel, the interpreting angel, the next three are symbolic visions, and the final one is basically a narrative of the miraculous restoration of 94 sacred books by Ezra (and five rapid writers, 14:24), 24 for the worthy and the unworthy, and 70 for the wise (distinguishing between the 24 books of the Hebrew canon and 70 unnamed revelatory works).

Added Christian introduction (1–2 = 5 Esdras)

- I. First vision (3:1–5:20)
  - A. Introduction (3:1–3)
  - B. Ezra questions God (3:4–36)
    1. From Adam to the fall of Jerusalem (3:4–27)
    2. Why have you spared the wicked (Babylon) and punished your people? (3:28–36)
  - C. Uriel's dialogue with Ezra (4:1–5:19)
    1. Human mind is limited (4:1–12)
    2. Parable of the forest and the sea (4:13–21)
    3. Ezra: Why have you forsaken your people? (4:22–25)
    4. God: The end of the age will bring recompense (4:26–32)
    5. Dialogue on when the new age will come (4:33–51)
    6. God on the signs of the end (4:52–5:13)

Relationships among Ezra/Esdras Texts

Hebrew Bible	Septuagint	Vulgate	Protestant Apocrypha
Ezra	2 Esdras	1 Esdras	
Nehemiah	3 Esdras	2 Esdras	
	1 Esdras	3 Esdras	1 Esdras
		4 Esdras	2 Esdras

- D. Conclusion of the vision (5:14–20)
- II. Second vision (5:21–6:34)
  - A. Ezra complains again to God (5:22–30)
  - B. Uriel's dialogue with Ezra (5:31–6:28)
  - C. Conclusion (6:29–34)
- III. Third vision (6:35–9:25)
  - A. Introduction (6:35–37)
  - B. Ezra summarized the creation in six days, concluding with Israel's domination by other nations (6:38–59)
  - C. Uriel's dialogue with Ezra (7:1–9:22)
    1. The way to the next world is difficult (7:1–24)
    2. The coming of the Messiah and the end of the world (7:25–44)
    3. Few will be saved (7:45–61)
    4. Ezra laments over the human race (7:62–74)
    5. The intermediate state to the final judgment (7:74–115)
    6. Ezra again laments over the human race (7:116–131)
    7. Ezra appeals to God's mercy (7:132–8:36)
    8. God will save the righteous and doom the wicked (8:37–62)
    9. Signs preceding the end (8:63–9:13)
    10. Few will be saved (9:14–22)
  - D. Conclusion (9:23–25)
- IV. Fourth vision (9:26–10:59)
  - A. Introduction (9:26–27)
  - B. Ezra's prayer on the permanence of the Law (9:28–37)
  - C. Vision of the mourning woman and her transformation into the rebuilt Jerusalem (9:38–10:27)
  - D. The interpretation of the vision (10:28–59a)
  - E. Conclusion (10:59b)
- V. Fifth vision (11:1–12:51)
  - A. Introduction (11:1a)
  - B. The eagle vision (11:1b–12:2a)
  - C. The interpretation of the vision (12:2b–49)
  - D. Conclusion (12:50)
- VI. Sixth vision (13:1–58)
  - A. Introduction (13:1a)
  - B. The vision of the man from the sea (13:1b–20)
  - C. The interpretation of the vision (13:21–56)
  - D. Conclusion (13:57–58)
- VII. Seventh Vision (14:1–48)
  - A. Introduction (14:1a)
  - B. God prepares Ezra for his departure (14:1b–18)
  - C. Ezra's miraculous restoration of Scripture (14:19–47)
    1. 24 for the worthy and the unworthy (14:45)
    2. 70 for the wise (14:46)
  - D. Conclusion (14:48)

Added Christian Conclusion (15–16 = 6 Esdras)

The relationship between 4 Ezra *and* 2 Baruch *and the Revelation to John.* While it is evident that some kind of intimate relationship exists between *4 Ezra* and *2 Baruch*, there is no agreement on the precise nature of this relationship. Charles (1896) and Violet (1910, 1) argued that *2 Baruch* used *4 Ezra* as a source, while Bogaert (1980, 54–56, 67) argued the opposite, even suggesting that *4 Ezra* in turn "appears to know" the Revelation to John, which was itself dependent on *2 Baruch*. Bogaert's theory of the relationship between these three compositions can be diagrammed as follows:

2 Baruch → Revelation to John
↓ ↓
4 Ezra

Charles argued that the author of Revelation was literarily dependent on several Jewish apocalyptic texts, including the *Testament of Levi, 1 Enoch,* and the *Assumption* (or *Testament*) *of Moses* (Charles 1920, 1.lxv, lxxxii–lxxxiii). The ten passages in *1 Enoch* on which he claims that Revelation is dependent include *1 Enoch* 9:4; 14:15; 18:13; 46:1; 47:3–4; 48:9; 51:1; 62:3, 5; 86:1; 99:7. His relatively early dating of the *Similitudes of Enoch* (either 94–79 B.C.E. or 70–64 B.C.E.), made it easy for him to suppose that the author of Revelation could have been literarily dependent on the *Similitudes.* Most scholars, however, have not thought it likely that Revelation was dependent on the texts of the *Similitudes, 4 Ezra,* or *2 Baruch.* Swete's critique of Charles's claims is still valid: "Here it is enough to say that they [i.e., the parallels] shew the writer of the Christian Apocalypse to have been familiar with the apocalyptic ideas of his age, they afford little or no clear evidence of his dependence on Jewish sources other than the books of the Old Testament" (Swete 1908, clviii).

Shared motifs can logically be explained in one of three ways: (1) Revelation is literarily dependent on a particular Jewish apocalypse, (2) a particular Jewish apocalypse is dependent on the Revelation, or (3) similar motifs shared by Revelation and other Jewish apocalypses are based on a common written or oral apocalyptic tradition. In the past, scholars have been quick to propose various theories of literary dependence. More recently, as a result of more stringent standards for judging quotations and allusions, relationships other than direct literary dependence have been more seriously entertained. The passages in Revelation that Charles and others have thought dependent on Jewish apocalypses provide the opportunity for evaluating the source of such parallel passages. One example of shared motifs is the "Cry for Vengeance and the *Numerus Iustorum* (or 'number of the just')" (Rev. 6:9–11; *1 Enoch* 47:1–4; *4 Ezra* 4:35–37; *2 Bar.* 23:4–5a):

> Rev. 6:9–11: When he broke the fifth seal, I saw underneath the altar the souls of those slain because of the word of God and because of the witness which they bore. They cried out loudly saying, "O Master, holy and true, how long will it be until you judge and avenge our deaths caused by those who dwell on the earth?" Then each of them was given a white robe, and they were told that they should rest a while longer until the number of their fellow servants, that is, their brothers who were to be killed as they were, would be complete.

> *1 Enoch* 47:1–4 (trans. Knibb): And in those days the prayer of the righteous and the blood of the righteous will have ascended from earth before the Lord of Spirits. [2]In these days the holy ones who dwell in the heavens above will unite with one voice, and supplicate, and pray, and praise, and give thanks, and bless in the name of the Lord of Spirits, because of the blood of the righteous which has been poured out, and (because of) the prayer of the righteous, that it may not cease before the Lord of Spirits, that justice may be done to them, and (that) their patience may not have to last for ever. . . . [4]And the hearts of the holy ones were full of joy that the number of righteousness had been reached, and the prayer of the righteous had been heard, and the blood of the righteous had been required before the Lord of Spirits.

> *4 Ezra* 4:33, 35–37 (NRSV): [33]Then I answered and said, "How long? When will these things be?" Why are our years few and evil?" . . . [35]"Did not the souls of the righteous in their chambers ask about these matters, saying, 'How long are we to remain here? And when will the harvest of our reward come?' [36]And the archangel Jeremiel answered and said, 'When the number of those like yourselves is completed.'"

> *2 Baruch* 23:4–5 (Charlesworth, *OTP* 1.629): For when Adam sinned and death was decreed against those who were to be born, the multitude of those who would be born was numbered. And for that number a place was prepared where the living ones might live and where the dead might be preserved. No creature will live again unless the number that has been appointed is completed. For my spirit creates the living, and the realm of death receives the dead. And further, it is given to you to hear that which will come after these times. For truly, my salvation which comes has drawn near and is not as far away as before.

A quick survey of these four passages indicates that they are linked by the motifs of the reward of the righteous dead and the death of the predestined number of the righteous as an event that must occur before God will act. In Rev. 6:9–11, *1 Enoch* 47:1–4, and *4 Ezra* 4:33–37, the righteous dead ask about their vindication or reward and are given an answer involving the future completion of the complete number of the righteous dead. In Rev. 6:9–11 and *1 Enoch* 47:1–4 the dead are the righteous who have been killed by their enemies and pray for vindication and are answered with the *numerus iustorum* formula. In *4 Ezra* 4:33–37 they are the righteous dead, while in *2 Bar.* 23:4–5 they are simply all the dead. Revelation 6:9–11 has a special formal link with *4 Ezra* 4:33–37 by an entreaty attributed to the righteous dead in direct discourse introduced by the phrase "How long?" commonly used in impatient prayer in the OT and early Jewish literature (Pss. 6:3–4; 13:1–2; 35:17; 74:9–10; 79:5; 80:4; 89:6; 1 Macc. 6:22) and also used in apocalyptic contexts about when the end will arrive (Dan. 8:13; 12:6; *2 Bar.* 21:19; 81:3 [MS c only]; *4 Ezra* 6:59). Stone considers *4 Ezra* 4:35–36a to reflect the author's use of a source, and the author may therefore have structured 4:33 on the "how long?" pattern of 4:35 (Stone 1990, 96–97), a proposal that is unnecessary. Bauckham suggests the following possible literary relationship between these texts: *1 Enoch* 37–71 → Revelation → *4 Ezra* → *2 Baruch*. He thinks that the relationship between these four texts is not the result of direct literary dependence but rather is a result of dependence on a common tradition that had already taken particular forms in the sources used by each apocalypse (Bauckham 1993, 54).

A second example of motifs shared by Revelation and other Jewish apocalypses is the "Leviathan-Behemoth Myth" (Rev. 13:1–18; *1 Enoch* 60:7–11, 24; *4 Ezra* 6:49–52; *2 Bar.* 29:4).

> Rev. 13:1–18: I saw a beast rising out of the sea, with ten horns and seven heads, with ten diadems upon its horns and a blasphemous name up on its heads. . . . [11]Then I saw another beast which rose out of the earth, and it had two horns like a lamb, and it spoke like a dragon.

> *1 Enoch* 60:7–11, 24 (trans. Knibb): And on that day two monsters will be separated from one another: a female monster, whose name (is) Leviathan, to dwell in the depths of the sea above the springs of the waters; [8]and the name of the male (is) Behemoth, who occupies with his breast an immense desert, named Dendayn, on the east of the garden where the chosen and righteous dwell, where my great-grandfather was received, who was the seventh from Adam, the first man whom the Lord of Spirits made. [9]And I asked that other angel to show me the power of those monsters, how they were separated on one day and thrown, one into the depths of the sea, and the other on to the dry ground of the desert. . . . [24]And the angel of peace who was with me said to me: "These two monsters, prepared in accordance with the greatness of the Lord, will be fed that the punishment of the Lord [lacuna in the text] in vain."

> *4 Ezra* 6:49–52 (NRSV): Then you kept in existence two living creatures; the one you called Behemoth and the name of the other Leviathan. [50]And you separated one from the other, for the seventh part where the water had been gathered together could not hold them both. [51]And you gave Behemoth one of the parts that had been dried up on the third day, to live in it, where there are a thousand mountains; [52]but to Leviathan you gave the seventh part, the watery part; and you have kept them to be eaten by whom you wish, and when you wish.

> *2 Baruch* 29:2–4 (trans. Charlesworth, *OTP*, 1.630): For at that time I shall only protect those found in this land at that time. [3]And it will happen that when all that which should come to pass in these parts has been accomplished, the Anointed One will begin to be revealed. [4]And Behemoth will reveal itself from its place, and Leviathan will come from the sea, the two great monsters which I created on the fifth day of creation and which I shall have kept until that time. And they will be nourishment for all who are left.

The beast from the sea and the beast from the land of Rev. 13 clearly reflect the Jewish myth of Leviathan, the female monster from the sea, and Behemoth, the male monster from the desert, even though the beasts are not given their traditional names in the text. Further, in Revelation, the myth of the beast from the sea and the beast from the land are combined with other motifs associated with the Eschatological Antagonist, so that the beast from the sea is depicted as a godless, tyrannical ruler, while the beast from the land is presented as a lying prophet. It is striking that the Leviathan-Behemoth myth is referred to in only three Palestinian Jewish apocalypses, *1 Enoch* 37–71, *4 Ezra,* and *2 Baruch* (all relatively late), where they are explicitly named and rudiments of the myth are mentioned. The Leviathan-Behemoth myth has both protological features (i.e., both monsters were created on the fifth day of creation) and eschatological features (they will serve as food for the righteous in the eschaton). More complete forms of this myth, inspired by Gen. 1:21, are found in the Talmud and midrashim and have been synthesized by Ginsberg. According to Gen. 1:21, the great sea monsters were created on the fifth day, when God separated the pair, appointing Leviathan to inhabit the sea (Job 41:1–34; Ps. 104:25–26; *Apoc. Abr.* 21:4; *Ladder of Jacob* 6:13) and Behemoth the land (Job 40:15–24; *4 Ezra* 6:51). Missing from Revelation, but present in our three focal Jewish apocalypses as well as in rabbinic versions of the story, is the expectation that Leviathan and Behemoth will ultimately serve as food for the righteous in the eschaton (*1 Enoch* 60:24; *4 Ezra* 6:52; *2 Baruch* 29:4; cf. b. B. Bat. 75a).

While literary dependence could be proposed for the passages focusing on the Leviathan-Behemoth myth in the *Similitudes of Enoch, 4 Ezra,* and *2 Baruch,* the vague and general reference to the myth in Rev. 13 indicates only that the author or his sources were aware of the traditional features of the myth.

*Apocalyptic

Box 1912; Breech 1973 (translation); Hamilton 1999; Harnisch 1969; Longenecker 1995; Myers 1974; Stone 1984, 412–14; 1990; A. L. Thompson 1977; Violet 1910 (text); Willett 1989

Fable, a transliterated form of the Latin words *fabella* or *fabula*, and a translation of the Greek words αἶνος, μῦθος, or λόγος. Theon defined the fable as λόγος ψευδὴς εἰκονίζων ἀλήθειαν, "a fictitious story picturing a truth" (*Progym.* 3), a definition that is simpler and more accurate than modern definitions, which (for example) defines a fable as "an anecdote of animal life with a moralizing application; it may, however, be drawn from inanimate nature or directly from human experience" (*OCD* 355). Vouga (1992, 176–77) unpacks the definition provided by Theon in three aspects: fictionality, educational, and explanatory. He describes both fables and *parables as "miniature narratives" (Vouga 1992, 177) but claims that while fables primarily convey conventional wisdom, the parables of Jesus challenge daily human experience, and fables further lack the comic trick ("komischer Dreh") that characterizes the parables (Vouga 1992, 178). Fables occur in such early Greek authors as Hesiod and Archilochus, and collections of fables were made by Demetrius of Phaleron (4th cent. B.C.E.; Diogenes Laertius 5.80), Phaedrus (1st cent. C.E.), and Babrius (2d cent. C.E.). Phaedrus published a collection of 93 fables in Latin verse, while slightly later Babrius published a collection of 144 fables in Greek in choliambic meter, probably in two books. Jülicher (1919, 94–101, esp. 98) thought that the majority of the parables of Jesus that are in narrative form are fables, like those of Stesichoros and Aesop. Since Jülicher there has been a tendency among interpreters of the parables of Jesus to limit the scope of fables to narratives involving animals, plants, and inanimate objects, and therefore have no direct relevance for understanding the parables (Boucher 1977, 13), though there are exceptions (Linnemann 1966, 18–21; Beavis 1990). Jülicher derived his threefold system of classifying the parables of Jesus into similitudes, parables, and example stories from Aristotle (*Rhet.* 2.20), where fictional παραδείγματα ("examples") include λόγοι ("fables," "stories") and παραβολαί ("comparisons"); see *Rhet.* 2.20.2–4. According to Perry (1965, xxiii), the term "fable" includes a variety of ancient literary forms, including the fairy tale, the aetiological nature myth, the animal story exhibiting the cleverness or stupidity of an animal, the novella, the myth about the gods, the debate between two rivals, and the exposition of the circumstances in which a sententious or witty remark was made. Quintilian (1.9.1) recommended that pupils learn composition by hearing, reciting, and recording the fables with which they were familiar in their own words. An example of a fable in the collection of Babrius (20) indicates that fables should not be stereotyped as simply animal stories with a moral (LCL trans., with modifications):

> An ox-driver was bringing his wagon home from the village when it fell into a deep ravine. Instead of doing something about it, as the situation required, he stood by idly and prayed for help to Heracles, of all the gods the one whom he really worshiped and held in honor. Suddenly the god appeared in person beside him and said: "Take hold of the wheels. Lay the whip on your oxen. Pray to the gods only when you are doing something to help yourself. Otherwise your prayers will be useless."

In Synoptic parables, supernatural intervention occurs in just two parables, the parables of the Rich Fool (Luke 12:13–21) and of the Rich Man and Lazarus (Luke 16:19–31).

Old Testament fables. A number of meshalim occur in the OT that have content similar to some of the fables of Aesop, such as "The Trees Choose a King" (Judg. 9:7–15), "The Thistle and the Cedar" (2 Kgs. 14:9), comparable to Greek fables such as "The Oak and the Reeds" (Babrius 36) and "The Fir Tree and the Bramble" (Babrius 64).

Many fables have a moral, called a προμύθιον when used to introduce a fable, and an ἐπιμύθιος when used to conclude a fable. These introductory or concluding statements often have a secondary character and sometimes do not fit the story very well (Beavis 1990, 482). In the fable in Babrius 20, quoted above, the ἐπιμύθιος is an essential part of the fable, since the moral is conveyed through the brief speech of Heracles with which it concludes. In a number of Synoptic parables, the concluding sayings (ἐπιμύθια) are often attributed to the main character (Matt. 18:32–33; 20:13–15; 25:12, 26–28; Luke 12:20; 13:8–9; 15:31–32; 16:30; 18:4–5). In the Synoptic Gospels, a number of the parables in Luke have a προμύθιον which includes a mini-interpretation, as in Luke 18:1: "And he told them a parable to the effect that they ought always to pray and not to lose heart" (see Luke 12:15; 18:9). Beavis (1990, 482) has called attention to the similarities between the προμύθια of some of the fables of Phaedrus and Luke: (1) "This story has a moral for miserly men, and for such as are of low birth but bent on getting a name for wealth" (Phaedrus 1.27; LCL trans.), (2) "When a certain man was complaining about his ill fortune Aesop invented the following story to comfort him" (Phaedrus

4.18), (3) "It is for good cause that riches are hated by the brave . . . , since a hoard of money prevents praise from reaching its proper object" (Phaedrus 4.12).

*Folklore, *Parable

Beavis 1990; Boucher 1977; Daly 1961; Hasubeck 1982; Jülicher 1919; Linnemann 1966; *OCD* 355; Perry 1965; Vouga 1992

Fairy tale (see *Folklore)

Farewell address, a literary form (when part of a longer narrative) that also developed into a separate literary genre, consisting of the deathbed discourse of a dying patriarch, usually including a strong paraenetic emphasis (with examples drawn from the speaker's earlier life) and often concluding with a prediction of the future, which in later texts includes apocalyptic features (Collins 1984b, 325). When the farewell address is used as an independent literary form, it is called a testament (Collins 1984b; Kolenkow 1975). Farewell addresses are attributed to central characters in the narrative who have reached the end of life, typically a father speaking to his sons or a leader to his people (Jacob in Gen. 49; Moses in Deut. 31–33; Joshua in Josh. 23–24; Samuel in 1 Sam. 12; Jesus in Luke 22:14–38; Paul in Acts 20:17–38).

Relatives and friends are typically summoned to the deathbed to hear the final words of the person about to die. This form is a stereotypical literary construct based on the idealized death of a family head or hero, who lives long enough to preside at a gathering of family and friends and is lucid enough to mediate simmering family conflicts and to resolve inheritance issues. Since it was thought that death was a time when prophetic knowledge was granted, predictions of the future are frequently included in farewell addresses.

Stauffer (1948, 321–24; 1955, 344–47) identified 26 characteristics of farewell speeches and farewell scenes, providing numerous examples of each. Segovia (1991, 7–8) repeats Stauffer's list with several changes: (1) He divides Stauffer's characteristics into 14 characteristics of the context of such speeches and 12 characteristics of the speech itself, claiming (incorrectly) that Stauffer does not differentiate between the farewell scene and the farewell speech. Actually, Stauffer has 18 characteristics of the farewell scene, and 8 characteristics of the farewell speech. (2) For some peculiar reason, Segovia substitutes "He blesses those remaining behind" for Stauffer's "He completes his final footwashing," though the latter would appear more appropriate for a discussion of John 13–17. (3) Segovia also changes the order of many of the characteristics of Stauffer's farewell scene. Here is Stauffer's taxonomy:

I. Characteristics of the farewell setting
   1. Heaven reveals the approach of death
   2. The person on the point of death gathers those whom he is leaving behind
   3. He completes his last footwashing
   4. He eats his final meal with them
   5. They fall down and worship
   6. He is transformed before them
   7. He rejects earthly food
   8. He parts from those remaining
   9. He speaks his last words
   10. He climbs a solitary hill
   11. He enters heaven by ascension of body and soul
   12. The soul is redeemed
   13. Those left behind mourn their loss
   14. Those left behind rejoice at his ascension

II. Characteristics of the farewell speech
   1. The person on the point of death announces his forthcoming ascension
   2. He explains that, though they will no longer see and associate with him, such a situation will benefit them
   3. He bids farewell to those he leaves behind with
      a. A theological review of history
      b. Revelations about the future
      c. Warnings and final injunctions
      d. Exhortations to keep his words and instructions
      e. Commandments to love
      f. Woes and controversies
      g. Words of consolation and promises
      h. Problems of intercession
      i. A prayer for those left behind
      j. The appointment of a successor

Many of the characteristics of farewell scenes and farewell speeches proposed by Stauffer are problematic. Most obviously, many characteristics are attested by only two or three texts, one or two Jewish and one or two Christian, e.g., "He completes his last footwashing (*T. Abr.* B

3; *T. Abr.* A3; John 13:5); "Exhortations to keep his words and instructions" (*1 Enoch* 94:5; 99:10; John 14:21, 23); "A prayer for those left behind" (*Jub.* 22:28ff.; *Ps.-Philo.* 21:2–6; Luke 22:32; John 17); "They fall down and worship" (*Ass. Mos.* 11:1; 12:1; *1 Enoch* 64:3–4; Matt. 28:9, 17); "He rejects earthly food" (*1 Enoch* 56:2; Luke 24:30–31; John 21:5, 21–22). Perhaps the main problem with Stauffer's analysis is that he does not clearly identify those texts that narrate a farewell scene and farewell discourse. For an overview of research on the farewell discourse, and a critique of Stauffer, see Segovia 1991, 5–20.

Perhaps the most satisfying approach to the analysis of the farewell speech in Judaism and early Christianity is the work of H.-J. Michel (1973), who first lists the appropriate passages in the OT and early Judaism (Jacob in Gen. 47:29–49:33; Moses in Deuteronomy; Joshua in Josh. 23:1–24:30; Samuel in 1 Sam. 12:1–25); David in 1 Kgs. and 1 Chr.; Tobit in Tob. 14:3–11; Mattathias in 1 Macc. 2:49–70; several examples in *Jubilees*; the *Testament of the Twelve Patriarchs*; the *Testament of Isaac and Abraham*; the *Life of Adam and Eve*; several examples in Ps.-Philo; *the Assumption of Moses*; Ezra in *4 Ezra* 14; several examples in *2 Baruch* and *2 Enoch*), and only then formulates a list of characteristics. Michel (1973, 54) finds four basic elements in farewell addresses: (1) the conception of the speaker; (2) the gathering of the audience; (3) admonitions and prophecies; (4) conclusion (farewell gestures, death). He lists thirteen motifs of farewell discourses (1973, 48–54, each with subdivisions and a wealth of examples: (1) confirmation of the nearness of death, (2) the circle of auditors, (3) paraenetic expressions, (4) prophetic part, (5) self-examination of the dying person, (6) selection of the successor, (7) the blessing, (8) prayer, (9) final instructions, (10) burial instructions, (11) promises and vows, (12) further gestures of departure, (13) the end (death).

In the NT, farewell addresses can be identified in Jesus' farewell address in Luke 22:14–38 (Kurz 1985; Neyrey 1985, 12–48; Katter 1993), Jesus' table talks with his disciples just before his passion in John 13–17 (Segovia 1991; see his bibliography of similar studies on this passage in 1991, 332–33), and Paul's farewell speech in Acts 20:17–38 (H.-J. Michel 1973; Lambrecht 1979).

In the analysis of Paul's farewell address in Acts 20:17–38), H.-J. Michel (1973, 68–71) identifies ten characteristics of the farewell addresses he has examined earlier (see above): (1) summoning of the circle of hearers (Acts 20:17); (2) account and depiction of Paul's exemplary behavior (20:18–21, 31, 33–35); (3) attestation of personal innocence (20:26); (4) announcement of death (20:22–25); (5) paraenesis (20:28, 31, 35); (6) prophecies (20:29–30); (7) successors in office (20:28); (8) blessing (20:32); (9) prayer (20:36); (10) further gestures of departure: drinking wine, hugging, and kissing (20:37).

In his analysis of John 13–17, Segovia (1991, 308–16) identifies six typical features of ancient farewell discourses: (1) the announcement of the approaching death of the hero, (2) paraenetic exhortation to those who will outline the dying hero, (3) prophecies or predictions of events following the death of the hero, (4) review of major events of the life of the hero, (5) establishment of the heirs or successors of the hero, and (6) final instructions for the family or followers of the hero.

**Adam and Eve, Lives of,* **Baruch, Second,* **Testaments of the Twelve Patriarchs,* *Timothy, Second Letter to

---

J. J. Collins 1984, 1986; Cortés 1976; Katter 1990; Kolenkow 1975, 1986; Kurz 1985, 1990; Lambrecht 1979; H.-J. Michel 1973; Munck 1950; Murphy 1985; Neyrey 1985, 5–48; von Nordheim 1980, 1985; Sayler 1984; Segovia 1991; Stauffer 1955, 344–47; Whitters 2002

Festal letters are open letters sent by Jewish or Christian authorities for the purpose of maintaining a uniform religious calendar and implementing a strict moral code. Festal letters had antecedents in the OT. 2 Chr. 30:1–9 is an embedded letter sent by Hezekiah to the tribes of Ephraim and Manasseh inviting all to celebrate the Passover in Jerusalem. Other festal letters include Esth. 9:20–32 (Whitters 2001, 274–79), 2 Macc. 1:1–9; 1:10–2:18 (Whitters 2001, 279–82), the Elephantine Passover Papyrus (Porten 1996, 125–26), and a doubtful example, *2 Baruch* 78–87 (Whitters 2001, 285–88). While festal letters constitute a type of letter with a relatively restricted function, they cannot be regarded as a literary genre (contra Whitters 2001, 273).

Aune 1987, 174–80; Whitters 2001

Fiction is a term typically used of a narrative account of events that appear realistic but may not in fact have happened. Fiction can be distinguished from history in that while the latter has a referent in the real world, the former has no such referent; it makes no sense, for example, to say that *Chariton, the author of the Greek novel *Chaereas and Callirhoë*, was mistaken about the actions of the hero and heroine (Konstan 1998, 6). The term "fiction," however, is ambiguous, for it could refer to imaginary events just as well as events that are depicted realistically but nevertheless never happened. Ancient literary theory placed narratives in three categories on the basis of the truth of their contents (Holzberg 1996, 15; Quintilian 2.4.2): (1) mythical: those narratives that deviate from the truth or are entirely fictional (μῦθος or *fabula*); (2) historical: those narratives that have happened and are consistent with the truth; (3) dramatic: those narratives that are fictional but still seem realistic (πλάσμα, πλασματικόν or *argumentum*). Despite the ostensibly fictional intentions of the authors, ancient Greek novels pretend to refer to events that actually happened, as in Chariton 1.1 (trans. Reardon 1989, 21): "My name is Chariton, of Aphrodisias, and I am clerk to the attorney Athenagoras. I am going to tell you the story of a love affair that took place in Syracuse" (here an allusion to the opening lines of Herodotus and Thucydides is apparent; see Konstan 1998, 11).

*Fable, *Mimesis, *Novels, *Parable

Bowersock 1994; Feeney 1993; Gill and Wiseman 1993; Konstan 1998

First-person plural is a stylistic feature reflected in the use of verbs and pronouns, which occurs frequently in the letters of the NT, such as the Pauline letters, though a striking number of *"we"-passages also occur in Acts and have been the object of intense study (Wedderburn 2002). The use of the first-person plural is also found in the six fragments making up 4QMMT (=4Q394–98), written from ca. 75 B.C.E. to ca. 50 C.E., a stylistic feature reflecting the fact that the author writes on behalf of a group with whom he agrees to an audience with which he has a great deal in common (Brooke 1995, 79). It is difficult to distinguish among the various possible functions of the first-person plural, particularly when (as in 1 and 2 Thess. and 2 Cor.) first-person singulars are used elsewhere in the same letter. The possible functions of the first-person plural include these (Byrskog 1996, 232): (1) It may indicate joint authorship of letters (the prescripts of most Pauline and Deutero-Pauline letters indicate more than one sender: 1 Cor. 1:1; 2 Cor. 2:1; Gal. 1:2 ["all the brothers who are with me"]; Phil. 1:1; 1 Thess. 1:1; 2 Thess. 2:1; Phlm. 1; only Romans mentions no cosender). (2) It may be the editorial "we" or literary plural (Dick 1900), although there appears to be little evidence for this in the Pauline letters: cf. 1 Cor. 15:30 (Byrskog 1996, 249). (3) The *pluralis sociativus* ("plural of association") includes the addressees or a group of the addressees (e.g., the phrase "we know that" in Rom. 2:2; 3:19; 7:14; 8:22, 28; 1 Cor. 8:4; 2 Cor. 5:1; 1 Tim. 1:8). (4) It may be a stylistic feature of diatribe style (Stowers 1981, 218 n. 65). Papyrus and Jewish letters include several senders only rarely (Byrskog 1996, 233–36). The main criteria for identifying which type of "we" is used in the text are the content and context in which the first-person plural occurs (Byrskog 1996, 232). However, there are no fixed rules for identifying which type of "we" is being used. In 1 Thess 1:1 there is mention of three senders (Paul, Silvanus, and Timothy), and the first-person plural used throughout, with the exception of the first-person singular referring to Paul in 2:18 ("I, Paul"), 3:5, and 5:27. Here the first-person plural is a deliberate device to include all the senders. The "we" is also used to associate the senders with the recipients (1 Thess. 3:11, 13; 4:14; 5:9, 23, 28). Galatians is dominated by the first-person singular, but the "we" is used as a means of associating Paul with those Galatians exposed to Judaizers (1:3–4; 3:13–14, 23–25; 4:3, 5, 6; 4:31–5:1, 25–26; 6:9–10, 14, 18). In Galatians (Byrskog 1996, 238–40) the first-person plural is rarely used for coauthorship (1:8–9; 2:4–5 includes Barnabas and Titus mentioned in 2:1), 9–10 (includes Barnabas). In 1 Corinthians, the first-person singular dominates the letter, and many occurrences of the "we" reflect Paul's identification with the recipients (1:2–3, 7–9, 10, 18, 30; 5:4, 7–8; 6:3, 11, 14; 8:1, 4, 6, 8; 9:10, 25; 10:1, 6, 8–9, 11, 16–17, 22; 11:16, 31–32; 13:9, 12; 15:3, 19, 32, 49, 51–52, 16:22). In 2 Corinthians, where Timothy is mentioned as coauthor, the plural dominates chapters 1–9, which Byrskog regards as a real plural representing coauthors (1996, 245; Murphy-O'Connor 1995, 24–30), but Carrez (1979–80), who ignores Timothy as a cosender, often construes as a "we" Paul's apostolic "I" (1:4–8; 5:11–15; 6:3–11; 7:2–13). The first-person singular clearly represents Paul (1:13, 15, 17, 23; 2:1–10, 12–13; 5:11; 6:13; 7:3–4, 8–9, 12, 14, 16; 8:3, 8, 10, 23; 9:1–5). In Philippians, although Timothy is mentioned as cosender in 1:1, first-person singulars dominate the letter, interspersed with plurals used by Paul to associate himself with the recipients (3:3, 15–16, 20–21; 4:20). The plural may include Timothy only in 3:17. Philemon mentions Timothy as cosender and the plural occurs in 1–3, but Paul uses the singular thereafter.

"We"-passages in Acts. These are passages characterized by the sudden appearance of the first-person plural in a predominantly third-person narrative: Acts 16:10–17 ("we" sailed from Troas to Philippi, via Samothrace and Neapolis); 20:5–15 ("we" sailed from Troas to Assos while Paul made the journey on foot, then with Paul "we" sailed to Miletus via Mitylene and Samos); 21:1–18 ("we" sailed from Miletus to Tyre, via Cos, Rhodes, and Patara; then overland to Ptolemais, Caesarea, and finally Jerusalem); 27:1–28:16 (Caesarea to Rome, via Sidon, Myra, Fair Havens, Cauda, Malta, Syracuse, Rhegium, and Puteoli). An additional "we"-passage, which is difficult to explain, occurs in 11:28 in the Western text. These passages were first noticed by Irenaeus (*Adv. haer.* 3.1.1; 3.10.1; 3.14.1–14). There are several ways of understanding this phenomenon, though none commands universal acceptance: (1) The author was a participant in those events narrated in the first-person plural, a view typically held by those who want to emphasize the historical trustworthiness of Acts (Hemer 1989, 312–34; Fitzmyer 1998, 103; Jervell 1998, 66). The "we"-passages do function as prima facie evidence for the fact that the writer claimed to be present at the events narrated, perhaps from the diary of the author. However, there are a number of Greek and Roman historians who participated in the events they narrate but used the third person in narrative (perhaps to emphasize their objectivity; see Norden 1956, 371), though an apparent exception is found in Ammianus Marcellinus. (2) The first-person plural passages were taken from an itinerary written by someone other than the author who participated in the events narrated (Dibelius 1956, 102–8). (3) The first-person plural was a literary device or stylistic convention meant to give the impression that the author was a participant in the events so narrated (a view criticized by Wedderburn 2002, 84–85). Wehnert (1989) argues that the combination of third-person and first-person narratives is a Jewish stylistic device found in Ezra and Daniel and that the inclusion of the first person is an attempt to guarantee trustworthiness, though the author—whom Wehnert thinks is Silas—was unaware of the pseudepigraphical character of such first-person narratives (Wehnert 1989, 183–89). Plümacher (1977) argues that historians were expected to speak from experience, particularly with regard to travel by sea. (4) Sea voyages were frequently narrated in the first-person plural (Norden 1956, 313–16; Robbins 1975; a view critiqued by Hemer 1985, 1989, 317–19). It may also be objected that sea voyages narrated in the third person were even more frequent (Praeder 1987), such issues cannot be decided statistically, which lessens the caution of Wedderburn (2002, 83): "Conventions of describing sea-journeys do not therefore seem to provide the key to the puzzling decision to write sometimes in the first person, sometimes in the third." Wedderburn also emphasizes the fact that the "we"-passages are not confined to sea voyages, but in fact such voyages are the focus of each of the four "we"-passages in Acts. (5) The first-person plural was intended to remind the reader of first-person plural passages in the *Odyssey* (MacDonald 1999). (6) The author, part of a Pauline "school," derived the "we"-passages (directly or indirectly) from traveling companions of Paul, i.e., based on *Erinnerungsberichte*, "recollections" (Wedderburn 2002, 94–98), though this view is in effect the most speculative of all, since it has no parallels on which to base such complex conjectures.

*Autobiography, *Coauthors, *Third-person plural, *"We"-passages

---

Askwith 1911; Byrskog 1996; Carrez 1979–80; Cranfield 1982; Dick 1900; von Dobschütz 1932; Haenchen 1965; Hemer 1985; 1989, 308–64; D.-A. Koch 1999; Lofthouse 1952–53; D. R. MacDonald 1999; Müller 1998; Murphy-O'Connor 1995; Plümacher 1977; Porter 1994; Praeder 1987; Richards 1991

Folklore, a term coined by William John Thoms in 1846 (Georges and Jones 1995, 35) for traditional lore passed on orally, by example or in written form (the latter emphasis is a controversial issue but one emphasized by Dundes 1999, 5–8), or various combinations of these. Folklore has been defined as "a collective term for those traditional items of knowledge that arise in recurring performances" (Abrahams 1968, 144). A similar definition sees folklore as traditional lore in process or performance (a modification of Niditch 1993, 3), with "lore" referring to narrative forms (folktales, oral histories, legends, myths, ballads, jokes), nonnarrative verbal forms or "folksay" (riddles, proverbs), dramatic forms (rituals, children's games), forms of material culture (handmade quilts, cooking, making canoes). Another definition of folklore has been proposed by Brunvand (1976, 2):

> As a working definition we may accept to begin with the common concept of folklore as consisting of materials in culture that are transmitted by word of mouth in "oral tradition" or by means of customary example. As a result of such transmission, folklore—whether verbal or in customary and material forms—tends to become stereotyped in style and structure, existing in many different variants that have mostly been dissociated from any specific named originator.

The folktale (or Märchen) is a major verbal type of folklore that has several characteristic features: (1) oral composition; (2) existence only in oral performance, often in interactive social contexts (oral tradition has durability after the moment of composition only in the memories of speaker and audience); (3) anonymity; (4) multiple versions in oral circulation; (5) variation; (6) patterned repetition; (7) stereotyped style and structure; (8) communal recreation; (9) cross-cultural occurrence of certain motifs and types; and (10) considered fiction by both speaker and audience, told primarily for entertainment value.

Some of these are more important than others. Dundes (1999, 18), for example, regards "multiple existence" and "variation" as the two most salient features of folklore (and he identifies biblical "doublets" as evidence of oral literature). The designation "folklore," however, does not indicate anything about the historicity of the traditional material (Dorson 1972; Culley 1972; Vansina 1985). Folklorists distinguish between free-phrase genres (e.g., legends, proverbs, and jokes, in which the basic elements of the plot are traditional but the wording or content varies in individual performances), and fixed-phrase genres (e.g., tongue twisters, folk similes, and poems, in which both the content and wording are traditional). The fairy tale, a type of folktale, may be defined as a short, imaginative traditional story with high moral and magical content.

The rich folklore of Judaism has been collected in a number of works, all of which tend to paraphrase legends found in postbiblical Jewish literature. The seven-volume work by Ginzberg (1909–38), however, contains not only paraphrases of the legends but also detailed notes and discussions of the sources and various aspects of each legend. The two collections of paraphrased legends by Bin Gorion, a six-volume work (1914–16), as well as a four-volume work (1913–26), like the three-volume collection of Rappoport (1928), which was later expanded by Raphael Patai in Rappoport and Patai (1966), contain few references to sources or explanatory material (though the introduction in Rappoport and Patai 1966, 5–16 is very helpful).

The existence of a rich folklore in the culture of ancient Greece, and to a lesser extent ancient Rome, is reflected extensively in both written texts and artistic representations. In his discussion of early childhood, Quintilian refers to "nursery tales" (*fabulae nutricularum*), which are succeeded by fables (*Inst.* 1.9.2). G. Anderson (2000) discusses fairy tales with motif-sequences similar to fairy tales collected in Europe from the beginning of the 19th cent., such as the Cinderella story, the Snow White story, Beauty and the Beast, and so on. Tertullian refers to the "towers of Lamia" (a cannibal ogress) and "combs of the sun" as part of a tale told to children to help them sleep (*Contra Val.* 2).

In exploring the possible relationships between the Bible and folklore (see the survey by Culley 1986), the textual or written character of the Bible has been a major issue. There has been a tendency among scholars to associate folklore only with oral tradition and to assume that once oral tradition has been written down, it no longer qualifies as folklore (a view maintained by Ong 1982 and Kelber 1983, and opposed by Niditch 1993, 7–9 and Dundes 1999, 9). It is striking that the founders of NT form criticism, Dibelius and Bultmann, did not conceive of a theoretical difference between oral and written speech (Thatcher 2000, 66). However, rather than regard the written Gospel texts as exhibiting oral features, they attributed certain characteristics of written texts, such as concrete existence like physical objects, a tendency which Thatcher calls the "objectification of oral utterance," to oral tradition (see the critique of Thatcher 2000, 66–71). However, an oral proverb when written down does not cease to be a proverb, nor does an oral legend when written cease to be a legend. Though the term "oral literature" is an oxymoron, it does preserve the insight that the Bible is to a large extent orally based but exists only in written form (Culley 1963, 118). Alternate terms for "oral literature" include "codified oral tradition" (Widengren 1959, 212), "codified folklore" (Dundes 1999, 12), "codified traditional literature" (Lord 1973), and "orally transmitted tradition written down" (Dundes 1999, 12).

The relationship between folklore and the Bible is an important issue for the literary study of the NT if written texts have preserved some of the stylistic features of oral transmission. Dundes (1999, 1–2) maintains not only that the Bible *contains* folklore, but that the Bible *is* folklore, a view that can be maintained only by ignoring large sections of the Bible (e.g., the prophetic books, the NT letters). Attempts to find folklore in the Bible have often focused on the OT (Frazer 1918; Gunkel 1961, 1987; Niditch 1987, 1993, 1996; Kirkpatrick 1988), a subject that is helpfully introduced by Niditch 1993.

Gunkel's work on the oral prehistory of traditional stories in the OT had an influential effect on the work of a number of NT scholars. The founders of NT "Formgeschichte" (usually translated as "form criticism") during the early part of the 20th cent. included Dibelius (1919; Eng. trans. 1936), Bultmann (1921; Eng. trans. 1963) and Albertz (1921). Since the canonical Gospels were written a generation after the death of Jesus, i.e., from 70–100 C.E., it seems obvious that oral tradition must have played a significant role in the transmission of Jesus traditions (Boman 1967; Henaut 1993). Some have erroneously characterized the canonical Gospels as folktale (Brewer 1979, 39). Since folktales are fictional by definition, the Gospels should rather be categorized as legends, and not as myths (Lord 1973, 5) or folktales (Dundes 1999, 18). Early form-critical scholars such as Dibelius (1936, 4) and Bultmann (1963, 4), heavily influenced by the work of Olrik (1908; Eng. trans. 1965), tended to speak of the "laws" of oral transmission. Olrik's "laws" include the presence of no more than two characters in a scene, a linear plot, the "law of three" (e.g., three blind mice, three men in a tub), and a slow entrance and exit from the story.

*Form Criticism, *Oral tradition

Abrahams 1968; G. Anderson 2000; Boman 1967; Brunvand 1976; Buxton 1994; Culley 1963, 1972, 1986; Dorson 1972; Dundes 1999; R. L. Fowler 2000; Frazer 1911–15; Gantz 1993; Georges and Jones 1995; Ginzberg 1909–38; Graf 1993; Henaut 1993; Lord 1973; Rank, Sommerset, and Dundes 1990; Rappoport 1928, 1937; Rappoport and Patai 1966; Vansina 1985; Vernant 2001; Widengren 1959

Folktale (see *Folklore)

Forensic rhetoric is one of the three Greco-Roman types of rhetoric (see *Rhetorical genres, *Rhetorical theory). The forensic speech had its primary setting in the court of law, where the issue was the decision of whether or not something had happened. The 1st cent. C.E. rhetorician Quintilian expressed the widely held view that the forensic speech consisted of five parts (*Inst. orat.* 3.9.1): (1) the *exordium,* or *prooemium*, preparing the audience to be receptive to the rest of the speech (Quintilian, *Inst. orat.* 4.1.1–4; Cicero, *Inv.* 1.15.20; *Ad Herennium* 1.4.6); (2) the statement of the facts, or *narratio* (Cicero, *Inv.* 1.13.18); (3) the proof, i.e., *probatio* or *pistis*; (4) the refutation (*refutatio*); and (5) the peroration (*peroratio*).

Kennedy 1972, 7–18

Formalism, a text-oriented type of *literary criticism (also called the New Criticism), is a type of literary criticism that repudiates both authorial intention (referred to as the "intentional fallacy") and the reader's freedom to construe a text in any way possible. Literary works are free of authorial intention, historical necessity, and the projections of the reader's values and meanings (Scholes 1982, 15). Formalist and New Critical schools of criticism deny any cognitive quality to literary texts, i.e., they have no context beyond their own verbal system or other texts that share that system (Scholes 1982, 23).

*Scholes 1982

Form criticism is a critical method concerned primarily with the identification and analysis of stereotypical types of discourse that were originally transmitted orally but have been codified and modified through incorporation into written texts. The term "form criticism" is an English translation of the German term "Formgeschichte" (literally "form history"), which was part of the title of a 1919 book by Dibelius (*Die Formgeschichte des Evangeliums*, "The Form Criticism of the Gospel"). Form criticism presupposes that all types of human verbal communication occur in well-defined patterns, i.e., in forms or genres. The identification of an oral or written form (an operation that is usually unconscious) determines the hearer's or reader's expectations regarding content, attitude toward content, understanding of the constituent words and sentences. The term "literary form" refers to those characteristics of vocabulary and style that enable a hearer or reader to categorize a unit of written or oral communica-

Oral Forms in the Synoptic Gospels

V. Taylor (1935, 1966, 78–89)	Bultmann (1963)	Dibelius (1934, 1971)
1. **Pronouncement stories** (1935, 63–87)	1. ***Apophthegmata,*** terse, pointed sayings that are "ideal" constructions, not historical reports (1963, 11–69)	1. **Paradigms,** *Paradigmen* or "examples" (1934, 37–69; 1971, 34–66), e.g., Mark 2:1–12, 18–22, 23–28; 3:1–5, 20–30, 31–35; 10:13–16; 12:13–17; 14:1–3
Form: (1) Sayings of Jesus, (2) set in short narrative contexts, (3) culminating in a saying expressing some ethical or religious precept.	Subtypes: (1) **Controversy sayings** (*Streitgespräche*) with hostile opponents and beginning with a controversy (e.g., Mark 3:1–6) (2) **School sayings** (*Schulgespräche*), i.e., friendly discussion, beginning with question asked by someone seeking knowledge (e.g., Mark 12:28–34) (3) **Biographical *apophthegmata***, purporting to contain some information about Jesus, "best thought of as edifying paradigms for sermons" (Luke 9:57–62)	Setting: Narratives of the deeds of Jesus used as examples in early Christian preaching to explain and support the message. Form: (1) Independent of literary context (2) Brief and simple (3) Religious rather than artistic coloring, style (4) Didactic style often emphasizing words of Jesus (5) Ending in a saying useful for preaching
2. **Stories about Jesus** (1935, 142–67) Form: Great variety, no particular structural form	2. **Historical stories and legends**, religious and edifying stories that are not properly miracle stories (e.g., Mark 1:9–11 and Mark 1:12–13)	2. **Legends**, *Legende* (1934, 104–32), e.g., Luke 2:41–49 "Religious narratives of a saintly man in whose works and fate interest is taken" (1934, 104)
3. **Sayings of Jesus** (1935, 89–100) Form: Sayings with no narrative framework	3. ***Herrenworte***, Dominical sayings, divided into three groups according to content (1963, 69–166) (1) **Logia** (Proverbs), have 3 forms: (a) declarative forms (Matt. 6:34; 12:34; 22:14; Luke 10:7), (b) exhortations in an imperative form (Matt. 8:22; Luke 4:23), (c) questions (Matt 6:27; Mark 2:19). (2) **Prophetic and Apocalyptic Sayings**, in which Jesus "proclaimed the arrival of the Reign of God and preached the call to repentance, promising salvation for those who were prepared and threatening woes upon the unrepentant" (1962, 56), (e.g., Mark 1:15; Luke 10:23–24; 6:20–21) (3) **Legal Sayings and Church Rules** (e.g., Mark 3:4; 7:15; Matt 18:15–17) (4) **I-Sayings**, in which Jesus speaks of himself, his work, his destiny (e.g., Matt. 5:17; 15:24; Mark 10:45) (5) **Similitudes** (i.e., Parables)	3. ***Paränese***, or Exhortations (1934, 233–65; 1971, 234–65). Dibelius uses ***Paradigmata*** to partially cover both ***Apophthegmata*** and ***Herrenworte*** in Bultmann's classification. Under **Paränese** he briefly mentions six forms: (1) maxims, (2) metaphor, (3) parabolic, (4) narrative, (5) prophetic address (beatitude, woe, eschatological preaching), (6) short commandment, and (7) extended commandment with reason provided.

(continued next page)

Oral Forms in the Synoptic Gospels *(continued)*

V. Taylor (1935, 1966, 78–89)	Bultmann (1963)	Dibelius (1934, 1971)
4. **Miracle stories** (V. Taylor 1935, 119–41) Form: (1) Circumstances (2) Healing (3) Impression of onlookers or confirmation of cure Examples: Mark 1:23–27, 29–31.	4. **Miracle stories**, *Wundergeschichten* (Bultmann 1963, 209–44), stories of healing and nature miracles focusing on the miracle as the main theme and is described in some detail.	4. **Tales** or *Novellen* (Dibelius 1934, 70–103), e.g, Mark 1:40–45; 4:35–41; 5:1–20, 21–43; 6:35–44, 45–62; 7:32–37; 8:22–26; 9:14–29; Luke 7:11–16 Stories of Jesus' miracles which originate in present form with storytellers and teachers. Form: (1) History of the illness (2) Technique of the miracle (3) Success of the miraculous act
5. **Parables** (1935, 100–105)	5. ***Gleichnisse***, Similitudes. See above under 3. (5)	5. ***Gleichnisse***, or "Similitudes" (categorized under "Exhortations" or *Paränesis* in Dibelius 1935, 233–65)
6. **Passion narrative** (V. Taylor 1935, 44–62)	6. **Passion narrative** (1963, 262–84)	6. **Passion story** (1935, 178–217)

tion within a particular literary type. A "literary type" is a characteristic form of oral or written expression found in a number of texts with similar style, vocabulary, expressions, and purpose. According to Collins (162): "Thus the first task of form criticism is the analysis of the literary form of a given document with the view of assigning it to a given literary type."

The threefold task of classical form criticism was to classify the Synoptic material by form, recover the original form, and determine the setting out of which the forms originated (V. Taylor 1935, 22–28). Form criticism typically assumes that each oral form arose within and was determined by a particular social situation. One of the difficulties of this view is that the social situation is often identified by circular reasoning. Ultimately the inability of form critics to identify the actual *Sitz im Leben* within which various oral forms arose has not added to the credibility of the method. Yet the rejection of the so-called "laws of tradition" emphasized by early folklorists such as Axel Olrik (1908; Eng. 1965) and Kaarle Krohn (upon whom both Bultmann and Dibelius were dependent) has freed form criticism (and folklore studies generally) from a preoccupation with historical, geographical, and genetic origins. Similarly, there is less concern among folklorists with the atomizing tendencies of the folktale types catalogued by S. Thompson (1955) and Aarne and Thompson (1961), and the extensive compendium of motifs produced by Thompson has been replaced with a concern for identifying either the diachronic or synchronic structures of folklore genres (particularly tales), inspired by Vladimir Propp (1960) on the one hand and by the French structuralists on the other (cf. Eleasar M. Meletinsky, "The Structural-Typological Study of the Folktale," *Genre* 4 [1971]: 249–79). This approach has become influential in the form-critical study of the Gospels, primarily through the innovative treatment of the miracle story in Theissen (1974).

Classification of oral forms in the Synoptic tradition. The comparative chart of terminology for the various oral forms identified in the Synoptic Gospels is based on V. Taylor 1935, Bultmann 1963, and Dibelius 1934.

In addition to the forms identified *(see table beginning on page 188)* by the classical practitioners of form criticism, other proposals have been made as well. Sellew has proposed the form-critical category "dominical discourse," which he defines as "a series of sayings of Jesus, sometimes of disparate origin, gathered in the oral tradition due to their thematic connection to a topic of importance to his followers" (1988,

98). As an example of this oral collection of sayings, he analyzes the Beelzebul pericope (Mark 3:22–30 and Q/Luke 11:14–23; Matt. 9:32–34; 12:22–30).

*Apophthegmata, *Chreiai, *Folklore, *Oral tradition, *Parables, *Pronouncement stories

---

Albertz 1921; Berger 1984a, 1984b; Bultmann 1963, 1967, 1971; Buss 1999; Dibelius 1934, 1971; Fascher 1924; Greenwood 1970; Hultgren 1979; Longman 1985; McKnight 1969; Meletinsky 1971; Tannehill 1981; V. Taylor 1935, 1966, 78–89

Forms, a term for relatively short literary units used as constituent elements of the genres that frame them (Aune 1987, 13; Bailey 1995, 197).

*Form criticism

Four Gospels, a general designation for the four canonical Gospels, conventionally arranged in the order Matthew, Mark, Luke, John, all composed between ca. 70 and 100 C.E. The earliest clear evidence for the existence of the fourfold Gospel is found in Irenaeus, late 2d cent. C.E. (quoted in Eusebius, *Hist. eccl.* 5.8.2–4):

> Matthew composed his Gospel among the Hebrews in their language, when Peter and Paul were preaching the Gospel in Rome and founding the church there. After their death, Mark, the disciple and interpreter of Peter, handed down to us the preaching of Peter in written form. Luke, the companion of Paul, set down the Gospel preached by him in a book. Finally John, the disciple of the Lord, who also reclined on his breast, himself composed the Gospel when he was living in Ephesus in Asia.

T. Heckel (1999, 327–29) argues that Justin (ca. 100–ca. 165) already knew a fourfold Gospel collection, and von Harnack (1960, 79, 84–85, 211, 249) argued that Marcion (who broke with the Roman church in the summer of 144 C.E.) already knew a fourfold Gospel as well. It is also possible that the creation of a fourfold Gospel about 150–175 C.E. was perhaps a reaction to the single Gospel of Marcion, either in Rome or Asia Minor (Campenhausen 1972, 171–72). Justin, who may have known a collection of the three *Synoptic Gospels (T. Heckel 1999, 327–29), probably did not know a collection of four Gospels since there is no clear evidence that he knew the Gospel of John. Two decades after Justin, Irenaeus argued that there cannot be either more or less than four Gospels (*Adv. haer.* 3.11.8–9). Irenaeus also tended to refer to the fourfold Gospel using the singular term "Gospel" (*Adv. haer.* 1.20.2; 3.5.1).

The titles of all four canonical Gospels are similar (e.g., "The Gospel according to Mark"), with the preposition κατά ("according to") taking the place of the regular and expected genitive of authorship (e.g., "The Gospel *of* Mark"). The oldest known form of this title was probably Κατὰ Μάρκον, "According to Mark," which should be understood as a way of indicating authorship. While Hengel (1985b, 65–67) argues for the originality of the longer form, he does not provide a convincing explanation for the supposed secondary origin of the shorter form. The similarity in form of the titles of all four Gospels suggests that they were originally added when the fourfold Gospel was assembled.

The plurality of the Gospels was perceived as a problem by some during the mid-2d cent. C.E. (Cullmann 1966, 548–65). The conflation of the four Gospels into one continuous composition, a "gospel harmony," was done by *Tatian, a student of *Justin Martyr, ca. 170 C.E. in Syria. Tatian's **Diatessaron,* first mentioned by Eusebius (*Hist. eccl.* 4.29.6), was compiled after the middle of the 2d cent. C.E. in Syria (for a comprehensive review of Diatessaron studies, see W. L. Petersen 1994). The *Diatessaron,* called the "Gospel of the Mixed" was canonical in Syria until the 5th cent.

*Diatessaron, *Harmonies of the Gospels, *Synoptic Gospels

Carroll 1954–55; Cullmann 1966; Farmer 1998; Grant 1965; Heckel 1999; Hengel 1984, 2000; von Campenhausen

Friendly letter A sample of a friendly letter is provided by Ps.-Demetrius, *Epistolary Types* 1 (trans. Malherbe 2000, 181):

> Even though I have been separated from you for a long time, I suffer this in body only. For I can never forget you or the impeccable way we were raised together from childhood up. Knowing that I myself am genuinely concerned about your affairs, and that I have worked unstintingly for what is most advantageous to you, I have assumed that you, too, have the same opinion of me, and will refuse me in nothing.

*Epistolography, *Philippians, *Thessalonians, First Letter to the

---

Malherbe 2000

Galatians, Paul's Letter to the

Authorship and destination. Paul is presented as the author of Galatians (1:1), and the letter is universally accepted as a genuine Pauline production. The letter is addressed to the churches of Galatia. Galatia is a problematic designation, however, for it can refer both to the ethnic region of north central Anatolia, where the Gauls settled after migrating from central Europe in the 3d cent. B.C.E. (perhaps visited by Paul according to Acts 16:6 and 18:23) and to the region in south central Anatolia that was incorporated as the Roman province of Galatia in 24 B.C.E. If the northern ethnic region is in view (the North Galatian theory), the letter was probably written after 52 C.E.; if the Roman Province of Galatia is in view (the South Galatian theory, or the province theory), the letter could have been written as early as ca. 47 or 48, not long after the first missionary journey of Paul (for arguments pro and con, see Guthrie 1970, 450–58; Kümmel 1975, 296–98). Though the cities in which these churches are located are not known, they may include Iconium, Lystra, and Derbe (Acts 14), if the letter was directed to the province of Galatia.

Purpose. The central message of this complex letter is freedom, and for that reason it has been called "the charter of Christian liberty." The freedom at issue is freedom from the necessity of observing the ritual requirements of the Mosaic law, particularly circumcision (5:2; 6:12) and a vague ritual calendar (4:10). The importance of the Mosaic ritual law was apparently emphasized by competing Jewish-Christian missionaries who arrived in Galatia after Paul and his associates had left. Paul expresses shock and outrage (see *Pathos) that they have turned from the gospel that he proclaimed to "another gospel," though there really is no such thing (1:6–7). In Paul's words (2:15–16): "We ourselves . . . are Jews by birth and not Gentile sinners, yet . . . know that a man is not justified by doing works of the law but through faith in Jesus Christ."

Here the phrase "works of the law" probably refers, not to the whole law, but rather to certain ritual requirements of the law, including circumcision, Sabbath observance, ritual purity, a kosher diet, and perhaps other social markers indicating allegiance to Judaism and Jewish ethnic identity. The main subject of Galatians, primarily a deliberative letter, put in terms of Roman declamation themes, is: "The Galatians deliberate whether Gentile believers in Christ should be circumcised" (Fairweather 1994, 5).

Epistolary analysis. Since Galatians is a letter, it exhibits a distinctive variation on of the typical epistolary opening and closing that Paul had adopted for his letters addressed to congregations. The epistolary prescript, found in 1:1–5, consists first of all of a superscription (1:1–2a) in which the sender and his qualifications are mentioned, along with his associates. The adscription in 1:2b is a simple address "to the churches of Galatia." The salutation (1:3–4) begins in typical Pauline form: "Grace to you and peace from God our Father and our Lord Jesus Christ." What is not so typical, however, is the fact that it continues with a participial phrase that describes the saving work of Jesus Christ. Also unusual is the absence of the typical Pauline thanksgiving period. The concluding mention of God the Father is also expanded by a relative clause to form a concluding *doxology: "to whom be the glory for ever and ever. Amen" (1:5).

The epistolary postscript (6:11–18) is also unusual in that the autographed greeting (v. 11), which is often found in the closing sections of Pauline letters, is followed by a summary of the argument of the main part of the letter (vv. 12–17). The typical Pauline grace benediction then concludes the letter (v. 18): "The grace of our Lord Jesus Christ be with your spirit, brethren. Amen."

A relatively simply outline of Galatians has been proposed by Légasse, who is aware of contributions to the rhetorical analysis of Galatians but essentially rejects them, since Galatians is a letter not a speech, and it is not an apology but an exhortation that has similarities to deliberative rhetoric (Légasse 2000, 36–39). The following thematic outline is based on Légasse (2000, 40), supplemented by the more detailed structure found in the body of his commentary:

I. Address (1:1–5)
II. Introduction (1:6–10)
III. Proof (1:11–5:12)
  A. Autobiographical argument (1:11–2:21)
    1. The thesis (1:11–12)
    2. Before revelation: Paul among the Jewish elite (1:13–14)
    3. After revelation: "Without consulting flesh and blood" (1:15–17)
    4. Paul's first visit to Jerusalem (1:18–20)
    5. Between the two visits to Jerusalem (1:21–24)
    6. The council of Jerusalem (2:1–10)

7. The incident at Antioch (2:11–14)
8. Commentary: Justification (2:15–21)

B. Appeal to reason (2:22–5:12)
1. Apostrophe: The experience of the Galatians (3:1–5)
2. First argument: Abraham, the law, and faith (3:6–14)
3. Second argument: Abraham and the promises (3:15–18)
4. Why the law? (3:19–25)
5. Third argument: Christians, as children of God, are freed from the law (3:26–4:7)
6. Fourth argument: Reminder and reproach (4:8–20)
7. Fifth argument: The law against the law; the two sons of Abraham (4:21–5:1)
8. Sixth argument: Circumcision separates one from Christ (5:2–12)

IV. Paraenesis: Instructions for the Christian life (5:13–6:10)
A. Introduction: The thesis (5:13–15)
B. The Spirit and the flesh in conflict in Christian existence (5:16–26)
C. Particular exhortations (5:27–6:10)

V. Postscript (6:11–18)

This outline has a basic similarity to the rhetorical outlines proposed below (*see p. 194*), even if Légasse has resisted the typical structures of deliberative rhetoric. He regards 1:11–12 as the thesis: "For I would have you know, brethren, that the gospel which was preached by me is not man's gospel. For I did not receive it from man, nor was I taught it, but it came through a revelation of Jesus Christ."

Rhetorical analysis. The publication of the detailed rhetorical analysis of Galatians by Betz (1974–75, 1979) stimulated a revival in interest in *rhetorical criticism of the NT (particularly the NT letters) that shows no signs of diminishing. Numbers of essays and monographs dealing with various aspects of the rhetoric of Galatians have been published in the last several decades, though there is little agreement on the *rhetorical genre and rhetorical structure of Galatians. Betz (1974–75, 1979), followed by others (Brinsmead 1982, 37–55; Hester 1984), has argued that Galatians is an apologetic letter (Kern 1998, 86 has Betz claim that Galatians is an "apologetic speech," though Betz's analysis is far more nuanced and subtle than that). Many others have preferred to regard Galatians as essentially deliberative (e.g., Kennedy 1984, 145; Hall 1987; Smit 1989; C. C. Black 1989, 255), and there are even a few who have opted to regard Galatians as belonging to the epideictic genre (Hester 1991, a change in viewpoint from his 1984 article; White 1993, critiqued by Kern 1998, 162–64). Some prefer to consider Galatians as a mixed rhetorical genre (Aune 1981; Longenecker 1990; Fairweather 1994; critiqued by Kern 1998, 157–61). Longenecker even identifies Gal. 4:12 as the specific passage marking the transition from forensic rhetoric to deliberative rhetoric. Each of these categorizations has its own problems. More recently a number of scholars have expressed skepticism about the relationship of Galatians to any of the three species of Greco-Roman rhetoric (Kern 1998, 166; R. D. Anderson 1999, 142–89; Légasse 2000, 36–41). Dunn (1993, 20) rejects the strictures that he perceives are inherent in a cookie-cutter rhetorical approach:

> [A]ttempts to label Galatians as a particular kind of letter or to determine its structure from conventional parallels are of questionable value. It is clear that Galatians does not accord closely with any ideal type, and there is a danger that analysis of the letter will be too much determined by fitting it on to a grid drawn from elsewhere rather than by the natural flow of the argument. More important, there is a danger that too much emphasis on rhetorical considerations may blur the extent to which the letter is driven by theological logic and passion.

Referring to the "exordium" of Galatians, Classen (2000, 23) observes:

> The address is followed by what one might call an *exordium* ("introduction"); but its unusual elements must be taken as a warning that what follows is not one of the three traditional types of *logos* distinguished by rhetorical theory; indeed neither a judicial nor a deliberative nor a demonstrative type of speech would have been appropriate here, as Paul is neither addressing a court of law from which he expects a verdict at the end, nor an assembly which will pass a resolution, let alone praising an individual or a group.

Finally, Kern (1998) maintains that "Galatians is not a classical oration," though Kern's arguments are frequently exaggerated, and his grasp of ancient rhetoric is problematic.

According to Betz (1974–75, 1979), the structure of Galatians is that of a juridical speech framed as a letter. Paul is being accused by a group of opponents in Galatia, and the Galatian Christians are placed by him in the role of judges. Paul defends himself as if before a jury. Betz views Galatians as an apologetic letter or letter of defense, framed by an epistolary prescript (1:1–5) and postscript (6:11–18), the latter also functioning as a *peroratio* or conclusion. The body of Galatians consists of five structural elements: (1) The *exordium* ("introduction"), in 1:6–11, contains a statement of the *causa*, the invocation of a curse, and the inclusion of a *transitus* or *transgressio* that introduces the next stage of argumentation, (2) the *narratio* ("statement of facts"), in 1:12–2:14. After stating the thesis in 1:12, "For I did not receive it [the Gospel] from man, nor was I taught it, but it came through a revelation of Jesus Christ," he outlines the events or facts on which his case rests (1:13–2:14). (3) The *propositio* ("proposition, theme") in 2:15–21 first states the point of agreement (2:15–16) and then the point of disagreement (2:17–18). (4) The *probatio* ("proofs") in 3:1–4:31, the main part of the letter, is divided into several parts: (a) the first argument, from indisputable evidence (3:1–5), (b) the second argument, from Scripture (3:6–14), (c) the third argument, from common practice (3:15–18), (d) a digression on Torah (3:19–25), (e) the fourth argument, from Christian tradition (3:26–4:11), (f) the fifth argument, from friendship (4:12–20), (g) the sixth argument, an allegorical argument from Scripture (4:21–31). (5) The *exhortatio* ("exhortation") in 5:1–6:10.

Since there are few if any examples of "apologetic letters" to which Galatians can be compared, an appeal to this "genre" is problematic. Kennedy (1984, 144–46; see also Classen 2000, 24–25) argues that Betz has overemphasized the narrative section (Gal. 1:12–2:14) by making it fit the pattern of judicial rhetoric (narratives are used for different purposes in the three genres of rhetoric) and underemphasized the role of exhortation (Gal. 5:1–6:10), which points in the direction of deliberative rhetoric. The term *exhortatio* applied to Gal. 5:1–6:10 is also problematic, since the term itself is not found in the ancient rhetorical handbooks, and it has been claimed that such a section is not found in any of the three types of rhetoric, nor is it discussed in the rhetorical handbooks. Betz (1979, 254) admits that "paraenesis plays only a marginal role in the ancient rhetorical handbooks." While Gal. 1–2 has an apologetic character, Gal. 3–4 is more deliberative. Vouga (1988) has defended Betz's analysis of Galatians, but as a deliberative rather than as an apologetic letter, by adducing the speech of Demosthenes entitled *On the Peace* as an example of a deliberative speech with a rhetorical structure similar to that of Galatians: (1) *exordium* (1–3), (2) *narratio* (4–12), (3) *propositio* (13–14a), (4) *probatio* (14b–23), (5) *exhortatio* (24–25). Chrysostom held the view that from a rhetorical perspective, Galatians was both apologetic and exhortatory, i.e., judicial and deliberative (Fairweather 1994, 6). The rhetorical analysis of Longenecker (1990) argues that Galatians is in part juridical and in part deliberative (see below).

Smit (1989), responding to Betz (1979), has proposed quite a different rhetorical analysis of Galatians, in which he omits the epistolary opening and closing of the letter as irrelevant for the purposes of rhetorical analysis. (1) *Exordium* (Gal. 1:6–12): (a) brings audience to a state of alarm by informing them that they are deserting God (vv. 6–7a); (b) arouses hostility against opponents (vv. 7b–9); (c) attempts to win sympathy for himself (vv. 10–12). (2) *Narratio* (Gal. 1:13–2:21): (a) brings up subject of Judaism (vv. 13–14); (b) indicates direction they should choose: God himself sent Paul to preach the gospel to the Gentiles (vv. 15–24); (c) provides two examples of how Christians cannot force non-Jewish Christians to accept circumcision and observe the Torah (2:1–10, 11–21); (d) story divided into four episodes: (i) Gal. 1:13–14: place: Judaism; opposition: Jews vs. Gentiles; (ii) Gal. 1:15–24: place: not-Jerusalem; opposition: God vs. humanity; (iii) Gal. 2:1–10: place: Jerusalem; opposition: Jews vs. Gentiles, i.e., the circumcised vs. the uncircumcised; (iv) Gal. 2:11–21: place: Antioch; opposition: Jews vs. Gentiles, i.e., the righteous observing the Torah vs. the lawless sinners. (3) Proof or *confirmatio* (Gal. 3:1–4:11): (a) introduction (3:1–5); Galatians acting foolishly and against their own interests; (b) first argument (3:6–14); (c) second argument (3:15–29); (d) third argument (4:1–7); (e) conclusion (4:8–11): Galatians acting against their own interests. (4) *Conclusio* (4:12–5:12) of three parts: (a) *conquestio* (4:12–20), an appeal to pity; (b) *enumeratio* (4:21–5:6), a brief summary of the speech; (c) *indignatio* (5:7–12), an incitement of the hearers to hate someone. [Gal. 5:13–6:10 is regarded by Smit as a later interpolation into the letter because it is so alien to the deliberative structure.] (5) *Amplificatio* (6:11–18), a transgression of normal deliberative structure, is an amplification, in 6:12–16, of the thought in Gal. 5:11 by means of antithesis, in the framework of an epistolary closing *(see following table)*.

Synopsis of Rhetorical Analyses of Galatians

Dispositio	Betz 1974–75, 1979	Brinsmead 1982, 49–54	Kennedy 1984	Hester 1984	Hall 1987	Smit 1989	Becker 1989, 288–94	Longenecker 1990
Epistolary prescript	1:1–5		1:1–5				1:1–5	1:1–5
Exordium or *proem*	1:6–11	1:6–10	1:6–10	1:6–10	1:1–5	1:6–12	1:6–9	1:6–10
Stasis		—		1:11–12				—
Transitio		—		1:13–14			1:10	—
Narratio	1:12–2:14	1:11–2:14		1:15–2:10		1:13–2:21	1:11–2:21	1:11–2:14
Propositio	2:15–21	2:15–21		—	1:6–9			2:15–21
Probatio or *confirmatio*	3:1–4:31	3:1–4:21	1:11–5:1	—	1:10–6:10	3:1–4:11	3:1–5:12	3:1–4:11
Refutatio		4:1–6:10						
Exhortatio or *paraenesis*	5:1–6:10		5:2–6:10	—			5:13–6:10	4:12–6:10
Peroratio or *conclusio*				—	6:11–18	4:12–5:12		—
Epistolary postscript or subscription	6:11–18		6:11–18	—			6:11–18	6:11–18
Amplificatio				—		6:11–18		

Both the agreements and disagreements in these rhetorical analyses of Galatians are of interest. While the epistolary opening and closing sections are relatively obvious, they coincide with rhetorical analyses only for those who regard the epistolary postscript as doing double duty and also functioning as a rhetorical *peroratio*. The beginning of the controversial paraenetic section is also problematic, and Becker (1989, 288–94) is one of the few who accepts the influential analysis of Merk (1969), who argues that the paraenesis begins in 5:13 (a view also found in John Chrysostom, *Galatians* 13.39).

*Epistolography, *Irony, *Letters, Pauline, *Rhetorical criticism

Becker 1989; Betz 1974–75, 1976, 1979; Brinsmead 1982; Classen 1992; Dolamo 1989; Fairweather 1994; Hall 1987; Hansen 1989; Hester 1984, 1993; Kern 1998; Légasse 2000; Longenecker, 1990; Lührmann, 1992; Martin 1995; Martyn, 1997; Merk 1969; Matera 1988; Nannos 2002; Porter 1999b; W. B. Russell 1993a, 1993b; Sänger 2002; Schlier 1962; Smit 1989; Vouga 1988; White 1993

Gattung, a German term frequently used in biblical scholarship for a literary *form or *genre (Bailey 1995, 197).

Genealogy, a list tracing the descent of a person from an ancestor or ancestors. In early Christian literature the most significant genealogies are those of Jesus in Matt. 1:1–17 and Luke 3:23–38, which display conventions characteristic of both Greco-Roman and biblical genealogies. In Greco-Roman literature, genealogies appeared in several different genres: biography (βίοι), history, scholia, mythology, epigrams, and inscriptions. Both Matthew and Luke conform to the Greco-Roman pattern of including a genealogy toward the beginning of a βίος. Matthew inserts a genealogy at the very beginning (cf. Plutarch, *Agis*, *Alcibiades*, *Pyrrhus*, *Solon*, *Themistocles*; Suetonius, *Lives of Caesars*; Josephus, *Life*; Quintilian 7.10). In the OT, Chronicles begins with genealogies, and Genesis is structured by them, but the closest parallels to Matthew's opening are Zephaniah 1:1 and especially Tobit 1:1–2. Other Greco-Roman βίοι parallel Luke's insertion of a genealogy after an introduction (cf. Plutarch, *Lycurgus* 1:4), though Luke's introductory narrative preceding the genealogy is unusually long. Luke may have been influenced by the LXX, where the genealogy of Moses does not occur until Exod. 6:14–17 (Kurz 1984, 172–75). The genealogies of Ezra and Judith also occur later in those works (Ezra 7:1–2, Jdt. 8:1). The purpose of beginning a βίος with a genealogy was either to highlight the subject's noble origins (as in Matthew and Luke) or to point to the subject's virtue in overcoming humble origins (Quintilian 3.7, 10); Matthew traces the descent of Jesus from the Davidic dynasty of Judah.

Matthew's genealogy is complicated by the inclusion of four female ancestors of ambiguous moral and social standing. The mention of women in a genealogy is unusual, though not unprecedented, either in the OT or Greco-Roman literature. Women's names are mentioned occasionally in OT genealogies (14 in 1 Chr. 2 alone). Greco-Roman genealogies could also include women. A late genealogy of Kodros, the last king of Athens, includes ten successive pairs of parents (Scholion to Plato, *Symp.* 208D [text in Green 1938, 63=*FGH* 4.125; Mussies 1986, 39):

> Kodros was descended from Deukalion, as Hellanikos says, for Hellen is born of Deukalion and Pyrrha, or according to some of Zeus and Pyrrha [female], of Hellen and Othreïs was born Xuthos, Aiolos, Doros and Xenopatra [female]; of Aiolos and Iphis [female] the daughter of Peneios was born Salmoneus, of Salmoneus and Alkidike [female] was born Tyro [female], of her and Poseidon Neleus was born, of Neleus and Chloris [female] Periklymenos; of Periklymenos and Peisidike [female], Boros was born; of Boros and Lysidike [female] Pentheilos was born; of Pentheilos and Anchirrhoe [female] Andropompos was born; of Andropompos and Henioche [female] (the daughter of Harmenios the son of Zuexippos the son of Eumelos the son of Admetos) Melanthos was born. He migrated from Messene to Athens when the Heraclidae came, and to him Kodros was born.

It is uncertain, however, why the evangelist included just these particular four women. All are Gentiles, and the sexual improprieties of three are narrated in the OT. However, their reputation was apparently rehabilitated in early Jewish biblical interpretation, allowing them to be understood as heroes of faith. Greco-Roman genealogies could use the term "son" in both the biological sense and in an adoptive, legal sense. Inscriptions refer to Marcus Aurelius as the descendant of all four previous emperors (Nerva, Trajan, Hadrian, and Antoninus Pius), though these emperors were not actually related; each was the adopted son of the former, thus forming a dynasty. Different genealogies could also be given for the same individual, based on either birth or adoption (Mussies 1986, 34–35). Furthermore, Greco-Roman as well as biblical genealogies could be abbreviated by skipping generations (Est. 2:5; Plutarch, *Agis* 3; Appian, *Mthr.* 16.112). The Matthean genealogy clearly skips generations (cf. Matt. 1:9 with 1 Chr. 3:11 and 26:11), and the genealogy of Luke probably does as well. Examples of both the ascending genealogical pattern in Luke (later to earlier) and the descending pattern in Matthew (earlier to later) occur in the OT and Greco-Roman literature. Descending genealogies are the rule in the OT, but examples are occasionally found in Greco-Roman literature (Plutarch, *Lycurgus* 1.4, *Pyrrhus* 1). Matthew's genealogy differs from these latter in the use of the Septuagint term "beget" (γεννᾶν). Ascending genealogies were the rule in Hellenistic literature (Speyer 1976, 1211). Close parallels to Luke's genealogy are to be found in Herodotus 7.204, 4.147, 7.11.2, 8.131 (Kurz 1984, 170), as well as in some of the apocrypha that originated in the Hellenistic period (Tob. 1:1–2; Jdt. 8:1). Both genealogies of Jesus are much longer than those typically found in Greco-Roman literature, but not unusual for readers familiar with the Septuagint (Kurz 1984, 170–71; Speyer 1976, 1158, 1169, 1172, 1174–75). Luke's tracing of the descent of Jesus back to God has no biblical precedent but resembles the custom among Greco-Roman aristocracy of reckoning the family ancestry from a god (Speyer 1976, 1172). Matthew explicitly structures his genealogy in sets of fourteen generations, while Luke has eleven sets of seven generations counting backwards toward Adam. Parallels for such numerological structuring of generations are uncommon but can be found (cf. Scholion on Euripides, *Orestes* 1648=*FGH* 323a F22a; Mussies 1986, 46).

Abel 1973; D. R. Bauer 1990; Broadbend 1969; Farrar 1955; Hammer 1980; Hood 1961; Johnson 1969; G. Kuhn 1923; Kurz 1980b, 1984; J. Masson 1982; Mussies 1986; Nolland 1996, 1997; Ramlot 1964; Schnider and Stenger 1979; Schöllig 1968; Speyer 1976; Weren 1997; Wilson 1977

JON BERGSMA

General Epistles or Catholic Epistles (ἐπιστολαὶ καθολικαί) refers to a group of seven letters found in the NT: James (1,735 words), 1 Peter (1,669), 2 Peter (1,103), 1 John (2,137), 2 John (245), 3 John (219), and Jude (456). These seven were called ἐπιστολαὶ καθολικαί by the 4th cent. C.E., particularly in the Eastern church. In the West they tend to be called *Canonicae* ("canonical") rather than *Catholicae*, certainly by the 6th cent. C.E. They are called "general" or "catholic epistles" because four of them are addressed not to specific local Christian communities, but either to Christians everywhere (Jas. 1:1: "To the twelve tribes in the Dispersion") or to Christians in a certain broad geographical area (1 Pet. 1:1b: "To the exiles of the Dispersion in Pontus, Galatia, Cappadocia, Asia, and Bithynia"). The Johannine letters have a different character. First John is a homily rather than a letter, and both 2 and 3 John have specific destinations. Second John is addressed "to the elect lady and her children," while 3 John is addressed to Gaius. The number of words in each of the general letters, together with their adscriptions, indicate that two collections have been combined, a collection of four letters arranged according to decreasing size (James, 1 Peter, 2 Peter, Jude), and a second group of Johannine letters similarly arranged according to decreasing size. In addition, Jude and 2 Peter have a literary relationship.

The order of the letters in the English Bible is the order in which they occur in many ancient witnesses (e.g., Codex Vaticanus and the Canon of the Synod of Laodicea, 363 C.E.; see Westcott 1889, 540–79). Eusebius, *Hist. eccl.* 2.23 referred to James as the first of the Catholic Letters. He also designates all but 1 Peter and 1 John as disputed books (*Hist. eccl.* 3.25.3): "Of the disputed books (ἀντιλεγομένων), which are, nevertheless, known to most are the Epistle called of James, that of Jude, the second Epistle of Peter; and the so-called second and third Epistles of John which may be the work of the evangelist or of some other with the same name."

Other ancient lists, however, use different orders: 1–2–3 John, 1–2 Peter, Jude, James; and 1–2 Peter, 1–2–3 John, James, and Jude (Hastings 1900, 1:359–60). As a group, the Catholic Letters sometimes are placed between Acts and the Pauline letters (e.g., Codex Vaticanus, Codex Alexandrinus), but in Codex Sinaiticus they are placed between the Pauline Letters (with Hebrews) and the Revelation to John, the order which we have in modern editions of the Greek NT.

*James, Letter of *John, First Letter of *John, Second Letter of, *John, Third Letter of, *Jude, Letter of *Peter, First Letter of, *Peter, Second Letter of

---

Hastings 1900; Westcott 1889

Genetic fallacy, the supposition that knowing about the sources of a document can take the place of interpreting the work itself (apparently coined by R. Martin 2000, 44).

Genre criticism is primarily concerned with the identification and analysis of groups of texts that appear related through a coherent and recurring pattern of literary qualities. They bear a family resemblance to one another. A part of the discipline of comparative literature, the task of genre criticism is to understand literary works in relationship to each other. Such related works constitute a literary genre, that is, a group of texts that exhibit a coherent and recurring pattern of qualities in terms of their form, content, and function (Aune 1987, 13). It has always been difficult, however, to arrive at satisfactory definitions and descriptions of individual genres, because so many different literary features can be involved. The general procedure in genre analysis is to construct a paradigmatic model by listing various generically salient features of apparently related types of texts in a hierarchical arrangement. In practice, however, this task is rarely undertaken systematically. One of the major problems of this paradigmatic approach is that the generic features of a given group of texts are often not formulated at a sufficiently high level of abstraction to take into account *all* of the texts of a particular type. However, the problem with describing a genre at a sufficiently abstract level is that the hermeneutical value of such generic patterns is thereby lessened. We may perhaps formulate a general rule that the hermeneutical value of a generic paradigm increases in proportion to the complexity of the paradigm. It also appears that the shorter the literary form, the greater the possibilities for a stable and complex formal structure. Further, it is to be expected that genres will differ in complexity, so that the view propounded by E. D. Hirsch, that the perception of genre is a necessary prerequisite for understanding and valid interpretation, is perhaps overly general.

According to Hirsch (1967, 76), "All understanding of verbal meaning is necessarily genre-bound," and Fowler (1982, 38) has observed that a genre is "a communication system for use of writers in writing, and readers and critics in reading and interpreting." The term "genre" is an English loanword from French, originally derived from the Latin term *genus* ("kind, type, sort"). Bailey (1995, 200) has defined genre as "the conventional and repeatable patterns of oral and written language, which facilitate interaction among people in specific social situations." Some ancient popular conceptions of literary form tended to focus on content to the exclusion of other features. Another problematic perspective is the almost metaphysical assumption that texts are not just the sum of their parts, but rather that the whole has a "gestaltist" unity. For example, E. D. Hirsch's notion of "intrinsic genre" is "that sense of the whole by means of which an interpreter can correctly understand any part in its determinacy." Essentially the same credo is represented by a very different critic, J. N. Ellis (1974, 202): "An interpretation, then, is a hypothesis about the most general organization and coherence of all the elements that form a literary text. The most satisfying interpretation will be that which is the most inclusive." Even texts that are apparently incoherent may eventually yield up their secrets to patient criticism (J. N. Ellis 1974, 208): "It cannot be ruled out that someone may still find the interpretation that can, to the satisfaction of other critics, absorb the recalcitrant parts of the text." Ancient historians and classicists have begun to look at genres as flexible, dynamic entities that were constantly changing and developing (Marincola 1999).

New Testament genres. Our consideration of literary genres in the NT is based on the view that the three primary "genres" found therein (gospel, letter, apocalypse) are most satisfactorily regarded as "inclusive" or "host" genres. Constituent forms are framed by these genres in various ways, and there are various degrees of tension between the whole and the part, a factor partially determined by the function of the text. Further the distinctive way of framing the constituent forms, i.e., the composition technique, is considered here to be an important formal generic feature. Again, our understanding of these genres and their constituent literary forms is such that they are regarded as the written expressions of social conventions permeating the world of Roman Hellenism, yet must be understood in terms of their adaptation and transformation by the various social groups in which they arose and the relationship between that group and the broadest segments of ancient society.

*Apocalypse, Literary genre of; *Gospel, literary genre of; *Epistolography; *Letters, literary genre of

———

Bailey 1995; Blomberg 1990a, 1991; Conte 1994; M. Davies 1990; Duff 2000; Fowler 1982; Hirsch 1967, 1974

Gloss (from the Greek word γλῶσσα or γλῶττα, "tongue, language, obscure word") is a term used for a word or very short phrase that explains the meaning of a word or idiomatic phrase (as in a dictionary) or for translation equivalents in one language for words or idiomatic phrases in another language (as in a lexicon). Aristotle used the term γλῶττα for an obscure or foreign word that required explanation (*Poetica* 1457b, 1459a, 1460b; see Pfeiffer 1.1968:12, 78–79). γλῶσσαι are contrasted to λέξεις (plural of λέξις, meaning words that are peculiar in form or significance). The term "gloss" is also used for a brief explanation or synonym of a difficult word, a correction or short interpretive note placed in the margin or between the lines of a handwritten manuscript and sometimes incorporated into the text by the author through the process of copying (Metzger 1992, 27, 194; Walker 2001, 22). Glosses were generally not intended to be taken as part of the text, but rather as an explanation of a particular feature in the text. Since scribes often corrected omissions in texts by adding them between the lines or in the margins of manuscripts, it is easy to understand how copyists have assumed that glosses are corrections and copied them into the new text. Glosses that have at one stage or another been included in the text, however, are evident in the manuscript tradition (e.g., John 5:3b–4; Rom. 8:1 [Metzger 1992, 194]). Other glosses that do not appear as textual variants may have entered into the text of manuscripts, though they cannot usually be identified with any certainty, e.g. 1 Cor. 1:16 (de Boer 1994, 241). Despite the lack of textual evidence, many passages in the NT and early Christian literature have been thought to be glosses for stylistic or theological reasons. Hagen (1980–81) considers Rom. 6:13 a gloss because it interrupts the thought of vv. 12 and 14, has a change of person and tense in the verbs, and shifts the theological perspective. He considers 6:19 a gloss for similar reasons. Frequently 1 Cor. 11:2–16 is judged a gloss (Cope 1978; Murphy-O'Connor 1976, 1980, 1988; Padgett 1988; Walker 1975), while 1 Cor. 13 is sometimes considered one (Titus 1959). First Corinthians 14:34–35 is also frequently considered a gloss (Fitzer 1963). Frequently 2 Cor. 6:14–7:1 is regarded as an interpolation (Grossouw 1951; Fitzmyer 1961b; Gnilka 1968; Betz 1973), though its authenticity is also defended (Fee 1977; Thrall 1977; Lambrecht 1978).

*Glossography, *Interpolations, *Scholia

———

DNP 4.1097–1101; Dyck 1987; Hagen 1980–81; O'Neill 1982

Glossography or glossary, collections of definitions of archaic and obscure words (see *gloss), including words in various Greek dialects used primarily in Greek poets, that were compiled by Alexandrian scholars in the Hellenistic period. Philitas (b. ca. 340 B.C.E.), the teacher of Zenodotus, wrote a work called Ἄτακται γλῶσσαι ("Miscellaneous Glosses"); see Pfeiffer 1968.90–91), and Zenodotos (b. ca. 325 B.C.E.), for example, wrote a work in two books that has not survived entitled Γλῶσσαι, a collection or glossography of definitions of Homeric words. The works of the γλωσσογράφοι ("glossographers"), frequently mentioned in scholia on the Homeric epics, apparently date back to the 3d cent. B.C.E. in Alexandria (Pfeiffer 1968, 79).

DNP 4.1097–1101; Dyck 1987; *OCD* 639–40; Pfeiffer 1968

Gnome, γνώμη (see *Maxim)

Gnomic quatrain is a generic term coined by Henderson (1991) to characterize the very specific form of seven aphoristic sayings of Jesus in the Gospels, with no apparent parallels in Hellenistic or Semitic poetry: (1) Mark 2:21–22b and par.; (2) Matt. 6:22=Luke 11:34–35 (36); (3) Luke 16:10–12; (4) Matt. 6:24=Luke 16:13; (5) Matt. 7:6; (6) Matt. 10:24–25 (Luke 6:40; John 3:16; 15:20); (7) Matt. 10:26b–27=Luke 12:2–3. The gnomic quatrain is a gnomic saying or aphorism following by a three-step argumentative development. Matt. 10:24–25 (NRSV) can serve as an example:

> A disciple is not above the teacher,
> nor a slave above the master;
> 25 it is enough for the disciple to be like the teacher,
> and the slave like the master.

Henderson regards this literary form as marginal in the sayings of Jesus, and does not think that it can be used as criterion of historicity. Rather, it is an example of early interpretation and amplification of the teachings of Jesus.

*Aphorisms

Henderson 1991

Gnomologia are collections of proverbs or maxims (Plato, *Phaedrus* 267c). Examples of gnomologies in the NT include Rom. 12:9–21 and Gal. 6:1–10, in which series of *maxims function as paraenesis.

Gnosticism, a term for a distinctive religious worldview espoused by a variety of sects that found themselves in conflict with early Christianity. Once texts are labeled as "gnostic" or "quasi-gnostic" by modern scholars, they are read in very particular ways. The problem of defining "gnosticism" was a major concern of scholars during the latter part of the 20th cent., and the focus of an international colloquium at Messina. Emerging from this discussion was a core definition of "gnosticism" which consisted of a microcosmic conception of the divided person corresponding to a macrocosmic conception of a divided cosmos. Just as the inner person was thought to have originated in the divine world and was trapped in an alien, material body, so the cosmos was divided into a transcendent divine world separated from the cosmos itself, the creation of an inferior ignorant demiurge. Labeling is an effective means of effacing the historical particularities of persons and documents in the interest of eliminating messy facts that may not easily fit existing categories. The terms "gnostic" and "gnosticism" are fuzzy categories used to describe the religious ideologies that characterize such texts as the *Gospel of Thomas* (Antti 1998) or the *Odes of Solomon*, or the Fourth Gospel, since they are used in such an elastic and unhistorical way. Grenfell and Hunt (1897, 20), in the editio princeps of what would become known as P.Oxy. 654, commented briefly on the suggestion that Logion 5 was "clearly Gnostic," and anticipated how other scholars would label other sayings in their newly discovered papyrus fragment: "And if the other new logia are to be branded as 'Gnostic,' it is difficult to see what might not be included under that convenient category." Recently, it has become increasing evident that even terms like "Judaism" and "Christianity" (even when their complex character is recognized through the plural forms "Judaisms" and "Christianities") are anachronistic labels not fully appropriate for the 1st-cent. C.E. realities they attempt to describe. M. A. Williams (1996) has recently argued at length that the "gnostic" label not only needs rethinking but also needs to be recognized for the dubious historical category it is. The abstract term "Gnosticism," an 18th-cent. neologism, is more problematic than the labels "Judaism" and "Christianity" in the 1st cent. C.E.

Antti 1998; M. A. Williams 1996

Gnostic literature (see *Nag Hammadi literature)

Golden Age (of Latin literature) extended from ca. 70 B.C.E. to 14 C.E. and included such men of letters as poets Catullus, Virgil, Horace, Lucretius, and Ovid and prose writers Julius Caesar, Cicero (rhetoric, philosophy), and Livy (history).

*Latin literature, *Silver age (of Latin literature)

———

Bloomer 1997; Classen 1998; Feeney 1998; Fuhrmann 1999; Habinek 1998; Hadas 1952; Kenney (ed.) 1982

Gorgianic figures, a translation of the phrase Γοργίεια σχήματα, used to refer to *antithesis, *homoioteleuton, and parisosis as used in the extant fragments of the sophist Gorgias of Leontini (ca. 485–380 B.C.E.). The distinctive style of Gorgias is evident in this English translation of a passage from his *Helen* (Schiappa 1999, 86):

> Becoming to a city is a goodly army; to a body beauty, to a soul wisdom, to an action excellence, to speech truth. But their opposites are unbecoming. Man and woman and speech and deed and city and event should be honored with praise if praiseworthy, but on the unworthy blame should be laid; for it is equal error and ignorance to blame the praiseworthy and to praise the blameworthy.

Gorgianic figures are also characteristic of Asianic rhetoric (see *Asianism), a style with which *Ignatius of Antioch is associated, and which also characterizes the style of 2 Peter and the Letter to Diognetus.

*Antithesis, *Asianism, *Diognetus, Letter to, *Ignatius of Antioch, *Peter, Second Letter of

———

Schiappa 1999, 85–132

Gospels, apocryphal can be broadly defined as that body of *pseudepigraphic (or anonymous), popular, extracanonical Jesus literature that arose from the 1st through the 5th cent. C.E. (and even later) that present themselves both as apostolic and therefore as equal in authority to the canonical Gospels.

Basic features. The apocryphal gospels share several characteristics: (1) They were frequently *pseudepigraphic*, i.e., written under the names of famous early Christian figures (such as Peter, Thomas, James, Mary and Bartholomew), often as a means of legitimating their special content and message. The appeals to apostolic authority by representatives of various types of Christianity was a central feature of early Christian polemic, so the identification of the authors of authoritative religious documents was of potentially great theological significance. Occasionally the unknown authors of ancient Jesus literature used the term "gospel" in the titles of their works. Some apocryphal gospels appear to have been written anonymously (e.g., *Gos. Eg.*, *Gos. Eb.*, *Gos. Heb.*), a feature they share with the canonical Gospels. (2) Many of them are *popular* in the sense that they were composed or circulated not by early Christian scholars but by ordinary Christians, and they often appear to represent the written preservation of early Christian folklore. (3) Though apocryphal gospels continued to be produced throughout the middle ages and even into the 20th cent., the period of concern must be limited to that of the early church from the late 1st cent. C.E. to the 3d cent. Sometimes this limit is somewhat arbitrary, as in the case of the *Apocr. Gos. John*, written during the early 11th cent. C.E., using earlier traditions. Unfortunately, it is often difficult, if not impossible, to determine when, where, and within what specific type of Christianity these documents were written. Further, most of these compositions were not simply copied verbatim but rather were revised and expanded so that the final product often represents the reworking of much earlier traditions, and sometimes even reflects revision by Christians with views radically different than those with whom the document originated.

Value and significance. The concern with determining whether there are authentic Jesus traditions present in the apocryphal gospels has provided a strong motivation for investigating these documents. The emphasis on verifying the authenticity of Jesus traditions (the major concern of Resch 1906, Ropes 1896, and Jeremias 1964) has often resulted in an atomistic approach to the apocryphal gospels, in which the primary interest is in the isolation of sayings of Jesus and the assessment of their possible historicity, to the exclusion of other historical, literary, and social concerns. The search for the authentic voice of Jesus, though certainly legitimate, has the effect of treating extracanonical Jesus literature as a quarry for earlier sources or stages of tradition, tacitly diverting attention away from the inherent value of such literature, as well as from the literary matrix and social settings within which such sayings were transmitted. The consequences of this atomistic approach are evident in this "important negative conclusion" of Joachim Jeremias, echoing the earlier sentiments of James Hardy Ropes (Jeremias 1964, 120): "[T]he extra-canonical literature, taken as a whole, manifests a surprising poverty. The bulk of it is legendary, and bears the clear mark of forgery. Only here and there, amid a mass of worthless rubbish, do we come across a priceless jewel."

While some of the Jesus traditions, despite the inevitable alterations that took place in the process of oral transmission, can be traced back to Jesus himself, there are also many traditions created by the Christian community through its preachers, teachers, prophets, and storytellers. The greater part of the narrative and discourse material in the canonical Gospel of John, for example, cannot be traced back to the historical Jesus, despite the efforts of many scholars. Since reliable criteria for making such judgments are unattainable, scholars are not in agreement. While NT scholars say that *many* of the Jesus traditions in the canonical Gospels were created by early Christians, *some* Jesus traditions are surely authentic. Since Jesus literature was transmitted through both oral and literary processes, each unit of text must be tested individually to determine whether it had a previous existence in written or oral form. More often than not, there are no foolproof methods for deciding such questions. It is important that the criteria of authenticity used to determine whether units of text reflect traditions that can be traced back to the historical Jesus (Boring 1985, 1988; Meier 1991, 167–95) be applied to the apocryphal gospels with the same vigor as to the canonical Gospels. Until quite recently the problem of literary history of the Gospels, as reconstructed by source, form, redaction, and tradition criticism, was construed largely as an intracanonical issue. The reason was simply that extracanonical Jesus literature was perceived as both late and derivative and therefore of little real value in writing a literary history of the gospel tradition.

Since the publication of three Nag Hammadi tractates containing Jesus traditions (*G.Thom.; Dial.Sav.; Ap.Jam.*) and the *Secret Gospel of Mark*, there is a growing tendency to regard some of these traditions as independent and perhaps even earlier than parallel traditions in the canonical Gospels. Further, Koester (1982, 2.163) and Crossan (1985, 125–81; 1988) have argued that the passion account in the *Gospel of Peter* is independent of the canonical accounts and perhaps even earlier, though this proposal has encountered stiff opposition (D. F. Wright 1985; R. E. Brown 1987). There is a growing tendency to expand the intratextual system of the New Testament canon to include the apocryphal gospels, i.e., to include all extant forms of ancient Jesus literature (Koester 1980; Crossan 1985). The dominant theory of the relationship between the Synoptic Gospels is called the Two Source theory, i.e., Matthew and Luke were dependent on two major sources, Mark and Q. A few scholars argue for the Griesbach hypothesis, i.e., that Matthew was the first Gospel, that Luke was dependent on Matthew, and that Mark is a conflation and condensation of Matthew and Luke. It has become increasingly clear with the discovery of the Coptic Jesus literature, particularly the *Gospel of Thomas,* the *Dialogue of the Savior,* and the *Apocryphon of James*, as well as the discovery of excerpts from *Secret Gospel of Mark* preserved by Clement of Alexandria, that the history of gospel tradition is far more complex than previously imagined. It is now reasonable to suppose, for example, that an irrecoverable Proto-Mark existed, and that Matthew and Luke each used different revisions of that work (i.e., $\text{Mark}^{\text{Matt}}$ and $\text{Mark}^{\text{Luke}}$); it is also reasonable to hypothecate that different versions of Q were used by Matthew and Luke respectively, i.e., Q^{Matt} and Q^{Luke} (Koester 1980; Davies and Allison 1988–97, 1.115–27). In addition, there was also a revision now called the *Secret Gospel of Mark* (see **Mark, Secret Gospel of*), and one used by the Carpocratians about which nothing specific is known.

Transmission and preservation. Apocryphal gospels have survived, some only fragmentarily, in a variety of different ways. (1) Several apocryphal gospels are known only from brief quotations in early Christian writers (e.g., *Gos. Eb., Gos. Heb., Gos. Eg.,* and *Gos. Barn.*). (2) Others have been discovered preserved on fragments of papyrus and parchment, almost exclusively from Egypt, such as the *Gospel of Peter* (see **Peter, Gospel of*), and **Papyrus Egerton 2.* (3) Yet other apocryphal gospels have been preserved by Christian copyists from early Christianity through the medieval period and have frequently been translated into many languages, such as the *Infancy Gospel of James.* (surviving in more than 30 Greek MSS and also in Syriac, Armenian, Coptic, and Old Slavonic), the *Infancy Gospel of Thomas* (preserved in Greek, Latin, Syrian, Armenian, and Georgian), and the *Acts of Pilate* (preserved in Latin, Syriac, Armenian, Coptic, and Arabic).

Popular vs. Heretical Origins. Traditionally the apocryphal gospels have been regarded as reflecting popular Christian beliefs at the time of their origins, from the 2d to the 5th cent. C.E., though they are often difficult to situate more specifically in space and time. Many apocryphal gospels arose within types of Christianity that were eventually branded heretical by the Great Church, though there was no clear distinction between orthodoxy and heresy in the 1st cent., and during the 2d cent. there were often only hazy distinctions among various regional variants of Christianity. Occasionally earlier forms of Christianity in particular areas were eventually regarded as unacceptable (the thesis of Bauer 1971, opposed by H. E. W. Turner 1954), so that the ancient model of an originally pure, orthodox Christianity from which later, heretical movements developed was often incorrect. Modern categories that supposedly correspond to ancient types of Christianity (e.g. "gnostic," "Jewish-Christian") are sometimes applied without careful nuancing to Christian documents such as the *Gospel of Thomas* (see **Thomas, Gospel of*) and the *Odes of Solomon*, which are labeled and written off as "heretical." Further, there is often a more positive understanding of the role and status of women in many of the apocryphal gospels (compared with the more scholarly Christian literature produced in more orthodox circles), particularly those that arose or were revised within gnostic circles (e.g., *G.Egy.; G.Mary; G.Thom.*; *Dial.Sav.*).

The term "gospel" is often used in the titles of apocryphal gospels, and many reflect some kind of relationship to the canonical Gospels and the tradition preserved in them. The fragmentary *Gospel of Peter*, though lacking a title, is generally thought to be the work referred to in Eusebius, *Hist. eccl.* 6.12.2 under the title εὐαγγελίον κατὰ Πέτρον, an imitation of the titles of the canonical Gospels. In some instances the titles are modern, e.g., the *Protevangelium of James*, the oldest manuscript of which has another title, reflecting two different reader responses to the contents: "The Birth of Mary, The Revelation of James." The literary relationships exhibited among the compositions of ancient Jesus literature are very complex. While there are clear examples of the dependence of apocryphal gospels upon the canonical Gospels (e.g. *G.Ebi.; G.Naz.; In.Jam.*), there are also some which are certainly independent (Q), some which are largely independent (*G.Thom.*), some which are possibly independent (P.Eger. 2, *Dial.Sav., G.Pet.*) or reflect an earlier stage of development than parallel traditions in the canonical Gospels. Vielhauer (1975, 936–39) argues that while P. Eger. 2 reflects familiarity with all four canonical Gospels, that familiarity is the result of the interaction of oral and written traditions. Crossan (1983, 65–87) argues that the question about tribute found in Mark 12:13–17 (and par.) exists in an earlier form in P. Eger. 2, 54–59.

Literary genre. While the four canonical Gospels belong to the same literary genre (see *Gospels, literary genre of), a distinctive Christian subtype of Greco-Roman biography (Aune 1987, 46–67), the label "apocryphal gospels" has been applied to a variety of compositions united only by the fact that they are literary extracanonical vehicles for the transmission of Jesus traditions. Schneemelcher has reiterated the traditional classification of the various types of apocryphal gospels into three categories (*NTA* 1.77–87): (1) writings closely connected with the canonical Gospels, usually dependent upon them; (2) gnostic revelatory Jesus literature, usually in the form of dialogues with, or discourses of, the risen Jesus; and (3) compositions that supplement the canonical Gospels, e.g., those that focus on the miraculous birth of Jesus (e.g., *In.Jam.)*, those which emphasize the childhood of Jesus, the infancy gospels (e.g., *In.Thom.*) and passion gospels (e.g., *Ac.Pil.*).

The various literary forms of ancient Jesus literature, however, are more complex than Schneemelcher's categories suggest. Biographical narratives of the life of Jesus analogous to the canonical Gospels are relatively rare (Tatian's *Diatessaron*; P.Oxy. 840; P.Eger.; *G.Naz.; G.Ebi.; G.Heb.; G.Pet.; Sec.Mk.*; *Apoc.Gos.Jn.*—three other fragments containing Jesus tradition probably belong to this category: P.Oxy. 1224; P.Cairensis 10.735; Fayyum fragment). Other literary forms that serve as vehicles for Jesus traditions include: (1) the letter (*Ep.Apost.; Abgar Legend*); (2) the revelatory dialogue (Freer Logion, an interpolation into the longer ending of Mark at Mark 16:14; *Dial.Sav.*; *Ap.Jam.*; *Th.Cont.*; *G.Mary*; *Soph.Jes.Chr.; G.Barth*); (3) collections of sayings (*G.Thom.*, *G.Phil.*); (4) aretalogies, or collections of miracle stories (*In.Thom.*; they dominate the *Apoc.Gos.Jn.*); (5) the homily (*G.Truth)*; (6) the mythic cosmogony (G.Egy.); and (6) the martyr act (Ac.Pil.). Some gospel-like tractates combine several genres. The *Apocalypse of James* and *the Letter of Peter to Philip* are both revelatory dialogues in an epistolary framework. The *Gospel of Bartholomew* is a revelatory dialogue with similarities to an apocalypse.

Revelatory dialogues and infancy gospels. Acts 1:3 briefly mentions the 40-day period between the resurrection and ascension of Jesus, when Jesus spoke to his disciples of the kingdom of God. This tradition provided an attractive gap for creative imagination to fill. Later Jesus literature expanded this interim period to 550 days (*Ap.John* I, 2.19–20) or even to 11 years (*Pistis Sophia* 1.1). The form of the revelatory dialogue, based on the question-and-answer scheme from ancient school tradition, was frequently used for these fictional postresurrection seminars chaired by Jesus. Such postresurrection revelatory dialogues were favored by gnostic Christians, who seem to have regarded the accounts about the apostles in the canonical Gospels as reflecting a period of ignorance and incompetence before the enlightenment that occurred with the resurrection, e.g., *G.Mary* 7,1–9,24 (Perkins 1980, 37–58; Luttikhuizen 1988), but were also current with other forms of Christianity as well (e.g., *Ep.Apos.* 10–51). The canonical Gospels contain very little information about the childhood of Jesus. Aside from the two quite different accounts of the virginal conception and subsequent birth of Jesus in Bethlehem in Matthew and Luke, only Luke records a brief summary of Jesus' early years in Nazareth (Luke 2:39–40) and the story of a visit of the boy Jesus with his family to the temple in Jerusalem when he was twelve for what Jews would later call a bar mitzvah (Luke 3:41–51). The apocryphal gospels take these holes in the story of Jesus' life as opportunities to develop their own more popular narrative theologies of Jesus as the superior, miraculous child (*In.Thom.* 6:1–7:4; 19:1–5). These elaborations on the themes of the virginal conception and the childhood of Jesus are based on traditions later than those found in the early chapters of Matthew and Luke.

Constituent literary forms. The episodic character of the Synoptic Gospels is largely reflective of the units of oral tradition that were incorporated into more encompassing narrative frameworks, transforming these oral traditions into literary forms. These were taken up and revised by subsequent authors, during which time oral and literary tradition continued to cross-fertilize each other. Since many of the literary forms that characterize the canonical Gospels continued to be used in extracanonical literature, it is important to characterize briefly each major type of literary form. Jesus traditions may be roughly divided into two major categories: (1) sayings traditions, which include aphorisms and parables, and (2) narrative traditions, which include pronouncement stories, miracle stories, and stories about Jesus.

Parables. One of the more distinctive features of the teaching of Jesus as presented in the Synoptic Gospels is the prevalence of **parables* (i.e., very short stories with a double meaning) and *similitudes* (i.e., descriptions of typical situations or recurring events with a double meaning). The parables of Jesus have always been a matter of vital interest for students of the NT, an interest stimulated by the discovery in 1945 of the Coptic *Gospel of Thomas,* which contains fourteen parables of Jesus, three of which were not previously known. Another recently discovered Coptic-Gnostic document, the *Apocryphon of James,* contains three parables of Jesus not previously known: the Date-Palm Shoot (*Ap.Jam.* 7.28–35), the Grain of Wheat (8.10–27), and the Ear of Grain (12.22–31). This is important evidence for the teaching of Jesus, in view of the fact that scholars generally agree that parables were characteristic of the historical Jesus but are rare in extracanonical sources (with the exceptions of *G.Thom.* and *Ap.Jam.*). Several Synoptic parables have parallels in the Apocryphal New Testament: (1) The parable of the Rich Man and Lazarus (Luke 16:19–31) is narrated in *Acts of John* 16. (2) The parable of the Talents (Matt. 25:14–30; Luke 19:12–27) is referred to in *G.Naz.* 18. (3) The parable of the Ten Virgins (Matt. 25:1–12) is summarized in *Ep.Apos.* 43. (4) The parable of the Unjust Steward (Luke 16:1–13) is alluded to in the *Book of John the Evangelist* (James 1924, 188). Jeremias (1963) used the parables in the *Gospel of Thomas* in reconstructing the literary history of the Synoptic parables. Jeremias occasionally judges parables in the *Gospel of Thomas* to reflect stages of tradition earlier than parallel versions in the Synoptic Gospels. Since Jeremias it has become virtually impossible to reconstruct the history of the parable tradition without serious recourse to the *Gospel of Thomas*. Though the relationship between the *Gospel of Thomas* and the Synoptic Gospels is still vigorously debated and can be resolved only through the careful exegesis of each saying (Fallon and Cameron 1988, 4213–24; Neller 1988–90, 1–18; Hedrick 1988–89, 39–56; Aune 2002c), there is strong evidence to suggest that the *Gospel of Thomas* preserves parables that are both independent of and reflect earlier stages of comparable tradition found in the Synoptic parables, since the *Gospel of Thomas* often lacks the redactional features of parables found in the Synoptic Gospels. For example, every saying from Mark 3:35–4:34 is represented in the *Gospel of*

Thomas with the exception of 4:13–20, the secondary allegorical interpretation of the parable of the Sower. In addition, Bauckham (1987) has argued that *Ac.Thom.* 146 alludes to a parable of Jesus about a vine (otherwise not extant), and that it has a good claim to authenticity because of similarity to the parables of the Mustard Seed (Mark 4:30–32; *G.Thom.* 20) and the Seed Growing of Itself (Mark 4:26–29).

Pronouncement stories. Pronouncement stories, often designated apophthegms or chreiai, are short narrative units, often with dialogical features, that culminate in a pithy or memorable saying of Jesus. There are as many as three dozen pronouncement stories in the Synoptic Gospels, and more than 40 in the apocryphal gospels and in quotations in the church fathers. Some 22 pronouncement stories are transmitted in the *Gospel of Thomas* alone, of which only six have Synoptic parallels (*G.Thom.* 72, 79, 99, 100, 104, 113). At least three pronouncement stories are found in the *Gospel of Philip* (34, 54, 55), and (based on the fragmentary evidence which survives) the Jewish Christian apocryphal gospels apparently also contained many pronouncement stories (*G.Naz.* 2, 16; *G.Ebi.* 5; *G.Heb.* 7; *G.Egy.* 1, 5; cf. *2 Clem* 12:2; P.Oxy. 840).

Miracle stories. While miracles performed by the apostles permeate the apocryphal acts (Achtemeier 1976), the surviving apocryphal gospels contain very few miracle stories attributed to the adult Jesus: (1) P.Eger. 2, 2 contains a story of Jesus healing a leper. (2) In P.Eger. 2, 4, Jesus causes a tree to grow instantly on the banks of the Jordan. (3) In *G.Naz.* 10 a mason (named Malchus, according to *G.Naz.* 29) pleads with Jesus to heal his withered hand (the conclusion of the miracle is not preserved). (4) In an apparent summary passage in *G.Naz.* 27, Jesus purportedly performed 53 miracles in Chorazin and Bethsaida. (5) In *G.Phil.* 63.25–30, Jesus reportedly went to the dye works of Levi and threw 72 colors into the vat; they all turned white (interestingly enough, the primary colors of light [red, green, and blue], become white when combined, while the three primary colors of pigment, red, yellow, and blue] become black when combined). (6) The resurrection of a rich young man, clearly a variant of the story of the raising of Lazarus in John 11, is narrated in *Sec.Mk.* (7) According to *G.Heb.* 3, the Holy Spirit carried Jesus off by the hairs of his head to Mount Tabor. (8) In *G.Naz.* 25, rays came forth from Jesus' eyes and frightened his adversaries. In the Greek version of *In.Thom.* (which is virtually an *aretalogy or collection of miracle stories), on the other hand, 16 miracles are attributed to the boy Jesus, who is depicted as a vain and spiteful youth often in conflict with adults. The story of the three-year-old Jesus making a dried fish become alive in a basin of water (*In.Thom.* 1) exists in a variant version in which the miracle is attributed to Peter (*Ac.Pet.* 13). Similarly in the *Gospel of Ps.-Matthew* (an 8th-cent. combination of *In.Jam.* and *In.Thom.* with some independent material in chapters 18–24), several miracles are attributed to the child Jesus in addition to those taken over from *In.Thom.*, e.g., the miracle of the date palm (20–21), the shortened journey (22), the falling down of the idols of Hermopolis, and the mass conversion of its citizens (23–24). According to the *Arabic Infancy Gospel*, the child Jesus transformed uncooperative playmates into three-year-old goats, and when they followed him on command some women who were watching affirmed his status as the good shepherd of Israel.

Often the label "gospel" appears to have been added by early copyists and revisers who understood the term more as a way of identifying the content than the form of the composition. Several of the Nag Hammadi Coptic treatises, for example, use the term "gospel" (*peuaggelion*) in their titles, including the *Gospel of Thomas* (II,2) (see **Thomas, Gospel of*), the *Gospel of Philip* (II,3), the *Gospel of Truth* (I,2; XII,2), and the *Gospel of the Egyptians* (III,2; IV,2). The *Gospel of Mary* (preserved in Papyrus Berolinensis 8502,1), also has its title in a subscription (19.3–5). The Coptic titles of the *Gospel of Thomas* (ΠΕΥΑΓΓΕΛΙΟΝ ΠΚΑΤΑ ΘΩΜΑΣ), the **Gospel of Philip* (ΠΕΥΑΓΓΕΛΙΟΝ ΠΚΑΤΑ ΦΙΛΙΠΠΟΣ), and the **Gospel of Mary* (ΠΕΥΑΓΓΕΛΙΟΝ ΠΚΑΤΑ ΜΑΡΙΖΑΜΜ), are obviously transliterations from a Greek original, the titles of which was clearly modeled after the later titles of the canonical Gospels. In the case of the *Gospel of Truth*, however, in the Coptic phrase ΠΕΥΑΓΓΕΛΙΟΝ ΝΤΜΗΕ from the incipit, the term ΝΤΜΗΕ ("of truth") is an epexegetical genitive, so that entire phrase "gospel of truth" means "the gospel, that is, the truth" (Grobel 1960, 33). The modern title "Gospel of Truth" is taken from the opening line or incipit of the Coptic text; the composition has no formal title. Yet since such incipits were often intended as titles, this work may be the one referred to under the name *Veritatis Evangelium* by Irenaeus (*Adv. haer.* 3.11.9). The term "gospel" in the *Gospel of Truth* refers to the content, rather than the form of the document, as is the case with the canonical Gospels. Much of the extant Jesus literature, however, is not designated as "gospel." Three gospel-like Nag Hammadi texts that are not explicitly called gospels are the *Apocryphon of James* (1,2; 11,1; 111,1; BG, 2), the *Book of Thomas the Contender* (11,7), and the *Dialogue of the Savior* (111,5). It is clear that early Christians did not understand the term "gospel" as a term for a literary genre as it is understood today. They do not appear to have distinguished generically between compositions that from our perspective look very different indeed.

*Gospel, genre of *Peter, Gospel of, *Secret Gospel of Mark *Thomas, Gospel of

---

Aune 2002c; Bauckham 1987; Bauer 1971; R.E. Brown 1987; Crossan 1985, 1988; Fallon and Cameron 1988; Hedrick, 1988–89; Koester 1982; Neller 1989–90; Resch 1906; Vielhauer 1975; Wright 1985

Gospels, literary genre of "Gospel" is an Old English word used to translate the Greek word εὐαγγέλιον, though "good news" is a more accurate translation. Though the first occurrences of the term εὐαγγέλιον in the NT refer to the oral proclamation of the Christian message of salvation, by the mid-2d cent. it was used of a certain type of literature, i.e., narratives of the life of Jesus emphasizing his sayings and deeds, such as Matthew, Mark, Luke, and John. Since the canonical Gospels share so many literary similarities, they have been thought to be *sui generis*, i.e., without comparable literary parallel in the ancient world. Some NT scholars even want to regard Mark as belonging to a genre different from that of Matthew or John (Vines 2002, 24–25), a proposal that ignores the many common literary features shared by those works. For those who regard the Gospels as *sui generis*, the attempts to define and describe the genre to which they belong is necessarily a non-issue. In recent years, however, there has been a willingness, particularly on the part of Anglo-American scholars, to regard the Gospels as a type of ancient βίος ("life") literature (Bryan 1993, 9–64). The view that the Gospels must have generic affinities with ancient literature is grounded in four converging sets of presuppositions: (1) Since literary criticism now understands genre both as a social convention and a communication code, the notion of a unique genre is problematic. (2) Literature should be defined, not in terms of supposed "intrinsic qualities" (see *Literature) but primarily as a social phenomenon. i.e., a text is "literary" when a given society uses it in such a way that the immediate context of its origin is ignored or regarded as irrelevant (Ellis 1974, 44). (3) The literary and linguistic implications of the pyramidal structure of ancient society have rendered the older dyadic social and literary model obsolete. The pyramid model suggests that the vertical bonds between people of different orders or classes took precedence over horizontal bonds and that the direction of cultural influences was from the top down, not from the bottom up. The literary culture of the highest strata of ancient society, according to this view, percolated down, usually in weakened, attenuated, and even eclectic forms to the lowest social and cultural levels of ancient society. The older categories of *Hochliteratur* and *Kleinliteratur* are therefore ideal types at opposite ends of a complex spectrum of linguistic and literary styles and levels. The Gospels are "unique" in the sense that no other ancient composition, Greco-Roman or Jewish, is precisely like them. Yet there are a great many other ancient "biographical" compositions, each of which is unique in the sense that it has no exact literary analogue. These include the anonymous life of Secundus the Silent Philosopher, Lucian's *Demonax,* Tacitus's *Agricola,* and Philostratus's *Life of Apollonius.* Categorizing ancient texts as "unique" tells us nothing significant about them. The Hellenistic period was a time when there was a great deal of experimentation in literature, with the emergence of "new" genres through the transformation and recombination of earlier forms and genres in novel ways. But does this mean that each of the literary works listed above is "unique"? Not really. In one sense, of course, they are unique (as every historical phenomenon is), but in another they are simply distinctive literary responses to new contexts, needs, and expectations. There are many significant similarities between the canonical Gospels and various types of Hellenistic biographical literature. There are also many significant differences. Despite the fact that Hellenistic biography encompasses such a large and diverse body of texts, the similarities nevertheless indicate generic affiliation with the Gospels. In my view, the most convincing solution is to regard the Gospels as a recognizable subtype of Hellenistic biography, distinctive because of their content (the unique character of the life of Jesus, largely articulated in Jewish and Christian categories), while in form and function they are primarily Hellenistic. The Gospels, no less than the other forms of early Christian literature, reflect the complexities of the syncretistic world within which they arose.

εὐαγγέλιον in Paul. Paul, the first extant Christian author, used εὐαγγέλιον as a terse abbreviation for "the good news [of the saving significance of the death and resurrection of Jesus]" (Rom. 1:9; 1 Cor. 9:23; 2 Cor. 2:12; Gal. 1:11), i.e., as a term for the oral proclamation of the distinctive Christian message of salvation. Paul also used the fuller expressions "gospel of God," referring to God as the source or authority for his message (Rom. 1:1; 15:16; 2 Cor. 11:7; 1 Thess. 2:2), and "gospel of Christ," referring to Christ as the content of his message (Rom. 15:19; 1 Cor. 9:12; 2 Cor. 9:13; Gal. 1:7); see Dunn 1998, 163–69.

εὐαγγέλιον in the Gospels. The term "gospel" (εὐαγγέλιον) occurs in the first sentence of Mark (1:1): "The beginning of the gospel of Jesus Christ, the Son of God." Though this sentence is frequently understood as the title of the entire work (Gnilka 1978–79, 1.42; Pesch 1977, 1.74–75), since it is not grammatically separated from what follows (the καθώς of 1:2 links vv. 2–3 with v. 1, not v. 4; Arnold 1977), it describes only the contents of the opening section, probably 1:2–15 (Arnold 1977; Guelich 1989, 3–5), perhaps 1:4–8 (Gundry 1993, 30–31). However, even though the "*beginning* of the gospel" refers to the first short section of Mark, the term "beginning of the *gospel*" suggests that the whole of Mark may be characterized by this term, even though its "beginning" is limited to 1:4–8 or 1:2–15. The term εὐαγγέλιον (used in transliterated form to mean "gospel" in most European languages), occurs seven times in Mark (1:1, 14, 15; 8:35; 10:29; 13:10; 14:9) and in every instance means "the message proclaimed about Jesus Christ." Further, Matthew uses εὐαγγέλιον four times (4:23; 9:35; 24:14; 26:13), while Luke omits it altogether (there are two occurrences in Acts, 15:7 and 20:24).

Second-century evidence. The wording of the titles of all four canonical Gospels is similar (e.g., "The Gospel according to Mark"), with the preposition κατά ("according to") taking the place of the regular and expected genitive of authorship (e.g., "The Gospel *of* Mark"). The oldest known form of this title was simply Κατὰ Μάρκον, "According to Mark," which should be understood as a way of indicating authorship. While Hengel (1985b, 65–67) argues for the originality of the longer form, he does not provide a convincing explanation for the supposed secondary origin of the shorter form (Trobisch 1996, 60). The similarity in form of the titles of all four Gospels suggests that they were originally anonymous compositions that had to be distinguished from each other by the addition of secondary titles after they had been collected to form a fourfold group, not later than ca. 125 C.E. (Hengel 1985b, 70). The term εὐαγγέλιον probably became part of the titles of the four Gospels through the influence of Mark 1:1. The problem of when the term εὐαγγέλιον is first used of a literary form or a book is problematic, though it appears that such a meaning occurs in Marcion and then in Justin Martyr (Koester 1989b; 1990, 1–40; Gundry 1996). The title of the revised version of Luke advocated by Marcion of Sinope (ca. 140 C.E.), attributed to no specific author (Tertullian, *Adv. Marc.* 4.2.3), was simply titled εὐαγγέλιον (Harnack 183*–84*). Justin Martyr (mid-2d cent. C.E.) refers to the Gospels as εὐαγγέλια, i.e., as "gospels" in the plural (*1 Apol.* 66.3; cf. *2 Clem.* 8:5), thus using the term of written documents. *2 Clem* 8:5 introduces a quotation of the words of Jesus with the statement "for the Lord says in the gospel [ἐν τῇ εὐαγγελίᾳ], 'If you did not guard something small, who will give you something great? For I say to you, whoever is faithful with very little is faithful with much,'" which probably refers to an oral tradition (Donfried 1974, 72–73; Gundry 1996, 324).

The genre of the Gospels in modern scholarship. As long as the Gospels were comfortably classified as *Kleinliteratur*, i.e., as the logical written expression of an oral kerygma, they could be regarded as constituting a new or unique genre. Yet once the Gospels are regarded as "literature," the problem of genre must be raised, for the notion that four documents can constitute all members of a genre is exceedingly problematic. Are the Gospels, or rather is Mark (or John) a unique form of literature, a "new genre"? It is occasionally claimed that a unique genre would be utterly incomprehensible, and so an antecedent impossibility (Wellek and Warren 1954, 245). During much of the 20th cent. it was widely held that Mark and the other canonical Gospels were *sui generis*, i.e., a unique literary type (Bultmann 1963, 371; Nineham 1977, 35–37; Guelich 1983). There are three variants of the unique-genre hypothesis, which maintain that the Gospel of Mark is (1) an expanded version of the oral kerygma ("proclamation") of early Christianity, reflected in Acts 2:14–39;

3:13–26; 10:36–43; 1 Cor. 15:1–7 (Gundry 1974; Guelich 1983); (2) an intentionally structured replacement for the Torah in early Christian liturgy (Carrington 1952; Goulder 1974, 1978; Guilding 1960 [for the Fourth Gospel]; this view is criticized by Morris 1964, 1983, and W. D. Davies 1962, 67–95); or (3) an unliterary form of "folk literature" that emerged naturally from the Christian community (Schmidt 1923).

More specific generic identifications have included Hellenistic romance or popular fiction (Tolbert 1989, 59–70; Beavis 1989, 35–37; Dowd 1991; Wills 1997); OT biographical narratives (Baltzer 1975; R. Brown 1971; Kline 1975); the Jewish novel (Vines 2002); Greek tragedy (Bilezekian 1977); and "an apocalyptic historical monograph" (Yarbro Collins 1992, 26–27). Recently the earlier view that Mark should be considered a form of Hellenistic biography or βίος (Votaw 1970, a reprint of 1915) has been argued more forcefully by a number of scholars (Talbert 1977; Aune 1987; Burridge 1992; Bryan 1993). The eclectic character of Mark is emphasized by some, arguing that the author drew from a pool of genres and narrative devices (Young 1999, 29). For Pedersen (1994) the attempt to label the genre of Mark is a hopeless enterprise, since it had different generic antecedents and was itself a parody of earlier forms.

*Biography, *Genre criticism, *Literature

———

Arnold 1977; Bryan 1993, 9–64; Burridge 1992; Guelich 1989; Gundry 1996; Hengel 1985b; Koester 1989, 1990; Shuler 1982; Votaw 1970; Wills 1997

Graffiti (singular graffito) the plural diminutive of the Italian *graffio* a "scratch" (from *graffiare* "to scratch," from the Latin *graphium*, "stylus," transliterated from the Greek γραφεῖον, "graving tool," from γράφειν, "to write"). Graffiti are the writing, scratching, and drawing of letters, words, and images on walls, vessels, potsherds, lamps, loom-weights, stones, statues, and various other expedient media. Both ancient and modern graffiti have been classified as public (created on exterior surfaces for mass viewing), private (created on surfaces or objects for individualized viewing, e.g., latrinalia), and personal (tattoos or scarification, e.g., Lev. 19:28) (Melhorn and Romig, 1985, 31–32). There is a widespread misconception that most graffiti are sexual or obscene in content (Deiulio 1978). Although some ancient graffiti expressed amorousness, revulsion, or obscenities, many ancient graffiti and ostraka (incised potsherds) served commercial, artistic, religious, or utilitarian functions. These graffiti and ostraka oftentimes served as the ancient equivalents of modern notes on scratch paper, requesting or promoting goods and services in locations such as the Athenian agora (Lang 1988) and Pompei (Canali and Cavallo 1991; *CIL* IV). Ancient graffiti assist in better understanding the history of literacy by providing evidence regarding the values and shapes of letters, writing direction, forms of abbreviation, and orthography (Lang 1988, 3). The frequently incorrect orthography of Greek graffiti also assists in reconstructing the phonetics of ancient Greek (for inscriptions, see Caragounis 1995) and are significant as one of the only forms of writing representative of lower-status people in the Greco-Roman world. Several graffiti have been especially useful for NT scholarship. A Greek graffito recovered on a wall located in Rome depicts a man showing reverence to a crucified figure with the head of a donkey and a caption reading "Alexamenos worships his god," thus expressing popular ridicule of Christian belief in a crucified Jewish hero (Smith 1978, 81–82; cf. 1 Cor. 1:18–31). In a graffito recovered from Pompei, a lovestruck young man has used gematria for a woman's name, "I love her whose number is 545 [φμε′]," an interesting analogue to the number of the beast, 666, in Rev. 13:18 (Deissmann 1908, 276).

———

Canali and Cavallo 1991; Caragounis 1995; Deissmann 1908; Deiulio 1978; M. L. Lang 1974, 1975, 1990; Melhorn and Romig 1985; Reisner 1971; M. Smith 1978

JOHN FOTOPOULOS

Grammatical person is the use of first-person singular and plural and third-person singular pronouns and verb forms to indicate some kind of authorial involvement in a narrative or in an expositional passage that is part of a narrative.

*First-person plural, *Third-person plural, *"We"-passages

Greek, a generic term for several related dialects that developed from a reconstructed Proto-Greek language, part of the Indo-European family of languages. The Greeks called themselves "Hellenes," recognizing mutual ties of history, language, and culture, and designated others as βαρβάροι ("non-Greeks"). The Romans called the Hellenes

Graeci (from the Greek term *Graikoi*, of uncertain etymology) and their language *Graecum* (Apollodorus 1.7.3; Aristotle, *Meteor.* 1.352a). During the late Republic and early Empire many Romans spoke disparagingly of Greeks as *Graeculi* (Cicero, *De orat.* 1.47; Pliny, *Ep.* 10.40.2); some Romans even referred disparagingly to the Philhellene emperor Hadrian as a *graeculus* or "Little Greek" (*Scriptores historiae Augustae, Hadrian* 1.5).

The language of the earliest extant Greek literature, the *Iliad* and *Odyssey*, is an artificial amalgam of words, constructions, and dialect forms from the Late Bronze Age (ca. 1600–1000 B.C.E.), based on a spoken form of Ionic. By the 5th cent. B.C.E., two major groups of Greek dialects appeared: *West Greek*, including "strict" Doric dialects (Laconian, Messenian, Cretan, Cyrenaean), "middle" Doric dialects (West Argolic, East Aegean Doric), and "mild" Doric dialects (Megarian, Corinthian, East Argolic, Northwest dialects), and *East Greek*, including Attic-Ionic (Attica, Euboea, the Cycladic islands, and the coast of Asia Minor), Aeolic (island of Lesbos, Thessalia, Boeotia), and Arcado-Cypriote or Achaean (spoken in central Peloponnesus and Cyprus). The Greeks themselves distinguished four dialects: Attic, Ionic, Doric, Aeolic (Strabo 8.1.2; 14.5.26).

The common Greek of the Hellenistic period (325–150 B.C.E.) and the Roman period (150 B.C.E.–300 C.E.) is called Koine, following the ancient designation ἡ κοινὴ διάλεκτος, "the common (dialect)." This common dialect was based on 4th-cent. B.C.E. Attic Greek and was in use until the mid-6th cent. C.E., when it developed into Byzantine Greek. The independence and isolation of the Greek city-states had encouraged the preservation of local dialects, but the formation of political leagues tended to foster linguistic homogenization. The key political and military role played by Athens in defeating the Persians in the early 5th cent. (490–479 B.C.E.) led to her formation and domination of the First Maritime League. Subsequently, because of Athenian dominance Attic replaced Ionic as the most prestigious Greek dialect; mercenaries in the Athenian army and fleet had to learn Attic, the language of command. After unifying Macedonia, Philip II of Macedon (382–336 B.C.E.) defeated the Athenians and the Thebans at the battle of Chaeronea, thereby forming an extensive Greco-Macedonian empire. Philip adopted Greek culture to provide cohesion to his empire, and made Attic Greek, the dialect of Athens, the official language of his court and his diplomatic correspondence, transforming what was primarily a local dialect in the 5th cent. into Imperial Attic, a new common dialect. This policy was continued by Alexander III (356–323), who succeeded Philip in 336 and immediately planned and expedited the invasion and conquest of the Persian Empire, whose official lingua franca was Aramaic. As he marched through Asia Minor, Syria-Palestine, and Egypt, and then proceeded east by means of the Fertile Crescent through Mesopotamia to India, Alexander established numerous city-states and military garrisons that were populated with Greek-speaking Macedonian soldiers, veterans, and thousands of Greek settlers, including artisans and merchants, from Macedonia and all other parts of the Greek world. They brought with them their native dialects, but Koine was the language of the army and the common speech of settlers, so these dialects disappeared by the third generation. Koine became the language of government, diplomacy, commerce, and education, the spoken and written language of the ruling elite and upper-class natives, because Greek language and culture was tacitly considered superior to other languages and cultures. In much of the Near East, literacy meant literacy in Greek, while the native languages were spoken by those who did not read or write. Aramaic was never completely displaced, however, as the bilingual Greek-Aramaic inscriptions from Kandahar and Mchet'a indicate (Altheim-Stiehl, 1960, 21–32, 243–61). Greeks who settled throughout the Near East, however, tended to be monolingual because of the high status of their language and culture. This was especially true of the upper class of the administrations and the royal families (Plutarch, *Antony* 27.3–4). Indigenous languages were correspondingly regarded as culturally inferior by both Greek immigrants and upper-class natives (λάοι). After the death of Alexander in 323 B.C.E., his successors διάδοχοι consolidated power in three great Hellenistic monarchies, Antigonid Macedonia, Seleucid Syria, and Ptolemaic Egypt, in addition to many petty kingdoms. Koine was the official language of all these Hellenistic kingdoms. During the 3d cent. B.C.E., the Seleucids controlled Syria, Mesopotamia, and much of Asia Minor, while Ptolemaic Egypt had a vast overseas empire including Cyprus, Cyrene, Cyrenaica, Coele-Syria, Syria, Phoenicia, Palestine, Lycia, Caria, Miletus, Ephesus, Samos, parts of Thrace and Samothrace, and a league of Aegean islands.

Written Koine was a uniform language that had no local dialects but rather exhibited only stylistic, lexical, and phonological variation. Hellenistic Koine became the standard language of Greece and was realized in many regional phonological substandards, i.e., Attic-Ionic Koine, Aegean Doric Koine, Achaean Doric Koine, Northwest Doric Koine, South-East Aegean Koine, Egyptian Koine, Syro-Palestinian Koine, Asia Minor Koine (Bubeník, 1989, 175–255). The uniform character of the written language appears to have contributed to the standardization of the spoken language. The transformation from Attic to Koine was characterized by a variety of linguistic developments that occurred throughout the Hellenistic and Roman periods: (1) The Attic preference for the double consonant *-tt-* (as in θάλλαττα, "sea") was bypassed by the Koine preference for -σσ- (as in θάλλασσα, "sea"); *-ss-* was actually an earlier preference of the Athenian tragedians and Thucydides. (2) In Koine there was an increasing tendency to ignore the Attic distinction between long and short vowels. Other trends were (3) the disappearance of the athematic aorist, (4) the obsolescence of the optative (5) the phasing out of the dative, and (6) the increased use of prepositions to indicate case relations. (7) During the period of the Roman Empire, one of the most frequent phonetic features of Koine Greek is iotacism, i.e., the Greek vowels or diphthongs ι, ει, η, οι, and υ were pronounced so similarly that they were frequently interchanged in orthography. (8) The sounds of ο and ω, ϵ and αι, ει and ι, ου and υ were confused orthographically.

Throughout the Hellenistic cities of Egypt and Syria-Palestine, the middle- and upper-class Greeks lived in relative isolation from the natives, so that the influence of indigenous languages (e.g., Demotic, Aramaic, Phoenician, Hebrew, and Arabic) was not strong. Greek continued to be spoken in the Hellenistic cities in the former Persian empire, such as Seleuceia on the Tigris and Susa.

In the 16 Roman provinces of the Greek East, the use of Greek, the language of local Roman administration, was dominant. Many Greeks, disregarding the existence of the Roman Empire, continued to divide humanity into two categories, Greeks and barbarians (Strabo 6.1.2; Dio Chrysostom, *Orations* 1.14; Josephus, *Antiquities* 18.20; Philo, *Legatio* 8, 83, 145, 292); Apollonius of Tyana is made to divide the Roman world up into Greek-speaking and Latin-speaking provinces (Philostratus, *Vita Apollonii* 5.36); Aelius Aristides wanted to modernize the Greek/barbarian division into a Roman/non-Roman one (*Orations* 26.63), and others wanted to expand the categories to Greeks, Romans, and barbarians (Cicero, *De finibus* 2.49; Plutarch, *On the Fortune of the Romans* 324B). In the Greek-speaking provinces, even official Roman decrees, letters and edicts, and honorary inscriptions to Roman magistrates, emperors, and members of the imperial family were routinely promulgated in Greek. However, most inscriptions on public works are in Latin, while about 30 percent are bilingual. Milestones are often bilingual, but almost always Latin in Syria and Arabia and many are exclusively in Greek in Asia Minor and Thrace. Two languages were used in the administration of eastern Roman provinces, Latin and Greek. Latin was the language of administration used for communication between the central government and Roman magistrates, between Roman magistrates and Roman colonies (as well as within Roman colonies), and in some respects as it involved Roman citizens. The language of the native population was nearly always Greek.

The preservation of nonliterary Greek papyri in Egypt from the 3d cent. B.C.E. through the 3d cent. C.E. provides an important avenue into the written Koine of this period, though the absence of comparable documentary material from other Mediterranean lands makes it impossible to detect the presence of distinctive dialects. Papyrus letters in Greek begin to appear in the 3d cent. B.C.E. Evidence for "Egyptian Koine" is found in documents produced by bilingual Egyptians (i.e., primarily those in the inferior local administration who held the office of κώμαρχος, "village chief," and κωμογραμματεύς, "village scribe") that exhibit linguistic interference. An example is the Demotic-Greek contracts from Soknopaiou Nesos in the northern Fayum (P. Ryl. 160–160D), which exhibit the interchange of voiced stops (b, d, g) with voiceless stops (p, t, k), and the interchange of the liquids (l, r). Some letters written by Greeks also exhibit a high degree of interference. Such orthographic confusion, however, reflects differences in phonology or accent rather than a difference in dialect. Josephus, for example, admitted that his native language (Aramaic) interfered with his pronunciation of Greek (*Ant.* 20.263–65); similar observations were made of native Cappadocians (Philostratus, *Vitae sophistarum* 2.13 [594]; *Vita Apollonii* 1.7). The evidence from inscriptions indicates little dialectal difference between the Koine of Egypt, Asia

Minor, Italy, and Syria-Palestine. Native Egyptians continued to speak Egyptian until the 3d cent. C.E. In the 2d cent. C.E., the Egyptian language, at this stage known as Coptic, began to be written using Greek characters and was heavily dependent on other aspects of Greek. As much as 20 percent of the Coptic lexicon, for example, consists of Greek loanwords, and some Greek verbs were adapted to Coptic morphology (e.g., the Greek verb πιστεύειν, "to believe," occurs in Bohairic as *af-er-pisteuin*, in Fayumic as *af-el-pisteuin*, and in Sahidic as *af-pisteue*). Upper-class administrators and aristocrats as well as the lower social classes (especially in Upper Egypt) were monolingual.

After the death of Alexander in 323 B.C.E., Coele-Syria, Syria, Phoenicia, and Palestine were controlled by Ptolemaic Egypt until conquered by the Seleucids in 201. From the 3d cent. on, most of the inscriptions found in Syria-Palestine are in Greek. Among the earliest Greek documents from Palestine are two of a cache of six ostraca, four in Aramaic, one in Greek, and one an Aramaic-Greek bilingual, found at Khirbet el-Qôm (12 km. west of Hebron), dated the 12th of Tammuz, year 6, probably the sixth year of Ptolemy II Philadelphus, i.e., 277 B.C.E. From 259 to 257 B.C.E. the Zenon papyri reflect the relationship between the Jew Tobias and Egyptian authorities. The next oldest dated inscription is from Jaffa in honor of Ptolemy IV and is dated to 217 B.C.E. Though there were enclaves of Hellenistic culture in the Hellenistic cities in Galilee such as Sepphoris, Beth Shean (Scythopolis), and the more northerly cities of the Decapolis, including Hippos, Abila, Gadara, and Pella, no clear picture has yet emerged regarding the complex relationship between Jewish and Hellenistic cultural worlds in Upper and Lower Galilee during the 1st cent. C.E. Existing evidence suggests that there was in fact a tension between Hellenistic cities such as Tyre and the Galilean hinterland upon which the city was dependent for its food supply.

The Phoenician coastal cities of Aradus, Byblos, Berytus, Sidon, Tyre, and Akko were profoundly affected by Hellenistic culture and became Greek cities. Many Greek settlers had arrived during the 3d cent. B.C.E. The traditional bilingualism of these cities was replaced with monolingualism in Hellenistic Koine, though inscriptions in Phoenician occur as late as the 1st cent. C.E. A treaty between Rome and the Maccabees is recorded in 1 Macc. 8:17–32. Palmyra in the Greco-Roman period was multilingual. The educated class was bilingual (Palmyrene Aramaic and Hellenistic Koine).

The use of Greek in Palestine during the Roman period has been intensely investigated because of the problem of the language(s) of Jesus and the more general problem of the degree to which Palestinian Judaism was Hellenized. It now seems clear that Hebrew was a spoken language in Palestine until the Mishnaic period, though it is not clear how widely it was spoken. However, rather than refer to Palestine as bilingual or trilingual, it is more useful to use the sociolinguistic terms diglossic and triglossic, i.e., using two or three languages for different kinds of social communication in a variety of social contexts. From this perspective, it is probable that Hebrew and Greek were *both* regarded as prestige languages *in different social contexts*. During the 2d and 1st cent. B.C.E., Hebrew was used at least as a literary language, for such compositions as Daniel, Ben Sira, and much of the Qumran literature. Hellenistic and Roman Palestine was a bilingual speech community; Hellenistic Koine was used by all social classes, not just the educated elite. Oddly, public and private Hellenistic Koine inscriptions do not display any Semitisms. Among the Dead Sea Scrolls are a number of Greek manuscripts dating from the mid-2d cent. B.C.E. to as late as the mid-1st cent. C.E., including fragments of four Septuagint scrolls from Cave 4 (4QLXXLev^a, pap4QLXX Lev^b, 4QLXXNum, 4QLXXDeut) and two other fragmentary Greek scrolls closely related to the Bible. A scroll of the Minor Prophets in Greek was found at Nahal Hever (perhaps late 1st cent. B.C.E.).

Two of the 15 Bar Kochba letters (written 132–35 C.E.) from Nahal Hever are written in Greek, while the other 13, together with nine Bar Kochba letters from Wadi Murabba'at, are in Hebrew and Aramaic. In addition, there is the Babatha archive from Nahal Hever, consisting of 36 or 37 documents written from ca. 93–132 C.E. in Nabatean, Aramaic, and Greek. The 221 Greek inscriptions from the 3d and 4th cent. C.E., discovered in the necropolis of Besara or Beth She'arim in Galilee, far outnumber those in Hebrew and Aramaic and reveal the extent to which the Greek language had penetrated Palestinian Jewish culture. Yet in the case of epitaphs there are sociolinguistic differences determined by whether the in-group language of the deceased is used (frequently in catacombs) or the out-group language of the observers (when the tomb is in public view). More than

60 percent of all Jewish funerary inscriptions in Palestine are written in Greek, and even in Jerusalem the percentage of epitaphs in Greek is approximately 40 percent. The fact that there are ca. 1500 Greek loanwords in Talmudic literature underlines the widespread use of Greek in the first centuries C.E.

*Greek literature

Altheim and Stiehl 1960; Buberink 1989

Greek literature consists of an extensive body of texts, beginning with the *Iliad* and *Odyssey* of Homer through to late antiquity (survey in Easterling and Knox (eds.) 1985). The language of the earliest extant Greek literature, the *Iliad* and *Odyssey*, is an artificial amalgam of words (including archaisms and neologisms), constructions, and dialect forms from the Late Bronze Age (i.e., the Late Minoan and Late Helladic periods, ca. 1600 B.C.E. to ca. 700 B.C.E.), based on a spoken form of Ionic. The language of Homer was formed and transmitted, at least initially, in a nonliterate oral environment. The invention of writing made it possible to freeze the ordinarily varied oral performances of the Homeric poems into what became their final, authoritative form in the late 7th cent. B.C.E. The dissemination of epic poetry throughout the Greek world resulted in the literary imitation of Homeric language by Hesiod of Boeotia for his didactic, moralizing poems, including the *Theogony* and *Works and Days*. Elegaic, iambic, and solo lyric poetry was developed in the 7th cent. by Ionian poets writing in Ionic in a modified form of epic hexameter and spread from there to the mainland. Important elegaic poets include Callinus of Smyrna, Tyrtaeus of Sparta, Mimnermus of Colophon, Solon of Athena, and Theognis of Megara, the only elegaic poet whose work has survived. Elegaic epitaphs became popular in the 6th cent. and continued to be written until the 4th cent. C.E. Archilocus of Paros was a 7th-cent. iambic poet and Sappho of Lesbos a lyric poet who wrote in Aeolic. Choral lyric poetry, written in the Doric dialect, arose in the Peloponnesus, Sicily, and Boeotia, the home of its most famous exponent, Pindar. Athenian tragedy of the 5th cent., written in Attic Greek and developed during the zenith of the Athenian empire, was an extremely popular form of entertainment. The important tragedians, some of whose works have survived, include Aeschylus, Sophocles, and Euripides. Old Comedy, emphasizing satire and phantasy, is represented primarily by Aristophanes, who wrote in an educated form of Attic. Middle Comedy, represented by Menander, served as a transition to the development of the realism of New Comedy.

Greek prose literature began to appear during the 5th cent. in Ionia with the work of the Ionian philosophers (Heracleitus, Democritus, Hippocrates), while the greatest philosophical and scientific writers lived in Athens, Plato and Aristotle. Herodotus was the first significant historian (ca. 485–425 B.C.E.). He wrote in the Ionic dialect for a largely Athenian audience, narrating the Persian Wars with the Greeks. He has been called the father of ancient historiography. Thucydides, the author of an incomplete account of the Peloponnesian War, was the first native Athenian historian. *Historiography became one of most important literary genres in the following centuries and spawned many subgenres, including local history, geography, and antiquarian history. Some of the more important later historians include Xenophon (4th cent. C.E.) and Polybius (2d cent. C.E.), both of whom provide evidence of different stages in the development of Koine; Diodorus Siculus (late 1st cent. B.C.E. to early 1st cent. C.E.); his contemporary Dionysius of Halicarnassus; and his imitator Flavius Josephus (late 1st to early 2d cent. C.E.).

By the end of the Republic (mid-1st cent. B.C.E.), Greeks dominated Roman education (grammar, rhetoric, philosophy); Greek literature, mythology, and history were basic to Roman education; and Greek was the first language of Roman education. By the 1st cent. B.C.E., young male Roman aristocrats were regularly educated in Greece. Educated Romans were privately bilingual but thought it inappropriate to boast of their knowledge of Greek language and literature publicly. By the 1st cent. C.E., perhaps only 10 percent of the residents of Rome were of Roman or Italian ancestry. Within Rome itself various national groups often maintained linguistic and cultural ghettos. The large Jewish community, for example, which numbered from 30,000 to 50,000, was a Greek-speaking community. Of the 534 Jewish catacomb inscriptions, 76 percent are in Greek, 23 percent are in Latin, with 1 percent in Aramaic.

*Greek

Easterling and Knox (eds.) 1985; Lesky 1966; Mussies 1976; Sevenster 1968; Spolsky 1983

Hapax legomenon, plural hapax legomena, a transliteration of the Greek phrase ἅπαξ λεγόμενον (the latter a present passive participle from λέγω [plural λεγόμενα] meaning "once said"), usually refers to words found only once in a particular text but it may also refer to words peculiar to a text no matter how many times they occur in that text (vocabulary). The phrase was first used by the Alexandrian Homeric scholars to designate words used only once in the Homeric epics (Martinazolli 1957). The first known attempt to label Homeric words as hapax legomena was by Zenodotus of Ephesus (ca. 325–234 B.C.E.), and after him the term came to be used regularly by Aristarchus of Samothrace (220–145 B.C.E.) and Apollonius the Sophist (late 1st cent. C.E.). The synonymous phrase ἅπαξ εἰρήμενον (the latter word a perfect passive participle from εἴρω) was also used interchangeably with ἅπαξ λεγόμενον. Some authors (e.g., Harrison 1921, 1964; criticized by Grayston and Herdan 1959–60) have used the pattern of hapax legomena to determine the problem of authorship of particular texts like the Pastorals. Harrison uses hapax legomena in the second sense mentioned above, i.e., words found only in one letter of Paul. One problem with hapax legomena is that the ratio of hapax legomena to pages or text or numbers of words in a text changes with increasing text length (Grayston and Herdan 1959–60, 5). A useful tool for checking frequency of vocabulary in the NT is Morgenthaler 1958.

*Stylometry

Grayston and Herdan 1959–60; Harrison 1921; Martinazoli 1957; Morgenthaler 1958

Hardship catalogues (see *Peristasis catalogues)

Harmonies (of the Gospels) are attempts to combine the text of two or more Gospels into a single narrative. *Synopses of the Gospels or Gospel parallels, on the other hand, typically arrange the text of the Gospels in parallel columns so that the similarities and differences between them is evident.

The plurality of the Gospels was recognized by some as a problem by the mid-2d cent. C.E. (Cullmann 1966, 548–65), and textual harmonization was one way of removing or neutralizing the differences between the Gospels. The most famous Gospel harmony in the early church was the **Diatessaron* of Tatian (first mentioned by Eusebius, *Hist. eccl.* 4.29.6), compiled after the middle of the 2d cent. C.E. in Syria (ca. 170) by Tatian, a student of Justin (for a comprehensive review of *Diatessaron* studies, see W. L. Petersen 1994). The *Diatessaron*, called in Syriac the "Gospel of the Mixed," was canonical in Syria until the 5th cent. The "Gospel of the Separated" replaced the *Diatessaron* beginning with the 5th cent. There is evidence that an earlier harmony or collection of some harmonized passages of the Synoptic Gospels (though not John) was used by Justin (Bellinzoni 1967, 139–42; Osborn 1973, 125–31); this was picked up by Tatian and incorporated into the *Diatessaron* (W. L. Petersen 1990, 1994, 346–48). W. L. Petersen has argued that Justin's harmony must be earlier than 160 C.E. and possibly earlier than 150 C.E. (1994, 348). Though the evidence is fragmentary, there appears to be evidence for other early Gospel harmonies as well. One likely candidate is the *Gospel of the Ebionites* (seven fragments quoted in Epiphanius, *Haer.* 30.13.2–8; 30.14.5; 30.16.4–5; 30.22.4; see Bertrand 1980). Several harmonies are mentioned that have not survived, such as that based on the four Gospels by Theophilus of Antioch (Jerome, *Ep.* 121.6.15).

Bellinzoni 1967; Bertrand 1980; Osborn 1973; W. L. Petersen 1990

Haustafeln (see *Household rules)

Hebraisms (see *Semitisms)

Hebrews, Letter to the, is an anonymous composition of uncertain date, though the last quarter of the 1st cent. C.E. seems likely. While *1 Clem.* 35:2–6 does allude to Heb. 1:3–15, the date of *1 Clement* is not secure, though it probably originated between 90 and 120 C.E. (Attridge 1989, 6–9). The origin and destination of the work are also uncertain, though many argue, partly on the basis of Heb. 13:24 ("those from Italy greet you"), that it was sent to a Christian congregation in Rome (Lane 1991, 1, lviii–lx). The actual title of the work, ΠΡΟΣ ΕΒΡΑΙΟΥΣ, "To the Hebrews," is not original but represents an early conjecture about its destination (Attridge 1989, 12).

Language and style. Hebrews contains 4,942 Greek words, with a vocabulary of 1,038 different words (Morgenthaler 1958, 164). The author has a rather large vocabulary, and his style is that of an educated person. He is really the only NT author who knows how to use *prose rhythm effectively (the most informed discussion of his use of prose rhythm is found in Moffatt 1924, lvi–lxiv). Hebrews 1:1 opens with the word πολυμερῶς ("in various ways" or "in various parts"), which must be scanned

˘˘˘- (ο=˘, υ=˘, ϵ=˘, ω=-), which is an instance of παιῶν καταληκτικός, i.e., a paeon ending with a long syllable, which theorists from Aristotle to Quintilian thought should *end* a sentence. But a παιὼν καταληκτικός does not occur at the end of a sentence in Hebrews until 11:3: γεγονέναι, i.e., ˘˘˘- (Moffatt 1924, lvi). For a brief discussion of prose rhythms in Hebrews, see Moffatt (1924, lvi–lix). The author of Hebrews prefers ˘˘-- as an ending (e.g., 7:28; 9:26; 10:34, 35; 11:13, 15, 28; 12:3). The resolved cretic (-˘˘-) occurs with some frequency as in the carefully composed passage in Heb. 4:8–10.

The author is fond of π-alliteration, which occurs five times in 1:1, five times in 11:28; four times in 12:11, and three times each in 2:2; 7:25, and 13:19. Hebrews 1:1 is particularly striking, where the initial letter "p" is repeated five times in a clause of twelve words, in a way impossible to reproduce in English: ***polymeros*** *kai* ***polytropos palai*** *ho theos lalesas tois* ***patrasin*** *en tois* ***prophetais***, "God spoke fragmentarily and in many ways to the fathers by the prophets." The author uses several long *periodic sentences: Heb. 1:1–4 (72 words); 2:2–4 (54 words); 12:18–24 (91 words); N. Turner (1976, 106) also mentions 2:14–15; 3:12–15; 4:12, 13; 5:1–3, 7–10.

Literary genre. Though Hebrews has often been categorized as a *letter, it lacks the typical features of the epistolary opening; it does have an epistolary conclusion. While the literary genre of the work has been debated, the author describes his work as a λόγος παρακλήσεως or "word of exhortation" (13:22), a phrase used in Acts 13:15 for the sermon of Paul that follows in Acts 13:16–41 (similar phrases are also found in Acts 2:40; 1 Macc. 10:24; 2 Macc. 5:11; 7:24; *Apost. Const.* 8.5).

Rhetorical genre. The rhetorical species or genre of Hebrews has been identifed as epideictic, more specifically a sermon or *homily (Attridge 1989, 14; 1990a; Lane 1991, 1, lxix–lxxv; Olbricht 1993, 378); as deliberative (Lindars 1989, a blanket assertion not backed up by a supporting rhetorical analysis; Übelacker 1989, 106–23, 214–29); and as a mixture of the two (C. Koester 2002, 104).

Analyzing Hebrews as deliberative, Übelacker (1989, 193–95) identified Heb. 2:17–18 as the thesis statement (Greek πρόθεσις; Latin *propositio*): "Therefore he had to be made like his brethren in every respect, so that he might become a merciful and faithful high priest in the service of God, to make expiation for the sins of the people. For because he himself has suffered and been tempted, he is able to help those who are tempted." He then proposes the following deliberative rhetorical structure in Hebrews (Übelacker 1989, 224):

I. *Prooemium* or *exordium* (1:1–4)
II. *Narratio* (1:5–2:18), with *propositio* (2:17–18)
III. *Argumentatio* with *probatio* and *refutatio* (3:1–12:29)
IV. *Peroratio* (13:1–21)
V. *Postscriptum* (13:22–25)

C. Koester (2002), who regards Hebrews as containing both deliberative and epideictic elements, emphasizes a standard or basic rhetorical structure consisting of introduction, arguments, and conclusion. He arranges Hebrews in the following rhetorical units: (1) Introduction or *exordium* (1:1–2:4): Framed by the periods in 1:1–4 and 2:2–4, this section deals with the Son as heir and creator of all things. There is no shift in subject after 1:4, for only after 2:4 does the emphasis on the suffering of Jesus become a matter of focal concern. This *exordium* is thus an indirect introduction to what follows. (2) Thesis or *propositio* (2:5–9): God's plans for humankind are accomplished through the death and exaltation of Christ, articulated by a quotation of Ps. 8:4–6 and a brief exposition of that text. (3) Arguments (2:10–12:27), including: (a) First series (2:10–6:20), [1] Argument: Jesus received glory through faithful suffering—a way that others are called to follow (2:10–5:10); [2] transitional digression: warning and encouragement (5:11–6:20); (b) Second series (7:1–10:39), including [1] Argument: Jesus' suffering is the sacrifice that enables others to approach God (7:1–10:25); [2] Transitional digression: warning and encouragement (10:26–39); (c) Third series (11:1–12:27), including: [1] Argument: People of God persevere by faith through suffering to glory (11:1–12:24); [2] Transitional digression: warning and encouragement (12:25–27). (4) Peroration (12:28–13:21). (5) Epistolary postscript (13:22–25).

Use of the OT. A complex form of typological interpretation of the OT is found in Hebrews (Synge 1959; Kistemacher 1961; Sowers 1965; Schröger 1968), a subject that has not been studied recently.

*Letters, General, *Homily

C. P. Anderson 1966; Attridge 1989; Bligh 1964; DeSilva 1995, 2000; G. Guthrie 1994; Lindars

1989; Swetnam 1969; Übelacker 1989, 1994; Vanhoye 1976; Watson 1997; Wrede 1906

Heliodorus (see *Novel)

Hendiadys, a transliteration of the Greek phrase ἓν διά δυοῖν, "one through two," is a rhetorical figure that uses two nouns connected with "and" to express a single idea rather by a noun and a modifier. Example: the phrase "in demonstration of the Spirit and power" (1 Cor. 2:4) is a hendiadys for "in demonstration of spiritual power."

Hermagoras of Temnos, active during the middle of the 2d cent. B.C.E., was an influential teacher of rhetoric who developed a complex *stasis theory and set a new direction in rhetorical theory (Quintilian 3.1.16). Though his own works have not survived (see the collection of fragments in Matthes 1962), his theories have been preserved by *Cicero (*De inventione*), *Quintilian, and Hermogenes. Hermagoras divided political questions into two classes (Kennedy 1963, 305): (1) θέσεις ("theses"), which do not involve individuals, such as "Should one marry?" "Should one participate in public life?" (examples given by Quintilian 3.5.8); (2) ὑποθέσεις ("hypotheses"), which involve specific controversies involving named persons and definite occasions, such as "Should Cato marry?" or "Did Orestes murder his mother?"

Cicero's *De inventione* is the clearest and most complete expression of Hermagoras's system of stasis theory. The most important part of *De inventione* is arguably the section on the doctrine of *constitutio causae*, or "determination of the issue," which is derived, with modifications, from Hermagoras (Hubbell 1949, xiii). Hermagoras's most influential work was on "invention" or "discovery" (εὕρεσις), which primarily included his stasis theory (Kennedy 1963, 313). Following Hermagoras, Cicero identified four issues, i.e., στάσεις or *status* (Jolivet 1997, 311–12): (1) The conjectural issue or the issue of fact (*coniectura*; στοχασμός) dealt with whether a person committed a particular act and was supported by conjectures and inferences. (2) The definitional issue (*definitiva*; ὅρος) involved the precise definition of an act—should a homicide be regarded as murder or manslaughter? (3) The qualitative issue (*generalis*; ποιότης) involved, in the case of homicide, whether there were extenuating circumstances such as self-defense or temporary insanity. (4) The translative issue (*translativa*; μετάληψις) involved procedural objections such as motions of dismissal because the wrong person was bringing the charge or the wrong penalty was sought for a particular time.

Hubbell 1949; Kennedy 1963, 303–21; Matthes 1958, 1962

Hexapla, a Greek term meaning "sixfold," referring to a lost work of Origen in which he assembled the Hebrew text of the OT, a Greek transliteration of the Hebrew texts, and four Greek translations of the OT—the LXX, Aquila, Symmachus, and Theodotion—all in parallel columns. Origen marked problem words and phrases in the text using the traditional marginal signs: the obelus, for marking words not occurring in the Hebrew, and the asterisk, for marking inserted words to show that they were additions from other versions in conformity with the Hebrew but absent from the LXX (Origen, *Commentary on Matthew* 15:14). Despite the length of the work, Eusebius claims that Origen left copies that were available in the library at Caesarea (*Hist. eccl.* 6.16).

Field 1964; Salveson 1998; Schenker 1982

Hiatus, in Greek prose (see *Prose rhythm), is the relationship between a vowel ending one word and a vowel beginning the next word. Hiatus can often be avoided by elision, i.e., by omitting the concluding vowel of the first word (e.g., ἀλλ', δέ) or by crasis, combining the vowels of two syllables into one long vowel or diphthong (e.g., κἄν for καὶ ἄν, or τοὔνομα for τὸ ὄνομα). Isocrates carefully avoided hiatus (Dionysius Hal., *De Isocr.* 2; *De elocutione* 23), as did Demosthenes (Cicero, *Orator* 151). It is often difficult, however, to know how phrases in the texts preserved in the manuscripts were actually pronounced. Cicero indicates that hiatus was unnatural in spoken Latin (*Orator* 150–52), and many ancient orators in addition to Isocrates and Demosthenes tried to avoid it (*Ad Herennium* 4.12.18).

*Crasis, *Ellision

McCabe 1968, 21–29; *OCD* 703–4; Reeve 1971; Stanforth 1967, 57–59

Historical criticism is the method or art of evaluating (ἡ κριτικὴ τέχνη) the evidence about past events (i.e., "history"), by comparing reports and applying verifiable standards for distinguishing or reconstructing what happened in the past, based on the careful analysis of the available sources. Since past events are irrevocably past, and most of the component factors can never be known in anything like their original complexity, only a very selective and approximate account of past events is possible. Accounts of the past can at best be only probable, never certain. The historian's task is one of interrogating the sources (written texts, oral tradition or remembered events, and material remains, such as archaeological excavations) in order to separate fact from fiction and truth from falsehood, much as an attorney interrogates a witness in court in order to elicit truth from his or her testimony.

The word "history" can be defined as (1) "a narrative of events connected with a real or imaginary object, person, or career," (2) "the events that form the subject matter of a history," or (3) "a systematic written account comprising a chronological record of events, and usually including a philosophical explanation of the cause and origin of such events" (*Webster's Third New International Dictionary*). Thus "history" can mean a narrative of real or imaginary events, a record of events, or the events themselves.

Historical method and abduction. Historical criticism is concerned not only with what probably happened in the past but also with causality, i.e., what factors are responsible for a particular chain of events. Of the three kinds of reasoning, deduction, induction, and abduction, only abduction can originate an idea (Hartshorne and Weiss 1960, §145: "Abduction consists in studying facts and devising a theory to explain them. Its only justification is that if we are ever to understand things at all, it must be in that way." Peirce's version of Aristotle's abductive argument has this form: (1) Facts of type B have been observed. (2) A true statement of the form "If A, then B" can explain B. (3) Therefore, A is probably true. Here is a slight expansion of abductive inference, showing its relevance for the formulation of scientific hypothesis: (1) D is a collection of data. (2) H (a hypothesis) would, if true, explain it. (3) No other hypothesis can explain D as well as H does. (4) Therefore, H is probably true. In the end it is obvious that "abductive reasoning" is a formalized version of a common form of thought that reflects the way people make choices in daily living, as well as the way in which historians propose hypotheses about causation in historical events. Abduction, then, is the basic method used by historians, to propose various theories of historical causation.

History of historical criticism. Historical criticism has its beginnings in 5th-cent. B.C.E. Athens and is reflected in the rigorous historical method of Thucydides, which appears again in the work of the 2d-cent. B.C.E. historian Polybius. Historical criticism in the modern period was revived in the Enlightenment, which began in the 17th cent. An essential feature of historical criticism is rationalism, which regards human reason as the sole basis for determining truth. In 1637 René Descartes (1596–1650) published his *Discourse on Method*, in which he argued that there are certain innate, self-evident principles from which all true knowledge necessarily follows. He had already formulated the method of universal methodological doubt, or methodological skepticism, which he systematically applied to all branches of knowledge as a kind of mathematical process starting from natural human intuition and proceeding by deduction.

Historical criticism of the Bible. The Bible, traditionally understood as the inspired, authoritative, and inerrant word of God, was particularly vulnerable to the new spirit of rationalism. The French Catholic priest Richard Simon (1638–1712) has been called "the father of biblical criticism." After writing "The Historical Criticism of the Old Testament" in 1678, he was expelled by his order and became a parish priest. In this work he dealt with various phenomena in the Pentateuch, including different styles, contradictions, and repetitions, issues that have continued to serve as bases for the source criticism of the Pentateuch.

The historical study of the Bible had several foci. One such focus was investigating the historical context in which the books of the Bible arose, by asking such questions as, Who was the author? What was his major concern? Why did he write? When did he write? Where did he write? While these questions seem harmless enough, more conservative scholars were alarmed when methodological skepticism was invoked and traditional ascriptions of authorship were denied. Another focus was the use of the Bible as one of many sources for the reconstruction of the historical events referred to in it.

Historical criticism and the Gospels. After the Enlightenment began in the 17th cent., the assumption that the dogma of divine inspiration guaranteed the historical and theological truth of Scripture was increasingly abandoned during the late 18th to mid-19th cents. by liberal Protestant academics in some European universities, notably Friedrich Schleiermacher (1768–1834) and F. C. Bauer (1792–1860).

During the 19th cent. confidence in the historical method encouraged scholars to attempt to separate fact from fiction in the Gospels with the object of producing a historically reliable biography of Jesus, e.g., the famous life of Jesus by David Friedrich Strauss (1837) and the life of Jesus by Ernst Renan (1863). The miracles of Jesus were problematic for rationalistic critics, who found naturalistic ways of explaining them or omitted them altogether as pious accretions. The Gospel of John, with its marked theological emphases and striking differences from the Synoptics, came to be regarded as having little historical value. Scholars became increasingly skeptical of the traditional identities of the Gospel authors and about the supposed "eyewitness" character of their reports. In 1906 Albert Schweitzer wrote a celebrated book exposing the subjective character of this "quest for the historical Jesus."

Rather than successfully separating the real Jesus from the legendary embellishments of early Christian piety and credulity, scholars unintentionally fabricated a "historical" Jesus reflecting (and thus justifying) their own theological and philosophical views. In effect, they fashioned a Jesus in their own image and likeness. The quest for the historical Jesus had reached an impasse, and many were skeptical about the possibility of writing a biography of Jesus at all. A contemporary of Schweitzer, Wilhelm Wrede, demonstrated that even Mark (the Gospel thought earliest and most historical) was a high theological (hence historically tendentious) interpretation of Jesus.

After World War I, a reaction to the idealism of liberal theology emerged as dialectical theology. Associated with such European Protestant theologians as Karl Barth, Emil Brunner, and Friedrich Gogarten, dialectical theology became influential for New Testament studies when combined with existentialism by Rudolf Bultmann. Despite the Bible's errors, imperfections, and mythic modes of thought, it was argued, the Bible and the gospel it conveys can mediate an encounter with the transcendent Word of God. With the kerygmatic Christ thus insulated from the possibility or necessity of historical qualification or disconfirmation, there was little reason to worry about the so-called historical Jesus.

*Historiography

Baird 1992; Dobbs-Allsopp 1999; Hatina 1999; Krentz 1977; Linnemann 1990, 1998; Neill 1988; J. G. Prior 1999

Historical present is the use of a verb in the present indicative to narrate action that takes place in the past and would normally be narrated using the aorist tense. While it has been argued that the use of the historical present is a *Semitism, reflecting the phenomenon of Semitic interference (Black 1967, 130; *BDF* §361; S. Thompson 1985, 35–37; N. Turner 1976, 20), the historical present was relatively common in classical Greek narrative, where it was used to highlight aspects of the narrative (Maloney 1989, 68). The historical present was avoided in literary Hellenistic Greek but used in *Atticism (Kilpatrick 1977). With few exceptions (7:40; 8:49; 11:37, 45), Luke avoids using the historical present (Cadbury 1920, 158–59). The historical present occurs 151 times in *Mark, 78 times in *Matthew, 4 or 6 times in *Luke, 13 times in *Acts (Hawkins 1968, 144–49), and 164 times in *John (O'Rourke 1974).

Kilpatrick 1977; Maloney 1989; O'Rourke 1974

Historiography, a transliterated form of the Greek word ἱστοριογραφία (found in an interpolation in Josephus, *Contra Apionem* 1.134, referring to the work of Berossus called ἡ τῆς ἀρχαιότητος ἱστοριογραφία, "History of Antiquity," but missing from the quotation of that passage in Eusebius), is based on the verb ἱστοριογραφέω, meaning "to write history" (Dionysius Hal., *De Thucydide* 42). "Historiography" refers to the writing of history in Greek and Roman antiquity based on the critical examination of sources, the sifting and selection of data from sources judged to be reliable, and the arrangement of the particulars into a chronological, ordered narrative framework. History was often closely connected with rhetoric, for historians were trained primarily in rhetoric rather than historiography. Cicero subsumes histories (*historiae*) under epideictic rhetoric (*Orator* 37; cf. 66). This rhetorical emphasis did not tend to produce accurate historiography on the Thucydidean or Polybian model (Cicero, *Brutus* 42; LCL trans.): "[T]he privilege is conceded to rhetoricians to distort history in order to give more point to their narrative." In the words of F. Young (1997, 80): "'History' as a literary genre, then, was closely akin to rhetoric and tragedy: there was more interest in fate and fortune, in moral lessons, in creative composition and effective style, than in historicity."

Jacoby's model of five historiographical genres. An appropriate starting point for understanding ancient Greek and Roman historiography is the important essay of Jacoby (1909), in which the author presented a taxonomy of Greek historiography, purportedly conforming to ancient conceptions, in preparation for a new edition of the fragments of the Greek historians (Jacoby 1923–58). Jacoby divided Greek historiography into five subgenres, arranged in the order of development: (1) mythology or genealogy, (2) ethnography, (3) chronography, (4) contemporary history (*Zeitgeschichte*), and (5) horography or local history. Reluctant to designate what the ancients wrote as "history," Jacoby considered all five subgenres forms of "historical writing," but none qualified as "history" per se. Jacoby (1909, 34; trans. Fornara 1981, 3) defined *Zeitgeschichte*, the closest to "history" as "all authors who, without restricting themselves to localities, portrayed the history of the community of the Hellenes in their own times or down to their own times."

Each of these subgenres requires some explanation (for the following, see Jacoby 1909; Fornara 1983, 1–46; Marincola 1997). 1. Mythography or genealogy (Jacoby 1909, 23–24; Fornara 1983, 1, 4–12; Aune 1987, 84–85; Lendle 1992, 10–25) records heroic traditions and tries to reconcile the contradictions in various sources (for some of these sources, see R. L. Fowler 2000).

1. Geneology. Though he may have had now-unknown predecessors, Hecataeus's *Genealogiai,* inspired by the poetry of Hesiod, is the first example of this subgenre and influenced its development. Herodotus distinguishes between mythological and historical periods (3.122), but may have derived this model from Hecataeus. Following Herodotus, there was a tendency to speak of the earliest times with the verbs μυθολογεῖν ("to tell mythic tales") and γενεαλογεῖν ("to trace descent"). Following the work of the mythographers, subsequent writers skipped over the earliest history (e.g., Ephorus) or used it as the first part of a more general history of Greece or the Mediterranean world (e.g., Diodorus).

2. Ethnography (Jacoby 1909, 26–27; Fornara 1983, 12–16; Aune 1987, 85), the hallmark of which is description, was one of the more important subgenres, beginning in the early 5th cent. B.C.E. and continuing down until late antiquity, and focused on a particular ethnic group and in its native habitat. Four types of descriptive information were characteristically included: (a) geography (i.e., the description of a region), (b) dynastic history (i.e., a narrative summary of the succession of native rulers), (c) the marvels or wonders of the area, and (d) an exposition of the customs of the inhabitants. Since ancients assumed that environment determined the character of a people (see Hippocrates, *Airs, Waters, Places*), geography was an important feature of this subgenre of historiography. While the earliest ethnography was the *Persika* of Dionysius of Miletus, one of most influential was the *Periēgēsis* or *Periodos Gēs* or "Journey around the Earth" by Hecataeus of Miletus, in two books, one on Europe and one on Africa. The shorter accounts of non-Greek lands, according to Jacoby, were developed into longer, more substantial treatments by Herodotus.

3. Chronography (Fornara 1983, 28–29; Aune 1987, 85–86; Marincola 1999, 286) began with the *Priestesses of Hera at Argos* by Hellanicus of Lesbos (*Fr.Gr.Hist.* 4 F 74–84), who gave the names of the priestesses of Hera in succession, dating events based on their tenure, though his narrative had a pan-Greek scope. In its simplest form chronography consisted of ordered lists of priests, priestesses, kings, magistrates, officials, and Olympic victors. These were used for dating by years. A year could be identified by officials who held office in that year (e.g., archons in Athens, ephors in Sparta, *stephanephoroi* in Miletus). By the 5th cent., the Greeks used numerical dating by olympiads (four-year periods starting with 776 B.C.E.). Absent a universal scheme for reckoning time, these synchronic devices were indispensable for writing local histories. While Jacoby (1909, 24–25) regarded chronography as a form of history, Fornara (1983, 29) assigns it a category of its own.

4. Contemporary history (*Zeitgeschichte*) (Fornara 1983, 29–38; Aune 1987, 87–89; Marincola 1999, 287) was for Jacoby the most important of the historical subgenres. He defined their authors as those "who without local restriction narrated the general Greek history of their own time or up to their own time" (Jacoby 1909, 34). This subgenre has three characteristic features: (a) the narrative centers primarily on the author's own time, (b) the viewpoint is Greek, (c) the scope is pan-Hellenic (including events in all Greek city-states). This subgenre first appears in Herodotus 7–9, and in Thucydides' history of the Peloponnesian War in the next generation, it comes to maturity. Following Thucydides, contemporary historians focused on individual wars or a particular period of time (e.g. Xenophon's *Hellenica*) or on particular individuals (Theopompus's *Philippica*).

5. Horography (Aune 1987, 85) or local history, i.e., literary accounts of individual Greek

Focalization Continuum

Individual → Group → City-state → Nation → Group of nations → Known world

city-states, did not yet exist in the mid-5th cent. B.C.E. when Herodotus collected material for his *Persian Wars*, though they did appear shortly thereafter, according to Jacoby. Horography had three distinguishing features: (a) fixed annalistic structure, (b) the inclusion of other social and cultural institutions (e.g., cultic), in addition to political and military events, and (c) a truly local emphasis, treating aspects of other Greek states only when they affected the city-state that was the focus of the monograph.

Critique of Jacoby's model. Humphreys (1997, 213) argues that a critique of Jacoby's scheme in *FGH* "must question not only its conception of the sub-genres of historical writing, but also its conception of the category 'history.'" There are several problems with Jacoby's proposals (Humphreys 1997; Schepens 1997; Marincola 1999, 290–301): (1) Jacoby's scheme as a whole is too teleological, since it is based on the development from "primitive" to "perfect" forms (e.g., in the case of "contemporary history" the perfect form is Thucydides' war monograph on the Peloponnesian War). (2) Jacoby's conception of individual historians as the microcosmic model for macrocosmic developments of Greek historiography generally is improbable. According to R. Fowler (1996, 68): "A theory in which all the characteristics of the first stage of historiography are found in one author, Hekataios, and all the characteristics of the logical second stage in another, Herodotos, and all of the logical third stage in another, Hellanikos, and all of the fourth stage, in another, Thucydides, all of whom fit together like ashlar blocks, squeezing out anyone caught in between, is inherently unlikely." (3) Jacoby's rigid categories do not cohere well with ancient categories and at times are anachronistic constructs based on modern criteria. For "contemporary history" and "ethnography," Jacoby could not find anything like consistent and distinctive ancient terminology (Marincola 1999, 295). Further, Jacoby distinguished "contemporary history" from "ethnography" based on a difference in focalization, the former on mainland Greece and important Greek city-states, the latter on individual Greek city-states or non-Greek lands. This is hardly the basis for generic differentiation. By defining works that treat foreign lands as "ethnography," Jacoby was implicitly defending his view that Herodotus was the first historian, though before Herodotus, Dionysius of Miletus wrote *Persika* (Merincola 1999, 297). "Jacoby clearly had difficulties," observes Marincola 1999, 298, "explaining why certain histories of specific areas were not really history . . . but rather ethnography." In Roman literature, there is no distinction between "annalist" and "historian," and the term *scriptor annalium* is used for all writers of history, and there cannot have been a subgenre of *annales* (Verbrugghe 1989). (4) Jacoby's conception of genre is generally static, though ancient writers valued both tradition and innovation (Marincola 1997, 12–19). The tendency of many ancient authors to break with the models and generic norms of the past has been explored by classical scholars using the perspective of *intertextuality. (5) Jacoby's fixed categories cannot accommodate certain works, which are then considered problematic.

The classification of historical works by genre may reveal only part, and perhaps not the most important part, of such works (Marincola 1999, 312). Rather than propose a new system of genres, Marincola (1999, 301–9) rather suggests five specific criteria when analyzing historical works (somewhat modified): (1) Type of discourse: Does the work use synchronic descriptive discourse or diachronic narrative discourse (or a combination of the two)? (2) Focalization: What is the focalization, or point of view, from which the story is told? The types of focalization are suggested in the table above, and they may be mixed. (3) Chronological limits: What are the chronological limits, since it is impossible to "begin at the beginning" and "end at the end," which can also be represented by the schematization in the table below. (4) Chronological arrangement: The structure of a historical work is determined by the chronological system underlying it, either an annalistic pattern, successions of kings or magistrates. A historian can also focus on particular theaters of action before moving to a different one. (5) Subject

Chronological Continuum

Origins → Early history → Recent history → Present day

matter: History can include not only political and military actions but social and cultural events and institutions, customs, and the lives of leading figures. Relegating authors who included such material (e.g., Berossus, Manetho, Timaeus, Posidonius) to the category of ethnography implies that what they were doing was something other than history. Further, the inclusion of the religious character and observances of the Roman people and the monuments of the city itself are part of Livy's history of Rome.

Surviving Greek historical works are few; the following fourteen cover a millennium of Greek historical writing: Herodotus and Thucydides (5th cent. B.C.E.), Xenophon (b. ca. 430 B.C.E.), Theopompus (4th cent. B.C.E.), Polybius (ca. 200–118 B.C.E.), Diodorus Siculus (early 1st cent. B.C.E.), Dionysius of Halicarnassus (late 1st cent. B.C.E.), Josephus (1st cent. C.E.), Arrian (86–160 C.E.), Appian (early 2d cent. C.E.), Cassius Dio (164–229 C.E.), Herodian (ca. 180–238 C.E.), Procopius (6th cent. C.E.), and Agathias Scholasticus (ca. 532–80 C.E.). Most Greek historical works have perished, but there are fragments of many lost works (Jacoby 1923–58, continued by Schepens 1998).

Literature and rhetoric were closely related in the ancient world, so closely, in fact, that many of our modern assumptions about ancient literature are misleading. The numerous (and entertaining) excursuses in the first six books of Herodotos's *History of the Persian Wars,* for example, appear to be there precisely because he wrote with the intention of public recitation. Further, Thucydides' reliance upon *speeches as a primary means for understanding the motivations of great men and their role in influencing historical events is scarcely conceivable in isolation from the great developments in rhetoric and oratory in the Athens of his day. Even though Thucydides criticized Herodotos for being too entertaining, the historians of the Hellenistic and Roman periods forsook the rules of evidence and accuracy for the qualities of readability and entertainment (Momigliano 1981, 164ff.). Runnalls (1997, 740 n. 7) argues that Josephus followed Greco-Roman oratorical conventions in crafting the 11 speeches in the *Bellum* and the 23 speeches in the *Antiquitates*.

Apologetic historiography. In a study of Philo of Byblos, Oden (1978) lists five typical features of "hellenistic historiography" practiced by those living in countries subjected to Hellenism, i.e., "apologetic historiography": (1) euhemerism, (2) a universal scale with extended chronological and geographical limits characterized by special pleading for the great antiquity of the historian's nation, (3) "patriotic cultural history" in which each historian claims humanity's cultural benefactors as the ancestors of his own nation, (4) a belligerent and defensive posture toward Greek civilization and mythography, and (5) a claim to have access to recently discovered archives of unimpeachable provenance and antiquity.

Based on Lucian of Samosata's essay *How to Write History*, a list of ten "rules" for Hellenistic historiography can be enumerated (L. Alexander 1998, 98–99): (1) noble subject, (2) public benefit, (3) *parrhesia* (lack of bias or partisanship), (4) fitting beginning and end, (5) collection of material, (6) selection and variety, (7) disposition and order, (8) *enargeia* (vividness of narration), (9) topographical details, (10) speeches suitable to speaker and occasion. Yet Alexander points out how difficult it is to understand precisely what Lucian had in mind with many of these "rules."

*Luke–Acts, *Prefaces

L. Alexander 1998; Fornara 1983; Humphreys 1997; Immerwahr 1966; Jacoby 1909, 1923–58; Mader 2000; Marincola 1999; Oden 1978; Sacks 1983; Schepens 1997; Sterling 1992; Verbrugghe 1989; F. Young 1997

Historiola, or "small story," is an abbreviated mythological narrative that is incorporated into magical spells and the verbal portions of exorcism and healing rituals (Frankfurter 1995, 458). The short narrative typically functions as a mythical paradigm for a desired magical action in Greek magical incantations, and is sometimes introduced with "just as," while the application is introduced with "so also" (formally similar to Homeric similes). An example of this latter type is found in *PGM* XXXIIa.1: "As Typhon is the adversary of Helios, so inflame the heart and soul of Amoneios." In an amulet dating from the 7th cent. C.E., recovered from a synagogue, this historiola appears: "As you have suppressed the sea by your horses and stamped the earth with your shoe, and as you suppress trees in winter days and the herb of the earth in summer days, so may [there be suppressed] [. . .] before Yose son of Zenobia" (Naveh and Shaked 1993, 45).

Aune 1980; Frankfurter 1995; Heim 1892, 495–507

Homer (in the Hellenistic and Roman period) is the traditional designation for the author of two hexameter epics, the *Iliad* and the *Odyssey*, the earliest extant Greek literary works. Homer was *the* Greek poet, and the memorization of large sections of the *Iliad* and the *Odyssey* was an integral part of the primary education of Greek children. According to Heraclitus, in a book on Homeric problems, perhaps written in the 1st cent. C.E. (*Quaest. Hom.* 1.5–7):

> From the earliest stage of life, our infant children in their first moments of learning are suckled on him; we are wrapped in his poems, one might also say, as babies, and nourish our minds on their milk. As the child grows and comes to manhood Homer is at his side, Homer shares his mature years, and the man is never weary of him even in old age. When we leave him, we feel the thirst again. The end of Homer is the end of life for us.

In Greco-Roman culture, the Homeric poems occupied an authoritative role roughly comparable to the Bible in the West and provided Greeks with the basis for their cultural identity.

Homeric hypertexts in the NT. Recently, MacDonald (2000) has argued that Mark is a prose epic modeled after the *Odyssey* and the end of the *Iliad.* MacDonald (2000b) has also proposed that there are literary similarities between the end of Luke (Luke 24), and the end of the *Odyssey* (*Odyssey* 24). The major flaw in MacDonald's method is to regard the similarity of parallel motifs, often with a folkloristic character, as suggestive of literary imitation.

*Allegory

Buffière 1958, 1962; H. Clarke 1981; Dawson 2000; Erbse 1969–88; Glockmann 1967, 1968; Grube 1965; Hofrichter 1992; Kindstrand 1973; Krause 1958; Lamberton 1986; Lamberton and Keaney 1992; Long 1992; MacDonald 1994, 1999, 2000a, 2000b; McNamee 1981; Pépin 1958; Pfeiffer 1968; Rengakos 1993; N. J. Richardson 1975; Russell 1981

Homily, a transliterated form of the Greek word ὁμιλία (ranging in meaning from "association, company" to "exhortation, lecture"). Sermons or homilies are normally speeches of exhortation, often using arguments based on the interpretation of biblical passages, directed to insiders. No rigid distinctions can be made between the sermonic or homiletic forms and styles used in early Judaism and early Christianity, since early Christianity only gradually emerged from Judaism (Boyarin [1999] pushes this separation into the 3d cent. C.E.).

The phrase "word of exhortation" (λόγος παρακλήσεως), which occurs in Acts 13:15 and Heb. 13:22 (cf. Acts 2:40; 1 Macc. 10:24; 2 Macc. 7:24; 15:11; *Apost. Const.* 8.5), is apparently one designation for the homily. Two early Christian texts place the synagogue homily in a narrative context, though both are literary constructs and both are adversarial. According to Luke 4:16–30, after standing up to read Isa. 61:1–2 (*haphtarah*), Jesus sat down and delivered a brief homily loosely linked to that text. In Acts 13:15, after the reading from the Law (*seder*) and the Prophets (*haphtarah*), the rulers of the synagogue in Pisidian Antioch asked Paul and his companions if they had any "word of exhortation" (λόγος παρακλήσεως; cf. Heb. 13:22) for the people, which Paul then presented in vv. 16–41. In *Spec. leg.* 2.61–62, Philo speaks of the synagogue as a school (διδασκαλεῖον) and the primary activity which goes on there every Sabbath as philosophizing (φιλοσοφεῖν). Someone with special experience stands and "sets forth what is the best and sure to be profitable and will make the whole life grow to something better." The homiletic exegesis of Scripture was certainly a characteristic feature of Judaism, but prior to the formation of the Mishnah (ca. 200 C.E.), fixed sermonic patterns did not exist. By the end of the Tannaitic period (ca. 200 C.E.), the proem homily was still not widely used and had not yet attained a fixed format. The Yelammedenu homilies are much later. The "discovery" of proem homilies in the NT (e.g., John 6:31–58; Acts 13:16–41; Rom. 1:17–4:25; 1 Cor. 1:18–3:20) is anachronistic and forced (Aune 1987, 202).

Acts 13:17–41. The speech in Acts 13:17–41 (the synagogue setting is introduced in vv. 13–15, and the effect of the speech on the audience is described in vv. 42–43) has attracted extensive scholarly attention and for that reason will be considered here in some detail. Four publications appeared in 1984 presenting analyses of the speech in this text, two by a single author and with none of the authors betraying any awareness of the work of the others (Wills 1984; Kennedy 1984; Berger 1984a, 1984b).

Wills (1984), using Paul's speech set in the synagogue in Pisidian Antioch as a prime example (Acts 13:13–41), has proposed that the Jewish or Christian homily has three parts: (1) The *exempla* are a reasoned exposition of the points to be made using examples from the past and biblical quotations for support (vv. 16b–37), consisting of an account of the Israelite captivity in Egypt, the exodus, and the conquest of Canaan through the appearance of Jesus and the announcement of the gospel (vv. 16b–33a), followed by citations from Scripture and the comparison of the resurrected Messiah to David (vv. 33b–37). (2) The *conclusion*, introduced with a conjunctive particle and based on the presentation made in the *exempla* section, tells the audience how it should think or act (vv. 38–39): "Let it be known to you therefore, brethren, that through this man forgiveness of sins is proclaimed to you, and by him every one that believes is freed from everything from which you could not be freed by the law of Moses." (3) The *exhortation*, a section based on the conclusion, uses the imperative or hortatory subjunctive (13:40–41): "Beware, therefore, lest there come upon you what said in the prophets [quotation of Hab. 1:5]."

There are several evident problems with this analysis. First, Acts 13:13–41 recounts a fictional speech placed in a fictional setting reflecting Luke's literary activity (Wilckens 1963, 99–100). Kennedy, however (with an optimism typical of classicists crossing the border into NT studies), regards this speech "as a typical example of the contents of Paul's preaching under similar conditions" (1984, 125). Second, the brevity of the speech underscores the fact that it was explicitly designed for this literary context. Third, a sermon or homily is normally a hortatory speech delivered to *insiders* (appeals to outsiders to convert is the province of protreptic; see *Protreptic literature). Fourth, this analysis in fact reveals very little of the structure of Acts 13:16–41, since Wills is unable to propose a structure for the largest part of the "sermon" in 13:16b–37. In part, this is owing to the fact that Wills concludes (correctly) that there is no close or obvious relationship between the speech of Paul in Acts 13 and the three species of Greco-Roman rhetoric (1984, 296).

Kennedy's (1984, 124–25) brief analysis of Acts 13:16–41 appeared the same year as Wills's article, so each was uninfluenced by the other. Kennedy characterizes Paul's speech as epideictic, fitting the request from the synagogue leaders (v. 15b) for an exhortation. The speech begins with a brief *proem*, since Paul did not know his audience (v. 16b). A *narratio* follows (vv. 17–25), consisting of a survey of events from the Egyptian captivity to John the Baptist, helping to establish Paul's basis for communication with the audience. Then comes the *propositio* (v. 26): "to us has been sent the message of this salvation," followed by a *proof* (vv. 27–37), explaining that through ignorance of prophecy, the Jews arranged Jesus' death. Nevertheless, God raised him from the dead in accordance with prophecy (Ps. 2:7; Isa. 55:3; Ps. 16:10). The epilogue (vv. 38–39 [surely he means vv. 38–41]) summarizes the message, warns against disregarding the prophecy.

In a critique of Wills's proposal, Black (2001, 119–26), building on Kennedy, argues that the speech in Acts 13 is actually closer to Greco-Roman rhetoric than Wills recognizes. To accomplish this, he has to emphasize the elasticity of rhetorical categories. However, unlike Kennedy, he does not categorize the speech as either epideictic, deliberative, or judicial. Black proposes the following analysis (2001, 123–25): (1) **exordium* (v. 16b), (2) *narratio* (vv. 17–25), (3) *propositio* (v. 26), (4) *probatio* (vv. 27–37), (5) epilogue (vv. 38–41). Yet Black's proposal is not without difficulties. First, the brief address "Men of Israel, and you that fear God, listen" (v. 16b) hardly fills the rhetorical function of an *exordium.* Second, Black retains Wills's description of the first part of the speech as "exempla," though calling it a *narratio. Exempla* (see *Example) or παραδείγματα constitute one of two main types of rational arguments, yet the narrative recounted in Acts 13:17–25 cannot be construed as an argument.

Finally, Berger's (1984a) brief discussion of Acts 13:16–41 is part of a section on *Reden* ("speeches"), which in turn is subsumed under the heading *Epideiktische Gattungen* ("epideictic forms"). In another article (1984b, 1363–71), in a section on *Predigten* ("Sermons"), Berger expresses extreme skepticism about what he considers anachronistic attempts to retroject "the sermon" form back into early Christian literature, yet his discussion of Acts 13:16–41 does precisely this. He provides a brief analysis of Acts 13:16–41, as consisting of three sections (Berger 1994a, 72 and 1994b, 1368; with slight discrepancies between the two): (1) *narratio*, a historical retrospective on Israel to the resurrection of Jesus (vv. 16–31), (2) *argumentatio*, scriptural proofs predicting the coming and the resurrection of Jesus (vv. 32–37 or vv. 32–39), and (3) *peroratio*, decisive arguments and threat (vv. 38–41 or vv. 40–41). Berger's analysis is generally convincing, though the fact that he waffles on parts 2 and 3 indicates an analytical uncertainty about the structure of those sections. Berger's analysis can be improved, once it is recognized that the author's direct references to the audience introduce the three main parts of the speech (Schneider 1980–82, 2.129; Fitzmyer 1998, 507): (1) "Israelite men, and those who fear God" (v. 16b, introducing vv.

17–25), (2) "Brothers, sons of the family of Abraham, and those among you that fear God" (v. 26a, introducing vv. 26b–37), (3) "Let it be known to you therefore, brethren" (v. 38a, introducing vv. 38b–41).

The speech falls neatly into three sections: (1) *narratio 1* (vv. 17–25), consisting of a review of the history of Israel beginning with the captivity in Egypt, the settlement of the land, the period of judges, culminating in the kingship of Saul and then in David. (2) *Narratio 2* (vv. 27–37), in which the review jumps from David to Jesus, the descendant of David who was presented by John the Baptist as a savior for Israel. This brief historical narrative is designed to focus on David and then shift the focus to Jesus (the implied Davidic Messiah) as culmination of Israel's salvation history. (3) Exhortation (vv. 38b–41): since the basis of forgiveness is through this man, along with freedom from the law of Moses, you resist belief at your peril.

The synagogue homily. The earlier history of the Jewish synagogue homily is shrouded in obscurity, for such homilies are preserved in Jewish literature only after 200 C.E. Two types of homilies are distinguished, the *proem* homily and the *yelammedenu rabbenu* homily. The *proem* homily exhibits a distinct pattern. It starts with an introductory text, not chosen from the *seder* (the basic Torah reading for the day) or from the *haftarah* (the second reading of the day, from the Prophets), but rather from some other part of Scripture (typically from the Kethubah or Writings, the third section of the Hebrew Bible). The *proem* text was intended to act as a bridge between the *seder* and *haftarah* readings, and had therefore to share a word with the *haftarah* reading so that the *proem* text had a formal link to the *haftarah* reading. The *yelammedenu rabbenu* (meaning "let our teacher instruct us") homily gets its name from the introduction to the homily that is formulated as a question, while the answer is introduced with the formula "thus our rabbis taught" (Stegner 1988, 53–54).

**Barnabas, Letter of*, **Clement, First Letter of*, *Hebrews, Letter to the, *Midrash

———

Attridge 1990a; Bacher 1913; Black 1988, 2001, 115–33; Borgen 1965; Bowker 1967; Ellis 1978; C. F. Evans 1970; Grelot 1989; Heineman 1971; Levine 2000; Osborn 1999; Overman 1992; von Rad 1966; Stegner 1988; Thyen 1955; Wilckens 1974; Wills 1984

Homoioteleuton, a transliteration of the Greek work ὁμοιοτέλευτος ("ending alike"), referring to the rhymed endings of clauses (Denniston 1952, 72; Stanforth 1967, 84–85). The *Letter to Diognetus* concludes with twelve short cola which exhibit homoioteleuton, with eleven lines ending in -ται (12:8b–9):

ὧν ὄφις οὐχ ἅπιε**ται**
[God] whom the serpent does not touch

οὐδὲ πλάνη συγχρωτίζε**ται**
nor error defile

οὐδὲ Εὔα φθείρε**ται**
nor Eve corrupt

ἀλλ' παρθένος πιστεύε**ται**
but a virgin is trusted

καὶ σωτήριον δείκνυ**ται**
and salvation is revealed

καὶ ἀπόστολοι συνετίζον**ται**
and the apostles are made to understand

καὶ τὸ κυρίου πάσχα προέρχε**ται**
and the Easter festival of the Lord approaches

καὶ καιροὶ συνάγον**ται**
and the seasons are brought together

καὶ μετὰ κόσμου ἁμόζον**ται**
and are harmonized with the world

The term is also used in textual criticism for discovering errors committed by a person copying who skipped lines because the eye jumped from one ending to the next, omitting the intervening line or phrase.

Household rules Codes of household rules (*Haustafeln*) are found in the later letters of the NT (Rom. 13:1–7; Col. 3:18–4:1; Eph. 5:22–6:9; Titus 2:1–10; 1 Tim. 2:1–15; 6:1–2; 1 Pet. 2:18–3:7). The oldest example, found in Col. 3:18–4:1 (see *Colossians, Letter to the), probably served as a source or model for later household codes (Crouch 1972, 36). Household rules consist of a group of exhortations directed toward people of various social statuses, all of whom are part of an ancient extended family or household (οἰκία). In Colossians, there are three pairs of exhortations, each addressed to people of a particular social status (wives and husbands, children and fathers, slaves and masters); each consists of a command and then a reason for the behavior. One of the obvious models for Christian household rules can be found in occurrences of the Hellenistic topos οἰκονομία ("household management"). The household was widely thought to constitute the basic unit of society, and a well-ordered household was the necessary prerequisite for a well-ordered state.

*Paraenesis

Balch 1981; Crouch 1973; Fiedler 1986; Kamlah 1964; Lührmann 1980–81; K. Müller 1983; Sampley 1971; Schroeder 1959; Schweizer 1979; Thraede 1980; Verner 1983; Vögtle 1936; Weidinger 1928; Wibbing 1959

Hymn, a transliterated form of the Greek word ὕμνος, meaning "hymn" or "ode [sung in praise of the gods]," primarily in cultic contexts. Hymns are typically poetic in form and are therefore sung or chanted, though prose hymns became increasingly common from the 2d cent. B.C.E. after (Aelius *Aristides composed several in the mid-2d cent. C.E.). Since Hebrew *poetry differs strikingly from Greek poetry, hymns from both spheres provide indispensable comparative data for understanding the forms and conventions of hymns in the NT and early Christianity.

Greco-Roman hymns. For Plato, hymns were songs in praise of the gods, while encomia were written in praise of people (*Rep.* 10.607a); elsewhere he characterizes hymns as prayers sung to the gods (*Laws* 700b). Dionysius Thrax defines the hymn in somewhat more detail as "a poem [ποίημα] comprising praises [ἐγκώμια] of the gods and heroes with thanksgiving [ἐχαριστίας]," indicating that a cultic hymn was a "poem," that the term "encomia" was used more broadly than Plato would have it, and that "thanksgiving" was an essential feature of a hymn (Furley and Bremer 2001, 9). Greek hymns are typically addressed to a god or a group of gods in the **du-Stil* (second-person singular direct address) or the **er-Stil* (third-person singular indirect address). While they are typically written in a poetic meter, there are no meters exclusive to such cultic poetry (Furley and Bremer 2001, 2). The cult hymn is a form of worship by a person directed towards obtaining the goodwill of a god as well as his or her winning a god's goodwill and securing his or her assistance. Hymns are very closely related in both form and content to prayers, which may be considered complementary forms of religious discourse (Furley and Bremer 2001, 3–4), though unlike prayers, hymns themselves were often regarded as a kind of sacrifice or votive offering to a god (Pulleyn 1997, 49–50).

Among the earliest Greek hymns written in meter are the 33 Homeric Hymns in hexameter, including four long hymns to Demeter, Apollo, Hermes, and Aphrodite (dating from 650–400 B.C.E.; cf. Kirk 1985, 111), as well as 29 relatively short ones that are probably later. The collection of 87 Orphic Hymns, also in hexameter (probably in imitation of Homeric Hymns), are among the latest products of pagan Greek religiosity and perhaps date from the late 3d cent. C.E. (Athanassakis 1977, viii), and possibly were connected to the the Temple of Demeter in Pergamon (Kern 1911). Prose hymns (i.e., ὑμνεῖν ἄνευ μέτρου, "to compose hymns without meter") as well as poetic hymnic texts were widely used in various liturgical contexts in the Greco-Roman world (Krenz 1995). Several "magical" hymns are found in the Greek magical papyri (e.g., the hymn to Proteus in PGM IV.939–48, the hymn to Helios in PGM I.315–25, and the hymn to the one immortal God in PGM XII.244–52; all discussed in Merkelbach and Totti 1990–91, 1.1–19).

Following one taxonomy, there were two main types of hymns in Greek literary tradition: the *cult* or *subjective* hymn and the *rhapsodic* or *objective* hymn (A. M. Miller 1986, 1–9). The function of the *cult* hymn was to persuade a god to act on behalf of the speaker; it was therefore framed in the so-called **du-Stil* (i.e., "thou [second-person singular] style") and consisted of three parts: (1) the invocation, with honorific epithets of the god addressed; (2) the *hypomnesis* or "reminder" recounting how the god has responded to the speaker's devotion in the past; and (3) the cult hymn, concluding with the actual request to which the first two parts have been leading. The *rhapsodic* hymn presupposed a human rather than a divine audience, was framed in the **er-Stil* ("he [third-person singular] style"), and consisted of three parts: (1) the *exordium,* announcing the speaker's intent to praise the god and including honorific epithets of the god; (2) the *midsection* (attached to the *exordium* by a relative pronoun, called the "hymnic relative"), consisting of either a general description of the god's nature (*descriptio*) or a narrative of a specific episode or sequence of episodes from the god's mythic experiences (*narratio*), though some hymns had both elements; and (3) the *epilogue,* containing a salutation and perhaps a request or the speaker's intention to compose another such hymn in the future.

The main problem with Miller's taxonomy of two types of hymn is simply that hymns composed for a cultic setting always involved audiences of various sizes, so that the composers would implicitly be aware of the context of the hymn. The more recent extensive discussion of Greek cult hymns by Furley and

Bremer provides a very similar but more satisfactory analysis of the basic structure of Greek hymns (2001, 50–63): (1) invocation (ἐπίκλησις), consisting of the following optional elements: (a) name(s), (b) attributes (epithets, titles), (c) genealogy, (d) place (abode, places of worship), (e) companion deities; (2) praise (εὐλογία), including the following possible elements: (a) predication of powers through relative clauses or participles, (b) repeated (anaphoric) addresses, (c) *hypomneseis* or "reminders" of earlier benefits conferred by the deity or earlier worship offered by the petitioners, (d) *ekphraseis*, or "descriptions" of the god, his or her haunts, actions, (e) narratives; (3) prayer (εὐχή).

"Hymns" in the NT and ECL. The singing or chanting of hymns was an important part of the worship of early Christians (1 Cor. 14:26; Col. 3:16; Eph. 5:1;9; Jas. 5:13; *Odes of Solomon*; Pliny, *Ep.* 10.96). Colossians 3:16 and Ephesians 5:19 refer to the singing of ψαλμοί ("psalms"), and ὕμνοι ("hymns") and ᾠδαὶ πνευματικαί ("spiritual odes," i.e., odes uttered under the influence of the Spirit of God), though these terms do not represent sharp distinctions among different genres or types of hymns (Kroll 1968, 4–6; Hengel 1987, 391).

It has become increasingly evident that the study of hymns embedded in the epistolary literature of the NT is methodologically problematic and needs thorough review. Several complexes of problematic issues are involved: (1) the problem of defining the formal compositional features of early Christian "hymns," including determining the propriety of the term "hymn," and the advisability of formulating a broader palette of generic categories; (2) the problem of the criteria available for identifying such "hymns" (or other preliterary forms) when they are embedded in epistolary literature and not explicitly identified by metatextual markers; (3) the problems attendant on reconstructing the *Sitz im Leben* or the original (or typical) context in which such a written or oral text was used.

The Lucan infancy hymns. Several hymns apparently based on OT models are embedded in the Lukan infancy narrative, including the Magnificat (Luke 1:46–55, the Benedictus (Luke 1:68–79), the Gloria in excelsis (Luke 2:14), and the Nunc dimittis (Luke 2:29–32); see Farris 1985. It is probable that Luke did not himself compose these hymns, but rather adapted them from an existing Jewish source.

The hymns of Revelation. An important feature of the heavenly throne-room ceremonial in Revelation is the inclusion of 16 hymns or hymnlike compositions at various points in the narrative set in the heavenly throne room (4:8c, 11; 5:9b–10, 12b, 13b; 7:10b, 12; 11:15b, 17–18; 12:10b–12; 15:3b–4; 16:5b–7b; 19:1b–2, 3, 5b, 6b–8). With the exception of a single independent hymn in 15:3b–5, all of these references are part of just seven antiphonal units (4:8–11; 5:9–14; 7:9–12; 11:15–18; 16:5–7; 19:1–4; 19:5–8). Scholars have debated whether these hymnic elements were adapted by the author from early Christian or early Jewish liturgical material, or whether the author composed these hymnic texts for the present context. The presence of some undeniably traditional liturgical elements, such as the hallelujah, the amen, the sanctus (4:8), doxologies (5:13; 7:10, 12; 19:1), and acclamations (4:11; 5:9, 12), suggests the former, while the fact that the hymns are used in the narrative to interpret the significance of eschatological events indicates the latter.

Hymns embedded in NT letters. Scholars have identified and analyzed a number of hymns or hymnic fragments embedded in early Christian literature (Schille 1965; R. Martin 1983, 39–52; Berger 1984a, 239–47; 1984b, 1149–71; Dormeyer 1993, 133–34). One of the first scholars to identify hymns and hymn fragments in the NT was Norden, who distingiushed several forms of hymnic rhetoric found in prose hymns in classical and Hellenistic literature as well as in the NT, including the **du-Stil* ("thou-style," i.e., the use of the second-person singular), addressed directly to the god (1956, 163), the *er-Stil* ("he-style," i.e., the use of the third person), also addressed to the god (1956, 163–66), and the participial predication or relative-clause predication (1956, 168–76). Norden discusses the hymnic features of Col. 1:12–20 (1956, 250–54) and 1 Tim. 3:16 (1956, 254–63).

Of the other hymns and hymnic fragments that have been identified in the letters of the NT, some are addressed to God (Rom. 11:33–36; 2 Cor. 1:3–4; Eph. 1:3–14; 1 Tim. 1:17; 1 Pet. 1:3–5; Col. 1:12–14), while others narrate the mission of Christ, frequently including preincarnation and postincarnation themes, particularly abasement and exaltation themes: John 1:1–14; Phil. 2:6–11; Eph. 2:14–16; 5:14; Col. 1:15–20; 1 Tim. 3:16 (W. Metzger 1979, 12); Heb. 1:3; 1 Pet. 2:21–25; Ignatius, *Eph.* 7:2; 19:1–3. Other candidates for embedded hymns are less well recognized: Phil. 3:20–21 (Reumann 1984).

Criteria for identifying NT hymns. For nearly a century, scholars have argued that certain texts in the epistolary literature of the NT are actually preexisting hymns embedded in their present contexts; hymns in narrative context such as the Gospel of Luke and the Revelation to John are usually more clearly demarcated and are normally given a clear literary function. However, the criteria for identifying hymns, or even the formal characteristics of such hymns and the setting in which they were purportedly originally used, have remained vague and problematic. Stauffer (1955, 338–39) proposed "Twelve Criteria of Credal Formulae in the New Testament," criteria that should also be useful in detecting the presence of hymnic material (prayers, hymns, and creedal statement cannot be rigidly distinguished): (1) Creedal materials or hymns are often inserted and introduced by such words as "deliver," "believe" or "confess" (cf. Rom. 10:9). (2) Contextual dislocations often mark creedal material, because when creedal material or hymns are inserted, either it or the context or both undergo compositional changes (e.g., 1 Tim. 3:16). (3) Frequently the creedal formula or hymn does not fit into the context syntactically (e.g., Rev. 1:4). (4) The creedal formula or hymn often exhibits a different linguistic usage, terminology, or style from its context (e.g., 1 Cor. 16:22). (5) Different passages sometimes repeat the same formula in very similar form (e.g., 2 Cor. 5:21). (6) Creedal formulas or hymns often exhibit simple syntax, avoiding particles, conjunctions, complicated constructions, preferring *parataxis to *hypotaxis, and the thought proceeds by thesis rather than argument (e.g., Acts 4:10). (7) Creedal formulas or hymns often stand out because of stylistic construction, i.e., they favor antithetic or anaphoral style (e.g., 1 Tim 3:16). (8) Creedal formulas or hymns are often rhythmical in form, by the number of stresses or even words (e.g., 1 Cor. 15:3). (9) Creedal formulas or hymns are often arranged in lines and strophes (e.g., Col 1:15ff.). (10) Creedal formulas or hymns are often marked by their preference for appositions and noun predicates (e.g., Ignatius, *Eph.* 7:2). (11) Creedal formulas or hymns frequently favor participles and relative clauses (e.g., Rom. 1:3). (12) Creedal formulas or hymns refer to the elementary truth and events of salvation history as norms (e.g., Ignatius, *Trall.* 9:1–2).

Christian hymns of the 2d to 4th cent. Metrical poetry appeared relatively late in early Christianity. The Christian *Sibylline Oracles,* often written in a defective hexameter, are among the earliest Christian metrical poetry; *Sib. Or.* 6 is a 28-line hymn to Christ that probably dates to the 3d cent., and *Sib. Or.* 8, a collection of oracles written by one or more Christian authors ca. 175 C.E. contains an acrostic poem in hexameter on judgment in lines 218–50; each line begins with a letter of the phrase ΙΗΣΟΥΣ ΧΡΕΙΣΤΟΣ ΘΕΟΥ ΥΙΟΣ ΣΩΤΗΡ ΣΤΑΥΡΟΣ, "Jesus Christ, son of God, savior, cross," a slightly expanded form of the ΙΧΘΥΣ ("fish") acrostic. Greek metrical poetry essentially begins in Christianity with Gregory Nazianzus, Amphilochius of Iconium, and Apollinaris of Laodicea, while Latin poetry begins with Hilarius and Ambrose (C. Schneider 1954, 2.51).

Analyzing early Christian hymns. Schattenmann argues that the authors of the prose hymns in the NT (e.g., Phil. 2:6–11; Col. 1:12–20) were not concerned with the vowel quantity of the syllables, i.e., short or long (see *Prose rhythm) but rather with the number of syllables; they did not use a meter but a kind of free rhythm (Schattenmann 1965, 3 n. 1). These hymns often consists of two parts, one about God and one about God's people, with a select word at the center dividing the two parts. In Phil. 2:6–11, for example, the first part is 2:6–8 (about the self-humbling of Jesus despite his equality with God), and the second part is 2:9–11 (about the exaltation of Jesus); the central word is σταυροῦ ("cross") at the end of 2:8 (Schattenmann 1965, 14). If the article τό before ὄνομα in 2:9 is omitted (as in several Greek manuscripts), then both halves consist exactly of 90 syllables. In Schattenmann's less satisfying analysis of Col. 1:12–20, on the other hand, he moves 1:13–14 after 1:18a (and omits τῆς ἐκκησίας as a gloss), and comes up with a two-part hymn: (1) Col. 1:12, 15–18a, a "Logos hymn," and (2) Col. 1:13–14, 18b–20; a "Christ hymn (Schattenmann 1965, 16–18) the first part has 78 words consisting of 151 syllables, while the second part has 75 words consisting of 151 syllables. The radical surgery Schattenmann uses is not justified by the results obtained.

Athanassakis 1977; Berger 1984a, 1984b; Bremer 1981; Charlesworth 1986; Chazon 1998; Deichgräber 1967; *DNP* 5.788–97; Frankowski 1982; Furley 1993, 1995; Furley and Bremer 2001; Hengel 1987; O. Kern 1911; D. R. Jones 1968; Kroll 1968; R. Martin 1983; W. Metzger 1979; A. M. Miller 1986; Reumann 1984; J. T. Sanders 1971; Schattenmann 1965; Schille 1965; Schuller 1993; C. Schneider 1954, 50–73; Wengst 1972

Hypertext, a term coined by Genette, is any text that somehow relies on a written antecedent or *hypotext (Genette 1982, 11–14).

Hypotaxis or hypotactic style (see *Periodic style)

Hypotext, a term coined by Genette, is any text which serves as an antecedent to a later written text or *hypertext (Genette 1982, 11–14).

Hypothesis (ὑποθέσις), a Greek rhetorical term (see *Thesis).

Hysteron/Proteron (two Greek words meaning "last-first"), a figure of speech in which there is a reversal of the logical sequence of events. Examples: John 1:51: "the angels of God ascending and descending," Rev. 5:5: "to open the book and to break its seals" (see also Rev. 3:3, 17; 6:4; 10:4, 9; 20:4–5, 12–13; 22:14).

———

Robertson 1934, 423

Idea-Theory is the formulation of critical judgments about texts based on a system of "virtues" (ἀρεταί) or "ideas" (ἰδέαι) of style, thought to characterize earlier texts, that serve as literary models.

*Second Sophistic, *Style

———

Rutherford 1998

Ignatius of Antioch, who also calls himself "Theophorus" in each of his letters, was a bishop of Syria (Ign., Rom. 2:2), probably in Antioch (*Philad.* 10:1; *Smyrn.* 11:1; *Polyc.* 7:1), the capital of the Roman province of Syria, and was remembered as the second bishop there following Euodius (Eusebius, *Hist. eccl.* 3.22, 36). Ignatius was arrested, tried, and condemned *ad bestias*, "to the wild animals" (*Eph.* 1:2; *Rom.* 4:2; *Trall.* 10:1) in Antioch and sent to Rome for execution, which took place very probably in the Amphitheatrum Flavium (later called the Colosseum), about 117 C.E. Despite his Roman name "Egnatius," he could not have been a Roman citizen, for citizens were not subject to being chained as Ignatius was (*Eph.* 11:2; *Smyrn.* 11:1), nor were they condemned *ad bestias*. During his forced journey to Rome, Ignatius wrote seven letters during a relatively brief period.

*Ignatius, Letters of

———

Bauer and Paulsen 1985; Corwin 1960; Schoedel 1985

Ignatius, Letters of The seven genuine letters of *Ignatius of Antioch (d. ca. 117 C.E.), were all written within a few short weeks under conditions of exceptional physical and emotional strain. Ignatius was under arrest and being escorted to Rome by a Roman cohort for the purpose of execution during the latter part of the reign of Trajan (98–117 C.E.). Ignatius mentions Paul twice by name (*Eph.* 12:2; *Rom.* 4:13) and reflects a knowledge of a collection of Pauline letters through verbal allusion and stylistic imitation (see the comparative tables of von der Goltz 1894, 99–118), though Schneemelcher (1964) argues (unpersuasively) that Ignatius lacked a firsthand acquaintance with any of the Pauline letters. Ignatius does not mention the name "John," even though the letter addressed to the church at Ephesus was written within a generation after the composition of the Gospel and Letters of John. Further, there is no conclusive evidence that Ignatius even knew the Fourth Gospel, even though his theology and language are often described as having a "Johannine ring" (J. N. Sanders 1943, 14; Grant 1942, 98), though some argue the contrary (Maurer 1949; F.-M. Braun 1959, 262–82).

Text. Letters originally written in Greek and attributed to Ignatius of Antioch exist in three recensions. The Middle Recension (Lightfoot 1889, II.1.328–430) consists of seven letters, which most scholars consider authentic and which were mentioned by Eusebius (*Hist. eccl.* 3.36): *Ephesians*, *Magnesians*, *Trallians*, *Romans*, *Philadelphians*, *Smyrnaeans,* and *Polycarp*. The Short Recension (Lightfoot 1889, II.1.280–327) consists of three letters (to *Polycarp, Ephesians,* and *Romans*) and is an epitome of those letters preserved in Syriac. The Long Recension (Lightfoot 1889, II.1.246–79) consists of 13 letters, six of which are spurious and, together with interpolations in the seven genuine letters, was produced toward the end of the 4th cent. C.E. The long recension of the letters of Ignatius of Antioch is found in *Codex Hierosolymitanus* 54 (completed on June 11, 1056 C.E. by a scribe named Leo, a MS which also contains the *Didache*, the *Epistle of Barnabas*, *1 Clement*, and *2 Clement*).

Rius-Camps (1979) regards only four of the letters of Ignatius as authentic. He regards the

Middle Recension as earlier than the Later Recension, but the Middle Recension is not what Ignatius wrote. Originally just four letters were written between 80 and 100 C.E.: *Romans*, *Magnesians*, *Trallians*, *Ephesians* (all written at Smyrna). A 3d-cent. reviser took material from them to write *Smyrnaeans*, *Polycarp,* and *Philadelphians* (the three Troas letters). The evidence about the Ignatian corpus in Polycarp, *Philippians* is the result of interpolation. *Romans* is the only letter fully preserved as Ignatius wrote it. For critiques, see Smulders 1981 and Trevett 1984.

The order of the genuine letters. The popularity of the seven genuine letters of Ignatius encouraged the addition of six spurious letters by a single unknown person in the 4th cent. C.E. The present collection of seven, arranged not in the order found in the MSS but in the order mentioned by Eusebius (*Hist. eccl.* 3.36.1–10), suggests that they originally formed two groups, those written from Smyrna (*Ephesians*, *Magnesians*, *Trallians*, *Romans*) and those written from Troas (*Philadelphians*, *Smyrnaeans*, *Polycarp*). Eusebius may be responsible for the fact that the letters are roughly arranged in order of decreasing length. The collection begins with *Ephesians* (the longest, at 1,778 words), and concludes with *Polycarp* (the shortest, at 785 words). Between them are *Magnesians* (1,063), *Trallians* (950), *Romans* (1,032), *Philadelphians* (1,019), and *Smyrnaeans* (1,147).

Literary features. The rhetoric of the letters of Ignatius has been linked to a florid Greek literary style called *Asianism (Perler 1949; Riesenfeld 1961; Schoedel 1985, 7–8), which was rejected by those who adopted an archaizing Atticistic style. Asianic rhetoric is a designation for an exuberant literary style emphasizing *pathos and consisting of plays on words, metaphors, parallelism and antithetical phrases, *Gorgianic figures, and rhythmic short cola. Asianic rhetoric apparently began in Pergamon in the late 4th and early 3d cent. B.C.E., and had a significant impact on Roman rhetoric, since many of the Greek teachers of rhetoric who came to Rome beginning with the 2nd cent. B.C.E. were Asiatic Greeks. Cicero distinguished two types of Asianism (*Brutus* 325; LCL trans.):

> Of the Asiatic style there are two types, the one sententious and studied, less characterized by weight of thought than by the charm of balance and symmetry. Such was Timaeus the historian; in oratory Hierocles of Alabanda in my boyhood, and even more so his brother Menecles, both of whose speeches are masterpieces in this Asiatic style. The other type is not so notable for wealth of sententious phrase, as for swiftness and impetuosity—a general trait of Asia at the present time—combining with this rapid flow of speech a choice of words refined and ornate. This is the manner of which Aeschylus of Cnidus and my contemporary Aeschines of Miletus were representatives. Their oratory had a rush and movement which provoked admiration, but it lacked elaborate symmetry of phrase and sentence.

Epistolary form. The opening and closing epistolary formulas used by Ignatius differ from the epistolary styles used in earlier Christian letters. The superscript in each letter is short and unpretentious: "Ignatius, also called Theophoros." The basic adscript, "to the church," is amplified by three structural elements: (1) passive participles describing the benefits each church has received from God (e.g., blessed, foreordained, united, elect); (2) adjectives describing the spiritual greatness of each church (e.g., worthy of blessing); and (3) mention of the location of each church. The following translation of the preface to *Ephesians* exhibits this structure through the italicizing of the participles and adjectives mentioned above:

Superscription:	Ignatius, also called Theophoros,
Adscription:	to her who is *blessed* with greatness by the fullness of God the Father, *foreordained* before the ages to be forever destined for enduring and unchangeable glory, *united* and *elected* in true suffering by the will of the Father and Jesus Christ our God, to the church *worthy of blessing* which is in Ephesus in Asia,
Salutation:	warmest greetings in Jesus Christ and with blameless joy.

The longest and most ornate adscript is found in *Romans*, where (among other flowery features), Ignatius has an asyndetic list (see *Asyndeton) of six compound adjectives, each beginning with ἀξιο- ("worthy"): "worthy of God, worthy of respect, worthy of blessing, worthy of praise, worthy of success, worthy of holiness." The use of unusual compound words, such as the 11 ἀξιο-compounds used by Ignatius, is one feature of Asianic rhetoric (Schoedel 1985, 39). Since *Romans* is basically a letter of request, Ignatius is obviously working on the assumption that flattery will get him somewhere.

The basic salutation favored by Ignatius is "warmest greetings" (πλεῖστα χαίρειν), a formula that first appears in papyrus letters of the 1st cent. B.C.E. He also uses "greetings with blameless joy" once (*Eph.* praef.) and "blameless greetings" once (*Rom.* praef.), and he omits the saluation altogether in *Philad.* praef., probably an oversight. Ignatius uses the ἀσπάζεσθαι (greetings) formula several times in epistolary adscriptions (*Magn.* praef., *Trall.* praef., *Rom.* praef., *Philad.* praef.), a formula Paul normally uses in the closing sections of his letters. While thanksgivings never occur after epistolary prescripts in his letters, Ignatius does include an epistolary thanksgiving toward the end of several letters, perhaps consciously modifying Pauline practice (*Eph.* 21:1; *Philad.* 11:1; *Smyrn.* 10:1).

The postscripts in the letters of Ignatius exhibit several formal features: (1) The typical Hellenistic epistolary closing, "farewell" (ἔρρωσθε), is expanded by various prepositional phrases, such as "in the Lord" (*Polyc.* 8:3) or (the longest), "in the concord of God possessing an unhesitating spirit which is Jesus Christ" (*Magn.* 15:2; cf. *Eph.* 21:2; *Rom.* 10:3; *Philad.* 11:2; *Smyrn.* 13:2). (2) Both personal and secondary greetings occur frequently (*Magn.* 5:1; *Trall.* 13:1; *Rom.* 9:3; *Philad.* 11:2; *Smyrn.* 11:1; 12:1; 13:1–2). Ignatius occasionally uses the first-person singular verb ἀσπάζομαι ("I send greetings"), a form attested only for the early 2d cent. C.E. and later (*Trall.* 12:1; *Smyrn.* 11:1; 12:2; 13:1, 2; *Polyc.* 8:2, 3). (3) Requests for prayer occur often (*Eph.* 20:1; 21:1–2; *Magn.* 14:1; *Rom.* 8:3; *Smyrn.* 11:1). (4) Ignatius regularly uses the verb γράφειν ("to write") in his postscripts and mentions the place of writing (an unusual feature in Hellenistic letters), e.g., *Eph.* 21:1; *Trall.* 12:1–3; *Rom.* 10:1; *Philad.* 11:2. (5) One postscript includes the date of writing (*Rom.* 10:3, unusual in Hellenistic letters, but probably intended to enable the Roman Christians to calculate the approximate time of Ignatius's arrival).

The opening sections of Ignatius's letters exhibit structural parallels to Hellenistic royal diplomatic correspondence, which typically begin with a section praising the recipients (i.e., a **captatio benevolentiae*). Most of the letters of Ignatius begin in this way. Apart from the *exordium,* the central sections of Ignatius's letters are primarily hortatory and consist of various types of paraenesis, including positive exhortation (*Eph.* 4, 10; *Magn.* 3–9); negative warnings (*Eph.* 5:2–3; *Magn.* 11; *Trall.* 7; *Philad.* 2–3; *Smyrn.* 6–7); positive examples (*Eph.* 12); and negative examples (*Eph.* 7). Ignatius's hortatory style is gentle, never authoritarian (*Trall.* 3:3). A characteristic way of summarizing his exhortations, for example, is the impersonal phrase "therefore it is proper for you to do (such-and-such)" (*Eph.* 2:2; *Magn.* 3:2; *Rom.* 12:2; *Smyrn.* 7:2; *Polyc.* 5:2). Following another low-key hortatory technique, Ignatius often urges readers to continue in what they are already doing (*Eph.* 4:1; *Trall.* 8:1; 12:1; *Smyrn.* 4:1). Ignatius is fond of rhetorical antithesis and, like Paul, makes extensive use of it in paraenesis (*Eph.* 12:1; *Magn.* 3:1; 7:1; 11:1; *Rom.* 4:1–3; *Philad.* 1:1). *Ephesians* 12:1 is an example (trans. Schoedel 1985):

> I know who I am and to whom I write:
> I am condemned, you have been shown mercy;
> I am in danger, you have been strengthened.

Ignatius characterizes several of his own letters as "appeals" or "exhortations" (using the verb παρακάλειν, "to exhort" in *Eph.* 3:2; *Magn.* 14:1; *Polyc.* 7:3), a term synonymous with paraenesis (*Magn.* 6:1; *Smyrn.* 4:1). Ignatius knows that an appeal (appropriate for those of approximately equal status) is a gentler and more effective approach than a command such as an apostle might give (*Eph.* 3:1; *Trall.* 3:3; *Rom.* 4:3). In *Phlm. 8–9, which Ignatius may have used as a model, Paul also *appeals* to Philemon rather than *command* him. One of the modes of exhortation by which he complements his soft style is the frequent use of first-person plural hortatory subjunctives, e.g., "Let *us* fear the long suffering of God" (*Eph.* 11:1); "Let *us* love him" (*Eph.* 15:3).

The substance of Ignatius's exhortations and advice varies little from letter to letter, a fact which suggests that the epistolary situation was primarily determined by Ignatius's own circumstances, rather than the circumstances of those to whom he wrote. In an ecclesiastical application of the subjection principle characteristic of *household codes, Ignatius advises Christians to respect and obey the bishop and the council of elders, earthly representatives of God or Jesus Christ and the apostles (*Eph.* 4:1–6:2; *Magn.* 6:1–7:2; *Trall.* 2:1–3:3; *Smyrn.* 8:1–9:2). "Concord," "unity," and "peace" are code words for subjection to the bishop (*Eph.*

13:1–2; *Philad.* 8:1–2), while "strife," "pride," and "division" are caused by those resisting such subjection (*Eph.* 8:1; *Magn.* 6:2). Ignatius also advises Christians to avoid deviant teachers peddling heresy (*Eph.* 9:1; 17:1; *Trall.* 6:1–2; *Smyrn.* 4:1) and to be examples, following the Lord, of gentleness, faith, love, humility, and endurance (*Eph.* 10:1–2; *Magn.* 1:2; *Trall.* 4:1–2). He has an overriding theological concern that true Christians fully accept the actual birth, suffering, and resurrection of Christ. He therefore frequently inserts creedal formulas summarizing correct belief (*Eph.* 7:2; 18:2; *Magn.* 11:1; *Trall.* 9:1–2; *Smyrn.* 1:1–2). The closest he comes to a list of vices is a list of those persons for whom heretics show no love (*Smyrn.* 6:2).

The letter to *Polycarp* is the only letter that Ignatius addresses to an individual. It is a pastoral letter addressed to the bishop of Smyrna with close similarities to two pseudo-Pauline pastoral letters, 1 Timothy and Titus (Wolter 1988, 157–61). All three letters are addressed to individuals who are themselves responsible for one or more Christian congregations.

*Asianism, *Apostolic Fathers, *Epistolography, *Ignatius of Antioch *Letter collections

---

Bauer and Paulsen 1985; M. P. Brown 1963; Corwin 1960; Lightfoot 1889–90; Maurer 1949; Mellink 2000; Perler 1949; Riesenfeld 1961; Rius-Camps 1979; Schoedel 1985; Sieben 1978; von der Goltz 1894

Iliad (see *Homer)

Implied author, a phrase coined by Booth (1983 [originally published in 1961], 70–76, 151), which refers to the image of the real *author which the reader infers through the text (1983, 74–75): "The 'implied author' chooses, consciously or unconsciously, what we read; we infer him as an ideal, literary, created version of the real man; he is the sum of his own choices." Booth also uses the alternate phrase "inferred author" (1983, 74–75). The implied author, unlike the *narrator, has no voice and does not communicate directly with the reader. The implied author is not the real author (who writes) or the *narrator (who tells). In works which represent collections or compilations of individual compositions by several real authors, there are as many implied authors as there are constituent documents (against Chatman 1978, 149). When Booth wrote *The Rhetoric of Fiction* in 1961, he maintained the validity of the "intentional fallacy" (an emphasis of the *New Criticism), yet adhered to the notion that literary works constituted intentionally structured normative worlds accessible to ethical criticism. The concept of the "implied author" enabled Booth to continue believing that he could interpret and criticize the normative worlds of literary works without transgressing the limits of the text and falling victim to the "intentional fallacy."

The notion of an "implied author" has been criticized from the point of view of description and interpretation (Kindt and Müller 1999). Descriptive narratology has no particular use for the implied author (Genette 1980, 265; 1988, 137). According to Genette (1988, 137), "narratology has no need to go beyond the narrative situation, and the two agents 'implied author' and 'implied reader' are clearly situated in that beyond." Bal (1981, 209), another narratologist, proposes that it would be better "to speak of the interpretation, or the overall meaning of the text" than of the implied author.

Thus for the context of description, the notion of the "implied author" should be abandoned, since it can play no descriptive role. For the context of interpretation (argue Kindt and Müller (1999), the use of the concept of the implied author also poses problems, because many of those who use the concept of the "implied author" for interpretive purposes also use detailed narratological descriptions, apparently unaware of the theoretical problems in combining descriptive and interpretive statements (e.g., Culpepper 1983). One way of solving the problem is simply to replace the concept of the "implied author" with the concept of the "author," in an intentionalist sense, but not wedded to a particular interpretive methodology. Those who wish to retain the concept of the "implied author" in a nonintentionalist sense might consider replacing that confusing term with a different one with less risk of confusion, might wish, as a first step, to adopt a different term, involving less risk of confusion with an intentionalist conception of meaning, such as "textual intention" or "narrative strategy."

*Authorship *Implied reader, *Literary criticism, *Narrator

Bal 1981; Booth 1983; Chatman 1978; Genette 1980, 1988; Kindt and Müller 1999

Implied reader is the counterpart to the *implied author, the audienced presupposed by the narrative itself (Chatman 1978, 149–50); an alternate designation is the "text-connoted reader" (R.A. Edwards 1997). An equivalent concept is "authorial audience," coined by Rabinowitz (1977, 126; 1989, 81–100) and subsequently used in an analysis of 1 Thessalonians by A. Smith (1995, 14, 22) and in an analysis of the parables in Matthew by Carter and Heil (1998). Smith defines "authorial audience" as the hypothetical audience Paul had in view when composing a letter. Carter and Heil (1998, 10–12) prefer the phrase "authorial audience" to "implied reader" because the latter suggests interacting with the text through reading a personal copy (but in the ancient world texts were normally read aloud and hence "heard" rather than "read") and because "authorial audience" is contextualized socially and historically, whereas "implied reader" is an ahistorical conception.

*Literary criticism, *Implied author

Booth 1983; Carter and Heil 1998; Culpepper 1983, 205–27; R. A. Edwards 1997; Fowler 1985; Iser 1974, 1978; Rabinowitz, 1977, 1989; Staley 1988

Incipit, a third-person singular present indicative of *incipere* ("to begin, undertake"), is a label for the opening words of a manuscript, which often functioned as a title.

*Explicit, *Titles of books

Inclusio, a Latin term meaning "imprisonment, confinement," is a modern literary term referring to two very similar phrases or clauses placed at the beginning and end of a relatively short unit of text as a framing device. In the study of the Fourth Gospel, von Wahlde has called this literary technique "repetitive resumption" (1976, 520) or a "framing repetition" (1989, 27). The standard German term for this literary technique is *Wiederaufnahme* (Boismard 1977, 235–41). Romans 1:16–2:11 is a textual unit framed by use of the phrase "[to] the Jew first and also [to] the Greek" (1:16; 2:10). This framing device is also used with *digressions, the second part used to pick up the argument or narrative where it was left before the digression. One example from Mark is the pericope on Jesus before the Sanhedrin (14:53–65), framed by the similar phrases "Peter . . . was warming himself" (14:54), and "seeing Peter warming himself" (14:67a), involving three pairs of identical words. A closely related seam or *inclusio* is found in the pericope on the inquiry before Annas in John 18:19–24, which is framed by the phrases "Peter was standing there keeping warm" (18:18b), and "Now Simon Peter was standing there keeping warm" (18:25a), involving six pairs of identical words. C. A. Evans (1982) argues that since the pericope frames are so dissimilar, these framing repetitions do not betray the use of sources, but rather reflect the storytelling device of digression and resumption. In the story of the healing of the paralytic in Mark 2:1–12, the interpolated pronouncement story in 2:5b–10 (Bultmann 1967, 12–13) is framed by the phrase "he said to the paralytic" (2:5a, 10b), the second of which is parenthetical. Justin's *1 Apology* is framed by the phrase τὴν προσφώνησιν καὶ ἔντευξιν, "this plea and petition" at the beginning (*1 Apol.* 1), and the closely similar phrase τὴν προσφώνησιν καὶ ἐξήγησιν, "this petition and explanation," at the end (*1 Apol.* 68.3). *Inclusios* can be very simple, such as the two verbs that frame Mark 2:13–17, ἐξῆλθεν, "he [Jesus] went out" (v. 13), and ἦλθον, "They came" (v. 17).

*Chiasmus, *Digression, *Ring composition

Boismard 1977; C. F. Evans 1982; Von Wahlde 1976, 1989

Indirect discourse, or indirect speech, attributes a purportedly original utterance to a reporting narrator and usually provides the content, though not the subjective aspect, of the speech (Banfield 1982, 62–63). Indirect discourse can range from a word-for-word reproduction of the "original" utterance, though with the necessary changes in pronouns and verb forms, to reproducing the gist of what was said on a particular occasion. Speech in the Homeric epics are normally presented as *direct discourse, though indirect discourse is used in certain marginal instances (de Jong 1987, 114–18).

*Direct discourse

Banfield 1982; de Jong 1987

Inscriptions include various type of texts in Greek and Latin inscribed or etched on stone and metal.

Greek inscriptions. Inscriptions can be categorized as either "public" inscriptions, whose language is determined by a magistrate or official body, i.e., decrees, dedications, honorary inscriptions, epitaphs (Lattimore 1962; Gibson 1978; van der Horst 1991), manumissions, mileposts or *miliaria*, or "private" inscriptions, whose language is determined by a private individual (funerary monuments, private dedications, manumissions, curse tablets). Our knowledge of "vulgar" Attic is primarily based on curse tablets and epitaphs. The survival locale of inscriptions, together with the use of dialect in comedies, provides the primary basis for our knowledge of dialects other than Attic and Ionic. The earliest Ionic inscription known is a graffito on a *kylix* from the 7th cent. B.C.E. found at Smyrna (*SEG* 12.480; see *Graffiti).

Among the important tools for the study of Greek inscriptions are the handbook of abbreviations used in ancient inscriptions in Oikonomides (1974) and the list of abbreviations of collections of inscriptions by Horsley and Lee (1994). The main corpora containing collections of Greek inscriptions include the following: (1) *CIG=Corpus inscriptionum graecarum.* Ed. A. Boeckh et al. Berlin: Reimer, 1828–77 (continued by IG); (2) *CIJ=Corpus inscriptionum judaricarum.* Ed. P. Jean-Baptiste Frey. 2 vols. Rome: Pontifical Institute of Christian Archaeology, 1936–1952. (3) *IG=Inscriptiones graecae.* Berlin: Reimer, 1873–1932; Berlin: Walter de Gruyter, 1932– (4) SEG=Supplementum epigraphicum graecum. Leiden, 1923–.

Latin inscriptions. Early Latin is represented by the earliest surviving inscriptions of the 6th cent. B.C.E., often resembling Greek letter forms and sometimes written in the so-called *boustrophedon* ("turning like oxen when plowing") style in which alternate lines written from left to right then right to left. An example is perhaps the earliest Roman inscription from possibly the 6th cent. B.C.E. (*Corpus Inscriptionum Latinarum* I^2, 1). While an early Latin inscription from Praeneste from the 7th cent. survives (*Inscriptiones Latinae Selectae* 8561), its authenticity is now doubtful (Gordon, 75f.); the Romans began to inscribe texts in the 6th cent. B.C.E., while most of the literary and inscriptional evidence for Latin begins to accumulate toward the end of the 3d cent. B.C.E. In addition to stone, bronze was commonly used, particularly for legal texts (Pliny, *Hist. nat.* 16.237; 34.99). More perishable wooden boards were frequently used for public notices, such as Caesar's famous short text displayed at his triumph in 47 B.C.E.: *VENI, VIDI, VICI,* "I came, I saw, I conquered" (Suetonius, *Caesar* 37.2). Vespasian tried to replace the more than 3,000 bronze tablets that were destroyed by a fire on the Capitoline in Rome in 69 C.E. (Suetonius, *Vespasian* 8.5). More than 300,000 Roman inscriptions are known; most are carved in "Roman Capitals," which reached a developmental high point toward the end of the 1st cent. C.E. The most extensive collection of Latin inscriptions is the *Corpus Inscriptionum Latinarum* (Berlin, 1862–), in 18 volumes, primarily arranged geographically. Dessau edited a selection of 9,000 texts published as *Inscriptiones Latinae Selectae* (Berlin, 1892–1916). The language of these inscriptions was primarily Latin in the western Mediterranean, while in provinces east and south of the Adriatic the language was chiefly Greek, the lingua franca of the Levant. The evidence for the use of Oscan is limited to ca. 200 inscriptions from the last two centuries B.C.E., while knowledge of Umbrian is largely restricted to the Iguvine tablets from the 1st cent. B.C.E.

The main categories of Latin inscriptions are (1) laws, treaties, and other public documents (frequently on bronze panels); (2) texts commemorating the construction of a building; (3) inscriptions commemorating individuals (often on a statue base); (4) altars and religious dedications; (5) gravestones; and (6) curse tablets.

Avi-Yonah 1940; Bérard and Feisel 1989; Cook 1987; Gibson 1968; Gordon 1983; Horbury and Noy 1992; Horsley and Lee 1994; Keppie 1991; Lattimore 1962; Oikonomides 1974; Omeltchenko 1977; van der Horse 1991; Woodhead 1981

Integrity, literary, a phrase used to indicate that a particular literary work is the product of a single author and not a compilation consisting of two or more sources that had an originally independent existence.

Intercalation (English designations include "dovetailed narratives" and "sandwiched narratives," while German tags include *Verschachtelung, Schachtelung, Perikopenverschränkung,* and *Schwalbenschwanz-Komposition*) is a literary technique in which a narrative segment is interrupted by the embedding of a second narrative segment (a *Zwischenepisode*) within the first, after which the threads of the first are picked up again, producing an ABA′ pattern of composition (von Dobschütz 1928; Pesch 1976, 1.24; Lambrecht 1967, 33 n. 4). There are often signals at the end of the first part of the outer narrative indicating that it is incomplete.

Intercalations occur at least six times in Mark (Neirynck 1988, 133; Van Oyen 1992; Shepherd 1995): (1) Within the narrative of the coming of Jesus' relatives (3:20–21, 31–35) is inserted an account of the accusation of the scribes that Jesus is possessed and sayings of Jesus on demons (3:22–30). This intercalation is omitted by Matthew, who separated Mark's inner story (12:22–32) from the outer story (12:46–50), and by Luke, who placed the outer story earlier in his narrative (8:19–21) than the inner story (11:14–23). (2) Within the outer account of the raising of Jairus's daughter (5:21–24, 35–43) is inserted the inner account of the healing of the woman with the hemorrhage (5:25–34). This intercalation is retained by Matthew (with 9:20–22 inserted within 9:18–19, 23–26 (much shortened), and Luke (with 8:43–48 inserted into 8:40–42a, 49–55). (3) Within the narrative of the sending out and return of the Twelve (6:7–13, 30–31) is intercalated the narrative of Herod's views of Jesus and the death of John the Baptist (6:14–29). Matthew has a truncated version of inner story of the death of John (14:1–12) but places the narrative of the sending out of the Twelve earlier, making no reference to their return (10:1–14). Luke retains a shortened version of the story of John's imprisonment (9:7–9) intercalated into the story of the sending out and return of the Twelve (9:1–6, 10). (4) Within the story of the cursing of the fig tree (11:12–14, 20–25) is inserted the story of the cleansing of the temple (11:15–19). Matthew arranges Mark's outer story into a single separate anecdote (21:18–22), while Luke omits it entirely. (5) Into the narrative of the conspiracy of the high priests with Judas against Jesus (14:1–2, 10–11), the author intercalates the story of Jesus' anointing at Bethany (14:3–9). (6) Into the narrative of Peter following Jesus to the session of the Sanhedrin and his betrayal of Jesus (14:53–54, 66–72) is inserted the story of Jesus before the Sanhedrin (14:55–65; omitted in Bultmann 1967, 365, but included in Bultmann 1971, 116). This is the only instance in which the outer and inner narrative occur simultaneously (Van Oyen 1992, 967–68). Matthew retains this intercalation, with 26:59–68 inserted into 26:57–75, while Luke reworks the intercalation in a distinctive way by inserting the story of Peter's betrayal (22:54b–62) into the narrative of Jesus being seized and led to the high priest's house (22:54a, 63–71).

Others have suggested other intercalations (e.g., J. R. Edwards 1989). Two of these are miracle stories (Kee 1977, 54–56), the healing of the paralytic (2:1–5a, 10b–12, into which is inserted a *pronouncement story on forgiveness (2:5b–10a), and the healing of the man with the withered arm (3:1–3, 5b–6), into which is placed a saying on healing on the Sabbath (3:4–5a). Moloney (2001, 647–50) argues that Mark 6:14–29 has been intercalated between Mark 6:13 and 6:30. In a more complex analysis, S. G. Brown (2002) argues that Mark 11:1–12:12 contains a triple intercalation: 11:1–11 and 11:15–19 frame 11:12–14, while 11:15–19 and 11:27–12:12 frame 11:20–25.

Literary functions. Intercalation, considered by most scholars as part of the narrative technique of Mark, may function in one of several ways (Van Oyen 1992, 951): (1) to strengthen the chronological link between the inner and outer stories, (2) to connect pericopes thematically by contrast or parallelism, (3) to frame emphases on the suffering and death of Jesus with discipleship material (Donahue 1973, 62), (4) to provide implicit authorial commentary on the text by implicitly directing the reader to read the inner story in light of the outer and vice versa (Fowler 1991, 142–44), (5) to produce a dramatized *irony between the main characters of the two stories and their actions (Shepherd 1995). Irony is clearly present in Mark 14:53–72 (J. R. Edward 1989, 212), where the bold confession of Jesus before the high priest (vv. 55–65) is contrasted with the cowardly denial of Peter in the courtyard outside (vv. 53–54, 66–72). (6) Intercalations reveal redactional insertions of Mark. Achtemeier (1970, 269–79), for example, argues that Mark inserted the story of the hemorrhaging woman into the story of Jairus's daughter. (7) While it is clear that intercalation was a literary technique of Mark, it is also possible that he found this technique in some of the sources he used (Meier 1994, 983 n. 52), such as the story of the raising of Jairus's daughter that frames the healing of the woman with the hemorrhage (Mark 5:21–43) and the cursing of the fig tree into which is inserted the cleansing of the temple (Mark 11:12–25).

Parallels. Within the NT, an analogous literary technique is found twice in Revelation. Revelation 7:1–17 (the description of the 144,000 and the innumerable heavenly host) is intercalated in 6:1–8:1 (the narrative of the opening of the seven seals), while a much longer text (10:1–11:14) is intercalated in 8:2–11:18. Schüssler Fiorenza (1977, 360–66) argues that diagraming or outlining successive sections of Revelation is virtually impossible because the author uses the technique of intercalation (examples referred to above). She regards the author's penchant for intercalation as a key to understanding the structure of the whole book, which she arranges as a sevenfold chiastic structure:

A. 1:1–8
  B. 1:9–3:22
    C. 4:1–9:21; 11:15–19
      D. 10:1–15:4
    C′. 15:1, 5–19:10
  B′. 19:11–22:9
A′. 22:10–22:21

The technique of intercalation is not common outside the NT, though two examples are found in 2 Maccabees: (1) 2 Macc. 8:30–38 (Judas's encounters with the forces of Timothy and Bacchides) is inserted into the story of Nicanor's invasion (2 Macc. 8:12–29, 34–36); (2) 2 Macc. 14:15–17 (the Jewish response to Nicanor's coming) and 14:37–46 (the suicide of Razis), are inserted into 2 Macc. 14:11–15:11 (the escalating conflict between Judas and Nicanor). Downing (2000) has made a relatively extensive search for the phenomenon of intercalation in Greek narrative literature but finds a sort of intercalation only in the Greek romances (e.g., Chariton 1.6, 8–9, intercalated with 1.7, and several episodes not specifically located in Xenophon of Ephesus and Achilles Tatius; Downing 2000, 114–16). Yet none of these examples is comparable to Markan intercalations, for they are simply narrative devices used to described simultaneous (or nearly simultaneous) events which cannot be narrated at the same time. There are some forms of (interlocking) intercalation in the *Testament of Solomon*, where the story of the old man and his son (20:1–21) is inserted between 19:3 and 21:1. An example of an "interlocking intercalation" in the same text is in the letter detailing the problem of the king of Arabia (22:1–5), followed by a mention of the problem of the huge cornerstone (22:6–8), followed by Solomon's solution of the king of Arabia's problem (22:9–15), again followed by the solution of how to move the gigantic cornerstone (22:16–24:5).

*Digression, **Inclusio*, *Interpolation, *Irony, *Mark, Gospel of

---

S. G. Brown 2002; Bultmann 1967, 365; Dobschütz 1928; Donahue 1973, 58–63; Downing 2000; J. Edwards 1989; Kee 1977, 54–56; F. J. Maloney 2001; Neirynck 1988; Schüssler Fiorenza 1977; Shepherd 1995; Van Oyen 1992; von Wahlde 1976

Interior monologue (see *Soliloquy)

Interpolation can be defined as one or more clauses or sentences consisting of "foreign material inserted deliberately and directly into the text of a document" (Walker 2001, 23). A carefully crafted related definition of an interpolation is found in Charlesworth 1977, 303: "Interpolations are insertions into the text that disrupt the flow of thought . . . . They can be removed because of their linguistic structure, which is usually genitival, parenthetical, or otherwise self-contained." According to tradition, Peisistratus interpolated various hexameter lines into the *Odyssey*; Plutarch (*Theseus* 20.2) claims that he inserted line 631 in Book 11 of the *Odyssey*, the so-called Nekyia. Aristarchus of Samothrace (ca. 216–144 B.C.E.), a learned Homeric scholar who became head of the Alexandrian library ca. 153 B.C.E., has frequently been charged with omitting genuine lines of Homer that he thought were interpolations. Apthorp (1980) has argued convincingly that Aristarchus was a conservative scholar who did not omit genuine Homeric lines, but that accidental omission during the post-Aristarchean period is a more plausible hypothesis for the shape of the text in the late Hellenistic period. A famous interpolation in Josephus's *Antiquitates* 18.63–64, the *Testimonium Flavianum* (Rajak 1984, 67, 131 n. 13; Bilde 1988, 22–33; K. A. Olson 1999), is still considered authentic by some scholars (Vicent Cernuda 1997) and as having an authentic core by others (Meier 1990, 1991, 59–69). The **Testaments of the Twelve Patriarchs* are thought by many to be basically Jewish documents that have been interpolated extensively by Christians (Ulrichsen 1991). H. C. Kee argues that *Test. Levi* 10.1–2 and 14.2 are just such Christian interpolations, because they interrupt the flow of thought, contain an idea in tension with the context, and can easily be removed (Charlesworth 1977, 302).

Interpolations in the NT. Numerous passages in the NT have been considered interpolations for various reasons; an extensive list of passages in the Pauline letters regarded by various scholars as interpolations is listed, with bibliographical references, in Walker 2001, 17–20. Walker also presents the most comprehensive discussion of the a priori probability of interpolations in Paul (2001, 26–43; see also Walker 1987; Munro 1990), the absence of relevant text-critical evidence (2001, 44–56), the burden of proof in the identification of interpolations (2001, 57–62), and the kinds of evidence appropriate for arguing for the presence of interpolations in the Pauline letters (2001, 63–90). Walker also presents the possibilities and probabilities of the presence of interpolated passages in the Pauline letters and the kinds of data necessary to demonstrate their presence: (1) Rom. 1:18–2:29 (Walker 2001, 166–89); (2) Rom. 16:25–27 (Walker 2001, 190–99; see also Munro 1990, 441–43); (3) 1 Cor. 11:3–16 (Walker 2001, 91–126); (4) 1 Cor. 2:6–16 (Walker 2001, 127–46); (5) 1 Cor. 13 (Walker 2001, 65); (6) 1 Cor. 14:33b–36, a passage that maintains women should keep silent in church, often considered an interpolation because it seems to contradict 1 Cor. 11:4–5, where women are expected to pray and prophesy publicly (Murphy-O'Connor 1986; R. A. Horsley 1998, 188; Newsom and Ringe 1998, 417–18; Walker 2002, 63–90). This has weak manuscript support, for vv. 34–35 are inserted after v. 40 by some Western witnesses, possibly a scribal attempt to find a more appropriate context for Paul's directive (Metzger 1994, 499–500). (7) Second Corinthians 6:14–7:1 in more recent scholarship has frequently been regarded as genuine and completely appropriate in its present context (Fee 1977; Thrall 1977; Lambrecht 1978; Murphy-O'Connor 1987), while it is also frequently judged a non-Pauline interpolation (Grossouw 1951; Fitzmyer 1961; Gnilka 1968; Walker 2001, 199–209) or even as a fragment derived from Paul's opponents (Betz 1973). There are also other passages in the Pauline letters that are widely regarded as interpolations, particularly 1 Thess. 2:13–15 (Pearson 1971; Boers 1975–76; Schmidt 1983), though Schippers (1966) has argued that 1 Thess. 2:13–16 is "pre-synoptic" tradition which Paul himself has reshaped for its present context.

*Gloss, *Scholia

K. Aland 1967; Apthorp 1980; Boers 1975–76; Bolling 1925; J. Edwards 1989; Kallas 1964–65; Munro 1990; Murphy-O'Connor 1986, 1987; O'Neill 1972, 1975, 1983; Pearson 1971; Schippers 1966; Schmidt 1983; Walker 1987, 2001

Intertextuality defined broadly "assumes that literary discourse is neither original nor particular to a given author, but is dependent on the prior existence both of individual texts and of general literary codes and conventions" (Jardine 1986, 387). Intertextuality accounts for the basic intelligibility of a text in terms of the codes and conventions by which it is read, and it may also play with those conventions through pastiche, plagiarism, imitation, allusion, parody, irony, and citation. Intertextuality can be construed as a theory of reading (Culler 1975, 1981). Each new "text" (oral or written) becomes part of a network of already existing texts by presupposing them in various ways. Though intertextuality is often reduced to a relationship between texts (Pfister 1985), it has also been applied to nonliterary art forms (Allen 2000, 174–81). Even Kristeva tends to restrict intertextuality to identifiable instances, which would resemble the conventional notions of source and influence in literary study. An appropriately flexible approach to intertextuality defines the intertext as anything from a single line in an earlier text, a proverb or cliché, to the general "rules" for an entire genre (Jardine 1986, 388). By the term "intertextuality," coined by Kristeva in 1969 (reprinted in 1986), she meant that "any text is constructed as a mosaic of quotations; any text is the absorption and transformation of another" (1986, 37; on Kristeva, see Bouissac 1998). From the standpoint of intertextuality, a particular text exists only as part of a larger literary tradition, or "canon." That is, a given text is part of a web of relationships including earlier texts that must be known in order fully to understand the focal text. An "intertext" is therefore a semantic or semiotic connection between any source text to a later text within a particular culture's semiotic universe. Kristeva (1984, 60) insists that intertextuality should not be limited to the mere study of sources. The guiding concept is that texts are necessarily written and read in light of the familiarity that both authors and readers have of earlier texts. The writers of texts use a variety of strategies as they write in the light of a circle of texts that they consider significant (Bloom 1973). Intertextuality is not as concerned with identifying the sources of a document as it is with understanding the impact and function of both earlier and contemporary texts on any given text. The numerous similarities between the apocryphal gospels and the canonical Gospels, for example, invite the reader to raise the question of the relationship of these texts to earlier texts. Intertextuality assumes that the "meaning" of a text lies both in its writing and its reading (see *Reader response criticism), i.e., a reader may understand more adequately factors in the communication process of which the author was not fully aware. There is also an implicit relationship between intertextuality and deconstruction (Mai 1991, 31).

Intertextuality in Greek and Roman literature. Students of ancient literature have embraced intertextuality and tried to utilize it in various ways in the interpretation of Greek and Latin texts. Some authors emphasize the tendency of ancient authors, particularly poets, to break with existing models or generic norms in often complex ways (Thomas 1999). Since ancient education focused on the primary texts, and there was a lesser proportion of secondary literature than in modern times, comparing primary texts with other primary texts fostered the awareness of intertextual relations.

Intertextuality in the NT and ECL. Focusing on the genuine Pauline letters, Hays (1989, 15) defines his intentions in the following words: "I propose instead to discuss the phenomenon of intertextuality in Paul's letters in a more limited sense, focusing on his actual citations of and allusions to specific texts. This approach is both possible and fruitful because Paul repeatedly situates his discourse within the symbolic field created by a single great textual precursor: Israel's Scripture." Hays is aware that larger literary entities are part of Paul's intertext, such as Job 13 in Philippians (Hays 1989, 21–24) and Deut. 32 in Romans (1989, 160–64). Hays (1989, 29–32) has suggested some criteria for determining whether allusions (particularly to the OT) are found in NT literature (he focuses on the letters of Paul): (1) *Volume*: What was the volume or the degree of explicit repetitions of words or grammatical patterns? (2) *Recurrence*: How often does the same author refer to the same text elsewhere? (3) *Prominence*: How distinctive or prominent is the precursor text? How much rhetorical stress does the reference receive in the author's discourse? (4) *Dissimilarity*: Are the thoughts in question dissimilar to other influences like Greco-Roman thought or Jesus traditions? Can the passage be distinguished from other Scripture texts? (5) *History of interpretation*: Have other reasons seen a reference to the particular text? (6) *Thematic coherence*: How well does the supposed primary text fit into the line of argument that the author develops? Does it illuminate the surrounding discourse?

Hays has been criticized for his focus on the intertextual echoes of Israel's Scripture in Paul, since this is a reduction of the broader sociocultural concerns of intertextuality. W. Green (1993, 59) accuses Hays of using "a minimalist notion of intertextuality." Other critics have observed than OT texts are always implicitly understood on the basis of later interpretive perspectives (Evans 1993). Yet surely a critic should be allowed to probe one significant aspect of the spectrum of intertextual possibilities.

*Architextuality, *Paratexts, *Quotations, *Testimonia, *Testimony book hypothesis, *Transtextuality

———

Aune 1991e; Boyarin 1990; Evans and Sanders 1993; Hatina 1999; Hays 1989; Hollander 1981; Jardine 1986; Mai 1991; Pfister 1985; Plett, 1991a, 1991b; Thomas 1999; Voelz 1995; Vorster 1989; Wolde 1989; Worton 1990

***Inventio*/invention** is the first of five parts of the duties of an orator that focuses on finding and elaborating arguments and whether the argument should be epideictic, deliberative, or juridical.

*Arrangement *Rhetorical theory

———

Heath 1997; Lanham 1991, 91–92; Lausberg 1998, 119–208

Irenaeus (ca. 130–202 C.E.), bishop of Lyons (ca. 178–202), a native of Asia Minor, spent some of his youth in Smyrna, where he became acquainted with *Polycarp, whence he moved to Gaul to assume leadership of the Christian community of Lyons (Lugdunum).

Writings. Only two complete works of Irenaeus survive: His extensive critique of Gnosticism entitled Ἔλεγχος καὶ ἀνατροπητῆς ψευδονόμου γνώσεως, "Exposé and Overthrow of What Is Falsely Called Knowledge," known as *Adversus haereses* or "Against Heresies." This work is partially extant in the original Greek, but complete in a Latin translation. A shorter work has also survived, entitled Ἐπιδείξις τοῦ ἀποστολικοῦ κηρύγματος, or "Proof of the Apostolic Preaching." Extant only in Armenian, this work is primarily catechetical, and therefore scholarship on Irenaeus generally has focused on the *Adversus Haereses*. References to Irenaeus's lost works can be found in Eusebius, *Hist. Eccl.* 5.20.1, 5.23.3, 5.24.11–17, and 5.26 (Quaesten 1950–60, 1.293). Modern critical editions of these works, with a facing French translation, are available in Rousseau, Doutreleau, and Mercer 1965–82, and Rousseau 1995. English translations are available in J. P. Smith 1952 and Unger and Dillon 1992. A comparatively recent French translation of *Adversus haereses* is available in Rousseau 1984, while recent German translations of *Adversus haereses* and *Epideixis* are those of Brox 1993, 2001.

Genre of Adversus haereses. Irenaeus called his major work an ἔλεγχος or "refutation" (Donovan 1984, 226–27; Reynders 1935, 6); it is comparable to other classical works that designate themselves as Ἔλεγχοι. Although the work is much longer than a speech, its organization and style follows typical Hellenistic rhetorical conventions for arguing a point in public debate or in court (Reynders 1935, Grant 1949, Perkins 1976, Schoedel 1959, Donovan 1984, 226–27, Overbeck 1995, 72–76). Within Christian generic categories, *Adv. haer.* is our first extant example of a "heresiology," since an earlier one, Justin's *Syntagma*, is lost (Vallée 1981, 5). As such, it had significant influence on the development of the genre.

Overview of Adversus haereses. Irenaeus wrote *Adv. haer.* ca. 180 C.E. to combat the rise of Gnosticism, particularly Valentinianism, not only in Gaul but throughout the Roman world. The work consists of five books. Book 1 gives an exposition of Gnostic doctrines as understood by Irenaeus. Book 2 consists of a refutation of these doctrines mostly through rational argumentation. In book 3, he begins a systematic attempt to marshal the testimony of the OT against gnostic teaching. Books 4 and 5 refute Gnosticism using the words of Christ, book 4 from the parables of Jesus and book 5 from his direct statements.

Structure of Adversus haereses. In the early 20th cent., strongly influenced by source-critical concerns (see *source criticism), scholars criticized Irenaeus for an apparent lack of organization and clarity of argument throughout his work (Harnack 1907a; Bousset 1915; Loofs 1930; Benoît 1960; Widmann 1957). *Adversus haereses* became longer than Irenaeus originally anticipated (*Adv. haer.* 3.12.9; Minns 1994, 6–7). This may account for the apparent lack of clear structure and progression of thought. Until the work of Bacq (1978), Irenaeus was often judged a mediocre thinker and an inept editor rather than an author. Recent scholarship has been more generous in its assessment of his work. Several scholars have demonstrated that *Adv. haer.* does, in fact, follow the structural scheme outlined in Hellenistic books of rhetoric for a speech, suitable for the legal court (Overbeck 1995, 74). Such speeches consist of an **exordium* (*Adv. haer.* 1. praef. 1–3), **narratio* (*Adv. haer.* 1.1–9), **divisio* (*Adv. haer.* 1.10.1–3), and an **argumentatio* (*Adv. haer.* books 2–5), which includes a **refutatio* (*Adv. haer.* 2) followed by a **confirmatio* (*Adv. haer.* 3–5) (Overbeck 1995, 72–75; cf. Reynders 1935, 5; Schoedel 1959, 27–28; Vallée 1980, 175–76). The only element missing is the final **peroratio*, which Irenaeus may have felt was unnecessary or which he lacked the time and energy to complete. Within the *argumentatio* (*Adv. haer.* 2–4), the author follows the rhetorical practice of progressing from weaker to stronger arguments (κατὰ αὔξησιν; see Theon, *Progymn.* 12; Schoedel 1959, 28). Thus, he first refutes the gnostics by reason, then by the words of Scripture, then by the words of Christ himself (Overbeck 1995, 74; Vallée 1980, 176). *Adversus haereses* 4 was frequently considered the best example of Irenaeus's disorganization of thought and poor editing of sources until the monograph by Bacq (1978) demonstrated that even this book has structure and system. Irenaeus follows a consistent sequential literary pattern: an *announcement* of a saying of Christ, a *citation* of the saying, and a *commentary* on it (cf. Donovan 1984, 222–23; 1997, 15). The pattern holds, even though elements of it may be as short as a paragraph or as long as a chapter. Moreover, the cited sayings of Christ are not chosen randomly but are linked by themes or keywords. The resulting composition has been described as forming "concentric circles" (Bacq 1978, 41–47) or *chiasmus (Donovan 1997, 17). Bacq's work has effectively demonstrated the literary and theological unity of *Adv. haer.* 4. Other recent works have done the same with *Adv. haer.* 1 (Perkins 1976) and *Adv. haer.* 5 (Overbeck 1995).

Style of Adversus haereses. At the beginning of the book, Irenaeus apologizes for his lack of literary and rhetorical skill, offering the excuse that he has been living among "barbarians" (Celts) for some time (1. Praef. 2–3). This statement has been variously evaluated in the course of scholarship. Under the influence of source critics (e.g., Harnack 1907; Bousset 1915) who disputed the unity and authorship of the work, scholars were inclined to agree with Irenaeus's self-evaluation. Recent scholarship, however, has been more sympathetic to Irenaeus. While no master of Greek rhetoric, his penchant for long and well-balanced sentences suggests more than an elementary education (Minns 1994, 6). However, such an apology for lack of rhetorical competence is itself a rhetorical cliché with parallels in Plato, *Apology* 17b; Lysias 19.1.2; Isaeus 10.1; and Hermogenes, *Id.* 2.6 (Grant 1997, 47; Schoedel 1959, 27). In fact, Irenaeus had enough rhetorical training that it influenced his theology: three of his key theological terms, ὑπόθεσις, οἰκονομία, and ἀνακεφαλαίωσις, are rhetorical terms. ὑπόθεσις referred to the plot of a play or narrative; οἰκονομία to its arrangement, and ἀνακεφαλαίωσις to a summary of it (Grant 1997, 47–53). Irenaeus applies these terms to aspects of the history of redemption. Within *Adv. haer.*, Irenaeus makes use of the standard dilemma, the (rhetorical) question, and the ad hominem technique, but also the syllogism (*Adv. haer.* 5.23.2, 32.2, cf. Overbeck 1995; 74, Orbe 1987; 485, idem 1988; 371, *pace* Reynders 1935; 8), the *enthymeme or ἐθύμημα (partially expressed syllogism), the ἐπιχείρημα (a fully expressed rhetorical syllogism e.g., *Adv. haer.* II 19.4), and the παράδειμα ("example," e.g. *Adv. haer.* III 25.5) (Schoedel 1959, 28–31). These and other examples, such as his use of irony and sarcasm (*Adv. haer.* 1.4.3–4; 1.11.4; 2.10.2), demonstrate that Irenaeus had adequate rhetorical training (Schoedel 1959, 27–32, Reynders 1935, Grant 1949, 47–51, Perkins 1976, 195–200).

Sources of Adversus haereses. Irenaeus was very familiar with the OT, though only in Greek translation. The form of his quotations often differs from the LXX, however, which has been cited by many scholars as evidence for his use of written *testimonia collections (Benoît 1960, 74–102). He was also familiar with the NT (Sanday and Turner 1923), citing from all the books of the NT except James, Jude, and 3 John. Irenaeus made significant and extensive use of the Pauline letters (Werner 1889; Balás 1992), the Johannine letters (Ferlay 1984), and the Gospel of Matthew (Bingham 1998). He was the first Christian writer to discuss the Gospels as a fourfold collection (Stanton 1999, 319–22; Blanchard 1993). He accepts the *Pastoral Letters, 1 *Peter, and *Revelation as apostolic, but disputes the Pauline authorship of Hebrews (Grant 1997, 34; Benoît 1960, 103–47). He also knows the works of *Papias, *Polycarp, Clement of Rome (see **Clement, First Letter of*), Hermas (see *Shepherd of Hermas), and *Justin Martyr (Grant 1997, 35–40; Benoît 1960, 15–27).

Relation to Justin. Irenaeus's relationship to Justin is particularly significant and has been much discussed in connection with the *testimonia hypothesis. Similarly, the choice and wording of scriptural proof texts in both Justin and Irenaeus suggest that they may have been dependent on a common testimonia collection (Starratt 1952, 101–7, 114–49; Prigent 1961, 183–88; Albl 1999, 112–14). Irenaeus takes over Justin's notion that the gnostic heresy began with Simon and Menander. Besides the *Apology*, Irenaeus knew Justin's now-lost *Syntagma*, "Against All Heresies" (Vallée 1981, 6, 9) and a polemical work against Marcion (Grant 1997, 39–40). However, the precise extent of Irenaeus's dependence on Justin is disputed (see Perkins 1976, 197–99). It is certain that Irenaeus had some gnostic texts at his disposal, but their identity and extent are difficult to determine. Irenaeus and the gnostic texts from Nag Hammadi portray the gnostic movement somewhat differently from each other, and the extent of these differences and how to account for them are debated (cf. Pagels 1974, Grant 1977, Donovan 1984, 226–27, Perkins 1976, Wisse 1971). Irenaeus had a good but not extensive knowledge of classical sources. In his use of philosophical sources, he was limited to what would have been available in contemporary *doxographies and philosophical handbooks. He shows evidence of particular dependence on the doxography of Ps.-Plutarch (Grant 1949, 43ff, Schoedel 1959, 23). In other classical literature, Irenaeus demonstrates some competence in Homer (e.g., *Adv. haer.* 1.9.4), knowledge of Aesop (*Adv. haer.* 2.11.1), and acquaintance with Hesiod (2.14.4, 21.2), Menander (2.18.5), Sophocles (5.13.2), Pindar (2.21.2), and Stesichorus (1.23.2) (Grant 1949, 48–49). The discovery of the remains of an elegant book roll of *Adv. haer.* in upper Egypt from the late 2d cent. indicates that *Adv. haer.* was well and widely received by churches around the Mediterranean within Irenaeus's lifetime. As a pioneer in the genre of heresiology, his work had a strong influence on Hippolytus's *Refutatio omnium haeresium* and Epiphanius of Salamis's *Panarion* (Vallée 1981, 1–8). It is mostly to the *Adv. haer.* that Irenaeus owes his subsequent reputation in the early church. He is praised for his wide knowledge, proximity to the apostles, and skill in refuting false doctrine by Tertullian (*Val.* 5), Eusebius (*Hist. Eccl.* 4.11.3), Augustine (*C. Jul.* 1.5 and elsewhere), and Basilius (*Spir.* 72). After the 4th cent., however, Irenaeus was eclipsed by Augustine in the West and by Clement of Alexandria and many others in the East. In the medieval period his work was neglected, perhaps because of his millenarian eschatological views, which were then considered suspect.

Epideixis. The *Epideixis*, known only from an Armenian translation of the 5th–6th cent., is a relatively short treatise addressed to a friend—but certainly intended for wider readership—aiming to give a concise and orderly summary of essential Christian doctrines with scriptural proofs. While not an exhaustive exposition of doctrine, it does focus on beliefs that the gnostics reject or distort. The treatise progresses in an orderly fashion, covering God, creation, and fall (1–16), the history of salvation (17–42), the presence of Christ in the old covenant (42–85), and Christ's establishment of the new covenant (86–100).

Genre of the Epideixis. The work is set in the form of a letter—as indeed is the *Adv. haer.*—but this is a literary device, and epistolary form is not reflected in the structure of the work. It has been called a "compendium" of theology (Weber 1912, xiv), a "catechism" (Harnack 1907b, 55, Drews 1907, 226–33), an "apologetic work" (Bardenhewer 1913–32, 1.411), and a "manual of theology" (Smith 1952, 21–22). The closest analogues to the *Epideixis* may be the **Constitutiones apostolicae* and Augustine's *De catechizandis rudibus*, supporting the classification "catechism" or "catechetical work" (Drews 1907, 226–33, Sagarda 1907, 487). Accordingly, this may be the best categorization (Albl 1999, 116). Irenaeus's sources for the *Epideixis* are largely the same as those mentioned for *Adv. haer.* Evidence for Irenaeus's dependence on Justin and testimonia collections are even stronger in *Epideixis* than in *Adv. haer.* (Smith 1952, 31–34, Albl 1999, 114–18) (see *Testimonia). The *Epideixis* provides little other literary or theological information about Irenaeus or early Christianity not already available in *Adv. Haer.* For this reason the work has been relatively neglected throughout church history, as the scarcity of manuscript witnesses attests.

*Justin Martyr

Bacq 1978; Bardenhewer 1913–32; Benoît 1960; Blanchard 1993; Bousset 1915; Donovan 1984, 1997; Drews 1907; Grant 1949, 1986, 1997; Harnack 1907a, 1907b; Lawson 1948; Loofs 1930; Minns 1994; Nielsen 1968; Overbeck 1995; Perkins 1976; Quasten 1950–60, 1.287–313; Reynders 1935; Sanday and Turner 1923; Schoedel 1959; Stanton 1999; Starratt 1952; Vallée 1981; Weber 1912; Widman 1957; Wingren 1959

JON BERGSMA

Irony, a transliterated form of the Latin word *ironia*, based on the Greek loanword εἰρωνεία, is a rhetorical *trope defined in the *Rhet. Alex.* 1434 in the following way: "Irony is saying something while pretending not to say it, or calling things by the opposite of their real names." A similar definition is offered by Quintilian: "Irony (*ironia*) is that figure of speech or trope in which something contrary to what is said is to be understood" (*Inst.* 9.22.44; cf. 6.2.15; 8.6.54); i.e., irony is saying something we mean by saying something contrary to it. The Greek term εἰρωνεία was used to denote sly, deceptive speech or conduct during the 5th and 4th cent. B.C., saying one thing and meaning another, though in irony the intended meaning is not necessarily the opposite of its apparent meaning, just different from its apparent meaning (Holland 1997, 235). In **Rhetorica ad Alexandrum* 21 (see *Rhetorical handbooks), εἰρωνεία is defined as "saying something while pretending not to say it or calling things by contrary names." Of the two cognates of εἰρωνεία, the verb εἰρωνεύομαι and the noun εἴρων, the latter is a term of abuse, meaning "dissembler, liar, deceiver, imposter" (Plato, *Phaedrus* 268a–b; Demosthenes, *1 Phil.* 7). Socrates was famous in antiquity for his use of irony, particularly in his disavowal of knowledge and teaching (Plato, *Apology* 21B–D; *Symp.* 216E, 218D; *Gorgias* 508E–509A; Aristotle, *Soph. El.* 183b; Aelius Aristides, *Orationes* 45.2; Cicero, *Acad.* 1.4.16; Plutarch, *Adv. Colotes* 1117D). Examples: (1) Eumaeios the swineherd to Odysseus in *Odyssey* 14.402: "Good repute and virtue I would have among men, if I were to kill you" (he means just the opposite). (2) 2 Cor. 11:8: "I robbed other churches by accepting support from them in order to serve you." Irony is frequently linked with *litotes* and exaggeration, i.e., with saying either less or more than what is actually meant. In 1 Cor. 4:8–13, Paul uses irony to contrast the "richness" of the Corinthians with the "wretchedness" of the apostles (Plank 1987, 44–62). The use of irony is evident in 1 Cor. 4:8, where the second sentence indicates that the first sentence cannot be taken at face value (Plank 1987, 45): "Without us you become kings! And would that you did reign!" 1 Cor. 4:10–13 contains a series of ironic antitheses in which Paul contrasts the blameworthy behavior of the Corinthians with the exemplary behavior of the apostles (Mitchell 1993, 220–21); 1 Cor. 4:10 is a sample of this section: "We are fools for Christ's sake, while you are sensible Christians! We are weak; you are powerful! You are honored; we are in disgrace!" Betz characterizes the *exordium* in Gal. 1:6–11 as "ironic and polemical" but does not further discuss Paul's use of rhetorical irony in this passage (1979, 46). Paul's use of the well-known term "gospel" (Gal. 1:7) to describe that "which is another gospel" (Gal. 1:6) but which in actually "is not another [gospel]" is a clear example of irony recognized by John

Chrysostom (Nikolakopoulos 2001, 200–201). Nannos (2002) argues that in this passage Paul is using the established rhetorical form of the "ironic rebuke." What Paul is really saying here, according to Nannos, is that Paul is neither "amazed," nor is it really a "gospel" to which the readers have been attracted. Again, in Gal. 2:6 the participle οἱ δοκοῦντες, "those who suppose" (see Gal. 6:3; 1 Cor. 10:12), is used in a kind of doubly ironical way, i.e., Paul actually meant the phrase ironically, but it is possible to read it in a nonironical sense (Nikolakopoulos 2001, 202–4); this "double irony" is also used elsewhere by Paul (1 Cor. 8:1; Gal. 5:15; Phil. 3:2). A third example of irony in Galatians is found in 5:11: "But if I, brethren, still preach circumcision, why am I still persecuted?" (Jónsson 1965, 267). Finally, in Gal. 5:12, Paul moves from the light irony of 5:11 to hard irony or sarcasm (Schlier 1962, 240; Betz 1979, 270; Longenecker 1990, 234; Nikolakopoulos 2001, 204–6): "I wish those who unsettle you would castrate themselves" (note the controversy of the Judaizing introduction of circumcision in the context).

*Sarcasm

Bergson 1971; Camery-Hoggatt 1992; Canter 1936; Duke 1985; Holland 1993, 1997; Jónsson 1965; Kierkegaard 1965; Lausberg 1998, §§582–85, 902–4; Muecke 1969; Nikolakopoulos 2001; Plank 1987; Van Oyen 1992; Vlastos 1991, 21–44

Isocolon, a transliteration of the Greek word ἰσόκωλος (Latin *conpar*), is two or more united cola that contain an almost equal number of syllables (*Rhetorica ad Herennium* 4.20.27).

Isocrates (see *Orators, Attic)

Itacism, or iotacism, a term derived from the Greek word ἰοτακισμός (meaning the doubling of ι, or the excessive use of ι), transliterated into late Latin as *iotacismus*, is used in Greek phonology and *textual criticism for the confusion between the sounds of seven different Greek vowels or diphthongs that all came to sound like iota, and for the erroneous substitution of one for the other in written manuscripts. In late Koine Greek (through to modern Greek), the vowels ι, η, and υ, as well as the diphthongs ει, οι, υι, and the improper diphthong ῃ, came to be all pronounced ē (as in the English words "be," "see," "eel"). Some examples (Metzger 1992, 191–92): (1) In Rev. 4:3, the ἶρις ("rainbow") which surrounds the throne was written ἱερεῖς ("priests") in two important Greek manuscripts, Alexandrinus (**A**) and Sinaiticus (**א**). (2) The term νῖκος ("victory") in 1 Cor. 15:54 is written as νεῖκος in several manuscripts. (3) In 2 Thess. 2:14, the phrase "he called you [ὑμᾶς]" is changed to "he called us [ἡμᾶς]" in the important manuscripts Alexandrinus (**A**) and Vaticanus (**B**).

*Etacism, *Textual criticism

Metzger 1992, 191–92

Itinerary is a literary genre consisting of a list of stopping places on a journey, often with mention of the intervening distances. The use of a written itinerary is one way of accounting for the so-called *"we"-passages in Acts (16:10–17; 20:5–15; 21:1–18; 27:1–28:16; cf. 11:28 in the Western text).

*"We"-passages

Norden 1956, 311–32; *OCD*[3], 775, 1141–42; Praeder 1984; Reumann 1989; Robbins 1975; Schille 1959

James, Letter of, one of a group of seven *General Epistles, or Catholic Epistles, so designated because of the general nature of their *adscriptiones* or intended recipients. James is addressed "to the twelve tribes in the Dispersion" (1:1). James is frequently regarded as pseudepigraphical and therefore dated relatively late in the 1st cent. C.E.

Authorship and date. James claims to have been written by "James, a servant of God and of the Lord Jesus Christ" (James 1:1), using the kind of slave epithet occasionally found in NT letters (Rom. 1:1a; Phil. 1:1a; Titus 1:1; 2 Pet. 1:1; Jude 1). There are two prominent figures named "James" in the NT, James the son of Zebedee (who was executed in 44 C.E., according to Acts 12:2) and James the brother of Jesus (who was lynched ca. 62 C.E. according to Hegesippus in Eusebius, *Hist. eccl.* 2.23; cf. Josephus, *Ant.* 20.9). A third James the son of Alphaeus, is also listed among the disciples of Jesus (Mark 3:17–18). The relatively high linguistic register of James has led some to conclude that the historical James (the brother of Jesus), a Palestinian Christian, could not be the author (Thyen 1955, 14). For a review of arguments that focus on the language issue, see Sevenster 1968, 4–21, who concludes (1968, 191): "the possibility can no longer be precluded that a Palestinian Jewish Christian of the first century A.D. wrote an epistle in good Greek."

If James was in fact written by James the Just, then the letter must be dated before his martyrdom. Moo (2000, 9–22, 25–27) argues that James was written by James the brother of the Lord in the mid-40s of the 1st cent. C.E., i.e., that it is the earliest surviving work in the NT (see Byrskog 2000, 167–75). Nevertheless, most critical scholars hold that James is a pseudepigraphic letter written during the latter part of the 1st cent. C.E..

Language and style. The Greek of James is generally recognized to be of a higher linguistic register than other NT books, with the exception of Hebrews. The language of James is not the language of ordinary speech (Wifstrand 1947, 175), i.e., it is neither common language nor a literary language but, rather, Koine Greek as it was written by people with some education; i.e., the stylistic home of James as of 1 Peter is "[t]he edifying language of the hellenized synagogue" (Wifstrand 1947, 180).

Epistolary analysis. James begins with a three-part epistolary prescript (1:1): (1) *superscriptio*: "James, servant of God and of the Lord Jesus Christ," (2) *adscriptio*: "to the twelve tribes in the Diaspora," and (3) *salutatio*: "greeting." The salutation, χαίρειν ("greetings") is the conventional Greek epistolary salutation but is found in the NT elsewhere only in two embedded letters in Acts (15:23; 23:26).

Francis (1970), responding to the claim of Dibelius that the epistolary prescript James lacks all the typical features of a letter, argues that the opening section (James 1:2–27) presents such themes as testing, steadfastness, perfect work or gift, reproaching, anger, wisdom/words, and rich-poor/doer, themes which are subsequently developed in the body of the letter. After a consideration of parallels, primarily in literary letters in Jewish sources, Francis (1970) argues that the opening period of James (vv. 2–21) has a twofold epistolary structure. The first part (vv. 2–11) is headed by the epistolary-liturgical term "joy," while the second part (vv. 12–21) is headed by the technical liturgical-epistolary term "blessed." In each part, the same three elements are introduced in the same order: (1) testing or steadfastness (vv. 2–4, 12–18), (2) wisdom-words/reproaching (vv. 5–8, 19–21), (3) rich-poor/doers (vv. 9–11, 22–25). A recapitulation, vv. 26–27, then closes this part. However, Francis has massaged parts two and three in both sections with the use of hyphenations, for the themes dealt with are in fact not the same in both parts.

Francis then argues that the material in James 2 constitutes a two-part diatribe, citing Dibelius (1964, 14). However Dibelius (1964, 14; 1975, 1, 124–25) argues that 2:1–3:12 consists of three expositions or treatises, each in the form of a diatribe. The three "treatises" Dibelius identifies are (1) 2:1–13, (2) 2:14–26, (3) 3:1–12. Francis then maintains that the remaining material in the body of the letter (3:1–5:6) is closely related to James 2. The final section of James, 5:7–20, is entitled "Closing admonitions" by Francis, who does not adduce arguments supporting this division, even though he specifically designates this section as "a recognizable epistolary close" (1970, 126).

Literary structure. Dibelius (1975, 2) is often castigated for claiming about James that "the entire document lacks continuity in thought," i.e., "the letter has no coherence of any sort." This view is essentially accepted by Moo (2000, 7), who observes that the body of the "letter" (1:2–5:20) is difficult to analyze, for it has no obvious structure or even a clearly defined theme. The opposite view, namely the coherence of James, is emphasized by Bauckham (1999, 63), who provides a simple analysis of the structure of James that hardly demonstrates its coherence: A. Prescript (1:1), B. Introduction (1:2–27), C. Exposition (2:1–5:20).

Genre. The fact that James begins like a letter does not mean that the question of genre is exhausted with the recognition of epistolary form, which may be used to frame very different kinds of literary genres. The very general character of the adscription, "to the twelve tribes in the Dispersion" (James 1:1), suggests that indications of a specific epistolary situation are missing precisely because the letter introduces a treatise or homily intended for anyone who reads it (Ropes 1916, 6). While a real letter is a substitute for conversation, the letter of James has a literary character that distances it from an instrument of personal communication.

Yet despite the absence of a clear indication of the historical situation to which James was directed, and despite the general nature of the audience, the author addresses his readers or hearers eleven times as "my brothers" (1:2, 16, 19; 2:1, 5, 14; 3:1, 10, 12; 5:12, 19), and four times as "brothers" (4:11; 5:7, 9, 10). In one instance he says, "Listen, my beloved brethren" (2:5). This is one of the reasons that James has often been characterized as a sermon or *homily (Baasland 1988, 3650–51; Moo 2000, 8–9), though this is problematic because the genre "homily" or "sermon" is a vague term. Baasland (1988, 3654) summarizes his detailed discussion of the genre of James as follows:

> Our results can be summarized in the following way: James is a written, protreptic, sapiental letter for the purpose of oral performance. The speech originated in diatribe instruction (perhaps in an academy) and was published in order to be read aloud in the (liturgical) assembly of the community. As an address to a community, who had a Hellenistic education, the work was constructed in accordance with rhetorical patterns. . . .

James has often been labeled "paraenesis" since the work of Dibelius (Mussner 1964, 23–24). Dibelius (1975, 3) identified James as paraenesis, i.e., "a text which strings together admonitions of general ethical content." The view that James is essentially paraenetic has been widely influential (Perdue 1981). Dibelius identified four characteristics of *paraenesis: (1) a focus on exhortation, (2) a general rather than a specific situation, (3) the use of traditional material, (4) loose organization. He further defined nine textual units in James: (1) 1:1, (2) 1:2–18, (3) 1:19–27, (4) 2:1–13, (5) 2:14–26, (6) 3:1–12, (7) 3:13–4:12, (8) 4:13–5:6, (9) 5:7–20. Some of these belong to clusters, such as the three expositions or treatises in 2:1–3:12 (each begins with an admonition or a rhetorical question that contains an admonition followed by an elaboration of that admonition) and the five series of sayings in 1:2–27 and 3:13–5:20. Berger (1984, 147), however, argued that the presence of invective (4:1–4 and 5:1–6), diatribe (2:14–26), and ekphrasis (3:1–12) does not fit the general designation of paraenesis. The paraenetic letter-type is described in some detail by Ps.-Libanius, *Characteres epistolici* 5:

> The paraenetic style is that in which we give someone paraenesis, persuading him to pursue something or avoid something. Paraenesis is divided into two parts, i.e., persuasion and dissuasion. . . . Paraenesis is paraenetic speech that does not admit a counter-statement. Thus, if someone should say, 'We must honor the divine,' no one contradicts this paraenesis, unless he is insane in the first place.

The paraenetic or hortatory character of James is revealed by the fact that it has the highest percentage of imperative verbs of any book in the NT, 58 in 108 verses (Baasland 1988, 3651).

The presence of *diatribe style in James has frequently been recognized. Ropes (1916, 10–16) described the whole of James as a diatribe (Ropes 1916), a view that Wifstrand (1947, 178) regards as a "grotesque overstatement." Dibelius identified 2:1–3:12 as the core of the letter, composed of three expositions or treatises written in the style of diatribe (Dibelius 1975, 1; see his identification of various diatribe features in this section in 1975, 124–206). The dialogical feature of the *diatribe includes questions like "Someone will say" (James 2:18) and the frequent use of rhetorical questions, often for emphasis, as in James 2:14–16, 20–21: "What does it profit, my brethren, if a man says he has faith but has not works? Can his faith save him? . . . What does it profit? . . . Do you want to be shown, you foolish fellow, that faith apart from works is barren? Was not Abraham our father justified by works, when he offered his son Isaac upon the altar?"

James, written "to the twelve tribes in the Dispersion" (1:1), has the character of an "open letter," similar to Acts 15:23–29, 1 Peter, Jude, 2 Peter, Revelation, *1 Clement*, and the *Martyrdom of Polycarp* (Tsuji 1997, 28–37). Niebuhr (1998) situates James in the generic context of early Jewish Diaspora letters, all of which were originally written in Greek and directed to Greek-speaking Jews in the Diaspora with the purpose of strengthening the identity of the addressees as members of the people of God: (1) the letter of Jeremiah to the elders and priests of the exile (Jer. 29; LXX 36); (2) the letters to the Jews in Egypt inserted by the epitomist in 2 Macc. 1:1–9, and 1:10–2:18, which both have epistolary openings but lack epistolary closings; (3) the letter of Baruch to the nine and one-half, tribes on the other side of the great river (*2 Bar.* 78–86), in which the address "my brothers" occurs several times (78:3; 79:1; 80:1, 4; 82:1); (4) the letter of Baruch from Jerusalem to the Babylonian exile in the *Paralipomena Jeremiae* 6.17–23).

There has also been the widespread view that James lacks compositional unity (Ropes 1916, 14). More recently, Johnson (1995, 16–24) has argued that James is a literarily coherent composition, written in correct Koine Greek with significant rhetorical features, that should be considered a *protreptic discourse in the form of a *letter.

Rhetorical analysis. James has not been the focus of much rhetorical analysis, despite the obvious micro-rhetorical features in the text. Berger regards James as a deliberative work (1984, 147). Two macro-rhetorical analyses, those of Wuellner (1978) and Baasland (1988), are compared in the following table:

Synopsis of Rhetorical Analyses of James

Arrangement	Wuellner 1978	Baasland 1988
Epistolary prescript	[1:1]	[1:1]
Exordium	1:2–4	1:2–15
Narratio	1:5–6	
Transitus		1:16–18
Propositio	1:12	1:19–27
Argumentatio	1:13–5:6	2:1–5:6
Peroratio	5:7–20	5:7–20

In this comparison, it is striking that Wuellner and Baasland agree only on the extent of the *peroratio*, though their *argumentatio* or *probatio* sections agree to a great extent.

Use of sources. James quotes or alludes to the OT rarely. There are just four explicit citations of the OT in James (Chaine 1927, lxi): (1) 2:8 (Lev. 19:18 according to the LXX); (2) 2:23 (Gen. 15:6, probably according to the LXX); (3) 4:6 (Prov. 3:34 according to the LXX; 4:5–6); (4) 5:20 (Prov. 10:12 according to the Hebrew). Three of these citations refer to the OT as γραφή, "Scripture" (2:8, 23; 4:5–6). There are, in addition, several allusions to the OT (Chaine 1927, lxi): (1) 1:10–11 (Isa. 40:6–7 according to the LXX); (2) 2:7 (Amos 9:12 according to the LXX); (3) 3:8 (Ps. 149 [MT 150]: 4 according to the LXX); (4) 5:4 (Isa. 5:8 according to the LXX). There are other possible allusions to the OT, but they are vague and uncertain (Chain 1927, lxi–lxii). The author of James also used OT figures as religious and moral paradigms, including Abraham (2:21–23), Rahab (2:25), the prophets (5:10), Job (5:11), and Elijah (5:17), all as interpreted by Jewish haggadah (Davids 1978; Bauckham 1988d, 306–8). On the Akedah (binding of Isaac) in James 2:21–23, see Jacobs 1975–76.

James has often been linked to sapiential traditions (Baasland 1982). James 1:19 contains the admonition "Let every one be quick to hear, slow to speak, slow to anger." This is a topos from Jewish Wisdom literature (Sir. 5:13; Eccl. 5:1, 7, 9; *Pirke Abot* 5.12).

Allusions to the Jesus traditions have frequently been identified in James, but without the use of quotation formulas. Byrskog (2000, 167–75) regards the author as James the brother of Jesus, and as a valuable transmitter of eyewitness oral tradition. A number of allusions to Matthew, particularly the Sermon on the Mount and the Q tradition, have been suggested: (1) 1:2–4, perfection (Matt. 5:48); (2) 1:5, ask for wisdom (Matt. 7:7); (3) 1:6, pray without doubting (Matt. 11:23–24); (4) 1:22, 25–26, love command, question of the law (Matt. 5:16–20; cf. Luke 16:17); (5) 2:5, kingdom of God is for the poor (Matt. 5:3; Luke 6:20–21); (6) 2:6–7, being dishonored (Matt. 5:11; Luke 6:22); (7) 3:13–18, wisdom from God (Matt. 11:25–26; Luke 10:21); (8) 3:18, humble behavior (Matt. 5:5, 7–9); (9) 4:12, do not judge (Matt. 7:1); (10) 5:12, swearing forbidden (Matt. 5:33–37); (11) 5:17, prayer of a righteous person (Matt. 5:34–37). Twenty-seven allusions to the Jesus tradition in the Gospels are listed by Mussner 1964, 48–50. Hartin (1991) has argued that the author of James used a Matthaean redaction of the Q document, while Shepherd (1956) argues that the author was directly dependent on Matthew. Both views are extremely doubtful.

*Diatribe, *Epistolography, *General Epistles, *Rhetorical criticism

Baasland 1982, 1988; Bauckham 1988d; 1999; Cantinat 1973; Cargal 1992; Chaine 1927; Davids 1978, 1982; Dibelius 1964, 1975; Francis 1970; Hartin 1991; I. Jacobs 1975–76; Johnson 1983, 1995; Moo 1985, 2000; Mussner 1964; Niebuhr 1998; Perdue 1981; Popkes 1986; Ropes 1916; Shepherd 1956; Sleeper 1998; Terry 1992; Tsuji 1997; Verseput 2000; Wachob 2000; Wall 1990, 1997; Watson 1993a, 1993c; Wifstrand 1947; Wuellner 1978; von Lips 1990, 409–38

John, First Letter of, the longest of the group of three short "letters" called the *"Johannine letters," has closer linguistic, literary, and conceptual links to the Gospel of John than the other letters in the corpus. The authorship, date, and provenance of 1 John are all problematic issues. The problem of genre is also a matter of debate.

Historical setting. The circumstances behind 1 John seem to involve a schism within a Christian community: the author speaks of those who "went out from us" and who did not really "belong to us" (2:19). Moreover, accusations are made against them: of "hating a brother" (2:9; 4:20) and of attempting to deceive the community (2:26; 3:7). The author also seems to label the same persons as "antichrists" (2:18), "liars" (4:20), "children of the devil" (3:10), and as "murderers" (3:15). Evidently, one major issue centered on whether or not Jesus Christ had come in the flesh (4:2), as well as on the significance of his baptism and crucifixion (5:6). It appears as if those who had left the community had made some special claim to the spirit of God (4:1–3); these persons the author labels "false prophets" (4:1). It has been argued that those who had left the community may have been adherents of a strain of Docetic thought that attempted to discount Jesus' coming in human flesh.

Literary genre. There is little agreement among scholars regarding the genre of 1 John. Despite its popular designation of "letter," and the fact that the phrase "I write to you" occurs frequently, 1 John does not exhibit the generic features typical of ancient letters, since it lacks a formal epistolary opening and closing. The genre of 1 John has been variously identified as that of a instructional tract (Perkins 1979, xvi), tractate, manifesto, circular epistle, homily (Aune 1987, 218), diatribe, epitome or enchiridion or instruction booklet for "applying the tradition in disturbing circumstances" (Grayston 1984, 4), pastoral encyclical (Brown 1982, 86–90), or community rule or church order (Hills 1991, 372–77). Many have regarded 1 John as a mixed genre and have characterized it as a *briefartige Homilie* (Strecker 1989, 49), i.e., "homilie in the form of a letter" (Strecker 1996, 3), or a *weisheitliches Gelegenheitstraktat*, or "sapiential occasional tractate" (Beutler 2000, 11). Brown (1982, 90) regards 1 John as a commentary on Gospel of John, a category which enjoys the support of a number of recent discussions of the question.

Literary analysis. The literary analysis of the structure of 1 John has proven to be problematic. It resists a structurally neat description of its contents, and it may be best simply to acknowledge the lack of an easily recognizable overarching structure. There have been a number of proposals: e.g., 1 John follows the structure of the Gospel; 1 John is defined by a chiastic or concentric structure (Thomas 1998, 372). There is, however, no one prevailing view. One way of structuring 1 John is by taking its style into account. A prominent feature of 1 John is its repetitiveness or the "spiraling" of themes throughout the letter. That is, the author often reiterates points made earlier in connection with new argumentative elements. Klauck (1990) proposes a simple threefold division: (1) Prologue: From the Word of Life (1:1–4); (2) Body: Instruction in the reality of love (1:5–5:12), (a) Community with God and knowledge of God (1:5–2:17), (b) Before the claim of the last hour (2:18–3:24), (c) Faith and Love put to the test (4:1–5:12); (3) Epilog: Conclusion of the book and postscript (5:13–21).

Rhetorical analysis. Watson (1993, 118–23) argues that 1 John is epideictic because this species of rhetoric is intended to increase the adherence of the audience to those values they already hold. Vouga (1990), followed by Klauck (1990, 209–13), on the other hand, regard 1 John as belonging rather to the *genus deliberativum*, an advisory address. Leaving aside the "epistolary prescript" (1:1–4) and the "epistolary conclusion" in 5:13–21, Klauck proposes the following rhetorical analysis of the letter with a brief explanation of each section:

1. *Captatio benevolentiae* (1:5–2:17)
2. *Narratio* (2:18–27)
3. *Propositio* (2:28–29)
4. *Probatio* (3:1–24)
5. *Exhortatio* (4:1–21)
6. *Peroratio* (5:1–12)

Klauck recognizes the problem of including the beginning and the end of 1 John in this analysis. It should be noted that he regards these textual units not as imitative of epistolary forms.

In a microstructural rhetorical analysis, Watson focuses on the repetitive and emphatic features of the letter and argues that they fit recognized techniques of amplification. Watson elsewhere (1989d; followed by Klauck 1990, 214–16) uses clues from Greco-Roman rhetorical to solve an exegetical problem in 1 John 2:12–14 which he regards as a digression:

> 12 I am writing to you, little children,
> because your sins are forgiven for his name's sake.
>
> 13 I am writing to you, fathers,
> because you know him who is from the beginning.
>
> I am writing to you, young men,
> because you have overcome the evil one.
>
> I am writing to you, children,
> because you know the Father.
>
> 14 I write to you, fathers,
> because you know him who is from the beginning.
>
> I write to you, young men,
> because you are strong,
> and the word of God abides in you,
> and you have overcome the world.

To whom do these various familial terms belong? One group? Three groups? The common view is that "children" is the inclusive term for those the author addresses, while "fathers" and "young" men represent a senior and junior division of the addressees. One problem is why the author presents two groups of parallel statements addressing children, fathers and young men. Watson argues that this is the figure of speech called *conduplicatio* or reduplication in combination with the figure of speech called *expolitio*, in which the same topic continues to be treated, yet the speaker appears to say something new (*Ad Herennium* 4.42.54; Quintilian 10.5.7, 9). For example, in v. 12, the author addresses children, "because your sins are forgiven for his name's sake," and in v. 13 he addresses them again, "because you know the Father," changing the idea slightly by changing the form (Watson 1989d, 102–3).

*General Epistles, *Homily, *John, the Letters of, *John, Gospel of, *John, Second Letter of, *John, Third Letter of

---

Brown 1982; Grayston 1984; Hills 1991; Klauck 1991; Painter 2002; Perkins 1983; Rensberger 1997; Schnackenburg 1992; Smalley 1984; Strecker 1996; Thomas 1998; Vouga 1990; Watson 1989d, 1993

P. J. KIM AND D. E. AUNE

John, Gospel of, one of the four canonical Gospels and part of the so-called Johannine corpus, which consists of five writings attributed to John the apostle since the 2d cent. C.E.: the Gospel of John, 1 John, 2 John, 3 John, and the Revelation to John. In reality, none of these works are by John the apostle. The Fourth Gospel and 1 John seem to have a common author or else arose in the same circle. Again, 2 John and 3 John seem to be by a common author, known only as "the elder." The Revelation to John is the only work in the Johannine corpus that actually claims in the text to be the work of a person named John, but this John cannot be identified with John the apostle and disciple of Jesus (see *Revelation to John).

Despite its apparent simplicity, the Fourth Gospel is one of the more problematic texts in the NT. The so-called "Johannine problem" involves such issues as the following: (1) Where was the Gospel of John written? While Ephesus is the most common answer, other possibilities are Antioch, Palestine, and Alexandria. (2) What is the source of the Jesus traditions in the Fourth Gospel? Though the *Synoptic Gospels and the Fourth Gospel share many Jesus traditions (which presumably go back to a common oral or written source), the relationship between John and the Synoptics and the tradition behind them is problematic, and the uniform language of John makes it difficult to identify oral forms that have been reduced to writing (as in the case of the Synoptic Gospels). The traditions of Jesus' words and deeds seem to have been reworked and homogenized through some unknown traditioning process. (3) It has been generally recognized among critical scholars since the mid-19th cent. that the Synoptic Gospels are more historically reliable than the Fourth Gospel, with some striking exceptions (the three-year ministry of Jesus; the geographical features of the pool of Bethesda in Jerusalem described in John 9). (4) The source of the dualistic theological and ethical system of the Fourth Gospel is problematic. The dualistic language of the Fourth Gospel includes such antitheses as "above" and "below," "descend" and "ascend," "light" and "darkness," "of this world" and "not of this world." Platonism, Gnosticism, and the dualism found in some works among the Dead Sea Scrolls have been candidates for the origin of this Johannine language (see Aune 2002b).

Text, language, and style. Parts of the text of John are preserved in 22 papyrus fragments (Comfort 1990, 625), more than of any other book of the NT, with 11 fragments dating from before 300 C.E. (𝔓5, 22, 28, 45, 52, 66, 75, 80, 90, 95). John contains 15,420 Greek words, with a vocabulary of 1,011 different words (Morgenthaler 1958, 164), a relatively restricted vocabulary. Earlier scholars thought that the Fourth Gospel was originally translated from Aramaic, as evidenced by the frequency of "Aramaisms" in the text. Colwell (1931), investigating this issue, compared the 54 "Semitisms" ("Aramaisms" or "Hebraisms") of the text of John with those of other Hellenistic authors, particularly Epictetus, and demonstrated that most of the so-called "Semitisms" in John were also found in Hellenistic literature and were therefore not "Semitisms" at all but colloquialisms characteristic of nonliterary Koine Greek (for a detailed discussion of the linguistic features of John, see Wellhausen 1908, 133–46). John heavily favors the historical present (see *Present, historical), which he uses 162 times (cf. Mark, where it occurs 151 times). The syntactic style of the Fourth Gospel is paratactic; syntactical *prolepsis occurs 12 times in John, a sufficient concentration to consider it a distinctive stylistic feature (4:35; 5:42; 7:27; 8:54; 9:8, 19, 29; 10:36; 11:31; 13:28; 14:17; 16:4). A number of studies, in reaction to the hypothesis that as many as three different sources were used in the composition of John (see below, under *Sources*), have emphasized the stylistic homogeneity of John (Schweizer 1965; Ruckstuhl 1951; Ruckstuhl and Dschulnigg

1991) in an attempt to preclude or invalidate source-critical analysis.

Authorship and date. Since the late 2d cent. C.E., the Fourth Gospel has been generally attributed to John the apostle, even though the work itself (apart from the later addition of the inscription) is anonymous. The epilogue of the final redaction of the Fourth Gospel (21:24–25) attributes the whole work to the "beloved disciple," a figure who occurs throughout the work (13:23–25; 19:26–27; 20:2–8) but is never named (Charlesworth 1995). He is associated with Peter, and it is possible that "the other disciple" (18:15–16) who knows the high priest and brings Peter into the palace of the high priest is identical with the beloved disciple. Yet the wording of John 19:35 makes it impossible to consider the beloved disciple the author of the Gospel. Charlesworth (1995) considers the beloved disciple to be Thomas, while Stibbe (1992, 81) revives the old view that Lazarus is the beloved disciple (see John 11:3), and that John the Elder was the author.

John is widely thought to have been written ca. 90 C.E., toward the end of the 1st cent. C.E. There are some that assign a relatively early date to John. Berger (1997), who regards John as the earliest of the Gospels, proposes that it was written ca. 50–60 C.E.

Title. The titles or *inscriptiones* of all four canonical Gospels are similarly phrased, with the preposition κατά ("according to") standing for the genitive of authorship: εὐαγγέλιον κατὰ Ἰωάννην, "The Gospel *of* John," the title uniformly used in modern translations of the NT into English in the form "The Gospel according to John." The shorter title Κατὰ Ἰωάννην ("According to John"), preferred by Nestle-Aland (1993), is attested to only by the second hand of the great 4th-cent. codices Vaticanus (**B**) and Sinaiticus (ℵ), the same two textual witnesses that have the identical form of title for the other four Gospels, in each case in a second hand. However, "The Gospel according to John" (εὐαγγέλιον κατὰ Ἰωάννην) is attested to by an impressive number of ancient witnesses, some older than Vaticanus and Sinaiticus, including 𝔓66 (ca. 200 C.E.) and 𝔓75 (3d cent. C.E.). Codex Alexandrinus (**A**) a 5th-cent. MS, has the phrase εὐαγγέλιον κατὰ Ἰωάννην as a title in the subscription, i.e., at the end of the manuscript (where the titles of all papyrus rolls were normally placed in antiquity). The longer title is also attested by six other *uncial manuscripts (**C, D, L, W, Θ,** and **Ψ**, as well as the Byzantine text and the Vulgate.

Relationship to Synoptic Gospels. Since the work of Gardner-Smith (1938), the literary independence of John and the Synoptic Gospels has been widely accepted, but this consensus began to disintegrate toward the end of the 20th cent. (for a history of research, see D. M. Smith 1992). Boismard and Lamouille (1987), Neirynck (1979), and de Solages (1979) are three scholars who argue in various ways that John was dependent on the Synoptics. A number of scholars have argued that there is an affinity between Johannine and Lukan traditions (Grant 1937), and some that John was directly dependent on Luke (Bailey 1963). Yet others deny any special relationship between John and Luke (Parker 1962–63) or argue that Luke was dependent on John (Cribbs 1971). F. C. Grant (1937) argues that John was not directly dependent on Luke, but that John probably knew Q, L (a special Lukan passion source), and Mark. There are some verbal agreements between Luke and John (listed in R. E. Brown 1966–70, 1.xlix–xlvii) that suggest some kind of literary relationship. Boismard (1962) proposed that Luke was the final redactor of John, a view that he later abandoned.

Source criticism. The modern discussion of the sources of the Fourth Gospel began with the three-source theory of Bultmann (1971b, 6–7): a miracle source, a gnostic revelation discourse source, and a *passion narrative (for a critique see D. M. Smith 1965). The miracle source and the passion narrative have proven most convincing to scholars, though H. Becker (1956), a student of Bultmann, tried to rework and refine Bultmann's revelation discourse source. Fortna (1970) has argued that the Signs Source, formally signaled in John 2:11; 4:54, and 20:30, was not just a collection of miracles, but that it concluded with the greatest sign of all, the resurrection of Jesus. Cope (1987, 19) argues that the Signs Gospel was the earliest of all the Gospels and suggests the possibility of the late 40s or early 50s for a date, but settles on the period of 55–60 as more cautious and credible (also the view of Berger 1997). More recently, Nordsieck (1998, 43–55) has proposed a more modest *Redenquelle* (discourse source), for which he prefers the term *Zoe-Quelle* ("life"-source), since the term "life" (a functional substitute for the Synoptic phrase "kingdom of God") is characteristic of this source. He identifies a relatively modest number of passages that he thinks are derived from this source (Nordsieck 1998, 47–49): 4:(10), 14; 5:24/8:51; 6:35a, 51b; 7:37b, 38; 8:12, 31b, 32; 10:7, 9b, 10b, 14, 15b, 28a; 5:25, 26; 11:25,

26; 3:36, 18; 15:1, 5b; 15:9, 10; 14:6, 16, 17a, 20 (17:11; 21:22); 14:19. Several studies have argued for the stylistic homogeneity of John (Schweizer 1965; Ruckstuhl 1951; Ruckstuhl and Dschulnigg 1991) as a way of rendering source criticism invalid.

Literary analysis. The literary structure of the Fourth Gospel, as in the case of many other NT compositions, is a debated subject. The Gospel of John has a defined prologue (1:1–18) that is completely different from the opening sections of any of the other canonical Gospels. Similarly, the last two verses of John form an epilogue (21:24–25): "[24]This is the disciple who is bearing witness to these things, and who has written these things; and we know that his testimony is true. [25]But there are also many other things which Jesus did; were every one of them to be written, I suppose that the world itself could not contain the books that would be written."

This epilogue falls into two parts. The first part (v. 24) is a brief commentary on the identity of the mysterious "beloved disciple," who is not identified but who is claimed (in the third person) to be the author of the Fourth Gospel (Culpepper 1983, 47; Haenchen 1984, 228; Painter 1993, 87–95; Charlesworth 1995, 26; opposed by Schnackenburg 1968–82, 3.379 and Beasley-Murray 1989, 5, who think that the beloved disciple is the witness behind the Fourth Gospel). (Many have speculated about the identity of the beloved disciple; for a full review of the history of research on this subject, see Charlesworth 1995, who concluded that Thomas should probably be identified as the beloved disciple.) The second part of the epilogue contains a striking hyperbole or topos. At the end of Valerius Alexandria's *On the Power of Nature*, he concluded: "If we were now to say all that could be said about this plant, an entire book would not be sufficient" (Boring, Colpe, and Berger 1995, 308; same for the next quote); again in Porphyry, *Life of Pythagoras* 29, after a list of the miracles of Pythagoras: "Ten thousand other things yet more marvelous and more divine are told about the man, and told uniformly in stories that agree with each other. To put it bluntly, about no one else have greater and more extraordinary things been believed." Even more striking than this topos is the occurrence of the first-person singular used by the author-editor: οἶμαι ("I think"), and it becomes immediately evident that the person who wrote the third-person comment in v. 24 is actually claiming to be the author of John 1–20. This is striking because a first-person singular reference to a Gospel author occurs elsewhere only in Luke 1:2: "It seemed good to *me* also . . . to write an orderly account for you, most excellent Theophilus." In neither John 21:25 nor Luke 1:2 (or their contexts) is the author identified.

Critical scholars are agreed that John 21 is a later addition to the book and that it falls into two parts, the third appearance of Jesus to his disciples (vv. 1–14), and the dialogue of Jesus and Peter, which concludes with a *narrative aside (vv. 15–23). John 21 is frequently called an epilogue, appendix, addition, or supplement to the Fourth Gospel. While it is almost certainly a later addition, John 21 does not in fact function as an epilogue to the final form of John. Rather, the passage quoted above, John 21:24–25, clearly serves as an epilogue to the expanded work (John 1:1–21:23).

Since John 21 was a later addition, it seems very likely that John 20:30–31 was the original epilogue of the work (another view on which most critical scholars are in agreement): "[30]Now Jesus did many other signs in the presence of the disciples, which are not written in this book; [31]but these are written that you may believe that Jesus is the Christ, the Son of God, and that believing you may have life in his name." The emphasis in this earlier or original epilogue on "signs" is appropriate for the work it concludes, since there is a special emphasis on seven signs that occur only in the first half of the work (John 2–12). The location and setting of the seven signs in fact serve to delimit the first half of John from the second half of John.

The two main sections of John clearly intended by the author are John 1:19–12:50, which narrates the public ministry of Jesus, and 13:1–20:29, which narrates Jesus' private ministry to his own disciples in preparation for his death (for a tripartite division of John consisting of 1:19–4:54, 5:1–10:42, and 11:1–20:29, see Giblin 1990). In these two main sections of the work the author develops a plot that centers on the conflict over the true identity of Jesus and his ultimate rejection. This plot has a tragicomic structure in that, while it does involve the death of Jesus, the hero (as in tragedy), that death is effectively negated by his resurrection, which signals the victory of the hero over his enemies (as in comedy).

The plot of John is similar to the plot of the Synoptic Gospels, though it is worked out in quite a different way. The prologue (1:1–18) provides believing readers with insight into the true identity of Jesus, identifying him as the preincarnate Word of God, the agent of whom the universe was created, who became a human being. The plot and even the structure of the gospel is anticipated in John 1:10–12: "[10]He was in the world, and the world was made through him, yet the world knew him not. [11]He came to his own home, and his own people received him not. [12]But to all who received him, who believed in his name, he gave power to become children of God." Here vv. 10–11 anticipate the ministry and rejection of Jesus by his people generally (narrated in 1:19–12:50), while v. 12 anticipates the acceptance of Jesus by a circle of followers (narrated in 13:1–17:26).

The first part concludes with John 12:36b–50, which provides the rationale for the end of Jesus' public ministry. Here is the beginning of the transition in John 12:36b–37: "When Jesus had said this, he departed and hid himself from them. Though he had done so many signs before them, yet they did not believe in him." The thematic parallels between this brief passage and the closing epilogue containing the general statement of the purpose of the original gospel in 20:30–31 (quoted above) is clear. Following John 12:36b–37 are quotations from Isa. 53:1 and Isa. 6:10 dealing with the lack of belief, spiritual blindness, and hardness of heart of Israel, all of which are understood as fulfilled in the generally negative response to the ministry of Jesus. Isaiah 6:9–10 is also quoted at the conclusion of Acts (28:25–29), where it is said to be fulfilled by the rejection of Paul's gospel by the Jews. This similar use of the Isa. 6 passage in both John 12:40 and Acts 28:26–27 suggests that it had become part of a common Christian prophetic apologetic for dealing with the rejection of Jesus by the Jews (see also the use of Isa. 6:9–10 in a fulfillment quotation in Matt. 13:14–15, and the allusion to Isa. 6:9 in Mark 4:12, followed closely by Luke 8:10b, dealing with the Jewish response to the ministry of Jesus). The plot is driven by the fact that Jesus (and his message) is "from above" and is "light", and is in conflict with the world ("below," which is in "darkness").

The first section of part one (1:19–4:54) is introduced with the testimony of John to Jesus (the testimony of John has already been mentioned in the prologue, 1:6–8) that Jesus is the Lamb of God (1:29, 36) and the Son of God (1:34). There is as yet no conflict between Jesus and his adversaries, but rather an increasing acceptance of Jesus and his message as signaled by the initial gathering of disciples (1:35–51). The next part of this section is framed by the two Cana miracles, the changing of water to wine—which had the appropriate effect on the disciples: they "believed in him" (2:1–11)—and the healing of the nobleman's son (4:46–54). These two signs frame the dialogue with Nicodemus (3:1–21), a further testimony of John to the true identity of Jesus (3:22–36), and the story of Jesus and the woman of Samaria, which elicits the faith of many Samaritans (4:1–45).

The second section of part one (5:1–6:61) begins with a journey of Jesus to Jerusalem, where he heals a paralytic on the Sabbath (5:1–18), which causes a conflict with the Jews, since they construed it as a violation of Sabbath law. The narrator reveals that the Jews intended to kill Jesus, indicating serious conflict between Jesus and the Jews that would result in Jesus' death. In response to Jewish antagonism, Jesus delivers a long monologue (5:19–47) in which he reveals his relationship to God, which is attested to by the testimony of John the Baptist (5:33–35) but even more clearly by the testimony of his own works (5:36). "I have come in my Father's name," he claims, "and you do not receive me" (5:43), echoing the words of the prologue (1:10–11). John 6 begins with the fourth and fifth miracles of Jesus, the feeding of the 5,000 (6:1–13), which concludes with the recognition that Jesus was the prophet destined to come into the world (6:14), and an unsuccessful attempt to make Jesus king (6:1–15). The fifth sign, Jesus' walking on the water (6:16–21), is narrated but plays a relatively unimportant role in the development of the plot.

The second part of this section is 6:22–59, which contains Jesus' discourse on the bread of life, an interactive homily sparked by the sign of the feeding of the 5,000. The discourse highlights Jesus' true identity as bread from heaven, analogous to the miracle of the provision of manna in the wilderness to the people of Israel. Allusions of the story of Israel in the wilderness include the "murmuring" (vv. 41, 43, 61; cf. Exod. 16:2–3) of the Jews at Jesus' claim, "I am the bread which came down from heaven" (6:41). The contrast between earthly and heavenly is underscored in John 6:49–51: "[49]Your fathers ate the manna in the wilderness, and they died. [50]This is the bread which comes down from heaven, that a man may eat of it and not die. [51]I am the living bread which came down from heaven; if any one eats of this bread, he will live for ever; and the bread which I shall give for the life of the world is my flesh." Doubtless for the Christian reader this constitutes an allusion to the Eucharist, but it also anticipated the death of Jesus.

The third part (6:60–71) is an ominous section that anticipates the falling action of John 18–21, for it is not the Jews, but Jesus' own disciples who take offense at his claims. At this juncture, those disciples who are not true disciples forsake Jesus, anticipating the rejection of Jesus that culminates at the end of John 12. The core group of faithful disciples, with Peter as their spokesperson, confess that Jesus is the Holy One of God (6:68–69), a counterpart to the confession of Peter in the Synoptics (Mark 8:27–33; Matt. 16:13–23; Luke 9:18–22). The betrayal of Jesus is anticipated by Jesus' closing words, "Did I not choose you, the twelve, and one of you is a devil?" (6:70). The narrator makes it clear that he "spoke of Judas the son of Simon Iscariot, for he, one of the twelve, was to betray him" (6:71).

The third section of part one (7:1–12:50) narrates the intensification of Jesus' conflict with those who rejected his message, and functions as the falling action. The section begins with another anticipation of Jesus' death: Jesus goes about in Galilee, but not Judea, "because the Jews sought to kill him" (7:1). Jesus then sends his disciples to the feast of Tabernacles in Jerusalem (7:2–9), but later goes there himself secretly (7:10–13). The divided reception of his message is made clear by the narrator: "While some said, 'He is a good man,' others said, 'No, he is leading the people astray'" (7:12; the same motif is repeated in 7:25–27, 31, 40–43). Jesus then teaches publicly in the temple, focusing on the why the people are so intent on killing him (7:14–24), a motif that continues to be reiterated throughout the remainder of the chapter (7:19, 25). In John 8 the conflict intensifies between Jesus and the Jews, and is filled with irony and sayings that function as riddles. When asked if he thinks he's greater than Abraham, he makes the astonishing claim, "Truly, truly, I say to you, before Abraham was, I am" (8:58). They then attempt to stone him, but he hides himself from them (8:59). John 9 contains the sixth sign, the healing of a man born blind (9:1–12), and the fact that he is healed by Jesus on the Sabbath day angers the Pharisees, who interrogate the man repeatedly (9:13–34). Jesus later finds the healed man and asks him if he believes in the Son of man (9:35), to which he responds "Lord, I believe" (9:38). The point of the episode is brought home when the Pharisees ask Jesus "Are we also blind?" (9:40), making the symbolic significance of the sign clear: the blind man, who believes in Jesus, has true sight, while the Pharisees, who do not believe, yet have physical sight, are spiritually blind. John 10 centers on the metaphor of Jesus as the good shepherd, who gives his life for his sheep, and includes a clear prediction of his death and resurrection (10:17): "For this reason the Father loves me, because I lay down my life, that I may take it again." When asked by the Jews if he is the Christ (10:24), he speaks of his sheep, which cannot be taken from him, and for some reason they again try to stone him, because he is a man who makes himself out to be God (10:31–33). Crossing the Jordan, he continues to inspire belief (10:40–42). John 11 narrates the seventh sign, the rising of Lazarus, which functions as a narrative anticipation of the resurrection of Jesus in John 20. When the Jewish authorities learn what has happened, they decide that Jesus must be executed (11:45–57). In the middle of the section, the high priest Caiaphas utters an ironic prophecy: "It is expedient for you that one man should die for the people, and that the whole nation should not perish" (11:50). John 12 begins with the anointing of Jesus by Mary with costly ointment, symbolizing his impending death (12:1–11). This is followed by the triumphal entry in which Jesus presents himself as Messiah to the people (12:12–19), but Jesus knows that his death is imminent. The first main part of the Fourth Gospel concludes with 12:36b–50, in which Jesus turns away from the people who have rejected him. This transitional section has two parts. In the first (12:36b–43), the narrator comments on the rejection of Jesus, which he sees foreshadowed by a prophecy in Isa. 6:9–10. In the second (12:44–50), Jesus himself gives a brief speech dealing the consequences of accepting and rejecting him.

The second main section of the Fourth Gospel (13:1–21:25), includes two major parts. The first part, called the Farewell Discourse of Jesus, includes table conversation relating to the significance of Jesus and the provisions he has made for the disciples following his death (John 13–17), while the second section narrates the death and resurrection of Jesus (John 18–21). John 13 opens with Jesus' recognition that "his hour had come to depart out of this world to the Father" (13:1), and includes a mention of Judas Iscariot, the betrayer of Jesus (13:2). At the meal (which is never characterized in John as the Last Supper), Jesus mentions that one of the disciples will betray him (13:21–30). The beloved disciple asks who the betrayer is, and Jesus gives him an obvious clue. Judas leaves at the request of Jesus, who then claims, "Now is the Son of man glorified, and in him God is glorified" (13:31). The farewell discourse itself extends from 14:1–17:26, ending with a lengthy prayer of Jesus.

The second half of part two (18:1–21:25) begins with a focus on the events surrounding the betrayal and arrest of Jesus, followed by his interrogation (18:1–40). The irony of dressing up Jesus in a crown of thorns and a purple robe and greeting him as the king of the Jews is clear to the reader of John and is found in the Synoptics as well, for the reader recognizes that Jesus is truly a king. The final condemnation, death, and burial of Jesus are narrated in 19:12–42. That these events were all part of God's plan is emphasized by the quotation of OT texts that are fulfilled in the death of Jesus (19:24, 36–37). John 20 narrates the circumstances following the resurrection of Jesus. Mary Magdalene visits the tomb early on the first day of the week (20:1); finding it empty, she reports to Peter and "the other disciple" (the beloved disciple?), who run to the tomb and Peter enters it while the other remains outside and believes, even though they do not yet know the Scripture that Jesus must rise from the dead (20:2–10). Jesus then reveals himself to Mary (20:11–18) and to the disciples (20:19–23). Thomas is absent and skeptical (20:24–25), but believes when Jesus appears to the disciples a second time (20:26–29). The original Gospel then concludes with a brief epilogue in John 20:30–31, emphasizing the purpose of the signs. They are to foster belief in Jesus as the Messiah, the Son of God.

Literary features. Narrative asides—various kinds of intrusive comments of the narrator, presenting essential information the reader needs in order to understand the narrative—occur frequently in John (Culpepper 1983, 15–49). Using various criteria, scholars have identified anywhere from 59 (Tenney 1960) to 165 (van Belle 1985) narrative asides in the Fourth Gospel, with O'Rourke (1979) identifying 109. Tenney (1960, 51–52) categorizes the function of the "footnotes" (i.e., "narrative asides") in John into ten types: (1) explanatory translations, (2) explanation of time or place of action, (3) explanation of customs, (4) reflections of the author, (5) recollections of the disciples, (6) explanations of situations or actions with respect to cause or consequence, (7) summary of enumerating footnotes, (8) identification of persons, (9) supernatural knowledge of Jesus, and (10) theological comments.

Van Belle (1985, 106–12) has expanded this list to 17 functions: (1) translations of Hebrew or Aramaic words (e.g., 1:38, 41, 42; 5:2; 9:7); (2) interpretation of Jewish customs (2:6; 4:9; 18:28; 19:40); (3) indication or description of persons (e.g., 1:6–8, 6.12c–13, 15, 24, 40, 42, 44); (4) indication or description of place (e.g., 1:28; 2:11; 3:23; 4:46, 54; 5:2); (5) indication of time (e.g., 1:39; 3:24; 4:6, 23; 5:9, 25); (6) interpretation of the words of Jesus or others (e.g., 2:21–22; 4:8, 9; 6:6, 64, 71); (7) interpretation of the acts of Jesus or others (e.g., 3:19, 23, 24; 4:44, 45; 5:13, 18); (8) incomprehension of the disciples or others (e.g., 2:9; 7:5; 8:27); (9) tardy comprehension of the disciples (2:21–22; 12:16); (10) fulfillment of the Scriptures or the words of Jesus (e.g., 1:23; 2:17; 6:31; 7:38; 12:14–16); (11) reference to a passage that precedes or follows (e.g., 1:24, 40; 2:22; 3:26; 4:2, 45); (12) corrections (e.g., 1:8; 3:33; 4:2, 23); (13) notice of conclusion (e.g., 1:28; 2:11; 4:54; 6:59; 7:9; 8:20); (14) reflection inserted after the fact in the narrative (e.g., 1:24, 28, 40, 44; 2:6; 3:24; 4:8); (15) longer theological reflection (e.g., 1:6–8, 15; 3:16–21, 31–36; 12:37–42); (16) "reference" to the author of the Gospel (1:14; 19:35; 21:20, 23, 24); (17) Jesus' supernatural knowledge (2:24–25; 6:6, 64; 13:11). Hedrick (1990) presents a list of 15 types of narrative asides, very similar to those of Tenney and van Belle.

The Fourth Gospel makes extensive use of *irony (Culpepper 1983, 165–80; 1996; Duke 1985; O'Day 1986; Staley 1988). Irony can be described as a two-level literary phenomenon: below is the apparent meaning, above is a meaning that is contradictory or incompatible with the meaning at the lower level (Culpepper 1983, 167). Readers must move from the lower level to the higher level (Culpepper 1983, 167, based on Booth 1974, 10–12): "In order to make the leap from one level to the other, the reader must take four steps: (1) reject the literal meaning, (2) recognize alternative interpretations, (3) decide about the author's knowledge or beliefs, and (4) choose a new meaning which is in harmony with the (implied) author's position." The dichotomous Johannine language of above/below corresponds with Johannine cosmology in which the dualistic language of above/below, heavenly/earthly, ascend/descend expresses the theologoumenon that truth is from above and error is from below. The prologue in John 1:1–18 places the readers in a privileged perspective on Jesus' true identity, which they share with the author.

The basic irony of the Fourth Gospel is that the Jews reject the Messiah whom they earnestly expected (Culpepper 1983, 169). In line with Johannine cosmology, Johannine irony tends to be corrective and is "stable irony" (a phrase coined by Booth); that is, the readers of John's Gospel are never victims of irony; irony is always directed at characters in the story (Culpepper 1983, 179; 1996, 195–99; Duke 1985, 30). Staley (1988, 110, 113, 116) disagrees and speaks of the central rhetorical effect of the Fourth Gospel as "the victimization of the reader." An example is John 3:22 and 4:2; in 3:22 the reader is told that Jesus is with his disciples baptizing in Judea, but in 4:2 the reader learns that Jesus does not in fact baptize anyone. Culpepper (1996, 199–201) has recently come to recognize the element of instability in Johannine irony. Thatcher (1999), building on Staley, argues that John 5:1–10 and 9:1–14 involve a form of the victimization of the reader, by withholding information from the reader, and therefore are examples of "unstable irony." (Thatcher 1999, 57). This notion of the "victimization of the reader," however, seems to be anachronistic in the sense that it is a modern literary strategy projected back onto the Fourth Gospel.

Types of Johannine irony include the following (Culpepper 1996, 195–96): (1) false claims to knowledge: "Is not this Jesus, the son of Joseph, whose father and mother we know? How can he now say, 'I have come down from heaven'?" (John 6:42; cf. 7:27; 7:41b-42, 52b; 9:29); (2) false assumptions: "Are you greater than our ancestor Jacob?" (4:12; cf. 7:15; 8:53, 57); (3) accusations of demon possession, Samaritan origins, violation of the law: "Give God the praise; we know that this man is a sinner" (9:24; cf. 7:19–20; 8:41; 9:16; 18:30); (4) suggestions of belief: "Can it be that the authorities really know that this is the Christ?" (7:26; cf. 7:47–48; 7:52); (5) unconscious prophecy and testimony: "If we let him go on thus, every one will believe in him, and the Romans will come and destroy both our holy place and our nation" (11:48–50; cf. 2:10; 7:3–4, 35–36; 8:22; 12:19).

Use of the OT. The author of the Fourth Gospel is less concerned with the fulfillment of individual passages from the OT than with the general fulfillment of Scripture itself (Beutler 1996), though there are four specific fulfillment quotations (12:38; 13:18; 15:25; 17:12). In John 13:18 the phrase "the Scripture will be fulfilled" is used with a quotation from Ps. 41:9, though the source of the quotation is referred to only as "Scripture" (for a similar general use of the term "fulfill," see 17:12; 19:24, 36). There are 17 passages in which quotations from the OT are introduced with a citation formula (all do not agree on the number, but this is the view of both Freed 1965 and Menken 1996): 1:23 (Menken 1996, 21–35); 2:17 (Menken 1996, 37–45); 6:31 (Menken 1996, 47–65); 6:45 (Menken 1996, 67–77); 7:38 (Menken 1996, 187–88); 7:42; 8:17; 10:34; 12:15 (Menken 1996, 79–97); 12:34, 38, 40 (Menken 1996, 99–122); 13:18 (Menken 1996, 123–38); 15:25 (Menken 1996, 139–45); 19:24, 36 (Menken 1996, 147–66); 19:37 (Menken 1996, 167–85) (cf. 17:12 and 19:28, quotation formulas without a specific quotation). There is a concentration of OT quotations where the end of Jesus' public ministry is narrated (12:15, 34, 38, 40) and where his crucifixion and death are narrated (19:24, 36, 37). Elsewhere, quotations of the OT are attributed to Jesus where he demonstrates that his ministry accords with Scripture (6:45; 7:38; 13:18; 15:25), and both Jesus and his adversaries quote Scripture in disputes over who he really is (6:31; 7:42; 8:17; 10:34; 12:34). The OT quotations in John do not agree precisely with any known version of the OT, whether the MT, the LXX, or other Greek versions (Menken 1996, 13). However, three quotations agree exactly with the LXX (10:34; 12:38; 19:24), and eight are relatively close (1:23; 2:17; 6:31, 45; 7:38; 12:15; 15:25; 19:36). A few quotations indicate a knowledge of the Hebrew text (7:38; 12:40; 13:18; 19:37; see Freed 1965, 126; Menken 1996, 205). A. T. Hanson, in his detailed study of the use of the OT in John, finds about 50 instances in which particular episodes that appear to have no historical basis can arguably be attributed to the influence of the OT on the narrative (1991, 242–45, et passim).

*Gospels, literary genres of, *John, First Letter of, *John, Second Letter of, *John, Third Letter of

---

Ashton 1994; Aune 2002b; Bailey 1963; Berger 1997; Beutler 1996; Boismard and Lamouille 1977; Both 1974; Carson 1978, 1988; Charlesworth 1995; Colwell 1931; Comfort 1990; Cope 1987; Culpepper 1983; De Solages 1979; Duke 1985; Freed 1965; Freed and Hunt 1975; Giblin 1990; Goodwin 1954; F. C. Grant 1937; A. T. Hanson 1991; Kysar 1973; Menken 1996; Neirynck 1979; O'Day 1986; Parker 1962–63; Reim 1974, 1995; Ruckstuhl 1951; Ruckstuhl and Dschulnigg 1991; Schuchard 1992; Schweizer 1939; D. M. Smith 1981, 1992; Staley 1988; Stibbe 1992; Thatcher 1999; Tilborg 1996; van Belle 2001; Wellhausen 1908

John, the Letters of Three New Testament documents that, with the Gospel of John and Revelation (together called the

Johannine corpus), early Christian writers associated with one of the twelve apostles, John, the son of Zebedee. Though the Johannine Letters have been part of the General Epistles or Catholic Letters (ἐπιστολαὶ καθολικαί) since at least the 3d cent. C.E., they do not have general addressees, as do James, 1 Peter, 2 Peter, and Jude. First John is not formally a letter and lacks an adscription, while 2 John is addressed to "the elect lady and her children," and 3 John is addressed to "Gaius." The three Johannine Letters did not form a naturally homogenous group like the Synoptic Gospels or the Pauline Letters but gradually were included together after the Acts of the Apostles in manuscripts of much of the NT (Strecker 1996, xxxii–xxxiii). Modern critical scholarship is in general agreement, however, that John the son of Zebedee is not the actual author of the writings traditionally attributed to him, and the letters themselves make no claim that John was their author. First John is anonymous, while 2 John and 3 John claim to be written by "the elder." Despite the ambiguity concerning authorship, the similarities in language, style, and thought between the Fourth Gospel and the Letters, especially in light of the rest of the New Testament, seem to reflect a common background and have led scholars commonly to posit a Johannine community or circle behind these texts. Similarities are particularly evident between the Gospel and 1 John. Indeed, 1 John seems to presuppose the existence of the Gospel, or at the very least, units of oral tradition now embedded within John. Some shared terminology includes life, love, light, darkness, Son, and truth. However, differences have been noted as well, e.g., concerning the significance of Jesus' death, which make a single author behind the Gospel and the Letters unlikely.

The Letters give no clear indication of the date of their final composition, nor is there complete agreement as to the order of their composition (Brown 1982, 30–36); it is only their relationship with the Gospel that enables approximate dating of the corpus as a whole. Modern scholarship tends to place them about a decade or so after the Gospel, which is often dated toward the end of the first century, thus placing the Letters ca. 90–110 C.E.

The Letters also do not inform of us their provenance. The earliest Christian tradition places 1 John in Asia Minor (Polycarp, *Phil.* 7.1). Asia Minor, and more specifically Ephesus, has traditionally been considered the place of origin for the Letters, again, because of their association with the Gospel.

*John, First Letter of, *John, Gospel of, *John, Second Letter of, *John, Third Letter of

---

Brown 1982; Grayston 1984; Klauck 1991, 1992; Lieu 1986; Rensberger 1997; Schnackenburg 1992; Smalley 1984; Strecker 1996

P. J. KIM

John, Second Letter of, which contains just 245 words, is the second longest of the so-called *Johannine letters (1 John is the longest, 3 John the shortest with 219 words), and clearly belongs to the epistolary genre in a formal sense. These three texts belong to the traditional corpus of Johannine literature, which also includes the Gospel of John and the Revelation to John. Second John, as well as the other two Johannine letters, are part of the seven-member group of *General epistles. Second John, like 3 John, claims to have been written by "the Elder," an anonymous figure apparently of some authority. The adscription, "the elect lady and her children," may well be a symbolic term for a church and its membership. This is in part confirmed by the epistolary conclusion in vv. 12–13, which consists of travel plans (v. 12), and then secondary greetings: "The children of your elect sister greet you." Like the other Letters of John, answers to the questions concerning authorship, date, and provenance of 2 John are problematic (see *John, the letters of). Second John and 3 John were probably written by the same author, to be distinguished from the author or authors of the Gospel of John and 1 John, though all these works emerged from the Johannine community (Strecker 1995).

Historical setting. The circumstances behind 2 John may have been similar to 1 John, since the former mentions the commandment to love (5; cf. 1 John 1:7) and the deceivers who do not hold that Jesus Christ came in human flesh (v. 7; cf. 1 John 4:2). Second John provides specific instructions for its addressees, whereas 1 John does not: 2 John urges the readers to guard themselves from deceivers who teach things that go beyond the teaching of Christ (vv. 8–9), and not to extend hospitality to them (vv. 10–11). Due to these rather "radical admonitions," it has been argued that 2 John may have been composed earlier than 1 John as an initial measure taken against "the elder's" opponents (Thomas 1995, 72).

Epistolary and rhetorical analysis. Second John opens with an epistolary prescription (vv. 1–3), consisting of a superscription: "The elder" (v. 1a), an adscription: "to the elect lady and her children . . . (vv. 1b-2), and a salutation (v. 3): "Grace, mercy, and peace will be with us, from God the Father and from Jesus Christ the Father's Son, in truth and love." The adscription is modified by a long relative clause that functions as a **captatio benevolentiae* as well: "whom I love in truth, and not only I, but also all who know the truth, because of the truth that abides in us and will be with us forever." The epistolary conclusion in vv. 12–13 consists of a brief apology for the shortness of the letter (v. 12a), which provides the basis for a vague indication of the author's future travel plans (v. 12b), followed by secondary greetings (v. 13: "The children of your elect sister greet you"). The common peace benediction found at the conclusion of most early Christian letters is conspicuously absent.

Similar to the other Letters of John, 2 John utilizes carefully constructed Greco-Roman rhetorical conventions (Watson 1989b, 110–29) in order to persuade its readers to continue in their faithfulness to the commandment to love, as taught by the tradition they had received, which the "deceivers" now threaten.

Watson (1989b; followed closely by Klauck 1990, 217–24) argues that 2 John should be categorized as deliberative rhetoric in which the author tries to persuade the addressees to pursue a particular course of action and avoid the alternative. He also proposes a rhetorical analysis of the letter, fully aware of the fact that rhetorical theory and epistolary theory were not integrated in antiquity:

1. *Praescriptio* as *Exordium* (vv. 1–3)
2. *Exordium* (v. 4)
3. *Narratio* (v. 5)
4. *Probatio* (vv. 6–11)
5. *Peroratio* (v. 12)
6. Epistolary Closing as *Peroratio* (v. 13).

The *narratio* proposed by Watson is found in v. 5: "But now, dear lady, I ask you, not as though I were writing you a new commandment, but one we have had from the beginning, let us love one another" (cf. John 13:34; 1 John 2:7; 3:11). This is problematic for two reasons. First, vv. 5–6 constitute a unit with "commandment" and "from the beginning" linking them together. Second, v. 5 hardly functions as a *narratio* in any conventional sense of the term, but simply an antithetical formulation (not . . . but) of the thesis of the letter. Watson (1989b, 117–18) more appropriately designates the *narratio* as essentially identical with the *partitio*, the proposition or propositions to be developed in the *probatio*.

*John, First Letter of, *John, letters of, *John, Third Letter of

———

Brown 1982; Grayston 1984; Klauck 1990, 1992; Lieu 1986; Painter 2002; Rensberger 1997; Schnackenburg 1992; Smalley 1984; Strecker 1996; Thomas 1995; Watson 1989b

P. J. KIM AND D. E. AUNE

John, Third Letter of The shortest book in the NT with 219 words, 3 John (like 2 John) was written by "the Elder," a figure about whom nothing is known. Though 3 John has been traditionally ascribed to John the Apostle, there is little evidence supporting this ancient view. Third John is addressed to "Gaius," another figure about whom we have no historical information outside of this letter. Third John together with 1 John and 2 John make up a short corpus of letters (arranged in order of decreasing size), which together with the Gospel of John and the Revelation to John constitute the Johannine corpus. The Johannine letters are also part of the seven *General Epistles which were grouped together under the name "Catholic Epistles" in the eastern church by the 4th cent. C.E., but were called "Canonical epistles" in the western church. Since 3 John, like 2 John, is addressed to a specific person or group, it does not share the general adscriptions found in James, 1 Peter, 2 Peter, and Jude.

Purpose. Unlike the first two Johannine letters, 3 John belies no hint of the christological controversies around which 1 and 2 John revolve, possibly because there is no such controversy behind 3 John (Rensberger 1997, 27). Instead, the matter seems to concern issues of hospitality and authority. In 3 John, "the Elder," likely the same elder of 2 John, writes to Gaius, commending him for his hospitality toward persons apparently associated with "the Elder" (vv. 5–8), and perhaps ingratiating himself in light of the ensuing criticism of Diotrephes (vv. 9–10) and exhortation (vv. 11–12). Diotrephes, apparently a figure of some authority, has not only refused the envoys of "the Elder" (v. 9) (cf. Mitchell 1998, 317–20), but also has spread false charges against him, has refused "the brethren," and has expelled from the church those who wanted to do otherwise (v. 10b). In response to Diotrephes, "the elder" states that, should he come, he will call attention to Diotrephes' slandering (v. 10a), and then exhorts Gaius not to "imitate what is evil" (v. 11) and to receive Demetrius favorably, presumably the person who delivered the message (v. 12).

Epistolary and rhetorical analysis. Like 2 John, 3 John is easily categorized as an ancient letter. Third John opens with an epistolary prescription which included a superscription (v. 1a): "The Elder," followed by an adscription (v. 1b): "to the beloved Gaius," followed by a short relative clause modifying "Gaus": "whom I love in truth." Unlike most NT letters, there is no salutation (cf. the salutation in 2 John 3). The prayer in v. 2a occupies the same slot as the Pauline thanksgiving periods, but is closer in content to the prayers found in the documentary papyri. The epistolary closing (vv. 13–15) has some similarity to that found in 2 John 13–14. The author concludes with an apology for the brevity of the letter (cf. 2 John 13a): "I have much to write to you, but I would rather not write with pen and ink." This is followed by vague travel plans (v. 14): "instead I hope to see you soon, and we will talk together face to face." Finally, the author includes a peace wish (v. 15a) followed by secondary greetings in v. 15b (cf. 2 John 14): "The friends send you their greetings. Greet the friends there, each by name."

In content, 3 John is a mixed letter (White 1986, 197–98) which, according to Watson (1989c, 482), combines features of letters of friendship, request, advice, commendation, praise, encouragement, vituperation, and accusation. Black (1998, 459) regards 3 John primarily as a letter of petition. Such letters have a standard format in the body of the letter (C. Black 1998, 459): (1) identification of the one recommended, (2) the sender's recommendation, (3) acknowledgment of the addressee's favor and the sender's promise to repay. As Black (1998, 459) observes, 3 John deviates from this basic pattern, but the reason is simply that 3 John is not a letter of petition.

It is clear that the body of the letter contains three main sections: (1) Gaius is praised for the hospitality he has shown to traveling Christians (vv. 5–9). (2) Diotrephes is blamed for his lack of hospitality (vv. 9–10). (3) Demetrius, presumably the emissary from the elder, is held up as an example to all (vv. 11–12).

Watson (1989c, 484–85; closely followed by Klauck 1990) regards 3 John as an epideictic letter "to increase Gaius' adherence to an honorable value he already holds: extending hospitality to traveling Christian missionaries. . . ." However, the most obvious epideictic features are the praise directed to Gaius (vv. 5–8) and the blame leveled at Diotrophes (vv. 9–10). Watson (1989c, 485–500, with discussion) proposed the following rhetorical analysis of 3 John (slightly rearranged):

1. *Praescriptio* as *Exordium* (v. 1)
2. *Exordium* (vv. 2–4)
3. *Narratio* (vv. 5–6)
4. *Probatio* (vv. 7–12)
5. *Peroratio* (vv. 13–14)
6. Postscript as *Peroratio* (v. 15)

Watson's analysis is problematic, not least because he insists on imposing a rhetorical template on a relatively simple private letter. Third John 5–6 hardly constitutes a narrative, just as vv. 13–14 hardly constitute a *peroratio*. Further, vv. 5–8 constitute a textual unite which Watson artificially divides in the middle.

Brown 1982; Grayston 1984; Klauck 1990; Lieu 1986; Mitchell 1998; Painter 2002; Rensberger 1997; Schnackenburg 1992; Smalley 1984; Strecker 1996; Watson 1989c

P. J. KIM AND D. E. AUNE

Josephus, often referred to as Flavius Josephus (because he was a client of the Flavian dynasty), was a Palestinian Jew of priestly descent on his father's side and Hasmonean royal descent on the side of his mother (*Vita* 1.1–2; 1.3). A participant in the Jewish revolt against Rome of 66–73 C.E., he surrendered to Vespasian early in the war. Thereafter he went to Rome as a client of the the three Flavian emperors (Vespasian, Titus, and Domitian), where he was granted Roman citizenship and a pension (*Vita* 422–30). Under Flavian patronage, Josephus wrote a number of works, including *Bellum* ("War of the Jews"), *Antiquities*, *Vita,* and *Contra Apionem*, all of which were preserved by Christians, not Jews. The famous paragraph mentioning Jesus, the *Testimonium Flavianum* (*Ant.* 18.63–64), is an interpolation by Christians, ca. 300 C.E. (Rajak 1984, 67, 131 n. 13; Bilde 1988, 22–23; Olson 1999), though some defend its partial authenticity (Meier 1990, 1991, 59–69). Given the transmission history, it is striking that more Christian interpolations were not made.

Bellum Judaicum. A work in seven books originally written in Aramaic (*Bellum* 1.3) between 75 and 79 C.E., it was sponsored by the emperors Vespasian and Titus and deposited in the imperial library in Rome. The Greek version, which described events to 75 C.E., was completed before the death of Vespasian in 79 C.E. However, the highly literary Greek style of *Bellum* does not exhibit "translation Greek." Josephus wrote the *Bellum* for several reasons: (1) to justify his transformation from Jewish general to Roman client; (2) to enhance the reputations of his patrons, the emperor Vespasian (69–79 C.E.) and his son and successor Titus (79–81 C.E.); and (3) to pin the blame for the Jewish revolt on the revolutionaries who incited it by victimizing the Jewish people (*Bellum* 1.9–10). Josephus's purpose in the *Bellum* has been summarized by Hubbard, based on *Bellum* 1.9–12 (1979, 1.60): "Divine providence favored Rome [2.390; 3.6; 4.622; 5.367, 412; 6.38], as various prophecies and portents attest [3.351–54; 4.385–88; 6.288–309, 312–13], whereas the revolutionaries totally disregarded their own religious and ethical standards [4.150, 155, 381–83] and thus got what they deserved [2.449–57; 6.108–10, 249–51]." *Bellum* contains numerous *speeches, composed in conformity with the general rules of Greco-Roman rhetoric, which the author used to convey his own theological and ideological evaluation of the conflict between the Jews and the Romans (Runnalls 1997, 738). There are eleven speeches in *Bellum* (Runnalls 1997, 740 n. 7): 1.73–79; 2.345–401; 3.362–82; 4.162–92, 237–69; 5.376–419; 6.34–53, 99–110, 323–50; 7.323–36, 341–88. These include seven deliberative speeches (2.345–401; 3.362–82; 4.162–92, 238–69; 5.376–419; 6.99–110; 7.323–88) and one forensic speech (6.328–50). Runnalls (746–50) provides a basic analysis of the structure of the five major deliberative speeches in *Bellum*: (1) 2.345–401: (a) *exordium* (345–47), (b) statement (348–57), (c) proofs (358–87), (d) peroration (388–401). (2) 3.362–82: (a) *exordium* (362–63, (b) statement (364–68), (c) proofs (369–78), (d) peroration (379–82). (3) 4.163–92: (a) *exordium* (163–71), (b) statement (172–75), (c) proofs (176–84), (d) peroration (185–92). (4) 4.238–69: (a) *exordium* (238–43), (b) statement (244–50), (c) proofs (251–64a), (d) peroration (264b–69). (5) 7.341–88: (a) *exordium* (341–42), (b) statement (343–48), (c) proofs (349–77), (d) peroration (378–88). Two speeches have just three parts, and Runnalls (1997, 750–53) regards these, both presented as speeches of Josephus himself, as "Jewish sermons": (1) 5.376–419: (a) introduction (376–78), (b) demonstration (379–414), (c) exhortation (415–19). (2) 6.99–110: (a) introduction (99–102), (b) demonstration (103–7), (c) exhortation (108–10).

Antiquitates Judaicae. *Judaean Antiquities*, Josephus's longest and most complicated work, constitutes a complex example of *rewritten Bible. Since *AJ* was arranged in 20 books by Josephus, it seems clear that he was using the *Antiquitates Romanae* of Dionysius of Halicarnassus, also arranged in 20 books, as a model (Thackeray 1929, 69). Josephus dates the publication of this work to the 13th year of the reign of Domitian (81–96 C.E.), and to the 56th year of his own life, i.e., to 93/94 C.E. (*Ant.* 20.267). Some scholars have identified two endings of the work, one in 20.258, 267–68 and the other in 20.259–66, suggesting that the second was added in the second edition of *AJ*, published about 100 C.E. (Thackeray 1929, 16–19; this proposal is convincingly rejected by Barish 1978). The *AJ* is widely recognized as having an apologetic purpose (see *Apologetic literature). Yet Mason (1995, 196–207) argues convincingly that an apologetic emphasis in the *AJ* does not exhaust the author's intentions, which include an emphasis on the attractiveness of Judaism, in that obedience to the law of God will result in happiness, the recognized goal of most ancient philosophical schools. The thesis of *CA* is stated in 1.14 (LCL trans.):

> But, speaking generally, the main lesson to be learned from this history by any who care to peruse it is that men who conform to the will of God, and do not venture to transgress laws that have been excellently laid down, prosper in all things beyond belief, and for their reward are offered by God happiness [εὐδαιμονία]; whereas, in proportion as they depart from the strict observance of these laws, things practicable become impracticable, and whatever imaginary good thing they strive to do ends in irretrievable disasters.

In writing history, Josephus makes it explicit that he wanted to communicate the truth in a pleasing way (*Ant.* 14.2–3; LCL trans.):

> For while the relation and the recording of events that are unknown to most people because of their antiquity require charm of exposition, such as is imparted by the choice of words and their proper arrangement and by whatever else contributes elegance to the narrative, in order that readers may receive such information with a certain degree of gratification and pleasure, nevertheless what historians should make their chief aim is to be accurate and hold everything else of less importance than speaking the truth to those who must rely upon them in matters of which they themselves have no knowledge.

Speeches in the Antiquitates Judaicae. The *AJ* contains at least 23 speeches (Runnalls 1997, 740 n. 7): 1.228–31; 2.140–58; 2.330–33; 3.300–302; 4.25–34, 40–50; 4.114–17; 4.177–93; 5.93–99; 6.20–21; 6.148–50; 8.111–17; 10.203–9; 11.38–56 (three speeches); 12.20–23; 13.198–200; 14.172–74; 15.127–46

(=*Bellum* 1.373–79); 15.382–87; 16.31–57; 17.110–20; 19.167–84. Five of these speeches are long enough to exhibit features of Greco-Roman rhetoric: 4.177–93; 15.127–46; 16.31–57; 17.110–20; 19.167–84. These include two deliberative speeches (4.177–93; 15.127–46 [=*Bellum* 1.373–79]), two forensic speeches (16.31–57; 17.110–20), and one epideictic speech (19.167–84). There is just one major deliberative speech with a four-part structure: 15.127–46: (a) *exordium* (127–28), (b) statement (129–30), (c) proofs (131–45), (d) peroration (146). Runnalls (1997, 750–53) considers the single deliberative speech with a three-part structure to be a "Jewish sermon": the speech of Moses in 4.177–93: (a) introduction (177–79), (b) demonstration (180–91a), (c) exhortation (191b–93).

Contra Apionem. Perhaps originally entitled "On the Antiquity of the Jews" (Origen, *Contra Celsum* 1.16; 4.11), this presents itself as a sequel to *AJ*. *Contra Apionem* was arranged by the author in two books, a format necessitated by the size of the composition, which required two papyrus rolls (*Contra Apionem* 1.320; Mason 1992, 79). Probably the last work which Josephus wrote during his long tenure in Rome, it was probably written 97–100 C.E. The work was intended for a Gentile audience in Rome, since the summary of Judaism in 2.180–219 would have been far too elementary for Jews (Mason 1996, 188; Goodman 1999, 51). Further, the emphasis on the unanimity of the Jews in 2.179–81 contradicts the variety of Jewish practices detailed in *Est.* 2.119–61 and *Antiquities* 18.11–21.

Literary genre of, Contra Apionem. When Josephus wrote *Contra Apionem*, he referred explicitly to his previous work, *Antiquitates Judaicae*, and claimed that he would now try to do what that previous work failed to do (*Contra Apionem* 1.1–5). As one of the few surviving Jewish apologetic works written as a defense against various accusations leveled against Judaism by non-Jews (see *apologetic literature), the importance of this work can hardly be overestimated. Josephus wrote the *CA* in part because he did not consider the apologetic purpose of *Antiquitates* as successful (1.2). In *CA* Josephus adopted a strikingly pro-Roman and anti-Greek stance (Goodman 1996; Haaland 1999), in attempting to demonstrate the antiquity of the Jewish people in reply to those who claim the opposite (*Contra Apionem* 1.2–5). In *CA* Josephus does not present Judaism as a "system of different philosophical schools" (as in *Bellum* 2.119–66; *Antiquities* 13.171–73; 18.11–25), "nor as 'the best philosophy' or '*the* philosophy', but rather a system superior to and beyond philosophy" (Haaland 1999, 292).

Rhetorical structure of Contra Apionem. The rhetorical structure of *CA* has close similarities to *forensic rhetoric, though it omits the *narratio (which is usually indispensable; see Quintilian 10.4.2.4–8). The work has the following structure: (1) the *exordium* (1.1–5), appropriately brief, outlines the theme of the work: the defense of Judaism against the attacks of outsiders, i.e., those who have attacked Josephus's *AJ* (particularly Apion), as well as other charges against the Jews including misanthropy, atheism, lack of inventiveness, and so on. (2) The first main section of the **probatio* (1.6–320) refutes the charge that Jews are not an ancient people. It begins, however, with a lengthy *digression (1.6–56; he specifically labels this as a παρέκβασις in 1.57) that does not function like a typical digression, since it suggests that everything worth saying was not written by Greeks (Mason 1992, 77–78). He provides a programmatic statement of his intentions in 1.58 (LCL trans.):

> I propose in the first place, to reply briefly to those critics who endeavor to prove the late origin of our constitution from the alleged silence of the Greek historians concerning us [1.60–68]. I shall then proceed to cite testimonies to our antiquity from external literature [1.69–218], and finally to show the utter absurdity of the calumnies of the traducers of our race [1.219–2.144].

(3) The second part of the *probatio* (2.1–286) contains rebuttals of various other charges against the Jews. This section is dominated by Josephus's attack on Apion (1.2–144), a Greco-Egyptian grammarian and lexicographer who taught rhetoric in Rome during the 1st half of the first cent. C.E. and wrote an anti-Jewish work called Αἰγυπτιακά in five books; see *DNP* 1.845–47. It is here that Josephus claims that Moses was the father of Greek philosophy and culture (2.168). Hay (1979, 2.89–90) suggests that another viable construal of the *probatio* is to understand 1.6–2.144 as a series of rebuttals of specific charges and 2.145–286 as a positive description of the Jews and their law (according to Quintilian 5.13.53, a refutation of charges followed by a positive statement is the appropriate sequence for a defense argument). In this section, Josephus emphasizes the qualities particularly appreciated by the Romans but unlike those of the fickle Greeks (Goodman 1996, 92–93): Jews oppose innovation (2.182),

encourage sobriety (2.95, 204), stress communal values (2.196), oppose homosexuality (2.199), keep their women submissive (2.201), honor their parents (2.206), love justice, embrace hard work, avoid extravagance and show courage in defensive war (2.291–92), occupy themselves with crafts and agriculture (2.294), have both practical and theoretical wisdom (2.173–74), have a serious attitude toward life, i.e., are willing to die for their laws (2.171–72). (4) In the *peroratio* (2.287–96), he concludes that all attacks on Judaism have now been successfully rebutted.

The similarities between Josephus's *Contra Apionem* and Philo's *Hypothetica* (fragments preserved only in Eusebius, *Praep.* 8.6–7) have led to the view that both Josephus and Philo were dependent on a common genre of Alexandrian Jewish apologetic (Goodman 1999, 48; S. Schwartz 1990, 23). Verbal similarities between certain passages in *Contra Apionem* (2.145–296, esp. 2.190–219) and *Hypothetica* further indicate that Josephus and Philo used a common source (Belkin 1936; Gerber 1997, 42–49), though that source need not have had the form of an apology. The primary concern of Josephus is rebutting denials that Jews are an ancient nation and refuting moral slanders made against the law of Moses. Josephus's arguments fall into three categories: (1) arguments about good and bad historiography; (2) arguments from historical events, typical or unique; and (3) arguments based on the content of the Mosaic law. The most reliable sources on the antiquity of the Jews are not Greek, but rather Egyptian, Phoenician, and Jewish (1.28–43). He refutes his adversaries by denigrating the quality of their historiography: (a) critics of the Jews frequently disagree among themselves about the same events (1.4, 22–26, 293); (b) they are often guilty of obvious absurdities (1.318–20; 1.17–18); (c) their motives for writing history are improper (1.24–25); (d) those who attack the Jews are intentionally lying (1.3; 2.295); (e) they rely on conjecture (1.15, 22, 46, 293) and dubious etymologies (1.22–27). There is evidence to suggest that the *Contra Apionem* was used as a model by early Christian apologists including Theophilus of Antioch, Ps.-Justin, Origen (Mizugaki 1987), Tertullian, and Eusebius (Hardwick 1996).

Vita *("Autobiography")*. In content, Josephus's "Life" has some of the features of an *autobiography, but most of the work (*Vita* 28–406) focuses on a controversial five-month period of Josephus's life. Josephus is responding to criticism leveled against his *Bellum* by Justus of Tiberias. The work is a sequel to *Bellum* but was apparently published as an appendix to *Antiquitates* (its position in all Greek manuscripts; it was cited by Eusebius, *Hist. eccl.* 3.10.8 as part of the *Antiquitates*) and is generally thought to have been written shortly after the completion of *AJ*. This is problematic, however, for the *Vita* assumes the death of Agrippa II (359–60), who apparently died during the third year of the reign of Trajan (97–117 C.E.), thus placing the *Vita* in about the year 100 C.E. (Barish 1978). Nevertheless, Josephus refers to Domitian in a way that indicates he is still living (*Vita* 428), suggesting that the work was completed before Domitian's assassination in September 96 C.E. The *Vita* itself has no preface but is introduced at the end of *Antiquitates* 20.266.

Relevance for NT and ECL. The two major historical works of Josephus, *Bellum* and *Antiquitates*, provide distinctive historical accounts that have many links to the narratives of the Gospels and Acts, serving as a kind of "Who's Who" for the NT world (Mason 1992, 85–150, 151–84). There are also numerous and significant affinities between the writings of Josephus and *Luke–Acts (Mason 1992, 185–229). Both *Bellum* and *Antiquitates*, on the one hand, and Luke–Acts, on the other, belong to the broad genre of Hellenistic *historiography, more specifically to the common subgenre of "apologetic historiography" (Sterling 1992). Luke places a *preface before each of the two books of his work (Luke 1:1–4; Acts 1:1).

*Apologetic literature, *Autobiography, *Historiography

Attridge 1976; Barish 1978; Bilde 1988; S. Cohen 1979; Franxman 1979; Gerber 1997, 1999; Goodman 1999; Haaland 1999; Hay 1979; Levison and Walker 1996; Mason 1991, 1992, 1996; K. A. Olson 1999; Rajak 1983; Runnalls 1997; Schreckenberg 1996; Sterling 1992; van der Horst 1996

Jude, Letter of, one of a group of seven *General epistles, widely thought to be *pseudonymous.

Authorship and date. The identity of the author and the possible use of *pseudonymity impinge upon questions concerning the date and the *Sitz im Leben*, which are equally uncertain (Bauckham 1988b, 3812–19). The ideological perspective of Jude has been described as Jewish apocalyptic (Lyle 1998, 69–87), especially in light of the citation of *1 Enoch* and the repetitive language of impending destruction for the ungodly (Bauckham 1983a, 8–11). German Protestant scholarship has understood the letter theologically as reflecting the "early Catholicism" of the late 1st and early 2d cent. rather than the supposedly earlier setting of Jewish apocalypticism (Perrin 1974, 260). This latter position is often supported by the belief that Jude is directed against some form of Gnosticism, the same group opposed by 2 Peter (Green 1987, 42–46; Kelly 1969, 231). However, despite the apparent use of Jude by 2 Peter, there is no conclusive evidence that these two letters are directed at the same audience (Knight 1995, 20–22).

Relationship to 2 Peter. Due to the many parallels in content and order evident in Jude and 2 Peter, there is a clear literary relationship between the two letters (see *Peter, Second Letter of). The common view in the 19th cent. and early 20th cent. was that Jude was dependent on 2 Peter (Bigg 1902, 216–24, 312–17). Some scholars have more recently argued that both letters are dependent on a common source (Reicke 1964, 148, 189–90; Green 1987, 58–64). Among the more idiosyncratic recent views, J. A. T. Robinson (1976, 192–95) proposed that Jude wrote his own letter and also was the agent who wrote 2 Peter under apostolic authority, and Soards (1988, 3828–40) argues that the Letter of Jude is one of several works of a Petrine school that is responsible for the production of the interrelated documents of 1 Peter, 2 Peter, and Jude. However, most scholars agree that the relationship is best explained by positing that 2 Peter is dependent on Jude (Bauckham 1983, 141–43; Kahmann 1989; Watson 1988, 160–87).

Sources. The content of Jude draws from the traditions of the OT (the exodus and wilderness wanderings, the story of the fallen angels, a haggadic expansion of Gen. 6:2–6, the destruction of Sodom and Gomorrah, the sin of Cain, Balaam's greed, the rebellion of Korah), two Pseudepigrapha (the *Assumption of Moses* and *1 Enoch*), and a saying of the apostles (vv. 17–18). The citation of *1 Enoch* 1:9 in verse 14 as an authentic prophecy has been part of the debate about the development of the canon (Bauckham 1988b, 3794–96).

Epistolary structure. Jude follows the typical three-part form of the letter in the ancient world (Aune 1987, 161–69): an opening consisting of sender, addressee, salutation, and wishes for health or good fortune (vv. 1–2); the body, containing the purpose of writing and information to be conveyed (vv. 3–23); and a conclusion using typical closing formulae (vv. 24–25).

Literary Analysis. The body has been divided into a variety of different subunits by scholars, but it seems clear that vv. 3–4 contain the purpose and vv. 5–16 serve as background to understand the appeal made by the climax of the argument in vv. 17–23 (Bauckham 1988b, 3802–3). The background in vv. 5–16 focuses on examples of previous destruction of the ungodly and the expectation of similar punishment for the "intruders." The direct address to the audience in v. 17 and again in v. 20 indicates how the author expects his readers to respond to this information. The exhortations in vv. 20–23 fulfill the purpose for writing that is stated in the letter's opening remarks. The conclusion takes the form of an elegant doxology (vv. 24–25) that may have been used in an early Christian liturgical setting before its incorporation into the letter (Neyrey 1993, 94–101).

Rhetorical analysis. Watson (1988, 34–78) has proposed the following rhetorical structure of Jude, which he considers to be an example of deliberative rhetoric (slight modifications):

I. Epistolary prescript (1–2)
II. *Exordium* (3)
III. *Narratio* (4)
IV. *Probatio* (5–16)
  A. First proof (5–10)
  B. Second proof (11–13)
  C. Third proof (14–16)
V. *Peroratio* (17–23)
  A. The *repetitio* (17–19)
  B. The *adfectus* (20–23)
VI. Doxology or "quasi-*peroratio*" (24–25)

Purpose. Like the genuine *Pauline Letters, Jude is occasional, i.e., written at a particular time for a particular purpose. The author states his purpose in vv. 3–4. He encourages his audience to "contend for the faith" against "intruders" among the community. He condemns these opponents, using defamatory language. This purpose accounts for the overt rhetorical nature of the letter, which is the focus of the most recent studies on Jude (Charles 1993; Lyle 1998; Reese 2000; Watson 1988). The letter has a *paraenetic thrust that has been termed variously as a *diatribe (Loisy 1935, 138), a *homily imbedded in a letter similar to the Letter to the Hebrews (Cantinat 1973, 270), a polemical tract (Kelly 1969, 228), and a homily containing a *midrash, i.e., a commentary on Scripture (Horrell 1998, 109; Bauckham 1983a, 3–5).

*General Epistles, *Peter, Second Letter of

Aune 1987; Bauckham 1983a, 1988b; Cantinat 1973; J. D. Charles 1990, 1991a, 1991b, 1993,

1997; Green 1987; Horrell 1998; Kelly 1969; Kahmann 1989; J. Knight 1995; Loisy 1935; Lyle 1998; Neyrey 1993; Perkins 1995; Reese 2000; Reicke 1964; J. A. T. Robinson 1976; Soards 1988; Watson 1988

STEVEN SCHWEITZER

Judicial rhetoric (see *Forensic rhetoric)

Justin Martyr, the most influential of the Christian *apologists of the 2d cent. (Chadwick 1966, 9–30), was born ca. 100 C.E. in Flavia Neapolis (present-day Nablus; ancient Shechem) in Samaria (*1 Apol.* 1.1) and died in Rome as a martyr ca. 165 C.E. Though he refers to himself once as a Samaritan (*Dial.* 120.6), it seems more likely that he was descended from Greek or Roman colonists after Flavia Neapolis was established by Vespasian in 72 C.E. Justin tells us (*Apol.* 1.1) that his father was named Priscus (a Greek name), and his grandfather Bacchius (a Latin name). Justin regarded himself as a philosopher (*Dial* 1.1; 8.1–2) and provides a stereotypical account at the beginning of his *Dialogue with Trypho* narrating his sampling of various philosophical schools; he studied, in turn, Stoicism, Aristotelianism, Pythagoreanism, and finally Platonism (*Dial.* 2). Justin became a Christian ca. 132–34 C.E., perhaps at Ephesus (*Dial.* 7–8), and later went to Rome, where he lived for about ten years the first time, ca. 140 to 150 C.E., and ten years the second time, ca. 155 to 165 (Eusebius, *Hist. eccl.* 4.11). In between he went back to Samaria. In Rome he opened a philosophical school, where the main curriculum was probably the Old Testament and its exegesis; the later Christian apologist Tatian became one of Justin's students. Justin was beheaded, with six other Christians, between 163 and 167 C.E. under the prefect of Rome, Junius Rusticus; the *Acts of Justin* contains historically reliable information about the trial and execution of Justin and his companions (see *Acts of the Christian Martyrs).

Justin was both a Christian and an eclectic Platonist who was convinced that Greek philosophy had a partial apprehension of truths found more completely in Christianity (Chadwick 1966, 15–20): (1) Justin used the Platonic doctrine of the transcendence of God effectively in arguing that the God who appeared to the patriarchs must be Christ as the preexistent divine Logos or Reason, since God the Father was far removed from the material world (this influential theologoumenon dominated christological discussion to the 4th cent.). (2) He argued that all rational beings share in the universal Logos or Reason, so that both Abraham and Socrates were Christians before Christ (*1 Apol.* 46).

Justin wrote a number of works (many are discussed in Eusebius, *Hist. eccl.* 4.18), though just three have survived, *1 Apology* and *2 Apology* as well as the lengthy *Dialogue with Trypho the Jew,* all in a single manuscript that Harnack (1882, 77–79) judged to be in desperate condition. The text of the *Dialogue* in this MS is corrupt, with the introduction missing, which must have had a dedication to Marcus Pomeius, as well as a section following *Dial.* 74.3. This manuscript also contains two other works falsely attributed to Justin, the *Cohortatio ad Graecos* and the *De monarchia* (see the critical editions in Marcovich 1990). Justin's style and composition have not always engendered much appreciation. According to Quasten (1950–60, 1.197): "The style of these [three surviving] works is far from pleasant. Not accustomed to adhere to a well-defined plan, Justin follows the inspiration of the moment. He digresses, his thought is disjointed, he has a failing for long-spun sentences. His whole manner of expression lacks force and seldom attains to eloquence or warmth of feeling."

The "two" Apologies. The two works by Justin conventionally designated as *1 Apology* (or *Apologia Maior*) and *2 Apology* (or *Apologia Minor*) exist essentially in a single MS, *Codex Parisinus graecus* 450, dated September 11, 6872=1363 (there is also an *apograph with no independent value, *British Museum Loan Nr. 36*, dated April 2, 1541, as well as *Codex Ottobonianus graecus 274*, a 16th-cent. MS containing an excerpt of *2 Apol.* 65–67 [72 lines] that is inferior to *Parisinus graecus 450*; see Marcovitch 1994, 5–7). In *Codex Parisinus graecus* 450 (and its apograph), the *2 Apology* (fol. 193r–201r) occurs before the *1 Apology* (fol. 201r–239r). This order was maintained in the editio princeps published by Robert Estienne in 1551 but reversed in favor of a chronological order following an edition published in 1742 (Munier 1994, 14).

The problem of the relationship between the two works has continued to challenge scholarship. There are three different proposals:

1. Since *1 Apology* exhibits a literary unity, there is a clear distinction between the two works (Ehrhardt 1953; Keresztes 1965a, 1965b). Eusebius explicitly mentions two separate works, a λόγος or "treatise" addressed to Antoninus Pius and a second apology

(δευτέρα ἀπολογία) addressed to the Roman Senate and Antoninus Verus (*Hist. eccl.* 4.18.2). Some arguments for compositional unity include the following (Marcovich 1994, 8): (a) The *1 Apology* is framed by the phrase τὴν προσφώνησιν καὶ ἔντευξιν, "this plea and petition," at the beginning (*1 Apol.* 1), and the closely similar phrase τὴν προσφώνησιν καὶ ἐξήγησιν,"this petition and explanation," at the end (*1 Apol.* 68.3). (b) *1 Apol.* concludes with a legal document, a *rescriptus* of Hadrian, appended to it (68.6–10). (c) The *2 Apology* is framed with the term σύνταξις at the beginning (*2 Apol.* 1.1) and τούσδε τοὺς λόγους συνετάξαμεν at the end (*2 Apol.* 15.2). (d) Each *Apology* ends with a *peroratio* (*1 Apol.* 68.1; *2 Apol.* 14.1 and 14.2).

2. The two apologies have never had a separate, independent existence but rather exhibit a single structure and design intended by the author (Holfelder 1977; Munier 1994, 29–40, 1995, 3–6). The statements of Eusebius regarding the apologies of Justin are problematic: (a) The second apology referred to by Eusebius is not the *2 Apology* that has survived (*Hist. eccl.* 4.18.2). (b) Eusebius cites passages from the *2 Apology* that are from our *1 Apology* (*Hist. eccl.* 4.17.1–13 cites extensively from *2 Apol.* 2 as being ἐν τῇ προτέρᾳ ἀπολογίᾳ, "in the First Apology"; *Hist. eccl.* 4.8.4 has a quotation from *1 Apol.* 31, while 4.8.5 quotes *2 Apol* 12 as being ἐν ταύτῳ, "in the same [work]"). Further arguments for unity: (a) Two key words that frame the entire work are εὐσεβεία and φιλοσοφία (*1 Apol.* 1.1; 2.1, 2; *2 Apol.* 15.5; see Hohlfelder 1977). (b) Both apologies are addressed to the same persons, the emperor Antoninus Pius and his adopted son the Caesar Marcus Aurelius (*1 Apol.* 1.1; *2 Apol.* 2.8, 16).

3. The prevailing solution is that the *2 Apology* is a *Nachtrag* or appendix to the *1 Apology* some time after it had been completed (Harnack 1958, 274; Quasten 1950–60, 1.199; Marcovich 1994, 8–11).

Genre and setting of the Two Apologies. Eusebius (*Eccl. hist.* 4.11.11; 4.18.2) refers to the *1 Apolology* as λόγοι ("discourse, oration"), and as a λόγος ("address"). Justin similarly refers to the *1 Apology* as a προσφώνησις, "address" (1.1), an ἔντευξις, "petition" (1.1), and an ἐξήγησις, "explanation" (68.3). All three terms suggest that the *1 Apology* is crafted as a deliberative address to advise the Roman rulers to change the current procedures used at trials involving Christians (Keresztes 1965a, 106). Formally, Justin calls the *2 Apology* a βιβλίδιον or *libellus* (14.1), i.e., a petition addressed to the emperor by a private person (F. Millar 1977, 563). The term *libellus* was applied to all kinds of petitions or letters addressed to a high official or to the emperor; such petitions would have been received by the *A libellis*, the head of the division of the imperial chancery which dealt with all kinds of petitions directed to the emperor (A. Berger 1953, 338; F. Millar 1977, 556–66). From the standpoint of ancient rhetoric, the two Apologies constitute a single *forensic speech with a discernible rhetorical structure (Munier 1994, 32–40).

One important issue, however, is whether or not the *1 Apology* and the *2 Apology* were actually addressed to the emperors or constitute a literary fiction. Munier (1987) thinks that the setting of the two apologies is a literary fiction. Munier's view is confirmed by peculiar features of the address found at the beginning of the *1 Apology* (trans. Fall 1965, 33):

> To the Emperor Titus Aelius Adrianus Antoninus Pius Augustus Caesar; to his son Verissimus the Philosopher; to Lucius the philosopher, by birth son of Caesar and by adoption son of Pius, an admirer of learning; to the sacred Senate and to the whole Roman people; in behalf of those men of every race who are unjustly hated and mistreated: I, one of them, Justin the son of Priscus and grandson of Bacchius, of the city of Flavia Neapolis in Syria-Palestine, do present this address and petition.

This address contains three conspicuous errors in protocol (Buck 2003, 51): (1) In the correct imperial titulature (which had to be present if one wanted the emperor to read the petition) the title for the Emperor Antoninus Pius placed "Caesar" immediately following "emperor." (2) The two adopted sons, Marcus Aurelius (here under the name Verissimus), and Lucius were not associated with Antoninus Pius in official titulature. (3) Justin fails to address Marcus Aurelius as Caesar, though he had been given the title ten years before the composition of the *1 Apology*.

Further, even though petitions to the emperor had to be tightly and economically argued, in 1 *Apol.* 54–67, Justin makes no less than four digressions (Buck 2003, 51–52): (1) In 55.1, the mention of the cross prompts a digression on the sign of the cross (55.1–8). (2) A passing reference to philosophers in 58.3 provokes a harangue on Plato's plagiarism (59.1–60.11). (3) The notion that his statements about the poets might seem unfair in 61.1 leads him into a lengthy discussion of Christian doctrine and practice (61.2–67.8). (4) The mention of Christ's instructions to Moses at the burning bush (62.3–4) stimulates a digression within a digression on the failure of the Jews to recognize the voice of Christ in the flames (63.1–17).

One can only conclude that, despite the form and content of *1 Apology* and *2 Apology*, they were not in fact originally addressed to the emperor, but their composition is a literary fiction (Munier 1987, 181–83; Buck 2003, 51–56). Justin wrote *1 Apology* between 150 and 154 C.E., but used the fictitious imperial address to situate it early in the reign of Antoninus Pius, ca. 139 C.E. Justin calls Marcus Aurelius "Verissimus" and Lucius both philosophers, so he can attack them because they do not live up to that designation (2.2). Literary models for abusive appeals to rulers are found in 1 Kgs. 21:20 and Mic. 3:1–2, but closer to home in the long Greek tradition of the *parrhesia* or "freedom" of expression allowed a philosopher to confront the moral lapses of rulers (Buck 2003, 58).

Dialog with Trypho. The *Dialogue*, which is also preserved in the single manuscript *Codex Parisimus graecus* 450, is essentially a defense of Christianity against Judaism. It purportedly reproduces a discussion in Ephesus between Justin and Trypho the Jew over a period of two days, dividing the *Dialogue* into two sections, 1–74 and 75–142. The *Dialogue* is in fact a literary fiction (van Winden 1971, 127), a fact made clear by the symbolic significance of the myterious "Old Man" who is instrumental in Justin's conversion (*Dial.* 8). The *Dialogue* probably represents a lifetime of arguing the superiority of Christianity over Judaism, honed in debates in Justin's philosophical schools in Rome and Samaria. In *Dial.* 80.3, Justin specifically promises to write down their whole discussion, a reference providing one reason for his later composition of the *Dialogue*. Trypho had fled Palestine following the Bar Kosiba revolt (132–35 C.E.), and was now primarily a resident of Corinth (*Dial.* 1.4). Very little is known about Trypho, assuming that he was a historical character, though later Christian writers describe him as one of the more prominent Jewish scholars of his day (Eusebius, *Hist. eccl.* 4.18.6; Jerome, *De viris illustribus* 23). Zahn (1885–86) identified him with the famous Rabbi Tarphon. Trypho is accompanied by proselytes, that is, pagans who have converted to Judaism (*Dial.* 10:4; 23–24; 85.6). Justin composed the *Dialogue*, an extremely long and rambling work, ca. 155–61 C.E. The work was probably dedicated to Marcus Pompeius (*Dial.* 141.5; cf. *Dial.* 8.4, where the Greek does not have the name Pompeius, but the Latin has "*carissime Pompei*"), though the dedication itself is missing. In the prologue to the *Dialogue*, Justin gives an autobiographical account of his journey to the true philosophy, Christianity (in the form of a stereotypical literary convention; see Droge 1989, 50–51), to which he is introduced by the mysterious figure of "the Old Man" (*Dial.* 2–8). The fact that the Old Man virtually disappears (*Dial.* 8.1) confirms the view that the dialogue is a literary fiction (van Winder 1971, 118). For Hyldahl (1966, 169) the Old Man represents "barbarian Wisdom," while for van Winden (1971, 118) he represents "the rediscovered primordial philosophy, i.e., Christianity," or a "Christian Socrates" (Skarsaune 1976, 69, who nevertheless thinks that the Old Man was an actual person, see 1976, 70). While van Winden and Skarsaune are probably correct in their construal of the symbolic import of "the Old Man," Hyldahl (1966, 162–72) has an extremely informative discussion of the stock figure of the Old Man, or πρεσβύτης, in Hellenistic philosophical and moral literature. The issue is whether Justin's conversion happened in the manner he relates at all, or whether what happened has been overlaid by "literary devices and following the conventions of conversion stories" (Osborn 1973, 67). One discrepancy that scholars pounce on is found in *Apol.* 2.12, where Justin gives as the reason for his conversion to Christianity from Platonism the profound impression made on him by the Christian martyrs. Many find *Dial.* 7 and *Apol.* 2.12 to be contradictory (Hyldahl 1966, 49).

The most satisfactory outline of the *Dialogue* is still that of Otto (1969, 1.lxxxii–xc), who argues that the *Dialogue* is divided into three sections: (1) the decline of the Old Covenant (10–47), (2) Jesus as the true Son of God who became a human being and was crucified for our sake (48–108), and (3) the calling of the Gentiles as the true people of God (109–41). It is apparent that the *Dialogue* has the macrostructure of a λόγος προτρεπτικός, or "speech of exhortation," intended to win converts and attract people to a particular way of life (see *Protreptic literature). The central function of λόγοι προτρεπτικοί was to encourage conversion, and they included both ἀποτρέπειν ("dissuasion") and ἐλέγχειν ("censure") intended to free the potential convert person from erroneous beliefs and practices. Protreptic speeches typically consist of three sections: (1) a negative section criticizing the rival sources of knowledge, ways of living, or schools of thought that reject philosophy (i.e., in the case of the *Dial.* 10–47, why the Law is obsolete and Christians do not obey it); (2) a positive section in which the truth claims of philosophical knowledge, schools of thought, and ways of living are presented, praised, and defended (i.e., why Christ is the true Messiah in *Dial.* 48–108); and (3) an optional section, consisting of a personal appeal to the hearer, inviting the immediate accepting of the exhortation (i.e., why Christians are the true heirs of the promises of God in *Dial.* 109–41, which includes explicit appeals to Trypho to repent in *Dial.* 118 and 137, as one would expect). Though more extensive outlines have been attempted (see Sagnard 1951, adopted by Dubois, Archambault et al. 1994, 96), they are frustrated by what has been called Justin's "remarkably bad organization of the material" (Skarsaune 1987, 135). More typically, the content of the *Dialogue* is conveyed by one-sentence descriptions of the content of each chapter. Here is the very basic outline of Otto (1969, 1.lxxxii–xc):

I. Prologue (1–9)
II. Why Christians do not obey the Torah (10–47)
III. Why Christ is the true Messiah (48–108)
IV. Christians are the true heirs of the divine promises (109–41)
V. Conclusion (142)

Other works. The *Syntagma* is a lost work of Justin to which he himself refers (*1 Apol.* 26.8) and which Irenaeus explicitly cites (*Adv. haer.* 4.6.2). Prigent (1964) argues that in the *Apology* and the *Dialogue,* Justin is primarily using excerpts from the lost *Syntagma*. Among the works incorrectly attributed to Justin are the *Cohortatio ad Graecos* (Riedweg 1994) and the *De resurrectione* (Heimgartner 2001), though Prigent (1964, 36–64) argues at length, and has convinced several others, that the *De resurrectione* should be attributed to Justin.

Use of sources: The NT. The writings of Justin provide abundant evidence that he knew the Gospels of Matthew and Luke (Köhler 1987, 258; T. Heckel 1999, 318). That he knew Mark, which is naturally difficult to demonstrate, given the fact that most of Mark is found in Matthew and Luke, is more problematic (Bellinzoni 1967, 139–42 is negative on this issue). Thornton (1993) argues that *Dial.* 106.3 (e.g., the reference to "sons of thunder," found only in Mark 3:17, and the Markan reference that the new name Peter replaces the old name Simon) is proof that Justin knew Mark. On this slim basis, then, it is possible to say that Justin knew Mark (T. Heckel 1999, 319–20). There is no convincing evidence, however, that Justin knew John (Bellinzoni 1967, 131–38; for contrary argument see T. Heckel 1999, 320–24). He refers to the Gospels as εὐαγγέλια, i.e., "gospels" in the plural (*1 Apol.* 66.3), and also as ἀπομνημονεύματα τῶν ἀποστόλων, "memoirs of the apostles" (*1 Apol.* 66.3; 67.3; *Dial.* 103.8; 106.3), clearly referring to written documents. Some have claimed that Justin was influenced by a Lukan tradition (O'Neill 1961, 10–58; Hyldahl 1966, 261–72). For O'Neill (1961, 29–44) this means: (1) Justin did not use Luke as a source, (2) Justin used sources used by Luke, (3) Luke harmonized his own source(s) with Matthew as he wrote, (4) Justin shared a number of unwritten traditions with the author of Luke–Acts, and (5) Marcion edited Luke's Gospel in light of Justin's other source(s).

Justin also appears to have been dependent on Paul (especially Rom. 2–4 and 9–11) for the text of the OT that he uses in quotations and allusions (Skarsaune 1987, 92–98), rather than quoting directly from an LXX text (see Werline 1999). In fact, of the 49 quotations and allusions to the OT in Romans, Justin has parallels to 14, i.e., 29 percent (Skarsaune 1987, 93).

The text of the Gospels that Justin cites often varies from known manuscript traditions. Scholars have tried to account for this by suggesting that he quoted largely from memory (an older view revived by Köhler (1987, 169–70, 172, 257), that he quoted from noncanonical gospels, or that he was dependent on a harmony of the Gospels (Bellinzoni 1967, 139–42; Osborn 1973, 125–31). According to some, this Gospel harmony of Justin was taken over by Tatian (a student of Justin in Rome), who incorporated Justin's harmony into the **Diatessaron* (W. L. Petersen 1990, 1994, 346–48). W. L. Petersen has argued that Justin's harmony must be earlier than 160 C.E., possibly earlier than 150 C.E. (1994, 348).

Use of sources: OT quotations and exegesis. The most striking thing about Justin's use of the OT is the great length of many of the passages that he quotes (49 quotations are five verses or more in length; Skarsaune 1987, 19 n. 2). In Greco-Roman antiquity, it was not necessary for educated writers to quote extensive passages, since any other educated person would recognize the quotation. What they would do is rework the passage in a mimetic way so that the reader would recognize both the original and the skillful and imitative reworking of the passage in its new content. This is not what Justin does with the OT. The Christian expropriation of the Jewish classical texts was inherently problematic, since Christians did not interpret them as the Jews did. Since culture resided in books, and "nothing could be both new and true" (F. Young 1997, 52), the apologetic stakes were high in demonstrating that the Jewish Scripture was really a Christian book. Justin's *Dialogue with Trypho* can be construed as a concentrated apologetic effort to showcase the truth and validity of the Christian interpretation of Scripture, which the Jew read in a completely wrong way. As an OT exegete, Justin presents his OT exegesis as based on received tradition (Aune 1966, 179–82; Skarsaune 1987, 11–13). Justin regards himself as an interpreter of the OT who was a student of the apostles, who in turn learned it from Christ *(Dial.* 53.5; 76.6; *1 Apol.* 49.5; 50.12).

Justin's use of the OT has been frequently studied (Katz 1957; Smit Sibinga 1963; Prigent 1964; Shotwell 1965; Aune 1966; Barnard 1967c, 175–76), though the large monograph by Skarsaune (1987) is the most comprehensive and focused analysis of Justin's exegetical methods and sources. Skarsaune (1987) concludes that authoritative *testimonia* collections were used by Justin's time, suggesting that they attained such status even earlier, and argues that Justin used both biblical manuscripts and *testimonia* collections. He argues that Justin's short, non-LXX quotations are not "free" quotations made from memory or taken from deviant biblical MSS, but rather are taken from written Christian sources. Further, the long LXX quotations in Justin are not secondary amplifications by scribes, but his own excerpts from the biblical manuscripts to which he had access (Skarsaune 1987, 8). An emerging consensus, then, seems to be that Justin's version of the LXX is not a Christian but a Jewish revision of the Greek OT (Skarsaune 1987, 20).

Skarsaune characterizes the testimony source common to the *Apology* and the *Dialogue* as a missionary document, a codex formulated for Christian use, a sort of notebook of Christianizing targums. The pattern for this source was the creed or kerygma, and it had great hermeneutical authority. The texts that Justin used are strikingly Jewish: Isa. 11:1–4; Mic. 5:1–4; Ps. 72:5–17. Justin treats as Messianic two texts that are also treated as Messianic in the Targum Onqelos but are not found in the NT: Gen. 49:10ff. and Num. 24:17. Skarsaune proposes that there is a repeated pattern in this Christian collection of interpreted texts: (1) the text is quoted, (2) an exposition of symbolic material is added, and (3) the fulfillment is reported. Justin's *1 Apol.* 32 provides an example of this pattern (from F. Young 1997, 124–25). Justin says that Moses, the first of the prophets, spoke these words (Gen. 49:10): "The sceptre shall not depart from Judah, nor a lawgiver from between his feet, until he come for whom it is reserved; and he shall be the expectation of the nations, binding his foal to the vine, washing his robe in the blood of the grape." Justin needs to determine how long Judah had a king and lawgiver of its own. Since Judah was the forefather from whom the Jews took their name, they had their own kingdom until the time of Jesus Christ. He was the one referred to in the phrase "until he come for whom it is reserved." The next phrase "he shall be the expectation of the nations," refers to the expectation of the Parousia, for there are some Christians who are part of all nations who await his second coming. The last parts are regarded as symbols of what was to happen to Christ. The "foal" refers to the animal that Jesus' disciples found for him to ride into the city, and "the blood of the grape" refers to his passion, while "his robe" refers to believers who are washed in his blood. F. Young (1997, 125) draws the following conclusions from this example:

> The pattern of text, explanation and application is evident, but the fundamental issue is one of reference, and to distinguish between a "literal" understanding of the first part of the text, where Justin does take the words more at their face value, and an "allegorical" treatment of the last part of the text, where the symbols are asking to be unpacked, does not help much in the characterisation of the exegetical process. The crucial move is to take the text as a "riddling" oracle and discover what its reference "really" is.

The example given above of Justin's exegesis, and the conclusions drawn by F. Young, make it clear that the usual categories of allegorical, typological, and literal interpretation do not really facilitate the understanding of Justin's exegetical method.

*Apologetic literature, *Irenaeus

Allert 2002; Aune 1966; Barnard 1967c; Bousset 1915; Chadwick 1966; Droge 1989; Erhardt 1953; Goodenough 1968; Goodspeed 1941; Guerra 1992; Harnack 1882, 1930;

Holfelder 1977; Hyldahl 1966; Katz 1957; Keresztes 1965a, 1965b; Munier 1986, 1987, 1994, 1995; Marcovich 1994, 1997; Osborn 1973; Otto 1969; Prigent 1964; Rudolf 1999; Shotwell 1965; Skarsaune 1976, 1987; Smit Sibinga 1963; Stylianpoloulos 1975; Thornton 1993; Winden 1971; Zahn 1885–86

Koine Greek (see *Greek)

Kunstprosa (see *Prose rhythm)

L, Special is a siglum for what some regard as the homogeneous material found only in the Gospel of Luke (see *Luke–Acts); this source was first suggested by B. Weiss, followed by Easton (1911) and B. H. Streeter. Special L consists primarily of pericopes that have no parallel in Mark or Matthew. More problematic is the material found only in Luke at the beginning or end of pericopes that have parallels in one or both of the other Synoptic Gospels (placed in brackets below). Rehkopf (1959, 87) has sought to delineate the linguistic style of Special L on the basis of six criteria that characterize a word, a word-group, or a syntactical construction: (1) it is seldom or never used independently by Luke; (2) it is extensive in Markan material or always avoided by Luke; (3) it is the opposite of a preferred Lukan usage with similar or identical content; (4) it betrays a clear Semitic linguistic background; (5) it is limited to the non-Markan material of Luke; and (6) it is shown in the rest of the NT to be a characteristic community formulation. The following list of material in Special L contains 222 unbracketed verses that together with the 39 bracketed verses make a total of 261 verses in special L:

1. 3:10–14	John replies to questioners
2. 3:23–38	Genealogy of Jesus
3. [4:17–22a, 25–30	Jesus' sermon at Nazareth]
4. 5:1–11	Call of Simon
5. 6:24–26	The woes
6. 7:11–17	Raising of the widow's son at Nain
7. [7:36–50	Jesus anointed by penitent woman]
8. [8:1–3	Women disciples of Jesus]
9. 9:52–56	Samaritan villagers reject Jesus
10. 10:29–37	Parable of Good Samaritan
11. 10:38–42	Mary and Martha
12. 11:5–8	The midnight request
13. 11:27–28	True blessedness
14. 12:13–15	Warning against avarice
15. 12:16–21	Parable of the Rich Fool
16. [12:32	"Fear not, little flock"]
17. [12:33	"Sell your possessions"]
18. 12:35–38	On watchfulness
19. 13:1–5	Repentance or destruction
20. 13:6–9	Parable of the Barren Fig Tree
21. 13:10–17	Healing of the crippled woman
22. 13:31–33	A warning against Herod
23. 14:1–6	Healing of the man with dropsy
24. 14:7–14	Teaching on humility
25. 14:28–33	Cost of discipleship
26. 15:8–10	Parable of the Lost Coin
27. 15:11–32	Parable of the Prodigal Son
28. 16:1–9	Parable of the Unjust Steward
29. 16:10–12	Faithfulness in small things
30. 16:14–15	Pharisees reproved
31. 16:19–31	Parable of the Rich Man and Lazarus
32. 17:7–10	Unworthy servants
33. 17:11–19	Cleansing of the ten lepers
34. 17:20–21	The coming of the kingdom
35. [17:31–34	Watch for the Parousia]
36. 18:1–8	Parable of the Unjust Judge
37. 18:9–14	The Pharisee and the publican
38. 19:1–10	Zacchaeus
39. 19:39–40	Jesus does not rebuke his disciples
40. 19:41–44	Jesus weeps over Jerusalem
41. [21:34–36	Exhortation to watch]
42. 22:31–32	Jesus addresses Simon
43. 22:35–38	The two swords
44. 23:6–12	Jesus before Herod
45. 23:27–31	Crowd follows Jesus to Golgotha

There are 15 parables in Special L, all but the first located in Luke's travel section (9:51–19:43).

1. The two debtors (7:41–42)
2. The Good Samaritan (10:30–36)
3. The Reluctant Friend at Midnight (11:5–8)
4. The Foolish Rich Man (12:16–20=GThom 63)
5. The Barren Fig Tree (13:6–9)
6. Not Seeking Honor at Table (14:8–10)
7. Inviting the Poor to Table (14:12–14)
8. Counting the Cost (14:28–33)
9. The Lost Coin (15:8–10)
10. The Prodigal Son (15:11–32)
11. The Dishonest Steward (16:1–8a)
12. The Rich Man and Lazarus (16:19–31)
13. The Dutiful Servant (17:7–10)
14. The Unrighteous Judge (18:2–5)
15. The Pharisee and the Tax Collector (18:10–14a)

*Example stories, *Luke–Acts, *Parables, *Soliloguy

Easton 1910, 1911; Grant 1957, 45–48, 61–62; Hawkins 1909, 194–97; Jeremias 1980; Petzke 1990; Rehkopf 1959; Streeter 1930, 198; Taylor 1926

Latin, a term derived from a group of related tribes called Latini who settled in the region of Latium, where Rome eventually came to occupy a significant position. The Latini originated in central Europe and settled in Latium by the 10th cent. B.C.E. Latin belongs to the Italic group of the Indo-European family of languages and is divided into two groups, Oscan-Umbrian and Latin-Faliscan. Oscan was the standardized common language of central Italy until the area was subjugated by the Romans. Originally the language of Latium and the city of Rome, Latin, eventually displaced the other Italic languages as a result of the increasing political and military power that Rome exerted first in central Italy, then throughout Italy. The perceived cultural superiority of Greek made it the preferred language of the Roman intelligentsia from the 1st cent. B.C.E. to the 1st cent. C.E. Marcus Aurelius (2d cent. C.E.), for example, chose to write his *Meditations* in Greek. By the 4th cent. C.E., however, most educated Romans in the West were monolingual and understood little or no Greek. The formal end of classical Latin may be dated to 813 C.E., when Charlemagne officially recognized the vernaculars.

The 21-letter Latin alphabet ultimately derived from the 26-letter Greek alphabet, via the 26-letter Etruscan alphabet. The Latin alphabet originally consisted of 20 letters, with *c* and *g* both represented by the letter *c* (*g* continued to be represented by *c* in abbreviations for the *praenomina* Gaius [C.] and Gnaeus [Cn.]), and *z* and *y* were added as phonemes in transliterated Greek words. Later the Latin alphabet added another letter, making a distinction between *c* and *g*. The Roman alphabet lacked *j* (the consonantal version of *i*), *u* (the vocal version of *v*), and *w*. During the 1st cent. C.E., Emperor Claudius attempted to add three new letters to the Latin alphabet, but for the most part these innovations did not long survive him (Quintilian 1.7.26; Suetonius, *Claudius* 41.3; Tacitus, *Annals* 2.13–14).

Latin was the main language of Rome (a multilingual city with a substantial Greek population), the colonies founded by Rome, the Roman army, and the Roman provincial civilian administrations, though Rome does not appear to have had a formal language policy. Though Italy had previously been multilingual, Latin increasingly predominated, until by the 1st cent. B.C.E. Latin was also the dominant language of the peninsula. In the Western empire outside Italy and the Roman colonies, the army was one of the main vehicles for the spread of Latin, through both contact with the local population and the learning of Latin by originally non–Latin-speaking auxiliaries. In Italy there were two different kinds of Latin, the formal, polished, correct Latin spoken by the educated and surviving in public speeches and most of the extant body of Latin literature, and common colloquial Latin (Plautus is a major exception). There were striking phonological differences between regional speakers of Latin in the various provinces (Cicero, *Brutus* 171–72; Jerome, *Epistles* 107.9; see Omeltchenko 1977; Whatmough 1970), i.e., there were a number of vulgar Latins. Though some of these vulgar forms of Latin developed into the Romance languages, it is hardly appropriate to speak of Latin "dialects" during the earlier period. The substrate language of various regions certainly influenced the phonology of Latin (*Historia Augusta Sept. Sev.* 19.9).

In many of the provinces where Latin was the language of the army, the administration, and culture, there were native languages that inevitably exerted influence on Latin phonology. In North Africa, the earliest native language was Libyan ("Berber," from the Greek term βαρβάροι, "foreign"), used from the 8th cent. B.C.E. on. Called by Augustine the "lingua Punica," it was a Semitic language based on Phoenician, the first language of both the emperor Septimus Severus (145–211 C.E.) and Augustine (354–430 C.E.). While there are some surviving inscriptions in Libyan, many in Punic, and some bilinguals in Punic-Latin and Libyan-Latin, the more than 30,000 Latin inscriptions from North Africa preponderate.

The relationship between Rome and the many Greek colonies in the western Mediterranean was complex. Many Greek colonies in Magna Grecia lost their Greek population and language through the conquests of the Samnites. Tarentum capitulated to Rome in the Pyrrhic War in 272 B.C.E., and it and many other cities were either destroyed or depopulated during the remainder of the Republican period, until the inauguration of Augustus's policy of the Romanization of Italy obliterated the remaining pockets of Greek culture and language. Neapolis was the last city in the western Mediterranean to abandon Greek as an official language, and public and private inscriptions were written in Greek until the late 1st cent. C.E., perhaps because Roman aristocrats found it convenient to have a Greek city near Rome. During the Hannibalic War, Sicily was captured and plundered by the Romans and later (132 B.C.E.) became the first Roman province. Later Augustus founded six colonies in Sicily in which Latin was the first language, and this was accompanied by a conscious program of Romanization that resulted in the gradual elimination of the Greek language during the first few centuries C.E. Before Augustus, most public inscriptions and legends on coins were in Greek; after him Latin was used almost exclusively. The replacement of Greek by Latin in old Greek colonies occurred primarily in the Augustan age. Outside of southern Italy and Sicily, the Romans had close contacts with Massilia (modern Marseilles), which was triglossic (Greek, Latin, and Celtic) until late antiquity (Justinus 43.3.4). The Romans also had close contacts with Emporion, a Greek colony of Massilia in Spain (Strabo 3.4.8; Livy 34.9).

Latin never achieved the position in the eastern Mediterranean held by Greek in the western Mediterranean. Some Romans began to immigrate to the Greek East during the 3d cent. B.C.E., with the movement peaking in the next century. Roman settlers were particularly encouraged by the founding of the free harbor at Delos in 166 B.C.E., as well as by the new opportunities provided by Roman conquests. The slaughter of Romans in 88 B.C.E. gives some idea of the magnitude of Roman colonization. The total number of Romans and Italians killed that year in Asia Minor by the Greeks, instigated by Mithridates, was between 80,000 (Valerius Maximus 9.2.4) and 150,000 (Plutarch, *Sulla* 24.4), while most of the 20,000 massacred at Delos were Romans (Appian, *Mithridates* 5.28). Romans who settled in the Greek East include (a) merchants and craftsmen, (b) soldiers and veterans (involved in military operations, providing garrisons in the provinces, and colonizing as veterans), (c) magistrates and civil servants in provincial administration, and (d) colonists. There were many Roman settlements (the technical term was *conventus civium Romanorum*) by the middle of the 1st cent. B.C.E. in Greece, Asia Minor, and Syria, with at least 41 settlements in Asia Minor alone.

Macedonia was the first Roman province in the East (148–147 B.C.E.). By the mid-1st cent. C.E., there were 16 Roman provinces in the East: 4 in Greece (Achaea, Epirus, Macedonia, Thracia), 6 in Asia Minor (Asia, Bithynia et Pontus, Galatia, Lycia et Pamphylia, Cilicia, Cappadocia), 4 in Syria (Syria, Iudaea, Mesopotamia, Arabia), Aegyptus and Creta et Cyrenaica. Official Roman colonization in the Greek East began in the mid-1st cent. B.C.E., and by 14 C.E. there were about 30 colonies, 4 in Greece, 15 in Asia Minor, 6 in Macedonia, 1 in Crete, and 2 in Syria. Latin was the first language of all Roman colonies. Though these colonies were eventually Hellenized, the colonists formed a socially separate, privileged group, while the native populations had an inferior social status, lacking Roman citizenship. Both public and private inscriptions, as well as legends on coins, were exclusively in Latin in such colonies.

Following the Roman conquest of Palestine in 63 B.C.E., Latin was used in Palestine primarily by the Romans, for whom it was the language of the army and the civilian administration. Inscriptional evidence for the presence of Latin includes dedicatory inscriptions on aqueducts and buildings, funerary inscriptions, inscriptions on milestones on Roman roads, and large numbers of brick and tile stamp–impressions of abbreviations for the Tenth Legion Fretensis. Caesarea Maritima, a seaport city built by Herod the Great (Josephus, *Ant.* 15.331–41; *War* 1.408–14), became the Roman provincial capital of Judaea in 6 C.E., the residence of the provincial governor (Acts 23:33; 25:1), and the main garrison of the Roman army. The excavations at Caesarea have uncovered many Latin inscriptions, including a dedicatory slab erected by Pontius Pilate (prefect of Judea ca. 26–36 C.E.) for a *Tiberieum*, i.e., a cult center for Tiberius, and a inscription of the Tenth Legion, which repaired the high-level aqueduct during the time of Hadrian. The multilingual character of Jerusalem is indicated by the signs posted in the temple in both Greek and Latin forbidding foreigners to enter the holy place (Josephus, *War* 5.193–94; 6.125; *Ant.* 15.417; Philo, *Legatio ad Gaium* 212). Two fragmentary Greek copies of this inscription have been found (*SEG* 8.169; 20.477). Appropriately for this trilingual context, John 19:20 mentions that the inscription on the cross of Jesus was written in Aramaic, Latin, and Greek. Julius Caesar reportedly sent a decree in 47 B.C.E. to the people of Sidon that was to be recorded on a bronze tablet in both Greek and Latin (Josephus, *Ant.* 14.191, 197), and Mark Antony similarly sent a bilingual edict in 41 B.C.E. to the people of Tyre (Josephus, *Ant.* 14.319). The reason for using Latin in these two Phoenician cities, however, is not immediately clear.

The Romans typically had contempt for Egyptians, often making no distinction between native Egyptians and Egyptian Greeks. Egypt had three Greek cities, Naucratis and Alexandria in Lower Egypt and Ptolemais in Upper Egypt. Alexandria was populated primarily by Greeks and Jews, who engaged in

intermittent conflict. The Greek language predominated in the administration of Roman Egypt. The papyri containing imperial constitutions, edicts, rescripts, and decrees are 75 percent Greek and 25 percent Latin. Generally, imperial rescripts sent to private individuals, including Romans, and those for public promulgation in Egypt, are written in Greek, while rescripts and mandates addressed to Roman officials and instructions to the army are written in Latin. Edicts of the Roman prefect of Egypt and other Roman magistrates in Egypt are almost exclusively promulgated in Greek. Egyptian provincials who were not Roman citizens always used Greek in legal documents. Roman citizens necessarily used Latin for many types of legal documents (e.g., birth certificates, marriage contracts, petitions to the prefect, and wills).
*Greek, *Latin literature

W. S. Allen 1965; Altheim 1951; Conte 1994a, 1994b; Fitzmyer 1979, 29–56; Omeltchenko 1977; Palmer 1954; Whatmough 1970;

Latin literature is customarily divided into three major periods: (1) the formative period (ca. 240–80 B.C.E.), i.e., Livius Andonicus to Cicero, (2) the classical period or *golden age of Latin literature (ca. 80 B.C.E.–14 C.E.), i.e., to the death of Augustus, and (3) the *silver period (14–180 C.E.), to the death of Apuleius (see the masterful survey in Conte 1994b).

The formative period (240–80 B.C.E.). Data for our knowledge of the Latin language is hampered by the fact that there are few texts that antedate the 3d cent. B.C.E. In the view of scholars both ancient (Cicero, *Brut.* 71–72; Quintilian 10.2.7) and modern, Latin literature began during the late 3d cent. B.C.E. with Livius Andronicus, a Greek from Tarentum, who became a school teacher in Rome and translated the *Odyssey* into Latin (in a native accentual meter called Saturnian) in order to have a school text. Gnaeus Naevius, a Greek from Sardinia, was trilingual (Greek, Oscan, Latin) and wrote an epic on the first Punic War between Carthage and Rome, in Latin, also using Saturnian meter. Another Greek, Quintus Ennius (239–169 B.C.E.), of Rudiae near Tarentum, was significant for adapting Greek metrical form to the Latin language. Latin prose has its beginning with Ennius's translation of Euhemerus, preserved by the Christian rhetorician Lactantius. Oddly, scarcely a single author of Latin prose or poetry actually came from the city of Rome. That means that no type of Latin literature is completely native. The earliest extensive body of literature that has survived, however, are the 21 plays of T. Maccius Plautus (late 3d to early 2d cent. B.C.E.), from Umbria, who became Rome's greatest dramatist. Terence (ca. 195–159), a native of North Africa, found a patron in the younger Scipio Africanus and wrote comedies based closely on Greek originals, particularly Menander. Latin prose began with M. Porcius Cato (234–149 B.C.E.), who wrote orations and essays, though only *De agricultura* has survived. Prose Roman history, which had its beginnings in the *Annales* or yearly records compiled by the current *pontifex maximus*, was written in Greek beginning in the late 3d cent. B.C.E. by Q. Fabius Pictor and his successors.

The golden age (80 B.C.E.–14 C.E.). The classical period of Latin literature began with the much-admired didactic poem of Lucretius (94–55 B.C.E.), *De rerum natura*, which focused on Epicurean physics. The most innovative litterateur of the period was Marcus Tullius *Cicero (106–43 B.C.E.), a politician and orator whose prose compositions, primarily speeches, letters, and philosophical essays, became literary and rhetorical models for later writers through the Renaissance and later. Other influential writers of this period include Cicero's contemporaries M. Terentius Varro (116–27 B.C.E.), who wrote the *Roman Antiquities* (lost) and one surviving work, *De re rustica* ("On agriculture"); Julius Caesar (100–44 B.C.E.), who wrote *De bello Gallico* ("On the Gallic War"), and *De bello civili* ("On the Civil War") in crisp, unadorned prose; and Sallust (86–35 B.C.E.), who also wrote historical works. Under the Empire, the poet of greatest stature was Virgil (70–19 B.C.E.), whose most important work was an epic, the *Aeneid*, a modernized *Iliad* and *Odyssey* that promulgated the ideals of the Augustan principate. Other eminent Latin poets include Horace (65–8 B.C.E.), Propertius (late 1st cent. B.C.E.), and Ovid (43 B.C.E.–17 C.E.), who wrote in elegaic meter. Livy (59 B.C.E.–17 C.E.) wrote a history of Rome in 142 volumes, of which 35 have survived.

The silver age (14–180 C.E.). During the early imperial period the Latin literature produced during the classical period became models to be both imitated and parodied during the following centuries. After varying degrees of intellectual and literary repression following the death of Augustus in 14 C.E., Latin literature again exhibited creativity from the end of the first to the middle of the second century C.E.

Some of the more important literary figures are Seneca (ca. 4 B.C.E.–65 C.E.), an important writer of literary tragedies, philosophical essays, and letters; his nephew Lucan (39–65 C.E.), who wrote *Pharsalia* (both were forced by Nero to commit suicide); Pliny the Elder (ca. 23–79 C.E.); Pliny the Younger (ca. 61–112 C.E.); Tacitus (b. ca. 56 C.E.), a historian who wrote *Germania*, *Agricola*, *Histories*, and *Annals*; and the accomplished comic novelist Apuleius (ca. 123–180 C.E.), author of the *Golden Ass*.

*Asianism, *Atticism, *Golden age, *Latin, *Silver age

———

Conte 1994b; Fuhrmann 1999; Kenny 1982

Lectionary refers to the ritual of reading selections or pericopes of Scripture at synagogal and ecclesial services of worship as well as to the books eventually compiled containing these readings. Some scholars have proposed that some books in the OT and the NT were composed to correspond in various ways with lectionary traditions (Carrington, 1952; Guilding 1960; Goulder 1974, 1978), while other argue that the evidence for fixed lectionary pericopes and cycles is too late for such use (Morris 1964).

Ezra 8 narrates the public reading of the Law (Torah) of Moses by Ezra the scribe (Deut. 31:10–14 prescribes the reading of the Law every seven years), and it is clear that readings of the Law and the Prophets (the latter came to be called *haftarah*, "completion") soon became an integral part of synagogue services (Luke 4:16–20; Acts 13:15; 15:21; Josephus, *Against Apion* 2.17.175; Philo, *On Dreams* 2.127). By the end of the 2d cent. C.E., there is evidence in the Mishnah for the systematic reading of the Law over a three-year period, for *m. Megillah* 4.2–4 prescribes that seven men will read not less than three verses from the Torah portion. Since the Masoretic Text of the Torah has 5,845 verses, it would take 278 Sabbaths of 21 verses each to complete the cycle of readings, though the average weekly lectionary was larger than the minimum (see *m. Taanit* 4.3). The Torah lections were also accompanied by oral translations in Aramaic by a *meturgeman*, which eventually became fixed as the Targums. By the end of the 6th cent., there was a Palestinian lectionary (triennial cycle of 154 *sedarim* or "sections") and a Babylonian lectionary (annual cycle), the latter still in use, consisting of 53 or 54 *parashiyot* or "pericopes" (*b. Megillah* 31b). It is not possible, however to retroject either the triennial or annual cycle of readings back to the 1st cent. C.E. (Heinemann 1968, 41–48).

Early Christians read letters sent to their congregations by Paul and others (1 Thess. 5:27; Col. 4:16; Rev. 1:3), and it appears that they also continued the Jewish practice of reading the OT in public worship, a practice that included the Gospels by the mid-2d cent. (Justin, *1 Apology* 67).

———

Carrington 1952; Colwell and Riddle 1933; Crocket 1966; Goulder 1974, 1978; Greeven 1951; Guilding 1960; Heinemann 1968; Mann 1971; Morris 1964; *Revised Common Lectionary* 1992; Wikgren 1963

Legend, from the Latin verb *legere* ("to read"), means "that which ought to be read." Legend, which is difficult to distinguish clearly from myth, can be defined as follows (Rappoport and Patai 1966, 1.xi):

> [A] typical legend differs from a myth in that it lacks the latter's charter character: it neither validates nor explains anything. Moreover, while it is, like the myth, traditional and religious, its protagonists are not divine beings and heroes, but saints, martyrs and other deeply pious men or women; although the story told in the legend is usually believed to be true, the acceptance of the legend as truth is not, as in the case of the myth, a religious imperative; and finally, the legend as a rule contains a moral lesson. Legend has, therefore, an historical or historicizing character, and can be regarded as semi-historical traditions (Kirk 1975, 23).

*Folklore, *Form criticism

———

Kirk 1970, 1974

Lesser to greater argument (Latin: *a minore ad maius*; Hebrew: קל וחמר; *qal wahomer*) is the argument that if something is true in a lesser case, it will much more obviously be true in a greater case. In the later Greek rhetorical tradition, the argument from the lesser to the greater (Aristotle refers to "the topic of lesser to greater," *Rhet.* 1.2.21, i.e., "lesser to greater" is a *topos, ὁ τοῦ μᾶλλον καὶ ἧττον τόπος) is often a source for particular forms of the *enthymeme. An example is found in Apsines, *Ars rhetorica* 8.2 (trans. Dilts and Kennedy 1997, 177): "Now the topic from the lesser is naturally amplificatory; it is so, for example, in the case of the man who destroyed the fleet and is brought to trial: 'Come now; for if it is illegal to destroy one ship, clearly it is much worse to destroy a whole fleet.'" The lesser to greater argument also occurs frequently in Christian literature (Keener 1999, 247 n. 231). Examples: (1) "For if many died through one man's trespass, much more have the grace of God and the free gift in the grace of that one man Jesus Christ abounded for many" (Rom. 5:15). (2) "Do you not know that the saints will judge the world? And if the world is to be judged by you, are you incompetent to try trivial cases?" (1 Cor. 6:2). (3) "Do you not know that we are to judge angels? How much more, matters pertaining to this life!" (1 Cor. 6:3). (4) "If God is for us, who is against us?" (Rom. 8:31). (5) "He who did not spare his own Son but gave him up for us all, will he not also give us all things with him?" (Rom. 8:32). For a further example from Paul, see Gal. 3:15–17. (6) "If you then, who are evil, know how of give good gifts to your children, how much more will your Father who is in heaven give good things to those who ask him!" (Matt. 7:11=Luke 11:13. Many find the lesser-to-greater argument as part of the preceding parable of the Friend at Midnight in Luke 11:5–8; see Snodgrass 1997, 512; Hultgren 2000, 238). According to Bultmann (1963, 188), this is the only example of the *a minore ad maius* argument in the Synoptic Gospels; however, other examples do occur in Matt. 6:30 (Davies and Allison 1988, 684); Matt. 10:25b; Heb. 12:9.

*Style, *Enthymeme

Encyclopedia Judaica 8.367; Snodgrass 1997

Letter collections, a literary genre popular primarily in Greek philosophical schools and then subsequently Roman political and rhetorical circles. The Romans were more avid writers and collectors of letters than the Greeks. The letters of famous Romans were often written with the intention of publishing or circulating them as collections, e.g., Cicero, Horace (W. Allen 1972–73), Ovid, Seneca (H. Cancik 1967), and Pliny (Sherwin White 1966). Such letters were thought worth preserving because of their literary, educational, and historical value.

Important collections of Latin letters are attributed to Cicero and Pliny the Younger. The 931 letters of Cicero's extant correspondence between 68 and 43 B.C.E. were published posthumously (ca. 60 C.E.) in four collections (*To Friends*, *To Atticus*, *To Quintus*, *To Brutus*). Cicero intended to publish a small selection of his letters (*To Atticus* 16.5) that would illustrate his literary abilities (*To Friends* 16.17.1), but he died without accomplishing this desire. Cicero kept copies of some of his letters (*To Friends* 7.25.1), and recipients such as Atticus retained them, perhaps pasting them together into rolls. Cornelius Nepos (*Atticus* 16.2–4) refers to 11 rolls of Cicero's letters owned by Atticus. They perhaps constituted 11 of the 16 books of letters to Atticus that were later published.

Pliny (61–112 C.E.) published nine books of 358 letters arranged chronologically. He usually limited letters to one theme, avoided excessive length, and used a style appropriate to the subject. The distinctive character of his letters suggests an origin in the oratorical digression, which characteristically treated the praise of persons or places, descriptions of places, and historical and legendary narratives (Quintilian 4.3.12). The literary character of Pliny's letters is also evident in his use of standardized opening phrases indicating the subject of his letters.

The first Greek author to publish a collection of his own letters was Gregory Nazianzus (ca. 329–89 C.E.). There are many other collections of Greek letters, however. Some important representative collections of ancient Greek letters include those by Isocrates, Demosthenes, Epicurus, Apollonius of Tyana, and Libanius. The letters of Aristotle (384–322 B.C.E.), surviving only in fragments, were collected and published after his death. A collection of nine letters of Isocrates (436–338 B.C.E.) is still extant, though the authenticity of several is debated. A collection of six letters of Demosthenes (384–322 B.C.E.) has been preserved, of which four are authentic and two doubtful (Goldstein 1968). Similarly, a collection of the letters of Epicurus (341–270 B.C.E.) became influential as models for philosophical letters. The 17th-cent. English classicist Richard Bentley persuasively demonstrated that ancient collections of Greek letters attributed to Phalarais, Themistocles, Socrates, and Euripides were forgeries. In consequence, the shadow of doubt has fallen on many other such collections, though some contain at least a few authentic letters.

A collection of 97 letters and letter fragments make up the correspondence of Apollonius of Tyana (d. ca. 97 C.E.). Some may be authentic (e.g., *Ep.* 71). In addition, 20 letters (*Ep.* 98–117, following Hercher's numbering) are quoted in Philostratus, *Life of Apollonius*. Philostratus claims to have used letters of Apollonius as sources (1.2, 23–24, 32). That suggests the existence of a collection that antedates the biography. Philostratus also knows a collection of letters that Apollonius exchanged with Euphrates (5.39; *Ep.* 1–8, 14–18, 60). While all the letters of Apollonius have abbreviated openings (i.e., the name of the recipient in the dative, or just the statement "to the same person"), closing salutations (ἔρρωσο or ἔρρωσθε) occur just four times (*Ep.* 14, 43, 47, 53).

One of the great letter writers of late antiquity was the Antiochean rhetorician Libanius, who wrote more than 1,600 letters (Seeck 1906; Liebeschuetz 1972, 17–23). Libanius and his educated friends wrote with a wider public in view, for they publicly read letters they received (*Ep.* 1264; *Or.* 1.175) and expected recipients of their letters to do the same. Libanius consciously tried to give his letters a timeless quality so that they might have a permanent value transcending the original circumstances of their composition.

*Epistolography, *Letters, literary genre of, *Pastoral letters

---

W. Allen 1972–73; H. Cancik 1967; Constable 1976; Goldstein 1968; Hercher 1873 (the most extensive collection of ancient Greek letters available); Liebeschuetz 1972, 17–23; Malherbe 1977a; Seeck 1906; Sherwin White 1966

Letter openings (see *Epistolography, *Prescriptions, epistolary; *Thanksgivings, epistolary)

Letters, literary genre of Genuine letters are written communications between two parties who are separated spatially and for whom the letter is a substitute for being personally present. Letters also serve to provide information, to make requests, to recommend, and to promote congenial relations between the sender and the addressee.

Since Deissmann, research on Greco-Roman letters has taken three different routes: formal literary analysis, thematic analysis, and rhetorical analysis. In addition, NT scholars have developed another method, form criticism, first applied to the Synoptic Gospels, to identify and analyze various types of fixed traditional forms, or preformed traditions both oral and written, that have been preserved in early Christian letters and homilies.

Formal literary analysis. The formulaic features of ancient letters, particularly documentary papyrus letters, have been extensively analyzed in comparison with NT letters (White 1986). Considerable progress has been made, not only with regard to opening and closing formulas, but also in the matter of epistolary forms, which tend to cluster at the beginning and end of the body or central section of ancient letters. Yet there are limitations in this approach, and the analysis of the central section remains problematic.

Since the Pauline Letters are the earliest and generally most complex early Christian letters (*1 Clement* is also extremely complex, though a generation later than the Pauline letters), epistolary conventions found in them can provide a framework for discussing early Christian epistolary formulas. These letters, like most ancient letters, have three basic elements: the opening and closing epistolary formulas and the larger central section which they bracket. In most Pauline letters, the basic elements of the epistolary *praescriptio* or prescript have each been expanded in distinctive ways. The body is the central section that often closes with travel plans and exhortation. The closing formulas typically consist of doxology, greetings, and benediction. Many of these features are derived from, or have parallels to, Greco-Roman and Jewish epistolary conventions. Here is an overview of the typical formal structure of the Pauline letter (Aune 1987, 183–91; White 1988, 97):

- I. Opening formulas
  - Epistolary prescription
    - Superscription
    - Adscription
    - Salutation
  - Thanksgiving [or benediction]
- II. Central section (Body of the letter)
  - Internal transitional formulas
    - Disclosure formulas
    - Parakalō formula
    - Confidence formula
  - Epistolary topoi
    - Business
    - Domestic events
    - Government matters
    - Health
    - Letter writing
    - Reunion with addressees
  - Autobiographical statements
  - Travel plans
  - Concluding paraenesis
- III. Closing formulas
  - Peace wish
  - Request for prayer
  - Secondary greetings
  - Holy kiss
  - Autographed greeting [various positions]

Opening formulas. The formulaic opening of the Pauline Letters consists of two basic elements: the *prescription (consisting of the superscription or sender, the adscription or addressee, and salutation), and the *thanksgiving.

In superscriptions, Paul usually identifies himself with epithets such as "apostle" and "servant" (lacking in 1 Thessalonians, 2 Thessalonians, Philippians, and Philemon). Most of Paul's letters list *cosenders (Romans, Ephesians, and the Pastorals are exception; of this group, only Romans is certainly authentic).

All Pauline letters with the exception of the Pastorals have similar salutations, found in simplest form in Paul's earliest letters: "Grace to you and peace" (1 Thess. 1:1). Paul may have used the term "grace" (χάρις) as a word play on the usual epistolary "greetings" (χαίρειν). The closest parallel is found in a pseudepigraphic letter attributed to Baruch, originally written in Hebrew ca. 100 C.E. (*2 Bar.* 78:2): "Mercy and peace to you." Paul's use of "peace" probably reflects the Hebrew and Aramaic salutation שלם, "shalom" or "peace." In NT letters, the simple χαίρειν ("greetings") occurs only in James 1:1 and in two embedded letters in Acts (15:23; 23:26). The salutation "grace to you and peace" was expanded by making the source of grace and peace explicit, as in Col. 1:2: "Grace to you and peace *from* God our Father"), and was further amplified in the other eight letters: "Grace to you and peace from God our/the Father and the/our Lord Jesus Christ." Galatians 1:3–5 is unusual, for the salutation is expanded into a doxology (in Rev. 1:5b–7, a doxology similarly follows the epistolary salutation).

All of the authentic Pauline letters except Galatians and 2 Corinthians insert a prayer of thanksgiving immediately after the salutation (e.g., Rom. 1:8–17; 1 Cor. 1:4–9; Phil. 1:3–11). In 2 Cor. 1:3–7 there is a benediction where a thanksgiving is expected. These prayers of thanksgiving all begin with the phrase "I give thanks to God always for you" (or the equivalent), using the Greek verb εὐχαριστεῖν ("to give thanks"), which quickly became a technical term for the Lord's Supper (Ignatius, *Eph.* 13:1; Justin, *1 Apol.* 65–66). The thanksgivings in two of the Pastoral Letters (1 Tim. 1:12–17; 2 Tim. 1:3–5) use an entirely different idiom, and the prayer in 1 Pet. 1:3–13 is really a eulogy or benediction, since it begins, like 2 Cor. 1:3–7, with the term εὐλογητός ("blessed"). Ephesians 1:3–4 is a eulogy followed by a thanksgiving (1:15–23).

The inclusion of a prayer or a religious expression of gratitude after the salutation has parallels in ancient letters. The *proskynema* formula follows the salutation in Greek papyri beginning with the 1st cent. C.E. Similar prayers are found in the same position in some Hellenistic Jewish letters (2 Macc. 1:1–9; 1:10–2:18, perhaps the closest parallel to the Pauline thanksgiving; *Par. Jer.* 6.19–25). Speeches occasionally begin with an expression of gratitude (Dio Chrysostom, *Or.* 48.1, thanking the city magistrate who permitted the assembly). Seneca begins a letter by expressing gratitude for receiving letters frequently from a friend (*Moral Epistles* 40.1).

The thanksgiving period is not just formal or ornamental. It often praises the recipients, functioning as an **exordium* aimed as securing their goodwill. As such it is a functional equivalent to introductory sections of official letters that praise the recipients. Pauline thanksgivings often encapsulate the main themes of letters, like the thanksgiving periods in papyrus letters and the *exordia* of speeches. The length of the thanksgiving reflects the degree of intimacy between the writer and recipients. The longer thanksgivings of Philemon and 1 Thessalonians reflect cordial relations. They are missing from Galatians and 2 Corinthians altogether, reflecting strained relations.

Closing formulas. Paul's letters always conclude with a χάρις ("grace") benediction. Before the grace benediction, optional epistolary formulas are often placed, usually in the following order: (1) peace wish, (2) request for prayer, (3) secondary greetings, (4) holy kiss, (5) autographed greetings (varied positions).

Paul replaces the usual Hellenistic formulas of final greeting with the grace benediction, "Grace [χάρις] be with you," characteristic of all Pauline letters but Ephesians (and just six other Christian letters through the 6th cent. C.E.). This benediction always comes last (except in 1 Cor. 16:23). The benediction contains three basic elements: (a) "grace," (b) the divine source of that grace, and (c) those who benefit from that grace. The benediction of Paul's earliest letter exhibits the basic pattern: "The grace / of our Lord Jesus Christ / be with you (1 Thess. 5:28; cf. Rom. 16:20; 1 Cor. 16:23; 2 Cor. 13:14; Gal. 6:18; Phil. 4:23; 2 Thess. 3:18; Phlm. 25). This Pauline pattern is also followed in Rev. 22:21 and *1 Clem.* 65:2. The latter joins the benediction to a doxology. Just two elements are found in Colossians and in several (other) non-Pauline letters: "Grace / be with you" (followed by several variations in 1 Tim. 6:21; 2 Tim. 4:22; Titus 3:15; cf. Heb. 13:25). A different form of blessing concludes *Barn.* 21:9: "May you be saved, children of love and peace. The Lord of glory and all grace [be] with your spirit."

A typical Pauline peace wish is found in Phil. 4:9: "and the God of peace will be with you." The formula is found near the end of all the Pauline letters except 1 Corinthians and Philemon.

A request for prayer occasionally is made at the end of Pauline and deuteropauline letters (Rom. 15:30–33; 1 Thess. 5:25; 2 Thess. 3:1; Col. 4:3; Eph. 6:18–20; cf. Heb. 13:18).

Secondary greetings (greetings conveyed to the addressee[s] by the author from others) are frequently found at the conclusion of Hellenistic letters after the 1st cent. B.C.E., using the ἀσπάζεσθαι ("to send greetings to") formula. Early Christian letters often use this form, e.g., Phlm. 23–24: "Epaphras, my fellow prisoner in Christ Jesus, sends greetings (ἀσπάζεται) to you, and so do Mark, Aristarchus, Demas, and Luke, my fellow workers." Secondary greetings occur in every authentic Pauline letter but Galatians; they are absent from the doubtful 2 Thessalonians and from the deuteropauline Ephesians and 1 Timothy. The longest section of secondary greetings is found in Rom. 16:3–16 (26 people are greeted); the shortest is 2 Cor. 13:13: "All the saints greet you." Among the non-Pauline NT letters, concluding secondary greetings occur in Heb. 13:23–24; 1 Pet. 5:13–14; 2 John 13; 3 John 15.

Several times the addressees of Paul's letters are told to greet each other with a "holy kiss" (Rom. 16:16; 1 Cor. 16:20; 2 Cor. 3:12; 1 Thess. 5:26). This uniquely Christian greeting, which elsewhere occurs only in 1 Pet. 5:14, is perhaps simply an enactment of Paul's greetings to each of them. The practice is later attested as part of the early Christian liturgy (Justin, *1 Apol.* 65; Tertullian, *On Prayer* 14). When Ignatius says "the love of X greets you" (*Trall.* 13:1; *Rom.* 9:3; *Philad.* 11:2), he may be alluding to this custom.

A personal "autographed greeting" is found at the end of five of Paul's letters (1 Cor. 16:21; 2 Thess. 3:17; Col. 4:18; Gal. 6:11; Phlm. 19), e.g., 1 Cor. 16:21: "I, Paul, write this greeting with my own hand." Many papyrus letters have final greetings written in a hand different from that of the rest of the letter, suggesting that it was added by the author rather than the scribe. Even literary letters reflect this practice (Cicero, *To Atticus* 12.32; 13.28; 14.21). Paul's statement in 2 Thess. 3:17 suggests that while he regularly made use of a secretary, he also validated his letters with his own closing greeting: "I, Paul, write this greeting with my own hand. This is the mark in every letter of mine; it is the way I write." Of course, this may be a strategy for legitimating a pseudonymous letter as well.

The central section. This section of the letter, the one containing the material that constitutes the purpose for which the letter was written, is also the section that has proven most resistant to formal analysis. The central section of ancient letters also contains formulaic phrases, some toward the beginning, serving as transitions from the opening to the central section, and others toward the end, serving as transitions from the main part to the closing. There are five types of material found in the central sections of early Christian letters: (1) internal transitional formulas, (2) epistolary topoi, (3) autobiographical statements, (4) travel plans, and (5) concluding paraenesis.

1. *Internal transitional formulas.* The central sections of two of Paul's letters begin with a disclosure formula: "I would have you know, brethren" (Gal. 1:11; Phil. 1:12); two others begin with the related phrase: "I/we do not want you to be ignorant" (Rom. 1:13; 2 Cor. 1:8). Both phrases can occur within letters as a way of moving into the discussion of an important issue.

Bjerkelund (1967) has argued that sentences beginning with "I appeal [παρακαλῶ] to you," or "I beseech [ἐρωτῶ] you," constitute fixed epistolary formulas of Greek origin found in both private and official letters. Such phrases occur 19 times in Paul (e.g., Rom. 15:30; 16:17; 1 Cor. 4:16; 16:15). The most revealing instance is perhaps Phlm. 8–10, in which Paul emphasizes the fact that he appeals to Philemon rather than commands him, i.e., he writes in a friendly rather than an authoritative manner. These sentences have a transitional function, indicating a change in subject and often disclosing the main purpose of the letter (2 Thess. 2:1; 1 Cor. 1:10; 1 Thess. 4:1–2, 10b–12). The closest parallels are found in the diplomatic correspondence of Hellenistic kings, in which the *parakalō*-clauses emphasize the friendly, personal dimension of the relationship between the king and his subjects. Though the formula can introduce paraenesis (Rom. 12:1; 1 Thess. 5:12, 14), it remains transitional, unrelated to the paraenesis itself.

The *confidence formula*, containing expressions of confidence, occurs several times in Paul (Rom. 15:14; 2 Cor. 7:4, 16; 9:1–2; Gal. 5:10; 2 Thess. 3:4; Phlm. 21). Typical is 2 Cor. 7:16: "I rejoice, because I have perfect confidence in you." There are four variations in these expressions of confidence, all of which have parallels in ancient papyrus letters: (1) confidence in the recipient's compliance (Gal. 5:10; 2 Thess. 3:4; Phlm. 21); (2) request based on confidence (2 Cor. 9:2); (3) pretended confidence as an excuse for making a request (Rom. 15:14; 2 Cor. 9:1–2); and (4) expression of confidence as a polite request (Rom. 15:24).

2. *Epistolary topoi* are the themes and constituent motifs used in stereotypical ways in ancient letters. A comparison between the nonliterary papyrus letters and early Christian letters reveals a number of common epistolary themes and motifs: (1) letter writing (Rom. 15:14; 1 Cor. 4:14; 5:9; 7:1; Phlm. 21); (2) health (1 Cor. 1:8–11; Phlm. 2:25–30; 2 John 12; 3 John 13); (3) business (1 Cor. 16:1–4; 2 Cor. 9:1–5; Phil. 4:14–18); (4) domestic events (1 Cor. 5:1–6:11; Phil. 4:2–4, 14–18); (5) reunion with addressees (Rom. 15:14–33; Phil. 3:19–24; 1 Thess. 2:17–3:13; 2 John 12b; 3 John 13–14); and (6) government matters (Rom. 13:1–7; Titus 3:1–2; 1 Pet. 2:13–17). In several of the hortatory sections of Paul's letters (Rom. 12:1–15:13; Gal. 5:13–16:10; Col. 3:5–4:6; 1 Thess. 4:1–5:22), the exhortations emphasize departing from evil and seeking good (cf. 3 John 11–12). These sections contain a number of topoi on stock themes. Romans 13, for example, contains a series of four topoi on authority (vv. 1–5), on paying tribute (vv. 6–7), on love (vv. 8–10), and a distinctively Christian topos on the eschatological hour (vs. 11–14). Similarly, in 1 Thess. 4:9–5:11 there are three separate topoi discussed and developed on the love of the brethren (4:9–12), on the fate of the Christian dead (4:13–18), and on times and seasons (5:1–11).

3. *Autobiographical statements*. Throughout his letters, Paul makes autobiographical statements (see *Autobiography). Three lengthy ones are found in 1 Thess. 1:2–3:13, Gal. 1:11–2:21, and 2 Cor. 1:12–2:17, continued in 7:5–16. Many of these statements are located toward the beginning of the letters, often following the thanksgiving (Rom. 1:14–16a; 2 Cor. 10:7–12:13; Phil. 1:12–26; 3:2–14). Such autobiographical statements (missing only from 1 Corinthians and Philemon) are often understood as attempts by Paul to defend himself and his gospel from the accusations of opponents. In Greco-Roman oratory an important type of argument was based on the establishment of the moral character (ἦθος) and conduct of the speaker (Aristotle, *Rhet.* 1415a; Cicero, *Divisions of Oratory* 6.22; 8.28; *Rhetorica ad Herennium* 1.4.8–5.1; see *Ethos). Character (ἦθος) was important for several reasons: (1) the speaker wished to project a likeable and trustworthy image of himself; (2) the speaker wished to foster the right impression (and therefore had to know the concerns and situation of his audience); and (3) the speaker wished to present the character of his opponents plausibly but so that his own version would be more persuasive.

According to Lyons (1985), the autobiographical section in Gal. 1:10–2:21 is structured in accordance with conventional autobiographical topoi: (1) *prooimion*: Paul's divine gospel (1:10–12); (2) *anastrophe* (behavior): Paul's character (a) as a persecutor (Gal. 1:13–14), (b) as a preacher of the gospel (1:15–17); (3) *praxeis* ("deeds"): Paul's conduct (1:18–2:10); (4) *epilogos* ("epilogue"): Paul does not reject God's grace (2:21). The rhetorical antitheses in this passage and in 1 Thess. 1:2–3:13 do not necessarily reflect a point-by-point rebuttal of hypothetical charges (Donfried 2000; Hoppe 2000).

4. *Travel plans*. Since letters are a primary means of communication between those who are separated, the topos of reunion occurs frequently. Funk (1967) has described an epistolary form that centers on such visitation talk, which he designates the "*apostolic parousia." It usually concludes the main part of Paul's letters. The three modes of Paul's apostolic presence are the letter, envoys, and personal presence. However, the absence of a consistent structure suggests that we are dealing with a topos of theme with a number of subordinate motifs. Funk defines the apostolic parousia in terms of five elements, some with several subordinate features: (1) mention of Paul's letter-writing activity, (2) mention of his relationship to the addressees, (3) statement of plans for paying a visit (desire to visit, delays in coming, sending an emissary, announcement of a visit), (4) invocation of divine approval and support for the visit, and (5) benefits of the impending visit. There are twelve examples of the apostolic parousia in Paul's letters, though few of them contain all the above elements (e.g., Rom. 1:8–15; 15:14–33; 1 Cor. 4:14–21; 16:1–11; Gal. 4:12–20; Phil. 2:19–30; 1 Thess. 2:17–3:13; Phlm. 21–22). Travelogues are found in several deuteropauline letters (Eph. 6:21–22; 2 Tim. 4:6–18; Titus 3:12–14), as well as in other Christian letters (Heb. 13:18–19, 22–23; 2 John 12; 3 John 13–14).

5. *Concluding paraenesis*. *Paraenesis means "advice" or "exhortation," and refers to general moral and religious instruction that falls between symbouleutic and epideictic rhetoric. Since Judaism, with its rich tradition of ethical

monotheism, and the major Hellenistic schools of philosophy (Stoics, Peripatetics, Platonists, Epicureans) all emphasized ethics, moral exhortation was a common phenomenon throughout the ancient world.

One of the distinctive features of the Pauline letter tradition is the presence of a concluding section of paraenesis (Rom. 12:1–15:13; Gal. 5:1–6:10; 1 Thess. 4:1–5:22; Col. 3:1–4:6). The frequent occurrence of lengthy paraenetic sections in the latter part of some Pauline letters has encouraged the division of the body of Paul's letters into two main sections, doctrinal and ethical. Yet there are other letters in which paraenesis is not concentrated in the concluding section but is woven throughout the composition (1 Corinthians, 2 Corinthians; Philippians; cf. James, Hebrews, 2 John, 3 John, *1 Clement*). Paraenesis is a complex subject that has recently been the focus of research. At this point, however, it is helpful to highlight between *epistolary paraenesis*, which is found in defined concluding sections of some Christian letters, and *paracretic styles*, which permeate letters (e.g., 1 Thessalonians, Galatians, Colossians).

Paraenesis has several important characteristics: (1) Paraenesis is traditional, reflecting conventional wisdom generally approved by society (Isocrates, *Nicocles* 40–41; Ps.-Libanius, *Epistolary Styles* 5; Phil. 4:8). (2) Paraenesis is applicable to many situations (Seneca, *Letters* 94.32–35). (3) Paraenesis is so familiar that it is often presented as a "reminder" (Seneca, *Letters* 13.15; 94.21–25; Dio Chrysostom, *Or.* 17.2.5; 1 Thess. 4:1–2; 2 Thess. 3:6; Phil. 3:1). (4) Paraenesis can be exemplified in exceptional people who are models of virtue (Seneca, *Letters* 6.5–6; 11.9–10; 95.72; 2 Thess. 3:7; Phil. 3:17; 4:9). Paraenesis is usually transmitted by people who are social and morally superior to those they address.

*Apostolic parousia, *Prescriptions, epistolary

Aune 1987, 158–225; Barr 1966, 1968; Bjerkelund 1967; Boers 1975–76; Doty 1973; Exler 1923; Koskenniemi 1956; Llewelyn 1995; Mullins 1973; O'Brien 1977; Sanders 1962; Schnider and Stenger 1987; Thraede 1970; White 1971a, 1971b, 1972a, 1972b, 1986, 1988

Levi, Testament of, is a pseudepigraphon in the form of a testament or first-person speech of a dying patriarch (see *Farewell address), in which Levi tells his sons what they should do and what will happen to them on the day of judgment. The structure of *T. Levi* is problematic. After an introduction in the first person in 1:1–2, the remainder of the testament is couched in the third person *T. Levi* 2–9 centers on two dream visions, both of which deal with the priesthood of Levi. In the first dream vision, after praying to God for deliverance from human sinfulness, Levi sees the heavens open and is invited by an angel to enter (2:1–6; cf. Rev. 4:1). He ascends through three heavens, each lighter and brighter than the previous one (for they are further away from the sinful earth), and is promised a vision of four more heavens even more brilliant (2:7–9). Finally he is told that he will stand before the Lord as his priest (2:10). The angelic guide then explains each of the seven heavens (3:1–10) and tells Levi that his prayer for deliverance is answered by the priestly office he will exercise in Israel, though he must warn his descendants not to reject the Lord when he comes (4:1–6). Thereupon the gates of heaven are opened, and Levi sees the Most High sitting on his throne (5:1). God himself then bestows upon him the priestly office (5:2). Returning to earth, he is given a shield and sword by the angel and commanded to avenge the rape of Dinah, after which he awakes (5:3–7). Levi and his brothers then kill Shechem and Hamor and destroy their city (6:1–7:4). In the second dream vision, Levi is given the vestments and insignia of a priest by seven angels and, upon awaking, is aware of the connection with the first dream vision (8:1–19). This section concludes with a visit with Jacob to Isaac and centers on Isaac's instructions to Levi regarding the priesthood (9:1–14).

Chapters 10–19 exhibit a less obviously unified pattern. Several sections with a hortatory character predict the sin, exile, and sometimes the return of Levi's descendants (10:1–5; 14:1–15:4; 16:1–5), the first two introduced with the stereotyped phrase "and now my children." A historical narrative describing Levi's marriage and children and the marriages of his children culminates with a chronology of Levi's life (11–12). The only purely horatory section is 13:1–9 (introduced with the phrase "and now my children"), where the consequences of obeying and disobeying the law of God are rehearsed. In 17:1–11 is the prediction of seven jubilees, during each of which a priest will predominate. In 18:1–14 is told the coming of the new priest. In 19:1–5, introduced with "and now my children," Levi presents his sons with the choice between light or darkness. They choose light, and Levi calls on the Lord and his angels as witnesses to their choice. Levi then dies.

Text: De Jonge 1978. Translations: Kee in *OTP* I, 775–828. Commentary: Hollander and de Jonge 1985

Library, a public or private collection of books and manuscripts for reading and research, was a phenomenon found throughout the ancient world. The Latin noun *librarius* meant either a "secretary, scribe" or "bookseller," while the adjectival form *libraria* could mean "bookshop." The Greek term βιβλιοθήκη means "repository for books." There were both public and private libraries in the Greco-Roman world. The epitomator of Athenaeus (1.3a) mentions the bibliophile Larensius and says of him that "he owned so many ancient Greek books that he surpassed all who have been celebrated for their large libraries including Polycrates of Samos, Peisistratus the tyrant of Athens, Eucleides, likewise an Athenian, Nicocrates of Cyprus, the kings of Pergamum, Euripides the poet, Aristotle the philosopher, Theophrastus, and Neleus, who preserved the books of the two last named."

Aristotle's library. One of the most famous and extensive of ancient private libraries was that of Aristotle. Aristotle reportedly purchased the small library of Speusippos, Plato's successor, for the huge sum of three Attic talents or 72,000 sesterces, a collection that may have included some of Plato's own autographs (Aulus Gellius 3.17.3; *Diogenes Laertius 4.5). Aristotle's library consisted of three categories of works (Blum 1991, 53): (1) copies of books by other authors that he had purchased; (2) personal copies of his own works, including the more polished, exoteric works intended for others and the less polished, esoteric works intended for Peripatetic consumption; and (3) his archives, consisting of notes, personal papers, letters. Aristotle willed this collection of works to Theophrastus (see Gottschalk 1972 and *Aristotle's *Rhetorica*). Theophrastus bequeathed his library and that of Aristotle to Neleus of Skepsis on his death in 286 B.C.E. (a transcript of his will is preserved in Diogenes Laertius 5.51–57). The collection was badly cared for and suffered damage until it was acquired by Appelikon of Teos, a wealthy book collector (Athenaeus 5.214d), who died ca. 84 B.C.E.). Shortly thereafter it was seized and sent to Rome by Sulla (Strabo 13.1.54). An alternate account (but one supported by Blum 1991, 58 and C. Lord 1986, 142–43) holds (on the evidence preserved in Athenaeus, *Deipn.* 1.3a) that Ptolemy II Philadelphus bought the libraries of Aristotle and Theophrastus from Neleus and took them to Alexandria. Long after Theophrastus died, the collection suffered damage and was eventually appropriated by Sulla, who sent it to Rome (Strabo 13.1.54; Plutarch, *Sulla* 26.1–2), where the works of Aristotle and Theophrastus were apparently edited by Andronikos of Rhodes.

The Alexandrian library. The Museion (from Μυσεῖον, "sanctuary of the Muses") at Alexandria, one of the largest libraries in the ancient world, was founded by Ptolemy I shortly before he died (283 B.C.E.) as a universal research institute (El-Abbadi 1990; MacLeon 2000; Casson 2001). The institution of the Museion had the form of a cult association, and its highest official was a priest appointed by the king (Strabo 17.1.8). The Museion was part of the royal palace complex, had facilities for members to dine together, and included walkways, porticoes, and exedras for scholarly conversation (Vitruvius, *De architectura* 5.11.2). The holdings of the library were made accessible by the *Pinakes* of *Callimachus, a bibliography of Greek literature and catalog of the Alexandrian library in 120 books. Callimachus organized this catalog in eight categories: oratory, rhetoric, poetry (two parts), law, philosophy, history, and miscellaneous. Ptolemy II Philadelphus reportedly had the Hebrew Bible translated into Greek for inclusion in the Museion (Josephus, *Ant.* 12.11–16). Ptolemy III decreed that all merchant ships anchored in the Alexandrian harbor must loan their manuscripts to the Museion for copying. The holdings of the Museion library were extremely large, though there is no ancient agreement about its size. Some authors put the figure as high as 700,000 books (Gellius), others have 400,000 (Orosius), and yet others have 70,000 (Isidorus); see the list of testimonies in F. Schmidt 1922, 4–15. The library was destroyed by fire in 47 B.C.E. The library of Theophrastus, himself a prolific author, presumably included his own works (232,808 stichoi in total length), which are found in an alphabetical catalogue in Diogenes Laertius 5.42–50 (which appears to be a composite list), which some regard as a catalogue produced by the Alexandrian library, while others think that it is an inventory of a number of separate Peripatetic collections (C. Lord 1986, 143). The role of Demetrius of Phaleron is mentioned specifically in the *Letter of Aristeas* 9–10, as the context in which Ptolemy II

Philadelphus commissioned the translation of the Hebrew Bible into Greek (trans. Hadas):

> When Demetrius of Phalerum was put in charge of the king's library he was assigned large sums of money with a view to collect, if possible, all the books in the world; and by arranging purchases and transcriptions he carried the king's design to completion as far as he was able. When he was asked, in my presence, about how many thousands of books were already collected, he replied, "Above two hundred thousand, Your Majesty; and in a short while I shall exert every effort for the remainder, to round out the number of half a million. I am informed that the laws to the Jews also are worthy of transcription and of being included in your library.

Roman libraries. After the burning of the famous library housed in the Museion in Alexandria in 47 B.C.E., Julius Caesar intended that the first public libraries in Rome be as magnificent as possible (Suetonius, *Caesar* 44; Plutarch, *Caesar* 49). In 39 B.C.E., C. Asinius Pollio incorporated libraries of Greek and Latin books into the reconstruction of the Atrium Libertatis adjacent to the Forum Iulium (Ovid, *Tr.* 3.1.71; Pliny, *Hist. nat.* 7.115; Dio Cassius 48.41.7). During the decade of the 20s B.C.E., Augustus included a collection of Greek and Latin books, stored in separate rooms, in the library facilities of the temple of Apollo Palatinus (Dio Cassius 53.1; *CIL* 6.2347–49; 4431–35; 5192) and the Porticus Octaviae were completed (Plutarch, *Marcellus* 30; Ovid, *Tr.* 1).

Libraries in Palestine. There were many libraries of which little or nothing is now known. Nicholas of Damascus during the reign of Herod I (37–4 B.C.E.) wrote a universal history in 144 books while living in Jerusalem. He must have had a substantial library at his disposal. There is no evidence to indicate the existence of libraries in Jerusalem, and none to suggest the existence of a central library in the temple in Jerusalem (Shavit 1994, 302–7). Josephus does not refer explicitly to a library anywhere in *Antiquities*, though he describes the temple in detail in books 5 and 15. Josephus reports that a building called the archives (τὸ ἀρχεῖον), the location of which is unknown (though apparently near the Akra and the Bouleuterion, or council chamber where the Sanhedrin met), was burned by the Jewish rebels in 70 C.E. (*Wars* 6.354), while the archives themselves (τὰ ἀρχεῖα), consisting of the bonds issued by moneylenders, were apparently burned in 66 C.E. (*Wars* 2.427). The building in which these records were houses is called the record depository (γραμματοφυλακεῖον) in *Wars* 2.427 (cf. 7.55, where it is clear that at Antioch τὰ αρχεία were housed in the γραμματοφυλακεῖον, both of which were destroyed by fire).

Blau (1902, 97–111) argued that there was once a library of Scripture in the temple in Jerusalem containing the standard text according to which all copies must be corrected, a question later reviewed by Klijn (1977), and the subject is also treated somewhat uncritically by Beckwith 1988, 40–45). The storing of texts in sanctuaries is attested quite early in Israel. The tables of the law (Exod. 25:16, 21; 40:20) and the book of Deuteronomy (Deut. 10:1–5; 31:24–26) were stored in or near the ark of the covenant. The book of the law, probably Deuteronomy, was discovered in the temple during the reign of Josiah (2 Kgs. 22:8; 23:2, 24; 2 Chr. 34:15, 30). The *Letter of Aristeas* (176–77) reports that 72 translators arrived from Jerusalem bringing scrolls of the Torah written in gold. This was because it had earlier been discovered that no copies of the Torah in Hebrew were found in the Alexandrian library (30). On the basis of this slim evidence, it is not possible to maintain that a library of biblical manuscripts existed in Jerusalem (Klijn 1977, 266). There is reference in 2 Macc. 2:13–15 to the founding of a library in Jerusalem by Nehemiah, in which were "collected books about the kings and prophets, the writings of David, and letters of kings about inventories of votive offerings." The historicity of this brief notice is problematic, though nothing is said about the presence of biblical books in the library (Klijn 1977, 267–68). In several places Josephus mentions that written works including biblical texts were to be found in the temple of Jerusalem (*Ant.* 3.38; 4.303; 5.61; *Life* 418; *War* 7.150; 7.162); though a special copy of the Torah was available in the temple (presumably the one carried off by Titus according to Josephus, *War* 7.162 and depicted on the arch of Titus), no exemplary significance is attached to this particular copy (Klijn 1977, 268–69). A variety of rabbinic sources also mentions the presence of a scroll of the Torah in the temple, but it is never claimed that it is superior to other texts (Klijn 1977, 269–72). Beckwith (1988, 44–45) suggests (on the basis of no convincing evidence) that the collection of the books of the Law, Prophets, and Writings in the temple archive provided the canonical standard: "the main test of the canonical reception of a book must have been whether or not it was one of those laid up in the Temple."

The fact that the remains of ca. 850 scrolls were found in the vicinity of Qumran has naturally led scholars to suppose that a large library was housed at Khirbet Qumran. Another hypothesis suggests that the Dead Sea Scrolls were not housed at Qumran, but represent a library (perhaps the temple library) that was removed from Jerusalem when it was under siege by the Romans (66–70 C.E.) and hidden in caves in the desert (Golb 1990). It is doubtless true that the Dead Sea Scrolls do not represent the homogenous literary productions of a single Jewish sect, suggesting that the scrolls consist of both sectarian and nonsectarian documents (Newsom 1990). Archaeologists have not discovered a room in the remains of Khirbet Qumran that would have been an appropriate storage place for parchment scrolls, though Stegemann has proposed that a thousand scrolls were stored in jars and baskets in the main building. There are no references within the scrolls themselves, nor in the ancient descriptions of the Essenes, that mention the existence of a library or even the writing and copying of books.

*Codex, *Papyrus

Blau 1902; Blum 1991, 52–64; Canfora 1989; Casson 2001; *DNP* 8.507–511; Gamble 1995, 144–202; MacLeod 2000; Müller-Graupa 1933; Klijn 1977; Pfeiffer 1968, 96–104; Oldfather 1938; R. W. Smith 1974; J. W. Thompson 1940; N. G. Wilson 1980

Lists, though one of "the most archaic and pervasive of genres," have not been given a great deal of attention by scholars (J. Z. Smith 1982, 44). A "list" is a comprehensive term to designate a series of items, whether ordered or unordered, just as the Greek term κατάλογος could refer to both ordered and unordered lists (Fitzgerald 1997, 276 n. 4). *Listwissenschaft,* or "the science of enumeration," including word lists (Westenholz 1985) and king lists (Jacobsen 1939), was widespread in the ancient Near East (Towner 1973, 2–3; for a bibliography see Fitzgerald 1997, 276–77 n. 5); in the Hebrew Bible, particularly in the form of genealogies (Eissfeldt 1965, 24–26; Roth 1965; Malamat 1968; Hartman 1972; Wilson 1977; Coxon 1986); and in early Jewish literature (Stone 1976; Towner 1973). Catalogues occur frequently in early Greek literature, particularly in the *Iliad* (e.g., the famous catalog of ships in *Iliad* 2.494–760, called a *neon katalogos* in Plutarch, *Solon* 10; the catalog of Nereids in *Iliad* 18.39–49; the catalog of gifts in *Iliad* 9.121–30) and Hesiod (e.g., the genealogy of the gods in the *Theogony*), and are now regarded as an important feature of pre-Homeric epic (Minton 1962; Lattimore 1959, 1–13; bibliography in Fitzgerald 1997, 278 n. 7). The list or catalog can be regarded as both a *style (in that they contrast with narratives) and a literary form, though it has no set structure for component parts. Catalogs often have the character of a *digression. A frequent function of catalogs, in either a narrative or explanatory context, is amplification (αὔξησις), which lends importance to the subject. Catalogs make frequent use of quantitative adjectives and adverbs and comprehensive terms like πᾶς ("all"). Paul uses a comprehensive "all" before a vice list in Rom. 1:29, and quantitative terms in a hardship catalog in 2 Cor. 11:23–26 ("far greater labors, far more imprisonments, with countless beatings, and often near death. Five times [lashed] . . . three times [beaten]," etc.). In the list of 28 types of merchandise goods denied to Rome listed in Rev. 18:11–13, the term "all" or "all kinds of" occurs three times. In 2 Cor. 11:23–28, Paul gives a catalog of hardships he has experienced (see *Peristasis catalogs), and they provide narrative of a specific hardship (vv. 32–33). Catalogs used as amplification "create the feeling of quantity, size, greatness, fullness, completeness, and thereby raise the significance of what is related" (Fitzgerald 1997, 287). The notion of massiveness becomes more important than individual items in the catalog. The amplification of individual items in a catalog indicates the importance of the item. In addition, catalogs function to provide an air of factuality and objectivity of what is being conveyed (Márot 1949, 43–49). They may also serve as a kind of proof of what is being narrated. In sum, catalogs can function to amplify, verify, and bestow objectivity (Fitzgerald 1997, 289).

*Amplification, *Asyndeton, *Climax, *Digression, *Polysyndeton, *Priamel

---

Fitzgerald 1997b; Jacobsen 1939; Lattimore 1959, 1–13; Márot 1949; Minton 1962; Race 1982, 24–27; Regenbogen 1941; Towner 1973; Westenholz 1985; Zaas 1988

Lists of vices and virtues (see *Catalogues of vices and virtues)

Literacy basically refers to the ability to read and write, though there are obviously wide variations in reading and writing skills. Literacy in Greco-Roman antiquity was largely restricted to a privileged minority. According to Harris (1989, 130–33, 141, 323–37), an average of about 10 percent of the population throughout the Greek, Hellenistic, and Roman imperial periods was literate, an average that never exceeded 15–20 percent at any given time. It has often been argued that the importance of Scripture in early Christianity meant that a relatively high percent of Christians was literate, but this is doubtful (Gamble 1995, 5). Christian leaders must have been able to read, since Scripture was read at services of worship (1 Tim. 3:13; Justin, *Apol.* 1.67). The earlier assumption that early Christians were largely drawn from the ranks of the illiterate lower classes has been shown to be without basis. The Hebrew Bible (and its Greek translation in the Western Diaspora) was of central importance in Judaism, and for that reason boys were taught to read in preparation for participation in the reading of the Torah in synagogue services (Josephus, *Contra Apionem* 2.204; *Antiquities* 4.211; Philo, *Ad Gaium* 115, 210; 2 Tim. 3:14–15; Safrai 1976, 2.945–70).

*Literary criticism, *Reading

Bar-Ilan 1988, 1992; Botha 1992; Bowman and Woolf 1994; Cole 1981; Culpepper 1983; Finnegan 1988; Gamble 1995; Harris 1989; Hezser 2001; Humphrey 1991; Millard 2000; R. Thomas 1992; J. Watson 2001

Literary criticism is actually an umbrella term for a spectrum of critical approaches to the reading and interpreting of literary texts. The term "criticism" itself, in fact, has tended to replace the terms "poetics" and "rhetoric" in the modern period. Literary criticism is essentially discourse about literature, i.e., metaliterary discourse, the major social and political function of which is inclusion and exclusion, leading inexorably to the construction of a canon of literary models (Loo 1998, 3–5). The English phrase "literary criticism" combines two critical activities differentiated in German with the terms *Literaturkritik* (a certain kind of journalism that reviews contemporary literature and the kind of cultural discourse found in popular magazines and newspapers) and *Literaturwissenschaft* (the scholarly, philological, and methodologically self-conscious evaluations of literature published in scholarly journals and books and taught in universities). More generally, literary criticism is understood to refer to a self-conscious act involving the technical and aesthetic appraisal of autonomous literary works by an individual. The term "criticism," etymologically based on the Greek word κρίνειν ("to judge, evaluate, decide, rule"), clearly implies an emphasis on the evaluation of literary works and hence is concerned with making value judgments, discriminating between the good, useful, just, and truthful, and (on the other hand) what is bad, useless, unjust, and false (Loo 1998, 10). In general, literary criticism suggests a focus on understanding the text itself in terms of its language and imagery, structure and development of thought, literary form, and (in the case of narratives) character and plot. Other relevant aspects essential to understanding a literary work include its relationship to earlier literary works (see *Intertextuality), the historical and cultural context in which it took shape, and the ways in which the work has been construed and affected yet other texts. Poetics, which remains a useful term, generalizes the uniqueness of a literary work in poetic language; textual analysis attempts to explain the uniqueness of a literary text (Riffaterre 1983, 2). A literary text is unique, according to Riffaterre (1983, 2), and "the literary experience is characteristically disorienting, an exercise in alienation, a complete disruption of our usual thoughts, perceptions, expressions."

Ancient literary criticism. The dividing line between ancient and modern literary criticism is generally located in the Enlightenment, which began in the mid-18th cent. (Wellek 1955, 5), in part because criticism then began to understand itself as freed from ancient classical authorities and standards (Berghahn 1988). Since metaliterary discourse can consist of a phrase or a sentence as well as an excursus or a treatise, the point at which metaliterary discourse actually begins in the Greek world is problematic. From the standpoint of intertextuality, all oral and written texts (the modes are combined in the *Iliad* and the *Odyssey*) were reactions to other oral and/or written traditions.

Since 1965 a number of books on the history of Greek and Roman literary criticism have appeared: Grube 1965; Pfeiffer 1968; Russell and Winterbottom 1972 (a useful anthology of texts in English translation of the major and minor ancient works on literary criticism); D. A. Russell 1981 (a topical treatment); Kennedy 1989; Russell and Winterbottom 1989 (a shortened version of their 1972 volume); Loo 1998. Many historians of ancient literary criticism regard Plato as the first thinker "to develop a theory of literature and of its place in society" (Grube 1965, 47), but of course it did not begin with Plato (Harriott 1969). In Plato, *Republic* 2–3, the role of poetry in the education of young citizens is emphasized (i.e., Socrates stresses the role of literature in influencing the character and nature of its audience, thereby determining the way a citizen will behave in society; cf. 395d–396c). In *Republic* 10, on the other hand, the author rejects literary and artistic imitation because it is inferior to the object it attempts to represent (i.e., the philosopher makes certain that mimetic narratives represent only virtuous individuals, such as citizens must be; 395c). One can get around this apparent contradiction if one recognizes that Plato accepts "good imitation" (a knowledgeable presentation of things as they are) but rejects "bad imitation" (that which fails to use a good, i.e., divine, paradigm); cf. Loo 1998, 59–62. The *Republic* functions as a work of criticism because it discriminates, i.e., it condemns and banishes poetry from the ideal state in favor of philosophy.

Literary criticism and the Bible. Literary criticism is a designation which biblical scholars have used to refer primarily to source criticism, that is, the study of the literary relationships between biblical texts (such as the Synoptic Gospels) and of the sources used by biblical authors, all part of what was once called "higher criticism." More recently (particularly since the 1970s) a variety of literary methods has been imported into biblical studies from other disciplines (primarily modern literary studies, linguistics, discourse analysis, and semiotics) and has been designed as "new criticism" (*IDBSup* 547) or "the new literary criticism" (S. Moore 1989, xv).

Literary criticism vs. historical criticism. Since modern literary theory is focused primarily on fiction, whether epic, novel, or short story (Booth 1983), the suitability of applying such theory to early Christian literature is debatable, unless that literature is regarded as fiction. The early Christian literary works at issue constitute a relatively modest corpus, including the Gospels, Acts, and the Revelation to John in the NT, as well as numbers of apocryphal gospels, acts, and apocalypses written from the 2d through the 4th cent. C.E. (and beyond). The central issue involves a collision between *historical criticism and literary criticism. Thus Young (1999) sets up his narrative approach to Mark 6:45–56 (the mysterious story of Jesus' walking on the sea and stilling the storm) by parading examples of scholars who use forms of historical criticism (including form and redaction criticism) to salvage the historical value of that narrative or to find symbolic meaning in a pre-Markan version of that narrative.

———

Beardslee 1971; Berghahn 1988; Booth 1961; Brooks 1984; Culler 1975, 1981; Andrew Ford 2002; Fowler 1981, 1985, 1991; Grube 1965; Kennedy (ed.) 1989; McKnight 1978, 1985, 1988; Moore 1989; Pearson 1997; Loo 1998; Petersen 1978a; Poland 1981; Russell 1981; Russell and Winterbottom 1972

Literature is the common English word for written compositions that have been removed from their original communication setting and are then susceptible to new and different lines of interpretation. Literature thus has no intrinsic qualities but is "literature" because of the perception of its enduring values to a particular community. Literature is traditionally thought to be distinct from written texts generally because of certain intrinsic qualities. Hirsch (1976, 134) contends that literature "comprises any linguistic word, written or oral, that has significant aesthetic qualities when described in linguistic categories."

Ancient literature. Out of approximately 2,000 known authors in Greek and Roman antiquity, the complete works of just 136 (6.8 percent) have been preserved, together with fragments of another 127 (6.3 percent); see Gerstinger 1948, 10. During the late 19th and early 20th cent., scholars were persuaded that two antithetical tiers of literary activity were distinguishable in the Greco-Roman world, *Hochliteratur* ("cultivated literature") and *Kleinliteratur* ("popular literature"), a dyadic model for conceptualizing the relationship between ancient literature and ancient society. This dyadic model received plausible support from a corresponding model of Hellenistic Greek which consisted of a "literary language," i.e., literary Koine, and an "everyday language," i.e., nonliterary Koine. Corroboration was also found in the elitist views of ancient literary critics and in the traditional assumption that true literature can be defined in terms of certain essential properties. K. L. Schmidt (1923) rescued the Gospels by assigning a positive value to their uniqueness and nonliterary character by understanding them as examples of *Volksliteratur*, a cultural category that had romantic associations at that time.

The New Testament as "literature." Influential classical and NT scholars of the late 19th and early 20th cent. agreed that "literature" was an inappropriate designation for any of the writings preserved in the NT. New Testament texts were categorized as *Kleinliteratur*, in contrast to the *Hochliteratur* produced by and for the educated upper classes of the Greco-Roman world. The social correlative of this typology was that Christians were thought to have been drawn almost exclusively from the lower classes, a view now widely regarded as inaccurate. The dichotomy between *Hochliteratur* and *Kleinliteratur* derived linguistic support from the widespread opinion current earlier in this century that the Greek language of the first century C.E. could conveniently be divided into two major types, literary and nonliterary Koine. Several scholars have since argued for a third kind of Hellenistic Greek between the extremes of nonliterary and literary Koine. Though there is some disagreement about its exact character, popular literary Greek is an appropriate designation for this middle type. The Swedish scholar Lars Rydbeck (1967) labeled this mediating type of Greek "professional" or "technical prose." As the written language of people with some education, it occurs in technical and scientific treatises, in popular philosophical literature, in some of the more literary papyri, and in the NT. Nigel Turner also regards the Greek of the NT as neither the common language of the papyri nor the language of cultured authors. Unlike Rydbeck, however, he regards the literature of the NT as biblical Greek, a dialect of Jewish Greek "innoculated" with Semitic style and syntax and with many ties to Septuagint Greek. These two differing perspectives ultimately depend on how the so-called "Semitic" features of NT Greek are evaluated (they are neglected by Rydbeck and exaggerated by Turner). More recent scholarship has made it increasing clear that many "Semitisms" (Hebrew or Aramaic modes of expression that appear awkward or uncharacteristic when expressed in Greek) in early Christian Greek can be construed as idiomatic features of a popular (as opposed to the elevated) literary style (Reiser 1984). The NT writings themselves represent various levels and qualities of popular literary Greek. Since the categories of *Hochliteratur* and *Kleinliteratur* are actually ideal types at opposite ends of a complex spectrum of linguistic and literary styles and levels, such a dyadic model is a grossly inadequate tool for dealing with relationships among ancient literary and social phenomena. Ancient social historians frequently conceptualize Greco-Roman society as a socioeconomic pyramid, with the emperor at the top, an enormous slave population at the bottom with various segments of the upper and lower classes layered in between. The pyramid model not only implies that vertical bonds between people of different orders or classes took precedence over horizontal bonds, but also that the direction of influence and authority was from the top down, never from the bottom up. This model emphasizes the unidirectional flow of linguistic and literary conventions from the top to the bottom of society. The literary culture of the highest strata of ancient society percolated down, usually in weakened, attenuated, and even eclectic forms to the lowest social and cultural levels of ancient society. This suggests that the inchoate category "popular literature" cannot be fully understood in isolation from the high literary culture of antiquity and that the analysis of representative members of a literary type inevitably sheds light on other members of that same type. In the Hellenistic world, biography and history (the two types of literature with which Luke and Acts are most frequently compared) are broad literary categories encompassing an enormous variety of compositions that at times appear to be linked by very slender literary features. Therefore, when Cadbury claims that Luke–Acts "does not fit the formal features of either category," one must ask just what constitute the formal features of biography or history. Asked in this way, it must be admitted that classical scholarship has only begun to explore the specifically literary qualities of the biographical and historical literature of antiquity.

Defining "literature." In modern times literary critics have often raised the question "What is literature?" only to respond with vague intuitive definitions (such as, "I can't define it, but I know it when I see it") or in terms of particular "literary" ingredients in texts, the "literary" organization of linguistic material in texts, or the "literary" authorship of texts. However, none of these last three criteria can in reality distinguish "literary" from "nonliterary" texts. "Literature" must be defined in terms of the occasions and situations in which a given society uses a text in a way not taken "as specifically relevant to the immediate context of its origin," i.e., literature is a social phenomenon (J. M. Ellis 1974, 44). In the area of NT studies, this means that critics who originated and perpetuated the distinction between *Hochliteratur* and *Kleinliteratur* were adopting the prescriptive approach to the definition of what constitutes "literature" held by the ancient educated elite, a tiny minority located at the top of the social pyramid in the Greco-Roman world. In more recent studies, particularly in connection with the redaction criticism of the Gospels and the rhetorical analyses of the Pauline Letters, NT scholars have been impressed by the "literary features" of some of the texts. In practice, these "literary features" are primarily suggested by the fact that it is now thought possible to propose hypotheses about the general organization and coherence of all of the elements that form a given text (J. M. Ellis 1974, 202). In the case of the Gospels, such pervasive themes as passion christology, the failure of discipleship, and the secrecy motif have been regarded as exhibiting the literary craftsmanship of Mark, while in the case of Galatians, the controlling schema into which all apparently disparate elements find coherence is the forensic speech of self-defense or the deliberative speech advocating a change in behavior. These and other studies suggest that while the NT texts may be designated as "literature," that designation is valid only with respect to the early Christian community, which rather quickly separated these documents from their original communication setting, and to the social acceptance of the Bible as literature in the Western world. Yet within the setting of particular social groups in the ancient world (however narrowly or broadly defined), groups of texts do not suddenly become "literature" by the process of mass conversion. An individual text becomes literature only gradually, when the community increasingly recognizes it as a paradigmatic expression of its own values. Yet genres as well as individual texts appear to be involved in this process of social validation, in the sense that texts within particular social frameworks may be grouped in terms of common features that may be contrasted with texts with a literary status in other social frameworks. For example, the apocalyptic genre appears largely confined to nativistic groups alienated by the Greek and Roman suppression of kingship traditions. At the other end of the social spectrum, epic continued to be composed in hexameter, though the intended audience of Apollonios Rhodios's *Argonautica* and Virgil's *Aeneid* was highly restricted. Though the world of Roman Hellenism can be considered a social and cultural unity, it nevertheless consisted also of numbers of heterogeneous social groups that stood in various relationships and postures to the tiny minority constituting the upper classes at the peak of the social pyramid. Judaism and early Christianity are two such social groups who stood in an ambiguous relationship, not only to society at large, but also to each other. In addition to sharing to various extents in the dominant culture of the day, each of these communities possessed its own special reasons for existence, ideologies, and literatures. Yet despite the obvious discontinuities between the literary cultures of the *honestiores* and those of the various groups that together constituted the *humiliores* in the world of Roman Hellenism, there are various indications of *continuity* that should not be ignored. Though society in the Greco-Roman world was pyramidal, there was for the most part no deep-seated unrest or antagonism between the upper and lower classes. Further, elevated literary forms and styles were not locked away in the libraries or salons of the very rich, but were on public display (van Groningen 1965, 41–46). During the 1st and 2d cent. C.E., for example, public performances by rhetoricians were in great demand, and they (like the Hollywood movie stars or the rock music stars of the modern period) received wealth and prestige along with fame. Not only were declamations common, but also the public recitation of literary works was popular. Thus all spectrums of the population of the Roman world were exposed to a variety of structures and styles found in the rhetoric, literature, and art on public display throughout the empire. While many of the sophisticated styles of the literature and rhetoric of the upper classes are for the most part absent from the literature of lower-class groups, such as the absence of linguistic Atticism from the NT writings (Wifstrand 1967, 29–30), there are some similar literary and rhetorical patterns or genres that penetrate all strata of ancient society. In spite of the evident differences in style and language between the literary letters of such ancient savants as Cicero, Seneca, and Pliny, for example, and the lowly papyrus letters recovered from ancient Egyptian garbage dumps, they exhibit a basically similar structure. Whether that structure deserves the designation "genre" is a matter for further discussion. Again, though there are evident differences between the style of the forensic speech of a polished rhetorician and that of a common citizen who has been hailed into court and must defend himself against the charges of his accusers, the basic structures remain the same. Therefore, at a more abstract level than comparable groupings of texts with similar features in particular social settings, literary genres in the ancient world are also social conventions that existed with the general acceptance and sanction of ancient society in general.

The whole and the part. In ancient Greek literature, as in the literature of ancient Israel preserved in the OT, there appears to have been an ongoing tension between literary compositions that exhibited a striking degree of unity of plot and structure (e.g., tragedy, comedy, epic, biblical books such as Ruth, Esther, and Jonah) and those that exhibited a looser, more episodic structure or were used as vehicles to frame other, shorter literary units in ways that often defy analysis (e.g., history, biography, "antiquities," and in the Bible, the "historical" section which runs from Genesis through to 2 Kings and from the Chronicles to Ezra-Nehemiah). In the Hellenistic and Roman periods this tension continued, though at the expense of the Aristotelian ideal of structural unity. This period was a time when literary innovation and experimentation went hand in hand with an archaism of both language and theme, based largely on literary models from the past (Bowie 1974). There was a greater exploitation during this period of the elastic and framing qualities of various genres, and the inclusion of a wide variety of constituent literary forms within larger, more encompassing "host" or "inclusive" genres became very common. The virtual "canonization" of particular texts from the classical past did not constrain even the literary circles of the upper classes to forgo generic experimentation. Indeed, this ongoing tension between the whole and the part appears to have been resolved often in terms of loosening the constraints of the whole to provide for the greater dominance of the part. While Virgil's *Aeneid* demonstrates that great epic could still be written, Apollonios's Rhodios *Argonautica* demonstrates equally well that technical perfection in details does not ensure the unity and coherence of the whole. This emphasis on the part at the expense of the whole as a feature of some ancient compositions is a quality that strikes many modern critics as a sign of mediocrity and decadence (van Groningen 1965, 41–56). Regardless of the merits of this critical judgment from a broader literary perspective, it is surely not invalid to attempt to understand the ancient perspectives on composition that produced works of such character.

*Gospels, literary genre of, *Greek literature, *Historiography, *Inscriptions, *Latin literature

---

Bowie 1974; J. M. Ellis 1974; Gerstinger 1948; Hirsch 1976; Reiger 1984; Rydbeck 1967; K. L. Schmidt 1923; Wifstrand 1967

Litotes, a transliterated form of the Greek word λιτοτής ("plainness, simplicity"), is a figure of speech using understatement, often by means of a negation. The figure of *litotes* was favored by Atticists and also by the author of Luke–Acts, who uses the phrase οὐκ ὀλίγος ("not a few"="many") eight times in Acts (12:18; 14:28; 15:2; 17:4, 12; 19:23, 24; 27:20; see Josephus, *War* 7.438); see Cadbury 1927, 120–21. The phrase "not many" (= "a few") occurs in the phrase "not many days" in Luke 15:13 and Acts 1:5 (the phrase occurs also in John 2:12; Josephus, *Ant.* 5.328; *Vita* 309). Paul (of Acts) also describes himself as "a citizen of no insignificant city," referring to Tarsus in Acts 21:39.

Cadbury 1927

Logos protreptikos (see *Protreptic literature)

Luke, Gospel of (see *Luke–Acts)

Luke–Acts, is a modern designation for the Gospel of Luke and the Acts of the Apostles (coined by Cadbury 1927), originally composed as a single literary work in two books; the title *Ad Theophilum* is more fitting. Luke wrote his work in *two* "books" (a "book" was identical with the content of one papyrus roll, a convention preserved in the English word "volume" from the Latin *volumen*, "papyrus roll"), probably using one roll for Luke of ca. 35 feet, and another for Acts of ca. 32 feet (papyrus rolls came in stock sizes with maximum lengths of 35 to 40 feet). An average 30-foot roll could contain about 100 columns of writing with 30 to 40 lines per column and 20 letters per line or stichos. Luke introduced his first book with a historical *preface or προοίμιον (Luke 1:1–4) addressed to his patron or friend "Theophilus" (a real, not a symbolic name, meaning "lover of God"), and included an optional secondary preface in Acts 1:1–2, reiterating the name "Theophilus." While Luke–Acts is generally thought to have been written ca. 90 C.E. (a view partly dependent on the conviction that "Luke" used the Gospel of Mark, which was written ca. 70 C.E.), some have pushed the composition of Luke–Acts to the mid-2nd cent. C.E. (O'Neill 1961), which is unnecessarily late.

Although this single work is normally treated as two different compositions (given separate entries in dictionaries of the Bible, separate commentaries, etc.), their separation is simply a historical accident (though admittedly, no ancient manuscript places Acts directly after Luke). They will therefore be treated here as two parts of a single literary work, though their bifurcation in scholarship, resulting in uneven treatment, makes this task difficult.

Titles. Though originally one work in two books, the early separation of Luke from Acts to facilitate the inclusion of the former in the collection of *four Gospels made it inevitable that each work would be given a separate title. The titles, or *inscriptiones*, of all four canonical Gospels are similarly phrased, with the preposition κατά ("according to") standing for the genitive of authorship: εὐαγγέλιον κατὰ Λουκᾶν, "The Gospel *of* Luke," attested by the 5th cent. uncial MS **A** (Alexandrius) and a number of other MSS (**D, L, W, Θ, =, Ψ**, the Byzantine text and the Latin text and a few other witnesses). The oldest form of this title was probably κατὰ Λουκᾶν, "According to Luke," though attested only by the second hand of two very important 4th cent. uncial MSS, ℵ (Sinaiticus) and **B** (Vaticanus), a phrase which should also be understood as indicating authorship. Hengel (1985b, 65–67) argues for the originality of the longer form, though he does not provide a convincing explanation for the origin of the shorter form. That all four Gospels have similarly phrased titles suggests that they were originally anonymous compositions which had to be distinguished from each other by the addition of secondary inscriptions after they had been collected to form a fourfold group, not later than ca. 125 C.E. (Hengel 1985b, 70). The term εὐαγγέλιον probably became part of the titles of the four Gospels through the influence of Mark 1:1. The title of the revised version of Luke advocated by Marcion of Sinope (ca. 140 C.E.) apparently did not attribute the work to a specific author (Tertullian, *Adv. Marc*. 4.2.3), but was simply titled εὐαγγέλιον (Harnack 183*-84*). Luke, mentioned three times in the NT as one of Paul's coworkers (Col. 4:14; Phlm. 24; 2 Tim. 4:11; cf. Rom. 16:21), is the traditional author of Luke–Acts. The name Λουκᾶς is a Greek hypocoristic form of Λούκιος, a transliterated form of the Latin name Lucius. The church fathers, beginning with Irenaeus, unanimously identified this Luke as the author of both the Gospel of Luke and the Acts of the Apostles. The "we" passages in Acts (16:10–17; 20:5–15; 21:8–18; 27:1–28:16; see *"We"-passages) have suggested to many (beginning with Irenaeus) that the author was a companion of Paul. There is, however, no sure way of linking the composition of Luke–Acts to this little-known figure.

The title "Acts of [all] the Apostles," *acta [omnium] apostolorum* first occurs in the *Canon Muratori (*Acta autem omnium Apostolorum sub uno libro scripta sunt*), though it was assigned no fixed title during the 2d cent. C.E. (G. Schneider 1980–82, 1.74). The Greek title Πράξεις, "Acts" is attested by the second hand of ℵ (Sinaiticus) and **1175**, while the longer (and probably more original) form Πράξεις Ἀποστολῶν, "Acts of the Apostles," is attested by the second hand of **B** (Vaticanus) and **D** (Beza), and by **Ψ** and a few *minuscules. The secondary title "Acts [of all the Apostles]" stuck because it appropriately characterized the work for ancient readers. Luke described his first book as dealing with "all that Jesus began to *do* and to teach" (Acts 1:1), and his second book deals with the deeds and teachings of the apostles. *Praxeis* ("deeds, achievements") was a term applied to entire historical works (Polybius 1.1.1; 9.1.5–6; Diodorus Siculus 1.1.1) or to portions of them (Xenophon, *Education of Cyrus* 1.2.16; Polbius 4.1.3; Josephus, *Ant*. 14.68; Diodorus Siculus 3.1.1; 16.1.1; Dio Cassius 62.29). The emperor Augustus wrote his own obituary summarizing his public achievements, called *Res gestae divi Agusti*, "Acts of the deified Augustus." The Latin phrase *res gestae* ("achievements") is translated πράξεις in a Greek translation of the inscription.

The term is also used as a title of three or four ancient works, including Callisthenes' *Acts of Alexander* (4th cent. B.C.E.), and Sosylus's *Acts of Hannibal* (2d cent. B.C.E.). Some scholars have maintained that *Praxeis* was an established literary form. *Praxeis* literature, unlike biography, does not treat character and development, but rather depicts the outstanding deeds of a prominent person, such as a king, general, or hero. *Praxeis* is a nontechnical, descriptive term for narratives of the accomplishments of noteworthy individuals or cities (whether legendary, historical, or fictional). The term offers little help in determining the genre of Acts.

Luke contains 19,404 Greek words (approximately 2,900 stichoi) with a vocabulary of 2,055 different words (Morgenthaler 1958, 164). Luke avoids the historical present found 151 times in Mark (Cadbury 1920, 158–59). Acts contains 18,374 Greek words (approximately 2,600 stichoi), with a vocabulary of 2,038 different words (Morgenthaler 1958, 164). The preface to Luke–Acts (Luke 1:1–4), a periodic sentence, signals the literary intentions of the author.

Literary sources. Luke refers to "many" others who had written narratives covering the events that he is covering (Luke 1:1–2), and it is reasonable to suppose that he incorporated some of these into his narrative. The fact that the three Synoptic Gospels exhibit a striking amount of verbal similarities in various parallel passages suggests that some kind of literary borrowing took place. On the bases of the widely held theory of the priority of Mark (see the arguments in Fitzmyer 1976–77; 1981–85, 1.65–106), the sources widely thought to be used by Luke in the first volume of Luke–Acts include *Mark, the Sayings Source Q (see *"Q" [Sayings Source]), and Special L (see *L, Special).

The material in Luke that has no parallels with the other canonical gospels, called Special L, may have constituted a coherent source with a consistent style (Rehkopf 1959, 87). Special L consists of from 222 to 261 verses (the sections bracketed below are not as certainly assigned to Special L):

1.	3:10–14	John replies to questioners
2.	3:23–38	Genealogy of Jesus
3.	[4:17–22a, 25–30	Jesus' sermon at Nazareth]
4.	5:1–11	Call of Simon
5.	6:24–26	The woes
6.	7:11–17	Raising of the widow's son at Nain
7.	[7:36–50	Jesus anointed by penitent woman]
8.	[8:1–3	Women disciples of Jesus]
9.	9:52–56	Samaritan villagers reject Jesus
10.	10:29–37	Parable of Good Samaritan
11.	10:38–42	Mary and Martha
12.	11:5–8	The midnight request
13.	11:27–28	True blessedness
14.	12:13–15	Warning against avarice
15.	12:16–21	Parable of the Rich Fool
16.	[12:32	"Fear not, little flock"]
17.	[12:33	"Sell your possessions"]
18.	12:35–38	On watchfulness
19.	13:1–5	Repentance or destruction
20.	13:6–9	Parable of the Barren Fig Tree
21.	13:10–17	Healing of the crippled woman
22.	13:31–33	A warning against Herod
23.	14:1–6	Healing of the man with dropsy
24.	14:7–14	Teaching on humility
25.	14:28–33	Cost of discipleship
26.	15:8–10	Parable of the Lost Coin
27.	15:11–32	Parable of the Prodigal Son
28.	16:1–9	Parable of the Unjust Steward
29.	16:10–12	Faithfulness is small things
30.	16:14–15	Pharisees reproved
31.	16:19–31	Parable of the Rich Man and Lazarus
32.	17:7–10	Unworthy servants
33.	17:11–19	Cleansing of the ten lepers
34.	17:20–21	The coming of the kingdom
35.	[17:31–34	Watch for the Parousia]
36.	18:1–8	Parable of the Unjust Judge
37.	18:9–14	The Pharisee and the publican
38.	19:1–10	Zacchaeus
39.	19:39–40	Jesus does not rebuke his disciples
40.	19:41–44	Jesus weeps over Jerusalem
41.	[21:34–36	Exhortation to watch]
42.	22:31–32	Jesus addresses Simon
43.	22:35–38	The two swords
44.	23:6–12	Jesus before Herod
45.	23:27–31	Crowd follows Jesus to Golgotha

Of the 661 verses in Mark, 350 are substantially similar to verses in Luke (Fitzmyer 1981–85, 1.68). Luke's use of Mark and the Markan order can be seen in this list of parallels, additions and omissions (Fitzmyer 1981–85, 1.67):

1. Mark 1:1–15 = Luke 3:1–4:15
2. Mark 1:21–3:19 = Luke 4:31–6:19
   [Luke's Little Interpolation: 6:20–8:3]
3. Mark 4:1–9:40 = Luke 8:4–9:50
   [At Luke 9:17, Luke's Big Omission: Mark 6:45–8:26]
   [At Luke 9:50, Luke's Little Omission: Mark 9:41–10:12]
4. Mark 10:13–13:32 = Luke 18:15–21:33
5. Mark 14:1–16:8 = Luke 22:1–24:12

In addition there are also verbal agreements between Luke and John (listed in R. E. Brown 1966–70, 1.xlix–xlvii) which suggest some kind of relationship as well (Cribbs 1971). Boismard (1962) considers Luke as the final redactor of John, a view for which there is little evidence.

The second volume of Luke–Acts is more problematic since there are no similar works with verbal parallels that might reveal the author's use of sources, though it is highly likely that he used some. There is no scholarly consensus on the problem of the sources of Acts (for a discussion of this issue, see Pesch 1986, 1.45–51). Linguistically, Acts falls into two sections, 1:1–15:35 and 15:36–28:31; Kennedy (1984, 127) argues that Acts 1:1–15:35 "seems to be a compositional unit and could be read as a complete work." The first section contains a striking number of Semitisms (Wilcox 1965, 171–79), suggesting that the author was dependent on sources which had been translated from Hebrew or Aramaic.

The Purpose of Luke–Acts. It has often been argued that Luke–Acts had an apologetic purpose (survey in Alexander 1999, 15–44; see *apologetic literature). This apologetic purpose has been construed along five different lines (Alexander 1999, 16–19): (1) as an inner-Christian apologetic (e.g., as anti-Gnostic; see Talbert 1966, 115), (2) as an apologetic directed toward Judaism, (3) as an apology directed to the Greeks (taking up the apologetics developed in Hellenistic Judaism), (4) as a political apologetic defending the innocence of Paul and hence all Christians against Roman charges, or (5) as an apologetic aimed at forging group identity (Sterling 1992), to explain and justify Christianity to the members of his [Luke's] community (Esler 1987, 222). While Josephus's *Antiquities* made his case directly to the Hellenistic world, Luke–Acts makes its case indirectly "by offering examples and precedents to Christians so that they can make their own *apologia*" (Sterling 1992, 386). However, since apologies constitute a subgenre of forensic speech, they are dominated by direct discourse, while Luke–Acts is dominated by narrative. However, there are a number of dramatic scenes in Acts, in which various characters defend themselves in forensic contexts with apologetic speeches (Pervo 1987, 34–50). Disputes with Judaism are relatively frequent in Acts. One series of encounters is dramatized in Acts 4–5, with the apostles forbidden to preach in the name of Jesus (4:18), which they disobey (5:28), appealing to God as the higher authority and blaming the Sanhedrin for the execution of Jesus (5:29–32). The longest defense speech in Acts is that of Stephen in the context of his defense before the Sanhedrin (7:2–60). Paul's speech at the Areopagus in Athens (17:16–34) has a philosophical character and involves both propaganda and defense. The most prominent apologetic speeches in Acts, however, are those of Paul defending himself in Roman judicial contexts, where it is concluded that "This man could have been set free if he had not appealed to Caesar" (Acts 26:32).

Literary genre. There are two main options in assessing the literary genre of Luke–Acts. Either the work was composed as a single work in a single genre, or two different genres have been linked together by the hyphen. Luke is commonly regarded as a "gospel" because of obvious similarities to the other Gospels, and Acts is widely categorized as "history," though lacking exact Hellenistic or Israelite-Jewish literary analogues. Dormeyer (1993, 212) regards each of the four Gospels as representing an independent branch of Hellenistic biography, continuing OT prophetic biography in a late Hellenistic form. He regards Acts as clearly separated from Luke by the introductions in Luke 1:1–4 and Acts 1:1–8, and claims without argument that Acts is an example of episodic tragic historiography (*die pathetische Geschichtsschreibung*) similar to 2 Maccabees (Dormeyer 1996, 228–30). Jervell (1998, 78 n. 156) holds that "Luke and Acts are two different literary forms," and Acts itself can appropriately be categorized as "tragische Geschichtsschreibung," with the proviso that his history is a part of biblical history which is a model for him and the reason that he imitates the style of the Septuagint; it is only this history that is normative for him (Jervell 1998, 78–9). The views of several "unitarians" have been published recently. Löning (1997–, 1.24–5) regards Luke–Acts as a literary unit, written in a single genre which he designates "an apologetic historical report" (*ein apologetischer Geschichtsbericht*). Cancik (1997, 263) supports the generic unity of Luke–Acts: "Luke–Acts is a history that narrates the origin and spread of an institution, a thesis that applies to both *logoi*; that is, the first *logos* is not a biography." The view of the generic unity of Luke–Acts is also shared by W. Stegemann (*DNP* 7:491–93), who proposes that Luke belongs to ancient genre of historiography, not biography.

By itself, Luke could (like *Mark, *Matthew, and *John) be classified as a type of ancient biography. But Luke, though it might have circulated separately, was subordinated to a larger literary structure. Luke, therefore, does not belong to a type of ancient biography, for it belongs with Acts, and Acts cannot be forced into a biographical mold.

1. *Luke–Acts as unique*. German New Testament scholarship in particular has continued to emphasize the unique literary character of both the Gospels and Acts; Acts particularly is singled out as a unique composition based on no models and having no imitators (Kümmel 1972, 37, 164–6; Vielhauer 1975, 90–112; Momigliano 1981, 178–79; Schneider 1980–82, 1.73–76). In the recent commentary on the Acts by Schneider (1980–82), the author accepts the unique and unparalleled literary character of Acts but proposes that the specific form of Acts can better be understood through considering partial analogies among the literary precursors and imitators of Acts.

2. *Luke–Acts as history*. The thesis that Luke–Acts belonged to Hellenistic historical writing generally was emphasized by Cadbury (1927, 133) who observed: "No doubt Luke's work is nearer to history than to any other familiar classification," placing the entire two-volume

composition in a single literary genre, "history." Cadbury was also insistent that Luke should not be formally categorized as a biography (1927, 132): "That Luke's gospel should not be counted a formal biography is further confirmed when one recalls that it is merely part of a longer work, and that its sequel, though full of biographical incident, is even less concerned with sketching the full career of its principal characters. . . . If we take Luke's work as a whole, and not by halves, biography is not the word for it." Cadbury finally distances Luke–Acts from formal historiographical categories in favor of the popular literature theory advocated by K. L. Schmidt (Cadbury 1927, 133–34; cf. K. L. Schmidt 1923). While Luke–Acts should be identified as "popular literature," Cadbury does not suggest that there are any discrete literary types within that amorphous category, but claims rather that this literature "never enjoyed the clear-cut subdivision which goes with conscious workmanship." In categorizing Luke–Acts as historiography, one must not confuse the issue of whether or not the author of Luke–Acts is a good, mediocre or bad historian or whether he is historically accurate in every or any detail, with the issue of whether he intended to write within the generic confines of Hellenistic historiography. These are two different questions. According to Pervo, "it is impossible to resolve disputes about accuracy by means of a generic classification." Working within the basic framework of Luke–Acts as historiography, Maddox (1982, 15–18) propose that the genre of Luke–Acts be designated "theological history," since it is "shaped by the style and technique of Greek historiography" and is "steeped in the motivation of biblical historiography." However, the adjective "theological" provides little insight into the generic problem, since virtually all ancient histories are ideologically driven.

3. *Luke–Acts as biography.* Based on the model of Diogenes Laertius, *Lives of the Philosophers*, Talbert (1974, 125–34) has argued that Luke–Acts is a *succession narrative*, a type of Greco-Roman biography. He argues that the lives of philosophers have three primary components: (1) Life of the founder: the founders of the Greek philosophical schools (e.g., Plato, Aristotle, Epicurus) were venerated as divine figures. (2) Narratives about disciples and successors: the successors of the founder formed a type of religious community "created and sustained by the divine figure," a community which possessed "many of the characteristics of a church" (1974, 126). (3) Summaries of the doctrine of the philosophical schools, "sometimes in the words of the founder, sometimes in the words of its disciples and successors" (1974, 127). He further suggests that it is necessary to determine the function which each of these three elements would have had independently of their combination in Diogenes Laertius (1974, 128): (1) The life of a philosopher defines the way of life of the school or group associated with him. (2) A succession list or narrative indicated where the true and living tradition of the school could be found. (3) The list of books and a summary of the master's teaching ensured an accurate view of the tradition.

L. Alexander found Talbert's thesis that Luke–Acts is a "biographical succession narrative" attractive, though ultimately inadequate. Taking a clue from Talbert, Alexander suggests that "The role of such biographical material within the school traditions should certainly be explored in any future investigation of the literary genre of Luke-Acts" (1993, 202–3). She finally concludes, however, that "the difficulties involved in treating the Gospel as a 'philosophical biography' suggest that we should be looking in a different direction" (L. Alexander 1993, 204).

While Talbert's proposal has the advantage of suggesting a generic analogy to the whole of Luke-Acts, it founders in several respects: (1) διαδοχαί ("successors") literature, based on the analogy with dynastic succession, was limited to the histories of philosophical schools. Despite the cultic features of Hellenistic philosophical schools and the divinity of their founders, and a superficial resemblance of early Christian groups to philosophical schools or "scholastic communities" (Judge 1960; see Malherbe 1983, 45–59), during the first century, Christian communities simply did not consider themselves philosophical schools. (2) Talbert observes that, although the biographical schema in the *Lives of the Philosophers* of Diogenes Laertius is topical rather than chronological, other ancient biographies exhibit the same arrangement (1974, 128). Luke–Acts, however, is a chronological narrative with a plot and has little resemblance to Diogenes Laertius's treatment of the lives of philosophers. Talbert argues that lives of philosophers "usually" consist of three elements (life + successors + teachings), though just six of the 82 lives exhibit this pattern (Aristippos, Plato, Zeno, Pythagoras, Pyrrho, Epicurus). (2) Talbert's contention that the succession narrative reveals where authentic tradition is found is not really confirmed in Diogenes Laertius, where the concern is rather who studies with whom and who succeeded whom, not with the legitimacy of their views. (3) The phrase "succession *narrative*" is an inappropriate designation for brief *lists* of students or successors.

4. *Acts as a novel.* Several scholars have argued that Acts belongs to the same genre as the ancient novels (Schierling and Schierling 1978; Praeder 1981; Pervo 1987). Praeder (1981, 282–88) lists seven generic criteria to which the ancient novel was expected to conform: (1) the mixture of historical and fictional characters in a story set in the eastern Mediterranean, (2) the biography of a main character with back-references to past events, (3) an alternation between summary and scene with the latter dominating, (4) the presence or absence of narrator from the narrative world as indicated by first- or third-person narration, (5) avoidance of reference to sources, (6) a depiction of Greco-Roman experience and imagination, and (7) the achievement of various intentions and effects through interesting and entertaining communication. Since all these generic features are found in Luke–Acts, it must be considered an ancient novel, or more exactly as a subgenre of the novel as a "Christian ancient novel." However, this list does not consist of generically distinctive features, but rather narrative techniques used in a wide variety of ancient narrative literature. It seems doubtful, given the author's use of historical *prefaces (in Luke 1:1–4 and Acts 1:1–2), in the first of which sources are referred to, that the ancient reader would read Luke–Acts as a novel (the criticism of Kany 1986, 89–90).

The generic affinities between Acts and the Greek novel have been argued in great detail by Pervo (1987); Acts lacks factual accuracy and should be classified as a historical novel, not as history. The primary purpose of Acts, he maintains, is edification in an entertaining package. The Acts of the Apostles shares this purpose with the Greek and Latin novels as well as with the Apocryphal Acts (see *Acts, Apocryphal). Luke achieves this using many of the same themes and motifs as the novelists. Pervo (1987, 18) finds 33 episodes in Acts (23 in Acts 13–28) that feature miraculous and exciting last-minute escapes from various perils (e.g., 14:2–6; 16:16–40; 22:22–24). These episodes, with close analogies in ancient novels, fall into five categories: (1) arrests and imprisonments (3:1–4:31; 5:12–42), (2) persecution and martyrdom (21:27–22:29), (3) mob scenes (eleven, including 16:19–23; 18:12–17; 19:23–41), (4) trial scenes (nine, including 4:5–22; 18:12–17; 25:6–12), (5) travel and shipwreck (e.g., 27:1–28:16). Pervo focuses on the fictional features of these and other elements in Acts and the links that they have with novelistic themes and motifs.

While Pervo is correct about the entertaining and edifying character of Acts, it is doubtful that Acts should be categorized as a historical novel with closer links to fiction than history. His arguments are problematic for several reasons: (1) Fiction can be distinguished from history in that while the latter has a referent in the real world, the former has no such referent; it makes no sense to say that Chariton, the author of the Greek novel *Chaereas and Callirhoë*, was mistaken about the actions of the hero and heroine (Konstan 1998, 6), but it would make sense to argue that Luke is wrong in having Paul claim Roman citizenship in Acts 22:25. (2) Though ancient historians wrote to entertain, they did not think truth and usefulness had to be sacrificed. (3) The term "historical novel" should be reserved for novels that follow a historical sequence of events (like Xenophon's *Education of Cyrus* or Ps.-Callisthenes' *Alexander Romance*), rather than applied to fictional narratives set in the real world. (4) The factual accuracy of Acts (variously assessed) is irrelevant to generic classification if the author of Luke–Acts intended to narrate actual events. Luke's use of historical prefaces (Luke 1:1–4; Acts 1:1–2), and his mention of sources are not found in novels. (5) Though Pervo isolates Luke from Acts and treats on the genre of the latter, there are strong arguments for regarding Luke–Acts as a single literary genre. (6) Many of the "novelistic" episodes Pervo mentions, far from being common to only ancient novels and Acts, are found in both factual and fictional narratives in the Hellenistic world. Schierling and Schierling (1978) are more accurate in referring to novelistic elements in Acts.

Speeches of Acts. Speeches played an important role in both Hellenistic histories and novels, often constituting from 20–35 percent of the narrative. There is some disagreement about the exact number of speeches in Acts, a disagreement based on how long a unit of direct discourse must be in order for it to be considered a speech. Schneider (1980–82, 1.96) is typical in identifying 24 speeches in Acts: (1) 1:16–22 (Peter); (2) 2:14–36, 38–39 (Peter); (3) 3:12–26 (Peter); (4) 4:8–12, 19–20 (Peter); (5) 5:29–32 (Peter); (6) 5:35–39 (Gamaliel); (7) 7:2–53 (Stephen); (8) 10:34–43 (Peter); (9) 11:5–17 (Peter); (10) 13:16–41 (Paul); (11)

14:15–17 (Paul); (12) 15:7–11 (Peter); (13) 15:13–21 (James); (14) 17:22–31 (Paul); (15) 19:25–27 (Demetrius); (16) 19:35–40 (Ephesian town clerk); (17) 20:18–35 (Paul); (18) 22:1–21 (Paul); (19) 24:2–8 (Tertullus); (20) 24:10–21 (Paul); (21) 25:24–27 (Festus); (22) 26:2–23 [25–27] (Paul); (23) 27:21–26 (Paul); (24) 28:17–20 (Paul). Kennedy (1984, 114–40) analyzes the speeches in Acts, and comes up with 25 of them, by adding three (the apostle's prayer in 4:24–30, the speech of the brethren to Paul in Jerusalem, 21:20–25, and the speech of Festus to Agrippa, 25:14–21, but omitting two (a speech of Paul, 14:15–17, and the speech of Demetrius, 19:25–27).

Soards (1994, 21–22) identifies no less than 36 speeches in Acts and devotes a brief commentary to each of them. Soards argues that the many speeches used throughout Acts contribute to the overall unity of the narrative. He is concerned particularly with repetitions in the speeches which contribute to the unity of the text, but which also serve to advance the action of the narrative or to emphasize a point of view (Soards 1994, 183). Repeated emphases are often found in the speeches, including: (1) divine authority, i.e., there is a transcendent God who acts in the world to realize his will (Soards 1994, 184–86), (2) God's will is realized in Jesus Christ (186–87), (3) mention of the plan of God occurs frequently and in varied ways (187–89), (4) temporal phrases are often used to indicate the time, often the critical nature of the present time during which the speaker addresses his audience (190–92), and (5) the theme of witness is strongly emphasized (192–200).

The 24 speeches in Acts (excluding short statements) make up approximately 25 percent of the narrative (following the enumeration of Schneider 1980–82, 1.96). Eight speeches are attributed to Peter, nine to Paul, and one each to Stephen and James. Five are attributed to those who are not followers of Jesus: Gamaliel, Demetrius, the town clerk in Ephesus, Tertullus, and Festus. While speeches occupy 24 percent of Thucydides, and 25 percent in Acts, they function in very different ways. The narrative settings of Thucydides' speeches are very brief. In Acts the narrative frameworks of the speeches are important; with the speeches they constitute 74 percent of the narrative. In Thucydides, speeches function as a commentary on events. In Luke–Acts, speeches are an essential feature of the plot itself, which centers on the spreading of the word of God.

Do the speeches of Acts represent approximations of what was actually said or were they freely composed by the author? If Luke was a typical Hellenistic historian, we could not expect the speeches to be verbatim reports, epitomes, or even approximations of what was actually said, but rather inventions restrained only by the necessity of suitability to speaker, audience, and occasion. It is, of course, difficult to prove that particular speeches could not have been given by those to whom they are attributed. Luke probably faced much the same problem as did Thucydides, or any historian of recent events. In Thucydides' time, speeches were not written down before they were delivered, nor were they typically transcribed and published after oral delivery. Hellenistic historians, however, found a wealth of discourse material in their sources and were faced with several options. They could omit them (usually unthinkable), faithfully transcribe them (almost unthinkable), or modify them. Most, like Dionysius of Halicarnassus, chose the last option. Since Luke wrote about events of the previous generation, it is unlikely that he found speeches in written sources. His options were three: (1) To interview those present or, if he himself was present, to recall the substance of what was actually spoken, (2) to freely improvise speeches according to the principle of appropriateness, or (3) to combine research and memory with free composition. Luke very likely followed the last route.

The speeches of Luke–Acts can be examined from at least two perspectives, historical criticism (are they historical?) and literary criticism (how do they function in the larger composition and are they contextually appropriate, i.e., appropriate in the historical setting which the author has created and appropriate in the literary context?). There are several important questions which must be considered in order to answer these questions.

1. Although the style of the speeches in Luke–Acts is not uniform, it is consistent with the author's general style. An apparent exception is Paul's speech to the elders of Ephesus (Acts 20:18–53), which is evocative of Paul's style as attested in his letters (Kennedy 1984,139). While most historians imposed their own style on speeches (e.g., Thucydides, Polybius, and Dionysius of Halicarnassus), there are important exceptions (e.g., Herodotus). Writing speeches in styles appropriate to various speakers was widely practiced by Hellenistic writers (Lucian, *History* 58; Theon, *Progymnasmata* 10).

2. The speeches of Acts exhibit considerable variety in form and content: (a) six are evan-

gelistic speeches to Jews and Gentile sympathizers, (b) two are evangelistic speeches to pagans, (c) five are forensic speeches, four by Paul and one by Tertullus.

Several observations can be made about each type: (a) According to Schweizer, the six evangelistic speeches (*Missionsreden*) to Jews (Acts 2:14–39; 3:12–26; 4:9–12; 5:29–32; 10:34–43; 13:16–41) exhibit a uniform structure: direct address, appeal for attention, mention of the problem of misunderstanding, initial quotation from Scripture, reference to the crucifixion and resurrection of Jesus, proof from Scripture, the proclamation of salvation, and the call to repentance. These similarities suggest that the author has composed the speeches, though there is no way of proving or disproving the antiquity of the core elements. Plümacher (1993) has argued (a point made earlier by Dibelius 1949) that the mission speeches are located at turning points in the narrative of Acts. (b) The two speeches to pagan audiences appropriately omit proofs from Scripture and instead quote a Greek poet (17:28). (c) None of the forensic speeches exhibit a complete traditional rhetorical structure (three are interrupted). The speech in Acts 22:1–21 begins with a short introduction, and consists of an autobiographical *narratio* (which also functions as an *argumentatio*) until it is interrupted. The speech of Tertullus (24:2–8 begins with a **captatio benevolentiae* (i.e., an *exordium* aimed at securing goodwill by flattering the governor) in vv. 2–4, followed by a twofold accusation (vv. 5–8: Paul is a ringleader of the troublesome Nazarenes, and has desecrated the Temple. Paul's response (24:10–21) begins also with a *captatio benevolentiae* (v. 10) and continues with a brief *narratio* ("statement of the facts," v. 11) and *propositio* ("proposition," v. 12). Paul's defense speech in 26:2–23 also begins with a *captatio benevolentiae* (26:2–3), continues with a *narratio* (vv. 4–18), followed by the *argumentatio* ("proof"), which is interrupted (vv. 19–23). All of these speeches suggest that Paul is familiar with the structures of forensic rhetoric.

3. Some of the speeches in Luke–Acts do not appear to be contextually appropriate (Plümacher 1974, 244–45). Stephen's outline of Israelite history in Acts 7:2–53 does not fit the charge in 6:13–14. The apologetic elements in Paul's farewell speech in Acts 20:18–35 (i.e., vv. 20–21, 27, 33–34) do not fit the setting. In Paul's Areopagus speech (Acts 17:22–31), v. 22 is in tension with the context (v. 16). Paul's speech to the crew in 27:21–26 belongs to the lierary convention of a storm at sea (the model for which was *Odyssey* 5.299–312, emulated by Virgil, *Aeneid* 1.92–101) and is appropriate literarily rather than historically. The tension between some speeches and their contexts may be due to the fact that the speeches were in all probability inserted at a final stage in composition, or to the fact that the author has focused on the speeches, giving less care to their narrative settings. Historians typically compiled a rough draft (*hypomnema*), later rewriting the whole according to accepted literary standards (Lucian, *History* 47–48; Josephus, *Contra Apionem* 1.49–50). Dramatic episodes and speeches were usually inserted at a final stage of composition, judging by their absence from "unfinished" portions of histories (speeches are entirely absent from Thucydides 5.10–83 and all of book 8; Herodian 5–8 contains just six speeches). This was probably Luke's procedure in compiling Acts.

Greek historians often reported speeches using *indirect discourse. Indirect discourse is a more accurate way of reporting speeches, while direct discourse is a more vivid and potentially dramatic medium. Some historians (e.g., Herodian) and most novelists used direct discourse almost exclusively, probably for its dramatic value. Indirect discourse is largely absent from speeches in the NT, though it occurs occasionally in Luke–Acts. The speeches of Acts, however, are almost entirely in direct discourse. Luke begins some speeches with indirect discourse and then switches to direct discourse (Luke 5:14; Acts 1:4; 17:3; 23:22–24; 25:4–5). The same phenomenon is found in classical authors such as Herodotus (1.118, 125, 153; 3.156.2–3; 5.31, 39; 6.1; 9.2) and Thucydides (only three speeches combine direct with indirect discourse, 1.137.4; 3.113; 8.53). Josephus also slides from indirect to direct discourse within single speeches (*Wars* 4.40–48; 4.238–69; 4.272–82), as do Herodian (8.3.4–6) and Arrian (*Anabasis* 5.11.4).

Luke uses two distinctive literary techniques in the speeches. First is *intentional interruption*, frequently because of anger or dissension (Luke 4:28; Acts 2:36; 4:1; 7:53; 10:44; 17:32; 19:28; 22:22; 23:7; 26:34). Such interruptions are literary devices common to historians and novelists. They heighten the drama of particular episodes (Josephus, *War* 1.629; 2.605; 3.485; 7.389; Herodian 2.5.8; Achilles Tatius 8.1.2; 8.7.1; 8.11.1). Second, Luke concludes some speeches by suggesting that further remarks were made but which are not included (Luke

24:27; Acts 2:40; 13:43; 15:12). This too is a literary device that shortened the length of a speech and suggests the transcriptional character of the part "quoted." Similar conclusions are found in the speeches of Hellenistic historians (Arrian, *Anabasis* 3.9.8; Josephus, *War* 1.638; 2.33; 3.383) and novelists (Longus 1.16).

*Direct discourse *Gospels, literary genre of, *Historiography, *Indirect discourse, *Itinerary, *Prefaces, *Speeches, *"We"-passages

---

Alexander 1993; Bovon 2002; Bruce 1942, 1974; Cadbury 1920, 1927; Callan 1985; Darr 1992; Dibelius 1949, 1956; Diefenbach 1993; Fitzmyer 1981–85; Haenchen 1971; Harrington 2000; Maddox 1982; Moessner 1999; Munck 1967; Palmer 1987, 1993; Pervo 1987; Pesch 1986; Plümacher 1972, 1974, 1978, 1979, 1998, 1999; Praeder 1981; Reasoner 1999; Schierling and Schierling 1978; D. Schmidt 1999; Soards 1994a, 1994b; W. Stegemann, *DNP* 7:491–93; Talbert 1974, 1996; Trites 1974; Verheyden 1999a, 1999b; Wilcox 1965; W. Wilson 2001; Witherington 1996

Macarism (see *Beatitude)

Magical papyri, a varied collection of ancient Greek, Demotic, and Coptic magical texts written from the 3d through the 6th cent. C.E., though often incorporating traditional materials and sources from much earlier. Most numerous is the corpus of Greek magical papyri, a growing collection currently numbering about 230 papyrus texts (Brashear 1995, 3389), most dating from the 3d to the 5th cent. C.E. (though a few are earlier and a few later), though many of them preserve older material. To this collection should be added the nine published Demotic magical texts (some of which have Greek passages and some of which were even translated from Greek). These papyri, which scholars have conventionally labeled as "magical," consist of three types of material: (1) magical handbooks, i.e., collections of magical procedures which once belonged to ancient magicians who would sell them to customers with particular problems; eight relatively extensive Greek magical handbooks have survived (Brashear 1995); (2) magical formularies, i.e., individual magical procedures of the type assembled in magical handbooks and which could be activated by the insertion of the name of the customer and/or those he or she wishes to affect; (3) individual magical texts which, like the master texts in the magical handbooks and formularies, were actually used by people for one of several purposes: (a) love magic (attracting a member of the opposite sex, even against their will), (b) revelatory magic (means of learning the unknown or the future), (c) protective apotropaic magic (warding off various kinds of disease and demonic influences), (d) aggressive and malevolent magic (attempts to harm or even kill your enemies), and (e) general-purpose procedures, such as those for procuring the services of an assisting deity (*paredros daimon*) as a permanent supernatural helper. For many reasons it is impractical to exclude the evidence provided by amulets from the magical papyri for the simple reason that magical handbooks often give instructions for writing or inscribing magical texts on a variety of materials as well as papyrus, including foil or lamellae, thin sheets of lead, copper, silver, and gold (typically folded and rolled up and inserted into small tubes to be worn as amulets), and semiprecious stones which could be inscribed and worn as amulets or mounted in rings. The chief problem with amulets is the difficulty of dating them since the vast majority of the more than 5,000 known amulets are not found in archaeological contexts. Eight of the more extensive magical papyri are books of magical recipes once owned by magical practitioners.

Magical papyri and magical books of various kinds were widely distributed throughout the ancient Mediterranean world (see Acts 19:19). Since nearly all the extant magical papyri were preserved by the dry climatical conditions of Egypt, they exhibit a Greco-Egyptian character and often reflect ancient Egyptian magical names, themes and traditions. Other important sources of Greco-Roman magic have been preserved on more durable materials, such as magical gems and amulets (ca. 5,000 pieces have survived), as well as lead curse tablets, the so-called *defixiones tabellae* (Gager 1992). Since these sources, together with a variety of references to magic in Greek and Latin literature, exhibit many similarities with the magical papyri, it is likely that the papyri represent a Greco-Egyptian variation of ancient Mediterranean magical practices (M. Smith 1979). The conservative nature of the rituals, formulas, prayers, and hymns preserved in the papyri indicate that Greco-Egyptian magic had taken on a fairly stable form by the 1st cent. C.E., the approximate date of the first surviving magical texts.

Most of the texts included in the major corpus of magical papyri contain detailed instructions for the performance of rituals involving the recitation of carefully prescribed formulas, prayers, and hymns, and the preparation of various concoctions, sacrifices, and paraphernalia, all for achieving very particular goals within private settings. The distinguishing features of all magical papyri are that they consist of religious texts containing instructions for the performance of private instrumental rituals. The procedures or spells (the Greek term is πράξεις, "actions") are designed to accomplish a variety of specific goals. There are five major categories of spells found in the magical papyri: (1) Erotic magic (Faraone 1999), (2) Revelatory magic (Hopfner 1921–24), (3) protective and apotropaic magic, the typical function of magical gems and amulets (Delatte and Derchain 1964), (4) aggressive and malevolent magic (Gager 1992), (5) general-purpose procedures, such as those for procuring the services of an assistant deity. These magical procedures are structured with three major sections: (1) preliminary preparations (including various types of purification), (2) invocation (ἐπίκλησις), and (3) sacrificial ritual (the πρᾶξις proper).

"Judaism" has influenced the Greek magical papyri in two specific ways: (1) Aspects of Jewish narrative traditions, cultic rituals and the crucially important use of names, including human names (Abraham, Jacob, Moses, Solomon), divine names (Iao, Sabaoth, Adonai), angelic names (Gabriel, Raphael, Suriel), and demonic names (Asmodaeus), both biblical and postbiblical, which have been borrowed and used in magical texts and images, though in their original contexts they were not associated with magic. (2) Jewish magical traditions preserved in books of magical recipes, including 4Q560, the earliest such handbook from Qumran, dating to the 1st cent. B.C.E. (Alexander 1997, 329–30; Naveh 1998), and a variety of magical texts and magical handbooks from the Cairo Genizah (Schiffman and Swartz 1992), including the Sepher ha-Razim (Margalioth 1966; Morgan 1983). In addition, there are the approximately 40 amulets in Hebrew and Aramaic found in Palestine and the surrounding regions (Naveh and Shaked 1985, 1993; McCollough and Glazier-MacDonald 1996; Hamilton 1996; Naveh 2001), and more than 30 Aramaic incantation bowls from Mesopotamia (Naveh and Shaked 1985, 216–40; 1993, 147–242).

There are several striking and pervasive features of the magical papyri and magical amulets which distinguish them from other types of religious texts, regardless of which eastern Mediterranean culture produced them: (1) the frequent use of voces magicae, i.e., lengthy sequences of vowels and consonants, some with no discernible meaning, others representing words from various languages and in various degrees of corruption, and some consisting of palindromes such as αβλαναθαναλβα, (2) the use of magical characters, i.e., strange stick letters with small circles where the serifs would be), and (3) the elaborate use of eclectic strings of divine names from a variety of religious traditions including Egyptian, Babylonian, Jewish, and Greek, as part of invocation rituals, reflecting either the ecumenical view that these names describe the same deity (e.g., the *interpretatio Graeca*, or well-known penchant of the Greeks to equate Egyptian deities with Greek ones), or playing. Many of these were borrowed from Judaism (M. Smith 1986), including the name "Iao" (Aune 1995).

*Historiola, *Testament of Solomon

Aune 1980, 1995; Betz 1992; Brashear 1995; Delatte and Derchain 1964; Faraone 1999; Gager 1992; Graf 1997; Hopfner 1921–24; Luck 1985; McCollough and Glazier-McDonald 1996; Meyer and Mirecki 1995; Montgomery 1913; Morgan 1983; Preisendanz 1993–94; Schiffmann and Swartz 1993; M. Smith 1979, 1986

Makarism (see *Beatitude)

Mandates (see *Edicts)

Marginal note, or *Randbemerkung* (see *Gloss)

Mark, Gospel of is, by critical consensus, the earliest of the canonical Gospels, written 65–70 C.E. Traditionally, the Gospel of Mark has been ascribed to John Mark, who is referred to eight times in the NT (Acts 12:12, 25; 15:37, 39; Col. 4:10; 2 Tim. 4:11; Phlm. 24; 1 Pet. 5:13), and it has also been linked historically with Peter (cf. 1 Pet. 5:13), for whom John Mark ostensibly served as an amanuensis or ἑρμενευτής (Eusebius, *Hist. eccl.* 3.39.15), and its place of origin was widely thought to have been Rome. However, there is no convincing historical basis for any of these traditions (Black 1994, 238–41 et passim). Whether Mark was familiar with *Q (the Sayings Source) remains a debated issue (*pro:* Mack 1991; Catchpole 1992; Lambrecht 1992; contra: Dunderberg 1995).

Language and style. Mark contains 11,229 Greek words, with a vocabulary of 1,345 different words (Morgenthaler 1958, 164). Mark's style was commented on by Papias (Eusebius, *Hist. eccl.* 3.39.15): "Mark became Peter's interpreter and wrote accurately all that he [Peter] remembered, thought not in order [οὐ μέντοι τάξει], of the things said or done by the Lord." The author uses the historic present 151 times (see the lists with parallels in Matthew and Luke in Hawkins 1909, 144–48 and in E. P. Sanders 1969, 242–46), a fact that accounts for his preference for λέγειν over εἶπειν, since the latter has no present form. Mark favors *parataxis, for independent clauses are coordinated with the conjunction καί ("and") 591 times and the postpositive conjunction δέ ("and") 113 times (E. C. Maloney 1981, 66). The statistically frequent use of paratactic καί suggests the influence of Hebrew or Aramaic (E. C. Maloney 1981, 67). Out of 88 total paragraphs in Mark, 80 begin with καί and six with δέ (Hawkins 1909, 151).

Title. The opening sentence of Mark, "The beginning of the gospel of Jesus Christ, the Son of God" (Mark 1:1), is frequently understood as the title of the entire work (Gnilka 1978–79, 1.42; Pesch 1977, 1.74–75; a possibility for K. L. Schmidt 1919, 19). This sentence has two problematic features (Meier 1994, 85 n. 112): it has a subject ("beginning") but no verb and no predicate, and a subordinate clause with no main clause (vv. 2–3, introduced with καθώς). If v. 1 is construed as a title, it is in the nominative absolute. Since there are no examples of books beginning with καθώς, it seems likely that v. 1 is not grammatically separated from what follows (the καθώς of 1:2 links vv. 2–3 with v. 1, not with v. 4; Arnold 1977). If so, vv. 2–3 cannot be taken to describe the contents of the work, but only the opening section, probably 1:2–15 (Arnold 1977; Guelich 1989, 3–5), perhaps 1:4–8 (Gundry 1993, 30–31). Guelich (1989, 5) refers to 1:1–3 as the "heading." However, even though the phrase "*beginning* of the gospel" refers to the first short section of Mark, the term "beginning of the *gospel*" suggests that the whole of Mark may be characterized by this term, even though its "beginning" is necessarily limited to 1:4–8 (K. L. Schmidt 1919, 18–19) or 1:2–15. While Marcus (2000, 143–46) claims that 1:1 is a title that introduces both the prologue (1:1–13 or 1:1–15) and the whole Gospel, with "the beginning" having a double reference, he does not present any supportive arguments.

Textual problems. The ending of Mark was extremely unstable in the manuscript tradition. Both Codex Vaticanus (**B**) and Codex Sinaiticus (א) conclude with 16:8. The so-called longer ending (16:9–20) is found in nearly 99 percent of the Greek manuscripts of Mark (Aland and Aland 1987, 287). The shorter ending is found in some manuscripts after Mark 16:8 in place of or together with the longer ending (16:9–20). A different interpolation in the longer ending of Mark is quoted by Jerome (*Adv. Pelag.* 2.15): "Afterward when the eleven sat at table, Jesus appeared to them and upbraided their unbelief and hardness of heart because they had not believed those who had seen him after his resurrection. And they made excuse saying, 'This age of iniquity and unbelief is under Satan who does not permit, through unclean spirits, that the true power of God be apprehended. Therefore, reveal even now your righteousness.'"

Genre. During the first half of the 20th cent. it was widely held that Mark was *sui generis*, i.e., without literary parallel (Bultmann 1963, 371; Guelich 1983). This view is still held by many scholars and is particularly popular in England and Germany. The *sui generis* proposal, however, is inherently problematic, since virtually all texts are written with some kind of response to other texts (see *Intertextuality, *Transtextuality). Two variants of the unique-genre hypothesis are that the Gospel of Mark either (1) is an expanded version of the oral kerygma ("proclamation") of early Christianity, reflected in Acts 2:14–39; 3:13–26; 10:36–43; 1 Cor. 15:1–7 (Gundry 1974; Guelich 1983); (2) is intentionally structured to replace the Torah in early Christian liturgy (Carrington 1952; Goulder 1974, 1978; Guilding 1960 [for the Fourth Gospel]; this view is criticized by Morris 1964, 1983, and W. D. Davies 1962, 67–95); or (3) is an unliterary form of "folk literature" that emerged naturally from the Christian community (Schmidt 1923). More specific generic identifications have included Hellenistic romance or popular fiction (Tolbert 1989, 59–70; Beavis 1989, 35–37; Dowd 1991; Wills 1997); OT biographical narratives (Baltzer 1975; R. Brown 1971; Kline 1975); the Jewish novel (Vines 2002); Greek tragedy (Bilezekian 1977); and "an apocalyptic historical monograph" (Yarbro Collins 1992, 26–27). Though recently the earlier view that Mark should be considered a form of Hellenistic biography or βίος (Votaw 1970, a reprint of 1915) has been argued more forcefully by a number of scholars (Talbert 1977; Aune 1987; Burridge 1992; Bryan 1993), the contrary

Pre-Markan Miracle Cantenae (Achtemeier 1970)

Catena I	Catena II
* + Stilling of storm (4:35–41)	* # Jesus walking on the sea (6:45–51)
* + Gerasene demoniac (5:1–20)	Blind man of Bethsaida (8:22–26)
* + Woman with hemorrhage (5:24b–34)	* Syrophoenician woman (7:24b–30)
* + Jairus's daughter (5:21–23, 35–43)	Deaf-Mute (7:32–37)
* + # Feeding of the 5,000 (6:34–44, 53)	* Feeding of the 4,000 (8:1–10)

view that Mark is *not* a biography still has defenders (Nineham 1977, 35–37). The eclectic character of Mark is emphasized by some, arguing that the author drew from a pool of genres and narrative devices (Young 1999, 29). For Pedersen (1994) the attempt to define the genre of Mark is a hopeless enterprise, since it had different generic antecedents and was itself a parody of earlier forms.

Constituent literary forms. Mark contains a number of literary forms, some of which may reflect the use of sources (Telford 1992). Many of these literary forms appear to be based on oral forms identified and categorized by *form criticism.

1. **Pronouncement stories* are brief narrative forms that culminate in a saying of Jesus. V. Taylor (166, 78–79) finds 19 pronouncement stories in Mark: 2:5–10a; 2:16–17; 2:18–20; 2:23–26; 3:1–6; 3:22–26; 3:31–35; 7:1–8; 7:9–13; 9:38–39; 10:1–9; 10:13–16; 11:27–33; 12:13–17; 12:18–27; 12:28–34; 12:35–37; 12:41–44; 13:1–2.

2. *Miracle stories* (17) include (a) *exorcisms* (3): [1] demoniac at Capernaum (1:23–28); [2] Gerasene demoniac (5:1–20); [3] the possessed boy (9:14–29); (b) *healings* (8): [1] Peter's mother-in-law (1:29–31); [2] healings in the evening (1:32–34); [3] a leper (1:40–45); [4] paralytic at Capernaum (2:1–4, 10b–12); [5] woman with the hemorrhage (5:25–34); [6] the deaf mute (7:31–37); [7] the blind man at Bethsaida (9:22–26); [8] blind Bartimaeus (10:46–52); (c) *raising the dead* (1): Jairus's daughter (5:21–24, 35–43); (d) *nature miracles* (5): [1] the storm on the sea (4:35–41; a rescue miracle; Meier 1994, 924–33); [2] feeding the 5,000 (6:35–44; a gift miracle, Meier 1994, 950–76); [3] walking on the water (6:45–52; an epiphany miracle; Meier 1994, 905–24, esp. 914); [4] feeding of the 4,000 (8:1–10; a gift miracle, Meier 1994, 950–76; [5] cursing the fig tree (11:12–14, 20–22; a curse miracle, Meier 1994, 884–96).

The four miracle stories found in Mark 4:35–5:43 are widely thought to have constituted a pre-Markan collection or cycle (Schmidt 1919, 150–52; Bultmann 1967, 224 [defining the unit as 4:37–5:43]; Theissen 1974, 103, 109 [later classified as a deliverance miracle in Theissen and Mertz 1998, 295]; Meier 1994, 924–25). Keck (1965) and Pesch (1976, 198, 277–81), followed with qualifications by Guelich (1989, 142–44, 261–63), have argued for a larger pre-Markan collection of six miracle stories introduced with the pre-Markan summary in 3:7–17 at the beginning, and concluding with the two miracle stories of the feeding of the 5,000 and Jesus walking on the water in 6:32–52. Kuhn (1972, 191–213), unaware of Keck (1965) and Achtemeier (1970), examined the possibility of a pre-Markan collection of six miracle stories in Mark 4:35–6:52, but is not certain that all six stories belonged to a single collection (1972, 208–10). Achtemeier (1970) argued for an even larger pre-Markan collection of two miracle catenas, consisting of ten miracle stories that formed two parallel series of five stories, each series with an initial sea miracle and an ending feeding miracle that frame three healing miracles (*=Matthean parallel; +=Lukan parallel; #=Johannine parallel): Achtemeier's identification of two pre-Markan miracle collections is supported by the fact that they are analogous to the pre-Johannine Signs Source utilized by the Fourth Evangelist. The distinctive feature of the ten miracle stories in Mark 4:35–8:26 is that they ignore the conflicts between Jesus and Jewish religious leaders and emphasize rather the supernatural power of Jesus, i.e., Jesus as divine man, a *theologia gloriae* or "theology of glory."

3. *Stories about Jesus* (29): (a) John the Baptist (1:1–8); (b) baptism of Jesus (1:9–11); (c) temptation of Jesus (1:12–13); (d) call of disciples (1:16–20); (e) departure to a lonely place (1:35–39); (f) call of Levi (2:13–14); (g) rejection at Nazareth (6:1–6a); (h) Syrophoenician woman (7:24–30); (i) demand for a sign (8:11–13); (j) confession of Peter (8:27–33); (k) transfiguration (9:2–8); (l) rich man's question (10:17–22); (m) conversation on riches (10:23–27); (n) question of rewards (10:28–31); (o) request of James and John (10:35–40); (p) entry into Jerusalem (11:1–11); (q) cleansing the

temple (11:15–19); (r) anointing (14:3–9); (s) preparations for supper (14:12–16); (t) Last Supper (14:22–25); (u) Gethsemane (14:32–42); (v) arrest (14:43–52); (w) trial before the priests (14:53–65); (x) denial of Peter (14:66–71); (y) trial before Pilate (15:1–15); (z) mocked by the soldiers (15:16–20); (aa) crucifixion (15:21–41); (bb) burial (15:42–47); (cc) visit to the tomb (16:1–8).

4. *Parables* (6): (a) sower (Mark 4:3–8); (b) seed growing secretly (4:26–29), (c) mustard seed (4:30–32), (d) the wicked tenants (12:1–12), (e) the fig tree (13:28–29), (f) the master's unexpected return (13:34–37).

5. *Sayings of Jesus* are those statements attributed to Jesus with no narrative framework, a category that technically includes both sayings of Jesus and parables. There are approximately 38 sayings of Jesus in Mark (Taylor 1966, 86–87): (a) patches and wineskins (2:21–22), (b) the Sabbath (2:27–28), (c) the strong man (3:27–29), (d) the purpose of the parables (4:10–12), (e) the lamp (4:21), (f) what is hidden (4:22), (g) ears to hear (4:23), (h) the measure you give (4:24), (i) the one who has (4:25), (j) on defilement (7:14–23), (k) on bearing one's cross (8:34), (l) whoever would save his life (8:35), (m) what shall it profit? (8:36), (n) what would a man exchange for his life? (8:37), (o) whoever is ashamed (8:38), (p) there are some here (9:1), (q) receiving little ones (9:37), (r) he who is not against us (9:40), (s) a cup of cold water (9:41), (t) causing little ones to stumble (9:42), (u) hand, foot, and eye (9:43–48), (v) salted with fire (9:51), (w) salt is good (9:50a), (x) have salt in yourselves (9:50b), (y) on adultery (10:11–12), (z) many that are first (10:31), (aa) on prayer (11:23–25), (bb) on the scribes (12:38–40), (cc) on persecution (13:9–15), (dd) signs before the Parousia (13:5–8, 24–27), (ee) on the abomination of desolation (13:14–20), (ff) false Christs and false prophets (13:21–23), (gg) this generation (13:30), (hh) heaven and earth (13:31), (ii) no one knows the day (13:32), (jj) take heed (13:33), (kk) the absent householder (13:34), (ll) be watchful (13:35–37).

6. *Editorial comments* include the various contributions of the author in putting the various components of his work together and making them contribute to the development of the narrative. There are 11 summary statements in Mark: (a) 1:14–15; (b) 1:21–22; (c) 1:39; (d) 2:13; (e) 3:7–12; (f) 5:21; (g) 6:6b; (h) 6:12–13; (i) 6:30–33; (j) 6:53–56; (k) 10:1. These statements are the contribution of the evangelist and function to both summarize and give direction to the narrative.

Redaction criticism. While early research devoted most of its energies to positing and analyzing these sources, the advent of redaction criticism (first applied to Mark by W. Marxsen 1969) led to an emphasis on the specific contributions that the author made in constructing the Gospel. Some argued that Mark is largely a work of fiction (Mack 1988). Others have sought a middle ground in their treatment of Mark, acknowledging Mark's dependence on borrowed traditions, while stressing the fact that the Gospel as it stands should be regarded as a literary unity, with all of the trademarks of a coherent story (Best 1983; Hooker 1991, 8–18).

Literary analysis. Mark is arranged in five sections (Marcus 2000, 64): (1) prologue (1:1–15); (2) Jesus' ministry (1:16–8:22); exposition on the nature of discipleship (8:23–10:52); the passion narrative (11:1–15:47); the resurrection (16:1–8). A very different literary analysis was carried out by F. G. Lang (1977) on the basis of symmetry and *stichometry, in which he proposed a five-part structure of Mark with an introduction: introduction (1:1–13; 29 lines); (1) Jesus' first appearance in Galilee (1:14–3:6; 155 lines); (2) the Sea of Galilee as the center of Jesus' saving activity (3:7–6:6a; 6:6b–8:21; 505 lines: 14 in 3:7–12; 246 in 3:13–6:6a; 245 in 6:6b–8:22); (3) the revelation of Jesus' nature and the journey (8:22–10:45; 264 lines); (4) the Jerusalem temple as the center of conflict (10:46–13:37; 280 lines); (5) Jesus' passion at Passover (14:1–16:8; 282 lines).

Narrative criticism of Mark. Narrative criticism focuses on reading the text as literature and is concerned with voice, plot, character, and structure, including the implied author and implied reader (Rhoads, Dewey, and Mitchie 1999, 137–38; Malbon 2000, 1–40). Reader-response criticism emphasizes the process of reading and how the reader experiences the text, creating meaning by filling in gaps (Fowler 1991).

Several important themes can be traced through Mark, including: (1) Jesus' conflicts with demonic powers, Jewish authorities, and his own disciples; (2) the identity of Jesus, including the titles Messiah, Son of Man, and Son of God; (3) the so-called messianic secret: (a) demons cast out are forbidden to speak (1:24–25, 34; 3:12); (b) the healed leper is instructed "to say nothing to any one" (1:43); (c) Jesus raises a young girl from the dead and orders "that no one should know this" (5:43); (d) after the healing of the deaf and dumb man (7:31–35), Jesus "charged them to tell no one;

but the more he charged them, the more zealously they proclaimed it" (7:36); (e) after Peter's confession, Jesus "charged them to tell no one about him" (8:30); (f) Mark 9:9 is particularly striking: "And as they were coming down the mountain, he charged them to tell no one what they had seen, until the Son of man should have risen from the dead." This messianic secret is finally revealed in Mark 14:62, where Jesus admits that he is the Son of God, an admission that leads to his condemnation.

What is the significance of the messianic secret? Wrede (1971) offered a historical solution: the historical Jesus did not require secrecy because he did not see himself as the messiah. Since Jesus' followers acknowledged him as Messiah after his death, the early church invented the secrecy motif to show that Jesus did not proclaim himself as messiah.

A more traditional historical explanation is that Jesus wanted to redefine his messianic role, not as a military messiah, but as a messiah who came to suffer and die. Jesus used the title "Son of man" as the neutral vehicle for defining his role, rejecting the traditional triumphalist conceptions of the messiah. The secrecy motif is basically historical, reflecting Jesus' attempts to dampen nationalistic messianism.

Turning to a literary rather than a historical solution, information in Mark is disseminated in two spheres, the inside and the outside. Outsiders have only a public experience of Jesus, and therefore their understanding is limited. In private, however, Jesus discloses further truth about his person and mission (4:10–11, 34). The meaning of Jesus is not disclosed to the one merely seeing the miracles, but faith sees Jesus correctly from the vantage point of the cross and resurrection.

The geographical settings used in Mark, once thought historical, have more recently been analyzed for their literary function (Malbon 1986). Mark's topography is invested with symbolic meaning. Galilee, for example, represents the place of Jesus' rejection, and is one of the place names that Mark added to his sources (Schmidt 1919, 43; Marxsen 1959, 36–37, 40; van Cangh 1972a). Jerusalem, on the other hand, is the place of Jesus' rejection and death (Lohmeyer 1936; Kümmel 1975, 88–89). This symbolism is reflected in Mark's two-part geographical outline (Mark 1–9: Galilee; Mark 10: trip to Jerusalem; Mark 11–16: Jesus in Jerusalem).

Other settings also seem to be tied to stock images. For example, each lake crossing is linked to a test of the disciples' faith (4:35–41, 6:45–52, 8:13–21), tests that they repeatedly fail. A contrast between private and public spheres is also present in Mark (Rhoads, Dewey, and Mitchie 1999, 70–71).

The dramatis personae in Mark are often divided into two general categories, "three-dimensional" and "two-dimensional," or "round" and "flat" (Forster 1974, 46–54, followed by Kingsbury 1988 and Malbon 2000, 10–11). Round characters have the potential for change and development; the readers or listeners are therefore more inclined to identify with them (Tannehill 1977, 392–93). Flat characters remain static throughout the narrative and serve primarily to advance the plot by eliciting different reactions from the round characters. The following presents a brief evaluation of the major characters in Mark (see Malbon 2000; Rhoads, Dewey, and Mitchie 1999, 98–135):

1. *Jesus* is the central character in the story. From the beginning the author presents him in a positive light. Not only is he declared to be the Messiah and Son of God in the first line, but the truth of this claim is supported by a voice from God during his baptism, "Thou art my Son, the Beloved, with thee I am well pleased" (1:11). Jesus is the gauge by which other characters will be evaluated, though the central protagonist is essentially a flat character. The consequence of this portrayal is an increased focus on how different characters respond to Jesus.

2. The *Jewish authorities* are presented negatively, in constant opposition to Jesus: they are hypocrites (7:6), they are concerned with their own reputations (12:38–40), they are legalists and manipulators of the law (7:1–13), and they put Jesus to the test (12:13–27).

3. Mark elicits from the readers a negative attitude toward the *family and friends of Jesus*; they are ignorant of who he is and of the purpose of his mission. This is developed in the following ways: (a) the antifamily episode (3:21, 31–34); (b) people from his hometown turning against him (6:1–3); (c) the disciples presented as ignorant and cowardly (4:13; 4:35–41; 6:30–44). After Jesus walks on water (6:45–51), Mark concludes (6:52): "they did not understand about the loaves, but their hearts were hardened." It is obvious that the disciples in Mark are presented as failures and function as negative examples (Tolbert 1996, 195–230; Weeden 1971, 26–51). They continually fail to understand the true nature of Jesus' identity and mission (6:51–52, 8:17–21, 10:13–14, etc.), they actively oppose the way of suffering that is so integral to Jesus' self-proclaimed destiny (8:32–33), they remain obtuse about the king-

dom principles of service and sacrifice (10:37), and finally, they abandon Jesus when he is arrested and put to death (14:49–50). Despite these failings, there are some positive features in their characterization (Best 1983, 44–48; Tannehill 1977, 386–405; Malbon 2000, 41–69). The disciples enjoy some successes (6:13), and as insiders they are told by Jesus: "To you has been given the secret of the kingdom of God" (4:11).

4. The *crowd* also responds both favorably and negatively to Jesus. They are perhaps best seen as a complement to the struggles of the disciples. They represent the full range of possible responses to Jesus and form the context within which the readers must make their own response to Jesus (Malbon 2000, 70–99).

Literary devices. A number of literary features are distinctive of the Gospel of Mark (Rhoads, Dewey, and Mitchie 1999, 47–61). 1. *Intercalation is a favorite Markan literary device (J. Edwards 1989; Shepherd 1995). He often sandwiches an episode between the beginning and end of another story, providing a context for both stories, drawing out contrasts or parallels between the subject matter and characters. For example, within the story of the cursing of the fig tree (11:12–14, 20–25) is inserted the story of the cleansing of the temple (11:15–19). Matthew arranges Mark's outer story into a single separate anecdote (21:18–22), while Luke omits it entirely.

2. The second evangelist also uses repetition with some frequency, sometimes to reinforce the importance of an idea. Jesus predicts his suffering, death, and resurrection three times (8:31; 9:30–31; 10:33–34). In each context these predictions are connected to teaching material in which discipleship is linked to Jesus' impending suffering and death. For analysis on Mark's use of dualities and triads, see F. Neirynck 1972, Rhoads, Dewey, and Mitchie 1999; for concentric parallelism see J. Dewey 1980.

3. Irony is another literary device of the author (Camery-Hoggatt 1992). Readers have knowledge denied to characters in the narrative, enabling them to see two layers of meaning in the statements and actions encountered in the story. For instance, while he hangs on the cross, Jesus is mocked by the chief priests and the scribes, who say, "He saved others; he cannot save himself" (15:31). The readers know that Jesus predicted his own death three times and did not try to avoid it.

4. The evangelist also uses symbolism. The two-step healing of the blind man (8:22–26) is widely understood as symbolizing of the blindness of Jesus' followers and their step-by-step progression toward an awareness of Jesus' true identity.

5. The *narrative asides function as direct commentary by the author to the readers. One of the most striking of these is found in the midst of the prediction of future tribulation in Mark 13: "But when you see the desolating sacrilege set up where it ought not to be (let the reader understand), then let those who are in Judea flee to the mountains" (13:14).

6. The evangelist relies heavily on quotations from and allusions to the Hebrew Scriptures (Miller and Miller 1990), though these are not generally used in terms of promise-and-fulfillment, Mark 14:27 is a partial exception. These flesh out his story, providing important historical, literary, and theological contexts. For example, in Mark, Jesus interprets his actions in the temple through the use of two OT quotations, Isa. 56:7 and Jer. 7:11, "Is it not written, 'My house shall be called a house of prayer for all nations'? But you have made it a den of robbers" (11:17). Jeremiah 7 contains warnings to unrighteous Jewish leaders not to put their trust in the temple, for just as God destroyed God's home at Shiloh, so too God will not hesitate to destroy the temple if it becomes a refuge of unrighteous rebels. Thus Jesus uses the quotation as a warning of divine judgment on the temple and its current leadership.

*Synoptic Gospels, *Historical present, *Intercalation

Achtemeier 1970, 1972; Anderson and Moore 1992; Aune 1987; Baltzer 1975; Beavis 1989; Best 1983; R. Brown 1971; Burridge 1992; Bryan 1993; Camery-Hoggatt 1992; Cancik 1984; Catchpole 1992; Dewey 1989; Dowd 1991; Dunderberg 1995; Fowler 1981, 1991; Gnilka 1978–79; Goulder 1974, 1978; Guelich 1983, 1989; Guilding 1960; Gundry 1974; Hatina 2002; Hengel 1985b; Hooker 1991; Kee 1977; Kelhoffer 2001; M. Klein 1975; Kürzinger 1977; Lambrecht 1992; Lohmeyer 1936; Mack 1988, 1991; Malbon 1986, 2000; E. C. Maloney 1981, 1989; Marcus 2000; Marxsen 1959, 1969; Miller and Miller 1990; Moore 1992; Morris 1964, 1983; Neirynck 1988; Nineham 1977; Orton 1999; Pesch 1977; Räisänen 1990; Reiser 1984a, 1984b; Rhoads, Dewey, and Mitchie 1999; Robbins 1981b; Shepherd 1995; Suhl 1965; Tannehill 1977; Telford 1999; Tolbert 1989; 1996; Trocmé 1975; van Cangh 1972a, 1972b; Vines 2002; Votaw 1915, 1970; Weeden 1971; Weiss 1903;

Wikgren 1942; Witherington 2001; Wrede 1971; Yarbro Collins 1990; Young 1999

BRIAN GREGG AND D. E. AUNE

Mark, Secret Gospel of This Greek text, discovered and published by the late Morton Smith, contains part of the "Secret Gospel of Mark" (SGM) quoted in a letter of Clement of Alexandria to Theodore. A detailed commentary on the text is available in Smith 1973a, and a popular account of the discovery is found in Smith 1973b. Theodore wishes to learn whether all the material in a Carpocratian version of Mark is really present in the SGM, used in the church in Alexandria. Clement observes that Mark wrote a public gospel, presumably canonical Mark, during Peter's sojourn in Rome, but after Peter's death he went to Alexandria, where he wrote an expanded secret gospel. The letter then quotes two sections from the SGM. The first fragment (located between Mark 10:34 and 10:35) is a story of Jesus' raising a rich young man from the dead who then begs to be with Jesus. After keeping Jesus in his house for six days, he receives a command from Jesus and meets him in the evening, with a linen cloth covering his naked body, and listens to Jesus teach the mystery of God's kingdom all night long. The second fragment (following Mark 10:46a) narrates Jesus' rejection in Jericho of the rich young man's sister and mother and Salome.

A variety of scholars has assessed SGM very differently: (1) Bruce (1974) argues that the quotations preserved by Clement of Alexandria from SGM are interpolations into canonical Mark based on a knowledge of the other canonical Gospels. (2) Koester (1983) proposes that a now unrecoverable original Proto-Mark was transformed into the very different revisions we now call Matthew and Luke. SGM was yet another stage in the revision of Mark. (3) Schenke (1984), like Koester, considers canonical Mark to be a purified version of the SGM, available for use only in the church of Alexandria.

*Gospels, Apocryphal

Bruce 1974; Gundry 1993, 603–23; Koester 1983, 1990, 34–36; Schenke 1984; Smith 1973a, 1973b, 1982

Martyrdom of Polycarp is a narrative account framed as a letter written by the church in Smyrna to the church in Philomelium in ca. 159/60 C.E., a year or so after the execution of Polycarp in Smyrna. The text, which claims the attestation of eyewitnesses (15:1), is important since it is the first extant martyr act (which became a literary pattern for later martyr acts), and contains the first mention of the cult of the martyrs (17:3; 18:3). The text dates the martyrdom of Polycarp to "the second day of the first half of the month of Xanthicus, the seventh day before the kalends of March, a great sabbath, at the eighth hour" (21:1), but does not indicate the year. The problem centers on when L. Statius Quadratus was proconsul; Grant (1970, 86–87) understands recent evidence to point to the year 156, though Schoedel (1967, 78–79) thinks that one cannot be more precise than 155–60, and Hartog (2001, 22–32) thinks it best to leave the date of Polycarp's martyrdom sometime between 155 and 167.

Text and translations. The text was written in Greek and is preserved in nine Greek manuscripts and fragments (listed Dehandschutter 1979, 27–34), and in addition a large part of the text is preserved in Eusebius (*Hist. eccl.* 4.15–25). The conclusion of the text is obviously a later addition, but provides a fascinating glimpse of the subsequent history of the transmission of the text (trans. Holmes (1989, 144):

> This account Gaius transcribed from the papers of Irenaeus, a disciple of Polycarp, who also lived with Irenaeus. And I, Socrates, wrote it down in Corinth from the copies of Gaius. Grace be with everyone. And I Pionius, wrote it down again from the previously mentioned copy, after making a search for it (for the blessed Polycarp showed it to me in a revelation, as I will explain in the sequel). I gathered it together when it was nearly worn out by age, that the Lord Jesus Christ might also gather me together with his elect into his heavenly kingdom; to whom be the glory with the Father and the Son and the Holy Spirit forever and ever. Amen.

The standard critical Greek text is Funk and Bihlmeyer (1956, xxxviii–xliv, 120–32). English translations are available in Lake, with the Greek text on facing pages (1912, 2.307–45), Glim, Marique, and Walsh (1947, 145–63), and Holmes (1989, 131–44).

Literary form. The *Mart. Polyc.* is framed as a letter (Dehandschutter 1979, 157–75), but contains a narrative martyr act (Dehandschutter 1979, 175–87). This combination, in the view of Dehandschutter (1979, 175–87) is not a generic feature of *acta martyrum*, but is accidental. There are, to be sure, a few other *acta martyrum*

Parallels between the Gospels and the Martyrdom of Polycarp

Gospel event	**Text(s)**	**Martyrdom of Polycarp**	**Text in *Martyrdom of Polycarp***
Jesus enters Jerusalem on a donkey	Mark 11:1–10; Matt. 21:1–11; Luke 19:28–36	Polycarp enters Smyrna on a donkey	8:1
Jesus prays for disciples	John 17:1–26	Prays for the churches	5:1
Betrayed by a disciple	Mark 14:10–11, 44–46; Matt. 26:14–16, 47–50; Luke 22:3–6, 47–49; John 18:2–5	Betrayed by two servants of his household after torture	6:1–2
Hosts a final meal	Mark 14:22–25; Matt. 26:26–29; Luke 22:15–20	Hosts a final meal	7:2
Prays before arrest	Mark 14:32–43; Matt. 26:36–46; Luke 22:40–46; John 17:1–26	Prays before arrest	7:2–3
Interrogated by Herod	Luke 23:6–12	Interrogated by Herod	8:2–3
Pilate interrogates Jesus	Mark 15:1–5; Matt. 27:11–14; Luke 23:2–7; John 18:28–19:11	Interrogated by the governor	9:1–11:2
Jews call for the death of Jesus	John 19:12–16; cf. Mark 15:9–15; Matt. 27:16–23; Luke 23:20–24	Jews call for the death of Polycarp	12:2–13:1
Crucifixion on a Friday	Luke 23:54; John 19:31	Polycarp arrested on Friday; executed on the Sabbath	7:1; 8:1
Body taken for burial	Matt. 27:57–61	Bones taken for safety	18:2–3

which are framed as letters, including the *Letter of the Churches of Lyons and Vienne*, and *The Testament of the Forty Martyrs*. The church in Smyrna wrote the *Martyrdom of Polycarp* at the request of the church in Philomelium, who asked for news about the death of Polycarp. The epistolary prescript contains all of the standard elements of a Christian letter (trans. Musurillo): [Superscription]: "The church of God dwelling in Smyrna, [Adscription]: to the church of God of Philomelium and to all the communities of the holy Catholic church everywhere: [Salutation]: may the mercy, peace, and love of God the Father and Jesus Christ our Lord be multiplied." The second element of the adscription serves to universalize the addresses, making it clear that this is an open letter intended for wider circulation (made explicit in 20:1). This same universalizing feature occurs already in 1 Cor. 1:2: "To the church of God that is in Corinth, to those sanctified in Christ Jesus called to be saints *together with all those who in every place call upon the name of our Lord Jesus Christ, both their Lord and ours*" [emphasis mine]. The scribe who wrote the letter is identified as Evaristus (20:2). It appears that Marcion (20:1) is the source for the historical account of the martyrdom, while Evaristus is the person who wrote the text (Dehandschutter 1979, 187–89).

Gospel parallels. The numerous clear and evident parallels between the passion of Jesus and the passion of Polycarp suggest that the author was intentionally structuring parts of his narrative in conformity to Gospel patterns (*see chart above*). The author is aware of the parallelism, for in *Mart. Polyc.* 6:2, when the name of the police chief "Herod" is mentioned, the author observes that "destiny had given him the same name, that Polycarp might fulfil the lot that was appointed to him." Jefford (1996, 95) has put these parallels in the form of a table *(see page 296)* which I have modified).

*Apostolic Fathers, *Polycarp to the Philippians

———

Buschmann 1994; Conzelmann 1978; Dehandschutter 1979; Grant 1970; Harfog 2001; Musurillo 1972; Schoedel 1967

Matthew, Gospel of, is one of four canonical gospels, all of which were originally anonymous, but all of which were assigned the names of apostles (Matthew and John) or men associated with the apostles (Mark and Luke), sometime during the 2d cent. C.E., perhaps when they were collected from ca. 125–150 C.E. to form a fourfold gospel.

Language and Style. Matt. contains 18,275 Greek words, with a vocabulary of 1,691 different words (Morgenthaler 1958, 164). The historical present occurs 78 times in Matt., agreeing with Mark in 21 instances (see the list in Hawkins 1909, 148–9). Though Matthew is dependent on Mark (see below), his style is smoother than that of Mark and there are frequent attempts to rewrite portions of Mark in a more succinct manner (Turner 1976, 38–41).

Title. The titles or *inscriptiones* of all four canonical Gospels are similarly phrased, with the preposition κατά ("according to") standing for the genitive of authorship: εὐαγγέλιον κατὰ Μαθθαίον, "The Gospel *of* Matthew," attested in that form only by MS **W,** though in the slightly different form εὐαγγέλιον κατὰ Ματθαίον by uncials **D** (Beza), **fam 13** and the Byzantine text. The oldest form of this title was probably κατὰ Μαθθαίον, "According to Matthew," (though attested only by the second hand of two very important 4th cent uncial MSS, ℵ (Sinaiticus) and **B** (Vaticanus), a phrase which should be understood as indicating authorship. Hengel (1985b, 65–7) argues for the originality of the longer form, e.g., εὐαγγελίον κατὰ Μαθθαίον, though he does not provide a convincing explanation for the origin of the shorter form. The shorter form of the inscription was not originally appended to this book by the author (literary works written on *papyrus rolls regularly had abbreviated forms of the titles at the end), but was in all probability affixed to the work when the four Gospels became a collection.

The opening sentence of the book, often intended to function as a title of the following work, is "The book of the genealogy [γένησις can also mean "origin"] of Jesus Christ, the son of David, the son of Abraham." Though a few have argued that this was the title of the entire work (Davies and Allison 1988, 149–54), the arguments are unconvincing. Matt. 1:1 should rather be regarded as the designation for the genealogy in Matt. 1:2–17 alone (Stanton 1992, 1189–90). There is thus no evidence that the original affixed a title to the text.

Authorship, date and setting. Matthew, like the other canonical Gospels was written anonymously, though the title was added later, when the four Gospels were collected to form a corpus ca. 125 C.E. Like Mark, but unlike Luke (1:1–4) and John (21:24), it contains no allusion to authorship. Early Christian writers were persuaded that Matthew the Apostle was the author of the work. There was a widespread tradition in the early church that Matthew wrote his gospel in Hebrew. Papias, in a famous passage preserved in Eusebius (*Hist. eccl.* 3.39.16) is remembered as having said that "Matthew collected the sayings [τὰ λόγια] in the Hebrew language, and everyone interpreted them as he was able." Similarly, Irenaeus (*Adv. haer.* 3.3.1; also quoted in Eusebius *Hist. eccl.* 5.8.2): "Matthew also published a book of the gospel among the Hebrews, in their own dialect, while Peter and Paul were preaching the gospel in Rome and founding the church." Eusebius (*Hist. eccl.* 3.24.5) preserves information about Matthew that has proven controversial: "Matthew, who preached earlier to the Hebrews, committed his gospel to writing in his native tongue, and so compensated by his writing for the loss of his presence." The difficulty with this persistent testimony is that Matthew exhibits no sure indication of having been translated from Hebrew (or Aramaic) into Greek, and when the author quotes the OT, he relies on the Greek Septuagint rather than on the Hebrew Bible. It appears that Papias was the source for all those writing on the subject after him. The same tradition in a slightly different form is attributed to Origen (Eusebius *Hist. eccl.* 6.25.4): "The first gospel was written by Matthew, who was once a tax collector, but who was afterwards an apostle of Jesus Christ, and it was prepared for the converts of Judaism, and published in the Hebrew language." For other similar testimonia, see Augustine, *On the Agreement of the Evangelists* 1.2.4 and Jerome, *On Famous Men* 3. One of the arguments against Matthaean authorship is the generally accepted fact of the literary dependence of Matthew on Mark. Would an eyewitness of the ministry of Jesus (Matthew), rely on the text of an early Christian who was not an eyewitness of that ministry (Mark)? Further, there is the interesting fact that while the tax collector called by Jesus in Mark 2:14 and Luke 5:27–28 is named "Levi," the parallel passage in Matt. 9:9 gives him the name "Matthew" rather than "Levi." The date assigned to the composition of Matthew is generally the end of the first cent. C.E., i.e., 80–90 C.E. Matthew is often associated with the area of Antioch, and the situation reflected in Matthew assumes tension with the Jewish synagogue. Some scholars place it comparatively late, i.e., between 90–100 C.E. (Hengel 2000, 170).

Matthew's Jewish-Christian community appears to be involved in controversy with Judaism, probably in the wake of the Jewish war and the Jewish restoration movement that followed it. This struggle is revealed in the woes pronounced on the scribes and Pharisees in Matt. 23:1–36. This tension appears also to be reflected in the parable of the Wicked Tenants in Matt. 21:33–43, which concludes: "Therefore I tell you that the kingdom of God will be taken from you and given to a people bearing its fruits." The task of Israel is always a universal one (Matt. 28:16–20), though there are passages that emphasize a restriction of the gospel to Judaism (10:5–6; 15:24). However, Jesus' mission to Israel was rejected, and has now been given to the Gentiles (Parable of the Vineyard; Mark 12:1–12; Matt. 21:33–46). Matthew regards the church as the true Israel; empirical Israel has misunderstood its mission and lost its election.

Literary Genre. Justin Martyr referred to the Gospels (presumably including Matt.) as ἀπομνημονεύματα τῶν ἀποστόλων, "memoirs of the apostles" (*1 Apol.* 66.3; 67.3; *Dial.* 103.8; 106.3). While there was a widespread view that prevailed from the late 19th through the late 20th cent. that the canonical Gospels were *sui generis,* i.e, a unique genre (e.g., Bultmann 1963, 371), during the last thirty years there has been an increasing recognition that the Gospels, including Matthew, belong to a subset of the genre of Hellenistic biography (Talbert 1977; Aune 1987, 46–76; Burridge 1992). While Stanton argued earlier that there were significant differences that separated the Gospels from Hellenistic biography (1974, 117–36; cf. 1989, 19–20), more recently he had concluded that "the gospels are a type of Greco-Roman biography" (1992, 1197–8), and the same view is now maintained by Kingsbury (1998, 9–13).

Shuler (1982) argues that the Gospel of Matthew is a type of Greco-Roman βίος or "biography," and more specifically that it was written in praise of its subject and that therefore it is epideictic oratory, more specifically, the *encomium (Shuler 1982, 37), or the "laudatory biographical genre" (Shuler 1982, 45). Shuler argues that Matthew is a biographical encomium by rehearsing the themes found in Matthew that are recommended in rhetorical handbooks for encomia (family background and genealogy, miraculous birth, upright earthy father, escape from death as an infant, stories of the baptism and temptation, topoi surrounding the death of Jesus [the plot by opponents, supernatural events, emphasis on innocense, and resurrection]). Shuler also discusses the techniques (the historicization of traditions, use of OT quotations, thematic organization of material, amplification, and comparison). However, none of these elements is distinctive of ancient encomia. Shuler is not successful in demonstrating that Matthew is an encomium or laudatory biography, because if that can be said of Matthew then it can also be said of virtually every other ancient biography that presents the human subject from an ideal perspective.

Literary analysis. The literary structure of Matthew continues to be a debated issue, and in consequence some prefer not to propose such structural analyses (Gundry 1982, 10; Keener 1999, 36–38). Matthew in part uses Mark as the narrative framework for his own gospel, choosing to transform Mark into a more biographical literary type by prefixing a genealogy of Jesus (Matt. 1:1–18, carefully divided up into three sections of fourteen generations each; some have proposed this strategy was based on the numerical value of the three consonants of the Hebrew name "David" (which together add up to 14), a birth narrative (Matt. 1:19–2:23), and by ending with stories of the resurrection and appearance of the risen Jesus (Matt. 28:1–20). In addition, Matthew inserted much of the material he used from the *Q document into five extensive discourses (see below).

In proposing a structure for Matthew, some have emphasized the structural clues that the Evangelist included in his work. Bacon (1918, 1930) argued that there are five discourses of Jesus in Matthew, each of which end with a stereotypical conclusion "when Jesus had finished these things" (7:28; 11:1; 13:53; 19:1; 26:1), suggesting an analogy with the five books of the Torah, and Jesus as the new Moses. The five discourses are:

1. The Sermon on the Mount (Matt. 5–7)
2. The Missionary Discourse (Matt. 10)

3. Parables of the Kingdom (Matt. 13)
4. Church order: humility and forgiveness (Matt. 18)
5. The Eschatological Discourse (24–25)

In addition to the pattern of the five books of the Pentateuch, the number five also served as an organizing principle for other groups of five in the Hebrew Bible, including the five books of the Psalms, and the five scrolls, or megilloth, for certain Jewish festivals (Ruth, Ecclesiastes, Song of Songs, Esther, and Lamentations). While there is general recognition of the fact that there are five discourses that end with a stereotypical expression, few accept Bacon's proposal that the author intentionally structured his work this way in order to serve as an analogy to and a replacement of the five books of the Torah (see the critique of Bacon's position in W. D. Davies 1964, 14–25, 61, 92–93). A problem with the five-discourse arrangement that few scholars have recognized is the fact that there is a rather lengthy discourse that does not fit the pattern—the Woe to the Scribes and Pharisees (23:1–39). Allison (1992) uses the five discourses that alternate with extensive narrative sections to propose a structure for the Gospel:

Narrative: Introduction to the main character: Jesus (Matt. 1–4)
Discourse: Jesus' demands on Israel (5–7)
Narrative: Jesus' deeds in and for Israel (8–9)
Discourse: Extension of Jesus' ministry through the words and deeds of others (10)
Narrative: Israel's negative response (11–12)
Discourse: Explanation of Israel's negative response (13)
Narrative: Establishment of the new people of God, the church (14–17)
Discourse: Instruction to the church (18)
Narrative: Commencement of the passion (19–23)
Discourse: The future: judgment and salvation (24–25)
Narrative: The passion and resurrection (26–28)

A simpler outline based on clues provided by the author is based on the threefold occurrence of the phrase "from then on," found in Matt. 4:17; 16:21 and 26:16 (Kingsbury 1973, 1975, 7–25). Kingsbury therefore argues for three main structural divisions of Matthew: (1) 1:1–4:16, (2) 4:17–16:20, and (3) 16:21–28:20. However, the phrase "from then on" is so common, that it is difficult not to regard Kingsbury's outline at "precariously based" (Davies and Allison 1988–97,1.61).

Rhetorical analysis. Kennedy (1984, 101–2) makes some surprising claims about the rhetorical sophistication of Matthew:

> Of the four Gospels, Matthew's makes the widest use of all aspects of rhetoric. He arranges his Gospel into distinct parts which perform specific rhetorical functions, and he is concerned not only to establish the ethos of Jesus' authority and the pathos of his suffering, but consistently to provide his readers with something close to logical argument. He appears to furnish reason to make what is said seem probable and to allow his audience to feel some intellectual security in his account.

According to Kennedy (1984, 102), Matthew begins with a clearly defined proem in 1:1–17 in which the author does not just state the Davidic ancestry of Jesus and hence his messianic qualifications, but goes on to prove it by providing an entire genealogy. Stories of Jesus' birth, his meeting with John the Baptist, his temptation and the gathering of disciples (1:18–4:16), provide a narrative setting for the proposition, which consists of Jesus' teaching in the Sermon on the Mount (5–7). Jesus must be the Messiah because his birth fulfilled the prophecy of the birth of the Messiah, he was proclaimed Messiah by John the Baptist, he was recognized as Messiah by God, he was tested and proved by the devil, the disciples responded immediately to his call, and he was able to heal the sick (Kennedy 1984, 103). "Taken together with the genealogy," argues Kennedy (1984, 103), "these episodes provide documentary evidence, witnesses, and signs, major forms of external proof." Matthew also uses the internal proof of logical argument, primarily in the form of *enthymemes, the first of which is "Do not fear to take Mary your wife, for that which is conceived in her is of the Holy Spirit" (1:20). A second enthymeme follows immediately: "She will bear a son, and you shall call his name Jesus, for he will save his people from their sins." Throughout Matthew, unlike Mark, external evidence is drawn into the narrative which cumulatively demonstrates that prophecy has been fulfilled with the birth of Jesus. The Sermon on the Mount then functions as a proposition for the Gospel as a whole, emphasizing the law, exhibiting an extensive use of enthymemes, and hostility to the Gentiles. At this point Kennedy cuts off his rhetorical analysis of Matthew and moves on to discuss the other gospels. Elsewhere, Kennedy (1984, 39–72) provides an extensive analysis of the Sermon on the Mount as an example of deliberative rhetoric.

Relationship to Mark and Q. There is widespread agreement that Matthew (like Luke) is literarily dependent on both Mark and the Q document, a view called the Two Source Theory (Davies and Allison 1988, 98–114). Mark is much shorter than Matthew (or Luke), and both Matthew and Luke regularly follow the order of events in Mark. Mark contains 661 verses, while Matthew has 1,068 verses; Matthew reproduces 606 of the 661 verses in Mark, though he used just 51 percent of the actual wording of Mark. Further, Matthew (as well as Luke) frequently improve the style of Mark. While Mark has 151 instances of the historic present, Matthew retains just 21 of them. Matthew uses and emphasizes Mark's theological perspectives on Galilee and Jerusalem. Matt. 4:15–16 is an OT quotation from Isa. 9:1–2 that shows Galilee as the land of fulfillment, and Jesus' entry into Jerusalem is illuminated by a quotation from Isa. 62:11 and Zech. 9:9. However, Matthew does not accept Mark's messianic secret (cf. Mark 6:51–52 and Matt. 14:33), for he does not want to veil the true nature of Jesus but to emphasize the paradox of his revelation that takes place in lowliness (Matt. 10:42; 11:25; 12;18ff.; 18:6, 10; 25:40, 45). After the baptism and temptation, Mark introduces Jesus' ministry with a series of miracles (Mark 1–2), while Matthew inserts the Sermon on the Mount (Matt. 5–7), followed by Miracles (Matt. 8–9), thus emphasizing the role of miracles as support for doctrine, which is more important.

Use of the OT. The Jewish character of Matthew is often emphasized by scholars (Buchanan 1997, 1055), and one aspect of this is the author's concern with the promise-and-fulfilment theme involving OT prophecy (see *Testimonia). The author of Matthew, according to Buchanan (1997, 1040), "has gone to considerable lengths in order to relate the life and teaching of Jesus to the Old Testament, and in particular to demonstrate that much that had been anticipated in the Old Testament Scriptures has been brought to fulfillment through the actions and words of Jesus." Gundry (1967, 208–9) argues that the Jesus of Matthew fills four roles prophesied in the OT: (1) the Messiah and (2) the Son of Man (Matt. 26:64; alluding to Dan. 7:13), (3) the Isaianic servant (Matt. 8:16–17, quoting Isa. 53:4; Matt. 12:17–21, quoting Isa. 42:1–4), (4) Yahweh (Matt. 1:22–23, quoting Isa. 7:14). A key promise-and-fulfillment passage is Matt. 5:17–20 in which the Christian exposition of the Law is set over against the rabbis, i.e., Jesus is the authoritative interpreter of the Law for the law-abiding community of the Sermon on the Mount.

The author's promise-and-fulfilment understanding of the mission and message of Jesus is clearly reflected in the eleven formulae quotations, each of which use the ἵνα πληρωθῇ ("that it might be fulfilled") formula: (1) Matt. 1:22–23 (Isa. 7;14): the virgin birth, (2) Matt. 2:15 (Hos. 11:1): the flight to Egypt, (3) Matt. 2:17–18 (Jer. 31:15): massacre of the innocents, (4) Matt. 2:23 (unknown; see Menken 2001): Jesus lives in Nazareth, (5) Matt. 4:14–16 (Isa. 9:1–2): Jesus moves to Capernaum, (6) Matt. 8:17 (Isa. 53:4): the healing ministry of Jesus, (7) Matt. 12:17–21 (Isa. 42:1–4): the healing ministry of Jesus, (8) Matt. 13:14–15 (Isa. 6:9–10): Jesus' reason for parables, (9) Matt. 13:35 (Ps. 78:2): Jesus' teaching in parables, (10) Matt. 21:4–5 (Isa. 62:11; Zech. 9:9): Jesus enters Jerusalem, (11) Matt. 27:9–10 (Zech. 11:12–13; Jer 18:1–3; 32:6–15): the fate of Judas.

Subsequent Influence. Matthew became the most quoted Gospel in early Christianity (Bingham 1998). *Ignatius of Antioch (died ca. 117 C.E.) was the first Christian author to allude to the Gospel of Matthew (Matt. 3:15 in Ignatius *Smyrn.* 1:1; Matt. 10:16b in Ignatius *Polycarp* 2:2; Matt. 2:1–13 in Ignatius *Eph.* 19:2–3).

*Biography, *Gospels, canonical, *Parables

Allison 1992; Bacon 1918, 1930; B. Bauer 1988; D. R. Bauer 1989; Bingham 1998; Buchanan 1996; Butler 1951; H. G. Green 2001; Gundry 1967; D. B. Howell 1990; Kingsbury 1973, 1975, 1988; Menken 2001; Moo 1983; Orton 1989; Schuler 1982; Stanton 1992

Maxim (a translation of the Greek word γνώμη) in general is a premise or conclusion of an *enthymeme, since it summarizes universal truths based on popular wisdom and introduces the ethical power necessary for persuasiveness (Aristotle, *Rhet.* 2.21.1–16; 1394a–1395b). Aristotle provides examples of maxims that can take on the form of enthymemes: "Do not nurse immortal anger" is a maxim that becomes an enthymeme when prefaced with the reason expressed as a contrary: "Being a mortal, do not nurse immortal anger" (*Rhetorica* 2.21.6; 1394b).

*Aphorism, *Enthymeme

Searby 1998

Melito of Sardis, *Peri Pascha* A homily consisting of 803 lines discovered by Bonner (1940). Bonner attributed the homily to Melito of Sardis based on the testimony of Eusebius (*Hist. eccl.* 4.26.3–11, 13–14; 5.24.2–6). Eusebius claims that Melito wrote an apology to the Emperor Marcus Aurelius (161–80 C.E.), that he wrote six books of excerpts from the OT, and that he wrote two paschal homilies. Both the Chester Beatty papyrus edited by Bonner (1940) and the Bodmer Papyrus Codex XIII edited by Testuz (1960) attributed the homily to Melito. Cohick (2000, 12–13) is skeptical of this attribution and suggests that either an author named Melito, but not the one mentioned by Eusebius, wrote the homily, or else the homily was anonymous and later attributed to Melito. Both hypotheses seem unnecessarily skeptical. The homily, which contains no allusions to the NT, can be dated from the mid-2d to early 3rd cent. C.E. The rhetorical style of the homily is characteristic of the Second Sophistic.

Bonner 1940; Cohick 2000; Sykes 1999; Testuz 1960

Metabasis, a transliteration of the Greek rhetorical term μετάβασις ("transition"), equivalent to the Latin term *aversio* ("distraction"), refers to "an abrupt change of subject or a return to the subject from a digression" (Rowe 1997, 145). Romans 8:1 can be understood as just such an abrupt transition.

Rowe 1997.

Metaphor, a transliteration of the Greek word μεταφορά ("transference")—for which the corresponding Latin rhetorical term is *translatio*—is a *trope in which a word, group of words, or a sentence is used to stand for something different from the literal reference but is linked to it by some perceived similarity. Aristotle defined μεταφορά as: "the application to a thing of a name that belongs to something else [ὀνόματος ἀλλοτρίου], the transference taking place from genus to species, from species to genus, from species to species, or proportionally" (*Poetica* 21.7; cf. *Rhetorica* 3.10.7). Aristotle's treatment of the metaphor has dominated subsequent discussion to a profound extent (Otto 1998, 53–219). There has been a surge in the modern study of the metaphor, particularly during the last thirty years (Van Noppen et al. 1985; Van Noppen and Hols 1990). Studies on metaphor have been produced by philosophers, linguists, psychologists and biblical scholars.

Defining metaphor as "the transfer of a name," with the emphasis on metaphor as an isolable word or phrase, is a faulty assumption that has restricted the theoretical discussion of metaphor ever since Aristotle (White 1996, 56–58). Even Ricoeur (1977, 66) accepts this restrictive assumption: "the real definition of metaphor in terms of statement cannot obliterate its nominal definition in terms of word or name, because word remains the locus of the effect of metaphorical meaning. It is the word that is said to take a metaphorical meaning." A familiar dominical saying, "Doubtless you will quote to me this proverb, 'Physician, heal yourself'" (Luke 4:23), expresses a *single* metaphorical thought in two words. A more appropriate definition of metaphor is proposed by R. M. White (1996, 79–80):

> [A] metaphor is a sentence that may be regarded as a sentence that has arisen from the conflation of two other, grammatically analogous, sentences. . . . One of these sentences, the primary sentence for the metaphor, is a sentence that would give a literary description of the actual situation. The other sentence would give a description of a situation with which the metaphor invites us to compare the actual situation. As a result of such a conflation, we are invited to explore a network of similarities and dissimilarities between the two situations, and see the one situation in terms of the other situation, to see it as if it were the other situation.

Quintilian discusses metaphor in 8.6.4–18. He defines metaphor as one of the tropes based on the substitution of one word for another (9.1.5) and suggests that an extended metaphor develops into an allegory (9.2.46).

*Metonymy, *Parable

R. D. Anderson 2000, 73–77; Byatt 1995; Caird 1980; Otto 1998; Ricoeur 1977; Soskice 1985; Van Noppen et al. 1985; Van Noppen and Hols 1990; R. M. White 1996

Meter (see *Poetry)

Metonymy, a transliteration of the Greek word μετωνυμία (a rhetorical synonym is ὑπαλλαγή, "change, exchange") is a *trope in which one term is used for another, sometimes *pars pro toto*, "the part for the whole." In the modern proverb "A watched pot never boils," the term "pot" represents the water in it.

R. D. Anderson 2000, 77; Fass 1997

Midrash, a transliteration of the Hebrew word מדרש, meaning "study, inquiry, interpretation" (*DCH* 5.150), from the verb דרש ("to seek, inquire"). The term מדרש is used twice in titles of lost literary works mentioned in 2 Chr. 13:22 and 24:27, though the precise meaning of the term is unclear (Wright 1966, 113–16). In Neh. 8:2–8, Ezra the scribe reads the Torah, and a group of thirteen Levites help the people to understand the law in a liturgical setting. The noun and verb occur several times in the Dead Sea Scrolls with those meanings, e.g., the phrase מדרש התורה (found in 1QS 6.6; 8.15; CD 6:7; 7:18; 20.6; 4QFlor 1.11), means "the study of the Torah." In rabbinic Hebrew, the verb דרש takes on the technical meaning "to expound Scripture," and מדרש means "interpretation of Scripture" (Baumgarten 1977, 31–32), referring to an exegetical approach to Scripture found in the rabbinic midrashim of the 3d through the early 5th cents. C.E., but this meaning is not found in the Dead Sea Scrolls. In rabbinic literature, מדרש continued to mean "study, inquiry," but it was primarily used of the interpretation of Scripture. More specifically, "midrash" was "the traditional form of literature that arranged the rabbinic material in biblical sequence around specific texts" (Wright 1966, 119).

Defining midrash is widely perceived by experts in the field as problematic. According to Seeligmann (1953, 181), "it is not easy to define the complex phenomenon which we have customarily called midrash." There are narrow (e.g., P. Alexander 1984a and others) and broad (e.g., Bloch 1971, Le Déaut 1955, 1978, and others) approaches to defining midrash. A narrower definition combines midrashic *form* and midrashic *method* (P. Alexander 1984, 3). The narrow definition centers on the recognition that midrash is *explicit* commentary, that is, the recognition of the books of the Hebrew Bible as both sacred and authoritative means for some that commentary must be separated from the text on which the interpretation is based (Doeve 1954, 52–55). A narrow definition of midrash is sometimes used in classifying exegetical works that are closely similar to rabbinic midrashim, such as the Qumran Pesharim (Brownlee 1951, 76; Silberman 1961, 23–35; Stendahl 1967, 184–85, 189–94), though the pesharim are two to three centuries older than the earliest written midrashim. A broader definition is the result of focusing exclusively on midrashic *method* and also including prerabbinic exegesis of Scripture. There are two primary midrashic methods, *peshat* (literal exegesis) and *derash* (homiletical exegesis); the former predominates in midrash halakah (legal midrash), and the latter in midrash haggadah (homiletical midrash).

Defining "midrash" narrowly. The narrow definition of midrash is based on an inductive descriptive of that corpus of early rabbinic midrashic texts designated by the rabbis as midrash and accepted by all modern scholars as midrash, which exhibit both midrashic form and midrashic method and which date from the early 3d through the early 5th cents. B.C.E.: the Mekilta of Rabbi Ishmael (on Exodus), Sifre (on Numbers and Deuteronomy), Sifra (on Leviticus), Genesis Rabbah, Tanhuma, Pesikta Rabbati, and Pesikta deRav Kahana (P. Alexander 1984a, 2; see Chilton 1983, 9). Restricting our consideration to this corpus of texts is appropriate, since the term "midrash," as a technical term in modern scholarship, is based on the rabbinic midrashim listed above. This corpus of texts can be distinguished from other rabbinic texts that exhibit midrashic method but not midrashic form, including the *Mishnah (late 2d cent. B.C.E.), and the Aramaic Targumim (4th through 6th cent. C.E.).

The basic literary form of midrash consists of lemma (a brief quotation of Scripture) + commentary. The lemma may be part of a continuous passage (e.g., Genesis Rabbah), or a catena of passages (e.g., Pesikta deRav Kahana). Nevertheless, midrash is an exegesis of biblical *verses,* not biblical books, so the context of the individual verse is that of the boundaries of the canon itself, i.e., there is a disregard for the biblical book in which the verse appears as a meaningful context for interpretation (Kugel 1986, 92). Interestingly, the lemma and the commentary are not formally separated with a "spacer" (Alexander's term), as they are in the earlier Qumran *pesharim. The commentary exhibits several formal features that distinguish midrash from other rabbinic literary genres (P. Alexander 1984a, 3–4): (1) Scripture is quoted as a proof text, introduced by standard citation formulae (e.g., ש-נאמר). (2) The midrashist typically strings verses of Scripture together. (3) The midrashist quotes authorities (e.g., Rabbi Ishmael, Rabbi Akiva). (4) The midrashist cites different, sometimes contradictory, interpretations of the same word, phrase, or verse, often introduced with the formula דבר אחר ("another interpretation"). (5) The midrashist frequently uses meshalim or parables to resolve theological problems. A typical example of rabbinic midrash is found in Genesis Rabbah 34:13, with the formal features in capitals:

> [LEMMA] "And they said, 'Come, let us build a city, and a tower'" [Gen. 11:4]. [COMMENT BEGINNING WITH CITING AN AUTHORITY] R. Judan said: The tower they built, but they did not build the city. [CONTRARY OPINION] An objection is raised: But is written, "And the Lord came down to see the city and the tower" [Gen. 11:5]? Read what follows, he replied: "And they left off to build the city" [Gen. 11:8], the tower, however, not being mentioned. [ANOTHER AUTHORITY] R. Hiyya b. Abba said: A third of this tower which they built sank (into the earth), a third was burnt, while a third is still standing. And should you think that it [the remaining third] is small—[ANOTHER AUTHORITY] R. Huna said in R. Idi's name: When one ascends to the top, he sees the palm trees below him like grasshoppers.

Another example is from the Mekilta to Exod. 20:9, though this brief text refrains from naming earlier authorities (Fraade 1998, 73):

> [LEMMA FROM TORAH] "Six days you shall labor and do all your work": [EXEGETICAL PROBLEM] But is it possible for a human being to do all his work in six days? [SOLUTION] It simply means: Rest on the Sabbath as if all your work were done. [CONTRARY OPINION] Another interpretation [דבר אחר]: Rest even from the thought of labor. [TEXT FROM THE PROPHETS] And it says: "If you turn away your foot because of the Sabbath (from pursuing your affairs on My holy day . . . And if you honor it and go not your own way nor look to your affairs, nor strike bargains)" [Isa. 58:13] and then it says "Then you shall delight yourself in the Lord," etc. [Isa. 58:13].

To these examples we can add a rare example of explicit legal (halakic) midrash that is found in CD 9.2–8, perhaps from the 2d cent. B.C.E. (Fraade 1998, 69):

> And as to that which he said (ואמר אמר), [LEMMA] "You shall not take vengeance nor keep a grudge against the sons of your people" [Lev. 19:18], [COMMENTARY] anyone of those who enter the covenant who brings a charge against his neighbor without proof before witnesses, but brings it in his burning wrath or tells it to his elders to put him to shame, is taking vengeance and bearing a grudge. [VERSE FROM THE PROPHETS] It is written only, "He [God] takes vengeance against his adversaries and keeps a grudge against his enemies" [Nah. 1:2]. If he was silent from day to day and in his burning wrath charged him with a capital offense, his iniquity is upon him, for he did not fulfill the ordinance of God which says to him, "You shall surely reprove your neighbor so that you do not bear sin because of him" [Lev. 19:17].

Midrashic method deals with Torah, and according to classic rabbinic thought, Moses received the Torah on Mount Sinai in two different forms equal in authority, the written Torah (Scripture) and the oral Torah (tradition); *m. Abot* 1.1 claims that the [oral and written] Torah was transmitted from Moses through a chain of tradition to the rabbis (Weingreen 1976, ix–x; on Oral Torah, see Safrai 1987). Midrash was a means of presenting tradition in the form of the interpretation of the Torah. According to P. Alexander (1984a, 6): "So although at a formal, superficial level it is Tradition that is accommodated to Scripture, at a deeper level Scripture is accommodated to Tradition." P. Alexander (1984a, 9–11) then proposes four general features of early rabbinic midrashic exegesis: (1) Midrash is not a substitute for Scripture. (2) Midrash is argumentative, i.e., contrary opinions are worked, through revealing how final interpretations were reached. (3) Midrash has a point of contact or "peg" in the biblical text on which it is dependent. (4) The midrashist, conscious of working within a tradition of scholarship in which the role of the individual was minimal, did not value originality but was content to transmit the tradition which they received (Neusner 1971, 3.3).

Wright (1966, 1967), reacting to the work of Bloch (1955, 1978), for whom midrash had become an umbrella term for diverse types of texts (glosses on Scripture, meditation on Scripture in the light of recent events, the interpretation of events or themes or persons in the light of Scripture, the presentation of material in OT language, embellished history, didactic fiction, sources underlying the Gospels, the redaction of OT texts, etc.), sets out to investigate midrash as a literary form (1966, 106–8). In discussing the literary structure of rabbinic midrashim, Wright (1966, 124) distinguishes between exegetical midrashim (usually labeled halakhic midrash), homiletic midrashim (usually labeled haggadic midrash), and narrative midrashim (or *rewritten Bible), and this is the extent of his analysis of the literary structure of midrash (1966, 133). He provides a summary definition at the end of his study (1966, 456):

> As the name of a literary genre, the word midrash designates a composition which seeks to make a text of Scripture from the past under-

> standable, useful and relevant for the religious needs of a later generation. It is, thus, a literature about a literature. Midrashim exist in three forms, exegetical, homiletic and narrative, and they are accomplished in two ways: explicitly (the biblical text is presented and additional homiletic material and comments are assembled at the side of the biblical text) and implicitly (the interpretive material is worked into the text by means of a paraphrase).

The most important part of Wright's definition of midrash genre, however, is clearly stated not here, but on the previous page (1966, 455): "The fundamental question is: do the narratives under discussion [i.e., the infancy narrative of Luke] actualize biblical texts?" Wright then sets out to provide examples of what he considers "pre-rabbinic midrash": the Midrash of the Passover Haggadah (3d to 4th cents. C.E.); the Qumran Pesharim, which he characterized as "haggadic midrash" (1966, 422); the *Biblical Antiquities* of Ps.-Philo (a narrative midrash); the Genesis Apocryphon (which he tentatively identifies as midrash); and several homilies in the NT (1966, 433), including John 6:31–58, Gal. 3:6–29 (on Gen. 15:6), and Rom. 4:1–25 (on Gen. 15:6). This survey of "pre-rabbinic midrash" is inherently problematic, however, since Wright's focus is midrash as a *literary genre*. Wright emphasizes midrashic *form*, i.e., the midrashic genre (which he never defines adequately) and does not regard midrashic *method* and techniques as major characteristics, and the contents of midrash enter into the picture only when Wright distinguishes between haggadic and halakhic midrash (Le Déaut 1971, 264).

Defining "midrash" broadly. The discipline of "comparative midrash," which deals with Jewish and Christian exegesis of Scripture, is possible only if the term "midrash" is understood in a very general and comprehensive way. Kugel (1986, 91) approaches midrash in this way: "At bottom midrash is not a genre of interpretation but an interpretative stance, a way of reading the sacred text, and we shall use it in this broad sense." In an influential article on midrash, Bloch (1955) defines rabbinic midrash as a homiletic reflection or meditation on Scripture that seeks to reinterpret or actualize a given text of the past for present circumstances.

In a lengthy review of Wright's narrow approach to midrash (1967, a monograph based on two articles published in 1966), Le Déaut espouses a broad approach to midrash (1971, 268–69):

> Midrash is in effect a whole world which can be discovered only by accepting its complexity at the outset. It is pervasive throughout the whole Jewish approach to the Bible, which could in its entirely be called midrash. Technique and method cannot be separated, even if they lead to different literary genres. Midrash may be described but not *defined*, for it is also a way of thinking and reasoning which is often disconcerting to us.

For Le Déaut (1971, 270–71), defining midrash as a literary genre is inherently problematic, since genres in Judaism were not rigorously limited. Several "genres" could be juxtaposed in a single work. Midrash is the most ancient form of oral tradition, often synonymous with "oral Torah." Methods are so tied to the world of midrash that Le Déaut thinks that exegetical method is a criterion more fundamental for midrash than literary form (1971, 273). For Le Déaut (1971, 278–79), midrash and targum both "involve a presentation of the Word of God by adapting it to the contemporary conditions of the people of God." In the end, Le Déaut (1971, 281–82 n. 85) does not propose another definition of midrash, but rather regards the two essential marks of midrash to be scriptural context and adaptation. He concludes (1971, 282): "Midrash has produced works having vastly different literary forms and is very mixed in its content. By preserving its broad meaning one can establish classifications according to many criteria, as well as a terminology which does justice to all its aspects according to the results of analysis." In short, for Le Déaut, midrash is an "attitude" (Boyarin 1990, viii).

Midrash and the NT. The category "midrash" has become a very important one in the field of NT and early Christian studies, but is used with the general meaning of "Jewish exegesis during the 1st cent. C.E. on which authors of the NT documents were dependent." While messianism was one factor among many in the development of rabbinic midrashic exegesis, Christ became a centrally important factor in Christian interpretation of the OT (Seeligmann 1953, 173–75). Le Déaut (1971, 275) uses the term "Christian midrash" of the christological approach to interpreting the OT in the early church. Hanson (1974, 205) defines midrash as a "written meditation on the significance of a passage of Scripture with a view to bringing out its full meaning." He points to a number of passages in the Pauline corpus that he thinks are midrashic (Hanson 1974, 167): Rom. 6:7; 8:19–21, 33–34, 34–39;

11:17–24; 1 Cor. 5:6–8; 10:14–21; 2 Cor. 4:13–14; 5:19–6:2; Gal. 3:18–20; Col. 2:14–15. This is an example of the broad definition of midrash.

Goulder (1974) argues that Matthew is a midrash on Mark, but his proposal is problematic for several reasons (P. Alexander 1984a, 12–15): (1) Since midrash is performed on a canonical text, is it possible that Matthew regarded Mark as Scripture? Midrash is not meant to replace Scripture but to stand beside it, yet it seems that Matthew was bent on improving Mark and replacing it. (2) According to Goulder, Matthew is responsible for most of his additions to Mark, yet this contradicts the basic conservative tendency of midrash. (3) Though Goulder fixes on midrash as a model for the relationship between Matthew and Mark, there are also "synoptic problems" in rabbinic literature that he might have considered, from short individual haggadot to extensive compositions (e.g., the problem of the relationship between the Mishnah and the Tosephta).

*Rabbinic literature

———

P. Alexander 1984a, 1984b, 1990; Baumgarten 1977; Bloch 1955, 1978; Boyarin 1990; Chilton 1983; Doeve 1954; Fraade 1991, 1998; Hans 1981; Le Déaut 1969, 1971; Neusner 1987; Perrin 1965–66; Porton 1981a; Safrai 1987; Seeligman 1953; Wright 1966, 1967

Minuscule, from the Latin term *minusculus*, "rather less," is a term used for a particular style of writing in a small cursive script, i.e., a running hand with ligatures, which began to be used in manuscript production in the late Byzantine period (ca. late 8th to early 9th cent. C.E.). Since minuscule letters were smaller and more compact, as well as connected with ligatures, text required less space on *parchment and scribes could write more rapidly. There are a number of identifiable minuscule styles, such as the Anastios Style, named after a scribe active at the end of the 9th cent. C.E., which was used in Greek circles in southern Italy from the 9th to the 10th cents. (*DNP* 1.658); the Bouletée Style, 10th cent. (*DNP* 2.758); the Pearl Script, second half of the 10th cent. through the 12th cent., named after the stringing together of a number of letters by ligatures (*DNP* 9.594); and the Beta Gamma Style, second half of the 13th cent. through the beginning of the 14th cent. (*DNP* 2.592). The oldest NT minuscule MS is the Codex Uspenski (minuscule 461), containing the *Tetraevangelion or four Gospels, dated in the colophon to May 7, 6343=835 (Zereteli 1900; Diller 1956). Minuscule manuscripts of the Greek NT number just under 3,000 and are catalogued by Arabic numbers beginning with 1 (Gregory 1907, 370–83; Aland and Aland 1987, 125–55; Metzger 1992, 61–66).

*Uncial

———

Allen 1920; *DNP* 11.249; Metzger 1992, 8–10

Mishnah, a transliteration of the Hebrew word משנה meaning "study" (*m. Abot* 3.7) and "oral teaching" (b. Erub 54b), from the Hebrew verb שנה meaning "to repeat" or (in a technical sense) "to learn" (*m. Abot* 2.4; 3.3). In the broad sense Mishnah designates the three branches of rabbinic tradition, midrash, halakot and haggadot (Stemberger 1996, 109). The Mishnah is the earliest codified rabbinic writing and the basic work of Oral Torah (Safrai 1987) and is thought to have been compiled in the late 2d cent. C.E. by Rabbi Yehuda ha-Nasi, referred to frequently as simply "Rabbi," at Zippori in Galilee (his tomb is in Bet She'arim). The Mishnah is written in a Hebrew similar to that of the later books of the Hebrew Bible, though it is influenced by Aramaic and foreign words. According to classic rabbinic thought, Moses received the Torah on Mount Sinai in two different forms equal in authority, the Written Torah (Scripture) and the Oral Torah (tradition). While the Sadducees rejected the notion of an Oral Torah, the Pharisees-rabbis (the historical continuity between these groups is problematic) insisted that their halakic or legal traditions be transmitted by rote in oral form. The Mishnah has been regarded as a legal textbook (Goldberg 1987, 243) or a binding code (the former seems more likely).

Arrangement and content. According to *Abot* 2.4; 3.3, the Mishnah is divided into six orders (*sedarim*), each dealing with a main area of halaka, with each order further divided into from 7 to 12 tractates (*massektot*), with a total of 63 tractates. Each tractate is divided into from 3 to 30 chapters (*perakim*). In each order, the tractates are arranged in order of decreasing size (Geiger 1836; Derenbourg 1881). This principle of arrangement was common in the ancient world and is true of the suras in the Qur'an, the prophetic books in the Latter Prophets, and the Pauline Letters.

Mishnah and Scripture. The focus of biblical interpretation in the Mishnah is on the literal meaning of the text: פשט (Frankel 1956). Some

The Mishnah

Order (*Seder*)	**Tractates**	**Subject**
Zeraim (Seeds)	1. *Berakhot* (Benedictions)	Agricultural laws
	2. *Pea* (Corner of the field)	
	3. *Demai* (Uncertain produce)	
	4. *Kilayim* (Mixed kinds)	
	5. *Sheviit* (7th year)	
	6. *Terumot* (Heave offerings)	
	7. *Maasrot* (Tithes)	
	8. *Maaser* Sheni (Second tithe)	
	9. *Halla* (Dough offering)	
	10. *Orla* (Banned fruit)	
	11. *Bikkurim* (First fruits)	
Moed (Festivals)	1. *Shabbat* (Sabbath)	Sabbath, holy days, fast days
	2. *Eruvin* (Fusion)	
	3. *Pesahim* (Passovers)	
	4. *Shekalim* (Shekels)	
	5. *Yoma* (Day of Atonement)	
	6. *Sukka* (Booth)	
	7. *Beitsa* (Egg)	
	8. *Rosh ha-Shanah* (New Year)	
	9. *Taanit* (Fast)	
	10. *Megilla* (Scroll)	
	11. *Moed Katan* (Minor festival days)	
	12. *Hagiga* (Festival sacrifice)	
Nashim (Women)	1. *Yevamot* (Levirate marriage)	Marriage and divorce
	2. *Ketubot* (Marriage deeds)	
	3. *Nedarim* (Vows)	
	4. *Nazir* (Nazirite oath)	
	5. *Sota* (Suspected adulteress)	
	6. *Gittin* (Bills of divorce)	
	7. *Kiddushin* (Betrothals)	
Nezikin (Damages)	1. *Nezikin* (Damages)	Civil and criminal law
	a. *Baba Kamma* (First gate)	
	b. *Baba Metsia* (Middle gate)	
	c. *Baba Batra* (Last gate)	
	2. *Sanhedrin* (Great court)	
	3. *Shebuot* (Oaths)	
	4. *Eduyot* (Testimonies)	
	5. *Aboda Zara* (Idolatry)	
	6. *Abot* (Fathers)	
Kodashim (Sacred things)	1. *Zebahim* (Animal offerings)	Temple sacrifices and offerings
	2. *Menahot* (Meal offerings)	
	3. *Hullin* (Nonsacrificial slaughtering)	
	4. *Bekhorot* (First fruits)	
	5. *Arakhin* (Valuation vows)	
	6. *Temura* (Substituted offerings	
	7. *Keritot* (Extirpations)	
	8. *Meila* (Sacrilege)	
	9. *Tamid* (Daily whole burnt offering)	
	10. *Middot* (Measurements)	
	11. *Kinnim* (Bird offerings)	
Toharot (Purifies)	1. *Kelim* (Vessels)	Ritual impurities and required purifications
	2. *Ohalot* (Tents)	
	3. *Negaim* (Leprosies)	
	4. *Para* (Heifer)	
	5. *Toharot* (Cleannesses)	
	6. *Mikvaot* (Ritual immersion pools)	
	7. *Nidda* (Menstruant)	
	8. *Makhshirin* (Predisposers)	
	9. *Zavim* (Flux sufferers)	
	10. *Tevul Yom* (One immersed that day)	
	11. *Yadayim* (Hands)	
	12. *Uktsin* (Stalks)	

of the principles of פשט include a narrow approach to the construal of the text (Rosenblatt 1935, 3–4): Unqualified plurals never included more than two. Injunctions concerning enumerated objects should not be extended to others. Precepts should be fulfilled exactly in the form stated. The order of the statement had significance, since the statement coming first was preferred, and special significance was attached to repetitions of words or thoughts.

*Rabbinic literature

Derenbourg 1881; Frankel 1956; Geiger 1836; Goldberg 1987; Rosenblatt 1935; Stemberger 1996, 108–48 (the best introduction to the Mishnah in English); Weingreen 1976

Mixtum compositum or "mixed genres." There is an important sense in which the attenuated literary styles and forms that percolated down the social strata of antiquity tended toward eclecticism. The phenomenon of the *mixtum compositum* in turn, of course, was not unknown to educated authors of antiquity. Dionysius of Halicarnassus, who taught rhetoric in Rome after 30 B.C.E. and wrote *Antiquitates Romanae*, is very conscious of the eclectic character of his history, which he describes at some length (*Ant. Rom.* 1.7.1–4). He wants to begin with the oldest myths (avoided by many historians) and bring the narrative (διήγησις) down to the First Punic War (264 B.C.E.). He includes foreign wars and civil strife during that period, showing their causes and the actions and arguments (speeches) that brought them to an end. He also discusses the various types of constitutions that evolved along with characteristic Roman laws and customs, i.e., the whole corporate life (bios) of the ancient Romans. He concludes (1.8.3, LCL trans.):

> As to the form I give this work, it does not resemble that which the authors who make wars alone their subject have given to their histories (i.e., Thucydides), nor that which others who treat of the several forms of government by themselves have adopted (e.g., Aristotle), nor is it like the annalistic accounts which the authors of the Attic histories have published (for these are monotonous and soon grow tedious to the reader), but it is a combination (μικτός) of every kind, forensic, speculative and narrative, to the intent that it may afford satisfaction both to those who occupy themselves with political debates and to those who are devoted to philosophical speculations, as well as to any who may desire mere undisturbed entertainment in their reading of history.

Luke–Acts and the letters of Paul, when compared with the stylistic and structural prescriptions of the literary theory and practice of the educated, are eclectic. Yet unlike Dionysius of Halicarnassus, if they were aware of their eclecticism, they betray no hesitation, nor do they feel the need to defend what they are doing.

*Genre, literary, *Mode

Mode While *genres are usually identified in noun form (e.g., "apocalypse," "letter," "church order," etc.), modal terms tend to be adjectival (e.g., "apocalyptic," "hymnlike," "encomiastic," "mythic," "satiric"). They are applied more widely and never imply a complete overall external form or structure, because they are based on a selection of the features of the genre with which they are most closely connected (Fowler 1982, 106–7). Modes are not independent structures that exist apart from the genre from which they take their incomplete inventory of features, and they include such examples as "comic," "tragic," and "romance" (Fowler 1982, 111).

*Genre, *Subgenre

Fowler 1982, 106–29

Moses, Testament of (see *Pseudepigrapha, OT)

Motif (of the folktale), a term used by folklorists to refer to standard classification systems of narrative elements in the *types or whole plots of folktales. S. Thompson regarded a motif as the smallest element in a tale with the capability of persisting in a tradition, and the motif index he and others compiled was an aid to tracing the geographical and historical origins of folktales (called the Finnish method), under the assumption that each folktale had an original version, which was modified as it was transmitted (monogenesis). The standard motif index for folktales is S. Thompson 1955, supplemented by Baughman 1966 and Hoffman 1973. The assumption that an original version of a folktale can be reconstructed has been largely abandoned and replaced with theories of polygenesis (i.e., the repeated reinvention of similar materials because of similar social and cultural situations), but the motif indices remain useful for the comparative study of folktales.

Working independently of folklore scholarship, Hartman (1966, 23–49) identified a sequence of five elements in Jewish apocalyptic texts that he sometimes designated "themes" (Hartman 1966, 23) and at other times "motifs" (Hartman 1966, 71), which occur in five "groups of constituents" (which constitute an eschatological scenario or type), based on the identification and survey of 65 texts: (A) The preliminary time of evil, (B) divine intervention, (C) judgment, (D) fate of the sinners, (E) joy of the elect. An example is found in *1 Enoch* 100:1–9 (Hartman 1966, 55):

A 1 And in those days in one place the fathers together with their sons shall be smitten and brothers one with another shall fall in death until there flows a stream of their blood. 2 For a man shall not withhold his hand from slaying his sons and his sons' sons, and the sinner shall not withhold his hand from his honored brother: from dawn until sunset they shall slay one another. 3 And the horse shall walk up to the breast in the blood of the sinners, and the chariot shall sink down to its height.

B 4 In those days the angels shall descend into the secret places and gather together into one place all those who brought down sin, and the Most High will arise on that day of judgment

C, D to execute great judgement amongst sinners.

E And over all the righteous and holy he will appoint guardians from amongst the holy angels to guard them as an apple of an eye, until he has made an end of all wickedness and all sin, and though the righteous sleep a long sleep they have nought to fear. 6 Then the wise men shall see the truth, and the children of the earth shall understand all the words of this book, and recognize that their riches shall not be able to save them in the overthrow of their sins.

D, A 7 Woe to you, sinners, when you afflict the righteous on the day of strong anguish.

Theissen (1974, 17), in an analysis of the miracle stories of the Gospels, distinguished between *Motive* ("motifs") and *Motivvarianten* ("motif variants"), with explicit reference to the work of Dundes (1962). For Theissen, *Motiven* represent the "motifemes" of Dundes, while the *Motivvarianten* represent "motifs" and "allomotifs." Theissen (1974, 17–18) uses the term "themes" for a group of motifs that organize individual motifs into a compositional whole. This formalist and structuralist approach has been applied to NT miracle stories by Kahl (1994), using the work of Greimas. The basic narrative program of a "restoration miracle," according to Kahl, involves the transformation from a situation of Lack to a situation of Lack Liquidated. The basic structure of *all* miracle narratives, according to Kahl (1994, 41–45), involves a sequence of only four motifemes (Lack, Preparedness Phase, Performance Phase, and Sanction Phase; abbreviated by Kahl as L, Prep, P, and S). The last three motifemes are three aspects of Lack Liquidated.

*Form criticism, *Orality, *Oral tradition, *Types (of the folktale)

Baughman 1966; Dundes 1962, 1964; Hoffman 1973; Kahl 1994; Theissen 1974; S. Thompson 1955

Motifeme, a term coined by Dundes (1964), formed on analogy with linguist Kenneth Pike's (1967) theory of the "tagmeme." Dundes defines a folktale as a sequence of motifemes, a term he prefers to the term "functions" of Propp (1961). Dundes distinguishes between motifs (etic units) and motifemes (emic units). Motifemes are structural slots in a folktale narrative that may be filled by various motifs and allomotifs (i.e., motifs that share the same or similar function). One type of folktale consists of two motifemes, what Dundes 1964, 62) calls the "Nuclear Two Motifeme Sequence": Lack and Lack Liquidated. An example of this pattern is the following: a monster keeps all the water from the world (Lack); a hero slays the monster and releases the water (Lack Liquidated). Another type of folktale consists of four motifemes: (1) interdiction, (2) violation, (3) consequence, (4) attempted escape.

*Motif

Dundes 1964; Pike 1967; Propp 1961

Myth, a transliterated form of the Greek word μῦθος ("story, myth, plot"), can be defined as a sacred narrative that explains how the world and humans came to be in their present state, and is one of many of folklore genres (Dundes 1984). It has also been defined more broadly as "a religious charter, validating laws, customs, rites, institutions and beliefs, or explaining socio-cultural situations and natural phenomena and taking the form of stories, believed to be true, about divine beings and heroes" (Rappoport and Patai 1966, 1.xi).

*Folklore, *Motifs (of folktales), *Types (of folktales)

Bremmer and Graf 1987; Buxton 1994; Dowden 1992; Dundes 1984; Edmunds 1990; Fowler 2000; Gantz 1993; Graf 1993; Kirk 1974; Rappoport and Patai 1966; Scheer 1993; Vernant 2001; Veyne 1988

Nag Hammadi literature The Nag Hammadi Library (NHL) of Coptic texts was discovered in Upper Egypt in 1945, about six miles outside the modern city of Nag Hammadi. The cache contained twelve codices, plus eight pages of a thirteenth, containing a total of 46 different texts in 52 manuscripts. These texts date from the 4th cent. C.E., and were probably produced at Pachomian monasteries in the area. Most of these texts were previously unknown. Several bear partial titles familiar from the NT, such as "gospels" (see *Gospel, literary genre), "acts," "apocalypse," and in one instance "letter." Several of these texts contain Jesus traditions, the most widely known of which is the *Gospel of Thomas* (see **Thomas, Gospel of*).

Tools for the study of the Nag Hammadi texts. Those who are not specialists in the study of the Nag Hammadi texts can gain access to them and various studies about them through the many study tools now available. One of the main obstacles to nonspecialists is the fact that the texts are written in Coptic dialects. Some of the more important tools are: (1) keys to abbreviations (see table next page); (2) bibliographies (Scholer 1971, 1997; a "Bibliographica Gnostica: Supplementum" appears annually since 1971 in *NovT*); (3) introductions (Rudolf 1983 is perhaps the best introduction to Gnosticism and gnostic literature; separate introductory articles to individual tractates are found, with Coptic texts and English translations, in J. M. Robinson [ed.] 2000; informative introductions also accompany the Coptic text and French translation in the individual volumes of the Bibliothèque Copte de Nag Hammadi, Section "Textes," or BCNH, ST); (4) texts and translations (J. M. Robinson [ed.] 2000; BCNH, ST 1977–); (5) reviews of research (Turner and McGuire 1997).

Under the direction of J. M. Robinson, these texts have been published both in an initial facsimile edition of 12 volumes (Robinson 1972–84) and a series of critical editions with English translations in 17 volumes (Robinson [ed.] 1975–), now republished in five volumes (Robinson [ed.] 2000). In addition to these texts, there are also four related Coptic-Gnostic tractates in the Codex Berolinensis 8502 (Till): the *Apocryphon of John*, the *Sophia of Jesus Christ* (versions of both were found in the NHL), the *Gospel of Mary* and the *Acts of Peter*. English translations of all these texts are available in Robinson 1988. Four additional Coptic Gnostic texts are found in the Bruce Codex (the "First and Second Books of Jeu" and the "Untitled Text") and the Askew Codex ("Pistis Sophia"). English translations are available in Robinson 1975–, vols. 13 and 9.

Contents of the Nag Hammadi Codices. Nag Hammadi tractates *(see table on page 310)* are usually referred to with the siglum "NHC" (meaning "Nag Hammadi Codex"), followed by the number of the codex as a Roman numeral, a comma, and the number of the tractate. The Nag Hammadi Codices consist of 13 leather-bound books, significant for the study of codicology (J. M. Robinson 1978, 1979). Five of the tractates are represented by two or more copies, including the *Gospel of Truth* (I,3; XII,2); the *Apocryphon of John* (II,1; III,1; IV,1); *On the Origin of the World* (II,5; XIII,2); the *Gospel of the Egyptians* (III,2; IV,2); *Eugnostos* (III,3; V,1).

In addition, there are four Coptic Gnostic treatises preserved in the Berlin Gnostic papyrus *(see page 311)*, which are referred to with the siglum BG (Berlin Gnostic), then the number of the tractate, then the title.

Literary genres. The Nag Hammadi Codices represent a number of different literary genres (Pearson, *ABD* 4.988–89), yet the emphasis on revelation means that the more general category of revelatory literature has several subheadings, including apocalypses, revelatory dialogues, and revelatory discourses.

Apocalypses (Fallon 1979). Five of the Nag Hammadi texts use the term "apocalypse" in their titles: *Apocalypse of Paul* (V,2), the *First Apocalypse of James* (V,3), the *Second Apocalypse of James* (V,4), the *Apocalypse of Adam* (V,4), and the *Apocalypse of Peter* (VII,3). However the use of the term "apocalypse" in the titles of these documents does not necessarily mean that they conform to what has come to be defined as the apocalypse genre in modern scholarship (see *Apocalypse, literary genre of). There are other Nag Hammadi texts, without the term "apocalypse" in their titles, that exhibit some of the defining characteristics of apocalypses: the *Apocryphon of John* (II,1),

Nag Hammadi Tractates

Codex and tractate	Pages and lines	Title	Abbreviation
I,1	A1–B10	*The Prayer of the Apostle Paul*	*Pr. Paul*
I,2	1,1–16,30	*The Apocryphon of James*	*Ap. Jas.*
I,3	16,31–43,24	*The Gospel of Truth*	*Gos. Truth*
I,4	43,25–50,18	*The Treatise on the Resurrection*	*Treat. Res.*
I,5	51,1–138,27	*The Tripartite Tractate*	*Tri. Trac.*
II,1	1,1–32,9	*The Apocryphon of John*	*Ap. John*
II,2	32,10–51,28	*The Gospel of Thomas*	*Gos. Thom.*
II,3	51,29–86,19	*The Gospel of Philip*	*Gos. Phil.*
II,4	86,20–97,23	*The Hypostasis of the Archons*	*Hyp. Arch.*
II,5	97,24–127,17	*On the Origin of the World*	*Orig. World*
II,6	127,18–137,27	*The Exegesis on the Soul*	*Exeg. Soul*
II,7	138,1–145,23	*The Book of Thomas the Contender*	*Thom. Cont.*
III,1	1,1–40,11	*The Apocryphon of John*	*Ap. John*
III,2	40,12–69,20	*The Gospel of the Egyptians*	*Gos. Eg.*
III,3	70,1–90,13	*Eugnostos the Blessed*	*Eugnostos*
III,4	90,14–119,18	*The Sophia of Jesus Christ*	*Soph. Jes. Chr.*
III,5	120,1–147,23	*The Dialogue of the Savior*	*Dial. Sav.*
IV,1	1,1–49,29	*The Apocryphon of John*	*Ap. John*
IV,2	50,1–81.2	*The Gospel of the Egyptians*	*Gos. Eg.*
V,1	1,1–17,18	*Eugnosts the Blessed*	*Eugnostos*
V,2	17,19–24,9	*The Apocalypse of Paul*	*Apoc. Paul*
V,3	24,10–44,10	*The (First) Apocalypse of James*	*1 Apoc. Jas.*
V,4	44,11–63,32	*The (Second) Apocalypse of James*	*2 Apoc. Jas.*
V,5	64,1–85,32	*The Apocalypse of Adam*	*Apoc. Adam*
VI,1	1,1–12,32	*The Acts of Peter and the Twelve Apostles*	*Acts Pet. 12 Apost.*
VI,2	13,1–21,32	*The Thunder: Perfect Mind*	*Thund.*
VI,3	22,1–35,24	*Authoritative Teaching*	*Auth. Teach.*
VI,4	36,1–48,15	*The Concept of our Great Power*	*Great Pow.*
VI,5	48,16–51,23	*Plato, Republic 588–589b*	*Plato Rep.*
VI,6	52,1–63,32	*The Discourse on the Eighth and Ninth*	*Disc. 8–9*
VI,7	63,33–65,14	*The Prayer of Thanksgiving*	*Pr. Thanks.*
VI,8	65,15–78,43	*Asclepius 21–29*	*Asclepius*
VII,1	1,1–49,9	*The Paraphrase of Shem*	*Paraph. Shem*
VII,2	49,10–70,12	*The Second Treatise of the Great Seth*	*Treat. Seth*
VII,3	70,13–84,14	*The Apocalypse of Peter*	*Apoc. Pet.*
VII,4	84,15–118,9	*The Teachings of Silvanus*	*Teach. Silv.*
VII,5	118,10–127,32	*The Three Steles of Seth*	*Steles Seth*
VIII,1	1,1–132,9	*Zostrianos*	*Zost.*
VIII,2	132,10–140,27	*The Letter of Peter to Philip*	*Ep. Pet. Phil.*
IX,1	1,1–27,10	*Melchizedek*	*Melch.*
IX,2	27,11–29,5	*The Thought of Norea*	*Norea*
IX,3	29,6–74,30	*The Testimony of Truth*	*Testim. Truth*
X	1,1–68,18	*Marsanes*	*Marsanes*
XI,1	1,1–21,35	*The Interpretation of Knowledge*	*Interp. Know.*
XI,2	22,1–39,9	*A Valentinian Exposition*	*Val. Exp.*
XI,2a	40,1–29	*On the Anointing*	*On Anoint.*
XI,2b	40,30–41,38	*On Baptism A*	*On Bap. A*
XI,2c	42,1–43,19	*On Baptism B*	*On Bap. B*
XI,2d	43,20–38	*On the Eucharist A*	*On Euch. A*
XI,2e	44,1–37	*On the Eucharist B*	*On Euch. B*
XI,3	45,1–69,20	*Allogenes*	*Allogenes*
XI,4	69,21–72,33	*Hypsiphrone*	*Hypsiph*
XII,1	1,1–34,28	*The Sentences of Sextus*	*Sent. Sextus*
XII,2	53,1–54, 28; 57,1–60, 30	*The Gospel of Truth*	*Gos. Truth*
XII,3	1A–1B; 2A–2B	*Fragments*	*Frm.*
XIII,1	35,1–50,24	*Trimorphic Protennoia*	*Trim. Prot.*
XIII,2	50,25 +	*On the Origin of the World*	*Orig. World*

Codex Berolinensis 8502—Berlin Gnostic Papyrus

Codex and tractate	Pages and lines	Title	Abbreviation
BG,1	7,1–19,5	*The Gospel of Mary*	*Gos. Mary*
BG,2	19,6–77,7	*The Apocryphon of John*	*Ap. John*
BG,3	77,8–127,12	*The Sophia of Jesus Christ*	*Soph. Jes. Chr.*
BG,4	128,1–141,7	*The Acts of Peter*	*Acts Pet.*

the *Hypostasis of the Archons* (II,4), the *Sophia of Jesus Christ* (III,4), the *Asclepius* (VI,8), the *Paraphrase of Shem* (VII,1), *Zostrianos* (VIII,1), the *Letter of Peter to Philip* (VIII,2), *Melchizedek* (IX,1), *Marsanes* (X,1), *Allogenes* (XI,4), and *Hypsiphrone* (XI,5). The *Apocryphon of John*, for example, contains a revelation discourse given by the risen Christ to John, and a commentary on Gen. 1–6 reworked as a dialogue between Jesus and John (Kragerud 1965).

The defining feature of a gnostic apocalypse is the emphasis on present salvation through knowledge (Fallon 1979, 125). The spoken word, in both discourse and dialogue, is the dominant medium of revelation in gnostic apocalypses, rather than dreams or visions (there are no allegorical visions).

Revelatory dialogues. The distinction between apocalypses and revelatory dialogues is simply that the latter lack a narrative account of the appearance of the revealer. There are three revelatory dialogues in the Nag Hammadi corpus: (1) the *Book of Thomas the Contender* (II,7), (2) the *Dialogue of the Savior* (III,5), and (3) the *Discourse on the Eighth and Ninth* (VI,6).

Revelatory discourses. There are several revelatory discourses in the Nag Hammadi texts: (1) *Thunder: The Perfect Mind* (VI,2), (2) the *Concept of Our Great Power* (VI,4), (3) the *Second Treatise of the Great Seth* (VII,2), (4) *Trimorphic Protennoia* (XIII,2). These are essentially speeches attributed to a supernatural being for the purpose of conveying revelatory, often secret, knowledge to worthy mortals.

Gospels. Four texts that have the term "gospel" in their titles are among the Nag Hammadi tractates: (1) the *Gospel of Truth* (I,3), (2) the *Gospel of Thomas* (II,2), (3) the *Gospel of Philip* (II,3), and (4) the *Gospel of the Egyptians* (III,2; IV,2). (5) The *Gospel of Mary* (BG,1), found in the Berlin Gnostic Papyrus, is generically closer to an apocalypse than a gospel. None of these consist of narratives of the career of Jesus until his death and resurrection. The term "gospel" is used in the general sense of "Jesus material."

Acts. There are two works that have the term "acts" in the title, The *Acts of Peter and the Twelve Apostles* (NHC VI,1), and the *Acts of Peter* (BG,4).

Letters. The single Nag Hammadi tractate that has the term "letter" in its title, the *Letter of Peter to Philip* (VIII,2), begins with a letter but then quickly becomes an apocalypse. Two others are "doctrinal letters": the *Treatise on the Resurrection* (I,4), and *Eugnostos* (III,3; VI,1); while the *Apocryphon of John* (II,1; III,1; BG,2) is framed as a letter.

Other literary forms. A number of other tractates fit into a variety of other categories, such as (1) doctrinal treatises: the *Tripartite Tractate* (I,5), the *Exegesis of the Soul* (II,6), the *Authoritative Teaching* (VI,3), *A Valentinian Exposition* (XII,2), *On the Origin of the World* (XIII,2); and (2) wisdom books: the *Sentences of Sextus* (XII,1) and the *Teachings of Sylvanus* (IX,4), neither of which is gnostic in origin. There are also a number of embedded prayers, homilies, and hymns in some of the tractates.

Relevance for NT and ECL. Perhaps the one Nag Hammadi text most discussed for its relevance to the study of the NT is the *Gospel of Thomas*. "New Testament and Gnosticism" is a category in the two bibliographies of Scholer (1971, 84–90; 1997, 189–201).

The figure of Jesus frequently occurs in the Nag Hammadi texts, though largely as a legendary or mythical construct. Franzmann (1996) has devoted a recent monograph to this subject, and makes the following claim (1996, 21): "The study in the next chapters will be an attempt to present a description of the Jesus/es one finds in the texts of Nag Hammadi. I see this as a valid investigation of the historical Jesus since the texts belong to one strand of the many interpretive traditions about him." The fact that nowhere in the book does Franzmann make use of any criteria for determining historicity suggests that her interest is not in the historical Jesus but in the early traditions and images about him. She explicitly denies, however, that these are two different enterprises, since "both the material about the 'real' Jesus and the early traditions are interpretations"

(1996, 20). While Franzmann knows the distinction between the "real Jesus" (unknown and unknowable) and the "historical Jesus" (recoverable using the modern tools of scientific historical research), she seems to regard the latter (if that indeed is what she means by the "real" Jesus) as indistinguishable from her own enterprise. While her own enterprise is certainly valid, her unwillingness to distinguish between the history of faith-images of Jesus and the historical reconstruction of the life and teachings of Jesus is problematic.

*Apocrypha, New Testament, *Gnosticism, **Thomas, Gospel of*

Fallon 1979; Franzmann 1996; Kragerud 1965; Layton 1987; Perkins 1980; Robinson (ed.) 2000; Rudolf 1983; Scholer 1971, 1997; Turner and McGuire (eds.) 1997

Narratio/narrative is the second part of a six-part speech (whether the type of oration is *juridical, *deliberative or demonstrative, or *epideictic), which Cicero defines as "an exposition of events that have occurred or are supposed to have occurred (*De inventione* 1.19.27). He also advises that the narrative will be clear if the events are presented in chronological sequence (*De inv.* 1.19.29). The narrative can be omitted if its inclusion is a hindrance or no advantage (*De inv.* 1.19.30).

*Rhetorical theory, **Exordium*

Lanham 1991, 103; Lausberg 1998, 119–208; Cicero, *De inventione* 1.19.27–30

Narrative asides (also referred to as *animadversiones interiectae*, "explanatory comments," "parentheses," "footnotes," and "*hermeneiai*") are various kinds of intrusive comments of the narrator in a text (see *Narrator), usually presenting essential information which the reader needs to understand the narrative. Narrative asides correspond to dramatic asides in which an actor addresses the audience but are not heard by the other actors on stage. Booth (1983, 16–19) proposed several functions of the narrator's voice, including: (1) direct address, (2) explicit judgments, (3) inside views, (4) reliable statements of any dramatized characters, and (5) summaries. Oddly, NT scholars who have focused on the functions of the narrative asides in biblical narratives have rarely made use of modern literary theory concerning the various functions of the narrator.

Hedrick (1990, 76), in a discussion of the Gospel of John, defined a narrative aside (which he designates a *hermeneia*) as "comprised of intrusive word(s), sentence(s), or paragraph(s) of explanatory or clarifying commentary included in the narrative as direct address to the reader." Sheeley (1992, 36) offers a carefully crafted definition:

> Narrative asides may be defined as parenthetical remarks addressed directly to the reader which interrupt the logical progression of the story, establishing a relationship between the narrator and the narratee which exists outside the story being narrated. They provide commentary on the act of telling the story or on some aspect of the story itself. They include such things as self-conscious narration, prologues, postscripts and appeals to the reader.

He proposes four different functions for narrative asides (Sheeley 1992, 37–38) (see below).

From the standpoint of traditional literary criticism, narrative asides have frequently been regarded as glosses or redactional insertions into the text (van Belle 1985, 187), while from more recent literary critical perspectives narrative asides have been evaluated as part of the narrative strategy of the author.

Ancient narratives. Sheeley has explored the variety of narrative asides found in (1) ancient novels (1992, 41–56), including Longus's *Daphnis and Chloe*, *The Golden Ass*, Achilles Tatius, *Leucippe and Clitophon*, (2) histories (1992, 56–78), including 1 Maccabees, 2 Maccabees, Josephus's *War*, Tacitus's *Annales*, and (3) biographies (1992, 78–93), including Suetonius's *Lives of the Caesars*, Philostratus's *Apollonius of Tyana*, Philo's *De vita Mosis*, Lucian's *Demonax*. He finds many examples which he has used to formulate a taxonomy of narrative asides (this varies from text to text somewhat): (1) Material necessary to understand the story: (a) explanation, (b) identification, (c) translation, (d) context, (e) commentary on the story, (f) custom. (2) General information: (a) etiology, (b) aphorisms or proverbs, (c) comment on human nature, (d) customs. (3) Inside views (of characters). (4) Self-conscious narration (narrator's relationship to the story); proem. Sheeley has demonstrated that the phenomenon of the narrative side is widely distributed in ancient literature.

Narrative asides in the Gospel of John. Using various criteria, divergent numbers of narrative asides have been identified in the Gospel of John: 59 (Tenney 1960), 109 (O'Rourke 1979), 165 (van Belle 1985).

Hedrick identifies 67 hermeneiai in Mark (1987). Tenney (1960, 51–52) categorized the function of the "footnotes" in John into ten types: (1) explanatory translations, (2) explanation of time or place of action, (3) explanation of customs, (4) reflections of the author, (5) recollections of the disciples, (6) explanations of situations or actions with respect to cause or consequence, (7) summary of enumerating footnotes, (8) identification of persons, (9) supernatural knowledge of Jesus, and (10) theological comments. Van Belle (1985, 106–12) has expanded this list to 17 functions: (1) Translations of Hebrew or Aramaic words (e.g., 1:38, 41, 42; 5:2; 9:7), (2) Interpretation of Jewish customs (2:6; 4:9; 18:28; 19:40), (3) Indication or description of persons (e.g., 1:6–8, 6.12c–13, 15, 24, 40, 42, 44), (4) Indication or description of place (e.g., 1:28; 2:11; 3:23; 4:46, 54; 5:2), (5) Indication of time (e.g., 1:39; 3:24; 4:6, 23; 5:9, 25), (6) Interpretation of the words of Jesus or others (e.g., 2:21–22; 4:8, 9; 6:6, 64, 71), (7) Interpretation of the acts of Jesus or others (e.g., 3:19, 23, 24; 4:44, 45; 5:13, 18), (8) Incomprehension of the disciples or others (e.g., 2:9; 7:5; 8:27), (9) Tardy comprehension of the disciples (2:21–22; 12:16), (10) Fulfillment of the Scriptures or the words of Jesus (e.g., 1:23; 2:17; 6:31; 7:38; 12:14–16), (11) Reference to a passage which precedes or follows (e.g., 1:24, 40; 2:22; 3:26; 4:2, 45), (12) Corrections (e.g., 1:8; 3:33; 4:2, 23), (13) Notice of conclusion (e.g., 1:28; 2:11; 4:54; 6:59; 7:9; 8:20, 20), (14) Reflection inserted after the fact in the narrative (e.g., 1:24, 28, 40, 44; 2:6; 3:24; 4:8), (15) Longer theological reflection (e.g., 1:6–8, 15; 3:16–21, 31–36; 12:37–42), (16) "Reference" to the author of the Gospel (1:14; 19:35; 21:20, 23, 24), (17) Jesus' supernatural knowledge (2:24–25; 6:6, 64; 13:11). Hedrick (1990) presents a list of 15 types of narrative asides, very similar to those of Tenney and van Belle.

Narrative asides in Mark. The presence of narrative asides in Mark has been occasionally discussed (Rhoads and Michie 1982, 38; Fowler 1981, 157–68). Hedrick (1987, 244–45) proposed a categorization of types of narrative asides (or *hermeneiai*) in Mark: (1) Disclose what actors are thinking to the reader, (2) Clarify the character of persons and things, (3) Explain why statements of actors are made, (4) Explain a statement in the narrative, (5) Clarify the narrative through the use of an OT quotation, (6) Explain the time of an event, (7) Explain the meaning of foreign words, (8) Explain personal information about actors in the narrative, (9) Warn the reader, (10) Translate Greek words into Latin equivalents, (11) Draw theological conclusions and make moralizing comments, (12) Clarify the location of an event, (13) Clarify the identity of persons in the narrative. An example of a Markan narrative aside is found in Mark 3:10: "For he healed so many that the sick all came crowding round to touch him" (see also 3:21; 5:28; 6:14, 17, 18, 20, 50; 9:6 [2x], 31; 10:22; 11:18 [2x]; 12:12; 14:2, 40).

Narrative asides in Luke–Acts. The presence of numerous narrative asides in Luke–Acts falsifies the claim that Acts (and by implication also Luke) lacks an "authorial voice" with the exception of the prefaces in Luke 1:1–4 and Acts 1 (Alexander 1999, 25). Fitzmyer (1981–85, 2.1482) provides a short list of what he called "inconsequential explicative notes" in Luke–Acts, including Luke 1:66; 2:50; 3:15; 8:29; 9:14; 12:1; 16:14; 20:20; Acts 1:15; 17:21; 23:8. An example of a narrative aside in Luke not mentioned by Fitzmyer is found in Luke 7:29–30: "When they heard him, all the people, including the tax-collectors, acknowledged the goodness of God, for they had accepted John's baptism; but the Pharisees and lawyers, who had refused his baptism, rejected God's purpose for themselves."

Sheeley (1992) analyzed the whole of Luke–Acts for narrative asides using his grid of four functions (though his identification of the asides sometimes lacks clarity and therefore I have sometimes modified the references, commented on the passages cited, and suggested that some be omitted as not qualifying as narrative asides): (1) Material necessary to understand the story, (a) explanations (2:23; 8:29; 9:14 ["For there were about four thousand men"]; (b) identification (2:1 ["This was the first enrollment when Quirinus was governor of Syria"]; 2:4; 6:16b; 17:16 [a proleptic reference to Judas' betrayal]; 20:27b; 22:1b; 23:19, 50–51 [omit; a description of Joseph of Arimathea]); (c) context (14:7 [should be omitted]); (d) commentary, [1] on the story (9:45; 18:1); [2] on the characters (3:23; 9:33; 23:50–51 [referred to twice; omit]); (e) custom (1:8–9 [omit]); 4:16 [omit]; (2) General information (etiology); 23:12; (3) Inside views (characters): 7:29–30; 9:45. Luke 7:29–30 can serve as an example (in the RSV it is placed in a parenthesis): "(When they heard this all the people and the tax collectors justified God, having been baptized with the baptism of John; but the Pharisees and the lawyers rejected the purpose of God for themselves, not having been baptized by him.)" (4) Self-conscious narration, (a) narrator's relationship to story (1:1–4; 2:22–23 [doubtful]), (b) narrator's relationship to reader (1:1–4; 14:35 [doubtful), (c) reader's relationship to story (1:1–4; 5:24).

Sheeley finds the following types of narrative asides in Acts: (1) Material necessary to understand the story, (a) explanation (1:15; 4:22; 5:17; 8:26; 20:16; 21:9; 21:29; 23:8; 27:37), (b) identification (6:9; 10:2), (c) translation (1:19; 4:36; 9:36; 13:8; 14:12), (d) context (8:32–33), (e) commentary on the characters (10:2; 10:36; 11:24; 17:21); (2) General information, etiology (1:18–19; 11:26), (3) Inside view of the characters (12:9), (4) Self-conscious narration, (a) narrators relationship to story (1:1–5 [Luke 1:1–4]), (b) narrator's relationship to reader (1:1–5 [Luke 1:1–4]).

After surveying the varied types of narrative asides in Luke and Acts, Sheeley (1992, 137–76) turns to a discussion of the function of narrative asides in relation to the plot, the narrator, and the audience of Luke–Acts. The plot of Luke, according to Sheeley involves two motifs, conflict and prophecy-fulfillment, while in the plot of Acts conflict and prophecy-fulfillment are again of importance along with the growth of the church. Narrative asides are used to emphasize or intensify events in context, adding impetus to the movement of the plot (Sheeley 1992, 148). The narrative asides are also important for the reader's perception of the reliability and authority of the narrator, while they were most often used to direct the reader into the correct interpretation and to read with anticipation and retrospection. Sheeley maintains that the narrator of Luke and the narrator of Acts have separate identities "even though they constitute a unified narrative" (1992, 182–83). This is a very strange claim indeed (since Luke 1:1–4 introduces Luke–Acts as a whole, the narrator whom we meet there *must* be the same as the narrator we later meet in Acts). One of the most important results of the study, claims the author, is the way in which asides are used by the "narrators" to affirm their authority as storytellers (1992, 183). On the face of it this is a relatively trivial result, since (despite some specious claims to the contrary, as Dawsey 1986), the unreliable narrator is a modern literary device.

*Literary criticism, *Narrator

Alexander 1999; Bjerkelund 1986; Carson 1982; Culpepper 1983; Dawsey 1986; Hedrick 1984, 1987, 1990; Neirynck 1989; O'Rourke 1979; Tenney 1960; Sheeley 1988, 1992; Thatcher 1994; van Belle 1985, 1992; Wead 1970.

Narrative commentary, a type of Biblical commentary based on the recent story-centered literary criticism of the Gospels called *narrative criticism. In the late 20th cent., literary concerns began to eclipse historical and theological concerns for many biblical scholars, and it was perhaps inevitable that the new literary criticism would play an important role in reshaping the traditional conception of a biblical commentary. What is narrative commentary? It may be defined as "any interdisciplinary commentary on biblical narrative which draws on literary theory or criticism" (S. D. Moore 1987, 54). For the early practitioners of narrative commentary, however, narrative criticism was a holistic approach to the biblical text which centers on the finished form of the biblical text, and focuses on internal coherence and consistency (S. D. Moore 1987, 31–35). The first narrative commentary on a biblical book appears to be Kelber, *Mark's Story of Jesus* (1979a), in which the author clearly distinguishes his task from those with more historical-critical concerns (1979a, 11):

> Because we have focused on the individual stories *in* Mark we have not really come to know the story *of* Mark. This book is designed to introduce the reader to a single coherent story, Mark's story of Jesus' life and death. From a literary perspective the reader is therefore advised to approach the Markan story as he or she would any other story. . . .

S. D. Moore (1987, 38) charges Kelber with abandoning this literary approach and focusing on reading Mark as an allegory of the historical situation in which it was written. Yet surely these two concerns need not be contradictory. Is not Jonathan Swift's novel *Gulliver's Travels* an example of a literary work which also embodies a satirical social message? A second popular narrative commentary which does not explore the symbolic dimensions of the story is R. A. Edwards, *Matthew's Story of Jesus* (1985), who uses the construct of a hypothetical reader reading the text for the first time. The earliest full-fledged a narrative commentary (according to Moore) is the two volumes of Tannehill, *The Narrative Unity of Luke–Acts* (1986–90), in which the author focuses on character and plot (1986–90, 1.1), and the overarching purpose of the author which unifies the narrative, i.e., "the unifying purpose of God behind the events which are narrated, and the mission of Jesus and his witnesses represents that purpose being carried out through human action" (1986–90, 1.2). Tannehill assumes a reader that has read through the text several times (1986–90, 1.6). His holistic approach leads him to develop a more thematic organization. S. D. Moore (1987, 42–43) observes that Tannehill's version of a narrative commentary is basically a retelling of a gospel emphasizing the movement of its plot.

Since S. D. Moore's description of some of the features of narrative commentary (1987), and his critique of the work of narrative critics, Tannehill's two-volume treatment of Luke–Acts (1986–90) remains as a monument to the idea of a narrative commentary. The problem is twofold. First, the conception of a "narrative *commentary*" rather than a critical narrative reading of one of the Gospels (or in the case Luke, Luke–Acts) is an attempt to save an old category ("commentary") by adapting it for a purpose for which it is ill-suited. Second, it appears somewhat naive to suppose that one could produce sophisticated critical readings of a Gospel before a lot of long and arduous analysis had taken place by many NT literary critics. Rhoads's (1979a, 11) critique of other forms of NT criticism (source, form, and redaction criticism) maintained that "Because we have focused on the individual stories *in* Mark we have not really come to know the story *of* Mark." That is precisely the path now taken by narrative criticism. Rather than treat any of the Gospel narratives holistically, narrative critics are focusing on particular literary aspects of the Gospels, such as characterization (Malbon and Berlin 1993; Edwards 1997; Rhoads and Syreeni [eds.] 1999), the implied reader in John (Staley 1988), irony in John (Duke 1985; O'Day 1986; Staley 1988; Culpepper 1996), and point of view in John (Tovey 1997).

*Commentary

R. A. Edwards 1985, 1997; Kelber 1979a; Malbon and Berlin 1993; Moore 1987; Tannehill 1986–90.

Narrative criticism, a term coined by Rhoads (1982), is a type of formalist literary criticism which typically approaches biblical texts as a unified whole (i.e., as a closed, internally consistent story-world), emphasizing plot, conflict, character, setting, event, narrator, point of view, standards of judgment, the implied author, ideal reader, style, and rhetorical techniques (Rhoads 1982, 412–13), while usually bracketing out historical and theological issues. There are four basic aspects of the approach of narrative criticism (Merenlahti 2002, 18–19): 1. Narrative has a two-level structure in which aspects of form and content (the "how" and the "what" of narrative can be distinguished. 2. Narrative criticism espouses the ideal of a distinctly *literary* aproach that investigates the gospels as *literature*. 3. Narrative criticism regards the text as "a closed literary object whose form can be observed empirically." 4. Narrative criticism maintains that formal analysis reveals the literary value of a text which is based on the narrative unity of the text.

Narrative unity. The demonstration of narrative unity has been a core value espoused by narrative critics, because it was assumed that the discovery of a certain degree of narrative unity implied that the Gospels had literary value, which in turn meant that literary analysis was a valid approach (Merenlahti 2002, 3). "By any standards, a strong emphasis on the inherent unity of the gospel narratives must be considered the most salient single feature of narrative criticism" (Merenlahti 2002, 23). In his detailed review and critique of the rise and development of narrative criticism, Moore (1989), who espouses a postmodernist approach to literature, is particularly critical of the focus on narrative unity that ideologically dominates the work of many NT narrative critics, such as Tannehill 1986–90, whose narrative commentary is programmatically entitled *The Narrative Unity of Luke–Acts*. The emphasis on narrative unity is problematic because it is a concern distinctive to NT narrative critics, a concern with no real counterpart in nonbiblical literary criticism (Merenlahti and Hakola 1999; Merenlahti 2002, 28). Further, narrative unity does not appear to have been a concern of ancient literary critics (Heath 1989).

The assumption of the unity of a literary text is not always shared by historical critics who are aware of aporias, breaks, and inconsistencies in the text that cannot simply be smoothed over in a harmonistic way (Merenlahti 2002, 25).

Holistic approach. Concerned that the traditional types of biblical criticism (e.g., source criticism, form criticism, and redaction criticism) approached the text of the NT in a piecemeal and fragmentizing fashion, Rhoads argues for a holistic, text-oriented approach in which one would analyze "the closed universe of the story-world" (Rhoads 1982, 413). This approach has obvious similarities to *New Criticism with its focus on the autonomous text. However, the atomistic approach to the text that Rhoads deplored is in part the path now taken by narrative criticism. Rather than treat any of the Gospel narratives holistically, narrative critics are focusing on particular perspectives or certain literary aspects of the Gospels, such as characterization (Malbon and Berlin 1993; Rhoads and Syreeni [eds.] 1999), the implied reader in John (Staley 1988), irony in John (Duke 1985; O'Day 1986; Staley 1988; Culpepper 1996), and point of view in John (Tovey 1997).

Fiction vs. nonfiction. Narrative criticism is a development within biblical scholarship which, though initially based on the theoretical studies of nonbiblical literary critics (e.g., Chatman 1978, Booth 1983), has incorporated a variety of insights from these critics which has evolved into an eclectic form of literary criticism with no direct counterpart in nonbiblical literary criticism. Literary critics such as Chatman (1978), Bakhtin (1981), and Booth (1983) are primarily concerned with a poetics of fiction and do not deal with the extant varieties of nonfictional literature. From the postmodernist perspective, however, language does not represent reality (which is unattainable), but rather replaces it (Derrida). "Sensitive to this trauma of absence," observes Merenlahti (2002, 10), "postmodern writing typically blurs the difference between fiction and non-fiction." Several narrative critics (obviously working from a different ideological perspective) have criticized this blurring of fiction with nonfiction as having an antihistorical bias and a postmodern antagonism toward referentiality (Stibbe 1992). Coming from a different perspective, Merenlahti (2002, 10) observes that pragmatic differences exist between fictional and nonfictional texts: "The textual features of a novel and a newscast, a poem and a weather report, a tragedy and a gospel are understood differently. This is in spite of the fact that there are no definite formal differences between non-fictional or 'factual' and fictional discourse." Fiction, argues Merenlahti (2002, 10–11; following Genette 1993, 70), is a game of make-believe in which the narrator is part of the fictive world and does not represent the author, whereas in factual narrative, the author assumes full responsibility for the assertions of his or her narrative and therefore allows no autonomy to any narrator. Facing the issue of referentiality, Konstan (1998, 6) argues that fiction can be distinguished from history in that while the latter has a referent in the real world, the former has no such referent; it makes no sense, for example, to say that Chariton, the author of the Greek novel *Chaereas and Callirhoë*, was mistaken about the actions of the hero and heroine.

The three basic foci of narrative criticism are the author (i.e., the author implied by the text rather than the "real" author), the message and the readers (i.e., those implied by the text who is constructed by the text and addressed by it, and the "free readers" apart from the implied reader inscribed in the text by the author who brings to the text a whole constellation of associations not anticipated by the author). Narrative criticism represents the influence of New Criticism on biblical literature, though unlike the New Criticism it identifies the meaning of a literary work with the intention of the author (Moore 1989, 9). "Many of them [narrative critics] are reacting against a tradition that abstracts a propositional or ideational content from the Gospels. Instead they assert the inseparability of an evangelist's thought and his narrative means. Indeed, some of them tend to reconceive of the gospel's content in terms not of thought but of story. But the paradox is that most of them attempt to abstract the story (plot, character, etc.) from the narrator's discourse that mediates it" (Moore 1989, 63). Even such veteran NT narrative critics as R. A. Edwards (1997) continue to emphasize the autonomy of the narrative world in his reconstruction of the "text connoted reader," his term for the *implied reader.

Narrative criticism and the Gospels. The four canonical Gospels, particularly the Gospel of Mark (Kelber 1979a; Rhoads and Michie 1982; Dewey, Michie, and Rhoads 1999), have been the focus of NT narrative critics. Merenlahti (2002), critical of narrative criticism as it has previously been practiced by NT scholars, proposes a *poetics of the Gospels which has a radically historical as well as hermeneutical character (2002, 7): "It will be concerned with how poetic forms function in texts, and with what conditions shape human understanding of poetic forms in different places and at different times." He proposes that the great popularity of Mark among narrative critics is based on the traditional dichotomy between the aesthetic (or the literary) and the ideological (2002, 36): "The literary qualities of the gospel are seen to exist *in spite of* or *in dissonance with* its ideological aims." The assumed modernity of Mark as literature makes sense from the perspective of the two principal modern aesthetic traditions: realism and modernism (Merenlahti 2002, 38). Thus, reading Mark from the standpoint of modern literary realism, we find "A story which claims to have universal—indeed cosmic—significance yet focuses on everyday reality, that is, on the personal failure of an average individual of low social rank [i.e., Simon Peter in Mark 14:53–54, 66–72], as witnessed by a group of servants" (Merenlahti 2002, 38).

*Fiction, *Composition criticism, *Implied author, *Implied reader *Literary criticism, *New Criticism

---

Bakhtin 1981; Booth 1974, 1983; Brooke and Kaestli 2000; Chatman 1978; de Boer 1992; Dewey, Mitchie, and Rhoads 1999; R. A. Edwards 1985 1997; Focant (ed.) 1993; Fowler 1981, 1991; Frei 1974; Genette 1993; Heath 1989; Kelber 1979a; Konstan 1998; Marquerat and Bourquin 1999; Merenlahti 2002; Merenlahti and Hakola 1999; Powell 1990; Rhoads 1982; Rhoads and Michie 1982; Sternberg 1985; Tolmie 1999; G. W. Young 1999

Narrative theology While theological claims are intentionally embedded in the narratives and descriptions of Revelation, as they are in the Gospels and Acts, stories and descriptions cannot easily be translated into ideas, nor is that translation necessarily desirable. The meaning of a concrete event (in history or in story) is the series of events with which it is causally related, not a supposedly "deeper" allegorical or symbolic reading of the events, characters, and actions that constitute a realistic narrative. The christological debates of the 4th and 5th cent. centered on metaphysical issues, including such ontological categories as the nature, substance, and being of Christ. There was, however, little focus on the work of Christ during this period, and it was precisely the work of Christ that was the primary concern of the New Testament authors. While the christological doctrines that emerged from this period have largely determined the perspective from which the church reads the Bible (Lindbeck 1984, 74), these categories are more at home in exposition and dialogue (the question-and-answer was an early format for theological discussion) than in either narration or description. Unless we wish to turn the Gospels and Revelation into something they are not, it is simply not acceptable to sever meaning from the mutual implications of events in the order of their narration.

The Gospels and Acts consist of what Hans Frei has designated "realistic narrative," i.e., they are historylike and set in a recognizable, real world. The narrative episodes of Revelation, however, are "mythical narratives," i.e., they are highly symbolic and imaginative stories placed in settings in heaven or in the future (or both), which the living have not yet experienced. "Realistic narrative" or "history-like narrative" for Frei is "mimetic" (following Erich Auerbach), a quality that has nothing to do with the common distinction between fiction and nonfiction (i.e., story and history), for "realistic narrative" is found in both categories. It is tempting to mistake the "realistic narrative" of the Gospels for history, a move which Frei thinks led to the "eclipse" of biblical narrative (Frei, *Eclipse*, 11–12). Since the visions of Revelation are not set in the real world, it is of course less tempting to read them (as many have) as history written in advance. Finally, for Frei, "realistic narrative" carries no hidden meaning, but simply means what it says. Events in "realistic narrative" are not interchangeable symbols. One of the central characteristics of "mythical narrative," however, is precisely the fact that events are interchangeable symbols, and the narrative embodies a subtext encoded in story form. This subtext is the Master Story.

Frei 1974; Lindbeck 1984

Narratology (see *Narrative criticism)

Narrator, the one who tells the story and who manipulates the point of view, as distinguished from both the real *author and the *implied author. The narrator is a rhetorical device that authors use in a variety of ways. The intrusive comments of the narrator have been called explanatory comments or *narrative asides. In ancient literature, narrators are always reliable; the phenomenon of the unreliable narrator is modern (Scholes and Kellogg 1966, 264).

Neo-Aristotelianism, or the "Chicago School" of literary criticism, was programmatically presented in an article by Crane (1967; originally published in 1935), in which literary critics were urged to abandon historical and biographical approaches and the issue of taste, and to focus rather on the literary work as a rhetorically structured whole. Neo-Aristotelianism is similar to the approach advocated by the *New Criticism (on the differences, see Schneider 1994), from which is differed primarily with regard to their rhetorical orientation and its insistence on viewing the literary text as a form of communication between writer and reader. While early Chicago school critics focused on the text and virtually ignored the relationship between the writer and the reader, the later Chicago school critics, the most important representative of whom is Booth, emphasized both. Booth wrote *The Rhetoric of Fiction* (1983; originally published in 1961) as a conscious reaction against some of the rigidities of the New Criticism (Booth 1983, 84–85):

A generation had come to accept without thinking that a true "poem" (including fiction) should not mean but be. With the author ruled out under the "intentional fallacy" and the audience ruled out under the "affective fallacy," with the world of ideas and beliefs ruled out under the "didactic heresy" and with narrative interest ruled out under the "heresy of plot" some doctrines of autonomy had become so desiccated that only verbal and symbolic interrelationships remained.

*New Criticism, *New Rhetoric, *Rhetoric

Crane 1967; Schneider 1994

New Criticism, a form of literary criticism dominating Anglo-American literary criticism from the 1930s through the 1950s, which rejected extrinsic forms of criticism (historical, biographical, sociological, philosophical) and focused on intrinsic criticism, regarding the literary work as an autonomous and unified object in itself. The first major work by a New Critic was Richards 1924, while one of the last was Frye 1957. The popular literary handbook by Wellek and Warren 1977 is written from the perspective of New Criticism. The focus on the historical causes of literature, they argued, runs the risk of reducing a work to a particular aspect of one of those causes (Wellek and Warren 1977, 73–74). Form and content are indissolubly mixed. New Criticism rejected the idea that the meaning of a literary work coincided with the intention of the author, an error they labeled the "intentional fallacy" (Wimsatt and Beardsley 1954). NT narrative criticism began by emphasizing the story as a self-contained narrative world (Rhoads and Michie 1982) under the influence of the New Criticism (Moore 1989, 9–11). One of the earlier NT narrative critics, R. A. Edwards, continues to maintain the autonomy of the narrative world in his analysis of the "text-connoted" reader in Matthew.

*Narrative Commentary, *Narrative Criticism

Beardslee 1971; Crossan 1973; R. A. Edwards; Frye 1957; Moore 1989; Poland 1985a, 1985b; Rhoads and Michie (1982) Richards 1924; Wellek and Warren 1977; Wimsatt and Beardsly

New rhetoric, was a revival of rhetoric which occurred in the mid-20th cent. which was associated initially with the seminal works of I. A. Richards (1936) and Kenneth Burke (1950, 1970). Richards was interested in how language in any kind of discourse functions to propagate understanding (or misunderstanding) in an audience. For Burke, the key concept for the "old rhetoric" was *persuasion*, while the key concept for the "new rhetoric" is *identification*, which could even include a partly unconscious factor in appeal (Corbett and Connors 1999, 538). Burke maintained that those who intend to elicit cooperation of various kinds from others must identify themselves with them and even become "consubstantial" with them. Burke proposed a "dramatist pentad" as a critical mechanism for analyzing the motivation of human acts which included act, agent, agency (means), scene (background), and purpose. The Belgian philosopher Chaim Perelman (whose work first became known in the United States in Perelman and Olbrechts-Tyteca, 1969) had become dissatisfied with the application of formal logic to the problem of human decision-making. Since most of the things about which people argue belong to the sphere of the contingent, the probable and the plausible, he maintained that "scientific" demonstration is often neither possible nor effective.

The New rhetoric understands epideictic more broadly (Perelman and Olbrechts-Tyteca 1969, 47–57) than it was understood by Aristotle and in the Greco-Roman rhetorical handbooks. Kennedy, who does not draw a hard and fast line between classical rhetoric and modern rhetoric is in agreement (1997a, 45):

> Epideictic is perhaps best regarded as including any discourse, oral or written, that does not aim at a specific action or decision but seeks to enhance knowledge, understanding, or belief, often through praise or blame, whether of persons, things, or values. It is thus an important feature of cultural or group cohesion.

According to Perelman, while written versions or revisions of juridical and deliberative speeches simply become literature once they are taken from their original oratorical context, epideictic has permanent significance (Perelman 1979, 6): ". . . the epideictic genre is not only important but essential from an educational point of view, since it too has an effective and distinctive part of play—that, namely, of bringing about a consensus in the minds of the audience regarding the values that are celebrated in the speech."

A number of NT scholars have been deeply influenced by the New Rhetoric, including Wuellner (1987) and Amador (1999).

*Epideictic, *Rhetoric, *Rhetorical criticism, *Rhetorical genres

———

Amador 1999; Burke 1950, 1962, 1966, 1970, 1973; Dearin 1969; Perelman 1979; 1980, 1997; Perelman and Olbrechts-Tyteca 1969; Wuellner 1987

New Testament, the traditional title of the collection of 27 early Christian writings composed ca. 50–125 C.E. and regarded as sacred and canonical by virtually all Christian denominations; also designated as "the Word" and "the Scriptures," though these latter terms are often understood to include the *Old Testament as well. The phrase "New Testament" or "New Covenant" is a translation of the phrase καινὴ διαθήκη, which has its origin in the Hebrew phrase ברית חדשה, "new covenant" used in Jer. 31:31–33 [LXX 38:31–33]:

> Behold, the days are coming, says the LORD, when I will make a new covenant [ברית חדשה] with the house of Israel and the house of Judah, not like the covenant which I made with their fathers when I took them by the hand to bring them out of the land of Egypt, my covenant which they broke, though I was their husband, says the LORD. But this is the covenant which I will make with the house of Israel after those days, says the LORD: I will put my law within them, and I will write it upon their hearts; and I will be their God and they shall be my people.

The term "covenant" itself refers to a formal agreement or treaty between two parties, though the agreement is understood as granted by a superior party (God) to an inferior party (the people of God). In the OT, the covenant with David was referred to as permanent (Ps. 89:3–4; cf. the prose version in 2 Sam. 7:12–14), while the covenant at Sinai was considered conditional upon the continued obedience of Israel (Hos. 1:6–11). The phrase "new covenant" was also used by the Qumran community in their sectarian writings and in the NT and early Christian literature; both Essenes and Christians saw themselves as the remnant of God's people, with whom God had made a "new covenant" to replace the covenant made with Israel at Sinai. In one literary context, 2 Cor. 3:1–18, Paul uses both phrases καινὴ διαθήκη, "new covenant" and παλαιὸς διαθήκη, "old covenant." In 2 Cor. 3:6, in a clear allusion to Jer. 31:33, Paul speaks of Christians as "ministers of a new covenant, not of the letter but of the Spirit." In 2 Cor. 3:14, he refers to the old covenant: "when they [Jews] read the old covenant," a phrase that refers to the reading of the Torah. The phrase "new testament," however, was not originally used of a collection of sacred writings.

The phrase ἡ καινὴ ἡδιαθήκη was remembered as having been used by Jesus during the Last Supper. In the version of the Eucharistic words of Jesus found in Luke 22:20 and 1 Cor. 11:25, Jesus calls the cup "the new covenant [ἡ καινὴ διαθήκη] in my blood," referring to a new relationship between Jesus (as the agent of God) and his followers. In Mark 14:24 and Matt 26:28, the cup is interpreted as "my blood of the covenant." In Mark 14:24 and Matt. 26:28, the cup is interpreted as "my blood of the covenant."

The author of Hebrews has a particular interest in the phrase ἡ καινὴ διαθήκη and uses it several times (Heb. 8:8, 13; 9:15), while the synonymous phrase νέα διαθήκη occurs just once (12:24). For him, as for Paul, the "new covenant," which is a "better covenant" (7:22), is not a collection of books but a new relationship to God that came into being through the death of Christ. He also refers to the Torah or the Hebrew Bible as πρώτη διαθήκη, "first covenant" (8:13; 9:15, 18). Hebrews 8:8–12 (cf. 10:16–17) quotes Jer. 31:31–34 [LXX 38:31–34] (which deals with the prophet's prediction of the necessity of a new covenant) and observes that "in speaking of a new covenant he treats the first as obsolete" (Heb. 8:13). The author later speaks of Jesus as "the mediator of the new covenant" (9:15; 12:24), playing with the legal meaning of διαθήκη ("last will and testament"). He argues that the death of Jesus has in fact freed people from the first covenant, since for a διαθήκη to come into for C.E., a death is necessary (Heb. 9:16–17). The phrase "new testament," while a biblical phrase, was not used of a collection of sacred writings until the 2d cent. C.E.

The designation ἡ καινὴ διαθήκη was used by *Clement of Alexandria (*Strom.* 2.29.2–3). *Irenaeus (though he does not always use the phrase in this way) refers to the "New Testament" as a collection of books (*Adv. haer.* 4.28.2), as do *Origen (*In Ioannem* 5.8) and Eusebius (*Hist. eccl.* 3.25.1), while the equivalent Latin phrase *novum testamentum* is used by *Tertullian (*De pud.* 1; *Contra Prax.* 15). From Tertullian (ca. 160–225) on, *Novum Testamentum* came to be the accepted technical term for the Christian sacred writings (*Adversus Marcionem* 4.1.1), while Tertullian himself preferred the phrase *Novum Instrumentum. Instrumentum* can mean "document," "resources," and "backing," making it more flexible than *testamentum,* with its legal overtones. The English term "testament," as well as the Latin term *testamentum*, means "that which is attested to," "will," or "final testament," terms not fully appropriate in English for designating the two parts of the Christian Bible.

Not all the early Christian literature written from 50–125 C.E. has survived; Paul wrote a letter to Laodicea that is no longer extant (Col. 4:16) and as many as four letters to Corinth, whereas just two have survived (1 Cor. 5:9; 2 Cor. 2:1–4). Some early Christian writings that have survived from ca. 50–125 C.E. are not included in the various Christian canons of Scripture: *1 Clement* (ca. 90 C.E.), *Didache* (ca. 80–120 C.E.), the Letters of Ignatius (ca. 110 C.E.), *Barnabas* (ca. 100–120 C.E.).

Marcion of Sinope (d. ca. 160 C.E.) rejected the Jewish Scripture and promulgated a two-part collection consisting of a single *Euangelion*, "Gospel," a heavily edited version of the Gospel of Luke, which he did not attribute to Luke (Tertullian, *Adv. Marc.* 4.3), and an *Apostolikon*, "Apostle," a collection of ten letters of Paul (without the Pastorals) (Irenaeus, *Adv. haer.* 1.27.2). Marcion directed a polemic against the 12 apostles and apostolic teaching that he considered corrupt (Irenaeus, *Adv. haer.* 1.27.2; 3.2.2; 3.13.2), arguing that Paul alone was a true apostle (3.13.1). Marcion's promulgation of the Gospel and Apostle has suggested to some that he was the creator of the Christian holy Scripture (Harnack, *Marcion*, 151). Marcion forced the Great Church to recognize that the OT represented a stage of salvation history that was finally fulfilled in Jesus Christ (Campenhausen, *Formation*, 166).

*Canon, biblical

Kinzig 1994; Trobisch 1996; van Unnik 1961

Novel The novel or romance, a relatively lengthy fictional prose narrative, typically involving the themes of love, travel, and violence (usually within the framework of a story of two lovers separated and finally reunited after many trials), first appeared in the late Hellenistic or early Roman imperial period (1st cent. B.C.E. to 1st cent. C.E.).

Ancient novels. The *Odyssey*, a kind of proto-novel, has many novelistic features, even though it is written in verse and exhibits a far more complicated structure than any extant Greek novel. The six Greek novels that have survived are (1) *Chariton, *Chaereas and Callirhoë* (1st cent. C.E.); (2) Xenophon, *Ephesiaka* (2d cent. C.E.); (3) Iamblichus, *Babyloniaka* (2d cent. C.E.); (4) Longus, *Daphnis and Chloe* (late 2d cent. C.E.); (5) *Achilles Tatius, *Leucippe and Cleitohon* (end of 2d cent. C.E.); and (6) Heliodorus, *Ethiopika* (4th cent. C.E.). The two surviving Latin novels are Apuleius, *Metamorphoses* (Winkler 1985) and Petronius, *Satyricon*. In addition, Ps.-Lucian, *The Ass* is an epitome of a lost Greek work used by Apuleius. There are also fragments of a number of other Greek novels (Stephens and Winkler 1995; Stephens 1996), among them the *Phoinikika* of Lollianos (Henrichs 1969, 1972). A complete English translation of the novels and many fragmentary novels is available in Reardon 1989.

The genre of the novel. The terms "novel" and "romance" are clearly modern literary categories, for the Greeks had no special generic term for the novel (Holzberg 1996a, 11; Ruiz-Montero 1996, 32), which they various designated as a "tale" (αἶνος, διήγημα), "story" or "fiction" (μῦθος), "narrative" (λόγος), "history" (ἱστορία), or "report" (ἄκουσμα). In later antiquity novels were commonly referred to as "fictitious tales" (πλασματικά), or "dramatic tales" (δραματικά), but neither of these is a generic term. Greek novels, unlike their Roman counterparts, seem never to have been really accepted in literary circles, despite the fact that the first novels were probably written for educated people in Hellenistic Asia Minor at a time when people looked back with nostalgia at the classical period (480–330 B.C.E.) (see *Archaism, *Atticism, and *Second Sophistic). In a letter written in 363 C.E., the Emperor Julian (*Ep.* 301b) seems to have novels in mind: "All made-up stories of the type published by writers of earlier ages in the shape of historical documents—love stories [ἐρωτικὰς ὑποθέσεις] and all that kind of narrative—are to be rejected." Most novels used the classical age as a chronological setting (though Xenophon's *Ephesiaka* is an exception). Ancient critics thought that poetry was a more appropriate literary vehicle for fiction and regarded imaginative narratives in which the elements of edification and instruction were absent as unsuitable for adult consumption (Macrobius, *Commentary on the Dream of Scipio* 1.2.6–16). While some scholars make no real attempt to define the genre of the novel (Hägg 1983), others assume that the category "novel" exists and even includes a number of distinguishable subtypes.

The origins of the novel are often considered an important and even necessary part of describing the genre of the novel (Ruiz-Montero 1996). Rohde (1914, 178–83) regarded epic poetry and travel narratives as the basic literary types from which the novel developed, but today the origins of the novel are regarded as much more complicated (Hägg 1983, 109–24). The Greek novel reflects the influence of such earlier genres as history, biography, fabulous travel descriptions, and erotic poetry. Helm (1956, 6) thought that ancient novels existed in many types, including historical novels, mythological novels, travel novels and utopias, erotic novels, Christian novels, biographies, parodies of the novel, and comic-satirical novels) and that all these constituted a single genre. Bakhtin (1984) has referred to the novel as the polyphonic genre par excellence, since it assimilates the voices of many other literary forms. More recently, the literary origins of the novel have been pushed back to literary traditions originating in the ancient Near East (G. Anderson 1984, 19–27), though his proposals have not been widely accepted. Perhaps one can conclude with Ruiz-Montero (1996, 85), "it is clear that the novel shares elements from many other genres, but is to be identified with none of them and, in consequence, to be derived from none."

Some virtually ignore the various possibilities for the origin of the novel and focus on the texts of the existing novels. Perry (1967, 29) regarded the Greek novel as the most formless of ancient literary forms, reflecting the open society within which it originated, and he also regarded it as a unique literary creation (1967, 175): "The first romance was deliberately planned and written by an individual author, its inventor. He conceived it on a Tuesday afternoon in July, or some other day or month of the year. It did not come into being by a process of development on the literary plane." Perry (1967, 335) regarded the cultural context rather than literary pedigree as the primary force that generated the novel. In basic agreement with Perry, Reardon argued that the novel functioned as the myth of Greco-Roman society, with its central theme of the lonely traveler searching for his beloved as an expression of the individual's sense of isolation in the world.

One modern way of classifying the novels is by characterizing the five Greek novels as "ideal romances," while Lucian's *Ass*, Apuleius's *Metamorphoses,* and Petronius's *Satyricon* can be considered "comic romances" (Perry 1967, 87–95). The plots of the five idealistic novels (Chariton, Xenophon, Achilles Tatius, Longus, and Heliodorus) exhibit a stereotypical plot centering on the theme of romantic love (Konstan 1994), using the basic structure of the search that overcomes separation with reunion (Ruiz-Montero 1996, 31): a handsome youth falls headlong in love with a beautiful girl and they pledge themselves to one another. But their happiness is short lived. They are separated, and experience a series of adventures while traveling by sea and land in various parts of the Mediterranean world, including storms, shipwrecks, trials, kidnapping, pirates, and robbers. They are eventually reunited and experience a blissful married life. The two Latin "comic-realistic" novels, on the other hand, do not have plots that resemble the Greek novels, though many of the adventures are similar (Holzberg 1996a, 14). The distinction between "ideal romance" and "comic romance" has become difficult to maintain in light of the discovery of papyrus fragments of novels that do not fit these categories. For example, the *Phoinikika* of Lollianos indicates that comic novels existed in Greek as well as Latin; Achilles Tatius has layers of parody; some have doubted the seriousness of Antonius Diogenes' *The Wonders beyond Thule* (Ruiz-Montero 1996, 29).

The generic problem, however, is the satisfactory treatment of novellike works of extended prose narrative fiction other than the seven or eight "canonical" novels (Holzberg 1996a, 1996b), including fictional biography (Xenophon, *The Education of Cyrus*; Ps.-Callisthenes, *The Alexander Romance*, the *Life of Aesop*; Philostratus, *Life of Apollonius*; and the Apocryphal Acts of the Apostles) and fictional autobiography (the Pseudo-Clementine *Recognitions*).

Constituent literary forms. Speeches are frequently placed in the mouths of the main characters in the novels. In Chariton, for example, many speeches are set in the theatre in Syracuse (1.5.3–6.2; 3.4.3–18; 8.7.1–11). In Babylon, in a forensic context, there are speeches of accusation and defense, and several speeches are included verbatim, such as that of Dionysius (5.6.1–10), and Mithridates (5.7.1–7). The speech of Dionysius is patterned after speeches of accusation: (1) introduction (Chariton 5.6.1–4), (2) statement of the case (5.6.5–8), (3) proof (5.6.9), and (4) conclusion (5.6.10).

Other constituent literary forms include letters (Achilles Tatius 5.18.3–6; 20.5), catalogues of hardships (Chariton 6.2.10).

Literary style. The 2d cent. C.E. was the period in which the *Second Sophistic became an influential intellectual movement in literature and rhetoric. Two of the earlier novels (Chariton and Xenophon, as well as the fragments of the *Iolaus* and the *Phoinikika* of Lollianos) have been influenced by the Second Sophistic to a lesser extent and so have been labeled "pre-sophistic" or "non-sophistic" (Hägg 1983, 34–35). On the other hand, Achilles Tatius, Longus, and Heliodorus have been labeled "sophistic." This categorization is not without problems, however, for Xenophon's *Ephesiaka* was written during the *Second Sophistic yet was relatively uninfluenced by contemporary linguistic and literary trends.

The novel reached the zenith of its popularity in the 2d and 3d cents. C.E., and it sometimes circulated in *codex form (i.e., in the form of a book as opposed to a roll), a possible indication of both its popularity and its lower social level. Of the 32 surviving novel fragments from the 1st to the 3d cents. C.E., two are in codex form: Achilles Tatius (one fragment from the 2d cent. C.E.), and the more recently discovered *Phoinikika* of Lollianus (2d cent. C.E.). The heroine is really the focal character in many novels, suggesting their popularity among women (a view disputed by Ruiz-Montero 1996, 84). Some may even have been written by women. Scobie has proposed that itinerant storytellers read novels to households or lower-class groups, though the evidence for this attractive proposal is slim (Quintilian, *Inst.* 5.11.19; Pliny, *Ep.* 2.20.1). The heyday of the Greek novel coincided with the popularity of Christian Apocryphal Acts (2d and 3d cents. C.E.), and many scholars, including von Dobschütz, Söder, and Pervo, have emphasized their generic relationship.

Through the influence of Rohde nearly a century ago, Greek novels were thought to be late (originating in the 5th or 6th cents. C.E.), mediocre, and serious. Subsequent research has revised all of these judgments. Rohde (1914, 521–22) dated Chariton to the 5th or 6th cent. C.E., but the discovery of papyrus fragments of Chariton (P. Oxy. 1019) dating to the 2d or 3d cent. C.E. suggest that it is one of the earliest novels, perhaps composed in the 1st cent. C.E.

Novels and early Christian literature. Hellenistic histories are vehicles for narrating events worthy of record. Hellenistic biographies focus on the lives of prominent people worth remembering and emulating. Hellenistic novels narrate stories worth telling. While historians and biographers had historical intentions (i.e., what they wrote could be confirmed or falsified if someone could just dig up the right evidence), novelists consciously narrated imaginary events that could have happened but did not. They had fictional intentions.

A number of scholars have proposed a generic relationship between Acts and ancient novels (Schierling and Schierling 1978; Praeder 1981; Pervo 1987). Praeder (1981, 282–88) lists seven criteria to which the ancient novel was expected to conform: (1) a mixture of historical and fictional characters in a story set in the eastern Mediterranean, (2) the biography of a main character with references to past events, (3) an alternation between summary and scene, with the latter dominating, (4) the presence or absence of the narrator from the narrative world, indicated by first or third person narration, (5) avoidance of reference to sources, (6) a depiction of Greco-Roman experience and imagination, and (7) the achievement of various intentions and effects through interesting and entertaining communication. Since all these generic features are found in Luke–Acts, Praeder maintains, it must be considered an ancient novel, or more exactly as a subgenre, a "Christian ancient novel." However, this list consists not of generically distinctive features, but rather of narrative techniques used in a wide variety of ancient narrative literature. It seems doubtful, given the author's use of historical *prefaces (in Luke 1:1–4 and Acts 1:1–2), in the first of which sources are referred to, that the ancient reader would read Luke–Acts as a novel (the criticism of Kany 1986, 89–90).

The generic affinities between Acts and the Greek novel have been argued in great detail by Pervo (1987). Since Acts lacks factual accuracy, he claims, it should be classified as a historical novel, not as history. The primary purpose of Acts, he maintains, is edification (the empirical demonstration that virtue is superior to vice) in an entertaining form. The canonical Acts shares this purpose with the Greek and Latin novels and the six earliest Apocryphal Acts. Luke achieves this using many of the same themes and motifs as the novelists. Pervo (1987, 18) finds 33 episodes in Acts (23 in Acts 13–28) that feature miraculous and exciting last-minute escapes from various perils (e.g., 14:2–6; 16:16–40; 22:22–24). These episodes, with close analogies in ancient novels, fall into five categories: (1) arrests and imprisonments (3:1–4:31; 5:12–42); (2) persecution and martyrdom (21:27–22:29); (3) mob scenes (11, including 16:19–23; 18:12–17; 19:23–41); (4) trial scenes (9, including 4:5–22; 18:12–17; 25:6–12); (5) travel and shipwreck (e.g., 27:1–28:16). Pervo focuses on the fictional features of these and other elements in Acts and the links they have with novelistic themes and motifs.

Pervo's main contention is correct: Acts *is* entertaining and edifying. That Acts should be categorized as a historical novel with closer links to fiction than history, however, is doubtful. His arguments are problematic for several reasons: (1) Though ancient historians wrote to entertain, they did not think truth and usefulness had to be sacrificed. (2) The term "historical novel" should be reserved for novels that follow a historical sequence of events (like Xenophon's *Education of Cyrus* or Ps.-Callisthenes' *Alexander Romance*, rather than applied to fictional narratives set in the real world. (3) The factual accuracy of Acts (variously assessed) is irrelevant to generic classification if the author of Luke–Acts *intended* to narrate actual events. Historical prefaces (Luke 1:1–4; Acts 1:1–2) and mention of sources, which Luke uses, are not found in novels. (4) Luke–Acts must be treated as a two-volume work in one genre, but Pervo treats them in isolation. (5) Many of the episodes he discusses, with their constituent themes and motifs, far from being uniquely shared by ancient novels and the canonical Acts, are found in both factual and fictional narratives in the Hellenistic world.

In addition to the Apocryphal Acts (see *Acts, Apocryphal), there is at least one Christian novel that seems to be an imitation of the Greek novel, the Clementine *Recognitions* (Bowersock 1994, 32).

*Novella

L. Alexander 1995; G. Anderson 1982, 1984; Bartsch 1989; Bowersock 1994; Bowie 1977, 1985, 1994; Bowie and Harrison 1993; Braun 1938; Burton 1998; Davidson 1977; Dowd 1991; Hägg 1971, 1983; Henrichs 1969, 1972; Hock 1988, 1997, 1998; Hock, Chance, and Perkins 1998; Holzberg 1995, 1996a, 1996b; Hunger 1980; Kany 1986; Konstan 1994, 1998; MacAlister 1996; Morgan and Stoneman 1994; J. N. O'Sullivan 1995; Perry 1967; Pervo 1987, 1996; Praeder 1981; Reardon 1971, 309–43, 1989, 1991; Reeve 1971; Rohde 1914; Ruiz-Montero 1996; Sandy 1993; Schierling and Schierling 1978; Schmeling (ed.) 1996; Stephens 1996; Stephens and Winkler 1995; Swain 1995b; Wills 1995; Winkler 1985

Novelistic letters are fictional, often pseudepigraphical attempts to present stories and anecdotes about great past personalities. Some of these letters probably originated as rhetorical exercises in **prosopopoiia*, i.e., writing a speech in character for a famous historical or mythical person. During the early imperial period (1st cent. C.E.), an unknown author proficient in Asianic rhetoric (see *Asianism) wrote several letters in imitation of Hippocrates. The author appears to have been both a physician and a rhetorician (*Ep.* 23.1); he is proficient in *prosopopoiia*. The letters of Ps.-Hippocrates are written with a basically apologetic motive, reflecting the rivalry between the medical schools at Cos and Cnidos, represented respectively by Hippocrates and Ctesias. The novelistic features of the Hippocratic letters are particularly evident in *Ep.* 3–5, which circulated in excerpt form apart from the main corpus. They were popular because of the image of the ideal physician represented by Hippocrates: Artaxerses writes to Hystanes offering a reward to Hippocrates if he will come to the Persian court (*Ep.* 3), and Hystanes relays the message to Hippocrates (*Ep.* 4). Hippocrates then responds to Hystanes, refusing the offer and adding that he will not help enemies of the Greeks (*Ep.* 5). Hippocrates' moral code, which motivates him to treat the destitute sick rather than the wealthy Persian king, made this exchange popular.

*Declamations, *Epistolography, *Prosopoiia

Philippson 1928; Sakalis 1983

Novella, a tale or short story. Novellas (or romantic tales) are short stories narrating the resolution of a dramatic tension. While novellas often consist of a single episode, they may include several. They were never fully independent literary forms but were placed in collections (e.g., Aristides, *Milesian Stories*) or inserted in such inclusive literary forms as dialogues (Lucian's *Toxaris* contains ten short stories illustrating friendship), in histories as digressions (e.g., Herodotus 2.121, the novella of the Clever Thief with three episodes), and in novels (e.g., in Apuleius's *The Golden Ass* 15 novellas, constituting 60 percent of the text, are inserted at various points in the narrative). The famous novella of the Dance of Salome a novella in Josephus (*Ant.* 18.36), is found in Matthew 14:6–12 and Mark 6:22–29 (though she is not named in Matthew and Mark). Novellas, like those in the *Vita Secundi* (see **Secundus, Life of*) and the *Synoptic Gospels, often center on erotic themes.

Dibelius 1934, 164–72; Trenker 1958; Winkler 1985

Old Testament, an English translation of the Latin term *Vetus Testamentum* ("Old Testament"). A relationship between God and people (whether individuals or groups) in the OT is called a *berit* ("covenant"). Several such covenants are narrated in the Old Testament: (1) The covenant between God and Noah (Gen. 6:18; 9:8–17); (b) the covenant between God and Abraham (Gen. 15:18; 17:1–21; Exod. 2:24d; 6:2–5); (c) most important, the covenant between God and Israel at Sinai (Exod. 19:5; 24:7–8; Deut. 4:13; 1 Kgs. 11:11; Isa. 24:5). Similarly, in 2 Cor. 3:14, Paul uses the term παλαιὸς διαθήκη (old covenant).

*Canon, biblical, *New Testament

Onomasticon (plural onomastica), from the Greek adjective ὀνομαστικός ("naming, vocabulary"), a list of names of things with similar characteristics.

Onymity (see *Authorship)

Oracle One of the most common short literary units of antiquity, comprised of two structural parts, the question or occasion and the response, was the responsory oracle. In the form of oracle stories (see *Oracle story) they permeated ancient Greek literature, circulated in collections, were perpetuated in temple archives, and were inscribed prominently on public buildings and monuments. It is primarily in oracle stories and inscribed oracles that the oracular inquiry has survived with its oracular response. Oracular responses were often of such a proverbial character that they were capable of independent circulation and so were detached from the oracular inquiry.

*Revelatory literature

Aune 1983

Oracle story, an anecdote in which the tension in the story is occasioned by an oracle that has been apparently falsified. In a thoroughly unexpected way, however, the prediction contained in the oracle is fulfilled. There are literally hundreds of "oracle stories" in Greek literature. Those familiar with Greek and Latin literature will recall how frequently unfulfilled oracles serve as the exciting force in the construction of plots (cf. C. H. Moore 1921, 99–175). The oracle story is a microcosm of much larger compositions in which oracles play a critical role. Here is an example, in two parallel versions, of an anecdote found in Josephus, the first in *War* 1.78–80 (LCL trans.):

> Another feature of this case which may well excite astonishment was the conduct of Judas. He was of Essene extraction, and his predictions had never once proved erroneous or false. On this occasion, seeing Antigonus passing through the court of the temple, he exclaimed to his acquaintances—a considerable number of his disciples were seated beside him—"Ah me! now were I better dead, since truth has died before me and one of my prophecies has been falsified. For yonder is Antigonus alive, who ought to have been slain to-day. The place predestined for his murder was Strato's Tower, and that is 600 furlongs from here; and it is already the fourth hour of the day. So time frustrates the prophecy." Having said this, the old man remained plunged in gloomy meditation. A little later came the news that Antigonus had been slain in the underground quarter, also called, like the maritime Caesarea, Strato's Tower. It was this identity of names which had disconcerted the seer.

The second version is found in Josephus, *Ant.* 13.311–12 (LCL trans.):

> And in this connexion one may well wonder at the story of a certain Judas of the Essene group, who had never been known to speak falsely in his prophecies, but when he saw Antigonus passing by the temple, cried out to his companions and disciples, who were together with him for the purpose of receiving instruction in foretelling the future, that it would be well for him to die as one who had spoken falsely, since Antigonus was still alive, although he had foretold that he would die at the place called Strato's Tower, and now he saw him alive; for the place where he had foretold that Antigonus would be murdered was some six hundred stades from where he now was, and the greater part of the day had already passed, so that his prophecy was unfortunately likely to prove false. But as he was saying this and lamenting, the news came that Antigonus had been killed in the underground passage, which was also called Strato's Tower—by the same name, that is, as Caesarea on the sea-coast. It was this fact, therefore, that had confused the prophet.

Philostratos, who inserts many pronouncement stories in his *Vita Apollonii*, observed that Apollonius often responded to queries "in an oracular manner" (ὥσπερ ἐκ τρίποδος, literally, "as if from the tripod"), a characteristic presumably in keeping with his supernatural wisdom (1.17; 1.2). Thus the pronouncement story, which often served as a vehicle for conveying and preserving conventional wisdom, must be regarded as having more than a casual relationship to the oracular inquiry and response, for wisdom to the Greeks was divine in both origin and nature. An oracle story in the NT is found in 2 Cor. 12:7–9: "And to keep me from being too elated by the abundance of revelations, a thorn was given me in the flesh, a messenger of Satan, to harass me, to keep me from being too elated. Three times I besought the Lord about this, that it should leave me; but he said to me, 'My grace is sufficient for you, for my power is made perfect in weakness.' I will all the more gladly boast of my weaknesses, that the power of Christ may rest upon me." This is an oracle story in which the oracular response to Paul's entreaties is made the basis of a brief exposition. The response attributed to the Lord is couched in a stereotypical oracular form (Betz 1969, 288–305). A second example is the pericope on the baptism of Jesus (Mark 1:9–11; Matt. 3:13–17; Luke 3:21–22; cf. John 1:29–34), in which a familiar oracular form is placed as the culmination.

*Oracle, *Revelatory literature

———

Aune 1983, 1987, 1989

Orality refers to spoken communication, often as unaffected by or in contrast to written communication. It is useful to distinguish between "primary orality," which involves communication by people completely unfamiliar with writing (Ong 1982, 6), and "secondary orality," the influence of oral tradition on written texts, as well as the influence of written texts on oral tradition.

*Oral tradition

———

Ong 1982; J. Watson 2001

Oral tradition refers to material transmitted in spoken rather than written form over a relatively extended period of time. In ancient Greece, compared with other societies, there is very little evidence to suggest that there were formal or official "memorialists" (i.e., those entrusted with transmitting the oral tradition of a community), with the consequence that oral tradition was very fluid and changeable (R. Thomas 1993, 225–26).

Models of orality and literacy. "Oral" and "written" are frequently opposed as two different forms of discourse. Speaking and writing are such different types of linguistic activities (Bakker 1999, 30) that it is not an exaggeration to claim that all literate societies have different conventions for speaking and for writing. This is also true for the ancient Mediterranean world. Nevertheless the simplistic opposition of "oral" to "written" is misleading. According to Bakker (1999, 35): "The idea of oral and literate composition as mutually exclusive is in line with the medial understanding of orality, in which a discourse is either spoken or written, but not both." On one level, "orality" can be opposed to "literacy," while on another level it is helpful to conceptualize written discourse on a continuum from "transcription" → "composition," i.e., an existing oral discourse can be "transcribed" into a written form, while "composition" involves the creative act of producing a written text that did not exist before it was written (Bakker 1999, 31). A similar model is proposed by Oesterreicher (1993) using the terms *Verschriftung* ("textification") and *Verschriftlichung* (textualization). As one moves along the continuum from "transcription" to "continuum," there is an increasing "fictionalization" of discourse, i.e., the less likely it is that actual spoken discourse preceded the written discourse (Bakker 1999, 32). Yet another model that distinguishes between different aspects of orality is that proposed by Finnegan (1977, 16–24; cf. Gentili 1988, 4–5): (1) oral transmission (without the involvement of any written text at all); (2) oral communication (which can coexist beside a written text, such as the Greek schoolchildren who used to memorize from written texts of the poets in order to recite them without the written text [Plato, *Protagorus* 325e]); and (3) oral composition (composition without any help from writing in the process of composition). The oversimplification of the oral/written antithesis characterized Alfred Lord's view of Homer's "oral" poetry: "The written technique . . . is not compatible with oral technique, and the two could not possibly combine, to form another, a third, a 'transitional technique'" (1960, 129). According to Cicero, orators rarely wrote out their speeches before giving them (*Brutus* 91); he also mentioned that while Sulpicius wrote no speeches himself, there were several of his speeches in circulation transcribed by Publius Cannutius (*Brutus* 205).

Models for orality. Lord (1960, 33; 1987) has isolated five characteristics of oral tradition: (1) It is additive rather than subordinate. (2) It is aggregative rather than analytic. (3) It is redundant rather than concise. (4) It is conservative rather than creative. (5) It is acoustically oriented rather than visually oriented. Lord has based these five characteristics exclusively on the content of oral tradition. Based on the study of oral tradition in the Middle East during the 20th cent., Bailey (1991) has proposed three types of orality: (1) informal, uncontrolled oral tradition (no identifiable teacher, student, or structure); (2) formal, controlled oral tradition (identifiable teacher, student, and structure); (3) informal, controlled oral tradition (no identifiable teacher or student, but with three degrees of fixity and flexibility: *no* flexibility in recitation of poems and proverbs; *some* flexibility in telling parables, stories, and historical narratives; *total* flexibility in the telling of jokes and news). Unlike Lord's taxonomy, Bailey's model combines two elements, social factors (teachers and students, or the lack of either or both) and stereotypical structures.

Parry's oral-formulaic theory. Parry (1971) proposed the "oral-formulaic theory" in which he argued that the Homeric epics were composed orally because of the occurrence of word-groups that correspond to the practice of oral epic poets, though not of literary imitations of Homeric style. For Parry, a "formula" is "a group of words which is regularly employed under the same metrical conditions to express a given essential idea" (Parry 1930, 80). While this theory has been criticized (Sale 2001), it still dominates Homeric studies (Russo 1997).

Stylistic features of oral literature. Some of the more important characteristics of oral literature that have been suggested are (1) brief sentences and *parataxis rather than *hypotaxis (Havelock 1986, 76), (2) absence of syntactic hyperbaton (a figurative construction inverting the normal order of words or clauses), (3) avoidance of the idiosyncratic use of the first person, (4) use of clear, concrete language for the exposition of ideas that would be immediately comprehensible to an audience and would hold their attention. The more specific stylistic features that have been proposed for oral literature include (Aune 1991b, 62): (1) formulas; (2) envelope patterns (Hieatt 1987, 245–58) or ring composition (Immerwahr 1966, 53–58; Beck 1971); (3) recapitulations (Hägg 1971, 332); (4) interruptions and asides (Scobie 1983, 37); (5) stylization of introductions, epilogues, and endings (Jacobs 1959, 220–24); (6) number patterns; (7) devices expressing distance, location, or date (Jacobs 1959, 228–32); (8) directional statements (Lang 1984, 1–5); (9) conformity to widely known and used tale-types (Aarne 1973); (10) stereotypical motifs found in oral literature (Thompson 1955–58).

Oral Jesus traditions. Many oral traditions originated during the ministry of Jesus and were transmitted orally by the followers of Jesus before his death and by increasing numbers of adherents to Christianity (both Jewish and Gentile) in the years following the crucifixion (see *Form criticism). Since most oral traditions are not memorized verbatim by those who transmit them, Jesus traditions were subject to varying degrees of transformation and invention, like all oral forms of folklore. Since Jesus was a teacher and his disciples were students, many of his *sayings* were deliberately remembered in accordance with learning techniques of the day (the essential insight of Gerhardsson 1961, 1964, 1986). The *narrative* traditions, on the other hand, were probably not "learned" in the same way, but "remembered" later, and therefore subject to more thorough transformation. The oral transmission of Jesus traditions continued even after the composition of the first written documents in which these traditions were fixed. One example is the famous saying of Jesus, "It is more blessed to give than to receive" (Acts 20:35), a saying not found in the Gospels, but preserved in the setting of a sermon attributed to Paul. The earliest surviving Gospel is the Gospel of Mark, usually dated ca. 70 C.E. Once some of the Jesus traditions were fixed in written form, they probably exerted influence over oral traditions, just as the *Deutsche Sagen* ("German Legends") published by the Grimm brothers in 1816–18 had an unexpected impact on oral folktales in Germany, as parents bought the books and read the literary versions to their children rather than rely on their memory as their parents and grandparents had. Yet oral Jesus traditions continued to circulate and often came to be written down only much later. This continuing oral transmission of Jesus traditions influenced the written Gospels, a fact demonstrated by many additions to the hand-copied manuscripts of the gospels (Delobel 1982b). While these additions have been called "extra-canonical" (Stroker 1989) or "agrapha" (Jeremias 1964), since they occur as variant readings in some manuscripts and versions but almost certainly were not part of the original text, they are best regarded as "non-received" sayings of Jesus (Delobel 1982b). Examples of such additions to the texts include the story of the woman charged with adultery, the so-called *Pericopae adulterae* (John 7:53–8:11), the shorter and longer endings of Mark and the Freer Logion, inserted between Mark 16:14 and 15 in Codex W (5th cent. C.E.), the request for the Holy Spirit in the Lukan version of the Lord's Prayer in Luke 11:2, and the reaction of the disciples against the Samaritans in Luke 9:54–56. A particularly striking example of an agraphon later inserted into the text of the Gospels is the chreia or anecdote that replaces Luke 6:5 in Codex Beza (an important, though peculiar, 5th-cent. MS): "On the same day, seeing some one working on the Sabbath, he [Jesus] said to him, 'Man, if indeed you know what you are doing, you are blessed; but if you do not know, you are cursed and a transgressor of the Law.'"

*Form criticism, *Orality

———

Achtemeier 1990; Aune 1991b; K. E. Bailey 1991; Bakker 1997, 1999; I. Beck 1971; Byrskog 2000; Connors 1986; M. W. Edwards 1986, 1988; 1992; Finnegan 1977; Gentili 1988; Gentili and Cerri 1978; Gerhardsson 1961, 1964, 1986; Hägg 1971; Harvey 2002; Havelock 1971, 1976, 1986; Jacobs 1959; Jeremias 1964; Kelber 1979b; 1983; G. S. Kirk 1976; Lord 1960, 1973, 1978; Mackay 1999; Niditch 1997; Ong 1967, 1982; Parry 1971; A. Scobie 1983; Stroker 1989; Thomas 1989, 1993; Vansina 1985; J. Watson 2001

Oratio variata, literally "varied discourse," is a term used, among other things, for switching between direct discourse (*oratio recta*) and indirect discourse (*oratio obliqua*).

———

Robertson 1934, 440–44

Orators, Attic The works of ancient Greek orators that have survived are largely limited to the so-called "Canon of Ten Attic Orators," a list of 4th-cent. figures including Antiphon, Andocides, Lysias, Isocrates, Isaeus, Demosthenes, Aeschines, Hyperides, Lycurgus, and Dinarchus. According to the exaggerated view of Cicero (*Brutus* 49), Athens was the only Greek city to emphasize and value oratory. This traditional list, which is neither alphabetical nor chronological, does not go back to the activity of the Alexandrian grammarians (Kennedy 1963, 125 gives this as a possibility), as most of the *Alexandrian Canon does, but rather to the 1st-cent. B.C.E. Augustan critic Caecilius of Kale Acte (Schmid and Stählin 1920–29, 2.28–29; Worthington 1994, 254–59; *DNP* 2.895). The thumbnail biographies of the ten orators by Ps.-Plutarch, *Vitae decem oratorum* (*Moralia* 832b–852e) is dependent on a lost work of Caecilius. Of the ten Attic orators, Demosthenes is often regarded as towering over the rest, as in Cicero, *Brutus* 35 (LCL trans.): "For the perfect orator and the one who lacks absolutely nothing you would without hesitation name Demosthenes" (cf. 141; *Orator* 23). Some of the ten orators, such as Lysias, were essentially "closet" orators in that they wrote speeches for others but did not deliver them themselves (Cicero, *Brutus* 35).

*Alexandrian canon, *Archaism, *Atticism, *Second Sophistic

———

Kennedy 1963, 125–263; Worthington 1994

Oxymoron, a transliteration of the Greek word ὀξύμωρος ("pointedly foolish, paradoxical"), is a trope or figure of speech that consists of a "closely tightened syntactic linking of contradictory terms into a unity that, as a result, acquires a strong contradictive tension" (Lausberg 1998, §807). A modern witty example of an oxymoron is the phrase "military intelligence." An example from Greek literature is νόμος ἄνομος, "a law that is no law" (Aeschylus, *Agamemnon* 1142, similar to ὁ νόμος ἁμαρτία, "is the law sin?" in Rom. 7:7a). According to Tertullian (*On the Flesh of Christ* 5.4): "The Son of God has been crucified; the fact evokes no shame because it is shameful."

———

Lausberg 1998, §807; Smyth 1956, §3035

Paleography is the study of the history of writing on perishable materials, such as papyrus, *parchment or *vellum, and paper. Paleography is interested in the types and styles of handwriting, and a comparative study of these types and styles makes it possible to assign approximate dates for handwritten materials. Paleographical analysis can have important implications for the study of the New Testament and early Christian literature. An example is the famous Rylands Fragment of John, designated 𝔓52, which was dated ca. 125 C.E. on paleographical grounds; but A. Schmidt (1989) has questioned this date, on a somewhat more sophisticated paleographical basis, and placed it at ca. 170 C.E.

*Minuscules

———

Kenyon 1899; Martin 1967; Glénison, Bompaire, and Irigoin 1977; A. Schmidt 1989; Schubert 1966; Wittek 1967

Palimpsest, a transliterated form of the Greek word παλίμψηστος, derived from πάλιν + ψάω = "to rub again," referred to the practice of erasing writing on *parchment or *vellum for the purpose of recycling the sheet (see Plutarch, *Mor.* 779c), particularly when writing material was in short supply. Some very important classical manuscripts are palimpsests, including the *De re publica* of Cicero (a 4th-cent. MS discovered by Angelo Mai in 1819 and published in the editio princeps in 1822) under a work by Augustine on the Psalms of the 7th cent. and a 5th-cent. manuscript of the *Institutes* of Gaius, overwritten with letters of Jerome and Gennadius (discovered by Georg Niebuhr in 1816, identified by Savigny, and published by Goeschen in 1820; see Gordon and Robinson 1988, 11–13). These and other MSS were discovered by using various types of chemical reagents (which often damaged the manuscripts) and in modern times by ultraviolet photography. The important 5th-cent. NT manuscript Codex Ephraemi rescriptus is a palimpsest (as the Latin epithet *rescriptus* indicates), discovered in 1692, for the biblical text was erased in the 12th cent. and replaced with a Greek translation of the sermons of St. Ephraem Syrus, a 4th-cent. church father (Kenyon 1912; Metzger 1968, 12). While Codex Ephraemi originally contained the entire Greek Bible, just 64 leaves of the OT and 145 of the NT survive; the rest was discarded or recycled. Codex Claromontanus, a 6th-cent. uncial MS of the Pauline Letters, was patched using two erased leaves of Euripides' *Phaethon* (with a papyrus fragment, that is all that survives of that play). Of the 250 manuscripts of the NT, 52 are palimpsests (listed in Metzger 1968, 12 n. 1). The recycling of manuscripts was so widespread that a synodal decree of 691 C.E. forbade the destruction of manuscripts of the Scriptures and of the Fathers.

Palimpsest is a term is used figuratively by Genette (1997a) for texts that incorporate earlier texts in a variety of ways.

DNP 9.188–89; Reynolds and Wilson 1974, 174–77; E. M. Thompson 1966, 75–77

Panegyric, a transliterated form of the Greek word πανηγυρικός, one of the three main types of *epideictic speeches, including the ἐγκώμιον, "praise," and the ἐπιτάφιος λόγος, the funeral oration.

*Rhetorical genres, *Epideictic rhetoric

Papyrus (*Cyperus papyrus*), an aquatic plant native to Egypt and found especially in the Nile valley called βύβλος (Herodotus 2.92; Strabo 17.1.15). The most widely used writing material in the Greco-Roman world, papyrus was used for that purpose in the ancient Near East from about 3000 B.C.E. In his *Natural History* (13.21–27), Pliny the Elder provides a detailed description of the manufacture of papyrus as a writing material. The pith of the plant was removed, and strips were laid parallel to one another. Then another layer of strips was placed on top of the first at right angles to it. The two layers were pressed or beaten together, releasing the natural juices of the plant, which acted as an adhesive. After the resulting product dried, it was smoothed with pumice and trimmed to size. An average sheet measured 25 cm. long (11.4 inches) and 18–20 cm. wide (8.2–9.1 inches). At this point individual sheets could be bound together to make a roll or scroll (Greek βίβλος or βιβλίον, derived from the term βύβλος, "papyrus"; Latin *volumen*), which was the standard form of ancient "books" until the advent of the codex, which probably appeared at the beginning of the 2nd cent. C.E. A papyrus scroll could be any length, but most seem to have been about 3.5 meters (4.4 yards) (Gamble 1995, 44–45).

Papyrus is a light and strong writing material, but only dry climactic conditions such as those that prevail in Egypt and certain areas of Palestine (e.g., the cliffs above the Dead Sea) allowed ancient papyri to be preserved to the present day. However, unusual circumstances sometimes preserved papyri; the eruption of Mount Vesuvius (79 C.E.) is responsible for the preservation of almost 1,800 papyrus manuscripts in the so-called "Villa of the Papyri" in Herculaneum.

While scrolls are mentioned sporadically throughout the NT, by far the greatest number of references to terms in the semantic domain "book, scroll" occur in the *Revelation to John. Two of the most noteworthy examples of these occurrences are (1) a scroll written "inside and behind" (Rev. 5:2) and (2) a little scroll (Rev. 10:2, 8–10). A little scroll also plays an important role in the *Shepherd of Hermas* 2.1.3–4; 2.4.1–3.

In the language of NT textual criticism, the term "papyri" signifies those MSS written on the medium of papyrus in either an *uncial or *minuscule hand. Significant collections of NT papyri include the Oxyrhynchus and Chester Beatty papyri. Papyrus was used for manuscripts of NT books until the 7th cent. *Parchment began to replace papyrus as a more elegant writing material during the 4th cent.

*Codex, *Minuscule, *Parchment, *Uncial

ABD 6:999–1081; Epp 1991; Gamble 1995; Lewis 1974, 1989; Oates et al. 1985; D. C. Parker 1997:9–12; Parkinson and Quirke 1995; Pliny, *Hist. nat.* 13.21–27; Rupprecht 1994; Turner 1980

LESLIE BAYNES

Papyrus Egerton 2, written ca. 150 C.E. (perhaps based on a text composed 80–120 C.E.), can either be judged as a pastiche of allusions to all four canonical Gospels (Vielhauer 1975), or (more probably) as an independent witness to a Jesus tradition from which both Synoptic and Johannine traditions were derived (Mayeda 1946, 94–95).

*Gospels, apocryphal

Mayeda 1946; Vielhauer 1977; D. F. Wright 1985

Parable, a transliteration of the Greek word παραβολή (Latin *similitudo, collatio*) meaning "set down beside," "comparison," is a figure of speech that can be generally defined as "a more or less developed comparison in which two things or processes from different fields are set side by side so that in virtue of the similarity the unknown may be elucidated from the known" (*TDNT* 5.745–46). παραβολή occurs 48 times in the Synoptic Gospels (17 times in Matthew; 13 in Mark; 18 in Luke), twice in Hebrews, twice in *Barnabas,* and several times in Hermas. παροιμία ("proverb"), a synonym, is used four times in John with the meaning "hidden, obscure speech" that needs interpretation: 10:16 (referring to the allegory of the shepherd), and three times in 16:25–26, 29 (describing all Jesus' words as obscure speech), and only in 2 Pet. 2:22 with the meaning "proverb."

The term παραβολή is a Greek rhetorical term for one of two types of proof in argumentation, the παράδειγμα or "example" (see *paradigm, *example, *similitude), on which Jülicher based his conception of the *Gleichnis* ("similitude"), and the ἐνθύμημα, or "argument" (see *enthymeme). There are two types of παράδειγμα, those that are true to life and those that are fictional. Fictional παραδείγματα include λόγοι ("fables") and παραβολαί ("comparisons"); see Aristotle, *Rhet.* 2.20.2–4. In a later rhetorical handbook, the parable (*similitudo*) is described as being used to embellish the presentation, to prove something, to say something more clearly, or to put something vividly before the eyes of the audience (*Ad Herennium* 4.45.59). The term παραβολή is also used in the LXX as a translation of the Hebrew word משל ("to be like"), which is used for expressions that involve a comparison, either explicitly or implicitly. משל is a comprehensive term used in the OT to refer to riddles, proverbs, and allegories. Many NT scholars are convinced that the evangelists did not follow classical rhetoric in their use of the term παραβολή, since its usage in the NT is fully comprehensible in the context of the OT and early Judaism (Boucher 1977, 12; Gerhardsson 1988, 340).

Defining and classifying parables. The parables of Jesus have been defined in various ways. According to Dodd (1935, 16), "the parable is a metaphor or simile drawn from nature or common life, arresting the hearer by its vividness or strangeness, and leaving the mind in sufficient doubt about its precise application to tease it into active thought." This largely functional definition ignores the formal features of the "parables" of Jesus, if various metaphorical sayings found in the Gospels can indeed be lumped together under that single rubric. According to Boucher (1977, 23; emphasis hers), a parable "is a structure consisting of *a tropical narrative, or a narrative having two levels of meaning;* this structure functions as *religious or ethical rhetorical speech.*" B. Scott (1989, 8) defines a parable as a "*mashal* that employs a short narrative fiction to reference a transcendent symbol." Jülicher (1899, 1.58–80, 92–111, 112–15) devised a threefold system for classifying the parables of Jesus: the similitude (*Gleichnis*), and the parable (*Parabel*), both comparisons, and the example story (*Beispielerzählung*), an example to be imitated. Jülicher identified 28 similitudes, 21 parables, and 4 example stories. He regarded a parable as an extended simile and an allegory as a series of metaphors. All three types of parabolic speech—similitudes, parables, and example stories—were literal speech when uttered by Jesus but were later taken by the evangelists as mysterious allegories. Jülicher derived his categories from Aristotle (and has been widely criticized for this; see Caird 1989, 161), for whom fictional παραδείγματα ("examples") included λόγοι ("fables," "stories") and παραβολαί ("comparisons"); see *Rhet.* 2.20.2–4. The "similitude" is a brief narrative of a typical or recurrent event from real life using verbs in the present tense; the "parable" tells a fictional story about an event that could have happened using verbs in past tenses; the "example story" presents a specific case illustrating a general principle using verbs in the past tense (Boucher 1981, 17, 19, 20). Jülicher (1899, 1.70) cites the master example given by Aristotle (*Rhet.* 2.20; 1393b) for a παραβολή:

> Comparison [παραβολή] is illustrated by the sayings of Socrates for instance, if one were to say that magistrates should not be chosen by lot [the main point], for this would be the same

> as [ὅμοιον introduces the image or figure] choosing as representative athletes not those competent to contend, but those on whom the lot falls; or as [ὅμοιον implied] choosing any of the sailors as the man who should take the helm, as if it were right that the choice should be decided by lot, not by a man's knowledge.

While this classification scheme has continued to be widely used, others have also been proposed. Fiebig (1904, 1912) examined rabbinic parables or *meshalim,* which he found to contain many stock metaphors (God as king, man as servant, etc.), and arranged them in three categories: (1) pure parables, (2) pure allegories, and (3) mixed parable-allegories. Since the Hebrew term *mashal* and the Aramaic term *matla* mean "comparison" or "likeness" and are used for a variety of figures of speech, Gerhardson (1988, 339–42; 1991) has proposed two categories for the parables of Jesus, aphoristic meshalim (i.e., aphorisms or maxims) and narrative meshalim (of which he finds 55 examples). He defines narrative meshalim as fictive stories in which the characters are anonymous (though Lazarus and Abraham are exceptions in the parable of the Rich Man and Lazarus) and includes all those sayings that Jülicher characterizes as similitudes, parables, and example stories.

Introductory and concluding formulas. Parables, like *fables, are often accompanied by an interpretation or moral, which can be used to introduce a parable as a προμύθιον or to conclude a parable as an ἐπιμύθιον. Some parables conclude without any kind of application (Mark 4:26–29; Luke 11:5–8; 13:6–9), while others end with a question to the audience (Matt. 21:31; Luke 7:42; 10:36). Several parables in Luke have a προμύθιον that includes a miniinterpretation, as in Luke 18:1: "And he told them a parable to the effect that they ought always to pray and not to lose heart" (see Luke 12:15; 18:9). Several Synoptic parables have concluding sayings (ἐπιμυθία) that are attributed to the main character (Matt. 18:32–33; 20:13–15; 25:12, 26–28; Luke 12:20; 13:8–9; 15:31–32; 16:30; 18:4–5).

The comparative function of parables is often signaled by an introduction by means of a comparative particle such as ὡς or ὥσπερ ("as, like"), as in Mark 4:26: "the kingdom of God is like a man . . ." (see also Matt. 25:14; Mark 4:31). The verb ὁμοιόω ("to be like, compare") and adjective ὅμοιος ("like, similar") are often used to introduce parables, as in Matt.13:24: "The kingdom of heaven is like [ὡμοιώθη] a man . . ." (Carson 1985, 277–82). More frequently we find the phrase ὁμοία ἐστίν, "the kingdom of heaven is like" (Matt. 7:24; 11:16; 13:24, 31, 33, 44, 45, 47, 52; 20:1; 25:1; Luke 13:18).

In the following discussions of the parables in the canonical Gospels and the *Gospel of Thomas,* it should be noted that there is no agreement precisely how many parables there are in these texts, a problem based on the fuzzy way in which "parables" are distinguished from other figures of speech.

Parables in Mark. There are six parables in Mark: (1) the Sower (Mark 4:3–8=Matt. 13:3–8=Luke 8:5–8=*G.Thom.* 9); (2) the Patient Farmer (4:26–29); (3) the Mustard Seed (4:30–32=Matt. 13:31–32=Luke 13:18–19= *G.Thom.* 20); (4) the Wicked Tenants (Mark 12:1–12=Matt. 21:33–44=Luke 20:9–18= *G.Thom.* 65); (5) Fig Tree (13:28–29= Matt. 24:32–33=Luke 21:29–31); (6) the Master's Unexpected Return (13:34–37=Luke 12:35–38).

Parables in Matthew. The term παραβολή occurs 17 times in Matthew, with 12 of these occurrences concentrated in Matt. 13 (vv. 3, 10, 13, 18, 24, 31, 33, 34 [2x], 35, 36, 53), the author's largest parable collection. Though some scholars have found as many as 61 parables in Matthew (Drury 1985, 70–72), this includes a variety of figures, metaphors, and similes that are not parables. The following list contains 22 Matthaean parables:

1. Going before the Judge (Matt. 5:25–26=Luke 12:58–59)
2. The Wise and Foolish Builders (7:24–27)
3. Children in the Market (11:16–19=Luke 7:31–35)
4. The Unclean Spirit (12:43–45=Luke 11:24–26)
5. The Sower (13:3b–9=Mark 4:3–9=Luke 8:4–8), with allegorical interpretation in 13:18–23=Mark 4:13–20=Luke 8:11–15)
6. The Wheat and the Tares (13:24–30= *G.Thom.* 57, with allegorical interpretation in 13:35–43)
7. The Mustard Seed (13:31–32=Mark 4:31–32=Luke 13:18–19)
8. The Leaven (13:33=Luke 13:20–21= *G.Thom.* 96)
9. The Treasure in a Field (13:44=*G.Thom.* 109)
10. The Merchant (13:45–46=*G.Thom.* 76)
11. The Net (13:47–50)
12. The Lost Sheep (18:12–14=Luke 15:4–7=*G.Thom.* 107)

13. Unforgiving Servant (18:23–35)
14. The Laborers in the Vineyard (20:1–16)
15. The Man with Two Sons (21:28–32)
16. The Wicked Tenants (21:33–46)
17. The Wedding Feast (22:1–14=Luke 14:16–24=*G.Thom.* 64)
18. The Thief (24:42–44=Luke 12:39–40=*G.Thom.* 21b, 103)
19. The Wicked Servant (24:45–51=Luke 12:42–46)
20. The Five Wise and Five Foolish Virgins (25:1–13)
21. The Talents (25:14–30=Luke 19:12–27)
22. The Last Judgment (25:31–46)

Parables in Luke. Luke contains a total of 28 parables, 15 of which occur only in the Gospel of Luke (i.e., *Special L), all but the first in Luke's travel section (9:51–19:34):

1. The Two Debtors (7:41–42)
2. The Good Samaritan (10:30–36)
3. The Reluctant Friend at Midnight (11:5–8)
4. The Foolish Rich Man (12:16–20=*G.Thom.* 63)
5. The Barren Fig Tree (13:6–9)
6. Not Seeking Honor at Table (14:8–10)
7. Inviting the Poor to Table (14:12–14)
8. Counting the Cost (14:28–33)
9. The Lost Coin (15:8–10)
10. The Prodigal Son (15:11–32)
11. The Dishonest Steward (16:1–8a)
12. The Rich Man and Lazarus (16:19–31)
13. The Dutiful Servant (17:7–10)
14. The Unrighteous Judge (18:2–5)
15. The Pharisee and the Tax Collector (18:10–14a)

Some scholars have regarded these parables as the creation of Luke (Drury 1985, 111–24), while others think that they are based on earlier traditions that Luke had collected (Parrot 1991, 506–7) and the L parables may have existed as a collection prior to their incorporation into the Gospel of Luke (Parrot 1991, 507). Parrot finds four literary devices that characterize many of the L-Parables (1991, 509–11): (1) interior dialogue or *soliloquy, (2) contrasting character types, (3) a conclusion with a question, (4) use of the lesser to greater argument. In addition to the 15 listed above, there are several parables in Luke that have Synoptic parallels:

16. Children in the Market (Luke 7:31–35=Matt. 11:16–19)
17. The Unclean Spirit (Luke 11:24–26=Matt. 12:43–45)
18. The Sower (Luke 8:5–8=Mark 4:3–8=Matt. 13:3–8=*G.Thom.* 9)
19. The Master's Unexpected Return (Luke 12:35–38=Mark 13:34–37).
20. The Thief (Luke 12:39–40=Matt. 24:42–44=*G.Thom.* 21b, 103)
21. Going before the Judge (Luke 12:58–59 =Matt. 5:25–26)
22. The Mustard Seed (Luke 13:18–19= Matt. 13:31–32=Mark 4:31–32= *G.Thom.* 20)
23. The Leaven (Luke 13:20–21=Matt. 13:33=*G.Thom.* 96)
24. The Wedding Feast (Luke 14:16–24=Matt. 22:1–14=*G.Thom.* 64)
25. The Lost Sheep (Luke 15:4–7=Matt. 18:12–14=*G.Thom.* 107)
26. The Talents (Luke 19:12–27=Matt. 25:14–30)
27. The Wicked Tenants (Luke 20:9–18=Mark 12:1–12=Matt. 21:33–44=*G.Thom.* 65)
28. The Fig Tree (Luke 21:29–31=Mark 13:28–29=Matt. 24:32–33)

Parables in the Gospel of Thomas. Before the discovery of the Nag Hammadi library, very few parables attributed to Jesus had been preserved in the apocryphal gospels and other early Christian literature. In fact, just three were known: (1) The parable of the Talents, known from Q 19:12–27, was preserved in a fragment of the *Gospel of the Nazaraeans* quoted by Eusebius *De theophania* 19. (2) Versions of the parable of the Sower (Mark 4:3–9; Matt. 13:3–9; Luke 8:5–8) were preserved in Justin, *Dial.* 125.1 and *1 Clem.* 24:5. (3) The parable of the Fig Tree was preserved in *Apocalypse of Peter 2.* Apart from the *Gospel of Thomas,* several other parables were preserved among the Nag Hammadi tractates: (1) the Date Palm (*Apoc. James* [NHC I, 2] 7.22–35), (2) the Grain of Wheat (*Apoc. James* [NHC I, 2] 8.16–27), (3) the Ear of Grain (*Apoc. James* [NHC I, 2] 12.22–30). Interestingly, the *Apocalypse of James* refers to several parables by shortened titles: the Shepherds, the Seed, the Building, the Lamps of the Virgins, the Wage of the Workmen, the Didrachmas, and the Woman ([NHC I, 2] 8.3–10), indicating a traditional form of reference.

There are 17 parables in the *Gospel of Thomas* (though not all scholars agree on the number). Eight of these are kingdom parables (20, 57, 76, 96, 97, 98, 107, 109), because they are either introduced with the Coptic phrase *tmntero mpeiōt estntōn,* "the Kingdom of the

Parables in the Gospel of Thomas and Parallels

G. Thom. Parable	Mark	Matthew	Luke	Other
Log. 8: Wise Fisherman		13:47–50		
Log. 9: Sower	4:3–9	13:3–9	8:5–8	*1 Clem. 24:5*
Log. 20: Seed	4:30–32	13:31–32	13:18–19	
Log. 21a: Children in a Field				
Log. 21b: The Expected Thief=Log. 103		24:43	12:39	
Log. 35: The Thief	3:27	12:29	11:21–22	
Log. 57: Wheat and Tares		13:24–30		
Log. 63: Rich Man			12:16–21	
Log. 64: Banquet		22:1–10	14:15–24	
Log. 65–66: Vineyard	12:1–8, 10	21:33–39, 42	20:9–15, 17	
Log. 76: Merchant		13:44–46; 6:20	12:33	
Log. 96: Leaven		13:33	13:20–21	
Log. 97: Cracked Jar				
Log. 98: Assassin				
Log. 103: The Robbers		24:43	12:39	
Log. 107: 100 Sheep		18:12–13	16:4–6	*G.Truth* 31–32
Log. 109: Treasure		13:44		

Father is like" (57, 76, 96, 97, 98), or *tmntero estntōn*, "the Kingdom is like" (107, 109).

Parable vs. allegory. Before the end of the 19th cent., the parables of Jesus were commonly interpreted allegorically (see the history of parable interpretation reviewed in Jülicher 1899, 1.203–322; Kissinger 1979, 1–67; Wailes 1987). The rejection of the allegorical method of parable interpretation was expedited by the work of A. B. Bruce (1882; see Kissinger 1979, 67–71) in the United Kingdom and Jülicher (1899; see Kissinger 1979, 71–77) in Germany. Examples of the allegorical interpretation of parables abound from the early patristic period through the medieval period (Wailes 1987) through the mid-19th cent. Examples of this method can be found in Tertullian and Augustine. Tertullian (*On Purity* 9; see Hunter 1960, 154) suggests how parables should be interpreted:

> We, however, do not take the parables as sources of doctrine, but rather we take doctrine as a norm for interpreting the parables. Therefore we make no effort to twist everything so that it fits our own explanation, striving to avoid every discrepancy. Why a "hundred" sheep? And why, indeed, "ten" drachmas? And what does that "broom" stand for? Well, when he wanted to show how pleased God is at the salvation of one sinner, he had to mention *some* numerical quantity from which *one* can be described as lost.

Augustine's interpretation of the parable of the Good Samaritan (*Quaestiones Evangeliorum*, II, 19; slightly abridged by Dodd 1961, 1–2) is a clear example of the way in which a theological system is read into a narrative by means of allegory (the bold print indicates words and phrases preserved from the original parable).

> **A certain man went down from Jerusalem to Jericho**; Adam himself is meant; **Jerusalem** is the heavenly city of peace, from whose blessedness Adam fell; **Jericho** means the moon, and signifies our mortality, because it is born, waxes, wanes, and dies. **Thieves** are the devil and his angels. **Who stripped him**, namely, of his immortality; **and beat him**, by persuading him to sin; **and left him half-dead**, because in so far as man can understand and know God, he lives, but in so far as he is wasted and oppressed by sin, he is dead; he is therefore called **half-dead**. The **priest** and **Levite** who saw him and passed by, signify the priesthood and ministry of the Old Testament, which could profit nothing for salvation. **Samaritan** means Guardian, and therefore the Lord Himself is signified by this name. The **binding of the wounds** is the restraint of sin. **Oil** is the comfort of good hope; **wine** the exhortation to work with fervent spirit. The **beast** is the flesh in which He deigned to come to us. The being **set upon the beast** is belief in the incarnation of Christ. The **inn** is the Church, where travellers returning to their heavenly country are refreshed after pilgrimage. The

> **morrow** is after the resurrection of the Lord. The **two pence** are either the two precepts of love, or the promise of this life and of that which is to come. The **innkeeper** is the Apostle (Paul). The supererogatory payment is either his counsel of celibacy, or the fact that he worked with his own hands lest he should be a burden to any of the weaker brethren when the Gospel was new, though it was lawful for him to live by the Gospel.

In contrast to this allegorical hermeneutic, Jülicher argued that the parables of Jesus make a single point, and after his work, parables and allegories came to be sharply distinguished: parables contain only a single *tertium comparationis,* and they make only one point. Jülicher understood that point to be a general religious or moral truth; Dodd (1961; 1st edition 1933) and Jeremias (1972; 1st edition 1947) while accepting the view that parables make a single point, saw that point to relate to the crisis inaugurated by Jesus' proclamation of the kingdom of God. Jeremias (1972, 113–14), in agreement with Jülicher, saw increasing allegorization as one characteristic of the transformation of the parables of Jesus by the early church, reflecting his conviction that the original parables of Jesus were nonallegorical. Crossan (1973, 25) has modulated the emphasis on a single point of interpretation emphasized by Jülicher: "The essential criterion by which the parable is distinguished from the allegory is not, at least primarily, that the parable has one central point, but that its many elements relate first of all to each other within the parable."

By the late 20th cent., the pendulum had begun to swing to the opposite extreme, and "allegory" began again to be regarded as defined by Boucher (1977, 20): "an extended metaphor in narratory form." Reflecting this viewpoint and in light of modern literary criticism, a number of scholars argue (against Jülicher), not that the parables are allegories (the view attributed to many scholars by Parris 2002), but that parables cannot be separated from allegories as neatly as Jülicher supposed (Boucher 1977; Drury 1985; Caird 1980, 160–67; Blomberg 1990b; Sider 1995). Not all features of the authentic cores of the parables of Jesus are realistic (Huffman 1978, 208–15), and this lack of realism is also a characteristic of allegory (Blomberg 1991, 52). Modern interpreters of parables find it difficult consistently to avoid allegorical interpretation, at least in the tendency to suggest that main characters in the parable represent something or someone (Black 1960; Blomberg 1991, 52). Further, interpreters often identify a variety of "single points" in the parable. An example is the parable of the Prodigal Son in Luke 15:11–32, in which the main point has been argued to be the generosity of the father's love, the opportunity for repentance for any prodigal, and the need to avoid the hard-hearted attitude of the elder brother (Blomberg 1991, 53). It is perhaps better to admit the polyvalent character of the parable. Based on a detailed study of more than 300 Tannaitic parables, Johnston (1978, 636–37) concludes that the distinction between parable and allegory is inappropriate.

Literary vs. historical criticism. The *historical* approach to parable interpretation regards the parables embedded in Gospel narratives as windows through which to view the parables reconstructed in the form in which they were originally uttered by the historical Jesus (supported by Hunter 1960, 18–20; Linnemann 1966, 41–47; Crossan 1973, 3), while the *literary* approach focuses on the parables in the form in which they have come down to us and as contextualized in the Gospels (on the conflict between these two approaches, see Sider 1983). For many recent interpreters of the parables, the central issue is the ways in which parables project narrative worlds and reverse the expectations of the audience (Parris 2002, 35). The historical reconstruction of the teaching of Jesus, including the parable, is a perfectly legitimate enterprise that cannot either replace or exclude the literary critical approach to interpreting the parables in their present form.

The historical attempt to reconstruct the original form of the parables is classically represented by two influential NT scholars, Dodd (1961) and Jeremias (1972). Jeremias proposed ten "laws" indicating how the parables were transformed between Jesus and the Gospels (1972, 103–4): (1) Translation into Greek involved an inevitable change in meaning. (2) For the same reason, culturally bound material is occasionally translated. (3) Pleasure in the embellishment of parable is noticeable early. (4) Occasionally OT passages and folkloristic themes have influenced the shaping of the material. (5) Parables originally addressed to opponents or the crowd are often applied to the early Christian community. (6) This led to an increasing shift of emphasis on the hortatory aspect, especially a shift from the eschatological to the hortatory. (7) The early church related and expanded the parables to fit its own situation, of which two important themes were missionary concerns and the delay of the Parousia. (8) To an increasing degree the primitive church interpreted the parables allegorically with a view to their hortatory use. (9) The early church made collections of parables, occasionally fusing two parables together. (10) The primitive church provided the parables with a setting, which often produced a change in meaning; by adding general conclusions, many parables acquired a universal meaning.

*Aphorisms, *Form criticism

Blomberg 1990b; Boucher 1977, 1981; A. Bruce 1882; Carlston 1975; Carter and Heil 1998; Carson 1985; Crossan 1979; Dodd 1961; Jeremias 1972; Klauck 1978; Gerhardsson 1988; Hedrick 1994; Hultgren 2000; Hunter 1960; Kissinger 1979; Parris 2002; B. Scott 1989; Sider 1983, 1995; R. H. Stein 1981; Wailes 1987

Paradigm, from the Greek word παράδειγμα (literally "side-show," more generally "pattern, model, example"), is a story that provides a pattern or example to be either imitated or avoided. The use of the preposition παρά suggests that παραδείγματα were originally so designated because they functioned as *digressions in narrative texts. The paradigm is a technical rhetorical term for an argument based on the use of example (Aristotle, *Rhetorica*); an example is the story of Niobe, who remembered to eat despite her grief over her dead children, which was told to Priam, grieving over his slain son Hector, to encourage him to eat (*Iliad* 24.6–2–17).

*Parable

Paraenesis, a transliteration of the Greek word παραίνεσις ("advice, counsel"), is a general term for the kind of moral exhortation that is widely accepted and is not subject to refutation (Quinn 1990a, 192). Paraenesis has often been understood as the linking together of traditional moral precepts and exhortation. Among paraenetic topoi are self-control, deploring flatterers, making friends, having a sound mind in a sound body, guarding speech, and coping with instability in life (Ps.-Isocrates, *Ad Demonicum* 21–42). An extensive paraenetic tradition developed in antiquity, including such elements as precepts, advice, supporting argumentation, modes of encouragement, and the use of examples (Stowers 1986, 23). First Thessalonians (see *Thessalonians, First Letter to the) is an example of a paraenetic letter that makes extensive use of rhetoric.

Characteristics of paraenesis. Paraenesis has several important characteristics: (1) Paraenesis is traditional, reflecting conventional wisdom generally approved by society (Isocrates, *Ad Nicoclem* 40–41; Ps. Libanius, *Epistolary Styles* 5; Phil. 4:8). (2) Paraenesis is applicable to many situations (Seneca, *Letters* 94.32–35). (3) Paraenesis is so familiar that it is often presented as a "reminder" (Seneca, *Letters* 13.15; 94.21–25; Dio Chrysostom, *Or.* 17.2.5; 1 Thess. 4:1–2; 2 Thess. 3:6; Phil. 3:1). (4) Paraenesis can be exemplified in exceptional people who are models of virtue (Seneca, *Letters* 6:5–6; 11.9–10; 95.72; 2 Thess. 3:7; Phil. 3:17; 4:9). (5) Paraenesis is usually transmitted by people who are regarded as socially and morally superior to those they address.

Paraenetic letters. This letter-type is described in some detail by Ps.-Libanius, *Characteres epistolici* 5:

> The paraenetic style is that in which we give someone paraenesis, persuading him to pursue something or avoid something. Paraenesis is divided into two parts, i.e., persuasion and dissuasion. . . . Paraenesis is paraenetic speech that does not admit a counter-statement. Thus, if someone should say, "We must honor the divine," no one contradicts this paraenesis, unless he is insane in the first place.

One of the distinctive features of the Pauline letter tradition is the presence of a concluding section of paraenesis (Rom. 12:1–15:13; Gal. 5:1–6:10; 1 Thess. 4:1–5:22; Col. 3:1–4:6). The frequent occurrence of lengthy paraenetic sections in the latter part of Pauline letters has encouraged the division of the body of Paul's letters into two main sections, doctrinal and ethical. Yet there are other letters in which paraenesis is not concentrated in the concluding section but is woven throughout the composition (1 Corinthians; 2 Corinthians; Philippians; cf. James, Hebrews). Paraenesis is a complex subject that has recently been the focus of research. At this point, however, it is helpful to distinguish between epistolary paraenesis, which is found in defined concluding sections of some Christian letters, and paraenetic styles, which permeate letters (e.g., 1 Thessalonians, Galatians, Colossians).

*Admonition, *Catalogues of virtues and vices; *James, letter of

---

ADB 5.922–23; Fiore 1986; Gammie 1990; Malherbe 1983; Perdue 1981; Quinn 1990; Sensig 1996; Stowers 1986; Vetschera 1911–12

Parallelism, or *parallelismus membrorum* ("parallelism of clauses or cola"), the fundamental mark of Semitic poetry (as well as an almost universal characteristic of poetry; see Preminger [ed.] 1965, 599), is based on various types of repetition, completion, addition, matching, intensifying, and symmetry at the primary level of the bicolon or tricolon. Parallelism is not limited to poetry, as Kugel has argued, but occurs in typically prose texts as well (1981, 59–68). Furthermore, ca. 12 percent of the corpus of early Hebrew poetry consists of nonparallel lines (Geller 1979, 30). The basic unit of Hebrew poetry, however, remains the bicolon or couplet (though monocolon units occur only very rarely; cf. Ps 1:1). Sometimes two lines constitute a "parallel" unit (bicolon=a two-colon unit), and less commonly, three lines constitute a "parallel" unit (tricolon=three-cola unit). The structure of a bicolon can be exemplified by Ps. 92:1:

> It is good to give thanks to the LORD, /
> to sing praises to thy name, O Most High. //

The pattern in this bicolon can be represented as follows: A: __________ / B: _________ //; i.e., the first colon ends with a short pause, while the second colon ends with a longer pause. Following the work of Lowth in the 18th cent., three major types of parallelism have been generally recognized: (1) synonymous, (2) antithetic, and (3) synthetic. Following the influential work of Kugel (1981), a number of proposals have been made for refining the understanding of Hebrew poetic "parallelism." Kugel himself understands parallelism as essentially "a pause sequence that establishes a subjunction of one statement to another; it is not sufficiently regular to be meter or to be analogous to meter; therefore, the term 'poetry' is misapplied to biblical texts" (Raphael 2002, 39). One of these refinements has been called "the parallelism of greater precision" (Clines 1987), i.e., line B of a parallel bicolon is often more precise or specific than line A; an example from Isa. 40:16 (Clines 1987, 77–78):

> Lebanon would not suffice for fuel, /
> nor are its beasts enough for a burnt offering //

Parallelism in the Gospels. According to Davies and Allison (1988, 1.94–95), the sayings of Jesus in Matthew show a higher degree of parallelism than do those in Mark and Luke, though the types of parallelism exhibited are not discussed. Riesner (1981, 392–93; 1982, 507) claims that of 247 originally isolated sayings of Jesus in the Synoptic tradition, 197 exhibit some kind of *parallelismus membrorum;* i.e., at least 80 percent of the Synoptic sayings of Jesus have poetic form. Manson (1979, 31–32), finds examples of synonymous and antithetic parallelism in the teachings of Jesus. Matthew 5:45 serves as an example of simple synonymous parallelism:

> He makes his sun rise on the evil and on the good,
> and sends rain on the just and on the unjust.

Matthew 7:17 is an example of antithetic parallelism:

> Every sound tree bears good fruit,
> but the bad tree bears evil fruit.

Manson also identifies more elaborate forms. He quotes Luke 11:9–10=Matt. 7:7–8 (Q) as an example of parallelism between two short three-line strophes:

> Ask, and it will be given you;
> seek, and you will find;
> knock, and it will be opened to you.
>
> For every one who asks receives,
> and he who seeks finds,
> and to him who knocks it will be opened.

Burney (1925) proved to be extremely influential in arguing that the sayings of Jesus exhibit the characteristics of Semitic poetry, including parallelism of lines and clauses, rhythm, and perhaps even rhyme. Burney found four types of parallelism in the Gospels (1925, 16–21): (1) synonymous, (2) antithetic, (3) synthetic or constructive, and (4) climactic. Dependent on Burney, Manson cites an example of step-parallelism or climactic parallelism in Mark 9:37 in an earlier work (1935, 52):

> Whoever receives one such child in my name receives me;
> and whoever receives me, receives not me but him who sent me.

Burney's proposals were accepted enthusiastically but uncritically by a series of influential NT scholars, including Manson (1935, 50–56; 1949, 30–33), V. Taylor (1935, 89–90, Jeremias (1971, 14–29), and Black (1967, 143–85). Since the subject of the poetic structure of the sayings of Jesus seems to have been neglected in recent years, satisfactory analyses of this aspect of the sayings of Jesus constitutes an important issue that urgently needs analysis.

In J. Weiss's (1897) analysis of Pauline rhetoric, he places the emphasis on the Pauline use of parallelism derived from his Jewish background. He focuses on Paul's construction of sentences (1897, 167). "A particularly essential feature of the Pauline style is the parallelism of expression and of members" (1897, 168). The basic element in Pauline rhetoric is the short clause or sentence that continues on in an unperiodic style with subordinate clauses introduced with ὅτι, ἵνα, ὅπως, etc. He goes on to give numerous examples of various kinds of parallelism in Paul, including synonymous parallelism (Rom. 1:21; 7:7; 9:2; 1 Cor. 4:5; 15:50; Weiss 1897, 169–70) and antithetical parallelism (1 Cor. 12:3, 26; 2 Cor. 9:6; Gal. 6:7, 8; Weiss 1897, 174–81).

*Antithesis, *Poetry, *Style and stylistics

———

Berlin 1985, 1992; Clines 1987; Fokkelman 2001; Geller 1979; Hiebert 2000; Horgan and Kobelski 1989; Kugel 1981; O'Connor 1980; Petersen and Richards 1992, 21–35; Preminger (ed.) 1965, 599; Riesner 1982

Paranarrative is a designation coined by Alden (2000) concerning the Homeric epics for the secondary narratives related by the poet's characters and also the interludes related in the poet's own voice. These function as subtle guides to the interpretation of the main narrative. Another designation for a closely related literary phenomenon, of which Alden seems unaware, is the phrase *mise en abyme* (from heraldry), given a literary meaning by André Gide in 1893 (Gide 1948, 41), i.e., "the mirroring within [part of] the work of the work as a whole" (Don Fowler 2000, 90). Example: The basic story line of the *Odyssey* revolves around a hero detained beyond the time agreed that his wife should wait for him. He eventually returns home, often aided by a sympathetic female figure, to find his wife about to be forced into marriage with another man. A paranarrative exhibiting a microcosmic version of the same story shape is found in the story of Demodicus about the love affair of Ares and Aphrodite (*Odyssey* 8.266–369; see Alden 2000, 2–4 with other examples). In this story, during the contrived absence of Hephaestus her husband, Aphrodite is constrained by Ares to be his partner in adultery. Hephaestus, catching them in the act, ties them to the bed, and they become a laughing stock for the assembled Olympian gods. Alden's use of the term paranarrative as a microcosmic version of the macrocosmic narrative is a useful analytic tool for conceptualizing the function of narratives (usually brief) that do not advance the main plot.

An example from the NT would be Jesus' sermon in the synagogue at Nazareth, which resulted in his near-lynching but surprising escape (Luke 4:16–30), as reflecting the overall plot of Luke.

*Paradigms

———

Alden 2000

Parataxis, paratactic style, is a stylistic structure in which clauses and sentences are strung together either without conjunctions or combined with coordinate conjunctions. This was called the λέξις εἰρομένη, or "running style" (Aristotle, *Rhet.* 3.9).

*Style or stylistics

———

Aejmelaeus 1982; Schwyzer 1950–71, 2.631–34; Smyth 1956, ¶2168–72

Parchment is a term for the skins of animals, primarily sheep and goats, dressed and prepared for use as material for writing, either sewn together to form a roll or folded into quires and bound together to form a *codex; the resultant material is light yellow in color (see *vellum). The term "parchment" itself is based on the medieval Latin word *pergamentum* ("parchment"), which is derived from Pergamon, the city in Mysia where the great Pergamon library was located. According to an apocryphal story, attributed to Varro, the technique for manufacturing parchment was "invented" in Pergamon during the reign of Eumenes II (197–158 B.C.E.), when Ptolemaic Egypt, in a move calculated to handicap the rival Pergamon library and support the Alexandrian Museion, stopped exporting papyrus (Pliny, *Hist. nat.* 13.70; Jerome, *Ep.* 7). Another Latin term, *membranum* ("skin, parchment") was largely displaced by *pergamentum* in the medieval period; the phrase *membrana Pergamena* ("Pergamene parchment") first occurs in an edict of Diocletian in 301 C.E. The great uncial manuscripts of the Bible are parchment codices (see *Textual criticism). In 2 Tim. 4:13, "Paul" asks Timothy to bring him a coat καὶ τὰ βιβλία μάλιστα τὰς μεμβράνας, "and the books, especially the parchment sheets [or the books made of parchment]." *Membranai* (a Latin loanword) is ambiguous; it could mean "parchment sheets," "rolls" (apparently the view of Theodoret 3.695), or "codices." Parchment replaced papyrus by the 4th cent. C.E. as a more distinguished material on which to copy NT documents, particularly the Gospels.

R. R. Johnson 1968; Skeat 1979

Parenesis (see *Paraenesis)

Parenthesis, a transliteration of the Greek word παρένθεσις ("insertion, parenthesis"), is a clause inserted into a sentence without syntactical connections with the encompassing sentence. The Latin equivalent is *interpositio* or *interclusio,* which Quintilian (9.3.23) defined as "the interruption of the continuous flow of our language by the insertion of some remark." An obvious parenthesis occurs in Mark 13:14 (=Matt. 24:15): "Let the reader understand." Parentheses, which are related to *narrative asides and *digressions, are relatively common in ancient Greek and Latin literature. In Longus 4.5, for example, we find this parenthesis: "This Eudromus (for that was his name, because he was a foot-page) they received and entertained with great kindness." Parentheses are extremely common in the NT and early Christian literature. Though Greek and Latin manuscripts, written as *scriptio continua* ("continuous writing," i.e., no spaces between words and little or no punctuation) do not formally indicate the presence of parentheses, they are frequently set off with parentheses or dashes in modern translations. For other examples of parenthetical remarks see Mark 2:10 (= Luke 5:24); 3:16; 14:8; Luke 9:28; 13:24; John 1:6; 3:1; 7:22; 10:12, 35; Acts 1:15; 12:3; 23:35; Rom. 5:12; 9:1, 11; 15:23–28; 1 Cor. 16:5; 2 Cor. 8:3; 10:10; Heb. 10:29. Longer parentheses are found in Luke 6:4; 23:51; Col. 1:21–22; 2 Pet. 2:8; 2 Cor. 9:12; Heb. 7:20–22.

*Anacolouthon, *Apostrophe, *Digression, *Narrative asides

Robertson 1934, 433–35

Parisosis, from the Greek word παρίσωις, means "making the two members of a period equal in length" (Aristotle, *Rhet.* 3.9.9 [1410a]).

Paroemiographer, a transliterated form of the term παροιμιογράφος (Zenobius 2.45), which means compiler of παροιμίαι ("proverbs") for philosophical or rhetorical purposes. The *Corpus paroemiographorum Graecorum* (Leutsch and Schneidewin 1958–61, 1), existed in the early Middle Ages in three parts: (1) the works of Zenobius (early 2nd cent. C.E.), (2) a collection of the proverbs of Plutarch used by the Alexandrians, and (3) an alphabetical list of popular proverbs.

*Aphorisms, *Proverbs,

Leutsch and Schneidewin 1958–61

Paronomasia, from a Greek word meaning "play upon words which sound alike," involves the use of two or more words in a relatively brief context that are either very similar in form (Cicero, *De oratore* 2, 256–57) or make use of different meanings of the same word (Blass-Debrunner 1961, §488). A famous example of paronomasia involving a shift in denotation in Matt. 16:18: "And I tell you, you are Peter [Πέτρος], and on this rock [πέτρα] I will build my church." In Rev. 22:18–19 the term ἐπιτίθημι is used twice, the first time meaning "add" (in the sense of adding something to an existing quantity) and the second time meaning "inflict on" (in the sense of subjecting some to a particular experience, normally by force); the term ἀφαιρέω is also used twice, the first time with the denotation "to remove," the second time with the denotation "to cause to cease" (in the sense that someone is no longer permitted to enjoy some state or activity):

> I warn every one who hears the words of the prophecy of this book:
> if any one adds [ἐπιθῇ] to them,
> God will add [ἐπιθήσει] to him the plagues described in this book,
> and if any one takes away [ἀφέλῃ] from the words of the book of this prophecy,
> God will take away [ἀφελεῖ] his share in the tree of life and in the holy city, which are described in this book.

For paronomasia elsewhere in the NT, see 2 Tim. 2:9 (δεσμῶν and δέδεται; Spicq 1947, 347).

*Assonance

Passion narrative (=PN) refers to both the oral and written traditions of the last days of Jesus, including his arrest, trial, condemnation, execution, and burial. Each of the Gospels in its own way places major emphasis on the passion of Jesus. Kähler (1964, 80), in an oft-quoted statement, claimed that Mark was "a passion story with a long introduction." The PNs constitute the longest series of connected narrative episodes in the canonical Gospels and the *Gospel of Peter* (Mark 14:1–15:47; Matt. 26:1–27:66; Luke 22:1–23:56; John 13:1–19:42). The PN is the only extended section of the Gospels where all four canonical Gospels are in significant harmony. The extent to which an extended PN existed in oral tradition between the death of Jesus (ca. 29 C.E.) and the composition of Mark, the first written Gospel (ca. 70 C.E.), is debated. The NT has passion traditions outside the Gospels: (1) 1 Cor. 11:23–26: (a) Jesus instituted the Lord's Supper; (b) Jesus was betrayed; (c) these events took place at night; (d) Jesus died. (2) 1 Cor. 15:3–5: (a) Christ died for our sins; (b) he was buried. (3) Heb. 5:7 (Gethsemane or crucifixion tradition: Jesus offered prayers and petitions with loud cries and tears to God who was able to deliver him from death).

*Form criticism

ADB 5:172–77; Borgen 1958–59; Brown 1994; Buse 1957–58; Crossan 1988; Dibelius 1971, 178–218; Donahue 1973, 1976; Dormeyer 1977; J. Green 1988; Harrington 2000; Kelber 1976; Linnemann 1970; Mohr 1982; Moo 1983; Nickelsburg 1980; Reinbold 1994; L. Schenke 1971; Schneider 1973; Schreiber 1969; Senior 1975, 1984; Soards 1987, 1991; Taylor 1972; Trocmé 1984; Yarbro Collins 1993

Pastoral Letters, a group of three closely related pseudepigraphic letters (see *Pseudepigrapha, NT) attributed to Paul, designated 1 Timothy, 2 Timothy, and Titus (see *Timothy, First Letter to; *Timothy, Second Letter to; *Titus, Letter to), probably written early in the 2nd cent. to solve the problem of competing forms of Christianity. Like Philemon, these letters are addressed to individuals, but unlike Philemon they have a focus on guiding or shepherding the Christian congregations where the addressees are working, and because of this practical purpose they have been designated "pastoral" letters. The Pastoral Letters are problematic in that it is difficult to determine who wrote them, when they were written, why they were written, and to whom they were written. The fact that Polycarp clusters allusions to the Pastorals in sections of his letter where he mentions the name "Paul" suggests that he is the earliest witness to the Pauline authorship of the Pastorals (Berding 1999).

Original order. The three Pastoral Letters form a minicollection of "Pauline" letters, probably produced when a larger collection of Pauline letters had already begun to be formed. The texts of the Pastorals first appear in canonical context in Codex Clarmontanus in the order 1 Timothy–2 Timothy–Titus, their present canonical order. This arrangement is based on decreasing size (1 Timothy=1,586 words; 2 Timothy=1,235 words; Titus=328 words). In the Muratorian Canon (line 60), however, they appear in the order Titus–1 Timothy–2 Timothy. Quinn regards this as the original order, arguing that the extremely long section in Titus 1:1–3 naming Paul as the sender, containing 48 words, provides an appropriate thematic introduction to the entire corpus of Pastoral Letters (Quinn 1978, 63–64, 78). However, Wolter (1988, 21–22) argues more convincingly for the order 1 Timothy–Titus–2 Timothy, pointing to the important introductory autobiographical section in 1 Tim. 1:12–17 as part of the total united image fostered in the Pastorals. Reicke (2001, 105–20), who regards the Pastorals as authentically Pauline, discusses the chronology of the Pastorals in the context of this presupposition, and concludes that 1 Timothy was written in 56 C.E., Titus in 58 C.E., and 2 Timothy in 60 C.E.

Authorship. There are several approaches to the problem of authorship: 1. Some argue that Paul is in fact the author of the Pastorals and that various mitigating factors account for the differences in language, style, and theology between the Pastorals and the other Pauline letters (Kelly 1963; Guthrie 1970, 584–634; Fee 1984, 1988; Reicke 2001, 52–56). Some argue that the high concentration of traditional materials is best accounted for by arguing that they were collected by Paul himself (Harnack 1958, 239–40 n. 3; Cannon 1983; Ellis 1987).

2. The common critical view is that the Pastorals were written by a single author who intended his work to be taken as genuinely Pauline (Dibelius and Conzelmann 1972). There is some disagreement about whether all three were written by the same unknown author, or whether 2 Timothy was written by one author and 1 Timothy and Titus by another (Murphy-O'Connor 1991a). In part, this argument is based on the fact that 2 Timothy contains personal information relating to Paul, while 1 Timothy and Titus contain very little such personal information. The argument for single authorship emphasizes the fact that all three letters presuppose the same false teachers, the same form of church organization, and similar conditions in the community (Kümmel 1975, 367).

3. Some argue that the Pastorals are the product of an author or authors who were part of a Pauline "school" and who collected and edited his teachings (P. N. Harrison 1921, 1964). Harrison (1964, 106–28) argues for the presence of three genuine Pauline fragments in the Pastorals: (a) Titus 3:12–15; (b) 2 Tim. 4:9–15, 20–21a, 22b; (c) 2 Tim. 1:16–18; 3:10–11; 4:1, 2a, 5b–8, 16–19, 21b, 22a.

4. Based on the similarities of language and style of Luke–Acts and the Pastorals, some scholars have argued unsuccessfully for common authorship (Moule 1965; Strobel 1969; Quinn 1978 [not supported in the posthumous Quinn and Wacker 2000]; Wilson 1979 [critiqued by Marshall 1981, who emphasizes the differences in diction]; Kaestli 1995). Quinn argues that the Pastorals were originally appended to Luke–Acts in the order Titus, 1 Timothy, 2 Timothy (1978, 68–75).

5. More recently, J. D. Miller (1997, 144–58) in a highly speculative study argues that the Pastorals should be attributed to neither Paul nor a pseudo-Paul. Rather, each letter is based on authentic core letters that were originally addressed by Paul to Timothy and Titus but have been expanded and amplified by a community of skilled scribes who valued Paul's memory and who worked in a school (i.e., seminary) for pastors. He speculates the "core" of each letter but offers a minimum of analysis (147–51): 1 Tim. 1:1–7; 1:18–20; 3:14–15; 6:20–21; Titus 1:1–5; 3:9–11; 3:12–15; 3:15c; 2 Tim. "A" (1:1–2; [1:3–5]; 1:15–18; 4:6–8; 4:22a); and 2 Tim. "B": (4:9; 4:10–18; 4:19–21; 4:22b).

Date. There are three different and widely spaced time slots suggested for the composition of the Pastorals: (1) Those who argue that the Pastorals were written by Paul must situate them before his death, most likely between 60 and 64 C.E. (Bernard 1899; M. Prior 1989; Spicq 1969, lxxiii–lxxxviii). (2) Some of those who are convinced that Paul could not have been responsible for these letters, because of the developed church order, domestic codes, and ministerial offices, situate them in the generation following Paul, i.e., 70–100 C.E. (Lock 1924, xxii). (3) Others, agreeing that they are not authentic, place them at an even greater distance from Paul, during the first third of the second century, i.e., 100–130 C.E. (Dibelius and Conzelmann 1972). Given the importance that Paul has for the unknown author, it is striking that there are no clear allusions to the Pauline letters. The proverb "for the clean everything is clean" (Titus 1:15), is close to Rom. 14:20 ("everything is indeed clean"), though not evidently dependent on it.

Rhetorical situation. Given the pseudepigraphical character of the Pastorals, both the author and the audience are anachronistic constructs of the late first or early second century. Thus the implied author "Paul" and the implied recipients "Timothy" and "Titus" all function as typological constructs of ideal Christian ministers. Similarly, the roles of various genders and age groups are discussed, all of which make up the surrogate household as a metaphor for the church (Titus 2:1, 3, 6, 9). The Letter of Titus delineates a "Pauline" program for Jewish-Christian congregations, for which the congregations in Crete are paradigms. The letter of 1 Timothy is concerned with the Christian congregations who were primarily converts from paganism in Ephesus, a major eastern Mediterranean metropolis. These Christians may be susceptible to Judaizing (1 Tim. 1:6–11).

Social Organization. There is a central concern that ministers at various levels will be appointed who are morally and spiritually qualified for ministry (1 Tim. 5:22; 2 Tim. 1:6; 2:2; Titus 1:5). The offices of bishop (1 Tim. 3:2–7; Titus 1:7–10), deacon (1 Tim. 3:8–10) and elder (1 Tim. 5:17–19; Titus 1:5–6) are mentioned, though their relationship is never specified.

Language and style. One-third of the vocabulary of the Pastorals (apart from some 55 proper nouns and adjectives) does not appear in the rest of the Pauline letters. The language of the Pastorals has a striking resemblance to the language of Luke–Acts (mentioned above). The author uses a variety of tropes, including assonance, alliteration, paronomasia, polysyndeton, and asyndedon. Quotations from a variety of sources occur with some frequency. Deuteronomy 25:4 is quoted in 1 Tim. 5:18a ("You shall not muzzle an ox when it is treading out the grain"), the same passage quoted by Paul in 1 Cor. 9:9. A proverb, "The laborer deserves his wages," is paired with the quotation from Deut. 25:4 in 1 Tim. 5:18b, but is found alone in the teaching of Jesus (Luke 10:7). Poetic pieces occur several times (1 Tim. 3:16; 2 Tim. 2:11–13; Titus 1:12). The style is paraenetic in the sense that the author urges his points rather than argues for them (Quinn and Wacker 2000, 6).

*Letter collections, *Timothy, First Letter to, *Timothy, Second Letter to, *Titus, Letter to

---

Barrett 1963; Berding 1999; Dibelius and Conzelmann 1972; J. K. Elliott 1968; Fiore 1986; Hanson 1966, 1982; P. N. Harrison 1921; L. T. Johnson 2001; Kaestli 1995; Lock 1924; Miller 1997; Murphy-O'Connor 1991a; M. Prior 1989; Quinn 1990; Quinn and Wacker 2000; Verner 1983; Wilson 1979; Wolter 1988

Pathos, a transliterated form of the Greek word πάθος ("emotion, passion"), corresponding to the Latin word *adfectus* (from which the modern English word "affect" is derived), is a general term for the emotions (the most important of which was anger), which were the subject of extended philosophical discussion (Harris 2002), in literary composition (Longinus 8.1) and in rhetoric, where it was used of the emotions of an audience and how to arouse them. For Aristotle, pathos was one of the three basic types of artificial rhetorical proofs (πίστεις ἄτεχνοι) making reasoned judgment (κρίσις) possible; the other two are *ethos or "character" and logos or "argument" (*Rhet.* 1.2.3–6). All three types of proof were together part of what later rhetoricians called *inventio,* the "discovery [of arguments]," one of three parts of Aristotle's *officia oratoris,* i.e., duties of an orator (*Rhet.* 3.1.1; 1403b), which for Aristotle were proofs, style, and arrangement. Aristotle's emphasis on the three types of proofs (πάθος, "emotion," ἦθος, "character," and τὸ πρᾶγμα, "the matter itself"), however, is only rarely found in later rhetorical traditions: *Rhetorica ad Alexandrum* 14.8–9; Dionysius Hal. *Lysias* 19; Cicero *De oratore* 2.114). Generally, however, ethos and pathos seem to have dropped out of rhetorical handbooks after Aristotle (Kennedy 1980, 80; Wisse 1989, 80–83), and certainly after Hermagoras of Temnos, fl. 150 B.C.E. (Solmsen 1974), due in part to Stoic influence, since the Stoics were very much interested in rhetoric, but rejected emotional appeals and therefore did not adopt Aristotle's scheme of the three proofs. The absence of ethos and pathos from rhetorical handbooks is reflected in a conversation attributed to the Academic philosopher Charmadas ca. 102 B.C.E. in Cicero *De oratore* 1.87 (LCL trans.; italics added):

> For he [Charmadas] was of opinion that the main object of the orator was that he should both appear himself, and to those before whom he was pleading, to be such a man as he would desire to seem (*an end to be attained by a reputable mode of life, as to which those teachers of rhetoric had left no hint among their instructions*), and that the hearts of his hearers should be touched in such fashion as the orator would have them touched (another purpose only to be achieved by a speaker who had investigated all the ways wherein, and all the allurements and kind of diction whereby, the judgment of men might be inclined to this side or to that); *but according to him such knowledge lay thrust away and buried deep in the very heart of philosophy, and those rhetoricians had not so much as tasted it with the tip of the tongue.*

In general, however, it is true to say that while ethos and pathos no longer existed as independent concepts under the task of *inventio,* ethos was primarily associated with the exordium of a speech and pathos with the epilogue (Cicero *De inventione* 1.98–109; *Rhetorica ad Herennium* 2.47).

In *Rhet.* 2.1.8 (trans. Kennedy 1991, 121), Aristotle explains why he includes pathos as a type of rhetorical proof:

> The emotions [πάθη] are those things through which, by undergoing change, people come to differ in their judgments and which are accompanied by pain and pleasure, for example, anger, pity, fear, and other such things and their opposites.

Pathos was used as a rhetorical concept before Aristotle, who in fact complains in the opening paragraphs of the *Rhetorica* about the misuse of emotional appeals in court (1.1.3–6), yet he apparently contradicts himself by turning around and devoting a substantial section of his *Rhetorica* to the subject (2.2–11). In this latter section, Aristotle discusses fifteen emotions in this section in terms of seven paired antithetical emotions, concluding with the solitary emotion "contempt": (1) anger, (2) mildness, (3) love or friendship, (4) hate, (5) fear, (6) lack of fear, (7) shame, (8) shamelessness, (9) favor or goodwill, (10) lack of goodwill, (11) pity, (12) indignation, (13) envy, (14) emulation, (15) contempt (2.2–11). The contradiction between the opening section (1.1.3–6) in which Aristotle criticizes the use of pathos and his extensive discussion of pathos in 2.1–11 is problematic and cannot be glossed over (Wisse 1989, 17–20). Aristotle's concept of pathos includes the gentle emotions (e.g., sympathy) as well as the stronger emotions. Aristotle's treatment of pathos, or the emotions, as one of three types of rhetorical proof does not intellectualize the emotions, but rather treats the subject of the emotions in a systematic and rational manner (Wisse 1989, 72–74). Both before and after Aristotle, pathos was primarily limited to the prologue and epilogue (Cicero *De inventione* 1.98–109; Quintilian 6.1.7–55). Each of the three rhetorical genres was associated with particular emotions. In judicial rhetoric, the accuser tries to rouse the jury to feel hatred toward the accused, while the defender tries to make the jury feel pity for the accused (Quintilian 6.1.9–11). In deliberative rhetoric, hope and fear are inculcated in the audience, while in epideictic rhetoric the focus is on love and hate.

After a short discussion of the reliability of the speaker's ἦθος or character, Aristotle has a lengthy discussion of πάθος, i.e., the emotional manipulation of the audience (2.1.8–2.11.7; 1378a–1388b). The widely accepted view (Grimaldi 1972, 148; Conley 1984, 168–9) that the premises of an *enthymeme can involve matters of character (ἦθος) and emotion (πάθος) in addition to reason (λόγος), however, is contradicted in *Rhetorica* 3.17.8; 1418a (trans. Kennedy):

> And when you would create pathos, do not speak in enthymemes; for the enthymeme either knocks out the pathos or is spoken in vain. (Simultaneous movements knock out each other and either fade away or make each other weak.) Nor should you seek an enthymeme when the speech is being 'ethical'; for logical demonstration has neither *ēthos* nor moral purpose.

In *De oratore,* Cicero treats ethos, pathos, and logos in Aristotelian fashion as the three types of proof under invention (*De oratore* 2.99–306), focusing first on rational argumentation (2.114–177), then on ethos (2.182–4), and then on pathos (2.185–211a); see Wisse 1989, 190–221. Cicero summarizes the role of each descriptively in *De oratore* 2.128, without using technical rhetorical terms:

> Under my whole oratorical system . . . lie three principles [*rationes*], as I said before, first the winning of men's favour [ethos], secondly their enlightenment [logos], thirdly their excitement [pathos].

Some (e.g., Solmsen 1974) have maintained that Cicero understood ethos as referring to the gentler, milder emotions, while pathos referred to the stronger and more vehement emotions (*De oratore* 2.183–184, 212). However, Wisse argues that ethos in Cicero should not be equated with the *leniores affectus* ("gentler emotions"), and pathos with the stronger emotions. This is rather the view of Quintilian, superimposed over Cicero; see a view found in Quintilian (6.2.8–10; LCL trans.):

> However, as we learn from our ancient authorities, there are two kinds of emotions. One is called *pathos* by the Greeks, and we correctly and properly translate this as "emotion" (*adfectus*). The second kind they call *ēthos*; in my view, Latin lacks any equivalent. . . . They have therefore spoken of one of the sets of emotions as violent, and the other as gentle and steady; in the one (they say) the passions are vehement, in the other subdued; the former command, the latter persuade; the former are powerful agents of disturbance, the latter of good will. Some say also that *ēthos* is permanent, *pathos* temporary.

Both Cicero and Quintilian maintain that the orator who intends to move an audience emotionally should exhibit the same emotions himself in order to maintain credibility (Cicero *De oratore* 2.189–94; Quintilian 6.2.26–36; J. Martin 1974, 161).

Relevance to NT & ECL. There have been a number of studies that have sought to illuminate the function of pathos in early Christian literature, primarily the NT letters (DiCicco 1995; Kraftchick 2001; Olbricht and Sumney [eds.] 2001). The chief difficulty in analyzing Paul's purported use of rhetorical pathos is the fact that the rhetorical prescriptions for the use of pathos were intended to be used in speeches delivered before real audiences. Evoking pathos is in part dependent on the gestures and the tone of voice of the speaker, not alone on the words that he speaks. In written texts, such as the NT letters and the letters of Ignatius, we are dealing with written texts that the speakers did not intend to deliver orally. Paul frequently made use of emotional appeals in his letters. In 2 Cor. 2:4, Paul claims that he wrote to the Corinthians "out of much affliction and anguish of heart and with many tear, not to cause you pain but to let you know the abundant love that I have for you." Fredrickson (2001) sees this reference to tears as a key to understanding the rhetoric of 2 Cor. 1–7. In 2 Cor. 7:8–13, Paul is aware that a letter he wrote to the Corinthians made them grieve (7:8), and stirred other emotions in them as well, including indignation, fear, and longing (7:11). Since their grief led to their contrition (7:9), Paul's letter was effective, and we can suspect that Paul intentionally used pathos to achieve precisely that objective. Again, Paul expresses anger toward the Galatians for how they have unwittingly embraced "another gospel" (Gal. 1:6–9; 3:1–5; cf. 4:12–20), yet it is more likely that Paul is here making use of rhetorical pathos in order to achieve his rhetorical objectives (Thurén 1999). Betz (1979, 200–201) argued that Gal. 4:12–20 consisted of a string of friendship commonplaces, and T. Martin (2001) argues rather successfully for Paul's use of pathos in this passage. Since pathos was primarily thought appropriate for the perorations of speeches, Wuellner (1991, 138–41) proposes that the pathos section of the peroration in Romans (15:14–16:23) is found in 15:30–16:23. Following the modern rhetorical model of P. C. Smith (1998), in which logos, ethos, and pathos are intertwined and inseparable in "original arguments" or "embodied arguments," Kraftchick (2001, 42) finds ethos and pathos arguments in Paul (specifically in Gal. 4:12–20), "not because some rhetorical handbook has suggested their use, but because they are necessary parts of a speech that seek to change the mind and actions of a community." Keck (2001) treats pathos in Romans, but after a fairly helpful and insightful introduction to the use of pathos in the work of the rhetoricians, he provides a brief, commonsense discussion of pathos in Romans with little or no reference to pathos in the rhetorical handbooks. Eriksson (2001) tries to identify Paul's use of pathos in 1 Cor. 15 and 16:13–24 (the latter is identified as the peroration of 1 Corinthians, where pathos would be appropriate), but is not successful, since it just is not there. Sumney (2001) is more successful in identifying Paul's use of pathos in 2 Cor. 1–9 and 10–13.

*Ethos, *Rhetorical criticism, *Rhetorical genres

Brinton 1988; Conley 1982–83; DiCicco 1995; Eriksson 2001; Frede 1996; Fredrickson 2001; Gill 1984; Gross and Walzer 2000; Harris 2001; Johanson 1987; Keck 2001; Kraftchick 2001; Martin 2001; Nussbaum 1996; Olbricht 2001; Olbricht and Sumney (eds.) 2001; Shivola and Engberg-Pedersen 1998; Solmsen 1974; Thurén 1999; Wisse 1989

Paul, a Jew and a Pharisee (whose Jewish name was Saul) who was transformed from an enemy of early Christians to one of their number through a visionary experience that he interpreted on analogy to a prophetic call (Gal. 1:7–12; 1 Cor. 9:1; 15:8; 2 Cor. 12:1–3; see *Commission stories), which the author of Luke–Acts presents three times in subtly different ways as a conversion experience (Acts 9, 22, 26). Paul was born in Tarsus (Acts 9:11; 21:39; 22:3), and in Acts 21:39 it is claimed that he was a citizen of that city (Légasse 1995, 367–68), a center of Greek philosophy, rhetoric, and education. According to Strabo 14.5.13 (LCL trans.):

> The people at Tarsus have devoted themselves so eagerly, not only to philosophy, but also the whole round of education in general, that they have surpassed Athens, Alexandria, or any other place that can be named where there have been schools and lectures of philosophers. . . . Further, the city of Tarsus has all kinds of schools of rhetoric.

According to Acts (21:40; 22:2; 26:14), Paul was probably trilingual, able to speak Greek, Hebrew, and Aramaic; his letters are written in colloquial Greek and his Bible was primarily the Septuagint. The quality of Paul's Greek implies that he must have read works written in Greek and would therefore have been familiar with the compositional and argumentative patterns in those works (Classen 2000, 6). Classen (2000, 29–44) also demonstrates that certain technical rhetorical terms occur in the Pauline letters, including κεφαλαιοῦν, "to recapitulate [the essential elements of a speech]" (Rom. 13:9), ἀλληγορεῖν, "to interpret allegorically" (Gal. 4:24), βεβαίωσις, "confirmation [of a statement by means of proofs]" (Phil. 1:7), μετασχηματίζειν, "to rearrange the form of a speech" (1 Cor. 4:6), μακαρισμός, "blessing" (Gal. 4:15); yet this is scarcely a rich harvest.

Though born in Tarsus, Paul left there at an early age for Jerusalem (note that Strabo [4.5.13] emphasizes the fact that people from Tarsus frequently completed their education abroad, unlike those from other cities, with the exception of Alexandria). He was educated in Jerusalem, beginning in a Jewish school and continuing in the academy of Gamaliel I (Acts 22:3), the grandson of Hillel, where the Torah was the primary text in the curriculum. Paul may have had a basic Hellenistic education and was certainly familiar with rhetoric, which permeated ancient society (Becker 1989, 53–59). However, though the early Christian fathers were not overly impressed with Paul's Greek language and style, they tended to regard that in a positive light; they regarded the power of God as antithetical to rhetorical and stylistic skill, rejected rhetoric in the church, and rejoiced that the NT texts were written by unlearned and ignorant men (Kern 1998, 167–203). According to Malherbe (1983, 34): "The Church Fathers, measuring Paul by the criteria of Classicism, were embarrassed by his rudeness of style." This antithesis between rhetoric and the truth of God may be viewed as part of the ancient antipathy between philosophy and rhetoric first articulated by Plato in the *Gorgias.* Paul pursued the trade of a leather worker or tent maker (Hock 1980), a profession that was relatively low on the social scale.

Paul is the author or coauthor of at least seven letters found in the NT (*Romans, 1 *Corinthians, 2 Corinthians, *Galatians, *Philippians, 1 *Thessalonians, *Philemon). His influence continued in various ways (some speak of a "School of Paul"), and a number of pseudepigraphal letters are attributed to him, including *Ephesians and the Pastorals (see *Pastoral Letters), and perhaps even *Colossians and 2 Thessalonians. Paul was familiar with συστατικαὶ ἐπιστολαί, "letters of recommendation" (2 Cor. 3:1), using the terminology of Ps.-Demetrius, *Formae epistolicae* 2 (see *Epistolography).

An important but problematic aspect of Paul as a speaker and writer is the extent to which he was educated in rhetoric. Since about 1975, the Pauline Letters have increasingly been regarded as speeches and therefore subject to rhetorical analysis in accordance with Greco-Roman rhetorical theory and practice (Watson and Hauser 1994, 120–25). Since various sophisticated juridical, demonstrative, and epideictic rhetorical structures have been identified in the major Pauline letters, what does this imply about Paul's education? According to J. Weiss (1897, 165): "The fact that Paul expressed in his letters, which are clearly dictated and intended for public reading, the prominent rhetorical features of his day is nothing new. The question is only how this rhetorical element ought to be explained and evaluated." For the most part, Weiss focuses on Paul's use of the individual clause or sentence, and particularly on the various types of parallelism he used, and he thought that Paul's style had much in common with the Cynic-Stoic diatribe (J. Weiss 1897, 167–68). Weiss shows no interest in determining whether the macrostructure of the Pauline letters was influenced by the three main types of speech, forensic, deliberative, and epideictic. While Weiss thinks that the features of Pauline style and rhetoric he has discussed should serve as a motivation for approaching the question of Paul's rhetorical education, he leaves that issue to scholars more knowledgeable in both Paul and ancient rhetoric. According to G. Kennedy (1980, 130): "Rhetorical schools were common in the Hellenized cities of the East when Paul was a boy, and he could have attended one; certainly he was familiar with the rhetorical conventions of speeches in Roman lawcourts, the oral teachings of Greek philosophers, and the conventions of Greek letter-writing." The problem with this statement, however, is the combination of formal education with the results of a kind of cultural trickle-down effect (for similar statements see Olbricht 1990, 221; Longenecker 1990, cxii–cxiii; Hughes 2000, 251–52). An informal theory of rhetorical absorption is articulated by Longenecker (1990, cxix):

> The persuasive modes of the classical rhetorical handbooks had become the common coinage of the realm in Paul's day. One did not have to be formally trained in rhetoric to use them. Nor did rhetoricians have proprietory [sic!] right on them. In his Galatian letter (as elsewhere in his writings), Paul seems to have availed himself almost unconsciously of the rhetorical forms at hand, fitting them into his inherited epistolary structures and filling them out with such Jewish theological motifs and exegetical methods as would be particularly significant in countering what the Judaizers were telling his converts.

Did Paul learn rhetorical formally, or did he absorb it from his cultural environment? Hellholm (1995, 178–79) makes the exaggerated claim that Paul's arguments in Rom. 6 are in accord with "the best of Hellenistic rhetoric" (178–79). This statement is problematic for at least two reasons: (1) Paul wrote letters, not speeches (even though aspects of the latter genre can be included in the former). (2) *Prose rhythm was an important component of Greek rhetoric, and despite the claims of Blass, Paul does not seem to make any use of the conventional prose rhythms (but see Rose 1924). While some NT scholars suppose that Paul received rhetorical training (Fitzgerald 1990, 193), for others there is no evidence that Paul was ever trained in ancient rhetoric (Weima 2000, 126). Paul did use the proem–narrative–argument–epilogue pattern, but this was a widely known and used pattern of composition (Fairweather 1994, 23–24). One of the more sustained (though flawed) arguments that Paul did *not* use classical rhetoric is argued by Kern (1998).

Pauline thought. The complexity of Paul's theological thought is made even more problematic by the fact that the primary evidence for his views is found in occasional letters written in a variety of specific contexts for the purpose of addressing particular problems and issues, i.e., they are historically contingent pastoral communications. Further, the basic seven-letter corpus can hardly be regarded as a representative sample of Pauline thought. Despite the difficulties, many attempts have been made to understand the coherence of Paul's thought and on that basis to identify the core or center of his thought. Some scholars have doubted whether Paul himself thought in terms of such a "core," or whether the evidence from seven occasional letters is adequate for such a task. The more important suggestions for identifying the central message of Paul's thought include (1) the gospel, (2) christology,

(3) the death and resurrection of Jesus, (4) the theme "in Christ" (participatory categories), (5) ecclesiology, (6) justification by faith (the traditional Lutheran view), and (7) anthropology. It is evident, however, that many of these topics are closely related, so that the choice of a core for Pauline thought becomes a matter of nuance. It is clear, for example, that Paul's polemical doctrine of justification by faith is an aspect of his christology, and that anthropology and ecclesiology are two ways of looking at individual Christians who are at the same time part of the people of God.

Other scholars have proposed that it is more important to identify the structure of Paul's thought. Two of the most important proposals include (1) salvation history, i.e., the belief that God, who is the central actor in history, has had an ultimate salvific goal for humanity from the beginning, originally centered on Israel and ultimately on all who believe in Christ (a structure particularly evident in Rom. 9–11) and (2) apocalyptic eschatology. However, salvation history and apocalyptic eschatology must not be considered antithetical, since the latter is simply a more specific and particular version of the former.

The Pauline heritage. During the 2d cent. there was a fierce battle by various Christian factions over the appropriation of the Pauline heritage (Wiles 1967; Pagels 1975; Barrett 1974; Lindemann 1979, 1999; D. R. MacDonald 1983; for an overview see Hughes 1989, 97–104, focusing on the deuteropauline letters). This is signaled by 2 Pet. 3:15b–16 (a document written ca. 125 C.E.): "So also our beloved brother Paul wrote to you according to the wisdom given him, speaking of this as he does in all his letters. There are some things in them hard to understand, which the ignorant and unstable twist to their own destruction, as they do the other scriptures." The Pauline heritage was claimed by a diverse spectrum of early Christian authors and texts: the author of Luke–Acts (end 1st cent. C.E.), the authors of the pseudepigraphal Pauline letters (Ephesians and the Pastorals; perhaps Colossians and 2 Thessalonians), Marcion, the Valentinians, and the authors of the *Acts of Paul* (including *3 Corinthians*) and the *Apocalypse of Paul.*

*Commission stories, *Pauline Letters

Barrett 1974; Fairweather 1994; Pagels 1975; Kern 1998; Légasse 1995; Lindemann 1979, 1999; D. R. MacDonald 1983; Malherbe 1983; Mills 1993; Pagels 1975; Rose 1924; J. Weiss 1897; Wiles 1967

Pauline Letters The NT contains thirteen letters attributed to Paul. There are several issues and problems connected with this Pauline corpus, including the issue of authenticity; the contexts in which pseudepigraphical Pauline letters arose; the reasons for the canonical order of the letters (and alternate earlier orders); the problem of where, when, and how the Pauline letters were collected; and whether or not the collection involved editorial activity including the combination of shorter letters or letter fragments into longer ones (e.g. 2 *Corinthians, *Philippians); Philippians has been regarded as a composite of two or three letters (Rathjen 1959–60; Koester 1982, 2.132; Sellew 1994, 17 n. 1), or in Bornkamm's view a collection of Pauline letters (1962b).

There is also the possibility that smaller units were interpolated into larger units when the collection was made (e.g., the addition of Rom. 16 to *Romans and the insertion of 2 Cor. 6:14–7:1 into 2 *Corinthians). In addition, there are an unknown number of Pauline letters which have not survived, unless they have been renamed or inserted into other letters. Colossians 4:16 refers to a letter to the Laodiceans (which has probably not survived, but that was Marcion's designation for *Ephesians), and in 1 Cor. 5:9 Paul states, "I wrote to you in my letter not to associate with immoral men," a letter predating 1 *Corinthians, and some have proposed that it appropriately describes 2 Cor. 6:14–7:1, a fragment which seems to have been sandwiched in between 2 Cor. 6:13 and 7:2. *Hebrews is a wildcard in the Pauline collection, for though it is now clear that it is not Pauline, nor does it pretend to be Pauline, it was included in early collections of the Pauline letters (e.g. 𝔓46).

The problem of authenticity. Seven of these letters are widely regarded as authentic (*Romans, 1 Corinthians, 2 Corinthians, *Galatians, *1 Thessalonians, *Philippians, and *Philemon. Of the remain six letters (often categorized as deuteropauline letters) two are possibly not by Paul (2 *Thessalonians, *Colossians), while four are probably not by Paul (*Ephesians, *1 Timothy, *2 Timothy, and *Titus); see Keck and Furnish 1984, 16–17. The hypothesis that those "Pauline" letters not actually written by Paul were the products of a "Pauline school" has occasionally been proposed, though the differences between 2 Thessalonians, Colossians, Ephesians and the Pastorals weaken this suggestion (Schmeller 2001, 25–27, 183–253).

The Pauline Corpus

Pauline letter	Words	Stichoi	Genuineness
Romans	7,094	920	Yes
1 Corinthians	6,807	870	Yes
2 Corinthians	4,448	590	Yes
Galatians	2,220	293	Yes
Ephesians	2,425	312	No
Phillipians	1,624	208	Yes
Colossians	1,577	208	Questionable
1 Thessalonians	1,472	193	Yes
2 Thessalonians	824	106	Questionable
1 Timothy	1,568	230	No
2 Timothy	1,235	172	No
Titus	663	97	No
Philemon	328	38	Yes

The collection of the Pauline letters. There are various hypotheses to account for the collection and dissemination of the Corpus Paulinum (C. P. Anderson 1966). Even apart from the Pastorals, the Pauline letters were too long to fit comfortably on a single papyrus role and would have taken at least two rolls (Knox 1935, 42; Kenyon 1932, 61–62), though the whole corpus could easily be accommodated in a codex. The beginnings of a letter collection can perhaps be seen in Col. 4:16, where the Colossians are encouraged by "Paul" to exchange letters with the Laodiceans. This process, if continued, would probably have resulted in the gradual collection of the Pauline letters (the view of Aland 1979, 348, was based on the evidence of Pauline MSS). A second possibility is that the Pauline corpus developed from several smaller collections. The third possibility is that the collection was intentionally made by a single person, who then "published" them. A close analogy to this process can be found in Polycarp, *Phil.* 13, which indicates that *Phil.* was written as a cover letter to accompany a collection of the letters of Ignatius, which Polycarp apparently already had made, and which he was about to send to the Philippian Church at their request. Early attestations to collections of two or more Pauline letters do not provide any details regarding which letters were included (2 Pet. 3:15–16; *1 Clem.* 47:1–2; Ignatius, *Eph.* 12:2; Polycarp, *Phil.* 11:3).

The theory of Goodspeed and Knox. Goodspeed (1933, 1951) proposed that Ephesians was a pseudepigraphical Pauline letter written for the express purpose of introducing a collection of seven Pauline letters (Romans, Corinthians, Galatians, Philippians, Colossians, Thessalonians, and Philemon). Since Acts does not know of the existence of a collection of Pauline letters (or even that Paul was a frequent letter-writer), Goodspeed thought that the composition of Acts, ca. 90 C.E., was the *terminus a quo* for the Pauline letter collection. Knox (1942, 53–73) proposed that Marcion's Pauline corpus could have been derived from the kind of collection proposed by Goodspeed, since Marcion used the designation "Laodiceans" for Ephesians, in the following order, including the number of stichoi or lines in each letter (Tertullian, *Adv. Marc.* 5.1.9; 5.21.1): Galatians (293), Corinthians (1,460), Romans (920), Thessalonians (299), Laodiceans (312), Colossians (208), Philippians (208), Philemon (38). Knox has an elaborate explanation for how Marcion's collection occupied two roles and was copied backwards to approximate the order of the collection proposed by Goodspeed. Buck (1949, 57) objects to the view of Goodspeed and Knox based on the fact that there is no evidence that a corpus of Pauline letters headed by Ephesians ever existed. Mitton (1955), however, was in essential agreement with the theory of Goodspeed and Knox.

Early lists and manuscript evidence. After Marcion's list of the Pauline letters, the next extant list of the Pauline corpus is found in the Muratorian fragment (ca. end of the 2nd cent. C.E.): Corinthians, Ephesians, Philippians, Colossians, Galatians, Thessalonians, Romans, and Philemon. It is perhaps noteworthy that the general tendency to arrange the letters in order of decreasing length in Marcion's list plays no role whatsoever in the order preserved in the Muratorian fragment.

The only papyrus manuscript to contain a substantial collection of Pauline letters is the Chester Beatty papyrus of the Pauline letters (abbreviated as 𝔓46), a codex dating from ca. 200 C.E. 𝔓46 contains the following order of letters: Romans (beginning with 5:17), Hebrews, 1 Corinthians, 2 Corinthians, Ephesians, Galatians, Philippians, Colossians, 1 Thessalonians (concluding with 5:28); the rest of the codex is missing. Since it has been calculated that seven double-sided pages are missing (i.e., 14 pages), there has been a great deal of speculation about how the MS ended.

Among the uncial manuscripts, the order Romans, 1–2 Corinthians, Galatians, Ephesians, Philippians, Colossians, 1–2 Thessalonians, Hebrews, 1–2 Timothy, Titus, and Philemon is attested, along with an order which omits Hebrews: Romans, 1–2 Corinthians, Galatians, Ephesians, Philippians, Colossians, 1–2 Thessalonians, 1–2 Timothy, Titus, and Philemon (the present canonical order). A third order that is also found is Romans, 1–2 Corinthians, Galatians, Ephesians, Colossians, Philippians, 1–2 Thessalonians, Philemon, and Hebrews. Codex Vaticanus appears to have had the following order: Romans, 1–2 Corinthians, Galatians, Hebrews, Ephesians, Philippians, Colossians, 1–2 Thessalonians (Trobisch 1989, 29–30).

Among the minuscule MSS of the Pauline letters, there are three different arrangements of the Pauline letters (Trobisch 1989, 14–17): (1) Romans, 1–2 Corinthians, Galatians, Ephesians, Philippians, Colossians, 1–2 Thessalonians, Hebrews, 1–2 Timothy, Titus, and Philemon; (2) Romans, 1–2 Corinthians, Galatians, Ephesians, Philippians, Colossians, 1–2 Thessalonians, 1–2 Timothy, Titus, Philemon, Hebrews (the present canonical order); and (3) Romans, 1–2 Corinthians, Galatians, Ephesians, Philippians, Colossians, 1–2 Thessalonians, Hebrews, 1–2 Timothy, Philemon, Hebrews.

The theory of Trobisch. Trobisch (1989), after an exhaustive analysis of the evidence, proposes a theory that the Pauline corpus arose in several stages.

1. At the earliest stage, a group of several letters, Romans, 1 Corinthians and 2 Corinthians (and perhaps Galatians), and a second, smaller group, Philippians and 1 Thessalonians, reflect a recension created by Paul himself.

2. In the second stage, which did not involve the author, two groups of letters crystallized: (1) To Romans, 1–2 Corinthians, were added Ephesians, Hebrews, and Galatians. (2) To Philippians and 1 Thessalonians were added others, some of which are doubtful or pseudepigraphical Pauline letters: Colossians, 2 Thessalonians, 1–2 Timothy, Titus, and Philemon.

3. The third stage involves (1) the "catholic" edition of the Pauline letters, including the addition of redactional elements which universalized the letters (Ephesians, Hebrews, Romans, and 1 Corinthians), and (2) the early collection in Ephesus (Romans, 1–2 Corinthians, and Galatians).

4. The fourth stage in the 13-letter collection is the result of the combination of the early collection (Romans, 1–2 Corinthians, and Galatians) with the other collection from the second stage (Philippians, 1 Thessalonians, Colossians, 2 Thessalonians, 1–2 Timothy, and Philemon). The fifth stage is the conflation of the 13-letter collection with the "catholic" edition.

*Letters, *Literary genre, *Paul, *Rhetorical theory

———

Aland 1979; Aletti 1992; Ellis 1957; Goodspeed 1933, 1951; Keck and Furnish 1984; Kennedy 1984; Koch 1986; Reed 1993; Schmithals 1960; D. M. Smith 1988; Stanley 1992; Trobisch 1989, 1994

Pericope (plural: pericopae), a transliterated Greek word used to refer to a relatively self-contained unit of text, particularly in the Gospels.

Period, a transliterated form of the Greek word περίοδος (literally, "a way around"), refers in metrical composition to the basic self-contained unit within which there is syntactic continuity, the conclusion of which is signaled by syntactic interruption (M. L. West 1982, 5). The metrical period is analogous to the sentence or periodic sentence in prose discourse. There are several variations in the definition of a prose period in ancient sources.

*Periodic sentence

———

M. L. West 1982

Periodic sentence, a transliteration of the Greek word περίοδος, literally "a way around," for which the Latin equivalents are *ambitus, circuitus, comprehensio, continuatio,* and *circumscriptio* (Cicero, *Orator* 204), is a carefully structured sentence in which a balance created by a combination of word order and syntax takes the reader or hearer on "the way around" (περί+ὁδός) a circle and then back to the point at which he or she began (see R. D. Anderson 2000, 94–101). Aristotle defined a periodic sentence simply as "a sentence that has a beginning and end in itself and a magnitude that can be easily grasped" (*Rhetorica* 3.9.3; see the whole discussion in 3.9.1–10.10). A similar definition is found in *Rhetorica ad Herennium* 4.19.27 (LCL trans., with modifications): "A period [*continuatio*] is a dense and uninterrupted group of words expressing a complete thought." In *Rhetorica* Aristotle discusses two styles (*Rhet.* 3.9.1–3), the λέξις εἰρομένη ("continuous style"), which is ἄρρυθμος ("nonrhythmic"), and the λέξις κατεστραμμένη ("compact style"), which is εὔρυθμος ("rhythmic, euphonous"), and it is the second that consists of periods. For Aristotle, a period is the basic unit and depends on the presence of rhythm, not on a combination of cola, so a period with one or two members is consistent with his view (*Rhet.* 3.9.5 [1409b]; quoted by Ps.-Demetrius, *On Style* 34), while according to Ps.-Demetrius, the colon (closely connected with a thought) is the basic unit, and when combined with other cola makes a period (see Schenkeveld 1964, 29–31, who argues that Ps.-Demetrius has clearly misunderstood Aristotle; for other views that line up with either Aristotle or Ps.-Demetrius, see Schenkeveld 1964, 31–33). According to Ps.-Demetrius, "Now the period is a combination of members [κώλων] or phrases [κομμάτων], arranged dexterously to fit the thought to be expressed" (*On Style* 10; LCL trans.). For Ps.-Demetrius, a period consists of a complete thought. Further, Ps.-Demetrius divides periods into short periods, which consist of two cola, and long periods, which consist of four cola, though periods of one and three cola are also possible (*On Style* 16–17). Ps.-Demetrius divides periodic sentences into three types, a division not found elsewhere in ancient criticism (Kennedy 1963, 288; Schenkeveld 1984, 39–41): "There are three kinds of period: for narrative, dialogue, and oratory" (*On Style* 19). A number of period sentences occur in those parts of the NT that exhibit a more elevated style: Luke 1:1–4 (42 words); Rom. 1:1–6 (93 words); Heb. 1:1–4 (72 words); 2:2–4 (54 words); 12:18–24 (91 words); 1 Pet. 1:3–12 (179 words [3 are textually uncertain]; Windisch 1951, 52; Achtemeier 1996, 90); Eph. 1:3–14; 4:11–16.

*Period, *Periodic style

———

DNP 9.575–76; Norden 1909, 295–99

Periodic style (λέξις κατεστραμμένη, involves the organization of a relatively large number of phrases and clauses into a single unified sentence. There are several periodic sentences in the NT including Luke 1:1–4 and Heb. 1:1–4 (*BDF* §464).

*Style, *Hypotaxis

Periploi (singular: *periplous*), a transliterated Greek word meaning "voyages around, circumnavigation," a generic term referring to narratives of voyages which follow the coastline naming ports, harbors, and other features of the trip.

*Itinerary

———

Casson 1989; Frisk 1927

Peristasis catalogues or "hardship catalogues" (the Greek term *peristasis* can mean "difficult circumstances") refers to passages in the Pauline Letters that detail the hardships and sufferings experienced by Paul (Rom. 8:35; 1 Cor. 4:10–13; 2 Cor. 4:8–9; 6:4–10; 11:23–33; 12:10; Phil. 4:12). Scholars have investigated the literary models Paul may have used (Fitzgerald 1988). The combination of boasting or self-praise with a list of hardships the speaker has experienced has been connected with parallel texts in diatribes, some of Cynic origin (Betz 1972, 97–100).

*Boasting

———

Betz 1972; Ebner 1991; Fitzgerald 1988; Fridrichsen 1928, 1929; Hodgson 1983; Pobee 1985; Schrage 1974; Willert 1995.

Peroration, a transliteration of the Latin rhetorical term *peroratio,* "concluding part of a speech" (the Greek term is ἐπίλογος). The *peroratio* had two major objectives (Lausberg 1998, §431): (1) to refresh the memory by summarizing the main arguments of the speech (*recapitulatio* or ἀνακεφαλαίωσις; see Lausberg 1998, §§434–35) and (2) to influence the emotions (Lausberg 1998, §§436–39). According to Quintilian (6.1.52): "It is in the peroration, if anywhere, that we must let loose the whole torrent of our eloquence. For, if we have spoken well in the rest of our speech, we shall now have the judges on our side, and shall be in a position, now that we have emerged from the reefs and shoals, to spread all our canvas."

*Rhetorical theory

———

Lausberg 1998, §§431–42

Pesharim, a designation for a type of biblical commentary found among the Dead Sea Scrolls. The term "pesher," from the Hebrew

פשר, "commentary, interpretation," occurs just once in the OT, in Eccl. 8:1. The plural form is "pesharim" (פשרים). The Aramaic cognate "peshar" (פשר) occurs 30 times in the Aramaic parts of Daniel. In addition to referring to a particular type of biblical commentary, "pesher" or "midrash pesher" is used to refer to a certain type of nonliteral biblical interpretation (Vermes in *IDBSup* 438–41), which some have categorized as midrashic or as a subtype of *midrash (Brownlee 1951, 76). Wright regards them as "haggadic midrash" (1966, 421–22).

Qumran pesharim. At least 18 texts from Qumran are continuous pesharim; many were written after 72 B.C.E. (Steudel 1993, 241–42), all of which exist in single copies only, possibly *autographs. The pesharim are all commentaries on prophetic books and the Psalms. The Psalms were probably included because they were widely regarded in Judaism as prophetic since they were written by David the prophet; see 1QPs[a] 27.11: "All these he [David] uttered through prophecy which was given him from before the Most High" (Kugel 1990). The Qumran pesharim include six fragmentary commentaries on Isaiah (3QIsaiah Pesher=3Q4; 4QIsaiah Pesher[a]=4Q161; 4QIsaiah Pesher[b]=4Q162; 4QIsaiah Pesher[c]= 4Q163; 4QIsaiah Pesher[d]= 4Q164; 4QIsaiah Pesher[e]=4Q165); two on Hosea (4QHosea Pesher[a]=4Q166; 4QHosea Pesher[b]=4Q167); two on Micah (1QMicah Pesher=1Q14; 4QMicah Pesher=4Q168); one on Nahum (4QNahum Pesher=4Q169; see the extensive study by Doudna 2001); one on Habakkuk (1QHabakkuk Pesher=1QpHab); two on Zephaniah (1QZephaniah Pesher= 1Q15; 4QZephaniah Pesher=4Q170); one on Malachi (5QMalachi Pesher=5Q10); and three on the Psalms (4QPsalms Pesher[a]=4Q171; 4QPsalms Pesher=4Q16; 4QPsalms Pesher[b]= 4Q173).

The interpretive procedure of the pesharim. For an example of a pesharim commentary, we can cite 1QpHab 7.1–8 (trans. García Martínez 1992, 200):

> And God told Habakkuk to write what was going to happen to the last generation, but he did not let him know the end of the age. And as for what he says [Heb. 2:2]: "So that the one who reads it may run." Its interpretation [פשרו על] concerns the Teacher of Righteousness, to whom God has disclosed all the mysteries [רזים] of the words of his servants, the prophets. [Hab 2:3]: "For the vision has an appointed time, it will have an end and not fail." Its Interpretation [פשרו]: the final age will be extended and go beyond all that the prophets say, because the mysteries [רזים] of God are wonderful.

Continuous pesharim, like 1QpHab, exhibit a fixed literary structure quite different from the midrashim, consisting of a quotation of the biblical text to be interpreted, followed by the commentary, typically bridged by a "spacer" (the term of P. Alexander 1984a, 16 n. 4), which consists of various formulaic phrases such as: פשרו ("its interpretation [is]"), or פשרו עשר ("its interpretation [is] that"), or אשרו על ("its interpretation concerns"), פשר הדבר ("the phrase means"). A distinctive formal feature of the comment is the fact that it focuses on comparatively recent historical events that are presaged by the portion of Scripture cited in the lemma and are assumed to have occurred at the end of the age. The older pesharim (e.g., 4QpIsa[c] and 4QpPs[a]) are less rigid in their form, i.e., quotations from other books are used, parts of the focal book are neglected, phenomena that do not occur in late pesharim such as 4QpNah (Steudel 1992, 538). There is a striking similarity between this literary structure and petirah midrash, in which the Aramaic root פתר is substituted for פשר (Silberman 1961, 327–31; Wright 1966, 421), and since פשר could be used for dream interpretation, Silberman finds a link between the pesher technique and the dream interpretation of Daniel.

The primary purpose of the anonymous authors of the pesharim was to show that portions of the Hebrew Bible, understood as prophecies, had been fulfilled or were now being fulfilled in the history and experience of the Qumran community. The commentators regarded the biblical text as a code or "mystery" (רז) that can be understood only by divine insight, sometimes referred to as "*charismatic exegesis" (Aune 1993). This is referred to above in the phrase "the mysteries of the words of his servants, the prophets." Very similar interpretive language is applied to the visions that Daniel interpreted through divine enablement (Bruce 1959, 59–65). Bruce (1959, 9) summarizes the principles of biblical interpretation implicit in the pesharim in three points: (1) God revealed his purpose to his servants the prophets, but this revelation could not be understood until it was disclosed to the Teacher of Righteousness. (2) All the words of the prophets refer to the time of the end. (3) The time of the end has arrived.

A more extensive list of thirteen principles implied in the interpretive method of the author of 1QpHab has been proposed by Brownlee (1951, 60–62; see also Horgan 1979, 244–46):

(1) Everything the prophet wrote has a veiled, eschatological meaning. (2) Since the prophet wrote cryptically, his meaning can often be determined by a forced or abnormal construction of the biblical text. (3) The prophet's meaning may be detected through the textual or orthographic peculiarities of the text, i.e., special readings. (4) Textual variants may assist interpretation. (5) The application of the features of a verse may be determined by analogous circumstance or (6) by allegorical propriety. (7) The full meaning of the prophet may mean construing his words as having more than one meaning. (8) Sometimes the prophet veiled his meaning to such an extent that only by exploring synonyms of the original word can the meaning be uncovered. (9) Sometimes the prophet veiled his message by substituting one word for another which the interpreter can recover by rearranging the letters of a word or (10) by substituting similar letters for one or more of the letters in the word of the biblical text. (11) Sometimes the prophet's meaning can be discovered by dividing one word into two or more parts and by explaining the parts. (12) Sometimes the prophet concealed his message by an abbreviation, the "notarikon." (13) Other passages of Scripture may illuminate the meaning of the prophet.

Yet another list of six major characteristics of the pesher technique is proposed by Fishbane, for which he finds precedence in ancient Egyptian and Mesopotamian texts (1977, 101–5), as well as in the Hebrew Bible itself (1977, 105–12), thus demonstrating how ancient the phenomenon of pesher interpretation is (1977, 98–100): (1) citation and atomization (the lemma is linked to the interpretation by a variety of expressions, and the link between the text and the interpretation is established by the repetition of a key word from the lemma in the interpretation); (2) multiple interpretations (sometimes more than one meaning is given to a word or phrase; cf. 1QpHab 2.1–10); (3) paronomasia (the interpretation plays with a homonymous root in the lemma); (4) symbols (many symbols with typological significance are found); (5) notarikon (this hermeneutical technique includes such approaches as interpreting each letter, or transposing letters); (6) gematria (this technique calculates the numerical values of letters of a word).

Following Dimant (1984, 504–5), three types of pesharim can be distinguished: (1) *continuous* pesharim (i.e., verse-by-verse commentaries on entire books, e.g. 1QpHab); (2) *thematic* pesharim, a phrase coined by Stegemann 1967, 213–17; cf. Carmignac 1970, 360–61; Steudel 1994, 537–38 (i.e., quotations from various biblical books grouped around a theme, e.g., 4QpIsa^{e}, 4QFlor 1–2 i 14; 11QMelch 12, 17; on 4QFlor=4Q174, see Brooke 1985; on 4Q174 and 4Q177, see Steudel 1994); and (3) *isolated or discontinuous* pesharim; see Carmignac 1970, 360–61 (the use of one or two verses from the Hebrew Bible interpreted using the pesher method and terminology, but within the framework of a larger composition, e.g., CD 19.5–13 on Zech. 13:7; 1QS 8.13–15 on Isa. 40:3; see Brooke 1994 and Bernstein 1994 on 4Q252).

The pesharim have a clear eschatological orientation (for an argument for the term "eschatololgical midrashim," see Steudel 1992, 536; 1994), since the phrase "in the last days" occurs in them with some frequency. As Steudel (1993, 231) has pointed out, in Qumran this phrase refers to the "last period of time directly before the time of salvation" but which covers aspects of the past, present, and future. The authors of the pesharim believed that "all prophetic scripture was concerned with the fulfilment of God's purpose in the end time, and that the key to the understanding of this purpose had been granted to their Teacher" (Bruce 1959, 68). These authors read prophecy as a forecast not only of eschatological events, but also of the details of the career of the Teacher of Righteousness and the many trials that he and his followers would have to endure (Bruce 1959, 18–27).

It has been claimed that the authors of the pesharim intentionally altered the biblical text in order better to accommodate their interpretations, or selected variant textual traditions as a conscious interpretive technique (Brownlee 1951, 60–62; Stendahl 1967, 185–90; Horgan 1979, 45; Brooke 1987, 1994; Lim 1997a). Doudna (2002, 67–70) has argued that no convincing example of either practice has been pointed out, while Longenecker (1999, 25) expresses a more mediating attitude.

Is pesher or midrash-pesher a genre or interpretive method (or both)? There is a running argument over whether the Qumran commentaries constitute a literary genre, a subgenre of midrash, or an interpretive method (or perhaps a combination of form and content). As a genre or interpretive method, "pesher" or "midrash pesher" (the latter term was apparently coined in 1953 by Brownlee 1979, 25) is usually related to midrash, as the compound designation "midrash pesher" suggests (earlier, Brownlee [1951, 76] preferred to label the pesharim as "midrash"). Wright (1966, 418–22) categorized the Qumran pesharim as haggadic midrash, while K. Elliger (1953, 163–64) regarded the pesharim as a type of commentary quite different from midrash since, unlike the midrashim, the interpretation of the pesharim is not derived from the text, and compared them to dream interpretation in Daniel. Stendahl (1967, 184) regarded the pesharim as a special type of midrash, "midrash pesher," alongside the midrash halakah and the midrash haggadah. Similarly Brownlee (1979, 24) thought that the pesharim differ so significantly from the closest rabbinic counterparts that they deserve a classification of their own, and proposed (in a 1953 paper) that they be designated "midrash pesher" (1979, 24). The view of M. Black (1971, 1) that "*Midrash-pesher* is a modern invention probably best forgotten," is a critique that should itself best be forgotten. After a review of research on the scholarly definitions of "Qumran pesher," (Brooke 1979, 502) concludes:

> In sum, providing it is recognized that midrash as literary genre is now a broad enough category to require qualification in every instance as to its provenance (e.g., rabbinic, New Testament, etc.), we may conclude that the [Qumran pesher] commentaries through their combination of primary (structural) and secondary (methodological) factors are to be properly classified as *Qumran midrash.* Consequently, to use the word pesher as a generic classification in association with midrash, in anything like its translation (i.e., "interpretation") is purely tautological.

More recenty, Steudel (1992, 536; 1994) has characterized 4QFlorilegium (=4Q174 or 4QMidrEschat[a], and 4Q177 or 4QMidrEschat[b]), as "a midrash on eschatology" (*der Midrasch zur Eschatologie*), a term conveying the distinctive eschatological orientation of Qumran commentaries that are close to the pesharim.

The pesharim and the NT. The conviction that the time of the end was somehow inaugurated with the coming of Jesus pervades early Christianity. Like the authors of the Qumran pesharim, many NT authors are convinced that what was previously hidden has now been revealed (Rom. 16:25–26; Col. 1:26; Eph. 3:4–6; 1 Pet. 1:10–12; see Bruce 1959, 66–77; Seeligmann 1953, 173–75); in Rom. 16:25–26, for example, Paul speaks of "the revelation of the mystery which was kept secret for long ages but is now disclosed and through the prophetic writings is made known to all nations." Many NT scholars have used the term "pesher" or "midrash pesher" as the label for an interpretive method and/or interpretive genre used by NT authors, including Paul (Ellis 1957, 139–47; Goldsmith 1968) and Matthew (Stendahl 1967, 35, 183–202; Hay in *IDBSup* 443–44), though other argue that pesharim, strictly defined, occur nowhere in the NT (Fitzmyer 1960–61, 298–99). Ellis (1957) argues that Paul conflated proof texts, fiddled with the grammar of the biblical text, and selected variant readings from existing texts and targumim.

*Charismatic exegesis, *Midrash, *Testimony book hypothesis

P. Alexander 1984a; Bernstein 1994; Black 1971; Brooke 1979–81, 1985, 1987; Brownlee 1951, 1979; Bruce 1959; Carmignac 1964, 1969–70, 1970; Dimant 1984; Doudna 2001; K. Elliger 1953; Ellis 1957; Fishbane 1977; Fitzmyer 1960–61; Goldsmith 1968; Horgan 1979; Kugel 1990; Lim 1997a, 1997b; Perrin 1965–66; Silberman 1961; Stegemann 1967; Steudel 1992, 1993, 1994; Vermes 1975; Wright 1966

Peter, First Letter of, is generally regarded as a pseudepigraphical letter by critical scholars, but the issue of authorship remains one of the dominant concerns in recent discussions of this letter. In his discussion of the canonical status of early Christian writings, Eusebius (*Hist. eccl.* 3.25.2) locates 1 Peter among the ὁμολογούμενα, i.e., the "accepted" or "acknowledged" books. The earliest attestation of 1 Peter is 2 Pet. 3:1: "This is now the second letter that I have written to you." For a detailed list of early references to 1 Peter, see Bigg 1901, 7–15.

Title. The oldest manuscript of 1 Peter, Codex Vaticanus (**B**) has the title Πέτρου α´ ("First [letter] of Peter"), while the other old uncials, Sinaiticus (א) and Coridethi (**C**), have Πέτρου ἐπιστολή α´ ("First Letter of Peter").

The role of Silvanus. According to 1 Pet. 5:12, "I am writing [epistolary aorist] to you διὰ Silvanus." Though many have assumed that this passage indicates that the author used "Silvanus" as a secretary, Richards (2000) argues (following Grudem 1988, 24; Michaels 1988, 306; Achtemeier 1996, 351–52), though in more detail, that the formula διὰ Σιλουανοῦ ἔγραψα, widely assumed to refer either to the secretary or the letter carrier, refers only to the letter carrier (in this Richards is correct). The formula διὰ + the genitive of a proper name +

ἔγραψα or γράφω or γράφω διά τινος also occurs in Ignatius, *Smyrn.* 12:1, *Philad.* 11:2 and Polycarp, *Phil.* 16; in these passages, Richards argues that the individual mentioned in the genitive is the emissary, not the secretary. However, Richards skates over the reference in Eusebius, *Hist. eccl.* 4.23.11, where Dionysius of Corinth refers to *1 Clement* as "written to you by Clement," a passage that refers to Clement as the writer, not as the bearer of the letter (Biggs 1901, 5). Other scholars have entertained the possibility that the ambiguity of the passage can mean that Silvanus was *both* the secretary and the emissary (Biggs 1901, 5).

Language and style. The Greek of 1 Peter is generally recognized to be of a higher linguistic register than other NT books with the exception of James and Hebrews. The language of 1 Peter is not the language of ordinary speech, and the frequent occurrence of the conjunctive participle is supporting evidence for this claim (Wifstrand 1947, 175). The language of 1 Peter is neither common language nor a literary language, but rather ordinary Koine Greek as it was written by people with some education, i.e., what Wifstrand's student Rydbeck (1967) called *Fachprosa* or *Zwischenprosa.* The letter contains 1,678 words, with a vocabulary of 545 words (Morgenthaler 1958, 164). First Peter contains 62 words not found in other NT books (listed in Bigg 1902, 2). The author inserts a long periodic sentence with many conjunctive participles in 1:17–21. The occurrence of the paired contrasting correlative particles μέν and δέ, where the inclusion of μέν throws the emphasis on δέ, occurs six times (1:20; 2:4, 14; 3:18; 4:6, 14). The definite article is used more in conformity to classical style than by any other author in the NT. For Bigg (1902, 4–5), the absence of such connective particles as ἄρα, γε, ἐπει, ἐπειδή, τε, δή, που, and πως, as well as the absence of ἄν, indicates that the author is not a native Greek speaker. The quality of the Greek of 1 Peter is often used as an argument against its attribution to Simon Peter the disciple of Jesus (Bigg 1901, 5). For Selwyn (1947, 26–27), the affinities of the Greek of 1 Peter are closer to literary Greek than to the vernacular Greek of the papyri (and for this reason he regards Silvanus as the one who drafted the letter). Wifstrand (1947, 175) identifies only one popular stylistic feature in 1 Peter, the use of εἰς ἥν for ἐν ᾗ (5:12).

Genre. While 1 Peter is clearly framed as a letter (see the epistolary analysis below), that does not exhaust the generic issue. Unlike most NT letters, 1 Peter is a circular letter sent to a large but specifically defined geographical area. Early in the 20th cent., the central theme of 1 Peter was thought to be baptism (see the allusions to baptism in 1:3, 23; 2:2; 3:21), and the letter was regarded as essentially a baptismal homily or liturgy. The importance of paraenesis in the letter then encouraged scholars to regard it as a paraenetic letter (Selwyn 1947; Lohse 1953; Michaels 1987; 1988, xlv–xlix).

Unity. Some have proposed that the doxology in 4:11 ("To him belong glory and dominion forever and ever. Amen") signaled the end of an original form of 1 Peter and was followed by the epistolary ending in 5:12–13, so that the existing letter was formed by joining two originally separate parts (Leaney 1964, 240). Moule (1956–57) proposed that 1:13–4:11 constituted the first edition of the letter. The doxology in 5:11 ("To him be the dominion forever and ever. Amen"), phrased very similarly to that in 4:11, suggests that the two doxologies are used to frame a later insertion consisting of 4:12–5:11. On the other hand, doxologies occur frequently in the body of NT letters when the name of God is mentioned and perhaps for the purpose of inserting a reading pause (Rom. 1:25; 9:5; 11:36; Gal. 1:5; Eph. 3:21; 1 Tim. 1:17; Rev. 1:6). The problem of suffering is treated as a future possibility in 1:13–4:11 but as a present reality in 4:12–5:11 (see a review of the issues in Achtemeier 1996, 58–62).

Epistolary Analysis. First Peter is framed as a letter, with an epistolary prescription 1:1–2, consisting of the superscript in v. 1a ("Peter, an apostle of Jesus Christ"), an elaborate adscript in vv. 1b–2 ("To the exiles of the Dispersion in Pontus, Galatia, Cappadocia, Asia, and Bithynia," etc.), and a salutation in v. 3 ("May grace and peace be multiplied to you"). The prescript is followed by a blessing in vv. 3–12 that begins in a manner identical to the blessing found in 2 Cor. 1:3–7: "Blessed [εὐλογητός] be the God and Father of our Lord Jesus Christ." There is not much disagreement about the structure of 1 Peter. Achtemeier (1996, 73–74), whose analysis is explicitly epistolary, proposes that the body of the letter consists of three parts: (1) body opening (1:13–2:10; cf. Thurén 1990, 84–86); (2) body middle (2:11–4:11); (3) body closing (4:12–5:11). The earlier analysis of Michaels (1988, xxxvii) identifies the identical main sections: (1) greeting (1:1–2); (2) the identity of the people of God (1:3–2:10); (3) the responsibilities of the people of God (2:11–4:11); (4) the responsibilities of a church and its elders (4:12–5:11); (5) final greetings and benediction constitute the epistolary ending (5:12–14).

Rhetorical analysis. Thurén (1995, 88–183) proposes a detailed rhetorical analysis of 1 Peter: (1) *exordium* (1:1–12), which consists of an epistolary prescript (1:1–2) or general introduction, followed by a section articulating the grounds for praise (1:3–5); (2) the first part of the *argumentatio* (1:13–2:10) or the continuation of the *exordium;* (3) the central *argumentatio* or part of the body middle (2:11–3:12); (4) modifications and clarifications (3:13–4:11); (5) the final phase (4:12–5:7; cf. Thurén 1990, 157–58), where there is a *recapitulatio* of the theses of 1:3–12; (6) *recapitulatio* (5:8–14), with a body closing in v. 12 and an epistolary closing in vv. 13–14. The strength of Thurén's analysis, which differs little from Achtemeier's epistolary analysis in main outlines, is that he is not wedded to a rhetorical macroform but uses insights from both ancient and modern "rhetorics" to analyze the argument of 1 Peter.

*Letters, General

Achtemeier 1996; Bigg 1902; Brox 1986; Goppelt 1978; Grudem 1988; Kraus 2001; Leaney 1964; Lohse 1954; Richards 2000; Selwyn 1947; Thurén 1990, 1995; Wifstrand 1947

Peter, Gospel of, a fragmentary *apocryphal gospel that consists of just nine papyrus codex leaves (P. Cairo 10759), dated to the 8th or 9th cent. C.E., was discovered in the grave of a monk in 1884 in Akhmim, in Upper Egypt, containing sections numbered from 1:1 to 14:60. In addition, there is the Greek papyrus fragment P. Oxy. 2949, which contains a fragmentary version of 2:3–5a. There are two other Petrine papyrus fragments that could be from the *Gospel of Peter* (P. Oxy. 4009 and P. Oxy. 1224), but this cannot be proven. The *Gospel of Peter* is probably earlier than 150 C.E. and has been dated from 70 to 150 C.E. It is the earliest noncanonical account of Jesus. The *Gospel of Peter* is mentioned by several Christian authors of the 3d and 4th cents. C.E., including Origen, *Hom. on Matt.* 10.17; Theodoret, *On heretical fables* 2.2 ("The Nazaraeans are Jews who know Christ as a righteous man, and use the Gospel called According to Peter"); Eusebius, *Hist. eccl.* 3.3.2. The *Gospel of Peter* focuses on the death and resurrection of Jesus; it circulated in some churches in Asia Minor when a bishop named Serapion (fl. 190 C.E., the latest possible date for the *Gospel of Peter*) informed the churches in the region that the *Gospel of Peter* was not in accordance with the true teachings of the Savior (Eusebius, *Hist. eccl.* 6.12.3–6). Serapion thought that the *Gospel of Peter* had been composed by docetists, since Jesus felt no pain when he hung on the cross. However, the specific passage reads (4:1): "And they brought two criminals and crucified the Lord between them. But he himself remained silent, as if in no pain." This seems to be part of the silence motif, for silence was expected of the Suffering Servant in Isa. 53:7.

The narrative of the resurrection in the Gospel of Peter is one of the few that actually describes the event:

> [9] Early in the morning, when the Sabbath dawned, a large crowd came from Jerusalem and the surrounding regions to see the sealed tomb. But during the night before the Lord's Day dawned, while the soldiers were keeping guard by two's in each watch, a great sound came from the sky. They saw the heavens opened and two men descend shining with a great light, and approached near to the tomb. The stone which had been set on the door rolled away by itself and moved to one side, and the tomb was opened and both of the young men went in. [10] Now when these soldiers saw that, they roused the centurion and the elders (who were also there keeping watch). While they were yet telling them the things which they had seen, they saw three men come out of the tomb, two of them sustaining the other one, and a cross following after them. They saw that the heads of the two reached up to heaven, but the head of the one led by them was beyond heaven. Then they heard a voice from heaven saying, "Have you preached to those who sleep?" The answer heard from the cross was, "Yes!"

Relationship to the canonical Gospels. Most scholars think that the *Gospel of Peter* exhibits dependence on all four canonical Gospels, though that view has been vigorously disputed in recent years. One of the tests used to determine whether an early Christian writing is dependent on the canonical Gospels is to examine whether or not what appear to be allusions to the canonical Gospels reflect redactional features characteristic of Matthew or Luke or from "Special L" or "Special M," indicating dependence on those texts. Crossan (1988) has argued that the *Gospel of Peter* contains what he called a "Cross Gospel," i.e., a very early passion story that was used by all four canonical Gospels. Alternatively, the *Gospel of Peter*'s source for the passion narrative may have been the same one used by both Mark and John.

*Gospels, Apocryphal

Brown 1987; 1994, 1.1317–49; Coles, Haslam, and Parsons 1994; Crossan 1988, 1998b; Denker 1975; Mara 1973; V. H. Stanton 1901; Swete 1892

Peter, Second Letter of, is rarely studied on its own account, especially in monographs (Charles 1997). More often, it is explained in relationship to other documents, especially 1 Peter and the Letter of Jude (Bigg 1902; Kelly 1969; Bauckham 1983a; Pearson 1989; Neyrey 1993; Knight 1995; Perkins 1995; Horrell 1998). This relationship has focused on a few primary issues: Petrine authorship and pseudepigraphy, literary connections to other writings, the redactional use of Jude by 2 Peter, the theological content of 2 Pet. 3, the formation of the New Testament canon, and defining the opponents criticized in 2 Pet. 2.

Style. A comparison with Jude, on which 2 Peter is thought to depend, suggests that a change of style is a central redactional feature of 2 Peter (Thurén 1996, 338). The vocabulary of 2 Peter is unusual in that it contains the highest proportion of *hapax legomena (words occurring one time only) in the NT (57 out of a total vocabulary of 401 words in a total word count of 1,103; see Morgenthaler 1958, 164). Three words are not found in any other Greek text: ἀκατάπαστος, ἐπαιγμονή, παραφρονία (Bauckham 1983a, 136). The style of 2 Peter has been widely criticized as bombastic or pretentious (Kelly 1969, 228; N. Turner 1976, 142), and a number of scholars have identified the style of 2 Peter as Asianic (Bauckham 1983a, 137; Green 1968, 18, 41; Reicke 1964, 146–47; Thurén 1996, 340 n. 65). Watson (1988, 146), however, is less convinced: "2 Peter is not the best example of Asian style, but does possess several of its characteristics." The historical issues surrounding the composition of 2 Peter are numerous and were the focus of scholarship during the 19th and early 20th cents. (Bauckham 1988a, 3713).

Relationship to Jude. The literary character of 2 Peter often centers around its relationship to the Letter of Jude. Jude 4–13, 16–18 closely parallels 2 Pet. 2:1–18; 3:1–3. These two texts share an unusual vocabulary, order of argument, and themes. However, their styles are very different, and exact linguistic repetition is exceptionally rare. The texts are related in some manner, although several options are possible. The common earlier view was that Jude was dependent on 2 Peter (Bigg 1902, 216–24, 312–17). While some have more recently argued that the letters share a common source (Reicke 1964, 148, 189–90; Green 1987, 58–64), most scholars now agree that 2 Peter is dependent on Jude (Bauckham 1983a, 141–43; Kahmann 1989; Watson 1988, 160–87). Regardless of the exact literary relationship, the polemic of Jude and that of 2 Peter are not necessarily directed at the same audience, as Bauckham notes (1988a, 3714–16, 3724–28).

Date. The pseudepigraphic nature of 2 Peter is a central issue in dating the letter. The variety of dates assigned by scholars, 60 to 170 C.E., makes 2 Peter one of the most widely dated documents in the NT (Bauckham 1988a, 3740–42). If Petrine authorship is accepted, then the letter must be dated prior to Peter's death, which has traditionally been located in the mid-60s C.E. (Bigg 1902, 242–47; J. A. T. Robinson 1976, 149; Green 1987, 39–42). If the letter is pseudonymous, then the relationship of Jude to 2 Peter is also involved. If 2 Peter was dependent on Jude, then the earliest possible date for Jude would determine the earliest possible date for 2 Peter. However, the date of Jude is uncertain, and numerous possibilities have been suggested (Bauckham 1988b, 3812–15). It should be noted that though 2 Peter was apparently known in the middle of the 2d cent., it was not a popular text (Kasemann 1964, 174; Horrell 1998, 135). Its popularity had increased by the 5th cent., although its inclusion in the canon was seriously disputed, as Eusebius suggests (*Eccl. hist.* 3.25.14). Petrine authorship was openly rejected by prominent Christian scholars such as Origen (preserved in Eusebius, *Hist. eccl.* 6.25) and Jerome (*Ep.* 120,11). Given these issues, the majority of modern scholars locate 2 Peter in the late 1st cent. or first two decades of the 2d cent. (Bauckham 1983, 157–58; Reicke 1964, 144; Kelly 1969, 235–37; Perkins 1995, 160; Horrell 1998, 137–38; Knight 1995, 57).

Genre. More recently, the issue of the genre of 2 Peter has been raised. Second Peter is obviously in the form of a letter. It follows the pattern of letters in the ancient world (Aune 1987, 161–69): an opening consisting of sender, addressee, salutation, and wishes for health or good fortune (1:1–2); the body containing the purpose of writing and information to be conveyed (1:3–3:18a); and a conclusion using typical closing formulas (3:18b). Instead of the typical epistolary ending, 2 Peter ends with a doxology (3:18b), as does Jude (24–25).

Another form used in 2 Peter is the *farewell address or testament (Bauckham 1983a,

131–35), a record of the last words of an important person to his or her successors (J. J. Collins 1984b, 325). The author mentions his approaching death in 1:12–15 and attests to the truth of his statements in 1:16–18, common elements of the testament. In addition, the author emphasizes his authority by mentioning an earlier letter sent to this same audience in 3:1 and by enlisting the apostle Paul, whose writings have apparently attained scriptural status, on his side of the dispute against the "scoffers" in 3:15–17.

Analysis. The body of the letter can be outlined in this manner: virtues and promises of the godly life (1:3–11); purpose of writing as a testament and a prophecy (1:12–21); condemnation of false teachers (2:1–22); encouragement to persevere (3:1–18a).

Constituent literary forms. A variety of literary forms and techniques is found in 2 Peter. One form that has received some attention is the catalog of virtues in 2 Pet. 1:5–7. These verses have been compared to similar lists in the New Testament and in the Hellenistic world (Easton 1932; Neyrey 1993, 154–55; J. D. Charles 1997). The text is clearly in the form of *sorites,* a rhetorical device that consists of placing items in a list that ascend to a climax (Fischel 1973, 119; Bauckham 1988a, 3735), but also has precedents in Jewish literature of the same period (Swanson 2000, 57–61). In addition, Danker has argued that this passage is part of a larger unit (1:3–11) that resembles imperial and civic decrees (1978), while Watson characterizes it as a homily (1988, 96–101).

Pseudepigraphy. Second Peter is widely considered a clear example of *pseudepigraphy, i.e., the author has assumed the name of "Peter" as the one from whom the work originated (Käsemann 1964, 169; Kelly 1969, 235–37; Bauckham 1988a, 3719–24, 3736–40). A few scholars argue against pseudonymity, including Bigg (1902, 242), Green (1968, 13–39), Guthrie (1970, 840), and Marín (1975). In general, reasons for using a pseudonym are varied and uncertain (Balz 1969; Metzger 1972; Hengel 1972; Meade 1986), and no clear reason can be asserted for its use in the case of 2 Peter (Bauckham 1988a, 3736).

*Catholic Letters, *Jude, Letter of, *Peter, First Letter of

Aune 1987; Balz 1969; Bauckham 1983a, 1988a, 1988b; Bigg 1902; J. D. Charles 1997; Easton 1932; Fischel 1973; Green 1987; Guthrie 1970; Hengel 1972; Horrell 1998; Kahmann 1989; Käsemann 1964; Kelly 1969; Knight 1995; Marín 1975; Meade 1986; Metzger 1972; Neyrey 1993; Pearson 1989; Perkins 1995; Reicke 1964; Thurén 1996; N. Turner 1976; Watson 1988

STEVEN SCHWEITZER

Philemon, Letter to, widely regarded as an authentic Pauline letter, Philemon is distinctive in two respects: it is the shortest of Paul's letters and is the only one addressed to an individual. Paul writes while in prison (vv. 1, 9), and Philemon is one of four prison letters of Paul (see also *Philippians, *Colossians, *Ephesians), perhaps written during Paul's period of house arrest in Rome from ca. 61–63 C.E.

Epistolary analysis. Philemon is a letter of mediation or intercession in the sense that one person is making a request of another regarding a third party (Stowers 1986, 153–65). In this case, Paul is making a request of Philemon on behalf of Onesimus. Kim (1972, 124) treats Philemon as a Greek letter of recommendation, with the body of the request in vv. 8–17, though he admits that it does not exhibit the same form and structure as papyrus letters of recommendation. Analysis: (1) The prescription (vv. 1–3) consists of a superscription naming both Paul and Timothy as coauthors (v. 1a), the adscription to Philemon, Apphis, and Archippus (vv. 1b–2), and a salutation (v. 3). (2) The thanksgiving period (vv. 4–7) functions as a **prooimion* introducing the themes of "love" in vv. 5, 7 (ἀγάπη; cf. ἀδελφὸν ἀγαπητόν, "beloved brother" in v. 16), "fellowship" in v. 6 (κοινωνία, cf. κοινωνός, "partner" in v. 17), and "refresh the heart" in v. 7 (ἀναπαύειν τὰ σπλάγχνα, note the identical expression in v. 20). (3) The body of the letter is a plea on behalf of Onesimus (vv. 8–21). (4) The epistolary closing includes an autograph (v. 19), a request for hospitality (v. 22), secondary greetings (vv. 23–24), and a grace benediction (v. 25).

Rhetorical structure. While the request section of Philemon (vv. 8–16) has some similarities to papyrus letters of petition, its structure and argument are generally thought to follow the conventions of deliberative rhetoric (Church 1978; Hock 1995, 75). Philemon is somewhat unusual among the Pauline letters in that it is dominated by one basic issue: whether or not Paul can convince Philemon to take Onesimus back, not simply as a returned runaway slave, but as a Christian brother. This simple *rhetorical situation lends itself nicely to analysis as deliberative rhetoric. Philemon consists of five parts (Church 1978, 21–31; Aune 1987, 211): (1) Prescript (vv. 1–3). (2) *Exordium* or introduction

(vv. 4–7). This is also a thanksgiving in which Paul accomplishes three things: (a) he praises Philemon, establishing goodwill between them; (b) he stresses the particular qualities of Philemon on which the outcome depends (i.e., his ἀγάπη); and (c) he alludes to details that are woven into the main section and the peroration of the letter, including: (i) love (vv. 5, 7, 9), (ii) "good" (vv. 6, 14), (iii) "fellowship" (vv. 6, 17), (iv) "heart" (vv. 7, 12, 20). (3) The proof (vv. 8–16). In vv. 8–14, in the form of an elaborate request (White 1971a, 35–36), Paul waives his authority (vv. 8–9a), relying on Philemon's willing compliance with his request to receive Onesimus back as a brother. (4) Peroration or concluding summary (vv. 17–22). Here Paul restates his request (v. 17), amplifies his argument (vv. 18–19), puts the recipient in an emotional frame of mind, using *pathos (v. 20), and secures the recipient's favor (vv. 21–22). (5) Postscript (vv. 23–25).

Paul's epistolary thanksgivings (here vv. 4–7) usually function to signal the main themes of his letters. Philemon 4–7 doubles as a **captatio benevolentiae* (an **exordium* securing the goodwill of the recipient). By praising Philemon, Paul establishes mutual goodwill and stresses the positive qualities of Philemon to which he can later appeal (e.g., Philemon's love, which refreshes the hearts of the saints). Using an emotional appeal in vv. 8–10, Paul claims that though he has the status appropriate for commanding Philemon, he chooses instead to appeal to his Christian love. He proposes that it is advantageous for Philemon to be reconciled to Onesimus using a pun. The Roman surname "Onesimus" (a common name for slaves in antiquity), based on the Greek adjective ὀνήσιμος, meaning "profitable, useful," is used as a play on words when Paul refers to Onesimus "once so useless [ἄχρηστον] to you, but now useful [εὔχρηστον] indeed both to you and to me" (v. 11). In vv. 12–14, Paul appeals to the honor of Philemon. In the peroration, he reiterates his request (v. 17), amplifies it (vv. 18–19), appeals to Philemon's emotions (v. 20), and secures his favor (vv. 21–22).

Chiastic structure? Chiastic arrangements have been proposed for Philemon by various scholars, including Lund (1942, 219) and Welch. Welch (1981, 225–26) identifies 20 units of text chiastically arranged with J (v. 14) and J' (v. 15) as a pair of units (which Welch calls "central comments") at the center of this chiastic structure, which is problematic because of its complexity. Heil (2001) proposes a chiastic structure of Philemon that not only indicates a balanced formal structure but also reveals "more precisely the purpose and meaning of this shortest and subtlest of Paul's letters" (Heil 2001, 178). For Heil, chiasm is a hermeneutical key to unlock the meaning of texts that otherwise seem obscure. He argues that there are nine identifiable units in Philemon forming an A B C D E D' C' B' A' pattern: A (vv. 1–3), B (vv. 4–7), C (vv. 8–10), D (vv. 11–13), E (v. 14), D' (vv. 15–17), C' (vv. 18–19), B' (vv. 20–22), A' (vv. 23–25). Heil regards v. 14 as the "central and pivotal point" of the chiastic structure (Heil 2001, 188, 198, 205): "but without your [i.e., Philemon's] consent, I resolved to do nothing, so that your good might not be as under compulsion but rather under benevolence." This passage, claims Heil (2001, 198) refers to all the preceding units (A through D), and also contains key parallels to other units (though some of these parallels seem trivial, e.g., ἵνα-clauses in v. 14 (E) as well as in v. 13 (D) and v. 15 (D'). It is striking that Welch (1981, 225–26) identifies vv. 14–15 as the center of the chiasm, very similar to Heil's analysis.

Reconstructing the story. Philemon was a Christian household head who lived in Colossae, since Paul's companion Tychicus had carried a letter from Paul to the Colossians and "with him comes Onesimus" (Col. 4:7–9). Since the time of John Chrysostom (Kümmel 1975, 348; Petersen 1987, 67; Dunn 1996, 302–3), the most common reconstruction of the situation lying behind the letter has been that the slave Onesimus, owned by Philemon, a Christian, ran away after stealing some money and valuables from his master. The fugitive slave, who was not a Christian, came into contact with Paul while Paul is in prison and became a convert to Christianity. Paul then sent him back to his master, along with a letter (canonical Philemon), pleading with Philemon to take his slave back, "no longer as a slave but . . . a beloved brother" (v. 16). There is no evidence whether or not Paul's pleading had the desired effect. Some dispute that Onesimus was in fact a slave, since the only evidence is v. 16 ("no longer as a slave"), and here "slave" could be understood metaphorically, describing levels of warmth with which Philemon might receive Onesimus (Callahan 1996, 10); this is unpersuasive. Though Onesimus very probably had been a slave, it is not probable that he had left his master illegally, for Paul does not refer to Onesimus as a runaway. It was a very serious criminal offense in the ancient world for a slave to run away from a master (including possibility of punishment by execution, Wilson 1997, 289), and there were legal terms for such a fugitive, but no such terms nor verbs of flight occur in the letter (Callahan 1996, 5; Fitzmyer 2001, 17–18). Why then did Paul write a conciliatory letter on behalf of Onesimus? Perhaps Onesimus had quarreled with Philemon and had gone to Paul—a friend of his master (*amicus domini*)—since, according to Roman law, a slave seeking a friend of his or her master is not considered a fugitive (Barclay 1997, 101; Fitzmyer 2001, 17–18).

Historical parallel. Strikingly similar to Paul's letter to Philemon is Pliny's letter to Sabinianus, written on behalf of an alienated freedman (*Ep.* 9.21; LCL trans.):

> The freedman of yours with whom you said you were angry has been with me, flung himself at my feet, and clung to me as if I were you. He begged my help with many tears, though he left a good deal unsaid; in short, he convinced me of his genuine penitence. I believe he has reformed, because he realizes he did wrong. You are angry, I know, and I know too that your anger was deserved, but mercy wins most praise when there was just cause for anger. You loved the man once, and I hope you will love him again, but it is sufficient for the moment if you allow yourself to be appeased. You can always be angry again if he deserves it, and will have more excuse if you were once placated. Make some concession to his youth, his tears, and your own kind heart, and do not torment him or yourself any longer—anger can only be a torment to your gentle self.
>
> I'm afraid you will think I am using pressure, not persuasion, if I add my prayers to his—but this is what I shall do, and all the more freely and fully because I have given the man a very severe scolding and warned him firmly that I will never make such a request again. This was because he deserved a fright, and is not intended for your ears; for maybe I *shall* make another request and obtain it, as long as it is nothing unsuitable for me to ask and you to grant.

Barclay 1997; Callahan 1997; Church 1978; Dunn 1996; Fitzmyer 2001; Heil 2001; Hock 1995; Kim 1972; Lund 1942; Nordling 1997; Petersen 1985; Welch 1981; J. L. White 1971a; A. Wilson 1997

Philippians, Letter to the, is undoubtedly a genuine letter of Paul written from prison (1:7, 13, 17), one of a group of four prison letters attributed to him (see *Philemon, *Colossians, *Ephesians). Philippi was a city in Macedonia that Paul evangelized on his "second" missionary journey (Acts 16) in ca. 49–50 C.E. Since several trips from Paul's undisclosed location to Philippi in the past or future are mentioned (2:19–24, 25–30; 4:18), the imprisonment in question may not be either of the two lengthiest ones at Caesarea (Acts 23:33–26:32) or Rome (28:16–31), but possibly one that occurred during his stay in Ephesus (since he speaks of many imprisonments in 2 Cor. 11:23). If Philippians was written from Ephesus, a ten-day journey from Philippi, it can be dated ca. 56 C.E. The letter was written in response to a gift the Philippians gave Paul through Epaphroditus, who had fallen ill and almost died either before he reached Paul or shortly thereafter.

Purpose. Throughout the letter Paul mentions pressures, suffering, and conflicts with which the Philippians are faced (1:28–30), and he warns them against Judaizers (3:2) as well as against Christians who are "enemies of the cross of Christ" and behave in a worldly manner (3:18–19). He even alludes to a rift between two Christian women, Euodia and Syntyche (4:2–3). Paul himself had been attacked and put in prison in Philippi (Acts 15:19–40), just as he is now in prison again elsewhere. The Philippians were witnesses to the conflicts Paul experienced (1:30) and know about his struggle. He is able to appeal to them on the basis of his own example to resist such internal and external pressures. There is no agreement on identifying the central theme of Philippians, and several themes pervade the letter, e.g., joy or rejoicing (1:18; 2:17, 18, 19, 25, 28, 29; 3:1; 4:1, 4), love (1:9; 2:1; 4:1), unity (1:27; 3:15; 4:2), and suffering (1:14, 17; 3:8, 12).

The problem of unity. Philippians is regarded as a single unified letter by a number of critical scholars (Jewett 1970; Kümmel 1975, 332–35; Lindemann 1979, 23–25; Garland 1985; Fitzgerald 1996, 321). A number of themes that pervade the letter, including elements of the friendship topos, suggest the unity of the letter. The abrupt introduction of invective in 3:2–19 is not so strange, but is a natural antithesis to praising one's friends.

The various partition theories that have been applied to Philippians are based on several problematic features found in the letter: (1) The radical shift in tone in 3:2 (Kümmel 1975, 333). (2) The fact that 3:1 fits together well with 4:4, making the intervening material from 3:2 through 4:3 appear to be a later *interpolation. (3) The inclusion of travel plans, normally part of the epistolary ending, at a midpoint in the letter (Phil. 2:25–30). (4) The unusual inclusion of Paul's expression of gratitude toward the end of the letter rather than the beginning in 4:10–20 (Osiek 2000, 16). (5) The striking change in the role of Ephaphroditus between 2:25–30 and 4:18. (6) Paul's awkward reference to "writing the same things" in 3:1 (R. P. Martin 1987, 38). (7) The term "finally" occurring twice (3:1; 4:8). (8) Paul abruptly addressing a person not previously mentioned or named in 4:3 with the phrase "I ask you, true fellow-worker to help these women." (9) Polycarp's letter to the Philippians (3:2), in which he reminds the church that "when he [Paul] was among you in the presence of the people of that time, taught accurately and steadfastly the word of truth, and also when he was absent wrote letters [ἐπιστολάς] to you, from the study of which you will be able to build yourselves up into the faith given you." The use of the plural "letters" (ἐπιστολάς) suggests that Polycarp knew that Paul had written more than one letter to the Philippians (Sellew 1994, 23–27).

Because of these factors, Philippians has sometimes been regarded as a composite of two or three letters (Rathjen 1959–60; Koester 1982, 2.132; Sellew 1994, 17 n. 1), or in Bornkamm's view a collection of Pauline letters (1962b). Three letters combined in Philippians have been identified as follows (e.g., Bornkamm 1962b, 194–95): Letter 1 (or A), a letter of thanks including a receipt for a monetary gift, stripped of its epistolary opening and closing (4:10–20); Letter 2 (or B), surviving largely intact (1:1–3:1; 4:4–9, 21–23); Letter 3 (or C) a *Kampfbrief* or polemical letter (3:2–4:3). More recently, rhetorical criticism has been used by a number of scholars to argue for the compositional unity of the letter (Watson 1988; Garland 1985; Brucker 1997, 280–300).

Constituent literary forms. The so-called Christ-hymn in Phil. 2:6–11 (see *Hymns), has been one of the most discussed texts in Philippians (for a detailed survey of research, see Deichgräber 1967, 118–33; R. P. Martin 1983).

Epistolary analysis. Philippians has been categorized as a hortatory letter of friendship Paul sent to a community that had helped him financially (L. M. White 1990; *ADB* 5.320; Fitzgerald 1996, 107–60), though this does not help to discover its structure, and it has also been compared to "family letters" (L. Alexander 1989). The inclusion of features of the friendship topos in Philippians support this view (Malherbe 2000, 180–81): expressions of a desire to see the addressees (Phil. 2:24), circumstances responsible for the delay (Phil. 2:23), the sending of emissaries (Phil. 2:19–25), the description of his converts as a "crown of boasting" (Phil. 2:16).

The letter opening consists of the three-part prescript mentioning the senders, Paul and Timothy, who are defined as "servants of Jesus Christ" (1:1a), the recipients, "to all the saints in Christ Jesus who are at Philippi, with the bishops and deacons" (1:1b), and the salutation: "Grace to you and peace from God our Father and the Lord Jesus Christ" (1:2). It is a mistake to regard the prescript as part of the *exordium* as some suggest (Watson 1997, 409–11). A relatively lengthy thanksgiving period follows (1:3–11), introduced by the formulaic "I thank my God in all my remembrance of you" (v. 3). This thanksgiving period also functions as an *exordium*, not only in the sense that it seeks the attention, receptivity, and goodwill of the recipients, but also in the sense that it contains themes that will be picked up and developed in the body of the letter. Paul mentions the fact that he is in prison by referring to "my bonds" (τὰ δεσμά μου) in v. 7, and three more times in vv. 13, 14, 17. The theme of "joy" (χαρά) in v. 4 is repeated four more times throughout the letter (1:25; 2:2, 29; 4:1).

The letter closing is found in Phil. 4:21–23 and consists of greetings (v. 21a), secondary greetings (vv. 21b–22), and a concluding grace benediction (v. 23).

There is disagreement about the structure of the letter. Hawthorne (1983, xlviii) maintains that there is no logical progression in the letter, but that the subject matter changes abruptly. The body of the letter extends from 1:13 through 4:20 and consists of several sections: (a) Paul's mention of the effects of his imprisonment on the progress of the gospel (1:12–26), (b) exhortations to the church (1:27–2:18), (d) a discussion of the emissaries Paul sends to Philippi (2:19–30), (d) a warning against opponents of the gospel (3:1–21), (e) concluding exhortations (4:1–9) and (f) a thank-you note (4:10–20). The letter concludes with an epistolary ending including secondary greetings (4:21–22) and a typical Pauline grace benediction.

Rhetorical analysis. Philippians has been categorized by some as *epideictic (Kennedy 1984, 77), while others argue that its primary rhetorical function is *deliberative (Watson 1988, 59; D. A. Black 1995, 16, 49). This lack of consensus raises general questions about the legitimacy of applying Greek rhetorical categories to the Pauline letters (Aune 1987, 203; see *rhetorical criticism). Watson (1988, 1997) uses rhetorical criticism to argue for the unity of Philippians, even suggesting that "the use of rhetorical conventions in the letters of Paul is pervasive" (Watson 1997, 403). Wuellner (1990, 117) essentially agrees, since he thinks it appropriate to subordinate epistolography to rhetoric. Watson, who construes Philippians as belonging to the deliberative genre, proposes the following rhetorical outline, which he thinks indicates the unity of the letter:

1. Epistolary prescript (1:1–2)
2. *Exordium* (1:3–26)
3. *Narratio* (1:27–30)
4. *Probatio* (2:1–3:21)
   a. First development (2:1–11)
   b. Second development (2:12–18)
   c. *Digressio* (2:19–30)
   d. Third development (3:1–21)
5. *Peroratio* (4:1–20)
   a. *Repetitio* (4:1–9)
   b. *Adfectus* (4:10–20)
6. Epistolary postscript (4:21–23)

A competing rhetorical analysis of Philippians has been proposed by Brucker (1997, 290–300), who also understands the work as basically symbouleutic or deliberative, and it reveals some striking contrasts:

1. Epistolary prescript (1:1–2)
2. *Exordium* / προοίμιον (1:3–11)
3. *Narratio* / διήγησις (1:12–26)
4. *Propositio* / πρόθεσις (1:27–30)
5. *Probatio* / πίστις (2:1–3:21)
   a. Excursus (2:19–30)
   b. *Exordium* (3:2–4a)
   c. *Narratio* (3:4b–7)
   d. *Propositio* (3:8–11)
   e. *Probatio* (3:12–14)
   f. *Refutatio* (3:15–16)
   g. *Peroratio* (3:17–21)
6. *Peroratio* (4:1–20)
7. Epistolary postscript (4:21–23)

In their analyses, Watson and Brucker agree on the extent of the *probatio* (2:1–3:21), on the digression or excursus in 2:19–30, and on the *peroratio* (4:1–20). Brucker seems not to have noticed that his construal of 3:2–21 as a mini-deliberative speech supports a partition hypothesis of Philippians. However, Watson and Brucker disagree sharply on the extent of the *exordium* and the *narratio*. On the face of it, this kind of disagreement is puzzling. Watson has identified a more defensible *exordium* (1:3–26) than Brucker (1:3–11). Further, neither 1:27–30 (Watson), nor 1:12–26 (Brucker) qualify as a *narratio* (which, after all, is characteristic primarily of juridical rhetoric, where the facts of the case must be established).

Chiastic analyses. Welch (1981, 226) and Thomson (1995, 25) do not find any macrochiastic structures, i.e., *chiasmus in larger textual units or even entire books, in Philippians, but for different reasons. Welch does not find them and Thomson is skeptical of the category. Two proposals for finding macrochiastic patterns in Philippians are the studies of Wick (1994) and Luter and Lee (1995). Wick (1994) analyzes the structure of Philippians into a series of parallel paragraphs:

A (1:12–26)=A' (3:1–16)
B (1:27–30)=B' (3:17–21)
C (2:1–11)=C' (4:1–3)
D (2:12–18)=D' (4:4–9)
E (2:19–30)=E' (4:10–20)

The analysis of Luter and Lee (1995) finds a more conventional macrochiastic arrangement, with the focus on 2:17–3:1a:

(1:1–2) Opening greetings
  A (1:3–11) Prologue: Partnership in the gospel
    B (1:12–26) Comfort (with example)
      C (1:27–2:4) Challenge
        D (2:5–16) Example / action
          E (2:17–3:1a) Midpoint: Caring models of gospel partnership
        D' (3:1b–21) Example / action
      C' (4:1–5) Challenge
    B' (4:6–9) Comfort / example
  A' (4:10–20) Epilogue
(4:21–23) Closing greetings

What is perhaps most striking in comparing these analyses is that, with the exception of Phil. 4:10–20, no textual units have the same content or extent. Since the identification of constituent textual units should be based on objective criteria found in the text itself, the widespread disagreement between Wick on the one hand and Luter and Lee on the other suggests that one or the other, perhaps both, have manipulated the data to fit a parallel or chiastic model.

*Pauline Letters

L. Alexander 1989; D. A. Black 1995; Bloomquist 1993; Bornkamm 1962b; Dalton 1979; Debanné 2002; Fitzgerald 1996; Garland 1985; Gnilka 1971b; Hawthorne 1983; Jewett 1970; Lindemann 1979; Luter and Lee 1995; Martin 1983; O'Brien 1974–75; 1977, 19–46; Osiek 2000; Rathjen 1959–60; Reed 1993, 1996; R. Russell 1982; Schenk 1984; Sellew

Synopsis of Rhetorical Analyses of Philippians

Arrangement	**D. A. Black 1995, 46–49 Deliberative**	**Watson 1997 Deliberative**	**Brucker 1997 Deliberative**
Epistolary prescript	1:1–2	1:1–2	1:1–2
Exordium	1:3–11	1:3–26	1:3–11
Narratio	1:12–26	1:27–30	1:12–26
Propositio			1:27–30
Argumentatio or Probatio	1:27–3:21	2:1–3:21	2:1–3:21
Excursus			2:19–30
Exordium			3:2–4a
Narratio			3:4b–7
Propositio	1:27–30		3:8–11
Probatio	2:1–30		3:12–14
Refutatio	3:1–21		3:15–16
Peroratio			3:17–21
Peroratio	4:1–9	4:1–20	4:1–20
Narratio	4:10–20		
Epistolary postscript	4:21–23	4:21–23	4:21–23

1994; Snyman 1993; Swift 1984; Watson 1988, 1997; Wick 1994; Witherington 1994; Wuellner 1990

Philo of Alexandria (ca. 20 B.C.E.–50 C.E.), a prolific Jewish biblical interpreter and philosopher from Alexandria, whose works have been preserved by Christians. The only firm date for his life is his participation in an embassy to Rome to the emperor Gaius, on behalf of the Jewish community in Alexandria in 39–40 C.E., narrated in his *De legatione ad Gaium.* Alexandria was home to the largest Jewish population outside Palestine, and Philo was a member of one of its more prominent families. Combining a Hellenistic education with a Jewish upbringing, Philo was strongly influenced by Middle Platonism (Dillon 1977, 139–83), as well as Stoicism, which he used to facilitate his exegesis of the Pentateuch. He was widely read in Greek literature and quotes 54 Greek authors in his works (Sandmel 1979, 15). Philo wrote a complex form of Koine Greek, and since he knew little or no Hebrew, his knowledge of the biblical text was based primarily on the Greek *Septuagint.

Rhetoric. Alexandria was one of the greatest literary and cultural centers in the Greco-Roman world, typified by the institution of the Alexandrian *library called the Museion (R. W. Smith 1974), and Philo had a first-class Hellenistic education involving training in rhetoric and literature (Manuel Alexandre 1999, 87–91). Philo's rhetorical skills are evident in his eulogistic biographical narrative *De vita Mosis,* a form of *epideictic narrative (for the following, see Manuel Alexandre 1999, 109–14). The two books of *De vita Mosis* have a five-part rhetorical structure: (1) *Exordium* (1.1–4). (2) *Narratio* (1.5–333), which basically presents Moses as the ideal king and includes the following sections: (a) birth and education (5–33), (b) Moses' attempts to help the suffering of the Jews in Egypt (34–46), (c) Moses' flight, marriage, and life as a shepherd (47–70), (d) Moses' call by God and return to Egypt (71–147), (e) his election as a sovereign ruler based on his virtue, nobility, humility, and wisdom (148–62), (f) the 40-year period in the wilderness (163–318), (g) the request by the two tribes and Moses' nouthetic discourse (319–333). (3) *Transitio* (1.334–2.7). (4) *Confirmatio* (2.8–247), where Philo follows a topical approach and characterizes Moses as an ideal legislator (2.8–65), high priest (2.66–186), and prophet (2.187–287). In *Quod omnis probus liber sit* ("Every Good Man Is Free"), Philo is widely thought to have used the genre of the *diatribe. (5) *Peroratio* (2.288–91).

Biblical exegesis and the allegorical method. During the last few decades, there has been a new recognition of Philo's primary role as an interpreter of Scripture, beginning with the work of Nikiprowetzky (1973, 1977). Further, it has become clear that Philo was the heir of a tradition of Jewish exegesis (Mack 1984b). While Hellenistic *allegory pervades his work (Christiansen 1969; Cazeaux 1973), Philo was a practicing Jew who refused to allegorize the ritual requirements of Jewish law. He was intolerant of those who neglected the obligations of circumcision or the observation of the Sabbath by regarding them exclusively as symbols of deeper truths (*De migratione Abrahami* 91–93). He found himself between the literalists (Shroyer 1936) and the extreme allegorists. Hay (1979–80, 45) oversimplifies the situation somewhat by referring to the fundamental hermeneutical division in Philo's day as between literalists and allegorists. The theme of "the migration of the soul" is the center of Philo's thought and dominates his exegetical works, and he regards Abraham as the paradigm of the journey toward God valid for every human person (Manuel Alexandre 1999, 94–95). This is inspired by Philo's concern for unity, harmony, and totality. The literal and allegorical interpretations of the Pentateuch are as inseparable as the body, which represented the literal meaning or τὸ ῥητόν, and soul, which represents the allegorical meaning, τὸ πρὸς διάνοιαν or τὸ συμβολικόν (*De migratione Abrahami* 93; LCL trans.): "Nay, we should look on all these outward observances as resembling the body, and their inner meanings as resembling the soul. It follows that, exactly as we have to take thought for the body, because it is the abode of the soul, so we must pay heed to the letter of the laws."

In some passages Philo appears to believe that the Torah was intentionally written in allegory (*De opificio mundi* 157; LCL trans.): "Now these are no mythical fictions, such as poets and sophists delight in, but modes of making ideas visible, bidding us resort to allegorical interpretation guided in our renderings by what lies beneath the surface."

Philo's formal exegetical procedure consists of several steps (Dillon 1983, 77–87): (1) The text to be interpreted is divided into short passages or *lemmata,* which are interpreted word by word or phrase by phrase, sometimes beginning with an overview of the meaning of the entire passage. (2) In the individual section of commentary (κεφάλαιον), first literal, then ethical, then the allegorical interpretations are given. (3) Toward the beginning of the individual section of commentary, there is criticism of previous interpreters and the solving of difficulties (ἀπορίαι) found in the text. (4) There is systematic etymologizing of proper names in the Pentateuch.

Philo's surviving writings total 49 treatises, about 75 percent of his total literary output. The surviving treatises fall into three major categories (Runia 1993, 37): (1) the *exegetical* writings: (a) the *Quaestiones in Genesim* and the *Quaestiones in Exodum* (6 treatises), (b) the Allegorial Commentary, based upon Gen. 2:1–41:24 (21 treatises), (c) the Exposition of the Law (12 treatises); (2) five *philosophical* treatises; and (3) four *historical-apologetical* treatises.

Philo and early Christianity. Philo's works were preserved and read by Christians, not Jews. He became a church father, as Runia (1993, 3) says, *honoris causa* (Jerome mentions Philo in *De viris illustribus,* a catalog of Christian writers). Philo's influence on the NT and early Christian literature beginning with Paul has been surveyed by Runia 1993. Philo has been used to illuminate the use of Platonism in Hebrews (Sowers 1965) and the term "logos" in the Gospel of John. Borgen (1965) used the designation *homily for John 6:31–58, where he identified homiletic structures similar to those in Philo (especially *Leg. alleg.* 3.162–68 and *Mut.* 253–63, with parallels in other parts of the NT, e.g., Gal. 3:6–29 and Rom. 4:1–22). The homiletic pattern Borgen describes consists of three main features: (1) the opening and closing of the homily correspond to each other; (2) there is always a main quotation from the OT some subordinate OT quotations; and (3) there is a repetition, paraphrase, or expansion of words from the text in the homily. Philo's use of allegorical exegesis, in terms both of method and content, has extensive analogies and similarities in the writings of the church fathers. Among the Christians over whom Philo had the greatest influence were Clement of Alexandria (van den Hoek 1988), Origen, Didymus the Blind, Cyril, Eusebius of Caesarea, Ambrose, and the Cappodocians.

*Allegory, *John, Gospel of

Text: Cohn and Wendland 1962; Text and translation: Colson, Whittaker, and Markus 1929–62. General studies: Manuel Alexandre 1999; Borgen 1986; Conley 1987; Dillon 1983; Hay 1979–80; Mack 1974–75, 1984a, 1984b, 1990; Radice and Runia 1988; Runia 1993, 1995; Sandmel 1979; Sowers 1965; Williamson 1970.

D. E. AUNE AND L. BAYNES

Philostratus, the name of four related Greek orators, of whom the most famous was L. Flavius Philostratus (ca. 170–245), the author of the *Life of Apollonius* and *Lives of the Sophists.* Two sets of *Imagines* or "Descriptions of Pictures," one written by a grandfather and the other by his grandson, both named Philostratus, also survive. They are all part of the rhetorical movement called the *Second Sophistic by Flavius Philostratus (*Lives of the Sophists* 1. praef.). The *Lives of the Sophists* documents the history of the First and Second Sophistic periods, naming Gorgias and Aeschines, respectively, their founders. Flavius Philostratus details the lives of the most notable *sophists down to his own period, including the lives of his distinguished teachers. The sophists were primarily teachers, often paid at public expense, who gained their greatest prestige in the 2d and 3d cents. C.E. They held as their ideal the revival of Greek religion and culture in the Roman world (see *Archaism). The *Life of Apollonius* details the life of the neo-Pythagorean philosopher Apollonius, supposedly based on the memoirs of Apollonius's disciple Damis (1.19). Philostratus was commissioned to write the work by Julia Domna, wife of the Roman emperor Septimius Severus (emperor 193–211 C.E.). Philostratus portrayed Apollonius as a favorite of the gods who stood up to tyrants (1.2, 4) and pursued wisdom even more eagerly than Pythagoras himself (1.2). The two primary aspects of Apollonius's life that Philostratus highlights are his religious reforms (i.e., 1.8–11) and his opposition to tyranny (i.e., book 8). The work seems to have as its main purpose a defense of Hellenism, not unlike the sophists' ideal (Swain 1999). Finally there are the two sets of *Imagines*, largely descriptions of paintings (see *Ekphrasis). The latter of these two authors compares painting to poetry, insofar as they both involve imagination in describing the subject's character (Prooemium 6). The earlier author stresses the realism of the paintings he describes and states that the purpose of description is to interpret and appreciate the contents of paintings (1.3).

Anderson 1986; Fairbanks 1931, 15–32; Petzke 1970; Swain 1999

ERIC STEWART

Plot is the temporal and causal arrangement of events in a story that is inseparably connected to *character. Characters are defined by the plot, and the plot becomes evident as characters act and interact. A functional definition is found in Abrams (1971, 127), who defines plot in a dramatic or narrative work as "the structure of its actions, as these are ordered and rendered toward achieving particular emotional and artistic effects."

*Character, *Literary criticism, *Narrative criticism

Abrams 1971; Culpepper 1983, 79–98; B. Richardson (ed.) 2002

Plutarch of Chaeronea, born ca. 45 C.E. in the city of Chaeronea in Boeotia, where he spent his life, was an encyclopedic scholar, Platonic philosopher (student of Ammonius), and prolific author. He produced an extensive series of paired biographies in which he compared famous Greek and Roman political and military figures (e.g., Demosthenes and Cicero, Alexander and Caesar), because of some significant similarities he perceived between the figures (Wardman 1974). Twenty-two sets of these paired lives and four separate lives survive (48 individual biographies).

He also wrote a large number of essays on a variety of religious, ethical, literary, historical, and political themes called the *Moralia* (78 treatises are extant; see the convenient list in *DNP* 9.1167–70). The Lamprias Catalogue (Sandbach 1969, 3–29) contains an incomplete list of 227 of Plutarch's works many of which have not survived. Plutarch wrote a number of essays that appear to be rhetorical exercises, including four *epideictic speeches, "On the Fortune of the Romans" (316C–326C), "On the Fortune or the Virtue of Alexander" (326D–333C and 333C–345D), in two parts, and "Were the Athenians More Famous in War or in Wisdom?" (345C–351B), the beginning and end of which are missing.

*Biography, *Comparison

Aune 1975, 1978; Betz (ed.) 1975, 1978; Hamilton 1969; Jeukens 1907; H. Martin 1997; Moles 1988; Sandbach 1969; Stadter 1989; Wardman 1974; Ziegler 1964

Poetics is traditionally understood as the theory of poetry, i.e., the system of conscious and unconscious aesthetic and technical principles that govern the production and interpretation of a literary composition. It is helpful to distinguish between primary poetics, as just defined, and secondary poetics, which involves ancient literary theory and criticism as well as the inductive reconstruction of the poetics based on the analysis of ancient literary works.

*Prosaics

Preminger 1965, 636–39

Poetry is a term for various forms of rhythmical, metrical, and symmetrical compositions in the Greco-Roman world, early Judaism, and early Christianity (see also *Parallelism, *Prose rhythm, and *Symmetrical structure). A primary issue in the study of ancient poetics is the problem of distinguishing poetry from prose, a problem that is particularly pressing in the identification of early Christian hymns.

Hebrew poetry. Until the 1980s, it was taken for granted that Hebrew poetry consisted of parallelism and meter (Gottwald 1962). Parallelism, designated **parallelismus membrorum* (parallelism of clauses), was widely thought (since Lowth 1962; originally published in 1787) to have three primary forms: synonymous, antithetic, and synthetic (though the last type was frequently recognized as a wastebasket category). It was generally recognized that the "meter" of Hebrew poetry was based not on vowel quantity (i.e., long and short vowels), as in Greek and Latin poetics, but rather on an alternating series of stressed and unstressed syllables (Fokkelman 2001, 21–27). Beginning in the 1980s, however, a series of studies have disputed the existence of any kind of regular meter (the view of Kugel 1981, 171–203) and have demonstrated the limitations of Lowth's categories of synonymous, antithetic, and complementary parallelism (O'Connor 1980; Kugel 1981; Fokkelman 2001, 24–27). One of the most comprehensive reassessments of the phenomena of "parallelism" and "meter" is that of the aforementioned Kugel (1981), who essentially rejects the existence of meter and heavily critiques the conception of parallelism that has dominated since Lowth. After calling attention to the fact that there are no words in biblical Hebrew for "poetry" (Kugel 1981, 69), Kugel makes the point that a distinction between poetry and prose is not emic in the Hebrew Bible, but is rather a Hellenistic imposition essentially foreign to the biblical text. On the basis of a stylistic analysis of biblical Hebrew, Kugel grants that some parts of the Bible have a more elevated style, a relatively formal organization, binary sentences, a concern for terseness, and a high degree of semantic parallelism, but he does not want to delimit such examples of elevated style by calling them "poetry," since there is a continuum between "elevated" style and "ordinary" style (Kugel 1981, 85, 94–95; cf. Petersen and Richards 1992, 13, 28). Much of this apparently springs from the fact that Kugel essentially rejects the notion that the Hebrew Bible, in whole or in part, should be regarded as "literature" (Kugel 1981, 303–4; Raphael 2002), and his negative attitude toward categorizing portions of the text as "poetry" coheres with this presupposition. Kugel summarizes his views toward the end of the book (1981, 302):

> It is not this study's contention that there is no difference between what has been called "biblical poetry" and "biblical prose," nor yet that the very idea of a "biblical poetry" is all one great mistake. Its argument is rather that the concepts of poetry and prose correspond to no precise distinction in the Bible, and that their sustained use has been somewhat misleading about the nature and form of different sections of the Bible, and about the phenomenon of parallelism. Of course there is some justification in speaking of the "poem of Job" and the like. But it should now be clear that there is also some distortion and risk. Though biblical poetry and its meters have an honored place in the history of scholarship, it might be wiser to restrict the use of these terms—to speak, in more neutral (and, alas, colorless) language, of biblical Hebrew's "high" or "rhetorical" style, and to call the Bible's songs simply songs, its prayers prayers, and its speeches speeches.

While Kugel is virtually alone in denying the existence of Hebrew poetry (Petersen and Richards 1992, 14), many basically agree with his critique of existing conceptions of meter and parallelism (O'Connor 1981; Berlin 1985, 1992; Fokkelman 2001, 24–27). Kugel's view, it seems, is that poetry must be metrical (though he never states this clearly), and since biblical "poetry" is not metrical, it is not really poetry (Kugel 1984, 114); see the critique in Landy 1984 and Raphael 2002. Since Hebrew is a dead language, its actual pronunciation at any time during its long history from the earliest parts of the Hebrew Bible to the Dead Sea Scrolls is simply not known with any degree of accuracy (the vowel signs of the Masoretic Text were probably added between 500 and 700 C.E.). Further, some of the problems of parallelism are evident in the fact that different translations of the OT arrange the stichoi of ostensibly poetic sections differently (Petersen and Richard 1992, 4–5). Brucker (1997, 31–35), an NT scholar, uses Kugel's critique of parallelism to justify ignoring parallelism in the Hebrew Bible as a background for understanding the characteristics of the Christ hymns in the NT (particularly Phil. 2:6–11), appealing instead to the phenomenon of parallelism in Greek rhetoric.

It is now more appropriate to refer to three basic characteristics of Hebrew poetry: parallelism (understood in a much more complex way than earlier), rhythm, and style (Petersen and Richards 1992, 14). Fokkelman (2001, 35) is one of the few who has formulated a definition of a Hebrew poem: "A poem is the result of (on the one hand) an artistic handling of language, style and structure, and (on the other hand) applying prescribed proportions to all levels of the text, so that a controlled combination of language and number is created." Fokkelman further presents a model for the hierarchical organization of a poetic text, moving from "texture" to "composition" (1998–2001, vol. 1, p. 4):

Texture	*Composition*
6. Verses	
5. Cola	11. Poem
4. Phrases	10. Sections
3. Words	9. Stanzas
2. Syllables	8. Substanzas
1. Sounds	7. Strophes

Fokkelman makes the important point that the bicolon and tricolon (very rarely the monocolon), while they are the basic units of Hebrew poetics, are nevertheless usually part of larger poetic structures that must be recognized as essential to Hebrew poetics. This arrangement is somewhat forced, however, since "8. Substanzas" and "10. Sections," appear to be unnecessary refinements that have no objective existence in poetic texts. An example of a transparently structured poem is Ps. 114, which exhibits strikingly symmetrical features: it consists of two halves that mirror each other (vv. 1–4, 5–8), and each half can again be divided in two (vv. 1–2, 3–4 and vv. 5–6, 7–8), so that this poem has two stanzas, four strophes, eight verses, and sixteen cola (Fokkelman 1998–2001, vol. 1, p. 1).

Greek and Latin poetry. The smallest metrical unit in Greek poetry is the "foot," which is usually equal to a μέτρον or "measure." A metrical foot must consist of at least three short vowels (⏑ ⏑ ⏑), and cannot exceed three long vowels (- - -). Metrics, according to Aristotle, included vowel quantity (long and short), sound quality or timber, and pitch-variation or melody (*Poetics* 20 [1456b]), all of which together constitute euphony (Stanford 1967, 6). Strong word stress was essentially absent from Greek (Stanford 1967, 48 n. 70), which had the effect of producing a smoother line of sound in Greek (Stanford 1967, 63). By the 1st cent. C.E., quantitative distinction between vowels began to gradually disappear, a development accompanied by the replacement of the pitch accent or tonal accent with a stress accent (W. S. Allen 1974, 88–89, 106–7; L. R. Palmer 1980, 176–77), a process that was essentially completed by the 3d cent. C.E. (W. S. Allen 1974, 89). For example, the confusion between ο and ω among Greek-speakers in Egypt during the 2d cent. C.E. became increasingly common.

Before late antiquity, both Greek and Latin had a quantitative vowel system that consisted of long and short vowels. Vowels could be long or short by nature, or position; in meter a long is equivalent to two shorts. Vowels that are "long" by nature include eta and omega, most diphthongs, and all vowels followed by two or more consonants. Vowels that are "short" by nature include epsilon and omicron, while vowels which can either be "long" or "short" are alpha, iota, and upsilon. Long vowels took twice as long to pronounce as short vowels, making them analogous to musical notations in which music written in 4/4 time means that there are four beats to a measure and a quarter note gets one beat, while an eighth note gets a half beat; thus a "long" vowel is analogous to a quarter note, while a "short" vowel is analogous to an eighth note. In modern English, "long" and "short" vowels are simply different phonemes, e.g., long "a" (phonetically represented as a) occurs in such words as "far" and "father," while short "a" (phonetically represented as ɒ), occurs in such words as "date" and "made."

In Greek poetry there are three different vowel patterns, long (-), short (⏑) and anceps (x), i.e., either long or short. Various Greek meters consist of regular patterns of long and short vowels that are rhythmic and in contrast with the regular patterns of speech (see *Prose rhythm). The oldest form of Greek poetry is dactylic hexameter, used in the earliest Greek epics, the *Iliad* and the *Odyssey,* as well as the late *Sibylline Oracles.* Dactylic hexameter consists of five metrical feet per line or stichos and can be constructed from spondees, two long vowels in succession (- -); dactyls, one long followed by two short vowels in succession (- ⏑ ⏑). The obligatory caesura, or pause in the middle of the stichos, often occurs in the third measure. While there are no examples of Greek meters used in poetic portions of the NT or ECL through the end of the 2d cent., there are some examples of the use of prose rhythm. On Greek meter, see Maas 1962, West 1982, 1987. A list of the Greek names for various metrical patterns follows:

˘ ˘ ˘	Tribrach
– ˘	Trochee, Choreus
˘ –	Iambic
˘ ˘ ˘ ˘	Tetrabrach
– ˘ ˘	Dactyl
˘ ˘ –	Anapaest
– –	Spondee
˘ – ˘	Amphibrach
˘ ˘ ˘ ˘	Pentabrach
– ˘ ˘ ˘	Paeon Protos
˘ – ˘ ˘	Paeon Deuteros
˘ ˘ – ˘	Paeon Tritos
˘ ˘ ˘ –	Paeon Tetratos
˘ – –	Bacheios
– ˘ –	Cretic
– – ˘	Palimbacheios
˘ ˘ – –	Ionic ap'elassonos
– – ˘ ˘	Ionic ap'meizonos
– ˘ ˘ –	Choriambos
˘ – – ˘	Anapaest
– – –	Molossos

Early Christian poetry. The earliest Christian poetry is based on the symmetrical and repetitive principle of parallelism, with examples in Luke 1:46–55; 1:68–79; 2:29–32; 1 Tim. 3:16; 2 Tim. 2:11–13; Rev. 5:9–10; 15:3–4 (see *Hymn). Poetic composition essentially begins in Christianity with Gregory Nazianzanus (ca. 329–90), who wrote more than 17,000 verses in classical Greek meter on Christian themes, including his autobiographical poetry; Amphilochius of Iconium; and Apollinaris of Laodicea, while Latin poetry begins with Hilarius and Ambrose (C. Schneider 1954, 2.51).

Are the sayings of Jesus poetic? The view that the sayings of Jesus in the Synoptic Gospels, when translated back into Aramaic (the native language of Jesus) exhibit Aramaic or Semitic poetic form goes back to the influential work of Burney (1925). Burney argued that the sayings of Jesus exhibit the characteristics of Semitic poetry, including parallelism of lines and clauses, rhythm, and perhaps even rhyme. Burney found four types of parallelism in the Gospels (1925, 16–21): (1) synonymous, (2) antithetic, (3) synthetic or constructive, and (4) climactic. In his re-translations of portions of the Gospels from Greek into Aramaic, Burney noted that they exhibited three types of rhythmic form: (1) four-beat, (2) three-beat, and the *qina* meter (3+2), based on what Burney called "the rules for stress-accentuation in Hebrew poetry" (1925, 43–62). Burney's proposals were accepted enthusiastically but uncritically by a series of influential NT scholars, including Manson (1935, 50–56; 1949, 30–33), Jeremias (1971, 14–29), and Black (1967, 143–85). More recently, the subject seems to have been largely ignored, though a number of scholars have made interesting proposals about poetic structures and devices in the Greek texts of the Gospels (di Lella 1987; Irigoin 1991; H. B. Green 2001). Manson (1949, 31–32), following Burney (1925), gave numerous examples of synonymous and antithetic parallelism in the teachings of Jesus (in Q, Special M, and Special L). As an example of simple synonymous parallelism Manson cites Matt. 5:45:

> He makes his sun to rise on the evil and the good,
> and sends rains on the just and the unjust.

He refers to Matt. 7:17 as an example of antithetic parallelism:

> Every sound tree bears good fruit,
> but the bad tree bears evil fruit.

More elaborate forms are identified as well. Manson quotes Luke 11:9–10=Matt. 7:7–8 (Q) as an example of parallelism between two short three-line strophes:

> Ask, and it will be given you;
> seek, and you will find;
> knock and it will be opened to you.
>
> For every one who asks receives,
> and he who seeks finds,
> and to him who knocks it will be opened.

Again, following Burney (1925), Manson cites an example of step-parallelism or climactic parallelism (see *Sorites) in Mark 9:37 (1935, 52):

> Whoever receives one such child in my name receives me;
> and whoever receives me, receives not me but him who sent me.

Jeremias drew heavily on Burney, and added a fourth type of rhythmic form, a two-beat rhythm, to Burney's three types (Jeremias 1971, 20–27). Burney's view (1925, 83–84) that antithetic parallelism was particularly characteristic of the teaching of Jesus, was also accepted by Jeremias (1971, 14–20), though it is a highly dubious criterion of historicity (Meier 1991, 179), since such texts are not un-Greek and could certainly have been composed in Greek. Black (1967, 143–60) was also heavily dependent on Burney and found other characteristic features of Semitic poetry outside the sayings of Jesus in the Gospels, including in the sayings attributed to John the Baptist and the Lucan infancy hymns.

In retrospect, the proposals of these scholars appears somewhat naive and simplistic. The recent debate over the nature of Hebrew poetry has called into question the validity of earlier conceptions of "parallelism" and "meter." Confident assessments of "Aramaic poetry," for which the corpus of extant texts is extremely limited compared with Hebrew poetic texts, are extremely vulnerable. Fitzmyer (1979, 16) is critical of Black's proposals:

> The subtle shifting back and forth between the adjectives 'Aramaic' and 'Semitic' in his [Black's] discussion is revealing, for the question arises whether such formal rhetorical elements as parallelism, rhythm, rhyme, alliteration, assonance, and paronomasia are really the specific elements of *Aramaic* poetry. Such things may not be the usual features of classic Greek poetry and were studied more in connection with rhetoric in classical antiquity than with poetry, and one wonders to what extent Hellenistic poetic forms may not be operative here.

Second- to fourth-cent. Christian hymns. Metrical poetry appeared relatively late in early Christianity. The Christian *Sibylline Oracles,* often written in a defective hexameter, are among the earliest Christian metrical poetry. *Sibylline Oracles* 6 is a 28-line hymn to Christ that probably dates to the 3d cent. *Sibylline Oracles* 8, a collection of oracles written by one or more Christian authors, ca. 175 C.E., contains an acrostic poem in hexameter on judgment in lines 218–50; each line begins with a letter of the phrase ΙΗΣΟΥΣ ΧΡΕΙΣΤΟΣ ΘΕΟΥ ΥΙΟΣ ΣΩΤΗΡ ΣΤΑΥΡΟΣ, "Jesus Christ, son of God, savior, cross," a slightly expanded form of the ΙΧΘΥΣ ("fish") coded phrase.

*Hymn, *Parallelism, *Rhythmic Prose

———

Alter 1985; Berlin 1985; Black 1967, 143–86; Burney 1925; Gottwald 1962; H. B. Green 2001; Horgan and Kobelski 1989; Irigoin 1991; D. R. Jones 1968; Kugel 1981, 1984; Landy 1984; Maas 1962; Manson 1935, 1949; O'Connor 1980; Petersen and Richards 1992; Raphael 2002; W. G. E. Watson 1984, 1994; West 1982, 1987

Point of view is a literary critical term used in several ways. From the perspective of descriptive narratology (which rejects the concept of an implied author), point of view or "focalization" is determined by whether the story is narrated from the inside (e.g., by the main character or an omniscient author) or the outside (e.g., by a minor character or the author as an observer); see Genette 1980, 186–90; Culpepper 1983, 20–34.

S. D. Moore's definition of "point of view" is formulated by a critic in the context of literary interpretation (1989, 181): Point of view is "the rhetorical activity of an author as he or she attempts, from a position within some socially shared system of assumptions and convictions, to impose a story-world upon an audience by the manipulation of narrative perspective." "Point of view," then, refers to the norms and values that the implied author establishes for understanding the story, i.e., how readers will evaluate the characters, events, and settings that make up the story (Powell 1990, 23–25). Tovey (1997) analyzes the point of view of the implied author in the Fourth Gospel.

*Implied author, *Implied reader, *Literary criticism, *Narrator

———

Booth 1983; Culpepper 1983, 20–34; Petersen 1978b; Powell 1990, 1995; Tovey 1997

Polycarp, *Letter to the Philippians* A letter written by Polycarp (ca. 70–156 C.E.), bishop of Smyrna, to the Christian church at Philippi, ca. 117–120 C.E. According to *Phil.* 13:1, it is unclear whether or not Ignatius is already dead (the date of his martyrdom is ca. 117 C.E.), which suggests that Polycarp wrote about that year. According to Irenaeus (*Adv. haer.* 3.3.4), as a young man he had met Polycarp, who he claims had been instructed by apostles and had been appointed bishop of Smyrna by apostles (Tertullian, *De praescr. haer.* 32.2, claims that Polycarp was appointed bishop of Smyrna by the apostle John). He also refers to an episode in which Polycarp met Marcion and called him the firstborn of Satan to his face (the phrase "firstborn of Satan" is also found in *Phil.* 8:1). Irenaeus also mentioned the letter that Polycarp had written to the Philippians. In a letter of Irenaeus to Florinus preserved by Eusebius (*Hist. eccl.* 5.20.5–8), he also mentions hearing the discourses of Polycarp when he was a young boy and refers to the letters that Polycarp wrote to various churches and groups of believers. Three epistolary documents relating to Polycarp have survived. Two of these are a letter addressed to Polycarp by *Ignatius of Antioch and a letter from the church of Smyrna to the church of Philomelium narrating the execution of Polycarp, ca. 156 C.E., traditionally entitled the **Martyrdom of Polycarp.* The letter was written as a cover letter to accompany a collection of the letters of Ignatius, which Polycarp apparently already had, which he was about to send to the Philippian church at their request. In addition, there is a *Life of Polycarp* which cannot have originated earlier than the 3d cent. C.E. (Lightfoot 1889–90, part 2, vol. 3.488–506).

Texts and translations. The complete text of Polycarp, *Philippians,* originally written in Greek, is preserved in nine late and defective Greek manuscripts all derived from the same archetype (each contains only Polycarp, *Phil.* 1-9, followed immediately by a defective form of the *Epistle of Barnabas,* which begins with 5:8), two long quotations in Eusebius which contains chapters 9–13 (*Hist. eccl.* 3.36.13–15), and nine manuscripts of a Latin translation, based on a Greek text which is generally superior to the nine defective Greek witnesses to chapters 1–9 mentioned above. Irenaeus mentions that Polycarp wrote several letters (*Adv. haer.* 5.33.4), though this letter alone survives. The Greek text is available in the edition of Lindemann and Paulsen (1992), which contains the Funk-Bihlmeyer text (Bihlmeyer 1956) with a German translation. The Greek text with an English translation is available in Lake (1912, 1.279–301), while English translations are available in Glimm, Marique, and Walsh (1947, 131–43), and a more recent translation in Holmes (1989, 119–34; a revision of Lightfoot and Harmer).

Integrity. Harrison (1936) argued that the conflict between chapters 9 and 13 of *Phil.* has never been satisfactorily harmonized, and proposed that the letter was in fact a combination of two letters written by Polycarp: Letter 1 consisted of chapter 13, and possibly 14 (written ca. 115 C.E., while Ignatius was still living), and was essentially a cover letter to accompany a collection of the letters of Ignatius requested by the Philippians, while Letter 2 consisted of chapters 1–12 (written ca. 135), written for the purpose of warning the Philippians about the heresy of Marcion. Barnard (1966, 31–39), while essentially agreeing with Harrison's thesis of two letters, and Harrison's dating of Letter 1, argued that Letter 2 was written not later than 120 C.E. More recently a number of scholars have argued for the unity of the letter (Schoedel 1967; Paulsen 1985), but none so convincingly or in such detail as Hartog (2001, 149–69).

Epistolary analysis. Polycarp uses a standard version of early Christian letter prescription to begin his letter (trans. Holmes 1989, 123): [Superscription]: "Polycarp and the presbyters with him" [Adscription]: "to the church of God that sojourns as Philippi:" [Salutation]: "may mercy and peace from God Almighty and Jesus Christ our Savior be yours in abundance." The letter then includes a section which consists of an extremely long sentence, the subject of which is the verb "I rejoice" (1:1–3), which praises the Philippian Christians for their exemplary faith. This is, in effect, a **captatio benevolentiae* which aims at securing the goodwill of the recipients.

The body of the letter consists of chapters 2–12 and is largely paraenetic, that is, it consists primarily of moral exhortation (Stowers 1986, 151; Dehandschutter 1989, 279), or since advice and paraenesis were not separated in ancient epistolary theory, the letter may be characterized as an "advisory paraenetic letter" (Hartog 2002, 124). Chapter 2 functions as a continuation of the *exordium* in 1:1–3, and introduces the main theme of righteousness (Hartog 2002, 135–45). Paul is then adduced as an exemplum (3:1–3), who taught the Philippians the word of truth and sent them letters to build them up in the faith when he was absent (Polycarp appears to be implicitly playing the same role that Paul played). The "household code" in 4:1–6:3 regards the extended family as part of the Christian community, for it begins with instructions to wives to love their husbands and properly educate their children, but then turns to widows (4:3) who are wards of the community. Instructions are then given to deacons (5:2), then the younger men, with a brief note appended for virgins (5:3), and finally there is a paraenetic section directed toward presbyters. The element of reciprocity, common in the NT household codes, is missing, partly because there is little attempt to develop the paired relationships involved. Further, the household code is framed by injunctions for all to walk worthy of the commandment. The brief warning against heresy (7:1) is grounded in exhortation to persevere, imitating Christ (7:2–8:2). Examples of perseverance are then listed (Ignatius, Zosimus, Rufus, and Paul [9:1–10:3]).

The epistolary conclusion is found in chapters 13–14, and consists first of business, arrangements regarding the collection of the letters of Ignatius (13) and mention of Crescens who may have acted as a scribe in writing the letter and was the person who delivered it to the Philippians (14:1). Finally, he concluded with a farewell preserved only in Latin (14:2; trans.

Holmes 1989, 130): "Farewell in the Lord Jesus Christ in grace, you and all those with you. Amen."

Intertextuality. Polycarp's *Phillipians* consists primarily of a pastiche of quotations and allusions to early Christian literature, and for that reason alone is of great value. Even though *Phillipians* is quite short, it alludes to a number of biblical books, including Psalms, Proverbs, Isaiah, Jeremiah, Ezekiel, Tobit (though his use of the OT was generally slight; see Grant 1946, 145); Matthew, Luke, Acts (doubtful), Romans, 1–2 Corinthians, Galatians, Ephesians, Philippians, 1–2 Timothy, 1 Peter, 1 John, *1 Clement* (Schoedel 1967, 4–5), and Harrison (1936, 7) included Philippians and 2 Thessalonians (Harrison 1936, 7). For a careful review of the evidence of Polycarp's allusions to biblical texts, see Hartog (2001, 170–90). Campenhausen (1951), on the basis of the style, content, and historical background, maintained that Polycarp was the author of the Pastoral Letters, though this proposal has not been widely accepted. Berding (1999) argued that Polycarp assumed that Paul was the author of 1–2 Timothy, because he alluded to these letters in various clusters associated with allusions to other Pauline letters.

In Polycarp's letter to the Philippians (3:2), he reminds the church that "when he [Paul] was among you in the presence of the people of that time, taught accurately and steadfastly the word of truth, and also when he was absent wrote letters [ἐπιστολάς] to you, from the study of which you will be able to build yourselves up into the faith given you." The use of the plural form of ἐπιστολάς "letters," has often been taken to mean that he wrote more than one letter to the Philippians (Sellew 1994, 23–27).

*Apostolic fathers, *Martyrdom of Polycarp

Barnard 1966; Bauer 1995; Berding 1999; Campenhausen 1951; Dehandschutter 1989; Grant 1946; P. N. Harrison 1936; Hartog 2001; Sellew 1994

Polysyndeton is the use of conjunctions between each item in a series or list. According to Quintilian (*Inst. or.* 9.3.54), both polysyndeton and *asyndeton "make our utterances more vigorous and emphatic and produce an impression of vehemence." Polysyndeton produces the effect of "extensiveness and abundance by means of an exhaustive summary" (Blass and Debrunner 1961, §460). In the list of 28 trade items in Rev. 18:12–13 linked by καί ("and"), polysyndeton emphasizes the conspicuous consumption of Rome (Aune 1997–98, 3.981). Further examples of polysyndeta in the NT using καί ("and"): Rom. 2:17–18; 9:4; Rev. 4:11; 5:12, 13; 7:12. Examples of polysyndeta in the NT using the connective particle ἤ ("or"): Rom. 8:35; Mark 13:35. Examples using μήτε ("nor"): Matt. 5:34–36; Luke 9:3; Acts 23:8; 2 Thess. 2:2; Jas. 5:12. Examples with οὔτε ("not"): Acts 24:12–13; Rom. 8:38–39; 1 Cor. 6:10. Examples with ἀλλά ("but"): 1 Cor. 6:11. In the Synoptic Gospels, there are examples where one Gospel uses a finite verb with καί, while another Gospel has a participle (E. P. Sanders 1969, 237–40), and one Gospel used asyndeton where another Gospel has a conjunction (E. P. Sanders 1969, 240–42).

*Asyndeton

Aune 1975, 308–9

Preaching (see *Homily)

Preface, a translation of the Greek term προοίμιον ("introduction, preamble, preface, beginning") transliterated into Latin as *prooemium,* an introduction to a literary work or speech that orients the readers or hearers to the overt and covert intentions of the author or speaker. Prefaces have been among the more closely studied features of ancient Greek and Latin literature, and there is therefore an enormous bibliography on the subject. There are, indeed, substantial monographs on individual prefaces or on closely related prefaces (Janson 1964, 7–14).

Rhetorical prefaces. According to Plato (*Phaedrus* 266d), a *prooimion* was an essential part of a speech. Aristotle treats the *prooimion* at some length in *Rhetorica* 3.14–15. The normal Latin term for the introduction to a speech is *exordium* or the more general *principium.* The Athenian orators began their speeches with prefaces that typically contained a brief statement about the contents of the speech, a discussion of reasons for delivering it, and sometimes an apology for the poor ability of the speaker. Isocrates wrote numerous political pamphlets and *panegyrics in the form of speeches, and so his works represent both rhetorical and literary features. His prefaces often have a metatextual function, in that they comment on various aspects of the speech itself. Prefaces to his *Helena* and *Busiris* are the earliest example of polemical prefaces. In the preface to the *Ad Nicoclem*—(the first *dedication in a preface), Isocrates states that since people give gifts to kings, he is presenting a treatise on the art of ruling, and he also expresses uncertainty about his ability to write well.

Literary prefaces. The Greek term for an introduction to a prose or poetic work is προοίμιον, while the normal classical Latin terms for the introduction to literary works are *prooemium* and *praefacio.* A preface in the form of a letter is simply called *epistula.* Early Greek poetic prefaces tend to begin with "I will sing of [such-and-such a god]," or "Sing, Muse, of . . . ," using the literary fiction of an inspiring deity. Hesiod mentions his own name in the prefaces to both the *Theogony* and *Works and Days,* and he also mentions a second person, his nephew Perses (10, 27) in the latter work (M. L. West 1978, 136–42).

Historical prefaces. History was the first type of prose writing to develop a distinctive form of preface or *prooimion* (see also *Historiography). There is a relatively late (ca. 166 C.E.) methodological discussion of the historical preface in Lucian's *Quomodo historia conscribenda sit* ("How to Write History"). In this work Lucian includes a discussion of prefaces (*Hist.* 52–54), which G. Avenarius (1956, 113–18) has shown is dependent on the rhetorical views of crafting *exordia,* with the exception that a historiographer need not be concerned about the reader's *benevolum,* "goodwill," but only that he or she is *docilem,* "receptive," and *attentum,* "attentive" (G. Avenarius 1956, 115). In the words of Lucian (*Hist.* 53; LCL trans.): "Whenever he does use a preface, he will make two points only, not three like the orators. He will omit the appeal for a favorable hearing and give his audience what will interest and instruct them. For they will give him their attention if he shows that what he is going to say will be important, essential, personal, or useful." The themes in the prose prefaces of the classical historians Herodotus and Thucydides became *topoi for subsequent historians (Lucian, *Hist.* 54) but apparently had little influence on the prefaces of other genres. These topoi include the praise of history, the claim of impartiality, and the permanent value of the subject. Prefaces in Xenophon's historical works consist primarily of an explanation of why the author chose the particular subject that he did. The formal characteristics of historical prefaces include (L. Alexander 1993, 26–31): (1) mention of the author's name, (2) mention of the subject of the work, usually in the first sentence, (3) the appropriate length (three to six pages on average), (4) an end that effects a smooth and appropriate transition to the narrative (Lucian, *Hist.* 55; Avenarius 1956, 117–18).

Three major topoi are used in the prefaces of the Roman historians, as summarized by Janson (1964, 66–67): (1) *Laudatio historiae* ("praise of history"): The author tends to praise his subject and to emphasize its usefulness, importance, beauty, and ability to confer immortality. (2) Reason for choice of the subject: After arguing for the usefulness of history generally, the author must indicate why the subject treated in this monograph requires treatment (e.g., it has not been treated adequately before). (3) The historian's attitude toward his work: The historian was expected to comment on his own situation and his relationship to his subject.

Scientific literature. Archimedes (287–212 B.C.E.) wrote technical scientific works and included prefaces in most of his writings (Janson 1964, 19–22). Most of his prefaces take the form of a letter addressed to a friend, containing a dedication of the work to that person and including some personal comments on the work. While the majority of Hellenistic scientific literature is lost, Janson (1964, 24) summarizes the basic features of the prefaces based on surviving works and fragments of lost works: (1) they are addressed to a certain person, to whom the work is thereby dedicated; (2) they are written in a personal tone; (3) the author usually states reasons for treating the subject; (4) the inclusion of praise for the person receiving the work is common; (5) mention is sometimes made that the dedicatee has requested the work; (6) prefaces may take the form of letters or as the prefaces to speeches. Prefaces were also used to introduce individual books of larger historical works, a practice known but rejected by Polybius (11.1). Seneca the Elder is the first of the Roman rhetorical writers to use an epistolary form for his prefaces (Janson 1964, 49).

One typical use of prefaces in works of two books or more was to recapitulate the previous book and summarize the next (e.g., Herodotus 1.42; 2.1.1–3; 3.1.1–3; 8.1.1–6). Further, when prefaces occur at the beginning of several books in a multivolume work, the first preface is usually the most important, since it contains a dedication and a presentation of the entire work (Janson 1964, 33, referring to Cicero, *De oratore* 1.1; cf. Luke 1:1–4 in *Luke–Acts). Prefaces to historical texts were a convention that exhibits a number of topoi, including (1) remarks on the importance of the subject, (2) the inadequacy of previous treatments, (3) the author's circumstances and the reason for writing, (4) the author's impartiality and concern only with the truth, (5) the author's intensive research efforts and the emphasis on eyewitness testimony, (6) the thesis of the author, including his view of the causes of the events he will narrate, and (7) a brief outline of the work's contents. According to Wheeldon (1990, 7), "the prefaces to ancient historiographical works influenced the reader's reaction to the narrative of events that followed by presenting an image of the writer as an authoritative source for these events." Lucian's *prooimion* to his *Verae historiae* is satirical, using negative forms of the typical introductory prefaces found in historical works, and concludes with these words: "Be it understood, then, that I am writing about things which I have neither seen nor had to do with nor learned from others—which, in fact, do not exist at all and, in the nature of things, cannot exist. Therefore my readers should on no account believe in them."

The preface of Luke–Acts. Luke–Acts is a two-volume work, each introduced with a preface (Luke 1:1–4; Acts 1:1). The dedication to "your excellency Theophilus" [κράτιστε Θεόφιλε] is mentioned in Luke 1:3 and repeated in Acts 1:1. Josephus dedicated his great historical work *Antiquitates* to Epaphroditus, who is mentioned in *Ant.* 1.8, but in *Vita,* an appendix to *Antiquitates* (see *Ant.* 20.266), the dedication of the work to Epaphroditus, who is here addressed as "the most excellent of men" (κράτιστε ἀνδρῶν), is a clear parallel to Luke 1:3. The dedication of Luke–Acts to Theophilus is a clear signal of the literary intentions of the author who is thereby seeking a larger public.

Luke 1:1–4 has routinely been identified as a historical preface, though this view has been questioned by L. Alexander (1986, 1993), who argues that despite Cadbury's detailed exegesis of Luke 1:1–4 (Cadbury 1922, 489–510), "there has never been a concerted attempt to find the right context for Luke's preface within the whole range of Greek literature" (1993, 9). Her intention was to test whether or not Luke's explanatory preface (specifying who the author is, what he is doing, why, and for whom) follows Greek historiographical tradition (Alexander 1993, 10). After formulating a useful objective description of the form, syntactical structure, topics, and style of Luke's preface for comparative purposes (1993, 13), Alexander examines Greek historical prefaces in terms of their general features, formal characteristics (author's name, dedication, subject matter, length of preface, and transition), and recurrent topics (magnitude of the subject, aims and value of history, and sources of information), concluding with a discussion of the convention of *autopsia* (1993, 23–41). She lists 21 authors of scientific treatises in an appendix, together with bibliographies (1993, 217–29).

One problem such an investigation faces is the fact that few Greek historical works actually survive, and fragmentary references to them preserved in later authors tended to omit prefaces. Surviving Greek historical works are few; the following 14 cover a millennium of Greek historical writing: Herodotus and Thucydides (5th cent. B.C.E.), Xenophon (b. ca. 430 B.C.E.), Theopompus (4th cent. B.C.E.), Polybius (ca. 200–118 B.C.E.), Diodorus Siculus (early 1st cent. B.C.E.), Dionysius of Halicarnassus (late 1st cent. B.C.E.), Josephus (1st cent. C.E.), Arrian (86–160 C.E.), Appian (early 2d cent. C.E.), Cassius Dio (164–229 C.E.), Herodian (ca. 180–238 C.E.), Procopius (6th cent. C.E.), and Agathias Scholasticus (ca. 532–80 C.E.). Most Greek historical works have perished, but there are fragments of lost works (Jacoby 1923–58, continued by Schepens 1998), as well as rhetorical treatises that deal with the subject of *prooimia.*

In comparing Greek historical prefaces with Luke 1:1–4, Alexander finds a number of contrasts (1993, 102): (1) Luke's single-sentence *prooimion* is shorter than the shortest Greek historical preface and is scarcely comparable in content (i.e., he does not clearly reveal what it is that he is writing about). (2) Luke does not give his own name, though Greek historians typically do. (3) Luke's dedication to Theophilus is unlike the practice of Greek historians, who avoided dedications. (4) Luke's style does not begin to compare with the elevated style characteristic of the prefaces of the Greek historians. (5) Luke's use of the first person contrasts with the Greek historians' use of the more impersonal third-person style. Alexander argues that the closest parallels to the preface of Luke are actually found in the prefaces of the scientific tradition, i.e., the tradition of technical or professional prose (*Fachprosa*), which began to proliferate in the 4th cent. B.C.E., and included treatises on medicine, philosophy, mathematics, engineering, rhetoric, and a variety of other subjects (1993, 21). Since Luke–Acts is not a scientific or technical treatise, this thesis poses a problem. Alexander must suppose that Luke was at the very least a reader of scientific treatises (1986, 66), which were characterized by "a sober, non-rhetorical presentation of fact, unembellished by literary allusion or rhetorical decoration" (1986, 64). Luke's preface provides a "firm link to the world of the crafts and professions of the Greek East *in general,* and makes all the more urgent a thorough investigation of the social dynamics of that world" (1986, 66). Since none of the scientific treatises Alexander has examined in her study are biographies, the biographical context presents another set of problems. She then suggests that the problem of the biographical character of Luke's work can be explained, not by looking to the scientific tradition for parallels (conspicuous by their absence) but to parallels in *function* (1986, 69); she concludes that the scientific treatises and the Gospel of Luke have in common the fact that they are school texts. She concludes, "In sum, then, I would argue that the biographical content of the Gospel and Acts is by no means an insuperable obstacle to viewing Luke as a writer set firmly within the context of the scientific tradition" (1986, 70).

There are several weaknesses in Alexander's proposal (Aune 2002d): 1. Since Luke is a single composition, one cannot expect it to conform only to the statistically common features of ancient prefaces rather than to statistically rare features. Any individual text can be an "outlier." A statistical study of the Greek historical works that have survived cannot claim to be representative. For example, when Alexander claims that "dedication was not normal practice among the classical historians" and that they are "exceptional" (1993, 27), the phrases "not normal practice" and "exceptional" do not mean that dedications never occurred in historical prefaces. It happens that, in the lengthy *prooimion* of Josephus *Antiquitates* 1.1–26, the first extant example of a dedicated historical work (1993, 27), there is a eulogy of "Epaphroditus," the person addressed as κράτιστε ἀνδρῶν 'Επαφρόδιτε ("most excellent of men, Epaphroditus") in Josephus, *Vita* 430, making it clear that the *Antiquities* was dedicated to him. Alexander also mentions several other indirect references to dedications in other historical prefaces (Diogenes Laertius 2.93; Dionysius of Halicarnassus, *Ant. Rom.* 1.4.3).

2. An examination of historical prefaces is hampered by the fact that few have survived, and of those which have, most are written by authors with a social status to which Luke could never have aspired and in an elevated style that he could never have emulated. There must have been literally hundreds of histories written in *Zwischenprosa* that the educated would have considered mediocre and that have been lost (Lucian, *Hist.* 2). One example, which specifically critiques a historical *prooimion,* is found in Lucian's ascerbic account (*Hist.* 16; LCL trans.):

> Another of them [i.e., a contemporary historian] has compiled a bare record of the events and set it down on paper, completely prosaic and ordinary, such as a soldier or artisan or pedlar following the army might have put together as a diary of daily events. However, this amateur was not bad—it was quite obvious at the beginning what he was, and his work has cleared the ground for some future historian of taste and ability. The only fault I found was this: his headings were too pompous for the place his books can hold—"Callimorphus, surgeon of the Sixth Lancers, History of the Parthian War, Book so-and-so"—there followed the number of each book. Another thing, his preface was very frigid: he put it like this: it was proper for a surgeon to write history, since Asclepius was the son of Apollo and Apollo was the leader of the Muses and lord of all culture; also because, after beginning in Ionic, for some reason I can't fathom he suddenly changed to the vernacular [κοινή], using indeed the Ionic forms of "medicine," "attempt," "how many," "diseases," but taking the rest from the language of everyday, most of it street-corner talk.

While little can be known about the prefaces in lost works, the available data, though fragmentary, suggests the existence of pedestrian historical prefaces written in an artificially elevated linguistic register, contrasting sharply with the body of the work itself.

3. While Alexander thinks she has demonstrated that Luke 1:1–4 is not a historical preface, she has not demonstrated what it *is,* beyond saying that it has many parallels in scientific or technical literature. That is, she fails to address directly the function of prefaces in scientific literature.

4. Although the Gospel of Luke has a scientific preface, according to Alexander, the work itself (part of the two-volume work Luke–Acts) is obviously not a scientific or technical treatise. The scientific literature she examines has no close generic parallels in form or content with the Gospel of Luke. Apart from the preface, Luke consists primarily of narrative discourse; apart from their prefaces, the scientific or technical treatises consist primarily of expository and descriptive discourse. She pro-

poses, however, that the biographical character of Luke links it to the scientific tradition.

While Alexander's careful and detailed comparison of the *prooimion* of the Gospel of Luke with those of 21 scientific or technical writers is a model of scholarly analysis, it may be that other surviving texts should be included in the comparative enterprise. It appears, for example, that some light can be shed on the problem of whether Luke 1:1–4 is a historical or scientific *prooimion* by considering one of *Plutarch's moral essays, *Septem sapientium convivium,* which is neither a technical nor scientific work but rather an example of belles lettres by a skilled and versatile author (Martin 1997). This work begins with an explanatory *prooimion* that introduces a narrative framed as a symposium (Aune 1978, 51–105). This *prooimion* exhibits a striking number of features in common with the *prooimion* in Luke 1:1–4. While there is little doubt that Plutarch is the actual author, the essay is in fact a literary tour de force, in the form of a pseudonymous composition attributed to Diokles, a mantis in the court of the 6th-cent. Corinthian tyrant Periander, though the reader is able to attach a name to the first-person narrator only well into the narrative (149D). The short *prooimion* consists of 105 words in three periodic sentences, the gist of which is that the author (whose name is not yet mentioned) was both present and a participant at the symposium of the Seven Sages, and desires to provide Nikarchos (the dedicatee) with a true account of what transpired on that famous occasion. The author thinks that this is an important task in view of the many false accounts of the symposium in circulation, and he wishes to relate his version of the event before old age impairs his memory. Here is a translation of this *prooimion:*

> Certainly the passing of time will contribute a great deal of obscurity and uncertainty to events, Nikarchos [ὦ Νίκαρχε], since already patently false fabricated accounts about new and recent events have gained credibility. For the symposium did not include, as you [ὑμεῖς] have heard, the Seven alone, but more than twice as many (among whom I myself was one, since I was a close friend of Periander because of my trade and I was also Thales' host, for he stayed with me by Periander's arrangement). Whoever relayed the details [ὁ διηγούμενος] to you [ὑμῖν] did not remember the conversations correctly, for it appears that he was not among those who were actually present. Since I now have a lot of free time, and old age is not trustworthy enough to delay telling my story [τοῦ λόγου], I will recount everything to you [ὑμῖν] from the beginning [ἀπ' ἀρχῆς ἅπαντα διηγήσομαι], since you are eager to listen.

This *prooimion* exhibits the following characteristics: (1) The author does not name himself, just as the author of Luke–Acts does not name himself in Luke 1:1–4. (2) Nikarchos is named as the dedicatee using the classical vocative expression ὦ Νίκαρχε. (3) The *prooimion* is written in the first person, just as Luke uses the pronoun κἀμοι ("and to me"), as a self-reference. (4) The term πολύ in the first sentence reflects the Greek rhetorical penchant for using πολύς and derivatives in the *prooimia* of compositions; the second word in Luke 1:1 is πολλοί (cf. Demosthenes, *Or.* 9.1; Dionysius of Halicarnasus, *De antiquis oratoribus* 1.1; cf. Sir. 1:1; Heb. 1:1) . (5) The author claims to have been present at the famous symposium where the Seven Sages gathered at the invitation of the tyrant Periander (627–587 B.C.E.) and thus writes an account based on personal experience (no counterpart in Luke 1:1–4). (6) The author uses the verb διηγέομαι ("to narrate," "to describe in detail") for his own decision to write an account of what happened, which he reserves for the last word of the last clause in the *prooimion:* ὑμῖν ἀπ ἀρχῆς ἁπάντα διηγέομαι. He uses the same verb in participial form for an inaccurate oral "informant" (ὁ διηγούμενος) he mentions. Luke chose to use the cognate διήγησις of accounts compiled by others in Luke 1:1, without labeling his own composition apart from referring to it later as a λόγος in Acts 1:1 (just as the author of the *prooimion* quoted above calls his account or story a λόγος). (7) The author mentions the existence of erroneous accounts (λόγοι ψευδεῖς) written by those who could not have been present at the symposium. Luke mentions other writers, but differing from the common practice of ancient historians, does not impugn the accuracy of their accounts. (8) The author refers to the subject of the following narrative in an oblique case (the dative) as τοῖς πράγμασι, "the matters," in a way comparable to Luke's use of the phrase περὶ τῶν πραγμάτων. (9) The author promises to narrate ἀπ' ἀρχῆς παντα, "everything from the beginning," a common cliché among ancient writers, though in Luke 1:2 the phrase is used to refer to those who were "eyewitnesses and ministers of the word from the beginning [ἀπ' ἀρχῆς]." (10) The author twice uses the plural pronoun ὑμῖν as an indirect object for those to whom an erroneous version of the symposium was recounted (e.g., ὑμῖν ἀπ' ἀρχῆς ἅπαντα διηγέομαι), indicating that Nikarchos is not intended to be the sole reader of the ensuing narrative. He also uses the plural pronoun in the phrase ὑμεῖς ἀκηκόατε, "you have heard." (11) The first sentence of the *prooimion* is alliterative, with seven words beginning with π; Luke uses four π- words in the first two clauses in Luke 1:1–2. (12) The first sentence in the *prooimion* is vague and general, and the actual subject of the following narrative is not mentioned until the second sentence. Luke is even more vague, since he never really tells us what his account is about in his *prooimion*.

Plutarch chose to introduce *Septem sapientium convivium* with an explanatory *prooimion* as part of a pseudepigraphic strategy to lend credence to the fictional account which followed, just as Luke chose to introduce his first book with an explanatory *prooimion* to assure Theophilus that the ensuing narrative would confirm the truth of what he had been taught. Plutarch's *prooimion* is essentially a cliché, i.e., a pastiche of elements that the ancient reader would reflexively recognize as an explanatory *prooimion* whose primary function would be to bolster the claim that the following account is the truth and nothing but the truth. The many parallels between Plutarch's *prooimion* and the scientific prefaces analyzed by Alexander, on the one hand, and Luke 1:1–4, on the other, should make it abundantly clear that the *prooimion* of the *Septem sapientium convivium* has numerous parallels to both. Both the author (whom we later learn is named Diokles) and Nikarchos (the one to whom he dedicates his narrative) are fictitious. The explanatory *prooimion* is part of Plutarch's strategy to lend credence and verisimilitude to a fictional account. The fictive author presents himself as an eyewitness and participant in the events and conversations in the narrative, which is based on an imaginative dramatization of legendary sayings and stories that clustered about the figures of the *Seven Sages.

When this comparison of the *prooimia* of Plutarch's *Septem sapientium convivium* and Luke–Acts are considered in light of Alexander's careful comparison of the *prooimia* of scientific or technical treatises and Luke 1:1–4, it begins to appear increasingly plausible that the distinction between historical and scientific *prooimia* is a false dichotomy. Marshall (1995, 375) was nearer the truth when he asked, in a review of Alexander's monograph: "May it not be claimed that readers of a 'scientific' writing would look for the kind of accuracy appropriate to the particular kind of writing within that tradition, and in the case of an account of a person's life and teaching, they would expect a historically accurate account of it?"

*Luke–Acts

Alexander 1986, 1993; Aune 2002; Callan 1985; Earl 1972; Hunger 1964; Janson 1964; Palmer 1987, 1993; Wheeldon 1990

Prescriptions, epistolary, are the formal features that introduce ancient letters. With a view to the general structure of epistolary prescriptions in the Pauline and other NT letters, they consists of three constituent elements: (1) the *superscriptio* (in which the sender[s] is/are named), (2) the *adscriptio*, (in which the recipient[s] is/are named), and (3) the *salutatio* or greeting.

Superscriptions. In the 13 NT letters ascribed to Paul, the superscriptions exhibit a variety of features. See table on p. 373.

Adscriptions. While the qualifiers in adscriptions are normally quite short, there are some notable exceptions in the NT (1 Cor. 1:2; 1 Pet. 1:1b–2a; 2 John 1b–2) and some extremely long qualifiers in the letters of Ignatius. As a rule, the longer the qualifier in an adscription, the more likely it is to have an important rhetorical function for the letter it introduces. See table on pp. 374–75.

Salutations. The table of salutations in NT letters (*see page 376*) is arranged in terms of increasing complexity. Only Jas. 1:1 in the NT has the typical salutation found in Hellenistic documentary letters (χαίρειν also occurs in the salutations of two embedded letters in Acts 15:23 and 23:26). The typical form of the salutation is "grace [to you] and peace," combining the term χάρις ("grace"), a play on words for the typical Greek greeting χαίρείν ("greetings"), since both are from the same Greek root, and "peace" a Greek translation of the Hebrew word שלום, "shalom" used in Hebrew and Aramaic letters. See table on p. 376.

*Epistolography, *Letters

Priamel, a germanicized form of the late Latin term *praeambulum* ("going before, preface"), is a modern term applied first to medieval German epigrams, then to a short, often poetic, literary form in Greek and Latin literature in which that which is most valued is

Superscriptions in Letters in the NT and Apostolic Fathers

Text	Sender 1	Qualifications	Sender 2 (and 3)	Qualifications
Rom. 1:1–6	Paul	a servant of Christ Jesus, called to be an apostle (72 Greek words)		
1 Cor. 1:1	Paul	called by the will of God to be an apostle of Christ Jesus	and Sosthenes	our brother
2 Cor. 1:1	Paul	an apostle of Christ Jesus by the will of God	and Timothy	our brother
Gal. 1:1	Paul	an apostle, not from men nor through man, but through Jesus Christ and God the Father, who raised him from the dead	and all the brothers	who are with me
Eph. 1:1a	Paul	an apostle of Christ Jesus by the will of God		
Phil. 1:1a	Paul		and Timothy	servants of Christ Jesus
Col. 1:1	Paul	an apostle of Christ Jesus by the will of God,	and Timothy	our brother
1 Thess. 1:1	Paul		and Silvanus and Timothy	
2 Thess. 1:1	Paul		and Silvanus and Timothy	
1 Tim. 1:1	Paul	an apostle of Christ Jesus by the command of God our Savior and of Christ Jesus our hope		
2 Tim. 1:1	Paul	an apostle of Christ Jesus by the will of God according to the promise of life that is in Christ Jesus		
Titus 1:1	Paul	a servant of God and an apostle of Jesus Christ, for the sake of the faith of God's elect (46 Greek words)		
Phlm. 1	Paul	a prisoner for Christ Jesus	and Timothy	our brother
Jas. 1:1	James	a servant of God and of the Lord Jesus Christ		
1 Pet. 1:1	Peter	an apostle of Jesus Christ		
2 Pet. 1:1a	Simon Peter	a servant and apostle of Jesus Christ		
2 John 1	The elder			
3 John 1	The elder			
Jude 1	Jude	a servant of Jesus Christ and brother of James		
Rev. 1:4a	John			
1 Clem pr.	The church of God	which sojourns in Rome		
Ign., *Eph.* praescr.	Ignatius	who is also called Theophorus		
Ign., *Magn.* praescr.	Ignatius	who is also called Theophorus		
Ign., *Trall.* praescr.	Ignatius	who is also called Theophorus		
Ign., *Rom.* praescr.	Ignatius	who is also called Theophorus		
Ign., *Philad.* praescr.	Ignatius	who is also called Theophorus		
Ign., *Smyrn.* praescr.	Ignatius	who is also called Theophorus		
Ign., *Polyc.* praescr.	Ignatius	who is also called Theophorus		
Polycarp, *Phil.*	Polycarp		and the elders with him	

Adscriptions in Letters in the NT and Apostolic Fathers

Letter	Addressee(s)	Qualifiers
Rom. 1:7a	to all God's beloved in Rome	who are called to be saints
1 Cor. 1:2	to the church of God to those sanctified in Christ Jesus	which is at Corinth called to be saints together with all those who in every place call on the name of our Lord Jesus Christ, both their Lord and ours.
2 Cor. 1:1b	to the church of God with all the saints	which is at Corinth who are in the whole of Achaia
Gal. 1:2b	to the churches of Galatia	
Eph. 1:1b	to the saints	who are also faithful in Christ Jesus
Phil. 1:1b	to all the saints in Christ Jesus who are at Philippi with the bishops and deacons	
Col. 1:1b	to the saints and faithful brethren in Christ at Colossae	
1 Thess. 1:1b	to the church of the Thessalonians	in God the Father and the Lord Jesus Christ
2 Thess. 1:1b	to the church of the Thessalonians	in God our Father and the Lord Jesus Christ
1 Tim. 1:2a	to Timothy	my true child in the faith
2 Tim. 1:2a	to Timothy	my beloved child
Titus 1:4	to Titus	my true child in a common faith
Phlm. 1b–2	to Philemon and Apphia and Archippus and the church in your house	our beloved fellow worker our sister our fellow soldier
Jas. 1:1b	to the twelve tribes	in dispersion
1 Pet. 1:1b–2a	to the exiles of the Dispersion in Pontus, Galatia, Cappadocia, Asia, and Bithynia	chosen and destined by God the Father and sanctified by the Spirit for obedience to Jesus Christ and for sprinkling with his blood
2 Pet. 1:1b	to those who have obtained a faith of equal standing with ours	in the righteousness of our God and Savior Jesus Christ
2 John 1b–2	to the elect lady and her children	whom I love in the truth, and not only I but also all who know the truth, because of the truth which abides in us and will be with us for ever
Jude 1b	to those who are called	beloved in God the Father and kept for Jesus Christ
Rev. 1:4b	to the seven churches that are in Asia	
1 Clem. pr.	to the church of God which sojourns in Corinth to those who are called and sanctified	 by the will of God through our Lord Jesus Christ
Ign., *Eph.* pr.	to the church in Ephesus of Asia	blessed with greatness through the fullness of God the Father, predestined before the ages for lasting and unchangeable glory forever, united and elect through genuine suffering by the will of the Father and of Jesus Christ our God, most worthy of blessing
Ign., *Magn* pr.	to the church at Magnesia on the Maeander	which has been blessed through the grace of God the Father in Christ Jesus our Savior

(*continued*)

Adscriptions in Letters in the NT and Apostolic Fathers

Letter	Addressee(s)	Qualifiers
Ign., *Trall.* pr.	to the holy church at Tralles in Asia,	dearly loved by God the Father of Jesus Christ, elect and worthy of God, at peace in flesh and spirit through the suffering of Jesus Christ, who is our hope when we rise to be with him
Ign., *Rom.* pr.	to the church in the land of the Romans	that has found mercy in the majesty of the Father most high and Jesus Christ his only Son, beloved and enlightened through the will of him who willed all things that exist, in accordance with faith in and love for Jesus Christ our God, worthy of God, worthy of honor, worthy of blessing, worthy of praise, worthy of success, worthy of sanctification, and presiding over love, observing the law of Christ, bearing the name of the Father,
Ign., *Philad.* pr.	to the church of God the Father and of Jesus Christ at Philadelphia in Asia	that has found mercy and is firmly established in godly harmony and unwaveringly rejoices in the suffering of our Lord, fully convinced of his resurrection in all mercy,
Ign., *Smyrn.* pr.	To the church of God the Father and of the beloved Jesus Christ at Smyrna in Asia,	mercifully endowed with every spiritual gift, most worthy of God, bearing holy things
Ign., *Polyc.* pr.	To Polycarp	bishop of the church of the Smyrnaeans, or rather who has God the Father and the Lord Jesus Christ as his bishop
Polycarp, *Phil.* pr.	To the church of God that sojourns at Philippi	
Barnabas 1:1	Sons and daughters	

compared with other things or qualities of lesser value. A prose example is found in Plato, *Lysis* 211d–e: "one man wants horses, another dogs, another money, another distinctions, but I want friends." A poetic example occurs in Ps. 20:7: "Some boast of chariots, and some of horses; but we boast of the name of the LORD our God." For a review and critique of definitions, see Race 1982, 17ff. One relatively inclusive definition of the priamel is that of Bundy (1962, 5): "The priamel is a focusing or selecting device in which one or more terms serve as foil for the point of particular interest." The priamel therefore consists of two parts, foil and climax. An NT example is Matt. 13:17 (par. Luke 10:24): "Truly, I say to you, many prophets and righteous men longed to see what you see, and did not see it, and to hear what you hear, and did not hear it." A short priamel is found in Matt. 22:14 (par. *Barn.* 4:14): "For many are called, but few are chosen." Romans 8:30 may also be classified as a priamel, though it also exhibits the more rigid structure of a *climax. First Corinthians 13:1–3, with focus on love in contrast to other qualities, is an extended priamel. Kirby (1985) proposes that the priamel is a subset of example as the a fortiori is a subset of the enthymeme.

*Catalogues, *Climax, *Example

Berger, 1984a, 212–13; 1984b, 1204–8; Bundy 1962, 1972; Fridrichsen 1940; Kirby 1985; Race 1982

Progymnasmata, a transliteration of the Greek word προγυμνάσματα, meaning "preliminary [rhetorical] exercises," intended for the early stages of a student's rhetorical training and graded for increasing difficulty (γυμνάσματα is also used; see Hermogenes, *Progym.* 12). Of the two Latin designations for these exercises, *praeexercitationes* and *praeexercitamina,* the latter became the standard term in the Middle Ages and the Renaissance. There are four extant manuals under the title *Progymnasmata:* (1) Aelius Theon (late 1st cent. C.E.), (2) Hermogenes of Tarsus (late 2d cent. C.E.), (3) Aphthonius of Antioch (late 4th cent. C.E.), and (4) Nicolaus of Myra (5th cent. C.E.). English translations of these texts

Salutations in Letters in the NT and Apostolic Fathers
(Arranged in order of complexity)

Letter	Salutation	Source
Jas. 1:1c	Greetings [χαίρειν]	
Barn. 1:1	Greetings [χαίρετε]	in the name of the Lord who loved us, in peace
Ign., *Eph.* pr.	Abundant greetings [πλεῖστα . . . χαίρειν]	in Jesus Christ and in blameless joy
Ign., *Magn.* pr.	Whom I greet [ἀσπάζομαι] Abundant greetings [πλεῖστα χαίρειν]	in God the Father and in Christ Jesus
Ign., *Trall.* pr.	Which I greet [ἀσπάζομαι] and offer abundant greetings [πλεῖστα χαίρειν]	in the fullness of God in the apostolic manner
Ign., *Rom.* pr.	Which I greet [ἀσπάζομαι] Abundant greetings [πλεῖστα χαίρειν]	in the name of Jesus Christ, the Son of the Father to those who are united in flesh and spirit in every one of his commandments, filled with the grace of God without wavering, and filtered clear from every foreign stain, in Jesus Christ our God, in blamelessness
Ign., *Philad.* pr.	I greet her [ἀσπάζομαι]	in the blood of Jesus Christ, which is eternal and abiding joy, especially if men be at one with the bishop, and with the presbyters and deacons, who together with him have been appointed according to the mind of Jesus Christ, and he established them in security according to his own will by his Holy Spirit
Ign., *Smyrn.* pr.	Abundant greetings [πλεῖστα χαίρειν]	in a blameless spirit and in the Word of God
Ign., *Polyc.* pr.	Abundant greetings [πλεῖστα χαίρειν]	
Col. 1:2b	Grace to you and peace	from God the Father
1 Thess. 1:1c	Grace to you and peace	from God the Father and the Lord Jesus Christ
2 Thess. 1:2	Grace to you and peace	from God the Father and the Lord Jesus Christ
Phil. 1:2	Grace to you and peace	from God our Father and the Lord Jesus Christ
Phlm. 3	Grace to you and peace	from God our Father and the Lord Jesus Christ
Rom. 1:7b	Grace to you and peace	from God our Father and the Lord Jesus Christ
1 Cor. 1:3	Grace to you and peace	from God our Father and the Lord Jesus Christ
2 Cor. 1:2	Grace to you and peace	from God our Father and the Lord Jesus Christ
Eph. 1:2	Grace to you and peace	from God our Father and the Lord Jesus Christ
Gal. 1:3a	Grace to you and peace	from God the Father and our Lord Jesus Christ
Titus 1:4b	Grace and peace	from God the Father and Christ Jesus our Savior
1 Tim. 1:2b	Grace, mercy, and peace	from God the Father and Christ Jesus our Lord
2 Tim. 1:2b	Grace, mercy, and peace	from God the Father and Christ Jesus our Lord
Polycarp, *Phil.* pr.	Mercy and peace be multiplied to you	from God Almighty and Jesus Christ our Savior
Jude 2	May mercy, peace, and love be multiplied to you	
2 John 3	Grace, mercy, and peace will be with us	from God the Father and from Jesus Christ the Father's Son in truth and love
1 Pet. 1:2b	May grace and peace be multiplied to you	
2 Pet. 1:2	May grace and peace be multiplied to you	in the knowledge of God and of Jesus our Lord
1 Clem. pr.	May grace and peace be multiplied to you	from God Almighty through Jesus Christ
Rev. 1:4b	Grace to you and peace	from him who is and who was and who is to come, and from the seven spirits who are before his throne, and from Jesus Christ the faithful witness, the firstborn of the dead, and the ruler of kings on earth

are available in Kennedy 2003. The earliest extant treatise on progymnasmata is by Theon of Smyrna, dating perhaps to the 1st cent. C.E., while the first rhetorical use of the term προγυμνάσμα is in *Rhetorica ad Alexandrum* 1436a, though this may be a later interpolation (Kennedy 1983, 55). Quintilian and Suetonius provide lists of exercises for use by the grammarian (Quintilian, *Inst.* 1.9; Suetonius, *De grammaticis* 4) and the rhetorician (Quintilian, *Inst.* 2.4; Suetonius, *De rhetoribus* 1). The progymnasmata have relatively simple content, consisting of a series of exercises, graded from the comparatively simple to the more complex. While none of the constituent exercises is intended to constitute an independent speech, they can be used as parts of speeches.

The exercises of Aphthonius (Spengel 1853–54, 2:21–53; Kennedy 2003, 89–127). Though there are variations in these exercises from author to author, the following 14 exercises are found in *Aphthonius (Kennedy 1983, 54–70; Heath 1995, 13–17; Hock 1997, 454): (1) *Fable* (μῦθος, *fabula;* Lausberg 1998, §§1107–10; Spengel 1853–54, 2.21): This first relatively simply exercise involved retelling a fable (Lausberg 1998, §1107). This could typically involve paraphrasing Aesop's fables and analyzing each verse, always changing the language (Quintilian 1.9.2). (2) *Narration* (διήγημα, *narratio;* Lausberg 1998, §§1111–16; Spengel 1853–54, 2.22): Since narrative plays an important role in a judicial speech, it was important to be able to compose a plausible account that would include six circumstantial elements: Who? What? When? Where? How? Why? (3) *Anecdote* (χρεία, *chreia;* Lausberg 1998, §1117–20; Spengel 1853–54, 2.23–24): A student was given an anecdote (an attributed saying in a brief narrative framework) and required to develop it into a moral essay. In this essay, the student was expected to follow a set pattern in developing the theme: (a) praise the figure to whom the saying is attributed; (b) paraphrase the anecdote; (c) support the truth of the anecdote by showing why it is true, by pointing to its opposite, by adducing analogies, by giving examples, and by citing other authorities for the same principle; and (d) conclude with an exhortation. (4) *Maxim* (γνώμη, *sententia;* Lausberg 1998, §1121; Spengel 1853–54, 2.25–27): A student was given a maxim (an unattributed aphorism) and required to develop it into a moral essay. (5) *Refutation* (ἀνασκευή, *refutatio;* Lausberg 1998, §1122–25; Spengel 1853–54, 2.27–30): This fifth exercise is the first part of an antithetical pair, preparing students to argue both sides of an issue. Here the student is given a standard argument and is expected to find it contradictory, implausible, immoral, and so forth. (6) *Confirmation* (κατασκευή; Spengel 1853–54, 2.30–32): The student can, for example, be given a story, he must defend in detail, but the treatment must be exactly the opposite of ἀνασκευή. (7) *Commonplace* (κοινὸς τόπος, *locus communis;* Lausberg 1998, §1126–28; Spengel 1853–54, 2.32–35): this is an exercise in *amplification, in which the student must elaborate on generalizations that apply to any particular instance of a given category; the common topics against tyrants or adulterers provide material for an attack against a particular tyrant or adulterer. The student was provided with a checklist of criteria for assessing an action: Is it legal? Is it honorable? Is it advantageous? (8) *Encomium* (ἐγκώμιον, *laus;* Lausberg 1998, §1129; Spengel 1853–54, 2.35–40): Antithetically paired with the next exercise (invective), encomium is the basis for epideictic oratory and is used in juridical oratory to treat motives and intentions, teaching students how to treat a subject in a good or bad light. Subjects can include, in addition to persons, things (e.g., justice), times (e.g., spring), places, animals, and growing things (e.g., the olive tree). The headings include *proemium, genos* (divided into nation, city, ancestors, and parents), upbringing (habits, art, and laws), deeds (those relating to soul, body, and fortune), favorable comparison with another, epilogue (e.g., a prayer). (9) *Invective* (ψόγος, *vituperatio;* Lausberg 1998, §1129; Spengel 1853–54, 2.40–42): This exercise focuses on attacking a specific person or thing rather than a type. The headings are identical with those under encomium. (10) *Comparison* (συγκρίσις, *comparatio;* Lausberg 1998, §1130; Spengel 1853–54, 2.42–44): This exercise combines the skills learned in encomium and invective; Aphtonius gives an example of the comparison of Hector and Achilles. This can be a double encomium or an encomium and an invective. (11) *Character representation* (ἠθοποιΐα or προσωποποΐα, *sermocinatio;* see **prosopopoiia*); Lausberg 1998, §1131–32; Spengel 1853–54, 2.44–46): The student must imagine what a particular individual might say in a particular situation. ἠθοποιΐα has three subdivisions: ἠθικαί ("disposition"): What would a person from the interior say when first seeing the sea; παθητικαί ("emotion"): What would Hecuba say as Troy lay in ruins; and μικταί ("mixed," i.e., a combination): What would Achilles say over the fallen Patroclus as he decides to go to war? (12) *Description* (ἔκφρασις, *descriptio;* see **ekphrasis*; Lausberg 1998, §1133; Spengel 1853–54, 2.46–49): the student is required to set a scene vividly before the imagination, a useful ability in making a significant impact on the audience. According to both Theon (*Prog.* 11) and Hermogenes (*Prog.* 10), an ekphrasis "is a descriptive composition that brings what is being disclosed vividly before the eyes." (13) *Thesis* (θέσις, *thesis;* Lausberg 1998, §1134–38; Spengel 1853–54, 2.49–53): The student is required to argue for or against a general proposition. (14) *Proposal of law* (νόμου εἰσφορά, *legis latio*; Lausberg 1998, §1139; Spengel 1853–54, 2.46–51): A student speaks for or against a particular law. This is useful in judicial oratory when a speaker must interpret a law. When students finished their course in progymnasmata, they then are able to make a transition from composing parts of speeches to composing whole speeches, i.e., *declamations (D. A. Russell 1983).

*Ekphrasis, *Rhetorical genres, *Rhetorical handbooks

Bonner 1977, 250–76; Clark 1957, 177–212; Heath 1995, 13–17; Hock and O'Neill 1986, 9–22; Kennedy 1983, 54–70; 2003

Prolepsis, a transliterated form of the Greek word πρόληψις (translated into Latin as *anticipatio*) is used in rhetoric for the defensive anticipation of the argument of the opponent (Lausberg 1998, §§855). In syntax, however, prolepsis is "the anticipation of the subject (object) of the subordinate clause by making it the object of the main clause" (BDR §476; a detailed discussion of syntactical prolepsis is found in van Belle 2001). An example of prolepsis is found in Rev. 3:9: ἰδοὺ ποιήσω *αὐτοὺς* ἵνα ἥξουσιν καὶ προσκυνήσουσιν ἐνώπιον τῶν ποδῶν σου, "Behold I will make *them* that they will come and will fall prostrate before your feet." Here the object of the main clause, αὐτοὺς ("them"), anticipates the subjects of the two verbs in the subordinate clause ἥξουσιν ("they will come") and προσκωνήσουσιν ("they will fall prostrate"). Prolepsis is one of the characteristic stylistic features of the Gospel of John (van Belle 2001), where it occurs 12 times (4:35; 5:42; 7:27; 8:54; 9:8, 19, 29; 10:36; 11:31; 13:28; 14:17; 16:4). Prolepsis also occurs three times in Matthew (6:28 [= Luke 12:27]; 10:25; 25:24), four times in Mark (1:24 [= Luke 4:34]; 7:2; 11:32; 12:34), seven times in Luke (4:34 [= Mark 1:24]; 9:31; 12:24, 27 [= Matt. 6:28]; 13:25; 19:3; 24:7), eight or nine times in Acts (3:10, 12; 4:13; 5:26; 9:20; 13:32–33; 15:36; 16:3 [var. lect.]; 26:5).

Boismard 1977a; Van Belle 2001

Pronouncement stories, short literary forms consisting of two characteristic parts, a story and a pronouncement that is the climactic element, were variously labeled by earlier form-critical scholars *apophthegmata (Bultmann 1963, 11–69; 1967, 8–73), *Paradigmen* (Dibelius 1934, 26, 37–69; 1971, 24–25, 34–66), or *Streitgespräche* (Albertz), but called "pronouncement stories" by Taylor (1935, 63–87). More recently, Kee has designated this form as an "aphoristic narrative" (1996, 133), while Robbins (1981a, 52 n. 5) prefers the designation "gnomic chreia." Tannehill has framed a useful definition of this literary form (1981, 1):

> A pronouncement story is a brief narrative in which the climactic (and often final) element is a pronouncement which is presented as a particular person's response to something said or observed on a particular occasion of the past. There are two main parts of a pronouncement story: the pronouncement and its setting, i.e., the response and the situation provoking that response. The movement from the one to the other is the main development in these brief stories.

Among the earlier proposals for a typology of apophthegmata was that of Bultmann, emphasizing differences in content (1963, 11–69; 1967, 8–73): (1) *Streitgespräche* (controversy dialogues), (2) *Schulgespräche* (scholastic dialogues), and (3) *biographische apophthegmata* (biographical apophthegms). Fascher provided a thorough critique of Bultmann's third category and concluded that a more apt designation might be *Anekdoten* (anecdotes) (Fascher 1924, 203). More recently, Tannehill proposed a sixfold typology that serves to discriminate between the various rhetorical functions of pronouncement stories (1981, 7–12): (1) corrections, (2) commendations, (3) objections, (4) quests, (5) inquiries, and (6) descriptions. Earlier, Aune (1978, 60–69) had classified a group of what he labeled as "wisdom stories," in Plutarch's *Banquet of the Seven Sages,* as gnomic wisdom stories, agonistic wisdom stories, and paradigmatic wisdom stories. Robbins (1981a) combined Tannehill's sixfold typology with Aune's threefold typology by suggesting three main types of pronouncement stories, each with two subtypes: (1) aphoristic pronouncement stories, (a) description, (b) inquiry; (2) adversative pronouncement stories, (a) correction, (b) dissent, [1] objection, [2] rebuff; (3) affirmative pronouncement stories, (a) commendation, (b) laudation.

The earlier identification, classification, historical analysis, and reconstruction of the *Sitz im Leben* ("life settings") of the pronouncement story were by form critics (see *Form criticism), whose primary interest lay in the preliterary origin and transmission of these traditional units. The pronouncement story exhibits a degree of discontinuity in its final literary settings, thereby maintaining its connection with its independent origins (much like the literary recontextualization of different folklore genres such as the riddle, proverb, or epigram). While Bultmann and other form critics were primarily interested in the pronouncement story in pre-Gospel tradition, Tannehill (1981, 5) was primarily concerned with their literary function as acts of communication between authors and their audiences. Pronouncement stories were thought appropriate for inclusion in a number of host genres, including ancient biography. There are collections of pronouncement stories, both as collections (e.g., Plutarch's *Regnum et imperatorum apophthegmata*) and as concentrations within other literary genres (cf. Petzke 1970, 111–18). Even within the same author the same pronouncement can be attributed to different individuals in different settings; in these cases (like similar attribution of the same saying to different rabbinic sages) the rhetorical focus is often on the encapsulated wisdom expressed in the pronouncement. It is important to know that rhetorical theorists placed such sayings *without* a narrative setting in the same category as sayings with a narrative framework, but also and primarily through the fact that *sententiae* or γνώμαι were not uncommonly given narrative frameworks when they were detached from oral speech and recontextualized in a literary setting with recognizable scenes and an appropriate cast of characters. This transition from oral to written, accompanied by the addition of a narrative framework, is a process folklorists have observed in the study of proverbs (cf. Abrahams and Babcock 1977). Tannehill's emphasis on the stylized character of pronouncement stories is well taken (1981, 3); it is precisely the stereotypical features of pronouncement stories—their essential anonymity and their existence and circulation in several versions—that make them appropriate objects for the application of folkloristic methods of analysis. The fact that the culminating sayings in many pronouncement stories can stand alone (and there is evidence that many did in fact circulate in that form) led Bultmann (1967, 49) to designate those apophthegmata in which the culminating saying is inseparable from the narrative framework as having a "unitary conception" (*einheitliche Konzeption*), and is further reflected in Hultgren's (1979, 67) analysis of Synoptic conflict stories under the rubrics of "Unitary Conflict Stories" and "Non-Unitary Conflict Stories."

Apocryphal gospels. Stroker (1981) emphasizes the relative paucity of pronouncement stories in the apocryphal gospels. Yet there are 22 pronouncement stories in the *Gospel of Thomas* (Perkins 1981, 122–23), of which only 6 have Synoptic parallels (*Gos. Thom.* 72, 79, 99, 100, 104, 113). At least 3 pronouncement stories are found in the *Gospel of Philip* (34, 54, 55), and the Jewish Christian apocryphal gospels apparently also contained many pronouncement stories based on the fragmentary surviving evidence (*Gos. Naz.* 2, 16; *Gos. Eb.* 5; *Gos. Heb.* 7; *Gos. Eg.* 1, 5; cf. *2 Clem.* 12:2; *P. Oxy.* 840.12).

*Chreia, *Conflict stories, *Form criticism, *Oral tradition

Abrahams and Babcock 1977; Aune 1978; Bultmann 1967; Dibelius 1934; Fascher 1924; Hultgren 1979; Perkins 1981; Petzke 1970; Robbins 1981a; Tannehill 1981; Taylor 1935

Pronouncements of Sacral Law, a translation of the German phrase *sätze heiligen Rechtes* coined by Käsemann in 1969. According to Käsemann, the characteristic features of "pronouncements of sacral law" include the following: (1) The pronouncement is structured in the form of a chiasmus (a b b a), a feature often more obvious in Greek than in English translation. (2) The same verb is found in both parts of the pronouncement. (3) The second part of the pronouncement deals with the eschatological activity of God, and the verb is often in the passive voice, functioning as a circumlocution for divine activity. (4) The principle of *ius talionis*, or "retributive justice" is a central feature of the pronouncement, expressing the intimate relationship between guilt and punishment, duty and reward. (5) The first part (the protasis) is introduced with the casuistic legal form "if any one" or "whoever," while the second part (the apodosis) is in the style of apodictic divine law (Käsemann 1969, 66–68)

Aune 1983, 237–40; Käsemann 1969

Prooimion, a transliterated form of the Greek word προοίμιον, meaning "introduction, prologue" (Latin *exordium*) a term for the first part of a speech (Cicero, *De inventione* 1.20–26). The function of the prooimion is to put the audience in the proper frame of mind to listen to the rest of the speech. One of the more important functions of the prooimion is the convincing presentation of the character or *ethos* (ἦθος) of the author. According to Cicero, "We shall win good-will from our own person if we refer to our own acts and services without arrogance" (*De inventione* 1.22). If the audience is hostile, this attitude must be changed through the prooimion before the argument can be presented (Cicero, *Inv.* 1.23). According to Smit (1989, 1–26), the prooimion or *exordium* of *Galatians is found in 1:6–12, where it serves the following functions: (1) Paul alarms his audience by informing them that they are deserting God (vv. 6–7a); (2) he arouses hostility against his opponents (vv. 7b–9); and (3) he tries to gain sympathy for himself (vv. 10–12).

*Exordium, *Preface, *Rhetorical theory

Prophetic call narrative (see *Call narrative)

Prosaics, a 20th-cent. neologism used as the counterpart to poetics, dealing with the theory of prose writing. Fokkelman (1998–2001, 1:2–3) presents a linguistic model for the various levels of complexity which constitute a narrative text:

Texture	*Composition*
6. Sentences	12. Book
5. Clauses	11. Section
4. Phrases	10. Act
3. Words	9. Story
2. Syllables	8. Scenes
1. Sounds	7. Sequences or speeches

*Narrative criticism, *Rhetorical handbooks

Fokkelman 2000; Morson and Emerson 1990

Prose Rhythm, or *numerosa oratio,* an aspect of *style (λέξις or *elocutio*), is the use of certain patterns or sequences of long and short vowels, frequently in the κῶλον or *clausula,* i.e., a clause within the sentence, often a clause at the end of a sentence, and a term for the rhythms used there to create a certain esthetic effect in the audience (Cicero, *Orator* 199). The term "rhythm" is a transliterated form of the Greek word ῥυθμός ("measured movement"), equivalent to the polysemous Latin term *numerus* and also the Latin term *rhythmus,* transliterated from Greek (Quintilian, *Inst.* 9.4.54). Prior to late antiquity, both Greek and Latin had quantitative vowel systems in which long vowels took twice as long to pronounce as short vowels. Thus Greek and Latin vowels were analogous to a musical notation system in which (for example) music written in 4/4 time means that there are four beats to a measure and a quarter note gets one beat, while an eighth note gets a half beat (thus a quarter note takes twice as long to sing as an eighth note). Similarly "long" vowels (eta and omega, most diphthongs, and all vowels followed by two or more consonants) took twice as long to pronounce as "short" vowels (epsilon and omicron), and those vowels which can either be "long" or "short" (alpha, iota, and upsilon). In modern English, on the other hand "long" and "short" vowels are simply different phonemes, e.g., long "a" occurs in such words as "far" and "father," while short "a" occurs in such words as "date" and "made." The observation of Maas (1962, 3) on the subject of prose rhythm in Greek is striking: "Scarcely any facet of the culture of the ancient world is so alien to us as its quantitative metric . . . [which has] now vanished not only from the literature, but from the speech of Europe." After ca. 400 C.E., the quantitative difference between long and short vowels in Greek was largely replaced with stress, as in modern English, French, and German. For Latin, however, the quantitative length of vowels lasted into the Middle Ages. Thus in classical and Hellenistic Greek, as in Latin, rhythm was unavoidable, which is why Dionysius of Halicarnassus insisted that *all* Greek words have some sort of rhythm (*De comp. verb.* 17). In Cicero's extensive discussion of prose rhythm (*Orator* 149–203), he comments on the fact that rhythm is characteristic of prose as well as poetry (*Orator* 188, 196–97; LCL trans.):

> For the foot, which is employed in rhythms, is of three types; it divides into two equal parts, or one part is twice as long as the other, or half again as long. Examples of these are, respectively, the dactyl [-⏑⏑; 2:2], the iambus [⏑- 1:2], the paean [⏑ ⏑ ⏑ - 3:2 or - ⏑ ⏑ ⏑; 2:3]. How can these feet fail to occur in prose? And when they are arranged in a systematic order the effect must be rhythmical. However, the question is raised as to which rhythm or which rhythms it is most desirable to use. All of them may occur in prose, as appears from the fact that we often

> make verses unintentionally in delivering a speech. . . . The iambus, for example, is most frequent in passages of a plain, simple conversational type; the paean is used in the more elevated style, and the dactyl in both. Therefore in a long speech with varying moods these rhythms must be mingled and blended.

Quintilian (*Inst.* 11.2.39) suggests that rhythmic prose is easier to remember than prose lacking rhythm, a feature that some relate to the poetic formulation of the teaching of Jesus (Gerhardsson 1979, 20–21; Riesner 1982, 507).

Greek and Latin literature. The most extensive ancient discussion of prose rhythm is found in Cicero, *Orator* 149–203 (a contribution of which he is fully aware; see 226). Theoretical discussions of prose rhythm emphasize two points (Landfester 1997, 166): (1) the entire sentence should be pleasing to the ear and have rhythmic content (Quintilian, *Inst.* 9.4.115–16; Cicero, *De oratore* 3.190), and (2) the way the sentence ends is particularly important (Aristotle, *Rhetorica* 3.8 [1409a]; Cicero, *De oratore* 3.192; Quintilian, *Inst.* 9.4.61–63). Isocrates (436–338 B.C.E.) was credited by his student Naucrates with being the first to introduce rhythm into prose (Cicero, *De inv.* 3.44.173; *Brutus* 32), but Cicero later learned that Thrasymachus was actually the inventor of prose rhythm and Isocrates who perfected it (Cicero, *Orator* 175). However, Greek notions of who first did what should always be viewed with skepticism because of the enormous importance they placed in understanding a phenomenon on the basis of its putative origin. Aristotle (*Rhetorica* 3.8.1–7 [1408b–1409a]) recommended that formal speech should neither be metrical (for that would make it poetry), or nonmetrical (for that would make it unpleasing and unlimited). He recommends the use of the paeon (i.e., an unresolved cretic [κρητικός]), because it is the one prose rhythm most likely to be undetected (*Rhetorica* 3.8.5 [1409b]). Similarly, Cicero (*Orator* 192; revised LCL trans.) argues that "those who neglect the paean fail to see that they are neglecting the rhythm which is most pleasant but at the same time most stately." And again (Cicero, *Orator* 194; LCL trans.): "the paean, however, is poorly adapted to verse, and therefore prose welcomes it gladly." The cretic and the choriambus are the two prose rhythms most like ordinary speech. While the normal cretic is a long, then a short, then a long (-˘-), the "unresolved" cretic (or paeon) has two forms ˘˘˘- (i.e., short, short, short, long) or -˘˘˘ (i.e., long, short, short, short), and Aristotle thought that the first type was appropriate for an ending, and the second for a beginning (according to Cicero, *Orator* 218; Aristotle; Theophrastus; Theodectes; and Ephorus, the paeon was best adapted to the beginning, middle, or end of a sentence, a judgment repeated in Quintilian, *Inst.* 9.4.107). Ps.-Demetrius (*De elocutione* 38–39) uses the terms παιὼν προαταρκτικός (i.e., first paeon) for a paeon with an initial long syllable (-˘˘˘), and παιὼν καταληκτικός (i.e., last paeon) for one ending with a long syllable (˘˘˘-). The choriambus exhibits a different pattern -˘˘-. After Demosthenes, three prose rhythmical patterns emerged as dominant (Norden 1909, 2.917): (1) the ditrochaic (διτρόχαιος): -˘- x (x = *anceps*, "ambivalent," i.e., either long or short; equivalent to the Greek term κοινή), (2) the cretic + cretic: -˘---˘- or -˘---˘x, (3) the cretic + the trochaic: -˘---x, and (4) the trochaic + trochaic: -˘-- x (this last metrical pattern is added by Dihle 1965, 2450–51). For an example of the cretic + trochaic (Landfester 1997, 169), see Plutarch, *Moralia* 346f: ἀλλ᾽ οὐκ ἂν οἶμαι . . . ἀνάσχοισθε τῶν προτιμώντων . . . τὸ μίμημα τῆς αληθείας [-˘---˘], "But I do not think . . . that you would tolerate those who prefer . . . the imitation of the truth."

The analysis of prose rhythm in Greek and Latin texts is usually carried out deductively rather than inductively, that is, certain rhythmic patterns are looked for in the clausulae (sentence endings) of classical texts. An extensive inductive study was carried out by de Groot (1919, 40–43) based on 12 sequences of 1,000 syllables in various classical authors. The patterns discovered in this way were then compared with the patterns found in clausulae, a procedure that revealed which statistically significant prose rhythms were used in clausulae. One result of this procedure is evidence for rhythmic patterns in clausulae favored and avoided by the authors examined. For example (de Groot 1919, table between 196 and 197), Josephus favors -˘˘-˘˘x and -˘--˘x, but avoids -˘˘-x, and ---x; Philo favors ˘˘˘-˘˘x, -˘-x, -˘-˘˘x, -˘˘˘x, -˘˘˘-x, -˘˘-˘x, -˘--˘x, and ˘˘˘--x, etc. (he also provides similar analyses of Thrasymachus, Thucydides, Plato [*Laws*], Isocrates, Demosthenes, Chariton, Plutarch, and Polemo).

Dionysius of Halicarnassus, a Greek teacher of rhetoric in 1st-cent. B.C.E. Rome, emphasizes the importance of prose rhythms in public speaking (*De comp. verb.* 18; LCL trans.): "it is rhythms which are noble and dignified, and possess majesty, that make composition dignified, noble and impressive, whereas it somehow lacks both majesty and gravity when ignoble or mean rhythms are used." He prefaces this statement with a relatively extensive explanation of the various Greek poetic meters (*De comp. verb.* 17). Dionysius emphasizes the importance of prose rhythms in speech (*De comp. verb.;* Bonner 1969, 73–74), arguing that all Greek words have some sort of rhythm (*De comp. verb.* 17); for example, a word of two syllables can have two longs or two shorts or one short and one long. According to "Blass's Law," Demosthenes (4th cent. B.C.E.) tended to avoid sequences of two short syllables, a rule that Blass used as a negative criterion of authenticity and as a criterion for emendation (for a scansion of numbers of cola in Demosthenes, see Norden 1909, 2.911–17). More recently, McCabe (1968) has argued convincingly that while Blass's Law was unknown to ancient literary critics (1968, 9–41), it is nevertheless generally valid (1968, 119–68) but should be racheted down from a "law" to a "strong tendency." According to Vogel (1923, 109; cf. McCabe 1968, 20), Aelius Aristides (2d cent. C.E.) was apparently the only rhetorician in antiquity to notice Blass's Law. There was an even greater tendency to avoid three short syllables in a row: ˘˘˘, a so-called trochee or tribrach (some confusion because the tribrach was called *trochaeus* in Latin; Quintilian, *Inst.* 9.4.66, 87, 105).

Latin prose rhythm was initially largely dependent on Greek notions of the subject. Cicero was one of the more influential authors for Latin prose rhythms (Primmer 1968). Cicero is the first rhetorician to treat clausulae at any length (*Orator* 207–26), a virtue of which he is fully aware (*Orator* 226), and Quintilian also has an extensive treatment of clausulae (*Inst.* 9.4.60–111). Quintilian (*Inst.* 9.4.97) claimed that Demosthenes liked to end sentences with a spondee (σπονδεῖος): -- (two long syllables).

NT and ECL. This subject is rarely treated by scholars of the NT and early Christian literature (Siegert 1993, 56–58), confirming Augustine's late 4th cent. C.E. observation that clausula-rhythm was largely absent in the Greek NT (*De doctrina Christ.* 4.41). While prose rhythm is admittedly rare in the Pauline letters, it is used with some frequency in Acts, where Paul is occasionally made to speak more elegantly than in his own letters (Siegert 1993, 51–54). Unfortunately Morgenthaler (1993), who discusses the subject of prose rhythm in Quintilian in the first half of his book, does not discuss the application of this matter to Luke–Acts with any specificity. Blass (1905, 43, 53) finds prose rhythms in 1 Corinthians, primarily in 1 Cor. 13 (but his proposals are faulted by Schmid and Stählin 1920–24, 2/2.1135 n. 4 and 1152 n. 1). Prose rhythm is also used in the letter of James, where Siegert (1993, 54) calls attention to a remarkable sequence of 23 long vowels in James 2:18, which the author uses to emphasize his thesis: δεῖξόν μοι τὴν πίστιν σου χωρὶς τῶν ἔργων, κἀγώ σοι δείξω'κ [the hiatus between ω and ε could be avoided by crasis, pronouncing the phrase δείξω ἐκ as δείξω'κ] τῶν ἔργων μου τὴν πίστιν, "show me your faith apart from works, and I will show you faith by my works." According to Ps.-Demetrius (*De elocutione* 39; LCL trans.): "the long syllable has in its very nature something grand." The author of Hebrews, however, begins in 1:1 with πολυμερῶς ("in various ways" or "in various parts"), which must be scanned ˘ ˘ ˘ - (ο=˘, υ=˘, ε=˘, ω=-). The ending recommended by theorists from Aristotle to Quintilian does not occur in Hebrews until 11:3: γεγονέναι, i.e., ˘˘˘- (Moffatt 1924, lvi). Blass discussed prose rhythm in Hebrews, which he regarded as a work in *Kunstprosa* (1902, 420), in some detail (1902, 1903). For a brief discussion of prose rhythms in Hebrews, see Moffatt (1924, lvi–lix). The author of Hebrews prefers ˘˘˘-- as an ending (e.g., 7:28, 29; 9:26; 10:34, 35; 11:13, 15, 28; 12:3). The resolved cretic (-˘˘-) occurs with some frequency as in this carefully composed section in Heb. 4:8–10. Rose (1924) has a detailed discussion of the rhythmic clausulae in the Pauline letters, which he uses as an argument for distinguishing authentic Pauline letters from pseudonymous Pauline letters.

*Atticism, *Asianism, *Metrical analysis, *Style

———

BDR §487; Blass 1901, 1902, 1903, 1905; Dihle 1965; Groot 1919; Landfester 1997, 166–70; Lausberg 1998, §§1006–51; Maas 1962; McCabe 1981; Morgenthaler 1993, 175–82; Norden 1909, 2.909–60; *OCD* 1260–62; Preminger 1965, 666–67; Primmer 1968; Rose 1924; Rowe 1997, 154; Schmid 1959; Siegert 1993

Prosopography, from προσώπον ("person"), is the study of the proper name (ὄνομα κύριον, *nomen proprium*) of an individual and the use of such onomastic evidence (ὀνομαστικός, "of naming," a term that includes topographical names) to determine regional origins, family connections (including marriage and adoption), clan connections, and tribal membership of individuals.

Fraser 1987–97

Prosopopoiia, a transliteration of the Greek word προσωποποιΐα, character delineation or "speech-in-character" (Stowers 1994), which normally introduces a specific character, whether person or thing (*ethopoiia,* or ἠθοποιΐα is a term reserved for a person) and allows it to speak. The person or thing that speaks is virtually always identified (Quintilian, *Inst.* 9.2.37), According to Demetrius, *Eloc.* 265: "Another figure of thought—the so-called 'prosopopoeia'—may be employed to produce energy of style, as in the words: 'Imagine that your ancestors, or Hellas, or your native land, assuming a woman's form, should address such and such reproaches to you.'" Stowers (1994) has identified several instances of *prosopopoiia* in Rom. 2:1–5, 17–29; 3:1–9; 3:27–4:2; 7:7–8:2 (these are not unproblematic, since in the last passage there is no indication that Paul has introduced another speaker or voice). While Stowers (1995) specifically identifies Rom. 7:7–25 as an instance of *prosopopoiia,* it appears rather to be a personal *paradeigma* or *example (R. D. Anderson 1999, 232). Athanasius of Alexandria uses *prosopopoiia* when he crafts a brief speech by the flesh giving an answer to a disputatious heretic (*Contra Arianos* 3.34):

> I indeed am mortal by nature, taken from the earth. In the latter days, however, I have become the flesh of the Logos, and he himself has borne my passions, impassible though he is. So I am free of them. I am no longer enslaved to them, for the Lord has set me free from them. If you object because I have been released from the corruption which is mine by nature, see to it that you raise no objection to the fact that the divine Logos took to himself my state of slavery. Just as the Lord became a human being when he put on a body, so we human beings, once we have been connected to him by way of his flesh, are divinized by the Logos, and from that point on we are the heirs of eternal life.

Again, Athanasius tries to capture the relationship between the Father and the Son (*Contra Arianos* 3.36):

> Suppose that the radiance itself says, "The light has given me all places to illumine, and I illumine not from myself but as the light wills." In saying this, the radiance does not indicate that at one time it did not possess light but rather asserts, "I am proper to the light and everything which belongs to the light is mine."

R. D. Anderson 2000, 106–7; Stowers 1994, 1995

Protoapocalyptic is a designation for those works and parts of works widely regarded as precursors of the *apocalypse genre. These works include Isa. 24–27 (the so-called "Isaiah apocalypse"), Isa. 40–55 ("Deutero-Isaiah"), Isa. 56–66 ("Trito-Isaiah"), Ezek. 38–39, Ezek. 40–48, Joel, Zech. 1–6, Zech. 9–14. Some of these texts are more proximate precursors of apocalypses because of their formal features, such as vision reports, and the use of the literary device of the *angelus interpres.*

Hanson 1979; Koch 1989; Millar 1976; Tigchelaar 1996

Protocanonical, a Roman Catholic term for those 24 books of the Old Testament or Hebrew Bible that were translated from Hebrew into Greek and then into Latin. The term *deuterocanonical is used for those books and revisions of books found in the Roman Catholic Old Testament canon of 46 books. This distinction was first made by Pope Sixtus of Sienna in 1561.

*Canon, biblical

Protreptic literature The λόγος προτρεπτικός, or "speech of exhortation," is a speech intended to win converts and attract young people to a particular way of life. The primary setting for the *logos protreptikos* was the philosophical school, where it was the primary rhetorical tool used to attract adherents by exposing the errors of alternate ways of living and demonstrating the truth claims of a particular philosophical tradition over its competitors. During the Hellenistic period, Jewish intellectuals often conceptualized Judaism as a philosophy and attempted to present it in philosophical guise to outsiders. Christianity inherited this conception (Jaeger 1961, 9–10).

In *rhetoric,* the terms τὸ προτρεπτικός ("persuasion") and τὸ ἀποτρεπτικός ("dissuasion"), refer to the two different purposes of *deliberative rhetoric. In *philosophical* contexts, on the other hand, τὸ προτρεπτικός is paired with ἐλεγχός ("censure") and refers to a single method consisting of encouragement and rebuke used to bring a person to embrace the truth. The λόγος προτρεπτικός, however, is rooted in both the rhetorical and philosophical protreptic traditions but must be distinguished from both. The central function of λόγοι προτρεπτικοί was to encourage conversion, but it included a strong component of ἀποτρέπειν ("dissuasion") and ἐλέγχειν ("censure") as well, aimed at freeing the person from erroneous beliefs and practices. In Lucian, *Nigrinus* 4, the author has created a protreptic confrontation between Nigrinus the Platonist and himself: "For he [Nigrinus] went on to praise philosophy and the freedom that it gives, and to ridicule the things that are popularly considered blessings—wealth and reputation, dominion and honor, yet also purple and gold—things accounted very desirable by most men, and til then by me also." In the *Hermotimus,* a parody of the protreptic genre, Lucian claims that adherents to particular philosophical traditions "persuade as many as they can to the same situation" (*Herm.* 75). Few philosophers, claims Lucian's character Lycinus, realize the error of their ways and try (like the skeptic Lucian himself) to dissuade others from such errors (*Herm.* 75). The fact that the λόγος προτρεπτικός is not discussed in any of the extant rhetorical handbooks makes it necessary to base our knowledge of the structure and argumentation used in protreptic speeches on an inductive study of the genre. The inductive analysis of the genre, however, is impeded by the survival of very few λόγοι προτρεπτικοί from the Hellenistic period. Most are known by name only, and a few others survive in fragmentary form, such as Aristotle's *Protrepticus* and Cicero's *Hortensius*. Those which have survived (e.g., Iamblichus's *Protrepticus,* come from the period of the Empire. λόγοι προτρεπτικοί existed in the form of oral discourses (with both epideictic and deliberative features) as well as written dialogues, discourses (in the form of monologues), and letters (on the latter, see Seneca, *Ep.* 60 and the *Letter to Menoeceus* of Epicurus (Diogenes Laertius 10.122–35). The earliest surviving λόγος προτρεπτικός, Plato's *Euthydemus,* is a dialogue, while Aristotle's *Protrepticus* (which is dependent on the *Euthydemus*) was written in the form of a discourse (Düring 1961, 29–32), with some use of diatribe style (Schneeweiss 1912, 238). This variety makes it difficult to claim generic status for the λόγος προτρεπτικός only if an artificially rigid view of the nature of oral and literary genres is maintained. There is an element of fluidity between these and related forms of discourse.

Philo of Larissa (ca. 159/8–84/3 B.C.E.). According to Philo of Larissa (Stobaeus, *Anth.* 2.7.2), a Platonist who verged on skepticism: "All protreptic consists of two parts, of which one is the demonstration of the value and profit of philosophy, whereas the other refutes the views of those adversaries who misrepresent or condemn this activity." An inductive approach suggests that ἐνδεικτικός ("demonstration") and ἀπελεγμός ("refutation") are characteristic of λόγοι προτρεπτικοί. For Philo of Larissa, protreptic is defined as "urging on to virtue." Gerhäuser (1912, 11–13), using the work of Philo, has outlined the negative and positive types of arguments used in protreptic. Ways of responding to adverse arguments take the form of responses to the following questions: (1) Is philosophy possible? (2) Is philosophy necessary? (3) Did not people at the dawn of civilization live without philosophy? (4) Does philosophy have value though lacking practical utility? (5) Is there not a contradiction between the theory and practice of philosophers? The positive arguments emphasize the fact that philosophy is the only road to happiness by (1) making a comparison (σύγκρισις) with other goods, (2) defining philosophy and the tasks included, (3) establishing its connections with other arts and sciences, (4) demonstrating that philosophy derives from the true nature of humanity, and (5) ultimately affirming philosophy by the divinization of the philosophers.

In a discussion of the generic characteristics of philosophical protreptic, Jordan (1986, 314–27) analyzes the structure of several λόγοι προτρεπτικοί, including Plato's *Euthydemus* and Aristotle's *Protrepticus.* He finds three stages in protreptic sections of the *Euthydemus* that he thinks are typical of later protreptic: (1) desire for good as a choice based on knowledge, (2) critique of rival sources of knowledge, (3) exhortation to choose philosophy, the only valid source of knowledge.

Gaiser (1959, 219–20), following Jaeger, found evidence suggesting the threefold structure of Aristotle's *Protrepticus* in the way Iamblichus arranged excerpts from this work (Iamblichus, *Protrepticus* 6, 7–8, 9–12). The threefold structural analysis of Aristotle's *Protrepticus* by Schneeweiss (1912, 231–35; cf. Düring 1961, 17–20) supports Gaiser's proposal: (1) epideictic section, (2) apelenktic section (the opponents are not actual; Aristotle has attributed objections to fictional opponents in a way similar to *diatribe style), (3) summary epideictic section.

*Lucian of Samosata (ca. 120–80 C.E.), wrote four dialogues focusing on conversion, one of which is a λόγος προτρεπτικός (*Nigrinus*), while the other three are parodies of λόγοι προτρεπτικοί (*Hermotimus, De parasito, De saltatione*); see Schäublin 1985, 117–31. Each concludes with a "conversion." In adapting protreptic to the dialogue form, the speeches of the partcipants focus first on dissuasion, then on persuasion. The *Nigrinus*, for example, is structured as a *synkrisis* comparing praiseworthy Athens with despicable Rome in light of the virtues appropriate for the philosophical life and vices inconsistent with the philosophical life (L. Müller 1929, 574–78; Bompaire 1958, 277).

This survey of the basic structure of a number of λόγοι προτρεπτικοί indicates that they characteristically consist of three features: (1) a negative section centering on the critique of rival sources of knowledge, ways of living, or schools of thought that reject philosophy; (2) a positive section in which the truth claims of philosophical knowledge, schools of thought, and ways of living are presented, praised, and defended; (3) an optional section, consisting of a personal appeal to the hearer, inviting the immediate accepting of the exhortation. In view of the fact that basic features of juridical rhetoric (persuasion and dissuasion) and *epideictic rhetoric (praise and blame) are *combined* in λόγοι προτρεπτικοί (they are not normally combined in either epideictic or juridical speeches), it is not surprising that the rhetorical strategy of σύγκρισις (*comparison) is frequently utilized. Further, the essentially propaedeutic character of the genre meant that the diatribe style was suitable for use in λόγοι προτρεπτικοί.

Relevance for NT and ECL. Several scholars have suggested that *Romans is a "persuasive discourse," or *logos protreptikos* (Berger 1984, 217; Stowers 1986, 112–14; Aune 1991b, 1991c; Guerra 1995, 1–22; Bryan 2000, 18–28). In the NT, Berger (1984, 217) suggests other NT passages with protreptic features: Matt. 7:13–27; 11:25–30; John 3:1–21; 1 Cor. 13; 1 Tim. 4:7b–10). Against Berger, however, appeals to conversion are not the only generic features of λόγοι προτρεπτικοί. The so-called *Letter to Diognetus* (see *Diognetus, Letter to*) is also a protreptic discourse in three main parts: (1) *Diognetus* 2–4 ridicules the two major non-Christian religious options, pagan idolatry (*Diogn.* 2) and Jewish superstition (*Diogn.* 3–4). (2) *Diognetus* 5–9, the προτρεπτικός proper, attempts to persuade the dedicatee by describing the positive moral character of Christians and summarizing the theological basis for Christian beliefs. (3) *Diognetus* 10 is an appeal to the dedicatee to become a convert to Christianity.

In the protreptic section that constitutes the introduction to the *Dialogus cum Tryphon*, *Justin Martyr recounts his philosophical journey through Stoicism, Aristotelianism, Pythagoreanism, and Platonism. He then recounts his discussion with an old man (a literary figure personifying wisdom, in this case Christianity). The old man first tries to demonstrate the errors of Platonism (*Dial.* 3.1–6.2), then attempts to persuade Justin that Christianity is the true philosophy, and concludes with an appeal for a response that eventually results in Justin's conversion (*Dial.* 7.1–9.3). Yet the entire *Dialogue* can be construed as a λόγος προτρεπτικός, or "speech of exhortation," intended to convert Trypho and his friends to Christianity. The fact that the setting for the *Dialogue* is entirely fictional does not contradict this view.

The most satisfactory basic outline of the *Dialogue* is that of Otto (1969, 1.lxxxii–xc), who argues that the *Dialogue* is divided into three sections: (1) the decline of the Old Covenant (10–47), (2) Jesus as the true Son of God who became a human being and was crucified for our sake (48–108), and (3) the calling of the Gentiles [as well as Jews] as the true people of God (109–41). It is apparent that the *Dialogue* has the basic structure of a λόγος προτρεπτικός, or "speech of exhortation," intended to win converts and attract people to a particular way of life. The *Dialogue* fits the three-part structure of protreptic speeches: (1) a negative section criticizing the rival sources of knowledge, ways of living, or schools of thought that reject philosophy (i.e., why the Law is obsolete and Christians do not obey it) (*Dial.* 10–47); (2) a positive section in which the truth claims of philosophical knowledge, schools of thought, and ways of living are presented, praised, and defended (i.e., why Christ is the true Messiah in *Dial.* 48–108); and (3) an optional section, consisting of a personal appeal to the hearer, inviting the immediate accepting of the exhortation (i.e., why Christians are the true heirs of the promises of God in *Dial.* 109–41, which includes explicit appeals to Trypho to repent in *Dial.* 118 and 137, as one would expect).

*Apologetic literature, *Barnabas, letter of, *Diatribe, *Diognetus, Letter to, *Romans, Paul's letter to the

Aune 1991c, 1991d; Berger 1984; Bompaire 1958; Bryan 2000; Gerhäuser 1912; Guerra 1995; Jaeger 1961; Jordan 1986; L. Müller 1929; Schneeweiss 1912; Stowers 1986

Proverbs. While Homer and the archaic Greek poets refer to proverbs with such terms as ἔπος, λόγος, and αἶνος, from the 5th cent. on, new terms are introduced, including ἀπόφθεγμα, γνώμη, παροιμία, and ὑποθήκη (Kindstrand 1978). In the Hellenistic period the most commonly used Greek terms for a proverb are γνώμη (which basically means a "way of knowing") and παροιμία ("proverb, maxim"), while the primary Latin term is *sententia* (basically meaning "way of thinking"). A proverb or maxim is a concise unattributed saying which gives pithy expression to an insight about life or moral truth, the validity of which is generally recognized and approved (see *Aphorism). Aristotle defined the maxim (γνώμη) in these words (*Rhet.* 2.21; 1394a): "A maxim is a statement that treats neither particulars—like what sort of fellow Iphicrates is—but things in general, not just anything in general—like the fact that the straight is the opposite of the crooked—but those things pertaining to human action, things that are to be chosen or avoided." A more succinct definition is found in the slightly earlier handbook of Anaximines (**Rhetorica ad Alexandrum* 11; 1430b): "The maxim is, in a word, an expression of one's personal conviction about some general principle of human action." *Rhetorica ad Herennium* is the earliest extant treatise in which *sententiae* is used as a technical rhetorical term (Sinclair 1993, 564), which he defines as "a declaration derived from social behavior, which succinctly presents either what is or what ought to be a fact of life" (4.24). For Quintilian (9.1.18), however, the *sententia* is not a rhetorical figure at all.

A proverb can also function as a premise or conclusion of an *enthymeme (which, with the example, functioned for Aristotle as the two primary forms of rhetorical proof), since it summarizes universal truths based on popular wisdom and introduces the ethical power necessary for persuasiveness (Aristotle, *Rhet.* 2.21.1–16; 1394a–1395b). Holloway (1998, 35–36) understands the γνώμη in Aristotle and Anaximines to be a rhetorical argument, yet initially ignores the fact that the proverb must be in the form of an enthymeme. Aristotle provides examples of proverbs that can take on the form of enthymemes: "Do not nurse immortal anger" is a proverb which becomes an enthymeme when prefaced with the reason expressed as a contrary: "Being a mortal, do not nurse immortal anger" (*Rhet.* 2.21.6; 1394b). "There is no man who is really free" becomes an enthymeme with the addition of "for he is the slave either of wealth or of fortune" (*Rhet.* 2.21.2; 1394b; from Euripides, *Hecuba* 864–65).

Holloway (1998, 46–52) identifies several *sententiae* in Paul (though not all the "examples" he cites are in fact proverbs, e.g. Rom. 4:26), including 1 Cor. 9:22: "To *all* men I have become *all* things that by *all* means I might save some." This maxim contains four words in each colon and uses forms of the word "all" three times, the figure of *paronomasia.

Sententiae or γνῶμαι could be given narrative frameworks when detached from oral speech or written collections and recontextualized in a narrative framework (see *Pronouncement story). This transition from oral to written, accompanied by the addition of a narrative framework, is a process that folklorists have observed in the study of proverbs (cf. Abrahams and Babcock 1977).

*Aphorisms, *Enthymeme, *Paroemiographers

Holloway 1998; Kindstrand 1978; Lardinois 2001; Mieder 1982, 1990, 1994, 1998; Mieder and Dundes 1981; Russo 1983; Searby 1998; Sinclair 1993

Psalms of Solomon (see Pseudepigrapha, OT)

Pseudepigrapha, NT, is used as a general designation for books of the NT ascribed to persons who are not the actual authors. "Pseudepigrapha," the neuter plural form of the Greek adjective ψευδεπίγραφος, was used for the first time by Serapion of Antioch (early 2d cent. C.E.), to refer to certain early Christian writings as τὰ ψευδεπίγραφα, i.e., as writings "with false superscriptions" (Eusebius, *Hist. eccl.* 6.12.3). The term was applied again to certain early Christian writings in the *Canones apostolorum* 60, from the 4th cent. C.E. Extracanonical early Christian writings analogous to the OT Pseudepigrapha have traditionally been designated NT Apocrypha (see *Apocrypha, NT).

Several letters attributed to Paul are widely regarded as pseudonymous. *Ephesians and the *Pastoral Letters (1 *Timothy; 2 *Timothy; *Titus), while 2 *Thessalonians and *Colossians are considered pseudonymous by some scholars. Among the Catholic Letters, *James, 1 *Peter, 2 *Peter, and *Jude are generally considered pseudonymous. The *Johannine letters, 1 John, 2 John, and 3 John, are attributed to "John" in titles added some time after their composition and, though they were not written by the apostle John, are anonymous rather than pseudonymous. Similarly, the four canonical Gospels are attributed to two disciples (Matthew and John) and two who are considered associates of disciples (Mark and Luke). Yet these ascriptions, like those on the Johannine letters, were added later, and so the Gospels are also anonymous rather than pseudonymous.

*Apocrypha, New Testament

Pseudepigrapha, OT, is a designation for a miscellaneous collection of religious writings of various genres (apocalypses, wisdom books, testaments, psalms, *rewritten Bible, epics, tragedies, and philosophical treatises) attributed to Jewish authors and editors who wrote between ca. 200 B.C.E. and C.E., written in Aramaic, Hebrew, and Greek (though typically preserved in Greek, Latin, Syriac, and Armenian translations). The OT Pseudepigrapha include all early Jewish compositions that are not part of other defined collections, such as the OT canonical books, the *Apocrypha, and the *Dead Sea Scrolls. Traditionally these books have been called "Apocrypha" by Roman Catholics and some Anglicans (for whom the Protestant label "Apocrypha" designates deuterocanonical books in the Roman Catholic OT canon), while Protestants (who label the Roman Catholic deuterocanonical books as "Apocrypha"), use the term "Pseudepigrapha" for noncanonical Jewish writings composed between 200 B.C.E. and 200 C.E.. "Pseudepigrapha" is the neuter plural form of the Greek adjective ψευδεπίγραφος, which was apparently used for the first time by Serapion of Antioch (early 2d cent. C.E.), a Christian author, who referred to certain early Christian writings as τὰ ψευδεπίγραφα, i.e., as writings "with false superscription" (Eusebius, *Hist. eccl.* 6.12.3). The term entered the theological vocabulary of the West when J. A. Fabricius (1722–33) published a work entitled *Codex pseudepigraphicus veteris testamenti.* The first German translation of these works (Kautzsch 1900) and the first English translation (R. H. Charles 1913) brought the term into common currency. The most recent and comprehensive collection of OT Pseudepigrapha is the translation edited by Charlesworth (1983–85), *The Old Testament Pseudepigrapha,* containing 52 documents. The Anglo-Catholic tradition of labeling this collection as Apocrypha is continued in Sparks (1984), *The Apocryphal Old Testament.* The term "Pseudepigrapha," however, is a misleading category, since many of the works so designated are anonymous, and further, writings with false attributions already occur in the OT itself (e.g., Daniel, Song of Songs), and some of the writings included in the Apocrypha are also pseudepigraphic (e.g., Wisdom of Solomon). Many Pseudepigrapha, however, are attributed to famous ancient Israelite figures such as Adam, Shem, Enoch, Noah, Abraham, Sedrach, Baruch, Ezra, and Daniel. The OT Pseudepigrapha are traditionally distinguished from the Apocrypha of the OT, many of which were included among the *deuterocanonical books of the Roman Catholic OT. However, the Jewish compositions in this category (like the *Septuagint, *Philo, and *Josephus) were transmitted by Christians, rather than Jews, and the transmission process sometimes involved not only copying, but also redaction and *interpolation (de Jonge 1995). While many Jewish compositions were transmitted by Christians with few if any Christian adaptations (1 *Enoch, *Josephus), others were only lightly or superficially interpolated (*Testaments of the Twelve Patriarchs), and still others were heavily rewritten (*Ascension of Isaiah, *Sibylline Oracles) or framed by extensive additions (4 *Ezra).

Earlier scholarship tended to identify various writings associated with the Pseudepigrapha of the OT with one of the four Jewish sects (Pharisees, Sadducees, Essenes, Zealots), though more recently that tendency has been largely abandoned, primarily because early Judaism was far more complex and varied than was once thought, so that the conception of a dominant "normative Judaism" is an illusion.

A comprehensive bibliography is found in DiTomaso 2001.

R. H. Charles 1913; Charlesworth 1981, 1983–85, 1985; Charlesworth and Evans 1993; Denis 1970; Di Tomaso 2001; Fabricius 1719, 1722–33; Herr 1990; Kautzsch 1900; Knittel 2002; Rost 1971; Russell 1987; Sparks 1984

Pseudepigraphy is the ascription of a written text to someone other than the actual author; the text itself is called a "pseudepigraphon." Following the work of Richard

Bentley in the late 17th cent., proving that the letters attributed to Phalaris, Themistocles, Socrates, and Euripides were forgeries, the canon of criticism for scholars was that literary letters from the ancient world must be considered forgeries unless they could be proven genuine (Stirewalt 1993, 30).

Functions of pseudepigraphy. The most common type of pseudepigraphy is the composition of works supporting particular positions, such as the Cynic epistles that attribute aspects of Cynic teaching to prominent Cynics or other famous figures of the past whom the authors want to portray as exhibiting Cynic tendencies, such as Crates, Diogenes, Heraclitus, and Socrates (Attridge 1976; Malherbe 1977b). Three literary techniques characteristic of pseudonymous works occur in the *prooimion* to Plutarch, *Septem sapientium convivium* (Speyer 1971, 44–84): (1) the use of the first person, (2) the emphasis on an eyewitness report, and (3) warnings against literary falsifications. One pseudonymous device missing is attribution to a famous person in antiquity.

Ancient attitudes toward pseudepigraphy. Though it pervaded the production of ancient literature, pseudepigraphy was often regarded negatively. According to Herodotus (*Hist.* 7.6), Onomacritus (a member of the court of Peisistratus in late 6th-cent. B.C.E. Athens) was found guilty of including an oracle that he had written in a collection of the oracles of Musaeus. In general, pseudepigraphy was viewed negatively in Christian circles (Donelson 1986, 16; J. D. Miller 1997, 5–7). This judgment is borne out by numerous references in early Christian texts regarding pseudepigraphy. Some disputed the authenticity of *1 Enoch,* finding it difficult to believe that it survived the flood (Tertullian, *De cultu fem.* 1; Metzger 1972, 15). Tertullian reports that the Asian presbyter who wrote the **Acts of Paul* was exposed and removed from office (Tertullian, *De baptismo* 17). According to Jerome, the authenticity of 2 Peter (see *Peter, Second Letter of) was disputed on the basis of differences in style with 1 Peter (see *Peter, First Letter of). Origen doubted the Pauline authorship of *Hebrews (which is anonymous) on stylistic criteria (Eusebius, *Hist. eccl.* 6.25.11–14). The Muratorian Canon (lines 63–67; Latin text in Westcott 1889, 521–38; text and translation in Theron 1958, 106–13) rejected the supposed Pauline letters to the Laodiceans and the Alexandrians as forgeries made in Paul's name for the Marcionites.

Pseudepigraphy in the OT and Judaism. While many of the writings of the OT are anonymous (see *Anonymity) rather than pseudonymous, several works attributed to Solomon, either directly or indirectly, qualify as pseudonymous, including Ecclesiastes, Song of Songs, and parts of Proverbs (10:1–22:16; 25:1–29:27). Pseudonymous works attributed to Solomon continued to be written, including the *Psalms of Solomon,* the *Odes of Solomon,* and the *Testament of Solomon.*

Pseudepigraphy is also found in the Qumran texts (Berstein 1999). 11QTemple is an example of *Rewritten Bible in which the third-person narrative of Pentateuchal texts is transposed into the first person, as if God were the speaker. Unlike typical pseudepigraphical authors, the writer does not attribute the work to a particular historical individual. For this reason, Wise (1990, 200) argues that 11Q Temple is not a pseudepigraphon.

*Apocryphal NT, *Pseudepigrapha, NT, *Pseudepigrapha, OT,

Bauckham 1988c; Baum 2001; Brox 1975, 1977; Chazon and Stone (eds.) 1999; J. Collins 1999; Donelson 1986; Guthrie 1962; Kiley 1986, 15–35; Meade 1986; Metzger 1972; Rist 1972; Rosenmeyer 2001; Speyer 1971, 1989, 1993; Stirewalt 1993, 27–42

Pseudo-Demetrius, *Epistolary Forms* is a handbook listing 21 types of letters (for details, see *Epistolography). While the work has been dated between 200 B.C.E. and 50 C.E. (Brinkmann 1909; 310–17), it seems more prudent to expand this possible range to between 200 B.C.E. and 300 C.E. (Malherbe 1988, 4).

*Epistolography

Brinkmann 1909; Malherbe 1988

Pseudo-Philo, *Biblical Antiquities* (see *Biblical Antiquities)

Publication in antiquity involved the production of a new work or *edition (Greek: ἔκδοσις; Latin *editio*) by an author who had one or more copies made of the original work for patrons and friends. This process is distinct from a critical edition of a text, which involves the task of publishing the original form of a text through choosing between textual variants of two or more manuscripts as well as conjectural emendation. In antiquity, the notion of "written publication" differed considerably from modern notions of "publication." In the case of Herodotus, for example, "publication" involved both an "oral publication" (i.e., a public reading of his work), based on a written text, and arranging to have copies made of the original text (Thomas 1993, 226–27). In philosophical schools, where the primary method was oral teaching or lecturing, the oral lectures were often regarded as a more authoritative source of knowledge than the written texts of the founder or head (L. Alexander 1990, 233–37). The copies that an author made of a work were just the beginning of the "publication" process, and the only part in which the author was directly involved (Van Groningen 1963, 4). Often the production of additional copies was arranged by the author from the original or a copy in order to sell them. Three important Greek terms relating to the process of publication in chronological order are ἔκδοσις ("publication"), διάδοσις ("distribution"), and παράδοσις ("transmission [of the text]"). The verb ἐκδίδωμι is frequently used with the meaning "to publish" (Dionysius Hal., *De Thucydide* 1; Plutarch, *Theseus* 20.2; *Romulus* 8.7; *Numa* 1.4; Athenaeus 4.168e; Diogenes Laertius 8.89; see Van Groningen 1963, 5–7). Dionysius of Halicarnassus composed his writings on criticism in the form of letters to various individuals, including friends, patrons, and students (Pritchett 1975, 47).

Illicit publication. In the *prooemium* to his *Institutio oratoria,* Quintilian mentions that part of his desire to write this work is based on two unauthorized books on the art of rhetoric circulating under his name (1. *praef.* 7–8). One of the books was a two-day lecture transcribed by some of his students, while the other consisted of notes taken by his students during a more extended course of study. "Consequently," he says, "in the present work although some passages remain the same, you will find many alterations and still more additions, while the whole theme will be treated with greater system and with as great perfection as lies within my power" (1. *praef.* 8; LCL trans.). During the Roman period, it was not uncommon to have in circulation written texts based on notes taken in lectures or copies made from other copies, neither of which were regarded by the author as his final version (Thomas 1993, 227). In *On prognosis* 9.8–9 (trans. A. E. Hanson 1998, 31), Galen (2d cent. C.E.) makes the following remarks: "Upon the emperor's return to Rome, I gave these treatises to my friends who asked for them, expecting that they would remain in their possession. If I had been aware then that they would be passed out to the unworthy, I would not have handed them out even to my friends."

Corruption. The author of the Revelation to John tried to prevent the alteration of his work by appending a curse (Rev. 22:19–20): "I warn every one who hears the words of the prophecy of this book: if any one adds to them, God will add to him the plagues described in this book, and if any one takes away from the words of the book of this prophecy, God will take away his share in the tree of life and in the holy city, which are described in this book."

The famous physician Galen (ca. 129–199 or 216 C.E.), a prolific author, was concerned for his postmortem reputation and therefore wrote two bibliographical essays on his own writings, *De libris propriis liber* ("On His Own Books"), which contained a descriptive catalog of his works (including a descriptive title and specifying the number of books), and *De ordine librorum suorum ad Eugenianum* ("On the Order of His Own Books to Eugenianus"). Galen mentioned the fact that many people had mutilated his writings in various ways; some read his works as their own, deleting things, or adding and changing other things (*De libr. prop, proemium* 1).

In *In Hipp. Epid. I comment.* 1 36, V 10.1 (trans. A. E. Hanson 1998, 25), Galen says that

> Sometimes I have written twice on a single matter, with one discussion in the text, but the other in one of the margins, so that I may consider the alternate and decide between them at leisure. The first one to copy the book, however, wrote out both versions, but since I neither paid attention to what happened, nor did I correct the error, the work, given out to many, remained without correction.

Tertullian claims that the first edition (*primum opusculum*) of his work *Adversus Marcionem* had been withdrawn in favor of a more complete edition of the work. This had been stolen (i.e., *excerpts were copied out of it) by a Christian who later became an apostate (*Adv. Marc.* 1.1). Tertullian replaced the second edition with a third edition that incorporated corrections and additions. He mentions all this "so that no one may be perplexed if in one place or another he comes across varying forms of it."

*Edition

L. Alexander 1990; Gamble 1995, 82–143; Marrou 1949; Most 1998; Pfeiffer 1968; Rengakos 1993; Thomas 1993; Van Groningen 1963

"Q" (Sayings Source). The so-called Sayings Source, designated Q (popularly, but incorrectly, understood as an abbreviation of the German word "Quelle," meaning "source"; it originated simply as an alphabetic *siglum* following "P"), is a lost but reconstructed document which consisted largely of sayings of Jesus compiled from ca. 40–75 C.E., probably in several stages, in Palestine or Syria. Q survives primarily and most obviously in the double tradition, i.e., in non-Markan parallels between Matthew and Luke, on the basis of which it has been argued that both evangelists were dependent on a common source, whether oral or written. Limiting Q to the non-Markan parallels between Matthew and Luke is the narrow definition of Q (Edwards 1976, 9–10). The maximal extent of Q includes additional sites for the location of possible Q material, including the triple tradition, singular Markan traditions, the special sources of Matthew and Luke, and the doublets (Broadhead 2001).

Tools and resources for the study of Q. Since the 1980s there has been, to judge from the scores of books and articles which have appeared on the subject, an increased scholarly interest in Q and the problems its presents. Since many scholars are convinced that the order of Q is preserved more closely in Luke than in Matthew, Q is often reconstructed in the order of the pericopes thought to belong to Q in Luke, and when such sigla as Q11:2b–4 occur it refers to Luke 11:2b–4 considered with its parallel in Matt. 6:9–13. The study of the content and wording of Q is facilitated by the synopsis of Q parallels constructed by Kloppenborg (1988), which contains the Greek text of the Matthaean and Lukan parallels, with a facing English translation. It also includes parallels, printing the Greek and Coptic texts, and a concordance to Q. A truly magnificent tool for Q research is *The Critical Edition of Q* (Robinson, Hoffmann, and Kloppenborg [eds.] 2000), laid out in eight parallel columns in Greek and Coptic, with translations of the critical Q text in English, German, and French (from left to right): (1) any Markan parallel to Matthew; (2) any Matthean doublet; (3) the Matthaean text derived from Q; (4) the critical text of Q (shaded); (5) the Lukan text derived from Q; (6) any Lukan doublet; (7) any Markan parallel to Luke; (8) any parallel from the *Gospel of Thomas*. A critical evaluation of this tool is a typically lengthy review by Neirynck with the critical text of Q as an appendix (2001a). A companion series called *Documenta Q: Reconstructions of Q Through Two Centuries of Gospel Research Excerpted, Sorted, and Evaluated* (Leuven: Peeters Press, 1996–), has already appeared in several volumes (the first volume is Carruth and Garsky 1996). An extremely useful volume is Neirynck 2001b (a revision of Neirynck 1995), which contains a Q synopsis (the Greek text of the double tradition with Matthew on the left-hand page, faced by the Luke, with the agreements in boldface type, as well as the Greek text of the critical edition of Q based on Robinson, Hoffmann and Kloppenborg (2000). The history of Q research is treated in detail with extensive bibliographical citations in Robinson, Hoffmann, and Kloppenborg (eds.) 2000, xix–lxxi.

Date and provenance. On the basis of the Two-Document Hypothesis (i.e., Matthew and Luke are both dependent on Mark and Q), the composition of Q must be earlier than the composition of either Matthew (ca. 80–85 C.E.) or Luke (ca. 85–90 C.E.). However, since these dates are only educated guesses and can vary ten years either way, this does little to pin down the date of Q, which has been widely dated ca. 50 C.E. as a result of the proposal of K. Lake (1909). Q seems to reflect the existence of a community of Jewish Christians in pre-70 C.E. Palestine.

Language and style. Some have proposed that Q was originally composed in Aramaic based on the detection of Aramaisms, e.g., words translated into Greek in two different ways, perhaps because of misreadings (Bussby 1954). Despite the fact that Q contains Aramaisms, proposals that Q was originally written in Aramaic and only later translated into Greek (Allison 1997, 47–49), there are convincing indications that Q was originally composed in Greek (Kloppenborg 1987, 59–64). As reconstructed (Robinson, Hoffmann, and Kloppenborg 2000, 563), Q has a total word count of 3,519 words (including more than 400 occurrences of the definite article) with a vocabulary of 760 words.

The genre of Q. Q is a collection of the sayings of Jesus which apparently began with the message of John the Baptist (Luke 3:7b–9= Matt. 3:7–10) and conclude with the saying on Judging the Twelve Tribes of Israel (Luke 22:28–30), consisting of at least 48 pericopes. There is no evidence that Q contained either passion predictions or a passion narrative. Nevertheless there are many narrative elements in Q (S. Hultgren 2002). It contained one story about Jesus, the temptation story (Luke 4:1–13; Matt. 4:1–11), and one miracle (Luke 7:1–10; Matt. 8:5–13). The genre of Q therefore differs from that of the canonical gospels, but is similar to that of the *Gospel of Thomas* in the basic sense that both are collections of the sayings of Jesus (Robinson 1986). It is therefore not a gospel in the sense that the four canonical gospels are (even though the title of Kloppenborg [ed.] 1995 refers to Q as "the Sayings Gospel Q," and C. Heil refers to "der Spruchevangelium Q," 2003). The genre of Q is a question which has only recently been raised (Robinson, 1964, 1971), though the compositional analysis of Q has been the subject of much discussion (for a review of research see Kirk 1998, 1–86).

1. *Q as sayings of the sages.* On the basis of the similarities between the *Gospel of Thomas* and Q, Robinson (1964, 1971; see also Kloppenborg 1987, 27–34) proposed that Q belonged to the genre, "sayings of the sages" or "words of the wise" (because such sayings collections were often associated with a sage) similar to Proverbs (particularly the collections in Prov. 22:17–24:22; 30; 31) and Pirke Aboth, to Lucian, *Demonax* and in addition to the *Gospel of Thomas,* similar to various collections of sayings in early Christian literature (e.g., *Did.* 1:3–2:1; *1 Clem.* 13:1–2; 46:7–8). While the genre of "sayings of the sages" quickly dropped out of much of early Christianity, it was preserved in certain Gnostic texts such as the *Book of Thomas the Contender* (NHC II, 7). Kloppenborg (1987, 30–31) observes that Q is a composite of a variety of types of sayings in addition to wisdom sayings, such as chriae, prophetic and apocalyptic words, and the temptation story, yet he thinks that this variety is compatible with the *Logoi Sophon* genre. His views changed, however, for in Kloppenborg 2000, 112–65, on the composition and genre of Q, the *Gospel of Thomas* is hardly mentioned. Some of the problems involved in comparing Q and the *Gospel of Thomas* have become evident. While the *Gospel of Thomas* is a random collection of the sayings of Jesus with some linking of individual sayings with catchwords, Q is a far more complex collection of material. Piper (1989) has demonstrated, for example, that a recurring compositional pattern recurs in several clusters of material in Q (6:27–35; 11:9–13; 12:2–12; 12:22–31). Each cluster begins with (1) a general aphoristic saying, followed by (2) a general maxim which supports the aphorism. These are followed by (3) two rhetorical questions employing striking images from life, illustrating the point of the opening aphorism and maxim, and the cluster culminates with (4) a concluding saying which summarizes the argument and applies it to the community. An example is found in Q 11:9–13 (Piper 1994):

1. Opening aphorism:
   "Ask and it shall be given to you, seek and you shall find, knock and it will be opened to you."

2. Supportive maxim:
   "For whoever asks receives, and whoever seeks finds, and whomever knocks it will be opened."

3. Two illustrative rhetorical questions:
   "What father among you, who when his son asks for a fish will instead of a fish give him a serpent? Or if he asks for an egg, will give him a scorpion?"

4. Concluding application:
   "If you then, being selfish know how to give good gifts to your children, how much more will your heavenly Father give good things to those who ask him?"

The compositional sophistication of Q means that macro-textual comparisons between Q and the *Gospel of Thomas* are problematic.

2. *Q as expanded instruction.* Kloppenborg himself designates Q^1 as "expanded instruction" (Kloppenborg Verbin 2000, 143–53, 154–65), which has a family resemblance to other examples of the "instruction" genre in ancient Near Eastern literature (e.g., Prov. 1–9, Sirach; 4Q185; 4QSapiential Work; the *Teachings of Silvanus* [NHC VII, 4], etc.). Kirk (1998), a student of Kloppenborg, has put the instructional speech genre of Q on a virtually unassailable foundation. The basic building block of "instruction" is the admonition, which contains an imperative with a motive clause. The formative instructional stratum (Q^1) was then provided with a narrative framework supplemented by Q^2 material, much of which was chriae, i.e., sayings set in a brief narrative framework.

3. *Q as a prophetic book.* Q has also been categorized as a "prophetic book" (Sato 1987), a macro-genre which had not been adequately investigated. Sato suggests four generic characteristics of "the prophetic book," all of which apply to Q (Sato 1987, 76–83): (1) the claim of divine origin for the oracles they contain, (2) identification of a human figure as the agent of divine oracles, (3) the use of constituent prophetic genres, and (4) evidence of original oral proclamation. Nevertheless Q differs from prophetic books in two respects (Sato 1987, 84): (1) it contains more wisdom sayings than a typical prophetic book, and (2) it has a sending narrative. The constituent prophetic genres

which Sato identifies in Q include: (1) the *Ankündigung,* or "announcement" (Q 3:16; 7:22; 10:9b, 15; 11:20; 12:10; 13:28–29; 17:34–35), (2) the *Unheilswort* or "judgment saying" (Q 11:31–32, 49–51; 13:34–35), (3) the *Heilswort* or "salvation saying" (Q 6:20b–21, 22–23; 12:11–12). The basic problem with Sato's generic proposal is that "Q lacks the principal generic markers of a prophetic book," and it is striking that God never speaks in Q (Kloppenborg Verbin 2000, 141).

4. *Q as biography.* Downing (1988, 1994) argues that Q is an example of Greco-Roman biography similar to Lucian's *Demonax,* and would have been understood by first-century Greeks as the biography of a Cynic teacher. Downing, following Burridge (1992), lists several features of Q that suggest to him proximity to the biography genre: (1) Q exhibits a strong focus on one person (1994, 7–8). (2) Most space is devoted to sayings and anecdotes leading to a pithy pronouncement by the sage (1994, 9). (3) Biographies often lack a continuous narrative but rather exhibit degrees of topical organization. (4) Lives ranges from 3,000 words (*Demonax*) to 82,000 words (Philostratus, *Life of Apollonius*); Q has about 3,500 words. (5) Philosophical biographies are restricted to the deeds and sayings of the subject, though some treat his relationship to predecessors (e.g., John the Baptist). (6) Virtually all philosophical lives are constructed from stories and anecdotes, some carefully and others more loosely composed. (7) Characterization depends on the words of the sage with no further commentary necessary, and often by comparison with other figures (1994, 13).

Composition and redaction. Q is based on the double tradition (non-Markan parallels between Matthew and Luke), and there are some passages with Markan parallels (e.g., the temptation story, the Beelzebul controversy). The problem of whether this material is based on a single document has been debated; most scholars now favor the unity of Q (Jacobson 1982, 1992, 61–76). On the basis of the theory of the priority of Mark, and the use that Matthew and Luke made of it, it is evident that they redacted the sources they used and that, just as they sometimes omit material from Mark, it is also probable that they omitted material from the version of Q which they used (on Luke's redaction of Q, see C. Heil 2003). In some of these cases what has been classified as "Special M" (material distinctive to Matthew) and "Special L" (material distinctive to Luke) may in fact be derived from Q. Further, it is unlikely that Matthew and Luke used identical versions of Q, and the distinction between these two versions can be represented by the sigla $Q^{Matt.}$ and Q^{Luke}. The probability that Q was not just a collection of the sayings of Jesus, but a collection which exhibited evidence of redactional activity, i.e., that it had a theology (particularly the opposition to "this generation"), was first demonstrated by Lührmann 1969 (see Jacobson 1992, 37–40; Kloppenborg 1995, 1). More recently, the important redactional features of Q have been regarded as the arrangements of the unit of tradition rather than modifications of individual units (Kloppenborg 1995, 7).

Kloppenborg Verbin (2000, 145–46), one of the more influential scholars who have focused their attention on Q, argues for two main strata in Q, the formative stratum (Q^1) and the main redaction (Q^2). To the formative stratum belongs six clusters of sayings which are united by paranetic, hortatory, and instructional concerns:

1. Q 6:20b–23b, 27–35, 36–45, 46–49
2. Q 9:57–60, (61–62); 10:2–11, 16 (23–24?)
3. Q 11:2–4, 9–13
4. Q 12:2–7, 11–12
5. Q 12:22b–31, 33–34 (13:18–19, 20–21?) and probably
6. Q 13:23; 14:26–27; 17:33; 14:34–35

On the other hand (Kloppenborg Verbin 2000, 118–22), the main redactional structures of Q includes the recurring motifs of *coming judgment* (in sayings that frame the collection: Q 3:7–9, 16–17; 17:23–34; 19:12–27; 22:28–30), *the Lot cycle* (Q 10:12; 17:28–30, 34–35), and *Deuteronomistic theology* (e.g., Q 6:23c; 11:47–51; 13:34–35). These three motifs suggest the thematic unity of Q. The five blocks of Q material incorporating these three motifs constitute the main redaction of Q, i.e., Q^2 (Kloppenborg 1987, 102–70; Kloppenborg Verbin 2000, 143–44):

1. Q 3:(2–3), 7–9, 16b–17, allusions to the story of Lot; John's announcement of judgment; call to repentance.
2. Q 7:1–10, 18–28, 31–35, shaming Israel by using a Gentile; the rejection of John and Jesus as prophets of Wisdom.
3. Q 11:4–5, 16, 17–26, (27–28), 29–32, 33–36, 39b–44, 46–52, instances of the nonrecognition of Jesus; announcement of judgment; prophets as envoys of Wisdom; calls to repentance.

4. Q 17:23–24, 37b, 26–30, 34–35; 19:12–27; 22:28–30, allusions to Lot cycle; announcement of judgment; judgment of Israel.
5. Q 12:39–40, 42b–46, 49, 50–53, 54–59, announcement of judgment; admonitions to readiness; call to recognition.

In addition, Kloppenborg (1987, 246–62, 325–27; Kloppenborg Verbin 2000, 152–53) proposes that there was a final recension of Q (Q^3), which consisted of the addition of the temptation story (Q 4:1–13), as well as two other sayings (Q 11:42c and 16:17). This addition is problematic and has been criticized by Hoffmann (2001, 285–86).

Essentially, the formative stratum of Q^1 has a sapiential focus (Kloppenborg 1987, 171–245), while the main stratum of Q^2 has a focus on apocalyptic judgment (Kloppenborg 1987, 102–70). This distinction is in part informed by the presupposition that wisdom and apocalypse are distinct and opposed traditions (Jacobson 1992, 35), a view that Jacobson finds problematic (1992, 50–51). Yet it would be a mistake to suppose that Kloppenborg Verbin separated out the formative from the main stratum of Q by placing sapiential sayings in one pot and apocalyptic sayings in another. As Kloppenborg Verbin (2000, 388) notes:

> To characterize Q as "sapiential" is not, therefore, to imply a depiction of Jesus as a teacher of this-worldly, prudential wisdom, or still less to imply an intellectual world that was hermetically sealed against eschatology, prophetic traditions, and the epic traditions of Israel. Q indeed contains elements that *might have developed* toward a completely contemporizing, noneschatological presentation of Jesus and his message.

Most scholars who have wrestled with Q are aware that both "wisdom" and "apocalyptic," when applied to the Q material, are categories which are complex and in fact interrelated. Kloppenborg arrived at his view of the composition history of Q by using literary critical indicators, not by assigning various components of Q to the sapiential or apocalyptic world of ideas.

In a book published the same year as Kloppenborg's dissertation on Q (1987), Sato (1987, 28–68; see Jacobson 1992, 57–59 and the critique by Kloppenborg Verbin 2000, 136–40) traced the redaction history of Q through three stages: (1) Redaction A (Q 3:2–7:28), which focuses on John the Baptist, (2) Redaction B (Q 9:57–10:24) is chronologically the next block of material, which focuses on the theme of the sending of the disciples, and (3) Redaction C includes the combination of Redactions A and B as well as the inclusion of more material (Q 7:31–34, 35; 11:14–32, 39–54; 13:23–35, and possibly 12:2–34 and 17:23–27). Two themes dominated Recension C, the announcement of judgment to "this generation," and the Sophia motif.

Reconstructing the contents and order of Q. The arguments that Q in its various versions (see below) was a written document are compelling (Kloppenborg Verbin 2000, 56–60), and that assumption underlies the critical edition of Q (Robinson, Hoffmann, and Kloppenborg [eds.] 2000). This critical edition contains 90 units or pericopes which probably belong to Q. There is no attempt to impose any unity on this critical reconstruction by arranging the pericopes in any kind of hierarchical arrangement. The following conservative reconstruction of Q is found in Grant (1957, 59–60), in which the unity of Q is indicated by the hierarchical arrangements of pericopes under eleven major headings:

1. The ministry and message of John the Baptist
   a. John's preaching of repentance (Luke 3:[2b], 3a, 7b–9=Matt. 3:1–10)
   b. John's prediction of the coming judge (Luke 3:16, 17=Matt. 3:11, 12)
2. The ordeal of the Messiah
   a. The Temptation (Luke 4:1b–12=Matt. 4:1–11)
3. Jesus' public teaching
   a. Sermon on the Plain (Luke 6:20–49= or Mountain Matt. 5:3–12, 39–48; 7:12, 1–5, 16–27; 10:24, 25; 12:33–35; 15:14)
4. Response to Jesus' preaching
   a. Centurion's faith (Luke 7:2, 6b–10= Matt. 8:5–13)
   b. John's emissaries and Jesus' words about John (Luke 7:18b, 19, 22–28, 31–35= Matt. 11:2–6, 7–19)
   c. Various followers (Luke 9:57b–60, 61, 62=Matt. 8:19–22)
5. Mission of the Twelve
   a. Mission of the disciples (Luke 10:2–16= Matt. 9:37, 38; 10:7–16, 40; 11:21–23)
   b. [Return of the Twelve (Luke 10:17b–20)]
6. Rejoicing of Jesus (Luke 10:21b–24=Matt. 11:25–27; 13:16, 17)

7. Jesus teaching about prayer
   a. Lord's Prayer (Luke 11:2–4=Matt. 6:9–13)
   b. [Parable of the friend at midnight (Luke 11:5–8)]
   c. Constancy in prayer (Luke 11:9–13=Matt. 7:7–11)
8. Controversy with the scribes and Pharisees
   a. Charge of collusion with Beelzebul (Luke 11:14–23=Matt. 12:22–30)
   b. Story of the unclean spirit (Luke 11:24–26=Matt. 12:43–44)
   c. The sign of Jonah (Luke 11:29b-32=Matt. 12:38–42)
   d. Jesus' sayings about light (Luke 11:33–36=Matt. 5:15; 6:22, 23)
   e. Controversy with the scribes and Pharisees (Luke 11:39b, 42, 43, [44], 46–52=Matt. 23:4–36)
9. Jesus' teaching about discipleship: the duties of disciples under persecution
   a. Testimony of disciples among adversaries (Luke 12:2–12=Matt. 10:26–33; 12:32; 10:19, 20)
   b. Freedom from care (Luke 12:22–31=Matt. 6:25–33)
   c. On treasure (Luke 12:33b, 34=Matt. 6:19–21)
   d. Three parables of watchfulness (Luke 12:39, 40, 42–46=Matt. 24:43–51a)
   e. Messianic divisions (Luke 12:49–53=Matt. 10:34–36)
   f. Signs of the times (Luke 12:54–56=Matt. 16:2, 3)
   g. Duty of speedy reconciliation (Luke 12:57–59=Matt. 5:25, 26)
   h. Parables of the mustard seed and the leaves; growth of kingdom despite opposition (Luke 13:18–21=Matt. 13:31–33)
   i. The narrow way (Luke 13:24–29=Matt. 7:13, 14; 7:22, 23; 8:11, 12)
   j. The fate of Jerusalem (Luke 13:34–35=Matt. 23:37–39)
   k. On self-exaltation (Luke 14:11=18:14=Matt. 18:4; 23:12)
   l. Parable of the great supper (Luke 14:16–23=Matt. 22:1–10)
   m. On hating one's next of kin and bearing the cross (Luke 14:26, 27=Matt. 10:37, 38)
   n. The saying on salt (Luke 14:34, 35=Matt. 5:13)
   o. Parable of the lost sheep (Luke 15:4–7=Matt. 18:12–14)
   p. [Parable of the lost coin (Luke 15:8–10]
   q. On serving two masters (Luke 16:13=Matt. 6:24)
10. Sayings about the law
    a. The Law and the Prophets until John; on divorce (Luke 16:16–18=Matt. 11:12, 13; 5:18, 32)
    b. On offenses (Luke 17:1, 2=Matt. 18:6, 7)
    c. On forgiveness (Luke 17:3, 4=Matt. 18:15, 21, 22)
    d. On faith (Luke 17:6=Matt. 17:20b)
11. The coming Parousia
    a. The Parousia (Luke 17:23, 24, 26–30, 34, 35, 37b=Matt. 24:26–28, 37–39; 10:39; 24:40–41, 28)
    b. Parable of the talents (Luke 19:12, 13, 15b-26=Matt. 25:14–30)
    c. [The apostles' thrones (Luke 22:28–30=Matt. 19:28)]

Amsler 2001; Bussby 1954; Carruth and Garsky 1996; Catchpole 1993; Downing 1988, 1994; Edwards 1976; Fleddermann 1995; A. E. Hanson 1998; Hoffmann 1972, 2001; Horsley 1991; Jacobson 1982, 1992; A. Kirk 1998; Kloppenborg 1987, 1988; Kloppenborg (ed.) 1994, 1995; Lake 1909; Lührmann 1969; Manson 1979, 1998; Neirynck 1995, 1998, 2001a, 2001b; Piper 1989, 1994, 1995; Robinson 1964, 1971, 1986; Robinson, Hoffmann, and Kloppenborg 2000; Sato 1987; Streeter 1930; Tuckett 1996a

Quadratus, a Christian apologist from Athens active ca. 125 C.E., during the reign of the Emperor Hadrian (117–138 C.E.), about whom very little is known. Just one fragment of his work has been preserved in Eusebius, *Hist. eccl.* 4.3.2: "But our Savior's works were permanent, for they were real. Those who had been cured or rose from the dead not only appeared to be cured or raised but were permanent, not only during the Savior's stay on earth, but also after his departure. They remained for a considerable period, so that some of them even reached our times."

*Apologetic literature, Christian

Quintilian, *Institutio oratoria.* M. Fabius Quintilianus (ca. 35–95 C.E.), taught rhetoric in Rome under the patronship of the Flavian emperors (ca. 71–91 C.E.). In retirement, he wrote *Institutio oratoria* ("On the Education of the Orator") in 12 books. The author's stated purpose "is the education of the perfect orator" (1. *praef.* 9). Book 1 of *Inst.* is preceded by a letter, the *Epistula ad Tryphonem,* from the author to his publisher, containing an report of Trypho's request that the finished work be published and of Quintilian's doubt over his competence to write such a work (Janson 1964, 51, 98–100). The author's expression of doubts about his ability and his apology for poor style function in two ways: if a reader finds something to criticize, the author has already protected himself with the introductory apology; if the reader finds the work excellent, the author has shown evidence of appropriate modesty (Janson 1964, 51). In the *prooemium* proper, Quintilian begins with three conventional topoi: (1) an account of a request by certain friends that he write on the art of oratory (1. *praef.* 1–2), (2) the expression of a lack of confidence to complete so formidable a task (1. *praef.* 3), and (3) a dedication to his friend Marcellus Victorius, who is encouraged to use it in the education of his son Gela (1. *praef.* 7). There was, in the words of Janson (1964, 54), "a general tendency and even an express rule for orators to deny as far as possible any rhetorical brilliance and stress the importance of the facts of the case." Quintilian wrote prefaces to seven of the twelve books (1, 4, 5, 6, 7, 8, 12).

Outline of the Institutes. The *Institutes* can be divided into five major sections (see Morgenthaler 1993, 16–82, with a schematic outline on 81–82; and particularly D. A. Russell 2001, 12–18). The basic framework of the *Institutes* is based on the five traditional duties or functions of an orator, *officia oratoris* or *vis oratoris* (Cicero, *Partitiones oratoriae* 5–26): (1) *inventio,* i.e., "discovery (of the resources appropriate for persuasion inherent in any oratorical setting)," (2) *dispositio* or *collocatio,* "arrangement," (3) *elocutio,* "style," (4) *actio* ("delivery"), and (5) *memoria* ("memory"). Of the five duties of the orator, *inventio* is clearly the most important to Quintilian, and under the category of *inventio*, forensic rhetoric receives the longest and most detailed treatment, indicating the relative unimportance of epideictic and deliberative rhetoric in his day.

Letter to Tryphon
Dedication to Victorius
- I. Introductory material (1.1–3.5)
  - A. The education of the orator (1.1–2.10)
  - B. Prolegomena to rhetoric (2.11–21)
  - C. History of rhetoric (3.1–5)
- II. Invention (3.6–6.5)
  - A. Issues (3.6)
  - B. Epideictic rhetoric (3.7)
  - C. Deliberative rhetoric (3.8)
  - D. Forensic rhetoric (3.9–6.5)
    1. Basic structure and strategies (3.9–11)
    2. Plan of the next book (4.1–5)
    3. The subject of proof (5)
       - a. Technical proofs (5.1–7)
       - b. Nontechnical proofs (5.8–14)
    4. The epilogue and emotions (6.1–5)
- III. Arrangement (7.1–10)
- IV. Elocution (8.1–11.1)
- V. Memory (11.2)
- VI. Delivery (11.3)
- VII. The finished orator: Moral issues (12)

*Arrangement, *Rhetoric, *Rhetorical handbooks

———

Janson 1964, 50–59; Morgenthaler 1993; D. A. Russell 2001

Quotations, citations, *allusions, and echoes of earlier literature (particularly the OT) frequently occur in early Christian literature. They function in a variety of ways: they can provide proofs for arguments and can embellish and beautify a narrative or exposition. The NT authors often quote passages from the OT as a sacred text or Scripture. In *citations,* a portion of text reproduced word for word from a source, often prefaced with an introductory formula such as "As it is written" (Rom. 9:13), "For the scripture says to Pharaoh" (Rom. 9:17), "Have you not read this scripture" (Mark 12:10–11). Distinguished from citations are *quotations,* word-for-word reproductions of a text without any introductory markers. *Allusions* are references that the writer assumes the reader will recognize (Morner 1991, 5), consisting of one or more words sufficiently distinctive to be traced to a known text, but not a verbatim reproduction of any part of that text (Paulien 1987, 170–71; Tenney 1957, 102; Hollander 1981, 64, 82). An *echo* is subtler than an allusion and is a relatively faint reference to a text (Hollander 1981, 62–63; Hays 1989, 24). The exact distinctions between these categories vary among scholars. Many would insist that to be considered a quotation, a borrowing must have at least an introductory formula, such as "it says" or "it is written." Others would omit this requirement, especially if the grammatical or stylistic features of the borrowing are sufficient to distinguish it from the surrounding text (Fox 1980, 416–17; Gordis 1949, 130; Hoek 1996, 228). Archer and Chirichigno (1983) have provided a complete survey of OT quotations in the NT, including the Hebrew texts of OT passages and the Greek text of LXX and NT passages, together with a commentary in the order in which quotations occur in the OT (an index of the NT passages discussed is found on pp. xix–xxi). This helpful tool has a grading system for categorizing quotations, though the authors are preoccupied with possible implications for the doctrine of the verbal inerrancy of Scripture (xxv–xxxii): A: reasonably complete and accurate renderings from the Masoretic Text to the LXX and then into the NT passage; B: NT quotation closely adhering to LXX wording, even when it deviates somewhat from the MT; C: quotations in which the NT adheres more closely to the MT than does the LXX; D: NT quotation adhering closely to the LXX, even when it deviates from the MT; E: quotations that give the impression of unwarranted liberties taken with the OT text in light of its context; F: close resemblance between the OT source and the NT application. A more recent tool is that of Hübner 1997, in which the target passage in the NT is cited in canonical order, with quotations of the relevant passages quoted or alluded to in the OT in both the LXX and Masoretic Texts.

While NT authors typically quote from the OT, they quote less often from the writings later classified as *apocrypha or *pseudepigrapha, occasionally from early Christian hymns or liturgy (though this is disputed; see Frankowski 1983). A few quotations of Greek authors occur in the NT, including Plato, *Apology* 29D: "Athenians, I respect and love you, but I shall obey God rather than you" (Acts 4:19; 5:29); Aratus, *Phaenomena* 5: "For we too are his offspring" (Acts 17:28); Thucydides 2.97.4: "Indeed, it was more disgraceful for a man not to give when asked than to ask and be refused" (Acts 20:35; cf. Kilgallen 1993); Euripides Bacchae 794–95: "than kick against the goads" (Acts 26:14; Hacket 1956).

The *Apostolic Fathers continue the heavy use of the Old Testament (noticeably *1 *Clement* and **Barnabas*) but apparently quote or allude to early Christian documents which were eventually included in the NT canon as well. This is a very prozblematic area, however, for there are often reasons for thinking that the quotations or allusions are from oral tradition rather than from written documents (Koester 1957, 1990). By the time of Clement of Alexandria (ca. 150–215 C.E.), Christian authors have begun to quote heavily from Greco-Roman literature in addition to Scripture.

The somewhat free adaptation of quoted texts practiced by early Christian authors—particularly in the NT—is entirely in keeping with the practices of their contemporaries, both Greco-Roman and Jewish (Stanley 1986, 348). Common methods of adapting quotations in antiquity included selective omissions of irrelevant parts of the quoted text, adjusting the grammar to suit the new context (e.g. person, number, case, etc.), conflating two or more texts from the same or different sources, replacing obscure words with ones more appropriate to the author's point, and the addition of interpretive words or phrases. These adaptations were motivated by a desire to make certain the quote fit smoothly in its new textual environment and conveyed the point the author wished to make (Stanley 1986, 338–60).

Quotations, particularly of the OT, have several different functions in early Christian literature (Ellis 1977, 199; Hartman 1972, 154). (1) Most often, quotations serve to obtain the support of an authority for the author's argument. Frequently, the older Scriptures are regarded as a "witness" (μαρτυρία) to the claims of the Christian community in a forensic or juridical sense (Albl 1999, 71). (2) Quotations are also used to provide *examples of the author's point (Albl 1999, 72), to produce a literary or stylistic effect, or to evoke a set of associations in the mind of readers familiar with the source texts (Ellis 1977, 199; Hays 1989, 21–24 et passim). (3) OT quotations are frequently used in a promise and fulfilment sense; OT passages are understood as fulfilled in aspects of the life, ministry, death, and resurrection of Jesus: e.g., 1 Cor. 15:3–4: "Christ died for our sins according to the scriptures . . . he was raised on the third day in accordance with the scriptures."

Since most early Christian literature is in Greek, it is not surprising that most quotations of the OT seem to favor the text of the *Septuagint. There is, however, evidence for the use of the proto-MT and other variant textual traditions of the Hebrew Scriptures. It also seems apparent that at times New Testament and early Christian authors made use of *testimonia collections, i.e., established lists of scriptural citations designed to support Christian claims in apologetic and pedagogical contexts (Albl 1999). The use of such collections helps to explain certain patterns of deviation between early Christian quotations and the known textual traditions of Scripture.

JON BERGSMA

*Intertextuality, *Testimonia

Albl 1999; Archer and Chirichingno 1983; Balentine 1981; Barrett 1970a; Beentjes 1982;

Carson and Williamson 1988; Dodd 1952; Ellis 1977; C. A. Evans 1982; Falcetta 2001; Fitzmyer 1961a; M. V. Fox 1980; Frankowski 1982; Gordis 1949; Hartman 1972; Hays 1989; Hollander 1981; van den Hoek 1996; Hübner 1997; H. Menken 1996; Morner 1991; Paulien 1987; Rendall 1964; D. M. Smith 1972; C. D. Stanley 1986; I. H. Thompson 1995; Wilcox 1977

Rabbinic literature, a term that encompasses a series of religious works produced by rabbinic sages beginning in the late 2d cent. C.E., each of which came to be regarded as an extension of Torah. The earliest rabbinic document is *Mishnah (meaning "repetition"), which was compiled at the end of the 2d cent. C.E. by Rabbi Judah ha-Nasi at Zippori in Israel (his tomb is located in the nearby necropolis of Beth She'arim). The Mishnah is followed, in the 3d and 4th cents. C.E., by the earliest midrashic collections, Sifre (on Numbers and Deuteronomy), Sifra or Torat-Kohanim (on Leviticus), all of which follow the order of the Torah. Later, two further midrashic compositions come into existence, Genesis Rabbah and Leviticus Rabbah (divided into 37 *parshiyyot,* each with 5 to 15 subdivisions) Sifre (on Numbers and Deuteronomy), Sifra or Torat-Kohanim (on Leviticus). The *Targumim are oral paraphrastic translations of the Torah and select other portions of the Hebrew Bible which were codified from the 4th to the 6th cent. C.E.

*Midrash, *Mishnah, *Talmud, *Targums

Chapman and Köstenberger 2000; Neusner 1994; Stemberger 1996

Reader response criticism recognizes the affective or subjective nature of criticism, a perspective which the *New Criticism rejected as the so-called affective fallacy. Reader response criticism argues that the reader plays an active role in producing the meaning of a text. The reader is important because an author consciously or unconsciously postulates the reader (i.e., the *implied reader) while he writes. When the literary work is completed, it is not autonomous, since its meaning does not effectively exist outside of a reader.

*Implied Reader, *Intertextuality, *Literary criticism, *Paratexts

---

Eco 1979; Iser 1978; Tompkins 1980

Reading refers to several differing activities, including the process of transforming written linguistic signs into the language that they represent, silently or aloud, publicly or privately. Reading can also be understood as the conscious and unconscious strategies with which the reader makes sense of a text. Reading, at least when a text is read for the first time, is a linear experience, that is, what the author is communicating occurs only sequentially and can be understood only sequentially. Some texts are certainly intended to be read more than once, so that clues and perspectives picked up the first time can be used as a vantage point from which to understand the text more thoroughly during subsequent and hence more sophisticated readings. Ancient readers could not grasp the notion of an "anachronistic reading," i.e., the propensity to understand earlier texts, not in terms of the historical circumstances in which they arose, but rather in terms of contemporary perspectives (F. Young 1997, 36, 81). Reading was an activity done publicly (Binder 1995) as well as privately, though determining the extent of ancient literacy is very difficult (Harris 1989 is a bit too pessimistic). Reading aloud publicly was particularly problematic since written manuscripts had no word division and little or no punctuation.

Written text and oral performance. Since ancients routinely read aloud (Baloghl 1927, 213; Knox 1968, 421–35), ancient authors arguably wrote with the expectation that their compositions would be read aloud (Kennedy 1963, 4). One of the features of ancient reading that links it to rhetoric is the fact that texts were almost always read aloud, and authors knew that their works would be so read (Stanforth 1967, 1–3). Two ancients who read "silently" (but with their lips moving) were Aristotle and Ambrose, exceptions that prove the rule (B. M. W. Knox 1968). Thus, in many ancient texts, the terms "hear" and "read" are often used as synonyms (Herodotus 1.48; Rev. 1:3; Augustine, *Ep.* 147; *Conf.* 10.3; Cassiodorus, *Inst. Divin. Lec.* 1.29; see Balogh 1927). The intimate relationship between written text and oral performance suggests that the *rhetorical handbooks of antiquity should be of considerable interest to the historian of ancient literature, both for what they treat and for what they do not treat. It is highly likely that all of the writings of the New Testament were written expressly for public, oral performance. This even appears to have been the case with such a quasi-literary document as the Shepherd of Hermas (*Vis.* 2. 4. 3; cf. 1. 3. 3–4). We also know that Paul used an amanuensis (Gal. 6:11; 1 Cor. 16:21; Col. 4:18; 2 Thess. 3:17; Phlm.

19), which means that his oral presentation, mediated by his letters, would be reenacted when his letters were publicly read. Orality also plays an explicit role in the Revelation to John, where each of the seven proclamations is dictated to the author (according to his account), along with other large segments of the book.

Reading sacred vs. secular texts. Reading a written text, whether aloud or silently, involves certain implicitly learned social skills and knowledge of which the reader is often unaware. The reading of *sacred* texts in early Judaism and early Christianity requires a different approach from secular texts. Biblical interpretation also presupposes certain reading strategies that the interpreter assumes.

In Jewish midrashic exegesis (see *Midrash), for example, the verse of Scripture that is the focus of the interpreter is not perceived to be part of its immediately "literary" context, nor indeed part of the book in which the passage is found; the context of each verse is delimited only by the boundaries of the canon of Scripture itself (Kugel 1986, 92). In the words of Sommer (1996, 231–32): "For the rabbinic exegete [and the modern orthodox Jew wanting to read Isaiah as Scripture] . . . These verses and pericopes must be shown to relate not foremost to other parts of Isaiah but to other parts of the canon, perhaps most of all to the Torah." What was true for the practitioners of Jewish midrashic exegesis was certainly true for the Jewish people present at the synagogue liturgy who heard interpretations of the Scripture linked to readings from the Torah and the Haphtarah.

Similarly, in early Christianity, at least from the 2d cent. on, "the unity of the Bible" and its witness to Christ was the assumption underlying its "reception" by readers and hearers in the "public assembly of the community" (F. Young 1997, 19). This unity of Scripture was called, among other things, the rule of faith (Osborn 1989). For Irenaeus, for example, this unity of the Bible could be expressed as the canon of truth or the rule of faith, *regula fidei* (*Adv. haer.* 1.1.15), while Athanasius of Alexandria was concerned with discerning the unitive διανοία ("mind") of Scripture. According to F. Young (1997, 21):

> Neither the Rule of Faith nor the creed was in fact a summary of the whole biblical narrative. . . . They provided, rather, the proper reading of the beginning and the ending, the focus of the plot, and the relations of the principal characters, so enabling the "middle" to be heard in it as meaningful. They provided the "closure" which contemporary prefers to leave open. They articulated the essential hermeneutical key without which texts and community would disintegrate in incoherence.

Thus, in early Christianity, as in Judaism, the canon of many books was functionally treated as a single book, so that the context for a particular verse was not only the immediate context or the particular writing but the bounds of the entire canon.

Reading practices are occasionally referred to in the NT. The author of Revelation intends his book to be read aloud before a group (Rev. 1:3), an early Christian ritual practice also reflected in Col. 4:16. Portions of the OT were read aloud in Jewish synagogues (Luke 4:16–20; Acts 13:15), and this practice was continued in early Christianity (Justin, *1 Apol.* 67).

*Literacy, *Scriptio continua

Balogh 1927; Binder 1995; Bobertz and Brakke 2002; Gamble 1995; Gavrilov 1997; Gilliard 1993; C. A. Hall 1998; Harris 1989; Knox 1968; McCartney 1948; *DNP* 2.815; Osborn 1989; Slusser 1992; Stanford 1967

Recto/verso, a pair of terms formerly used to refer to the two sides of a *papyrus roll, the recto referring to the side with horizontal fibers of the split papyrus stalk used as a writing surface, while the verso referred to the side with vertical fibers (E. G. Turner 1980, 4–5). This use of recto/verso has proven confusing, however, for fragments of papyrus *codices have been discovered with writing on the verso. Turner has therefore argued that the terms "front/back" be used for a sheet of papyrus and "inside/outside" for a papyrus roll.

E. M. Thompson 1901; E. G. Turner 1980

Redaction criticism is a form of criticism that focuses on the alterations made in the traditional material used by a writer as a key to his or her theological viewpoint. The German word *Redaktionsgeschichte,* meaning "redaction history" or "editorial history," was coined by Marxsen in 1969. Redaction criticism is primarily interested in the editorial stages that led to the production of the final composition, i.e., it attempts to reconstruct the theology of the author-editors of various biblical compositions, a task accomplished by separating tradition from redaction. Redaction criticism, with its emphasis on the evangelists as authors, has served to shift the focus of interest from the constituent form to the encompassing genre of the Gospels. "Redaction and composition critics, then, attempt to recover the theology of the evangelists; to do so they paradoxically recast that narrative theology in a systemic and topical form alien to it" (Moore 1989, 63). The classical redaction critical studies of the Gospels include Marxen (1959, 1969) on Mark, Bornkamm, Barth, and Held (1963) on Matthew, and Conzelmann (1961) on Luke. Redaction criticism, when applied to biblical narratives such as the Gospels and Acts, abstracts a propositional content from the narratives. "In this perspective, redaction criticism (preoccupied with theological point of view) seems more discourse-oriented, more true to the generic, verbal-narrative trait of mediacy, and to that extent more literary than much narrative criticism (typically preoccupied with action and character)" (Moore 1989, 63).

*Criticism, biblical, *Form criticism

Bornkamm, Barth, and Held 1963; Conzelmann 1961; Conzelmann 1961; Marxsen 1959, 1969; Moore 1989; Perrin 1969

Redactions are revisions of earlier passages reworked and embedded into the fabric of a document so that they cannot be removed or even distinguished from earlier sections (Charlesworth 1977, 303; Walker 2001, 23–24).

Referential fallacy is a literary critical term for confusing the world of the text with the real world. This fallacy may lead to taking stylistic features such as "vividness of narration" in the canonical Gospels as an indication of historicity or even using them as arguments for historicity.

Repetition is a figure of Greek prose style, whether of a word, a phrase, or a main clause. Seven rhetorical functions of repetition are enumerated by Anderson (1994, 44): (1) to highlight or draw attention, (2) to establish or fix in the mind of the implied reader, (3) to emphasize the importance of something, (4) to create expectations, increasing predictability and assent (anticipation), (5) to cause review and reassessment (retrospection), (6) to unify disparate elements, (7) to build patterns of association or contrasts.

*Anaphora, *Style

Anderson 1994; Denniston 1952, 78–98; Snyman and Cronje 1986, 115–18.

Rescripts (see *Edicts)

Revelation to John, the only *apocalypse in the NT, is generally thought to have been written ca. 95 C.E. in the southwest part of Roman Asia to seven Christian communities in the area.

Date. While most scholars date Revelation to the latter part of the reign of the Roman emperor Domitian, i.e., ca. 95 C.E. (Aune 1997–98, 1.lvi–lxx), some propose a date a bit later, during the reign of Trajan (98–117 C.E.), while others argue that it was written earlier, soon after the death of Nero in 68 C.E. During much of the 19th cent., the prevailing view was that Revelation was composed between 64 C.E. (following the Neronian persecution) and 70 C.E. (the destruction of Jerusalem). This view was primarily based on the enigmatic list of seven kings in 17:9–11, under the assumption that the sixth king, "who is living," was the reigning emperor when Revelation was written. Beginning the count with Julius Caesar, the sixth king would be Nero (54–68 C.E.), while beginning with Augustus, the sixth king would be Galba (June 68–Jan. 69 C.E.). Either possibility supports the early date of the Revelation. However, scholars have construed this passage in a bewildering number of ways (Yarbro Collins, 58–64), by omitting the three emperors of 68–69 C.E. or by starting enumeration with emperors other than Julius Caesar or Augustus. Toward the end of the 20th cent. there was a marked tendency to interpret the seven kings as symbols of the complete period of the reign of evil.

There was a significant shift in opinion in dating the Revelation by the beginning of the 20th cent., placing its origins toward the end of the reign of the emperor Domitian, i.e., ca. 95 C.E. (following the supposed Domitianic persecution). Since the theme of persecution and suffering pervades Revelation, a date in the late 60s or late 90s provided an appropriate setting for the persecutions reflected in the book. The Domitianic date for the Revelation is supported by Irenaeus (*Adv. haer.* 5.30.3), where he claims that the Revelation was seen toward the end of the reign of Domitian, i.e., ca. 95 C.E. During the last quarter of the 20th cent., however, the historicity of the supposed Domitianic persecution has come under increasing attack and has been largely abandoned (L. L. Thompson 1990). The pressure against Christians in Roman Asia toward the end of the 1st cent. and at the beginning of the 2d cent. C.E. is now considered purely local, random, and sporadic, similar to the situation reflected in the exchange of letters by Pliny and Trajan on the Christian problem in Bithynia in 111 C.E. (Pliny, *Ep.* 10.96–97). In Roman Asia, as in Bithynia, the requirement to sacrifice to the imperial cult forced Christians to choose between Christ and Caesar, resulting in their prosecutions (Price 1984), not to mention the antagonism of fellow citizens. Despite the debunking of the supposed Domitianic persecution (L. L. Thompson 1990) the late 90s continues to be favored by scholars as the most appropriate date for the composition of Revelation, but on a different basis. Arguments supporting the date of ca. 95 C.E. include the symbolic use of the name Babylon as a cipher for Rome (14:6; 16:19; 17:4; 18:2, 10, 21), used elsewhere only in texts later than 70 C.E. (1 Pet. 5:13; *4 Ezra* 3:1–2, 28–31; *2 Baruch* 10:1–3; 11:1; 67:7; *Sib. Or.* 5.143, 159; see Huntzinger 1965), and the presence of the Nero *redivivus* or *redux* myth in Rev. 13 and 17, a myth that developed and circulated during the years following Nero's suicide on June 9, 68. Given the likelihood that some version of the revision and fragmentary hypotheses are correct, it appears likely that both the earlier and later dates for the production of Revelation are partially correct, since the composition and compilation of Revelation are probably an extended editorial process that began in the 60s and only concluded in the late 90s, or perhaps during the beginning of Trajan's reign (98–117 C.E.).

Authorship. Though most Jewish and Christian apocalypses are pseudonymous, it is likely that Revelation was in fact written by "John" (1:1, 4, 9; 22:8). This reveals little, since the Greek name 'Ιωάννης is a transliterated form of the Hebrew name יוחנן, "Yohanan," a theophoric name meaning "Yahweh is [or, has been] gracious," and was common among Jews in the Hellenistic and Roman period. The author appears to be a Palestinian Jew, a conclusion suggested by several factors: (1) Revelation contains more than 300 allusions to the OT (usually the Hebrew text, occasionally a Greek translation); (2) the author uses the literary genre apocalypse as a vehicle for his message, a genre used in Judaism almost exclusively in Palestine; (3) the author exhibits familiarity with the temple in Jerusalem and its cult (8:3–4; 11:1–2, 19); (4) the author is familiar with motifs found in other, nearly contemporary, Jewish apocalypses (see below).

Many early Christian authors assumed that the author also wrote the Gospel of John (see *John, Gospel of) and the Johannine letters, was John, the son of Zebedee, one of twelve disciples of Jesus (Justin, *Dial.* 81.4; Irenaeus, *Adv. haer.* 4.20.11; Tertullian, *Adv. Marc.* 3.14.3; 3.24.4; Clement Alex., *Quis Dives* 42; Eusebius, *Hist. Eccl.* 3.18.1; 4.18.8). This identification is questionable, however, since the author of Revelation does not refer to himself as an apostle in the epistolary superscription in 1:4 and elsewhere refers to the Twelve apostles as past founder figures (18:20; 21:14; cf. Eph. 2:20). Dionysius of Alexandria (d. ca. 264–65 C.E.) argued on the basis of language and style that Revelation could not have been written by the same person who wrote the Gospel of John and the Johannine Letters (Eusebius, *Hist. eccl.* 7.25.6–8.12–16.22), a line of argument that most critical scholars have accepted since the mid-19th cent. Revelation has sometimes been attributed to a shadowy figure named John the Elder, a person distinguished by Papias and Eusebius from John the apostle (Eusebius, *Hist. Eccl.* 3.39.2–4). Eusebius attributed the Gospel of John to John the apostle, but Revelation to John the Elder (Eusebius, *Hist. eccl.* 7.25.12–16). More recently it has been proposed that John the Elder (author of 2 John and 3 John) was the founder of the Johannine school, or that he wrote Revelation in 68–70 C.E., and it was later rewritten by his disciples (Hengel 1993). However, most critical scholars think that Revelation was written by neither figure, but by an otherwise unknown Jewish Christian from Palestine who apparently emigrated to the Roman province of Asia in the wake of the first Jewish revolt (66–73 C.E.).

Important data about the social identity of this otherwise unknown figure can be inferred from Revelation itself. Though the author does not explicitly claim to be a prophet, the fact that he designates his work as a "prophecy" (1:3), and a "prophetic book" (22:7, 10, 18–19) clearly carries that implication. The specific commission with which Revelation begins (1:9–20), and the more general commission narrated in 10:1–11, which contains clear allusions to the call of Ezekiel in Ezek. 2:8–3:3, suggest that both passages function on analogy to the OT prophetic call narratives (Jer. 1:4–10; Isa. 6:1–13; 40:1–11). The author all but identifies himself as a prophet in the words of the *angelus interpres* in 22:9: "I am your fellow servant with you and your brethren the prophets," suggesting that John is a member of a prophetic group (perhaps analogous to the group headed by the prophetess Jezebel of Thyatira (2:20–23). Revelation 22:16 again indicates that John was one of a number of Christian prophets who constituted a prophetic circle or guild: "I Jesus have sent my angel to you [ὑμῖν, a plural pronoun probably indicating prophets] with this testimony for the churches." The fact that the author seems to have had inside knowledge of the communities he addressed (Hemer 1986) may suggest that he was an itinerant prophet who had ministered to them in the past.

The Corpus Johanneum consists of five NT writings attributed to John (understood in the ancient church to be identical with John, son of Zebedee), namely, the Gospel of John, the Johannine letters, and Revelation, though the latter is the only work that explicitly claims to have been written by a person named John. Further, while these works have often been regarded as products of several different members of the same school (Strecker 1986), Revelation has the fewest connections to the rest of the Johannine literature and is at best peripheral to the school (Schnelle 1995). Even though a detailed attempt has been made to suggest links between Revelation and the rest of the Corpus Johanneum at the final redactional level (Frey in Hengel 1993, 326–429), there are very few literary, stylistic, or thematic features that suggest that the author of Revelation was part of a Johannine community in any meaningful sense (Heinze 1998).

Genre. The generic term "apocalypse" was derived from the first sentence of the Revelation to John, Ἀποκάλυψις Ἰησοῦ Χριστοῦ, "the revelation of Jesus Christ" (Rev. 1:1). In this context, however, ἀποκάλυψις (which occurs only twice in the entire book; here and in the superscription) is not a *generic* designation, but rather a description of the *contents* of the work. The inscription, ἀποκάλυψις Ἰωάννου, "the Apocalypse of John" (presumably a 2d-cent. C.E. formulation originally placed at the end of the book but then moved to the beginning with the transition from roll to codex), is simply a shortened form of the title or first sentence of the book, with descriptive rather than generic intentions. However, whether through the influence of the Revelation to John or other documents which have not survived, the designation ἀποκάλυψις came to be used relatively quickly in a quasigeneric sense of works with a revelatory character, though such works rarely conform to the modern generic conception of "apocalypse." While the modern designations "apocalypse" and "apocalyptic" then really represent modern conceptions applied to ancient texts and ideologies, i.e., they are etic rather than emic designations (Malina 1995, 12), which does not mean that these designations are unhelpful. Revelation shares the generic features of other Jewish works categorized as "apocalypses," including Dan. 7–12, *1 *Enoch* (a composite text containing five originally separate apocalypses), *4 *Ezra, 2 *Baruch, 2 Enoch, 3 Enoch,* the *Apocalypse of Abraham, Testament of Levi* 2–5, *3 *Baruch,* and the *Apocalypse of Zephaniah.*

Revelation is clearly an apocalypse and conforms to the following definition (Aune 1987, 230): In *form* an apocalypse is a first-person prose recital of revelatory visions or dreams, framed by a description of the circumstances of the revelatory experience, and structured to emphasize the central revelatory message. The *content* of apocalypses involves, in the broadest terms, the communication of a transcendent, often eschatological, perspective on human experience. Apocalypses exhibit a threefold *function:* (1) to legitimate the message (and/or the messenger) through an appeal to transcendent authorization, and (2) to create a literary surrogate of revelatory experience for hearers or readers, (3) so that the recipients of the message will be motivated to modify their views and behaviors to conform to transcendent perspectives.

The hermeneutical significance of the literary genre of biblical books has become increasingly obvious, for the meaning conveyed by the generic packaging of texts provides the indispensable context for understanding the constituent parts of a composition. Revelation is usually assigned to the literary genre apocalypse. It is the only book in the NT which belongs to this genre, though it is hardly a typical apocalypse, for it is framed as a letter by 1:4–5a and 22:21 (Karrer 1986). The name for the genre was derived from Rev. 1:1, where the author uses the Greek word ἀποκάλυψις (found only here) to describe, not the literary genre, but rather the revelatory character of the book and its divine origin as "the revelation *from* Jesus Christ" (subjective genitive). In the same context the author describes his work as a προφητεία, "prophecy" (1:3), and in the epilogue he refers to his work four times as a "prophetic book" (22:7, 10, 18–19), thus linking it with early Christian prophecy. Further, at the close of the commission narrative in Rev. 10:1–11, the author uses the verb προφητεύω, "to prophesy" in a heavenly command to him to "prophesy about many peoples and nations and tongues and kings" (10:11). Thus there is no doubt that the author's conception of his literary task involved the communication of a divine revelation using language derived from the OT prophetic writers, whether that literary task is labeled prophecy or apocalypse. Apocalypse is a modern generic designation for early Jewish and early Christian literary works that resemble Revelation in both form and content. Most Jewish apocalypses were written between 200 B.C.E. and 100 C.E.; they include Dan. 7–12, the only OT apocalypse, and *1 Enoch, 2 Enoch, 2 Baruch, 3 Baruch, 4 Ezra,* and the *Apocalypse of Abraham.* Apocalyptic traditions found in some of these works were known and used by the author of Revelation. After Revelation, the earliest Christian apocalypses include the Shepherd of Hermas, written in stages between 90 and 150 C.E., the *Book of *Elchasai,* early 2d century C.E., and the *Apocalypse of Peter,* mid-2d cent. C.E., though these three works are markedly different from Revelation in form and content.

The typical Jewish apocalypse, like Revelation, is a first-person narrative written in a fictive rhetorical setting and attributed to a famous OT figure of the distant past (such as Adam, Enoch, Abraham, Baruch, or Ezra), relating one or more revelatory visions about the future and/or the heavenly world. These revelatory narratives are typically based on earthly visions or during a heavenly journey. Jewish apocalypses often reflect a sharp distinction between the present evil age and imminent future age of blessing. The conflict between a righteous minority (generally Israel or an oppressed minority within Israel) and their enemies is understood to represent a cosmic clash between God and Satan. After a period of intense suffering, God is expected to intervene decisively in human history, sometimes through a messianic agent to vindicate and reward his people and to defeat and punish their oppressors. Jewish apocalypses frequently include mythological themes based on ancient Israelite royal ideology, historically frustrated and intensified by long periods of subjection to and domination by foreign nations. A stock figure of Jewish apocalypses who plays a relatively minor role in Revelation is the **angelus interpres* or "interpreting angel," a heavenly being who escorts the seer around the visionary world and provides detailed explanations of the hidden meaning of the seer's visions (Reichelt 1994). Since descriptions of the apocalypse genre are based on an ideal summary of literary traits shared by existing apocalypses, it is not surprising that Revelation goes beyond the generic features of the apocalypse in several significant respects: (1) It is not pseudonymous, but is written under the name of the actual author, nor was it placed in a fictive rhetorical setting, but reflects the actual circumstances of a group of Christian communities in the Roman province of Asia. (2) It is framed as a letter, though the extent to which the letter genre has affected the main composition is debated (Karrer 1986). (3) It has abandoned a focus on a particular ethnic group constitutive of the righteous and instead substitutes a universalism that coheres with developments in Christian thought in the Pauline and deuteropauline letters by including in the people of God those from every tribe, language, people, and nation (5:9; 7:9; 11:9; 13:7; 14:6; 17:15). (4) Though paraenesis occurs rarely in Jewish apocalypses, it is strikingly present in Revelation, particularly in the chapters that frame the book (1–3, 22). (5) Unlike visions in typical apocalypses, the visions in Revelation have few if any allegorical features, and the *angelus interpres* is largely absent from the narrative. In view of the distinctive features of Revelation, many of which exhibit a prophetic character, it is appropriate to regard the work as a prophetic apocalypse.

Language and style. Revelation was originally written in a very distinctive Greek style, which has Semitic features but does not incorporate the typical syntactical structures found in the translation Greek of the Septuagint (Mussies 1971). The text of Revelation contains 337 sentences (Nestle-Aland punctuation), of which 245 (73.79 percent) begin with the connective particle καί. Particular sections of Revelation exhibit a strikingly different paratactic style. Specifically, Rev. 2–3 contains 44 sentences, of which just 10 begin with καί (22.7 percent). This statistical features suggest that the author of Revelation has set the speeches of the risen Jesus in a slightly higher linguistic register. Proposals that Revelation was translated from a Hebrew or Aramaic source (Torrey 1958) are not persuasive. R. H. Charles's (1920, cxliii) thought that the language of Revelation was unique, since the author thought in Hebrew but wrote in Greek, a view essentially repeated by S. Thompson (1986, 108), who regards Revelation as written in a Christianized form of Jewish Greek (critiqued by Porter 1989).

Constituent literary forms. Apocalypses typically function as host genres to a variety of shorter literary forms, many of which have been incorporated into Revelation. The book is, e.g., punctuated with a number of liturgical or quasiliturgical forms including amens (1:6; 19:1; 22:21), hallelujahs (19:1, 3, 4, 6), doxologies (1:5b; 4:9; 5:13–14; 7:12; 19:1), the

Trisagion (4:8), and 16 hymns or hymnlike compositions (many antiphonal) set in heavenly throne–room scenes that provide a theological commentary on narrative developments (4:8c, 11; 5:9b–10.12b, 13b; 7:10b, 12; 11:15b, 17–18; 12:10b–12; 15:3b–4; 16:5b–7b; 19:1–4.5–8). The seven "letters" of Rev. 2–3 are really proclamations that have formal similarities both to imperial edicts and to prophetic speeches and serve to further the opposition between God and Christ (as the true sovereigns over against Rome) and her emperors as instruments of Satan (Müller, 57–107).

Most intriguing of all are the series of 11 relatively self-contained texts that are embedded at various points in Revelation, differing from each other in style and genre and appearing to have been composed for other settings prior to their inclusion in Revelation: (1) the sealing of the 144,000 (7:1–18), patterned after a military roster; (2) the angel with the little scroll (10:1–11), a commission narrative; (3) the two witnesses (11:1–13), a prophetic homily; (4) the woman, child, and dragon (12:1–18), an interpretation of constellations in terms of Hellenistic combat myths; (5) the beasts from the sea and the land (13:1–18), a literary vision expanding on the Leviathan-Behemoth myth; (6) the whore of Babylon (17:1–18), based on an ἔκφρασις or description of a work of art, a sestertius minted under Vespasian depicting Dea Roma seated on seven hills (Aune 3.919–26); (7) the fall of Babylon (18:1–24), a unified combination of three poetic forms; (8) the rider on the white horse (19:11–16), a symbolic description; (9) the final defeat of Satan (20:1–10); (10) the judgment of the dead (20:11–15); and (11) the vision of the New Jerusalem (21:9–22:5).

Literary sources. The question of whether more extensive literary sources lie behind Revelation in its present form remains a complex and debated issue. Three types of source-critical theories have been proposed: compilation theories (the combination of two or more originally separate apocalypses), revision theories (a single apocalypse later revised and expanded), and fragmentary theories (shorter units of tradition were combined to form the present text). Compilation theories of Revelation were popular in the late 19th and early 20th cents., but are now generally out of favor except for several French scholars under the influence of Boismard (1949), including Rousseau and Stierlin (1972) in the late 60s and early 70s. By the last third of the 20th cent., Anglo-American scholarship generally favored the compositional unity of Revelation, (the combined revision and fragmentary theory proposed by Aune 1997–98 is an exception, and criticized in detail by Prigent 2001, 84–92). The unity of Revelation is similarly emphasized among Continental scholars, with the exception of revision theories proposed by Kraft and Prigent, while variations of the fragmentary theory proposed by Bousset have been advocated by Bergmeier.

Structure. The author has imposed an artificial literary unity on his work by presenting the whole as a single, extensive vision report that is introduced in 1:9 and concludes somewhat uncertainly at 22:20. The external narrative unity provided by this overarching vision report does not guarantee the unity of the episodes that constitute it. Further, this lengthy vision report is framed as a letter with an epistolary prescript (1:4–5a), and concludes with an epistolary grace benediction (22:21). Despite recent arguments to the contrary, this does not mean that the material framed by these formal epistolary elements is either epistolary in character or is significantly affected by the epistolary framework (Karrer 1986). This letter framework is further subordinated to a metatextual introduction (1:1–3) that is "meta" because it self-consciously refers to the text that follows, much as a title prefixed or suffixed to a literary work. This introductory paragraph in Rev. 1:1–3, which has no analogies in ancient letters, is an auctorial innovation that overrides the formal epistolary features and signals that what follows is a vision narrative rather than a letter.

Though there is little agreement among scholars on the structure of Revelation, any structural analysis must privilege the organizational signals and patterns present in the text itself. In general, the prologue (1:1–8) and epilogue (22:10–21), with their epistolary features, frame three substantial units of text: (1) John's earthly vision of Christ and the dictation of seven proclamations to the churches (1:9–3:22); (2) John's ascent to heaven followed by a series of three heptadic visions narrating three waves of plagues sent to punish the inhabitants of the earth (4:1–16:21); (3) John's visions of the fate of Babylon and the supernatural enemies of God's people, followed by the full realization of eschatological salvation for God's people (17:1–22:9).

The number seven (used 53 times) provides a basic organizational principle for four heptads: (1) seven proclamations (2–3), (2) seven seals (4:1–8:1), (3) seven trumpets (8:2–11:18), and (4) seven libation bowls (15:1–16:21). The possibility that some segments of the text recapitulate other segments was broached by Victorinus of Petau (d. ca. 304), who proposed that the seven bowl plagues of 15:1–16:21 do not sequentially follow the seven trumpet plagues (8:2–11:18) as part of a continuous series, but are rather parallel accounts or recapitulations of the same events. This theory was revived in a more sophisticated form in the 20th cent. by Bornkamm (1937), followed by others (e.g., Yarbro Collins 1976).

While these heptads dominate the formal structure in chaps. 2–16, they have little to do with the several texts that are often labeled intercalations or enlargements: (1) the sealing of the 144,000 (7:1–17), sandwiched between the 6th and 7th seals; (2) the angel with the little scroll (10:1–11) and (3) the two witnesses (11:1–13), similarly sandwiched between the 6th and 7th trumpets; (4) the woman, child, and dragon (12:1–17); (5) the beasts from the sea and the land (13:1–18) and (6) a miscellany of visions and auditions (14:1–20), somewhat awkwardly inserted between the heptads of trumpets and bowls. Each of these six texts has a strikingly independent character, with a different literary form and lacking significant references to previous or subsequent segments of the text. Each of these texts appears to be more important to the author-editor than the heptads themselves and probably originated in another context before incorporation in the final text of Revelation.

In Rev. 17:1–22:9, a completely different formal compositional pattern dominates (Giblin 1974). The author uses two parallel angelic revelations (17:1–19:10 and 21:9–22:9), which begin and end with close parallels (17:1–3=21:9–10; 19:9–10=22:6–8), to frame and emphasize 19:11–21:8, which deals with a series of climactic eschatological events. These include the Parousia of Christ and his defeat of the hosts opposed to God (19:11–21), the temporary imprisonment of Satan (20:1–3), the resurrection of the martyrs (20:4–6), the final defeat and punishment of Satan and the armies of Gog and Magog (20:7–10), the judgment of the dead (20:11–15), and the salvific promise of the new Jerusalem (21:1–8). These very different types of formal organization barely conceal the tensions that continue to exist between the overarching literary framework and the constituent partial texts, where the author's focal concerns lie.

Use of the OT. Several kinds of sources are reflected in Revelation. The author shows an intimate familiarity with the OT, which he never formally quotes but to which he alludes more than 300 times (often following the Hebrew text but occasionally the Greek). Allusions numerically favor the prophetic books of Isaiah, Jeremiah, Ezekiel, and Daniel. There is disagreement with regard to whether the author is interpreting the OT with contextual integrity (Fekkes 1994, Beale 1998), or (more probably) whether his allusions are used to clothe his own ideas with scriptural language and authority (Ruiz 1989, Moyise 1995) and not interpreting the OT at all. Some argue that certain OT books, particularly Daniel (Beale regards Rev. 4–5, 13, and 17 as midrashes on Daniel) and Ezekiel (Vanhoye 1962, Ruiz 1989) are used to structure major sections of the book. In contrast with other early Christian authors, the language of promise and fulfillment is almost completely absent from Revelation.

Revelation and "contemporary" Jewish apocalypses. Revelation shares a number of motifs with some early Jewish apocalypses, particularly those which are nearly contemporary, including *1 Enoch* 37–71 (the *Similitudes of Enoch*), *4 Ezra,* and *2 Baruch,* though there is no clear evidence that he actually read these texts. Examples of shared motifs include: (1) the terror of humanity before the throne of judgment (Rev. 6:15–16=*1 Enoch* 62:3–5); (2) the Messiah seated on the throne of God judging the wicked (Rev. 3:21; 6:16; 22:1, 3=*1 Enoch* 45:3; 51:1; 55:4; 61:8; 62:2.5; 69:26–29); (3) the cry for vengeance and the *numerus iustorum* (Rev. 6:9–11=*1 Enoch* 47:1–4; *4 Ezra* 4:35–37; *2 Bar.* 23:4–5a); (4) eastern kings supernaturally instigated to march on the holy city (Rev. 16:12–16; 19:19–21; 20:7–10=*1 Enoch* 56:5–7); (5) the Leviathan-Behemoth myth (Rev. 13:1–18=*1 Enoch* 60:7–11.24; *4 Ezra* 6:49–52; *2 Bar.* 29:4); (6) the New Jerusalem (Rev. 21:9–22:9=*4 Ezra* 7:26; 8:52; 10:25–27a, 44; 13:36; *2 Bar.* 4:1–7; cf. the New Jerusalem fragments from Qumran, including 11Q19; 5Q15; 4Q554). The author's use of these and other common apocalyptic motifs indicates that he moved in Palestinian apocalyptic circles before emigrating to Roman Asia.

An example of shared motifs between Revelation and *1 Enoch* is the motif of the "terror of humanity before the throne of judgment" (Rev. 6:15–16; *1 Enoch* 62:3–5).

> Rev. 6:15–16: The kings of the earth and the great men and the generals and the rich and the strong and every one, slave and free, hid in the caves and among the rocks of the moun-

tains, calling to the mountains and rocks, "Fall on us and hide us from the face of him who is seated on the throne, and from the wrath of the Lamb; for the great day of their wrath has come, and who can stand before it?"

1 Enoch 62:3–5 (trans. Knibb): And on that day all the kings and the mighty and the exalted, and those who possess the earth, will stand up; and they will see and recognize how he sits on the throne of his glory . . . and pain will come upon them as (upon) a woman in labour for whom giving birth is difficult. . . . And one half of them will look at the other, and they will be terrified, and will cast down their faces, and pain will take hold of them when they see that Son of a Woman sitting on the throne of this glory.

These two passages exhibit similarities and differences. Similarities: (1) They share the apocalyptic motif of the terror of all humankind before the throne of judgment. (2) In *1 Enoch* 37–71, the phrase "the kings and the mighty and the exalted and those two dwell on the earth" (62:3) is a stereotypical phrase referring to everyone (62:1, 3, 6, 9; 63:1, 12; 67:8). A very similar phrase occurs in Rev. 6:15: "The kings of the earth and the great men and the generals and the rich and the strong and every one, slave and free" (similar lists occur twice elsewhere in Revelation with essentially the same meaning: 13:16; 19:18). These phrases may allude to the LXX text of Isa. 34:12 where the phrase "the kings and rulers and great ones" (with nothing corresponding to it in the Masoretic text) is found in a context of judgment. (3) In Rev. 6:15–16, God occupies the throne of judgment, though the Lamb is somehow also involved in judgment (see the next section below). In *1 Enoch* 62:3–5, God is initially seated on the throne of judgment (62:2–3), while the Son of Man is suddenly referred to as "sitting on the throne of his glory." There is one major difference between these passages: Different OT passages are alluded to: Rev. 6:15–16 is based on allusions to Isa. 2:19–21 and Hos. 10:6, while *1 Enoch* 62:3–5 alludes to the image of the woman in labor in Isa. 13:8.

The allusions to different OT passages in these two texts discourages the hypothesis of a direct literary relationship between them. However, the three impressive similarities suggest that both texts are dependent on a relatively fixed oral or written source or tradition. Since the existence of an *oral* apocalyptic tradition cannot easily be substantiated, it appears more likely that both Revelation and the *Similitudes of Enoch* are dependent on a common *written* source, which each author partially reformulated in a distinctive way.

A second example of motifs shared between Revelation and *1 Enoch* is the motif of the "kings from the east supernaturally instigated to march on the holy city" (Rev. 16:12–16; 19:19–21; 20:7–10; *1 Enoch* 56:5–7).

Rev. 16:12–16: The sixth angel poured his bowl on the great river Euphrates, and its water was dried up, to prepare the way for the kings from the east. [13] And I saw, issuing from the mouth of **the dragon from the mouth of the beast and from the mouth of the false prophet,** three foul spirits like frogs [14] for they are demonic spirits, performing signs, who go abroad to the kings of the whole world, to assemble them for the battle on the great day of God the Almighty. . . . [16] And they assembled them at the place which is called in Hebrew Armageddon.

Rev. 19:19–21: And I saw the beast and the kings of the earth with their armies gathered to make war against him who sits upon the horse and against his army. **And the beast was captured, and with it the false prophet who in its presence had worked the signs by which he deceived those who had received the mark of the beast and those who worshiped its image. These two were thrown alive into the lake of fire that burns with brimstone.** And the rest were slain by the sword of him who sits upon the horse, the sword that issues from his mouth; and all the birds were gorged with their flesh.

Rev. 20:7–10: And when the thousand years are ended, Satan will be loosed from his prison [8] and will come out to deceive the nations which are at the four corners of the earth, that is, God and Magog, to gather them for battle; their number is like the sand of the sea. [9] And they marched up over the broad earth and surrounded the camp of the saints and the beloved city; but fire came down from heaven and consumed them, [10] **and the devil who had deceived them was thrown into the lake of fire and brimstone where the beast and the false prophet were, and they will be tormented day and night for ever and ever.**

1 Enoch 56:5–7 (trans. Knibb): And in those days the angels will gather together, and will throw themselves towards the east upon the Parthians and Medes; they will stir up the kings, so that a disturbing spirit will come upon them, and they will drive them from their

> thrones; and they will come out like lions from their lairs, and like hungry wolves in the middle of their flocks. [6] And they will go up and trample upon the land of my chosen ones, and the land of my chosen ones will become before them a tramping-ground and a beaten track. [7] But the city of my righteous ones will be a hindrance to their horses, and they will stir up slaughter among themselves, and their (own) right hand will be strong against them; and a man will not admit to knowing his neighbour or his brother, nor a son his father or his mother, until through their death there are corpses enough, and their punishment—it will not be in vain. [8] And in those days Sheol will open its mouth and they will sink into it; and their destruction—Sheol will swallow up the sinners before the face of the chosen.

Of the three passages in Revelation cited above, the first two constitute a single source that has been interrupted in order to accommodate an extensive section on Babylon in Rev. 17–18. The first fragment in Rev. 16:12–16 ends without narrating the actual assembly of the king and the ensuing eschatological battle, while the second fragment in Rev. 19:19–21 provides both. Together these passages constitute a doublet of Rev. 20:7–10; the bold phrases are probably the additions to the source used by the author of Revelation. The same eschatological scenario characterizes the two passages: a malevolent supernatural being or beings instigates the kings of the east to assemble and march to the holy city, where they are supernaturally defeated by God and/or his Messiah.

This same scenario characterizes *1 Enoch* 56:5–7, which designates the enemy specifically as the Parthians and the Medes. This identification has been the basis of attempts to date the *Similitudes.* Sjöberg argued that this text was written shortly after the capture of Jerusalem by the Parthians in 40–37 B.C.E. (Sjöberg 1946, 39), while J. C. Hindley argued that it reflected Trajan's campaign against the Parthians in 113–17 C.E. (Hindley 1968–69, 551–65). These are just two of many proposals, none of which has proven decisive. *First Enoch* 56:5–7 also reflects the defeat of the enemy before the holy city, and therefore appears to be based on Sennacherib's abortive campaign against Jerusalem in 701 B.C.E. (Isa. 36:1–37:38=2 Kgs. 18:13–19:37). The motif of "trampling" on the holy land is applied to the holy city in LXX Zech. 12:3 ("and Jerusalem will be trampled on by the Gentiles until the times of the Gentiles are fulfilled"), a passage that is alluded to in both Luke 21:24 and Rev. 11:2. In *1 Enoch* 56:5–7, the holy city is inviolate. The fate of the enemy host is depicted through a combination of two traditions, one emphasizing the self-destruction of the enemy forces and the other saying that Sheol opens up and swallows them.

A comparison of the use of this motif in the *Similitudes* and the Revelation to John suggests that no mutual literary dependence is probable, but rather that both texts have used this motif in distinctive ways.

*Apocalypse, literary genre of

Aune 1997–98; Bauckham 1993; Beale 1998; Bergmeier 1984; Boismard 1949; Bornkamm 1937; R. H. Charles 1920; Fekkes 1994; Giblin 1974; Giessen 1997, 2000; Heinze 1998; Hemer 1986; Hengel 1993; Hindley 1968–69; Huntzinger 1965; Karrer 1986; Klauck 1992; Knight 1997; Lambrecht (ed.) 1990; Malina 1995; Moyise 1995; Müller 1975; Mussies 1971; Porter 1989; Price 1984; Prigent 2001; Resseguie 1998; Reichelt 1994; Roloff 1984; Ruiz 1989; Schnelle 1995; Sjöberg 1946; Stierlin 1972; Strecker 1995; L. L. Thompson 1990; S. Thompson 1986; Yarbro Collins 1976

Revelatory dialogue (see *Dialogue)

Revelatory literature All of the cultures of the ancient Mediterranean world and the Near East had a revelatory worldview. It was assumed that communication between the divine and human worlds was necessary for achieving and maintaining the welfare of the nation, the city, the tribe, the clan, the family, and the individual. This need for special knowledge, unavailable through conventional channels, lies behind the widespread phenomenon of divination, which can be defined as the interpretation of symbolic messages from the gods. Oracular or prophetic divination, messages from the gods in human language, became the basis for many types of revelatory literature. "Oracle" is a term derived from the Latin word *oraculum,* used both for a divine pronouncement about the unknown or the future and for the place where such pronouncements were given. The terms "prophecy" and "prophet" are derived from a family of Greek words based on the stem προφήτ-, used to translate the Hebrew root נבא ("prophet," "to prophesy"). Both Judaism and Christianity tended to avoid using the term μάντις, the pagan Greek term for prophet. The term "oracle" has come down to us through Greek and Latin literature and is often associated with inspired reponses to inquiries. The words "prophet" and "prophecy," on the other hand, have been transmitted through Judeo-Christian tradition and are often connected with unsolicited inspired speech. Actually, "oracle," "prophet," and "prophecy" all refer to the same cross-cultural phenomenon, though reflecting different cultural idioms. Modern anthropological studies of third-world cultures use the terms interchangeably.

Israelite-Jewish revelatory literature. In ancient Israel, prophecy was an oral phenomenon until the 8th cent. B.C.E., when the great classical prophets arose, beginning with Amos and Hosea in Israel, and Micah and Isaiah in Judah. These prophets were not typically authors but had followers who wrote down individual sayings and speeches that were later organized into larger compositions that in turn became the basis for the formation of OT prophetic books (Isa. 8:1; 30:8; Jer. 30:2; Ezek. 43:11). One of the original reasons for recording prophetic oracles was to authenticate the words of the prophets in anticipation of their fulfillment (Isa. 8:16–22; 29:11–12; 30:8–14; Hab. 2:2–3; Jer. 30:2–3). Another reason was to provide a substitute for the presence of the prophet (see Jeremiah's three prophetic letters, Jer. 29:1–23, 26–28, 31–33). Prophecy functioned in several ways, for there were court prophets (salaried by the king), temple prophets (salaried by temple authorities), and freelance prophets who were independent of both court and temple. The heyday of the free prophets extended from the 8th to the 6th cents. B.C.E., when Israel was profoundly and negatively affected by her expansionist neighbors, Assyria, Babylonia, and Persia. Free prophecy was partly a conservative protest movement attempting to revitalize ancient theocratic ideals they thought were endangered by a compromising monarchy that sought entangling foreign alliances in the interests of national security. Thus the free prophets whose oracles are preserved in the OT constituted a powerful political and social force in Israel with no real analogue in Greek or Roman culture.

By the 2d cent. B.C.E., the prophetic writings had received the kind of sacrosanct status that had earlier been accorded to the Pentateuch (see *Canon, Old Testament). At this point Jewish apocalyptic works (portions of *1 Enoch* and Dan. 7–12) began to be written. The prophetic section of the Jewish Scriptures was revered not out of antiquarian curiosity but because the ambiguity associated with prophecy made these books a continuing source of revelation (note the use of Jeremiah in Dan. 9:2 and the eschatological reinterpretation of Habakkuk in the Qumran commentary on Habakkuk (1QpHab; see *Pesharim). *Philo of Alexandria, author of extensive biblical commentaries, regarded the Pentateuch as a collection of oracles. The Jewish Scriptures thus served as a paradigm for written revelation in a way unique in the ancient world.

The relationship between prophecy and *apocalyptic in Judaism continued to be debated. Some emphasize the alien character of apocalyptic and propose foreign (usually Iranian) influence, while others view apocalyptic as an Israelite phenomenon that developed either out of mantic wisdom (as distinguished from proverbial wisdom) or out of prophecy itself. *Mantic wisdom* included skill in dream interpretation, attributed to sages like Joseph and Daniel in the OT, while *proverbial wisdom* is exemplified by the aphorisms of conventional wisdom found in the books of Proverbs and Sirach. The strong Jewish presence in the eastern Diaspora (Babylonia) for more than a millennium, beginning with the early 6th cent. B.C.E., served as a conduit for Mesopotamian traditions in Palestinian Judaism (e.g., the Enoch traditions). It is now widely recognized that prophecy did not cease with the last of the canonical Israelite prophets (Haggai, Zechariah, and Malachi) but simply took different forms appropriate to changing social and political circumstances. Apocalyptic writers often claimed inspiration, either explicitly or implicitly (*1 Enoch* 91:1; 93:1; *2 Enoch* 22:4–13; *4 Ezra* 14 [the legend of Ezra's miraculous reconstitution of 94 revelatory books]; *2 Bar.* 6:3; 10:1–3), but this should not necessarily be understood as a challenge to the status of the "canonical" scriptures.

Revelatory literature in early Judaism is largely limited to genres closely associated with apocalyptic eschatology: (1) apocalypses (the central characteristic of which is a dream or vision report, sometimes included in host genres, such as the testament), (2) revelatory discourses, (3) revelatory dialogues, and (4) revelatory revisions of Scripture (see *Rewritten Bible).

A *testament* (see *Farewell address), or speech of a dying patriarch modeled after Joseph's deathbed speech (Gen. 49), can stand alone or be incorporated into other genres (cf. the testament of Abraham in *Jub.* 20–22). Testaments consist of three basic elements: (1) a biography of the patriarch, (2) exhortation to his descendants, and (3) a deathbed forecast of the future. This is obviously related to the threefold structure of legends, visions, and admonitions, characteristic of many apocalypses (e.g., *2 Enoch* and *2 Baruch;* Daniel lacks admonitions, Revelation lacks legends), and reveals a basic compatibility between the testament and the apocalypse. Testaments with pronounced apocalyptic or eschatological segments include the *Testaments of the Twelve Patriarchs,* the *Testament of Abraham,* and the *Testament of Moses.* The *Testament of Levi* contains the following constituent elements: (1) a narrative of an otherworldly vision (2–5), (2) a narrative of a this-worldly vision (8), (3) a section of admonitions (10–13), and (4) a prophecy of the future (14–18), all framed and punctuated by biographical legends (1, 6–7, 9, 19).

A *revelatory discourse* is a "prophetic" speech that may contain a historical review presented as a prediction of future events and/or an eschatological description of the events immediately preceding and following the end of the age. It is not an apocalypse because it is not presented as a dream or vision report. Revelatory discourses are usually part of the testament form found in each of the *Testaments of the Twelve Patriarchs* (*T. Simeon* 5:4–6; *T. Levi* 14–18; *T. Judah* 22–25; *T. Issachar* 6; *T. Zebulon* 9), and in *T. Moses* 2–10; *T. Adam* 3:1–12; *T. Sol.* 15:8–12), though not in the testaments of Abraham, Isaac, Jacob, and Job. They can also be included in revelatory revisions of Scripture (see *Jub.* 23). In the NT, the Olivet discourse of Jesus found in Mark 13 and parallels has this form.

A *revelatory dialogue* is a conversation between a human recipient of revelation and a supernatural revealer, not necessarily to express a variety of opinions or offer a dialectical process of finding the truth in a Socratic manner, but rather to use the human recipient as a foil for the presentation of the revelatory message. Revelatory dialogues are sometimes found in the context of prophetic *call narratives, particularly those that feature the motif of the reluctant emissary (Moses in Exod. 3:7–4:17; Gideon in Judg. 6:11–24; Saul in 1 Sam. 9:15–21; Jeremiah in Jer. 1:4–7; cf. *Acts of Thomas* 1–3), i.e., the one called expresses hesitation and needs to be convinced by God. Dialogues are appropriate in the context of visionary guided tours of heaven or hell or the cosmos (cf. *1 Enoch* 21–36; *Apoc. Abraham* 12–14) or symbolic visions (Dan. 7:15–28; 8:15–27). The substantial use of dialogue in *4 Ezra* and *2 Baruch* between the seer and an angel of God, in which real problems are raised by the seers in a discussion focusing on theodicy, does not appear to be a straight-line development from early Jewish revelatory dialogues but shows Greco-Roman influence.

Revelatory revision of Scripture (see *Charismatic exegesis; Rewritten Bible) is a creative way of dealing with the normative status of the Torah and the Prophets, which left only limited ways of justifying dissident views and practices. These include *eisegesis* (manipulating the meaning of the text to reflect the opinion of the interpreter and his community), *modification* (attempting to change the sacred text, by additions, deletions, or composing documents that might supplement the collection) or actual *revision* (rewriting the offensive portions so they will reflect "correct" opinion).

Greco-Roman revelatory literature. The revelatory literature of the Hellenistic and Roman periods is largely based on oracles. The Romans, heir to the elaborate Etruscan science of divination, made little use of oracles, while the Greeks placed a high value on them, though they also used many other forms of divination. Oracles could be assembed in collections (analogous to the early stages in the formation of the OT prophetic books) and expanded into oracular discourses or oracular dialogues. These four literary types presuppose the phenomenon of the possession trance, i.e., possession by a supernatural being, enabling the medium to speak on behalf of the god. A fifth literary form, the vision report (the central feature of Jewish and Christian apocalypses), is based on the phenomenon of the vision trance, i.e., visions, hallucinations, and out-of-body experiences.

Greek *oracles* were usually short (two to four lines) pronouncements in verse or prose, expressed in the first person, of the inspiring deity (usually Apollo) in response to inquiries made at oracle shrines by individuals or representatives of states. When some Greeks had problems digging a canal, they sent messengers to Delphi to ask Apollo the reason. He reportedly replied in verse (Herodotus 1.174):

> The isthmus neither fence with towers nor dig through,
> for Zeus would have made it an island, had he so desired.

Most oracles dealt with matters of ritual, as does the following prose oracle quoted by the Athenian orator Demosthenes (*Or.* 21.53): "The prophet of Zeus in Dodona commands: To Dionysus pay public sacrifices and mix a bowl of wine and set up dances; to Apollo the Averter sacrifice an ox and wear garlands, both free men and slaves, and observe one day of rest; to Zeus, the giver of wealth, a white bull."

Often the inquirer would receive a written copy of the oral response. If the inquirer were an emissary of a city-state, the response might be deposited in state archives. The staff at oracle shrines sometimes deposited oracular responses in temple archives. Particularly important oracles might be engraved on stone for all to see, and many of these have survived, though none from Delphi, the most important of the ancient oracle sanctuaries of Apollo. Most of the preserved oracles were placed in literary settings as *oracle stories, a form favored by Herodotus, but unfortunately these are the least historically reliable. The ambiguity of oracles provided a market for professional oracle interpreters, who operated in the vicinity of oracle sanctuaries.

Many *oracle collections* existed in the ancient world, but none have survived intact. Since the inherently ambiguous meaning of oracles meant that their fulfillment was uncertain, oracles were collected by intinerant oracle expounders (χρησμόλογοι), who provided readings and interpretations. The collections, which circulated under the pseudonyms of Orpheus, Musaeus, and the various Sibyls and Bakides, were not collections of responses, but rather unsolicited oracles believed uttered by those after whom the collections were named. In form, many sections of the surviving *Sibylline Oracles* are really revelatory discourses. The Romans kept an official collection of Sibylline Oracles for consultation in times of national emergency. The legendary character of the various Sibyls (more than 40 were distinguished by the end of antiquity) means oracles attributed to them were really pseudonymous literary products.

The *oracular dialogue* has a complicated literary pedigree as one of the many types of the *dialogue that developed in Greco-Roman culture. The philosophical dialogues of Plato and Aristotle became literary models throughout the rest of antiquity. They were emulated in Rome during the 1st cent. B.C.E. and later by Plutarch and Lucian. Many dialogues are essays cast into an artificial dialogical form. As an independent literary form, dialogues are usually placed in a conventional setting (e.g., temple dialogues occur in or near a sanctuary, symposia are dinner dialogues, and peripatetic dialogues place conversation in the framework of a stroll). One special form of the dialogue is the *erotapokrisis* ("question-and-answer"), a didactic form modeled on teacher-student conversation. This type of dialogue typically minimized the importance of the setting and was adapted as a literary vehicle for revelatory teaching by a supernatural being in a catechetical style (e.g., the many Hermetic tractates and the three Coptic-Gnostic dialogues, *Hypostatis of the Archons, Thomas the Contender,* and *Dialogue of the Savior* (see *Nag Hammadi literature). Rather than developing directly from conventional question-and-answer dialogues, or *erotapokriseis,* oracular dialogues derived from the simple question-and-answer scheme. Oracle questions often had two parts, e.g., "Shall I or shall I not do such-and-such?" and "To which god or goddess shall I sacrifice to ensure success?" (e.g., Thucydides 1.134.4; Xenophon, *Ways and Means* 6.2–3; *Anabasis* 3.1.5–7; Dionysius Hal., *Ant. Rom.* 1.23.4). Lucian has preserved an oracular dialogue between a wealthy Roman and the oracular deity Asklepios-Glykon (*Alexander* 43). Many of the revelatory spells in the *magical papyri provide instructions on conducting question-and-answer dialogues with supernatural revealers. A literary adaptation of the oracular dialogue is found in Vergil, *Aeneid* 6, in which the hero Aeneas receives a guided tour of hades by the Sibyl and his deceased father Anchises and asks about some of the sights. Vergil used as a model *Odyssey* 11, where Odysseus, without a guide, holds conversations with a succession of ghosts in hades. Though the dialogue form is not really present in the Revelation to John, it is found in a highly developed form in the Shepherd of Hermas.

The *oracular discourse* was another way of expanding conventional oracular responses. The oracular discourse could easily be changed into an oracular dialogue, which is reflected in the composition history of some Coptic-Gnostic dialogues (see *Nag Hammadi literature). Fictional prophetic speeches occur frequently in Greek literature, like the doom oracle of Theoclymenus (*Odyssey* 20.351–57) and the underworld speeches predicting the future adventures of various epic heroes (e.g., *Odyssey* 11.90–137; Vergil, *Aeneid* 6.756–859). Book 3 of the *Sibylline Oracles* (mid-2d cent. C.E.), contains several oracular discourses (97–161, 162–95, 196–294, 350–80, 381–87, 388–400, 401–88, 545–656, 657–808). There tend to be two types of oracular discourses, those that predict judgment, frequently connected with a historical review presented as a forecast (e.g., *Sib. Or.* 3.97–161, 4.188), and those that exhibit a two-part scheme, the prediction of tribulation followed by deliverance (e.g. *Sib. Or.* 3.350–80; 545–656, the potter's oracle).

Reports of dreams or visions are common in Greco-Roman literature and exhibit striking similarities to those of ancient Near Eastern cultures. Revelatory experiences could take place in an earthly setting (as in most dreams) or could involve ascent to heaven or descent to the underworld. Further, they tended to be narrated in direct discourse and inserted into a variety of host genres, such as history, biography, novels, and letters (e.g., Dionysius Hal., *Ant. Rom.* 1.57.3–4; Plutarch, *Lucullus* 12.1–2; *Eumenes* 6.4–7; Philostratus, *Life of Apollonius* 4.34).

One type of literary form that has many points of similarity to Jewish and Christian apocalypses is the narrative of an ascent or descent to the supernatural world. These accounts are all fictional pseudonymous narratives, either reported in the first person or secondarily related by a supposedly reliable informant providing hearsay evidence. Examples are Plato's Myth of Er (*Rep.* 10.13–16), the Dream of Scipio (Cicero, *Rep.* 6.9–26), the visions of Timarchus (Plutarch, *On the Genius of Socrates* 21–22), Thespesius (Plutarch, *On the Delays of Divine Justice* 22–31), and Menippus (Lucian, *Icaromenippus*). Most of these "apocalypses" consist of journeys in which the postmortem rewards of the righteous or the punishments of the wicked are seen and reported for the purpose of instilling a fear that motivates correct behavior when these experiences are narrated (Diodorus 1.2.2; LCL trans.):

> For if it be true that the myths which are related about Hades, in spite of the fact that their subject-matter is fictitious, contribute greatly to fostering piety and justice among men, how much more must we assume that history, the prophetess of truth, she who is, as it were, the mother-city of philosophy as a whole, is still more potent to equip men's character for noble living!

These guides' tours to the other world are always constituent elements of larger literary forms, unlike their Jewish and Christian analogues (though the Dream of Scipio was preserved separately because of the commentary on it by Macrobius).

*Apocalyptic, *Farewell address, *Oracle, *Oracle story, *Revelatory dialogue, *Testament

Rewritten Bible is a modern designation (coined by Vermes 1973, 126) for a spectrum of early Jewish and early Christian literature that relates in a variety of ways to earlier literary exemplars or models. Other designations for Rewritten Bible include "narrative exegesis," i.e., reworking the biblical narrative with exegetical aims (Fröhlich 1998), and "parabiblical works." Rewritten Bible refers to a type of biblical interpretation exhibited in a number of early Jewish writings that present biblical books in a revised and rewritten form, attributing to them an authority close to, if not identical with, existing biblical books, thus attesting to the status held by such works. Using transcultural terminology, Rewritten Bible is a form of "*hypertext" that is transparently connected to an earlier "*hypotext" (using the language of Genette's structuralist poetics, 1997a), *but always so that the model on which the reconfigured text is based is clearly recognizable.* A literary theory related to Genette's *hypertextuality is *intertextuality, which maintains that "every work is formed and finds meaning in relation to other literary works, every text is viewed as conditioned by other texts, through similarity or differentiation" (Conte 1994b). This reconfiguration of the text called Rewritten Bible or narrative exegesis, like hypertextuality and intertextuality, can involve similarity (expansions, additions, clarifications) or differentiation (deletions, emendations, corrections, reactions, and contradictions). Greek and Roman literary culture valued both tradition and innovation, and the tension between these two values resulted in the continual transformation of literary genres.

The phrase Rewritten Bible (RB) is somewhat problematic, because what the phrase describes is a process common to all literary cultures, though the term "Bible" indicates that the hypotext has a sacrosanct status that would make a qualitative distinction between Rewritten Bible and rewritten literature, though the phenomena at issue are essentially the same. Although RB texts can often follow the authoritative hypotext verbatim (as do translations) and can clarify and expand important sections (as do the Targums) and interpret the Bible (as does midrash), they are not merely translations, nor *targums nor *midrashim *sensu stricto.* They are retellings that often seamlessly interweave Scripture, tradition, and auctorial creativity. In so doing they constitute entirely new compositions that have their own distinct genres, literary frames, historical settings, redactional tendencies, and theological perspectives. While RB can be a fuzzy category, several clear examples of the phenomenon can be found within the Bible and the literature of early Judaism and early Christianity. Within the OT, the phenomenon of rewriting is already apparent in both legal and narrative material. The author of Deuteronomy rewrites Exod. 20–23 and portions of Numbers and Leviticus, while the author of Chronicles both truncates and expands the Deuteronomistic History, especially the books of 1–2 Samuel and 1–2 Kings, in an attempt to construct his own postexilic account of the sacred history of Israel. Sometimes it is unclear which is the hypertext and which the hypotext (e.g., Isa. 36–39 and 2 Kgs. 18–20; many Psalm doublets, e.g., Pss. 14 and 53; Ps. 18 and 2 Sam. 22; Pss. 40:13–17 and 70; 57:7–11 and 108:1–5; 60:5–12 and 108:6–13; 115:4–8 and 135:15–18); see Evans 1988, 156. Also significant are the expanded versions of the books of Daniel and Esther in the LXX, which clearly follow the form and content of the Hebrew and Aramaic originals, often word for word, but supplement these originals with considerable expansions.

Examples of RB are more frequent in early Jewish and early Christian literature. One of the earliest instances of this interpretive technique is found in *1 Enoch* 6–11, which is a reworking of Gen. 6:1–4 with several new features (Nickelsburg 2001, 29; see also Dimant 2002): (1) The Hebrew version is elaborated in Aramaic. (2) To the basic myth about divine-human mating, a story about a heavenly rebellion has been added. (3) Genesis 6:1–4 has been linked to the flood story in such a way that God's judgment is directed against the giants' offenses against humanity. *First Enoch* 106 is a free reworking of Gen. 5:28–29. The stories of Genesis have been reworked in *Jubilees* and the *Genesis Apocryphon* from Qumran, lQapGen (Fitzmyer 1971), as well as in 4Q252 (Lim 1992; Brooke 1994; Bernstein 1994) and CD 2.2–3.12 (Fröhlich 1998). These texts have some common features (Fröhlich 1998, 82): (1) they follow the order of the biblical text and often include additions (sometimes rather long ones) to the biblical text; (2) they retell only certain stories and omit others; (3) they are discontinuous narratives that jump from one story to another, often ignoring links between the episodes; and (4) the reader can understand the narrative only on the basis of the text of Genesis. The *Genesis Apocryphon* includes some word-for-word translations in the manner of the *Targums, as well as some imaginative embellishments resembling haggadic *midrash (on the genre of the *Genesis Apocryphon,* see Fitzmyer 1971, 5–12, who regards it as a prototype of midrash). However, since the *Genesis Apocryphon* does not distinguish text from commentary, it does not belong to the midrash genre (C. A. Evans 1988). The fragmentary *Genesis Apocryphon* retells the stories of the patriarchs Lamech, Noah, Abraham, and others narrated in Genesis. Other examples of the RB technique include the **Testament of Moses* (based on Deut. 31–33), parts of the **Testaments of the Twelve Patriarchs,* the *Testament of Abraham,* the *Testament of Job,* the Books of *Adam and Eve, the Targumim, certain works categorized as *pseudepigrapha, such as *Jubilees* (a lengthy rewriting of Gen. 1:1 through Exod. 12:50 that presents itself as a revelation given to Moses by an angel on Mount Sinai). The *Temple Scroll,* another work from Qumran, is a detailed description of the temple moving from the inside to the outside, and from col. 50 on, it follows the order and content of Deut. 12–26. Other early Jewish examples of RB include Pseudo-Philo's *Biblical Antiquities,* which includes a sometimes brief, sometimes full retelling of biblical history from Adam to David (though the ending may be lost; see Nickelsburg 1984, 107 n. 102). The first ten books of Josephus's *Antiquities* is also a rewriting of biblical history supplemented by a rewriting of postbiblical works bringing the narrative down to his own time following the destruction of the temple in 70 C.E. The *Assumption of Moses* is a rewriting of the farewell speech of Moses in Deut. 31–34 that ends with an apocalypse of Israel's future. *Esdras* is a selective rewriting of biblical history from Josiah to Ezra that focuses on, among other things, the reform of the temple cult. Among the works of Philo, *On Abraham* is an excellent example of RB (Harrington 1976, 165; cf. Sandmel 1979, 18).

In addition to these examples, we also possess (1) fragmentary works that may well have represented (in their full original form) retellings of the Bible and (2) examples of the phenomenon of rewriting Scripture in works that may not themselves be appropriately classified as "Rewritten Bible." The former category is represented primarily by fragmentary Hellenistic Jewish rewritings of the Bible that attempt to recast the biblical narratives in forms that might appeal to the tastes of Hellenistic Jews (Nickelsburg 1984, 118–30). For example, Philo the Epic Poet's *On Jerusalem* probably rewrote the stories of the patriarchs Abraham and Joseph. Theodotus's epic hexameter poem, *On the Jews*, retells the rape of Dinah and the sack of Shechem (Gen. 33–34). Finally, Ezekiel the Tragedian's *Exagoge* probably retold various portions of stories from Genesis and Exodus.

The second category is represented by works that contain examples of the phenomenon of rewriting the Bible "less obviously keyed to the structure and flow of the biblical narrative" (Harrington 1986, 246). For example, the book of *1 Enoch* is hardly a close retelling of the book of Genesis, but at least one portion of it is clearly a rewriting of the story of the Watchers from Gen. 6:1–4 (see *1 En.* 6–11). Similarly, the *Life of Adam and Eve* is clearly inspired by Genesis 1–3, but is so extensive in its expansions that it moves far beyond the realm of mere "rewriting."

Basic techniques of rewriting. In order to further delineate the category of RB, it is important to list some of the techniques of rewriting utilized in examples (Nickelsburg 1984). While many of these techniques are common to most, if not all of the works, no one of them stands out above the rest as definitive or determinative for the category—unless the common practice of following the general order of the biblical narrative should be considered a "technique" of rewriting. Rather, the presence of several of these together as the key compositional features of a book is what justifies the categorization of any given text as Rewritten Bible. Some of the major techniques are as follows: (1) *Verbatim reproduction.* Even examples of RB that contain major expansions (such as the *Genesis Apocryphon*) often follow the biblical text word for word, thereby revealing their use of Scripture as a primary source of composition. (2) *Paraphrase.* This is the technique that most closely links examples of RB with the later Jewish Aramaic Targums; it is utilized, for example, by Pseudo-Philo to summarize or shorten portions of Scripture that are less pertinent to his task. (3) *Additions.* Additions to the source text can come in many forms, including the interpolation of prayers, speeches, narrative expansions, entirely new stories, substantial revision of old stories, added frameworks, halakic insertions, calendrical emendations, and eschatological additions. (4) *Deletions.* Most examples of RB show no hesitation to delete large portions of the text if the passages in question are irrelevant to the task at hand. For example, Pseudo-Philo deletes most of the legal material in Exodus and Numbers and almost the entire book of Leviticus, as well as the story of the Israelite conquest in Josh. 3–21 (Nickelsburg 1984, 107). The combined effect of these techniques is to interpret the source material and explain difficulties in the original text while at the same time creating an altogether new document.

Rewritten Bible vs. midrash and Targumim. In the past, scholars have often understood examples of RB in terms of later Jewish Targumim and midrash (see, e.g., Vermes 1973; Bloch 1955; Patte 1975; Porton 1981; Haas 1981; Wright 1967). On the one hand, this is a reasonable assumption, since Rewritten Bible literature does paraphrase Scripture (as do the Targums) and does interpret Scripture (as do the midrashim). Moreover, the traditions that work their way into RB literature as expansions and additions often have striking parallels in the haggadic traditions of later Jewish midrashim and Targumim. Thus, the phenomenon of RB is in many ways similar to the activity of Jewish scribes in the production of the Targumim and midrash. On the other hand, some scholars have questioned the identification of RB texts with later Jewish Targumim and midrash (Harrington 1986; Fitzmyer 1971; Evans 1988, 1993).

Several arguments have been levied against equating the rewriting of the Bible with targumic and midrashic activity. (1) *Implicit vs. explicit interpretation.* The strongest argument against categorizing RB as midrash is that interpretation in RB is "implicit," while interpretation in the Qumran pesharim and rabbinic midrash is "explicit." This distinction has been utilized both by Evans in his discussion of "explicit" vs. "implicit interpretation" and by Perrot in his understanding of *texte expliqué* and *texte continua* (Evans 1993; Perrot 1976). For Perrot, the *texte expliqué* is the focus of midrash, which explicitly exegetes a text, while *texte continua,* the story of Scripture, is the focus of an RB text like the *Biblical Antiquities.*

Explicit interpretation is characterized by a formal distinction between text and commentary. The integrity of the text is respected and cannot be altered or rewritten. If the text is altered or rewritten, it is done so out of a conviction that the original reading is thereby restored. The text is to be interpreted, whether we are talking about midrash, pesher, typology, or allegory. But not all interpretation is explicit. Some interpretation is implicit. When interpretation is implicit, the author's interpretation is interwoven with the text. Interpretation and story are merged (Evans 1993, 171). It is this interweaving of text and interpretation that is characteristic of RB texts. They are not strict "exegesis" of Scripture in the same way as the midrashim, because they do not alert the reader to the presence or authority of the source being utilized. Although some scholars have ventured to categorize early forms of "rewritten Bible" as "midrash," the rabbinic midrashim display an important difference from earlier works like *Jubilees,* Pseudo-Philo, and the *Genesis Apocryphon.* "The Midrashim clearly distinguish text from interpretation, and so in a certain sense are forerunners of the modern commentary" (Evans 1988, 165).

"Radical paraphrase" vs. targumic paraphrase. On the one hand, RB texts are by all accounts very similar to later Jewish Targumim, because both RB texts and Targumim engage in translation and paraphrase and the interpretive processes that are necessarily part of these activities. Thus, both RB texts and Targumim engage in implicit interpretation. In this sense they are the same kind of work. On the other hand, RB goes beyond Targum. In the strict sense, Targumim are first and foremost paraphrastic *translations* that aim on some level to *reproduce* the biblical text. By contrast, rewritten Bible texts are *entirely new literary products* that have as their goal the *creation* of a new work rather than the reproduction—however loose—of an original. They are, in the words of Craig Evans, "radical paraphrase": "'Radical paraphrase' is not translation (though translation is often involved). Radical paraphrase involves the retelling of the biblical story. . . . [Rewritten bible texts] are not commentaries, not anthologies, nor actual histories. They are *literary contributions* to the sacred story. They might be regarded, as some of their authors no doubt intended, as semi-Scripture" (Evans 1993, 173–74 [emphasis added]). In this sense RB texts are examples of radical paraphrase rather than paraphrastic translation or "targumic paraphrase." Of course, this is a generalization, since even among the premier Jewish Targumim, Targum Pseudo-Jonathan is as "radical" in its paraphrase of the biblical text as any earlier RB.

Is Rewritten Bible a genre? In light of the strong affinities shared by many of the RB texts, it is tempting to suggest that together they constitute a "genre." But do they? Or, as Nickelsburg suggests, do they employ a variety of subgenres (1984, 89–90)? One major factor weighs against the suggestion of a single genre: Rewritten Bible texts quite clearly belong to *different* literary genres. For example, while both *Jubilees* and the *Assumption of Moses* are premier examples of RB, in terms of form they are both apocalypses, and the latter also probably belongs to the testamentary genre (Harrington 1986, 243). The books of Chronicles, 1 Esdras, and Josephus's *Antiquities* are first and foremost historiography, a genre that for Evans is a subdivision or "part of the Jewish rewritten Bible" (1993, 175). The fragmentary Hellenistic writings of Philo the Epic Poet, Theodotus, and Ezekiel the Tragedian definitely rewrite the Bible but are, in terms of genre, dramas. Other fragmentary texts, such as the *Genesis Apocryphon* and the *Temple Scroll,* are more difficult to classify, since their damaged condition has robbed us of the literary frameworks that would provide essential information about the genre of the works. In light of this generic diversity within the category of RB, "it seems better to view rewriting the Bible as a kind of activity or process than to see it as a distinctive literary genre of Palestinian Judaism. . . . In conclusion, it is tempting to place all these books, as well as others, under the broad literary genre of 'rewritten Bible,' but unfortunately the diversity and complexity of the materials will not allow it" (Harrington 1986, 243).

Rewritten Bible and the canon. The very terminology of "Rewritten Bible" assumes that a fully canonical text existed when individual texts were subject to rewriting. If so, one can follow scholars who suggest that the phenomenon of RB has its origins in the canonization of the biblical texts. From this perspective, RB texts "represent early biblical interpretation that is conscious of the canonical status and stablization of sacred tradition" (Evans 1988, 165). In similar fashion, Nickelsburg suggests that the tendency of RB "to follow the ancient texts more closely may be seen as a reflection of [the biblical texts'] developing canonical status" (Nickelsburg 1984, 89). The problem with this perspective is that the phenomenon of RB antedates the "canonization" of many of the texts that were being rewritten. As Vanderkam points out, the "biblical period" had not yet ended when many of these RB texts (such as 1–2 Chronicles and *Jubilees*) were being composed (1993). This makes the intentions and self-understanding of the rewriter much less clear than the above perspective allows. Do RB texts have as their purpose the supplementation of Scripture, such that they are meant to be read alongside it (Evans 1988, 164), or are they supposed to *replace* a text that may or may not have acquired "biblical" status? For example, does the author of Chronicles intend to supplement or displace the Deuteronomistic History that is his primary source? Can we know with certainty that the latter had acquired "biblical" status by the time of the composition of the former? Probably not. While Nickelsburg is correct to point out that the close following of a source text may be an indicator of canonical status, it is not necessarily so

(1984, 89). Other reasons, such as lack of other sources and recognition of the quality of the narrative framework provided by a source, may have been the main motivating factors. In any case, VanderKam is more precise when he states that "the term 'biblical' would not have had the precision that was later given it" (1993, 97). In light of this fact, perhaps the language of "Rewritten Bible" is itself inappropriate, and we should replace it with "Rewritten Scripture" or some such term that indicates that sacred (but not necessarily canonical) texts are being rewritten and possibly replaced. All we really know is that these works were interpreting *"older authoritative compositions* at a time when the bounds of the Hebrew Scriptures were not set" (VanderKam 1993, 97). Moreover, the revelatory claims of some of these texts, such as the *Temple Scroll* and the book of *Jubilees,* should make us very hesitant to describe them as mere rewritings or retellings of an already stabilized canon or "Bible." We may very well be obscuring the character of some of these texts by using a generic term such as "Rewritten Bible" despite the fact that it is inherently anachronistic and controlled by later theological and historical developments.

Rewritten Bible in the New Testament? If we prescind for a moment from the view of RB as a genre and see it instead as more of an activity, then RB can also be found in the NT, although no NT book can be said to represent a full-scale example of "rewritten Bible." Some scholars have suggested that the Gospels themselves be seen as examples of the process of rewriting of the Bible. Downing holds that retelling of OT history contained in the Gospels is similar to that of Josephus (Downing 1980). Chilton likewise views this retelling process as "cognate" with that which takes place in the later Jewish Targums (Chilton 1980, 125). Finally, Evans describes Luke–Acts as "an example of the 'historical hagiographa'" (i.e., sacred history or historical Scripture), a genre that is part of the Jewish RB (Evans 1993). Methodologically the predecessor of Luke is *Jubilees,* and his contemporaries are Pseudo-Philo's *Liber antiquitatum biblicarum,* Josephus's *Jewish Antiquities,* and the Gospel of Matthew (175). Evans holds that Luke–Acts should be compared with Jewish RB for several reasons, primarily because of parallel techniques in biblical rewriting and his view of the gospel story as "sacred tradition, if not in some sense as Scripture itself" (175). The primary parallels to the Lukan rewriting strategies can be found in the techniques of the Chronicler, 1 Esdras, *Jubilees, Antiquities,* and Pseudo-Philo (199).

BRANT PITRE

Adam and Eve, Lives of, *Apocrypha, *Josephus, *Antiquities of the Jews,* *Midrash, *Pesharim, *Pseudepigrapha, *Targum

---

Ackroyd 1972; P. Alexander 1988; Attridge 1976a, 1984; Bauckham 1983b; Bernstein 1994; Bloch 1955; Brooke 1994; Charlesworth 1987; Chilton 1980; Dimant 1988; Downing 1980; Endres 1987; C. A. Evans 1988, 1993; Feldman 1988; Fishbane 1980; Fitzmyer 1966, 1971; Franxman 1979; Fröhlich 1998; Hans 1981; Harrington 1976, 1985, 1986; Hayward 1990; Kratz, Krüger, and Schmid 2000; Kugel and Greer 1986; Lim 1992; Nickelsburg 1984, 2001, 29–30; Patte 1975; Perrot 1976; Porton 1981a; Sandmel 1961, 1979; VanderKam 1993; Vermes 1973; Wright 1967

Rhetoric, a transliterated form of the Latin word *rhetorica* based on the Greek term ῥητορική, can be defined in a number of ways (various definitions are discussed in Quintilian, *Inst.* 2.15.1–38). For Aristotle, philosophy and rhetoric were not separable. Plato and Aristotle both insisted that the purpose of each branch of rhetoric was a good, such as the expedient, the noble, or the just (*Rhetorica* 2.19.26 [1393a]). Rhetoric was considered an art (τέχνη), i.e., "Zeno said that τέχνη is a systematic collection of cognitions ordered by practice for some goal advantageous in life" (von Arnim 1968, 1.21; Long and Sedley 1987, 1.259). Aristotle traced the beginnings of rhetoric to two Sicilians, Corax and Tisias, who developed the earliest rhetorical theory (Cicero, *Brutus* 46). Rhetoric was a source of conflict between the Sophists and the Philosophers. The basis of the conflict was the attitude toward truth. Hermogenes (*On Issues* 29.4–6) reflected the rhetorical side of the conflict when he began his work with this disclaimer: "It is not the function of rhetoric to investigate what is really and universally just, honourable, etc." (Heath 1995, 28). Plato made a distinction between "true" and "false" rhetoric. Aristotle defined rhetoric as the "faculty of discovering the possible means of persuasion in reference to any subject whatever" (*Rhetorica* 1.2.1 [1355b]), while Quintilian (*Inst.* 2.17.37) preferred the broad definition *ars bene dicendi,* "the art of speaking well." A more lengthy definition is provided by the author of the **Rhetorica ad Herennium* (1.2):

"The task of the public speaker is to discuss capably those matters which law and custom have fixed for the uses of citizenship, and to secure as far as possible the agreement of his hearers." Cicero intentionally tried to bridge the gap between the philosopher and the orator in his *De oratore,* in which he played both roles.

From a modern perspective, rhetoric is often defined as the art of speaking or writing effectively or the study of speaking or writing as a means of communication and persuasion. Aristotle defined rhetoric simply as the art of persuasion. The recent definition of Classen (2000, 45) emphasizes the role of language, though it lacks specificity: "the deliberate, calculated use of language for the sake of communicating various kinds of information in the manner intended by the speaker (and the theory of such a use)." A more complete definition, proposed by Corbett, self-consciously reflects the Aristotelian tradition (1990, 3): "the art or the discipline that deals with the use of discourse, either spoken or written, to inform or persuade or motivate an audience" (whether an individual or a group).

For the student of the NT and early Christian literature, there are two main categories of rhetorical theory: classical rhetoric, or "old rhetoric" (elaborated in Greek and Latin rhetorical handbooks from antiquity through the middle ages and then tapering off in influence from the 17th to the 19th cent.), and modern rhetoric, developed in the 20th cent. Modern rhetoric itself has two main phases, *neo-Aristotelianism (which developed during the first half of the 20th cent.) and the "new rhetoric" (a development during the second half of the 20th cent.). While some scholars focus on Greek and Roman rhetorical theory (i.e., classical rhetoric) as a tool for understanding the composition of early Christian literature (Betz 1974–75, 1979; R. D. Anderson 1999), others argue that there is no good reason that a text should be analyzed only according to categories known (or possibly known) to the author (Amador 1999; Classen 2000, 5).

*New Rhetoric, *Rhetorical criticism, *Rhetorical handbooks

Classen 2000; Corbett 1990; Lanham 1991, 131–35

Rhetoric, divisions of, or the *partes artis.* Since rhetoric is that aspect of discourse by which a speaker or writer tries to accomplish his or her purposes, referred to as the "duties of the orator" (*officia oratoris* or *vis oratoris*), rhetorical criticism as a historical method focuses on those features of rhetorical theory and practice that were central to the Greeks and Romans, consisting of five parts (Cicero *Partitiones oratoriae* 5–26): (1) **inventio,* i.e., the art of finding the materials of discourse, particularly arguments, by using common or specific topoi or "topics" (Heath 1997); (2) **dispositio,* or *collocatio,* the arrangement or order of the discourse (Wuellner 1997); (3) **elocutio,* the style including phrases and terms (Rowe 1997); (4) **memoria,* the art of memorizing a speech (Olbricht 1997b); (5) **actio,* the art of delivering a speech (Olbricht 1997b).

Heath 1997; Lausberg 1998, §§255–1091; Olbricht 1997b; Porter (ed.) 1997

Rhetorica ad Alexandrum, a rhetorical handbook written during the 4th cent. B.C.E. (the reference in 8.8 to the expedition of the Corinthians under Timoleon provides a *terminus post quem* of 341 B.C.E.), is a typical product of early rhetorical theory (Kennedy 1963, 81), particularly representative of sophistic rhetoric (Kennedy 1963, 115). Earlier attributed erroneously to Aristotle, the handbook was actually compiled by Anaximines of Lampsacus (380–320 C.E.), an instructor of Alexander the Great (to whom the work is addressed); this was suggested by Quintilian (3.4.9) and is generally supported by modern scholarship (Kennedy 1963, 114–15), though strong arguments against this attribution are presented by Buchheit (1960, 189–98, 205–7). It is likely that the *Rhetorica ad Alexandrum* was composed before the *Rhetorica* (Grimaldi 1972, 75–77), and there is no evidence that the author of the *Rhetorica ad Alexandrum* had read Aristotle's *Rhetorica* (Mirhady 1994, 55–56).

Rhetorical theory. While most *rhetorical handbooks focus on *forensic rhetoric, the *Rhet. Alex.* contains one of the more extensive discussions of *deliberative rhetoric (1.1421b–2.1425b) but virtually ignores *epideictic. After referring to the three genres of oratory, the author lists the seven species into which these are subdivided: exhortation, dissuasion, encomium, vituperation, accusation, defense, and investigation (1421b). Eight different lines of argument should be followed under exhortation (1421b): the cause should be presented as just (δίκαιον), legitimate (νόμιμον), convenient (συμφέρον), noble (καλόν), pleasant (ἡδύ), accessible (ῥάδιον), possible (δυνατόν), and necessary (ἀναγκαῖον). In dissuasion, the opposite of each of these should be argued. The first step in argumentation, the author maintains, is to reflect these eight values. He presents a second list of three arguments used in presenting each of the eight lines of argument (1422a–1423a): (1) the analogy (τὸ ὅμοιον), (2) the contrary (τὸ ἐνάτίον), and (3) previous judgments (τὰ κεκριμένα). There is no discussion in this handbook of *prose rhythm.

*Rhetorical handbooks

Kennedy 1963, 114–24; Mirhady 1994

Rhetorica ad Herennium, an anonymous rhetorical handbook written between 86 and 82 B.C.E. (Matthes 1958, 82; Achard 1989, xxxiv), wrongly ascribed to Cicero in the manuscript tradition, but thought by some to have been written by Cornificius (W. R. Roberts 1927, 262). Quintilian cites Cornificius in several places (3.1.21; 5.10.2; 9.2.27; 9.3.64–71; 9.3.98), and "Cornificius" says the same things found in *Ad Herennium* 4 (D. A. Russell 2001, 6). It may have emerged from the school of Plotius Gallus and seems to have influenced Cicero in his formative years. There is no evidence that the work was circulated or read before the 4th cent. C.E., when Jerome and others first refer to it and ascribe it to Cicero. While it may reflect the state of rhetorical theory in Rome by the mid-1st cent. B.C.E., it had no discernible influence on the subsequent history of rhetoric to the 4th cent. C.E. (but see the remarks on "Cornificius" above), though from the Carolingian period on, it became quite influential. It is closely related to Cicero's *De inventione* in that both go back to a Greek tradition of Hellenistic rhetorical theory. While Cicero's *De inventione* is somewhat earlier than the *Rhetorica ad Herennium,* the verbal similarities of these two works suggests dependence on a common Latin work that in turn was a translation of a Greek work, produced in Rhodes, by *Hermagoras of Temnos (Matthes 1958, 81–100; Janson 1964, 48). The *De inventione* and the *Ad Herennium* are the first works on rhetorical theory to survive in the 250-year period following the composition of Aristotle's *Rhetorica,* assuming that the *Rhetoric ad Alexandrum* was slightly earlier.

The work is written in four books, each of which has a preface and an epilogue, each addressed to Herennius, whether by name or in the second person. The preface functions as an apology for composing a rhetorical work since in early 1st cent. B.C.E., literary activity was regarded negatively as an inappropriate occupation by the Roman aristocracy, and the generally negative Roman attitude toward the Greeks meant that the writer downplayed his dependence on Greek rhetoricians (Janson 1964, 27–32).

The *Rhetorica ad Herennium* is the first extant rhetorical work arranged in accordance with the five ἔργα τοῦ ῥήτορος, "tasks of the orator," the *officia oratoris* (*DNP* 8.1119–20), or functions of the rhetor, which are discussed under the five topics of invention, arrangement (3.16–18), delivery (3.19–27), memory (3.28–40), and λέξις or style (book 4). Book 4 contains the earliest mention of the threefold division style that became standard in rhetorical theory: *gravis* ("grand"), *mediocris* ("middle"), and *adtenuata* ("plain").

*Cicero, *De inventione,* *Rhetorical criticism, *Rhetorical handbooks, *Style

---

Achard 1989; R. D. Anderson 1999, 71; Clarke 1953, 23–37; *DNP* 10.958; Matthes 1958; *OCD,* 1314–15; Kennedy 1972, 110–34; Ruch 1958

Rhetorical criticism, a phrase introduced by Muilenberg (1969, 8) into biblical studies (particular OT studies), which has been extended by NT scholars to refer to a method of analyzing argumentative texts based on the assumption that the works of early Christian authors were written using the compositional and argumentative standards, categories, and assumptions of Greco-Roman rhetoric (whether consciously or unconsciously) and/or modern rhetoric (e.g., Perelman and Olbrechts-Tyteca 1969; see *New criticism). Clines and Exum (1993, 16), provide a definition of the rhetorical criticism of the Hebrew Bible that is largely applicable to the NT and early Christian literature as well:

> Rhetorical criticism, sharing the outlook of new criticism about the primacy of the text in itself, and often operating under the banner of "the final form of the text," concerns itself with the way the language of the text is deployed to convey meaning. Its interests are in the devices of writing, in metaphor and parallelism, in narrative and poetic structures, in stylistic features. In principle, but not often in practice in Hebrew Bible studies, it has regard to the rhetorical situation of the composition and promulgation of ancient texts and to their intended effect upon the audience. But, like new criti-

cism, its primary focus is upon the texts and their own internal articulation rather than upon their historical setting.

There are two distinct foci of rhetorical criticism (R. D. Anderson 1999, 26): (1) structural rhetoric (macrorhetoric or architectonic rhetoric), which is concerned with identifying the form or genre of a text and its division into parts, and (2) textual rhetoric (microrhetoric or stylistic rhetoric), focusing on style and the development of argumentation. The latter is more directly useful for exegesis, since it focuses on the argumentative texture of the text.

There are two different tendencies in the rhetorical criticism practiced by New Testament scholars since 1970, *diachronic* and *synchronic* rhetorical criticism.

1. *Diachronic rhetorical criticism.* Some rhetorical critics regard rhetorical criticism as an aspect of *historical criticism and try to understand the rhetorical features of early Christian discourse within the context and categories of Greco-Roman rhetoric (Betz 1979, xv; Mitchell 1991, 6–17; R. D. Anderson 1999). For Mitchell (1991, 100; 2002, xxi; see also C. C. Black 1989, 69), rhetorical criticism is a subset of historical criticism and can therefore be designated "historical rhetorical analysis," which can be defined as "an examination of ancient Christian documents in the light of contemporary rhetorical conventions and possibilities as known from both actual rhetorical products and rhetorical handbooks" (Mitchell 2002, xxi n. 12). Watson and Hauser (1994, 110), state the obvious when they say that rhetorical criticism of the NT uses "only Greco-Roman rhetoric as an historical enterprise."

2. *Synchronic rhetorical criticism.* Other rhetorical critics reinterpret Greco-Roman rhetorical tradition as a subset of literary criticism. Some regard Greco-Roman rhetoric as an attempt to describe universal rhetorical categories (Kennedy 1984, 10–11), while others understand rhetoric in terms of the more comprehensive "new rhetoric," which emphasizes modes of human communication and argumentation generally (Perelman and Olbrechts-Tyteca 1969; Wuellner 1987; Mack 1990; Thurén 1990, 47; Amador 1999; Classen 2000), sometimes using ancient rhetoric in ways more creative than the prescriptions found in *rhetorical handbooks. For Kennedy (1984, 10–11), Aristotle attempted to describe rhetoric as a universal phenomenon, and Kennedy himself regards Greek rhetoric not only as a means for understanding the rhetoric of its time but also as a universal system (see also C. C. Black 1989, 257; Kern 1998, 63). Kennedy explores this perspective in a work on comparative rhetoric (1998). Numerous modern studies combine ancient with modern rhetoric (Corbett 1990; Brandt 1970; Corbett and Connors 1999).

Procedure of rhetorical criticism. The practice of rhetorical criticism can involve the following steps recommended by Kennedy (1984, 33–38; cf. Mitchell 1991, 6–17; Black 2001, 7–8 construes Kennedy's approach in six steps): (1) The determination of the extent of the rhetorical unit (i.e., a rhetorically coherent compositional whole), which must constitute an independent or embedded unit (roughly corresponding to the pericope in form criticism). One could add to Kennedy's description that the rhetorical unit should have analogies in ancient rhetorical handbooks, speeches, and letters. (2) The identification of the *rhetorical situation (roughly corresponding to the *Sitz im Leben* of form criticism), which sometimes involves a major rhetorical problem (real or perceived). (3) The determination of the rhetorical problem (i.e., the audience may not perceive the speaker as having appropriate authority or may even be hostile to him or her). Also involved here may be *status (i.e., the particular question at issue), and the three species of rhetoric (judicial or forensic, deliberative, and epideictic): judicial seeks to bring about a decision about events of the past, deliberative aims to affect decisions about the future, and epideictic either celebrates or condemns someone or some thing. (4) The identification of the arrangement of material in the text, its subdivisions and how these parts meet (or fail to meet) the rhetorical situation, involving a line-by-line analysis of the argument. (5) Analysis of each part for its invention (the crafting of arguments based on the three types of proofs: *logos, ethos,* and *pathos.* (6) At the conclusion of the process of analysis, review of the unit to determine its success in meeting the rhetorical problem and what the implications are for speaker and audience. Is the detailed analysis consistent with the overall impact of the rhetorical unit? It should be noted that in the preceding series of steps, Kennedy does not emphasize the identification of the rhetorical genre. "In general," he observes, "identification of genre is not a crucial factor in understanding how rhetoric actually works in units of the New Testament" (Kennedy 1984, 33).

R. D. Anderson (1998, 28) criticizes Kennedy's "virtually self-explanatory" method for making no distinction between the general study of the rhetoric of argumentation and the relationship (or contribution) of ancient rhetoric to understanding the unit: "There appears to be no distinction made between the study of the rhetoric or argumentation of a unit in general, and the relationship or contribution of *ancient* rhetoric to the unit." This, he argues, is the result of Kennedy's unwillingness to distinguish clearly between ancient and modern rhetoric. Anderson and Kennedy represent the opposed positions found in the academy, Anderson representing "historical or diachronic rhetorical analysis," and Kennedy representing synchronic rhetorical analysis. The application of Kennedy's program to individual texts is sometimes problematic. For example, Black's (2001, 12–22) application of these steps to the analysis of the dialogue between Jesus and the Samaritan woman in John 4:1–42 (essentially fictional speeches in a fictional context) is stretched and does not seems particularly useful or helpful.

The application of rhetorical criticism to early Christian literature has often assumed, incorrectly, that partial texts can be analyzed as if they were independent speeches. This tendency was apparently encouraged by Kennedy (1984, 34; cf. Porter 1997b, 362–67), who begins with the identification of "the rhetorical unit," which could be an entire composition or just a section of one. It also leaves open the possibility that the rhetorical situation of one rhetorical unit in a composition can be quite different from the rhetorical situation of another rhetorical unit in the same work. While this procedure showcases the creativity of the critic in applying the canons of rhetorical criticism to a given text, more often than not it reads into the text categories and patterns that are not there. Examples of this procedure include rhetorical analyses of Rom. 8:31–39 as epideictic rhetoric (Snyman 1988); 1 Cor. 1:10–4:21 (Bünker 1983, 51–59); 1 Cor. 13 (Smit 1991); 1 Cor. 15 (judicial rhetoric according to Bünker 1983, 59–72; Mack 1990, 56–59; D. Watson 1993b); Gal. 2:14b–21 (Becker 1989, 292: [a] *exordium* [2:14b], [b] *narratio* [2:15–16], [c] *propositio* [2:17], [d] *probatio* [1:18–20], [e] *peroratio* [2:21]; Jas. 2:1–13 and 2:14–26 as deliberative rhetoric (Watson 1993a); Jas. 3:1–12 (Watson 1993c). See the critique of R. D. Anderson (1999, 251–54). Exceptions exist if can be demonstrated that originally independent letters (in whole or in part) were incorporated into larger epistolary contexts, such as 1 Cor. 8 and 1 Cor. 9 (Betz 1985). Kern (1998, 142–46) regards the identification of partial texts as rhetorical units with particular functions as problematic (a persuasive text is deliberative, a defensive text is forensic, etc.). How, Kern (1998, 146) claims that "functional analyses of rhetoric were not part of the critical arsenal of the ancients." This statement is not strictly true, however, for in the 2nd-cent. C.E. rhetorical handbook by Ps.-Aristides, *Ars Rhetorica* 1.149–50 (Patillon 2002, 1.155), the author gives an example of a κρᾶσις or μῖξις (both Greek words mean "mixture") of genres in a speech of Demosthenes in which judicial, deliberative, and epideictic rhetoric are all present, and he discusses where in the oration each type of rhetoric is represented.

*Criticism, biblical, *Rhetorical genres, *Progymnasmata

R. D. Anderson 1999; 2000; C. C. Black 1989; E. Black 1965; Bünker 1983; Classen 1992, 2000; N. Elliott 1990; Greenwood 1970; Kennedy 1984, 1998; Kern 1998; Mack 1990; Olbricht 1997a; Porter 1993, 1997; Reed 1993; Smit 1991; Stamps 1995; Watson and Hauser 1994; Wuellner 1987.

Rhetorical genres, i.e., the τρία γένη τῶν λόγων or *tria genera causarum,* refers to the various types or species (Greek: γένη, or εἶδη; Latin: *genera*) of speeches required by particular social contexts in the city-state. The two primary settings for oratory were the law courts and the assemblies (Plato, *Gorgias* 454e), and according to Quintilian (*Inst.* 3.4.9), Anaximines (who wrote a rhetorical handbook in the mid-4th cent. B.C.E.) divided rhetoric into two types, judicial and deliberative. The classical division of rhetoric into three genres is found in Aristotle (*Rhetorica* 1. 3.1–3 [1358a–b]; LCL trans.):

> The kinds [εἶδη] of rhetoric are three in number, corresponding to the three kinds of hearers. For every speech is composed of three parts: the speaker, the subject of which he treats, and the person to whom it is addressed, I mean the hearer, to whom the end or object of the speech refers. Now the hearer must necessarily be either a mere spectator or a judge, and a judge either of things past or of things to come. For instance, a member of the general assembly is a judge of things to come; the dicast, of things past; the mere spectator, of the ability of the speaker. Therefore there are necessarily three kinds of rhetorical speeches,

Three Types of Rhetoric / τρία γένη τῶν λόγων / *Tria Genera Causarum*

	γένος δικανικόν	γένος συμβουλευτικόν	γένος ἐπιδεικτικόν
Subject matter	right or wrong	advantage or disadvantage	honor or dishonor
Function	accuse or defend	hortatory or admonitory recommend or dissuade	praise or blame
Temporal aspect	past	future	present (sometimes past or future)
Guiding end (type of argument)	Enthymemes* (mainly)	Examples* (mainly)	Amplification (mainly)
Communication situation	oration in court	oration before assembly	oration before a audience
Given end	the just	the useful	the noble

*Maintained only by Aristotle

> deliberative [συμβουλευτικόν], forensic [δικανικόν], and epideictic [ἐπιδεικτικόν].

This threefold schema was generally attributed to Aristotle in antiquity (Cicero, *De oratore* 2.10; *De inventione* 1.5.7; *Rhetorica ad Herennium* 1.2; Quintilian, *Inst.* 2.21.23; 3.3.14–15; Hinks 1936).

Each of the three types of rhetoric identified by Aristotle had a similar basic structure or *arrangement, the *partes orationis* (Cicero, *De inventione* 1.5.7): (1) *Deliberative rhetoric (Greek γένος συμβουλευτικόν; Latin *genus deliberativum*), the rhetoric of the legislative assembly, whose purpose was *protreptic ("persuasion") or *apotreptic ("dissuasion") of an audience about a future course of action. (2) *Judicial rhetoric (Greek γένος δικανικόν; Latin *genus iudiciale*), the rhetoric of the law court, whose purpose was to accuse or defend a person and to convince judges about whether or not certain events of the past had occurred and whether the accused was therefore guilty or innocent. (3) *Epideictic rhetoric or *panegyric rhetoric (Greek γένος ἐπιδεικτικόν or γένος πανηγυρικόν; Latin *genus demonstrativum*), the rhetoric of the stage or lectern, whose purpose was to entertain, i.e., provide pleasure in the present through praise or blame.

The overview of the most important features of the three rhetorical genres has been summarized by Hellholm (in Bakke 2001, 34; see also Hinks 1936) into which some modifications have been introduced *(see table above)*.

The three genres proposed by Aristotle were an attempt to describe the existing types of oratory of his day, each of which had a particular setting in the life of the polis. The three categories were anomalous, however, for judicial and deliberative speeches were directed to the listener as a decision-maker (κριτής), while epideictic speeches were directed to the listener as a spectator (θεωρός); see Aristotle, *Rhetorica* 1.3. Further, there were speeches that did not fit the settings of the court, the assembly, or the ceremonial occasion, such as the hortatory speech of a general pumping up his troops on the eve of battle, a teacher lecturing his or her students on ethics (using the *diatribe style), or religious speeches that were hortatory in nature (Hicks 1936, 174). Since the setting to which Paul addressed his letters was that of religious communities, and his overarching objective was to correct and strengthen them in their continued adherence to the gospel (Johanson 1987, 41), it is not necessary that the genre of his letters be limited to one of the three species.

The most problematic of these three types is *epideictic, which is essentially a general category for speeches that do not fit either of the other two types. The *New Criticism understands epideictic more broadly (Perelman and Olbrechts-Tyteca 1969, 47–57), as, in the words of Kennedy (1997a, 45), "including any discourse, oral or written, that does not aim at a specific action or decision but seeks to enhance knowledge, understanding, or belief, often through praise or blame, whether of persons, things, or values. It is thus an important feature of cultural or group cohesion."

The problem of mixed genres was recognized in antiquity (see *Mixtum compositum*). In the 2d-cent. C.E. rhetorical handbook by Ps.-Aristides (*Ars rhetorica* 1.149–50 [Patillon 2002, 1.155], the author gives an example of a κρᾶσις or μῖξις (both Greek words mean "mixture") of genres in a speech of Demosthenes in which judicial, deliberative, and epideictic rhetoric are all present. Yet the crucial element, the *setting,* is the court, making the entire speech judicial despite the admixture of other elements. The possibility of a speech in a **mixtum compositum* makes it possible to argue that early Christian letters are mixtures of rhetorical as well as epistolary genres (e.g., Longenecker 1990, who argues that Galatians is part judicial and part deliberative, with the dividing point at Gal. 4:11).

Subtypes. Each of the three main genres or types of oratory has two or three subtypes. A forensic or juridical speech can consist either of κατηγορία, "accusation," or ἀπολογία, "defense." A deliberative speech can consist either of προτρεπτικὸς λόγος, "persuasion" or ἀπροτρεπτικὸς λόγος, "dissuasion." An epideictic speech has at least three types: ἐγκώμιον, "praise," πανηγυρικὸς λόγος, a festival speech, or ἐπιτατφιος λόγος, a funeral oration.

*Arrangement, *Rhetoric, *Rhetorical criticism, *Rhetorical handbooks

---

Andersen 2002; Desbordes 1996; Hinks 1936; Kennedy 1997a; J. Martin 1974; Volkmann 1885

Rhetorical handbooks are texts in Greek (from the 4th cent. B.C.E.) and Latin (from the 1st cent. B.C.E.) that provide instruction in the art of rhetoric as a means of oral public persuasion. The important role of classical rhetorical handbooks in NT scholarship means that the proper purpose and function of these handbooks needs careful evaluation. It must be emphasized that a great deal of ancient "rhetoric" was never included in the handbooks. For example, the *diatribe, whether considered a literary genre or style, is *never* discussed in these handbooks (Watson 1993), nor are the various uses of *chiasmus or *ring composition, so widely used in ancient speaking and writing.

The two oldest handbooks, both originating in the 4th cent. B.C.E. and both complete, are *Aristotle's *Rhetorica,* and the **Rhetorica ad Alexandrum,* attributed to Anaximines of Lampsacus (380–320 B.C.E.); the latter is the sole surviving pre-Aristotelian manual of rhetoric, since it is likely that *Ad Alexandrum* was composed before Aristotle's book (Grimaldi 1972, 75–77). Aristotle had collected a number of rhetorical handbooks in a work in two books now lost: τεχνῶν συναγωγή (Diogenes Laertius 5.24). All the handbooks produced after the two mentioned above until the 1st cent. B.C.E., i.e., the time of *Cicero, who wrote *De inventione,* and of the composition of the anonymous *Rhetorica Ad Herennium,* are lost (i.e., from ca. 320–80 B.C.E.). It is not until the 2d and 3d cent. C.E. that additional Greek rhetorical handbooks are preserved, including the Anonymous Seguerianus and Apsines of Gadara (Dilts and Kennedy 1997), and Ps.-Aristides, *Ars Rhetorica* (Patillon 2002). However, one of the earliest handbooks in Latin, the *Rhetorica ad Herennium,* is almost entirely dependent on Greek rhetorical theory (M. L. Clarke 1953, 14). Between the composition of Alexander's *Ars Rhetorica* on the one hand, and the *Rhetorica ad Alexandrum* and Cicero's *De inventione* on the other, rhetoric underwent a number of changes: (1) Of Aristotle's three kinds of proofs or πίστεις, λόγος, ἦθος, and πάθος (*Rhet.* 1.2.3–6 [1356a]), the last two were essentially eliminated as acceptable forms of persuasion in argumentation (McBurney 1974, 132–34). (2) The importance of the enthymeme and the example as part of the proof (πίστις) were not recognized. (3) The division of the parts of the rhetorical art, the "duties of the orator" (*officia oratoris*), were increased from three to five: to εὕρεσις ("invention"), τάξις ("order, arrangement") and λέξις ("style, diction"), were added ὑπόκρισις ("delivery") and μνήμη ("memory"). (4) The number of the parts of a speech was expanded from two or four to six (see *Arrangement). Aristotle thought that speeches should consist of two to four parts (*Rhet.* 3.13 [1414a–b]): (a) προοίμιον ("introduction"), (b) πρόθεσις ("statement"), (c) πίστις ("proof"), and (d) ἐπίλογος ("epilogue"). The exigencies of the situation might require the elimination of the introduction and the epilogue. Sometime before Cicero, two more parts were added, making a total of six (Cicero, *De inventione* 1.14.19): (a) *exordium,* (b) *narratio,* (c) *divisio* or *partitio,* (d) *confirmatio,* (e) *confutatio* or *reprehensio,* and (f) *peroratio* or *conclusio.* (5) The internal structure of argumentation was reworked and amplified, with special attention to the parts of an argument. (6) *Stasis theory, worked out by *Hermagoras of Temnos in the mid-2d cent. B.C.E., became the basis for the study of rhetorical invention by the time of Cicero. Since Aristotle's *Rhetorica* had no systematic discussion of stasis theory, it had become became virtually obsolete by the 1st cent. B.C.E. (Kennedy 1996, 422), though it was known only in restricted circles in Rome at that time. In the *Rhetorica ad Herennium* (2.28–30), for example, the author suggests elaborating an argument in five parts (Manuel Alexandre 1999,

59): (1) *propositio* (a summary exposition of what one intends to prove), (2) *ratio* (the reason that the proposition is plausible) (3) *confirmatio* (additional reasons that corroborate the *ratio,* completing the basic structure of the primary proof) (4) *exornatio* (complementary supporting arguments provided for the established proof) and (5) *complexio* (the developed argument briefly summarized). For a more detailed discussion of the individual handbooks, see the appropriate entry listed below.

The use and abuse of handbooks. There are several potential problems involving the utilization of rhetorical handbooks. 1. The tendency to read the extant rhetorical theorists synchronically, without due regard for development over the centuries (see the brief sketch of historical developments in rhetoric mentioned above), is problematic (see *rhetorical criticism, *enthymeme). The widely influential synthesis of ancient rhetoric by Lausberg (1998), and to a lesser extent the syntheses of Volkmann (1885) and J. Martin (1974), encourage the synchronic conception of rhetorical theory.

2. There is a tendency to read rhetorical handbooks as though their contents were widely known throughout antiquity, despite the evidence that some of them were scarcely known or used at all (e.g., Aristotle's *Rhetorica* and the *Rhetorica ad Herennium*).

3. The tendency to base rhetorical analyses on the synthetic and systematic accounts of ancient rhetorical theory, such as those compiled by Volkmann (1885), Martin (1974), and Lausberg (1998), rather than on the basis of a reading of the rhetorical handbooks themselves, can lead to the assumption that all of the options present in such syntheses are potentially present for the speaker in any and every rhetorical situation.

4. Doubts have been raised about the propriety of using rhetorical handbooks, in the way that modern NT rhetorical critics do, namely, for analyzing an existing speech in terms of its genre and parts, rather than for constructing a speech using the suggestions in the handbooks as a guide. What these handbooks were *not* used for in antiquity was as a guide for analyzing existing speeches and essays, precisely the way they are used in modern NT scholarship (Kern 1998, 22–23). While Kern (1998, 71 n. 171), argues that Galatians is *not* a classical oration and that rhetorical handbooks were not intended as tools for analyzing speeches, he attempts to show the weaknesses of Betz's approach to the rhetorical analysis of Galatians and to show that Betz does not always understand the handbooks correctly or that he creates new categories (Kern 1998, 91–119). Kern damages his own cause, however, since Betz clearly does not use rhetorical theory as a cookie-cutter. It is true that ancient critics rarely if every analyzed a speech in terms of the *tria genera causarum,* or three rhetorical genres, or in terms of the *divisiones* of the speech. Yet there are hundreds of examples cited by the authors of the handbooks illustrating various rhetorical devices and arguments. Quintilian (10.1.48), in a discussion of the function of *exordia,* for example, tells us that in the opening or introductory lines of the *Iliad,* "He [Homer] secures the good will (*benevolum*) of the audience by invoking the goddesses believed to preside over poets, its attention (*intentum*) by his statement of the importance of his subject, and its readiness to learn (*docilem*) by his brief summary of the facts." This is, of course, an analysis of a Greek composition by means of the conventions of rhetorical handbooks.

5. Serious questions have been raised about the applicability of ancient rhetorical categories to the NT epistolary literature in general and the Pauline letters in particular (Porter 1993; Classen 1992, 2000, 1–28; Kern 1998; Reed 1993; Stamps 1995). These handbooks, as Porter suggests (1997, 250, 253), "present what is in effect courses on how to become rhetors, designed to instruct those interested in becoming persuasive speakers." That is, rhetorical handbooks were guides for making *speeches,* not for writing essays, and for this reason epistolary rhetoric was never part of the classical rhetorical handbook tradition.

6. There is a tendency to use Latin rhetorical handbooks from the Western Empire, particularly Quintilian, as tools for analyzing Greek compositions written in the Eastern Empire (i.e., the letters of Paul), because they are from the 1st cent. C.E., assuming that Greek and Latin rhetoric must be essentially identical. This is an obviously problematic assumption. While Betz (1979) uses three authors of rhetorical handbooks as tools for analyzing the composition of Galatians (**Rhetorica ad Herennium,* Cicero, and Quintilian), it is doubtful that Paul was directly influenced by any of these (Olbricht 1990, 221).

**Rhetorica ad Alexandrum* (Anaximenes), *Aristotle's *Rhetorica,* *Cicero, *De inventione,* *Cicero, *De oratore,* *Cicero, *De optimo genere oratorum,* *Quintilian, *Institutio oratoria,* **Rhetorica ad Herennium*

R. D. Anderson 1999, 2002; Classen 1992, 2000; Grimaldi 1972; Kennedy 1959; Kern 1998;

Lausberg 1998; Porrter (ed.) 1997; Stamps 1995; Vickers 1988, 12–52; Volkmann 1885.

Rhetorical questions, (Greek terms: ἐρώτησις ἐπερώτησις, or πύσμα; Latin: *interrogatio*), is a modern designation for clauses in the form of questions that do not normally expect an answer. While rhetorical questions are typically left unanswered by the speaker (sometimes the speaker does not reveal his or her own point of view, *Demetrius, *On Style* 279), in some cases they are answered. While rhetorical questions have the form of questions, they are often equivalent to emphatic declarations. The use of rhetorical questions often reflects the conviction of a speaker or writer that the audience is in agreement (e.g., Rom. 8:31–35). Rhetorical questions are a regular feature of *diatribe style (Bultmann 1910, 55). Rhetorical questions are sometimes used in series to heighten the effect. In Rom. 10:14–15, Paul uses an argumentative *climax (κλῖμαξ) consisting of a series of four rhetorical questions, each introduced by the interrogative particle πῶς ("how"): "But how are men to call upon him in whom they have not believed? And how are they to believe in him of whom them have never heard? And how are they to hear without a preacher? And how can men preach unless they are sent?" At the beginning of the *Letter to *Diognetus,* the author fires away with a series of 19 rhetorical questions, the first 12 of which begin with a negative particle (2:2–7). Elsewhere the same author has a series of four (4:2–5) and three (7:5–7, though the text here is problematic) rhetorical questions. Rhetorical questions can also be used to hammer away at one of two alternatives, as in Tertullian, *On the Flesh of Christ* 5.1: "What is more demeaning to God, what is more shameful—getting born or dying? To carry flesh or to carry a cross? To be circumcised or to be hanged? To be fed at the breast or to be buried? To be laid in a manger or shut up in a tomb? It would be wiser for you [Marcion] not to believe these things either."

*Diatribe

Anderson 2000, 51–52; Lanham 1991, 71; Wuellner 1986a.

Rhetorical self-consciousness is a term for the realization that there is (or can be) a discrepancy between speech and truth, i.e., between what is said to be true and what is actually true. This perceived gulf between rhetoric and reality was a characteristic of 5th-cent. B.C.E. Athenian thought (Kerford 1981, 78–82), as it is of modern Western thought. The power of rhetoric became particularly evident during the last half of the 5th cent. B.C.E. in the sophistic movement (see *Sophists, sophistic movement). Since, according to the sophists, knowledge is based on opinion (δόξα) rather than on absolute truth (which cannot be known), reason (λόγος) is able to manipulate opinion, since it is always distinct from true knowledge and therefore is relatively easy to change (Plato, *Gorgias* 449d–457c). There is, then, a radical distinction between λόγος and that to which it refers, so that λόγος can produce deception (ἀπατή). The power of λόγος can make small things seem large and large things seem small (Plato, *Phaedrus* 267a). The effect of λόγος on the soul is comparable to the use of drugs on the body. The power of rhetoric over people's souls is called ψυχαγωγία, the "guidance of souls" (Plato, *Phaedrus* 261a).

*Sophists, sophistic movement

Kerford 1981

Rhetorical situation, a phrase introduced by Bitzer (1968) referring to the specific historical context of discourse, consisting of persons, events, objects, and relations, in response to which a speaker formulates an oral or written discourse. Bitzer (1968, 6) provides this definition:

> Rhetorical situation may be defined as a complex of persons, events, objects and relations presenting an actual or potential exigence which can be completely or partially removed if discourse, introduced into the situation, can so constrain human decision or action as to bring about a significant modification of the exigence.

There are then, according to Bitzer, three constituent features of any rhetorical situation: (1) an *exigence* (i.e., an imperfection marked by an urgency that can be changed only by the intervention of discourse), (2) an *audience* (capable of being influenced by discourse and being mediators of change), and (3) *constraints* (persons, events, objects, and relations that are part of the situation because they are able to constrain the decision and action needed to modify the exigence.

Other theorists have referred to the "rhetorical situation" in different ways. Bakhtin (1986; originally published 1952–53), while regarding individual speech acts as unique and unrepeatable, nevertheless argues that the thematic content, style, and compositional structure of individual utterances are determined by the social context of communication (what Bitzer will later refer to as the "rhetorical situation"), since certain social contexts recur regularly and generate utterances or "speech genres" that follow the same rules. Todorov (1978, 9) proposes the following definition: "Discourse is a concrete manifestation of language, and it is produced, necessarily, in a specific context that involves not only linguistic elements but also the circumstances of the production: the interlocutors, the time place, the relations prevailing among these extralinguistic elements." Todorov proposes two levels of meaning in a discourse, the *direct* (which relates to the sentence nature of the discourse) and the *indirect* (which relates to the contextual nature of the discourse, i.e., the situational meaning that an audience infers). The indirect aspect of discourse he calls "verbal symbolism." The two types of discourse, direct and indirect (or symbolic), call for the audience to juggle two mental operations: they understand discourses first and foremost as language units but also interpret them as symbols (Todorov 1978, 18). Audiences reflexively look for meaning and coherence in discourse. If this is not evident (i.e., if the discourse is "impertinent"), the "pertinence" of the discourse may be revealed through some less obvious interpretation (Todorov 1978, 28).

Basing his reflections on the theoretical work of Jakobson, Bakhtin, Bitzer, and Todorov (though offering critiques of none of them), Thatcher (2000, 102) defines a "speech genre" or "oral form" as "that set of parameters which governs the verbal interaction between composer and audience in a rhetorical situation." For Thatcher, then, there are genres of rhetorical situations rather than genres of oral texts. Genre is a set of observable relations among "the empirical realities in the rhetorical situation" (Thatcher 2000, 102). He concludes (Thatcher 2000, 102):

> When rhetorical situations become "typical," uniting similar discourse participants in similar contexts on multiple occasions, a certain uniformity of surface structure, or "style," may be observable across multiple performances. In this sense, "style" as a typical use of language in similar situations becomes an element, more specifically an accident of genre, an empirical byproduct which reveals the presence of certain rules of verbal interaction.

In the context of Thatcher's critique of the founders of form criticism, he finds support for the functional approach of Dibelius, who begins with typical situations in the life of the church and regards "texts as products of the language functions which operate in these situations" (Thatcher 2000, 103). However, Thatcher maintains, Dibelius erred in making form a product of abstract laws rather than the dialogical and ideological aspects of these settings. Bultmann comes off worse than Dibelius in the judgment of Thatcher, since his form-critical method was based not on an explicit theory of genre but rather on an inductive approach to the similarities in the surface structure of the Gospel pericopae, sometimes focusing on form and at other times on content. One weakness of Thatcher's argument, however, is precisely that (like Dibelius) it involves *speculation* (rather than informed knowledge) about the community situations in which forms were created. That is, speech situations are *inferred* from the formal features of speech genres "which might have arisen under such conditions" (Thatcher 2000, 104).

While some have regarded the rhetorical situation as well defined and determinative (Bitzer 1968; followed by Kennedy 1984, 34–36), others place a greater emphasis on the indeterminacy of the situation and the creativity of the speaker in conceptualizing the situation, formulating the problem and the rhetorical solution. Vatz (1973), arguing from a post-structuralist perspective, challenges Bitzer's historical approach to the rhetorical situation, arguing that meaning is not inherent in events, facts, people, or situations, as Bitzer had proposed. Meaning is not discovered in rhetorical situations, according to Vatz (1973, 157), but created by speakers. In other words, the rhetorical situation is not something that waits to be discovered in the historical event of the speech situation, but rather lies in the creative activity of the rhetor. T. Martin (2000, 6) rightly judges the differences between Bitzer and Vatz to lie in changes in modern hermeneutical theory:

> Traditionally, interpreters assume that an author instills meaning in a text and conceive of their task as the discovery or recovery of this meaning. Recent hermeneutical theorists reject this assumption and assert that the interpreter creates the meaning in the encounter with the text. Thus, traditional hermeneutics locates meaning in the interaction of author and text whereas recent hermeneutical theory situates meaning in the interaction of text and reader.

Wuellner (1991c) uses the term "intentionality" in place of "rhetorical situation," seeking to free the rhetorical situation from the historical situation. Yet the concept of "intentionality" itself is not unproblematic as the identification of "the intentional fallacy" by "New Criticism" suggests.

Vatz has a point, but not because postmodernist hermeneutics is "right" and traditional hermeneutics is "wrong." It is clear that Bitzer has overly objectified the "rhetorical situation." While there are significant differences between a speech and a text, there are also similarities, particularly in the case of recorded or transcribed speeches and written texts (cf. Isocrates who *wrote* but did not actually deliver his speeches orally). In both cases, the speaker or writer presents himself or herself in a particular way or under a particular persona (unconsciously, consciously, or a combination of the two), i.e., inscribes himself or herself in the speech or text in a way not to be confused with the actual historical speaker or writer. Many literary critics since Booth (1983) refer to the "implied author" and this can be extended to refer to the "implied speaker" (in an oral context). Similarly, the transcribed speech or text presupposes a particular conception of the audience, again, not the historical audience but the "implied audience." Thus we must refer, not simply to "the rhetorical situation" as if it were a historical reality, but to "the *implied* rhetorical situation," created by the actual speaker or author in communication with an actual audience (neither of which can ever be "known" with any historical certainty). In this vein, Thurén (1990, 70–71), refers to "the picture of the audience which the author seems to presuppose, of the audience's premises and expectations, and as a result thereof, of the intended effects of the text." This also seems to be what Stamps (1993, 199) means when he refers to the "entextualization of the situation" in NT letters:

> While it may be granted that any text, and an ancient New Testament epistle in particular, stems from certain historical and social contingencies which contribute to the rhetorical situation of the text, it is also true that a text presents a selected, limited and crafted entextualization of the situation. The entextualized situation is not the historical situation which generates the text and/or which the text responds to or addresses; rather, at this level, it is that situation embedded in the text and created by the text, which contributes to the rhetorical effect of the text.

"Entextualization" is an important concept, because the text is all that exists of an ancient communication situation. Of course, teasing out the implied rhetorical situation is a relatively subjective enterprise that gives the reader control over the text. Yet the "implied author," the "implied rhetorical situation," and the "implied audience" are historical realities in an ideological sense, not to be confused with the real author, the real rhetorical situation, and the real audience.

The rhetorical situation can be understood, then, in two quite different senses: (1) It can be understood as the "implied rhetorical situation" inscribed in the text by the implied author (i.e., as a "historical" reality insofar as it represents a particular situation). (2) It can be understood in terms of the stereotypical pattern of recurring social situations that determine the genre of oral and written communication in such settings, what Berger (1977, 113–14) refers to as *typische Situationen des frühchristlichen Lebens* (typical situations in early Christian life), or *typische Interaktionsbereichen* (typical interactive situations). Aristotle's conception of forensic and deliberative speeches, for example, were genres linked to specific, recurring social contexts: the law court and the political assembly (epideictic speeches were less specific but restricted by Aristotle to ceremonial occasions). There were, of course, speech situations that Aristotle did not include in his scheme of three rhetorical species. These include the hortatory speech of a general to his troops before battle and speeches focusing on ethics delivered in a school situation. Lausberg (1998, §239) suggests that a forensic speech and a deliberative speech, heard by one who is not authorized to make a decision, becomes an epideictic speech:

> Since the topic of the speech does not concern him, he cannot participate in the serious aim of the main audience. The observer "abstracts" from this serious aim; he instead lets the speech affect him as a work of art and assesses it according to its level of artistry. Thus for him the object of evaluation is not the juridical or legislative issue (which constitutes the subject of the speech), but the speech itself: *the observer views the speech as an oratorical display.*

The situations in early Christianity in which Paul and others addressed letters to Christian congregations tended to center on the concern of a Christian authority figure that a Christian congregation think and live in ways appropriate to the gospel. Melanchthon, who knew a great deal about classical rhetoric, proposed a fourth rhetorical genre for the Pauline letters, the *genus didacticum,* the "didactic genre" (Classen 2000, 11, 126). Similarly, Olbricht (1990, 225–27) argues that, rather than force 1 Thessalonians into an alien rhetorical genre, a new rhetorical genre, "church rhetoric" should be added to the traditional three, a rhetoric that takes into consideration (as Aristotle did not) the acts of God in a Christian community: "The text's power lies in declaring the action of God, Christ, and the Holy Spirit—past, present, and future—rather than exhibiting the universal principles and friendship factors of Aristotle's civilization" (Olbricht 1990, 236).

In compositions in which readers must extrapolate the rhetorical situation from the text, there is always a problem of the circular argument if a historical conception of the rhetorical situation is in view (for an example of such circularity, see the analysis of Jas. 2 in Watson 1993a). Similarly, circular reasoning is also involved in the reconstruction of the social settings of oral forms incorporated into the Gospels by form critics such as Dibelius (see *Form criticism), though the problem is mitigated by the fact that form critics were interested, not in the specific social context in which a tradition about Jesus was performed, but rather in the general, recurring situation in which such performances appeared plausible. Attempts to determine the rhetorical situation of a portion of a letter of Paul, even though the portion can with some confidence be considered a rhetorical unit, are extremely problematic.

*Implied author, *Implied reader, *Rhetorical theory

Amador 1999, 27–31; Bakhtin 1986; Bitzer 1968, 1980; Brinton 1981; Consigny 1974; Jamieson 1973; Kennedy 1984, 34–36; Kirby 1988; T. W. Martin 2000; Schüssler-Fiorenza 1987; Snyman 1988; Stamps 1993; Thatcher 2000; Todorov 1978; Vatz 1973; J. N. Vorster 1994; Wuellner 1991c

Rhetorical species (see *Rhetorical genre)

Riddle may be defined as "a concise, interrogative unit of language that intentionally and at once conceals and reveals its referent with a single set of signs" (Thatcher 2000, 179). An example of one of the more famous riddles found in Sophocles' *Oedipus Rex* is the riddle of the sphinx:

> What goes on four legs in the morning,
> two legs in the afternoon,
> and three legs in the evening?

The answer is "a human being," who crawls as a child, walks upright as an adult, and walks with the aid of a cane in old age. The term "leg" is used with four meanings, two of which are metaphorical. "Four legs" refers to both the knees and hands of a crawling infant, while "three legs" refers to two physical legs and a cane referred to metaphorically as a "leg." The common meaning "support" links all these meanings together. Another ancient riddle is the following:

> The beginning of eternity,
> the end of time and space,
> the beginning of every end,
> and the end of every place.

The unexpectedly simply answer to this series of apparently profound statements is "the letter e." A final modern example is the following:

> There was a green house.
> Inside the green house there was a white house.
> Inside the white house there was a red house.
> Inside the red house there were lots of babies.

As in the last riddle, the question implied is "What is it?" In this case the answer is a watermelon. Perhaps the most famous biblical riddle is the riddle of Samson (Judg. 14:14):

> Out of the eater came something to eat.
> Out of the strong came something sweet.

The answer, of course, was the lion that Samson had killed and in whose carcass he later found a honeycomb.

There have been a number of approaches to the study of riddles, typically focusing on aspects of the riddle most interesting to the disciplinary perspective of the scholar. The structural and linguistic approaches to the riddle tend to focus on the text of the riddle in isolation from its social and performance context (Georges and Dundes 1963; C. T. Scott 1965), while anthropological approaches tend to focus on the social and cultural context rather than on the content and form of the riddle (Hart 1964).

The structural analysis of riddles focuses on morphological characteristics, since definitions based on style have proven inadequate (Georges and Dundes 1963, 113). Georges and Dundes, seeking a universal riddle structure underlying all riddles, and ignoring the specific social contexts in which riddles are performed

(1963, 111), identify a minimum unit of analysis that they call "the descriptive element." Each descriptive element consists of a "topic" (the apparent referent, i.e., the subject of the riddle question) and a "comment" (an assertion about the form, function, or action of the topic). They then define the riddle as "a traditional verbal expression which contains one or more descriptive elements, a pair of which may be in opposition; the referent is to be guessed" (Georges and Dundes 1963, 113).

C. T. Scott (1965) approaches the genre of the riddle from the perspective of both language and style. His analysis involves two steps, "definition" and "description." He argues that riddles have a binary construction, a question and answer, involving two participants. He therefore defines a riddle as "a unit of discourse consisting of an obligatory proposition slot filled by an utterance *p* and an obligatory answer slot filled by an utterance *a*" (C. T. Scott 1965, 69). By "slot" he is referring to Pike's theory of the tagmeme or "slot-class correlate units," i.e., slots that can be filled by a restricted number of linguistic items. According to Scott (1965, 73), "partially obscured semantic fit between two utterances is attributable to an unusual or unexpected collocation of the allosemes of one utterance with the allosemes of the second utterance." A "sememe" (a term coined by Bloom and sometimes called a "semanteme") is the smallest analysable unit of linguistic meaning (e.g., a word or affix), analogous to a "morpheme," the smallest meaningful unit in the grammar of a language. An "alloseme" is one of two or more complementary semes that manifest a sememe in an utterance. Thatcher (2000, 126–27), who summarizes Scott's views, makes a serious error in claiming that the sememe is a combination of smaller units called allosemes. Acting on this misunderstanding, he argues that the words "Humpty Dumpty sat on a wall" are a combination of allosemes that together create a meaningful unit, a sememe. But of course, each word in that sentence is a sememe, since sememes are the smallest units of linguistic meaning.

Identifying riddles. Thatcher (2000, 181–82), in the context of a study of riddles in the Fourth Gospel, proposes four criteria for identifying riddles in a literary text: (1) "A saying is a riddle if the narrator informs the audience that it is intentionally ambiguous, regardless of its surface form" (Thatcher 2000, 183). Example: Following the parable of the sheepfold in John 10:1–5, the author comments: "This figure (παροιμία) Jesus used with them, but they did not understand what he was saying to them" (John 10:6). (2) "A saying is a riddle when the speaking character signals that [his or] her words are intentionally ambiguous." Example: Samson says, "Let me now put a riddle to you; if you can tell me what it is, within seven days of the feast, . . ." (Judg. 14:12). (3) A saying is a riddle when the response of the character hearing the riddle may indicate that the reference of the remark is confusing or intentionally unclear. Example: "You will seek me and you will not find me; where I am you cannot come" (John 7:34). In the context the Jews say to each other, "Where does this man intend to go that we shall not find him?" (John 7:35). (4) A saying is a riddle when the discourse of a character seems inherently contradictory within the normal conventions of language or challenges conventional logic. Example: "He who comes after me ranks before me, for he was before me" (John 1:15).

Riddles in the NT and ECL. Perhaps one of the more famous riddles found in the NT is the numerical symbol for the number of the Beast (Rev. 13:18): "This calls for wisdom: let him who has understanding reckon the number of the beast, for it is a human number, its number is six hundred and sixty-six." Using the device of gematria, in which letters of the Greek or Hebrew alphabet are used in place of numbers, this riddle must be solved by finding a name that is equal in value to 666. Another riddle is found in Rev. 17:9–10, where the explanation of a verbal puzzle (a woman seated on a beast with seven heads and ten horns in v. 7) provides a context for putting a new riddle:

> This calls for a mind with wisdom: the seven heads are seven hills on which the woman is seated; they are also seven kings, five of whom have fallen, one is, the other has not yet come, and when he comes he must remain only a little while. As for the beast that was and is not, it is an eighth but it belongs to the seven, and it goes to perdition.

The new problem lies in determining *which* seven kings are being referred to, who the five are who have "fallen," and who the one is who is present, and who the one is who is to come.

Using the criteria enumerated above, Thatcher (2000, 184–87) identifies 38 riddles in the Fourth Gospel, often uttered in the context of a "riddling session." Though not all of these are equally convincing, here is a selection from the list compiled by Thatcher that includes some of his more convincing examples: (1) "My hour has not yet come" (2:4b); (2) "Destroy this temple, and in three days I will raise it up" (2:19); (3) "Our friend Lazarus has fallen asleep" (11:11); (4) "I, when I am lifted up from the earth, will draw all men to myself" (12:32); "A little while, and the world will see me no longer, but you will see me" (14:19). An example of a riddling session is found in John 8:18–29 (Thatcher 2000, 196–97):

Riddle 1: "I bear witness to myself, and the father who sent me bears witness to me" (8:18)
Confusion: "Where is your father?" (8:19)
Answer: "You know neither me nor my Father" (8:19)

Riddle 2: "Where I am going you cannot come" (8:21)
Confusion: "Will he kill himself?" (9:22)
Answer: "You are from below, I am from above" (8:23)

Riddle 3: "You will die in your sins unless you believe that I am he" (8:24)
Confusion: "Who are you?" (8:25)
Answer: "What have I told you from the beginning?" (8:25)

Riddle 4: "I declare to the world what I have heard from [the one who sent me]" (8:26)
Confusion: Narrator: They did not understand that he spoke to them of the Father (8:27)
Answer: "When you have lifted up the Son of man, then you will know that I am he" (8:28)

The structure which Thatcher elucidates in this analysis is helpful because of the obvious compositional pattern he has identified in the text. A longer riddling session in John 13:5–12 consists of seven riddles, each followed (for the most part) by an expression of confusion followed by an answer (Thatcher 2000, 202–3).

Thatcher thinks that the recognition of the presence of riddling sessions answers many of the perceived aporias, and hence source-critical hypotheses advanced to solve these textual awkwardnesses. He regards John 13–17 as an extending riddling session and finds that the central problematic verse in 14:31—"Rise, let us go hence"—does not signal awkward composition or the introduction of sources, or a literary seam but rather "this abrupt transition reinforces the ambiguity which has been building throughout the riddling session, leaving the disciples bewildered about the true nature of Jesus' departure" (Thatcher 2000, 205). Thatcher then categorizes and discusses four types of riddles in John (2000, 210–11, 213–94): (1) Dramatic riddles, which built dramatic or ironic tension in the narrative (John 6:5; 11:11; 11:23; 13:10; 13:21; 21:18; 21:22); (2) neck riddles, riddles posed by Jesus to save himself or his reputation (John 4:20; 7:23; 8:4–5; 9:2; 10:34–36); (3) mission riddles, riddles which play on the Johannine understanding of the identity and mission of Jesus (John 2:4b; 2:16; 2:19; 4:32; 8:18; 8:24; 8:26; 8:31–32; 8:51; 8:56; 9:39; 10:1–5; 12:32; 13:33; 14:4; 14:7); (4) salvation riddles, riddles which play on the Johannine understanding of the relationship between believers and God (John 3:3–5; 4:7–10; 6:32; 6:51; 7:37–38; 11:25–26; 14:19; 16:16).

Thatcher's proposals are very interesting, but they run the risk of leveling all types of metaphorical speech into riddles, including parables (e.g., John 10:1–5), allegories, and jokes. Nevertheless the literary structures that he has discovered and which he designates as "riddling sessions" provide new insights into problematic passages in John.

*Aphorism, *Proverb

Bryant 1983; Georges and Dundes 1981; Hart 1964; Kallen 1981; Schechter 1890; C. T. Scott 1965; A. Taylor 1976; Thatcher 2000

Ring composition, a term for introductory and concluding or summarizing phrases or sentences at the beginning and end of sections of a narrative, i.e., "framing sentences" (Immerwahr 1966, 12) also called an "envelope." Ring composition is formally similar to **inclusio,* which involves the framing of relatively short sections of text with noticeably similar phrases or sentences. The phrase "ring composition" as a type of composition tends to be favored by classical scholars, while NT scholars favor the term *chiasmus. D. S. Williams discusses a very similar "encircling pattern" in which 1 Macc. 1:11 is framed by 1:9 and 1:52 (2001). Waters (1985, 62) defines ring composition as "a return at the end of a section (digressive or otherwise) to the subject announced at the beginning, in a formulating phrase" and calls it "conspicuous epic mannerism." By establishing the presence of framing sentences, the compositional units of compositions like the history of Herodotus can be determined (Immerwahr 1966, 14). An example is the account or *logos* in Herodotus describing the ends of the world (3.106.1–116.3), which begins (3.106.1):

> The ends of the world possess the most beautiful things, just as Greece possesses seasons most beautifully mixed.

This segment then concludes (3.116.3):

> The ends of the world, which enclose the rest and hold it within, appear to possess what seems to us the most beautiful and the rarest.

These framing statements do not summarize the most important idea of the *logos* (the difficulty of acquiring precious goods); they do not correspond exactly to one another but are purposely varied (Immerwahr 1966, 54–55).

Ring composition pervades the *Iliad* and the *Odyssey,* and its function has been the subject of extended debate. Some have argued that it is evidence of oral composition, functioning as a mnemonic device for the oral bard (Minchin 1995) or that it functions as an aesthetic structuring device in literature (Stanley 1993). Some have regarded it as a framing device that focuses attention on a central element or as a device for delineating a *digression (Mackay, Harrison, and Masters 1999, 115). In his work on the *Iliad,* Whitman argues that ring composition was used as an architectonic principle consistent with the conventions of geometric art (Whitman 1958, 253; Lewis 1981; Mackay, Harrison, and Masters 1999). He argues that "the principle of circularity, including concentricity, or framing by balanced similarity and antithesis, is one of the chief dynamic forces underling the symmetry of geometric vase design" (1958, 55). Ring composition is evidenced, for example, in *Iliad* 5 (T. S. W. Lewis 1981, 93):

A Diomedes with Athena
   1. Domedes worsted by Pandarus
   2. Athena comes to his assistance
   3. Diomedes, with Athena's help, kills Pardarus
B Diomedes vs. Aeneas: Wounding of Aphrodite (Greeks have the advantage)
C Diomedes turned back by Apollo
B' Diomedes vs. Sarpedon and Hector, led by Ares (Trojans have the advantage)
A' Diomedes with Athena:
   1. Diomedes worsted before Ares
   2. Athena comes to his assistance
   3. Diomedes with Athena's help wounds Ares

Ring composition (usually under the name "chiasmus" or "envelope") occurs frequently in early Christian literature (see *chiasmus).

*Chiasmus, *Inclusio, *Symmetrical structure

I. Beck 1971; Dettmer 1980; Immerwahr 1966, 54–58; Murgatroyd 1986; Niles 1979; Nimis 1999; Mackay, Harrison, and Masters 1999; Minchin 1995; Scanlon 1988; Slater 1983; Stanley 1993; Traill 1981; Van Otterlo 1944

Romance (see *Novel)

Romans, Paul's Letter to the, is the longest of the authentic letters of Paul and, in accordance with ancient practices, has often been placed first in the collection of Pauline letters for that reason. Romans is one of the most distinctive and influential of the Pauline letters. It is the only genuine letter of Paul addressed to Christian urban house churches that he himself had neither visited nor founded. Though Melanchthon's view that Romans is a compendium of Christian doctrine is now widely rejected, it does contain an important element of truth, since the main section of the letter (1:16–11:36) consists of a chain of interconnected theological arguments and positions for which little if any connection can be found with what is known about the situation of the Christian communities in Rome. This fact demands an explanation. One of the central issues in Romans scholarship has been just this: Did Paul write the letter in response to an actual situation in Rome or was his primary purpose to present his views on important issues without any direct connection with local issues and problems? While there is some validity in both positions, the significance of the main part of the letter should not be subordinated to any supposed concrete situation teased out of the concluding paraenetic section (esp. 14:1–15:13).

Historical setting. Romans was probably written from Corinth during Paul's three-month residence there (Rom. 15:25; Acts 20:2–3), perhaps in the spring of 55 or 56 C.E. Paul did not found any of the Christian congregations in Rome (in fact, little is known of the origins and organization of Roman Christianity). When Paul arrived in Rome at the end of Acts, there were numbers of Christians already there (Acts 28:15). That there were several household churches in Rome is implied by the peculiar form of the adscription in 1:7a ("to all God's beloved in Rome") and by the mention of several house churches (Rom. 16:5, 14–15; Wedderburn 1988, 45–46; Lampe 1999, 332).

Purpose. Why Paul wrote Romans is not completely clear. In Rom. 1:11, Paul says that he desires to see the Romans and share a spiritual gift with them to strengthen them. This implies that the letter was in some sense a temporary substitute for his future visit (Kettunen 1979, 146–47; R. D. Anderson 1999, 208). Though Paul has preached the gospel from Jerusalem to Illyricum, he has not yet come to Rome because he did not found the churches there (15:18–21), but he hopes nevertheless to stop there on his way to Spain (15:24, 28–29). Romans 1–11 can be understood as an extensive statement of the gospel Paul had preached throughout the Mediterranean world (15:20–21). The purpose of Romans in indicting the Jewish Christians, whom he refers to as "the weak" (Rom. 14:1–4), "was to show that possession of and adherence to Torah was not legitimate grounds for passing judgment on the Gentile converts to Christianity who were also members of the Roman church" (Jolivet 1997, 335). Paul wrote to the Roman Christians in order to convince them (or remind them) of the truth of *his* version of the gospel (Rom. 2:16; cf. 16:25; Gal. 1:6–9; 2:1) and to spell out the particular lifestyle and encourage the kind of commitment he regarded as consistent with his gospel (Aune 1991c, 91). With this objective in mind, Romans is also a letter of self-introduction (Jervis 1991, 158, 164).

Unity. Though the unity of Rom. 1–15 is widely accepted (for exceptions, see Kümmel 1975, 314 n. 30), Schmithals (1995), in typical fashion, has proposed that it is in fact a combination of two originally separate letters. Just how this could have occurred, however, is difficult to imagine (Aland 1979, 349–50; Wedderburn 1988, 25–28). Others have proposed different partition schemes, but none has proven convincing. There is a textual problem toward the end of the letter indicated by the doxology in 16:25–27 which is found at the end of the letter in some manuscripts (𝔓[61], א, **B**, **C**, **D**, vulgate), after 14:23 and again after 16:23 in **A** and **P**, after 14:23 in the Byzantine text, and after 15:33 in 𝔓[45]. The movable doxology has been accounted for by crediting Marcion with excising chapters 15–16, but this is unlikely (Harnack 1960, 49, 164*–65*; Clabeaux 1989, 37). Chapter 16 was once widely regarded as a fragment of a Pauline letter to Ephesus later appended to Romans during the editorial process connected with the collection and dissemination of the earliest collection of Pauline letters (Gamble 1977, 36–55). However, in recent years the pendulum has swung the other way, and it is no longer fashionable to regard Rom. 16 in this manner (Gamble 1977, 127–42).

Genre. Romans is formally framed as a letter (see *Epistolary analysis* below), and may (following Stirewalt 1991, 1993, 18–20; cf. Bryan 2000, 15–18) be categorized as a letter essay. The letter essay, representing a transition from letter to monograph in literary circles, either supplements a previously published work or substitutes for one not yet written and often functions to instruct the recipients (Stirewalt 1993, 18). Jewett (1982) has argued that Romans is an "ambassadorial letter," and ambassadorial speeches are normally categorized as epideictic. However, since ambassadorial speeches were presented to rulers and included praise of the ruler, Romans does not appear to be an appropriate match for this category (R. D. Anderson 1999, 192).

Epistolary analysis. In spite of its unusual length (compared to pagan literary letters), Romans is still a letter, or a "letter-essay" (Stirewalt 1991). The epistolary prescript in 1:1–7, with the superscription or sender in vv. 1–6, the adscript or recipients in v. 7a, and a salutation in v. 7b, has unique features (Dahl 1977, 74–75): First, Paul expands the superscription (vv. 1–6) in such a way that it virtually functions as an *exordium* for the letter: he identifies himself as an apostle set apart for the gospel, promised in the OT, concerning God's Son, who was descended from David and then recognized as Son of God through the resurrection, who has chosen Paul as an apostle to evangelize the nations, including the Romans (N. Eliott 1990, 69). This is the longest opening of all known Greco-Roman letters (Schnider and Stenger 1987, 12–13). Second, he does not address the church in Rome, but "all God's beloved in Rome" (1:7a). This is followed by a thanksgiving (1:8–15). The body of the letter extends from 1:16 to 15:13. The epistolary conclusion follows in 15:14–33, and the letter concludes with an elaborate section of greetings (16:3–16) and a grace benediction (16:20b), followed by secondary greetings (16:21, 23), which frame the personal greetings of the scribe Tertius (16:22)—and perhaps concluding with a textually problematic doxology (16:25–27).

Rhetorical analysis. Romans has been frequently subject to rhetorical analysis, an approach encouraged by the fact that it has the longest sustained argumentation of any Pauline letter. It has been occasionally considered an example of epideictic rhetoric (Wuellner 1976;

Jewett 1982; Kennedy 1984, 152). According to Wuellner (1976, 337), the role Paul expects the Romans to perform is not to deliberate on anything (deliberative or symbouleutic rhetoric), nor to adjudicate (judicial or dicanic rhetoric), "but to affirm the communal values which Paul and the Romans share in being agents of faith throughout the world" (epideictic or demonstrative rhetoric). Yet for this function of epideictic Wuellner was primarily dependent, not on ancient rhetorical categories, but on the New Rhetoric (Jewett 1991, 266 n. 6).

It is clear that Romans consists of two main parts: Rom. 1–11 consists of an extended theological argument, while Rom. 12:1–15:13 centers on *paraenesis. The prescript (Rom. 1:1–7) functions both as an epistolary opening and as an *exordium* (Byrskog 1997). The rhetorical structure of Romans as an epideictic speech (Kennedy 1984, 153–54) can be construed as follows: (1) The proem (1:8–15) seeks the goodwill of the Romans by giving thanks for their renown as people of faith and by expressing his goodwill and desire to visit them. (2) The proposition is stated in 1:16–17: "For I am not ashamed of the gospel: it is the power of God for salvation to every one who has faith, to the Jew first and also to the Greek. For in it the righteousness of God is revealed through faith for faith; as it is written [Hab. 2:4], 'He who through faith is righteous shall live.'" (3) The narration in 1:18–2:16 centers on the power of God for salvation or damnation. (4) Then come various headings centering on the situation of the Jew (2:17–4:25) and then the Gentile (5–6). Romans 9:1–11:36 is addressed to Gentiles to help them understand the situation of Jews. (5) Pastoral topics (12:1–15:13). (6) Epilogue (15:14–33).

Despite different rhetorical approaches, there is general agreement that Rom. 1:16–17 is a πρόθεσις ("statement [of a case], thesis"), which is then explained and justified in the entire *probatio.* In fact, Paul proceeds by relatively short argumentative units (1:18–4:25; 5–8; 9–11) that, though strongly connected, nevertheless each have a *dispositio* that is complete and independent, including an introduction, some subpropositions, several proofs, and a conclusion (Aletti 1997, 295). Ancient discourses had just a single *exordium, narratio,* etc. Does 1:18–5:21 or 1:18–4:25 constitute a rhetorical unit? While the lexical and theological criteria are not decisive, the rhetorical argument is conclusive (Aletti 1991, 38–49).

The disposition of Rom. 5–8 can be outlined as follows (Aletti 1977, 305):

1. Introduction to the section (5:1–11)
2. Preparation of the argumentation (5:12–21) *synkrisis* Adam/Christ prepares for two types of humanity
3. Propositio 5:20–21
4. Proofs (6:1–8:30) *synkrisis* man-under-sin/the baptized; *sarx/pneuma*
   a. 6.1–23 (positive) the baptized and Christ, 7.1–6 *exemplum* and (*sub*)*peroratio*
   b. 7:7–25 (negative) man under the Law, prisoner of sin, swayed by the *sarx*
   c. 8:1–30 (positive) the baptized and the gift of the Spirit
5. Conclusion of the section (8:31–39)

Recently, the rhetorical analysis of the Pauline letters has come under fire, since they are not orations in the proper sense of the term, but rather combine rhetorical with epistolary features. Du Toit (1989), for example, argues convincingly that Romans is primarily a letter with rhetorical features. N. Elliott (1990, 64) finds it difficult to identify Romans with any of the three rhetorical species. These scholarly judgments reflect a growing trend that Romans should not be regarded as strictly deliberative, forensic, or epideictic, though topics from all three species of ancient rhetoric are evident in the argumentation (Jolivet 1997, 310). The standard four-part rhetorical scheme of *exordium, narratio, probatio,* and *peroratio* simply does not fit Rom. 1–11. It will take some time before these problems are properly sorted out.

Another type of rhetorical analysis is that which identifies Romans as a λόγος προτρεπτικός, or "speech of exhortation" (see *Protreptic literature), intended to win converts and attract people to a particular way of life. Several scholars have suggested that Romans is just such a "persuasive discourse" (Berger 1984, 217; Stowers 1986, 112–14; Aune 1991b, 1991c; Guerra 1995, 1–22; Bryan 2000, 18–28). The central section of Romans (1:16–15:13) is set within an epistolary framework (1:1–15 and 15:14–16:27). The body of Romans is so complex that it seems obvious that Paul must have worked and reworked the material found here many times in many different teaching, preaching, and debating situations.

λόγοι προτρεπτικοί characteristically consist of three parts: (1) a negative section centering on the critique of rival sources of knowledge, ways of living, or schools of thought that reject philosophy (cf. Rom. 1:16–4:25); (2) a positive section in which the truth claims of philosophical knowledge, schools of thought, and ways of living are presented, praised, and defended (cf. Rom 5:1–8:39); (3) an optional section, consisting of a personal appeal to the hearer, inviting the immediate accepting of the exhortation (cf. Rom. 12:1–15:13). The proposal that Romans is a λόγος προτρεπτικός provides a satisfactory explanator for the distinctive form and content of Rom. 1:16–15:13. Though the main section of Romans is not identical to other surviving examples of the λόγος προτρεπτικός, that is due to the flexibility of the genre and to the fact that Paul has effectively Christianized the λόγος προτρεπτικός by adapting it as a means for persuading people of the truth of his gospel.

Romans is protreptic on two levels. First, large sections of text (1:16–2:11; 2:12–4:25; 5:1–8:39; 9:1–11:36) show signs of having been developed orally during many years of Paul's preaching, teaching, and debating. In their original setting—and here the presumption is that Paul is reusing material he had carefully honed over many years—three of the four sections (Rom. 9–11 is the exception), appear to have had an originally protreptic character and function. Second, these originally protreptic sections have been linked together to form a relatively coherent λόγος προτρεπτικός in their present context in Romans. Paul's main purpose is to present the Roman Christians concrete examples of the way in which he presents the gospel in a variety of settings to a variety of people. By doing so, he is also presenting his gospel to the Roman Christians, i.e., in his view, he is imparting to them a spiritual gift (Rom. 1:11). Romans 9–11, though it has some links with what precedes, functions as a digression that focuses on the problem of Jewish unbelief and makes an uncharacteristically concentrated use of OT exegesis. Since exegesis was an important feature of Hellenistic school activity, this section exhibits yet another aspect of the Pauline curriculum. The complex paraenetic section in 12:1–15:13 form an appropriate conclusion to the main protreptic section, for they provide examples of the kind of concrete moral behavior expected of Christians.

Romans 1:16–15:13, the central section of Romans, contains four main units. (1) The first section (1:16–4:25) is a major textual unit that functions *negatively* as a protreptic ἐλεγτικός, or "censure" of those who are "outside," including both pagans (1:18–2:11) and Jews (2:12–4:25). (2) The second textual unit (5:1–8:39) functions in a largely *positive* manner, focuses on the life of the Christian "insider" who has been justified by faith, and functions as an ἔνδεικτικός or positive demonstration of the Christian way of life as proclaimed in the Pauline gospel. (3) The third textual unit is Rom. 9–11, in which Paul deals with the problem of Jewish unbelief in contrast to Gentile belief, arguing that the former is a temporary measure that is part of God's overall plan. The unity of this section (which suggests that the exegetical arguments contained in it had been worked out by Paul much earlier), together with the fact that it is difficult to account for its placement after Rom. 5:1–8:39, makes it probable that it should be considered a digression in its present context. (4) The fourth textual unit is Rom. 12:1–15:13, which is an extensive paraenetic section, introduced by 12:1–2 (which functions as a conclusion to 1:16–11:36) and itself concludes in 15:14–15. The protreptic appeal to the Romans that they dedicate themselves completely to God (12:1–2) provides a fitting conclusion to the presentation of his gospel in 1:16–8:39, only slightly interrupted by the digression in Rom. 9–11. In Rom. 15:14–15, Paul comments on what he has just written: "I have written to you boldly in part [of this letter] to remind you." That is, he is referring to the paraenetic section which he has just concluded (12:1–15:13).

Paul has brought the reader through the problems confronted by outsiders to the Christian gospel, whether Gentiles or Jews (1:18–4:25), and he has further presented with great clarity his view of the nature of the Christian life as a life lived from the perspective of the Spirit rather than the flesh (5:1–8:39). He now appeals to the readers (12:1–2), no matter what their status, to devote themselves fully to God. The paraenesis which follows in 12:3–15:13 describes in very particular terms just how Paul understands the abstract implications of 5:1–8:39 in terms of the duties and obligations of Christians living in community.

Use of the OT. Paul uses quotations and allusions to the OT most frequently in Romans, Galatians, and 1 Corinthians. There are 48 quotations or allusions or clusters of quotations or allusions to the OT (Skarsaune 1987, 93–95): (1) Rom. 1:17 (Hab. 2:4), (2) 2:24 (Isa. 52:5b, non-LXX); (3) 3:4 (Ps. 51:4); (4) 3:10–18 (Ps. 14:1–3; Ps. 5:9; Ps. 140:3; Ps. 10:7; Isa. 59:7–8; Ps. 36:1); (5) 3:20 (Ps. 143:2); (6) 4:3; cf. 4:9 (Gen. 15:6); (7) 4:7–8 (Ps. 32:1–2; LXX); (8) 4:17 (Gen. 17:5); (9) 4:18 (Gen.

15:5); (10) 7:7 (Exod. 20:17); (11) 8:36 (Ps. 44:22); (12) 9:7 (Gen. 21:12); (13) 9:9 (Gen. 18:10–14); (14) 9:12 (Gen. 25:23); (15) 9:13 (Mal. 1:2–3); (16) 9:15 (Exod. 33:19); (17) 9:17 (Exod. 9:16); (18) 9:20 (Isa. 29:16); (19) 9:21 (Jer. 18:6); (20) 9:25–26 (Hos. 2:25; 2:1); (21) 9:27–28 (Isa. 10:22–23); (22) 9:29 (Isa. 1:9, LXX); (23) 9:33; cf. 10:11 (Isa. 28:16; 8:14); (24) 10:5 (Lev. 18:5); (25) 10:6–8 (Deut. 30:12–14); (26) 10:13 (Joel 3:5); (27) 10:15 (Lev. 18:5); (28) 10:16 (Isa. 53:1); (29) 10:18 (Ps. 19:5); (30) 10:19 (Deut. 32:21); (31) 10:20–21 (Isa. 65:1–2); (32) 11:2 (Ps. 94:14); (33) 11:3–4 (1 Kgs. 19:10, 14, 18, non-LXX); (34) 11:8 (Deut. 29:3; Isa. 29:10); (35) 11:9–10 (Ps. 69:23–4; Ps. 35:8); (36) 11:26–27 (Isa. 59:20–21; Jer. 31:33–34; Isa. 27:9); (37) 11:34–35 (Isa. 40:13; Job 15:8); (38) 12:17 (Prov. 3:4); (39) 12:19 (Deut. 32:35); (40) 12:20 (Prov. 25:21–22); (41) 13:9 (Exod. 20:13–15, 17; Lev. 19:18); (42) 14:11 (Isa. 49:18; Isa. 45:23); (43) 15:3a (Ps. 69:10); (44) 15:3b (Ps. 18:50); (45) 15:10 (Deut. 32:43); (46) 15:11 (Ps. 117:1); (47) 15:12 (Isa. 11:10); (48) 15:21 (Isa. 52:15).

*Letters, Pauline, *Protreptic literature

Aletti 1990, 1992; Aune 1991b, 1991c; Barrett 1962; Bryan 2000; Byrskog 1997; Campbell 1992; du Toit 1989; Elliott 1990; Fraikin 1986; Gamble 1977; Guerra 1986, 1988, 1995; Hellholm 1993; Jervis 1991; Jewett 1982, 1991; Kennedy 1984, 152–56; Lampe 1999; Schmithals 1975; Siegert 1985; Snyman 1984, 1988; Stirewalt 1991; Stowers 1994; Wuellner 1976, 1991b

Rhythmic prose (see *Prose rhythm)

Sätze heiligen Rechtes (see *Pronouncements of sacral law)

Sayings of Jesus (see *Aphorisms, *Form criticism, *Thomas, Gospel of, *Pronouncement stories

Scholion (pl. scholia), a transliteration of the Greek word σχόλιον, refers to annotations written in the margins or between the lines of a text, primarily of an exegetical or critical nature. Scholia can be random notes, or they can constitute a continuous commentary. Scholia on classical Greek authors (Berkowitz and Squitier 1990, 344–56) are more extensive than scholia on classical Latin authors. There are published collection of scholia on a number of important Greek works, including the *Iliad* (Erbse 1969–88), the *Odyssey,* Aristophanes, Aeschuylus, Apollonius Rhodius, Dionysius Thrax, Euripides, Hesiod, Lucian, Pindar, Sophocles, and Theocritus. The most important scholia on Latin works focus on Virgil. There are also collections of scholia on certain early Christian authors such as Clement of Alexandria (*Scholia in protrepticum et paedagogum;* Stählin and Treu 1972, 295–340), Eusebius of Caesarea (*Scholia in praeparationem evangelicam* in Mras 1954, 1956), and Tatian (*Scholia in orationem ad Graecos* in Schwartz 1988, 44–47). The scholia are mines of information and include thousands of quotations and allusions to earlier authors that have not survived. Meijering (1987) has systematically investigated the scholia on the subject of literary and rhetorical theory, a source largely neglected.

*Commentary

Erbse 1969–88; Meijering 1987; *OCD* 1368; Schlunk 1974

Scriptio continua, a Latin phrase meaning "continuous writing," i.e., the common practice among the Greeks (but not the Romans) of writing words and sentences without the use of spaces or punctuation. Reading was therefore done syllable by syllable (Metzger 1992, 13). One example of the textual problems caused by *scriptio continua* is Mark 10:40, where the sequence of letters ΑΛΛΟΙΣ can be divided as ἀλλ' οἷς, "but for those" (i.e., an *elision for ἀλλὰ οἷς) or ἄλλοις, "for others" (Aland and Aland 1987, 277–78).

*Elision

Scriptorium, the neuter form of the Latin adjective *scriptorius* ("of, or connected with, writing"), first coined in the late 18th cent., was an ancient copying room for the mass production of manuscripts. A reader would stand in front of a group of scribes working at desks and slowly dictate the text of a work to be copied. This method of production, used until the invention of the printing press in 1454, led to many errors of faulty hearing (Metzger 1992, 190–92), since scribes did not actually see and read the text they were copying.

Scripture refers to a sacred body of literature that is regarded as authoritative and revelatory.

Beckwith 1985; Sundberg 1964

Seam, literary or editorial (see **Inclusio*)

Second Sophistic, an intellectual movement that began in the 2d cent. C.E. concerned more with language and rhetoric than with philosophy, in which the works of the sophists (see *Sophists, sophistic movement) were highly valued (Kerford 1981, 36). The Second Sophistic is a continuation of the *Atticism and classicism which began in late 1st cent. B.C.E. Rome (where educated Romans were bilingual), in part as a reaction again *Asianism, with *Dionysius of Halicarnassus and his contemporary Caecilius of Kale Akte. The literary models for this movement were the great prose writers of the 5th and 4th cent. B.C.E., Thucydides, Plato, Xenophon, and Demosthenes (see *Orators, Greek). Flavius Philostratus, a member of the intellectual circle sponsored by Empress Julia Domna, wrote *Lives of the Sophists* (3d cent. C.E.). It seems that some of the orators and writers who were part of the Second Sophistic thought themselves able to surpass the models of the past (Rutherford 1998, 102). Aelius *Aristides reports a dream in which he is told that he has surpassed Demosthenes in dignity (*Hieroi Logoi* 4.19).

*Archaism, literary and linguistic, *Aristides, *Atticism, *Philostratus, *Sophists, sophistic movement

---

G. Anderson 1986, 1993; Behr 1968; Bowersock 1969, 1974; Kerford 1981; Lesky 1966, 829–45; Kennedy 1972, 553–613; Reardon 1971; Rutherford 1998

Secretary In several NT letters there are clear indications that the authors wrote with the assistance of a secretary or amanuensis (Rom. 16:22; 1 Cor. 16:21; Gal. 6:11; Col. 4:18; 2 Thess. 3:17; Phlm. 19; Silvanus, 1 Pet. 5:12). The influence that these secretaries had on the substance of the Pauline letters is difficult to assess; they could be authors (though one would expect them to be listed as *coauthors), drafters, or simply scribes taking dictation. The only intrusive comment from such a secretary is found in Rom. 16:22: "I Tertius, the writer of this letter, greet you in the Lord" (cf. *Mart. Polyc.* 20.2, where Evarestus claims to be the writer). Three times Paul mentions that he writes the concluding greeting with his own hand (1 Cor. 16:21; Col. 4:18; 2 Thess. 3:17), and once he exclaims "see with what large letters I am writing to you with my own hand" (Gal. 6:11), indicating that the rest of these letters had been penned by someone else. The excellent Greek of 1 Peter has sometimes been ascribed to Silvanus (1 Pet. 5:2), but the phrase "through Silvanus I have written briefly" can also be construed as a reference to the one who delivered the letter (Achtemeier 1996, 350). There are at least three possibilities: (1) the secretary wrote in longhand when dictated to (Cranfield 1975, 1.4–5); (2) the secretary wrote in shorthand and later wrote the letter out longhand (Sanday and Headlam 1902, lx); and (3) the secretary composed the letter in accordance with the instructions of the authority behind the letter (Roller 1933, 14–15, 295–300).

*Cosenders, *First-person plural

Achtemeier 1996, 349–51; Byrskog 1996; Cranfield 1975, 1.2–5; Longenecker 1974, 281–97; M. Müller 1998; E. R. Richards 1995; Roller 1933.

Secret Gospel of Mark (see **Mark, Secret Gospel of*)

Secundus, Life of The *Vita Secundi,* or *Life of Secundus the Silent Philosopher,* written anonymously in Greek toward the end of the 2d cent. C.E., is generally regarded as a popular biography, i.e., a biography not written by and for, nor preserved by and for, the educated elite of antiquity. It is important because few such popular biographies have survived. It is also of interest because of the very distinctive character of its structure. The work was widely disseminated during the medieval period and was translated into (and amplified in) Latin, Syriac, Armenian, Arabic, and Ethiopic.

Authorship. The identity of this philosopher (assuming that he was an actual person) is unknown, though there was a 2d-cent. Athenian sophist or rhetorician named Secundus, a teacher of Herodes Atticus (Philostratus, *Lives of the Sophists* 1.26; 2.1). "Secundus" (originally meaning "second born") was a common Roman cognomen or family name during the imperial period, and it is quite possible that there was a 2d-cent. philosopher with the name Secundus, contemporary with Hadrian (117–138 C.E.), unknown from any other source.

Literary genre. The *Life of Secundus* is a type of *biography that has no close literary parallels in Greco-Roman literature (Aune 1988b). To that extent it is "unique."

Content. The *Life of Secundus* consists of four interrelated sections, each constituting an independent literary form. Each has parallels in

Hellenistic literature, though the entire composition has no close analogies. The first section is a *novella that provides the reason why Secundus maintained the life-long practice of silence by narrating the fateful reunion of Secundus with his mother. This novella is constructed around the theme of the man who, after a lengthy time away, returns home incognito to test members of his household (including the folklore motifs of the chastity test and the recognition scene). In Greek literature this theme first occurs in the *Odyssey,* where Penelope proves true to her long-absent husband, as do Telemachus the son of Odysseus and a handful of servants.

The second section focuses on the testing of the resolve of Secundus by the emperor Hadrian, who threatens him with death if he refuses to speak. The emperor, however, has secretly arranged to have him executed if he does speak, but rescued if he remains silent. The literary form of this section is the *martyrology, even though the narrative does not conclude with the death of Secundus. Secundus is depicted as one who accepts death willingly rather than compromise his principles. Among the closer literary parallels to this section are the so-called **Acts of the Pagan Martyrs* (Musurillo 1954, 1961) and the generically related acts of the Christian martyrs (Musurillo 1972); cf. *Acts of the Christian Martyrs. Closely related are stories of persecution and vindication of innocent people in Jewish literature (Nickelsburg 1980).

The third section consists of a scene before Hadrian that centers in a *diatribe written for Hadrian by Secundus. The purpose of this section is to prepare Hadrian for instruction by showing how weak and foolish humans are when compared with animals and to attack Hadrian's vanity and pride. The diatribe is in classroom style, consisting of a dialogical speech in which a teacher (usually a philosopher) addresses a student. In this speech Secundus uses some of the characteristic stylistic features of the diatribe, such as rhetorical questions, hypothetical objections, false conclusions, censure, and examples.

The fourth part consists of a question-and-answer dialogue in which Secundus submits written answers to a list of 20 questions formulated by Hadrian. This "dialogue" is also a popular literary form with parallels in Greco-Roman literature. Though some scholars have proposed that this section circulated independently, all the evidence suggests that it was originally composed for inclusion at this particular point in the narrative. The 20 independent sets of questions and answers exhibit no overall logical arrangement. The questions—all involving definitions and all introduced with the interrogative phrase "what is?" (Greek: τί ἐστι; Latin: *qui est?*), conform to one of the three distinctive types of Pythagorean *akousmata* ("oral teachings") formulated as questions and answers, i.e., (1) definitions (τί ἐστι, "what is?"), (2) superlatives (τί μάλιστα, "what is the most. . . .?"), (3) duties and obligations (τί πρακτέον, "what must one do . . . ?"). The content of the 20 sets of questions and answers has no particularly close relationship to Pythagoreanism or to any other ancient philosophical tradition. They are repartees that function more to underscore the wisdom of Secundus than to provide an elementary philosophical catechism for popular consumption.

As an example, let me quote question 20 with its 11 answers:

> 20. What Is Death?
>
> Eternal sleep, the dissolution of the body, the desire of the distressed, the desertion of the spirit, the fear of the rich, the desire of the poor, the slackening of the limbs, the flight from, and loss of, life, the father of sleep, an appointment truly prearranged, the end of all.

The answers are striking in that they are not the single best answers (appropriate in a philosophical context) but rather each "answer" consists of from 7 (No. 2) to 21 (No. 10) "answers" to each question, averaging 11 answers per question. The fact that the questions posed by Hadrian are paired with answers attributed to Secundus) indicates that we are dealing with chreiai ("anecdotes" or "aphorisms"). The closest literary parallel to part 4 is the *Altercatio Hadriani Augusti et Epicteti Philosophi* ("Dialogue between the Emperor Hadrian and Epictetus the Philosopher"), an anonymous treatise composed in the 2d or 3d cent. C.E., containing 73 questions posed by Hadrian and answered by the Stoic philosopher Epictetus. These answers too are clever and witty responses largely devoid of philosophical content. Unlike the question-and-answer dialogue in the *Life of Secundus,* most of the 73 questions are paired with single answers (exceptions: Nos. 24, 29, 32, 35, 37, 38, 52, 59, 67). In his *Banquet of the Seven Sages,* Plutarch includes nine written questions sent to Thales by Niloxenus, the emissary of Amasis, king of Egypt (153A–D). The first question is "What is the oldest thing?" The answer of Thales is

"God, for he has no beginning." Other question-and-answer "dialogues" similar to the fourth section of the *Life of Secundus* are the *Questions and Answers in Genesis and Exodus* of *Philo of Alexandria (mentioned in Eusebius, *Hist. eccl.* 2.18.1, but extant only in Armenian) and Plutarch's *Table Talks,* which consist of short dialogues, each of which is a discussion aimed at finding a solution for a particular problem, often phrased as a question, stated at the outset. In the so-called *Certamen Homeri et Hesiodi* ("Contest of Homer and Hesiod), one of the late Homerica, the famous bards engage in a wisdom contest by posing different questions to each other (315–21), none of which are logically related.

Relevance to NT and ECL. Though very different from the canonical Gospels, in a number of ways the *Vita Secundi* and the Gospels generically illuminate one another: 1. While all extended narratives are episodic, in Hellenistic biography the episodes characteristically consist of constituent literary forms that can have a separate, independent existence. Ancient biography is an inclusive literary form that provides a framework or setting for various types of shorter forms, including anecdotes (which Greek rhetoricians called chreiai), maxims (γνῶμαι). and reminiscences (ἀπομνημονεύματα). Chreiai are essentially sayings or actions (or a combination of the two) set in a brief narrative framework (e.g., the question-and-answer section of the *Life of Secundus*). γνῶμαι are proverbial sayings that lack attribution or a narrative framework, and ἀπομνημονεύματα are expanded chreiai thought to be transmitted by memory. In the case of the Gospels, form criticism has isolated and categorized a variety of forms that appear to have existed independently in oral form (pronouncement stories, sayings of Jesus, parables, stories about Jesus, and miracle stories). Examples of longer literary forms that can be included in biographies are novellas, speeches, and dialogues (as in the *Vita Secundi*).

2. The first two sentences of the *Vita Secundi* place Secundus in the marginal social role of a Pythagorean philosopher: "Secundus was a philosopher. The entire time that he pursued the philosophic life, he practiced silence, following the Pythagorean life style." Throughout the entire composition he is presented as an ascetic whose behavior is thoroughly consistent with his beliefs. Similarly, the first two Gospels begin with statements which place Jesus in the appropriate religious categories. For Mark he is "Jesus the Messiah, [the son of God]," and for Matthew he is "Jesus the Messiah the son of David, the son of Abraham." The burden of both Gospels is to demonstrate the truth of those roles despite any apparent evidence to the contrary. Hellenistic biography was primarily concerned with famous people as representative types (i.e., as representatives of group values) rather than as unique individuals, and was therefore more idealistic than realistic. Individual personalities were assumed to be as fixed and unchanging as the kinship groups and the social and political units within which they were enmeshed. Consequently, the subjects of most ancient biographies are depicted as static personalities, presented as paradigms of either traditional virtues or vices, rarely as a mixture of both. The subjects thought most suitable for biographical description were men prominent in public life (i.e., those active in the assembly, the marketplace, the gymnasium, the theater, the battlefield, and the law court) whose lives appropriately reflected the norms and values of the state (e.g., generals, politicians, kings, philosophers, poets, orators). In the late Hellenistic period there was a tendency to assign certain types of philosophers (primarily Pythagoreans and Cynics) and holy men to the margins of society. An ascetic lifestyle dramatized their rejection of conventional social values.

3. The chronological framework used in ancient biography was the means of organizing the external facts of the subject's life, not for tracing the development of his personality (which was assumed to be static). Unlike many Hellenistic biographies, the birth and forebears of Secundus are not mentioned, and his education is barely touched. Mark and John mention virtually nothing about Jesus' origins, while Matthew and Luke, doubtless influenced by biographical conceptions, include both birth stories and genealogies, though Luke alone includes a story from Jesus' youth. In linking the novella to the martyrology, the author used the phrase "at about this time," which gives the impression that this story follows the previous one chronologically. The Gospels contain many such temporal formulas used to introduce new pericopes and place them in apparent chronological order with preceding pericopes.

4. Ironically, had Secundus broken his vow of silence in order to live, he would have been executed. His victory over the threat of death provides a kind of ultimate legitimation for his wisdom as a philosopher. Though Secundus is functionally marginal to the society in which he lives and works, a willing death (the ultimate form of asceticism) would validate the truth of his teaching. That is to say, the truth of the

philosopher's wisdom is validated not only by his lifestyle, but also (and supremely) by his death. Though Secundus does not actually die, his indifference to life makes physical death unnecessary to the plot. For dramatic purposes his victorious confrontation with death must precede his interview with Hadrian. It is impossible to read the *Vita Secundi* without thinking of the tradition of Socrates' death, a tradition that must also have shaped the response of many Christians to the account of the death of Jesus. Some scholars have insisted that the Gospels differ from Hellenistic biography in that the former have a dramatic structure, while the latter do not. Such a distinction is more apparent than real. The *Vita Secundi* has a plot, though one that differs from those patterns found in the Gospels. Indeed, Hellenistic biographies in general consist of sequences of narrative episodes through which "stories" (events in their time sequence) are transformed through the introduction of "plot" (a sequence of events placed in causal relationships). The story of a person who dies in a tragic or untimely way or who has been unjustly executed by the state or killed by his or her enemies has inherent dramatic possibilities that have been universally exploited in all forms of literature. Much of this literature (including the Gospels) has arisen within a religious setting, where the problem of death is a theme of central importance. The Gospels themselves devote a great deal of space to narrating the events associated with the last days of Jesus, so much so that the Gospel of Mark has been aptly described as a passion story with an extended introduction, a characterization that applies also to the other Gospels, though to a lesser extent. The passion narrative doubtless existed prior to inclusion in Mark 14–16, perhaps in written form. Despite the earlier development of the theologia crucis ("theology of the cross") in Paul, it is remarkable that such an interpretation of the significance of the death of Jesus has not affected the Gospels in a more thorough way. In Mark the interpretation of Jesus' death in terms of atonement occurs just once (10:45; a saying reproduced in Matt. 20:28 but omitted by Luke). In Luke that view is missing altogether (despite the objections of Fitzmyer). Luke understands Jesus as a prophet-martyr whose death is due to divine necessity. This apologetic emphasis on the divine necessity of the death of Jesus is found in all the Gospels, though it is accented in Luke. The passion narrative was also read in other ways, as we know from scattered passages in the epistolary literature that emphasize the exemplary character of Jesus' suffering and death (1 Pet. 2:21–23; 1 Tim. 6:13; Heb. 2:10; 5:8; 12:1–4). In the light of the way that the *Vita Secundi* was intended to be understood, it is also likely that the nature of Jesus' death would have provided both authority and legitimation for his teaching. The passion narrative, in other words, provided a validation for the meaning of Jesus' life.

Even though the origin of biography has some connection with death as celebrated in epitaphs and eulogies, Greco-Roman biographies generally are not as interested in the deaths of their subjects as the Gospels are in the death of Jesus. Yet during the very period when the Gospels were in process of formation, there was a notable increase in the emphasis on death (particularly martyrdom) in Hellenistic biographical literature. Nero, like other Roman autocrats, had ordered the executions and suicides of many members of the Roman nobility. Short lives emphasizing the demise of famous men (a kind of martyr literature), a subgenre of biography, were fashionable at the end of the 1st cent. C.E. While their works have perished, we know of two contemporaries of Pliny who specialized in such biographies. Gaius Fannius wrote about the deaths of famous men executed under Nero (Pliny, *Letters* 5.5.1–3), and Titinius Capito (who wrote *Exitus illustrium virorum* ("Departure of Famous Men"), also focused on death scenes. The same fashion was followed by Tacitus (cf. his narratives of the final days of Seneca (*Annals* 15.60–64), and of Thrasea and Soramus (*Annals* 16.21–35). One of the forerunners of biography was the epic traditions celebrating the valiant deeds of the hero whose death had rescued him from oblivion and made him memorable, thereby giving him "individuality." The Greeks therefore placed a high value on the "good" death of the hero (*Iliad* 9.410–16). The exemplary death of Socrates had a powerful impact on ancient martyr literature, both Greco-Roman and Christian. Particularly for Stoics, many of whom died under Nero, the view of Seneca was typical: "To die well is to die willingly" (*Ep. Mor.* 63). Among pagans and Christians, calmness and courage in the face of death was celebrated (cf. Mark 14:32–42, 53–65; 15:2–5 and par.; John 18:29–38: 19:2–15), particularly as a prelude to voluntary suicide rather than public execution (Pliny, *Ep.* 3.16; Tacitus, *Annals* 11.3). The focus on the death of Jesus that characterizes all of the Gospels, then, is a theme characteristic of a development in Greco-Roman biography of the 1st cent. C.E. While this emphasis on the way an individual's life concludes is a logical way to end a biography (according to an ancient Greek conception, a person's life could be evaluated only when completed by death, cf. Herodotus 1.30–32), it is also clear that we are dealing with a complex literary topos that has not received the detailed study it deserves. This is reflected in the many anonymous lives of Greek poets who are often depicted as dying lonely or tragic deaths (e.g., Euripides was torn to pieces by dogs; Sophocles strained his voice while reading *Antigone* and died). Lefkowitz (1981) has demonstrated the extent to which the data in these biographies have been extrapolated from the subject's extant literary works, so that they are largely fictional products of anonymous biographers. The emphasis on death is also found in the late work on the lives of philosophers by *Dionysius Laertius, as well as in the thumbnail sketches of Israelite prophets in the anonymous *Vitae Prophetarum* (ca. 1st cent. C.E.), a work thoroughly Hellenistic in form. At the turn of the century Plutarch wrote the life of Cato the Younger, focusing on the nobility and resolve of his suicide in the Stoic tradition (and, according to Plutarch, in apparent emulation of Socrates). Among the counter-cultural literature written by and for members of the lower classes, the popular *Acta Alexandrinorum* ("Acts of the Pagan Martyrs") as well as the many acts of Christian martyrs that flourished in the 2d and 3d cent. C.E. also focused on the moral triumph of the persecuted innocent over the injustice and cruelty of magistrates or even emperors representing repressive regimes. The values inherent in these melodramatic plots also find expression in the anonymous *Life of Secundus the Silent Philosopher* in which he unwittingly avoids execution by stubbornly maintaining a vow of silence.

*Biography, *Gospel, literary genre

Aune 1988b; Leftkowitz 1981; Musurillo 1954, 1972; Nickelsburg 1980; Perry 1964

Semiotics can be defined as "the systems that enable human beings to perceive certain events or entities as signs, bearing meaning" (Scholes 1982, ix). Here is a chart representing Roman Jakobson's semiotic model of communication:

CONTEXTS
TEXT
AUTHOR - - - - - - - - - - - - - - - - - - READER
MEDIUM
CODES

Semiotic literary criticism tries to incorporate aspects of the typical emphasis on the author, the text, and the audience: (1) Authors are creatures of culture who through language attain a human subjectivity. What they produce as literary text has constraints of generic and discursive norms. Other voices speak through them (some cultural, some public). "An author is not a perfect ego but a mixture of public and private, conscious and unconscious elements, insufficiently unified for use as an interpretive base" (Scholes, 14). (2) Readers are structured like authors: "divided psyches traversed by codes" (Scholes, 14). Students need to acquire the interpretive codes of their culture and also to understand them as codes. (3) Texts, in contrast to the autonomous "work" of Formalism or the *New Criticism, are open, incomplete, insufficient, i.e., "a text is a piece of writing [which] must be understood as a product of a person or persons, at a given point in human history, in a given form of discourse, taking its meanings from the interpretive gestures of individual readers using the grammatical, semantic, and cultural codes available to them" (Scholes 1982, 15–16).

Scholes 1982

Semitism can be defined as a "deviation from genuine Greek idiom due to literal rendering of the language of a Semitic [Hebrew or Aramaic] original" (Moulton and Howard 1929, 14). The term "secondary Semitism" is used by Moulton and Howard (1929, 15) for the "overuse" of constructions that are rare in Greek but are also found in Hebrew or Aramaic. Semitisms should be distinguished from *Septuagintisms, which are the result of the imitation of the style of the LXX by early Christian and early Jewish authors.

Beyer 1962; E. C. Maloney 1981; Moulton and Howard 1929, 14–34, 413–85; Wilcox 1965, 1984, 1994

Sententia (see *Maxims)

Septuagint, from the Latin term *septuaginta,* "70" (abbreviated LXX), is a general designation for the translation of the Jewish Scriptures into the Greek language. The number 70 refers to a legend found in the *Letter of Aristeas* that the Pentateuch was translated by 70 Jewish scholars, each isolated from his fellows. Upon the completion of their task, each of their translations was purportedly identical with the others. Historically, the Pentateuch was probably translated during the first half of the 3d cent. B.C.E. (N. L. Collins 1992), while the rest of the Hebrew Bible, with various additions and modifications, was translated from the late 3d through the 2d cent. B.C.E. The LXX is a heterogeneous collection of documents, most of which were translated from Hebrew, though some were original compositions in Greek. The Pentateuch is the earliest part of the LXX and exhibits a certain unity, though it is likely that each of the five books was the work of a different translator. The linguistic problem presented by the LXX is that it is both a document written in Koine Greek and a document that consists largely of translation Greek. The peculiarities of LXX syntax have been attributed by some to translation methods and by others to a distinctive form of "Jewish Greek" spoken in Egypt in the 3d and 2d cent. B.C.E., though the "Jewish Greek" hypothesis has fallen on hard times (Lee 1983, 11–30; G. H. R. Horsley 1989, 5–40).

The LXX and the Hebrew text. Though the Septuagint is a translation, it is also a form of biblical exegesis, since all translations are interpretations (Le Déaut 1984). In a number of books in the LXX, the Greek text is significantly shorter than the Hebrew text. This is true for both Jeremiah and Ezekiel. The LXX text of Ezekiel is 4–5 percent shorter than the MT and, in the judgment of Tov (1986), a more original version.

The LXX is the main source quoted or alluded to in the NT and early Christian literature (see *Quotations, *Allusions), though some early Christian authors referred to the Hebrew text.

*Old Testament, *Semitism, *Septuagintisms

———

Aejmelaeus 1982; Conybeare and Stock 1905; T. V. Evans 2000; Fernández-Marcos 2000; Helbing 1907; G. H. R. Horsley 1989; Jellicoe 1968; Jones and Silva 2000; Le Déaut 1984; Lee 1983; Thackeray 1909; Tov 1986, 1997

Septuagintisms are imitations of the distinct linguistic patterns of the Greek *Septuagint, the Bible of Greek-speaking Jews from the late 3d cent. B.C.E. on. A tighter definition has been proposed by D. Schmidt (1991, 594): "syntactical peculiarities that are not reflective of Semitic syntax, but used to render Semitic constructions into Greek in one of the translation styles of the Septuagint." Schmidt is here following Beyer (1962, 11), who defines Septuagintisms as expressions not actually used in Hebrew. Fitzmyer (1981–85, 1.114–16) provides a list of 23 of the more common Septuagintisms in Luke.

*Semitisms, *Septuagint

———

Beyer 1962; D. Schmidt 1991

Sermon (see *Homily)

Seven Sages, a traditional Greek grouping of seven wise men who reportedly flourished during the early 6th cent. B.C.E.; the number seven became canonical in the early 5th cent. They include four from Ionia (Thales of Mileltus, Bias of Priene, Cleobulus from Lindos on Rhodes, Pittacus of Mitylene) and three from mainland Greece (Solon of Athena, Chilon of Sparta, and Periander the Corinthian tyrant). This standard list can be traced back to Demetrius of Phaleron (Stobaeus, *Eclogae* 3.1.172). While no one ever called this group of Seven Sages (no more, no less) into question, the sages counted among the seven as many as 23 different figures (Diogenes Laertius 1.41–42). Hermippus of Smyrna, who wrote a work *On the Seven Sages* (Radicke 1999, 24–33; §1026, F9–20), argued that there was a pool of 17 sages out of which various authors selected the canonical number of seven (F10).

———

Fehling 1985; Radicke 1999, 168–77; Snell 1938

Shepherd of Hermas, a Christian *apocalypse that seems to have begun with a narrative of four visions (ca. 90 C.E.), which were later expanded by a transitional fifth vision and the addition of extensive sections containing parables and mandates until the work reached its present size ca. 150 C.E. The *Shepherd* differs from Jewish apocalypses in two major respects: it is not a pseudepigraphon, and it does not make learned and complex allusions to the OT. In its final form, the *Shepherd* comprises three sections containing five visions, 12 mandates, and ten parables.

Occasion and purpose. The *Shepherd* reflects a blend of Jewish and Hellenistic traditions. The central theme of the work is the possibility of a second (and final) repentance (Joly 1958, 22–30). Traditionally, repentance was regarded as a once-for-all act connected with baptism (*Mand.* 4.3.1), but to Hermas was revealed the possibility of a second repentance (*Vis.* 2.2.4–5; *Mand.* 4.4.4). The *Shepherd* represents the victimized poor (the "pious poor" of Jewish tradition have an analogue in the "innocent poor" over against the "unjust rich," stock figures in Greco-Roman *declamations); he condemns those who are wealthy, involved in business, and socially ambitious and calls for a new and final repentance involving the rejection of "double-mindedness." The theme of the second repentance links the older section in *Vis.* 1–4 and the latter additions in *Vis.* 5 and the *Mandates* and *Similitudes.* The document purports to consist of a series of divine revelations granted to Hermas, first by an old woman, then by an angel in the form of a shepherd; from this last figure the name of entire work derives.

The message of this apocalypse is summarized in a statement by God himself in *Vis.* 2.2.5–7, though in indirect discourse, announcing a final opportunity for repentance to those who have denied him in the past (trans. Holmes 1989; the bold type indicates the speech of God):

> For the Master has sworn by his own glory regarding his elect, **that if sin still occurs, now that this day has been set as a limit, they will not find salvation, for repentance for the righteous is at an end; the days of repentance for all the saints are over, although for the heathen there is the possibility of repentance until the last day.** [6] So speak, therefore, to the officials of the church, in order that they may direct their ways in righteousness, in order that they might receive the promises in full with much glory.

Literary visions? A work like the *Shepherd of Hermas* poses the question of whether the visions and auditions Hermas claims to have experienced were entirely literary creations based on the conventions of Jewish and Christian *apocalyptic and *revelatory literature or (in addition to the undoubted presence of literary artifice) whether they had some basis in the author's religious experience. In posing this problem, it must at once be admitted that there is no effective method for clinically separating accounts of authentic experience from the later overlays of literary conceptualization or even complete literary fabrication (this kind of separation was tried without striking success by Lindblom 1968).

Authorship. What is known about Hermas, the ostensible author of the *Shepherd* in whole or in part, is found only in this work (on the social identity of Hermas, see W. J. Wilson 1927; Jeffers 1991, 21–25); he is not the Hermas mentioned in Rom. 16:14, identified by Origen (*Commentary on Romans* 10.31). He was a freedman, perhaps of Greek origins, who had been abandoned as a child, raised as a slave, and sold to a wealthy Roman woman named Rhoda. As an adult, he was apparently engaged in some kind of business and had suffered a financial setback (*Vis.* 2.3.1; 3.6.7). He was not an elder but does claim divine authority through his visions (*Vis.* 2.4.3), perhaps the authority of a prophet (*Mand.* 11; see Reiling 1973).

Date. The *Shepherd* is widely thought to have been written between 95 and 140 C.E. (Jeffers 1991, 21). The author mentions "Clement" in *Vis.* 2.4.3; if this person is identical with the Clement to whom *1 Clement* is ascribed, then a date late in the 1st cent. C.E. is appropriate. The *Shepherd* is mentioned in the Muratorian Fragment, which dates perhaps to the end of the 2d cent. C.E. The author denies apostolic authority to the *Shepherd,* which he claims was written recently by the brother of bishop Pius I (140–55):

> In the city of Rome, Hermas composed the *Shepherd* most recently, in our times, while his brother Pius was sitting in the chair of the church of the city of Rome. And for that reason it is appropriate that it be read, but not publicly among either the prophets, since their number is complete, nor among the writings of the apostles, until the end of times.

However, a number of scholars have rejected the veracity of the Muratorian Canon and have placed composition of both parts of the *Shepherd* ca. 95–100 C.E. (W. J. Wilson 1927, 50–59).

Texts and translations. The *Shepherd* was originally written in Greek, though no single manuscript contains the entire document. There are four Greek witnesses: (1) Codex Sinaiticus (א), a 4th-cent. copy of the Bible, contains the oldest text of the *Shepherd,* preserving only *Vis.* 1.1–*Man.* 4.3 (1.1–31.6); however, in 1975, twelve more leaves from the end of Sinaiticus were discovered in St. Catherine's monastery in the Sinai; these pages, which include more text of the *Shepherd,* have not yet been published; (2) Papyrus Michigan 129, from the 3d cent. C.E., contains *Sim.* 2.8–9.4.1 (51.8–82.1); (3) Bodmer Papyrus XXXVIII, a papyrus codex from the 4th or 5th cent. C.E. (Carlini 1991, 123–24), preserves most of *Vis.* 1–3 (1–21); (4) Codex Athous, 14th–15th cent., is the most complete Greek text of the *Shepherd,* containing *Vis.* 1.1–*Sim.* 9.29 (1.1–107.2). There are, in addition, 13 papyrus and vellum fragments, two in roll form from the 2d and 3d cent., and 11 in codex form (Whittaker 1956, xxv).

Sources and composition. The view that several authors contributed to the *Shepherd* (e.g., Giet 1963), is now less popular than the position that a single author was the editor of many sources (W. J. Wilson 1927, 33–34; Henne 1992). Giet (1963, 280–305) proposed that *Vis.* 1–4 was the work of Hermas, late in the 1st cent. C.E.; *Sim.* 9 was written by the brother of bishop Pius of Rome, as attested in the Muratorian Fragment, before the middle of the 2d cent. C.E., while *Vis.* 5 to *Sim.* 8 and *Sim.* 10 were written somewhat later. Generally *Vis.* 1–4 are thought to be the earliest part of the work, dating to the end of the 1st cent. C.E., while *Vis.* 5 (which serves as an introduction to the rest of the work) through the *Mandates* and *Similitudes* is widely thought to come from a later period. It is probable that the *Shepherd* was "published" in two stages, the first stage consisting of *Visions* 1–4, and the second of the entire work as it has come down to us in three sections (Joly 1958, 14–16). In the Greek MSS, the superscription to *Vis.* 5 is Ἀποκάλυψις ε' ("Revelation 5") in Codex Sinaiticus, but this is changed to ὅρασις ε' in Codex Athous (Giet 1963, 71 supposes that Sinaiticus changed the title from an original ὅρασις ε' to Ἀποκάλυψις ε'. The fact that *Sim.* 9.1.1–3 provides a summary of the entire *Shepherd* is an argument that the book was compiled by a single author (W. J. Wilson 1927, 33):

> 1 After I had written down the commandments and the parables of the shepherd, the angel of repentance, he came to me and said to me, "I want to explain to you what the Holy Spirit, which spoke with you in the form of the Church, showed you [*Vis.* 2.4.1]; for that Spirit is the Son of God. 2 For since you were too weak in the flesh, it was not explained to you by an angel; but when you were given power by the Spirit, and grew strong in your strength, so that you could even see an angel, then the building of the tower was revealed to you through the Church [*Vis.* 3.3–7]. You saw all things well and reverently, as from a young girl [*Vis.* 4.2–3]; but now you see it from an angel [*Vis.* 5], though by the same spirit.

It is of course also possible that this is an attempt by a redactor to tie the *Visions* more tightly to the rest of the work.

Osiek 1998 adds a few wrinkles by taking seriously the possibility of the oral as well as the literary character of the *Shepherd.* Writing is involved in *Vis.* 1–2, where Hermas is given a little book that takes him two weeks to understand. He is instructed to make copies for distribution to other churches through Clement and to the widows through Grapte. In *Vis.* 3–4 there are dialogical sections where Hermas receives visions and interpretations from a female supernatural revealer, with no mention of writing. Finally in *Vis.* 5 Hermas is commanded to write the commands and the parables so that they can be read orally to others. Because of this oral basis of the *Shepherd,* Osiek (1998, 161) suggests that what has survived in the manuscripts of the *Shepherd* is not the text, but a full outline, and there was no such thing as an original version, since each oral performance would be different from the last.

Genre. Is the *Shepherd* an apocalypse? Most scholars agree that it is (Joly 1958, 11–12; Yarbro Collins 1979, 75; Osiek 1986, 115), and the author apparently designated "Apocalypse 5" (the title in Codex Sinaiticus) the part later called "Vision 5." Although it has been labeled a "pseudo-apocalypse" because it lacks eschatological themes typical of many Jewish apocalypses and the Revelation to John, it fits the definition of the apocalypse genre (Aune 1987, 230):

> In *form* an apocalypse is a first-person prose recital of revelatory visions or dreams, framed by a description of the circumstances of the revelatory experience, and structured to emphasize the central revelatory message. The *content* of apocalypses involves, in the broadest terms, the communication of a transcendent, often eschatological, perspective on human experience. Apocalypses exhibit a threefold *function:* (1) to legitimate the message (and/or the messenger) through an appeal to transcendent authorization, and (2) to create a literary surrogate of revelatory experience for hearers or readers, (3) so that the recipients of the message will be motivated to modify their views and behaviors to conform to transcendent perspectives.

Like the Revelation to John, the *Shepherd* is not pseudonymous and was written to be read before congregations, unlike its Jewish analogues, but like its Greco-Roman counterparts (*Vis.* 1.3.3–4; 2.4.3; cf. Rev. 1:3; 22:18). Composed in an episodic style typical of apocalyptic literature, the *Shepherd* contains two apocalypses, *Vis.* 1–4 (Jefford 1996, 136) and *Vis.* 5 through *Sim.* 10. *Visions* 1–4 begins with a novelistic introduction (1.1.1–2), followed by reports of four visions on earth, each with several elements: (1) rapture by a spirit to the place of revelation, (2) preparation for revelation (prayer, fasting), (3) the vision itself, consisting of a dialogue between the revealer and Hermas. The stupidity of Hermas's questions is emphasized in the dialogues.

The second apocalypse, *Vis.* 5 through *Sim.* 10, begins with an extensive vision in which the Shepherd appears to Hermas and commands him to write the *Mandates* and *Similitudes* that follow. As in the Revelation to John (1:17b–18), the revealer introduces himself with an "I am" predication and concludes the inaugural interview with a conditional blessing and curse on those who hear the commands. The *Mandates* are largely paraenetic, as their name implies. *Mandates* 1–2, 9 are in the form of revelatory discourses by the Shepherd, while the rest are revelatory dialogues. The *Similitudes* contains six visions (2–4, 5, 6, 7–8, 9, 10), in which the Shepherd suddenly appears to Hermas and through dialogue explains the allegorical significance of various natural phenomena (an elm and a vine, *Sim.* 2; leafless trees, *Sim.* 3) or a story (the parable of the Vineyard, *Sim.* 5.2–7).

Outline. The outline of the *Shepherd* that follows is based on a reworking of Brox (1991, 7–9) and Jefford (1996, 154). *Vision* 5 was written later than *Vis.* 1–4 for the purpose of introducing the next two sections of the *Mandates* and the *Similitudes* (Hellholm 1980, 12); the terms ἐντολαί ("commandments, mandates") and παραβολαί ("parables, similitudes") first occur in *Vis.* 5.5.

- I. The Visions (*Vis.* 1–5)
  - 1. First vision
    - a. Hermas's sin (1.1–2)
    - b. "Rhoda" reveals Hermas's sin (1.3–2.1)
    - c. Threats and promises for Hermas (2.2–4.3)
  - 2. Second vision
    - a. Hermas copies the book of the elderly woman (2.1)
    - b. Hermas enabled to read the book and its message of a second repentance (2.2–3)
    - c. Young man reveals that the elderly woman is the Church (2.4.1)
    - d. Elderly woman appears again and commissions Hermas (2.4.2–3)
  - 3. Third vision
    - a. Hermas instructed about pleasing God (3.1.1–2.3)
    - b. Parable of the tower (3.2.4–9.10)
    - c. Meaning of the woman's three forms (3.10.1–13.4)
  - 4. Fourth vision: the coming great tribulation
  - 5. Revelation five: The Shepherd appears and commissions Hermas to write down the commandments and parables.
- II. Commandments or mandates
  - 1. Faith and continence
  - 2. Purity
  - 3. Truth
  - 4. Sexual purity, divorce, second marriage
  - 5. Patience and anger
  - 6. Faith
  - 7. Fear
  - 8. Sexual purity
  - 9. Doubt and indecision
  - 10. Sorrow
  - 11. True and false prophets and prophecy
  - 12. Evil desires (12.1.1–3.1)
  - 13. Epilogue to the commands (12.3.2–6.5)
- III. Parables or similitudes
  - 1. Parable of two cities
  - 2. Parable of the elm and the vine
  - 3. Parable of trees in winter
  - 4. Parable of trees in summer
  - 5. Parable of the vineyard worker
  - 6. Parable of the two shepherds
  - 7. Effect of the angel of punishment on Hermas
  - 8. Parable of the willow tree
  - 9. Parable of the mountains and the tower
  - 10. Final instructions

Systems of reference to the Shepherd. There are two ways of referring to passages in the *Shepherd.* The traditional way divides the work up into three sections, each containing a number of chapters, which in turn are divided into sections: (1) *Visions* (1–5), (2) *Mandates* (1–12), (3) *Similitudes* (1–10). The new numbering system divides the whole work into 114 chapters (*see the table at top of page 442*).

Literary features. Some have argued that the *Shepherd of Hermas* contains *ekphraseis* ("descriptions of a work of art"), centering on the allegorical moralizing interpretation of female figures, dependent on Cebes' *Tabula* (see *Cebes, *Tabula*), particularly in Hermas, *Vis.* 3.8 and *Sim.* 6.2–4; 9.15 (C. Taylor 1901, 1903a, 1903b, Joly 1963; Hilhorst 1976, 47). In *Vis.* 3.8.2, for example, Hermas sees seven women around the tower whose names are Faith, Self-Control, Sincerity, Knowledge, Innocence, Reverence, and Love. They are an allegory for the interrelationship of the virtues. According to 3.8.7 (trans. Holmes 1988), "From Faith is born Self-Control, from Self-

Concordance of the Old and New Reference Systems to the *Shepherd of Hermas*

Old	New	Old	New	Old	New
Vision 1.1–4	1–4	*Mandate* 1	26	*Similitude* 1	50
Vision 2.1–4	5–8	*Mandate* 2	27	*Similitude* 2	51
Vision 3.1–13	9–21	*Mandate* 3	28	*Similitude* 3	52
Vision 4.1–3	22–24	*Mandate* 4.1–4	29–32	*Similitude* 4	53
Vision 5	25	*Mandate* 5.1–2	33–34	*Similitude* 5.1–7	54–60
		Mandate 6.1–2	35–36	*Similitude* 6.1–5	61–65
		Mandate 7	37	*Similitude* 7	66
		Mandate 8	38	*Similitude* 8.1–11	67–77
		Mandate 9	39	*Similitude* 9.1–33	78–110
		Mandate 10.1–3	40–42	*Similitude* 10.1–4	111–114
		Mandate 11	43		
		Mandate 12.1–6	44–49		

Control, Sincerity, from Sincerity, Innocence, from Innocence, Reverence, from Reverence, Knowledge, from Knowledge, Love" (see also the chain of vices in Hermas, *Mand.* 5.2.4). This is an example of the rhetorical figure *sorites. Despite the shared features common to the *Shepherd* and Cebes' *Tabula* (e.g., the moral allegory of female figures), it is not necessary to suppose that the former is literarily dependent on the latter (Brox 1991, 53–54; Osiek 1999, 25). The main issue, however, is whether Hermas adapted the *ekphrasis* genre by basing literary vision reports on allegorical interpretations of pictures or sculpture. The static character of at least one of Hermas's visions (*Vis.* 4), suggests that this may well be an *ekphrasis* based on a unknown work of art.

The *Shepherd* contains a variety of constituent literary forms. Several types of prophetic oracles, identifiable on form-critical grounds, have been embedded in the *Shepherd* (Aune 1983, 299–310). This provides further evidence for the connection between prophecy and apocalypse in early Christianity. Four salvation-judgment oracles are found in the *Visions* (2.2.6–8; 2.3.4; 3.8.11–9.10; 4.2.5–6), each with conditional threats and promises, and all using the coming persecution as a sanction. *Vision* 2.2.6–8 will serve as an example *(see table below).*

In addition, there are two oracles of assurance preserved in the *Mandates* (12.4.5–7; 12.6.1–3), while six paraenetic salvation-judgment oracles are embedded in the *Similitudes* 6.1.4; 9.23.5; 9.24.4; 9.28.5–8; 9.31.3–32.5; 9.33.1). Parables or allegories were also used in Jewish apocalypses (*1 Enoch* 37–71; *4 Ezra; 2 Baruch*), and they play an

Salvation-Judgment Oracle in *Shepherd, Vis.* 2.2.6–8

Commission formula	You shall say, therefore, to the leaders of the church that they reform their ways in righteousness, that they receive in full the promises with great glory:
Admonition	"You, therefore, who work righteousness must remain steadfast and not be double-minded
Reasons:	
1. Conditional promise	that your way might be with the holy angels. Blessed are you, as many as endure the great persecution which is coming, and as many as shall not deny their life.
2. Conditional threat	For the Lord has sworn by his Son that those who have denied their Christ have been rejected from their life, that is, those who shall now deny him in the days to come.
3. Conditional promise	But those who denied him formerly have obtained forgiveness through his great mercy.

important role in the *Shepherd.* The term "parable" occurs more than 30 times, and functions both to reveal and to conceal divine truth (*Man.* 10.1.3–6; cf. Mark 4:11–12).

*Apostolic Fathers, *Ekphrasis

Aune 1983; Brox 1991; Carlini 1991; Coleborne 1970; Dibelius 1923; Giet 1963; Hellholm 1980; Henne 1992; Hilhorst 1976; Jeffers 1991; Jefford 1996, 134–58; Joly 1958, 1963, 1968; Osiek 1983, 1986, 1999; Reiling 1973; C. Taylor 1901, 1903a, 1903b, 1910; Whittaker 1956; W. J. Wilson 1927; Yarbro Collins 1979

Shorthand, or tachygraphy, the use of codes or abbreviations for words in order to be able to write more rapidly. The Greek terms σημειογράφος and ταχυγράφος (Eusebius, *Hist. eccl.* 6.23.2) mean "shorthand writer." Boge (1977, 99) defines "tachygraphy" as a special form of writing with short signs that departs from the alphabetical script used in normal writing. Greek inscriptions used a confusing variety of abbreviations that have been collected and arranged by Avi-Yonah 1940 (in Oikonomides 1974).

*Abbreviations, *Dictation, *Secretary

Boge 1977; Hurtado 1998; Oikonomides 1974; Strycker 1977

Sibylline Oracles, a designation for collections of oracles that circulated widely in the ancient world and were attributed to a "sibyl," an ecstatic prophetess. The Christian *Sibylline Oracles,* often written in a defective hexameter, are among the earliest Christian metrical poetry. *Sibylline Oracles* 6, a 28-line hymn to Christ, probably dates to the 3d cent.; *Sib. Or.* 8, a collection of oracles written by one or more Christian authors ca. 175 C.E., contains an acrostic poem in hexameter on judgment in lines 218–50, where each line begins with a letter of the phrase ΙΗΣΟΥΣ ΧΡΕΙΣΤΟΣ ΘΕΟΥ ΥΙΟΣ ΣΩΤΗΡ ΣΤΑΥΡΟΣ, "Jesus Christ, son of God, savior, cross," a slightly expanded form of the ΙΧΘΥΣ ("fish") coded phrase. Immediately following, in *Sib. Or.* 8.251–336, is a poem on Christ. *Sibylline Oracles* 11–14 date to the 3d cent. C.E., and narrate a history that begins with the flood and ends with the Arab conquest.

*Pseudepigrapha, OT

Collins 1983; Geffcken 1902

Signs source, a source theory proposed for the Gospel of *John, maintains that the seven miracles the Fourth Evangelist narrated in the first half of the work (John 1–12) are derived from a collection of signs attributed to Jesus, conventionally referred to in German works as the SQ (*Semeia Quelle,* "signs source"). A distinctive feature of the Fourth Gospel is the use of the word "sign" (σημεῖον) to refer to the miraculous deeds of Jesus. Two of these miracles, the miracle of wine at Cana (2:1–11) and the raising of Lazarus (11:1–44), are without parallel in other Gospels. Indications of this source are found in the enumeration of the first (2:11) and second (4:54) miracles performed by Jesus, even though other miracles are mentioned (2:23; 4:45; 12:37). Reference to the fact that "Jesus did many other signs in the presence of his disciples, which are not written in this book" (20:30) reads like a conclusion to the Gospel, even though it is followed by chap. 21. During the 20th cent., the most popular form of the Johannine signs source theory was proposed by Bultmann (Cope 1987, 19), who argued that the Signs Gospel was the earliest of all the Gospels, and suggested the possibility of the late 40s or early 50s for a date, but settled on the period of 55–60 as more cautious and credible. The signs source is often considered the first of several editions of the Fourth Gospel. For von Wahlde (1989, 13–14), the Fourth Gospel came out in three editions. (1) The first edition narrated Jesus' ministry from the baptism to the resurrection, focusing on the miracles of Jesus and the reactions they engendered, and took shape in the 70s or 80s (a view nearly identical with Fortna 1970, 1988). (2) The second edition appeared ca. 90 C.E. when the Johannine community was expelled from the synagogue. (3) The third edition was issued because of a misinterpretation of the second edition.

*John, Gospel of, *Source criticism

Bultmann 1971; Carson 1978; Cope 1987; Fortna 1970, 1988, 1992; Kysar 1973; Nicole 1972; D. M. Smith 1965, 1976a, 1976b; Teeple 1974; van Belle 1975; von Wahlde 1989

Silver age (of Latin literature) is the period following the reign of Augustus, i.e., 14–138 C.E., from the beginning of the reign of Tiberius (14–37 C.E.) to the end of the reign of Hadrian (117–38 C.E.). Writers during this period include (during the early part of the period under Tiberius through Claudius, 14–54 C.E.) the elder Seneca, Valerius Maximus, Velleius

Paterculus, Q. Curtius Rufus, Celsus, and Phaedrus. Writers during the Neronian period (54–68 C.E.) include Columella (on agriculture), Petronius (novelist and poet), Seneca (philosophy, poetry, satire), Persius (satire), Lucan (history), and Calpurnius Siculus (poetry). During the Flavian dynasty (69–96) important authors include the elder Pliny (science, antiquities), Quintilian (rhetoric), Frontinus (technical prose), and the poets Valerius Flaccus, Silius Italicus, Statius, and Martial. From Nerva through Hadrian (96–138 C.E.), the most prominent men of letters included Pliny the Younger (rhetoric, letters), Tacitus (history), Juvenal (poetry), Suetonius (grammarian, rhetorician, biographer) and Florus (poet, rhetorician, and historian).

*Golden age (of Latin literature), *Latin literature

Bloomer 1997; Classen 1998; J. W. Duff 1964; Feeney 1998; Fuhrmann 1999; Habinek 1998; Hadas 1952; Kenney (ed.) 1982; Sullivan 1985

Similitude, one of three types of parables of Jesus identified by Jülicher (1899), along with the *parable proper and the *example story. Jülicher himself (1899, 1.80) defined the similitude (*Gleichnis*) as "those figures of speech in which the meaning of a clause (thought) is determined through juxtaposition with a similar clause, belonging to another area, whose meaning is certain." The similitude can be defined as a brief narrative of a typical or recurrent event from real life.

Jülicher (1899, 2.3–259) identified 28 similitudes: (1) the Physician and the Sick (Mark 2:17=Matt. 9:12–23=Luke 5:31–32); (2) the Bridegroom (Mark 2:18–20=Matt. 9:14–15= Luke 5:33–35); (3) Patching Garments and Wineskins (Mark 2:21–22=Matt. 9:16–17= Luke 5:36–39); (4) Beelzebul (Mark 3:22–27= Matt. 12:22–30, 43–45=Luke 11:14–26); (5) Going to a Judge (Luke 12:57–59=Matt. 5:25–26); (6) the Lamp on the Lampstand (Mark 4:21=Matt. 5:14a, 15–16=Luke 8:16, 11:33); (7) Revealing the Hidden (Mark 4:22=Matt. 10:26–27=Luke 8:17, 12:2–3); (8) the True Source of Impurity (Mark 7:14–23=Matt. 15:10–20); (9) Children and Dogs (Mark 7:27–28=Matt. 15:26–27); (10) on Salt (Mark 9:49–50=Matt. 5:13=Luke 14:24–25); (11) the Fig Tree (Mark 13:28–29=Matt. 24:32–33=Luke 21:29–31); (12) the Master Returns Late (Mark 13:33–37=Luke 12:35–38); (13) the City on a Hill (Matt. 5:14b); (14) Scribes Trained for the Kingdom (Matt. 13:52); (15) Physician Heal Yourself (Luke 4:23); (16) the Blind Leading the Blind (Luke 6:39=Matt. 15:14); (17) Teachers and Students (Luke 6:40=Matt. 10:24–25); (18) the Tree and Its Fruit (Luke 6:43–46=Matt. 7:16–20, 12:33–37); (19) Children in the Market (Luke 7:31–35=Matt. 11:16–19); (20) the Asking Son (Luke 11:11–13=Matt. 7:9–11); (21) the Eye as the Light of the Body (Luke 11:34–36=Matt. 6:22–23); (22) Banquet Seating (Luke 14:7–11, 12–14); (23) Building Towers and Waging War (Luke 14:28 [25]–33); (24) the Double-Minded Servant (Luke 16:13=Matt. 6:24); (25) the Thief (Luke 12:39–40=Matt. 24:43–44); (26) the Faithful and Unfaithful Stewards (Luke 12:41–48=Matt. 24:45–51); (27) We Are Unprofitable Servants (Luke 17:7–10); (28) the Body and the Vultures (Luke 17:37=Matt. 24:28).

It is striking that Jülicher does *not* regard as similitudes precisely those narratives which other scholars routinely refer to as "similitudes," such as the Sower (Mark 4:3–9), the Seed (Mark 4:26–29), and the Mustard Seed (Mark 4:30–32); Jülicher categorizes all of these as parables (1899, 2.514–38, 546–63, 569–81). Boucher (1977, 3), discussing the views of Jülicher, gives three examples of similitudes (the Patient Farmer, Mark 4:26–29, the Lost Sheep and the Lost Coin, Matt. 18:12–14; Luke 15:3–10), yet these are all explicitly classified and discussed as *Parabeln* by Jülicher (1899, 2.538–46, 314–33).

*Parables

Boucher 1977; Jülicher 1899

Soliloquy refers to a dramatic monologue which is a speech to one's self. In the Homeric epics, heroes sometimes speak to themselves ("dispute in their hearts") to express their deepest emotions, frequently fear (Achilles in *Iliad* 22.385). In Hellenistic epic and novels, women are sometimes presented as having interior monologues, e.g. Medea (Apollonius Rhodius, *Argonautica* 3.772–801), Dido (Virgil, *Aeneid* 4.534–52); see also Ovid, *Metam.* 6.170–202; 10.319–33; Xenophon of Ephesus, *Ephesiaca* 1.4.1–7; Longus, *Daphnis* 1.14, 18). Interior monologues occur occasionally in Greek fables, which are closely related to the narrative parables of Jesus (Jülicher 1899, 98). An example is found in Babrius 131 (LCL trans.): "Hearing the bird faintly twittering, the youngest said to himself, 'What need have I now for extra clothing? Behold, here is a swallow. That means warm weather.' So saying, he went off and joined in the dice game, and, after playing a little, was beaten and forfeited his only garment."

The interior monologue is a device used in six parables in Luke (12:17–19 [=*G.Thom.* 92]; 12:45 [=Matt. 24:48]; 15:17–19; 16:3–4; 18:4–5; 20:13 [=Mark 12:6]) to provide access to the reader or hearer of a person's inner thoughts (Donahue 1988, 126; Parrot 1991, 509–10; Sellew 1992, 239). The soliloquy is occasionally found in other contexts in the Gospels (Mark 2:7–8=Matt. 9:3). and in other biblical contexts as well. In Rev. 18:7, personified Babylon "says in her heart" that she is a queen, not a widow, and she will never experience sorrow. This is a hybris soliloquy, a specific form of the soliloquy that provides a window into the pride and insolence of "Babylon." Revelation 18:7 is modeled after a similar hybris soliloquy in Isa. 47:8: "Now therefore hear this, you lover of pleasures, who sit securely, who say in your heart, 'I am, and there is no one beside me; I shall not sit as a widow or know the loss of children'" (Aune 1997–98, 3.995). Other examples of the hybris soliloquy are found in Ezek. 28:2; Jer. 5:12; *Sib. Or.* 5.173; Rev. 3:17; *2 Targ. Esther* 1.1: "Nebuchadnezzar became self-conceited and said, 'There is no king or ruler but I'" (Grossfeld 1991, 98). A very close parallel to the parables of Luke with an interior monologue is the Jewish story in Sir. 11:14–20, which is framed by a προμύθιον and an ἐπιμύθιος indicated by italics (see *Fable):

> *Good things and bad, life and death, poverty and wealth, come from the Lord. The gift of the Lord endures for those who are godly, and what he approves will have lasting success.* There is a man who is rich through his diligence and self-denial, and this is the reward allotted to him: when he says, "I have found rest, and now I shall enjoy my goods!" he does not know how much time will pass until he heaves them to others and dies. *Stand by your covenant and attend to it, and grow old in your work.*

Interior monologue occurs occasionally in the Apocryphal Acts (see *Acts, Apocryphal). An example is the *Acts of Andrew* (P. Copt. Utrecht I; *NTA* 2.125): "The young magician said within himself: 'If I have spent twenty years under the instruction of my master until I was taught this skill, behold! Now this is the beginning of my skill; if I do not prevail upon this virgin, I shall not be able to do any work." In the *Acts of Thomas* 99 (*NTA* 2.377): "Charisius . . . reflected, saying to himself: 'If the great despair that is about me should compel me to go now to the king, who will bring me into him? [etc.]."

———

Beavis 1990; Donahue 1988; Marshall 1978, 523; Sellew 1992

Solomon, Testament of, is a pseudepigraphical work attributed to Solomon, but written in the 2d or 3d cent. C.E. There are three pseudonymous works in the OT, attributed directly or indirectly to Solomon: Ecclesiastes, the Song of Songs, and parts of Proverbs (10:1–22:16; 25:1–29:27). Later pseudepigraphical works attributed to Solomon include the *Psalms of Solomon,* the *Odes of Solomon,* the *Testament of Solomon* and the medieval *Clavicula Salomonis.* The title of the work, Διαθήκη Σολομῶνος ("Testament of Solomon"), indicates that the work was written at a time when the literary genre "testament" enjoyed great prestige. Nevertheless the *Testament of Solomon* does not imitate genuine testaments (several major characteristic features of which are missing), but reflects the continuing reputation and authority of the testamentary form (Nordheim 1980, 185–93). The work is essentially Jewish with a few Christian interpolations (e.g., "Christ as Savior" in 17:4 and "the son of the virgin, the one crucified" in 22:20). The place of origin for the *Testament of Solomon* is a difficult question. Two of the main possibilities are Palestine and Egypt (Preisendanz 1956b, 690).

Contents. Solomon, wishing to protect a favored temple worker who is plagued by a demon, is given a magic ring in answer to his prayers. Using the ring, Solomon calls the offending demon before him and subsequently learns the powers and activities of all the demons, including the formula or angelic name that controls each. These demons are then compelled to work on various aspects of the construction of the temple. The story ends with a narrative of Solomon's for a Shunamite girl, his fall, and subsequent loss of power over the demons.

*Farewell address, *Magical papyri

———

Conybeare 1898; Delatte 1927; Duling 1975, 1983, 1987, 1988; Giversen 1972; Haelewyck 2002; Jackson 1988; McCown 1922a, 1922b; Nordheim 1980, 185–93; Preisendanz 1956a, 1956b; Torijano 2002; Whittaker 1984

Sophists, sophistic movement The Greek term σοφιστής (from σόφος, "wise," and σοφία, "wisdom") means "wise man." The sophist movement flourished in Athens 450–400 B.C.E. under the patronage of Perikles (Kerford 1981, 17–19; cf. Plutarch, *Pericles* 36.2), and it was particularly during this period that the sophists became professionals, i.e., they charged fees for their teaching (Plato, *Hippias maior* 282c), which some thought reprehensible (Xenophon, *Memorabilia* 1.2.7–8). The names of 26 sophists are known who were active 460–380 B.C.E., including Protagoras, Gorgias, Prodicus, Hippias, Antiphon, Thrasymachus, Callicles, Critias, Euthydemus, and Dionysodorus (Kerford 1981, 42–54). The real objection to the sophists, however, appears to center on the kind of people ("all kinds of people," Plato, *Hippias maior* 282d) who could have access to what the sophists had to offer, i.e., teaching people about affairs of state so that they could become powerful and influential in the city (Kerford 1981, 26). They were condemned by Socrates (who was himself part of the sophistic movement, cf. Kerford 1981, 55–57), and later by Plato and Aristotle. Plato has two main treatments of the sophists (*Gorgias* 462b–465e; *Sophist*). Aristotle also regarded the sophists negatively, referring to the sophistic art as consisting of apparent wisdom that is not real wisdom and to the sophist as one who makes money from apparent but not real wisdom (*Sophistici elenchi* 165a). This negative view of the sophistic movement, which lasted until their role was partially rehabilitated in the 19th cent. by the work of Hegel, Grote, and Zeller, and consisted of two basic criticisms (Kerford 1981, 6): (1) sophists were not serious thinkers and had no role within the history of philosophy, and (2) their teachings were profoundly immoral.

Sophists had three main spheres of activity: (1) public lectures, (2) public debates, and (3) private classes, where the educational methods included learning arguments based on the question-and-answer method (the Socratic tradition), prepared lectures on set themes, and rhetorical exercises for training future speakers in law courts and assemblies (Kerford 1981, 28–30).

Kerford (1981, 85–86) argues that a famous statement attributed to Protagoras conveys the basis for the entire sophistic movement: "Man is the measure of all things, of things that are as to how they are, and of things that are not as to how they are not" (Diogenes Laertius 9.51; Diels-Kranz 1952, 253 [80A1]). Though widely debated, this saying seems to mean that the individual person (not the human race) is the one who "measures," and what is "measured" about things is not their existence or nonexistence, but how things appear (as Plato says when he quotes this statement in *Theatetus* 152a): "each group of things is to me such as it appears to me, and is to you such as it appears to you." The example given is that of the wind, which can seem warm to one person and cold to another. Further, perceptions are "infallible," that is, each perception in each individual is true for them and cannot be "corrected" by a different perception of another individual.

*Second Sophistic

Bowersock 1969; Classen 1976; Guthrie 1971; Kerford 1981

Sorites, from the Greek term σωρίτης ("heaped up"), a term used in logic for a chain of syllogisms, the conclusion of each of which is used as a premise for the next. As a rhetorical *trope (in addition to σωρίτης, terms for this trope include κλῖμαξ and ἐπιπλοκή, while the Latin equivalents include *gradatio* [Lausberg 1998, §623], *ascensus,* and *catena*), it refers to a chain of paired terms, the second of which is used as the first member of the next pair, resulting in an A . . . B, B . . . C, C . . . D pattern (Fischel 1973, 119). Thus σωρίτης or *gradatio* is a progressive elaboration of the trope ἀναδίπλωσις ("repetition") or *reduplicatio,* in which a last word in one clause is immediately repeated, forming the first word of the next clause (Lausberg 1998, §619). A famous example from Demosthenes, *De corona* 179 is cited in **Rhetorica ad Herennium* 4.34 and Quintilian 9.3.55: "I did not conceive this without counseling it; I did not counsel it without myself at once undertaking it; I did not undertake it without completing it; nor did I complete it without winning approval of it." There are several examples in early Jewish sources (Wis. 6:17–20; *m. Sota* 9.15; see Fischel 1973, 132). A famous example of sorites is found in *Iliad* 2.102–7, where the descent of the royal scepter of Mycenae is traced: "Hephaestus gave it to king Zeus, son of Cronos, and Zeus gave it to the messenger Argeïphontes [an epithet for Hermes]; and Hermes, the lord, gave it to Pelops, driver of horses, and Pelops in turn gave it to Atreus, shepherd of the host; and Atreus at his death left it to Thyestes, rich in flocks, and Thyestes again left it to Agamemnon to bear." Sorites is also a natural trope to use in genealogies, as in this fragment from an unknown Roman tragedian (Quintilian 9.3.57): "From Jove, so runs the tale, was Tantalus sprung, from Tantalus Pelops, and of Pelops seed sprang

Atreus, who is sire of all our line." This same pattern is used in the genealogy of Jesus in Matt. 1:2–16: "Abraham was the father of Isaac, and Isaac the father of Jacob, and Jacob the father of Judah, and his brothers [etc.]."

Several examples of sorites are found in the NT and early Christian literature: (1) Rom. 8:30: "Those whom he predestined he also called; and those whom he called he also justified; and those whom he justified he also glorified" (see also Rom. 5:3–5; 10:14–15). (2) The *catalog of virtues in 2 Pet. 1:5–7 is in the form of sorites (Fischel 1973, 119; Bauckham 1983a, 175), but also has precedents in Jewish literature of the same period (Swanson 2000, 57–61):

> 5For this very reason make every effort to supplement your faith with virtue,
> and virtue with knowledge,
> 6and knowledge with self-control,
> and self-control with steadfastness,
> and steadfastness with godliness,
> 7and godliness with brotherly affection,
> and brotherly affection with love.

See also *G.Thom.* 2:

> Jesus said: He who seeks
> must not stop seeking until he finds;
> and when he finds, he will be bewildered;
> and if he is bewildered, he will marvel,
> and will be king over the All.

A variant version of this saying is quoted in Clement of Alexandria, *Strom.* 5.14.96 (trans. Cameron 1982, 86):

> He that seeks will not rest until he finds,
> and he that has found shall marvel;
> and he that has marveled shall reign;
> and he that has reigned shall rest.

In Hermas, *Vis.* 3.8.2, Hermas sees seven women around the tower whose names are Faith, Self-Control, Sincerity, Knowledge, Innocence, Reverence, and Love. They are an allegory for the interrelationship of virtues. According to 3.8.7 (trans. Holmes 1988), "From Faith is born Self-Control, from Self-Control, Sincerity, from Sincerity, Innocence, from Innocence, Reverence, from Reverence, Knowledge, from Knowledge, Love" (see also the chain of vices in Hermas, *Mand.* 5.2.4).

Bauckham 1983a, 175–76; Cameron 1982; Fischel 1973; Lausberg 1998, §621, 623

Source criticism is the attempt to determine the shape and character of oral or written sources that have been incorporated into written documents. There are eight commonly used indicators of the presence of sources in a text: (1) unevenness, (2) glosses (additions), (3) resumption, (4) interruption of the context, (5) doublets, (6) choice of words and style, (7) divergent theologies, and (8) textual criticism.

Source criticism of the Synoptic Gospels. The three canonical Gospels, Matthew, Mark, and Luke, exhibit stretches of text with some very close textual similarities, suggesting some kind of literary relationship. The majority of scholars agree that Matthew and Luke reused much of Mark independently of each other (a hypothesis called "the priority of Mark") and also that Matthew and Luke reused a source, now lost, called the Sayings Source or *Q. Matthew and Luke probably used slightly different versions of Mark (indicated by the sigla $Mark^M$ and $Mark^L$) as well as slightly different versions of Q (indicated by the sigla Q^M and Q^L).

*Aporia, *Criticism, biblical, *Interpolations

Breytenbach 1992; Fortna 1970, 1988; Gamble 1975; Kysar 1973; Martyn 1971; W. Michaelis 1958; J. D. Miller 1997; Schmithals 1972; Schwartz 1907, 1908; D. M. Smith 1976a, 1976b; Teeple 1974; Telford 1992; Von Wahlde 1976, 1989

Special L (see *L, Special)

Species of rhetoric (see *Rhetorical genres)

Speeches History for the ancient Greeks consisted of actions (πράξεις) and speeches (λόγοι); Homer was the model for both. Dirct speech in the Homeric epics occupies fully one-half of the *Iliad* and three-fifths of the *Odyssey,* and plays an important dramatic role by presenting past events as if present. In this and other respects, Homer exerted a lasting influence on Greek historiography. In content, Homeric single and paired speeches (all obviously fictional) involve *commands* (*Iliad* 1.321–25; 4.192–97), *advice* (2.23–34; 5.347–51), *appeals* including prayers (1.36–42; 3.250–58), and *announcements* (1.442–45; 5.102–5). Speeches not only dramatize relationships but show how and why people act as they do. Speeches of command, advice, and appeal usually function to motivate action, i.e., to show why people did what they did. Speeches of announcement, on the other hand, usually explain the speaker's actions or foreshadow coming events. In epic, tragedy, comedy, and Herodotean history, characterization does not include linguistic individualization; direct speech uniformly reflects the author's style (note the inappropriately elegant speech of the savage cannibal giant Polyphemus in *Odyssey* 9.447–60).

Direct discourse plays a significant role in Herodotus, the first historian to use direct speech for dramatization. According to Lang, his history contains 861 speeches in both direct and indirect discourse. Less than half (47.5 percent) are direct discourse. The important role of indirect discourse in Herodotus contrasts with the preference for direct discourse in Homer (as in OT narrative). The use of discourse in historiography reached a new and significant level of development in Thucydides, at a time when oratory began to develop in Athens. By earlier reckoning there are 41 speeches in direct discourse in Thucydides (24 percent of the narrative), uniformly reflecting his own language and style. According to West, there are 52 speeches in direct discourse and 85 in indirect discourse (three combining indirect with direct discourse). In an endlessly debated passage, Thucydides comments on his use of speeches (1.22.1):

> With reference to the speeches in this history, some were delivered before the war began, others while it was going on; some I heard myself, others I got from various quarters; it was in all cases difficult to carry them word for word in one's memory, so my habit has been to make the speakers say what was in my opinion demanded of them by the various occasions, of course adhering as closely as possible to the general sense of what they really said.

Thucydides proposes to give a reliable account of what the original speakers needed to say to accomplish their objectives with particular audiences in particular situations. There is little doubt, however, that he did not fully carry out his intentions. The language of the speeches is uniformly Thucydidean. The analysis of the speeches themselves, some of which are clearly anachronistic or inappropriate, suggests that they are neither historical nor authentic, but are rather vehicles for commenting on historical situations from various perspectives.

During the 4th and 3d cent. B.C.E., there was a reaction to the rationalistic historicism of Thucydides. Historians like Ephorus wrote more inclusive histories following the model of Herodotus. Speeches were inventions displaying the writer's rhetorical ability rather than the actual or epitomized remarks of the speakers. They also served as oratorical models. Polybius reacted against this feature of dramatic history and revived what he thought was the Thucydidean standard of accuracy. Like all ancient historians, he too used speeches frequently (about 50 in the surviving parts of his history). In 12.25a.5–25b.1, he comments on the proper use of speeches in a polemic against Timaeus (modified LCL translation):

> For he [Timaeus] has not set down the words spoken nor the sense of what was really said, but having made up his mind as to what ought to have been said, he recounts all these speeches and all else that follows upon events like a man in a school of rhetoric attempting to speak on a given subject, and shows off his oratorical power, but gives no report of what was actually spoken. The peculiar function of history is to discover, in the first place, the words actually spoken, whatever they were, and next to ascertain the reason why what was done or spoken led to failure or success.

Here Polybius faults Timaeus for freely composing speeches based on situational probability rather than setting down the substance of the actual speeches themselves. For Polybius the difference is between the possibility of tragedy, "what *could* happen," and the actuality of history "what *did* happen" (Polybius 2.56.10; cf. Aristotle *Poetica* 1451a–b). Elsewhere Polybius seems to say that the historian must *choose* the arguments appropriate to a speaker in a given situation, apparently contradicting the view quoted above (12.25i.3–9). Yet here Polybius is probably concerned with the editing or epitomizing of actual speeches, i.e., with selecting arguments in the actual speeches (or epitomes of them) for inclusion in his narrative. Since Polybius apparently avoided presenting speeches as rhetorical models (the penchant of the tragic historians), many of his speeches lack appropriate rhetorical structure and do not always focus on a main point.

Apart from Thucydides and Polybius, speeches composed for historical works were not based on actual speeches but were rhetorical compositions judged suitable for the person to whom they were ascribed in the particular situation envisaged. Hellenistic armchair historians found speeches in their sources and freely adapted them for their own compositions. *Dionysius of Halicarnassus was a practicing rhetorician and historian who favored the use of speeches (they constitute 30 percent of his *Roman Antiquities*). He criticized the speeches of Thucydides as rhetorically unsuitable (*On Thucydides* 37–41). Diodorus Siculus criticized the *excessive* use of rhetoric in framing speeches, but thought that rhetorical embellishment did have a place in historiography (20.1–2). Lucian suggests that speeches should first fit the person and subject, and only then be shaped to reflect the historian's rhetorical abilities (*History* 58).

*Declamations, *Luke–Acts, *Prosopoiia, *Rhetorical criticism

Bruce 1942, 1974; Fornara 1983, 142–68; Gomme 1937; Lang 1984; Soards 1994; Stadter (ed.) 1973; Walbank 1965

Stasis, or stasis theory, from the Greek word στάσις (Quintilian 3.6.3; Cicero, *Topica* 93), a rhetorical term meaning "issue" (Latin terms include *status* [Quintilian 3.6.1; Cicero, *Topica* 93] and *constitutio* [Quintilian 3.6.2]), deals with attempts to describe what an argument was about; an equivalent to the "who, what, when, where, why" of modern journalism (Lanham 1991, 93). Stasis theory, a highly systematized scheme of classifying rhetorical topics and arguments according to the "issues," sought to classify the various types of disputes that speakers had to address and to develop appropriate strategies for addressing them (Heath 1995, 2). This scheme was developed by Hermagoras of Temnos in the mid-2d cent. B.C.E. (though there were antecedents in earlier works, including those of Aristotle; see W. N. Thompson 1974) and thereafter constituted the basis of Greek and Roman rhetorical teaching and practice into the 2d cent. C.E. and beyond (Kennedy 1963, 318; Nadeau 1959). Cicero's *De inventione* is the clearest and most complete expression of Hermagoras's system of stasis theory. The most important part of *De inventione* is arguably the section on the doctrine of *constitutio causae,* or "determination of the issue," which is derived, with modifications, from the work of Hermagoras (Hubbell 1949, xiii). Hermagoras's most influential work was on "invention" or "discovery" (εὕρεσις), which primarily included his stasis theory (Kennedy 1963, 313). Following Hermagoras, Cicero identified four issues, i.e., στάσεις or *status* (Jolivet 1997, 311–12): (1) the conjectural issue or the issue of fact *(coniectura;* στοχασμός) dealt with whether a person committed a particular act and was supported by conjectures and inferences. (2) The definitional issue *(definitiva;* ὅρος) involved the precise definition of an act—should a homicide be regarded as murder or manslaughter? (3) The qualitative issue *(generalis;* ποιότης) involved, in the case of homicide, whether there were extenuating circumstances such as self-defense or temporary insanity. (4) The translative issue *(translativa;* μετάληψις) involved procedural objections such as motions of dismissal because the wrong person was bringing the charge or the wrong penalty was sought for a particular crime. After determining the issues of a controversy, Cicero advises that one should determine whether the dispute turns on general reasoning or on written documents (*De inventione* 1.13.17; LCL trans.): A dispute about a document arises from the nature of a written document.

> Of this there are five kinds (*genera*), which are separate from the 'issues' (*constitutionibus*). In one case it seems that there is a variance between the actual words and the intent of the author; in another, that two or more laws disagree; again, that what is written has two or more meanings; again, that from what has been written something is discovered which has not been written; finally, that there is a question about the meaning of a word, i.e., on what the meaning depends, as if it were in the definitional issue. Therefore the first class is said to be concerned with the letter and the intent, the second with the conflict of laws, the third with ambiguity, the fourth with reasoning by analogy, and the fifth with definition.

*Rhetorical theory, *Hypothesis, *Thesis

Dieter 1950; Hubbell 1949; Lausberg 1998, §§79–138; Matthes 1958, 1962; Nadeau 1959, 1964; W. N. Thompson 1974

Stichos (pl. stichoi), stichometry The transliterated Greek term στίχος (=Latin *versus*) means a line of poetry or prose serving as the unit of measure by which the length of manuscripts was calculated, by which copyists were paid for their work (usually calculated per hundred lines), and by which the commercial value of a manuscript was determined (Harris 1893, 26; Thackeray 1967, 73). In Alexandria, the term ἔπη (singular: ἔπος) was used for lines in poetic works, while στίχοι (singular: στίχος) was reserved for lines of prose. Frequently, however, these terms were synonymous (cf. Lucian, *Hist. conscr.* 28). The term "stichometry" is a modern designation for this ancient practice. Since a line of Homeric hexameter (earlier called an ἔπος, later a στίχος) consisted of about 15–17 syllables, a στίχος of prose was regarded as consisting of 15–17 syllables (34–38 letters) regardless of the length of the line in manuscripts (Diels 1882, 379), i.e., the conversion was based on estimates (Blumer 1991, 157–58). The average number of letters in a στίχος is 35.75 (Birt 1882, 197). The number of στίχοι was placed at the end of manuscripts, sometimes with subtotals every 50 or 100 lines in the left margins. The presence of stichometric figures in a manuscript indicates that it was copied professionally and paid for (E.G. Turner 1980, 95). Dionysius of Hal. (*De Thuc.* 13, 19, 33) refers to one section of Thucydides as consisting of 300 lines (στίχοι), another of 500 lines, and yet another of 100 lines. At the conclusion of Josephus, *Antiquitates* 20.267, the author notes: "With this I shall conclude my *Antiquitates,* contained in twenty books with sixty thousand lines." This notice is unusual in that the number of stichoi found in a work was normally placed as a separate note at the end of a text (Thackeray 1967, 73). Some papyri contain stichometric indications (Ohly 1928, 31–71).

The term στίχος also was used of the lines of manuscripts written for public reading. The reference to line numbers in works of prose occurs infrequently: Diogenes Laertius 7.187–88; Asconius's commentaries on Cicero; a scholiast on Oribasius (referring to works of Galen); Eustathius on Origin (referring to the Gospel of John), and Hegemonius against the Manichees (Ohly 1928, 109–17). $\mathfrak{P}^{46}$ contains stichometric indications for Romans, Hebrews, 2 Corinthians (illegible), Ephesians, Galatians, Philemon, and Colossians (illegible). Between Philemon and Hebrews, Codex Clarmontanus (copied in the 6th cent. C.E.), a Greek and Latin bilingual manuscript of portions of the NT, has a Latin list of the books of the Bible, including some OT and NT apocrypha and pseudepigrapha, giving the approximate number of stichoi for each composition (Tischendorf 1852, 468–69):

Matthew	2,600
John	2,000
Mark	1,600
Luke	2,900
Romans	1,040
1 Corinthians	1,060
2 Corinthians	970
Galatians	350
Ephesians	375
1 Timothy	209
2 Timothy	289
Titus	140
Colossians	251
Philemon	50
1 Peter	200
2 Peter	140
James	220
1 John	220
2 John	20
3 John	20
Jude	60
Ep. Barnabas	850
Revelation	1,200
Acts	2,600
Hermas	4,000
Acts of Paul	3,560
Apoc. of Peter	270

In a very different application of symmetrical stichometry to the NT, F. G. Lang (1977) proposed a five-part structure of Mark with an introduction: Introduction (1:1–13; 29 lines); (1) Jesus' first appearance in Galilee (1:14–3:6; 155 lines); (2) the Sea of Galilee as the center of Jesus' saving activity (3:7–6:6a; 6:6b–8:21; 505 lines: 14 in 3:7–12; 246 in 3:13–6:6a; 245 in 6:6b–8:22); (3) the revelation of Jesus' nature and the journey (8:22–10:45; 264 lines); (4) the Jerusalem temple as the center of conflict (10:46–13:37; 280 lines), (5) Jesus' passion at Passover (14:1–16:8; 282 lines).

*Colometry

Birt 1882, 133–57, 309–31; Diels 1882; Harris 1893; *DKP* 1979, 5.371; F. G. Lang 1977, 1999; Menken 1985, 12–16; Metzger 1981, 38–40; *OCD* 1443; Ohly 1928; E. M. Thompson 1901, 78–82; Wendel 1949, 33–44, 111–15.

Stobaeus, Joannes, the author of an anthology of excerpts called *Eklogae* or *Anthologium* ("selections"), compiled during the 5th cent. C.E. Many snippets of works otherwise lost are preserved in Stobaeus, though he avoids works produced by the *Second Sophistic and also preserves no fragments of Christian authors, suggesting that he himself was a pagan.

Text: Wachsmuth and Hense 1884–1912

Stories about Jesus The category of "stories about Jesus," or legends (see *Form criticism), is a relatively flexible narrative form with a miniplot in which the element of tension that begins the story is resolved at the end. While these stories may contain a saying of Jesus, the emphasis is rather on the event or action narrated. Crossan (1986, 172–221) collects 98 stories of Jesus, excluding only those containing *sayings of Jesus. In addition to the Matthaean and Lukan infancy stories and the episodes in the Synoptic passion narrative, there are 18 stories about Jesus in Mark and 11 in Luke (Taylor 1935, 142–65; Bultmann 1963, 244–74, 1967, 260–329). The stories about Jesus in Mark include: (1) the preaching of John (1:5–8), (2) the baptism of Jesus (1:9–11), (3) the temptation (1:12–13), (4) the call of the disciples (1:16–20), (5) the call of Levi (2:14), (6) Peter's confession (8:27–30), (7) the transfiguration (9:2–8), (8) the triumphal entry (11:1–10).

Stories of Jesus (the exception is the temptation story in Lk. 4:1–13 and Matt. 4:1–11) are almost entirely absent from *Q and the *Gospel of Thomas,* since both are instructional collections of "sayings of the wise," which normally exclude narrative forms. For similar reasons legends are seldom transmitted in the context of revelatory dialogues such as the *Dialogue of the Savior.* While miracle stories are the primary concern of the *Infancy Gospel of Thomas,* four legends are also found: (1) Jesus and the teacher Zacchaeus (6:1–7:4), (2) Jesus at school (15:1–4), (3) Jesus' trip to Jerusalem (19:1–2a), (4) Jesus in the temple (19:2b–5). Many legends are found in the *Infancy Gospel of James,* in which the infancy stories of Matthew and Luke are both embellished and expanded with the inclusion of many additional legends exhibiting common folklore motifs (cf. P. Cairensis 10.735); Similarly, numerous legends are included in the passion narratives found in *Gospel of Peter* and the *Acts of Pilate.* The narrative character of the Jewish Christian extracanonical gospels (the *Gospel of the Hebrews,* the *Gospel of the Ebionites,* the *Gospel of the Nazarenes*) provided an appropriate framework for the inclusion of many legendary motifs. These include the call of the disciples, transformed into a first-person narrative attributed to Jesus (the *Gospel of the Ebionites* 1), the baptism of John (*Gospel of the Ebionites* 2–3), and Jesus carried off by the hair to Mt. Tabor (*Gospel of the Hebrews* 3).

*Controversy stories, *Form criticism, Pronouncement stories

Bultmann 1963, 1967; Taylor 1935.

Style, or stylistics, refers to the distinctive manner of linguistic expression that characterizes the way individuals express themselves in written texts, i.e., *how* something is said as well as what is said. The most effective way of dealing with particular stylistic features is to regard them as defined by their general communicative and persuasive role as well as the rhetorical situation in which they occur (Thurén 1996, 338). There are several terms for "style" in Greek, including λέξις (Aristotle, *Rhetorica* 3.12.1 [1413b], et passim), χαρακτήρ (Ps.-Demetrius, *On Style* 2.36, et passim), and ἑρμηνεία (Dionysius of Halicarnassus, *Comp.* 1). The main Latin term for style is *elocutio* (**Rhetorica Ad Herennium* 4.1).

Linguistic register. One of most general stylistic features of a writer is the linguistic register used. During the first few centuries C.E., Hellenistic Greek was the lingua franca of the eastern Mediterranean. The speech patterns of people of Jewish origins was often characterized by various degrees of Semitic interference (see *Semitisms) in which locutions more characteristic of Hebrew or Aramaic are translated somewhat literally into Hellenistic Greek, the receptor language. *Septuagintisms, imitations of the distinct linguistic patterns of the Greek *Septuagint, the Bible of Greek-speaking Jews from the late 3d cent. B.C.E. on, are a closely related linguistic phenomenon. A quite different tendency for native speakers of Hellenistic Greek was *Atticism, an archaizing attempt to impose the characteristic linguistic features of Attic Greek of the 5th and 4th cent. B.C.E. on the Hellenistic Greek of the late 1st and early 2d cent. C.E. Greek and Roman rhetorical theorists paid primary attention to microlevel structures as well as macrolevel structures (subsumed under *Rhetorical theory).

The four virtues of style. Classical theory enumerated four "virtues or qualities of style," ἀρεταί τῆς λέξεως: (1) Correctness, i.e., ἑλληνισμός, "purity of grammar and diction," emphasizing two areas of grammatical error that should be avoided, barbarisms and solecisms (Rowe 1997, 122–23); (2) clarity (σαφήνεια), i.e., the immediate understanding of what a speaker has to say even by the inattentive (Rowe 1997,123–24); (3) ornamentation (Rowe 1997, 124–54); (4) propriety (πρέπον), "appropriateness of subject matter and setting," when all the parts of an oration form an organic unity (Rowe 1997, 154–56).

Taxonomies of style. The earliest division of classes or types of style is found in the threefold division of the *Rhetorica ad Herennium: gravis, mediocris, extenuatus* (4.8.11), similar to the threefold division of Cicero (*De oratore* 3.45.177; 3.52.199; 3.55.212): *gravis, medius, subtilis.* Cicero's *Orator* is primarily a detailed presentation of the three rhetorical styles, the "plain" style (75–90), illustrated by Cicero's speech for Caecina (102); the "middle" style (91–96), illustrated by Cicero's speech for the

Manilian Law (102); and the "grand" (*grandiloquus*) style (97–99), illustrated by Cicero's speech in defense of Rabirius (102). Most orators, according to Cicero, have a repertoire limited to one of the three styles, though he and Demosthenes are masters of all three (106–11). A twofold division of style is found in Cicero, *Brutus* 201: simple and concise (*attenuate presseque*), and elevated and abundant (*sublate ampleque*). In Dionysius of Halicarnassus (*De comp. verb.* 22), the designations for the three are (1) γλαφυρός (23), (2) εὔκρατος (24), (3) αὐστηρός ὑψηλός, μέσος, and ἰσχνός (25), though he claims that he has not been able to find authentic designations for these, so he has coined his own (21). The second and most extensive part of the treatise of Ps.-Demetrius, *On Style* focuses on the four styles (2.36–4.239): (1) χαρακτὴρ μεγαλοπεπὴς: the grand or elevated style (2.38–113), whose opposite is the frigid [ψυχρότης] style (2.114–27); (2) χαρακτὴρ γλαφυρός: the elegant style (3.128–85), whose opposite is the affected style (3.186–89); (3) χαρακτήρ: the plain style (4.190–235), whose opposite is the arid (ξηρός) style (4.236–39); and (4) χαρακτὴρ δεινός: the forceful style (240–301), and its opposite, the unpleasant style (302–4).

Stylistics in the second century C.E. What some have called "idea-theory" (Rutherford 1998) is already found in a highly developed form in Dionysius of Halicarnassus (1st cent. B.C.E.) but was developed further in the 2d cent. C.E. in the context of the *Second Sophistic. The most complex treatise on ideal-theory is the Περὶ ἰδεῶν of Hermogenes of Tarsus. Hermogenes discusses six main categories of ideas or stylistic qualities, several of which are subdivided further, making a total of 17 ideas (Rutherford 1998, 8):

1. Clarity (σαφήνεια)
   a. Purity (καθαρότης)
   b. Distinctiveness (εὐκρίνεια)
2. Grandeur (μέγεθος)
   a. Solemnity (σεμνότης)
   b. Envelopment (περιβολή)
   c. Brilliance (λαμπρόης)
   d. Roughness (τραχύτης)
   e. Vehemence (σφοδρόης)
   f. Peak (ἀκμή)
3. Beauty (κάλλος)
4. Agility (γοργότης)
5. Character (ἦθος)
   a. Plainness (ἀφέλεια)
   b. Sweetness (γλυκύτης)
   c. Pungency (δριμύτης)
   d. Reasonablcncss (ἐπιείκεια)
   e. Veracity (ἀλήθεια)
   f. Gravity (βαρύτης)
6. Power (δεινότης)

Hermogenes has three interrelated theses about the works of Demosthenes, who forms the main model for idea-theory (Rutherform 1998, 18): (1) Demosthenes uses *all* the *ideai.* (2) Demosthenes uses all the *ideai* perfectly. (3) Demosthenes' perfect use of all the *ideai* takes the form of combining them

*Anacolouthon, *Asianism, *Asyndeton, *Atticism, *Greek, *Hypotaxis, *Idea theory, *Latin, *Parallelism, *Periodic style, *Polysyndeton, *Repetition, *Rhetorical questions

---

Ø. Anderson 2002, 80–90; Botha 1991a, 1991b; Enkvist 1974, 1985; Kayser 1948; Kennedy 1980; Landfester 1997; Martin 1974, 245–345; Norden 1909; Rowe 1997; Spencer 1984; Schenkeveld 1964, 51–148; Volkmann 1885, 393–562

Stylometry, as defined by Kenny (1986, 1), "is the study of quantifiable features of a written or spoken text." For some, this is a controversial issue, for "Literary art cannot be reduced to a mathematical equation" (Guthrie 1957, 214, arguing against the method of Harrison [1921], who concluded that Paul did not write the *Pastorals). One reason for undertaking such a study is to determine the authenticity of a text or group of texts on the basis of a statistical comparison of various common "unconscious" features of style (and so, in a sense, the opposite of stylistics), typically with the aid of computer-assisted text analysis. Stylometry has been applied frequently to the problem of the authorship of the plays of Shakespeare, as well as to the problem of the chronology of the dialogues of Plato. One type of stylometry focuses on vocabulary frequency and the occurrence of **hapax legomena* (words that occur only once) for or against theories of authorship (Kenny 1986, 2). Harrison (1921, 18–66) argued, for example, on the basis of the number of *hapax legomena* per page in the Pastorals that do not occur in the rest of the NT or the Pauline letters. Another type, "positional stylometry" (Morton 1978, 110–14, 180–83), examines the relative frequency of specific words in certain positions in the sentence such as the initial particles in a Greek sentence or last words (Michaelson and Morton 1972). This is based on the supposition that works of a single author will exhibit more stylistic similarities than comparisons of the works of different authors. Morton, in a series of stylometric analyses of the Pauline letters, argues that only the four main letters, Romans, 1 Corinthians, 2 Corinthians, and Galatians, should be attributed to Paul (1978, 168, 183). Michaelson and Morton (1972) use stylometry to argue that Galatians and 1 Corinthians were Pauline, that Rom. 1 and 15–16 were non-Pauline, that 2 Corinthians was probably fabricated from Pauline material, that neither Ephesians, nor Philippians, nor Colossians is Pauline, that 1 and 2 Thessalonians were written by a single person but not Paul, and the Pastorals are non-Pauline. They were sharply criticized for their statistical method, however, by P. F. Johnson (1974). Mealand (1989) used positional stylometry (καί as the first word; δέ as the second word; γάρ as the second word; εἰ as the first word) to argue for the authenticity of seven Pauline letters (Romans, 1 and 2 Corinthians, Galatians, 1 and 2 Thessalonians, Philippians). Kenny concludes much more cautiously that there is no reason to reject the hypothesis that twelve of the Pauline letters are the work of a "single, unusually versatile author" (1986, 100). The main problem with stylometric analysis lies in the extent of the texts available. Short texts (even the longest of the Pauline letters are relatively short texts) do not usually prove long enough to arrive at statistically accurate assessments of the use of various stylistic features.

In an application of one form of stylometry to the **Shepherd of Hermas,* Colborne (1970) used the occurrence of various verb forms, which he found coincided with the following sections that he argued were probably composed by several authors: (1) *Visions* 1–5, (2) *Vision* 5, (3) *Mandates* 1–12.3.3, (4) *Mandates* 12.3.4 to the end of *Mandates,* (5) *Similitudes* 1–7, (6) *Similitude* 8, (7) *Similitude* 9. However, Colburne betrays no awareness of other stylometric studies, and his own results are presented in such an abbreviated form that it is impossible to critique it.

*Style, stylistics

———

Coleborne 1970; Grayston and Herdan 1960; Johnson 1974; Kenny 1966, 1986; Mealand 1988, 1989; Michaelson and Morton 1972, 1973; Morgenthaler 1958; Morton 1965, 1966, 1978; Morton and Winspear 1971; Wake 1948, 1957; C. B. Williams 1970

Subgenre, the subtypes into which a genre can be divided. There are, for example, several subgenres of the ode: anacreontic, epithalamic (wedding), or genethliac (birthday). According to Fowler (1982, 112): "Division of kinds into subgenres normally goes by subject matter or motifs. In fact, they are formed in just the opposite way from that which produces modes: subgenres have the common features of the kind—external forms and all—and, over and above these, add special substantive features." The Gospels are sometimes regarded as a subgenre of Greco-Roman biography, just as Acts or Luke–Acts is regarded as a subgenre of the Greek *novel or of Hellenistic *historiography.

*Genre, *Mode

———

A. Fowler 1982, 111–18

Succession literature (see *Diogenes Laertius)

Synkrisis (see *Comparison)

Symbouleutic rhetoric (see *Deliberative rhetoric)

Symmetrical structure in literary composition may consist of four main types (Bar-Efrat 1980): (1) The parallel pattern, as in *parallelismus membrorum* (e.g., A - A'), (2) the ring pattern (e.g., A - B - A'), (3) the chiastic pattern (A - B - B' - A'), and (4) the concentric pattern (A - B - C - B' - A'). One can argue (Menken 1985, 3) that just two basic types are involved here, the parallel pattern (A - A') and the concentric pattern (A - B - A').

*Chiasmus, *Parallelism, *Ring composition

———

Bar-Efrat 1980; Menken 1985

Synecdoche, a transliteration of the Latin word *synecdoche,* borrowed from the Greek word συνεκδοχή ("understanding one thing with another"), a figure of speech in which a part represents the whole, the cause the effect, or the effect the cause. In the LXX, the term σῶμα, "body," is used as a synonym for the personal pronoun με, "me" (Gen. 47:12; Job 6:4). Similarly, σῶμα can be used to refer to the whole person in the LXX (Zeisler 1983, 138–43). When Paul says that he preached circumcision, he meant that he was an advocate of Torah observance (Gal. 5:11). Paul and other early Christian authors frequently use the term "foreskin" (ἀκροβυστία) to refer to the Gentiles (Rom. 2:26; 3:20, 30; 4:9–11; Gal. 2:7; Col. 3:11; Eph. 2:11; *Barn.* 13:7) and "circumcision" (περιτομή) to refer to Jews (Rom. 3:30; 4:9, 12; 15:8; Gal. 2:7–9; Col. 3:11).

Mitchell 1994

Symposium, originally the Greek social custom of "drinking together" just before a banquet attended by men only, included lively conversation, entertainment, perhaps drunkenness and lewdness, and was held in the ἀνδρών ("male apartment") found in nearly every Greek home. In Rome the host frequently met his guests at the baths before bringing them to his home. The symposium was developed into a loosely structured literary form used to frame table conversation, dialogues, discourses, and other short literary forms. The symposium form was used by many ancient authors, including Plato, Xenophon, Aristotle, Plutarch, Lucian, and Athenaeus. While the Gospels mention meals shared by Jesus and his followers, only Luke and John have used the symposium as a short constituent literary form (Aune 1987, 122). Luke took over or shaped existing Synoptic tradition into five symposia: (1) 5:29–39; (2) 7:36–50; (3) 11:37–54 (Steele 1984); (4) 14:1–24 (de Meeüs 1961; Donahue 1988, 140; Braun 1995); (5) 22:14–38. In the Fourth Gospel, John 13–16 is an extensive dialogue between Jesus and his disciples that constitutes a symposium, with Jesus himself functioning as the host (13:5–12). The dramatis personae in a symposium include the host, a person who functions as the chief guest or guest of honor, and other lesser guests, while the structure may include the gradual disclosure of the identity of the guests and an action or statement that provokes comment and a main discourse (adapted from Steele 1984). Particularly gracious hosts anoint their guests with perfume (Xenophon, *Sym.* 2.3–4; Luke 7:44–46). One of the favorite themes of symposium literature was love (e.g., Plato, *Symposium;* Xenophon, *Symposium;* Luke 7:42, 47; John 13:34–35; 14:23–24; 15:9–13).

Aune 1978, 53–54; 1987, 122; Berger 1984a, 256; 1984b, 1310–15; Braun 1995; Delobel 1966; Heil 2000; Martin 1931; de Meeüs 1961; Murray (ed.) 1990; Steele 1984; Sterling 1992, 370–71

Synopses of the Gospels, or Gospel parallels, typically arrange the text of the Synoptic Gospels (sometimes the Gospel of John is also included) in parallel columns so that the similarities and differences between them is evident. One of the more recent and highly specialized of such synopses is *The Critical Edition of Q* (Robinson, Hoffmann, and Kloppenborg [eds.] 2000). Earlier, one of the more elaborate synopses is that by Robert W. Funk, *New Gospel Parallels,* 2 vols. (Philadelphia: Fortress, 1985). Funk treats each of the Gospels in turn as a primary text in the left-hand column with parallels located in columns spread to the right. He not only treats each of the canonical Gospels in this way, but he also does the same for the *Gospel of Thomas,* the *Dialogue of the Savior,* the *Apocryphon of James,* the *Infancy Gospel of Thomas,* the *Infancy Gospel of James,* the *Gospel of Peter,* the *Acts of Pilate,* and the various fragmentary gospels. This tool is extremely helpful, though limited by the fact that it publishes all texts in English translation only.

Synoptic Gospels is a modern designation for the first three canonical Gospels, *Matthew, *Mark, and *Luke. The fact that Matthew is first in the traditional canonical arrangements reflects the view that Matthew was the first of the Gospels to be written, held by the fathers of the church from the 2d cent. on (Irenaeus, *Adv. haer.* 3.11.7; Eusebius, *Hist. eccl.* 5.8.2–4; see Goodacre 2001, 76–81). Origen actually held that the Gospels were written in the order Matthew, Mark, Luke, John (Origen in Eusebius, *Hist. eccl.* 6.25; Augustine, *De consensu evangelistarum* 1.1.3: "primus Mattheus, deinde Marcus, tertio Lucas, ultimo Iohannes"). Clement of Alexandria, on the other hand, regarded Mark as having been written after Matthew and Luke (Eusebius, *Hist. eccl.* 6.14.5–7).

*Gospels, literary genre of, *Titles

Goodacre 2001

Targum (pl. Targumim), a transliterated form of the Hebrew word that means "translation." Targumim may be defined as oral paraphrastic Aramaic translations of the Torah that were eventually written from the 4th through the 6th cent. C.E. They are categorized by some scholars as translations, by others as a type of midrash, and by yet others as a unique type of Jewish biblical interpretation.

Origins of the Targumim. As a result of the conquest of Judah by the Neo-Babylonian empire in 586 B.C.E., many inhabitants of Judah were taken into exile, where Aramaic, the lingua franca of the ancient Near East and the official language of the Persian Empire, already known among some strata of Judean society

(2 Kgs. 18:26–28=Isa. 36:11–13), became the first language of the Jewish exiles (cf. Neh. 13:24), eclipsing Hebrew, which continued to be used in liturgy. However, the later books of the OT, together with the many Hebrew works among the Dead Sea Scrolls, indicate that Hebrew was still spoken and used, at least in some circles. Since people could no longer understand Hebrew well, the reading of the Torah in Hebrew in synagogues came to be accompanied by an oral paraphrastic translation of the Hebrew text in Aramaic by a *meturgeman* ("translator"). Nehemiah 8:2–8, where Ezra the scribe reads the Torah and a group of 13 Levites helped the people to understand the law in a liturgical setting, is regarded in rabbinic Judaism as the origin of the Targum (*b. Meg.* 3a). The rabbinic rules for delivering Targumim in the synagogue emphasize the distance between Torah and Targum. Scripture was read in Hebrew, while the Targum was recited orally in Aramaic by the *meturgeman,* and two different people had to perform these two functions. The Sabbath reading of the Torah and the Prophets was already established in the 1st cent. C.E., as two passages in the NT attest. According to Luke 4:16–30, after standing up to read Isa. 61:1–2 (later called *haphtarah*), Jesus sat down and delivered a brief homily loosely linked to that text. In Acts 13:15, after the reading from the Law (later called *parasha*) and the Prophets (*haphtarah*), the rulers of the synagogue in Pisidian Antioch ask Paul and his companions if they have any "word of exhortation" for the people, which Paul presents in vv. 16–41. The Mishnah (*Meg.* 4) contains the earliest description of the reading of Scripture in the synagogue. Each reader was accompanied by a translator (*meturgeman*), who provided from memory an oral paraphrastic translation following the reading of each verse of the Torah and after the reading of every third verse of the Prophets.

Character of the Targumim. Targumim are *implicit* interpretations of Scripture (like the types of *Rewritten Bible), in which no distinction is made between the original text and the paraphrastic additions of the translator. Implicit interpretation may be contrasted to *explicit* interpretation (e.g., the Qumran *pesharim and rabbinic *midrash) in which the text of Scripture is quoted followed by a commentary.

There are Targumim on the Torah (the most important), the Prophets, and the Writings, though the Targumim are by no means a unified corpus of rabbinic literature (Le Déaut 1989, 584). Targums vary considerably with respect to whether they are literal (i.e., no more than an Aramaic translation of the biblical text, like the Qumran Targumim) or paraphrastic. The targumic technique, according to Le Déaut (1989, 585), exhibits a twofold concern: (1) to make the biblical text immediately comprehensible and (2) to make it alive and relevant to the audience in a synagogue. Targumic methods include the following (Ribera 1994; Le Déaut 1989, 584–89): (1) The syntax of the Hebrew text can be modified. (2) Obscure words and expressions are interpreted. (3) In the interest of clarity the literal meaning of a metaphor or allegory can be given. (4) Questions that might arise in the mind of the listener are sometimes answered in the paraphrastic translation itself. (5) Anthropomorphic conceptions of God are avoided, as is the pronunciation of the divine name (terms like *Memra* ["Word"], *Kabod* ["Glory"], and *Shekinah,* ["Presence"], are used as substitutions for the divine name). (6) In the interests of making the text contemporary and relevant, conceptions involving messianism, eschatology, and angelology are folded into the text. (7) Sometimes paraenetic material is inserted into the text.

Targumim exist for all parts of the Hebrew Bible except Ezra–Nehemiah and Daniel. The Targum Onkelos or Babylonian Targum is the Aramaic paraphrastic translation and interpretation of the Torah that had the highest status in Judaism. The Palestinian Targumim of the Pentateuch, which did not exist in a single unified recension, has two forms. The complete form is called Pseudo-Jonathan or the Targum Yerushalmi I, in the recension of Codex Neofiti 1. The incomplete form consists of about 850 verses and is called the Fragmentary Targum or the Targum Yerusalmi II.

Dating the Targumim. While targumic literature was written down from the 4th cent. C.E. to the Middle Ages, the origins of much of the content of the Targumim may be much earlier. The discovery of fragments of written Targumim among the Dead Sea Scrolls (including 4QtgLev, 4QtgJob, and 11QtgJob (Sokoloff 1974), the latter an Aramaic "translation" of Job 17:14–42:11, not much longer than the Hebrew text, in 38 fragmentary columns, written in the mid-1st cent. C.E., but perhaps dating from the 2d cent. B.C.E.) indicates that Targumim existed much earlier than was once thought.

*Midrash, *Pesharim, *Rabbinic literature

Beattie and McNamara (eds.) 1994; Diéz Merino 1994; Le Déaut 1982, 1989; McNamara 1966, 1972; Ribera 1994; Sokolof 1974

Testament literature (see *Farewell address)

Testament of Moses (see *Pseudepigrapha, OT)

Testaments of the Twelve Patriarchs is a collection of twelve pseudepigraphical testaments attributed to the twelve sons of Jacob. The *Testaments* are problematic because they were composed as Jewish religious literature (perhaps by the mid-2d cent. C.E.) but were taken over and given a Christian redaction and transmitted exclusively by Christians. Several fragments of testament literature in Qumran have been discovered, including the Aramaic *Testament of Judah* (4QTestament of Judah=3Q7; 4QApocryphon of Judah=4Q538); the Aramaic *Testament of Joseph* (4QApocryphon of Joseph=4Q539); the Aramaic *Testament of Levi* (1QAramaic Levi=1Q21; 4QAramaic Levi[a]=4Q213; 4QAramaic Levi[b]=4Q214; 4QAaronic Text A=Testament of Levi[c]=4Q540; 4QAaronic Text A=Testament of Levi[d]=4Q541); and the Hebrew *Testament of Naphtali* (4QTestament of Naphtali=4Q215). The Aramaic *Levi,* at least, may go back to the 2d cent. B.C.E. (de Jonge 1979–80, 514–15). The present text of the *Testaments,* however, was written in Greek (de Jonge 1979–80, 516).

The *Testaments* were written with a primarily paraenetic purpose, with the lives of the individual patriarchs providing examples to be followed or avoided. Predictions of the future reveal what will happen to those who obey and those who disobey the commandments of God, and it is here that the obviously Christian features occur frequently. There is no mention of Sabbath observance, dietary laws, or circumcision. The author warns against the dangers of women. De Jonge has argued that a Sin-Exile-Return pattern (originally a Deuteronomic pattern) is found in the *Testaments* (e.g., *T. Asher* 7:1–7; *T. Levi* 10, 14–15, 16). The opening and closing sections of each of the *Testaments* were influenced by Gen. 49:1–2, 29–33, and 50:24–26.

*Farewell address, *Peter, Second Letter of, *Pseudepigrapha, OT, *Timothy, Second Letter to, **Levi, Testament of*

Becker 1970; Charles 1908; de Jonge 1975, 1993, 1995; Hultgård 1977; Jervell 1969; Kee 1977–78; Slingerland 1977; Ulrichsen 1991.

Testimonia are discrete passages of OT texts selected in their value for demonstrating that aspects of the life and ministry of Jesus were prophetically anticipated in the OT as occurring at the end of days, transmitted both orally and in writing. This is the promise-and-fulfillment understanding of the OT. Such compilations may have been useful in a variety of contexts (e.g., teaching, preaching, apologetics, debate). Two documents from Qumran that are analogous collections of messianic texts are 4Q Testimonia (an anthology of biblical passages including Deut. 5:28; 18:18–19; Num. 24:15–17; Deut. 33:8–11; Josh. 6:26) and 4QFlorilegium (2 Sam. 7:10–14; Ps. 1:1; 2:1–2; see Fitzmyer 1974c). The meaning scholars have given to the term testimonia has varied. In recent usage, distinctions are drawn between an individual testimonium and a collection of them called a testimonia collection; and between testimonia—which "prove" a theological claim—and *extracta,* which are simply excerpts of Scripture serving nonforensic purposes (Albl 1999, 7). There is abundant evidence that both Greco-Roman and Jewish authors in antiquity composed collections of excerpts from authoritative works for a variety of purposes, often for use in their own subsequent compositions (cf. Xenophon, *Memorabilia* 1.6.14; Plutarch, *Moralia* 457D–E; Cicero, *De inventione* 2.4; 4QTestimonia [4Q175]; 4QTanhumim [4Q176]). While there is no direct evidence for the existence of Christian testimonia collections before the 3d cent. C.E., the use of such collections has been surmised, based on the presence in the NT and patristic writings of OT quotations that are composite, are falsely attributed, deviate from the LXX and other known versions, occur in the same order in independent authors, contain interpretive comments, or are taken out of context. These characteristics support the claim that the authors are not working directly from manuscripts of Scripture but from an intermediary document, i.e., a testimonia collection. Such a hypothesis is plausible, given the widespread practice of creating collections of excerpts in antiquity and the practical benefits such collections would hold for early Christian leaders; e.g., they would be easier to carry and copy than scrolls containing portions of the OT (Albl 1999, 66–67). Although testimonia frequently deviated from the exact wording of known OT texts, they seem to have carried the same authority, as can be seen from the fact that many NT books (Matthew, the Pauline Epistles, 1 Peter) appear to cite them frequently.

R. J. Harris argued for a single "Testimony Book" used by the early church (Harris 1916–20), while C. H. Dodd (Dodd 1952) and

B. Lindars (Lindars 1961) conceived of the testimonia as circulating only orally. These theses have been discarded in favor of the existence of many small written collections of testimonia. Such collections may have consisted of bare lists of OT passages or lists with commentary and exegesis, or even as dialogues, homilies, and hymns.

Much of the scholarship on testimonia has focused on their apologetic use in Christian debate with the Jewish community, i.e., in an effort to prove from Scripture that Jesus was the Messiah (Lindars 1961). This function has probably been overemphasized. Testimonia likely functioned in a variety of settings, including evangelism, catechesis, worship, and composing new texts.

*Anthological style, *Quotations, *Testimony book hypothesis

Albl 1999; Barnard 1967b; Daniélou 1966; Dodd 1952; Fitzmyer 1957, 1974c; Gamble 1995, 24–28; Glasson 1975; J. R. Harris 1916–20; Hodgson 1979; Hommes 1935; R. Kraft 1960; Lindars 1961, 1964; Plooij 1932; Prigent 1961; Skarsaune 1987; Sundberg 1959

JON BERGSMA

Testimony book hypothesis The hypothesis that written, authoritative collections of scriptural excerpts (*extracta*) underlay NT and patristic writings was first proposed by Hatch (1889). The hypothesis was well received in Britain (Albl 1999, 16–17) and by some German scholars (Harnack 1890; Vollmer 1895), although many others responded quite negatively (Wrede 1891; Ungern-Sternberg 1913). Ungern-Sternberg dismissed the possibility of written *extracta* collections and proposed instead that OT texts were transmitted by oral tradition clustered around two topics: the person of Christ (*de Christo*), and Christian claims vis-à-vis the Jews (*de Evangelio*). Bousset (1915) extended Ungern-Sternberg's arguments by stressing the "school" setting in which he supposed the oral tradition was transmitted.

British scholarship. Growing British support for the idea of written collections, designated testimonia by Burkitt (1907), culminated in the influential work of Harris (1916–20), who proposed the existence of a single "Testimony Book" used by early Christian authors. Accepting the popular British identification of Papias's enigmatic Matthean "logia" as a testimonia collection, Harris argued that a "Testimony Book" was composed by Matthew and circulated under his authority. In support of his theory, Harris cited patristic writings that showed topical arrangement of scriptural proof texts, and called attention to the unusual form of many patristic and NT quotations, suggesting that the authors were not copying directly from any known version of the OT but from an intermediary source. Harris was supported by several English and Dutch scholars (Findlay 1933; Plooij 1932; Bakker 1933), though German scholars were less receptive (Hommes 1935; Michel 1929), pointing out that Harris could not demonstrate the existence of a single testimony book, and the deviant OT quotations in the NT could also be attributed to the creativity of the NT writers.

After World War II, the testimonia debate picked up again. Hunt (1951) argued that the testimonia collections were written and served as the underlying structure for the composition of the Gospels. Hunt's work, however, was eclipsed by the work of C. H. Dodd (1952), who rejected the notion of Harris and others that the testimonia constituted written sources. Dodd emphasized the role of oral tradition and argued that the OT context from which a testimonium was taken was often significant for interpreting the citation in its new context.

Krister Stendahl. The discovery and publication of the Dead Sea Scrolls had a profound influence on the testimonia debate and revised notions of early Jewish and early Christian OT exegesis, particularly the publication of the Qumran pesher commentary on Habakkuk (1QpHab). Stendahl used 1QpHab as the model for the exegetical practice of a Matthean "school," which he hypothesized was responsible for the composition of the first Gospel (this aspect of his work has been widely rejected). Stendahl rejected the notion of written or oral testimonia collections, instead ascribing the unique deviations of Matthean quotations to the "school's" creative exegesis. Ironically, the work of Dodd and Stendahl moved interest away from written testimonia collections, just when the Dead Sea Scrolls were providing analogies for such works. The publication of 4QTestimonia (Allegro 1956) and subsequent commentary on it and similar finds (Fitzmyer 1957) renewed interest in possible written sources for the early Christian quotations. Lindars (1961) disregarded such finds, choosing instead to build on Dodd's model of oral tradition. Lindars placed the development of the testimonia firmly in the life setting of Christian-Jewish debate. He thought that up to four layers of oral tradition—corresponding to slightly different life settings and theological developments—could be recovered from the present form of OT quotations in the NT.

Patristic scholarship. New support for written *testimonia* collections came from the work of patristic scholars. Prigent (1961) and others (Barnard 1967b, Kraft 1960) working on the *Epistle of Barnabas* argued for the existence of written, authoritative testimonia collections as early as the NT writings, although there was no agreement on how they were produced. Daniélou (1966) synthesizing the findings of previous scholars, placed the testimonia within the life setting of "Jewish Christianity," positing that the authoritative collections of OT passages had Jewish precedents. These were used by NT authors but became more developed by the time of Cyprian (ca. 200–250 C.E.). Against Lindars, Daniélou argued that the testimonia functioned in a wide variety of settings—liturgy, catechesis, teaching—and not just in apologetics.

By the 1970s interest had waned in the testimonia debate, until Hodgson (1979) argued for written testimonia collections, based on the Qumran evidence and the criteria for determining such sources dating back to Harris and Hatch, focusing on some NT letters. He later argued for the dependence of Q on a testimonia collection (Hodgson 1985). Skarsaune (1987), in a lengthy monograph on *Justin Martyr, concluded that authoritative *testimonia* collections were used by Justin's time and suggested that they attained such status even earlier. By suggesting that Justin used both biblical manuscripts and *testimonia* collections, Skarsaune moved the debate past a false either-or debate.

Other scholars dealt with the NT texts more directly. Juel (1988) proposed that the first testimonia were collected around the concept of Jesus as the royal (Davidic) messiah and that subsequent testimonia were added on other themes, providing the basis for the composition of the Gospels. Crossan (1988), impressed with the possibilities of testimonia collections as a source for narrative composition, dismissed any historical basis for the passion narratives, regarding them instead as free literary compositions inspired by collected prophetic texts.

The work of Martin Albl. Albl (1999) devoted a monograph to the form and function of the *testimonia* collections, bringing greater clarity to the debate by insisting on careful distinctions (a) between *midrash and the use of testimonia, and (b) between testimonia, which serve an apologetic purpose (proof of Christian doctrine), and *extracta*, which do not. After careful investigation of several testimonia traditions in the NT and patristic writings, Albl concludes that written testimonia collections were in existence already from the time of Jesus' earliest followers. They functioned in a variety of life settings and continued in use throughout the patristic period.

*Quotations, *Testimonia

Albl 1999; Allegro 1956; A. Bakker 1933; Barnard 1967b; Bousset 1915; Burkitt 1907; Crossan 1988; Daniélou 1966; Dodd 1952; Findlay 1933; Fitzmyer 1957; Glasson 1975; Harnack 1890; Hatch 1889; Hodgson 1979, 1985; Hommes 1935; Hunt 1951; Juel 1988; Kraft 1960; Lindars 1961, 1964; O. Michel 1929; Plooij 1932; Prigent 1961; Skarsaune 1967; Stendahl 1968; Sundberg 1959; Ungern-Sternberg 1913; Vollmer 1896; Wrede 1891

JON BERGSMA

Tetraevangelium, a collective designation for the fourfold Gospel or the collection of the four Gospels that must have occurred ca. 125 C.E.

Textual criticism is usually understood as the discipline that endeavors, as far as possible, to recover the original wording of a document, the actual words of an author (Renehan 1969, 2). Since all the books of the NT were written by hand and continued to be copied by hand until after the invention of movable type in the 15th cent., errors were frequently introduced. This conception is problematic, however, in cases in which there is no "original" text, such as in several of the plays of Shakespeare and the compositions of Mozart, each of whom made numerous changes in individual works (D. C. Parker 1997, 4–7). There are three categories of material used by textual critics: (1) Greek manuscripts (including papyri, uncials or majuscules, cursives or minuscules, and lectionaries), (2) versions, and (3) patristic citations.

*Critical editions, *Minuscules, *Papyrus, *Uncials, *Versions

---

Aland and Aland 1989; Aland and Delobel (eds.) 1994; Birdsall 1992; Greetham 1992; Maas 1958; Metzger 1992; D. C. Parker 1977, 1997; Renehan 1969.

Thanksgiving, epistolary In the Pauline letters, the epistolary thanksgiving is not simply a formal element; since it often praises the recipients, it simultaneously functions as an **exordium* securing their goodwill

(Aune 1987, 186). According to Schubert (1939, 173), the thanksgivings in the Pauline letters are examples of a widely used epistolary form in the Hellenistic world. Schubert proposed two types of thanksgiving in Paul (Ia and Ib), with four syntactical units or short cola common to both types (1939, 63): (1) the main verb εὐχαριστεῖν ("to give thanks"), (2) the personal object τῷ θεῷ ("to God"), (3) a temporal phrase or adverb, and (4) a pronominal object phrase περί or ὑπὲρ ὑμῶν ("for you").

The first type of thanksgiving period (Ia) adds three more syntactical units or short cola (Schubert 1939, 53–62): (5) temporal participial clause with a temporal adverbial phrase, (6) a causal participial clause or adverbial phrase, (7) a subordinate final clause introduced by ἵνα, ὅπως or εἰς + infinitive. Examples of the first type include Phlm. 4–7; 1 Thess. 1:2–5; Rom. 1:10; Eph. 1:15–16; Col. 1:3–4, 9–10; Phil. 1:3–11; 1 Thess. 3:9–10; 2 Thess. 1:11–12; 2 Cor. 1:11.

The second type of thanksgiving period (Ib), a variant of the first, does not have participial clauses, and its final clause is introduced by the causal ὅτι (Schubert 1939, 51–53). Examples of the second type include: 1 Cor. 1:4–5; Rom. 1:8; 2 Thess. 1:2–3; 2:13; 1 Thess. 2:13.

The thanksgiving section in 1 Thessalonians has proven extraordinarily difficult to analyze. Schubert (1939, 23–26) argued for a thanksgiving section in 1 Thess. 1:2–3:13, which he regarded as highly complex, extremely long, and with some extraneous matter in 2:14–16 (see *Interpolation), and which constituted the main body of the letter. There are, in fact, three thanksgivings in 1 Thessalonians (1:2–10; 2:13; 3:10–11). J. T. Sanders (1962, 355–56) argued that the thanksgiving section was confined to 1 Thess. 1:2–10.

*Letters, literary genre of

———

Artz 1994; Aune 1987, 185–86; Lambrecht 2000; O'Brien 1977; J. T. Sanders 1962; Schubert 1939

Theon of Alexandria, or Aelius Theon, probably flourished in the 1st cent. C.E. (Kennedy 1972, 616) and was the author of a number of rhetorical works, all of which have perished with the exception of the **Progymnasmata,* a somewhat mutilated work of introductory rhetorical exercises; it has been rearranged by a later hand and the end is missing. An Atticist (see *Atticism), his *Progymnasmata* consists of 15 exercises intended to prepare the student for *declamation as well as writing history and poetry. This is the oldest existing collection of elementary exercises and the most important surviving rhetorical manual of Alexandrian origin (Manuel Alexandre 1999, 83).

*Rhetorical handbooks, *Progymnasmata

———

Hock and O'Neill 1986, 2002; Kennedy 2003, 1–72

Theophany means "appearance of a god," is related to such other terms as "epiphany" and "hierophany" ("manifestation of the sacred"), and refers to traditional literary descriptions of the "coming" of God and its consequences. Theophanies are typically structured in two parts: the first speaks of God's coming, while the second describes the upsetting of the natural order (Jeremias 1965, 15). Theophanies in the OT are associated with sacred places, including springs, rivers, and trees, but particularly mountains, which were widely thought to represent links between the human world and the divine world (Clifford 1972). In the OT theophanies are linked to seismic and atmospheric phenomena, i.e., earthquakes, volcanic eruptions, fire, smoke, thunder, lightning, hail and rain, with the thunderstorm as the most prominent form in the older Israelite literature (Jörg Jeremias 1965, 100–111). In prophetic literature the thunderstorm is often the basis of theophanic imagery (Amos 1:2; Nah. 1:2–4; Zeph. 1:14–16). In the NT, theophanies take a quite different form. The theophany of the one like a son of man in Rev. 1:12–16 is based on descriptions of divine and angelic figures in Dan. 7:12–14 and 10:5–6, giving theophanic language intertextual links with the OT. The transfiguration scene narrated in Mark 9:2–13 and parallels depicts the transformation of Jesus, revealing him to be a divine figure both through the use of light imagery and by linking this transformation to the appearance of Elijah and Moses. Theophanies describe revelatory vision experiences in traditional imagery.

———

Clifford 1972; Jörg Jeremias 1965

Thesis, a transliteration of the Greek word θέσις ("laying down, situation, position"), is a Greek rhetorical term for the basic question at issue formulated in an abstract manner, i.e., a *quaestio infinita* or *quaestio generalis* ("general question"). Quintilian (3.5.5–11) gives an example of a θέσις ("Should a person marry?), in contrast with a ὑποθέσις or basic question at issue formulated as a *quaestio finita* or "particular question" ("Should Cato marry?"). θέσεις were primarily the concern of philosophy (Cicero, *De inventione* 1.8; Lausberg 1998, §70). In general, rhetorical theorists were more interested in ὑποθέσεις than θέσεις for the purpose of training orators. By the 1st cent. C.E., θέσεις became a standard exercise in the progymnasmata (Quintilian 2.4.24–32; Theon, *Progym.* 12; Aphthonius, *Progym.* 13). A declamation on a "thesis" could have eight parts (Mack 1990, 42): (1) introduction, (2) proposition, (3) reason, (4) opposite (contrary), (5) analogy (comparison), (6) example, (7) citation (authority), (8) conclusion.

*Declamation, *Progymnasmata

R. D. Anderson 2000, 63–65; Lausberg 2000, §§68–78

Thessalonians, First Letter to the, is probably the earliest of the Pauline letters, written ca. 49 C.E., from Corinth. Paul intended that the letter be read to the congregation (5:27), and he therefore crafted it for recitation in both an oral and liturgical context.

Authorship. First Thessalonians is a genuine letter of Paul, and apparently the earliest one he wrote. Modern scholars generally accept the authenticity of the letter, though F. C. Baur and some of his students rejected it as inauthentic. The superscript of 1 Thessalonians names Paul, Silvanus, and Timothy as *cosenders (all were involved in the founding of the church at Thessalonica according to Acts 17:1–15, if "Silas"="Silvanus"). The only cue to the importance of Paul in this group is the fact that he is listed first. The first-person plural is used throughout, with the exception of the first-person singular referring to Paul in 2:18 ("I, Paul"), 3:5 ("when I could bear it no longer, I sent that I might know your faith"), and 5:27 ("I adjure you by the Lord that this letter be read to all the brethren"). The last reference conforms to Paul's practice of adding a personal postscript to letters (1 Cor. 16:21–24; Gal. 6:11–18; Phlm. 19–25). Timothy is referred to in the third person in 3:2, 6 as a deliberate device to include all the senders. According to Byrskog (1996, 236–38), the shifts to the first-person singular reflect a deliberate choice to single out one person, just as the use of the first-person plural is a deliberate move to include others; all uses of the first-person plural are "real" (i.e., not editorial) and and are used in two ways: (1) to associate the senders with the recipients (3:11a, 13; 4:14; 5:9b, 23c, 28) and (2) to include the senders (all other instances).

Epistolary analysis. First Thessalonians can be characterized as a paraenetic letter (Malherbe 1983; 1992, 292; Stowers 1986, 96; Aune 1987, 203). According to Malherbe (1992, 292),

> 1 Thessalonians 1–3 thus exhibits the characteristics of a paraenetic letter. The description of the readers as μιμηταί ["imitators"], the theme of remembrance of what is already known, expressed by οἴδατε ["you know"] and μνημονεύετε ["remember"], the description of Paul himself in antithetical style, the theme of *philophronesis,* all contribute to this conclusion.

Some have characterized 1 Thess. as a letter of friendship (Schoon-Janssen 1991, 39–47; 2000, 182–90), while Chapa (1994) regards it, with some hesitation, as a letter of consolation, as does Johanson (1987, 165–66, 189). First Thessalonians begins with an epistolary prescript (1:1) that is relatively brief for a Pauline letter. The prescript consists of three constituent elements (see *Prescriptions, epistolary): (1) *superscriptio:* "Paul, Silvanus, and Timothy"; (2) *adscriptio:* "to the church of the Thessalonians in God the Father and the Lord Jesus Christ"; (3) *salutatio:* "Grace to you and peace." Since 1 Thessalonians is very probably the earliest of Paul's letters, the source of the elements in this epistolary prescript is an important yet puzzling question to which no satisfactory answer is possible. The superscript, which contains three names with no epithets, is identical to that found in 2 Thess. 1:1. Other superscriptions in the Pauline letters (whether authentically Pauline or not), with the exception of Phil. 1:1, include various epithets that identify the sender(s). Romans 1:1–6 has the longest qualifying phrases among the genuine Pauline letters, while Titus 1:1 has the longest among the Pauline pseudepigrapha.

The thanksgiving period, which begins in v. 2, is difficult to analyze. Schubert (1939, 23–26) argued that it extended from 1:2 to 3:13 and regarded it as highly complex, and extremely long, with some extraneous matter in 2:14–16 (see *Interpolation). In fact, he regarded the thanksgiving as constituting the body of 1 Thessalonians, i.e., "the thanksgiving *is* the letter" (Schubert 1939, 26). J. T. Sanders (1962, 355–56) argued that the thanksgiving section should be confined to 1 Thess. 1:2–10 but then blends into a narrative that continues from 2:1 to 3:8 and ends with a thanksgiving in 3:9–10. The ending recapitulates the earlier thanksgiving in 1:2–10 and also refers back to the reference to "seeing the face" of the Thessalonians in 2:17. The whole section from 1:2 to 3:13 is very skillfully put together.

Outline and structure. The structure of 1 Thessalonians is also problematic. According to Krenz (*ABD* 6.515), there are three major parts in 1 Thessalonians: (1) the epistolary opening (1:1–5); (2) the body of the letter (1:6–5:22), which falls into two parts (Lambrecht 2000, 136–37): (a) Paul's relationship to the church at Thessalonica (1:6–3:13) and (b) Paul exhorting the recipients to live in a way pleasing to God, aware that Christ may return momentarily (4:1–5:22); (3) the epistolary ending (5:23–28). The strength of this outline lies in part in the fact that each section concludes with a prayer (3:11–13 and 5:23–24). The first prayer (3:11–13) contains three aorist optatives, the second (5:24–25) two. The term "blameless" occurs in both prayers, as does the phrase "at the coming of our Lord Jesus." The probable function of these prayers within the letter is to signal the end of one emphasis, thus providing formal conclusions for each of the two main sections of the letter.

The outline discussed above is problematic as well, however, in that the epistolary opening is restricted to 1:1–5. As mentioned above, the thanksgiving period in this letter has proven extraordinarily difficult to analyze. While it clearly begins in 1:2 (following the epistolary superscript in 1:1), it has no natural ending until 1:10, where a new textual unit is indicated at 2:1 by the phrase "For you yourselves know" (J. T. Sanders 1962, 355–56; J. L. White 1972, 68–91). Sanders finds a second thanksgiving that begins in 2:13 and ends at 3:13. The first section of the letter (1:2–3:13), then, is dominated by a extensive narrative section (1:2–3:10), which is framed as a thanksgiving (1:2–10 and 3:9–10) and concludes with an intercessory prayer (3:11–13). Within the larger narrative (1:2–3:10), the first part (1:2–2:16) deals with the positive experiences that Paul and his coworkers had in Thessalonica, and the second part (2:17–3:10), framed by references to "seeing the face" of the Thessalonians (2:17 and 3:10), narrates the experiences of Paul and his coworkers after they left Thessalonica for Athens. In fact this absence from Thessalonica, combined with Paul's concern for their welfare, constitutes the reason for writing the letter. Part of the earlier narrative in the first section (1:2–2:16) had been traditionally understood as an apology (specifically 2:1–12), with the antithetical style present in vv. 3–8 understood as reflecting Paul's clash with opponents; but this reading was overturned by the proposal that Paul's language was based on the topos of a philosopher depicting himself as a model to be imitated (Malherbe 1970, 1989a, 35–48). The apologetic interpretation of 1 Thess. 2:1–12 is now widely rejected (Donfried 2000; Hoppe 2000), and the mirror reading of antithetical language is treated with more caution than previously (Lyons 1985, 184; Walton 1995, 244).

Rhetorical analysis. Regardless of what type of letter 1 Thessalonians is, Wuellner argues that in the analysis of 1 Thessalonians epistolography should be subordinated to rhetoric (1990, 117), a position that is problematic in view of the obviously epistolary features of the letter. Lyons (1985, 219–21), Jewett (1986, 72–76), Hughes (1900), Wuellner (1990), Wanamaker (1990, 48–50), Walton (1995, 250), and Schoon-Jansen (2000, 192–93) have argued that 1 Thessalonians belongs to the epideictic genre, because epideictic focuses on praise and blame; in 1 Thessalonians the author frequently praises the recipients for their exemplary behavior (1:2–3, 6–10; 2:13–14, 19–20; 3:6–9; 4:1–2, 9–10). Kennedy (1984, 102) regards it as a deliberative letter, while Johanson (1987, 165–66, 189) regards 1 Thessalonians as a letter emphasizing consolation with corrrection without reproof (cf. Chapa 1994), and thus basically deliberative. This kind of disagreement is symptomatic of the rhetorical approach to the Pauline letters and reflects the inability of such an approach to deal with their epistolary and rhetorical complexities. In this case, Lambrecht (2000, 177) is correct in arguing that on the basis of the situation in Thessalonica (see *Rhetorical situation), a choice between epideictic and deliberative language is unnecessary and should be avoided. Others have questioned the analysis of a *letter,* such as 1 Thessalonians, using the categories of *oral rhetorical discourse* (G. L. Green 2002, 69–72; see also Kern 1998 on Galatians). One problem with ancient *epistolography, however, is that while it labels various kinds of letters ("thankful," "friendly," "consoling," "apologetic," etc.), no particular *dispositio,* i.e., structure or *arrangement is discussed or recommended by the epistolary theorists (Classen 2000, 7, 19).

Integrity. While there is no doubt that this letter was written by Paul, 2:13–15 is regarded by a number of scholars as a non-Pauline interpolation (Pearson 1971; Boers 1975–76; Schmidt 1983), though Schippers (1966) has argued that 1 Thess. 2:13–16 is "pre-synoptic"

Comparing the Two Intercessory Prayers of 1 Thessalonians

1 Thess. 3:11–13	1 Thess. 5:23–24
[11] Now may our God and Father himself, and our Lord Jesus, direct [κατευθύναι] our way to you, [12] and may the Lord make you increase πλεονάσαι and abound [περισσεύσαι] in love to one another and to all men, as we do for you,	[23] Now may the God of peace himself sanctify ἁγιάσαι wholly;
[13] so that he may establish your hearts *unblamable* in holiness before our God and Father, *at the coming of our Lord Jesus* with all his saints.	and may your spirit and soul and body be kept [τηρηθείη] sound and *blameless at the coming of our Lord Jesus* Christ. [24] He who calls you is faithful; and he will do it.

tradition that Paul himself has reshaped for its present context.

A more serious issue is whether 1 Thessalonians is really a combination of two Pauline letters. Eckart (1961) maintained, without argument, that 1 Thess. 3:11–13 is an epistolary conclusion, while Schmithals (1965) argued that 1 Thess. 3:10–4:1 constitutes the epistolary conclusion. The argument turns on the comparative analysis of Pauline epistolary conventions and is therefore of some significance. Demke (1973), working with the two-letter hypothesis proposed in different ways by Eckard and Schmithals, and thinking to overcoming the negative critique of Kümmel (1962), argued that in the postapostolic period an unknown author took two letters of Paul and joined them, making a two-part composition. The first part (1:2–3:13) focuses on the apostle as witnessed to by the church, while the second part (4:1–5:28) uses apostolic tradition to provide encouragement for faithful perseverance.

*First-person plural, *Letters, Pauline, *Thessalonians, Second Letter to the

———

Boers 1975–76; Byrskog 1996; Chapa 1994; R. F. Collins 1984, 1990; Demke 1973; Donfried 2000; Donfried and Beutler (eds.) 2000; Eckart 1961; Frame 1912; G. L. Green 2002; Hester 1996; Holtz 2000; Hoppe 2000;

Synopsis of Rhetorical Analyses of 1 Thessalonians

Rhetorical Arrangement	**Kennedy 1984, 142–44**	**Jewett 1986, 72–76**	**Olbricht 1990**	**Wuellner 1990, 128–35**	**Wanamaker 1990, 48–50**	**Hughes 1990; 109–16**
	Deliberative	**Epideictic**	**"Church Rhetoric"**	**Epideictic: Paradoxon Encomoion**	**Epideictic**	**Epideictic**
Epistolary Prescript	1:1	1:1–5	1:1		1:1	1:1–10
Exordium	1:2–10		1:2–3	1:1–10 (*insinuatio*)	1:2–10	
"Statement"			1:4–10			
Refutation of charges	2:1–8					
Narratio	2:9–3:13	1:6–3:13			2:1–3:10	2:1–3:10
Partitio or *Transitus*					3:11–13 *Transitus*	3:9–10 *Partitio*
Probatio or Headings	4:1–5:22	4:1–5:22	2:1–5:11	2:1–5:22	4:1–5:22	4:1–5:3
Peroratio or Epilogue	5:23–24	5:23–28	3:14–16	5:25–28	5:23–28	5:4–11
Exhortation	—		—			5:12–22
Epistolary Postscript	5:25–28		5:25–28			5:23–28

Hughes 1990; Jewett 1986; Johanson 1987; Koester 1979; Kümmel 1962; Lambrecht 2000; Lyons 1985; Malherbe 1983, 1987, 2000; Olbricht 1990; Pearson 1971; J. T. Sanders 1962; Schippers 1966; Schmithals 1965; Schoon-Janssen 1991, 2000; Schubert 1939; Walton 1995; Wanamaker 1990, 2000; Weima and Porter 1998; Winter 1993; Wuellner 1990

Thessalonians, Second Letter to the, a letter claiming to be written by Paul, Silvanus, and Timothy, is a letter closely related to *1 Thessalonians. The letter was apparently written to refute the false teaching of the disorderly members of the congregation, to reinterpret Paul's eschatological teaching (assuming that the letter is pseudepigraphical), and to bring peace to the congregations by enforcing obedience to Pauline tradition (Holland 1988, 129).

Authorship. While this letter has the same superscription as 1 Thessalonians, it is nevertheless widely thought to be a pseudepigraphical Pauline letter modeled after 1 Thessalonians. Much of the work on 2 Thessalonians has focused on the problem of authorship. First Thessalonians has often been regarded as a model for 2 Thessalonians (Marxsen 1982; Holland 1988, 152–54). The problem has been solved by reversing the order of composition of the two letters, but that only creates yet other problems (see Marxsen 1968, 41–42).

Integrity. The issue of the integrity of 2 Thessalonians is not frequently discussed. While Schmithals (1964) thinks that 2 Thessalonians is Pauline, he thinks that it has been produced by combining two separate Pauline letters: Letter A: 1:1–12+3:6–16; Letter B: 2:13–14+2:1–12+2:15+2:16–3:5+3:17–18 (Schmithals 1964, 307–8). The problem of the integrity of 2 Thessalonians revolves about the second thanksgiving in 2:13 (Marxsen 1982, 37–39). Sumney (1990) argues that 2 Thess. 1:3–3:5 fits the ABA pattern, which he argues, following Hurd, is a Pauline pattern of epistolary composition. Basically he argues that 2 Thess. 1:3–12 and 2:13–3:5 frame 2:1–12, which fits the ABA pattern and thus supports not only the integrity of the letter but also its authenticity.

Content and literary analysis. Second Thessalonians is framed as a letter, with the letter opening in 1:1–12, including the prescript (vv. 1–2) and the extensive thanksgiving (vv. 3–12), and the letter closing in 3:17–18. The body of the letter extends from 2:1 to 3:16. The first part of this main section (2:1–3:5) focuses on the problem of the imminent coming of Christ, while the second part is given over to paraenesis (3:6–16).

There is a striking similarity between 1 Thessalonians and 2 Thessalonians in both form and content (Bailey 1978, 133):

One of the problems of this analysis is Bailey's view that the benediction comes at the end of the body or central section of the letter, for then the sections on paraenesis in 2 Thess. 3:1–15 and 1 Thess. 4:1–5:22 are excluded from the body of the letter.

Rhetorical analysis. Hughes (1989, 51–74; see especially his rhetorical summary on 68–73) proposes a rhetorical analysis of 2 Thessalonians as a letter of deliberative rhetoric (which I present in abbreviated form):

I. *Exordium* (1:1–12)
   A. Epistolary prescript (1:1–2)
   B. Thanksgiving prayer (1:3–10)
   C. Intercessory prayer (1:11–12)
II. *Partitio* (2:1–2)
   A. Subjects to be dealt with in the *probatio* (2:1–2)

Bailey's Synopsis of the Structure of 1 Thessalonians and 2 Thessalonians

Letter Structure	2 Thessalonians	1 Thessalonians
A. Letter opening	1:1–12	1:1–10
1. Prescript	1:1–2	1:1
2. Thanksgiving	1:3–12	1:2–10
B. Letter body	2:1–16	2:1–3:13
1. Thanksgiving in the middle	2:13	2:13
2. Benediction at the end	2:16	3:11–13
C. Letter closing	3:1–18	4:1–5:28
1. *Paraenesis*	3:1–15	4:1–5:22
2. Peace wish	3:16	5:23–24
3. Greetings	3:17	5:26
4. Benediction	3:18	5:28

B. Point of disagreement (heresy to be refuted) (2:2)
III. *Probatio* (2:3–15)
A. First proof (*refutatio*) (2:3–12)
B. Second proof (2:13–15)
IV. *Peroratio* (stated as an intercessory prayer) (2:16–17)
A. Orant: Paul (2:16)
B. Persons prayed for: readers
C. Deities invoked
D. Aretalogy
E. Petitions
V. *Exhortatio* (3:1–15)
A. Command to pray for Paul (3:1–4)
B. Intercessory prayer (3:5)
C. Command to work (3:6–15)
VI. Epistolary postscript (3:16–17)
A. Intercessory prayer (3:16)
B. Authentication (3:17)
C. Final blessing (3:18)

Hughes recognizes that the exhortation in 3:1–15 is not a traditional part of a speech in the Greek and Latin rhetorical handbook tradition (1989, 63–66). He argues, following Kennedy (1984, 144–47), that deliberative rhetoric consists of exhortation and dissuasion, which makes it possible to account for the presence of exhortation.

Independently of Hughes, Holland (1988, 6–58; with detailed outline on 8–24) also proposed a rhetorical analysis of 2 Thessalonians, which he regarded as a deliberative letter:

I. Epistolary prescript (1:1–2)
A. Name of the principal sender
B. Names of the cosenders
C. Naming of the addressees
D. Salutation
II. *Exordium* (1:3–4)
A. Description of an act of thanksgiving
B. Description of an act of boasting
III. *Narratio:* Episode in the last judgment (1:5–12)
A. Evaluation of the narrative
B. The narrative: episode in the last judgment
C. Report of a prayer intercession
IV. *Probatio* (2:1–17)
A. Topic of *probatio* in the form of a doctrinal exhortation
B. Proofs of the falsehood of the disturbing message
C. Description of an act of thanksgiving
D. Conclusion
V. *Exhortatio* (3:1–13)
A. Request for intercessory prayer by addressees on behalf of author
B. Exhortation against the -τάκτοι
V. *Peroratio* (3:14–16)
A. Command for enforcing the content of the letter upon the congregation
B. Intercessory prayer wish for the peace of the congregation
VI. Epistolary postscript (3:17–18)
A. A formula of epistolary authentication
B. Explanation

A synopsis that compares the basic features of both Hughes (1989) and Holland (1988) with Jewett (1986) is presented in the table below (a modified version of Krentz, *ABD* 6.518). While these analyses all divide 2 Thessalonians into the five standard parts of an oration, some of the analyses appear to have forced the text of 2 Thessalonians into the Latin rubrics of this rhetorical structure. First, to label 1:5–12 (the second coming of Christ in judgment) a *narra-*

Synopsis of Rhetorical Analysis of 2 Thessalonians

Rhetorical Section	Jewett (1986, 82–85)	Holland (1988, 8–33)	Hughes (1989, 68–73)
Epistolary prescript		1:1–2	[1:1–2; part of *exordium*]
Exordium	1:1–12	1:3–4	1:1–12
Partitio	2:1–2		2:1–2
Narratio		1:5–12	
Probatio	2:3–3:5	2:1–17	2:3–15
Peroratio			2:16–17
Exhortatio	3:6–15	3:1–13	3:1–15
Peroratio	3:16–18	3:14–16	see above
Epistolary Postscript		3:17–18	3:16–17

tio is problematic, since it describes a *future,* not a past event. Further, it functions as an argument, providing a reason that those who afflict the Thessalonians will not go unpunished. Second, none of the three authors agrees on the textual boundaries of the *probatio* and *exhortatio* sections. The basis for making such decisions appears to have been relatively subjective.

*Letters, Pauline, *Thessalonians, Paul's First Letter to the

---

Bailey 1978; Holland 1988; Hughes 1989; Jewett 1986; Malherbe 2000; Marxsen 1982; Sumney 1990; Weima and Porter 1998; Wanamaker 1990

Third-person plural According to Wheeldon (1990, 37), the use of the third-person plural was a way of preserving "the impression of authority created in the preface and sustained the reader's expectation of an objective account of events."

*First-person plural, *"We"-passages

Wheeldon 1990

Thomas, Gospel of. The *Gospel of Thomas* (*Gos. Thom.*) is a collection of 114 sayings of Jesus that is part of the Nag Hammadi Codices (II,2); see *Nag Hammadi literature. This work has had a profound and lasting impact on the study of the sayings of Jesus in the canonical Gospels, and has also provided important insight into the problem of the genre of Q.

Coptic and Greek versions. The Coptic version is a collection of 114 logia or "sayings" of Jesus in Coptic, discovered among the books in the *Nag Hammadi Library. Greek was very probably the original language of the work. The three extant Greek fragments of the *Gospel of Thomas* are P. Oxy. 1, 654, and 655. While there is little doubt that the Coptic text and the Greek papyrus fragments are versions of the same work, the Coptic text was translated from a different Greek version than that represented by the extant Greek fragments (Valantasis 1997, 4).

Date and place of writing. Nag Hammadi Codex II, which contains the *Gospel of Thomas,* was dated ca. 350 to 425 C.E. by the original editors, who proposed that the Sahidic Coptic version was a translation and adaptation of an earlier text written in Greek no later than ca. 140 C.E., which in turn was based on even earlier sources (Guillaumont 1959, vi). The Greek fragment of *Thomas,* P. Oxy 1 is generally dated ca. 200 C.E., and the earliest clear quotation of *Thomas* is a variant of logion 4 quoted by Hippolytus (*Haer.* 5.7.20). While ca. 140 C.E. is the most widely held date for the composition or compilation of *Thomas* (and therefore when used involves no special pleading), Koester (1982, 2.152; 1989, 39; Blatz 1991, 1.113) and others have proposed pushing the date earlier, to within the 1st cent. C.E., arguing that "the absence of any influence from the canonical Gospels and the location of the Thomas tradition in Syria are strong arguments for this date and provenance." According to Blatz (1991, 1.113): "We can only say that there is much in favour of the view that Thomas originated about the middle of the 2d century in eastern Syria, although admittedly the collected sayings material may in part go back even into the 1st century." Grenfell and Hunt (1897, 18), the first editors of the Greek fragments, suggested a date of ca. 100 C.E. for the origin of the collection represented by the fragments. Davies (1983, 3, 16–17) has proposed dating the *Gospel of Thomas* to the mid-1st cent. (ca. 50–70 C.E.), since it shares the "sayings collection" genre with Q and presumably the same *Sitz im Leben;* he thinks a date later than 90 C.E. doubtful because of the relatively short life of oral tradition. Ménard (1975, 2–3) suggested that the work was composed "avant le début du IIIe siècle" (and in turn influenced the *Acts of Thomas,* composed between 200 and 250 C.E. in Edessa). Dates suggested for the *Gospel of Thomas* thus range between 60 and 200 C.E., though a reasonably likely date would be ca. 100–110 C.E. (Valantasis 1997, 13). The date of the composition of the Gospel of Thomas may have been as early as the late first century, while the place of origin is probably Syria.

Title. The *incipit of the work is "These are the secret sayings which the living Jesus spoke and which Didymus Judas Thomas wrote down," while the subscription at the end of the work reads "The Gospel according to Thomas," probably in imitation of the secondary titles of the canonical Gospels (Koester 1990, 20). While the majority of scholars regard the Synoptic Gospels as the precursors of the *Gospel of Thomas,* that is not the only way of construing their intertextual relationship. Some students of the *Gospel of Thomas,* for example, regard it as independent of the Synoptic Gospels (MacRae 1978).

Compilation theories. Since the *Gospel of Thomas* contains 114 random sayings, 51 of which (45 percent) have no significant verbal parallels in the Synoptics or John, the question of how the *Gospel of Thomas* was compiled is an important issue for research. The fact that there are many doublets in the *Gospel of Thomas* is indicative of a complex compositional history (3=113, 38=92, 48=106, 55=101, 56=80, 87=112). The possibility that it came into existence in stages is an issue that needs serious consideration (Schenke 1998; DeConick 2002). Crossan's bifurcation of *Thomas* into two strata recognizes the compositional and redactional complexity of the work. However, Crossan nowhere explains just what he means by *Gospel of Thomas* I and II, except for the general observation that one layer of *Thomas* was composed by the 50s C.E., and a second layer was added during the 60s or 70s "under the aegis of the Thomas authority" (Crossan 1991, 427). However, it is possible to fill in the blanks by consulting his data base at the end of the book (Crossan 1991, 427–50: "Appendix 1: An Inventory of the Jesus Tradition by Chronological Stratification and Independent Attestation"). By *Gospel of Thomas* I, Crossan apparently means the 66 logia (of a total of 114) that (in whole or in part) are listed in his data base as belonging to the first stratum of Gospel tradition (30–60 C.E.). All but one of these 66 logia have close parallels in the Synoptics or John. Of the remaining logia, 32 are assigned to *Gospel of Thomas* II (Crossan's second stratum, 60–80 C.E.), none of which has significant parallels in the Synoptics or John. To put it simply, *Gospel of Thomas* I contains sayings of Jesus with canonical parallels, while *Gospel of Thomas* II contains sayings of Jesus which do not have canonical parallels. This is an extremely simplistic way of analyzing the compositional stratigraphy of the *Gospel of Thomas.*

Genre. The genre of the *Gospel of Thomas* is the "sayings collection" or "chreia collection," which has a Christian generic analogy in the Q document, though no other generically similar self-contained collections of Jesus' sayings have come down to us in addition to Q and *Thomas.* However, when it is argued that since Q originated in the 50s of the 1st cent. C.E., *Thomas* must be equally early (Davies 1983, 3), certain differences between Q and *Thomas* have been overlooked. Though both documents are sayings collections, *Thomas* is a random collection of sayings with occasional catchword associations linking two or more logia, while Q is a more intentional literary composition made up of several complexes of carefully structured sayings (Kloppenborg 1987, 89–101; Piper 1989, 1994; Kirk 1998; Kloppenborg Verbin 2000). Thus while *Thomas* gives the impression of being a more primitive sayings collection than Q, that is an insufficient basis on which to place them in relative chronological order. The sayings of Jesus in the *Gospel of Thomas* have an order completely independent of the order of Jesus' sayings in the Synoptic Gospels (de Solanges 1979). This suggests that sayings in *Thomas* with parallels in the Synoptic Gospels have not been derived from them.

Thomas and early Christian literature. The *Gospel of Thomas* is conventionally divided into 114 sayings, or logia, most (but not all) of which begin with the introductory phrase "Jesus said." The arrangement of the stichoi in the manuscript is such that there was apparently a pronounced tendency on the part of the scribe to attempt to conclude sayings at the end of a stichos as much as possible. This occurs 47 times using the conventional enumeration of 114 logia (or 41 percent), and 64 times using the division into constituent sayings of 143 units (or 42.66 percent). Since sayings material from various sources is combined in many of the logia of *Thomas,* I have indicated this fact by dividing individual sayings into two or more constituent elements, which are labeled (for example 3a, 3b, and 3c), followed by the page and line numbers of the original Coptic manuscript. If each of the constituent sayings is counted (the six "Ears to Hear" sayings are separately listed, but not separately counted), there are 143 sayings units in *Thomas.* Of these 143 sayings, 70 (46.97 percent) have no reasonably close parallels in the canonical Gospels, but 7 have reasonably close extracanonical parallels. Sticking with the conventional logia divisions, of the 114 logia, 64 (56.14 percent), in whole or in part, have no reasonably close parallels in the canonical Gospels. Logion 38b is the only unit which has a reasonably close verbal parallel to the Gospel of John (7:34a, 36a).

*Gospels, Apocryphal, *Gospels, literary genre of

———

Aune 2002d; R. E. Brown 1962–63; Cameron (ed.) 1982; S. Davies 1983; DeConick 2002; Desjardins 1992; de Solanges 1979; Doran 1987; Fallon and Cameron 1988; Fieger 1991; Fitzmyer 1974a; Gärtner 1961; Hedrick 1989–90; Kaestli 1979; Kloppenborg 1987; B. Lincoln 1977; MacRae 1960; Ménard 1975; Riley 1994; Schenke 1998; Schrage 1964; Snodgrass 1989–90; Valantasis 1997; Wilson 1960

Gospel of Thomas Parallels in Early Christian Literature

* = No parallels in the canonical Gospels.
+ = Partial canonical parallels
# = Noncanonical parallels
// = Parallels elsewhere in *G.Thom.*

r = Redactional feature of a particular Gospel
Underlined: Close verbal parallels to *G.Thom.*

G.Thom. Logion	Contents	Parallels
***1** (80.12–14) =P. Oxy 654.1–5	**Interpreting these words**	Cf. John 8:51, 52b
***#2** (80.14–19) =P. Oxy 654.5–9	**Seeking and finding**	//*G.Thom.* 92a, 94; *Gospel of the Hebrews* 4b, 4a (Clement of Alexandria *Strom.* 5.14.96; 2.9.45)
***3a** (80.19–24) =P. Oxy 654.9–15	**Location of kingdom**	//*G.Thom.* 113
3b (80.25–26) =P. Oxy 654.15–16	**Kingdom is within**	L: Luke 17:21b (Tradition: J. Jeremias 1980, 266)
***3c**(80.26–81.5) =P. Oxy 654/16–21	**Know yourselves**	
***4a** (81.5–9) = P. Oxy 654.21–25	**The old ask the young**	//Hippolytus 5.7.20 (referring to the Gospel attributed to Thomas);
4b (81.9–10) =P. Oxy 654.25–7	**First last, last first**	T: Mark 10:31=Matt. 19:30 [first last, last first]=Luke 13:30 [last first, first last]; Matt. 20:16 [last first, first last]
***5a** (81.10–11) =P. Oxy 654.27–28	**Know what you see**	
5b (81.12–14) =P. Oxy 654.28–31	**Revealing the hidden**	//*G.Thom.* 6b (line 1) and *G.Thom.* 5b (line 2): verbatim agreement with Luke 8:17; Luke 12:2=Matt.10:26b; Mark 4:22=Luke 8:17
***6a** (81.14–17) =P. Oxy 654.32–36	**Four rules**	//*G.Thom.* 14a
***6b** (81.18–20) =P. Oxy 654.36–38	**Do not lie or hate**	
6c (81.21–23) =P. Oxy 654.38–40	**Revealing the hidden**	//*G.Thom.* 5; Lk 12:2=Matt. 10:26b; Mark 4:22=Luke 8:17
***7** (81.23–28) =P. Oxy 654.40–42	**Blessed is the lion**	
8a (81.28–82.2)	**Wise fisherman**	M: Matt. 13:47–50
8b (82.2–3)	**Ears to hear**	//*G.Thom.* 21.d; 24.b; 63.b; 65.b; 96.b; Mark 4:9=Matt. 13:9=Luke 8:8b; Mark 4:23=Matt. 13:43b; Matt. 11:15; Luke 14:35b; Rev. 2:7, 11, 17, 29; 3:6, 13, 22; 13:9
9 (82.3–13)	**The sower**	T: Mark 4:3–9=Matt. 13:3–9=Luke 8:5–8; *1 Clement* 24:5
10 (82.14–16)	**Fire on the earth**	L: Luke 12:49 (Tradition: J. Jeremias 1980, 223)
***11** (82.16–24)	**Dead or alive**	
***12** (82.25–30)	**James replaces Jesus**	
***13a** (82.30–83.7)	**Who is Jesus?**	Cf. Mark 8:27–30=Matt. 16:13–16=Luke 9:18–21;

Gospel of Thomas Parallels in Early Christian Literature (*cont.*)

G.Thom. Logion	Contents	Parallels
***13b** (87.7–14)	**Three words to Thomas**	Acts of Thomas 47 (perhaps dependent on //*G.Thom.*: Klijn 1962, 240).
***14a** (83.15–19)	**Three rules**	//*G.Thom.* 6a; cf. Matt. 6:1–8, 16–18
14b (83.19–23)	**Eat what is set before you**	Luke 10:8–9 (Tradition: J. Jeremias 1980, 185)
14c (83.24–27)	**Defilement comes from within**	Mark 7:15=Matt. 15:11
***15** (83.27–31)	**The unborn father**	
r16 (83.31–84.4)	**No peace for the Earth**	H [Q] Luke 12:51–53a=Matt. 10:34–35 [Luke 12:52 redactional addition to Q: Robinson 2000, 382–83=*G.Thom.* 16b (83.36–84.4); βάλειν 2x in Matt. 10:34–35 and *G.Thom.* 16a (83.31–36]].
***17** (84.5–9)	**What eye has not seen**	1 Cor. 2:9a; 1 Clem. 34:8 ; cf. Luke 10:24=Matt. 11:17; 1 John 1:1 ("and touched with our hands")
***18** (84.9–17)	**The beginning and the end**	
***19a** (84.17–18)	**Blessed is he who was**	Cf. John 8:58
***19b** (84.19–25)	**Becoming disciples**	Cf. Matt. 3:9b=Luke 3:8b
20 (84.26–33)	**The mustard seed**	Mark 4:30–32=Matt. 13:31–32=Luke 13:18–19
***21a** (84.34–85.6)	**Children in a field**	
21b (85.6–15)	**Expecting the thief**	//*G.Thom.* 103; Luke 12:39=Matt. 24:43
***21c** (85.15–18)	**Harvesting the fruit**	Cf. Mark 4:29; Rev. 14:15–16, 18b–19
21d (85.19)	**Ears to hear**	//*G.Thom.* 8b; 24.b; 63.b; 65.b; 96.b; Mark 4:9=Matt. 13:9=Luke 8:8b; Mark 4:23=Matt. 13:43b; Matt. 11:15; Luke 14:35b; Rev. 2:7, 11, 17, 29; 3:6, 13, 22; 13:9
+22a (85.20–24)	**Entering kingdom like children**	Mark 10:13–15=Matt. 19:13–14=Luke 8:15–17; Matt. 18:3; cf. John 3:4–5
***#22b** (85.24–34)	**Making the two one**	*2 Clem.* 12:2 (interpreted in vv. 3–6); *Gospel of the Egyptians* frag. f (Clement of Alex., *Stromata* 3.13.92): "and when the two become one and the male with the female is neither male nor female"
***#23** (86.1–3) 3.134;	**One in a thousand**	Irenaeus, *Adv. haer* 1.24.6; *Pistis Sophia*
***24a** (86.4–6) =P. Oxy 655, fr. d	**Show us where you are**	Cf. Matt. 5:14; John 8:12
24b (86.6–7)	**Ears to hear**	//*G.Thom.* 8b; 21.d; 63.b; 65.b; 96.b; Mark 4:9=Matt. 13:9=Luke 8:8b; Mark 4:23=Matt. 13:43b; Matt. 11:15; Luke 14:35b; Rev. 2:7, 11, 17, 29; 3:6, 13, 22; 13:9
+24c (86.7–10)	**Light within**	Matt. 5:14a; Luke 11:34–36=Matt. 6:22–23
***25** (86.10–12) =P. Oxy 1.1–4	**Love your brother**	Cf. *Barn.* 19:19b

Gospel of Thomas Parallels in Early Christian Literature (*cont.*)

G.Thom. Logion	Contents	Parallels
26 (86.12–17)	**The mote and the beam**	Luke 6:41–42=Matt. 7:3–5
***27** (86.17–20) =P. Oxy 1.4–11	**Fasting and keeping the Sabbath**	
***28** (86.21–31) =P. Oxy 1.11–21	**Jesus the messenger**	Cf. John 1:14
***29** (86.31–87.2) =P. Oxy 1.22	**Flesh and spirit**	Cf. 2 Cor. 8:9
***30** (87.2–5) =P. Oxy 1.23–27	**Three gods**	Cf. Matt. 18:20
r31a (87.5–6) =P. Oxy 1.30–33	**Prophet**	T[L]: Mark 6:4=Matt. 13:57=Luke 4:24 [δεκτός only in Luke and //*G.Thom.*]; John 4:44
***31b** (87.6–7) =P. Oxy 1.33–35	**Physician**	
32 (87.7–10) =P. Oxy 1.36–41	**The city on a mountain**	//*G.Thom.* 21; M: Matt.5:14
33b (87.10–12) =P. Oxy 1.41–42	**Proclaim from the housetops**	Q: Luke 12:3b = Matt. 10:27b
33b (87.13–17)	**Lamps on lampstands**	H: Mark 4:21=Luke 8:16 [Q]; Q: Luke 11:3=Matt. 5:15
34 (87.18–20)	**Blind leading the blind**	Q: Luke 6:39=Matt. 15:14
35 (87.20–23)	**Strong man's house**	Q: Mark 3:27=Matt. 12:29=[cf. Luke 11:21–22]
36 (87.24–26) =P. Oxy 655.i.1–17	**Take no thought**	Q: Luke 12:22=Matt. 6:25
***#37**(87.27–88.1) =P. Oxy 655.i.17–ii.1	**Undressing without shame**	*Gospel of the Egyptians* frag. f (Clement of Alex. *Stromata* 3.13.92): "When you have trampled on the garment of shame."
38a (88.2–5) =P. Oxy 655.ii.2–7	**Hearing my words**	Q: Luke 10:24=Matt. 13:17
38b (88.5–7) =P. Oxy 655.ii.8–11	**Seeking and not finding**	John 7:34a, 36a; cf. John 8:21
39a (88.7–10) =P. Oxy 655.ii.11–23	**Keys of knowledge**	//*G.Thom.* 102; Q[L]: Luke 11:52 ["key of knowledge"]=Matt. 23:13
39b (88.11–13)	**Serpents and doves**	M: Matt. 10:16b; Ignatius, *Polycarp* 2:2; *Gospel of the Nazareans* 7.
40 (88.13–17)	**Alien vines**	M: Matt. 15:13; cf. Ignatius, *Trall.* 11:1; *Philad.* 3:1 (the phrase φυτεία πάτρος occurs in both passages).
41 (88.17–18)	**Giving and taking away**	Luke 19:26=Matt. 25:29; Mark 4:25=Matt. 13:12=Luke 8:18
***42** (88.19)	**Become passers by**	Cf. John 8:25; Matt. 12:33
44 (88.26–31)	**Blaspheming the Holy Spirit**	44a: Luke 12:10a=Matt. 12:32a; 44b: Mark 3:29=Matt. 12:32b=Luke 12:10b; cf. *Did.* 11:7
45 (88.31–89.5)	**No grapes from thorns**	Luke 6:43–45=Matt. 7:16–20; Matt. 12:34b

Gospel of Thomas Parallels in Early Christian Literature (*cont.*)

G.Thom. Logion	Contents	Parallels
46 (89.6–12)	**None superior to John**	Luke 7:28=Matt. 11:11
r47a (89.12–17)	**Serving two masters**	Luke 16:13=Matt. 6:24 [οἰκέτης, "servant" only in Luke (where it belongs to the Lukan redaction: J. Jeremias 1980, 258; Robinson 2000, 462–63), and //*G.Thom.* (Coptic: *hmhal*); *2 Clem.* 6:1 [also οἰκέτης]; cf. Clement of Alex., *Strom.* 3.26.2; 3.81.2.
r47b (89.17–18)	**Drinking old wine**	Luke 5:39
47c (89.19–23)	**Old wineskins**	Mark 2:22=Matt. 9:17=Luke 5:37–38
48a (89.24–25)	**When two agree**	//*G.Thom.* 106a; Matt. 18:19
48b (89.25–26)	**Moving mountains**	//*G.Thom.* 106b; Matt. 17:20b; Mark 11:23=Matt. 21:21; cf. *Didascalia* 3.6
***49** (89.27–30)	**Blessed are the solitary**	
***50** (89.31–90.7)	**Origin in light**	
***51** (90.7–12)	**The new world is present**	
***52** (90.13–18)	**Concerning the prophets**	Cf. John 5:39–40
***53** (90.18–23)	**True circumcision**	Cf. Rom. 2:28, 29; Phil. 3:3 ["true circumcision"].
54 (90.23–24)	**Blessed are the poor**	Matt. 5:3=Luke 6:20; Polycarp, *Phil. 2:3*
r?55 (90.25–29)	**Taking up the cross**	//*G.Thom.* 101; Luke 14:26–27=Matt.10:37–38 [Matt. and //*G.Thom.* have ἄξιος; not clear what was in Q: Robinson 2000, 452–55; cf. Mark 8:34b=Matt. 16:24=Luke 9:23
***56** (90.30–32)	**The world is a corpse**	Cf. //*G.Thom.* 80
57 (90.33–91.7)	**Wheat and weeds**	Matt. 13:24–30
***58** (91.7–9)	**Blessed are those who suffer**	Cf. Jas. 1:12; 1 Pet. 3:14
***59** (91.9–12)	**Looking on the Living One**	
***60** (91.12–22)	**The samaritan and the lamb**	
61a (91.23–25)	**Two on one bed**	Luke 17:34 (Tradition: J. Jeremias 1980, 270)
***61b** (91.25–34)	**Conversation with Salome**	91.28–30: "I was given one of the things of my father": Luke 10:22=Matt.11:27; John 3:35; 13:3a
+62a (91.34–92.1)	**Revealing mysteries**	Mark 4:11=Matt. 13:11=Luke 8:10; cf. Secret Mark f2r10
62b (92:1–2)	**Don't let the left hand know**	Matt. 6:3
63a (92.2–9)	**The rich farmer**	Luke 12:16–21 [the interior monologue with "What shall I do" is a Lukan redactional feature not found here: J. Jeremias 1980, 215–16]
63b (92.9–10)	**Ears to hear**	//*G.Thom.* 8b; 21.d; 24.b; 65.b; 96.b; Mark 4:9=Matt. 13:9=Luke 8:8b; Mark 4:23=Matt. 13:43b; Matt. 11:15; Luke 14:35b; Rev. 2:7, 11, 17, 29; 3:6, 13, 22; 13:9

Gospel of Thomas Parallels in Early Christian Literature (*cont.*)

G.Thom. Logion	Contents	Parallels
64 (92.10–35)	**The banquet**	Luke 14:16–24=Matt. 22:1–10
65a (93.1–15)	**Vineyard**	Mark 12:1–8=Matt. 21:33–39=Luke 20:9–15
65b (93.16)	**Ears to hear**	//*G.Thom.* 8b; 21.d; 24.b; 63.b; 96.b; Mark 4:9=Matt. 13:9=Luke 8:8b; Mark 4:23=Matt. 13:43b; Matt. 11:15; Luke 14:35b; Rev. 2:7, 11, 17, 29; 3:6, 13, 22; 13:9
66 (93.16–19)	**The rejected stone**	Mark 12:10–11=Matt. 21:42=Luke 20:17; cf. 1 Pet. 2:7b; *Barn.* 6:4; *T. Sol.* 23:4 [quotations of Ps. 118:22].
***67** (93.19–20)	**Knowing oneself**	
68 (93.21–24)	**Blessed are the hated**	//*G.Thom.* 69a; Luke 6:22=Matt. 5:10–11 [Matt. and //*G.Thom.* (68 and 69a) have διώκειν twice; Luke has hate and persecute together]; Polycarp, *Phil.* 2:3; cf. 1 Pet. 3:14; 4:14
69a (93.24–27)	**Blessed are the persecuted**	//*G.Thom.* 68; Luke 6:22=Matt. 5:10–11 [Matt.and //*G.Thom.* (68 and 69a) have διώκειν twice; Luke has hate and persecute together];
69b (93.28–29)	**Blessed are the hungry**	Luke 6:21a=Matt. 5:6
***70** (93.29–33)	**Bringing forth what is within**	
71 (93.34–35)	**Destroy this house**	Mark 14:58=Matt. 26:61 [shares first-person sing. with //*G.Thom.*]; Mark 15:29=Matt. 27:40; Acts 6:14; John 2:19
72 (94.1–6)	**Disputed inheritance**	L: Luke 12:13–14 [largely traditional: J. Jeremias 1980, 215]
73 (94.6–9)	**Harvest is great**	Q: Luke 10:2=Matt. 9:37
***#74** (94.9–11)	**Around the well**	Origen, *Contra Celsum* 8.16: "How is it that there are many around the well, but no one goes into it?"
***75** (94.11–13)	**Many at the door**	
76a (94.13–18)	**The merchant and the pearl**	M: Matt. 13:45–46
76b (94.19–22)	**Permanent treasure**	Q: Luke 12:33=Matt. 6:19–20a
***77a** (94.23–26)	**I am the light; I am the all**	Cf. *Martyrdom of Peter* 10
***77b** (94.26–28) =P. Oxy 1.27–30	**I am everywhere**	
78 (94.28–95.2)	**A shaken reed**	Q: Luke 7:24–25=Matt. 11:7b-8
79a (95.3–10)	**Blessed is the womb**	L: Luke 11:27–28 (Tradition: J. Jeremias 1980, 203)
79b (95.10–11)	**Blessed is the barren womb**	L: Luke 23:29 (Tradition: J. Jeremias 1980, 305)
***80** (95.12–14)	**The world is a body**	//*G.Thom.* 56
***81** (95.15–17)	**Renouncing power**	//*G.Thom.* 110; cf. 1 Cor. 4:8

Gospel of Thomas Parallels in Early Christian Literature (*cont.*)

G.Thom. Logion	Contents	Parallels
***#82** (95.17–19)	**Near Jesus, near the fire**	Origen, *Hom. in Jer.* 3.3: *"qui iuxta me est, iuxta ignem est; qui longa est a me, longa est a regno"*; Ps.-Ephrem, *Exposition of the Gospel* 83
***83** (95.19–24)	**The image of the Father**	
***84** (95.24–29)	**Seeing your likenes**	
***85** (95.29–34)	**Adam was unworthy**	
86 (95.34–96.4)	**Foxes have holes**	Q: Luke 9:58=Matt. 8:2
***87** (96.4–7)	**Wretched is the body**	//*G.Thom.* 112
***88** (96.7–12)	**Angels and prophets get theirs**	
89 (96.13–16)	**Washing the outside**	Q: Luke 11:39–41=Matt. 23:25–26
90 (96.16–19)	**Come to me**	M: Matt. 11:28–30
91 (96.20–25)	**Reading the sky**	96:22–25: Luke 12:56=Matt. 16:3b
92a (96.26)	**Seek and find**	//*G.Thom.* 2, 94; Q: Luke 11:9a=Matt. 7:7a
***92b** (96.26–29)	**Don't ask**	Cf. John 16:4–5; 16:23a
93 (96.30–33)	**Dogs and swine**	M: Matt. 7:6; *Did* 9:5 [only dogs]; cf. Hippolytus, *Ref.* 5.8.33
94 (96.33–34)	**Seek and find**	//*G.Thom.* 2, 92a ; Q: Luke 11:10=Matt. 7:8
95 (96.35–97.2)	**Don't lend with interest**	Q: Luke 6:30=Matt. 5:42; Luke 6:35b; *Did.* 1:4e, 5a
96a (97.2–5)	**Woman with the leaven**	Q: Luke 13:20–21=Matt. 13:33
96b (97.6)	**Ears to hear**	//*G.Thom.* 8b; 21.d; 24.b; 63.b; 65.b; Mark 4:9=Matt. 13:9=Luke 8:8b; Mark 4:23=Matt. 13:43b; Matt.11:15; Luke 14:35b; Rev. 2:7, 11, 17, 29; 3:6, 13, 22; 13:9
***97** (97.7–14)	**The cracked jar**	
***98** (97.15–20)	**The assassin**	
99 (97.21–26)	**Jesus' true family**	T: Mark 3:32b–35=Matt. 12:47–50= Luke 8:20–21; *Gospel of the Ebionites* 5; *2 Clem.* 9:11
100 (97.27–31)	**Caesar and God**	T: Mark 12:13–17=Matt. 22:15–22= Luke 20:20–26; P. Eger 2, fr. 2.43–55
101a (97.32–33)	**Hating father and mother**	//*G.Thom.* 55; L: Luke 14:26a; cf. Mark 10:29=Matt. 19:29=Luke 18:29b
***101b** (97.34–98.1)	**Loving father and mother**	
***102** (98.2–5)	**A dog in a manger**	Cf. Matt. 23:23
103 (98.5–10)	**Prepared for the thieves**	Q: Luke 12:39=Matt. 24:43
***104a** (98.11–13)	**Praying and fasting**	
104b (98.14–16)	**When the bridegroom comes**	T: Mark 2:20=Matt. 9:15b=Luke 5:35
***105** (98.16–18)	**Son of a harlot**	

Gospel of Thomas Parallels in Early Christian Literature (*cont.*)

G.Thom. Logion	Contents	Parallels
***#106a** (98.18–20)	**When the two become one**	//*G.Thom.* 48a; *Gospel of the Egyptians* 3 [Clement of Alex., *Strom.* 3.13.92]; cf. Matt. 18:19
106b (98.20–22)	**Moving mountains**	//*G.Thom.* 48b; M: Matt. 17:20b; Mark 11:23=Matt. 21:21
107 (98.22–27)	**The lost sheep**	Q: Luke 16:4–6=Matt. 18:12–13; *Gospel of Truth* 31.35–32.17 (with exegesis)
***108** (98.28–30)	**Drinking from Jesus' mouth**	
109 (98.31–99.3)	**The hidden treasure**	M: Matt. 13:44
***110** (99.4–5)	**Denying the world**	
***111** (99.6–10)	**The heavens will be rolled up**	
***112** (99.10–12)	**Woe to the flesh**	//*G.Thom.* 87
113 (99.12–18)	**When will the kingdom come?**	L: Luke 17:20
***#114** (99.18–26)	**Women entering the kingdom**	Cf. Clement of Alex., *Excerpta ex Theodoto* 21.3

Three, rhetorical use of The use of groups of three, or triplets, is a widespread rhetorical feature in the ancient world. Neirynck has identified 23 "series of three" (three people, things, or phrases used in a series) which are characteristic of the narrative style of Mark (1972, 110–12), and Robbins (1981) has identified several three-step progressions in Mark that cover two or three pericopes. The short letter of *Jude contains 20 sets of triplets (J. D. Charles 1991), including (1) a group of three exempla in vv. 5–7 (some saved in the exodus were later destroyed; angels who left their proper dwellings are imprisoned until judgment; Sodom and Gomorrah were punished for immorality); (2) false teachers who (a) defile the flesh, (b) reject authority, and (c) revile the glorious ones (v. 8); (3) false teachers also (a) walk in the way of Cain, (b) abandon themselves to Balaam's error, and (c) perish in Korah's rebellion (v. 11); (4) false teachers also are (a) grumblers, (b) malcontents, (c) loud-mouthed boasters (v. 16).

———

J. D. Charles 1991b; Neirynck 1988; Robbins 1981b

Throne vision (see *Call naratives)

Timothy, First Letter to. A doubly pseudonymous paraenetic letter (see *paraenesis) in that both sender and receiver are fictitious (Stenger 1974), part of a set of three letters called the *Pastoral Letters. First Timothy contains 1,586 Greek words, with a vocabulary of 541 words (Morgenthaler 1958, 164).

Date and authenticity. Like the rest of the Pastoral Letters attributed to Paul, 1 Timothy has been regarded as a letter actually written by Paul (Reicke 2001, 51–52), as a pseudonymous letter that preserves fragments of Pauline material, and as a wholly pseudonymous product. Reicke, who holds the first view, dates the composition of 1 Timothy to 56 C.E. and argues that the pseudonymous view is unlikely: "The other alternative does not seem very reasonable, because it implies that representatives of a later orthodoxy and hierarchy must have unearthed or fabricated Pauline names and dates in order to promote the so-called early Catholicism, without using the older Pauline letters in a consistent way as models for their vocabulary and message" (Reicke 2001, 53).

Epistolary analysis. 1. The opening epistolary formulas in 1 Timothy include an epistolary prescript that mentions Paul as the sender (1:1) and Timothy as the recipient (1:2a), and a salutation (1:2b): "Grace, mercy, and peace from God the Father and Christ Jesus our Lord." Unlike most Pauline letters, however, there is no thanksgiving period or blessing following.

2. The body of the letter extends from 1:3 through 6:21a. (a) The first installment of Timothy's commission is given in 1:3–3:13, followed by (b) a core of prophetic and hymnic

texts pertaining to the Christian community, under the metaphor of the household of God (3:14–4:5), in which the apostolic parousia in 1 Tim. 3:14–16 is adopted in a new form, namely that Paul is present in the manifold shapes of offices in the postapostolic period (Stenger 1974). The body ending consists of (c) the second installment of Timothy's commission (4:6–6:21a).

3. The epistolary ending omits the customary primary and secondary greetings (J. D. Miller 1997, 1–2) and consists of a very short grace benediction: "Grace be with you" (6:21b). While the letter is addressed to "Timothy," the final grace wish contains a second-person plural pronoun that indicates that the recipients are also communities (1 Tim. 6:22: "Grace be with you [ὑμῶν]").

Rhetorical situation. The fictional rhetorical situation presented by this letter involves the absence of "Paul" from "Timothy" (1 Tim. 1:2), who is in Ephesus (1:3). "Timothy" is in a situation where true Christianity is perverted by wayward Christians who teach and behave in ways at variance with "Paul's" gospel (1:11), but "Timothy" has the ability to refute these dissenters (1:3–7; 4:1–6; 6:2b-10, 20–21).

*Pastoral Letters, *Pauline Letters, *Pseudepigrapha, NT, *Timothy, Second Letter to

---

Dibelius and Conzelmann 1972; A. T. Hanson 1966; P. N. Harrison 1921; L. T. Johnson 2001; J. D. Miller 1997; Murphy-O'Connor 1991a; M. Prior 1989; Reicke 2001; Quinn and Wacker 2000; Stenger 1974; Verner 1983

Timothy, Second Letter to A doubly pseudonymous paraenetic letter (see *paraenesis) in that both sender and receiver are fictitious (Stenger 1974), belonging to a set of three letters called the *Pastoral Letters (see also *Timothy, First Letter to, and *Titus, Letter to).

Language and style. Second Timothy contains 1,235 Greek words, with a vocabulary of 458 (Morgenthaler 1958, 164). It contains some distinctive features when compared with 1 Timothy and Titus, namely, a thanksgiving period (1:3–5), references to suffering and the expression of personal concerns about and appeals to the recipient (M. Prior 1989, 62–64, 67). The form of 2 Timothy exhibits many features of the *testament (S. C. Martin 1997), purportedly written by Paul just before his death.

Epistolary analysis. (1) The opening epistolary formulas consist of a prescript with mention of Paul as the sender (1:1), an adscript directed to Timothy (1:2a), a salutation (1:2b), and a long thanksgiving period (1:3–14). (2) The body of the letter, in the form of a *testament (2:1–4:8), is sandwiched between a description of Paul's situation (1:15–18) and arrangements for his associates (4:9–18). (3) The concluding epistolary formulas include primary and secondary greetings (4:19–21) and a final grace benediction (4:22).

*Pastoral Letters, *Pauline Letters, *Pseudepigrapha, NT, *Timothy, First Letter to, *Titus

---

Dibelius and Conzelmann 1972; A. T. Hanson 1966; P. N. Harrison 1921; L. T. Johnson 2001; Murphy-O'Connor 1991a; M. Prior 1989; Stenger 1974; Verner 1983

Titles of books Titles of prose works in classical antiquity were derived from the text itself (Schmalzriedt 1970, 32–50). The opening sentence contained an extremely abbreviated description of the contents next to the name and origin of the author, e.g., "This is the publication of the investigation of Herodotus of Halicarnassus" (Herodotus 1.1) and "Thucydides of Athens composed the history of the war of the Peloponnesians and Athenians" (Thucydides 1.1; cf. Plutarch, *Moralia* 605c). In contrast to the titles of modern books, titles (from the Latin word *titulus,* "title, inscription, heading") used for books in antiquity refer to two literary phenomena, the *inscriptio* or the *superscriptio* (a short description of the work, usually in one or two words with a shortened form of the author's name in the genitive of authorship) and the **incipit* (the opening words of a manuscript), which often functioned as a more descriptive "title" than the *inscriptio* or *superscriptio.* In addition to being placed in the *inscriptio* or the *superscriptio,* the title could also be written on a strip of papyrus or vellum called the σίλλυβος or σίττυβος in Greek or *titulus* or *index* in Latin (Thompson 1901, 39; Cicero, *Ad Atticum* 79 [IV.4a]). The title of a papyrus roll was invariably placed at the *end* of the roll, where it was called a *subscriptio* (Oliver 1951, 243–48; Thompson 1966, 57; the Arethas Codex, Parisinus Graecus 451, has the work attributed to the 2d-cent. C.E. Christian apologist Athenagoras, *De resurrectio,* with the subscription ΑΘΗΝΑΓΟΡΑΣ ΠΕΡΙ ΑΝΑΣΤΑΣΕΩΣ, but the superscription is ΤΟΥ ΑΥΤΟΥ ΠΕΡΙ ΑΝΑΣΤΑΣΕΩΣ ΝΕΚΡΩΝ). The title could, in addition, be placed at the beginning of a roll, called an *inscriptio* (Cicero,

Topica 1; Pliny, *Hist. nat.* praef. 24; Quintilian 2.17.15). In addition, an external title could be written on a label called a γλῶσσα or γλωσσάριον (Thompson 1966, 57; Turner 1971, 34). In general, the first sentence of a book served as the title, making a separate title (at least at the beginning of the book) unnecessary (Nachmanson 1941, 7–8). Herodotus already refers to the *Iliad* (2.116–17) and the *Odyssey* (4.29) using those titles.

Titles of the Gospels. The titles or *inscriptiones* of the four canonical Gospels are similarly phrased (e.g., "The Gospel according to Mark"), with the preposition κατά ("according to") standing for the genitive of authorship (e.g., "The Gospel *of* Mark"). The oldest form of this title was probably, e.g., Κατὰ Μάρκον, "According to Mark," which should be understood as indicating authorship, though this short form in all the Gospels is attested only by the second hand of two 4th-cent. uncials, ℵ (Sinaiticus) and **B** (Vaticanus). Hengel (1985b, 65–67) argues for the originality of the longer form, e.g., εὐαγγέλιον κατὰ Μάρκον, though he does not provide a convincing explanation for the origin of the shorter form. The fact that all four Gospels have similar titles suggests that they were originally anonymous compositions that had to be distinguished from each other by the addition of secondary titles after they had been collected to form a fourfold group, not later than ca. 125 C.E. (Hengel 1985b, 70). The term εὐαγγέλιον probably became part of the titles of the four Gospels through the influence of Mark 1:1. The title of the revised version of Luke advocated by Marcion of Sinope (ca. 140 C.E.), did not attribute the work to a specific author (Tertullian, *Adv. Marc.* 4.2.3), but was simply titled εὐαγγέλιον (Harnack 183*–84*). The fragmentary *Gospel of Peter,* though lacking a title, is generally thought to be the work referred to in Eusebius, *Hist. eccl.* 6.12.2 under the title εὐαγγελίον κατὰ Πέτρον, an imitation of the titles of the canonical gospels.

Titles of other works in the NT and ECL. The Acts of the Apostles, the second book of the two-volume work Luke–Acts, was separated early from the first book, the Gospel of Luke (the two are never found together in any manuscript). The title "Acts of [all] the Apostles," *acta [omnium] apostolorum,* first occurs in the Canon Muratori (*Acta autem omnium Apostolorum sub uno libro scripta sunt*), though it appears to have been assigned no fixed title during the 2d cent. C.E. (G. Schneider 1980–82, 1.74). The Greek title Πράξεις, "Acts," is attested by the second hand of ℵ (Sinaiticus) and **1175**, while the longer (and probably more original) form Πράξεις Ἀποστολῶν, "Acts of the Apostles," is attested by the second hand of **B** (Vaticanus) and **D** (Beza), and by **Y** and a few *minuscules.

*Explicit, *Incipit

Fredouille, Goulet-Cazé, Hoffmann, and Petitmengin 1997; Genette 1997, 55–103; Hengel 1985; Munck 1963; Nachmanson 1941; Oliver 1951; Schmaltzriedt 1970; Schröder 1999; Thompson 1901; Zilliacus 1938; Pliny, *Hist. nat.* praef. 24–27

Titus, Letter to, a doubly pseudonymous letter in that both sender and receiver are fictitious (Stenger 1974), part of a set of three letters called the *Pastoral Letters, closely linked in style and forming a *letter collection. While the letter is addressed to "Titus," the second-person plural pronoun in the final clause in Titus 3:15 ("Grace be with you all [πάντων ὑμῶν]"), indicates that communities are also addressed, though this may be an early universalizing interpolation.

Date and authenticity. Titus, like the other Pastoral Letters, is regarded either as having been actually written by Paul (Reicke 2001, 68–73), as being pseudonymous but preserving genuine fragments of Pauline teaching, or as pseudonymous with no attempt to preserve authentic material from Paul. Placing Titus in the framework of the known events of Paul's life, Reicke (2001, 68–73) dates the letter to 58 C.E. Titus contains 663 Greek words, with a vocabulary of 303 words (Morgenthaler 1958, 164).

Fictive rhetorical setting. There is no obvious reason for placing "Titus" in Crete, except to allow the author to quote the proverb "Cretans are always liars, evil beasts, lazy gluttons" (1:12; Callimachus, *Hymn to Zeus* 8: "Cretans are confirmed liars"). The fictional rhetorical situation presented by this letter involves the absence of "Paul" from "Titus" (1:4), who is in Crete (1:5). "Titus" is in a situation where true Christianity is perverted by wayward Christians who teach and behave in ways at variance with "Paul's" gospel (1:3), but has the ability to refute these dissenters (1:9–16; 3:9–11).

Epistolary analysis. (1) The opening epistolary formula consists of the customary three-part prescript with an extremely long sender section (48 words) that appears to reflect the fact that Titus was the first letter in the collection and therefore the prescript articulates the purpose for the entire collection of Pastoral letters (see *Prescriptions, epistolary). The recipient is Titus (1:4a), and the salutation is phrased in the common Pauline form: "Grace and peace from God the Father and Christ Jesus our Savior" (1:4b), differing slightly from the saluation in 1 Tim. 1:1:2b and 2 Tim. 1:2b. (2) The body of the letter, found in 1:5–3:11, contains two different types of material: (a) a series of orders to appoint elders and bishops in the towns of Crete, together with a specification of their moral and spiritual qualities (1:5–16), (b) paraenesis for the entire Christian congregation (2:1–3:11). (3) The epistolary closing consists of travel arrangements for Paul's associates (3:12–14), a short section of secondary and primary greetings (3:15a), followed by a concluding grace benediction: "Grace be with you all" (3:15b).

*Pastoral Letters, *Pauline Letters, *Pseudepigrapha, NT, *Timothy, First Letter to, *Timothy, Second Letter to

---

Dibelius and Conzelmann 1972; A. T. Hanson 1966; P. N. Harrison 1921; Murphy-O'Connor 1991a; M. Prior 1989; Quinn 1990b; Stenger 1974; Verner 1983

Topos (plural topoi), from the Greek term τόπος (Latin *locus;* plural *loci*), literally meaning "place," is a rhetorical term used for one of the main duties of the orator (*officia oratoris*), i.e., *inventio,* or "discovery," with at least three metaphorical spatial meanings: (1) Topoi can refer to "themes" or "commonplaces," consisting of a complex of statements relating to a single commonplace topic such as "friendship." (2) Topos was used in the 4th cent. B.C.E. to refer to a "place" or "site" of discourse, i.e., stock arguments or ready-made arguments available to the speaker to select those most appropriate to the present rhetorical situation, i.e., "pidgeonholes for locating already existing ideas" (C. R. Miller 2000, 132). For example, a speaker might want to either enhance or minimize the trustworthiness of a witness. Aristotle's innovation was to replace this "ready-made-argument" system with an abstract argumentative structure (Solmsen 1974, 40), discussed next. (3) Topos, according to Aristotle (who never actually defines what his innovative way of using τόπος means), constitutes an "abstract argumentative structure" to be applied to specific issues in deductive syllogisms (as in Aristotle's *Topica*) and in rhetorical syllogisms or *enthymemes (as in Aristotle, *Rhetorica* 2.23, where 28 topoi are listed), i.e., "generative patterns of thought or methods of analysis" (C. R. Miller 2000, 132); see table on page 477.

Aristotle's topoi. For Aristotle a topos is a pattern or structure of a convincing argument rather than a "commonplace" which can be used in various kinds of arguments (Ryan 1984, 11). According to Aristotle, topoi are principles of a dialectical or rhetorical nature divided into two groups: (1) ἴδιοι τόποι ("particular topics"), topics that concern particular subjects and are specifically appropriate to the three genres of rhetoric (Aristotle, *Rhet.* 1.14–15; Quintilian 5.10.20; 10.5.12); (2) κοίνοι τόποι ("general topics"), characteristically rhetorical topics, general principles rather than having specific content so that they apply to all genres of discourse. The table on the following page is based partly on Cooper 1932, 159–72) and Warnick (2000, 120–28).

Topoi as commonplaces. In a paraenetic context, Bradley (1953, 240) has defined a topos as "the treatment in independent form of the topic of a proper thought or action, or of a virtue or a vice, etc." Bradley, however, deals largely with content, while Mullins (1980) has recognized the importance of dealing with form and has proposed three formal elements of a topos; (1) an injunction, (2) the reason for the injunction, (3) a discussion of its consequences. Brunt (1985) argues that the topos phenomenon as such indicates that such advice was not directed to a specific situation.

Bradley 1953; Brunt 1985; D'Angelo 1984; Grimaldi 1972, 115–35; C. R. Miller 2000; Mullins 1980; Ryan 1984; Solmsen 1974; Warnick 2000

Transtextuality a term coined by Genette for his general scheme of poetics, includes the following five elements arranged in an ascending order of abstraction: (1) intertextuality, (2) paratextuality (Genette 1997), (3) metatextuality, (4) hypertextualilty, and (5) architextuality. **Intertextuality,* as defined by Genette, is more restricted than the concept used in poststructuralism, i.e., "a relationship of co-presence between two texts or among several texts" and is "the actual presence of one text within another" (Genette 1997a, 1–2). *Paratextuality* refers to those elements on the "threshold" of the text which direct and control the reception of that text by the readers. The two aspects of paratexts include "peritexts" (titles, chapter titles, preface, notes) and "epitexts" (interviews, reviews, relevant private letters) that are outside the text itself but contextualize the text.

The 28 Aristotelian Topoi from *Rhetorica* 2.23

	Topic	Definition
1.	From opposites	Like reciprocity, but from opposing conditions or situations
2.	Inflections	Statement using one form of a word changed to allow another form of the same word
3.	From correlatives	Agent or reference in both cases must be the same; equivalent treatment applied to both
4.	More and less	If the lesser thing is true, the greater is also
5.	Time	If an agreement was made in the past, it should be honored in the present
6.	Opponents's utterance	
7.	Definition	Grasps essence of a thing; draws syllogistic conclusions about a subject; shows *what* something is, not *that* it is
8.	Ambiguous terms	Varied meanings of a word; assumes necessity of stability of terms across premises (*Topica* 106a–b; 130a)
9.	From division	At each stage take elements only from the essence; divide consecutively; leave out nothing; as in induction the inference must be added
10.	Induction	Example is a kind of induction; use of multiple examples to establish a general principle
11.	Existing decisions	Argument from authority
12.	From the parts	Of those things of which the genus is predicated; one of its species must also be predicated (*Topica* 111a)
13.	Simple consequences	Idea that something good and bad follows from the same cause
14.	Crossed consequences	Exhortation or dissuasion on two contrasting matters
15.	Between thoughts and actions	When people do not praise openly what they praise secretly
16.	Proportional results	If you would do X in Y case, then you should do its opposite in the opposite case
17.	Identical results	If some result is the same, so are the things from which it resulted
18.	Altered choices	Not always choosing the same thing before and after an event
19.	Attributed motives	The purpose for which something might exist or happen is the cause for which it does exist or has happened
20.	Incentives and deterrents	What turns the mind in favor of or against something; considers whether an action was possible, easy, advantageous, or harmful to enemies; if punishable, whether the punishment is less than the reward of the action
21.	Incredible occurrences	What seems improbable is probable
22.	Conflicting facts	Contradictions in dates, actions, and words applied to the opponent
23.	How to meet slander	Pointing up act or person misinterpretations
24.	Cause	If cause exists, so does effect; no cause, no effect
25.	Course of action	Is there a better plan of a different kind that will be more advantageous?
26.	Actions compared	When future action contrary to past action; look at them together
27.	Previous mistakes	To accuse and defend based on mistakes that have been made
28.	Meaning of names	Name represents character

Metatextuality is when a text has the relationship of commentary to another text, i.e., "It unites a given text to another, of which it speaks without necessarily citing it . . . sometimes even without naming it" (Genette 1997a, 4). *Hypertextuality* involves "any relationship uniting a text B (which I shall call the *hypertext*) to an earlier text A (I shall, of course, call it the *hypotext*), upon which it is grafted in a manner that is not that of commentary" (Genette 1997a, 5). Genette's "hypotext" is what many other critics call the "intertext," though he means self-conscious and intended relations between texts. *Architextuality* refers to those particular persistent and enduring modes (like narration and discourse), themes (like love, death), and formal features (e.g., meter), when linked in a persistent and enduring way. For Genette, "genre" is a literary category, while "mode" involves aspects of language itself and can be divided into "narration" (the recounting of facts or events without placing emphasis on the one recounting) and "discourse" (placing the focus on the person speaking and the situation in which he or she speaks).

*Transtextuality

Genette 1992, 1997a, 1997b

Triple tradition, or *traditio triplex,* refers to the pericopae in the Synoptic Gospels that have parallels in Matthew, Mark, and Luke.

Trope, from the Latin word *tropus* ("figure of speech"), derived from the Greek word τρόπος ("turn, turning"), refers to a word that has been "turned" from its normal meaning and hence is a "figure of speech." Quintilian defines *tropus* as "the artistic alteration of a word or phrase from its proper meaning to another" (8.6.1). The most common trope is the metaphor (Quintilian 8.6.4), but other tropes include metonymy, autonomasia, metalepsis, synecdoche, catachresis, allegory, hyperbole, and periphrasis (Quintilian 9.1.5–6).

R. D. Anderson 2000, 121; Quintilian, *Inst.* 8.6.1–76.

Two-ways tradition The metaphor of the two ways or two paths was widely used in ancient ethical instruction to indicate that a life of vice or virtue was based on choice and to indicate the consequences of the way of virtue as the way of life and the way of vice as the way of death. The two-ways tradition is found in the ancient Egyptian *Book of Two Ways* (Lesko 1972), in Greek and Roman literature (Hesiod, *Works and Days* 286–92; Xenophon, *Memorabilia* 2.1.21–33 [the story of Hercules at the crossroads]; Cebes, *Tabula*), the OT (Deut. 30:15; Jer. 21:8; Ps. 1:1, 6; Prov. 2:12–15), and Judaism (Sirach 15:11–17; 21:10; *T. Asher* 1–6; 1QS 3.13–4.26; *2 Enoch* 30:15). 1QS 3.13–4.26 is also connected to the two-ways tradition (Duhaime 1977, 1987; Murphy-O'Connor 1984). The beginning of the two-ways tradition in *Barn.* 18:1–2 has a close similarity to 1QS 3.13–4.26:

> There are two ways of teaching and power, one of light and one of darkness. And there is a great difference between the two ways. For over the one are set light-bringing angels of God, but over the other angels of Satan. And the one is the Lord from eternity and the other is the ruler of the present time of iniquity.

The same dualism is evident in *T. Judah* 20:1–5 (trans. Hollander and de Jonge):

> [1]Recognize, therefore, my children, that two spirits devote themselves to man, the spirit of truth and the spirit of deceit, [2]and in the midst is the spirit of understanding of the mind (to which it belongs) to turn wheresoever it wishes. [3]And the works of truth and the works of deceit are written upon the breast of man, and the Lord knows each of them; [4]and there is no time at which the works of men can be hidden, because on his own breast they have been written down before the Lord. [5]And the spirit of truth testifies all thngs and accuses all; and the sinner is burnt up from out of his own heart and cannot raise his face to the judge.

The two-ways tradition is first found in the NT in the metaphor of the wide and narrow gates in Matt. 7:13–14, the former leads to destruction and the latter to life. In Matt. 21:32 the phrase "way (ὁδός) of righteousness" is used of the life of John the Baptist and clearly presupposes the two-way motif. Both *Did.* 1–6 and *Barn.* 18–21 are based on a two-ways source, and both begin, "There are two ways, one of life and one of death, and there is a vast difference between the two ways" (*Did.* 1:1; *Barn.* 18:1). The two-ways motif also occurs in Hermas, *Mand.* 6.1–2–5 (cf. *Vis.* 3.7.1–2).

A comparison of *Didache* 1–5 with *Barnabas* 18–20 suggests that the two are related through a common written source, not only with the use of a two-ways schema. Didache 1:3b–2:1 does not occur in the *Doctrina XII apostolorum* (Schlecht 1901) or the *Canons of the Holy Apostles* (Schermann 1914). This section is found in the *Apostolic Constitutions* (7.2.2–6), which is therefore dependent on the *Didache* and not on an earlier two-ways source. The two-ways section of *Barnabas* (18–20) is very similar to the 1QS 3.13–4.26.

Betz 1994, 520–23; Brock 1990; Duhaime 1977, 1987; Kraft 2000; Lesko 1972; Murphy-O'Connor 1984; Rordorf 1972; Schermann 1914; Schlecht 1901; Suggs 1972; *TDNT* 5.43–48, 69–75, 93–96.

Types (of the folktale), a term used by folklorists to refer to standard classification systems of whole plots of folktales. The basic type index for folktales is Aarne and Thompson 1961, supplemented by Baughman 1966. The type index of Aarne and Thompson is based largely on content and tends to ignore form.

*Form criticism, *Motifs (of the folktale), *Orality, *Oral tradition

---

Aarne and Thompson 1961; Baughman 1966

Typology, a modern term based on the Greek word τύπος ("pattern, symbol, model"), referring to a kind of biblical interpretation that establishes "historical connexions between certain events, persons or things in the Old Testament and similar events, persons or things in the New Testament" (Lampe and Woollcombe 1957, 39). A "type" is usually reserved for what occurred earlier in history, which corresponds to that which occurs later, called an "antitype" (ἀντίτυπος, "that which corresponds to something else, copy, representation"). Typology is very similar to analogy and has antecedents in inner biblical exegesis. The miraculous parting of the Jordan in Josh. 4:22–24 is modeled after the miraculous parting of the Reed Sea in Exod. 14 (Fishbane 1985, 358–59). Creation is used as a prototype for future redemption in Isa. 65:17: "For, behold, I create new heavens and a new earth" (Fishbane 1985, 354). Allusions to the period of wandering in the desert for 40 years are found in the prophets (Jer. 16:14–15; Hos. 2:16–17; Mic. 7:14; Fishbane 1985, 361–68; Talmon 1966). The term παραβολή ("symbol") closely overlaps in meaning with τύπος in Heb. 9:9. Thus in 1 Pet. 3:21 the fact that Noah's family was saved in the ark that was borne up by water is a type of baptism, which is the "antitype" (here the term ἀντίτυπος is used). Thus the higher reality of baptism is foreshadowed by Noah's deliverance in the flood. Similarly, in Rom. 5:14 Adam is understood as a "type" of the one who was to come (i.e., Christ as ἀντίτυπος). The term τύπος is used again in an exegetical sense in 1 Cor. 10:6. Paul refers in 1 Cor. 10:1–4 to the Israelites under Moses in such a way that the typological significance of their experience is made patent: they passed through the sea and were "baptized" into Moses, who all ate the same supernatural food and drank from the supernatural rock that followed them, i.e., Christ. Nevertheless God was displeased with most of them and they died in the wilderness. Referring to this brief narrative, Paul says (1 Cor 10:6): "Now these things are warnings [τύποι, frequently translated 'examples'] for us, not to desire evil as they did." Thus the whole passage is a warning against idolatry. The promise-and-fulfillment schema is essential for typology: the OT is a book of prophetic promise that foretold an age of salvation that was to come, and for early Christians this age, the period of fulfillment, had arrived with Jesus of Nazareth and the early church. Typology occurs frequently elsewhere in Paul also. In Rom. 3:25, where Paul says that "God has publicly set him [Christ Jesus] as the *place of expiation* [ἱλαστήριον] through faith in his blood" (author's trans.), he is using a typological interpretation of Christ's death based on the ritual of atonement centering in his interpretation of the typological meaning of ἱλαστήριον (Roloff in *EDNT* 2.186).

*Allegory, *Barnabas, Letter of, *Exegesis, patristic biblical, *Justin Martyr

---

Aageson 1987; Baker 1976; Blair 1986; Buchanan 1987; Davidson 1981; Eichrodt 1963; Fishbane 1985, 1986; Goppelt 1982; Hvalvik 1996, 102–36; Lampe and Woolcombe 1957; Ostmeyer 2000; T. W. Martin 1992, 85–121.

Uncial, from the Latin word *uncia* ("a twelfth part of something," i.e., letters that occupied a twelfth part of a line), refers to the literary style of writing in separate, large capital letters. The uncial MSS of the Greek NT, also called majuscules, produced from the 3d to the 6th cent. C.E., are indicated by Arabic numerals preceded by "0." The siglum for Codex Sinaiticus, for example, is א or 01; Codex Alexandrinua is **A** or 02; Codex Vaticanus is **B** or 03 (Gregory 1907, 329–69; Aland and Aland 1989, 102–25; Metzger 1992, 42–61). The term "biblical uncial" is used for the script of the great biblical codices produced in the 4th and 5th cent. (Cavallo 1967). There are about 170 uncial manuscripts of the Gospels. In the late 8th to early 9th cent. C.E. there was a rapid transition from uncial to *minuscule script in the Byzantine Empire.

*Minuscules, *Papyri, *Textual criticism

Cavallo 1967; Gregory 1907, 329–69; Hatch 1935; Metzger 1992, 8–10; D. C. Parker 1997, 9–11

Understatement, a figure of speech (see *Litotes)

Unity, literary, is the notion that a literary composition ought to exhibit a central organizing principle so that all of its parts are integrated into an organic whole. Each of the major features or devices of a literary work can be used to unify the composition (plot, character, form, theme, symbolism). Modern readers are strongly inclined to assume the unity of a literary work and to base that assumption on modern expectations. In the case of ancient texts, however, such assumptions and expectations may have a limited validity. Centripetal or centrifugal unity inquires into the meaning of the whole and asks how the various parts contribute to this meaning. In the *Phaedrus* (264A–C; see Heath 1989, 12–27), Plato provides several criteria for judging whether a speech is good or bad: random arrangement is not acceptable, for every discourse should be like a living organism with a body, head, and limbs, all in the proper relationship to each other; i.e., completeness is essential. However, Plato provides no substantive criteria that indicates the proper order for the appropriate elements in a discourse, apart from the suggestion that a discourse should begin with a definition of disputed terms. The type of unity expected of a text, however, depends on the genre. Greco-Roman rhetorical theorists used several criteria to evaluate literary unity: συνεχαία ("continuity"), τὸ ὅλον ("completeness"), σύναγις ("connection"), συμμετρία ("symmetry") and σύστασις ("order"). Along with unity, many theorists also advocated "variety" (ποικιλία), which relieved boredom and provided pleasure (Isocrates, *Antidosis* 15.46–47); though Plato was usually opposed to ποικιλία, he could make a concession to popular expectations (Plato, *Laws* 665C).

Heath 1989; Orsini 1975; Ruckstuhl 1951

Unreliable narrator, a phrase introduced by Booth in 1961 (Booth 1983, 158–59): "For lack of better terms, I have called a narrator *reliable* when he speaks for or acts in accordance with the norms of the work (which is to say, the implied author's norms), and *unreliable* when he does not." According to Scholes and Kellogg (1966, 264–65): "The unreliable or semi-reliable narrator in fiction is quite uncharacteristic of primitive or ancient narrative. The author of an *apologia* is expected to be presenting himself in the best possible light, and thus is to be taken *cum grano salis,* but the idea of creating an unreliable fictional eyewitness is the sophisticated product of an empirical and ironical age." Moore (1989, 33–34) reviews the work of Dawsey (1986) on the Gospel of Luke, suggesting that he attributes to the author "a narrative technique and a matching audience response almost two millennia out of time."

Though the narrator of Mark is typically regarded as "reliable" (Juel 1999, 34), Young (1999, 146–60), argues that the *narrative aside in Mark 6:52 is the use of the device of the unreliable narrator. Mark 6:45–52 contains an epiphany miracle in which Jesus comes to the disciples by walking on the water. When he climbs into the boat, the wind ceases, and they express astonishment. The narrator then comments, "for they did not understand about the loaves, but their hearts were hardened." The negative judgment of the narrator is unexpected and is clearly inappropriate for the narrative context, as others have also observed (Bassler 1986, 163–65), but the problem with Young's reading is that the narrator who makes the value judgment in the aside in Mark 6:52 is the same narrator who speaks to the reader throughout Mark. In Mark 6:52, therefore, the narrator is not so much unreliable as simply inconsistent.

Further, though Young (1999, 158–60) makes an attempt to propose the existence of the device of the unreliable narrator in ancient literature, he is not successful. His only example does not inspire confidence (Young 1999, 160): Odysseus in the *Odyssey* "is constantly referred to by the Homeric narrator as 'deep and devious,' 'many sided,' as one who speaks 'crooked and shifty words,' here with particular reference to his speeches to Aclinous and his court (ch. 15)." First "Alcinous" is misspelled. Second, Odysseus's speech to Alcinous is found in *Odyssey* 7, not 15. Third, the speeches of Odysseus in *Odyssey* 7, first to Alcinous (7.207–25), then to Arete and Alcinous (7.240–97) are in a narrative by a character in the story, not by the narrator of the *Odyssey.* Fourth, in both speeches Odysseus tells the truth in full accord with what the reader learns from the narrator. In short, Young's proposal fails to convince.

Bassler 1986; Cuddon 1998, 535–36; Booth 1983; Dawsey 1986; Harmon and Holman 2000, 534–35

Vaticinia ex eventu, literally, "prophecies after the event," is a literary technique frequently used in *apocalypses, such as the *Apocalypse of Weeks* (*1 *Enoch* 93:1–10;

91:11–17) in which historical review of past events is presented as if were a prophecy of the future. This technique is often used when the ostensible author is an ancient Israelite worthy such as Adam, Enoch, Abraham, or Moses (see *Pseudepigraphy). In the NT, some see the prediction of the destruction of Jerusalem in Mark 13:2 and the prediction of the coming of deceivers in 13:5b–6 as *vaticinia ex eventu* (for 13:5b–6, see Yarbro Collins 1996, 10–14).

*Apocalypse, genre of

———

Osswald 1963

Vellum, a fine, high-quality type of *parchment manufactured from the skin of young animals such as calves, lambs, and kids.

*Parchment, *Papyrus

Versions, translations of all or part of the books of the OT and NT into languages other the originals, are useful for reconstructing early forms of the Hebrew and Greek text itself.

*Textual criticism

———

Tov 1997

Vices and virtues (see *Catalogues of vices and virtues)

We (see *First-person plural)

"We"-passages (in Acts) include those passages characterized by the sudden appearance of the first-person plural in a predominantly third-person narrative: Acts 16:10–17 ("we" sailed from Troas to Philippi, via Samothrace and Neapolis); 20:5–15 ("we" sail from Troas to Assos while Paul makes the journey on foot, then with Paul "we" sail to Miletus via Mitylene and Samos); 21:1–18 ("we" sail from Miletus to Tyre, via Cos, Rhodes, and Patara; then overland to Ptolemais, Caesarea, and finally Jerusalem); 27:1–28:16 (Caesarea to Rome, via Sidon, Myra, Fair Havens, Cauda, Malta, Syracus, Rhegium, and Puteoli). An additional "we"-passage, which is difficult to explain, occurs in 11:28 in the *Western text. These passages were first noticed by Irenaeus (*Adv. haer.* 3.1.1; 3.10.1; 3.14.1–14). There are several ways of understanding this phenomenon, though none is generally accepted:

1. The author was a participant in those events narrated in the first-person plural, a view typically held by those who want to emphasize the historical trustworthiness of Acts (Hemer 1989, 312–34; Fitzmyer 1998, 103; Jervell 1998, 66). The "we"-passages do function as *prima facie* evidence for the fact that the writer claimed to be present at the events narrated, perhaps from the diary of the author. However, there are a number of Greek and Roman historians who participated in the events they narrate but used the third person in narrative (perhaps to emphasize their objectivity; see Norden 1956, 371), though an apparent exception is found in Ammianus Marcellinus.

2. The first-person plural passages were taken from an itinerary written by someone who participated in the events narrated (Dibelius 1956, 102–8).

3. The first-person plural is a literary device or stylistic convention meant to give the impression that the author was a participant in the events so narrated (a view criticized by Wedderburn 2002, 84–85). Wehnert (1989) argues that the combination of third-person and first-person narratives is a Jewish stylistic device found in Ezra and Daniel, and that the inclusion of the first person is an attempt to guarantee trustworthiness, though the author—whom Wehnert thinks is Silas—was unaware of the pseudepigraphical character of such first-person narratives (Wehnert 1989, 183–89). Plümacher (1977) argues that historians were expected to speak from experience, particularly with regard to travel by sea.

4. Sea voyages were frequently narrated in the first-person singular (Norden 1956, 313–16; Robbins 1975; a view critiqued by Hemer 1985, 1989, 317–19). Though it may be objected that sea voyages narrated in the third-person were even more frequent (Praeder 1987), such issues cannot be decided statistically, which lessens the caution of Wedderburn (2002, 83): "Conventions of describing sea-journeys do not therefore seem to provide the key to the puzzling decision to write sometimes in the first person, sometimes in the third." Wedderburn also emphasizes the fact that the "we"-passages are not confined to sea voyages, but in fact such voyages are the focus of each of the four "we"-passages in Acts.

5. The first-person plural is intended to remind the reader of first-person plural passages in the *Odyssey* (MacDonald 1999).

6. The "we"-passages were derived by the author (directly or indirectly), part of a Pauline "school," from traveling companions of Paul, i.e., based on *Erinnerungsberichte,* "recollections" (Wedderburn 2002, 94–98). This view is in effect the most speculative of all, since it has

no parallels on which to base such complex conjectures.

*Acts of the Apostles, *First-person plural, *Itinerary

———

Dibelius 1956, 102–8; Haenchen 1965; Hemer 1985; 1989, 308–64; D.-A. Koch 1999; D. R. MacDonald 1999; Norden 1956, 311–32; Plümacher 1977; Porter 1994; Praeder 1984, 1987; Reumann 1989; Robbins 1975, 1978; Wedderburn 2002; Wehnert 1989

Wisdom of Solomon (see *Apocrypha, OT)

Xenophon of Ephesus (see *Novel)

Bibliography

Aageson, J. W.
1987 "Typology, Correspondence, and the Application of Scripture in Rom. 9–11," *JSNT* 31:51–72.

Aarne, A., and S. Thompson
1961 *The Types of the Folktale.* Helsinki: Suomalainen Tiedakatemia.

Abegg, M., P. Flint, and E. Ulrich
1999 *The Dead Sea Scrolls Bible.* Edinburgh: T. & T. Clark.

Abel, E. L.
1973 "The Genealogies of Jesus Ο ΧΡΙCΤΟC." *NTS* 20:203–10.

Abrahams, R. D.
1968 "Introductory Remarks to a Rhetorical Theory of Folklore." *JAF* 81:143–58.

Abrahams, R. D., and B. A. Babcock
1977 "The Literary Use of Proverbs." *JAF* 90:414–29.

Abrams, M. H.
1971 *A Glossary of Literary Terms.* 3rd ed. New York: Holt, Rinehart and Wilson.

Acerbi, A.
1989 *L'Ascensione di Isaia: Cristologia e profetismo in Siria nei primi decenni del II seculo.* Milano: Vita e Pensiero.

Achard, G.
1988 *Rhétorique à Herennius.* Paris: Les Belles Lettres.

Achtemeier, P.
1970 "Toward the Isolation of Pre-Markan Miracle Catenae." *JBL* 89:265–91.
1972 "The Origin and Function of the Pre-Markan Miracle Catenae." *JBL* 91:198–221.
1975 *Mark.* Proclamation Commentaries. Philadelphia: Fortress Press.
1976 "Jesus and the Disciples as Miracle Workers in the Apocryphal New Testament." In Schüssler Fiorenza (ed.) 1976, 149–86.
1979 *Society of Biblical Literature: 1979 Seminar Papers.* 2 vols. Missoula, Mont.: Scholars Press.
1990 "*Omne Verbum Sonat*: The New Testament and the Oral Environment of Late Western Antiquity." *JBL* 109:3–27.
1996 *1 Peter: A Commentary on 1 Peter.* Hermeneia. Minneapolis: Fortress Press.

Ackroyd, P.
1972 "The Chronicler as Exegete." *JSOT* 2:2–32.

Adkins, A. W. H.
1969 "*Euchomai, Euchole,* and *Euchos* in Homer." *CQ* 19:20–33.

Aigrain, R.
2000 *L'Hagiographie: ses sources, ses méthodes, son histoire.* Subsidia hagiographica 80. Brussels: Société des Bollandistes.

Aland, B., and J. Delobel (eds.)
1994 *New Testament Textual Criticism, Exegesis, and Early Church History: A Discussion of Methods.* The Netherlands: Kampen.

Aland, K.
1967 "Glosse, Interpolation und Komposition in der Sicht der neutestamentlichen Textkritik," *Studien zur Überlieferung des Neuen Testaments und seines Textes.* Berlin: de Gruyter.
1979 "Die Entstehung des Corus Paulinum." Pp. 302–50 in *Neutestamentliche Entwürfe.* Munich: Kaiser Verlag.

Aland, K., and B. Aland
1987 *The Text of the New Testament: An Introduction to the Critical Editions and to the Theory and Practice of Modern Textual Criticism.* Trans. E. F. Rhodes. Grand Rapids: Eerdmans; Leiden: Brill.

Albertz, M.
1921 *Die synoptische Streitgespräche: Ein Beitrag zur Formengeschichte des Urchristentums.* Berlin: Trowitzsch.

Albl, M. C.
1999 *"And Scripture Cannot Be Broken": The Form and Function of the Early Christian Testimonia Collections.* NovTSup 96. Leiden: Brill.

Alden, M.
2000 *Homer Beside Himself: Para-Narratives in the Iliad.* Oxford: Oxford University Press.

Aldridge, R. E.
1999 "The Lost Ending of the *Didache.*" *VC* 53:1–15.

Aletti, J.-N.
1990 "La présence d'un modèle rhétorique en Romains: Son rôle et son importance." *Biblica* 71:1–12.
1991 *Comment Dieu est-il juste? Clefs pour interpréter l'épître aux Romains.* Paris: Le Seuil.
1992 "La *dispositio* rhétorique dans le épîtres pauliennes. Proposition de méthode." *NTS* 38:385–401.
1996 "Romans 7,7–25: Rhetorical Criticism and Its Usefulness," *SEÅ* 61:77–95.
1997 "The Rhetoric of Romans 5–8." In Porter and Olbricht 1997, 294–308.

Alexander, L.
1986 "Luke's Preface in the Context of Greek Preface-Writing." *NovT* 28:48–74.
1989 "Hellenistic Letter-Forms and the Structure of Philippians." *JSNT* 37:87–101.
1990 "The Living Voice: Scepticism Towards the Written Word in Early Christian and in Greco-Roman Texts." In Clines (ed.) 1990, 221–47.
1993 *The Preface to Luke's Gospel: Literary Convention and Social Context in Luke 1.1–4 and Acts 1.1.* SNTSMS 78. Cambridge: Cambridge University Press.
1995 "'In Journeyings Often': Voyaging in the Acts of the Apostles and in Greek Romance." In Tuckett (ed.) 1995, 17–49.
1998a "Ancient Book Production and the Circulation of the Gospels." In Bauckham (ed.) 1998, 71–105.
1998b "Marathon or Jericho? Reading Acts in Dialogue with Biblical and Greek Historiography." In Clines and Moore (eds.) 1998, 92–125.
1999 "The Acts of the Apostles as an Apologetic Text." In Edwards, Goodman, Price, and Rowland (eds.) 1999, 15–44.

Alexander, P. S.
1983–85 "3 (Hebrew Apocalypse of) Enoch." In Charlesworth (ed.) 1983–85, 223–315.
1984a "Midrash and the Gospels." In Tucket (ed.) 1984, 1–18.
1984b "The Rabbinic Hermeneutical Rules and the Problem of the Definition of Midrash." *Proceedings of the Irish Biblical Association* 8:97–125.
1988 "Retelling the Old Testament." Carson and Williamson (eds.) 1988, 99–121.
1990 "Quis Athenis et Hierosolymis? Rabbinic Midrash and Hermeneutics in the Graeco-Roman World." In Davies and White (eds.) 1990, 101–24.

Alexandre, M.
1998 "Apologétique judéo-hellénistique et premières apologies chrétiennes." In Pouderon and Doré (eds.) 1998, 1–40.
1999 *Rhetorical Argumentation in Philo of Alexandria.* Studia Philonica Monographs 2. Atlanta: Scholars Press.

Allegro, J. M.
1956 "Further Messianic References in Qumran Literature." *JBL* 76:147–87.

Allen, T. W.
1920 "The Origin of the Greek Minuscule Hand." *JHS* 40:1–12.

Allen, W.
1940 "The Epyllion: A Study in the History of Literary Criticism." *TAPA* 71:1–26.
1972–73 "Horace's First Book of *Epistles* as Letters." *CJ* 68:119–33.

Allen, W. S.
1965 *Vox Latina.* Cambridge: Cambridge University Press.
1974 *Vox Graeca: A Guide to the Pronunciation of Classical Greek.* Cambridge: Cambridge University Press.

Allert, C. D.
2002 *Revelation, Truth, Canon, and Interpretation: Studies in Justin Martyr's Dialogue with Trypho.* VCSup 64. Leiden: Brill.

Allison, D. C., Jr.
1987 "The Structure of the Sermon on the Mount." *JBL* 106:423–45.
1992 "Matthew: Structure, Biographical Impulse and the *Imitatio Christi.* In F. van Soegbroek (ed.) 1992, 2.1205–21.

Alsup, J. E.
1981 "Type, Place, and Function of the Pronouncement Story in Plutarch's *Moralia.*" *Semeia* 20:15–27.

Alter, R.
1978 "Mimesis and the Motive for Fiction." *Tri-Quarterly* 42:228–49.
1985 *The Art of Biblical Poetry.* New York: Basic Books; London: George Allen & Unwin.

Altheim, F.
1951 *Geschichte der Lateinischen Sprache von den Anfängen bis zum Beginn der Literatur.* Frankfurt am Main: Klostermann.

Altheim, F., and R. Stiehl
1960 *Die aramäische Sprache un der den Achaimeniden.* Frankfurt am Main: Klostermann.

Amador, J. D. H.
1999a *Academic Constraints in Rhetorical Criticism of the New Testament: An Introduction to a Rhetoric of Power.* JSNTSupp 174. Sheffield: Sheffield Academic Press.
1999b "The Unity of 2 Corinthians: A Test Case for a Re-discovered and Re-invented Rhetoric." *Neot* 33:411–32.
2000 "Revisiting 2 Corinthians: Rhetoric and the Case for Unity." *NTS* 46:92–111.

Ammassari, A.
1996 *Bezae Codex Cantabrigiensia: Copia esatta del manoscritto onciale greco-latino dei quattro Vangeli e degli Atti degli Apostoli scritto all'inizio del V secolo e presentato da Theodore Beza all'Università di Cambridge nel 1581.* Vatican City: Libreria Editrice Vaticana.

Amsler, F.
1999 *Acta Philippi: Commentarius.* Corpus Christianorum, Series Apocryphorum 12. Turnhout: Brepols.
2001 *L'évangile inconnu: la source des paroles de Jesus (Q): traduction, introduction et annotation.* Geneva: Labor et Fides.

Amsler, F., F. Bovon, and B. Bouvier
1996 *Acts de l'apôtre Philippe: Introduction, traduction et notes.* Turnhout: Brepols.

Andersen, Ø.
1987 "Mündlichkeit und Schriftlichkeit im frühen Griechentum." *Antike und Abendland* 33:29–44.
2002 *I retorikkens hage.* 4th ed. Oslo: Universitetsforlaget.

Anderson, B. W.
1982 "The Problem and Promise of Commentary." *Interpretation* 36:341–55.

Anderson, C. P.
1966 "The Epistle to the Hebrews and the Pauline Letter Collection." *HTR* 59:429–38.

Anderson, G.
1984 *The Novel in the Ancient World.* Totowa: Barnes & Noble.
1986 *Philostratus: Biography and Belles Lettres in the Third Century A.D.* London: Croom Helm.
1993 *The Second Sophistic: A Culture Phenomenon in the Roman Empire.* New York: Routledge.
2000 *Fairy Tale in the Ancient World.* London: Routledge.

Anderson, G. A., and M. E. Stone (eds.)
1999 *A Synopsis of the Books of Adam and Eve.* 2nd rev. ed. SBL Early Judaism and Its Literature 17. Atlanta: Scholars Press.

Anderson, G. A., M. Stone, and J. Tromp (eds.)
2000 *Literature on Adam and Eve: Collected Essays.* Studia in Veteris Testamenti Pseudepigrapha 15. Leiden: Brill.

Anderson, J. C.
1994 *Matthew's Narrative Web: Over, and Over, and Over Again.* Sheffield: JSOT Press.

Anderson, J. C., and S. Moore (eds.)
1992 *Mark and Method.* Minneapolis: Fortress Press.

Anderson, R. D.
1999 *Ancient Rhetorical Theory and Paul.* Revised edition. Leuven: Peeters.
2000 *Glossary of Greek Rhetorical Terms Connected to Methods of Argumentation, Figures, and Tropes from Anaximenes to Quintilian.* Leuven: Peeters.

Andriessen, P.
1947 "The Authorship of the Epistula ad Diognetum." *VC* 1:129–36.

Andrieu, J.
1954 *Le dialogue antique, structure et présentation.* Paris: Les "Belles Lettres."

Antti, M.
1998 "Is *Thomas* a Gnostic Gospel?" Pp. 107–39 in *Thomas at the Crossroads: Essays on the* Gospel of Thomas. Ed. Risto Uro. Edinburgh: T. & T. Clark.

Apthorp, M. J.
1980 *The Manuscript Evidence for Interpolation in Homer.* BKA 2.71. Heidelberg: Winter.

Archer, G. L., and G. C. Chirichigno
1983 *Old Testament Quotations in the New Testament: A Complete Survey.* Chicago: Moody.

Argall, R. A., B. A. Bow, and R. A. Werline (eds.)
2000 *For a Later Generation: The Transformation of Tradition in Israel, Early Judaism, and Early Christianity.* Harrisburg: Trinity Press International.

Argyle, A. W.
1974 "The Greek of Luke and Acts." *NTS* 20:441–45.

Arnim, J. von (ed.)
1978 *Stoicorum veterum fragmenta.* 4 vols. Stuttgart: Teubner.

Arnold, G.
1977 "Mk 1,1 und Eröffnungswendungen in

griechischen und lateinischen Schriften." *ZNW* 68:121–27.

Artz, P.
1994 "The 'Epistolary Introductory Thanksgiving' in the Papyri and in Paul." *NovT* 36:29–46.

Ascough, R. S.
1996 "Narrative Technique and Generic Designation: Crowd Scenes in Luke–Acts and Chariton." *CBQ* 58:69–81.

Ashton, J.
1994 *Studying John.* Oxford: Clarendon Press.

Askwith, E. H.
1911 "'I' and 'We' in the Thessalonian Epistles." *ExpTim* 8:149–59.

Assmann, J.
1979 "Weisheit, Loyalismus und Frömmigkeit." Pp. 12–72 in *Studien zu altägyptischen Lebenslehren.* Edited by E. Hornung and O. Keel. OBO 28. Fribourg: Universitätsverlag; Göttingen: Vandenhoeck & Ruprecht.

Athanassakis, A. N.
1977 *The Orphic Hymns.* Missoula, Mont.: Scholars Press.

Attridge, H. W.
1976a *The Interpretation of Biblical History in the Antiquitates Judaicae of Flavius Josephus.* Missoula, Mont.: Scholars Press.
1976b *First-Century Cynicism in the Epistles of Heraclitus.* HTS 29. Missoula, Mont.: Scholars Press.
1984 "Historiography." In Stone (ed.) 1984b, 157–84.
1989 *The Epistle to the Hebrews: A Commentary on the Epistle to the Hebrews.* Hermeneia. Philadelphia: Fortress Press.
1990a "Paraenesis in a Homily (*logos paraklêseôs*): The Possible Location of, and Socialization in, the 'Epistle to the Hebrews.'" *Semeia* 50:211–26.
1990b "The Original Language of the Acts of Thomas." In Attridge, Collins, and Tobin (eds.) 1990, 242–50.

Attridge, H. W., J. J. Collins, and T. H. Tobin (eds.)
1990 *Of Scribes and Scrolls: Studies on the Hebrew Bible, Intertestamental Judaism, and Christian Origins.* Lanham, Md.: United Press of America.

Aubriot-Sévin, D.
1992 *Prière et conceptions religieuses en Grèce ancienne jusqu'à la fin du Ve siècle av. J.-C.* Lyon: Maison de l'Orient méditerranéen.

Audet, J.-P.
1958 *La Didachè: Instructions des Apôtres.* Paris: J. Gabalda.

Aune, D. E.
1966 "Justin Martyr's Use of the Old Testament." *BETS* 9:179–97.
1975 "De Esu Carnium Orationes I and II (Moralia 993A–999B)." In Betz (ed.) 1975:301–24.
1978 "Septem Sapientium Convivium (Moralia 146B–164D)." In Betz (ed.) 1978:51–105.
1980 "Magic in Early Christianity." In *ANRW* II, 23/2, 1507–57.
1981a "The Problem of the Genre of the Gospels: A Critique of C. H. Talbert's *What Is a Gospel.*" In France and Wenham (eds.) 1981, 9–60.
1981b Review of Betz, *Galatians. RSR* 7:322–27.
1983 *Prophecy in Early Christianity and the Ancient Mediterranean World.* Grand Rapids: Eerdmans Publishing Co.
1987a *The New Testament in Its Literary Environment.* Philadelphia: Westminster Press.
1987b "Oracles." Vol. 11, pp. 81–87 in *The Encyclopedia of Religion.* 16 vols. Ed. M. Eliade. New York: Macmillan.
1988 "Greco-Roman Biography." In Aune (ed.) 1988, 107–26.
1989 "Oracles." Pp. 206–216 in *Hidden Truths: Magic, Alchemy and the Occult.* Ed. L. E. Sullivan. New York: Macmillan.
1991a "Oral Tradition and the Aphorisms of Jesus." In Wansbrough (ed.) 1991, 211–65.
1991b "Prolegomena to the Study of Oral Tradition in the Hellenistic World." In Wansbrough (ed.) 1991, 59–106.
1991c "Romans as a *Logos Protreptikos.*" In Donfried (ed.) 1991, 278–96.
1991d "Romans as a Logos Protreptikos in the Context of Ancient Religious and Philosophical Propaganda." In Hengel and Heckel (eds.) 1992, 91–121.
1991e "Intertextuality and the Genre of the Apocalypse." Pp. 142–60 in *Society of Biblical Literature 1991 Seminar Papers.* Ed. E. H. Lovering, Jr. Atlanta: Scholars Press.
1991f "On the Origins of the 'Council of Javneh' Myth." *JBL* 110:491–93.
1993 "Charismatic Exegesis." In Charlesworth and Evans (eds.) 1993, 126–50.
1995 "Iao." Vol. 17, cols. 1–12 in *Reallexikon*

für Antike und Christentum. Stuttgart: Anton Hiersemann, 1995.
1997 "Greek." *OEANE* 1.434–40.
1997–98 *Revelation.* WBC. 3 volumes. Nashville: Thomas Nelson.
1998 "Jesus and the Romans in Galilee: Jews and Gentiles in the Decapolis." In Yarbro Collins (ed.) 1998, 230–51.
1998–99 "Qumran and the Book of Revelation." In Flint and Vanderkam (eds.) 1998–99, 622–48.
1999 "Diatribe." In *Religion in Geschichte und Gegenwart.* 4. Aufl. Tübingen: Mohr-Siebeck, 2:832–33.
2002a "God and Time in the Apocalypse of John." In Matera and Das (eds.) 2002, 229–48.
2002b "Dualism in John and the Dead Sea Scrolls: A Reassessment of the Problem." In Aune, Seland, and Ulrichsen (eds.) 2002, 281–303.
2002c "Assessing the Historical Value of the Apocryphal Jesus Traditions: A Critique of Conflicting Methodologies." Pp. 243–72 in *Der historische Jesus. Tendenzen und Perspektiven der gegenwärtigen Forschungen.* Ed. J. Schröter and R. Brucker. BZNW 114. Berlin and New York: Walter de Gruyter.
2002d "Luke 1:1–4: Historical or Scientific *Prooimion*?" Pp. 138–48 in *Paul, Luke and the Greco-Roman World.* Ed. A. Christophersen, C. Claussen, J. Frey and B. Longenecker. JSNTSup. 217. Sheffield: Sheffield Academic Press.

Aune, D. E. (ed.)
1972 *Studies in New Testament and Early Christian Literature: Essays in Honor of Allen P. Wikgren.* Leiden: Brill.
1988 *Greco-Roman Literature and the New Testament.* Atlanta: Scholars Press.
2001 *The Gospel of Matthew in Current Study.* Grand Rapids: Eerdmans.

Aune, D. E., T. Seland, and J. Ulrichsen (eds.)
2002 *Neotestamentica et Philonica: Studies in Honor of Peder Borgen.* NovTSup 106. Leiden: Brill.

Ausfeld, C.
1903 *De Graecorum precationibus quaestiones.* Neue Jahrbücher Suppl. 28:502–47.

Austin, N.
1966 "The Function of Digressions in the *Iliad.*" *GRBS* 7:295–312.

Avenarius, G.
1956 *Lukians Schrift zur Geschichtsschreibung.* Meidenheim am Glan: Anton Hain.

Avi-Yonah, M.
1940 *Abbreviations in Greek Inscriptions.* London: Humphrey Milford; reprinted, Chicago: Ares, 1974.

Ayres, L., and G. Jones (eds.)
1998 *Community.* London and New York: Routledge.

Baarda, T.
1982 "2 Clement 12 and the Sayings of Jesus." In Delobel (ed.) 1982, 529–56.
1993 *Text and Testimony: Essays on the New Testament and Apocryphal Literature in Honor of A. F. J. Klijn.* Kampen: Kok.
1994 *Essays on the Diatessaron.* Kampen: Kok Pharos.

Baasland, E.
1982 "Der Jakobusbrief als neutestametliche Weisheitsschrift." *Studia Theologica* 36:119–39.
1986 "Zum Beispiel der Beispielerzählungen." *NovT* 28:193–219.
1988a "Die *peri*-Formel und die Argumentationssituation des Paulus." *ST* 42:69–87.
1988b "Literarische, Form, Thematik, und geschichtliche Einordnung des Jakobusbriefes." Part II, vol. 25.5, pp. 3646–84 in *Aufstieg und Niedergang der römischen Welt.* Ed. W. Haase and Hildegard Temporini. Berlin: Walter de Gruyter.

Bacher, W.
1913 *Die Proömien der alten jüdischen Homilie: Beitrag zur Geschichte der jüdischen Schriftauslegung und Homiletik.* BWAT 12. Leipzig: J. C. Hinrichs.

Bachmann, M.
1992 *Sünder oder Übertreter: Studien zur Argumentation in Gal 2, 15ff.* WUNT 59. Tübingen: Mohr-Siebeck.

Bacon, B. W.
1918 "The 'Five Books' of Matthew against the Jews." *The Expositor* 15:55–66.
1930 *Studies in Matthew.* London: Constable.

Bacq, P.
1978 *De l'ancienne à la nouvelle Alliance selon S. Irénée: Unite du livre IV de IV de l'Adversus haereses.* Paris: Lethielleux.

Bahr, G. J.
1966 "Paul and Letter Writing in the First Century." *CBQ* 28:465–77.
1968 "The Subscriptions in the Pauline Letters." *JBL* 87:27–41.

Bailey, J. A.
1963 *The Traditions Common to the Gospels of Luke and John.* NovTSup 7. Leiden: Brill.
1978 "Who Wrote II Thessalonians?" *NTS* 25:131–45.

Bailey, J. L.
1995 "Genre Analysis." In Green (ed.) 1995, 197–221.

Bailey, J. L., and L. D. Vander Broek
1991 *Literary Forms in the New Testament: A Handbook.* Louisville, Ky.: Westminster/John Knox.

Bailey, K. E.
1991 "Informal Controlled Oral Tradition and the Synoptic Gospels." *Asia Journal of Theology* 5:34–54.

Baird, W.
1992 *A History of New Testament Research.* Minneapolis: Fortress Press.

Baker, D. L.
1976 "Typology and the Christian Use of the Old Testament." *SJT* 29:137–57.

Bakhtin, M. M.
1981 *The Dialogic Imagination: Four Essays.* Austin: University of Texas Press.
1986 "The Problem of Speech Genres." In *Speech Genres and Other Late Essays.* Edited by C. Emerson and M. Holquist. Translated by V. W. McGee. Austin: University of Texas Press.

Bakke, O. M.
2000 *"Concord and Peace": A Rhetorical Analysis of the First Letter of Clement with an Emphasis on the Language of Unity and Sedition.* WUNT 2.143. Tübingen: Mohr-Siebeck.

Bakker, A.
1933 "Testimony-Influence in the Old Latin Gospels." Pp. 1–14 in *Amicitiae Corolla: A Volume of Essays Presented to James Rendel Harris, D. Litt., on the Occasion of His Eightieth Birthday.* Ed. H. G. Wood. London: University of London.

Bakker, E. J.
1997 *Poetry in Speech: Orality and Homeric Discourse.* Ithaca, N.Y.: Cornell University Press.
1999 "How Oral Is Oral Composition?" In Mackay (ed.) 1999, 29–47.

Bakker, W. F.
1966 *The Greek Imperative: An Investigation into the Aspectual Difference between the Present and Aorist Imperatives in Greek Prayer from Homer up to the Present Day.* Amsterdam: A. M. Hakkert.

Balás, D. L.
1992 "The Use and Interpretation of Paul in Irenaeus's Five Books *Adversus Haereses.*" *SecCent* 9:27–39.

Balch, D. L.
1981 *Let Wives Be Submissive: The Domestic Code in 1 Peter.* SBLDS 26. Chico, Calif.: Scholars Press.
1988 "Household Codes." In Aune (ed.) 1988, 25–50.

Balch, D. L., E. Ferguson, and W. A. Meeks (eds.)
1990 *Greeks, Romans, and Christians: Essays in Honor of Abraham J. Malherbe.* Minneapolis: Fortress Press.

Balentine, S. E.
1981 "The Interpretation of the Old Testament in the New Testament." *SwJT* 23:41–57.

Balogh, J.
1927 "Voces Paginarum." *Philologus* 84:84–109, 202–40.

Baltzer, K.
1968 "Considerations Regarding the Office and Calling of the Prophet." *HTR* 61:567–81.

Balz, H. R.
1969 "Anonymität und Pseudonymität im Urchristentum." *ZTK* 66:403–36.

Banfield, A.
1982 *Unspeakable Sentences: Narration and Representation in the Language of Fiction.* Boston: Routledge & Kegan Paul.

Barclay, J. M. G.
1997 *Colossians and Philemon.* Sheffield: Sheffield Academic Press.

Bardenhewer, O.
1913–32 *Geschichte der altkirchlichen Literatur.* 5 vols. Freiburg im Breisgau: Herder.

Bardy, G.
1932 "La littérature patristique des 'quaestiones et responsiones' sur l'Écriture Sainte." *RB* 41:210–36, 341–69, 513–37.
1933 "La littérature patristique des 'quaestiones et responsiones' sur l'Écriture Sainte." *RB* 42:14–30, 211–29, 328–50.
1934 "Commentaires patristiques de la Bible." *DBSup* 2.73–103.

Bar-Efrat, S.
1980 "Some Observations on the Analysis of Structure in Biblical Narrative." *VT* 30:154–73.

Bar-Ilan, M.
1988 "Scribes and Books in the Late Second

Commonwealth and Rabbinic Period." In Mulder (ed.) 1988, 21–38.
1992 "Illiteracy in the Land of Israel in the First Centuries C.E." In Fishbane and Schoenfeld (eds.) 1992, 246–61.

Barish, D. A.
1977 "The *Autobiography* of Josephus and the Hypothesis of a Second Edition of his *Antiquities*." *HTR* 71:61–75.

Barker, A.
1976 "The Digression in the *Theaetetus*." *JHP* 14:457–62.

Barnard, L. W.
1965 "Epistle ad Diognetum: Two Units from One Author?" *ZNW* 56:130–37.
1967a "St. Clement of Rome and the Persecution of Domitian." Pp. 5–18 in *Studies in the Apostolic Fathers and Their Background*. Edited by L. W. Barnard. New York: Schocken.
1967b "The Use of Testimonies in the Early Church and in the Epistle of Barnabas." Pp. 109–13 in *Studies in the Apostolic Fathers and Their Background*. Edited by L. W. Barnard. New York: Schocken.
1967c *Justin Martyr: His Life and Thought*. Cambridge: Cambridge University Press.
1976 "Athenagoras: De Resurrectione. The Background and Theology of a Second Century Treatise on the Resurrection." *ST* 30:1–42.

Barnes, J.
1981 "Proof and the Syllogism." In *Aristotle on Science: The "Posterior Analytics": Proceedings of the Eighth Symposium Aristotelicum*. Edited by E. Berti. Padova: Antenore.
1984 *The Complete Works of Aristotle: The Revised Oxford Translation*. 2 vols. Princeton: Princeton University Press.
1994 *Aristotle* Posterior Analytics. 2d ed. Oxford: Clarendon Press.

Barnett, A. E.
1997 *Paul Becomes a Literary Influence*. Chicago: University of Chicago Press.

Barnett, P.
1997 *The Second Epistle to the Corinthians*. NICNT. Grand Rapids: Eerdmans.

Barrett, C. K.
1962 *A Commentary on the Epistle to the Romans*. London: Adam & Charles Black.
1963 *The Pastoral Epistles*. Oxford: Clarendon Press.
1970 "The Interpretation of the Old Testament in the New." Pp. 377–422 in *The Cambridge History of the Bible*. Edited by P. R. Ackroyd and C. F. Evans. Cambridge: Cambridge University Press.
1974 "Pauline Controversies in the Post-Pauline Period." *NTS* 20:229–45.
1976 *A Commentary on the First Epistle to the Corinthians*. 2d ed. London: Adam & Charles Black.
1978 *The Gospel according to St. John*. 2nd ed. Philadelphia: Westminster Press.
1980 "Galatians as an 'Apologetic Letter,'" *Interpretation* 34:414–17.
1993 *The Climax of Prophecy: Studies on the Book of Revelation*. Edinburgh: T. & T. Clark.

Bartsch, S.
1989 *Decoding the Ancient Novel: The Reader and the Role of Description in Heliodorus and Achilles Tatius*. Princeton: Princeton University Press.

Bates, W. H.
1965–66 "The Integrity of II Corinthians." *NTS* 12:56–69.

Bauckham, R.
1983a *Jude, 2 Peter*. Word Biblical Commentary 50. Waco: Word.
1983b "The Liber Antiquitatum Biblicarum of Pseudo-Philo and the Gospels as 'Midrash.'" In France and Wenham (eds.) 1983, 33–76.
1987 "The Parable of the Vine: Rediscovering a Lost Parable of Jesus." *NTS* 33:84–101.
1988a "2 Peter: An Account of Research." *ANRW*, II, 25/5, 3713–52.
1988b "The Letter of Jude: An Account of Research." *ANRW* II, 25/5, 3791–3826.
1988c "Pseudo-Apostolic Letters." *JBL* 107:469–94.
1988d "James, 1 and 2 Peter, Jude." In Carson and Williamson (eds.) 1988, 303–17.
1990 "Early Jewish Visions of Hell." *JTS* n.s. 41:355–85.
1993 "The *Acts of Paul* as a Sequel to Acts." In Winter and Clarke (eds.) 1993, 105–52.
1994 "The *Apocalypse of Peter*: A Jewish Christian Apocalypse from the Time of Bar Kokhba." *Apocrypha* 5:7–111.
1997 "The *Acts of Paul*: Replaces Acts or Sequel to Acts?" *Semeia* 80:159–68.
2000 "The Qumran Community and the Gospel of John." In Schiffman, Tov, and VanderKam (eds.) 2000, 105–15.

Bauckham, R. (ed.)
1993 "The Use of Apocalyptic Traditions." Pp. 38–91 in *The Climax of Prophecy:*

Studies on the Book of Revelation. Edinburgh: T. & T. Clark.
1995 *Palestinian Setting*. Vol. 4 of *The Book of Acts in Its First-Century Setting*. Edited by B. W. Winter. Grand Rapids: Eerdmans; Carlisle: Paternoster.
1998 *The Gospels for All Christians: Rethinking the Gospel Audiences*. Grand Rapids: Eerdmans.
1999 *James: Wisdom of James, Disciple of Jesus the Sage*. London and New York: Routledge.

Bauer, B.
1988 *The Structure of Matthew's Gospel*. JSNTSupp 31. Sheffield: JSOT Press.

Bauer, D. R.
1990 "The Literary Function of the Genealogy in Matthew's Gospel." Pp. 451–68, in *Society of Biblical Literature Seminar Papers*. Atlanta: Scholars Press.

Bauer, J. B.
1997 *Studien zu Bibeltext und Väterexegese*. Stuttgart: Verlag Katholisches Bibelwerk.

Bauer, W.
1925 *Das Johannesevangelium*. 2. Aufl. Tübingen: Mohr-Siebeck.

Bauer, W., and H. Paulsen
1985 *Die Briefe des Ignatius von Antiochia und der Polykarpbrief*. HNT 18. Tübingen: Mohr-Siebeck.

Baughman, E. W.
1966 *Type and Motif Index of the Folktales of England and North America*. The Hague: Mouton.

Baum, A. D.
2001 *Pseudepigraphie und literarische Fälschung im frühen Christentum*. WUNT 2.138. Tübingen: Mohr-Siebeck.

Baumeister, T.
1988 "Zur Datierung der Schrift an Diognet." *VC* 42:105–11.

Baumgarten, J. M.
1977 "The Unwritten Law in the Pre-Rabbinic Period." *Studies in Qumran Law*. Leiden: Brill.

Baumlim, J. S. and T. F. Baumlin (eds.)
1994 *Ethos: New Essays in Rhetorical and Critical Theory*. Dallas: Southern Methodist University.

Beale, G. K.
1998 *John's Use of the Old Testament in Revelation*. JSNTSup 166. Sheffield: Sheffield Academic Press.

Beardslee, W. A.
1967 "The Wisdom Tradition in the Synoptic Gospels." *JAAR* 35:231–40.
1970 "Uses of the Proverb in the Synoptic Gospels." *Interpretation* 35:231–40.
1971 *Literary Criticism of the New Testament*. Philadelphia: Fortress Press.
1972 "Proverbs in the Gospel of Thomas." In Aune (ed.) 1972, 92–103.

Beare, F. W.
1981 *The Gospel according to Matthew*. Oxford: Blackwell.

Beasley-Murray, G.
1978 "Romans 1:3f.: An Early Confession of Faith in the Lordship of Jesus." *TynBul* 31:147–54.
1989 *John*. WBC. Dallas: Word.

Beattie, D. R. G., and M. J. McNamara (eds.)
1994 *The Aramaic Bible: Targums in Their Historical Context*. JSOTSup 166. Sheffield: JSOT Press.

Beaujeu, J.
1973 *De deo Socratis, De Platone et eius dogmate, De mundo. Apulée, opuscules philosophiques et fragments*. Paris: Société d'Édition "Les Belles Lettres."

Beavis, M. A.
1989 *Mark's Audience: The Literary and Social Setting of Mark 4:11–12*. JSNTSup 33. Sheffield: JSOT Press.
1990 "Parable and Fable." *CBQ* 52:473–98.

Beck, B. E.
1976–77 "The Common Authorship of Luke and Acts." *NTS* 23:346–52.

Beck, D.
2001 "Direct and Indirect Speech in the Homeric *Hymn to Demeter*. *TAPA* 131:53–74.

Beck, I.
1971 *Die Ringkomposition bei Herodot und ihre Bedeutung für die Beweistechnik*. Hildesheim: Olms.

Becker, A. S.
1990 "The Shield of Achilles and the Poetics of Homeric Description." *AJP* 111:139–53.
1994 *The Shield of Achilles and the Poetics of Ekphrasis*. Lanham, Md.: Rowman & Littlefield.

Becker, J.
1970 *Untersuchungen zur Entstehungsgeschichte des Testamente der Zwölf Patriarchen*. *AGJU 8*. Leiden: Brill.
1989 *Paulus: Der Apostel der Völker*. Tübingen: Mohr-Siebeck.

Beckwith, R. T.
1985 *The Old Testament Canon of the New Testament Church and Its Background in Early Judaism*. London: SPCK.
1988 "Formation of the Hebrew Bible." In Mulder (ed.) 1988, 39–86.

Beentjes, P. C.
1982 "Inverted Quotations in the Bible: A Neglected Stylistic Pattern." *Bib* 63: 506–23.

Behr, C. A.
1968 *Aelius Aristides and the Sacred Tales.* Amsterdam: Hakkert.
1973 *Aristides I.* LCL. Cambridge: Harvard University Press.

Belkin, S.
1936 *The Alexandrian Halakah in Apologetic Literature of the First Century C.E.* Philadelphia: Jewish Publication Society.

Belleville, L. L.
1987 "Continuity or Discontinuity: A Fresh Look at 1 Corinthians in the Light of First-Century Epistolary Forms and Conventions." *EvQ* 59:15–37.

Benko, S.
1980 "Pagan Criticism of Christianity during the First Two Centuries A.D." *ANRW* II, 23.2, 1055–1118.

Benner, M.
1975 *The Emperor Says: Studies in the Rhetorical Style in Edicts of the Early Empire.* Göteborg: Acta Universitatis Gothoburgensis.

Benoît, A.
1960 *Saint Irénée: Introduction à l'Étude de sa Théologie.* Paris: Presses Universitaires de France.

Bérard, F., and D. Feissel
1989 *Guide de l'épigraphiste: Bibliographie choisie des épigraphies antiques et médiévales.* 2nd ed. Paris: Presses de l'Ecole Normale Supérieur.

Berding, K.
1999 "Polycarp of Smyrna's View of the Authorship of 1 and 2 Timothy." *VC* 53:349–60.

Berger, A.
1953 *Encyclopedic Dictionary of Roman Law.* Transactions of the American Philosophical Society, 43.2. Philadelphia: American Philosophical Society.

Berger, K.
1970–71 "Zu den sogennanten Sätze heiligen Rechts." *NTS* 17:10–40.
1974 "Apostelbrief und apostolische Rede." *ZNW* 65 (1974):190–231.
1977 *Exegese des Neuen Testaments.* Heidelberg: Quelle & Meyer.
1984a *Formgeschichte des Neuen Testaments.* Heidelberg: Quelle & Meyer.
1984b "Hellenistische Gattungen im Neuen Testament." *ANRW* II, 25.2, 1031–1432, 1831–85.
1997 *Im Anfang war Johannes: Datierung und Theologie des vierten Evangeliums.* Stuttgart: Quell.

Berghahn, K.
1988 "From Classicist to Classical Literary Criticism, 1730–1806." In Hohendahl (ed.) 1988, 13–98.

Bergholz, T.
1995 *Der Aufbau des lukanischen Doppelwerkes: Untersuchungen zum formalliterarischen Character von Lukas-Evangelium und Apostelgeschichte.* Frankfurt: P. Lang.

Bergman, J.
1976–77 "Zum Zwei-Wege Motiv: Religionsgeschichtliche und exegetische Bemerkungen." *SEÅ* 41–42:27–56.

Bergmeier, R.
1984 "Jerusalem du hochgebaute Stadt." *ZNW* 75:86–106.
1988 "Die Erzhure und das Tier: Apk 12:8–13:18 und 17f. Eine quellen- und redaktionskritische Analyse." *ANRW* II, 25/5, 3899–3916.

Bergren, T. A.
1990 *Fifth Ezra: The Text, Origin, and Early History.* SBLSCS 25. Atlanta: Scholars Press.

Bergson, L.
1971 "Eiron and Eironeia." *Hermes* 99:409–22.

Berkowitz, L., and K. A. Squitier
1990 *Thesaurus Linguae Graecae: Canon of Greek Authors and Works.* 3d ed. New York and Oxford: Oxford University Press.

Berlin, Adele
1985 *The Dynamics of Biblical Parallelism.* Bloomington: Indiana University.
1992 "Parallelism." *ABD* 5:155–62.

Bernard, J. H.
1899 *The Pastoral Epistles.* Cambridge: Cambridge University Press.

Bernstein, M. J.
1994 "4Q252: From Re-Written Bible to Biblical Commentary." *JJS* 45:1–27.
1998 "Pseudepigraphy in the Qumran Scrolls." In Stone and Chazon (eds.) 1998, 1–26.

Bertrand, Daniel A.
1979 "*L'Évangile des Ebionites*: Une Harmonie Évangélique antérieure au *Diatessaron*." *NTS* 26:548–63.

Best, E.
1998 *A Critical and Exegetical Commentary on Ephesians.* ICC. Edinburgh: T. & T. Clark.

Betz, H. D.
1969 "Eine Christus-Aretalogie bei Paulus (2 Kor 12,7–10)." *ZTK* 66:288–305.
1972 *Der Apostel Paulus und die sokratische Tradition.* BHT 45. Tübingen: Mohr-Siebeck.
1973 "2 Cor. 6:14–7:1: An Anti-Pauline Fragment?" *JBL* 92:88–108.
1974–75 "The Literary Composition and Function of Paul's Letter to the Galatians." *NTS* 21:353–79.
1975 *Plutarch's Theological Writings and Early Christian Literature.* SCHNT 3. Leiden: Brill.
1975 *Paul's Apology: II Corinthians 10–13 and the Socratic Tradition.* Protocol of the 2nd Colloquy. Edited by W. Wuellner. Berkeley: Center for Hermeneutical Studies in Hellenistic and Modern Culture.
1976 "In Defense of the Spirit: Paul's Letter to the Galatians as a Document of Early Christian Apologetics." In Schüssler Fiorenza (ed.) 1976, 99–114.
1978 *Plutarch's Ethical Writings and Early Christian Literature.* SCHNT 4. Leiden: Brill.
1978 "De laude ipsius (Plut. *Mor.* 539A–547F)." Pp. 367–93 in *Plutarch's Ethical Writings and Early Christian Literature.* Ed. H. D. Betz. SCHNT 4. Leiden: Brill.
1979 *Galatians: A Commentary of Paul's Letter to the Churches in Galatia.* Hermeneia. Philadelphia: Fortress Press.
1985a *2 Corinthians 8 and 9: A Commentary on Two Administrative Letters of the Apostle Paul.* Hermeneia. Philadelphia: Fortress Press.
1985b *Essays on the Sermon on the Mount.* Trans. L. L. Welborn. Philadelphia: Fortress Press.
1986 "The Problem of Rhetoric and Theology according to the Apostle Paul." In Vanhoye (ed.) 1986, 16–48.
1992 *The Greek Magical Papyri in Translation.* 2d ed. Chicago: University of Chicago Press.
1995 *The Sermon on the Mount.* Hermeneia. Minneapolis: Fortress Press.
1995 *The Sermon on the Mount: A Commentary on the Sermon on the Mount, including the Sermon on the Plain (Matthew 5:3–7:27 and Luke 6:20–49.* Hermeneia. Minneapolis: Fortress Press.

Beutler, J.
1995 "The Use of 'Scripture' in the Gospel of John." In Culpepper and Black (eds.) 1996, 147–62.
2000 *Die Johannesbriefe.* RNT. Regensburg: Friedrich Pustet.

Beyer, K.
1962 *Semitische Syntax im Neuen Testament.* Göttingen: Vandenhoeck & Ruprecht.
1984 *Die aramäischen Texte vom Toten Meer samt den Inscriften aus Palästina, dem Testament Levis aus der Kairoer Genisa, der Fastenrolle und den alten talmudischen Zitaten.* Göttingen: Vandenhoeck & Ruprecht.

Bickermann, Elias
1952 "La chain de la tradition Pharisienne." *RB* 59:44–54.
1967 *Four Strange Books of the Bible.* New York: Schocken.

Bieder, W.
1954 "Die sieben Seligpreisungen in der Johannes." *TZ* 10:13–30.

Bieringer, R. (ed.)
1996 *The Corinthian Correspondence.* BETL 125. Leuven: Peeters.

Bigg, C.
1902 *The Epistles of St. Peter and St. Jude: A Critical and Exegetical Commentary.* 2d ed. ICC. Edinburgh: T. & T. Clark.

Bihlmeyer, K.
1956 *Die apostolischen Väter: Neubearbeitung der Funkschen Ausgabe.* Part 1: *Didache, Barnabas, Klemens I und II, Ignatus, Polycarp, Papias, Quadratus, Diognetbrief.* Tübingen: Mohr-Siebeck.

Bilde, Per
1988 *Flavius Josephus between Jerusalem and Rome: His Life, His Works, and Their Importance.* JSPSup 2. Sheffield: JSOT Press.

Bilezekian, Gilbert G.
1977 *The Liberated Gospel: The Gospel of Mark and Greek Tragedy.* Grand Rapids: Baker Book House.

Bingen, J., and G. Nachtergael (eds.).
1979 *Actes du XVe Congrés International de Papyrologie.* Papyrologica Bruxellensia 16–19. 4 vols. Brussels: Fondation égyptologique Reine Elisabeth.

Bingham, D. J.
1998 *Irenaeus' Use of Matthew Gospel in* Adversus Haereses. Traditio Exegetica Graeca 7. Leuven: Peeters.

Bin Gorion, M. J.
1914–19 *Der Born Judas: Legenden, Märchen, und Erzählungen.* 6 vols. Leipzig: Insel-Verlag.
1913–26 *Die Sagen der Juden.* 4 vols. Frankfurt am Main: Kütten and Loening.

Birdsall, J. N.
1992 "The Recent History of New Testament Textual Criticism (from Westcott and Hort, 1881 to the Present)." *ANRW,* II, 26/1, 99–197.

Bittner, S.
1999 *Ciceros Rhetorik: Eine Bildungstheorie.* Frechen: Bodem Verlag.

Bitzer, L.
1968 "The Rhetorical Situation." *PR* 1:1–18.
1974 "Aristotle's Enthymeme Revisited." In Erickson 1974, 141–55 (reprinted from *QJS* 45 (1959): 399–408.
1980 "Functional Communication: A Situational Perspective." Pp. 21–38 in *Rhetoric in Transition: Studies in the Nature and Uses of Rhetoric.* Edited by E. While. University Park: Pennsylvania State University Press.

Bjerkelund, C. J.
1967 *Parakalo: Form, Function, und Sinn der Parakalo-Sätze in den paulinischen Briefen.* Oslo: Universitetsforlaget.
1986 *Tauta Egeneto: Die Präzisierungssätze im Johannesevangelium.* Tübingen: Mohr-Siebeck.

Black, C. C.
1988 "The Rhetorical Form of the Hellenistic Jewish and Early Christian Sermon: A Response to Lawrence Wills." *HTR* 81:1–18.
1994 *Mark: Images of an Apostolic Interpreter.* Columbia: University of South Carolina Press.

Black, D. A.
1995 "The Discourse Structure of Philippians: A Study in Textlinguistics." *NovT* 37:16–49.

Black, M.
1960 "The Parables as Allegory." *BJRL* 42:273–87.
1967 *An Aramaic Approach to the Gospels and Acts.* 3d ed. Oxford: Oxford University Press.
1970 *Apocalypsis Henochi Graece.* PVTG 3. Leiden: Brill.
1971 "The Christological Use of the Old Testament in the New Testament." *NTS* 18:1–14.
1976 "The Throne-Theophany Prophetic Commission and the 'Son of Man': A Study in Tradition History." Pp. 57–73 in *Jews, Greeks, and Christians: Religious Cultures in Late Antiquity.* Edited by R. Hamerton-Kelly and R. Scroggs. Leiden: Brill.
1985 *The Book of Enoch or I Enoch: A New English Edition with Commentary and Textual Notes.* SVTP 7. Leiden: Brill.
1992 "The Messianism of the Parables of Enoch: Their Date and Contributions to Christological Origins." In Charlesworth (ed.) 1992, 145–68.

Blanchard, A.
1974 *Sigles et abbréviations dans les papyrus documentaires grecs: Recherches de paléographie.* London: Institute of Classical Studies.
1989 *Les débuts du codex.* Bibliologia 9. Turnhout: Brepols, 1989.

Blanchard, Y.-M.
1993 *Le témoinage d'Irénéé.* Paris: Cerf.

Blanck, H.
1992 *Das Buch in der Antike.* Munich: C. H. Beck.

Blass, F.
1901 *Die Rhythmen der attischen Kunstprosa: Isokrates, Demosthenes, Platon.* Leipzig: B. G. Teubner.
1902 "Die rhythmische Komposition des Hebräerbriefs." *Theologische Studien und Kritiken* 75:420–61.
1903 *Brief an die Hebräer: Text mit Angabe der Rhythmen.* Halle: Max Niemeyer.
1905 *Die Rhythmen der asianischen und römischen Kunstprosa: Paulus, Hebräerbrief, Pausanius, Cicero, Seneca, Curtius, Apuleius.* Leipzig: A. Deichert.

Blass, F., and A. Debrunner
1961 *A Greek Grammar of the New Testament and Other Early Christian Literature.* Translated by R. W. Funk. Chicago: University of Chicago Press.

Blass, F., A. Debrunner, and F. Rehkopf
1984 *Grammatik des neutestamentlichen Griechisch.* 16. Auflage. Göttingen: Vandenhoeck & Ruprecht.

Blatz, B.
1991 "The Coptic Gospel of Thomas." In Schneemelcher (ed.) 1991, 1.110–33.

Blau, L.
1902 *Studien zum althebräischen Buchwesen I: Studien zum althebräischen Buchwesen und zur biblischen Literaturgeschichte.* Strassburg: K. J. Trübner.

Bligh, J.
1964 "The Structure of Hebrews." *Heythrop Journal* 5:170–77.

Blinzler, J., O. Kuss, and F. Mussner (eds.)
1963 *Neutestamentliche Aufsätze: Festschrift für Prof. Josef Schmid.* Regensburg: F. Pustet.

Bloch, H. (ed.)
1956 *Abhandlungen der griechischen Geschichtsschreibung.* Leiden: Brill.

Bloch, R.
1955 "Midrash." *DBSup* 5.1263–81.
1978 "Midrash." Pp. 29–50 in *Approaches to Ancient Judaism: Theory and Practice.* Edited by W. S. Green. BJS 1. Missoula, Mont.: Scholars Press.

Blomberg, C. L.
1989 "The Structure of 2 Corinthians 1–7." *Criswell Theological Review* 4:4–8.
1990a "New Testament Genre Criticism for the 1990s." *Themelios* 15:40–49.
1990b *Interpreting the Parables.* Leicester: Apollos.
1991 "Interpreting the Parables of Jesus: Where Are We and Where Do We Go from Here?" *CBQ* 53:50–78.

Blomqvist, J.
1979 *Das sogennante KAI adversativum: Zur Semantik einer griechischen Partikel.* SGU 13. Stockholm: Almqvist & Wiksell.

Bloom, H.
1973 *The Anxiety of Influence: A Theory of Poetry.* New York: Oxford University Press.
1998 *Shakespeare: The Invention of the Human.* New York: Riverhead Books.

Bloomer, W. M.
1997 *Latinity and Literary Society at Rome.* Philadelphia: University of Pennsylvania Press.

Bloomquist, L. G.
1993 *The Function of Suffering in Philippians.* JSNTSup 78. Sheffield: JSOT Press.
1997 "Methodological Considerations in the Determination of the Social Context of Cynic Rhetorical Practice: Implications for our Present Studies of the Jesus Traditions." In Porter and Olbricht (eds.) 1997, 200–231.
1999 "Rhetorical Argumentation and the Culture of Apocalyptic: A Socio-Rhetorical Analysis of Luke 21." In Porter and Stamps (eds.) 1999, 173–209.

Blowers, P. M.
1997 *The Bible in Greek Christian Antiquity.* Notre Dame: University of Notre Dame Press.

Blum, R.
1991 *Kallimachos: The Alexandrian Library and the Origins of Bibliography.* Madison: University of Wisconsin Press.

Bobertz, C. A., and D. Brakke
2002 *Reading in Christian Communities: Essays on Interpretation in the Early Church.* Notre Dame: University of Notre Dame Press.

Boers, H.
1975–76 "The Form-Critical Study of Paul's Letters: 1 Thessalonians as a Case Study." *NTS* 22:140–58.

Bogaert, P.
1969 *Apocalypse de Baruch, introduction, traduction du Syriaque et commentaire.* SC 144, 145. Paris: Les Éditions du Cerf.
1980 "Les Apocalypses contemporaines de Baruch, d'Esdras et de Jean." In Lambrecht (ed.) 1980, 47–68.

Boge, H.
1977 "Die Überlieferung der griechischen Tachygraphie." In Treu (ed.) 1977, 99–108.

Boismard, M.-E.
1949 "'L'Apocalypse' ou 'les apocalypses' de S. Jean." *RB* 56:507–27.
1962 "Saint Luc et la rédaction du quatrième évangile." *RB* 69:185–211.
1977 "Une procédé rédactionnel dans le quatrième évangile: la Wiederaufnahme." Pp. 235–41 in *L'Évangile de Jean: Sources, rédaction, théologie.* Leuven: University Press.

Boismard, M.-E., and A. Lamouille
1987 *L'Évangile de Jean: Commentaire.* 2d edition. Vol. 3 of *Synopse des quatre Évangiles en français.* Paris: Éditions du Cerf.

Bollansée, Jan
1999 *Hermippos of Smyrna.* Fascicle 3, IV. A Biography. Part Four (of *FGrHist* cont.): Biography and Antiquarian Literature. Edited by G. Schepens. Leiden: Boston, and Cologne: Brill.

Bolling, G. M.
1925 *The External Evidence for Interpolation in Homer.* Oxford: Clarendon Press.

Boman, T.
1967 *Die Jesus-Überlieferung im Lichte der neueren Volkskunde.* Göttingen: Vandenhoeck & Ruprecht.

Bompaire, J.
1958 *Lucian écrivain: Imitation et création.* Paris: Boccard.

Bonner, C.
1937 *The Last Chapters of Enoch in Greek.* London: Christophers.

1940 *The Homily on the Passion by Melito Bishop of Sardis and Some Fragments of the Apocryphal Ezekiel.* Philadelphia: University of Pennsylvania Press.

Bonner, S. F.
1949 *Roman Declamation in the Late Republic and Early Empire.* Berkeley: University of California Press.
1969 *The Literary Treatises of Dionysius of Halicarnassus: A Study in the Development of Critical Method.* Amsterdam: Hakkert.
1977 *Education in Ancient Rome.* Berkeley: University of California Press.

Bonnet, M. (ed.)
1898 *Acta Joannis. Acta apostolorum apocrypha* 2.1. Leipzig: Mendelssohn; reprinted Hildesheim: Olms, 1975.

Bonz, M. P.
2000 *The Past as Legacy: Luke–Acts and Ancient Epic.* Minneapolis: Fortress Press.

Booth, W.
1961 "Distance and Point of View: An Essay in Classification." *Essays in Criticism* 11:60–79.
1974 *A Rhetoric of Irony.* Chicago: University of Chicago Press.
1983 *The Rhetoric of Fiction.* 2d ed. Chicago: University of Chicago Press.

Borgen, P.
1958–59 "John and the Synoptics in the Passion Narrative." *NTS* 5:246–59.
1965 *Bread from Heaven: An Exegetical Study of the Concept of Manna in the Gospel of John and the Writings of Philo.* NovTSup 10. Leiden: Brill.

Borgen, P., and S. Giversen (eds.)
1986 *Philo, John, Paul: New Perspectives on Judaism and Early Christianity.* BJS 131. Atlanta: Scholars Press.
1995 *The New Testament and Hellenistic Judaism.* Aarhus: Aarhus University.

Boring, M. E.
1985 "Criteria of Authenticity: The Lucan Beatitudes as a Test Case." *Forum* 1:3–38.
1988 "The Historical-Critical Method's 'Criteria of Authenticity': The Beatitudes in Q and Thomas as a Test Case." *Semeia* 44:9–44.
1995 "The Gospel of Matthew: Introduction, Commentary, and Reflections." Vol. 8, pp. 87–505 in *The New Interpreter's Bible.* 12 vols. Nashville: Abingdon Press.

Bornkamm, G.
1937 "Die Komposition der apokalyptischen Visionen in der Offenbarung Johannis." *ZNW* 36:132–49.
1962a "The History of the Origin of the So-called Second Letter to the Corinthians." *NTS* 8:258–64.
1962b "Der Philipperbrief als paulinische Briefsammlung." Pp. 192–202 in *Neotestamentica et Patristica.* NovTSup 6. Leiden: Brill.
1977–78 "Der Aufbau der Bergpredigt." *NTS* 24:419–31.

Bornkamm, G., G. Barth and H. J. Held
1963 *Tradition and Interpretation in Matthew.* Philadelphia: Westminster Press.

Botha, J. E.
1991a *Jesus and the Samaritan Woman: A Speech Act Reading of John 4:1–42.* Leiden: Brill.
1991b "Style in the New Testament: The Need for Serious Reconsideration." *JSNT* 43:71–87.

Botha, P. J. J.
1992 "Greco-Roman Literacy as Setting for New Testament Writings." *Neot* 26:195–215.

Boucher, M.
1977 *The Mysterious Parable: A Literary Study.* CBQMS 6. Washington, D.C.: Catholic Biblical Association of America.

Bouissac, P. (ed.)
1998 *Encyclopedia of Semeiotics.* Oxford: Oxford University Press.

Boulanger, A.
1968 *Aelius Aristide et la Sophistique dans la Province d'Asie au IIe siècle de notre ère.* Paris: Éditions E. de Boccard.

Bousset, W.
1901 "Die Himmelsreise der Seele." *ARW* 4:136–69, 229–73.
1915 *Jüdischchristlicher Schulbetrieb in Alexandria und Rom: Literarische Untersuchungen zu Philo und Clemens von Alexandria, Justin und Irenäus.* FRLANT n.F. 6/23. Göttingen: Vandenhoeck & Ruprecht.

Bouttier, M.
1991 *L'Épître de Saint Paul aux Éphésiens.* Geneva: Labor et Fides.

Bovon, F.
1987 "Vers une nouvelle édition de la littérature apocryphe chrétienne." *Augustinianum* 23:373–78.
1988 "The Synoptic Gospels and the Noncanonical Acts of the Apostles." *HTR* 81:19–36.
1999 *Harvard Studies in the Apocryphal Acts*

of the Apostles. Cambridge: Harvard University Press.

2000 "John's Self-Presentation in Revelation 1:9–10." *CBQ* 62:693–700.

2002 *Luke 1.* Hermeneia. Minneapolis: Fortress Press.

Bovon, F., B. Bouvier, and F. Amsler (eds.)

1999 *Acta Philippi: Textus.* Corpus Christianorum, Series Apocryphorum 11. Turnhout: Brepols.

Bovon, F., A. G. Brock, and C. R. Matthews (eds.)

1999 *The Apocryphal Acts of the Apostles.* Harvard Divinity School Studies. Cambridge: Harvard University Press.

Bovon, F., and P. Geoltrain

1997 *Écrits apocryphes chrétiens.* Bibliothèque de la Pléade 442. Paris: Gallimard.

Bowe, B. E.

1988 *A Church in Crisis: Ecclesiology and Paranesis in Clement of Rome.* HDR 23. Minneapolis: Fortress Press.

Bowersock, G. W.

1969 *Greek Sophists in the Roman Empire.* Oxford: Oxford University Press.

1974 *Approaches to the Second Sophistic.* University Park, Pa.: American Philological Association.

1994 *Fiction as History: From Nero to Julian.* Berkeley: University of California Press.

Bowie, E. L.

1974 "Greeks and Their Past in the Second Sophistic." In *Studies in Ancient Society.* Edited by M. I. Finley. London: Routledge & Kegan Paul.

Bowie, E. L., and S. J. Harrison

1993 "The Romance of the Novel." *JRS* 83:159–78.

Bowker, J. W.

1967 "Speeches in Acts: A Study in Proem and Yelammedenu Form." *NTS* 14:96–111.

Bowman, A. K., and G. Woolf (eds.)

1994 *Literacy and Power in the Ancient World.* Cambridge: Cambridge University Press.

Box, G. H.

1912 *The Ezra-Apocalypse.* London: Sir Isaac Pitman & Sons.

Bowra, C. M.

1964 *Pindar.* Oxford: Clarendon Press.

Boyarin, D.

1990 *Intertextuality and the Reading of the Midrash.* Bloomington and Indianapolis: Indiana University Press.

1994 *A Radical Jew: Paul and the Politics of Identity.* Berkeley: University of California Press.

1999 *Dying for God: Martyrdom and the Making of Christianity and Judaism.* Stanford, Calif.: Stanford University Press.

Boyle, A. J. (ed.)

1993 *Roman Epic.* London: Routledge.

Bradley, D. G.

1953 "The *Topos* as a Form in the Pauline Paraenesis." *JBL* 72:238–46.

Bradshaw, P. F.

1982 *The Search for the Origins of Christian Worship: Sources and Methods for the Study of Early Liturgy.* New York and Oxford: Oxford University Press.

Brandes, P. D.

1989 *A History of Aristotle's* Rhetoric. Metuchen and London: Scarecrow Press.

Brandt, W. J.

1970 *The Rhetoric of Argumentation.* New York: Bobbs-Merrill.

Branick, V. P.

1982 "Source and Redaction Analysis of 1 Corinthians 1–3." *JBL* 101:251–69.

Brashear, W. M.

1995 "The Greek Magical Papyri: An Introduction and Survey; Annotated Bibliography (1928–1994)." Pp. 3380–3684 in *ANRW* II,18.5.

Braun, F.-M.

1959 *Jean le Théologien et son Évangile dans l'Église ancienne.* Vol. 1. Paris: J. Gabalda.

Braun, M.

1938 *History and Romance in Graeco-Oriental Literature.* Oxford: Basil Blackwell.

Braun, W.

1995 *Feasting and Social Rhetoric in Luke 14.* SNTSMS 85. Cambridge: Cambridge University Press.

Breck, J.

1987 "Biblical Chiasmus: Exploring Structure for Meaning." *BTB* 17:70–74.

Breech, E.

1973 "These Fragments I Have Shored against My Ruins: The Form and Function of 4th Ezra." *JBL* 92:267–74.

Bremmer, J. M.

1981 "Greek Prayer." In *Faith, Hope, and Worship.* Edited by H. S. Versnel. Leiden: Brill.

1995 *The Apocryphal Acts of John.* Leuven: Peeters.

1996a *The Apocryphal Acts of Paul and Thecla.* Leuven: Peeters.

1996b "Magic, Martyrdom, and Women's Liberation in the Acts of Paul and Thecla." In Bremmer (ed.) 1996a, 36–59.

1998 *The Apocryphal Acts of Peter: Magic, Miracles, and Gnosticism.* Leuven: Peeters.

1999 *The Apocryphal Acts of Andrew.* Leuven: Peeters.

Bremmer, J., and F. Graf

1987 *Interpretations of Greek Mythology.* Totowa, N.J.: Barnes & Noble.

Brent, A.

1999 "Diogenes Laertius and the Apostolic Succession." Pp. 159–99 in *Norms of Faith and Life.* Edited by Everett Ferguson. New York and London: Garland.

Brewer, D. I.

1992 *Techniques and Assumptions in Jewish Exegesis before 70 C.E.* Tübingen: Mohr-Siebeck.

Breytenbach, C.

1992 "Vormarkinische Logientradition: Parallelen in der urchristlichen Briefliteratur." In Van Segbroeck (et al.) 1992, 725–49.

Brinkmann, L.

1909 "Der älteste Briefsteller." *Rheinisches Museum* 64:310–17.

Brinsmead, B. H.

1982 *Galatians—Dialogical Response to Opponents.* SBLDS 65. Chico, Calif.: Scholars Press.

Brinton, A.

1981 "Situation in the Theory of Rhetoric." *PR* 14:234–48.

1988 "Pathos and the 'Appeal to Emotion': An Aristotelian Analysis." *History of Philosophy Quarterly* 5:207–19.

Broadbent, M.

1969 *Studies in Greek Genealogy.* Leiden: Brill.

Broadhead, E.

2001 "The Extent of the Sayings Tradition (Q)." In Lindemann (ed.) 2001, 719–28.

Brock, A. G.

1994 "Genre of the *Acts of Paul*: One Tradition Enhancing Another." *Apocrypha* 5:119–36.

Brock, S.

1990 "The Two Ways and the Palestinian Targum." Pp. 138–52 in *A Tribute to Geza Vermes: Essays on Jewish and Christian Literature and History.* Edited by P. R. Davies and R. T. White. JSOTSup 100. Sheffield: Sheffield Academic Press.

Broer, I.

1985 *Die Seligpreisen und der Bergpredigt.* BBB 61. Bonn: Peter Hanstein.

Brooke, A. E.

1967 *The Fragments of Heracleon.* 1891; reprint, Nendeln: Kraus.

Brooke, G. J.

1979–81 "Qumran Pesher: Towards the Redefinition of a Genre." *RevQ* 10:483–503.

1985 *Exegesis at Qumran: 4QFlorilegium in Its Jewish Context.* JSOTSup 29. Sheffield: JSOT Press.

1987 "The Biblical Texts in the Qumran Commentaries: Scribal Errors or Exegetical Variants." Pp. 85–100 in *Early Jewish and Christian Exegesis: Studies in Memory of William Hugh Brownlee.* Edited by C. A. Evans and W. F. Stinespring. Atlanta: Scholars Press.

1994 "The Genre of 4Q252: From Poetry to Pesher." *DSD* 1:160–79.

1995 "Luke–Acts and the Qumran Scrolls." In Tuckett (ed.) 1995, 72–90.

1998 "Shared Intertextual Interpretations in the Dead Sea Scrolls and the New Testament." In Stone and Chazon (eds.) 1998, 35–57.

Brooke, G. J., and J.-D. Kaestli (eds.)

2000 *Narrativity in Biblical and Related Texts; La narrativité dans la Bible et les textes apparentés.* BETL 149. Leuven: Leuven University and Uitgeverij Peeters.

Brooke, G. J., and B. Lindars (eds.)

1992 *Septuagint, Scrolls and Cognate Writings.* Atlanta: Scholars Press.

Brooks, P.

1984 *Reading for the Plot: Design and Intention in Narrative.* New York: Vintage.

Brouwer, Wayne

2000 *The Literary Development of John 13–17: A Chiastic Reading.* SBLDS 182. Atlanta: Society of Biblical Literature.

Brown, M. P.

1963 *The Authentic Writings of Ignatius: A Study of Linguistic Criteria.* Durham: Duke University Press.

Brown, R. E.

1962–63 "The Gospel of Thomas and St. John's Gospel." *NTS* 9:155–77.

1966–70 *The Gospel according to John.* AB 29, 29A. 2 vols. Garden City, N.Y.: Doubleday.

1971 "Jesus and Elijah." *Perspective* 12:85–104.

1982 *The Epistles of John.* AB 30. Garden City, N.Y.: Doubleday.

1987 "The *Gospel of Peter* and Canonical Gospel Priority." *NTS* 33:321–43.

1994 *The Death of the Messiah, From Gethsemane to the Grave: A Commentary on the Passion Narratives in the Four Gospels.* 2 vols. New York: Doubleday.

Brown, S.
1970 "Concerning the Origin of *Nomina Sacra.*" *SPap* 9:7–19.

Brown, S. G.
2002 "Mark 11:1–12:12: A Triple Intercalation?" *CBQ* 64:78–89.

Brownlee, W. H.
1951 "Biblical Interpretation among the Sectaries of the Dead Sea Scrolls." *BA* 14:54–76.

Brox, N.
1975 *Falsche Verfasserangaben: Zur Erklärung der frühchristlichen Pseudepigraphie.* Stuttgarter Bibelstudien 79. Stuttgart: Katholisches Bibelwerk.
1978 *Pseudepigraphie in der heidnischen und jüdisch-christlichen Antike.* Wege der Forschung 484. Darmstadt: Wissenschaftliche Buchgesellschaft.
1986 *Der erste Petrusbrief.* 2d ed. Zurich: Benziger.
1991 *Der Hirt des Hermas: Übersetzt und erklärt.* Göttingen: Vandenhoeck & Ruprecht.
1993 *Epideixis; Adversus haereses = Darlegung der apostolischen Verkündigung: Gegen die Häresien.* Fontes Christiani 8. Freiburg and New York: Herder.
2001 *Adversus haereses = Gegen die Häresien von Irenäus von Lyon.* Fontes Christiani 8/5. Freiburg: Herder.

Bruce, A. B.
1882 *The Parabolic Teachings of Christ: A Systematic and Critical Study of the Parables of Our Lord.* London: Hodder & Stoughton.

Bruce, F. F.
1942 *The Speeches in the Acts of the Apostles.* London: Tyndale.
1959 *Biblical Exegesis in the Qumran Texts.* The Hague: Van Keulen.
1974 "The Speeches in Acts—Thirty Years After." Pp. 53–68 in *Reconciliation and Hope: New Testament Essays on Atonement and Eschatology.* Edited by R. Banks. Grand Rapids: Eerdmans.
1974 *The "Secret" Gospel of Mark.* London: University of London.
1988 *The Canon of Scripture.* Glasgow: Chapter House.

Brucker, R.
1997 *Christus-Hymnen oder "Epideiktische Passagen"?* FRLANT 176. Göttingen: Vandenhoeck & Ruprecht.

Brunt, J. C.
1984 "More on *Topos* as a New Testament Form." *JBL* 104:495–500.

Brunvand, J. H.
1976 *Folklore: A Study and Research Guide.* New York: St. Martin's.

Bryan, C.
1993 *A Preface to Mark: Notes on the Gospel in Its Literary and Cultural Settings.* Oxford: Oxford University Press.
2000 *A Preface to Romans: Notes on the Epistle in Its Literary and Cultural Setting.* Oxford: Oxford University Press.

Bubenik, V.
1989 *Hellenistic and Roman Greece as a Sociolinguistic Area.* Amsterdam and Philadelphia: J. Benjamins.

Buchanan, G. W.
1996 *The Gospel of Matthew.* Lewiston, N.Y.: Edwin Mellen.

Buchheit, V.
1960 *Untersuchungen zur Theorie des Genes Epideiktikon von Gorgias bis Aristoteles.* Munich: Hueber.

Buck, C. H.
1949 "The Early Order of the Pauline Corpus." *JBL* 68:351–57.

Buck, P. L.
2003 "Justin Martyr's Apologies: Their Number, Destination and Form." *JTS* 54:45–59.

Buell, Denise K.
1999 *Making Christians: Clement of Alexandria and the Rhetoric of Legitimacy.* Princeton: Princeton University Press.

Buffière, F.
1958 *Les Mythes d'Homère et la pensée grecque.* Paris: Société d'Édition Les Belles Lettres.
1962 *Héraclite, Allégories d'Homère.* Paris: Société d'Édition Les Belles Lettres.

Bujard, W.
1973 *Stilanalytische Untersuchungen zum Kolosserbrief als Beitrag zur Methodik von Sprachvergleichen.* SUNT 11. Göttingen: Vandenhoeck & Ruprecht.

Bultmann, R.
1910 *Der Stil der paulinischen Predigt und die kynisch-stoische Diatribe.* FRLANT 13. Göttingen: Vandenhoeck & Ruprecht.
1963 *The History of the Synoptic Tradition.* Translated by John Marsh. New York: Harper & Row.
1967 *Die Geschichte der synoptischen Tradi-*

tion. 7th ed. Göttingen: Vandenhoeck & Ruprecht.
1971a *Die Geschichte der synoptischen Tradition: Ergänzungsheft.* Edited by G. Theissen and P. Vielhauer. 4th ed. Göttingen: Vandenhoeck & Ruprecht.
1971b *The Gospel of John: A Commentary.* Translated by G. R. Beasley-Murray, et al. Philadelphia: Westminster Press.

Bundy, E. L.
1962 *Studia Pindarica I and II.* Berkeley: University of California Press.
1972 "The Quarrel between Kallimachos and Apollonios, Part I: The Epilogue of Kallimachos' *Hymn to Apollo.*" CSCA 5:39–94.

Bünker, M.
1983 *Briefformular und rhetorische Disposition im 1.Korintherbrief.* GTA 28. Göttingen: Vandenhoeck & Ruprecht.

Burgess, T. C.
1902 *Epideictic Literature.* Chicago: University of Chicago Press.

Burke, Kenneth
1950 *A Rhetoric of Motives.* New York: Prentice-Hall.
1962 *A Grammar of Motives and a Rhetoric of Motives.* Cleveland: World Publishing.
1966 *Language as Symbolic Action: Essays on Life, Literature, and Method.* Berkeley: University of California Press.
1970 *The Rhetoric of Religion: Studies in Logology.* Los Angeles and London: University of California Press.
1973 *The Philosophy of Literary Form: Studies in Symbolic Action.* 3d ed. Berkeley: University of California Press.

Burkert, W.
1975 "Aristoteles im Theater: Zur Datierung des 3. Buch der *Rhetoric* und der *Poetik,*" *Museum Helveticum* 32:67–72.

Burkitt, F. C.
1907 *The Gospel History and Its Transmission.* 2d ed. Edinburgh: T. & T. Clark.

Burney, C. F.
1925 *The Poetry of Our Lord.* Oxford: Clarendon Press.

Burnyeat, M.
1994 "The Enthymeme: Aristotle on the Logic of Persuasion." In Furley and Nehamas (eds.) 1994, 3–55.
1996 "Enthymeme: Aristotle on the Rationality of Rhetoric." In Rorty (ed.) 1996, 85–115.

Burridge, R. A.
1992 *What Are the Gospels? A Comparison with Graeco-Roman Biography.* SNTSMS 70. Cambridge: Cambridge University Press.

Burton, J. B.
1998 "Reviving the Pagan Greek Novel in a Christian World." *GRBS* 39:179–216.

Buschmann, G.
1994 *Martyrium Polycarpi—eine formkritische Studie: Ein Beitrag zur Frage nach der Entstehung der Gattung Märtyrerakte.* BZNW 70. Berlin and New York: Walter de Gruyter.

Buse, Ivor
1957–58 "St. John and the Marcan Passion Narrative." *NTS* 4:215–19.

Buss, M. J.
1999 *Biblical Form Criticism in Its Context.* JSOTSup 274. Sheffield: Sheffield Academic Press.

Bussby, F.
1954 "Is Q an Aramaic Document?" *ExpT* 65:272–75.

Butler, B. C.
1951 *The Originality of St. Matthew.* Cambridge: Cambridge University Press.

Buxton, R. G. A.
1994 *Imaginary Greece: The Contexts of Mythology.* Cambridge and New York: Cambridge University Press.

Byatt, A.
1995 *New Testament Metaphors: Illustrations in Word and Phrase.* Edinburgh: Pentland.

Byrskog, S.
1996 "Co-Senders, Co-Authors, and Paul's Use of the First Person Plural." *ZNW* 87:230–50.
1997 "Epistolography, Rhetoric and Letter Prescript: Romans 1.1–7 as a Test Case." *JSNT* 65:27–46.
2000 *Story as History—History as Story: The Gospel Tradition in the Context of Ancient Oral History.* WUNT 123. Tübingen: Mohr-Siebeck.

Cadbury, H. J.
1920 *The Style and Literary Method of Luke.* Cambridge: Harvard University Press.
1922 "Commentary on the Preface of Luke." Pp. 2.489–510 in *The Acts of the Apostles,* Part I of *The Beginnings of Christianity.* Edited by F. J. Foakes Jackson and Kirsopp Lake. London: Macmillan.
1927 *The Making of Luke–Acts.* New York: Macmillan.
1968 "Four Features of Lucan Style." In Keck and Martyn (eds.) 1968, 89–101.

Caird, G. B.
1980 *The Language and Imagery of the Bible.* Philadelphia: Westminster Press.
Callahan, A. D.
1997 *The Embassy of Onesimus: The Letter of Paul to Philemon.* Valley Forge, Pa.: Trinity Press International.
Callan, T.
1985 "The Preface of Luke–Acts and Historiography." *NTS* 31:576–81.
Callebat, L.
1993 "Formes et modes d'expression dans les oeuvres d'Apulée." In *ANRW* II, 34/2, 1600–1664.
Cameron, A. (ed.)
1990 *History as Text: The Writing of Ancient History.* Chapel Hill: University of North Carolina Press.
Cameron, P. S.
1990 "The Structure of Ephesians." *Filologia Neotestamentaria* 3:3–17.
Cameron, R. (ed.)
1982 *The Other Gospels: Non-Canonical Gospel Texts.* Philadelphia: Westminster Press.
Camery-Hoggatt, J.
1992 *Irony in Mark's Gospel: Text and Subtext.* Cambridge: Cambridge University Press.
Campbell, D. A.
1992 *The Rhetoric of Righteousness in Romans 3:21–26.* JSNTSup 65. Sheffield: JSOT Press.
1994 "Determining the Gospel through Rhetorical Analysis in Paul's Letter to the Roman Christians." In Jervis and Richardson (eds.) 1994, 315–36.
Campenhausen, H. von
1972 *The Formation of the Christian Bible.* Translated by J. A. Baker. Philadelphia: Fortress Press.
Canali, L., and G. Cavallo.
1991 *Graffiti Latini: scrivere sui muri a Roma antica.* Milano: Bompiani.
Cancik, Hildegard
1967 *Untersuchungen zu Seneca Epistulae Morales.* Hildesheim: Olms.
Cancik, Hubert
1984a *Markus Philologie: Historische, literaturgeschichtliche und stilistische Untersuchungen zum zweiten Evangelium.* WUNT 33. Tübingen: Mohr-Siebeck.
1984b "Die Gattung Evangelium: Das Evangelium des Markus im Rahmen der antike Historiographie." In Hubert Cancik 1984a.
1997 "The History of Culture, Religion, and Institutions in Ancient Historiography: Philological Observations Concerning Luke's History." *JBL* 116:673–95.
Cancik, Hubert, H. Lichtenberger, and P. Schäfer (eds.)
1996 *Geschichte-Tradition-Reflexion: Festschrift für Martin Hengel zum 70. Geburtstag.* 4 vols. Tübingen: Mohr-Siebeck.
Canfora, L.
1990 *The Vanished Library: A Wonder of the Ancient World.* Translated by M. Ryle. Berkeley and Los Angeles: University of California Press.
Cannon, G. E.
1983 *Traditional Materials in Colossians.* Macon, Ga.: Mercer University Press.
Canter, H. V.
1931 "*Digressio* in the Orations of Cicero." *AJP* 52:351–61.
1936 "Irony in the Orations of Cicero." *AJP* 57:354–61.
Cantinat, J.
1973 *Les épîtres de Saint Jacques et de Saint Jude.* SB. Paris: Gabalda.
Caragounis, C. C.
1995 "The Error of Erasmus and Un-Greek Pronunciations of Greek." *Filologia Neotestamentaria* 8 (1995): 151–85.
Carey, G.
1999 *Elusive Apocalypse: Reading Authority in the Revelation to John.* Studies in American Biblical Hermeneutics 15. Macon: Mercer University.
Cargal, J.
1992 *Restoring the Diaspora: Discursive Structure and Purpose in the Epistle of James.* Atlanta: Scholars Press.
Carleton Paget, J.
1994 *The Epistle of Barnabas: Outlook and Background.* WUNT 2/64. Tübingen: Mohr-Siebeck.
Carlini, A.
1991 *Erma: Il Pastore (Ia–IIIa visione).* Papyrus Bodmer 38. Cologny-Genève: Fondation Martin Bodmer.
Carlston, C.
1975 *The Parables of the Triple Tradition.* Philadelphia: Fortress Press.
1980 "Proverbs, Maxims, and the Historical Jesus." *JBL* 99:87–105.
Carmignac, J.
1964 "Le genre littéraire du 'pesher' dans 'Pistis Sophia.'" *RevQ* 4:497–522.
1970 "Le document de Qumrân zur Melkisédek." *RevQ* 7:343–78.

Carozzi, C.
1994 *Eschatologie et Au-delà: Recherches sur l 'Apocalypse de Paul'.* Aix-en-Provence: Université de Provence.

Carrez, M.
1979–80 "Le 'Nous' en 2 Corinthiens: Paul parle-t-il au nom de toute la communauté, du groupe apostolique, de l'équipe ministérielle ou en son nom personnel? Contribution à l'étude de l'apostolicité dans 2 Corinthiens." *NTS* 26:474–86.

Carrington, P.
1952 *The Primitive Christian Calendar: A Study in the Making of the Markan Gospel.* Cambridge: Cambridge University Press.
1960 *According to Mark.* Cambridge: Cambridge University Press.

Carroll, K. L.
1954–55 "The Creation of the Fourfold Gospel." *Bulletin of the John Rylands Library* 37:68–77.

Carruth, S., and A. Garsky
1996 *Q11:2b-4.* Documenta Q. Leuven: Peeters Press.

Carson, D. A.
1978 "Current Source Criticism of the Fourth Gospel: Some Methodological Questions." *JBL* 97:411–29.
1985 "The ΟΜΟΙΟΣ Word-Group as Introduction to Some Matthean Parables." *NTS* 31:277–82.
1988 "John and the Johannine Epistles." In Carson and Williamson (eds.) 1988, 245–64.

Carson, D. A., P. T. O'Brien, and M. A. Seifrid (eds.)
2001 *Justification and Variegated Nomism.* Vol. 1: *The Complexities of Second Temple Judaism.* Tübingen: Mohr-Siebeck; Grand Rapids: Baker Academic.

Carson, D. A., and H. G. M. Williamson (eds.)
1988 *It Is Written: Scripture Citing Scripture.* Cambridge: Cambridge University Press.

Carter, W.
1992 "Kernels and Narrative Blocks: The Structure of Matthew's Gospel." *CBQ* 54:463–81.

Carter, W., and J. P. Heil
1998 *Matthew's Parables: Audience-Oriented Perspectives.* CBQMS 30. Washington, D.C.: Catholic Biblical Association of America.

Casey, M.
1998 *Aramaic Sources of Mark's Gospel.* Cambridge: Cambridge University Press.

Casson, L.
1989 *The Periplus Maris Erythraei.* Princeton: Princeton University Press.
2001 *Libraries in the Ancient World.* New Haven, Conn.: Yale University Press.

Catchpole, D. R.
1993 *The Quest for Q.* Edinburgh: T. & T. Clark.

Cavallo, G.
1967 *Richerche sulla Maiuscola Biblica.* Florence: Le Monnier.

Cazeaux, J.
1973 "Aspects de l'exégèse philonienne." *RSR* 47:262–69.

Cerfaux, L., and J. Tondriau
1957 *Le culte des souverains dans la civilisation gréco-romaine.* Tournai, 1957.

Chabert, S.
1897 *L'Atticisme de Lucien.* Paris: Lecene, Oudin, et cie.

Chadwick, Henry
1959 *The Sentences of Sextus: A Contribution to the History of Early Christian Ethics.* Cambridge: Cambridge University Press.
1966 *Early Christian Thought and the Classical Tradition: Studies in Justin, Clement, and Origen.* New York: Oxford University Press.
1998 *Pagane und christliche Allegorese: Activa und Passiva im antiken Umgang mit der Bibel.* Berlin: Walter de Gruyter.

Chaine, J.
1927 *L'Épître de Saint Jacques.* Paris: J. Gabalda.

Chance, J. B.
1991 "Fiction in Ancient Biography: An Approach to a Sensitive Issue in Gospel Interpretation." *Perspectives in Religious Studies* 18:125–42.

Chapa, J.
1994 "Is First Thessalonians a Letter of Consolation?" *NTS* 40:150–60.

Chapman, D. W., and A. J. Köstenberger
2000 "Jewish Intertestamental and Early Rabbinic Literature: An Annotated Bibliographic Resource." *JETS* 43:577–618.

Charles, J. D.
1990 "'Those' and 'These': The Use of the Old Testament in the Epistle of Jude." *JSNT* 38:109–24.
1991a "Jude's Use of Pseudepigraphic Source-Material as Part of a Literary Strategy." *NTS* 37:130–45.
1991b "Literary Artifice in the Epistle of Jude." *ZNW* 82:106–24.
1993 *Literary Strategy in the Epistle of Jude.*

Toronto, London and Scranton: Associated University Presses.

1997 *Virtue amidst Vice: The Catalog of Virtues in 2 Peter 1.* JSNTSup 150. Sheffield: Sheffield Academic Press.

Charles, R. H.

1896 *The Apocalypse of Baruch: Translated from the Syriac.* London: A. & C. Black.

1906 *The Ethiopic Version of the Book of Enoch.* Oxford: Clarendon Press.

1908 *The Greek Versions of the Testaments of the Twelve Patriarchs.* Oxford: Clarendon Press.

1912 *The Book of Enoch or 1 Enoch.* Oxford: Clarendon Press.

1913 *Apocrypha and Pseudepigrapha of the Old Testament.* 2 vols. Oxford: Oxford University Press.

1920 *A Critical and Exegetical Commentary on the Revelation of St. John.* 2 vols. Edinburgh: T. & T. Clark.

Charlesworth, J. H.

1977 "Reflections on the SNTS Pseudepigrapha Seminar at Duke on the Testaments of the Twelve Patriarchs." *NTS* 23:296–304.

1981a "Christian and Jewish Self-Definition in Light of the Christian Additions to the Apocryphal Writings." Pp. 27–55 in E. P. Sanders, A. I. Baumgarten, and A. Mendelson (eds.). *Jewish and Christian Self-Definition.* Vol. 2: *Aspects of Judaism in the Graeco-Roman Period.* Philadelphia: Fortress Press.

1981b *The Pseudepigrapha and Modern Research: With a Supplement.* SCSS 7. Chico, Calif.: Scholars Press.

1982 "A Prolegomenon to a New Study of the Jewish Background of the Hymns and Prayers in the New Testament." *JJS* 33:264–85.

1985 *The Old Testament Pseudepigrapha and the New Testament.* SNTSMS 54. Cambridge: Cambridge University Press.

1986 "Jewish Hymns, Odes, and Prayers (ca. 167 B.C.E.–135 C.E.)" In Kraft and Nickelsburg (eds.) 1986, 411–36.

1987a *The New Testament Apocrypha and Pseudepigrapha: A Guide to Publications, with Excursuses on Apocalypses.* Metuchen, N.J.: American Theological Library Association.

1987b "The Pseudepigrapha as Biblical Exegesis." In Evans and Stinespring (eds.) 1987, 139–52.

1995 *The Beloved Disciple: Whose Witness Validates the Gospel of John?* Valley Forge, Pa.: Trinity Press International.

Charlesworth J. H. (ed.).

1983–85 *The Old Testament Pseudepigrapha.* 2 vols. Garden City, N.Y.: Doubleday.

1985 *The Old Testament Pseudepigrapha and the New Testament: Prolegomena for the Study of Christian Origins.* SNTSMS 54. Cambridge: Cambridge University Press.

1991 *Graphic Concordance to the Dead Sea Scrolls.* Tübingen: Mohr-Siebeck; Louisville: Westminster/John Knox Press.

1992 *The Messiah: Developments in Earliest Judaism and Christianity.* Minneapolis: Fortress Press.

1994– *The Dead Sea Scrolls: Hebrew, Aramaic, and Greek Texts with English Translations.* 10 vols. Tübingen: Mohr-Siebeck; Louisville, Ky.: Westminster John Knox Press.

Charlesworth, J. H., and C. A. Evans (eds.).

1993 *The Pseudepigrapha and Early Christian Biblical Interpretation.* SNTSSup 14. Sheffield: JSOT Press.

Chatman, S.

1978 *Story and Discourse: Narrative Structure in Fiction and Film.* Ithaca, N.Y.: Cornell University Press.

Chazon, Esther G.

1998 "Hymns and Prayers in the Dea Sea Scrolls." In Flint and Vanderkam (eds.) 1998, 1.244–70.

Chihocka, H.

1975 "Die Konzeption des Exkurses im Geschichtswerk des Ammianus Marcellinus." *Eos* 63:329–40.

Childs, B.

1979 *Introduction to the Old Testament as Scripture.* Philadelphia: Fortress Press.

1994 *The New Testament as Canon: An Introduction.* Philadelphia: Fortress Press.

Chilton, B. D.

1980 "Targumic Transmission and Dominical Tradition." In France and Wenham (eds.) 1980, 21–46.

1983 "Varieties and Tendencies of Midrash: Rabbinic Interpretations of Isaiah 24.23." In France and Wenham (eds.) 1983, 9–32.

Chilton, B. D., and C. A. Evans (eds.)

1999 *Authenticating the Words of Jesus.* NTTS 28.1. Leiden: Brill.

Chiron, P.

1993 *Démétrios, Du Style.* Budé. Paris: Les Belles Lettres.

Christiansen, I.
1969 *Die Technik der allegorischen Auslegungswissenschaft bei Philon von Alexandrien.* Tübingen: Mohr-Siebeck.

Church, F. F.
1978 "Rhetorical Structure and Design in Paul's Letter to Philemon." *HTR* 71–72:17–33.

Cirillo, L.
1984 *Elchasai e gli Elchasaiti: Un contributo alla storia delle comunità giudeoristiane.* Cosenza: Marra.

Clabeaux, J. J.
1989 *A Lost Edition of the Letters of Paul: A Reassessment of the Text of the Pauline Corpus Attested by Marcion.* CBQMS 21. Washington, D.C.: Catholic Biblical Association of America.

Clark, A. C.
1933 *The Acts of the Apostles.* Oxford: Clarendon Press.

Clark, D. J.
1975 "Criteria for Identifying Chiasm." *Lingistica Biblica* 35:63–72.

Clark, D. L.
1957 *Rhetoric in Greco-Roman Education.* New York: Columbia University Press.

Clarke, A. D.
1993 *Secular and Christian Leadership in Corinth: A Socio-Historical and Exegetical Study of 1 Corinthians 1–6. AGJU* 18. Leiden: Brill.

Clarke, H.
1981 *Homer's Readers: A Historical Introduction to the Iliad and the Odyssey.* Newark: University of Delaware Press.

Clarke, M. L.
1953 *Rhetoric at Rome: A Historical Survey.* London: Cohen & West.
1996 *Higher Education in the Ancient World.* 3d ed. London: Routledge & Kegan Paul.

Classen, C. J.
1976 *Sophistik.* Weg der Forschung 187. Darmstadt: Wissenschaftliche Buchgesellschaft.
1992 "St. Paul's Epistles and Ancient Greek and Roman Rhetoric." *Rhetorica* 10:319–44.
1993 "St. Paul's Epistles and Ancient Greek and Roman Rhetoric." In Porter and Olbricht (eds.) 1995, 271–77.
1994–95 "Philologische Bemerkungen zur Sprache des Apostles Paulus," *Wiener Studien* 107–8:321–35.
1998 *Zur Literatur und Gesellschaft der Römer.* Stuttgart: Franz Steiner.
2000 *Rhetorical Criticism of the New Testament.* WUNT 128. Tübingen: Mohr-Siebeck.

Clifford, R. J.
1972 *The Cosmic Mountain in Canaan and the Old Testament.* Cambridge: Harvard University Press.

Clines, D. J. A.
1987 "The Parallelism of Great Precision: Notes from Isaiah 40 for a Theory of Hebrew Poetry." In Follis (ed.) 1987, 77–100.
1990 *The Bible in Three Dimensions.* Sheffield: Sheffield Academic Press.

Clines, D. J. A., and S. Moore (eds.)
1998 *Auguries: The Jubilee Volume of the Sheffield Department of Biblical Studies.* JSOTSup 269. Sheffield: Sheffield Academic Press.

Coggins, R. J., and J. L. Houlden (eds.)
1990 *Dictionary of Biblical Interpretation.* Philadelphia: Trinity Press International.

Cohen, B.
1966 *Jewish and Roman Law: A Comparative Study.* Vol. 1. New York: Shulsinger Bros.

Cohen, S.
1979 *Josephus in Galilee and Rome: His Vita and His Development as a Historian.* Leiden: Brill.

Cohick, L. H.
2000 *The Peri Pascha Attributed to Melito of Sardis: Setting, Purpose, and Sources.* BJS 327. Providence: Brown Judaic Studies.

Cohn, L., and P. Wendland.
1896–1930 *Philonis Alexandrini opera quae supersunt.* 7 vols. in 8. Berlin: Georg Reimer.

Cole, S. G.
1981 "Could Greek Women Read and Write?" In Foley (ed.) 1981, 219–45.

Coleborne, W.
1970 "*The Shepherd* of Hermas: A Case for Multiple Authorship and Some Implications." In Cross (ed.) 1970, 1.65–70.

Coleman, G. B.
1976 *The Phenomenon of Christian Interpolations into Jewish Apocalyptic Texts: A Bibliographical Survey and Methodological Analysis.* Ph.D. dissertation, Vanderbilt University.

Coles, R. A., M. W. Haslam, and P. J. Parsons (eds.)
1994 "4009. Gospel of Peter?" Vol. 60, pp. 1–5 in *The Oxyrhynchus Papyri.* London: Egypt Exploration Fund.

Collins, J. J.
1973 "The Date and Provenance of the

Testament of Moses." In Nickelsburg (ed.) 1973, 15–32.
1979 *Apocalypse: Morphology of a Genre. Semeia* 14. Missoula, Mont.: Scholars Press.
1982 "The Apocalyptic Technique: Setting and Function in the Book of Watchers." *CBQ* 44:91–111.
1983 *Between Athens and Jerusalem: Jewish Identity in the Hellenistic Diaspora.* New York: Crossroad.
1984a *The Apocalyptic Imagination: An Introduction to the Jewish Matrix of Christianity.* New York: Crossroad.
1984b "Testaments." In Stone (ed.) 1984, 325–55.
1986 "The Testamentary Literature in Recent Scholarship." In Kraft and Nickelsburg (eds.) 1986, 268–85.
1997 *Apocalypticism in the Dead Sea Scrolls.* London and New York: Routledge.
1998–99 "Apocalypticism and Literary Genre in the Dead Sea Scrolls." In Flint and VanderKam (eds.) 1998–99, 2.403–30.
1999 "Pseudepigraphy and Group Formation in Second Temple Judaism." In Chazon and Stone (eds.) 1999, 43–58.

Collins, J. J., and J. H. Charlesworth (eds.)
1991 *Mysteries and Revelations: Apocalyptic Studies since the Uppsala Colloquium.* JSOTSup 9. Sheffield: Sheffield Academic Press.

Collins, N. L.
1992 "281 B.C.E.: The Year of the Translation of the Pentateuch into Greek under Ptolemy II." In Brooke and Lindars (eds.) 1992, 403–503.

Collins, R. F.
1984 *Studies on the First Letter to the Thessalonians.* BETL 66. Leuven: Leuven University.
1990 *The Thessalonian Correspondence.* BETL 87. Leuven: Leuven University.
1996 "1 Corinthians as a Hellenistic Letter." In Bieringer (ed.) 1996, 39–61.
1999 *First Corinthians.* SP 7. Collegeville, Minn.: Liturgical Press.

Colson, F. H., G. H. Whittaker, and R. Marcus.
1929–62 *Philo, with an English Translation.* 10 vols. and 2 supplementary vols. LCL. Cambridge: Harvard University Press; London: Heinemann.

Colwell, E. C.
1931 *The Greek of the Fourth Gospel: A Study of Its Aramaisms in the Light of Hellenistic Greek.* Chicago: University of Chicago Press.

Colwell, E. C., and D. W. Riddle
1933 *Prolegomena to the Study of the Lectionary Text of the Gospels.* Chicago: University of Chicago Press.

Combrink, H. J. B.
1982 "The Macrostructure of the Gospel of Matthew." *Neot* 16:1–20.
1983 "The Structure of the Gospel of Matthew as Narrative." *TynBul* 34.

Comfort, P. W.
1990a *Early Manuscripts and Modern Translations of the New Testament.* Grand Rapids: Baker Book House.
1990b "The Greek Text of the Gospel of John according to the Early Papyri." *NTS* 36:625–29.

Conley, T. M.
1982–83 "Πάθη and πίστεις Aristotle 'Rhet'. II 2–11," *Hermes* 110:300–315.
1984 "The Enthymeme in Perspective." *QJS* 70:168–87.
1987 *Philo's Rhetoric: Studies in Style, Composition, and Exegesis.* Berkeley: Center for Hermeneutical Studies.

Connolly, R. H.
1929 *Didascalia Apostolorum: The Syriac Version Translated and Accompanied by the Verona Latin Fragments.* Oxford: Clarendon Press.
1935 "The Date and Authorship of the Epistle to Diognetus." *JTS* 36:347–53.

Connors, R. J.
1986 "Greek Rhetoric and the Transition from Orality." *Philosophy and Rhetoric* 19:38–65.

Connors, R. J., L. S. Ede, and A. A. Lunsford (eds.)
1984 *Essays on Classical Rhetoric and Modern Discourse.* Carbondale: Southern Illinois University Press.

Consigny, S.
1974 "Rhetoric and Its Situations." *PR* 7:175–86.

Constable, G.
1976 *Letters and Letter Collections,* Turnhout: Brepols.

Conte, G. B.
1994a *Genres and Readers: Lucretius, Love Elegy, Pliny's Encyclopedia.* Translated by G. W. Most. Baltimore: Penguin.
1994b *Latin Literature: A History.* Translated by J. B. Solodow. Revised by D. Fowler and G. W. Most. Baltimore and London: Johns Hopkins University Press.

Conybeare, F. C.
1898 "The Testament of Solomon." *JQR* 11:1–45.

Conzelmann, H.
1961 *The Theology of St. Luke.* New York: Harper & Row.
1978 *Bemerkungen zum Martyrium Polycarps.* Nachrichten der Akademie der Wissenschaften in Göttingen, Philologisch-Historische Klasse 2. Göttingen: Vandenhoeck & Ruprecht.

Conzelmann, H., and A. Lindemann
1988 *Interpreting the New Testament: An Introduction to the Principles and Methods of N.T. Exegesis.* Translated by S. S. Schatzmann. Peabody, Mass.: Hendrickson.

Cook, B. F.
1987 *Greek Inscriptions.* Berkeley and Los Angeles: University of California Press and the British Museum.

Cope, O. L.
1976 *Matthew: A Scribe Trained for the Kingdom of Heaven.* CBQMS 5. Washington, D.C.: Catholic Biblical Association.
1978 "1 Cor. 11:2–16: One Step Further." *JBL* 97:435–36.

Copenhaver, B. P.
1992 *Hermetica: The Greek Corpus Hermeticum and the Latin Asclepius in a New English Translation with Notes and Introduction.* Cambridge: Cambridge University Press.

Corbett, E. P. J.
1990 *Classical Rhetoric for the Modern Student.* 3d ed. Oxford: Oxford University Press.

Corbett, E. P. J., and R. J. Connors
1999 *Classical Rhetoric for the Modern Student.* 4th ed. New York and Oxford: Oxford University Press.

Corley, B. (ed.)
1983 *Colloquy on New Testament Studies: A Time for Reappraisal and Fresh Approaches.* Macon, Ga.: Mercer University Press.

Cornilliat, F. and R. Lockwood (eds.)
2000 *Èthos* et *Pathos*: Le statut du sujet rhétorique. Paris: Honoré Champion Éditeur.

Cortés, E.
1976 *Los Discursos de Adiós de Gn 49 a Jn 13–17.* Barcelona: Herder.

Corwin, V.
1960 *St. Ignatius and Christianity in Antioch.* New Haven, Conn.: Yale University Press.

Cosby, M. R.
1988 "The Rhetorical Composition of Hebrews 11." *JBL* 107:257–73.

Cotelier, J. C.
1672 *Sanctorum Patrum qui temporibus apostolicus floruerunt, Barnabae, Clementis, Hermae, Ignatii, Polycarpi, opera edita et inedita, vera et supposititia.* Antwerp: Huguetanorum sumtibus.

Court, J. M.
1981 "The Didache and St. Matthew's Gospel." *SJT* 34:97–107.

Cowley, R. W.
1974 "The Biblical Canon of the Ethiopian Orthodox Church Today." *Ostkirchliche Studien* 23:318–23.

Cox, S. L.
1993 *A History and Critique of Scholarship concerning the Markan Endings.* Lewiston, N.Y.: Mellen.

Coxon, P. W.
1986 "The 'List' Genre and Narrative Style in the Court Tales of Daniel." *JSNT* 35:95–121.

Crane, R. S.
1994 *Literaturkritik und Bildungspolitik.* R.S. Crane, die Chicago (Neo-Aristotelian) Critics und die University of Chicago. Heidelberg: Winter.

Cranfield, C. E. B.
1975–79 *The Epistle to the Romans.* 2 vols. Edinburgh: T. & T. Clark.
1982 "Changes of Person and Number in Paul's Epistles." In Hook and Wilson (eds.) 1982, 280–89.

Creed, J. M.
1930 *The Gospel according to St Luke.* London: Macmillan.

Crenshaw, J. L.
1974 "Wisdom." Pp. 225–64 in *Old Testament Form Criticism.* Edited by J. H. Hayes. San Antonio: Trinity University Press.
1981 *Old Testament Wisdom: An Introduction.* Atlanta: John Knox Press.

Crocket, L.
1966 "Luke IV.16–30 and the Jewish Lectionary Cycle: A Word of Caution." *JJS* 17:13–46.

Cross, F. L. (ed.)
1970 *Studia Patristica.* vol. 10. TU 107. Berlin: Akademie-Verlag.

Cross, F. M.
1995 *The Ancient Library of Qumran.* 3d ed. Sheffield: Sheffield Academic Press.

Crossan, J. D.
1971 "The Parable of the Wicked Husbandmen." *JBL* 90:451–65.
1973 *In Parables: The Challenge of the Historical Jesus.* New York: Harper & Row.

1979 *Finding Is the First Act.* Philadelphia: Fortress Press.

1983 *In Fragments: The Aphorisms of Jesus.* San Francisco: Harper & Row.

1985 *Four Other Gospels: Shadows on the Contours of the Canon.* Philadelphia: Fortress Press.

1986 *Sayings Parallels: A Workbook for the Jesus Tradition.* Philadelphia: Fortress Press.

1988 *The Cross That Spoke: The Origins of the Passion Narrative.* San Francisco: Harper & Row.

1991 *The Historical Jesus: The Life of a Mediterranean Jewish Peasant.* San Francisco: HarperSanFrancisco.

1998a *The Birth of Christianity: Discovering What Happened in the Years Immediately Following the Resurrection.* San Francisco: HarperSanFrancisco.

1998b "The Gospel of Peter and the Canonical Gospels." *Forum* n.s. 1:7–51.

Crouch, J. E.

1973 *The Origin and Intention of the Colossian Haustafel.* Göttingen: Vandenhoeck & Ruprecht.

Croy, N. C.

2001 "Where the Gospel Text Begins: A Non-Theological Interpretation of Mark 1:1." *NovT* 43:105–27.

Crump, M. M.

1931 *The Epyllion from Theocritus to Ovid.* Oxford: Clarendon Press.

Cuddon, J. A.

1998 *A Dictionary of Literary Terms and Literary Theory.* Revised by C. E. Preston. 4th ed. Oxford: Blackwell.

Culianu, I. P.

1983 *Psychanodia I: A Survey of the Evidence Concerning the Ascension of the Soul and Its Relevance.* EPRO 99. Leiden: Brill.

Culler, Jonathan

1975 *Structuralist Poetics: Structuralism, Linguistics, and the Study of Literature.* Ithaca, N.Y.: Cornell University Press.

1981 *The Pursuit of Signs: Semiotics, Literature, Deconstruction.* London: Routledge & Kegan Paul.

Culley, R. C.

1963 "An Approach to the Problem of Oral Tradition." *VT* 13:113–25.

1972 "Oral Tradition and Historicity." Pp. 102–16 in *Studies on the Ancient Palestinian World.* Edited by J. W. Wevers and D. B. Redford. Toronto: University of Toronto Press.

1986 "Oral Tradition and Biblical Studies." *Oral Tradition* 1:30–65.

Cullmann, O.

1966 "Die Pluralität der Evangelien als theologisches Problem im Altertum." Pp. 548–65 in *Vorträge und Aufsätze 1925–62.* Edited by K. Fröhlich. Tübingen: Mohr-Siebeck.

Culpepper, R. A.

1983 *Anatomy of the Fourth Gospel: A Study in Literary Design.* Philadelphia: Fortress Press.

Dabourne, W.

1999 *Purpose and Cause in Pauline Exegesis: Romans 1:16–4:25 and a New Approach to the Letters.* Cambridge: Cambridge University Press.

Dahl, N. A.

1962 "The Particularity of the Pauline Epistles as a Problem in the Ancient Church." Pp. 261–71 in *Neotestamentica et Patristica.* Leiden: Brill.

1977a *Studies in Paul: Theology for the Early Christian Mission.* Minneapolis: Augsburg.

1977b "A Fragment and Its Context: 2 Cor. 6.14–7.1." In Dahl 1977a, 62–69.

1989 "Ephesians." Pp. 1212–19 in *Harper's Bible Commentary.* Edited by J. L. Mays. San Francisco: Harper & Row.

2000 *Studies in Ephesians.* Edited by D. Hellholm, V. Blomkvist and T. Fornberg. WUNT, 131. Tübingen: Mohr-Siebeck.

Dahood, M.

1976 "Chiasmus." *IDBSup,* 145.

D'Alton, J. F.

1931 *Roman Literary Theory and Criticism.* London and New York: Longmans, Green.

Dalton, W. J.

1979 "The Integrity of Philippians." *Bibl* 60:97–102.

Daly, L. W.

1961 *Aesop without Morals.* London: Thomas Yseloff.

D'Angelo, F.

1984 "The Evolution of the Analytic Topoi: A Speculative Inquiry." In Connors, Ede, and Lunsford (eds.) 1984, 50–68.

Daniélou, J.

1966 *Études d'exégèse judéo-chrétienne (Les Testimonia).* Théologie Historique 5. Paris: Beauschesne.

Danker, F. W.

1991 "Paul's Debt to the *De Corona* of Demosthenes: A Study of Rhetorical

Techniques in 2 Corinthians." Pp. 262–80 in *Persuasive Artistry: Studies in New Testament rhetoric in Honor of George A. Kennedy.* Edited by D. Watson. JSNTSup 50. Sheffield: Sheffield Academic Press.

Darr, J.
1992 *On Character-Building: The Reader and the Rhetoric of Characterization in Luke–Acts.* Louisville, Ky.: Westminster John Knox.

Daube, D.
1949 "Rabbinic Methods of Interpretation and Hellenistic Rhetoric." *HUCA* 22:239–64.

Davids, P. H.
1979 "Tradition and Citation in the Epistle of James." In Gasque and LaSor (eds.) 1978, 113–26.
1980 *The Epistle to James: A Commentary on the Greek Text.* NIGTC. Grand Rapids: Eerdmans.

Davidson, M.
1977 "The Thematic Use of Ekphrasis in the Ancient Novel." In *Erotica Antiqua: Acts of the International Conference on the Ancient Novel.* Bangor: University of Wales.

Davies, M.
1990 "Genre." In Coggins and Houlden 1990, 256–58.

Davies, P. R.
2001 "Didactic Stories." In Carson, O'Brien, and Seifrid (eds.) 2001, 99–134.

Davies, P. R., and R. T. White (eds.)
1990 *A Tribute to Geza Vermes: Essays on Jewish and Christian Literature and History.* JSOTSup 100. Sheffield: JSOT Press.

Davies, S. L.
1980 *The Revolt of the Widows: Women in the Stories of the Apocryphal Acts.* New York: Seabury Press.
1983 *The Gospel of Thomas and Christian Wisdom.* New York: Seabury Press.
1986 "Women, Tertullian and the Acts of Paul." *Semeia* 38:139–43.

Davies, W. D.
1948 *Paul and Rabbinic Judaism.* London: SPCK.
1962 *Christian Origins and Judaism.* Philadelphia: Westminster Press.
1964 *The Setting of the Sermon on the Mount.* Cambridge: Cambridge University Press.

Davies, W. D., and D. C. Allison
1988–97 *Matthew.* ICC. Vol. 1: 1988; Vol. 2: 1991; Vol. 3: 1997. Edinburgh: T. & T. Clark.

Davies, W. D., and L. Finkelstein (eds.)
1989 *The Cambridge History of Judaism.* 2 vols. Cambridge: Cambridge University Press.

Davila, J. R.
2000 *Liturgical Works.* ECDSS 6. Grand Rapids: Eerdmans.

Dawsey, J. M.
1986 *The Lukan Voice: Confusion and Irony in the Gospel of Luke.* Macon, Ga.: Mercer University Press.
1989 "The Literary Unity of Luke–Acts: Questions of Style—A Task for Literary Critics." *NTS* 35:48–66.

Dawson, D.
1992 *Allegorical Readers and Cultural Revision in Ancient Alexandria.* Berkeley: University of California Press.
1998 "Allegorical Reading and the Embodiment of the Soul in Origen." In Ayres and Jones (eds.) 1998, 26–43.
2000 "Plato's Soul and the Body of the Text in Philo and Origen." In Whitman (ed.) 2000, 89–107.

Dean-Otting, M.
1984 *Heavenly Journeys: A Study of the Motif in Hellenistic Jewish Literature.* Frankfurt, Bern, and New York: Peter Lang.

Debanné, M. J.
2002 "An Enthymematic Reading of Philippians: Towards a Typology of Pauline Arguments." In Porter and Stamps (eds.) 2002, 481–503.

de Boer, M. C.
1992 "Historical Criticism and the Gospel of John." *JSNT* 47:35–48.
1994 "The Composition of 1 Corinthians." *NTS* 40:229–45.
2000 "The Narrative Function of Pilate in John." In Brooke and Kaestli (eds.) 2000, 141–58.

DeConick, A. D.
2002 "The Original *Gospel of Thomas.*" *VC* 56:167–99.

de Faye, E.
1925 *Gnostiques et gnosticisme: Étude critique des documents du gnosticisme chrétien aux IIe et IIIe siècles.* Paris: Leroux.

Dehandschutter, B.
1979 *Martyrium Polycarpi: Een literairkritische studie.* BETL 52. Leuven: Leuven University.

Deichgräber, R.
1967 *Gotteshymnus und Christushymnus in*

der frühen Christenheit: Untersuchungen zu Form, Sprache und Stil der frühchristlichen Hymnen. Göttingen: Vandenhoeck & Ruprecht.

Deissmann, A.
1908 *Light from the Ancient East.* Translated by L. R. M. Strachan. New York and London: Harper & Bros.

Deiulio, A.
1978 "Of Adolescent Cultures and Subcultures." *Educational Leadership* 35: 518–19.

de Jong, I. J. F.
1987 *Narrators and Focalizers: The Presentation of the Story in the Iliad.* Amsterdam: B. R. Grüner.

De Lacy, P. H. and B. Einarson (trans.).
1959 *Plutarch's Moralis VII 523c–612b.* LCL. Cambridge: Harvard University; London: William Heinemann.

del Agua, A.
1993 "Jewish Procedures of Biblical Interpretation in the Gospels: A Proposal for Systematic Classification." *EstB* 51:77–106.

Delatte, A.
1927 "Testament de Salomon." Pp. 211–27 in *Anecdota Atheniensia.* Bibliothèque de la Faculté de Philosophie et Lettres de l'Université de Liège 36. Liège and Paris: Édouard Champion.

Delatte, A., and P. Derchain
1964 *Les intailles magiques gréco-égyptiennes.* Paris: Bibliothèque Nationale.

del Cerro, G.
1993 "Los Hechos Apócrifos de los Apóstoles su género literario." *EstB* 51:207–32.

Delehaye, H.
1921 *Les Passions des martyrs et les genres littéraires.* Brussels: Bureaux de la Société des Bolandistes.
1955 *Les Legendes Hagiographiques.* 4th ed. Brussels: Societe des Bollandistes.

Delft, L. van
1993 *Littérature et anthropologie: nature humaine et charactère à l'âge classique.* Paris: Presses universitaires de France.

Delobel, J.
1966 "L'onction par la pecheresse." *ETL* 42:415–75.
1982a *Logia: Les Paroles de Jésus—The Sayings of Jesus. Mémorial Joseph Coppens.* ETL 59. Leuven: Leuven University.
1982b "The Sayings of Jesus in the Textual Tradition: Variant Readings in the Greek Manuscripts of the Gospels." In Delobel (ed.) 1982a, 431–57.

DeMaris, R.
1994 *The Colossian Controversy: Wisdom in Dispute at Colossae.* JSNTSup 96. Sheffield: Sheffield Academic Press.

Demke, C.
1973 "Theologie und Literarkritik im 1. Thessalonicherbrief. Ein Diskussionsbeitrag." Pp. 103–24 in *Festschrift für Ernst Fuchs.* Edited by G. Ebeling et al. Tübingen: Mohr-Siebeck.

Denis, A.-M.
1970 *Introduction aux pseudépigraphes grecs d'Ancient Testament.* SVTP 1. Leiden: Brill.

Denker, J.
1975 *Die theologiegeschichtliche Stellung des Petrusevangeliums: Ein Beitrag zur Frühgeschichte des Doketismus.* Berne: Herbert Lang.

Denniston, J. D.
1934 *The Greek Particles.* 2d ed. Oxford: Clarendon Press.
1952 *Greek Prose Style.* Oxford: Clarendon Press.

Depew, M.
1997 "Reading Greek Prayers." *Classical Antiquity* 16:229–58.

Derenbourg, J.
1881 "Les sections and les traités de la Mischnah." *REJ* 3:205–10.

Desbordes, F.
1996 *La Rhétorique Antique.* Paris: Hachette.

Descamps, A., and A. de Halleux (eds.)
1970 *Mélanges Bibliques en hommage R. P. Béda Rigaux.* Duculot: Gembloux.

DeSilva, D. A.
1993 "Measuring Penultimate against Ultimate Reality: An Investigation of the Integrity and Argumentation of 2 Corinthians." *JSNT* 52:41–70.
1995 *Despising Shame: Honor Discourse and Community Maintenance in the Epistle to the Hebrews.* SBLDS 152. Atlanta: Scholars Press.
2000 *A Socio-Rhetorical Commentary on the Epistle to the Hebrews.* Grand Rapids: Eerdmans.

Desjardins, M.
1992 "Where Was the Gospel of Thomas Written?" *TJT* 8:121–22.

De Solanges, B.
1979a "L'Évangile de Thomas et les Évangiles Canoniques: L'Ordre des Péricopes." *Bulletin de littérature ecclésiastique* 80:102–8.

1979b *Jean et les synoptiques.* Leiden: Brill.

Dettmer, H.
1980 "The Arrangement of Tibullus Book 1 and 2." *Philologus* 124:68–82.

Dewey, J.
1973 "The Literary Structure of the Controversy Stories in Mark 2:1–3:6." *JBL* 92:394–401.
1980 *Markan Public Debate: Literary Technique, Concentric Structure, and Theology in Mark 2:1–3:6.* Missoula, Mont.: Scholars Press.
1991 "Mark as Interwoven Tapestry: Forecasts and Echoes for a Listening Audience." *CBQ* 53:221–36.

Dewey, J., D. Michie, and D. M. Rhoads
1999 *Mark as Story: An Introduction to the Narrative of a Gospel.* 2d ed. Minneapolis: Fortress Press.

Dexinger, F.
1977 *Henochs Zehnwochenapokalypse und offene Probleme der Apokalyptikforschung.* Studia Post Biblica 29. Leiden: Brill.

Dibelius, M.
1923 *Der Hirt des Hermas.* Tübingen: Mohr-Siebeck.
1934 *From Tradition to Gospel.* Translated by B. L. Woolf. New York: Charles Scribner's Sons.
1949 *Die Reden der Apostelgeschichte und die Antike Geschichtsschreibung.* Sitzungsberichte der Heidelberger Akademie der Wissenschaften, Philosophisch-historische Klasse 1949.1. Heidelberg: Carl Winter Universitätsverlag.
1956 *Studies in the Acts of the Apostles.* Translated by M. Ling. London: SCM; New York: Scribner.
1964a *Der Brief des Jakobus.* 11th ed. Revised by H. Greeven. Göttingen: Vandenhoeck & Ruprecht.
1964b *A Commentary on the Epistle of James.* Revised by H. Greeven. Hermeneia. Philadelphia: Fortress Press.
1971 *Die Formgeschichte des Evangeliums.* 6th ed. Tübingen: Mohr-Siebeck.
1975 *A Commentary on the Epistle of James.* Revised by H. Greeven. Hermeneia. Philadelphia: Fortress Press.

Dibelius, M., and H. Conzelmann
1972 *The Pastoral Epistles.* Hermeneia. Philadelphia: Fortress Press.

DiCicco, M. M.
1995 *Paul's Use of Ethos, Pathos, and Logos in 2 Corinthians 10–13.* Lewiston, N.Y.: Mellen.

Dick, K.
1900 *Der schriftstellerische Plural bei Paulus.* Halle: Niemeyer.

Diefenbach, M.
1993 *Die Komposition des Lukas-Evangeliums unter Berücksichtigung antiker Rhetorikelemente.* FTS 43. Frankfurt am Main: Verlag Josef Knecht.

Diels, H.
1879 *Doxographi Graeci: collegit recensuit prolegomenis indicibusque instruxit.* Berlin and Leipzig: Walter de Gruyter.
1882 "Stichometrisches." *Hermes* 17:377–84.

Dieter, O. A. L.
1950 "Stasis." *Speech Monographs* 17:345–69.

Diéz Merino, L.
1994 "Targum Manuscripts and Critical Editions." In Beattie and McNamara (eds.) 1994, 51–91.

Dihle, Albrecht
1956 *Studien zur griechischen Biographie.* AAWG, Phil.-Hist. Kl. Dritte Folge, 37. Göttingen: Vandenhoeck & Ruprecht.
1965 "Prosarhythmus: Griechisch." *Lexikon der Alten Welt.* Zurich and Stuttgart: Artemis Verlag.
1991 "The Gospels and Greek Biography." In Stuhlmacher (ed.) 1991, 361–86.

Diller, A.
1956 "A Companion to the Uspenski Gospels." *Byzantinische Zeitschrift* 49:332–35.

Dillon, J.
1977 *The Middle Platonists.* Ithaca, N.Y.: Cornell University Press.
1983 "The Formal Structure of Philo's Allegorical Exegesis." In Winston and Dillon (eds.) 1983, 77–87.

Dilts, M. R., and G. A. Kennedy (eds.)
1997 *Two Greek Rhetorical Treatises from the Roman Empire: Introduction, Text, and Translation of the Arts of Rhetoric attributed to Anonymous Segunerianus and to Apsines of Gadara.* Mnemosyne 168. Leiden: Brill.

Dimant, D.
1984 "Qumran Sectarian Literature." In Stone (ed.) 1984b, 483–550.
1988 "Use and Interpretation of Mikra in the Apocrypha and Pseudepigrapha." In Mulder 1988, 379–419.
1995 "The Qumran Manuscripts: Contents and Significance." In Dimant and Schiffman (eds.) 1995, 23–58.

2002 "1 Enoch 6–11: A Fragment of a Parabiblical Work." *JJS* 53:223–37.

Dimant, D., and U. Rappaport (eds.)
1992 *The Dead Sea Scrolls: Forty Years of Research.* Leiden: Brill; Jerusalem: Magnes.

Dimant, D. and L. Schiftman (eds.)
1995 *Time to Prepare the Way in the Wilderness: Papers on the Qumran Scrolls.* STDJ 16. Leiden and New York: Brill.

Dirichlet, G. L.
1914 *De veterum makarismus.* Giessen: A. Töpelmann.

DiTommaso, L.
2001 *A Bibliography of Pseudepigrapha Research 1850–1999.* JSPSup 39. Sheffield: Sheffield Academic Press.

Dix, G.
1937 *The Treatise of the Apostolic Tradition.* London: SPCK.
1945 *The Shape of the Liturgy.* Westminster: Dacre.

Dobbs-Allsopp, F. W.
1999 "Rethinking Historical Criticism." *Biblical Interpretation* 7:235–71.

Dobschütz, E. von
1902 "Der Roman in der altchristlichen Literatur." *Deutsche Rundschau* 111:87–106.
1928 "Zur Erzählerkunst des Markus." *ZNW* 27:193–98.
1932 "Wir und Ich bei Paulus." *ZST* 10:251–77.

Dodd, C. H.
1952 *According to the Scriptures: The Substructure of New Testament Theology.* London: Nisbet.
1961 *The Parables of the Kingdom.* Rev. ed. New York: Charles Scribner's Sons.
1963 *Historical Tradition in the Fourth Gospel.* Cambridge: Cambridge University Press.
1968 "The Beatitudes: A Form-critical Study." *More New Testament Studies.* Grand Rapids: Eerdmans.

Dolamo, R. T. H.
1989 "Rhetorical Speech in Galatians." *Theologia Viatorum* 17:30–37.

Dominik, W. J. (ed.)
1997 *Roman Eloquence: Rhetoric in Society and Literature.* London and New York: Routledge.

Donahue, J. R.
1973 *Are You the Christ? The Trial Narrative in the Gospel of Mark.* SBLDS 10. Missoula, Mont.: Scholars Press.
1976 "From Passion Traditions to Passion Narrative." In Kelber (ed.) 1976, 1–20.
1988 *The Gospel in Parable: Metaphor, Narrative, and Theology in the Synoptic Gospels.* Philadelphia: Fortress Press.

Donelson, L. W.
1986 *Pseudepigraphy and Ethical Argument in the Pastoral Epistles.* Tübingen: Mohr-Siebeck.

Donfried, K. P.
1974 *The Setting of Second Clement in Early Christianity.* NovTSup 38. Leiden: Brill.
1991a *The Romans Debate: Revised and Expanded Edition.* Peabody, Mass.: Hendrickson.
1991b "False Presuppositions in the Study of Romans." In Donfried (ed.) 1991a, 102–27.
2000 "The Epistolary and Rhetorical Context of 1 Thessalonians 2:1–12." In Donfried and Beutler (eds.) 2000, 31–60.

Donfried, K. P., and J. Beutler (eds.)
2000 *The Thessalonians Debate: Methodological Discord or Methodological Synthesis.* Grand Rapids: Eerdmans.

Donfried, K. P., and P. Richardson (eds.)
1998 *Judaism and Christianity in First-Century Rome.* Grand Rapids: Eerdmans.

Donovan, M. A.
1984 "Irenaeus in Recent Scholarship." *SecCent* 4:219–41.
1997 *One Right Reading? A Guide to Irenaeus.* Collegeville, Minn.: Liturgical Press.

Doran, R.
1987 "A Complex of Parables: Gth 96–98." *NovT* 29:347–52.

Dorandi, T.
1991 "Den Autoren über die Schulter geschaut: Arbeitsweise und Autographie bei den antiken Schriftstellern." *ZPE* 87:11–33.
1993 "Zwischen Autographie und Diktat: Momente der Textualität in der antiken Welt." In Kullmann and Althoff (eds.) 1993, 71–83.

Dormeyer, D.
1974 *Die Passion Jesu als Verhaltensmodell.* NTAbh NF 11. Münster: Aschendorff.
1993 *Das Neue Testament im Rahmen der antiken Literaturgeschichte: Eine Einführung.* Darmstadt: Wissenschaftliche Buchgesellschaft.
2001 *Das Markusevangelium als Idealbiographie von Jesus Christus.* SBB 43. Stuttgart: Katholisches Bibelwerk.

Dorson, R. M.
1972 "The Debate over the Trustworthiness of Oral Traditional History." Pp. 199–224 in *Folklore: Selected Essays.* Edited by R. M. Dorson. Bloomington: Indiana University Press.

Doty, W. G.
1969 "The Classification of Epistolary Literature." *CBQ* 31:183–99.
1973 *Letters in Primitive Christianity.* Philadelphia: Fortress Press.

Doudna, G. L.
2001 *4Q Pesher Nahum: A Critical Edition.* JSPSup 35; Copenhagen International Series 8. Sheffield: Sheffield Academic.

Dowd, S. E.
1991 "The Gospel of Mark as Ancient Novel." *LTQ* 26:53–59.

Dowden, K.
1992 *The Uses of Greek Mythology.* London: Routledge.

Downey, G.
1959 "Ekphrasis." *RAC* 4:921–44.

Downing, F. G.
1980 "Redaction Criticism: Josephus' Antiquities and the Synoptic Gospels." *JSNT* 8:46–65, and 9:29–48.
1988 "Quite like Q: A Genre for 'Q': The 'Lives' of Cynic Philosophers." *Biblica* 69:196–225.
1994 "A Genre for Q and a Socio-Cultural Context for Q: Comparing Sets of Similarities with Sets of Differences." *JSNT* 55:3–26.
1998 "Deeper Reflections on the Jewish Cynic Jesus." *JBL* 117:97–104.
2000 "Markan Intercalation in Cultural Context." In Brooke and Kaestli (eds.) 2000, 105–18.

Draper, J. A. (ed.).
1996a *The Didache in Modern Research.* Leiden: Brill.
1996b "The Jesus Tradition in the *Didache.*" In Draper (ed.) 1996a, 72–91.

Drews, P.
1907 "Der literarische Charakter der neuentdeckten Schrift des Irenäus 'Zum Erweise der apostolischen Verkündigung." *ZNW* 8:226–33.

Droge, A. J.
1983 "Call Stories in Greek Biography and the Gospels." *SBLSP* 12:245–57.
1989 *Homer or Moses? Early Christian Interpretations of the History of Culture.* Tübingen: Mohr-Siebeck.
1992 "Apologetics, NT." *ADB* 1.302–7.

Drury, J.
1985 *The Parables in the Gospels.* London: SPCK.

DuBois, J.-D.
1984 "The New *Series Apocryphorum* of the *Corpus Christianorum.*" *SecCent* 4:29–36.

DuBois, J.-D., G. Archambault, L. Pautigny, and É. Gauche
1994 *Justin Martyr: Oeuvres complètes.* Paris: Migne.

Duff, D. (ed.)
2000 *Modern Genre Theory.* Harlow and London: Longman.

Duff, J. W.
1964 *A Literary History of Rome in the Silver Age: From Tiberius to Hadrian.* 3d ed. Edited by A. M. Duff. Westport, Conn.: Greenwood.

Duff, P. B.
1994 "2 Corinthians 1–7: Sidestepping the Division Hypothesis Dilemma." *BTB* 24:16–26.

Duhaime, J.-L.
1977 "L'Instruction sur les deux esprits et les interpretations dualistes à Qumrân (1QS III,3-IV,26)." *RevB* 84:584–87.
1987 "Dualistic Reworking in the Scrolls from Qumran." *CBQ* 49:32–56.

Duke, P. D.
1985 *Irony in the Fourth Gospel.* Atlanta: John Knox Press.

Duling, D. C.
1975 "Solomon, Exorcism, and the Son of David." *HTR* 68:235–52.
1983 "The Testament of Solomon." Vol. 1, pp. 935–87 in *The Old Testament Pseudepigrapha.* Edited by J. H. Charlesworth. Garden City, N.Y.: Doubleday.
1987 "The Eleazar Miracle and Solomon's Magical Wisdom in Flavius Josephus's *Antiquitatae Judaicae* 8.42–49." *HTR* 78:1–25.
1988 "The Testament of Solomon: Retrospect and Prospect." *JSP* 2:87–112.

Dunderberg, I.
1995 "Q and the Beginning of Mark." *NTS* 41:501–11.

Dundes, A.
1962 "From Etic to Emic Units in the Structural Study of Folktales." *JAF* 75:95–105.
1964 *The Morphology of North American Indian Folktales.* Helsinki: Suomalainen Tiedakatemia.
1965 *The Study of Folklore.* Englewood Cliffs, N.J.: Prentice-Hall.

1980 *The Hero Pattern and the Life of Jesus.* Berkeley, Calif.: Center for Hermeneutical Studies, 1977.
1984 *Sacred Narrative: Readings in the Theory of Myth.* Berkeley: University of California Press.
1999 *Holy Writ as Oral Lit: The Bible as Folklore.* Lanham, Md.: Rowman & Littlefield.

Dunn, J. D. G.
1993 *The Epistle to the Galatians.* BNTC. London: A. & C. Black.
1996 *The Epistles to the Colossians and to Philemon: A Commentary on the Greek Text.* Grand Rapids: Eerdmans.
1998 *The Theology of Paul the Apostle.* Grand Rapids: Eerdmans.

Dunn, P.
1996 "The Influence of 1 Corinthians on the *Acts of Paul.*" *SBLSP 1996*:438–54.

Dupont, J.
1958–73 *Les béatitudes.* Vol. 1: *Le probléme littéraire. Les deux versions du Sermon sur la Montagne et des Béatitudes.* 2d ed. Bruge: Abbaye de Saint André, 1958. Vol. 2: *Les béatitudes: La Bonne nouvelle.* Paris Gabalda et Cie, 1969. Vol. 3: *Les béatitudes: Les Évangelistes.* Paris: Gabalda et Cie, 1973.
1969 "Béatitudes égyptiennes." *Bib* 47:185–222.

Durham, D. B.
1938 "Parody in Achilles Tatius." *CP* 33:1–19.

Düring, I.
1957 *Aristotle in the Ancient Biographical Tradition.* Göteborg: Göteborgs Universitetet.
1961 *Der Protreptikos des Aristoteles.* Studia Graeca et Latina Gothoburgensia 12. Göteborg: Acta Universitatis Gothenburgensis.

du Toit, A. B.
1989 "Persuasion in Romans 1:1–17." *BZ* 33:192–209.

Dyck, A. R.
1987 "The Glossographoi." *HSCP* 91:119–60.

Earl, D.
1972 "Prologue-Form in Ancient Historiography." II, 1/2, 842–56.

Easterling, P. E., and B. M. W. Knox (eds.)
1985 *Greek Literature.* Vol. 1 of *The Cambridge History of Classical Literature.* Cambridge: Cambridge University Press.

Easton, B. S.
1910 "Linguistic Evidence for the Lucan Source L." *JBL* 29:139–80.
1911 "The Special Source of the Third Gospel." *JBL* 30:78–103.
1932 "New Testament Ethical Lists." *JBL* 51:1–12.
1934 *The Apostolic Tradition of Hippolytus.* New York: Macmillan.

Eckart, K. G.
1961 "Der Zweite echte Brief des Apostels Paulus an die Thessalonicher." *ZTK* 58:30–44.

Eco, U.
1980 *The Role of the Reader: Explorations in the Semiotics of Texts.* Bloomington: Indiana University Press.

Edmunds, L. (ed.)
1990 *Approaches to Greek Myth.* Baltimore: Johns Hopkins University Press.

Edwards, J.
1989 "Markan Sandwiches: The Significance of Interpolations in Markan Narratives." *NovT* 31:193–216.

Edwards, M. J., M. Goodman, S. Price, and C. Rowland (eds.)
1999 *Apologetics in the Roman Empire: Pagans, Jews, and Christians.* Oxford: Oxford University Press.

Edwards, M. W.
1986 "Homer and Oral Tradition: The Formula, Part I." *Oral Tradition* 1:171–230.
1988 "Homer and Oral Tradition: The Formula, Part II." *Oral Tradition* 3:11–60.
1992 "Homer and Oral Tradition: The Type-Scene." *Oral Tradition* 7:284–330.

Edwards, R. A.
1976 *A Theology of Q: Eschatology, Prophecy, and Wisdom.* Philadelphia: Fortress Press.
1985 *Matthew's Story of Jesus.* Philadelphia: Fortress Press.
1997 *Matthew's Narrative Portrait of Disciples.* Harrisburg: Trinity Press International.

Egger, W.
1976 *Frohbotschaft und Lehre: Die Sammelberichte des Wirkens Jesu im Markusevangelium.* Frankfurt: Knecht.

Ehrhardt, A. A. T.
1953 "Justin Martyr's Two Apologies." *JEH* 4:179–205.

Ehrman, B. D., and M. W. Holmes (eds.)
1995 *The Text of the New Testament in Contemporary Research: Essays on the Status Quaestionis.* Studies and Documents 46. Grand Rapids: Eerdmans.

Eichrodt, W.
1963 "Is Typological Exegesis an Appropriate Method?" In Westermann (ed.) 1963, 224–45.

Eissfeldt, O.
1965 *The Old Testament: An Introduction.* New York and Evanston: Harper & Row.

El-Abbadi, M.
1990 *The Life and Fate of the Ancient Library of Alexandria.* Paris: UNESCO.

Elliger, K.
1953 *Studien zum Habakkuk-Kommentar vom Toten Meer.* Tübingen: Mohr-Siebeck.

Elliger, W.
1975 *Die Darstellung der Landschaft in der griechischen Dichtung.* Berlin and New York: Walter de Gruyter.

Elliott, J. K. (ed.).
1968 *The Greek Text of the Epistles to Timothy and Titus.* Salt Lake City: University of Utah Press.
1993 *The Apocryphal New Testament.* Oxford: Clarendon Press.
1996 *The Apocryphal Jesus: Legends of the Early Church.* Oxford: Oxford University Press.

Elliott, N.
1990 *The Rhetoric of Romans: Argumentative Constraint and Strategy and Paul's Dialogue with Judaism.* JSNTSup 45. Sheffield: JSOT Press.

Ellis, E. E.
1957a *Paul's Use of the Old Testament.* Grand Rapids: Eerdmans.
1957b "A Note on First Corinthians 10:4." *JBL* 76:53–56.
1977 "How the New Testament Uses the Old." Pp. 199–219 in *New Testament Interpretation: Essays on Principles and Methods.* Edited by I. H. Marshall. Exeter: Paternoster; Grand Rapids: Eerdmans.
1978 "Midrashic Features in the Speeches of Acts." Pp. 198–208 in E. E. Ellis, *Prophecy and Hermeneutic in Early Christianity: New Testament Essays.* Grand Rapids: Eerdmans.
1987 "Traditions in the Pastoral Epistles." In Evans and Stinespring (eds.) 1987.

Ellis, E. E., and E. Grässer (eds.)
1975 *Jesus und Paulus: Festschrift für Werner Georg Kümmel.* Göttingen: Vandenhoeck & Ruprecht.

Ellis, J. M.
1974 *The Theory of Literary Criticism: A Logical Analysis.* Berkeley and Los Angeles: University of California Press.

Emmet, A.
1981 "Introductions and Conclusions to Digressions in Ammianus Marcellinus." *Museum Philologum Londiniense* 5:15–33.

Endres, J. C.
1987 *Biblical Interpretation in the Book of Jubilees.* CBQMS 18. Washington, D.C.: Catholic Biblical Association.

Engberg-Pedersen, T. (ed.)
1995 *Paul in His Hellenistic Context.* Minneapolis: Fortress Press.

Enkvist, N. E.
1974 *Stilforskning och stilteori.* Lund: Gleerup.
1985 "Text and Discourse Linguistics, Rhetoric, and Stylistics." Pp. 11–38 in *Discourse and Literature.* Edited by T. A. Van Dijk. Amsterdam: John Benjamins.

Enos, R. L. and K. R. Schnakenberg
1994 "Cicero Latinizes Hellenic *Ethos,*" in Baumlin and Baumlin 1994:191–209.

Enos, T.
1996 *Encyclopedia of Rhetoric and Composition: Communication from Ancient Times to the Information Age.* New York: Garland.

Enroth, A.-M.
1990 "The Hearing Formula in the Book of Revelation." *NTS* 36:598–608.

Epp, E. J.
1991 "New Testament Papyrus Manuscripts and Letter Carrying in Greco-Roman Times." In Pearson (ed.) 1991, 35–56.
1995 "The Papyrus Manuscripts of the New Testament." In Ehrman and Holmes (eds.) 1995.

Epp, E. J., and G. MacRae (eds.)
1989 *The New Testament and Its Modern Interpreters.* The Bible and Its Modern Interpreters 3. Atlanta: Scholars Press.

Erbetta, M. (ed.)
1966 *Atti e leggende: Versione e commento.* Vol. 2 of *Gli Apocrifi del Nuovo Testamento.* Turin: Marietti.

Erbse, H.
1969–88 *Scholia Graeca in Homeri Iliadem (scholia vetera).* 7 vols. Berlin: Walter de Gruyter.

Erickson, A., T. H. Olbricht, and W. Übelacker (eds.).
2002 *Rhetorical Argumentation in Biblical Texts: Essays form the Lund 2000 Conference.* Harrisburg: Trinity Press International.

Erickson, K. V. (ed.)
1974 *Aristotle: The Classical Heritage of Rhetoric.* Metuchen, N.J.: Scarecrow Press.

Eriksson, A.
2001 "Fear of Damnation: *Pathos* Appeal in 1 Corinthians 15 and 16." Olbricht and Sumney (eds.) 2001:115–26.

Erlemann, K.
1998 "Die Datierung des Ersten Klemensbriefes—Anfragen an eine Communis Opinio." *NTS* 44:591–607.

Ernesti, J. C. G.
1795 *Lexicon technologiae Graecorum rhetoricae.* Leipzig: Fritsch.

Esler, P. F.
1987 *Community and Gospel in Luke–Acts.* SNTSMS 57. Cambridge: Cambridge University Press.
1994 *The First Christians in Their Social Worlds: Social-Scientific Approaches to New Testament Interpretation.* London and New York: Routledge.

Esler, P. F. (ed.).
1995 *Modelling Early Christianity: Social-Scientific Studies of the New Testament in Its Context.* London and New York: Routledge.

Evans, C. A.
1982a "'Peter Warming Himself': The Problem of an Editorial Seam." *JBL* 101:245–49.
1982b "On the Quotation Formulas in the Fourth Gospel." *BZ* 26:79–83.
1988 "The Genesis Apocryphon and the Rewritten Bible." *RevQ* 13:153–65.
1993 "Luke and the Rewritten Bible: Aspects of Lukan Historiography." In Charlesworth and Evans (ed.) 1993, 170–201.
1998–99 "Jesus and the Dead Sea Scrolls." In Flint and VanderKam (eds.) 1998–99, 2.573–98.

Evans, C. A., and S. E. Porter (eds.)
1997 *New Testament Backgrounds.* Sheffield: Sheffield Academic Press.

Evans, C. A., and J. A. Sanders (eds.)
1993 *Paul and the Scriptures of Israel.* Sheffield: Sheffield Academic Press.

Evans, C. A., and W. F. Stinespring (ed.)
1987 *Early Jewish and Christian Exegesis.* Atlanta: Scholars Press.

Evans, C. A., R. L. Webb, and R. A. Wiebe (eds.)
1993 *Nag Hammadi Texts and the Bible: A Synopsis and Index.* Leiden: Brill.

Evans, C. F.
1970 "'Speeches' in Acts." In Descamps and Halleux (eds.) 1970, 207–302.

Evans, E. C.
1948 "Literary Portraiture in Ancient Epic." *HSCP* 58–59:189–217.

Evans, T. V.
2000 *Verbal Syntax in the Greek Pentateuch: Natural Greek Usage and Hebrew Interference.* Oxford: Oxford University Press.

Exler, F. X.
1923 *The Form of the Ancient Greek Letter: A Study in Epistolography.* Washington, D.C.: Catholic University of America.

Fabricius, A. A.
1719 *Codex apocryphus Novi Testamenti.* 3 vols. Hamburg: Schiller & Kisner.
1722–33 *Codex pseudepigraphicus Veteri Testamenti.* Hamburg: T. C. Felginer.

Fairbanks, A.
1931 "Introduction: Philostratus the Elder." In *Philostratus* Imagines *and Callistratus* Descriptions. LCL. Cambridge: Harvard University Press.

Fairweather, J.
1994 "The Epistle to the Galatians and Classical Rhetoric." *TynBul* 45:1–38, 213–44.

Falcetta, A.
2001 "A Testimony Collection in Manchester: Papyrus Rylands Greek 460." *BJRL* 83:3–19.

Falk, D. K.
1998 *Daily, Sabbath, and Festival Prayers in the Dead Sea Scrolls.* STDJ 27. Leiden: Brill.

Falk, D. K., F. García Martínez, and E. Schuller (eds.)
2000 *Sapiential, Liturgical, and Poetical Texts from Qumran.* STDJ 35. Leiden: Brill.

Fallon, F. T.
1979 "The Gnostic Apocalypses." In J. J. Collins (ed.) 1979, 123–47.

Fallon, F. T., and R. Cameron
1988 "The Gospel of Thomas: A *Forschungsbericht* and Analysis." In *ANRW* II.25/6, 2195–251.

Falls, T. B. (trans.)
1965 *Saint Justin Martyr.* Washington, D.C.: Catholic University of America Press.

Fantham, E.
1973 "Ciceronian *Conciliare* and Aristotelian *Ethos,*" *Phoenix* 27:262–75.

Faraone, C. A.
1999 *Ancient Greek Love Magic.* Cambridge: Harvard University Press.

Farmer, W. R.
1998 "Further Reflections on the Fourfold

Gospel Canon." In Malherbe, Norris, and Thompson 1998, 107–13.

Farrell, T. B.
2000 "Aristotle's Enthymeme as Tacit Reference." In Gross and Walzer (eds.) 2000, 93–106.

Farrer, A. M.
1955 "Note: The Genealogies of Christ." Pp. 87–88 in *Studies in the Gospels.* Edited by D. E. Nineham. Oxford: Blackwell.

Farris, S.
1985 *The Hymns of Luke's Infancy Narratives.* JSNTSup 9. Sheffield: JSOT Press.

Fascher, E.
1924 *Die formgeschichtliche Methode.* BZNW 2. Giessen: Töpelmann.

Fass, Dan
1997 *Processing Metonymy and Metaphor.* London, England and Greenwich, Conn.: Ablex.

Faw, C. E.
1952 "On the Writing of First Thessalonians." *JBL* 71:217–25.

Fee, G.
1977 "II Corinthians vi.14–vii.1 and Food Offered to Idols." *NTS* 23:140–61.
1984 *1 and 2 Timothy, Titus.* San Francisco: Harper & Row.
1987 *The First Epistle to the Corinthians.* NICNT. Grand Rapids: Eerdmans.
1988 *1 and 2 Timothy, Titus.* Peabody, Mass.: Hendrickson.
2001 *To What End Exegesis? Essays Textual, Exegetical, Theological.* Grand Rapids: Eerdmans.
2002 *New Testament Exegesis: A Handbook for Students and Pastors.* Louisville, Ky.: Westminster John Knox Press.

Feeney, D. C.
1993 "Towards an Account of the Ancient World's Concepts of Fictive Belief." In Gill and Wiseman (eds.) 1993, 230–44.
1998 *Literature and Religion at Rome: Cultures, Contexts, and Beliefs.* New York: Cambridge University Press.

Fehling, D.
1985 *Der sieben Weisen und die frühgriechische Chronologie: eine traditionsgeschichtliche Studie.* Bern and New York: Peter Lang.

Fekkes, J.
1994 *Isaiah and Prophetic Traditions in the Book of Revelation.* JSNTSup 93. Sheffield: Sheffield Academic Press.

Feldman, L. H.
1984 *Josephus and Modern Scholarship 1937–1980.* New York: Walter de Gruyter.
1988 "Use, Authority, and Exegesis of Mikra in the Writings of Josephus." In Mulder (ed.) 1988, 455–518.
1990 "Origen's 'Contra Celsum' and Josephus' 'Contra Apionem': The Issue of Jewish Origins." *VC* 44:105–35.
1998 *Studies in Josephus' Rewritten Bible.* JSJSup. 58. Leiden: Brill.

Feldman, L. H., and G. Hata (eds.)
1987 *Josephus, Judaism, and Christianity.* Leiden: Brill.

Feldman, L. H., and J. R. Levison (eds.)
1996 *Josephus' Contra Apionem: Studies in Its Character and Context.* Leiden: Brill.

Ferguson, E.
1997 *Encyclopedia of Early Christianity.* 2d ed. 2 vols. New York and London: Garland.

Ferlay, P.
1984 "Irénéé de Lyon exégète du quatrième évangile." *NRT* 106:222–34.

Fernández-Marcos, N.
2000 *The Septuagint in Context: An Introduction to the Greek Versions of the Bible.* Translated by W. G. E. Watson. Leiden: Brill.

Festugière, A.-J.
1954 *Personal Religion among the Greeks.* Berkeley: University of California Press.
1983 *La Révélation d'Hermès Trismégiste.* 4 vols. Paris: Société d'Édition Les Belles Lettres.

Fiedler, P.
1986 "Haustafel." *RAC* 103:1063–73.

Fiedrowicz, M.
1998 *Prinzipien der Schriftauslegung in der Alten Kirche.* Bern and New York: Lang.

Fieger, M.
1991 *Das Thomasevangelium: Einleitung, Kommentar, und Systematik.* Münster: Aschendorff.

Field, F.
1964 *Origenis Hexaplorum quae supersunt: sive Veterum interpretum graecorum in totum Vetus Testamentum fragmenta.* 2 vols. 1875; reprint, Hildesheim: Olms.

Findlay, J. A.
1933 "The First Gospel and the Book of Testimonies." Pp. 57–71 in *Amicitiae Corolla: A Volume of Essays Presented to James Rendel Harris, D. Litt., on the Occasion of His Eightieth Birthday.*

Edited by H. G. Wood. London: University of London.

Finegan, J.
1956 "The Original Form of the Pauline Collection." *HTR* 49:85–103.

Finnegan, R.
1988 *Literacy and Orality: Studies in the Technology of Communication.* Oxford: Basil Blackwell.

Fiore, B., S.J.
1986 *The Function of Personal Example in the Socratic and Pastoral Epistles.* Rome: Biblical Institute.

Fischel, H. A.
1973 "The Uses of Sorites (Climax, Gradatio) in the Tannaitic Period." *HUCA* 44:119–51.

Fishbane, M.
1977 "The Qumran-Pesher and Traits of Ancient Hermeneutics." Vol. 1, pp. 97–114 in *Proceedings of the Sixth World Congress of Jewish Studies.* Jerusalem: Jerusalem Academic Press.
1980 "Revelation and Tradition: Aspects of Inner-Biblical Exegesis." *JBL* 99:343–61.
1985 *Biblical Interpretation in Ancient Israel.* Oxford: Clarendon Press.
1986 "Inner Biblical Exegesis: Types and Strategies of Interpretation in Ancient Israel." Pp. 19–37 in *Midrash and Literature.* Edited by S. Budick and G. Hartmann. New Haven, Conn.: Yale University Press.

Fishbane, M., and S. Schoenfeld (eds.)
1992 *Essays in the Social Scientific Study of Judaism and Jewish Society.* Hoboken, N.J.: KTAV.

Fishwick, D.
1987 *The Imperial Cult in the Latin West: Studies in the Ruler Cult of the Western Provinces of the Roman Empire.* EPRO 108. Leiden: Brill.

Fitzer, G.
1963 *Das Weib schweige in der Gemeinde: Über den unpaulinischen Charakter der mulier-taceat-Verse in 1. Korinther 14.* Munich: Kaiser.

Fitzgerald, J. T.
1988 *Cracks in an Earthen Vessel: An Examination of the Catalogues of Hardships in the Corinthian Correspondence.* Atlanta: Scholars Press.
1990 "Paul, the Ancient Epistolary Theorists, and 2 Corinthians 10–13." Pp. 190–200 in *Greeks, Romans, and Christians: Essays in Honor of Abraham J. Malherbe.* Edited by D. L. Balch, E. Ferguson, and W. A. Meeks. Minneapolis: Fortress Press.
1992 "Virtue/Vice Lists." *ABD* 6:857–59.
1996 *Friendship, Flattery, and Freedom of Speech.* NovTSup. Leiden: Brill.
1997a *Greco-Roman Perspectives on Friendship.* SBLSBS. Atlanta: Scholars Press.
1997b "The Catalogue in Ancient Greek Literature." In Porter and Olbricht (eds.) 1997, 275–93.

Fitzgerald, J. T., and L. M. White
1983 *Tabula of Cebes.* SBL Texts and Translations 24. Chico, Calif.: Scholars Press.

Fitzmyer, J. A.
1957 "4QTestimonia and the New Testament." *TS* 18:513–38.
1960–61 "The Use of Explicit Old Testament Quotations in Qumran Literature and in the New Testament." *NTS* 7:297–333.
1961 "Qumran and the Interpolated Paragraph in 2 Cor. 6:14–7:1." *CBQ* 23:271–80.
1970 "The Priority of Mark and the 'Q' Source in Luke." In D. Miller (ed.) 1970, 1.131–70.
1971 *The Genesis Apocryphon of Qumran Cave 1: A Commentary.* 2d ed. BibOr 18A. Rome: Biblical Institute.
1974a "The Oxyrhynchus Logoi of Jesus and the Coptic Gospel according to Thomas." Pp. 355–433 in *Essays on the Semitic Background of the New Testament.* Missoula, Mont.: Scholars Press.
1974b "Qumran and the Interpolated Paragraph in 2 Cor. 6:14–7:1." Pp. 205–15 in *Essays on the Semitic Background of the New Testament.* Missoula, Mont.: Scholars Press.
1974c "4Q Testimonia and the New Testament." Pp. 59–89 in *Essays on the Semitic Background of the New Testament.* Missoula, Mont.: Scholars Press.
1979 *A Wandering Aramean: Collected Aramaic Essays.* SBLMS 25. Missoula, Mont.: Scholars Press.
1981–85 *The Gospel according to Luke.* AB 28, 28A. Garden City, N.Y.: Doubleday.
1992 "A Palestinian Collection of Beatitudes." In Van Segbroeck et al. 1992, 509–15.
1998–99 "Paul and the Dead Sea Scrolls." In Flint and VanderKam (eds.) 1998–99, 2.599–621.
2000 *The Letter to Philemon: A New Translation with Introduction and Commentary.* AB, 34C. New York: Doubleday.

Fleddermann, H. T.
1995 *Mark and Q: A Study of the Overlap Texts*. BETL 122. Leuven: Leuven University Press and Uitgeverij Peeters.

Flemming, J.
1902 *Das Buch Henoch: Äthiopischer Text mit Einleitung und Commentar.* Leipzig: J. C. Hinrichs.

Flint, P. W. (ed.)
2001 *The Bible at Qumran: Text, Shape, and Interpretation.* Grand Rapids: Eerdmans.

Flint, P. W., and J. C. VanderKam (eds.)
1998–99 *The Dead Sea Scrolls after Fifty Years: A Comprehensive Assessment.* 2 vols. Leiden: Brill.

Foat, G. W. G.
1901 "On Old Greek Tachyography." *JHS* 21:210–25.

Focant, C.
1993 *The Synoptic Gospels: Source Criticism and the New Literary Criticism.* Louvain: Peeters.
1996 "1 Corinthiens 13: Analyse rhétorique et analyse de structures." In Bieringer (ed.) 1966, 199–245.

Fokkelman, J. P.
1998–2001 *Major Poems of the Hebrew Bible: At the Interface of Hermeneutics and Structural Analysis.* 3 vols. Assen: Van Gorcum.
2000 *Reading Biblical Narrative.* Louisville, Ky.: Westminster John Knox Press.
2001 *Reading Biblical Poetry: An Introductory Guide.* Louisville, Ky.: Westminster John Knox Press.

Foley, H. P. (ed.)
1981 *Reflections of Women in Antiquity.* New York: Gordon & Breach.
1994 *The Homeric* Hymn to Demeter: *Translation, Commentary, and Interpretive Essays.* Princeton: Princeton University Press.

Follis, E. R. (ed.)
1987 *Directions in Biblical Hebrew Poetry.* JSOTSup 40. Sheffield: JSOT Press.

Fonrobert, C. E.
2001 "The *Didascalia Apostolorum*: A Mishnah for the Disciples of Jesus." *JECS* 9:483–509

Forbes, C.
1986 "Comparison, Self-Praise, and Irony: Paul's Boasting and the Conventions of Hellenistic Rhetoric." *NTS* 32:1–30.

Ford, A.
2002 *The Origins of Criticism: Literary Culture and Poetic Theory in Classical Greece.* Princeton: Princeton University Press.

Fornara, C. W.
1983 *The Nature of History in Ancient Greece and Rome.* Berkeley: University of California Press.

Forster, E. M.
1955 *Aspects of the Novel.* San Diego, New York, and London: Harcourt Brace Jovanovich.

Fortenbaugh, W. W.
1988 "*Benevolentum conciliare* and *animos permovere*: Some Remarks on Cicero's *De Oratore* 2.178–216," *Rhetorica* 6:259–73.

Fortenbaugh, W. W., and D. C. Mirhady (eds.)
1994 *Peripatetic Rhetoric after Aristotle.* New Brunswick and London: Transaction Publishers.

Fortna, R. T.
1970 *The Gospel of Signs: A Reconstruction of the Narrative Source Underlying the Fourth Gospel.* SNTSMS 11. Cambridge: Cambridge University Press.
1988 *The Fourth Gospel and Its Predecessor.* Philadelphia: Fortress Press.
1992 "Signs/Semeia Source." *ADB* 6:18–22.

Foucault, Michel
1979 "What Is an Author?" In Harari (ed.) 1979, 141–60.

Fowl, S.
1990 *The Story of Christ in the Ethics of Paul: An Analysis of the Function of the Hymnic Material in the Pauline Corpus.* Sheffield: Sheffield Academic Press.

Fowler, A.
1982 *Kinds of Literature: An Introduction to the Theory of Genres and Modes.* Oxford: Clarendon Press.

Fowler, D. P.
1991 "Narrate and Describe: The Problem of Ekphrasis." *JRS* 81:25–35.

Fowler, R. L.
1996 "Herodotus and His Contemporaries." *JHS* 116:62–87.
2000 *Early Greek Mythography.* Oxford: Oxford University Press.

Fowler, R. M.
1981 *Loaves and Fishes: The Function of the Feeding Stories in the Gospel of Mark.* SBLDS 54. Chico, Calif.: Scholars Press.
1985 "Who Is 'the Reader' in Reader Response Criticism?" *Semeia* 31:5–23.
1991 *Let the Reader Understand: Reader-Response Criticism and the Gospel of Mark.* Minneapolis: Fortress Press.

Fox, M. V.
1980 "The Identification of Quotations in Biblical Literature." *ZAW* 92:416–31.

Fraade, S. D.
1991 *From Tradition to Commentary: Torah and Its Interpretation in the Midrash Sifre to Deuteronomy.* Albany: State University of New York Press.
1998 "Looking for Legal Midrash at Qumran." In Stone and Chazon (eds.) 1998, 59–79.

Fraikin, D.
1986 "The Rhetorical Function of the Jews in Romans." In Richardson and Granskou (eds.) 1986, 91–105.

Frame, J. E.
1912 *A Critical and Exegetical Commentary on the Epistles of St. Paul to the Thessalonians.* ICC. Edinburgh: T. & T. Clark.

France, R. T., and D. Wenham (eds.)
1980 *Studies of History and Tradition in the Four Gospels.* Gospel Perspectives 1. Sheffield: JSOT Press.
1981 *Studies of History and Tradition in the Four Gospels.* Gospel Perspectives 2. Sheffield: JSOT Press.
1983 *Studies in Midrash and Historiography.* Gospel Perspectives 3. Sheffield: JSOT Press.

Francis, F. O.
1970 "The Form and Function of the Opening and Closing Paragraphs of James and 1 John." *ZNW* 61:110–26.

Frankel, I.
1956 *Peshat (Plain Exegesis) in Talmudic and Midrashic Literature.* Toronto: La Salle.

Frankemölle, H.
1988 *Evangelium: Begriff und Gattung: Ein Forschungsbericht.* Stuttgart: Katholisches Bibelwerk.

Frankfurter, D.
1995 "Narrating Power: The Theory and Practice of Magical *Historiola* in Ritual Spells." In Meyer and Mirecki (eds.) 1995, 457–76.

Frankowski, J.
1982 "Early Christian Hymns Recorded in the New Testament: A Reconsideration of the Question in the Light of Hebrews 1:3." *BZ* 27:183–94.

Franxman, T. W.
1979 *Genesis and the "Jewish Antiquities" of Flavius Josephus.* Biblica et Orientalia 35. Rome: Biblical Institute.

Franzmann, M.
1996 *Jesus in the Nag Hammadi Writings.* Edinburgh: T. & T. Clark.

Fraser, P. M., and E. Matthews (eds.)
1987–97 *A Lexicon of Greek Personal Names.* 3 vols. Oxford: Clarendon Press. Vol. I: *The Aegean Islands, Cyprus, Cyrenaica,* Edited by P. M. Fraser and E. Matthews (1987); vol. II: *Attica.* Edited by M. J. Osborne and S. G. Byrne (1994); vol. IIIA: *The Peloponnese, Western Greece, Sicily and Magna Graecia.* Edited by P. M. Fraser and E. Matthews (1997).

Frazer, J. G.
1911–15 *The Golden Bough.* 3d ed. 12 vols. London: Macmillan.
1918 *Folklore in the Old Testament.* 3 vols. London: Macmillan.

Frede, D.
1996 "Mixed Feelings in Aristotle's *Rhetoric.*" Rorty (ed.) 1996.

Fredrickson, D. E.
2001 "'Through Many Tears' (2 Cor 2:4): Paul's Grieving Letter and the Occasion of 2 Corinthians 1–7." Olbricht and Sumney (eds.) 2001:161–79.

Freed, E. D.
1965 *Old Testament Quotations in the Gospel of John.* NovTSup 11. Leiden: Brill.

Freed, E. D., and Russell B. Hunt
1975 "Fortna's Signs-Source in John." *JBL* 94:563–79.

Frei, H.
1974 *Eclipse of Biblical Narrative: A Study in Eighteenth and Nineteenth Century Hermeneutics.* New Haven and London: Yale University Press.

Frend, W. H. C.
1965 *Martyrdom and Persecution in the Early Church.* Oxford: Basil Blackwell.
1984 *The Rise of Christianity.* Philadelphia: Fortress Press.

Freund, E.
1987 *The Return of the Reader.* London and New York: Methuen.

Fridh, A.
1968 *Le problém de la Passion des saintes Perpétue et Félicité.* Göteborg: Acta Universitatis Gothoburgensis.

Fridrichsen, A.
1928 "Zum Stil des paulinischen Peristasenkatalogs, 2 Cor. 11." *SO* 7:25–29.
1929 "Peristasenkatalog und Res gestae." *SO* 8:78–82.
1940 "La priamèle dans l'enseignement de Jésus." *Coniectanea neotestamentica* 4:9–16.

Friedländer, Moriz
1903 *Geschichte der jüdischen Apologetik als*

Vorgeschichte des Christenthums. Zurich: Caesar Schmidt.

Friesen, S. J.

1993 *Twice Neokoros: Ephesus and the Cult of the Flavian Imperial Family.* EPRO 116. Leiden: Brill.

Frisk, H.

1927 *Le Périple de la mer Érythrée suivi d'une étude sur la tradition et la langue.* Göteborg: Elanders Boktryckerie.

Fritz, K. von.

1945–46 "Greek Prayer." *Review of Religions* 10:5–39.

1972 *Pseudepigrapha I: Pseudopythagorica, Lettres de Platon, littérature pseudepigrapha juive.* Geneva: Fondation Hardt.

Fröhlich, I.

1998 "'Narrative Exegesis' in the Dead Sea Scrolls." In Stone and Chazon (eds.) 1998, 81–99.

Frösén, J.

1974 *Prolegomena to a Study of the Greek Language in the First Centuries A.D.: The Problem of Koiné and Atticism.* Helsinki: Frösén.

Frye, Northrup

1957 *Anatomy of Criticism: Four Essays.* Princeton, N.J.: Princeton University Press.

Frye, Northrup, et al. (eds.)

1997 *The Harper Handbook to Literature.* 2d rev. ed. New York: Longman.

Fuentes González, P. P.

1998 *Les* Diatribes *de* Télès*: introduction, texte revu, traduction et commentaire des fragments (avec en appendice une traduction espagnole).* Sorbonne: Librairie Philosophique J. Vrin.

Fuhrmann, Manfred

1999 *Geschichte der römischen Literatur.* Stuttgart: Reclam.

Funk, F.

1967 "The Apostolic *Parousia*: Form and Significance." Pp. 249–68 in *Christian History and Interpretation.* Edited by W. R. Farmer, C. F. D. Moule, and R. R. Niebuhr. Cambridge: Cambridge University Press.

Funk, F. X.

1905–6 *Didascalia et Constitutiones apostolorum.* Paderborn: Schoeningh.

Funk, F. X., and K. Bihlmeyer

1956 *Die apostolischen Väter: Neubearbeitung der Funkschen Ausgabe.* 2. Aufl. von Wilhelm Schneemelcher. Tübingen: Mohr-Siebeck.

Furley, D. J.

1987 *The Formation of the Atomic Theory and Its Earliest Critics.* Vol. 1 of *The Greek Cosmologists.* Cambridge: Cambridge University Press.

1989 "The Cosmological Crisis in Classical Antiquity." Pp. 223–35 in *Cosmic Problems.* Cambridge: Cambridge University Press.

Furley, D. J., and A. Nehamas (eds.)

1994 *Aristotle's Rhetoric: Philosophical Essays.* Princeton, N.J.: Princeton University.

Furley, W. D.

1993 "Types of Greek Hymns." *Eos* 81:21–41.

1995 "Praise and Persuasion in Greek Hymns." *JHS* 115:29–36.

Furley, W. D., and J. M. Bremer

2001 *Greek Hymns: Selected Cult Songs from the Archaic to the Hellenistic Period.* 2 vols. SAC 9. Tübingen: Mohr-Siebeck.

Furnish, V.

1984 *II Corinthians.* AB. Garden City, N.Y.: Doubleday.

Fyfe, W. H., and W. R. Roberts

1927 *Aristotle* The Poetics; *"Longinus"* On the Sublime, *and Demetrius* On Style. LCL. Cambridge: Harvard University Press; London: William Heinemann.

Gabba, Emilio

1991 *Dionysius and the History of Archaic Rome.* Berkeley, Los Angeles, and Oxford: University of California Press.

Gager, John G.

1992 *Curse Tablets and Binding Spells from the Ancient World.* New York: Oxford University Press.

Gaiser, J. H.

1969 "Digressions in the *Iliad* and the *Odyssey.*" *HSCP* 73:1–43.

Galef, D.

1993 *The Supporting Cast: A Study of Flat and Minor Characters.* University Park: Pennsylvania State University Press.

Gamble, H. Y.

1975 "The Redaction of the Pauline Letters and the Formation of the Pauline Corpus." *JBL* 94:403–18.

1977 *The Textual History of the Letter to the Romans.* Studies and Documents 42. Grand Rapids: Eerdmans.

1985 *The New Testament Canon: Its Making and Meaning.* Philadelphia: Fortress Press.

1995 *Books and Readers in the Early*

Church: A History of Early Christian Texts. New Haven and London: Yale University Press.

Gammie, J. G.
1976 "The Classification, Stages of Growth, and Changing Intentions in the Book of Daniel." *JBL* 95:191–204.
1990 "Paraenetic Literature: Toward the Morphology of a Secondary Genre." *Semeia* 50:41–47.

Gantz, T.
1993 *Early Greek Myth: A Guide to Literary and Artistic Sources.* Baltimore: Johns Hopkins University Press.

García Martínez, F.
1996 *The Dead Sea Scrolls Translated: The Qumran Texts in English.* 2d ed. Leiden: Brill.

García Martínez, F., and E. J. C. Tigchelaar
1989 "The Books of Enoch (1 Enoch) and the Aramaic Fragments from Qumran." *RevQ* 14:131–46.
1997–98 *The Dead Sea Scrolls Study Edition.* 2 vols. Leiden: Brill.

García Martínez, F., and J. Trebolle Barrera
1995 *The People of the Dead Sea Scrolls: Their Writings, Beliefs, and Practices.* Leiden: Brill.

Gardiner, C. P.
1987 *The Sophoclean Chorus: A Study of Character and Function.* Iowa City: University of Iowa Press.

Gardner-Smith, P.
1938 *St. John and the Synoptic Gospels.* Cambridge: Cambridge University Press.

Garitte, G.
1960 "Les 'Logoi' d'Oxyrhynque et l'apocryphe copte dit 'Évangile de Thomas.'" *Le Muséon* 73:151–72.

Garland, D. E.
1985 "The Composition and Unity of Philippians: Some Neglected Literary Factors." *NovT* 27:141–73.

Garrett, S. R.
1990 "Exodus from Bondage: Luke 9:31 and Acts 12:1–24." *CBQ* 52:656–80.

Gärtner, B.
1961 *The Theology of the Gospel of Thomas.* Translated by E. J. Sharpe. London: Collins.

Garver, E.
1994 *Aristotle's Rhetoric: An Art of Character.* Chicago and London: University of Chicago Press.
2000 "La découverte de l'*èthos* chez Aristotle." Cornilliat and Lockwood (eds.) 2000:15–35.

Gasque, W.
1975 *A History of the Criticism of the Acts of the Apostles.* Tübingen: Mohr-Siebeck.

Gaster, T. H.
1981 *Myth, Legend, and Customs in the Old Testament.* 2 vols. Gloucester: Peter Smith.

Gaventa, B. R.
1986 "Galatians 1 and 2: Autobiography as Paradigm," *NovT* 28:309–26.

Gavrilov, A. K.
1997 "Techniques of Reading in Classical Antiquity." *CQ* 47:56–73.

Geerard, M. (ed.)
1983 *Patres Antenicaeni.* Vol. 1 of *Clavis Patrum Graecorum.* Brepols: Turnhout.

Geiger, A.
1836 "Einiges über Plan und Anordnung der Mischnah." *Wissenschaftliche Zeitschrift für jüdische Theologie.* 2:489–92.

Geller, S. A.
1979 *Parallelism in Early Biblical Poetry.* HSM 20. Missoula, Mont.: Scholars Press.

Genette, G.
1988 *Narrative Discourse Revisited.* Ithaca: Cornell University Press.
1992 *The Architext: An Introduction.* Translated by Jane E. Lewin. Berkeley, Los Angeles, and Oxford: University of California Press.
1997a *Palimpsests: Literature in the Second Degree.* Translated by C. Newman and C. Doubinsky. Lincoln: University of Nebraska Press.
1997b *Paratexts: Thresholds of Interpretation.* LCT 20. Translated by J. E. Lewin. Cambridge: Cambridge University Press.
1993 *Fiction and Diction.* Translated by C. Porter. Ithaca: Cornell University Press.

Gentili, B.
1988 *Poetry and Its Public in Ancient Greece.* Baltimore: Johns Hopkins University Press.

Gentili, B., and G. Cerri
1981 "Written and Oral Communication in Greek Historiographical Thought." In Havelock and Hershbell (eds.) 1978, 137–55.

Georges, R. A., and A. Dundes
1963 "Toward a Structural Definition of the Riddle." *JAF* 76:111.

Georges, R. A., and M. D. Jones
1995 *Folkloristics: An Introduction.* Bloomington and Indianapolis: Indiana University Press.

Gerber, C.
1997 *Ein Bild des Judentums für Nichtjuden von Flavius Josephus: Untersuchungen zu seiner Schrift Contra Apionem.* *AGJU* 40. Leiden: Brill.
1999 "Des Josephus Apologie für das Judentum: Prolegomena zu einer Interpretation von C 2:145ff." In Kalms and Siegert (eds.) 1999, 251–69.

Gerdmar, A.
2001 *Rethinking the Judaism-Hellenism Dichotomy: A Historiographical Case Study of Second Peter and Jude.* ConBNT 36. Stockholm: Almqvist & Wiksell International.

Gerhardsson, B.
1979 *The Origins of the Gospel Traditions.* Philadelphia: Fortress Press.
1988 "The Narrative Meshalim in the Synoptic Gospels." *NTS* 34:339–63.

Gerstinger, H.
1948 *Bestand und Überlieferung der Literaturwerke des griechisch-römischen Altertums.* Graz: J. A. Kienreich.

Gevaryahu, H. M. I.
1975 "Biblical Colophons: A Source for the 'Biography' of Authors, Texts, and Books." Pp. 42–59 in *Congress Volume.* VTSup 28. Leiden: Brill.

Giblin, C. H.
1976 "Structural and Thematic Correlations in the Theology of Revelation 16–22." *Biblica* 5:487–504.
1990 "The Tripartite Narrative Structure of John's Gospel." *Biblica* 71:449–67.

Gibson, E.
1978 *The "Christians for Christians" Inscriptions of Phrygia.* HTS 32. Missoula, Mont.: Scholars Press.

Giesen, H.
1997 *Die Offenbarung des Johannes.* RNT. Regenburg: Pustet.
2000 *Studien zur Johannesapokalypse.* SBA 29. Leipzig: Katholisches Bibelwerk.

Giet, S.
1970 *L'Énigme de la Didaché.* Paris: Ophrys.

Gill, C.
1984 "The Ethos/Pathos Distinction in Rhetorical and Literary Criticism," *CQ* 78:149–66.

Gill, C., and T. P. Wiseman (eds.).
1993 *Lies and Fiction in the Ancient World.* Austin: University of Texas Press.

Gill, D. W. J., and C. Gempf (eds.)
1994 *The Book of Acts in Its First-Century Setting.* Vol. 2: *Graeco-Roman Setting.* Grand Rapids: Eerdmans.

Gilliard, F. D.
1992 "More Silent Reading in Antiquity: *Non Omne Verbum Sonabat.*" *JBL* 112:689–94.

Ginzberg, L.
1909–38 *Legends of the Jews.* 7 vols. Philadelphia: Jewish Publication Society of America.

Giversen, S.
1972 "Solomon und die Dämonen." Pp. 16–21 in *Essays on the Nag Hammadi Texts in Honor of Alexander Böhlig.* Edited by M. Krause. NHS 3. Leiden: Brill.

Gjörgemanns, H.
1997 "Autobiographie." *Der neue Pauly* 2:348–53.

Gladigow, B.
1967 "Der Makarismus des Weisen." *Hermes* 95:404–33.

Glasson, T. F.
1975 "Old Testament Testimonies and Their Transmission." *ExpTim* 87:21–22.

Glénison, J., J. Bompaire, and J. Irigoin (eds.)
1977 *La paléographie grecque et byzantine.* Paris: Éditions du Centre national de la recherche scientifique.

Glimm, F. X., J. M.-F. Marique, and G. G. Walsh (trans.)
1947 *The Apostolic Fathers.* FC. New York: Cima.

Glockmann, G.
1967 "Homer in der christlichen Apologetik des zweiten Jahrhunderts." *Orpheus* 14:33–40.
1968 *Homer in der frühchristlichen Literatur bis Justinus.* TU 105. Berlin: Akademie-Verlag.

Glover, R.
1958–59 "The Didache's Quotations and the Synoptic Gospels." *NTS* 5:12–29.
1985 "Patristic Quotations and Gospel Sources." *NTS* 31:228–47.

Gnilka, J.
1968 "2 Cor. 6:14–7:1 in the Light of the Qumran Texts and the Testaments of the Twelve Patriarchs." Pp. 48–68 in *Paul and Qumran.* Edited by J. Murphy-O'Connor. London: Chapman.
1971a *Der Epheserbrief.* Freiburg: Herder.
1971b *The Epistle to the Philippians.* New York: Herder & Herder.
1978–79 *Das Evangelium nach Markus.* 2 vols.

Zurich: Benziger; Neukirchen-Vluyn: Neukirchener Verlag.

Gnuse, R. K.
1996 *Dreams and Dream Reports in the Writings of Josephus: A Traditio-Historical Analysis. AGJU* 36. Leiden: Brill.

Gold, B. K. (ed.)
1982 *Literary and Artistic Patronage in Ancient Rome.* Austin: University of Texas Press.

Goldberg, A.
1987 "The Mishna—A Study Book of Halakha." In Safrai (ed.) 1987a, 211ff.

Goldhill, S.
1994 "The Naive and Knowing Eye: Ekphrasis and the Culture of Viewing in the Hellenistic World." In *Art and Text in Ancient Greek Culture.* Edited by Simon Goldhill and Robin Osborne. Cambridge and New York: Cambridge University Press.

Goldsmith, D.
1968 "Acts 13:33–37: A Pesher on II Sam. 7." *JBL* 87:321–24.

Gomme, A. W.
1937 "The Speeches in Thucydides." Pp. 156–89 in A. W. Gomme. *Essays in Greek and History and Literature.* Oxford: Basil Blackwell.

Goodacre, M. C.
2001 *The Synoptic Problem: Entering the Maze.* London and New York: Sheffield Academic Press.
2002 *The Case against Q: Studies in Markan Priority and the Synoptic Problem.* Harrisburg: Trinity Press Inernational.

Goodenough, E. R.
1968 *The Theology of Justin Martyr.* Amsterdam: Philo.

Goodman, M.
1999 "Josephus' Treatise *Against Apion.*" In Edwards, Goodman, Price, and Rowland (eds.) 1999, 45–58.

Goodspeed, E. J.
1912 "The Vocabulary of Luke and Acts." *JBL* 31:92–94.
1914 *Die ältesten Apologete: Texte mit kurzen Einleitungen.* Göttingen: Vandenhoeck & Ruprecht.
1933 *The Meaning of Ephesians.* Chicago: University of Chicago.
1950 *The Apostolic Fathers.* New York: Harper & Bros.
1951 "Ephesians and the First Edition of Paul." *JBL* 70:285–91.
1960 *Index Patristicus sive Clavis Patrum Apostolicorum Operum.* Naperville, Ill.: Allenson. Corrected reprint of the 1907 edition.

Goodwin, C.
1954 "How Did John Treat His Sources?" *JBL* 73:61–75.

Goold, G. P. (ed.)
1995 Chariton, *Callirhoe.* LCL. Cambridge: Harvard University Press.

Goppelt, Leonhard
1981 *Typos: The Typological Interpretation of the Old Testament in the New.* Grand Rapids: Eerdmans.

Goppelt, L.
1978 *Der erste Petrusbrief.* Edited by F. Hahn. Göttingen: Vandenhoeck & Ruprecht.

Gordis, R.
1949 "Quotations as a Literary Usage in Biblical, Oriental, and Rabbinic Literature." *HUCA* 22:157–219.

Gordon, A. E.
1983 *Illustrated Introduction to Latin Epigraphy.* Berkeley: University of California Press.

Gordon, W. M., and O. F. Robinson
1988 *The Institutes of Gaius.* Ithaca, N.Y.: Cornell University Press.

Gorman, M. J.
2001 *Elements of Biblical Exegesis: A Basic Guide for Students and Ministers.* Peabody, Mass.: Hendrickson.

Gottschalk, H. B.
1972 "Notes on the Wills of the Peripatetic Scholars." *Hermes* 100:314–42.
1982 "Diatribe Again." *Liverpool Classical Monthly* 7:91–92.
1983 "More on DIATRIBAI." *LCM* 8:91–92.

Gottwald, N.
1962 "Poetry, Hebrew." *IDB* 3.829–38.

Goulder, M.
1974 *Midrash and Lection in Matthew.* London: SPCK.
1978 *The Evangelists' Calendar: A Lectionary Explanation of the Development of Scripture.* London: SPCK.
1991 "The Visionaries of Laodicea." *JSNT* 43:15–39.

Graf, F.
1991 "Prayer in Magic and Religious Ritual." Pp. 188–213 in *Magika Hiera: Ancient Greek Magic and Religion.* New York: Oxford University Press.
1993 *Greek Mythology: An Introduction.* Baltimore: Johns Hopkins University Press.
1997 *Magic in the Ancient World.* Cambridge: Harvard University Press.

Graham, W. A.
1987 *Beyond the Written Word: Oral Aspects of Scripture in the History of Religion.* Cambridge: Cambridge University Press.

Grant, F. C.
1937 "Was the Author of John Dependent upon the Gospel of Luke?" *JBL* 56:285–307.
1957 *The Gospels: Their Origin and Growth.* New York, Evanston, and London: Harper & Row.

Grant, R. M.
1942 "The Fourth Gospel and the Church." *HTR* 35:95–116.
1949 "Irenaeus and Hellenistic Culture." *HTR* 42:41–51.
1954 "Athenagoras or Pseudo-Athenagoras." *HTR* 47:121–29.
1964 *Introduction.* Vol. 1 of *The Apostolic Fathers: A New Translation and Commentary.* London and Toronto: Thomas Nelson.
1965 *The Formation of the New Testament.* New York: Harper & Row.
1985 "'Holy Law' in Paul and Ignatius." Pp. 65–71 in D. E. Groh and R. Jewett (eds.), *The Living Text: Essays in Honor of Ernest W. Saunders.* Lanham, Md.: University Press of America.
1986 "Carpocratians and Curriculum: Irenaeus' Reply." *HTR* 79: 127–36.
1988a *Greek Apologists of the Second Century.* Philadelphia: Westminster Press.
1988b "Five Apologists and Marcus Aurelius." *VC* 42:1–17.
1997 *Irenaeus of Lyons.* New York: Routledge.

Grant, R. M., and H. Graham.
1964 *First and Second Clement.* Apostolic Fathers 2. New York: Thomas Nelson & Sons.

Grant, R. M., and D. Tracy
1984 *A Short History of the Interpretation of the Bible.* 2nd ed. London: SCM.

Grayston, K.
1984 *The Johannine Epistles.* Grand Rapids: Eerdmans; London: Marshall, Morgan & Scott.

Grayston, K., and G. Herdan
1959–60 "The Authorship of the Pastorals in the Light of Statistical Linguistics." *NTS* 6:1–15.

Green, E. M. B.
1967 *The Second Epistle General of Peter and the General Epistle of Jude.* Grand Rapids: Eerdmans.

Green, G. L.
2002 *The Letters to the Thessalonians.* PNTC. Grand Rapids: Eerdmans.

Green, H. B.
1968 "The Structure of St. Matthew's Gospel." *Studia Evangelica IV.* Berlin: Akademia.
2001 *Matthew, Poet of the Beatitudes.* JSNTSup 203. Sheffield: Sheffield Academic Press.

Green, J. B.
1988 *The Death of Jesus: Tradition and Interpretation in the Passion Narrative.* Tübingen: Mohr-Siebeck.
1995 *Hearing the New Testament: Strategies for Interpretation.* Grand Rapids: Eerdmans.
1997 *The Gospel of Luke.* NICNT. Grand Rapids: Eerdmans.

Green, M.
1987 *The Second Epistle General of Peter and the General Epistle of Jude.* 2d ed. Grand Rapids: Eerdmans.

Green, W.
1993 "Doing the Text's Work for It: Richard Hays on Paul's Use of Scripture." In Evans and Sanders (eds.) 1993.

Greene, W. C.
1938 *Scholia Platonica.* Philological Monographs 8. Haverford: Haverford College Press.

Greenfield, J., and E. Qimron
1992 "The Genesis Apocryphon Col. XII." Abr-Nahrain Supplement 3:70–77.

Greenfield, J. C., and M. E. Stone
1977 "The Enochic Pentateuch and the Date of the Simlitudes." *HTR* 70:51–65.

Greenspoon, L.
1981 "The Pronouncement Story in Philo and Josephus." *Semeia* 20:73–80.

Greenwood, D.
1970 "Rhetorical Criticism and Formgeschichte: Some Methodological Considerations." *JBL* 89:418–26.

Greetham, D. C.
1992 *Textual Scholarship: An Introduction.* New York: Garland.

Greeven, H.
1951 "Die Textgestalt der Evangelienlektionäre." *TLZ* 76:513–22.

Grelot, P.
1958a "La géographie mythique d'Hénoch et ses sources orientales." *RB* 65:33–69.
1958b "La légende d'Hénoch dans les apocryphes et dans la bible: origine et signification." *RSR* 46:5–26, 181–220.
1989 *Homélies sur l'Écriture à l'Époque*

Apostolique. Vol. 8 of *Le Nouveau Testament.* Tournai: Desclée.

Grenfell, B. P., and A. S. Hunt
1897 ΛΟΓΙΑ ΙΗΣΟΥ*: Sayings of Our Lord.* London: Henry Frowde.

Grese, W. C.
1979 *Corpus Hermeticum XIII and Early Christian Literature.* SCHNT 5. Leiden: Brill.

Griffiths, J. G.
1975 *Apuleius of Madauros: The Isis-Book (Metamorphoses, Book XI).* EPRO 39. Leiden: E. J. Brill.

Grimaldi, W. M. A.
1972 *Studies in the Philosophy of Aristotle's Rhetoric.* Hermes Einzelschriften 25. Wiesbaden: Franz Steiner.
1980 *Aristotle, Rhetoric I: A Commentary.* New York: Fordham University Press.
1988 *Aristotle, Rhetoric II: A Commentary.* New York: Fordham University Press.

Grobel, K.
1960 *The Gospel of Truth: A Valentinian Meditation on the Gospel.* New York and Nashville: Abingdon Press.

Groningen, B. A. van
1963 "*EKDOSIS.*" *Mnemosyne* 4:1–17.

Groot, A. W. de
1919 *A Handbook of Antique Prose-Rhythm.* Groningen and The Hague: J. B. Wolters.

Gross, A. G., and A. E. Walzer (eds.)
2000 *Rereading Aristotle's Rhetoric.* Carbondale: Southern Illinois University Press.

Grossfeld, B.
1991 *The Two Targums of Esther.* ArBib 18. Wilmington, Del.: Glazier.

Grossouw, W. K. M.
1951 "Over de echtheid van 2 Cor. 6:14–7:1." *Studia Catholica* 26:203–6.

Grube, G. M. A.
1961 *The Greek Critic: Demetrius on Style.* PhoenixSup 4. Toronto: University of Toronto Press.
1964 "The Date of Demetrius on Style." *Phoenix* 18:294–302.
1965 *The Greek and Roman Critics.* Toronto: University of Toronto Press.

Gruber, W. E.
1993 *Missing Persons: Character and Characterization in Modern Drama.* Athens: University of Georgia Press.

Grudem, W.
1988 *The First Epistle of Peter: An Introduction and Commentary.* Grand Rapids: Eerdmans.

Guelich, R. A.
1982 *The Sermon on the Mount: A Foundation for Understanding.* Waco: Word.
1983 "The Gospel Genre." In Stuhlmacher (ed.) 1983, 183–219.
1989 *Mark 1–8:26.* WBC 34A. Dallas: Word Publishing.

Guerra, A. J.
1986 *Romans 3:29–30 and the Apologetic Tradition.* Ann Arbor, Mich.: University Microfilms.
1988 "Romans 4 as Apologetic Theology." *HTR* 81:251–70.
1992 "The Conversion of Marcus Aurelius and Justin Martyr: The Purpose, Genre, and Content of the First Apology." *SecCent* 9:171–87.
1995 *Romans and the Apologetic Tradition: The Purpose, Genre, and Audience of Paul's Letter.* SNTSMS 81. Cambridge: Cambridge University Press.

Guilding, A.
1960 *The Fourth Gospel and Jewish Worship.* Oxford: Clarendon Press.

Gundry, R. H.
1967 *The Use of the Old Testament in St. Matthew's Gospel.* Leiden: Brill.
1974 "Recent Investigations into the Literary Genre 'Gospel.'" In Longenecker and Tenney (eds.) 1974, 97–114.
1993 *Mark: A Commentary on His Apology for the Cross.* Grand Rapids: Eerdmans.
1995 "ΕΥΑΓΓΕΛΙΟΝ*: How Soon a Book?*" JBL 115:321–25.

Guthrie, D.
1962 "The Development of the Idea of Canonical Pseudepigraph in New Testament Criticism." In *Vox Evangelica.* Edited by R. Martin. London: Epworth.
1970 *New Testament Introduction.* 3d ed. Downers Grove, Ill.: Inter-Varsity.

Guthrie, G. H.
1994 *The Structure of Hebrews: A Textlinguistic Analysis.* NovTSup 73. Leiden: Brill.

Guthrie, W. K. C.
1952 "The Presocratic World Picture." *HTR* 45:87–104.
1972 *The Sophists.* Cambridge: Cambridge University Press.

Güting, E. W., and D. L. Mealand
1998 *Asyndeton in Paul: A Text-Critical and Statistical Enquiry into Pauline Style.* Lewiston, N.Y.: Mellen.

Gutzwiller, K. J.
1981 *Studies in the Hellenistic Epyllion.*

Beiträge zur klassischen Philologie 114. Königstein: Hain.

Haacker, K.
1999 *Der Brief des Paulus an die Römer.* THKNT 6. Leipzig: Evangelische Verlaganstalt.

Haaland, G.
1999 "Jewish Laws for a Roman Audience: Toward an Understanding of Contra Apionem." In Kalms and Siegert (eds.) 1999, 282–304.

Habel, N.
1965 "The Form and Significance of the Call Narrative." *ZAW* 77:297–323.

Habinek, T. N.
1998 *The Politics of Latin Literature: Writing, Identity, and Empire in Ancient Rome.* Princeton: Princeton University Press.

Hackett, J.
1956 "Echoes of the Bacchae of Euripides in Acts of the Apostles?" *ITQ* 23:219–27.

Hadas, M.
1952 *A History of Latin Literature.* New York: Columbia University Press.

Hadas, M., and M. Smith
1965 *Heroes and Gods: Spiritual Biographies in Antiquity.* New York: Harper & Row.

Haelewyck, J.-C.
2002 "La reine de Saba et les apocryphes salomoniens (*Testament de Salomon* et *Questions de la reine de Saba*)." *Graphè* 11:83–99.

Haelst, J. van
1976 *Catalogue des papyrus littéraires juifs et chrétiens.* Paris: Publications de la Sorbonne.
1982 "Les origines du codex." In A. Blanchard (ed.) 1989, 13–35.

Haenchen, E.
1965 "Das 'Wir' in der Apostelgeschichte und das Itinerar." Pp. 227–64 in *Gott und Mensch: Gesammelte Aufsätze.* Tübingen: Mohr-Siebeck.
1971 *The Acts of the Apostles: A Commentary.* Philadelphia: Westminster Press.
1984 *John.* 2 vols. Hermeneia. Philadelphia: Fortress Press.

Hafemann, S.
1990 "'Self-Commendation' and Apostolic Legitimacy in 2 Corinthians: A Pauline Dialectic?" *NTS* 36:66–88.
1998 "Paul's Use of the Old Testament in 2 Corinthians." *Interpretation* 52:246–57.

Hage, W.
1974 *Die griechische Baruch-Apokalypse.* Gütersloh: Gerd Mohn.

Hagen, W. H.
1980–81 "Two Deutero-Pauline Glosses in Romans 6." *ExpTim* 92:364–67.

Hägg, T.
1971 *Narrative Technique in Ancient Greek Romances. Studies in Chariton, Xenophon Ephesius, and Achilles Tatius.* Stockholm: Almqvist & Wiksell.
1983 *The Novel in Antiquity.* Berkeley: University of California Press.

Hagner, D. A.
1973 *The Use of the Old and New Testaments in Clement of Rome.* NovTSup 34. Leiden: Brill.

Hahneman, G.
1992 *The Muratorian Fragment and the Development of the Canon.* Oxford: Clarendon Press.

Hall, C. A.
1998 *Reading Scripture with the Church Fathers.* Downers Grove, Ill.: InterVarsity.

Hall, R. G.
1987 "The Rhetorical Outline for Galatians: A Reconsideration." *JBL* 106:277–87.
1988 "The 'Christian Interpolation' in the *Apocalypse of Abraham.*" *JBL* 107:107–10.
1990 "The Ascension of Isaiah: Community, Situation, Date, and Place in Early Christianity." *JBL* 109:289–306.

Hall, S. G.
1966 "Repentance in 1 Clement." Pp. 30–43 in *Studia Patristica.* Edited by F. L. Cross. Vol. 8, part 2. TU 93. Berlin: Akademie Verlag.
1979 *Melito of Sardis on Pascha and Fragments.* Oxford: Clarendon Press.

Hallow, W. W. and K. L. Younger (eds.)
2000 *Monumental Inscriptions from the Biblical World.* Vol. 2 of The Context of Scripture. Leiden, Boston and Köln: Brill.

Hamilton, A.
1999 *The Apocryphal Apocalypse: The Reception of the Second Book of Esdras (4 Ezra) from the Renaissance to the Enlightenment.* Oxford: Clarendon Press.

Hamilton, J. R.
1969 *Plutarch, Alexander: A Commentary.* Oxford: Oxford University Press.

Hamm, M. D.
1990 *The Beatitudes in Context: What Luke and Matthew Meant.* Wilmington: Glazier.

Hamman, A.-G., and M.-H. Congourdeau
1997 *Lire la Bible a l'ecole des Pères de Justin martyr à S. Bonaventure.* Paris: Migne.

Hammer, W.
1980 "L'intention de la généalogie de Matthieu." *ETR* 55.2:305–6.

Hammond Bammel, C. P.
1995 *Tradition and Exegesis in Early Christian Writers.* Aldershot and Brookfield: Variorum.

Hans, L.
1981 "Bibliography on Midrash." Pp. 93–103 in *The Study of Ancient Judaism I: Mishnah, Midrash, Siddur.* Edited by J. Neusner. New York: KTAV.

Hansen, G. W.
1989 *Abraham in Galatians: Epistolary and Rhetorical Contexts.* Sheffield: Sheffield Academic Press.

Hanson, A. E.
1998 "Galen: Author and Critic." In Most (ed.) 1998, 22–53.

Hanson, A. T.
1966 *The Pastoral Letters.* Cambridge Bible Commentary. Cambridge: Cambridge University Press.
1982 *The Pastoral Epistles.* London: SPCK.
1991 *The Prophetic Gospel: A Study of John and the Old Testament.* Edinburgh: T. & T. Clark.

Hanson, P. D.
1976 "Apocalypticism." *IDBSup*:28–34.
1979 *The Dawn of Apocalyptic: The Historical and Sociological Roots of Jewish Apocalyptic Eschatology.* Revised edition. Philadelphia: Fortress Press.

Hanson, R. P. C.
1959 *Allegory and Event.* London: SCM.

Harari, J. V.
1979 *Textual Strategies: Perspectives in Post-Structuralist Criticism.* Ithaca, N.Y.: Cornell University Press.

Hardwick, M. E.
1996 "Contra Apionem and Christian Apologetics." In Feldman and Levison (eds.) 1996, 369–402.

Harlfinger, D. (ed.)
1980 *Griechische Kodikologie und Textüberlieferung.* Darmstadt: Wissenschaftliche Buchgesellschaft.

Harlow, D. C.
1996 *The Greek Apocalypse of Baruch (3 Baruch) in Hellenistic Judaism and Early Christianity.* SVTP 12. Leiden: Brill.

Harmon, W., and C. H. Holman (eds.)
2000 *A Handbook to Literature.* 8th ed. Upper Saddle River, N.J.: Prentice Hall.

Harnack, A. von
1882 *Die Überlieferung der griechischen Apologeten des zweiten Jahrhunderts in der alten Kirche und im Mittelalter.* Texte and Unterschungen 1:1–2. Leipzig: J. C. Hinrichs.
1890 "Review of Edwin Hatch, *Essays in Biblical Greek.*" *TLZ* 15:297–301.
1901 "Patristische Miszellen." TU 20:102–6.
1905 "Zum Ursprung des sog. 2. Clemensbriefs." *ZNW* 6:67–71.
1907a "Der Presbyter-Prediger des Irenäus (IV, 27, 1–32,1), Bruchstücke und Nachklänge der ältesten exegetisch-polemischen Homilien." Pp. 1–38 in *Philotesia zu Paul Kleinert zum LXX. Geburtstage dargebracht.* Berlin.
1907b *Des heiligen Irenaeus Schrift zum Erweise der apostolischen Verkündigung in armenischer Version entdeckt, herausgegeben und ins Deutsche übersetzt von D. Karapet Ter Mekerttschian und Lic. D. Erwand Ter Minaaeantz, mit einem Nachwort und Bemerkungen von Ad. Harnack.* TU 31:1. Leipzig: J. C. Hinrichs.
1930 *Judentum und Judenchristentum in Justins Dialog mit Tryphon.* Leipzig.
1958 *Geschichte der altchristlichen Literatur bis Eusebius.* 2d ed. Teil II: *Die Chronologie.* Band 1: *Die Chronologie der Literatur bis Irenäus nebst einleitenden Untersuchungen.* Leipzig: J. C. Hinrichs.
1960 *Marcion: Das Evangelium vom fremden Gott: Eine Monographie zur Geschichte der Grundlegung der katholischen Kirche.* Darmstadt: Wissenschaftliche Buchgesellschaft. Originally published in 1923 and 1924.

Harnisch, W.
1969 *Verhängnis und Verheissung der Geschichte: Untersuchungen zum Zeit- und Geschichtsverständnis im 4. Buch Esra und in der syr. Baruchapokalypse.* FRLANT 97. Göttingen: Vandenhoeck & Ruprecht.

Harrington, D. J.
1976 "Abraham Traditions in the Testament of Abraham and in the 'Rewritten Bible' of the Intertestamental Period." In Nickelsburg (ed.) 1976, 165–72.

1985 "Pseudo-Philo." In Charlesworth (ed.) 1985, 2.297–377.

1986 "The Bible Rewritten (Narratives)." In Kraft and Nickelsburg (ed.) 1986, 239–47.

1996 *Wisdom Texts from Qumran.* London: Routledge.

Harrington, J. M.

2000 *The Lukan Passion Narrative: The Markan Material in Luke 22,54–23,25, A Historical Survey: 1891–1997.* NTTS 30. Leiden: Brill.

Harriott, R.

1969 *Poetry and Criticism before Plato.* London: Methuen.

Harris, J. R.

1893 *Stichometry.* London: C. J. Clay & Sons.

1916–20 *Testimonies.* 2 Vols. Cambridge: Cambridge University Press.

Harris, L. L.

1990 *Characters in 20th-Century Literature.* Detroit: Gale Research.

Harris, W. V.

1989 *Ancient Literacy.* Cambridge: Harvard University Press.

2001 *Restraining Rage: The Ideology of Anger Control in Classical Antiquity.* Harvard: Harvard University.

Harrison, P. N.

1921 *The Problem of the Pastoral Epistles.* London: Oxford University Press.

1936 *Polycarp's Two Epistles to the Philippians.* Cambridge: Cambridge University Press.

1964 *Paulines and Pastorals.* London: Villiers.

Harrison, S. J.

1996 "Apuleius." *OCD*: 131–32.

2000 *Apuleius: A Latin Sophist.* Oxford: Oxford University Press.

Hart, D. V.

1964 *Riddles in Filipino Folklore: An Anthropological Analysis.* Syracuse: Syracuse University Press.

Härter, A.

2000 *Digressionen: Studien über das Verhältnis von Ordnung und Abweichung in Rhetorik und Poetik.* Munich: Fink.

Hartin, P. J.

1991 *James and the Q Sayings of Jesus.* Sheffield: Sheffield Academic Press.

Hartman, G. H., and S. Budick (eds.)

1986 *Midrash and Literature.* New Haven, Conn.: Yale University Press.

Hartman, L.

1966 *Prophecy Interpreted: The Formation of Some Jewish Apocalyptic Texts and of the Eschatological Discourse of Mark 13 Par.* Lund: Gleerup.

1972 "Scriptural Exegesis in the Gospel of Matthew and the Problem of Communication." Pp. 131–52 in *L'Évangile selon Matthieu.* Edited by M. Didier. Gembloux, Belgium: J. Duculot.

1979 *Asking for a Meaning: A Study of 1 Enoch 1–5.* Lund: Gleerup.

Hartman, T. C.

1972 "Some Thoughts on the Sumerian King List and Genesis 5 and 11B." *JBL* 91:25–32.

Hartog, P.

2001 *Polycarp and the New Testament.* WUNT 2.134. Tübingen: Mohr-Siebeck.

Hartshorne, C., and P. Weiss (eds.)

1960 *Collected Papers of Charles Sanders Peirce.* Vol. 2: *Elements of Logic.* Vol. 5: *Pragmatism and Pragmaticism.* Cambridge: Harvard University Press.

Harvey, J. D.

1998 *Listening to the Text: Oral Patterning in Paul's Letters.* Grand Rapids: Baker Books.

2002 "Orality and Its Implications for Biblical Studies." *JETS* 45:99–109.

Hastings, J. (ed.)

1900 *A Dictionary of the Bible.* 3 vols. New York: Scribner's Sons.

Hasubek, P. (ed.)

1982 *Die Fabel: Theorie, Geschichte und Rezeption einer Gattung.* Berlin: Erich Schmidt.

Hatch, E.

1889 *Essays in Biblical Greek.* Oxford: Clarendon Press.

Hatch, W. H. P.

1935 "The Origin and Meaning of the Term 'Uncial.'" *CP* 30:247–54.

Hatina, T. R.

1999 "Intertextuality and Historical Criticism in New Testament Studies: Is There a Relationship?" *Biblical Interpretation* 7:28–43.

2002 *In Search of a Context: The Function of Scripture in Mark's Narrative.* JSNTSup 232. Sheffield: Sheffield Academic Press.

Havelock, E. A.

1971 *Prologue to Greek Literacy.* Cincinnati: University of Cincinnati Press.

1976 *The Literate Revolution in Greece and Its Cultural Consequences.* Princeton: Princeton University Press.

1986 *The Muse Learns to Write: Reflections on Orality and Literacy from Antiquity to the Present.* New Haven, Conn.: Yale University Press.

Havelock, E. A., and J. P. Hershbell (eds.)
1978 *Communication Arts in the Ancient World.* New York: Hastings House.

Hawkins, J. C.
1909 *Horae Synopticae: Contributions to the Study of the Synoptic Problem.* Oxford: Clarendon Press.

Hawthorn, J.
1994 *A Glossary of Contemporary Literary Theory.* 2d ed. London: Edward Arnold.

Hawthorne, G. F.
1983 *Philippians.* WBC 43. Waco, Tex.: Word.

Hay, D. M.
1979 "What Is Proof?—Rhetorical Verification in Philo, Josephus, and Quintilian." In Achtemeier (ed.) 1979, 2.87–100.
1979–80 "Philo's References to Other Allegorists." *SPhilo* 6:41–75.
2000 *Colossians.* Nashville: Abingdon.

Hayes, J. L., and C. Holladay
1987 *Biblical Exegesis: A Beginners Handbook.* Rev. ed. Atlanta: John Knox Press.

Hays, R. B.
1989 *Echoes of Scripture in the Letters of Paul.* New Haven, Conn.: Yale University Press.

Hayward, C. T. R.
1990 "Rewritten Bible." Pp. 595–98 in *A Dictionary of Biblical Interpretation.* Edited by R. J. Coggins and J. L. Houlden. London: SCM Press; Philadelphia Trinity Press International.

Head, P. M.
1991 "A Text-Critical Study of Mark 1.1, 'The Beginning of the Gospel of Jesus Christ.'" *NTS* 37:621–29.

Heath, M.
1989 *Unity in Greek Poetics.* Oxford: Clarendon Press.
1995 *Hermogenes* On Issues: *Strategies of Argument in Later Greek Rhetoric.* New York: Oxford University Press.
1997 "Invention." In Porter (ed.) 1997a, 89–119.

Heckel, T. K.
1999 *Vom Evangelium des Markus zum viergestaltigen Evangelium.* WUNT 120. Tübingen: Mohr-Siebeck.

Heckel, U.
1993 *Kraft in Schwachheit: Untersuchungen zu 2. Kor 10–13.* WUNT 2.56. Tübingen: Mohr-Siebeck.

Hedrick, C. W.
1984 "The Role of 'Summary Statements' in the Composition of Mark: A Dialog with Karl Schmidt and Norman Perrin." *NovT* 26:289–311.
1987 "Narrator and Story in the Gospel of Mark: *Hermeneia* and *Paradosis.*" *Perspectives in Religious Studies* 14:239–58.
1988 "The Tyranny of the Synoptic Gospels." *Semeia* 44:1–8.
1989–90 "Thomas and the Synoptics: Aiming at a Consensus." *SecCent* 7:39–56.
1990 "Authorial Presence and Narrator in John: Commentary and Story." In *Gospel Origins and Christians Beginnings.* Edited by J. E. Goehring, C. W. Hedrick, and J. T. Sanders. Sonoma: Polebridge.
1994 *Parables as Poetic Fictions: The Creative Voice of Jesus.* Peabody, Mass.: Hendrickson.
1998 "Conceiving the Narrative: Colors in Achilles Tatius and the Gospel of Mark." In Hock, Chance, and Perkins (ed.) 1989, 177–97.

Heiden, B.
1998 "The Placement of 'Book Divisions' in the *Iliad.*" *JHS* 118:68–81.

Heil, C.
2003 *Lukas und Q: Studien zur lukanischen Redaktion das Spruchevangeliums Q.* BZNW 111. Berlin and New York: Walter de Gruyter.

Heil, J. P.
2000 *The Meal Scenes in Luke-Acts: An Audience-Oriented Approach.* Atlanta: Society of Biblical Literature.
2001 "The Chiastic Structure and Meaning of Paul's Letter to Philemon." *Biblica* 82:178–206.

Heim, R.
1892 *Incantamenta Magica Graeca Latina.* Jahrbücher für classische Philologie Supplement 19. Pp. 463–576. Leipzig: Teubner.

Heimgartner, M.
2001 *Pseudojustin-Über die Auferstehung: Text und Studie.* PTS 54. Berlin and New York: Walter de Gruyter.

Heinemann, J.
1968 "The Triennial Lectionary Cycle." *JJS* 19:41–48.
1971 "The Proem in the Aggadic Midrashim: A Form-Critical Study." *Scripta Hierosolymitana* 22:100–200.

Heinze, A.
1998 *Johannesapocalypse und johanneische*

Schriften. BWANT 142. Stuttgart: Kohlhammer.

Hellholm, D.
1989 *Apocalypticism in the Mediterranean World and the Near East: Proceedings of the International Colloquium on Apocalypticism, Uppsala, August 12–17, 1979.* 2d ed. Tübingen: Mohr-Siebeck.
1993 "Amplificatio in the Macro-structure of Romans." In Porter and Olbright (eds.) 1993, 123–51.
1995 "Enthymemic Argumentation in Paul: The Case of Romans 6." In Engberg-Pedersen (ed.) 1995, 119–79.

Hemer, C. J.
1985 "First Person Narrative in Acts 27–28." *TynBul* 36:79–109.
1986 *The Letters to the Seven Churches of Asia in Their Local Setting.* JSNTSup 11. Sheffield: JSOT.
1988 *The Book of Acts in the Setting of Hellenistic History.* Edited by C. Gempf. WUNT 49. Tübingen: Mohr-Siebeck.

Henaut, B. W.
1993 *Oral Tradition and the Gospels: The Problem of Mark 4.* Sheffield: Sheffield Academic Press.

Henderson, I. H.
1991 "Gnomic Quatrains in the Synoptics: An Experiment in Genre Definition." *NTS* 37:481–98.
1996 *Jesus, Rhetoric, and Law.* BIS 20. Leiden, New York, and Cologne: E. J. Brill.

Hendrix, H.
1988 "On the Form and Ethos of Ephesians." *Union Seminary Quarterly Review* 42:3–15.

Hengel, M.
1972 "Anonymität, Pseudepigraphie und literarische Fälschung in der jüdisch-hellenistischen Literatur." In Fritz (ed.) 1972, 231–308.
1985a *Studies in the Gospel of Mark.* Philadelphia: Fortress.
1985b "The Titles of the Gospels and the Gospel of Mark." Pp. 64–84 in *Studies in the Gospel of Mark.* Philadelphia: Fortress Press.
1987 "Das Christuslied im frühesten Gottesdienst." Pp. 357–404 in *Weisheit Gottes—Weisheit der Welt: Festschrift für Joseph Kardinal Ratzinger zum 60. Geburtstag.* 2 vols. St. Ottilien: EOS Verlag.
1993 *Die johanneische Frage: Ein Lösungsversuch.* WUNT 67. Tübingen: Mohr-Siebeck.
2000 *The Four Gospels and the One Gospel of Jesus Christ.* Harrisburg, Pa.: Trinity Press International.

Hengel, M., and U. Heckel (eds.)
1992 *Paulus und das antike Judentum.* Tübingen: Mohr-Siebeck.

Hengel, M., and H. Löhr (eds.).
1994 *Schriftauslegung im Antiken Judentum und im Urchristentum.* WUNT 73. Tübingen: Mohr-Siebeck.

Henne, P.
1992 *L'Unité du Pasteur d'Hermas: Tradition et rédaction.* Paris: J. Gabalda.

Hennecke, E., and W. Schneemelcher (eds.)
1963–65 *New Testament Apocrypha.* Translated by R. McL. Wilson. 2 vols. Philadelphia: Westminster Press.

Henrichs, A.
1969 "Lollianos, Phoinikika: Fragmente eines neuen griechischen Romans." *ZPE* 4:205–15.
1972 *Die Phoinikika des Lollianos.* Papyrologische Texte und Abhandlungen 14. Bonn: R. Habelt.

Herbert, M., and M. McNamara
1989 *Irish Biblical Apocrypha: Selected Texts in Translation.* Edinburgh: T. & T. Clark.

Hercher, R.
1873 *Epistolographi Graeci.* Paris: Didot.

Herczeg, P.
1996 "New Testament Parallels to the Apocryphal Acta Pauli Documents." In Bremmer (ed.) 1996, 142–49.

Herr, M. D.
1990 "Les raisons de la conservation des restes de la littérature juive de l'Époque du Second Temple." Pp. 219–30 in *La faible apocryphe I.* Edited by P. Geoltrain, E. Junod, and J.-C. Picard. Turnhout and Paris: Brepols.

Hester, J. D.
1984 "The Rhetorical Structure of Galatians 1:11–2:14." *JBL* 88:1–18.
1986 "The Use and Influence of Rhetoric in Galatians 2.1–14." *TZ* 42:386–408.
1993 "Placing the Blame: The Presence of Epideictic in Galatians 1 and 2." In Watson (ed.) 1993, 281–307.
1996 "The Invention of 1 Thessalonians: A Proposal." In Porter and Olbricht (eds.) 1996, 251–79.

Heubeck, A., S. West, and J. B. Hainsworth
1988 *A Commentary on Homer's Odyssey.* Vol. 1. Oxford: Clarendon Press.

Hezser, C.
2001 *Jewish Literacy in Roman Palestine.* TSAJ 81. Tübingen: Mohr-Siebeck.

Hieatt, C. B.
1987 "On Envelope Patterns and Nonce Formulas." In *Comparative Research on Oral Traditions: A Memorial for Milman Parry.* Edited by J. M. Foley. Columbus, Ohio: Slavica.

Hiebert, T.
2000 "Poetry." *EDB,* 1065–68.

Hijmans, B. L.
1987 "Apuleius, Philosopher Platonicus." *ANRW* 36/1, 395–475.
1993 "Apuleius Orator: 'Pro se de Magia' and 'Florida.'" *ANRW* II, 34/2, 1708–84.

Hilgenfeld, A.
1884 *Die Ketzergeschichte des Urchristentums urkundlich dargestellt.* Leipzig: Fues.

Hilhorst, A.
1976 *Sémitismes et Latinismes dans le Pasteur d'Hermas.* Nijmegen: Dekker & Vande Vegt.
1996 "Tertullian on the Acts of Paul." In Bremmer (ed.) 1996, 150–63.

Hills, J. V.
1990 "Proverbs as Sayings of Jesus in the *Epistula Apostolorum.*" *Semeia* 49:7–34.
1991 "A Genre for 1 John." In Pearson (ed.) 1991, 367–77.
1994 "The Acts of the Apostles in the *Acts of Paul.*" *SBLSP* 33:24–54.
1997 "The *Acts of Paul* and the Legacy of the Lukan Acts." *Semeia* 80:145–58.

Himmelfarb, M.
1983 *Tours of Hell: An Apocalyptic Form in Jewish and Christian Literature.* Philadelphia: University of Pennsylvania Press.
1993 *Ascent to Heaven in Jewish and Christian Apocalypses.* New York and Oxford: Oxford University Press.

Hindley, J. C.
1968–69 "Towards a Date for the Similitudes of Enoch. An Historical Approach." *NTS* 14:551–65.

Hinks, D. A. G.
1936 "Tria genera causarum." *CQ* 30:170–76.

Hirsch, E. D.
1967 *Validity in Interpretation.* New Haven: Yale University Press.
1976 *Aims of Interpretation.* Chicago: University of Chicago Press.

Hobbs, E. C. (ed.)
1978 *The Commentary Hermeneutically Considered.* Colloquy 31 of the Center for Hermeneutical Studies in Hellenistic and Modern Culture. Berkeley: The Center for Hermeneutical Studies.

Hochman, B.
1985 *Character in Literature.* Ithaca: Cornell University Press.

Hock, R. F.
1980 *The Social Context of Paul's Ministry: Tentmaking and Apostleship.* Philadelphia: Fortress Press.
1988 "The Greek Novel." In Aune (ed.) 1988a, 127–46.
1997 "The Rhetoric of Romance." In Porter (ed.) 1997, 445–65.
1998 "Why New Testament Scholars Should Read Ancient Novels." In Hock, Chance, and Perkins (eds.) 1998, 121–38.

Hock, R. F., J. B. Chance, and J. Perkins (eds.).
1998 *Ancient Fiction and Early Christian Narrative.* SBLSymS 6. Atlanta: Scholars Press.

Hock, R. F., and E. N. O'Neil
1986 *The Chreia in Ancient Rhetoric.* Vol. 1: *The Progymnasmata.* Atlanta: Scholars Press.
2002 *The Chreia and Ancient Rhetoric: Classroom Exercises.* Atlanta: Society of Biblical Literature.

Hodgson, R.
1979 "The Testimony Hypothesis." *JBL* 98:361–78.
1983 "Paul the Apostle and the First Century Tribulation Lists." *ZNW* 74:59–80.
1985 "On the *Gattung* of Q: A Dialogue with James M. Robinson." *Bib* 66:73–95.

Hoek, A. van den
1988 *Clement of Alexandria and His Use of Philo in the Stromateis.* Leiden: Brill.
1996 "Techniques of Quotation in Clement of Alexandria: A View of Ancient Literary Working Methods." *VC* 50:223–43.

Hoffman, F.
1973 "Motif Index of Erotic Literature." In *Analytical Survey of Anglo-American Traditional Erotica.* Bowling Green, Ohio: Bowling Green University Popular Press.

Hoffmann, M.
1966 *Der Dialog bei den christlichen Schriftstellern der ersten vier Jahrhunderte.* Berlin: Akademie-Verlag.

Hoffmann, P.
1972 *Studien zur Theologie der Logienquelle.* Munich: Aschendorff.
2001 "Mutmassungen über Q: Zum Problem der literarischen Genese von Q." In Lindemann (ed.) 2001, 255–88.

Hofius, Otfried
1983 "Unbekannte Jesusworte." In Stuhlmacher (ed.) 1983, 355–82.
Hofmann, Norbert
2000 *Die Assumptio Mosis: Studien zur Rezeption massgültiger Überlieferung.* Leiden: Brill.
Hofrichter, P.
1993 "Parallelen zum 24. Gesang der Ilias in den Engelerscheinungen des lukanischen Doppelwerkes." *Protokolle zur Bibel* 2:60–76.
Hohendahl, P. U. (ed.)
1988 *A History of German Literary Criticism, 1730–1980.* Lincoln: University of Nebraska Press.
Holfelder, H. H.
1977 "Εὐσεβεία καὶ φιλοσοφία: Literarische Einheit und politischer Kontext von Justins Apologie." *ZNW* 68:48–66, 231–51.
Holladay, C. R.
1989 *Poets: The Epic Poets Theodotus and Philo and Ezekiel the Tragedian.* Vol. 2 of *Fragments from Hellenistic Jewish Authors.* Atlanta: Scholars Press.
1995 *Aristobulus.* Vol. 3 of *Fragments from Hellenistic Jewish Authors.* Atlanta: Scholars Press.
1996 *Orphica.* Vol. 4 of *Fragments from Hellenistic Jewish Authors.* Atlanta: Scholars Press.
Holland, G. S.
1988 *The Tradition That You Received from Us: 2 Thessalonians in the Pauline Tradition.* Tübingen: Mohr-Siebeck.
1993 "Speaking Like a Fool: Irony in 2 Corinthians 10–13." In Porter and Olbright (eds.) 1993, 250–64.
1997 "Paul's Use of Irony as a Rhetorical Technique." In Porter and Olbricht (eds.) 1997, 234–48.
Hollander, H. W., and M. de Jonge.
1985 *The Testaments of the Twelve Patriarchs: A Commentary.* SVTP 8. Leiden: Brill.
Hollander, J.
1981 *The Figure of Echo: A Mode of Allusion in Milton and After.* Berkeley: University of California Press.
Holloway, P. A.
1998 "Paul's Pointed Prose: The *Sententia* in Roman Rhetoric and Paul." *NovT* 40:32–53.
2001a *Consolation in Philippians: Philosophical Sources and Rhetorical Strategy.* SNTSMS 112. Cambridge: Cambridge University Press.
2001b "The Enthymeme as an Element of Style in Paul." *JBL* 120:329–42.
Holmberg, B.
1990 *Sociology and the New Testament: An Appraisal.* Minneapolis: Fortress Press.
Holmes, M. W. (ed.)
1989 *The Apostolic Fathers.* Translated by J. B. Lightfoot and J. R. Harmer. 2d ed. Grand Rapids: Baker Book House.
1992 *The Apostolic Fathers: Greek Texts and English Translations of Their Writings.* Translated by J. B. Lightfoot and J. R. Harmer. 2d rev. ed. Grand Rapids: Baker Book House.
Holzberg, N.
1995 *The Ancient Novel: An Introduction.* Translated by C. Jackson-Holzberg. London: Routledge.
1996a "The Genre: Novels Proper and the Fringe." In Schmeling (ed.) 1996, 11–28.
1996b "Novel-Like Works of Extended Prose Fiction II." In Schmeling (ed.) 1996, 619–53.
Hommes, N. J.
1935 *Het Testimoniaboek: Studien over O.T. Citaten in het N.T. en bij de Patres. Met Critische Beschouwingen over de Theorieen van J. Rendel Harris en D. Plooy.* Amsterdam: Noord-Hollandsche Uitgevers-Maatschappij.
Hood, R.T.
1961 "The Genealogies of Jesus." Pp. 1–15 in *Early Christian Origins.* Edited by A. Wikgren. Chicago: Quadrangle.
Hooker, M. D.
1991 *The Gospel according to St. Mark.* BNTC. London: A. & C. Black.
Hooker, M. M., and S. G. Wilson (eds.)
1982 *Paul and Paulinism: Essays in Honour of C. K. Barrett.* London: SPCK.
Hope, R.
1930 *The Book of Diogenes Laertius, Its Spirit and Its Method.* New York: Columbia University Press.
Hopfner, T.
1921–24 *Griechisch-ägyptischer Offenbarungzauber.* 2 vols. Leipzig: H. Haessel.
Hoppe, R.
2000 "The Epistolary and Rhetorical Context of 1 Thessalonians 2:1–12: A Response to Karl P. Donfried." In Donfried and Beutler (eds.) 2000, 61–68.
Horbury, W., and D. Noy (eds.)
1992 *Jewish Inscriptions of Graeco-Roman*

Egypt. Cambridge: Cambridge University Press.

Horgan, M. P.
1979 *Pesharim: Qumran Interpretations of Biblical Books*. CBQMS 8. Washington, D.C.: Catholic Biblical Association.

Horgan, M. P., and P. J. Kobelsky (eds.)
1989a *To Touch the Text: Biblical and Related Studies in Honor of Joseph A. Fitzmyer, S.J.* New York: Crossroad.
1989b "The Hodayot (1QH) and New Testament Poetry." In Horgan and Kobelski (eds.) 1989, 179–93.

Horrell, D. G.
1998 *The Epistles of Peter and Jude*. Epworth Commentaries. Peterborough: Epworth.

Horsfall Scotti, M. T.
1990 "Apuleio tra magia e filosophia: la riscoperta di Agostino." Pp. 295–320 in *Dicti studiosus: scritti di filologia offerti a Scevola Mariotti*. Urbino: QuattroVenti.

Horsley, G. H. R., and J. A. L. Lee.
1994 "A Preliminary Checklist of Abbreviations of Greek Epigraphical Volumes." *Epigraphica* 66:129–69.

Horsley, R. A.
1991 "Logoi Prophêtôn? Reflections on the Genre of Q." In Pearson (ed.) 1991, 195–209.
1998 *1 Corinthians*. ANTC. Nashville: Abingdon Press.

Horst, P. W. van der
1978 *The Sentences of Pseudo-Phocylides*. Leiden: Brill.
1996 "The Distinctive Vocabulary of Josephus' *Contra Apionem*." In Feldman and Levison (eds.) 1996, 83–93.

Hovhanessian, V.
2000 *Third Corinthians: Reclaiming Paul for Christian Orthodoxy*. New York: Peter Lang.

How, W. W., and J. Wells
1912 *A Commentary on Herodotus*. 2 vols. Oxford: Clarendon Press.

Howell, D. B.
1990 *Matthew's Inclusive Story*. JSNTSup 42. Sheffield: JSOT.

Howell, E. B.
1964 "St. Paul and the Greek World." *GR* 11:7–29.

Hubbard, B. J.
1977 "Commissioning Stories in Luke–Acts: A Study of Their Antecedents, Form, and Content." *Semeia* 8:103–26.
1978 "The Role of Commissioning Accounts in Acts." In Talbert (ed.) 1978, 187–98.

Hubbell, H. M.
1949 *Cicero, De Inventione*. LCL. Cambridge: Harvard University Press.

Hübner, H.
1984 "Der Galaterbrief und das Verhältnis von antiker Rhetorik und Epistolographie." *TLZ* 109:241–50.
1997a *An Philemon, An die Kolosser, An die Epheser.* HNT 12. Tübingen: Mohr-Siebeck.
1997b *Vetus Testamentum in Novo*. Vol. 2: *Corpus Paulinum*. Göttingen: Vandenhoeck & Ruprecht.

Hughes, F. W.
1989 *Early Christian Rhetoric and 2 Thessalonians*. JSNTSup 30. Sheffield: JSOT.
1990 "The Rhetoric of 1 Thessalonians." Pp. 94–116 in *The Thessalonian Correspondence*. Edited by R. F. Collins. BETL 87. Leuven: Peeters and Leuven University.
1991 "The Rhetoric of Reconciliation: 2 Corinthians 1:1–2:13 and 7:5–8:24." In Watson (ed.) 1991, 246–61.
1997 "Rhetorical Criticism and the Corinthian Correspondence." In Porter and Olbricht (eds.) 1997, 336–50.
2000 "The Rhetoric of Letters." In Donfried and Beutler (eds.) 2000, 194–240.

Hultgård, A.
1977 *L'Eschatologie des Testaments des Douze Patriarches*. Uppsala: Almqvist & Wiksell.

Hultgren, A.
1979 *Jesus and His Adversaries: The Form and Function of the Conflict Stories in the Synoptic Tradition*. Minneapolis: Augsburg Press.
2000 *The Parables of Jesus: A Commentary*. Grand Rapids: Eerdmans.

Hultgren, S.
2002 *Narrative Elements in the Double Tradition: A Study of their Place within the Framework of the Gospel Narrative*. BZNW 113. Berlin and New York: Walter de Gruyter.

Humphrey, J. H. (ed.)
1991 *Literacy in the Roman World*. Journal of Roman Archaeology Supplement 3. Ann Arbor, Mich.: Journal of Roman Archaeology Supplementary Series.

Humphreys, S.
1997 "Fragments, Fetishes, and Philosophies: Towards a History of Greek Historiography after Thucydides." In Most (ed.) 1997, 207–54.

Humphreys, W. L.
1985 "Novella." Pp. 82–96 in *Saga, Legend, Tale, Novella, Fable.* Edited by G. W. Coats. Sheffield: JSOT.

Hunger, H.
1980 *Antiker und byzantischer Roman.* Heidelberg: C. Winter.

Hunt, A. S., and C. C. Edgar (eds.)
1932–34 *Select Papyri.* 2 vols. Cambridge: Harvard University Press.

Hunt, B. P. W. S.
1951 *Primitive Gospel Sources.* New York: Philosophical Library.

Hunter, A. M.
1960 *Interpreting the Parables.* Philadelphia: Westminster Press.

Huntzinger, C.
1965 "Babylon als Deckname für Rom und die Datierung des 1. Petrusbriefes." Pp. 67–77 in *Gottes Wort und Gottes Land.* Edited by H. G. von Reventlow. Göttingen: Vandenhoeck & Ruprecht.

Hurd, J. C.
1983 *The Origin of 1 Corinthians.* 2d ed. Macon, Ga.: Mercer University Press.
1994 "Good News and the Integrity of 1 Corinthians." In Jervis and Richardson (eds.) 1994, 38–62.

Hurley, P. J.
1988 *A Concise Introduction to Logic.* 3d ed. Belmont: Wadsworth Publishing.

Hurtado, L. W.
1998 "The Origin of the *Nomina Sacra*: A Proposal." *JBL* 117:655–73.

Hvalvik, R.
1996 *The Struggle for Scripture and Covenant: The Purpose of the Epistle of Barnabas and Jewish-Christian Competition in the Second Century.* WUNT 2.82. Tübingen: Mohr-Siebeck.

Hyldahl, N.
1966 *Philosophie und Christentum: Eine Interpretation der Einleitung zum Dialog Justins.* Copenhagen: Munksgaard.

Imber, M.
2001 "Practised Speech: Oral and Written Conventions in Roman Declamation." In J. Watson (ed.) 2001, 199–216.

Immerwahr, H. R.
1966 *Form and Thought in Herodotus.* Cleveland: Western Reserve University Press.

Irigoin, J.
1991 "La composition rhythmique des cantiques de Luc." *RB* 98:5–50.

Iser, W.
1974 *The Implied Reader.* Baltimore: Johns Hopkins University Press.
1978 *The Act of Reading: A Theory of Aesthetic Response.* Baltimore: Johns Hopkins University Press.

Jackson, C. N.
1913 "The Latin Epyllion." *HSCP* 24:37–50.

Jackson, H. M.
1988 "Notes on the Testament of Solomon." *JSJ* 19:19–60.

Jacobs, I.
1975–76 "The Midrashic Background for James ii.21–3." *NTS* 22:457–63.

Jacobs, M.
1959 *The Content and Style of an Oral Literature: Clackamas Chinook Myths and Tales.* Chicago: University of Chicago Press.

Jacobsen, A.
1982 "The Literary Unity of Q." *JBL* 101:365–89.

Jacobsen, T.
1939 *The Sumerian King List.* Chicago: University of Chicago Press.

Jacobson, A.
1992 *The First Gospel: An Introduction to Q.* Sonoma, California: Polebrige Press.

Jacoby, F.
1909 "Über die Entwicklung der griechischen Geschichtsschreibung und den Plan einer neuen Sammlung der griechischen Historikerfragmente." *Klio* 9:80–123. Reprinted in Bloch (ed.) 1956.
1923–58 *Die Fragmente der griechischen Historiker.* 3 vols. in 15. Leiden: Brill. Reprinted 1954–69.

Jaeger, W.
1961 *Early Christianity and Greek Paideia.* Cambridge: Harvard University Press.

James, M. R.
1924 *The Apocryphal New Testament.* Oxford: Clarendon Press.

Jamieson, K. H.
1973 "Generic Constraints and the Rhetorical Situation." *PR* 6:162–70.

Jansen, H. L.
1939 *Die Henochgestalt: Eine vergleichende religionsgeschichtliche Untersuchung.* Oslo: Dybwad.

Janson, T.
1964 *Latin Prose Prefaces: Studies in Literary Conventions.* Acta Universitatis Stockholmiensis: Studia Latina Stockholmiensia 13. Stockholm, Göteborg, Uppsala: Almqvist & Wiksell.

Jardine, A.
1986 "Intertextuality." Vol. 1, pp. 387–89 in *Encyclopedic Dictionary of Semiotics.* 3 vols. Edited by T. A. Sebeok. Berlin: Mouton de Gruyter.

Jeffers, J. S.
1991 *Conflict at Rome: Social Order and Hierarchy in Early Christianity.* Minneapolis: Fortress Press.

Jefford, C. N.
1989 *The Sayings of Jesus in the Teaching of the Twelve Apostles.* Leiden: Brill.
1995 *The Didache in Context: Essays on Its Text, History, and Transmission.* Leiden: Brill.
1996 *Reading the Apostolic Fathers: An Introduction.* Peabody, Mass.: Hendrickson.

Jeremias, Joachim
1953 *Die Briefe an Timotheus und Titus.* Göttingen: Vandenhoeck & Ruprecht.
1958 "Chiasmus in den Paulusbriefen." *ZNW* 49:145–56.
1964 *Unknown Sayings of Jesus.* Translated by Reginald H. Fuller. 2d ed. London: SPCK.
1972 *The Parables of Jesus.* 2d ed. New York: Charles Scribner's Sons.
1980 *Die Sprache des Lukasevangeliums: Redaktion und Tradition im Nicht-Markusstoff des dritten Evangeliums.* KEK. Göttingen: Vandenhoeck & Ruprecht.

Jeremias, Jörg
1965 *Theophanie: Die Geschichte einer alttestamentlichen Gattung.* WMANT 10. Neukirchen-Vluyn: Gerd Mohn.

Jervell, J.
1969 "Ein Interpolator interpretiert: Zu der christlichen Bearbeitung der Testamente der zwölf Patriarchen." Pp. 30–61 in *Studien zu den Zwölf Patriarchen.* Edited by C. Burchard, J. Jervell, and J. Thomas. Berlin: Töpelmann.

Jervis, L. A.
1991 *The Purpose of Romans: A Comparative Letter Structure Investigation.* JSNTSup 55. Sheffield: Sheffield Academic Press.

Jervis, L. A., and P. Richardson (eds.)
1994 *Gospel in Paul: Studies on Corinthians, Galatians, and Romans for Richard N. Longenecker.* JSNTSup 108. Sheffield: Sheffield Academic Press.

Jeukens, R.
1907 *Plutarch von Chaeronea und die Rhetorik.* Strassburg: Trübner.

Jewett, R.
1970 "The Epistolary Thanksgiving and the Integrity of Philippians." *NovT* 12:40–53.
1971 *Paul's Anthropological Terms: A Study of Their Use in Conflict Settings. AGJU* 10. Leiden: Brill.
1978 "The Redaction of 1 Corinthians and the Trajectory of the Pauline School." *JAAR* 46:389–444.
1982 "Romans as an Ambassadorial Letter." *Interpretation* 36:5–20.
1986 *The Thessalonian Correspondence: Pauline Rhetoric and Millenarian Piety.* Philadelphia: Fortress Press.
1991 "Following the Argument of Romans." In Donfried (ed.) 1991, 265–77.

Jocelyn, H. D.
1982 "Diatribes and Sermons." *LCM* 7:3–7.
1983 "'Diatribes' and the Greek Book-title *Diatribai.*" *LCM* 8:89–91.

Johanson, B. C.
1987 *To All the Brethren: A Text-Linguistic and Rhetorical Approach to 1 Thessalonians.* Coniectanea biblica 16. Stockholm: Almqvist & Wiksell.

Johnson, L. T.
1983 "James 3:13–4:10 and the Topos *Peri Phthonou.*" *NovT* 25:327–47.
1989 "The New Testament's Anti-Jewish Slander and the Conventions of Ancient Polemic." *JBL* 108:419–41.
1995 *The Letter of James.* AB 37A. New York: Doubleday.
2001 *The First and Second Letters to Timothy.* AB 35A. New York: Doubleday.

Johnson, M. D.
1969 *The Purpose of the Biblical Genealogies with Special Reference to the Setting of the Genealogies of Jesus.* SNTSMS 8. Cambridge: Cambridge University Press.
1983–85 "Life of Adam and Eve." In Charlesworth (ed.) 1983–85, 2.249–95.

Johnson, P. F.
1974 "The Use of Statistics in the Analysis of the Characteristics of Pauline Writings." *NTS* 20:92–100.

Johnson, R. R.
1968 "The Role of Parchment in Greco-Roman Antiquity." Ph.D. dissertation, University of California at Los Angeles.

Johnston, R.
1978 "Parabolic Interpretation Attributed to the Tannaim." Ph.D. dissertation, Hartford Seminary.

Jolivet, I. J.
1997 "An Argument from the Letter and Intent of the Law as the Primary Argumentative Strategy in Romans." In Porter and Olbricht (eds.) 1997, 309–35.

Joly, R.
1958 *Hermas, Le Pasteur.* SC 53. Paris: Les Éditions du Cerf.
1963 *Le tableau de Cébès et la philosophie religeuse.* Collection Latomus 61. Brussells-Berchem: Latomus.

Jones, D. R.
1968 "The Background and Character of the Lukan Psalms." *JTS* 19:19–50.

Jones, F. S.
1996 "The Genre of the Book of Elchasai: A Primitive Church Order, Not an Apocalypse." Pp. 87–104 in *Historische Wahrheit und theologische Wissenschaft: Gerd Lüdemann zum 50. Geburtstag.* Edited by A. Özen. Frankfurt am Main: Peter Lang.

Jones, F. S., and P. A. Mirecki
1995 "The Transformation of Moral Exhortation in Didache 1–5." In Jefford (ed.) 1995.

Jonge, M. de.
1978 *The Testaments of the Twelve Patriarchs: A Critical Edition of the Greek Text.* PVTG I,2. Leiden: Brill.
1979–80 "The Main Issues in the Study of the Testaments of the Twelve Patriarchs." *NTS* 26:508–24.
1993 "The Transmission of the Twelve Patriarchs by Christians." *VC* 47:1–28.
1995 "The so-called Pseudepigrapha of the Old Testament and Early Christianity." Borgen and Giversen (eds.) 1995, 59–71.

Jonge, M. de (ed.)
1975 *Studies on the Testaments of the Twelve Patriarchs: Text and Interpretation.* SVTP 3. Leiden: Brill.

Jonge, M. de, and J. Tromp
1997 *The Life of Adam and Eve and Related Literature.* Guides to Apocrypha and Pseudepigrapha. Sheffield: Sheffield Academic Press.

Jónsson, J.
1965 *Humor and Irony in the New Testament, Illuminated by Parallels in Talmud and Midrash.* Reykjavik: Bókaúgáfa Menningarsjóls.

Joose, P.
1999 "An Introduction to Arabic Diatessaron." *Oriens-Christianus* 83:74–129.

Jordan, M. D.
1986 "Ancient Philosophical Protreptic and the Problem of Persuasive Genres." *Rhetorica* 4:309–33.

Judge, E. A.
1960 "The Early Christians as a Scholastic Community." *JRH* 1:4–15, 125–37.
1968 "Paul's Boasting in Relation to Contemporary Professional Practice," *Australian Biblical Review* 16:37–50.
1972 "St. Paul and Classical Society." *JAC* 15:19–36.

Juel, D.
1988 *Messianic Exegesis: Christological Interpretation of the Old Testament in Early Christianity.* Philadelphia: Fortress Press.
1999 *The Gospel of Mark.* Nashville: Abingdon Press.

Jülicher, A.
1886–89 *Die Gleichnisreden Jesu.* 2 vols. Tübingen: Mohr-Siebeck. 2d ed. 1899–1910. Reprinted, Darmstadt: Wissenschaftliche Buchgesellschaft.

Junod, E.
1983 "Apocryphes du NT ou apocryphes chrétiens anciens? Remarques sur la désignation d'un corpus et indications bibliographiques sur les instruments de travail récents." *Études théologiques et religieuses* 58:409–21.

Junod, E., and J.-D. Kaestli (eds.)
1983 *Acta Iohannis.* CCSA. Turnhout: Brepols.

Kaestli, J.-D.
1979 "L'Évangile de Thomas: Son importance pour l'étude des paroles de Jésus et du gnosticisme chrétien." *ETR* 54:375–96.
1995 "Luke–Acts and the Pastoral Epistles: The Thesis of a Common Authorship." In Tuckett (ed.) 1995, 110–26.

Kahl, W.
1994 *New Testament Miracle Stories in Their Religious-Historical Setting: A Religionsgeschichteliche Comparison from a Structural Perspective.* FRLANT 163. Göttingen: Vandenhoeck & Ruprecht.

Kähler, M.
1964 *The So-Called Historical Jesus and the Historic, Biblical Christ.* Philadelphia: Fortress Press.

Kahmann, J.
1989 "The Second Letter of Peter and the Letter of Jude: Their Mutual Relationship." In Sevrin (ed.) 1989, 105–21.

Kallas, J.
1964–65 "Romans XIII.1–7: An Interpolation." *NTS* 11:365–74.

Kallen, J. L.
1981 *Linguistics and Oral Tradition: The Structural Study of the Riddle.* Dublin: Trinity College.

Kalms, J. U. (ed.)
2000 *Internationales Josephus-Kolloquium, Aarhus 1999.* Münster: LIT Verlag.

Kalms, J. U., and F. Siegert (eds.)
1999 *Internationales Josephus-Kolloquium Brüssel.* Münster: LIT Verlag.

Kamlah, E.
1964 *Die Form der katalogischen Paränese im Neuen Testament.* WUNT 7. Tübingen: Mohr-Siebeck.

Kampen, J. I.
1998–99 "The Diverse Aspects of Wisdom in the Qumran Texts." In Flint and VanderKam (ed.) 1998–99, 1.211–43.

Kany, R.
1986 "Der lukanische Bericht von Tod und Auferstehung Jesus aus der Sicht eines hellenistischen Romanlesers." *NovT* 28:75–90.

Karadimas, D.
1996 *Sextus Empiricus against Aelius Aristides: The Conflict between Philosophy and Rhetoric in the Second Century* A.D. Lund: Lund University.

Karrer, M.
1986 *Die Johannesoffenbarung als Brief.* FRLANT 140. Göttingen: Vandenhoeck & Ruprecht.

Karris, R. J.
1973 "The Background and Significance of the Polemic of the Pastoral Epistles." *JBL* 92:549–64.

Käsemann, E.
1964 "An Apologia for Primitive Christian Eschatology," Pp. 169–95 in *Essays on New Testament Themes.* SBT 41. London: SCM Press.
1969 "Sentences of Holy Law in the New Testament." Pp. 66–81 in *New Testament Questions of Today.* Philadelphia: Fortress Press.

Kassel, R.
1958 *Untersuchungen zur griechischen und römischen Konsolationsliteratur.* Zetemata 18. Munich: Beck.

Katter, C. K.
1990 "Luke 22:14–38: A Farewell Address." Ph.D. dissertation, University of Chicago.

Katz, P.
1957 "Justin's Old Testament Quotations and the Greek Dodekapropheton Scroll." Studia Patristica 1. *Texte und Untersuchungen (series 63).* Berlin: Akademie-Verlag.

Kautzsch, E.
1900 *Die Apokryphen und Pseudepigraphen des Alten Testaments.* Tübingen: Mohr-Siebeck.

Kayser, W.
1948 *Das sprachliche Kunstwerk.* Bern: Francke.

Keck, L., and J. L. Martyn (eds.)
1968 *Studies in Luke–Acts.* Nashville: Abingdon Press.

Keck, L. E.
2001 "*Pathos* in Romans? Mostly Preliminary Remarks." Olbricht and Sumney (eds.) 2001:71–96.

Kee, H. C.
1973 "Aretalogy and Gospel." *JBL* 92:402–22.
1975a *Aretalogies, Hellenistic "Lives," and the Sources of Mark's Gospel.* Protocol of the Twelfth Colloquy: December 8, 1974. Center for Hermeneutical Studies in Hellenistic and Modern Culture.
1975b "The Function of Scriptural Quotations and Allusions to Mark 11–16." In Ellis and Grässer (eds.) 1975.
1977 *Community of the New Age: Studies in Mark's Gospel.* Philadelphia: Fortress Press.
1977–78 "The Ethical Dimension of the Testaments of the XII as a Clue to Provenance." *NTS* 24:259–71.
1996 *Jesus in History: An Approach to the Study of the Gospels.* 3d ed. Fort Worth: Harcourt Brace.

Kelber, W.
1976 *The Passion in Mark.* Philadelphia: Fortress Press.
1979a *Mark's Story of Jesus.* Philadelphia: Fortress Press.
1979b "Mark and Oral Tradition." *Semeia* 6:7–55.
1983 *The Oral and the Written Gospel.* Philadelphia: Fortress Press.

Kelhoffer, J.
2001 "The Witness of Eusebius' *Ad Marinum* and Other Christian Writings to Text-Critical Debates concerning the Original Conclusion to Mark's Gospel." *ZNW* 92:78–112.

Kelly, J. N. D.
1963 *A Commentary on the Pastoral Epistles.* London: Adam & Charles Black.
1969 *The Epistles of Peter and Jude.* New York: Harper & Row.

Kennedy, G. A.
1959 "The Earliest Rhetorical Handbooks." *AJP* 80:169–78.
1963 *The Art of Persuasion in Greece.* Princeton: Princeton University Press.
1968 "The Rhetoric of Advocacy in Greece and Rome." *AJP* 89:419–36.
1972 *The Art of Rhetoric in the Roman World.* Princeton: Princeton University Press.
1980 *Classical Rhetoric and Its Christian and Secular Tradition from Ancient to Modern Times.* Chapel Hill: University of North Carolina Press.
1984 *New Testament Interpretation through Rhetorical Criticism.* Chapel Hill: University of North Carolina Press.
1989 *Classical Criticism.* Vol. 1 of *The Cambridge History of Literary Criticism.* Cambridge: Cambridge University Press.
1991 *Aristotle on Rhetoric: A Theory of Civic Discourse.* New York: Oxford University Press.
1996 "The Composition and Influence of Aristotle's *Rhetoric.*" In Rorty (ed.) 1996, 416–24.
1997a "The Genres of Rhetoric." In Porter (ed.) 1997a, 43–50.
1997b "Historical Survey of Rhetoric." In Porter (ed.) 1997a, 3–41.
1998 *Comparative Rhetoric: An Historical and Cross-Cultural Introduction.* Oxford: Oxford University Press.
2003 *Progymnasmata: Greek Textbooks of Prose Composition and Rhetoric.* Atlanta: Society of Biblical Literature.

Kennel, G.
1995 *Frühchristliche Hymnen? Gattungskritische Studien zur Frage nach den Liedern der frühen Christenheit.* WMANT 71. Neukirchen-Vluyn: Neukirchener Verlag.

Kennett, R. H.
1899 *The Epistles of St. Clement to the Corinthians in Syriac.* London.

Kenney, E. J.
1974 *The Classical Text: Aspects of Editing in the Age of the Printed Book.* Berkeley, Los Angeles, and London: University of California Press.
1982 *Latin Literature.* Part 2 of *Cambridge History of Classical Literature.* Cambridge and New York: Cambridge University Press.

Kenny, A.
1986 *A Stylometric Study of the New Testament.* Oxford: Clarendon Press.

Kenyon, F. G.
1912 *Handbook to the Textual Criticism of the New Testament.* 2d ed. Grand Rapids: Eerdmans.
1951 *Books and Readers in Ancient Greece and Rome.* 2d ed. Oxford: Clarendon Press.
1970 *The Palaeography of Greek Papyri.* Chicago: Argonaut.

Keppie, L.
1991 *Understanding Roman Inscriptions.* Baltimore: Johns Hopkins University Press.

Keresztes, P.
1965a "The Literary Genre of Justin's First Apology." *VC* 19:99–110.
1965b "The 'So-called' Second Apology of Justin." *Latomus* 24:858–69.

Kerferd, G. B.
1981 *The Sophistic Movement.* Cambridge: Cambridge University Press.

Kermode, F.
1979 *The Genesis of Secrecy: On the Interpretation of Narrative.* Cambridge: Harvard University Press.

Kern, O.
1910 "Das Demeterheiligtum von Pergamon und die orphischen Hymnen." *Hermes* 46:431–36.

Kern, P. H.
1998 *Rhetoric and Galatians: Assessing an Approach to Paul's Epistle.* SNTSMS 101. Cambridge: Cambridge University Press.

Kettunen, M.
1979 *Abfassungszweck des Römerbriefes.* Helsinki: Suomalainen Tiedeakatemia.

Keyes, C. W.
1935 "The Greek Letter of Introduction." *AJP* 56:28–44.

Kierkegaard, S.
1965 *The Concept of Irony.* Translated by L. Capel. Bloomington: Indiana University Press.

Kiley, M.
1986 *Colossians as Pseudepigraphy.* Sheffield: JSOT.

Kilpatrick, G. D.
1963 "Atticism and the Text of the Greek

New Testament." In Blinzler, Kuss, and Mussner (eds.) 1963, 125–37.
1977 "The Historical Present in the Gospels and Acts." *ZNW* 68:258–62.

Kindstrand, J. F.
1973 *Homer in der zweiten Sophistik.* Uppsala: University of Uppsala.
1978 "The Greek Concept of Proverbs." *Eranos* 76:71–85.

Kindt T., and H.-H. Müller
1999 "Der 'implizite Autor.' Zur Explikation und Verwendung eines umstrittenen Begriffs." Pp. 273–87 in: *Rückkehr des Autors. Zur Erneuerung eines umstrittenen Begriffs.* Edited by F. Jannidis, G. Lauer, M. Martinez, S. Winko. Tübingen: Niemeyer 1999, 273–87.

Kingsbury, J. D.
1973 "The Structure of Matthew's Gospel and His Concept of Salvation History." *CBQ* 35:451–74.
1975 *Matthew: Structure, Christology, Kingdom.* Philadelphia: Fortress Press.
1988 *Matthew as Story.* 2d ed. Philadelphia: Fortress Press.

Kinneavy, J. L.
1987 *Greek Rhetorical Origins of Christian Faith.* New York: Oxford University Press.

Kinzig, W.
1989 "Der 'Sitz im Leben' der Apologie in der Alten Kirche." *ZKG* 100:291–317.
1994 "Ἡ καινὴ διαθήκη: The Title of the New Testament in the Second and Third Centuries." *JTS* 45:519–44.

Kirby, J. T.
1968 *Ephesians: Baptism and Pentecost: An Inquiry into the Structure and Purpose of the Epistle to the Ephesians.* London: SPCK.
1985 "Toward a General Theory of the Priamel." *CJ* 80:142–44.
1988 "The Rhetorical Situations of Revelation 1–3." *NTS* 34:197–207.

Kirk, A.
1977 *The Composition of the Sayings Source: Genre, Synchrony, and Wisdom Redaction in Q.* NovTSup 91. Leiden: Brill.

Kirk, G. S.
1970 *Myth: Its Meaning and Functions in Ancient and Other Cultures.* Berkeley and Los Angeles: University of California Press.
1974 *The Nature of Greek Myths.* Harmondsworth: Pelican.
1976 *Homer and the Oral Tradition.* Cambridge: Cambridge University Press.
1985 "The Homeric Hymns." In Easterling and Knox (eds.) 1985, 110–16.

Kirkpatrick, P. G.
1988 *The Old Testament and Folklore Study.* Sheffield: Sheffield Academic.

Kissinger, W. S.
1979 *The Parables of Jesus: A History of Interpretation and Bibliography.* Metuchen, N.J.: Scarecrow.

Kistemacher, S.
1961 *The Psalm Citations in the Epistle to the Hebrews.* Amsterdam: W. G. van Soest.

Kister, M.
1998 "A Common Heritage: Biblical Interpretation at Qumran and Its Implications." In Stone and Chazon (eds.) 1998, 101–11.

Klauck, H.-J.
1978 *Allegorie und Allegorese in synoptischen Gleichnistexten.* Münster: Aschendorf.
1990 "Zur rhetorischen Analyse der Johannesbriefe." *ZNW* 81:205–224.
1992 "Das Sendschreiben nach Pergamon und der Kaiserkult in der Johannesoffenbarung." *Bib.* 73:153–82.

Klein, M.
1977 "The Old Testament Origins of the Gospel Genre." *WJT* 38:1–27.

Klijn, A. F. J.
1962 *The Acts of Thomas: Introduction, Text, and Commentary.* NovTSup 5. Leiden: Brill.
1963 "The Apocryphal Correspondence between Paul and the Corinthians." *VC* 17:2–23.
1970 "The Sources and Redaction of the Syriac Apocalypse of Baruch." *JSJ* 1:65–76.
1976 *Die syrische Baruch-Apocalypse.* Gütersloh: Gerd Mohn.
1977 "A Library of Scriptures in Jerusalem?" In Treu (ed.) 1977, 265–72.
1983 "2 Baruch." *OTP* 1.615–52.

Kloppenborg, J. S.
1979 "Didache 16:6–8 and Special Matthaean Tradition." *ZNW* 70:54–67.
1987 *The Formation of Q: Trajectories in Ancient Wisdom.* Philadelphia: Fortress Press.
1988 *Q Parallels: Synopsis, Critical Notes & Concordance.* Sonoma, Calif.: Polebridge Press.
1995a "Conflict and Invention: Recent Studies on Q." In Kloppenborg (ed.) 1995, 1–14.

1995b "Moral Exhortation in *Didache* 1–5." In Jefford (ed.) 1995, 88–109.

2000 *Excavating Q: The History and Setting of the Sayings Gospel.* Minneapolis: Fortress Press.

Kloppenborg, J. S. (ed.)

1994 *The Shape of Q: Signal Essays on the Sayings Gospel.* Minneapolis: Fortress Press.

1995 *Conflict and Invention: Literary, Rhetorical, and Social Studies on the Sayings Gospel Q.* Valley Forge, Pa.: Trinity Press International.

Knibb, M. A.

1978 *The Ethiopic Book of Enoch: A New Edition in the Light of the Aramaic Dead Sea Fragments.* 2 vols. Oxford: Clarendon Press.

1979 "The Date of the Parables of Enoch: A Critical Review." *NTS* 25:345–59.

Knight, D.

1985 "Cosmogony and Order in the Hebrew Tradition." Pp. 133–57 in *Cosmogny and Ethical Order.* Edited by R. Lovin and E. Reynolds. Chicago: University of Chicago Press.

Knight, G. W.

1979 *The Faithful Sayings in the Pastoral Letters.* Grand Rapids: Baker Book House.

Knight, J. M.

1995 *2 Peter and Jude.* NTG. Sheffield: Sheffield Academic Press.

1997 "Apocalyptic and Prophetic Literature." In Porter (ed.) 1997a, 467–88.

Knittel, T.

2002 *Das griechische "Leben Adams und Evas": Studien zur einer narrativen Anthropologie im frühen Judentum.* Tübingen: Mohr-Siebeck.

Knox, B. M. W.

1968 "Silent Reading in Antiquity." *GRBS* 9:421–35.

Knox, J.

1935 *Philemon among the Letters of Paul: A New View of Its Place and Importance.* Chicago: University of Chicago Press.

1942 *Marcion and the New Testament.* Chicago: University of Chicago Press.

Koch, D.-A.

1986 *Die Schrift als Zeuge des Evangeliums: Untersuchungen zur Verwendung und zum Verständnis der Schrift bei Paulus.* BHT 69. Tübingen: Mohr-Siebeck.

1999 "Kollektenbericht, 'Wir'-Bericht und Itinerar: Neue (?) Überlegungen zu einem alten Problem." *NTS* 45:367–90.

Koch, K.

1970 *The Rediscovery of Apocalyptic.* Naperville, Ill.: Allenson.

1989 "Vom prophetischen zum apokalyptischen Visionsbericht." In Hellholm (ed.) 1989, 413–46.

Koester, H.

1957 *Synoptische Überlieferung bei den apostolischen Väter. TU* 65. Berlin: Akademie-Verlag.

1979 "1 Thessalonians: Experiment in Christian Writing." In *Continuity and Discontinuity in Church History.* Edited by F. F. Church and T. George. Leiden: Brill.

1980a "Apocryphal and Canonical Gospels." *HTR* 73:105–30.

1980b "Gnostic Writings as Witnesses for the Development of the Sayings Tradition." In Layton 1980, 238–61.

1982 *Introduction to the New Testament.* 2 vols. Philadelphia: Fortress Press; Berlin and New York: Walter de Gruyter.

1983 "History and Development of Mark's Gospel (from Mark to Secret Mark to Canonical Mark)." In Corley (ed.) 1983, 35–57.

1989a "Introduction." In Layton (ed.) 1989, 38–49.

1989b "From the Kerygma-Gospel to Written Gospels." *NTS* 35:361–81.

1990 *Ancient Christian Gospels: Their History and Development.* Philadelphia: Trinity Press International.

Kofsky, A.

2000 *Eusebius of Caesarea against Paganism.* JCPS 3. Leiden: Brill.

Köhler, W.-D.

1987 *Die Rezeption des Mattäusevangeliums in der Zeit vor Irenäus.* WUNT 2/24. Tübingen: Mohr-Siebeck.

Kolenkow, A. B.

1975 "The Genre Testament and Forecasts of the Future in the Hellenistic Milieu." *JSJ* 6:57–71.

1986 "The Literary Genre 'Testament.'" In Kraft and Nickelsburg (eds.) 1986, 259–67.

Koller, H.

1954 *Die Mimesis in der Antike: Nachahmung, Darstellung, Ausdruck.* Bern: A. Francke.

Konstan, D.

1994 *Sexual Symmetry: Love in the Ancient Novel and Related Genres.* Princeton: Princeton University Press.

1998 "The Invention of Fiction." In Hock, Chance, and Perkins (ed.) 1998, 3–17.

Koskenniemi, H.
1956 *Studien zur Idee und Phraseologie des griechische Briefes bis 400 N. Chr.* Helsinki: Suomalainen Tiedeakatemia.

Kraft, H.
1963 *Clavis Patrum Apostolicorum: Konkordanz zu den Schriften der Apostolischen Väter.* Munich: Kösel.

Kraft, R. A.
1960 "Barnabas' Isaiah Text and the 'Testimony Book' Hypothesis." *JBL* 79:336–50.
1961 "The Epistle of Barnabas, Its Quotations and Their Sources." Ph.D. dissertation, University of Manchester.
1965 *Barnabas and the Didache.* Apostolic Fathers 3. New York: Thomas Nelson.
1978 "Christian Transmission of Greek Jewish Scriptures: A Methodological Probe." Pp. 207–26 in *Paganisme, Judaïsme, Christianisme: Mélange offerts à Marcel Simon.* Edited by A. Benoît. Paris: de Boccard.
2000 "Early Developments of the 'Two-Ways Tradition(s),' in Retrospect." In Argall, Bow, and Werline (eds.) 2000, 136–43.

Kraft, R. A., and G. W. E. Nickelsburg (eds.)
1986 *Early Judaism and Its Modern Interpreters.* Philadelphia: Fortress Press; Atlanta: Scholars Press.

Kraftchick, S. J.
2001 "Πάθη in Paul: The Emotional Logic of 'Original Argument'." Olbricht and Sumney (eds.) 2001:39–68.

Kragerud, A.
1965 "Apocryphon Johannis: En formanalyse." *NTT* 66:15–38.

Kratz, R. G., T. Krüger, and K. Schmid (eds.)
2000 *Schriftauslegung in der Schrift: Festschrift für Odil Hannes Steck zu seinem 65. Geburtstag.* BZAW 300. Berlin: De Gruyter.

Kraus, C. S. (ed.)
1999 *The Limits of Historiography: Genre and Narrative in Ancient Historical Texts.* Mnemosyne Supplements 191. Leiden, Boston, and Cologne: Brill.

Kraus, T. J.
2001 *Sprach, Stil und historischer Ort des zweiten Petrusbriefes.* WUNT 2.136. Tübingen: Mohr-Siebeck.

Krause, W.
1958 *Die Stellung der frühchristlichen Autoren zur heidnischen Literatur.* Vienna: Herder.

Kremendahl, D.
2000 *Die Botschaft der Form: Zum Verhältnis von antiker Epistolographie und Rhetorik im Galaterbrief.* NTOA 46. Freiburg: Universitätsverlag; Göttingen: Vandenhoeck & Ruprecht.

Kremer, J.
1997 *Der erste Brief an die Korinther.* RNT. Regensburg: Friedrich Pustet.

Kremer, J. (ed.).
1979 *Les Actes des Apôtres: Traditions, rédaction, théologie.* BETL 48. Gembloux: J. Duculot; Leuven: Leuven University.

Krentz, E.
1977 *The Historical-Critical Method.* Philadelphia: Fortress Press.
1982 "New Testament Commentaries: Their Selection and Use." *Interpretation* 36:371–82.

Kristeva, J.
1980 *Desire in Language: A Semiotic Approach to Literature and Art.* Edited by L. S. Roudiez. New York: Columbia University Press.
1984 *Revolution in Poetic Language.* Translated by M. Waller. New York: Columbia University Press.
1986 *The Kristeva Reader.* Translated by Toril Moi. New York: Columbia University Press.

Krohn, K. L.
1971 *Folklore Methodology.* Austin: University of Texas Press.

Kroll, J.
1968 *Die christliche Hymnodik bis zu Klemens von Alexandreia.* 2. Aufl. Darmstadt: Wissenschaftliche Buchgesellschaft.

Krüger, G., and G. Ruhbach (eds.)
1965 *Ausgewählte Märtyrerakten.* 4th ed. Tübingen: Mohr-Siebeck.

Küchler, M.
1979 *Frühjüdische Weisheitstraditionen: Zum Fortgang weisheitlichen Denkens im Bereich des Frühjüdischen Jahweglaubens.* OBO 26. Göttingen: Vandenhoeck & Ruprecht.

Kugel, J. L.
1981 *The Idea of Biblical Poetry.* New Haven: Yale University Press.
1984 "Thoughts on Future Research." *JSOT* 28:107–17.
1986 "Two Introductions to Midrash." In Hartman and Budick 1986, 77–103.

1990 "David the Prophet." Pp. 45–55 in *Poetry and Prophecy.* Edited by J. Kugel. Ithaca, N.Y., and London: Cornell University Press.

Kugel, J. L., and R. A. Greer
1986 *Early Biblical Interpretation.* Library of Early Christianity. Philadelphia: Westminster Press.

Kuhn, G.
1923 "Die Geschlechtsregister Jesu bei Lukas und Matthäus nach ihrer Herkunft untersucht." *ZNW* 22:206–28.
1992 "The Impact of the Qumran Scrolls on the Understanding of Paul." In Dimant and Rappaport (eds.) 1992, 327–39.

Kuhn, H.-W.
1971 *Ältere Sammlungen im Markusevangelium.* SUNT 8. Göttingen: Vandenhoeck & Ruprecht.

Kühner, R., and B. Gerth
1890–1904 *Ausführliche Grammatik der griechischen Sprache.* 3d edition. 2 vols. Hannover and Leipzig: Hahn. Reprinted as 2 vols. in 4. Hannover: Hahn, 1963.

Kullmann, W., and J. Althoff (eds.)
1993 *Vermittlung und Tradierung von Wissen in der griechischen Kultur.* Tübingen: Gunter Narr.

Kümmel, W. G.
1962 "Das literarische und geschichtliche Problem des ersten Thessalonicherbriefes." Pp. 213–27 in *Neotestamentica et Patristica. Freundesgabe O. Cullmann zum 60. Geburtstag überreicht.* NovTSup 6. Leiden: Brill.
1975 *Introduction to the New Testament.* Rev. ed. Translated by H. C. Kee. Nashville: Abingdon Press.

Kurz, W. S.
1980a "Hellenistic Rhetoric in the Christological Proof of Luke–Acts." *CBQ* 42:171–95.
1980b "Luke–Acts and Historiography in the Greek Bible." *SBLSP* 19:283–300.
1984 "Luke 3:23–38 and Greco-Roman and Biblical Genealogies." Pp. 169–87 in *Luke–Acts: New Perspectives from the Society of Biblical Literature Seminar.* Edited by C. H. Talbert. New York: Crossroad.
1985 "Luke 22:14–38 and Greco-Roman and Biblical Farewell Addresses." *JBL* 104:251–68.
1990 *Farewell Addresses in the New Testament.* Collegeville, Minn.: Liturgical Press.

Kürzinger, J.
1977 "Die Aussage des Papias von Hierapolis zur literarischen Form des Markusevangeliums." *BZ* 21:245–64.

Kusemann, E.
1964 "A Primitive Christian Baptismal Liturgy." Pp. 149–68 in *Essays on New Testament Themes.* London: SCM Press.

Kysar, R.
1973 "The Source Analysis of the Fourth Gospel: A Growing Consensus?" *NovT* 15:134–52.

Laeuchli, S.
1952 "The Polarity of the Gospels in the Exegesis of Origen." *Church History* 21:215.

Lake, K.
1909 "The Date of Q." *Expositor* 7:494–507.
1912 *The Apostolic Fathers with an English Translation.* LCL. Cambridge: Harvard University Press.

Lalleman, P. J.
1998 *The Acts of John: A Two-Stage Initiation into Johannine Gnosticism.* Leuven: Peeters.

Lamberton, R.
1986 *Homer the Theologian.* Berkeley: University of California Press.
2000 "Language, Text, and Truth in Ancient Polytheistic Exegesis." In Lamberton and Keaney (eds.) 1992, 73–88.

Lamberton, R., and J. J. Keaney (eds.)
1992 *Homer's Ancient Readers: The Hermeneutics of Greek Epic's Earliest Exegetes.* Princeton: Princeton University Press.

Lambrecht, J.
1967 *Die Redaktion der Markus-Apokalypse: Literarische Analyse und Strukturuntersuchung.* AB 28. Rome: Päpstliches Bibelinstitut.
1978 "The Fragment 2 Cor vi 14–vii 1: A Plea for Its Authenticity." Pp. 143–61 in *Miscellanea Neotestamentica.* Vol. 2. Edited by T. Baarda, A. F. J. Klijn, and W. C. van Unnik. NovTSup 47. Leiden: Brill.
1979 "Paul's Farewell-Address at Miletus (Acts 20, 17–38)." In Kremer (ed.) 1979, 307–30.
2000 "Thanksgivings in 1 Thessalonians 1–3." In Donfried and Beutler (eds.) 2000, 135–62.
2001 "The Fool's Speech and Its Context: Paul's Particular Way of Arguing in 2 Cor. 10–13." *Bib* 82:305–24.

Lambrecht, J. (ed.).
1990 *L'Apocalypse johannique et l'Apocalyptique dans le Nouveau Testament.*

BETL 53. Gembloux: J. Duculot; Leuven: University Press.

Lampe, G. W. H. (ed.)
1961 *A Patristic Greek Lexicon.* Oxford: Clarendon Press.

Lampe, G. W. H., and K. J. Woollcombe
1957 *Essays on Typology.* SBT 11. Naperville, Ill.: Alec R. Allenson.

Lampe, P.
1999 *The Christians of Rome in the First Centuries.* England: Burns & Oates.

Landfester, M.
1997 *Einführung in die Stilistik der griechischen und lateinischen Literatursprachen.* Darmstadt: Wissenschaftliche Buchgesellschaft.

Landy, F.
1984 "Poetics and Parallelism: Some Comments on James Kugel's *The Idea of Poetry.*" *JSOT* 28:61–87.

Lane, W. L.
1974 *The Gospel according to Mark.* Grand Rapids: Eerdmans.
1991 *Hebrews.* WBC 47A, 47B. 2 vols. Dallas: Word.

Lang F. G.
1977 "Kompositionsanalyse des Markusevangeliums." *ZTK* 74:1–24.
1999 "Schreiben nach Mass. Zur Stichometrie in der antiken Literatur." *NovT* 41:40–57.

Lang, M. L.
1974 *Graffiti in the Athenian Agora.* Princeton, N.J.: American School of Classical Studies at Athens.
1975 *Graffiti and Dipinti.* Vol. 21 of *The Athenian Agora.* Princeton, N.J.: American School of Classical Studies at Athens.
1984 *Herodotean Narrative and Discourse.* Cambridge: Harvard University Press.
1990 *Ostraka.* Vol. 25 of *The Athenian Agora.* Princeton, N.J.: American School of Classical Studies at Athens.

Lanham, R. A.
1991 *A Handlist of Rhetorical Terms.* 2d ed. Berkeley and Los Angeles: University of California Press.

Lardinois, A.
2001 "The Wisdom and Wit of Many: The Orality of Greek Proverbial Expressions." In J. Watson (ed.) 2001, 93–107.

Larson, E. W.
2001 *The Translation of Enoch from Aramaic into Greek.* Minneapolis: Fortress Press.

Lattimore, R.
1959 *Hesiod.* Ann Arbor: University of Michigan Press.
1962 *Themes in Greek and Latin Epitaphs.* Urbana: University of Illinois Press.

Lauro, E. A. D.
2001 "The Temporal Means to the Eternal Hope: The Rehabilitation of Origen's Two Higher Senses of Scriptural Meaning." Ph.D. dissertation, University of Notre Dame.

Lausberg, H.
1998 *Handbook of Literary Rhetoric: A Foundation for Literary Study.* Edited and translated by D. E. Orton and R. D. Anderson. Leiden: Brill.

Lauther, H.
1998 *Creating Characters: A Writer's Reference to the Personality Traits That Bring Fictional People to Life.* Jefferson, N.C.: McFarland.

Lawlor, H. J.
1897 "Early Citations from the Book of Enoch." *Journal of Philology* 25:164–222.

Lawson, J.
1948 *The Biblical Theology of Saint Irenaeus.* London: Epworth.

Layton, B.
1968 "The Sources, Date, and Transmission of *Didache* 1.3b–2.1." *HTR* 61:343–83.
1980–81 *The Rediscovery of Gnosticism: Proceedings of the International Conference on Gnosticism at Yale, New Haven, Connecticut, March 28–31, 1978.* 2 vols. Leiden: Brill.
1987 *The Gnostic Scriptures.* Garden City, N.Y.: Doubleday.
1989 *Gospel according to Thomas, Gospel according to Philip, Hypostasis of the Archons, and Indexes.* Vol. 1 of *Nag Hammadi Codex II,2–7.* Nag Hammadi Studies 20. Leiden: Brill.

Leach, E. W.
1988 *The Rhetoric of Space: Literary and Artistic Representations of Landscape in Republican and Augustan Rome.* Princeton: Princeton University Press.

Leaney, A. R. C.
1964 "1 Peter and Passover: An Interpretation." *NTS* 10:238–51.

Le Déaut, R.
1971 "Àpropos a Definition of Midrash." *Interpretation* 25:259–82.
1982 *The Message of the New Testament and the Aramaic Bible (Targum).* SB 5. Rome: Biblical Institute.
1984 "La Septante, un Targum?" Pp. 151–53 in *Études sur le Judaïsme hellénistique.*

Lectio Divina 119. Paris: Éditions du Cerf.
1989 "The Targumim." In Davies and Finkelstein (eds.) 1989, 563–90.

Lee, J. A. L.
1983 *A Lexical Study of the Septuagint Version of the Pentateuch.* Chico, Calif.: Scholars Press.

Lefkowitz, M. R.
1982 *Lives of the Greek Poets.* Baltimore: Johns Hopkins University Press.

Légasse, S.
1995 "Paul's Pre-Christian Career according to Acts." In Bauckham (ed.) 1995, 365–90.
2000 *L'Épître de Paul aux Galates.* Paris: Les Éditions du Cerf.

Leiman, S. Z.
1976 *The Canonization of Hebrew Scripture: The Talmudic and Midrashic Evidence.* Hamden: Archon.

Lendle, O.
1992 *Einführung in die griechische Geschichtsschreibung von Hekataios bis Zosimus.* Darmstadt: Wissenschaftliche Buchgesellschaft.

Leo, F.
1901 *Die griechisch-römische Biographie nach ihrer literarischen Form.* Leipzig: B. G. Teubner.

Leopold, J.
1983 "Rhetoric and Allegory." In Winston and Dillon (eds.) 1983, 155–70.

Lesko, L. H.
1972 *The Ancient Egyptian Book of Two Ways.* Berkeley: University of California Press.

Lesky, A.
1966 *A History of Greek Literature.* Translated by J. Willis and C. de Heer. New York: Crowell.

Leutsch, E. L., and F. G. Schneidewin
1958–61 *Corpus Paroemiographorum Graecorum.* 3 vols. Hildesheim: Georg Olms.

Levine, L. I.
2000 *Ancient Jewish Synagogues: The First Thousand Years.* New Haven, Conn.: Yale University Press.

Levison, J. R.
1988 *Portraits of Adam in Early Judaism.* JSPSup 1. Sheffield: Sheffield Academic Press.
1989 "The Exoneration of Eve in the Apocalypse of Moses 15–30." *JSJ* 20:135–50.
1992 "Adam and Eve, Life of." *ADB* 1:64–66.
2000 *Texts in Transition: The Greek Life of Adam and Eve.* Early Judaism and Its Literature 16. Atlanta: Scholars Press.

Levison, J. R., and J. R. Walker
1996 "Introduction: The Character and Context of Josephus' *Contra Apionem.*" In Feldman and Levison (eds.) 1996, 1–48.

Lewis, J. P.
1964 "What do we mean by Jabneh?" *JBR* 32:125–32.

Lewis, N.
1974 *Papyrus in Classical Antiquity.* Oxford: Clarendon Press.
1989 *Papyrus in Classical Antiquity: A Supplement.* Papyrologica Bruxellensia 23. Brussels: Fondation Egyptologique Reine Elisabeth.

Lewis, R. G.
1993 "Imperial Autobiography, Augustus to Hadrian." *ANRW* II.34.2, pp. 629–706.

Lewis, T. S. W.
1981 "Homeric Epic and the Greek Vase." Pp. 81–102 in *The Greek Vase: Papers Based on Lectures Presented to a Symposium Held at Hudson Valley Community College at Troy, New York, in April of 1979.* Latham: New York. Hudson-Mohawk Association of Colleges and Universities.

Lichtenberger, H.
1992 "The Dead Sea Scrolls and John the Baptist: Reflections on Josephus' Account of John the Baptist." In Dimant and Rappaport (eds.) 1992, 340–46.

Lieberman, S.
1950 *Hellenism in Jewish Palestine.* New York: Jewish Theological Seminary.

Liebeschuetz, J. H. W. G.
1972 *Antioch: City and Imperial Administration in the Later Roman Empire.* Oxford: Clarendon Press.

Lietzmann, H.
1979 *Mass and Lord's Supper: A Study in the History of the Liturgy.* Leiden: Brill.

Lieu, J. M.
1986 *The Second and Third Epistles of John.* Edinburgh: T & T Clark.

Lightfoot, J. B.
1889 *The Apostolic Fathers.* Part 2: *S. Ignatius, S. Polycarp.* 3 vols. 2d ed. London: Macmillan. Reprint, Grand Rapids: Baker Book House, 1981.
1900 *The Apostolic Fathers:* Part 1; *S. Clement of Rome.* 2 vols. London: Macmillan.
1981 *St. Paul's Epistle to the Galatians.* 1865; reprint, Peabody, Mass.: Hendrickson.

Lilienfeld, F. von
1971 "Die christliche Unterweisung der *Apophthegmata Patrum*." *Bulletin de la Société d'Archéologie Copte* 20:85–110.

Lim, T. H.
1992 "The Chronology of the Flood Story in a Qumran Text (4Q252)." *JJS* 43:288–98.
1997a *Holy Scripture in the Qumran Commentaries and Pauline Letters.* Oxford: Clarendon Press.
1997b "Midrash Pesher in the Pauline Letters." In Porter and Evans (eds.) 1997, 280–92.

Lincoln, A.
1990 *Ephesians.* WBC 42. Dallas: Word.
2000 "The Letter to the Colossians." Pp. 551–669 in *The New Interpreter's Bible.* Vol. 11. Edited by L. Keck. Nashville: Abingdon Press.

Lincoln, B.
1977 "Thomas-Gospel and Thomas-Community: A New Approach to a Familiar 'Text.'" *NovT* 19:65–76.

Lindars, B.
1961 *New Testament Apologetic: The Doctrinal Significance of the Old Testament Quotations.* Philadelphia: Westminster Press.
1964 "Second Thoughts IV. Books of Testimonies." *ExpTim* 75:173–75.
1989 "The Rhetorical Structure of Hebrews." *NTS* 35:382–406.

Lindbeck, G.
1984 *The Nature of Doctrine: Religion and Theology in a Postliberal Age.* Philadelphia: Westminster Press.

Lindblom, J.
1962 *Prophecy in Ancient Israel.* Oxford: Basil Blackwell.
1968 Gesichte und offenbarungen: Vorstellungen von göttlichen Weisungen und ürbernatürlichen Erscheinungen im ältesten Christentum. Lund: Gleerup.

Lindemann, A.
1979 *Paulus im ältesten Christentum.* BHT 58. Tübingen: Mohr-Siebeck.
1992 *Die Clemensbriefe.* Handbuch zum Neuen Testament 17. Die Apostolischen Väter I. Tübingen: Mohr-Siebeck.
1999 *Paulus: Apostel und Lehrer der Kirche: Studien zu Paulus und zum frühen Paulusverständnis.* Tübingen: Mohr-Siebeck.

Lindemann, A. (ed.)
2001 *The Sayings Source Q and the Historical Jesus.* BETL 158. Leuven: University Press; Leuven, Paris, and Sterling, Virginia: Uitgeverij Peeters.

Lindemann, A., and H. Paulsen
1992 *Die Apostolischen Väter: Griechisch-deutsche Parallelausgabe.* Tübingen: Mohr-Siebeck.

Lindenberger, J.
1994 *Ancient Aramaic and Hebrew Letters.* SBLWAW 4. Atlanta: Scholars Press.

Linnemann, E.
1966 *Parables of Jesus: Introduction and Exposition.* London: SPCK.
1970 *Studien zur Passionsgeschichte.* Göttingen: Vandenhoeck & Ruprecht.
1990 *Historical Criticism of the Bible: Methodology or Ideology?* Grand Rapids: Baker Book House.
1998 *Biblical Criticism on Trial: How Scientific Is "Scientific Theology"?* Grand Rapids: Kregel.

Lipsius, R. A., and M. Bonnet (eds.)
1891–1903 *Acta Apostolorum Apocrypha.* 3 vols. Leipzig: Hermann Mendelssohn.

Litfin, D.
1994 *St. Paul's Theology of Proclamation: 1 Corinthians 1–4 and Greco-Roman Rhetoric.* SNTSMS 79. Cambridge: Cambridge University Press.

Llewelyn, S. R.
1995 "Sending Letters in the Ancient World: Paul and the Philippians." *TynBul* 46:337–56.

Lloyd, G. E. R.
1975 "Greek Cosmologies." Pp. 198–224 in *Ancient Cosmologies.* Edited by C. Blacker and M. Loewe. London: Allen & Unwin.

Loan, T. O. (ed.)
2001 *Encyclopedia of Rhetoric.* Oxford: Oxford University Press.

Lock, W.
1924 *A Critical and Exegetical Commentary on the Pastoral Epistles (I & II Timothy and Titus).* Edinburgh: T. & T. Clark.

Lofthouse, W. F.
1952–53 "'I' and 'We' in the Pauline Letters." *ExpT* 64:241–45.

Logan, A. H. B.
1991 "John and the Gnostics: The Significance of the Apocryphon of John for the Debate about the Origins of the Johannine Literature." *JSNT* 43:41–69.

Logan, A. H. B., and A. J. M. Wedderburn (eds.)
1983 *The New Testament and Gnosis: Essays in Honour of Robert McLachlan Wilson.* Edinburgh: T. & T. Clark.

Lohfink, G.
1974 "Kommentar als Gattung." *Bibel und Leben* 15:1–16.
1984 *Die Himmelfahrt Jesu: Untersuchungen zu den Himmelfahrts- und Erhöhungstexten bei Lukas.* Munich: Kösel.
Lohmeyer, E.
1936 *Galiläa und Jerusalem.* Göttingen: Vandenhoeck & Ruprecht.
Lohr, C.
1961 "Oral Techniques in the Gospel of Matthew." *CBQ* 23:403–35.
Lohse, E.
1954 "Paränese und Kerygma im I. Petrusbrief." *ZNW* 45:68–89.
1971 *Colossians and Philemon.* Hermeneia. Philadelphia: Fortress Press.
Loisy, A. F.
1935 *Remarques sur la littérature épistolaire du Nouveau Testament.* Paris: Nourry.
Lona, H. E.
2000 "Zur Structur von Diog 5–6." *VC* 54:32–43.
Long, A. A.
1992 "Stoic Readings of Homer." In Lamberton and Keaney (eds.) 1992, 41–66.
Long, A. A., and D. N. Sedley
1987 *The Hellenistic Philosophers.* 2 vols. Cambridge: Cambridge University Press.
Longenecker, B. W.
1995 *2 Esdras.* Sheffield: Sheffield Academic Press.
Longenecker, R. N.
1974 "Ancient Amanuenses and the Pauline Epistles." In Longenecker and Tenney (eds.) 1974, 281–97.
1990 *Galatians.* WBC 41. Dallas: Word.
1999 *Biblical Exegesis in the Apostolic Period.* 2d ed. Grand Rapids: Eerdmans.
Longenecker, R. N., and M. C. Tenney (eds.)
1974 *New Dimensions in New Testament Study.* Grand Rapids: Zondervan.
Longman, T.
1985 "Form Criticism, Recent Developments in Genre Theory, and the Evangelical." *WJT* 47:46–67.
Löning, K.
1997– *Das Geschichtswerk des Lukas.* 3 vols. Stuttgart: W. Kohlhammer.
Loofs, F.
1930 *Theophilus von Antiochen Adversus Marcionem und die anderen theologischen Quellen bei Irenäus. TU* 46.2. Leipzig: Hinrichs.
Lord, Alfred
1960 *The Singer of Tales.* Cambridge: Harvard University Press.
1973 "The Gospels as Oral Tradition Literature." In Walker (ed.) 1973, 33–91.
1987 "Characteristics of Orality." *Oral Tradition* 2:54–62.
Lord, C.
1986 "On the Early History of the Aristotelian Corpus." *AJP* 107:137–61.
Lösch, S.
1933 *Deitas Jesu und Antike Apotheose: Ein Beitrag zur Exegese und Religionsgeschichte.* Rottenburg: Bader.
Lowth, R.
1962 *De sacra poesi Hebraeorum.* 2 vols. Hildesheim: G. Olms. Orig. published 1678.
Lucchesi, E., and H. D. Saffrey (eds.)
1984 *Mémorial André-Jean Festugière: antiquité païenne et chrétienne: vingtcinq études.* Geneva: P. Cramer.
Luck, G.
1985 *Arcana Mundi: Magic in the Occult in the Greek and Roman World.* Baltimore: Johns Hopkins University Press.
Lührmann, D.
1969 *Die Redaktion der Logienquelle.* Neukirchen-Vluyn: Neukirchener Verlag.
1980 "Neutestamentliche Haustafeln und antike Ökonomie." *NTS* 27:83–97.
1987 *Das Markusevangelium.* Tübingen: Mohr-Siebeck.
1992 *Galatians: A Continental Commentary.* Minneapolis: Fortress Press.
Lund, N.
1942 *Chiasmus in the New Testament: A Study in the Form and Function of Chiastic Structures.* Chapel Hill: University of North Carolina Press.
1992 *Chiasmus in the New Testament: A Study in the Form and Function of Chiastic Structures.* Edited by D. M. Scholer and K. N. Snodgrass, 1942; reprint with new introduction, Peabody, Mass.: Hendrickson.
Luter, A. B., and M. V. Lee
1995 "Philippians as Chiasmus: Key to the Structure, Unity, and Theme Questions." *NTS* 41:89–101.
Luttikhuizen, G. P.
1985 *The Revelation of Elchasai: Investigations into the Evidence of a Mesopotamian Jewish Apocalypse of the Second Century and Its Reception by Judaeo-Christian Propagandists.* TSAJ 8. Tübingen: Mohr-Siebeck.
1987 "The Book of Elchasai: A Jewish Apocalypse." *Aula Orientalis* 5:101–6.

1988 "The Evaluation of the Teaching of Jesus in Christian Gnostic Revelation Dialogues." *NovT* 30:158–68.

1996 "The Apocryphal Correspondence with the Corinthians and the Acts of Paul." In Bremmer (ed.) 1996, 75–91.

Lyle, K. R., Jr.

1998 *Ethical Admonition in the Epistle of Jude.* SBL 4. New York: Peter Lang.

Lynch, D.

1998 *The Economy of Character: Novels, Market Culture, and the Business of Inner Meaning.* Chicago: University of Chicago Press.

Lyons, G.

1985 *Pauline Autobiography.* SBLDS 73. Atlanta: Scholars Press.

Maas, P.

1958 *Textual Criticism.* Oxford: Clarendon Press.

1962 *Greek Metre.* Oxford: Clarendon Press Press.

MacAlister, S.

1996 *Dreams and Suicides: The Greek Novel from Antiquity to the Byzantine Empire.* London and New York: Routledge.

MacDonald, D. R.

1990 *The Acts of Andrew and the Acts of Andrew and Matthias in the City of the Cannibals.* Atlanta: Scholars Press.

1992 "*The Acts of Paul* and *The Acts of Peter*: Which Came First?" *SBLSP,* 214–24.

1993a "*The Acts of Paul* and *The Acts of John*: Which Came First?" *SBLSP,* 506–10.

1993b "*The Acts of Peter* and *The Acts of John*: Which Came First?" *SBLSP,* 623–26.

1994a *Christianizing Homer: The Odyssey, Plato, and the Acts of Andrew.* New York: Oxford University Press.

1994b "Luke's Eutychus and Homer's Elpenor: Acts 20:7–12 and Odyssey 10–12." *JHC* 1:5–24.

1997 "Which Came First? Intertextual Relationships among the Apocryphal Acts of the Apostles." In Stoops (ed.) 1997, 11–41.

1998 "Secrecy and Recognitions in the *Odyssey* and Mark." In Hock, Chance, and Perkins 1998, 139–53.

1999 "The Shipwrecks of Odysseus and Paul." *NTS* 45:88–107.

2000a *The Homeric Epics and the Gospel of Mark.* New Haven, Conn.: Yale University Press.

2000b "The Ending of Luke and the Ending of the *Odyssey.*" In Argall, Boy, and Werline (eds.) 2000, 161–68.

MacDonald, M. Y.

1988 *The Pauline Churches: A Socio-Historical Study of Institutionalization in the Pauline and Deutero-Pauline Writings.* Cambridge: Cambridge University Press.

2000 *Colossians and Ephesians.* Sacra Pagina 17. Collegeville: Liturgical Press.

Mack, B. L.

1974–75 "Exegetical Traditions in Alexandrian Judaism: A Program for the Analysis of the Philonic Corpus." *SPhilo* 3:71–112.

1984a "Decoding Scripture: Philo and the Rules of Rhetoric." Pp. 81–115 in *Nourished with Peace: Studies in Hellenistic Judaism in Memory of Samuel Sandmel.* Chico, Calif.: Scholars Press.

1984b "Philo Judaeus and Exegetical Traditions in Alexandria." *ANRW* II, 21/1. Göttingen: Vandenhoeck & Ruprecht.

1988 *A Myth of Innocence: Mark and Christian Origins.* Philadelphia: Fortress Press.

1990 *Rhetoric and the New Testament.* Minneapolis: Fortress Press.

1995 *Who Wrote the New Testament? The Making of the Christian Myth.* San Francisco: HarperSanFrancisco.

Mack, B. L., and V. K. Robbins

1989 *Patterns of Persuasion in the Gospels.* Sonoma, Calif.: Polebridge.

Mackay, E. A.

1999 *Signs of Orality: The Oral Tradition and Its Influence in the Greek and Roman World.* Mnemosyne Supplements 188. Leiden: Brill.

MacLeod, R. (ed.)

2000 *The Library of Alexandria: Center of Learning in the Ancient World.* London and New York: Tauris.

MacRae, G. W.

1960 "The Gospel of Thomas—*Logia Iesou*?" *CBQ* 22:56–70.

1978 "Nag Hammadi and the New Testament." Pp. 144–57 in *Gnosis: Festschrift für Hans Jonas.* Edited by Barbara Aland et al. Göttingen: Vandenhoeck & Ruprecht.

Maddox, R.

1982 *The Purpose of Luke–Acts.* Edinburgh: T. & T. Clark.

Mader, G.

2000 *Josephus and the Politics of Historiography.* Mnemosyne Supplements 205. Leiden: Brill.

Mai, H.-P.
1991 "Bypassing Intertextuality." In Plett (ed.) 1991, 30–59.
Malamat, A.
1968 "King Lists of the Old Babylonian Period and Biblical Genealogies." *JAOS* 88:163–73.
Malbon, E. S.
1986 *Narrative Space and Mythic Meaning in Mark.* San Francisco: Harper & Row.
Malbon, E. S. and A. Berlin (eds.)
1993 *Characterization in Biblical Literature.* Semeia 63. Atlanta: Scholars Press.
Malherbe, A. J.
1970 "'Gentle as a Nurse': The Cynic Background to 1 Thess ii." *NovT* 12:203–17.
1977a "Ancient Epistolary Theorists." *Ohio Journal of Religious Studies* 5:3–77. Reissued as *Ancient Epistolary Theorists.* SBLSBS 19. Atlanta: Scholars Press, 1988.
1977b *The Cynic Epistles.* Missoula, Mont.: Scholars Press.
1980 "ΜΗ ΓΕΝΟΙΤΟ and the Diatribe in Paul." *HTR* 73:231–40.
1983a "Exhortation in First Thessalonians." *NovT* 25:238–56.
1983b *The Social Aspects of Early Christianity.* 2d ed. Philadelphia: Fortress Press.
1986 *Moral Exhortation: A Greco-Roman Sourcebook.* Philadelphia: Westminster Press.
1987 *Paul and the Thessalonians: The Philosophic Tradition of Pastoral Care.* Philadelphia: Fortress Press.
1988 *Ancient Epistolary Theorists.* SBS 19. Atlanta: Scholars Press.
1989a *Paul and the Popular Philosophers.* Minneapolis: Fortress Press.
1989b "*Mē Genoito* in the Diatribe and Paul." In Malherbe 1989a, 25–33.
1992 "Hellenistic Moralists and the New Testament." *ANRW,* II, 26/1, 267–333.
2000 *The Letters to the Thessalonians: A New Translation with Introduction and Commentary.* AB 32B. New York: Doubleday.
Malherbe, A. J., F. W. Norris, and J. W. Thompson (eds.)
1998 *The Early Church in Its Context: Essays in Honor of Everett Ferguson.* NovTSup 110. Leiden: Brill.
Malina, B. J.
1981 *The New Testament World: Insights from Cultural Anthropology.* Atlanta: John Knox Press.
1995 *On the Genre and Message of Revelation: Star Visions and Sky Journeys.* Peabody, Mass.: Hendrickson.
1998 *Social-Science Commentary on the Gospel of John.* Minneapolis: Fortress Press.
Malina, B. J., and J. J. Pilch
2000 *Social-Science Commentary on the Book of Revelation.* Minneapolis: Fortress Press.
Malina, B. J., and R. Rohrbaugh
1992 *Social-Science Commentary on the Synoptic Gospels.* Minneapolis: Fortress Press.
Maloney, E. C.
1981 *Semitic Interference in Marcan Syntax.* SBLDS 51. Chico, Calif.: Scholars Press.
1989 "The Historical Present in the Gospel of Mark." In Horgan and Kobelski (eds.) 1989, 67–78.
Maloney, F. J.
2001 "Mark 6:6b–30: Mission, the Baptist, and Failure." *CBQ* 63:647–63.
Man, R. E.
1984 "The Value of Chiasm for New Testament Interpretation." *BSac* 141:146–57.
Mann, J.
1971 *The Bible as Read and Preached in the Old Synagogue.* New York: KTAV Publishing House.
Mansfeld, J.
1994 *Prolegomena: Questions to Be Settled before the Study of an Author or a Text.* PA 61. Leiden: Brill.
Manson, T. W.
1935 *The Teaching of Jesus: Studies in Its Form and Content.* Cambridge: Cambridge University Press.
1949 *The Sayings of Jesus as Recorded in the Gospels according to St. Matthew and St. Luke Arranged with Introduction and Commentary.* London: SCM.
Manzi, F.
2002 *Seconda Lettera al Corinzi: Nuova versione, introduzione e commenta.* Cinisell. Balsamo: Edizione Paoline.
Mara, M. G. (ed.)
1973 *Évangile de Pierre.* Paris: Les Éditions du Cerf.
Marcovich, M.
1988 "The Wedding Hymn of Acta Thomae." Pp. 156–73 in *Studies in Graeco-Roman Religions and Gnosticism* by M. Marcovich. Leiden: Brill.
1990 *Pseudo-Iustinus Cohortatio ad Graecos, de Monarchia, Oratio ad Graecos.*

PTS 32. Berlin and New York: Walter de Gruyter.
1994 *Iustini Martyris Apologiae Pro Christianis.* PTS 38. Berlin and New York: Walter de Gruyter.
1995 *Tatiani Oratio ad Graecos, Theophili Antiocheni ad Autolycum.* PTS 43–44. Berlin and New York: Walter de Gruyter.
1997 *Dialogus cum Tryphone, Iustini Martyris.* PTS 47. Berlin and New York: Walter de Gruyter.
1999 *Diogenis Laertii Vitae philosophorum.* Stuttgart: B. G. Teubner.

Marguerat, D. and Y. Bourguin
1999 *An Introduction to Narrative Criticism.* London: SCM.

Marincola, J.
1997 *Authority and Tradition in Ancient Historiography.* Cambridge: Cambridge University Press.
1999 "Genre, Convention, and Innovation in Greco-Roman Historiography." In C. S. Kraus (ed.) 1999, 281–324.

Márot, K.
1949 "La fonction poétique de l'énumération épique." *Cahiers de littérature comparée* 1:41–44.

Marrou, H. I.
1949 "La technique de l'édition à l'époque patristique." *VC* 3:208ff.
1964 *A History of Education in Antiquity.* New York: Mentor.
1965 *A Diognète. Introduction, édition critique, traduction et commentaire.* SC 33. 2d ed. Paris: Les Éditions du Cerf.

Marshall, I. H.
1978 *The Gospel of Luke: A Commentary on the Greek Text.* NIGTC. Grand Rapids: Eerdmans.
1987 "Apg 12—ein Schlüssel zum Verständnis der Apostelgeschichte." Pp. 192–220 in *Das Petrus Bild in der neueren Forschung.* Edited by C. P. Thiede. Wuppertal: Brockhaus.

Marshall, P.
1987 *Enmity in Corinth: Social Conventions in Paul's Relations with the Corinthians.* Tübingen: Mohr-Siebeck.

Martin, F.
1988 *Narrative Parallels to the New Testament.* Atlanta: Scholars Press.

Martin, J.
1931 *Symposion: Die Geschichte einer literarischen Form.* Paderborn: Schöningh.
1974 *Antike Rhetoric.* Handbuch der Altertumswissenschaft 2:3. Munich: Beck.

Martin, R. P.
1976 *James.* WBC. Waco: Word.
1983 *Carmen Christi: Philippians 2:5–11 in Recent Interpretation and in the Setting of Early Christian Worship.* 2d ed. Grand Rapids: Eerdmans.
1986 *2 Corinthians.* WBC 40. Waco: Word Books.
1987 *The Epistle of Paul to the Philippians: An Introduction and Commentary.* Leicester: InterVarsity.
1989 *Reconciliation: A Study of Paul's Theology.* London: Marshall, Morgan & Scott.
1991 *Ephesians, Colossians, and Philemon.* Interpretation. Atlanta: John Knox Press.

Martin, S. C.
1997 *Pauli Testamentum: 2 Timothy and the Last Words of Moses.* Rome: Editrice Ponticifia Università Gregoriana.

Martin, T. W.
1992 *Metaphor and Composition in 1 Peter.* SBLDS 131. Atlanta: Scholars Press.
1994 "Apostasy to Paganism: The Rhetorical Stasis of the Galatian Controversy." *JBL* 114:437–61.
2000 "Entextualized and Implied Rhetorical Situations: The Case of 1 Timothy and Titus." *BR* 45:5–24.
2001 "The Voice of Emotion: Paul's Pathetic Persuasion (Gal 4:12–20)." Olbricht and Sumney (eds.) 2001:181–202.

Martinazzoli, F.
1957 *Hapax Legomenon.* Vol. 1, part 2. Rome: Casa editrice Gismondi.

Martyn, L.
1971 "Source Criticism and *Religionsgeschichte* in the Fourth Gospel." In vol. 1, pp. 247–73 of *Jesus and Man's Hope.* Pittsburgh: Pittsburgh Theological Seminary.
1997 *Galatians: A New Translation with Introduction and Commentary.* AB 33A. New York: Doubleday.

Marxsen, W.
1955 "Redaktionsgeschichtliche Erklärung der sogenannten Parabeltheorie des Markus." *ZTK* 52:255–71.
1959 *Der Evangelist Markus: Studien zur Redaktionsgeschichte des Evangeliums.* Göttingen: Vandenhoeck & Ruprecht.
1968 *Introduction to the New Testament.* Translated by G. Buswell. Oxford: Basil Blackwell.
1969 *Mark the Evangelist: Studies on the Redaction History of the Gospel.* Trans-

lated by James Boyce et al. Nashville and New York: Abingdon Press.
1982 *Der zweite Thessalonicherbrief.* ZB. Zürich: Theologischer Verlag.

Maschke, T.
1992 "Prayer in the Apostolic Fathers." *SecCent* 9 (1992):103–18.

Mason, H. J.
1993 "Greek and Latin Versions of the Ass-Story." *ANRW* 34/2, 1665–1707.

Mason, S.
1991 *Flavius Josephus on the Pharisees: A Composition-Critical Study.* Leiden: Brill.
1992 *Josephus and the New Testament.* Peabody, Mass.: Hendrickson.
1996 "The *Contra Apionem* in Social and Literary Context: An Invitation to Judean Philosophy." In Feldman and Levison (eds.) 1996, 187–228.

Masson, J.
1982 *Jésus fils de David dans les généalogies de Saint Matthieu et de Saint Luc.* Paris: Téqui.

Matera, F.
1987 "The Plot of Matthew's Gospel." *CBQ* 49:233–253.
1988 "The Culmination of Paul's Argument to the Galatians: Gal. 5:1–6:10." *JSNT* 32:79–91.

Matera, F., and A. Das (eds.)
2002 *The Forgotten God: Essays in Honor of Paul J. Achtemeier.* Louisville, Ky.: Westminster John Knox Press.

Matthes, D.
1958 "Hermagoras von Temnos, 1904–1955." *Lustrum* 3:58–214.
1962 *Hermagorae Temnitai Testimonia et fragmenta.* Teubner. Leipzig: B. G. Teubner.

Matthews, C. R.
2002 *Philip: Apostle and Evangelist: Configurations of a Tradition.* NovTSup 105. Leiden: Brill.

Maurer, C.
1949 *Ignatius von Antiochien und das Johannesevangelium.* Zurich: Zwingli.

May, H. H.
1979 "The *Ethica Digressio* and Cicero's *Pro Milone.*" *CJ* 74:243–44.

May, J. M.
1988 *Trials of Character: The Eloquence of Ciceronian Ethos.* Chapel Hill: University of North Carolina Press.
2002 *Brill's Companion to Cicero: Oratory and Rhetoric.* Leiden and Boston: Brill.

May, J. M., and J. Wisse (eds.)
2001 *Cicero on the Ideal Orator (De Oratore).* New York: Oxford University Press.

Mayeda, G.
1945 *Das Leben-Jesu-Fragment Papyrus Egerton 2 und seine Stellung in der urchristliche Literaturgeschichte.* Bern: Haupt.

Mayer, A. C.
2002 *Sprache der Einheit in Epheserbrief und in der Ökumene.* WUNT 150. Tübingen: Mohr-Siebeck.

McArthur, H. K.
1973 "Son of Mary." *NovT* 15:38–58.

McBurney, J. H.
1974 "The Place of the Enthymeme in Rhetorical Theory." In Erickson (ed.) 1974, 117–40.

McCabe, D. F.
1981 *The Prose-Rhythm of Demosthenes.* New York: Arno.

McCall, M. H.
1969 *Ancient Rhetorical Theories of Simile and Comparison.* Cambridge: Harvard University Press.

McCartney, E. S.
1948 "On Reading and Praying Audibly." *CP* 43:184–87.

McCollough, T,. and B. Glazier-McDonald
1996 "An Aramaic Bronze Amulet from Sepphoris." *'Atiqot* 28:161–65.

McCown, C. C.
1922a "The Christian Tradition as to the Magical Wisdom of Solomon." *JPOS* 2:1–24.
1922b *The Testament of Solomon.* Leipzig: J. C. Hinrichs.
1925 "Hebrew and Egyptian Apocalyptic Literature." *HTR* 18 (1925):387–411.
1941 "Codex and Roll in the New Testament," *HTR* 34:219–50.

McDonald, L. M.
1995 *The Formation of the Christian Biblical Canon.* Rev. ed. Peabody, Mass.: Hendrickson.

McEleney, N. J.
1974 "The Vice Lists of the Pastoral Epistles." *CBQ* 36:203–19.

McGaughy, Lane
1999 "Infancy Narratives and Hellenistic Lives: Luke 1–2." *Forum* 2:25–39.

McKenna, M.
1999 *Blessings and Woes: The Beatitudes and the Sermon on the Plain in the Gospel of Luke.* Maryknoll: Orbis Books.

McKnight, E. V.
1969 *What Is Form Criticism?* Philadelphia: Fortress Press.

1978 *Meaning in Texts: The Historical Shaping of a Narrative Hermeneutic.* Philadelphia: Fortress Press.

1985 *The Bible and the Reader: An Introduction to Literary Criticism.* Philadelphia: Fortress Press.

1988 *Postmodern Use of the Bible: The Emergence of Reader-Oriented Criticism.* Nashville: Abingdon Press.

McNamara, M.

1966 *The New Testament and the Palestinian Targum to the Pentateuch.* Rome: Pontifical Biblical Institute.

1972 *Targum and Testament: Aramaic Paraphrases of the Hebrew Bible: A Light on the New Testament.* Grand Rapids: Eerdmans.

McNamee, K.

1981a "Aristarchus and 'Everyman's' Homer." *GRBS* 22:247–55.

1981b *Abbreviations in Greek Literary Papyri and Ostraca.* Chico, Calif.: Scholars Press.

McVey, K.

1998 "The *Chreia* in the Desert: Rhetoric and the Bible in the *Apophthegmata Patrum.*" In Malherbe, Norris, and Thompson 1998, 245–55.

Meade, D.

1986 *Pseudonymity and Canonicity: An Investigation into the Relationship of Authorship and Authority in Jewish and Early Christian Tradition.* WUNT 39. Tübingen: Mohr-Siebeck.

Mealand, D. L.

1989 "Positional Stylometry Reassessed: Testing a Seven Epistle Theory of Pauline Authorship." *NTS* 35:266–86.

Meecham, H. G.

1949 *The Epistle to Diognetus: The Greek Text with Introduction, Translation, and Notes.* Manchester: University of Manchester.

Mees, M.

1971 "Die Bedeutung der Sentenzen und ihrer Auxesis für die Formung der Jesuworte nach Didache 1:3b–2:1." *Vetera christianum* 8:55–76.

Meeüs, X.

1961 "Composition de Luc., XIV et Genre Symposiaque." *ETL* 37:847–70.

Meier, J. P.

1990 "Josephus on Jesus: A Modest Proposal." *CBQ* 52:76–103.

1991 *The Roots of the Problem and the Person.* Vol. 1 of *A Marginal Jew: Rethinking the Historical Jesus.* New York: Doubleday.

1994 *Mentor, Message, and Miracles.* Vol. 2 of *A Marginal Jew: Rethinking the Historical Jesus.* New York: Doubleday.

2001 *Companions and Competitors.* Vol. 3 of *A Marginal Jew: Rethinking the Historical Jesus.* New York: Doubleday.

Meijering, R.

1987 *Literary and Rhetorical Theories in Greek Scholia.* Groningen: Egbert Forsten.

Meiser, M.

2000 "Frühjüdische und frühchristliche Apologetik." In Kalms (ed.) 2000, 155–84.

Mejer, J.

1978 *Diogenes Laertius and His Hellenistic Background.* Hermes Einzelschriften 40. Wiesbaden: Franz Steiner.

Meletinsky, E. M.

1971 "The Structural-Typological Study of the Folktale," *Genre* 4:249–79.

Melhorn, J. J., and R. J. Romig

1985 "Rest Room Graffiti: A Descriptive Study." *Emporia State Research Studies* 34:29–45.

Ménard, J.-É.

1975 *L'Évangile selon Thomas.* NHS 5. Leiden: Brill.

Menken, M. J. J.

1985 *Numerical Literary Techniques in John: The Fourth Evangelist's Use of Numbers of Words and Syllables.* NovTSup 55. Leiden: Brill.

1996 *Old Testament Quotations in the Fourth Gospel: Studies in Textual Form.* Kampen: Kok Pharos.

2001 "The Sources of the Old Testament Quotation in Matthew 2:23." *JBL* 120:451–68.

Merk, O.

1969 "Der Beginn der Paränese im Galaterbrief." *ZNW* 60:83–104.

Merenlahti, P.

2002 *Poetics for the Gospels? Rethinking Narrative Criticism.* SNTW. London and New York: T. & T. Clark.

Merenlahti, P., and R. Hakola

1999 "Reconceiving Narrative Criticism." In Rhoads and Syreeni (eds.) 1999, 13–48.

Merkelbach, R.

1977 *Die Quellen des griechischen Alexanderromans.* 2d ed. Munich: Beck.

Merklein, H.

1984 "Die Einheitlichkeit des ersten Korintherbriefes." *ZNW* 75:153–83.

Metso, S.
1998–99 "Constitutional Rules at Qumran." In Flint and Vanderkam (eds.) 1998–99, 1.186–210.

Metzger, B. M.
1972 "Literary Forgeries and Canonical Pseudepigrapha." *JBL* 91:3–24.
1981 *Manuscripts of the Greek Bible: An Introduction to Palaeography.* New York and Oxford: Oxford University Press.
1987 *The Canon of the New Testament: Its Origin, Development, and Significance.* Oxford: Clarendon Press.
1992 *The Text of the New Testament: Its Transmission, Corruption, and Restoration.* 3d ed. New York and Oxford: Oxford University Press.
1994 *A Textual Commentary on the Greek New Testament.* 2d ed. New York: United Bible Societies; Stuttgart: Deutsche Bibelgesellschaft.

Meyer, B. F.
1999 "How Jesus Charged Language with Meaning: A Study in Rhetoric." In Chilton and Evans (eds.) 1999, 81–96.

Meyer, M. W.
1984 *The Secret Teachings of Jesus: Four Gnostic Gospels.* New York: Random House.

Meyer, M. W., and P. Mirecki (eds.)
1995 *Ancient Magic and Ritual Power.* Leiden: Brill.

Michaelis, C.
1968 "Die π-Alliteration der Subjektsworte in der ersten 4 Seligpreisungen in Mt. V 3–6 und ihre Bedeutung für die Ausbau der Seligpreisungen bei Mt., Lk. und in Q." *NovT* 10:148–61.

Michaelis, W.
1958 "Teilungshypothesen bei Paulusbriefen." *TZ* 14:321–26.

Michaels, J. R.
1987 "Jewish and Christian Apocalyptic Letters: 1 Peter, Revelation, and 2 Baruch 78–87." *SBLSP* 26:268–75.
1988 *1 Peter.* WBC 49. Waco: Word.

Michaelson, S., and A. Q. Morton
1972 "Last Words: A Test of Authorship for Greek Writers." *NTS* 18:192–208.

Michel, H. J.
1973 *Die Abschiedsrede des Paulus an die Kirche Apg 20.17–38.* SANT 35. Munich: Kösel Verlag.

Michel, O.
1929 *Paulus und seine Bibel.* BFCT 2/18. Gütersloh: Bertelsmann.

Mieder, W.
1982 *International Proverb Scholarship: An Annotated Bibliography.* New York: Garland.
1990 *International Proverb Scholarship: An Annotated Bibliography, Supplement.* New York: Garland.
1994 *Wise Words: Essays on the Proverb.* New York: Garland.
1998 *"A House Divided": From Biblical Proverb to Lincoln and Beyond.* Burlington: University of Vermont Press.

Mieder, W., and A. Dundes (ed.)
1981 *The Wisdom of Many: Essays on the Proverb.* New York: Garland.

Mieke Bal, M.
1981 "The Laughing Mice—or: On Focalization," *Poetics Today* 2:202–10.

Milik, J. T.
1976 *The Books of Enoch: Aramaic Fragments of Qumrân Cave 4.* Oxford: Clarendon Press.

Millar, F.
1977 *The Emperor in the Roman World (31 BC–AD 337).* Ithaca: Cornell University Press.

Millar, W. R.
1976 *Isaiah 24–27 and the Origin of Apocalyptic.* HSM 11. Missoula, Mont.: Scholars Press.

Millard, A.
1994 "Ancient Abbreviations and the Nomina Sacra." Pp. 221–26 in *The Unbroken Reed: Studies in the Culture and Heritage of Ancient Egypt in Honour of A. F. Shore.* Edited by C. Eyre, A. Leahy, and L. M. Leahy. London: Egyptian Exploration Society.
2000 *Reading and Writing in the Time of Jesus.* Sheffield: Sheffield Academic Press.

Miller, A. M.
1986 *From Delos to Delphi: A Literary Study of the Homeric Hymn to Apollo.* Leiden: Brill.

Miller, C. R.
2000 "The Aristotelian *Topos*: Hunting for Novelty." In Gross and Walzer 2000, 130–46.

Miller, D. (ed.)
1970 *Jesus and Man's Hope.* 2 vols. Pittsburgh: Pittsburgh Theological Seminary.

Miller, D., and P. Miller
1990 *The Gospel of Mark as Midrash on Earlier Jewish and New Testament Literature.* Lewiston, N.Y.: Mellen.

Miller, J. D.
1997 *The Pastoral Letters as Composite Documents.* SNTSMS 93. Cambridge: Cambridge University Press.

Mills, W. E.
1993 *An Index to Periodical Literature on the Apostle Paul.* NTTS 16. Leiden: Brill.

Minchin, E.
1995 "Ring-Patterns and Ring-Composition: Some Observations on the Framing of Stories in Homer." *Helios* 22:23–33.

Minns, D.
1994 *Irenaeus.* Washington D.C.: Georgetown University Press.

Minton, W. W.
1962 "Invocation and Catalogue in Hesiod and Homer." *TAPA* 93:188–212.

Mirhady, D. C.
1994 "Aristotle, the *Rhetorica ad Alexandrum,* and the *tria genera causarum.*" In Fortenbaugh and Mirhady (eds.) 1994, 54–65.

Misch, G.
1951 *A History of Autobiography in Antiquity.* 2 vols. Cambridge: Harvard University Press.

Mitchell, M. M.
1989 "Concerning PERI DE in 1 Corinthians." *NovT* 31:229–56.
1991 *Paul and the Rhetoric of Reconciliation: An Exegetical Investigation of the Language and Composition of 1 Corinthians.* HUT 28. Tübingen: Mohr-Siebeck.
1995 "Rhetorical Shorthand in Pauline Argumentation: The Functions of 'the Gospel' in the Corinthian Correspondence." Pp. 63–88 in L. A. Jervis and P. Richardson (eds.). *Gospel in Paul: Studies on Corinthians, Galatians, and Romans for Richard N. Longenecker.* JSNTSupp 108. Sheffield: Academic Press.
2002 *The Heavenly Trumpet: John Chrysostom and the Art of Pauline Interpretation.* Louisville, Ky.: Westminster John Knox Press.

Mitton, C. L.
1951 *The Epistle to the Ephesians.* Oxford: Oxford University Press.
1955 *The Formation of the Pauline Letter Corpus.* London: Epworth.

Mizugaki, W.
1987 "Origen and Josephus." In Feldman and Hata (eds.) 1987, 325–37.

Moessner, D. P. (ed.)
1999 *Jesus and the Heritage of Israel: Luke's Narrative Claim upon Israel's Legacy.* Luke the Interpreter of Israel 1. Harrisburg, Pa.: Trinity Press International.

Moffatt, J.
1924 *A Critical and Exegetical Commentary on the Epistle to the Hebrews.* ICC. Edinburgh: T. & T. Clark.

Mohr, T. A.
1982 *Markus- und Johannespassion: Redaktions- und traditionsgeschichtliche Untersuchung der markinischen und johanneischen Passionstradition.* ATANT 70. Zurich: Theologischer Verlag.

Momigliano, A.
1981 "History and Biography." *The Legacy of Greece: A New Appraisal.* Edited by M. I. Finley. Oxford: Clarendon Press.
1984 *Settimo contributo all storia degli studi classici e del mondo antico.* Rome: Edizioni di Storia e Letteratura.
1993 *The Development of Greek Biography.* Expanded edition. Cambridge: Harvard University Press.

Montanari, F.
1998 "Zenodotus, Aristarchus, and the *Ekdosis* of Homer." In Most (ed.) 1998, 1–21.

Moo, D. J.
1983 *The Old Testament in the Gospel Passion Narratives.* Sheffield: Almond.
1985 *The Letter of James: An Introduction and Commentary.* Grand Rapids: Eerdmans.
2000 *The Letter of James.* Grand Rapids: Eerdmans.

Moore, C. H.
1921 "Prophecy in the Ancient Epic." *HSCP* 32 (1921):99–175.

Moore, G. F.
1927–30 *Judaism in the First Centuries of the Christian Era: The Age of the Tannaim.* 3 vols. Cambridge: Harvard University Press.

Moore, S. D.
1987 "Narrative Commentaries on the Bible: Context, Roots, and Prospects." *Forum* 3:29–62.
1989 *Literary Criticism and the Gospels: The Theoretical Challenge.* New Haven and London: Yale University Press.

Moores, J. D.
1995 *Wrestling with Rationality in Paul: Romans 1–8 in a New Perspective.* SNTSMS 82. Cambridge: Cambridge University Press.

Moraldi, L. (ed.)
1971 *Apocrifi del Nuovo Testamento.* 2 vols. Turin: Unione Tipografico-Editrice.

Moraux, P.
1951 *Les listes anciennes des ouvrages d'Aristote.* Leuven: University of Leuven.

Morgan, J. R., and R. Stoneman (eds.)
1994 *Greek Fiction: The Greek Novel in Context.* London: Routledge.

Morgan, M. A.
1983 *Sepher ha-Razim: The Book of the Mysteries.* Chico, Calif.: Scholars Press.

Morgenstern, M., E. Qimron, and D. Sivan
1995 "The Hitherto Unpublished Columns of the Genesis Apocryphon." *Abr-Nahrain* 33:30–52.

Morgenthaler, R.
1958 *Statistik des neutestamentlichen Wortschatzes.* Zurich and Frankfurt am Main: Gotthelf-Verlag.
1993 *Lukas und Quintilian: Rhetorik als Erzählkunst.* Zurich: Gotthelf-Verlag.

Morner, K.
1991 *NTC's Dictionary of Literary Terms.* Lincolnwood, Ill.: National Textbook Company.

Morray-Jones, C. R. A.
1992 "Transformational Mysticism in the Apocalyptic-Merkabah Tradition." *JJS* 43:1–31.

Morris, L.
1964 *The New Testament and the Jewish Lectionaries.* London: Tyndale.
1983 "The Gospels and the Jewish Lectionaries." In France and Wenham (eds.) 1983, 129–56.

Morson, G. S., and C. Emerson
1990 *Mikhail Bakhtin: Creation of a Prosaics.* Stanford: Stanford University Press.

Morton, A. Q.
1965 *The Authorship of the Pauline Epistles: A Scientific Solution.* Saskatoon: University of Saskatchewan Press.
1966 *Paul, the Man and the Myth: A Study in the Authorship of Greek Prose.* London: Hodder & Stoughton.
1978 *Literary Detection: How to Prove Authorship and Fraud in Literature and Documents.* New York: Scribner's.

Morton, A. Q., and A. D. Winspear (eds.)
1971 *It's Greek to the Computer.* Montreal: Harvest House.

Most, G. W.
1982 "Neues zur Geschichte des Terminus 'Epyllion.'" *Philologus* 126:153–56.

Most, G. W. (ed.)
1997 *Collecting Fragments = Fragmente sammeln.* Aporemata 1. Göttingen: Vandenhoeck & Ruprecht.
1998 *Editing Texts=Texte Edieren.* Aporemata 2. Göttingen: Vandenhoeck & Ruprecht.
2001 *Historicization=Historisierung.* Aporemata 5. Göttingen: Vandenhoeck & Ruprecht.

Moule, C. F. D.
1965 "The Problem of the Pastoral Epistles: A Reappraisal." *BJRL* 3:430–52.

Moulton, C.
1977 *Similes in the Homeric Poems.* Göttingen: Vandenhoeck & Ruprecht.

Moulton, J. H., and W. F. Howard
1929 *A Grammar of New Testament Greek.* Vol. 2: *Accidence and Word-Formation.* Edinburgh: T. & T. Clark.

Mouton, E.
1996 "The Communicative Power of the Epistle to the Ephesians." In Porter and Olbricht (eds.) 1996, 280–307.

Mowry, L.
1944 "The Early Circulation of Paul's Letters," *JBL* 63:73–86.

Moyise, S.
1995 *The Old Testament in the Book of Revelation.* JSNTSup 115. Sheffield: Sheffield Academic.

Mras, K.
1954 *Die Praeparatio evangelica.* Vol. 8 of *Eusebius Werke.* GCS 43.1. Berlin: Akademie Verlag.
1956 *Die Praeparatio evangelica.* Vol. 8 of *Eusebius Werke.* GCS 43.2. Berlin: Akademie Verlag.

Muecke, D. C.
1969 *The Compass of Irony.* London: Methuen

Muellner, L. C.
1978 *The Meaning of Homeric euchomai through Its Formulas.* Innsbruck: Inst. für Sprachwissenschaft der Universität Innsbruck.

Muilenberg, J.
1969 "Form Criticism and Beyond." *JBL* 88:1–18.

Mulder, J. M. (ed.)
1988 *Mikra.* CRINT 2.1. Assen: Van Gorcum; Philadelphia: Fortress Press.

Mullen, E. T., Jr.
1980 *The Divine Council in Canaanite and Early Hebrew Literature.* Cambridge: Harvard University Press.

Müller, H. P.
1971 "Mantische Weisheit und Apokalyptik."

Pp. 268–93 in *Congress Volume, Uppsala 1971*. Leiden: Brill.

Müller, K.
1983 Die Haustafel des Kolosserbriefes und das antike Frauenthema: Eine kritische Rückschau auf alte Ergebnisse." Pp. 263–319 in G. Dautzenberg et al. *Die Frau im Urchristentum*. QD 95. Freiburg: Herder.

Müller, L.
1929 "De Luciani dialororum rhetoricorum compositione." *Eos* 32:574–78.

Müller, M.
1998 "Der sogenannte 'schriftstellischer Plural'—neu betrachtet. Zur Frage der Mitarbeiter als Mitverfasser der Paulusbriefe." *BZ* 42:181–201.

Müller, U. B.
1972 *Messias und Menschensohn in jüdischen Apokalypsen und in der Offenbarung des Johannes*. Gütersloh: Gerd Mohn.
1975 *Prophetie und Predigt im Neuen Testament: Formgeschichtliche Untersuchungen zur urchristlichen Prophetie*. SNT 10. Gütersloh: Gerd Mohn.

Müller-Graupa, E.
1933 "Museion." *RE* Halbband 31, 797–821.

Mullins, T. Y.
1962 "Petition as a Literary Form." *NovT* 5:46–54.
1964 "Disclosure: A Literary Form in the New Testament." *NovT* 7:44–60.
1968 "Greeting as a New Testament Form." *JBL* 87:418–26.
1973 "Visit Talk in New Testament Letters." *CBQ* 35:350–54.
1976 "New Testament Commission Forms, Especially in Luke–Acts." *JBL* 95:603–14.
1980 "Topos as a New Testament Form." *JBL* 99:541–47.

Munck, J.
1950 "Discours d'adieu dans le Nouveau Testament et dans la littérature biblique." Pp. 155–70 in *Aux Sources de la Tradition chrétienne: Mélanges offerts à M. Maurice Goguel à l'occasion de son soixante-dixiéme anniversaire*. Neuchâtel: Delachaux; Paris: Niestlè.
1963 "Evangelium Veritatis and Greek Usage as to Book Titles." *ST* 17:133–38.
1967 *The Acts of the Apostles*. Revised by W. F. Albright and C. S. Mann. AB 31. Garden City: Doubleday.

Munier, C.
1986 "La structure litteraire de l'*Apologie* de Justin." *RevScRel* 60:34–54.
1987 "'A propos des apologies de Justin." *RevScRel* 61:171–86.
1994 *L'Apologie de Saint Justin, Philosophe et Martyr.* Paradosis 38. Fribourg: Éditions Universitaires Fribourg Suisse.
1995 *Saint Justin, Apologie pour les Chrétiens: Édition et traduction*. Paradosis 39. Fribourg: Éditions Universitaires Fribourg Suisse.

Munro, W.
1990 "Interpolation in the Epistles: Weighing Probability." *NTS* 36:431–43.

Murgatroyd, P.
1986 "Ring-structure in Bacchylides' Epinikion 3." *Liverpool Classical Monthly* 11:138.

Murphy, F. J.
1985 *The Structure and Meaning of Second Baruch*. SBLDS 78. Atlanta: Scholars Press.

Murphy, R.
1981 *Wisdom Literature: Job, Proverbs, Ruth, Canticles, Ecclesiastes, Esther.* FOTL 13. Grand Rapids: Eerdmans.

Murphy-O'Connor, J.
1970 "An Essene Missionary Document CD II,14–VI,1." *RB* 77:201–29.
1976 "The Non-Pauline Character of 1 Corinthians 11:2–16" *JBL* 95:615–21.
1980 "Sex and Logic in 1 Corinthians 11:2–16." *CBQ* 42:482–500.
1981 "Tradition and Redaction in 1 Cor. 15:3–7." *CBQ* 43:582–89.
1986 "Interpolations in 1 Corinthians." *CBQ* 48:81–94.
1987 "Relating 2 Corinthians 6.14–7.1 to Its Context." *NTS* 33:272–75.
1988 "1 Corinthians 11:2–16 Once Again." *CBQ* 50:265–74.
1991a "2 Timothy Contrasted with 1 Timothy and Titus." *RB* 98:403–418.
1991b *The Theology of the Second Letter to the Corinthians*. Cambridge: Cambridge University Press.
1995 *Paul the Letter-Writer: His World, His Options, His Skills*. Collegeville, Minn.: Liturgical Press.

Murphy-O'Connor, J., and J. H. Charlesworth (eds.)
1990 *Paul and the Dead Sea Scrolls*. New York: Crossroad.

Murray, O. (ed.)
1990 *Sympotica: A Symposium on the Symposion*. Oxford: Clarendon Press.

Mussies, G.
1971 *The Morphology of Koine Greek as Used in the Apocalypse of John: A Study in Bilingualism.* NovTSup 27. Leiden: Brill.
1972 *Dio Chrysostom and the New Testament.* SCHNT 2. Leiden: Brill.
1976 "Greek in Palestine and the Diaspora." Vol. 2, pp. 1040–64, in *Compendia Rerum Iudaicarum ad Novum Testamentum.* Section 1: *The Jewish People in the First Century.* Philadelphia: Fortress Press.
1986 "Parallels to Matthew's Version of the Pedigree of Jesus." *NovT* 28/1:32–47.

Mussner, F.
1964 *Der Jakobusbrief.* HTKNT. Freiburg, Basel, and Vienna: Herder.

Musurillo, H. (ed.).
1954 *Acts of the Pagan Martyrs: Acta Alexandrinorum.* Oxford: Clarendon Press.
1961 *Acta Alexandrinorum.* Bibliotheca Teubneriana. Leipzig: B. G. Teubner.
1972 *Acts of the Christian Martyrs.* Oxford: Clarendon Press.

Myers, J. M.
1974 *I and II Esdras.* AB 42. New York: Doubleday.

Nachmanson, E.
1941 "Der griechische Buchtitel: Einige Beobachtungen." *Göteborgs Högskolas Årskrift* 47:1–52.

Nadeau, R.
1959 "Classical Systems of Staseis in Greek: Hermagoras to Hermogenes." *GRBS* 2:53ff.
1964 "Hermogenes' *On Staseis*: A Translation with an Introduction and Notes." *Speech Monographs* 31:361–424.

Nannos, M. D.
2002 *The Irony of Galatians: Paul's Letter in First-Century Context.* Minneapolis: Fortress Press.

Narducci, E.
2001 *Dell'oratone.* Milan: Biblioteca Universale Rizzoli.

Naveh, J., and S. Shaked
1985 *Amulets and Magic Bowls: Aramaic Incantations of Late Antiquity.* Jerusalem: Magnes Press.
1993 *Magic Spells and Formulae: Aramaic Incantations of Late Antiquity.* Jerusalem: Magnes Press.

Neill, S., and T. Wright
1988 *The Interpretation of the New Testament, 1861–1986.* Rev. ed. Oxford and New York: Oxford University Press.

Neirynck, F.
1988a *Duality in Mark: Contributions to the Study of the Markan Redaction.* 2d ed. Leuven: Leuven University Press.
1988b "APO TOTE ERXATO and the Structure of Matthew." *ETL* 64:21–59.
1995 *Q-Synopsis: The Double Tradition of Passages in Greek.* Rev. ed. Leuven: Leuven University Press and Uitgeverij Peeters.
1998 *The Gospel of Matthew and the Sayings Source Q: A Cumulative Bibliography 1950–1995.* BETL 140. Leuven: Leuven University Press and Peeters.
2001a "The Reconstruction of Q and IQP / CritEd Parallels." In Lindemann (ed.) 2001,53–147.
2001b *Q-Parallels: Q-Synopsis and IQP/CritEd Parallels.* Leuven: Leuven University Press and Uitgeverij Peeters.

Neller, K. V.
1989–90 "Diversity in the Gospel of Thomas: Clues for a New Direction?" *SecCent* 7:1–18.

Nestle, W.
1936 "Legenden vom Tod der Gottesverächter." *Archiv für Religionswissenschaft* 33:246–69.

Neugebauer, O.
1981 *The 'Astronomical' Chapters of the Ethiopic Book of Enoch (72–82): Translation and Commentary, with Additional Notes on the Aramaic Fragments* by M. Black. Copenhagen: Munksgaard.

Neuschäfer, B.
1987 *Origenes als Philologe.* Basel: Friedrich Reinhardt.

Neusner, J.
1971 *The Rabbinic Traditions about the Pharisees before 70.* 3 vols. Leiden: Brill.
1972 "Types and Forms in Ancient Jewish Literature: Some Comparisons." *HR* 11:354–90.
1975 *Christianity, Judaism, and Other Greco-Roman Cults: Studies for Morton Smith at Sixty.* 4 vols. Leiden: Brill.
1987 *What Is Midrash?* Philadelphia: Fortress Press.
1994 *Introduction to Rabbinic Literature.* ABRL. New York: Doubleday.

Neusner, J., and E. S. Frerichs (eds.)
1987 *Judaic and Christian Interpretation of*

Texts: Contents and Contexts. Lanham, Md.: University Press of America.

Neusner, J., P. Borgen, E. S. Frerichs and R. Horsley (eds.)
1988 *The Social World of Formative Christianity and Judaism.* Philadelphia: Fortress.

Newsom, C.
1980 "The Development of 1 Enoch 6–19: Cosmology and Judgment." *CBQ* 42:310–29.
1985 *Songs of the Sabbath Sacrifice: A Critical Edition.* Atlanta: Scholars Press.

Neyrey, J. H.
1993 *2 Peter, Jude: A New Translation with Introduction and Commentary.* AB 37C. Garden City, N.Y.: Doubleday.

Nickau, K.
1977 *Untersuchungen zur textkritischen Methode des Zenodotos von Ephesos.* UALG 16. Berlin and New York: Walter de Gruyter.

Nickelsburg, G. W. E.
1972 *Resurrection, Immortality, and Eternal Life in Intertestamental Judaism.* HTS 26. Cambridge: Harvard University.
1977a "Apocalyptic and Myth in 1 Enoch 6–11." *JBL* 96:383–405.
1977b "The Apocalyptic Message of *1 Enoch* 92–105." *CBQ* 39:309–28.
1980 "The Genre and Function of the Markan Passion Narrative." *HTR* 73:154–84.
1981 *Jewish Literature between the Bible and the Mishnah: A Historical and Literary Introduction.* Philadelphia: Fortress Press.
1984 "The Bible Rewritten and Expanded." In Stone (ed.) 1984, 89–156.
1991 "The Apocalyptic Construction of Reality in *1 Enoch.*" In Collins and Charlesworth (eds.) 1991, 51–64.
2001 *1 Enoch 1: A Commentary on the Book of 1 Enoch, chapters 1–36; 81–108.* Hermeneia. Minneapolis: Fortress Press.

Nickelsburg, G. W. E. (ed.).
1973 *Studies on the Testament of Moses.* SCS 4. Cambridge, Mass.: SBL.
1975 *Studies on the Testament of Joseph.* SCS 5. Missoula, Mont.: Scholars Press.
1976 *Studies on the Testament of Abraham.* SCS 6. Missoula, Mont.: Scholars Press.

Nida, E. A., et al.
1983 *Style and Discourse with Special Reference to the Text of the Greek New Testament.* Cape Town: Bible Society.

Niditch, S.
1987 *Underdogs and Tricksters: A Prelude to Biblical Folklore.* San Francisco: Harper & Row.
1993 *Folklore and the Hebrew Bible.* Minneapolis: Fortress Press.
1996 *Oral World and Written Word: Ancient Israelite Literature.* Louisville, Ky.: Westminster John Knox Press.

Niederwimmer, K.
1993 *Die Didache.* 2. Aufl. Kommentar zu den Apostolischen Vätern. Göttingen: Vandenhoeck & Ruprecht.
1998 *The Didache.* Hermeneia. Minneapolis: Fortress Press.

Neilsen, E.
1954 *Oral Tradition.* Naperville, Ill.: Allenson.

Nielsen, J. T.
1969 *Adam and Christ in the Theology of Irenaeus of Lyons.* Assen: Van Gorcum.

Neirynck, F.
1979 *Jean et les synnoptiques: Examen critique de l'exégèse de M.-E. Boismard.* BETL 49. Leuven: Leuven University.

Niebuhr, K.-W.
1998 "Der Jakobusbrief im Licht frühjüdischer Diasporabriefe." *NTS* 44:420–43.

Nikiprowetzky, V.
1973 "L'Exégèse de Philon d'Alexandrie." *Revue d'Histoire et de Philosophie Religieuses* 53:309–29.
1977 *Le commentaire de l'écriture chez Philon d'Alexandrie.* ALGHJ 11. Leiden: Brill.

Nikolakopoulos, K.
2001 "Aspekte der 'paulinischen Ironie' am Beispiel des Galaterbriefs." *BZ* 45:193–208.

Niles, J. D.
1979 "On the Design of the Hymn to Delian Apollo." *CJ* 75:36–39.

Nilsson, M.
1946 "The New Conception of the Universe in Late Greek Paganism." *Eranos* 44:20–27.
1969 *Greek Piety.* New York: W. W. Norton.

Nimis, S. A.
1999 "Ring-Composition and Linearity in Homer." In Mackay (ed.) 1999, 65–78.

Nineham, D.
1977 *Saint Mark.* Philadelphia: Westminster Press.

Nitzan, B.
1994 *Qumran Prayer and Religious Poetry.* Leiden: Brill.

Nock, A. D.
1933 *Conversion: The Old and the New in*

Religion from Alexander the Great to Augustine of Hippo. Oxford: Oxford University Press.
1972 "Greek Magical Papyri." Vol. 1, pp. 176–94 in *Essays on Religion and the Ancient World.* Edited by Z. Stewart. 2 vols. Oxford: Clarendon Press.

Nock, A. D., and A.-J. Festugière.
1954–60 *Corpus Hermeticum.* 4 vols. Paris: Société d'Édition "Les Belles Lettres."

Nolland, J.
1996 "Genealogical Annotation in Genesis as Background for the Matthean Genealogy of Jesus." *TynBul* 47:115–22.
1997 "The Four (Five) Women and Other Annotations in Matthew's Genealogy." *NTS* 43:527–39.

Norden, E.
1909 *Die antike Kunstprosa.* 2 vols. Berlin: Teubner.
1956 *Agnostos Theos: Untersuchungen zur Formgeschichte religiöser Rede.* Leipzig and Berlin: Teubner.

Nordheim, E. von.
1980 *Die Lehre der Alten.* Vol. 1: *Das Testament als Gliedgattung im Judentum der Hellenistisch-Römischen Zeit.* ALGHJ 13. Leiden: Brill.
1985 *Die Lehre der Alten.* Vol. 2: *Das Testament als Literaturgattung im Alten Testament und im Alten Vorderen Orient.* ALGHJ 18. Leiden: Brill.

Nordling, J. G.
1997 "*Onesimus Fugitivus*: A Defense of the Runaway Slave Hypothesis in Philemon." In Evans and Porter (eds.) 1997.

Norris, F. W.
1976 "Ignatius, Polycarp, and 1 Clement: Walter Bauer Reconsidered." *VC* 30:23–44.

North, H.
1979 *From Myth to Icon: Reflections of Greek Ethical Doctrine in Literature and Art.* Ithaca, N.Y.: Cornell University Press.

Nussbaum, M.
1996 "Aristotle on Emotions and rational Persuasion." Pp. 303–23 in *Essays on Aristotle's* Rhetoric. Edited by A. O. Rorty. Berkeley, Los Angeles and London: University of California.

Nuttall, A. D.
1992 *Openings: Narrative Beginnings from the Epic to the Novel.* Oxford: Clarendon Press.

Oates, J. F., R. S. Bagnall, W. H. Willis, and K. A. Worp
1985 *Checklist of Editions of Greek Papyri and Ostraca.* 3d ed. Atlanta: Scholars Press.

O'Brien, P. T.
1974–75 "Thanksgiving and the Gospel of Paul." *NTS* 21:40–53.
1977 *Introductory Thanksgivings in the Letters of Paul.* NovTSup 49. Leiden: Brill.
1979 "Ephesians I: An Unusual Introduction to a New Testament Letter." *NTS* 25:504–16.

O'Connor, M. P.
1983 *Hebrew Verse Structures.* Winona Lake, Ind.: Eisenbraun.

O'Day, G. R.
1986 *Revelation in the Fourth Gospel.* Philadelphia: Fortress Press.

Oden, R. A., Jr.
1978 "Philo of Byblos and Hellenistic Historiography." *PEQ* 110:115–26.
1992 "Cosmogony, Cosmology." *ADB* 1:1162–71.

Oesterreicher, W.
1993 "Verschriftung und Verschriftlichung im Kontext medialer konzeptioneller Schriftlichkeit." Pp. 265–90 in *Schriftlichkeit im frühen Mittelalter.* Edited by U. Schaefer. Tübingen: G. Naar.

Ogden, G. S.
1979 "The 'Better'-Proverb (Tôb-Spruch), Rhetorical Criticism and Qoheleth." *JBL* 96:489–505.

Ohlert, K.
1979 *Rätsel und Rätselspiele der alten Griechen.* 2d ed. 1912; reprint, Hildesheim: Olms.

Ohly, K.
1928 *Stichometrische Untersuchungen.* Leipzig: O. Harrassowitz.

Oikonomides, A. N.
1974 *A Manual of Abbreviations in Greek Inscriptions, Papyri, Manuscripts, and Early Printed Books.* Chicago: Ares.

Olbricht, T. H.
1990 "An Aristotelian Rhetorical Analysis of 1 Thessalonians." In Balch, Ferguson, and Meeks (eds.) 1990, 216–36.
1993 "Hebrews as Amplification." In Porter and Olbricht (eds.) 1993, 375–87.
1996 "The Stoicheia and the Rhetoric of Colossians: Then and Now." In Porter and Olbricht (eds.) 1996, 308–28.
1997a "The Flowering of Rhetorical Criticism in America." In Porter and Olbricht (eds.) 1997, 79–102.
1997b "Delivery and Memory." In Porter (ed.) 1997a, 159–67.

2001 "*Pathos* as Proof in Greco-Roman Rhetoric." Olbricht and Sumney 2001:7–22.

Olbricht, T. H., and J. L. Sumney (eds.)
2001 *Paul and Pathos.* Atlanta: Society of Biblical Literature.

Oliver, R. P.
1950 "The First Medicean MS of Tacitus and the Titulature of Ancient Books." *TAPA* 82:232–61.

Oliver, J. H.
1953 "The Ruling Power." *TAPA* 43:871–1003.

Ollrog, H.
1979 *Paulus und seine Mitarbeiter.* Neukirchen-Vluyn: Neukirchener Verlag.

Olrik, A.
1909 "Epic Laws of Folk Narrative." In Dundes 1965:129–41.

O'Rourke, J. J.
1974 "The Historical Present in the Gospel of John." *JBL* 93:585–90.
1979 "Asides in the Gospel of John." *NovT* 21:210–19.

Olson, K. A.
1999 "Eusebius and the *Testimonium Flavianum.*" *CBQ* 61:305–22.

Olson, S.
1984 "Epistolary Uses of Expressions of Self-Confidence." *JBL* 103:585–97.

Olsson, Birger
1974 *Structure and Meaning of the Fourth Gospel.* Lund: Almqvist & Wiksell.

Omeltchenko, S. W.
1977 *A Quantitative and Comparative Study of the Vocalism of the Latin Inscriptions of North Africa, Britain, Dalmatia, and the Balkans.* Chapel Hill: University of North Carolina Press.

O'Neill, J. C.
1961 *The Theology of Acts in Its Historical Setting.* 2d ed. London: SPCK.
1972 *The Recovery of Paul's Letter to the Galatians.* London: SPCK.
1975 *Paul's Letter to the Romans.* Harmondsworth: Penguin.
1983 "Glosses and Interpolations in the Letters of St. Paul." TU 126, *Studia Evangelica* 7. Berlin: Akademie-Verlag.

Ong, W.
1967 *The Presence of the Word: Some Prolegomena for Cultural and Religious History.* New Haven, Conn.: Yale University Press.
1982 *Orality and Literacy: The Technologizing of the Word.* London: Methuen.

Orlinsky, H.
1989 "The Septuagint and Its Hebrew Text." In Davies and Finkelstein (eds.) 1989, 534–62.

Orsini, G. N. G.
1975 *Organic Unity in Ancient and Later Poetics.* Carbondale: University of Illinois Press.

Orton, D. B.
1989 *The Understanding Scribe.* JSNTSupp 25. Sheffield: JSOT Press.
1999 *The Composition of Mark's Gospel: Selected Studies from Novum Testamentum.* Leiden: Brill.

Osborn, E. F.
1973 *Justin Martyr.* BHT 47. Tübingen: Mohr-Siebeck.
1989 "Reason and the Rule of Faith in the Second Century A.D." In R. Williams (ed.) 1989, 40–61.

Osborn, R. E.
1999 *Folly of God: The Rise of Christian Preaching.* St. Louis: Chalice.

Osiek, C.
1983 *Rich and Poor in the Shepherd of Hermas: An Exegetical-Social Investigation.* CBQMS 15. Washington, D.C.: Catholic Biblical Association of America.
1986 "The Genre and Function of the *Shepherd of Hermas.*" *Semeia* 36:113–21.
1998 "The Oral World of Early Christianity in Rome: The Case of Hermas." In Donfried and Richardson (eds.) 1998, 151–72.
1999 *Shepherd of Hermas: A Commentary.* Hermeneia. Minneapolis: Fortress Press.
2000 *Philippians, Philemon.* ANTC. Nashville: Abingdon Press.

Osswald, E.
1963 "Zum Problem der *vaticinia ex eventu.*" *ZAW* 75:27–44.

Ostmeyer, K.-H.
2000 *Taufe und Typos: Elemente und Theologie der Tauftypologien in 1. Korinther 10 und 1. Petrus 3.* WUNT 2/118. Tübingen: Mohr-Siebeck.

O'Sullivan, J. N.
1995 *Xenophon of Ephesus: His Compositional Technique and the Birth of the Novel.* Berlin: Walter de Gruyter.

O'Sullivan, N.
1997 "Caecilius, the 'Canons' of Writers, and the Origins of Atticism." In Dominik (ed.) 1997, 32–49.

Otranto, G.
1979 *Esegesi biblica e storia in Giustino*

(Dial. 63–84). Quaderni di "Vetera Christianorum" 14. Bari: Istituto di Letteratura Cristiana Antica.

Otto, A.
1971 *Die Sprichwörter und sprichwörtlichen Redensarten der Römer.* Hildesheim: Georg Olms (originally published 1890).

Otto, D.
1998 *Wendungen der Metapher: Zur Übertragung in poetologischer, rhetorischer und erkenntnistheoretischer Hinsicht bei Aristoteles und Nietzsche.* Munich: Wilhelm Fink.

Otto, J. K. T.
1969 *Iustini philosophi et martyris opera.* 3d ed. 5 vols. Wiesbaden: Martin Sandig [originally published 1876–81].

Overbeck, F.
1965 "Über den pseudojustinischen Brief an Diognet." Pp. 1–92 in *Studien zur Geschichte der Alten Kirche.* Darmstadt: Wissenschaftliche Buchgesellschaft.

Overbeck, W.
1995 *Menschwerdung: Eine Untersuchung zur literarischen und theologischen Einheit des fünften Buches 'Adversus Haereses' des Irenäus von Lyon.* Basler und Berner Studien zur historischen und systematischen Theologie 61. Bern, Frankfurt, New York, and Paris: Peter Lang.

Overman, J. A.
1992 "Homily Form (Hellenistic and Early Christian)." *ADB* 3.280–82.

Padgett, A.
1984 "Paul on Women in the Church: The Contradictions of Coiffure in 1 Cor. 11:2–16." *JSNT* 23:69–86.

Pagels, E.
1973 *The Johannine Gospel in Gnostic Exegesis: Heracleon's Commentary on John.* Nashville: Abingdon Press.
1975 *The Gnostic Paul: Gnostic Exegesis of the Pauline Letters.* Philadelphia: Fortress Press.
1980 *The Gnostic Gospels.* New York: Random House.

Painter, J.
1993 *The Quest for the Messiah: The History, Literature, and Theology of the Johannine Community.* 2d. ed. Nashville: Abingdon Press.
2002 *1, 2, and 3 John.* Sacra Pagina 18. Collegeville: The Liturgical Press.

Palm, J.
1965–66 "Bemerkungen zur Ekphrase in der griechischen Literatur." *Årsbok.* Uppsala: Kungliga Humanistika Vetenskaps-Samfundet.

Palmer, D. W.
1987 "The Literary Background of Acts 1:1–14." *NTS* 33:427–38.
1993 "Acts and the Ancient Historical Monograph." Pp. 1–29 in *The Book of Acts in Its First Century Setting.* Vol. 1: *Ancient Literary Setting.* Edited by B. Winder and A. Clarke. Grand Rapids: Eerdmans.

Palmer, L. R.
1954 *The Latin Language.* London: Faber and Faber.
1980 *The Greek Language.* Atlantic Highlands, N.J.: Humanities Press.

Palmer Bonz, M.
2000 *The Past as Legacy: Luke–Acts and the Ancient Epic.* Minneapolis: Fortress Press.

Papanikolaou, A. D.
1973 *Chariton-Studien: Untersuchungen zur Sprache und Chronology der griechischen Romance.* Göttingen: Vandenhoeck & Ruprecht.

Parker, D. C.
1992 *Codex Bezae: An Early Christian Manuscript and Its Text.* Cambridge: Cambridge University Press.
1997 *The Living Text of the Gospels.* Cambridge: Cambridge University Press.

Parker, D. C., and C.-B. Amphoux (eds.)
1997 *Codex Bezae: Studies from the Lunel Colloquium June 1994.* NTTS 22. Leiden: Brill.

Parker, P.
1962–63 "Luke and the Fourth Evangelist." *NTS* 9:317–36.

Parkinson, R., and S. Quirke
1995 *Papyrus.* Austin: University of Texas Press.

Parris, D. P.
2002 "Imitating the Parables: Allegory, Narrative and the Role of Mimesis." *JSNT* 25:33–54.

Parry, M.
1930 "Studies of the Epic Technique of Oral Verse-Making. I. Homer and the Homeric Style." *HSCP* 41:73–147.
1971 *The Making of Homeric Verse.* Edited by Adam Parry. Oxford: Oxford University Press.

Patillon, M. (ed.)
2002 *Pseudo-Aelius Aristide, Arts Rhétoriques.* 2 vols. Paris: Les Belles Lettres.

Patte, D.
1975 *Early Jewish Hermeneutic in Palestine.* SBLDS 22. Missoula, Mont.: Scholars Press.
1995 *Ethics of Biblical Interpretation: A Reevaluation.* Louisville, Ky.: Westminster John Knox Press.

Patterson, S. J., and C. N. Jefford
1989–90 "A Note on *Didache* 12,2a (Coptic)." *SecCent* 9:65–75.

Paulien, J.
1987 *Decoding Revelation's Trumpets: Literary Allusions and the Interpretation of Revelation 8:7–12.* Andrews University Seminary Doctoral Dissertation Series, 11. Berrien Springs, Mich.: Andrews University Press.

Pearson, B. A.
1971 "1 Thessalonians 2:13–16: A Deutero-Pauline Interpretation." *HTR* 64:79–94.
1989 "James, 1–2 Peter, Jude." In Epp and MacRae (eds.) 1989, 371–406.

Pearson, B. A. (ed.)
1991 *The Future of Early Christianity: Essays in Honor of Helmut Koester.* Minneapolis: Fortress Press.

Pearson, B. W. R.
1997 "New Testament Literary Criticism." In Porter (ed.) 1997, 241–66.

Pelletier, A.
1962 *Flavius Josèphe, adaptateur de la Lettre d'Aristée. Une réaction atticisante contre la Koine.* Etudes et Commentaires 45. Paris: Librairie C. Klincksieck.

Pépin, J.
1967 "Remarques sur la théorie de l'exégèse allégorique chez Philon." Pp. 138–68 in *Philon d'Alexandrie.* Paris: Éditions du Centrenational de la recherche scientific.
1976 Mythe et allégorie: Les origines grecques et les contestations judéo-chrétiennes. 2d ed. Paris: Études Augustiniennes.

Perdue, L. G.
1981 "Paraenesis and the Epistle of James." *ZNW* 72:241–56.
1986 "The Wisdom Sayings of Jesus." *Forum* 2.3:3–35.

Perelman, C.
1979 *The New Rhetoric and the Humanities: Essays on Rhetoric and Its Applications.* Boston: Reidel.
1980 *Justice, Law, and Argument: Essays on Moral and Legal Reasoning.* Boston: Reidel.
1982 *The Realm of Rhetoric.* Notre Dame and London: University of Notre Dame Press.
1997 *L'Empire rhétorique: Rhétorique et argumentation.* Paris: J. Vrin.

Perelman, C., and L. Olbrechts-Tyteca
1969 *The New Rhetoric: A Treatise on Argumentation.* Translated by J. Wilkinson and P. Weaver. Notre Dame and London: University of Notre Dame Press.

Perkins, P.
1976 "Irenaeus and the Gnostics: Rhetoric and Composition in *Adversus Haereses* Book One." *VC* 30:193–200.
1979 *The Johannine Epistles.* Wilmington, Del.: Michael Glazier.
1980 *The Gnostic Dialogue: The Early Church and the Crisis of Gnosticism.* New York: Paulist Press.
1981 "Pronouncement Stories in the Gospel of Thomas." *Semeia* 20:121–32.
1995 *First and Second Peter, James, and Jude.* Louisville, Ky.: Westminster John Knox Press.

Perler, O.
1949 "Das vierte Makkabäerbuch, Ignatius von Antiochien und die ältesten Märtyrerberichte." *Revista di Archeologia Christiana* 87:47–72.

Pernot, L.
1993 *La rhétorique de l'éloge dans le mond gréco-romain.* 2 vols. Paris: Institut d'Études Augustiniennes.

Perrin, N.
1969 *What Is Redaction Criticism?* Philadelphia: Fortress Press.
1976 *Jesus and the Language of the Kingdom: Symbol and Metaphor in New Testament Interpretation.* Philadelphia: Fortress Press.

Perrot, C.
1976 *Pseudo-Philon: Les Antiquités Bibliques.* Tome 2. SC 230. Paris: Cerf.

Perry, B. E.
1964 *Secundus the Silent Philosophy: The Greek Life of Secundus.* Philological Monographs 22. Ithaca, N.Y.: Cornell University Press, for the American Philological Association.
1965 *Babrius and Phaedrus.* LCL. Cambridge: Harvard University Press.
1967 *The Ancient Romances: A Literary-Historical Account of Their Origins.* Berkeley: University of California Press.

Pervo, R. I.
1987 *Profit with Delight: The Literary Genre of the Acts of the Apostles.* Minneapolis: Fortress Press.

1996 "The Ancient Novel Becomes Christian." In Schmeling (ed.) 1996, 685–711.
1997 "A Hard Act to Follow: The *Acts of Paul* and the Canonical Acts." *JHC* 2:3–32.

Pesch, R.
1968 *Naherwartungen: Tradition und Redaktion in Mk. 13.* HTKNT 2.1–2. Düsseldorf: Patmos Verlag.
1977 *Das Markusevangelium.* 2 vols. Freiburg: Herder.
1986 *Die Apostelgeschichte.* 2 vols. EKK. Zürich, Einsiedeln, and Köln: Benziger Verlag; Neukirchen-Vluyn: Neukirchener Verlag.

Peter, H.
1901 *Der Brief in der römischen Literatur: Litterargeschichtliche Untersuchungen und Zusammenfassung.* Leipzig: Teubner.

Petersen, D. L., and K. H. Richards
1992 *Interpreting Hebrew Poetry.* Minneapolis: Fortress Press.

Petersen, N. R.
1978a *Literary Criticism for New Testament Critics.* Philadelphia: Fortress Press.
1978b "'Point of View' in Mark's Narrative." *Semeia* 12:97–121.
1985 *Rediscovering Paul: Philemon and the Sociology of Paul's Narrative World.* Philadelphia: Fortress Press.
1993 *The Gospel of John and the Sociology of Light: Language and Characterization in the Fourth Gospel.* Valley Forge, Pa.: Trinity Press.
1994 "Can One Speak of a Gospel Genre?" *Neot* 28:137–58.

Petersen, W. L.
1994 *Tatian's Diatessaron: Its Creation, Dissemination, Significance, and History in Scholarship.* Supplements to Vigiliae Christianae 25. Leiden: Brill.

Petersen, W. L. (ed.).
1989 *Gospel Traditions in the Second Century: Origins, Recensions, Text, and Transmission.* Notre Dame: University of Notre Dame Press.
1990 "Textual Evidence of Tatian's Dependence upon Justin's ἈΠΟΜΝΗΜΟΝΕΥΜΑΤΑ." *NTS* 36:512–34.

Peterson, D. N.
2000 *The Origins of Mark: The Markan Community in Current Debate.* BIS 48. Leiden: Brill.

Peterson, E.
1926 *Heis Theos: Epigraphische, formgeschichtliche und religionsgeschichtliche Untersuchungen.* FRLANT n.s. 24. Göttingen: Vandenhoeck & Ruprecht.

Petitmengin, P., and B. Flusin
1984 "Le livre antique et la dictée: Nouvelles recherches." In Lucchesi and Saffrey 1984, 247–62.

Petzke, G.
1970 *Die Traditionen über Apollonius von Tyana und das Neue Testament.* Leiden: Brill.
1990 *Das Sondergut des Evangeliums nach Lukas.* Zurich: Theologischer Verlag.

Pfann, S. J.
2000 "The Writings in Esoteric Script from Qumran." In Schiffman, Tov, and VanderKam (eds.) 2000, 177–90.

Pfeiffer, R.
1968 *History of Classical Scholarship: From the Beginnings to the End of the Hellenistic Age.* Oxford: Clarendon Press.

Pfister, M.
1985 "Konzepte der Intertextualität." Pp. 1–30 in *Intertextualität: Formen, Funktionen, anglistische Fallstudien.* Edited by U. Broich and M. Pfister. Tübingen: Max Niemeyer.

Phillips, E. D.
1952 "A Hypochondriac and His God." *GR* 21:23–36.

Philippson, O.
1928 "Verfasser und Abfassungszeit der sogenannten Hippokratesbriefe." *Rheinisches Museum* 77:293.

Philonenko-Sayar, B., and M. Philonenko.
1982 *Die Apocalypse Abrahams.* Gütersloh: Gerd Mohn.

Picard, J. C.
1967 *Apocalypsis Baruchi Graece.* PVTG 2. Leiden: Brill.
1970 "Observations sur l'Apocalypse grecque de Baruch I: Cadre historique et efficacité symbolique," *Semitica* 20:77–103.

Pike, K.
1967 *Language in Relation to a Unified Theory of the Structure of Human Behavior.* 2d ed. The Hague: Mouton.

Pilch, J.
1998 "No Jews or Christians in the Bible." *Explorations* 12:3.

Pilhofer, P.
1990 *Presbyteron kreitton: Der Altersbeweis der jüdischen und christlichen Apologeten und seine Vorgeschichte.* WUNT 2.39. Tübingen: Mohr-Siebeck.

Pinnick, A.
2001 *The Orion Center Bibliography of the Dead Sea Scrolls (1995–2000).* STDJ 41. Leiden: Brill.

Piovanelli, P.
1993 "Les origines de l 'Apocalypse de Paul' reconsidérées." *Apocrypha* 4:25–64.

Piper, R. A.
1989 *Wisdom in the Q-Tradition: The Aphoristic Teaching of Jesus.* SNTSMS 61. Cambridge: Cambridge University Press.
1994 "Matthew 7:7–11 par. Luke 11:9–13: Evidence of Design and Argument in the Collection of Jesus' Sayings." In Kloppenborg (ed.) 1994, 131–37.
1995 *The Gospel behind the Gospels: Current Studies on Q.* NovTSup 75. Leiden: Brill.

Plank, K. A.
1987 *Paul and the Irony of Affliction.* Semeia Studies. Atlanta: Scholars Press.

Plett, H. F.
1991a *Intertextuality.* Berlin and New York: Walter de Gruyter.
1991b "Intertextuality." In Plett 1991a.

Plezia, M.
1970 "L'histoire dialoguée dans la littérature patristique grecque." In Cross (ed.) 1970, 146–50.

Ploebst, W.
1911 *Die Auxesis (Amplificatio): Studien zur ihrer Entwicklung und Anwendung.* Munich: C. Wolf.

Plooij, D.
1932 *Studies in the Testimony Book.* Verhandelingen der Koninklijke Akadamie van Wetenschappen te Amsterdam, Literature Sect. 32/2. Amsterdam: Noord-Hollandsche Uitgevers-Maatschappij.

Plümacher, E.
1971 *Lukas als hellenistischer Schriftsteller.* Göttingen: Vandenhoeck & Ruprecht.
1974 "Lukas als griechischer Historiker." PW Supplementband 14:235–55.
1977 "Wirklichkeitserfahrung und Geschichtsschreibung bei Lukas: Erwägungen zu den Wir-Stücken der Apostelgeschichte." *ZNW* 69:2–22.
1978 "Apostelgeschichte." Vol. 3, pp. 483–528 in *Theologische Realenzyklopädie.* Berlin and New York: Walter de Gruyter.
1979 "Die Apostelgeschichte als historische Monographie." Pp. 457–66 in *Les Acts des Apôtres. Traditions, rédaction, théologie.* Edited by J. Kremer. BETL 48. Leuven: Leuven University.
1998 "TEPATEIA. Fiktion und Wunder in der hellenistisch-römischen Geschichtsschreibung und in der Apostelgeschichte." *ZNW* 89:66–90.
1999 "Cicero und Lukas. Bemerkungen zu Stil und Zweck der historischen Monographie." Pp. 759–75 in *The Unity of Luke–Acts.* Edited by J. Verheyden. BETL 142. Leuven: Leuven University and Peeters.

Pobee, J. S.
1985 *Persecution and Martyrdom in the Theology of Paul.* JSNTSup 6. Sheffield: JSOT Press.

Pogoloff, S.
1992 *Logos and Sophia: The Rhetorical Situation of 1 Corinthians.* SBLDS 134. Atlanta: Scholars Press.

Poland, L. M.
1985a *Literary Criticism and Biblical Hermeneutics: A Critique of Formalist Approaches.* Chico, Calif.: Scholars Press.
1985b "The New Criticism, Neoorthodoxy, and the New Testament." *JR* 65:459–77.

Popkes, W.
1986 *Adressaten, Situation und Form des Jakobusbriefes.* SBS 125/126. Stuttgart: Verlag Katholisches Bibelwerk.
1996 *Paränese und Neues Testament.* SBS 168. Stuttgart: Katholisches Bibelwerk.

Porten, B., et al.
1996 *The Elephantine Papyri in English: Three Millennia of Cross-Cultural Continuity and Change.* Leiden: Brill.

Porter, S. E.
1989 "The Language of the Apocalypse in Recent Discussion." *NTS* 35:582–603.
1990 "Romans 13:1–7 as Pauline Political Rhetoric." *Filologia Neotestamentaria* 3:115–37.
1991 "The Argument of Romans 5: Can a Rhetorical Question Make a Difference?" *JBL* 110:655–77.
1993 "The Theoretical Justification for Application of Rhetorical Categories to Pauline Epistolary Literature." In Porter and Olbricht (eds.) 1993, 100–122.
1994 "The 'We' Passages." In Gill and Gempf 1994, 545–74.
1997a "Paul of Tarsus and His Letters." In Porter (ed.) 1997a, 533–85.
1997b "Ancient Rhetorical Analysis and Discourse Analysis of the Pauline Corpus." In Porter and Olbricht (eds.) 1997, 249–74.
1999 "Paul as Epistolographer *and* Rhetorician? Implications for the Study of the Paul of Acts." In Porter (ed.) 1999, 98–125.

Porter, S. E. (ed.)
1997a *Handbook of Classical Rhetoric in the Hellenistic Period, 330* B.C.–A.D. *400.* Leiden: Brill.
1997b *Handbook to Exegesis of the New Testament.* NTTS 25. Leiden, New York, and Cologne: Brill.
1999 *The Paul of Acts: Essays in Literary Criticism, Rhetoric, and Theology.* WUNT 115. Tübingen: Mohr-Siebeck.

Porter, S. E., and K. D. Clarke
1997 "Canonical-Critical Perspective and the Relationship of Colossians and Ephesians." *Bib* 78:57–86.

Porter, S. E., and C. A. Evans (eds.)
1997 *The Scrolls and the Scriptures: Qumran Fifty Years After.* JSPSup 26. Sheffield: Sheffield Academic.

Porter, S. E., and T. H. Olbricht (eds.).
1993 *Rhetoric and the New Testament: Essays from the 1992 Heidelberg Conference.* JSNTSup 120. Sheffield: Sheffield Academic.
1996 *Rhetoric, Scripture and Theology: Essays from the 1994 Pretoria Conference.* JSNTSup 131. Sheffield: Sheffield Academic.
1997 *The Rhetorical Analysis of Scripture: Essays from the 1995 London Conference.* JSNTSup 146. Sheffield: Sheffield Academic.

Porter, S. E., and J. T. Reed
1998 "Philippians as a Macro-Chiasm and Its Exegetical Significance." *NTS* 44:213–31.

Porter, S. E., and D. L. Stamps (eds.)
1999 *The Rhetorical Interpretation of Scripture: Essays from the 1996 Malibu Conference.* JSNTSup 180. Sheffield: Sheffield Academic.
2002 *Rhetorical Criticism and the Bible.* JSNTSup 195. Sheffield: Sheffield Academic.

Porter, S. E., and D. Tombs (eds.).
1995 *Approaches to New Testament Study.* JSNTSup 120. Sheffield: Sheffield Academic.

Porton, G. G.
1979 "Midrash: Palestinian Jews and the Hebrew Bible in the Greco-Roman Period." *ANRW* II, 19/2, 103–38.
1981a "Defining Midrash." Pp. 55–92 in *The Study of Ancient Judaism.* Edited by J. Neusner. Vol. 1. New York: KTAV.
1981b "The Pronouncement Story in Tannaitic Literature: A Review of Bultmann's Theory." *Semeia* 20:81–99.
1985 *Understanding Rabbinic Midrash.* Hoboken: KTAV.

Pouderon, B., and J. Doré
1998 *Les apologistes chrétiens et la culture grecque.* Paris: Beauchesne.

Poulos, P. N.
1981 "Form and Function of the Pronouncement Story in Diogenes Laertius' *Lives.*" *Semeia* 20:53–63.

Poupon, G.
1988 "Les "Actes de Pierre" et leur remaniement." *ANRW* II, 25/6, 4363–83.
1998 "L'Origine africaine des *Actus Vercellenses.*" In Bremmer (ed.) 1998, 192–99.

Powell, M. A.
1990 *What Is Narrative Criticism?* Minneapolis: Fortress Press.

Praeder, S. M.
1981 "Luke–Acts and the Ancient Novel." *SBL 1981 Seminar Papers.* Edited by K. H. Richards. Chico, Calif.: Scholars Press.
1984 "Acts 27:1–28:16: Sea Voyages in Ancient Literature and the Theology of Luke–Acts." *CBQ* 46:683–706.
1986 "The Problem of First Person Narration." *NovT* 29:193–218.

Preisendanz, K.
1956a "Ein Wiener Papyrusfragment zum Testamentum Salomonis." *Eos: Commentarii Societatis Philologae Polonorum* 48:161–67.
1956b "Salomo." Pauly-Wissowa Supplement 8:660–704.
1973–74 *Papyri Graecae Magicae: Die griechischen Zauberpapyri.* Ed. A. Hinrichs. Stuttgart: B. G. Teubner.

Preminger, A. (ed.)
1965 *An Encyclopedia of Poetry and Poetics.* Princeton: Princeton University Press.

Price, S. R. F.
1984 *Rituals and Power: The Roman Imperial Cult in Asia Minor.* Cambridge: Cambridge University Press.

Prieur, J.-M.
1989 *Acts Andreae.* CCSA 5–6. Turnhout: Brepols.
1995 *Actes de l'Apôtre André: présentation et traduction du latin, du copte et du grec.* Turnhout: Brepols.

Prigent, P.
1964 *Justin et l'Ancient Testament.* Paris: Librarie Lecoffre.
1971 *Épître de Barnabé.* SC 172. Paris: Les Éditions du Cerf.
2001 *Commentary on the Apocalypse of St. John.* Tübingen: Mohr-Siebeck.

Prigent, P., and R. A. Kraft.

1961 *Les testimonia dans la christianisme primitif: L'épitre de Barnabe I-XVI et ses sources.* Paris: Gabalda.

Primmer, A.

1968 *Cicero Numerosus: Studien zum antiken Prosarhythmus.* Vienna and Graz: Böhlau in Kommission.

Prior, J. G.

1999 *The Historical Critical Method in Catholic Exegesis.* Rome: Pontifical Gregorian University.

Prior, M.

1989 *Paul the Letter-Writer and the Second Letter to Timothy.* JSNTSupp 23. Sheffield: JSOT.

Pritchett, W. K.

1975 *Dionysius of Halicarnassus on Thucydides.* Berkeley, Los Angeles, and London: University of California Press.

Probst, H.

1990 *Paulus und der Brief: Die Rhetorik des antiken Briefes als Form der paulinischen Korintherkorrespondenz (1 Cor. 8–10).* Tübingen: Mohr-Siebeck.

Propp, V.

1960 *The Morphology of the Folktale.* Austin: University of Texas.

1984 *Theory and History of Folktales.* Translated by A. Martin and R. Martin. Edited by A. Liberman. Minneapolis: University of Minnesota Press.

Puech, E.

1993 "The Collection of Beatitudes in Hebrew and Greek" (4Q525 1–4 and M & 5, 3–12). Pp. 353–68 in *Early Christianity in Context.* Edited by F. Manns and E. Alliata. Jerusalem: Franciscan Printing Press.

Quasten, J.

1950–60 *Patrology.* 3 vols. Utrecht and Antwerp: Spectrum.

Quinn, Jerome D.

1974 "𝔓46—The Pauline Canon?" *CBQ* 36: 379–85.

1990a "Paraenesis and the Pastoral Epistles: Lexical Observations Bearing on the Nature of the Sub-Genre and Soundings on Its Role in Socialization and Liturgies." *Semeia* 50:189–210.

1990b *The Letter to Titus.* AB 35. New York: Doubleday.

Quinn, J. D., and W. C. Wacker

1978 "The Last Volume of Luke: The Relation of Luke-Acts to the Pastoral Epistles." In Talbert (ed.) 1978, 62–75.

2000 *The First and Second Letters to Timothy.* Eerdmans Critical Commentary. Grand Rapids: Eerdmans.

Rabinowitz, P. J.

1977 "Truth in Fiction: A Reexamination of Audiences." *Critical Inquiry* 4:121–42.

1989 "Whirl without End: Audience-Oriented Criticism." In *Contemporary Literary Theory.* Edited by G. D. Atkins and L. Morrow. Amherst: University of Massachusetts Press.

Race, W. H.

1980 "Some Digressions and Returns in Greek Authors." *CJ* 76:1–8.

1982 *The Classical Priamel from Homer to Boethius.* Leiden: Brill.

Rad, G. von

1966 "The Levitical Sermon in *I and II Chronicles.*" Pp. 267–80 in *The Problem of the Hexateuch and Other Essays.* New York: McGraw-Hill.

1972 *Wisdom in Israel.* Nashville: Abingdon Press.

Radice, R., and D. T. Runia

1988 *Philo of Alexandria: An Annotated Bibliography 1937–1986.* Leiden: Brill.

Radicke, J.

1999 *Imperial and Undated Authors.* Fascicle 7 of IV A: *Biography,* of Part 4, *Biography and Antiquarian Literature* of Felix Jacoby. *FGH.* Leiden, Boston, and Cologne: Brill.

Radl, W.

1983 "Befreiung aus dem Gefängnis: die Darstellung eines biblischen Grundthemas in Apg 12." *BZ* 27:81–96.

Räisänen, H.

1990 *The 'Messianic Secret' in Mark.* Edinburgh: T. & T. Clark.

Rajak, T.

1984 *Josephus: The Historian and His Society.* Philadelphia: Fortress Press.

Ramlot, M.-L.

1964 "Les généalogies bibliques: Un genre littéraire oriental." *BVC* 60:53–70.

Rank, O., F. R. Sommerset, and A. Dundes

1990 *In Quest of the Hero.* Princeton: Princeton University Press.

Raphaell, R.

2002 "That's No Literature, That's My Bible: On James Kugel's Objections to the Idea of Biblical Poetry." JSOT 27:37–45.

Rappoport, A. S.

1937 *The Folklore of the Jews.* London: Soncino.

Rappoport, A. S., and R. Patai
1966 *Myth and Legend of Ancient Israel.* 3 vols. New York: KTAV.

Rathjen, B. D.
1959–60 "The Three Letters of Paul to the Philippians." *NTS* 6:167–73.

Reardon, B. P.
1971 *Courants littéraires Grecs des I^e et IIIe siècles après J.-C.* Paris: Les Belles Lettres.
1989 *Collected Ancient Greek Novels.* Berkeley, Los Angeles, and London: University of California Press.
1991 *The Form of the Greek Romance.* Princeton: Princeton University Press.

Reasoner, M.
1999 "The Theme of Acts: Institutional History or Divine Necessity in History?" *JBL* 118:635–59.

Reed, J. T.
1993 "Using Ancient Rhetorical Categories to Interpret Paul's Letters: A Question of Genre." In Porter and Olbricht (eds.) 1993, 297–314.
1996 "Philippians 3:1 and the Epistolary Hesitation Formulas: The Literary Integrity of Philippians, Again." *JBL* 115:63–90.
1997 "The Epistle." In Porter (ed.) 1997a, 171–93.

Reese, R. A.
2000 *Writing Jude: The Reader, the Text, and the Author in Constructs of Power and Desire.* BIS 51. Leiden: Brill.

Reeve, M. D.
1971 "Hiatus in Greek Novelists." *CQ* 21:514ff.

Regenbogen, O.
1941 "Pinax." PW 20:1409–82.

Regnault, L.
1974 "The Beatitudes in the *Apophthegmata Patrum.*" *Eastern Churches Review* 6:23–43.

Rehkopf, F.
1959 *Die lukanische Sonderquelle: Ihr Umgang und Sprachgebrauch.* WUNT 5. Tübingen: Mohr-Siebeck.

Reichelt, H.
1994 *Angelus Interpres—Texte in der Johannes-Apokalypse.* Frankfurt am Main: Peter Lang.

Reicke, B.
1964 *The Epistles of James, Peter, and Jude.* AB 37. Garden City, N.Y.: Doubleday.
2001 *Re-Examining Paul's Letters: The History of the Pauline Correspondence.* Edited by D. P. Moessner and I. Reicke. Harrisburg: Trinity Press International.

Reiling, J.
1973 *Hermas and Christian Prophecy: A Study of the Eleventh Mandate.* NovTSup 37. Leiden: Brill.

Reim, G.
1974 *Studien zum alttestamentlichen Hintergrund des Johannesevangeliums.* SNTSMS 22. Cambridge: Cambridge University Press.
1995 *Jochanan: Erweiterte Studien zum alttestamentlichen Hintergrund des Johannesevangeliums.* Erlangen: Verlag der Ev.-Luth. Mission.

Reinbold, W.
1994 *Der älteste Bericht über den Tod Jesu: literarische Analyse und historische Kritik der Passionsdarstellungen der Evangelien.* Berlin and New York: Walter de Gruyter.

Reinsch, D.
1980 "Bemerkungen zu byzantinischen Autorenhandschriften." In Harlfinger (ed.) 1980, 629–44.

Reiser, M.
1984a "Der Alexanderroman und das Markusevangelium." In Hubert Cancik (ed.) 1984, 131–64.
1984b *Syntax und Stil des Markusevangeliums im Licht der hellenistischen Volksliteratur.* WUNT 2.11. Tübingen: Mohr-Siebeck.
1999 "Die Stellung der Evangelien in der antiken Literaturgeschichte." *ZNW* 90:1–27.

Reisner, R.
1971 *Graffiti: Two Thousand Years of Wall Writing.* Chicago: Regnery.

Rendall, R.
1964 "Quotation in Scripture as an Index of Wider Reference." *EvQ* 36:214–21.

Renehan, R.
1969 *Greek Textual Criticism: A Reader.* Cambridge: Harvard University Press.
1975 *Greek Lexicographical Notes.* Hypomnemata 45. Göttingen: Vandenhoeck & Ruprecht.

Rengakos, A.
1993 *Der Homertext und die hellenistischen Dichter.* Hermes Einzelschriften 64. Stuttgart: Franz Steiner.

Rensberger, D.
1997 *1 John, 2 John, 3 John.* ANTC. Nashville: Abingdon Press.

Resch, A.
1906 *Agrapha: Ausserkanonische Schrift-*

fragmente gesammelt und untersucht. TU 15.3–4. Leipzig: J. C. Heinrichs.

Resseguie, J. L.
1998 *Revelation Unsealed: A Narrative Critical Approach to John's Apocalypse.* Leiden: Brill.

Reumann, J.
1984 "Philippians 3:20–21—A Hymnic Fragment?" *NTS* 30:593–609.
1989 "The 'Itinerary' as a Literary Form in Classical Literature and the Acts of the Apostles." In Horgan and Kobelski 1989, 335–57.

Revell, E. J.
1996 *The Designation of the Individual: Expressive Usage in Biblical Narrative.* Kampen: Kok Pharos.

Revised Common Lectionary
1992 Nashville: Abingdon Press.

Reynders, D. B.
1935 "La polémique de saint Irénée: Méthode et principes." *RTAM* 7:5–27.

Reynolds, L. D., and N. G. Wilson
1974 *Scribes and Scholars: A Guide to the Transmission of Greek and Latin Literature.* 2d ed. Oxford: Clarendon Press.

Rhoads, D.
1982 "Narrative Criticism and the Gospel of Mark." *JAAR* 50:411–34.
1994 "Jesus and the Syrophoenician Woman in Mark: A Narrative-Critical Study." *JAAR* 62:343–75.

Rhoads, D., and D. Michie
1982 *Mark as Story: An Introduction to the Narrative of a Gospel.* Philadelphia: Fortress Press.

Rhoads, D., and K. Syreeni (eds.).
1999 *Characterization in the Gospels: Reconceiving Narrative Criticism.* JSNTSup 184. Sheffield: Sheffield Academic Press.

Ribera, J.
1994 "The Targum: From Translation to Interpretation." In Beattie and McNamara (eds.) 1994, 218–25.

Richards, E. R.
1992 *The Secretary in the Letters of Paul.* WUNT 42. Tübingen: Mohr-Siebeck.
2000 "Silvanus Was Not Peter's Secretary: Theological Bias in Interpreting διὰ Σιλουανοῦ . . . ἔγραψα in 1 Peter 5:12." *JETS* 43:417–22.

Richardson, B. (ed.)
2002 *Narrative Dynamics: Essays on Time, Plot, and Frames.* Columbus: Ohio University Press.

Richardson, N. J.
1974 *The Homeric Hymn to Demeter.* Oxford: Clarendon Press.
1975 "Homeric Professors in the Age of the Sophists." *Proceedings of the Cambridge Philological Society* 21:65–81.

Richardson, P., and D. Granskou
1986 *Anti-Judaism and the Gospels.* Vol. 1: *Paul and the Gospels.* Waterloo, Ont.: Wilfrid Laurier University.

Ricoeur, P.
1975 "Biblical Hermeneutics." *Semeia* 4:29–148.
1977 *The Rule of Metaphor.* Toronto: University of Toronto Press.
1984–88 *Time and Narrative.* 3 vols. Translated by K. Blamey, K. McLaughlin, and D. Pellauer. Chicago: University of Chicago Press.

Riedweg, C.
1994 *Ps.-Justin (Markell von Ankyra?), Ad Graecos De Vera Religione (bisher "Cohortatio ad Graecos"): Einleitung und Kommentar.* 2 vols. Basel: Friedrich Reinhardt.

Riesenfeld, H.
1961 "Reflections on the Style and Theology of St. Ignatius of Antioch." *Studia Patristica* 4:312–22.

Riesner, R.
1982 "Der Ursprung der Jesus-Überlieferung." *TZ* 38:493–513.

Rigaux, B.
1962 *Saint Paul et ses lettres: État de la question.* Paris and Bruges: Desclée de Brouwer.

Riggi, C.
1987 "Lettura dell'Ad Diognetum secondo il codice F." Pp. 521–29 in *Texte und Textkritik.* Berlin: Akademie Verlag.

Riley, G. J.
1994 "The *Gospel of Thomas* in Recent Scholarship." *CurBS* 2:227–52.

Rist, J. M.
1989 *The Mind of Aristotle: A Study in Philosophical Growth.* Toronto: University of Toronto Press.

Rist, M.
1972 "Pseudepigraphy and the Early Christians." In Aune (ed.) 1972a, 75–91.

Rius-Camps, J.
1979 *The Four Authentic Letters of Ignatius, the Martyr.* Rome: Pontificium Institutum Orientalium Studiorum.
1988 "L'Epistolari d'Ignasi d'Antioquia (II): Carta d'Ignasi als Romans." *Revista Catalana de Teologia* 13:275–314.

Rizzi, M.
1989 *La questione dell' unità dell' 'Ad Diognetum'*. Milan: Università Cattolica del Sacro Cuore.

Robbins, V. K.
1975 "The We-Passages in Acts and Ancient Sea Voyages." *BR* 20:5–18.
1978 "By Land and by Sea: The We-Passages and Ancient Sea Voyages." Pp. 215–42 in *Perspectives on Luke-Acts*. Edited by C. H. Talbert. Edinburgh: T. & T. Clark.
1981a "Classifying Pronouncement Stories in Plutarch's *Parallel Lives*." *Semeia* 20:29–52.
1981b "Summons and Outine in Mark: The Three-Step Progression." *NovT* 23: 97–114.
1988a "The Chreia." In Aune (ed.) 1988, 1–23.
1988b "Pronouncement Stories from a Rhetorical Perspective." *Forum* 4:3–32.
1996a *Exploring the Texture of Texts: A Guide to Socio-Rhetorical Interpretation.* Valley Forge, Pa.: Trinity Press International.
1996b *The Tapestry of Early Christian Discourse: Rhetoric, Society and Ideology.* London: Routledge.
1998a "Socio-Rhetorical Hermeneutics and Commentary." Pp. 284–97 in *EPI-TOAYTO: Essays in Honour of Petr Podkorny—on His Sixty-Fifth Birthday.* Prague-Trebenice: Mln.
1998b "From Enthymeme to Theology in Luke 11.1–13." Pp. 191–214 in *Literary Studies in Luke-Acts: Essays in Honor of Joseph B. Tyson.* Edited by R. P. Thompson and T. E. Phillips. Macon, Ga.: Mercer University Press.

Robbins, V. K., and B. L. Mack.
1987 *Rhetoric in the Gospels: Argumentation in Narrative Elaboration.* Philadelphia: Fortress Press.

Roberts, C. H.
1954 *The Codex.* London: British Academy.
1970 "Books in the Greco-Roman World and in the New Testament." Vol. 1, pp. 48–66 in *Cambridge History of the Bible.* Cambridge: Cambridge University Press.
1979 *Manuscript, Society, and Belief in Early Christian Egypt.* London: British Academy.

Roberts, C. H., and Skeat, T. C.
1983 *The Birth of the Codex.* Oxford: Clarendon Press.

Roberts, D. H., F. M. Dunn, and D. Fowler (eds.)
1997 *Classical Closure: Reading the End of Greek and Latin Literature.* Princeton: Princeton University Press.

Roberts, J. H.
1986 "Pauline Transitions to the Letter Body." In Vanhoye (ed.) 1986.

Roberts, W. R.
1927 "Demetrius on Style." In Fyfe and Roberts (eds.) 1927, 255–487.

Robertson, D. S.
1971 *Apulée, Les Métamorphoses.* 3 vols. Paris: Société d'Édition "Les Belles Lettres."

Robinson, J. A. T.
1976 *Redating the New Testament.* Philadelphia: Westminster Press.

Robinson, J. M.
1962 "The Formal Structure of Jesus' Message." Pp. 91–110 in *Current Issues in New Testament Interpretation.* Edited by W. Klassen and G. Snyder. New York: Harper & Row.
1964 "Zur Gattung der Spruchquelle Q." Pp. 77–97 in *Zeit und Geschichte. Dankesgabe an Rudolf Bultmann.* Tübingen: Mohr-Siebeck.
1971 "Logoi Sophon: On the Gattung of Q." In Robinson and Koester (eds.) 1971, 71–113.
1972–84 *The Facsimile Edition of the Nag Hammadi Codices.* 12 vols. Leiden: Brill.
1975– *The Coptic Gnostic Library.* 17 vols. Leiden: Brill.
1978 "The Future of Papyrus Codicology." Pp. 23–70 in *The Future of Coptic Studies.* Edited by R. McL. Wilson. Coptic Studies 1. Leiden: Brill.
1979 "Codicological Analysis of Nag Hammadi Codices V and VI and Papyrus Berolinensis 8502." Pp. 9–49 in *Nag Hammadi Codices V, 2–5 and VI with Papyrus Berolinensis 8502, 1 and 4.* Edited by D. M. Parrott. NHS 11. Leiden: Brill.
1983 "The Nag Hammadi Library and the Study of the New Testament." In Logan and Wedderburn (eds.) 1983, 1–18.
1986 "On Bridging the Gulf from Q to the Gospel of Thomas (or Vice Versa)." Pp. 127–76 in *Nag Hammadi: Gnosticism and Early Christianity*. Edited by C. W. Hedrick and R. Hodgson. Peabody, Mass.: Hendrickson.
1988 *The Nag Hammadi Library in English.* Rev. ed. San Francisco: Harper & Row.
2000 *The Coptic Gnostic Library: A Complete Edition of the Nag Hammadi Codices.* 5 vols. Leiden: Brill.

Robinson, J. M., and H. Koester (eds.)
1971 *Trajectories through Early Christianity.* Philadelphia: Fortress Press.

Robinson, J. M., P. Hoffmann, and J. S. Kloppenborg (eds.)
2000 *The Critical Edition of Q.* Minneapolis: Fortress Press; Leuven: Peeters.

Robinson, T. M.
1995 *Plato's Psychology.* 2d ed. Toronto: University of Toronto Press.

Rohde, Erwin
1914 *Der griechische Roman und seine Vorläufer.* 3d ed. Leipzig: Breitkopf & Härtel.

Roller, O.
1933 *Das Formular der paulinischen Briefes: ein Beitrag zur Lehre vom antiken Briefe.* Stuttgart: Kohlhammer.

Roloff, J.
1984 *Die Offenbarung des Johannes.* Zurich: Theologischer Verlag.

Ropes, J. H.
1895 *Die Sprüche Jesu: Die in den kanonischen Evangelien nicht überliefert sind.* TU 14. Leipzig: Hinrichs.
1916 *A Critical and Exegetical Commentary on the Epistle of St. James.* ICC. Edinburgh: T. & T. Clark.

Rordorf, W.
1972 "Un chapître d'éthique judéo-chrétienne: les deux voies." *RSR* 60:109–28.
1991 "Does the Didache Contain Jesus Tradition Independently of the Synoptic Gospels?" In Wansbrough (ed.) 1991, 394–423.
1993a "Hérésie et Orthodoxie selon la Correspondance apocryphe entre les Corinthiens et l'Apôtre Paul." *Cahiers de la Revue de Théologie et de Philosophie* 17:21–63.
1993b "In welchem Verhältnis stehen die apokryphen Paulusakten zur kanonischen Apostelgeschichte und zu den Pastoralbriefen?" In Baarda (ed.) 1993.
1993c *Lex Orandi, Lex Credendi: Gesammelte Aufsätze zum 60. Geburtstag.* Paradosis 36. Freiburg, Switzerland: Universitätsverlag.
1998 "The Relation between the *Acts of Peter* and the *Acts of Paul*: State of the Question." In Bremmer (ed.) 1998, 178–91.

Rordorf, W., and A. Tuilier.
1978 *La Doctrine des Douze Apôtres (Didachè).* SC 248. Paris: Les Éditions du Cerf.

Rorty, A. O.
1996 *Essays on Aristotle's* Rhetoric. Berkeley, Los Angeles, and London: University of California Press.

Rose, H. J.
1924 "The *Clausulae* of the Pauline Corpus." *JTS* 25:17–43.

Rosenblatt, S.
1935 *The Interpretation of the Bible in the Mishnah.* Baltimore: Johns Hopkins University Press.

Rosenmeyer, P. A.
2001 *Ancient Epistolary Fictions: The Letter in Greek Literature.* Cambridge: Cambridge University Press.

Rosner, B. S.
1995 *Understanding Paul's Ethics: Twentieth Century Approaches.* Grand Rapids: Eerdmans.

Rost, L.
1971 *Einleitung in die alttestamentlichen Apokryphen und Pseudepigraphen einschliesslich der grossen Qumran-Handschriften.* Heidelberg: Quelle & Meyer.

Rousseau, A. (ed.)
1984 *Contre les hérésies: dénonciation et réfutation de la gnose au nom menteur, Irénéé de Lyon.* Paris: Éditions du Cerf.
1995 *Irénéé de Lyon: Demonstration de la prédication apostolique.* SC 406. Paris: Éditions du Cerf.

Rousseau, A., L. Doutreleau, and C. Mercier (eds.)
1965–82 *Irénéé de Lyon: Contre les hérésies.* SC 34 (replaced by 210 and 211), 100, 152, 153, 210, 211, 263, 264, 293, 294. Paris: Éditions du Cerf.

Rowe, G. O.
1997 "Style." In Porter (ed.) 1997a, 121–57.

Rowland, C.
1982 *The Open Heaven: A Study of Apocalyptic in Judaism and Early Christianity.* New York: Crossroad.

Ruch, M.
1958 *Le préambule dans les oeuvres philosophiques de Cicéron: Essai sur la genèse et l'art du dialogue.* Paris: Société d'Édition: Les Belles Lettres.

Ruckstuhl, E.
1951 *Die literarische Einheit des Johannesevangeliums: Der gegenwärtige Stand der einschlägigen Forschungen.* Freiburg: S. Paul.

Ruckstuhl, E., and P. Dschulnigg
1991 *Stilkritik und Verfasserfrage im Johannesevangelium: die johanneischen*

Sprachmerkmale auf dem Hintergrund des Neuen Testaments und des zeitgenössischen hellenistischen Schrifttums. Freiburg: Universitätsverlag; Göttingen: Vandenhoeck & Ruprecht.

Rudberg, G.
1911 "Zu den Sendschreiben der Johannes-Apokalypse." *Eranos* 11:170–79.

Rudolph, K.
1983 *Gnosis: The Nature and History of Gnosticism.* San Francisco: Harper & Row.

Ruiz, J. P.
1989 *Ezekiel in the Apocalypse: The Transformation of Prophetic Language in Revelation 16,17–19,10.* Bern: Peter Lang.

Ruiz-Montero, C.
1996 "The Rise of the Greek Novel." In Schmeling (ed.) 1996, 29–85.

Runia, D. T.
1984 "The Structure of Philo's Allegorical Treatises: A Review of Two Recent Studies and Some Additional Comments." *VC* 38:209–56.
1987 "Further Observations on the Structure of Philo's Allegorical Treatises." *VC* 41:105–38.
1993 *Philo in Early Christian Literature: A Survey.* Minneapolis: Fortress Press.
1995 *Philo and the Church Fathers: A Collection of Papers.* Leiden: Brill.

Runnalls, D. R.
1997 "The Rhetoric of Josephus." In Porter (ed.) 1997, 737–54.

Rupprecht, H.-A.
1994 *Kleine Einführung in die Papyruskunde.* Darmstadt: Wissenschaftliche Buchgesellschaft.

Russell, D. A.
1981 *Criticism in Antiquity.* Berkeley: University of California Press.
1983 *Greek Declamation.* Cambridge: Cambridge University Press.
2001 *Quintilian, The Orator's Education.* 5 vols. LCL. Cambridge: Harvard University Press.

Russell, D. A., and N. G. Wilson
1981 *Menander Rhetor.* Oxford: Clarendon Press.

Russell, D. A., and M. Winterbottom (eds.)
1972 *Ancient Literary Criticism: The Principal Texts in New Translations.* Oxford: Oxford University Press.
1989 *Classical Literary Criticism.* Oxford: Oxford University Press.

Russell, D. S.
1964 *The Method and Message of Jewish Apocalyptic.* Philadelphia: Westminster Press.
1987 *The Old Testament Pseudepigrapha: Patriarchs and Prophets in Early Judaism.* Philadelphia: Fortress Press.

Russell, R.
1982 "Pauline Letter Structure in Philippians." *JETS* 25:295–306.

Russell, W. B.
1993a "Rhetorical Analysis of the Book of Galatians, Part 1." *Bibliotheca Sacra* 150:341–58.
1993b "Rhetorical Analysis of the Book of Galatians, Part 2." *Bibliotheca Sacra* 150:416–39.

Russo, J.
1983 "The Poetics of the Ancient Greek Proverb." *JFR* 20:121–30.

Rutherford, I.
1998 *Canons of Style in the Antonine Age:* Idea-*Theory in Its Literary Context.* Oxford: Clarendon Press.

Ryan, E. E.
1982 *Aristotle's Theory of Rhetorical Argumentation.* Montréal: Les Éditions Bellarmin.

Rydbeck, L.
1967 *Fachprosa, Vermeintliche Volkssprache und Neues Testament.* Uppsala: Acta Universitatis Upsaliensis.

Ryle, H. E.
1909 *The Canon of the Old Testament.* 2d ed. London: Macmillan.

Sacks, K. S.
1983 "Historiography in the Rhetorical Works of Dionysius of Halicarnassus." *Athenaeum* 60:68–87.

Safrai, S.
1976 "Education and the Study of the Torah." Vol. 2, pp. 945–70 in *The Jewish People in the First Century.* CRINT sec. 1. Edited by S. Safrai and M. Stern. Philadelphia: Fortress Press.
1987a *The Literature of the Sages.* First Part: *Oral Tora, Halakha, Mishna, Tosefta, Talmud, External Tractates.* CRINT II.3.1. Philadelphia: Fortress Press; Assen and Maastricht: Van Gorcum.
1987b "Oral Torah." In Safrai (ed.) 1987a, 35–119.

Sagnard, F. M. M.
1951 "Y-a-t-il un plan du *Dialogue avec Tryphon*?" Pp. 171–82 in *Mélanges J.*

de Ghellinck. Vol. 1. Gembloux: J. Ducalot.

Sakalis, D. T.
1983 "Beiträge zu den Pseudo-Hippokratischen Briefen." Pp. 499–514 in *Formes de pensée dans la collection Hippocratique.* Edited by F. Lasserre and P. Mudry. Geneva: Librairie Droz.

Sale, M.
2001 "The Oral-Formulaic Theory Today." In J. Watson (ed.) 2001, 53–80.

Salveson, A.
1998 *Origen's Hexapla and Fragments: Papers Presented at the Rich Seminar on the Hexapla.* Tübingen: Mohr-Siebeck.

Sampley, J. P.
1971 *And the Two Shall Become One Flesh: A Study of Traditions in Ephesians 5:21–33.* Cambridge: Cambridge University Press.
1988 "Paul, His Opponents in 2 Corinthians 10–13, and the Rhetorical Handbooks." Pp. 162–77 in *The Social World of Formative Christianity and Judaism.* Edited by J. Neusner, P. Borgen, E. S. Frerichs and R. Horsley. Philadelphia Fortress.

Sanday, W., and A. C. Headlam
1902 *A Critical and Exegetical Commentary on the Epistle to the Romans.* ICC. 5th ed. Edinburgh: T. & T. Clark.

Sanday, W., and C. H. Turner
1923 *Novum Testamentum Sancti Irenaei Episcopi Lugdunensis.* Oxford: Clarendon Press.

Sandbach, F. H.
1969 *Plutarch's Moralia.* Vol. 15: *Fragments.* Cambridge: Harvard University Press; London: Heinemann.

Sanders, E. P.
1966 "Literary Dependence in Colossians." *JBL* 85:28–45.
1969 *The Tendencies of the Synoptic Tradition.* Cambridge: Cambridge University Press.

Sanders, J. A.
1972 *Torah and Canon.* Philadelphia: Fortress Press.

Sanders, J. N.
1943 *The Fourth Gospel in the Early Church: Its Origin and Influence on Christian Theology up to Irenaeus.* Cambridge: Cambridge University Press.

Sanders, J. T.
1962 "The Transition from Opening Epistolary Thanksgiving to Body in the Letters of the Pauline Corpus." *JBL* 81:348–62.
1966 "Paul's 'Autobiographical' Statements in Galatians 1–2," *JBL* 81:348–62.
1971 *The New Testament Christological Hymns.* SNTSMS 15. Cambridge: Cambridge University Press.

Sandmel, S.
1961 "The Haggada within Scripture." *JBL* 80:105–22.
1979 *Philo of Alexandria: An Introduction.* New York: Oxford University Press.

Sandt, H. van de, and D. Flusser
2002 *The Didache: Its Jewish Sources and Its Place in Early Judaism and Christianity.* CRINT III.5. Assen: Royal Van Gorcum; Minneapolis: Fortress Press.

Sandy, G. N.
1993 "Apuleius' 'Metamorphoses' and the Ancient Novel." *ANRW* 34/2, 1511–74.

Sandys, J. E.
1967 *A History of Classical Scholarship.* 3 vols. New York: Hafner.

Sänger, D.
2002 "'Vergeblich bemüht' (Gal. 4.11): Zur paulinischen Argumentsstrategie im Galaterbrief." *NTS* 48:377–99.

Sato, M.
1987 *Q und Prophetie: Studien zur Gattungs- und Traditionsgeschichte der Quelle Q.* WUNT 2.29. Tübingen: Mohr-Siebeck.

Sattler, W. M.
1947 "Conceptions of Ethos in Ancient Rhetoric." *Speech Monographs* 14:55–65.

Saw, I.
1995 *Paul's Rhetoric in 1 Corinthians 15: An Analysis Utilizing the Theories of Classical Rhetoric.* Lewiston, N.Y.: Mellen.

Saxer, V.
1980 *Morts, martyrs, reliques en Afrique chrétienne aux premiers siècles.* Paris: Editions Beauchesne.

Sayler, G. B.
1984 *Have the Promises Failed?* SBLDS 72. Atlanta: Scholars Press.

Scanlon, T. F.
1988 "Textual Geography in Sallust's War with Jugurtha." *Ramus* 17:138–76.

Schäferdiek, K.
1992 "The Acts of John." In *NTA,* 152–212.

Schattenmann, J.
1965 *Studien zum neutestamentlichen Prosahymnus.* Munich: Beck.

Schäublin, C.
1983 "Konversionen in antiken Dialogen?" *Catalepton. Festschrift für Bernhard*

Wyss. Edited by C. Schäublin. Basel: Seminar für Klassische Philologie.

Schechter, S.

1890 "The Riddles of Solomon in Rabbinic Literature." *Folklore* 1:349–58.

Scheer, T. S.

1993 *Mythische Vorväter: Zur Bedeutungen griechischer Heroenmythen im Selbstverständnis kleinasiatischer Städte.* Munich: Maris.

Schenk, W.

1969 "Der 1. Korintherbrief als Briefsammlung." *ZNW* 60:219–43.

1984 *Die Philipperbriefe des Paulus.* Stuttgart: Kohlhammer.

Schenke, H.-M.

1984 "The Mystery of the Gospel of Mark." *SecCent* 4:65–82.

1998 *On the Compositional History of the Gospel of Thomas.* Institute for Antiquity and Christianity Occasional Papers 40. Claremont, Calif.: Institute for Antiquity and Christianity.

Schenke, L.

1971 *Studien zur Passionsgeschichte des Markus: Tradition und Redaktion in Markus 14,1–42.* Würzburg: Echter Verlag; Stuttgart: Katholisches Bibelwerk.

Schenker, A.

1982 *Psalmen in den Hexapla: Erste kritische und vollständige Ausgabe der hexaplarischen Fragmente auf dem Rande der Handschrift Ottobonianus graecus 398 zu den Ps. 24–32.* Vatican: Biblioteca apostolica vaticana.

Schenkeveld, D. M.

1964 *Studies in Demetrius on Style.* Amsterdam: A. M. Hakkert.

Schepens, G.

1997 "Jacoby's *FrGrHist*: Problems, Methods, Prospects." In Most (ed.) 1997, 144–72.

Schermann, T.

1914–16 *Die allgemeine Kirchenordnung, frühchristliche Liturgien und kirchliche Überlieferung.* Paderborn: F. Schöningh.

Schierling, S. P., and M. J. Schierling

1978 "The Influence of the Ancient Romances on Acts of the Apostles." *Classical Bulletin* 54:81–88.

Schiffman, L. H.

1994 *Reclaiming the Dead Sea Scrolls.* Philadelphia and Jerusalem: Jewish Publication Society.

Schiffman, L. H., and J. C. VanderKam (eds.)

2000 *Encyclopedia of the Dead Sea Scrolls.* 2 vols. New York: Oxford University Press.

Schiffman, L. H., E. Tov, and J. C. VanderKam (eds.)

2000 *The Dead Sea Scrolls: Fifty Years after Their Discovery: Proceedings of the Jerusalem Congress, July 20–25, 1997.* Jerusalem: Israel Exploration Society and the Shrine of the Book.

Schiffman, L., and M. D. Swartz

1992 *Hebrew and Aramaic Incantation Texts from the Cairo Geniza: Selected Texts from Taylor-Schechter Box K1.* Sheffield: Sheffield Academic Press.

Schildgen, B. D.

1998 *Crisis and Continuity: Time in the Gospel of Mark.* Sheffield: Sheffield Academic.

Schille, G.

1959 "Die Fragwürdigkeit eines Itinerars der Paulusreisen." *TLZ* 84:165–74.

Schippers, R.

1966 "The Pre-Synoptic Tradition in 1 Thessalonians II 13–16." *NovT* 8:223–34.

Schlecht, J.

1901 *Doctrina XII apostolorum: Die Apostellehre in der Liturgie der katholischen Kirche.* Freiburg im Breisgau: Herder.

Schlier, H.

1962 *Der Brief an die Galater.* KEK. 12th ed. Göttingen: Vandenhoeck & Ruprecht.

Schlunk, R. R.

1974 *The Homeric Scholia and the Aeneid: A Study of the Influence of Ancient Literary Criticism on Vergil.* Ann Arbor: University of Michigan Press.

Schmeling, G. L. (ed.)

1996 *The Novel in the Ancient World.* Mnemosyne 159. Leiden: Brill.

Schmeller, T.

1987 *Paulus und die "Diatribe": Eine vergleichende Stilinterpretation.* Münster: Aschendorf.

2001 *Schulen im Neuen Testament? Zur Stellung des Urchristentums in der Bildungswelt seiner Zeit.* Freiburg, Basel, Vienna, Barcelona, Rome, and New York: Herder.

Schmid, W.

1887–97 *Der Atticismus in seinen Hauptvetretern.* 4 vols. Stuttgart: W. Kohlhammer.

Schmid, W.

1959 *Über die klassische Theorie und Praxis des antiken Prosarhythmus.* Wiesbaden: F. Steiner.

Schmid, W., and O. Stählin

1920–29 *Geschichte der griechischen Literatur.*

Part 1 (1929); part 2, vol. 1, 6th ed., 1920; part 2, vol. 2, 6th ed., 1924. Munich: C. H. Beck.

Schmidt, A.
1989 "Zwei Anmerkungen zu P.Ryl III." *Archiv für Papyrusforschung* 35:11–12.

Schmidt, C.
1903 *Die alten Petrusakten im Zusammenhang der apokryphen Apostelliteratur nebst einem neuentdeckten Fragment.* Leipzig: Hinrichs.
1905 *Acta Pauli: Übersetzung, Untersuchungen, und koptischer Text.* 2. Aufl. Leipzig: Hinrichs.
1930 "Zur Datierung der alten Petrusakten." *ZNW* 29:150–55.
1936 ΠΡΑΞΕΙΣ ΠΑΥΛΟΥ*: Acts Pauli nach dem Papyrus der Hamburger Staats- und Universitätsbibliothek.* Glückstadt and Hamburg: J. J. Augustin.

Schmidt, D. D.
1991 "Semitisms and Septuagintalisms in the Book of Revelation." *NTS* 37:592–603.
1999 "Rhetorical Influences and Genre: Luke's Preface and the Rhetoric of Hellenistic Historiography." In Moessner (ed.) 1999, 27–60.

Schmidt, J. M.
1976 *Die jüdische Apokalyptik: die Geschichte ihrer Erforschung von den Anfängen bis zu den Textfunden von Qumran.* 2d ed. Neukirchen-Vluyn: Neukirchener Verlag.

Schmidt, K. L.
1919 *Der Rahmen der Geschichte Jesu.* Berlin: Trowitsch.
1923 "Die Stellung der Evangelien in der allgemeinen Literaturgeschichte." Pp. 50–134 in *Eucharisterion. Hermann Gunkel zum 60. Geburtstag.* Edited by H. Schmidt. Göttingen: Vandenhoeck & Ruprecht.

Schmithals, W.
1960 "Zur Abfassung und Ältesten Sammlung der paulinischen Hauptbriefe." *ZNW* 51:225–45.
1964 "Die Thessalonicherbriefe als Briefkompositonen." *Zeit und Geschichte: Festschrift R. Bultmann.* Edited by E. Dinkler. Tübingen: Mohr-Siebeck.
1965 "Die historische Situation der Thessalonicherbriefe." Pp. 89–157 in *Paulus und die Gnostiker: Untersuchungen zu den kleinen Paulusbriefen.* TF 35. Hamburg-Bergstedt: Herbert Reich.
1969 "Die Korintherbriefe als Briefsammlung." *ZNW* 60:219–43.
1971 *Gnosticism in Corinth: An Investigation of the Letters to the Corinthians.* Translated by J. E. Steely. Nashville and New York: Abingdon Press.
1972 "On the Composition and Earliest Collection of the Major Epistles of Paul." Pp. 239–74 in *Paul and the Gnostics.* Translated by J. E. Steely. Nashville and New York: Abingdon Press.
1975 *Der Römerbrief als historisches Problem.* Gütersloh: Gerd Mohn.

Schnackenburg, R.
1968–82 *The Gospel according to St. John.* 3 vols. New York: Crossroad.
1992 *The Johannine Epistles.* Translated by R. and I. Fuller. New York: Crossroad.

Schneemelcher, W.
1964 "Paulus in der griechischen Kirche des zweiten Jahrhunderts." *ZKG* 75:1–20.
1991–92 *New Testament Apocrypha.* 2 volumes. Translated by R. McL. Wilson. Louisville: Westminster John Knox Press.

Schneeweiss, G.
1912 *Der Protrepticos des Aristoteles.* Munich: C. Wolf & Sohn.

Schneider, C.
1954 *Geistesgeschichte des antiken Christentums.* Munich: C. H. Beck 1954.

Schneider, G.
1973 *Die Passion Jesu nach den drei älteren Evangelien.* Munich: Kösel.
1980–82 *Die Apostelgeschichte.* 2 vols. Freiburg, Basel, Vienna: Herder.

Schneider, N.
1970 *Die rhetorische Eigenart der paulinischen Antithese.* Tübingen: Mohr-Siebeck.

Schnelle, U.
1995 "Die johanneische Schule." Pp. 198–217 in *Bilanz und Perspektiven gegenwärtiger Auslegung des Neuen Testaments: Symposion zum 65. Geburtstag von Georg Strecker.* Edited by F. Horn. BZNW 75. Berlin: Walter de Gruyter.
1998 *The History and Theology of the New Testament Writings.* Translated by M. E. Boring. Minneapolis: Fortress.

Schnider, F., and W. Stenger
1979 "Die Frauen im Stammbaum Jesu nach Mattäus: Strukturale Beobachtungen zu Mt. 1, 1–17." *BZ* 23.2:187–96.
1987 *Studien zum Neutestamentlichen Briefformular.* NTTS 11. Leiden: Brill.

Schoedel, W. R.
1959 "Philosophy and Rhetoric in the *Adversus Haereses* of Irenaeus." *VC* 13:22–32.

1972 *Legatio and De Resurrectione.* Oxford: Oxford University Press.
1984 "Theological Method in Irenaeus (*Adversus Haereses* 2.25–28)." *JTS* n.s. 35:31–49.
1985 *Ignatius of Antioch: A Commentary on the Letters of Ignatius of Antioch.* Philadelphia: Fortress Press.
1989 "The Apostolic Fathers." In Epp and MacRae 1989, 457–98.

Schoedel, W. R., and R. L. Wilken (eds.)
1979 *Early Christian Literature and the Classical Intellectual Tradition: In Honorem Robert M. Grant.* Paris: Éditions Beauchesne.

Scholer, D. M.
1971 *Nag Hammadi Bibliography: 1948–1969.* NHS 1. Leiden: Brill.
1997 *Nag Hammadi Bibliography: 1970–1994.* NHMS 32. Leiden: Brill.

Scholes, R. E.
1982 *Semiotics and Interpretation.* New Haven, Conn.: Yale University Press.

Scholes, R. E., and R. Kellogg.
1966 *The Nature of Narrative.* New York: Oxford University Press.

Schöllgen, G.
1985 "Die Didache—ein frühes Zeugnis für Landgemeinden?" *ZNW* 76:140–43.
1991 *Didache—Zwölf-Apostel-Lehre. Einleitung, Übersetzung, und Kommentar.* Freiburg: Herder.
1996 "The Didache as a Church Order: An Examination of the Purpose for the Composition of the Didache and Its Consequences for Interpretation." In Draper (ed.) 1996, 43–71.

Schoon-Jansen, J.
1991 *Umstrittene "Apologien" in den Paulusbriefen: Studien zur rhetorischen Situation des 1. Thessalonicherbriefes, des Galaterbriefes und des Philipperbriefes.* Göttingen: Vandenhoeck & Ruprecht.
2000 "On the Use of Elements of Ancient Epistolography in 1 Thessalonians." In Donfried and Beutler (eds.) 2000, 179–93.

Schrage, W.
1964 *Das Verhältnis des Thomas-Evangeliums zur synoptischen Tradition und zu den koptischen Evangelienübersetzungen.* BZNW 29. Berlin: Töpelmann.
1974 "Leid, Kreuz und Eschaton: Die Peristasenkataloge als Merkmale paulinischer theologia crucis und Eschatologie." *EvT* 34:141–75.
1991–2001 *Der erste Brief an die Korinther.* EKKNT. 4 vols. Neukirchen-Vluyn: Neukirchener Verlag, Zürich and Braunschweig: Benziger Verlag.
1995 "The Formal Ethical Interpretation of Pauline Paraenesis." In Rosner (ed.) 1995, 301–35.

Schreiber, J.
1969 *Die Markuspassion: Wege zur Erforschung der Leidengeschichte Jesu.* Hamburg: Furche.

Schröder, B.-J.
1999 *Titel und Text: Zur Entwicklung lateinischer Gedichtüberschriften. Mit Untersuchungen zu lateinischen Buchtiteln, Inhaltsverzeichnissen und anderen Gliederungsmitteln.* Berlin and New York: Walter de Gruyter.

Schröger, F.
1968 *Der Verfasser des Hebräerbriefes als Schriftausleger.* Regensburg: F. Pustet.

Schubart, W.
1962 *Das Buch bei den Griechen und Römern.* 3d ed. Edited by Erberhard Paul. Heidelberg: Lambert Schneider.
1966 *Palaeographie.* Munich: C. H. Beck.

Schubert, P.
1939 *Form and Function of the Pauline Thanksgivings.* BZNW 20. Berlin: Töpelmann.

Schuchard, B. G.
1992 *The Interrelationship between Form and Function in the Explicit Old Testament Citations in the Gospel of John.* SBLDS 133. Atlanta: Scholars.

Schuller, E.
1993 "Prayer, Hymnic and Liturgical Texts from Qumran." In Ulrich and VanderKam (eds.) 1993, 153–71.

Schürer, E.
1973–87 *The History of the Jewish People in the Age of Jesus Christ.* Revised by G. Vermes et al. 3 vols. Edinburgh: T. & T. Clark.

Schüssler Fiorenza, E.
1976 *Aspects of Religious Progaganda in Judaism and Early Christianity.* Notre Dame: University of Notre Dame Press.
1977 "Composition and Structure of the Book of Revelation." *CBQ* 39:344–66.
1987 "Rhetorical Situation and Historical Reconstruction in 1 Corinthians." *NTS* 33:386–403.

Schwartz, D. R.
1990 *Agrippa I: Last King of Judea.* Tübingen: Mohr-Siebeck.

Schwartz, E.
1888 *Tatiani oratio ad Graecos.* TU 4.1. Leipzig: Hinrichs.
1907 "Aporien im vierten Evangelium." Pp. 342–72 in *Nachrichten von der königlichen Gesellschaft der Wissenschaften zu Göttingen,* Göttingen: Dieterich.
1908 "Aporien im vierten Evangelium." Pp. 115–88, 497–560 in *Nachrichten von der königlichen Gesellschaft der Wissenschaften zu Göttingen,* Gottingen: Dieterich.

Schwartz, S.
1990 *Josephus and Judaean Politics.* Leiden: Brill.

Schweizer, E.
1965 *Ego eimi: die religionsgeschichtliche Herkunft und theologische Bedeutung der johanneischen Bildreden, zugleich ein Beitrag zur Quellenfrage des vierten Evangeliums.* 2d ed. FRLANT, n.s. 38. Göttingen: Vandenhoeck & Ruprecht.
1972–73 "Formgeschichtliches zu den Seligpreisungen Jesu." *NTS* 19:121–26.
1976 *Der Brief an die Kolosser.* EKK. Zürich, Einsiedeln, Köln: Benziger Verlag; Neukirchen-Vluyn: Neukirchener Verlag.
1979 "Traditional Ethical Patterns in the Pauline and Post-Pauline Letters and Their Development (Lists of Vices and Housetables)." Pp. 195–209 in *Text and Interpretation: Studies in the NT Presented to Matthew Black.* Edited by E. Best and R. McL. Wilson. Cambridge: Cambridge University Press.
1982 *The Letter to the Colossians.* London: SPCK.

Schwenn, F.
1927 *Gebet und Opfer.* Heidelberg: C. Winter.

Schwyzer, E.
1950–71 *Griechische Grammatik auf der Grundlage von Karl Brugmanns griechischer Grammatik.* 4 vols. Munich: C. H. Beck.

Scobie, A.
1983 *Apuleius and Folklore.* London: Folklore Society.

Scott, B. B.
1989 *Hear Then the Parable: A Commentary on the Parables of Jesus.* Minneapolis: Fortress Press.

Scott, C. T.
1965 *Persian and Arabic Riddles: A Language-Centered Approach to Genre Definition.* Bloomington: Indiana University Press.

Scott, K.
1936 *The Imperial Cult under the Flavians.* Stuttgart and Berlin: W. Kohlhammer.

Scourfield, J. H. D.
1993 *Consoling Heliodorus: A Commentary on Jerome "Letter 60".* Oxford: Clarendon Press.

Searby, D. M.
1998 *Aristotle in the Greek Gnomological Tradition.* Uppsala: Uppsala Universitetet.

Seeck, O.
1906 *Die Briefe des Libanius zeitlich geordnet.* TU 30. Leipzig: Hinrichs.

Seeligmann, I. L.
1948 *The Septuagint Version of Isaiah.* Leiden: Brill.
1953 "Voraussetzungen der Midraschexegese." Pp. 150–81 in *Congress Volume: Copenhagen 1953.* VTSup 1. Leiden: Brill.

Segal, A.
1980 "Heavenly Ascent in Hellenistic Judaism, Early Christianity, and Their Environment." *ANRW* II, 23/2, 1333–94.
1990 *Paul the Convert: The Apostolate and Apostasy of Saul the Pharisee.* New Haven, Conn: Yale University Press.

Segbroeck, F. van, and C. Tuckett (eds.)
1993 *The Four Gospels 1992: Festschrift Frans Neirynck.* 3 vols. Leuven: Peeters.

Segovia, F.
1991 *The Farewell of the Word: The Johannine Call to Abide.* Minneapolis: Fortress Press.

Seid, T. W.
1999 "Synkrisis in Hebrews 7: The Rhetorical Structure and Strategy." Porter and Stamps (eds.) 1999, 322–47.

Sellew, P.
1988 "Beelzebul in Mark 3: Dialogue, Story, or Sayings Cluster?" *Forum* 4.3:93–108.
1992 "Interior Monologues as a Narrative Device in the Parables of Jesus." *JBL* 111:239–53.
1994 "Laodiceans and the Philippians Fragments Hypothesis." *HTR* 87:17–28.

Sellin, G.
1990 "1 Korinther 5–6 und der 'Vorbrief' nach Korinth: Indizien für eine Mehrschichtigkeit von Kommunikationsakten im ersten Korintherbrief." *NTS* 37:535–58.

Selwyn, E. G.
1947 *The First Epistle of St Peter.* 2d ed. London: Macmillan.

Senior, D.
1975 *The Passion Narrative according to Matthew.* BETL 39. Leuven: Leuven University.
1984 *The Passion of Jesus in the Gospel of Mark.* Wilmington, Del.: Michael Glazier.

Sensig, T. R.
1996 "Towards a Definition of Paraenesis." *RQ* 38:145–58.

Sevenster, J. N.
1968 *Do You Know Greek? How Much Greek Could the First Jewish Christians Have Known?* NovTSup 19. Leiden: Brill.

Sevrin, J.-M. (ed.)
1989 *The New Testament in Early Christianity / La réception des écrits néotestamentaires dans le christianisme primitif.* BETL 86. Leuven: Leuven University.

Sharrock, A.
2000 "Intratextuality: Texts, Parts, and (W)holes in Theory." In Sharrock and Morales 2000, 1–39.

Sharrock, A., and H. Morales (eds.)
2000 *Intratextuality: Greek and Roman Textual Relations.* Oxford: Oxford University Press.

Shaw, G.
1983 *The Cost of Authority: Manipulation and Freedom in the New Testament.* Philadelphia: Fortress Press; London: SCM.

Sheeley, S. M.
1988 "Narrative Asides and Narrative Authority in Luke–Acts." *BTB* 18:102–17.
1992 *Narratives Asides in Luke–Acts.* Sheffield: JSOT.

Shepherd, M. H.
1956 "The Epistle of James and the Gospel of Matthew." *JBL* 75:40–51.

Shepherd, T.
1994 "The Narrative Function of Markan Intercalation." *NTS* 41:522–40.

Sherk, R. K.
1967 *Roman Documents from the Greek East: Senatus Consulta and Epistulae to the Age of Augustus.* Baltimore: John Hopkins University Press.

Sherwin-White, A. N.
1966 *The Letters of Pliny: A Historical and Social Commentary.* Oxford: Clarendon Press.

Shotwell, W. A.
1965 *The Biblical Exegesis of Justin Martyr.* London: SPCK.

Shroyer, M. J.
1936 "Alexandrian Jewish Literalists." *JBL* 55:261–84.

Shuler, P. L.
1982 *A Genre for the Gospels: The Biographical Character of Matthew.* Philadelphia: Fortress Press.

Shuvola, J., and T. Engberg-Pedersen (eds.)
1998 *The Emotions in Hellenistic Philosophy.* Dordrecht: Kluwer.

Sider, J. W.
1983 "Rediscovering the Parables: The Logic of the Jeremias Tradition." *JBL* 102:61–83.
1995 *Interpreting the Parables.* Grand Rapids: Zondervan.

Sieben, H. J.
1978 "Die Ignatianen als Briefe: Einige formkritische Bemerkungen." *VC* 32:1–18.

Siegert, F.
1980 *Drei hellenistisch-jüdische Predigten: Ps.-Philon, 'Über Jona,' 'Über Simson.'* WUNT 20. Tübingen: Mohr-Siebeck.
1985 *Argumentation bei Paulus gezeigt an Röm. 9 bis 11.* WUNT 34. Tübingen: Mohr-Siebeck.
1993 "Mass Communication and Prose Rhythm in Luke–Acts." In Porter and Olbricht (eds.) 1993, 42–58.

Sigountos, J. G.
1994 "The Genre of 1 Corinthians 13." *NTS* 40:246–60.

Silberman, L. H.
1961 "Unriddling the Riddle: A Study of the Structure and Language of the Habakkuk Pesher." *RevQ* 3:323–64.

Silverstein, T., and A. Hilhorst
1997 *Apocalypse of Paul: A New Critical Edition of Three Long Latin Versions.* Cahiers d'Orientalisme 21. Geneva: Cramer.

Simonetti, M.
1995 *Biblical Interpretation in the Early Church: An Historical Introduction to Patristic Exegesis.* Edinburgh: T. & T. Clark.

Simpson, M.
1976 *Gods and Heroes of the Greeks: The Library of Apollodorus.* Amherst: University of Massachusetts Press.

Sinclair, P.
1993 "The *Sententia* in *Rhetorica ad Herennium*: A Study in the Sociology of Rhetoric." *AJP* 114:561–80.

Sjöberg, E.
1946 *Der Menschensohn im äthiopischen Henochbuch.* Lund: Gleerup.

Skarsaune, O.
1976 "The Conversion of Justin Martyr." *ST* 30:53–73.
1987 *The Proof from Prophecy. A Study in Justin Martyr's Proof-Text Tradition: Text-Type, Provenance, Theological Profile.* NovTSup 56. Leiden: Brill.

Skeat, T. C.
1956 "The Use of Dictation in Ancient Book-Production." *Proceedings of the British Academy* 42:179–208.
1970 "Early Christian Book-Production: Papyri and Manuscripts." In vol. 1, pp. 54–79 of *Cambridge History of the Bible.* Cambridge: Cambridge University Press.
1979 "Especially the Parchments: A Note on 2 Timothy 4:13." *JTS* 30:173–77.
1982 "The Length of the Papyrus Roll and the Cost Advantage of the Codex." *ZPE* 45:169–75.
1997 "The Oldest Manuscript of the Four Gospels?" *NTS* 43:1–34.

Skydsgaard, J. E.
1968 *Varro the Scholar.* Copenhagen: E. Munksgaard.

Slater, W. J.
1983 "Lyric Narrative: Structure and Principle." *CA* 2:117–32.

Sleeper, C. F.
1998 *James.* Nashville: Abingdon Press.

Slingerland, H. D.
1977 *The Testaments of the Twelve Patriarchs: A Critical History of Research.* Missoula, Mont.: Scholars Press.

Slusser, M.
1992 "Silent Reading in Antiquity." *JBL* 111:499.

Smid, H. R.
1965 *Protevangelium Jacobi: A Commentary.* Assen: Van Gorcum.

Smit, J.
1989 "The Letter of Paul to the Galatians: A Deliberative Speech." *NTS* 35:1–26.
1991 "The Genre of 1 Corinthians 13 in the Light of Classical Rhetoric." *NovT* 33:193–216.
1993 "Argument and Genre of 1 Corinthians 12–14." In Porter and Olbricht (eds.) 1993, 211–30.

Smith, B.
1921 "Gorgias: A Study in Oratorical Style." *QJS* 7:335–59.

Smith, D. E.
2002 *The Canonical Function of Acts: A Comparative Analysis.* Collegeville, Minn.: Liturgical Press.

Smith, D. M.
1965 *The Composition and Order of the Fourth Gospel.* Yale: Yale University.
1972 "The Use of the Old Testament in the New." In *The Use of the Old Testament in the New and Other Essays.* Edited by J. Efird. Durham, N.C.: Duke University Press.
1976a "The Milieu of the Johannine Miracle Source: A Proposal." Pp. 164–88 in *Jews, Greeks, and Christians: Religious Cultures in Late Antiquity. Essays in Honor of W. D. Davies.* Edited by R. Hamerton-Kelley and R. Scroggs. Leiden: Brill.
1976b "The Setting and Shape of a Johannine Narrative Source." *JBL* 95:231–41.
1981 "John and the Synoptics: Some Dimensions of the Problem." *NTS* 27:287–94.
1988 "The Pauline Literature." In Carson and Williamson (eds.) 1988, 265–91.

Smith, J. P.
1952 *St. Irenaeus: Proof of the Apostolic Preaching.* ACW 16. Westminster: Newman; London: Longmans, Green.

Smith, J. Z.
1975 "Good News Is No News: Aretalogy and Gospel." In Neusner (ed.) 1975, 1.21–38.
1982 *Imagining Religion: From Babylon to Jonestown.* Chicago and London: University of Chicago Press.

Smith, M.
1971 "Prolegomena to a Discussion of Aretalogies, Divine Men, the Gospels, and Jesus." *JBL* 90:174–99.
1973a *Clement of Alexandria and a Secret Gospel of Mark.* Cambridge: Harvard University Press.
1973b *The Secret Gospel: The Discovery and Interpretation of the Secret Gospel according to Mark.* New York: Harper & Row.
1978 *Jesus the Magician.* New York: Harper & Row.
1979 "Relations between Magical Papyri and Magical Gems." *Papyrologica Bruxellensia* 18:129–36.
1982 "Clement of Alexandria and Secret Mark: The Score at the End of the First Decade." *HTR* 75:449–61.
1983 "On the History of ΑΠΟΚΑΛΥΠΤΩ and ΑΠΟΚΑΛΥΨΙΣ." Hellholm (ed.) 1983, 9–20.
1986 "The Jewish Elements in the Magical Papyri." Pp. 455–62 in *Society of Biblical Literature 1986 Seminar Papers.*

Edited by Kent H. Richards. Atlanta: Scholars Press.

Smith, R. W.
1974 *The Art of Rhetoric in Alexandria: Its Theory and Practice in the Ancient World.* The Hague: Nijhoff.

Smith, W. S.
1993 "Style and Character in the 'Golden Ass': 'Suddenly and Opposite Appearance.'" *ANRW* 34/2, 1575–99.

Smit Sibinga, J.
1963 *The Old Testament Text of Justin Martyr.* Vol. 1: *The Pentateuch.* Leiden: Brill.

Smulders, P.
1981 "De echte Ignatius?" *Bijdragen* 42:300–308.

Smyth, H. W.
1956 *Greek Grammar.* Revised by G. M. Messing. Cambridge: Harvard University Press.

Snell, B.
1938 *Leben und Meinungen der Sieben Weisen.* Munich: E. Heimeran.

Snodgrass, K.
1989–90 "The Gospel of Thomas: A Secondary Gospel." *SecCent* 7:19–38.
1997 "*Aneideia* and the Friend at Midnight (Luke 11:8)." *JBL* 116:505–13.

Snyder, G. F.
1976–77 "The *Tobspruch* in the New Testament." *NTS* 23:117–20.

Snyman, A. H.
1984 "Style and Meaning in Romans 8:31–9." *Neot* 18:94–103.
1988 "Style and the Rhetorical Situation of Romans 8:31–39." *NTS* 34:218–31.
1993 "Persuasion in Philippians 4.1–20." In Porter and Olbricht (eds.) 1993, 325–37.

Snyman, A. H., and J. v. W. Conje
1986 "Toward a New Classification of the Figures (ΣΧΗΜΑΤΑ) in the Greek New Testament." *NTS* 32:113–21.

Soards, M. L.
1987 *The Passion according to Luke: The Special Material of Luke 22.* JSNTSup 14. Sheffield: JSOT.
1991 "Oral Tradition before, in, and outside the Canonical Passion Narratives." In Wansbrough (ed.) 1991, 334–50.
1994a *The Speeches of Acts: Their Content and Concerns.* Louisville, Ky.: Westminster John Knox Press.
1994b "The Speeches in Acts in Relation to Other Pertinent Ancient Literature." *ETL* 70:65–90.

Söder, R.
1932 *Die apocryphen Apostelgeschichten und die romanhafte Literatur der Antike.* Stuttgart: Kohlhammer.

Solmsen, F.
1931 "ΠΕΡΙ ΕΡΜΕΝΕΙΑΣ und sein peripatetisches Quellenmaterial." *Hermes* 66:241–67.
1974 "The Aristotelian Tradition in Ancient Rhetoric." In Erickson (ed.) 1974, 278–309, reprinted from *AJP* 62 (1941):35–50, 167–90.
1976 "Review of *Studies in the Philosophy of Aristotle's Rhetoric,* by William M. A. Grimaldi, S.J.," *Classical Philology* 71:175.

Sommer, B. D.
1996 "The Scroll of Isaiah as Jewish Scripture, Or, Why Jews Don't Read Books." In *SBLSP 1996,* 225–42.

Soskice, J. M.
1985 *Metaphor and Religious Language.* Oxford: Clarendon Press.

Sowers, S. G.
1965 *The Hermeneutics of Philo and Hebrews.* Richmond: John Knox Press.

Sparks, H. D. F.
1984 *The Apocryphal Old Testament.* Oxford: Clarendon Press.

Spencer, A. B.
1984 *Paul's Literary Style.* Jackson: Evangelical Theological Society.

Spengel, L.
1853–4 *Rhetores Graeci.* 2 vols. Leipzig: Teubner.

Speyer, W.
1971 *Die literarische Fälschung im heidnischen und christlichen Altertum: Ein Versuch ihrer Deutung.* Handbuch der klassischen Altertumswissenschaft I.2. Munich: Beck.
1976 "Genealogy." Vol. 9, cols. 1145–1268 in *RAC.* Edited by T. Klauser. Stuttgart: Anton Hiersemann.
1989 "Religiöse Pseudepigraphie und literarische Fälschung im Altertum." Pp. 21–58 in *Frühes Christentum im antiken Strahlungsfeld.* Tübingen: Mohr-Siebeck.
1993 *Italienische Humanisten als Kritiker der Echtheit antiker und christlicher Literatur.* Mainz: Akademie der Wissenschaften und der Literatur; Stuttgart: F. Steiner.

Spicq, C.
1969 *Les Épîtres Pastorales.* Paris: Gabalda.

Spolsky, B.
1983 "Triglossia and Literacy in Jewish Palestine of the First Century." *International Journal of the Sociology of Language* 42:95–109.

Sprute, J.
1975 "Topos und Enthymem in der aristotelischen Rhetorik." *Hermes* 103:78.
1982 *Die Enthymemtheorie in der aristotelischen Rhetorik.* Göttingen: Vandenhoeck & Ruprecht.

Stadelmann, L.
1970 *The Hebrew Conception of the World.* Rome: Pontifical Biblical Institute.

Stadter, P. A.
1989 *A Commentary on Plutarch's Pericles.* Chapel Hill and London: University of North Carolina Press.

Stadter, P. A. (ed.)
1973 *The Speeches in Thucydides.* Chapel Hill: University of North Carolina Press.

Staley, J. L.
1988 *The Print's First Kiss: A Rhetorical Investigation of the Implied Reader in the Fourth Gospel.* SBLDS 82. Atlanta: Scholars Press.

Stamps, D. L.
1995 "Rhetorical Criticism of the New Testament: Ancient and Modern Evaluations of Argumentation." In Porter and Tombs (eds.) 1995, 129–69.

Standaert, B.
1986 "La rhétorique ancienne dans Saint Paul." In Vanhoye 1986.

Stanford, W. B.
1967 *The Sound of Greek: Studies in the Greek Theory and Practice of Euphony.* Berkeley and Los Angeles: University of California Press.

Staniforth, M. (trans.).
1968 *Early Christian Writings: The Apostolic Fathers.* New York: Penguin Books.

Stanley, C. D.
1990 "Paul and Homer: Greek and Roman Citation Practice in the First Century A.D." *NovT* 32:48–78.
1992 *Paul and the Language of Scripture: Citation Technique in the Pauline Epistles and Contemporary Literature.* SNTSMS 74. Cambridge: Cambridge University Press.

Stanley, K.
1993 *The Shield of Homer: Narrative Structure in the Iliad.* Princeton, N.J.: Princeton University Press.

Stanton, G.
1974 *Jesus of Nazareth in New Testament Preaching.* SNTSMS 27. Cambridge: Cambridge University Press.
1985 "Aspects of Early Christian-Jewish Polemic and Apologetic." *NTS* 31:377–92.
1987 *The Gospels and Jesus.* Oxford: Oxford University Press.
1992 "Matthew: *BIBLOS, EUAGGELION,* or *BIOS.* In Van Segbroeck et al. 1992, 1187–1201.
1999 "The Fourfold Gospel." In Ferguson (ed.) 1999, 1–30.

Stanton, V. H.
1901 "The 'Gospel of Peter': Its Early History and Character Considered in Relation to the History of the Recognition in the Church of the Canonical Gospels." *JTS* 2:1–25.

Staratt, A. B.
1952 *The Use of the Septuagint in the Five Books against the Heresies by Irenaeus of Lyons.* Ph.D. diss., Harvard University.

Stauffer, E.
1955 *New Testament Theology.* London: SCM Press.

Steele, E. S.
1984 "Luke 11:37–54—a Modified Hellenistic Symposium?" *JBL* 103:379–94.

Steele, T.
1990 *Missing Measures: Modern Poetry and the Revolt against Meter.* Fayetteville: University of Arkansas Press.

Stegemann, H.
1967 "Weitere Stücke von 4QpPsalm 37, von 4QPatriarchal Blessings and Hinweis auf eine unedierte Handschrift aus Höhle 4Q mit Exzerpten aus dem Deuteronomium." *RevQ* 6:193–227.

Stegemann, W.
1999 "Lukas." *DNP* 7:491–93.

Stegner, W. R.
1988 "The Ancient Jewish Synagogue Homily." In Aune (ed.) 1988, 51–69.

Steimer, B.
1992 *Vertex Traditionis: Die Gattung der altchristlichen Kirchenordnung.* BZNW 63. Berlin and New York: Walter de Gruyter.

Stein, M.
1992 *Definition und Schilderung in Theophrasts Charakteren.* Beiträge zur Altertumskunde 28. Stuttgart: B. G. Teubner.

Stein, R. H.
1981 *Introduction to the Parables of Jesus.* Philadelphia: Westminster Press.

Steinrück, M.
1992 *Rede und Kontext: zum Verhältnis von Person und Erzähler in frühgriechischen Texten.* Bonn: R. Habelt.

Stemberger, G.
1996 *Introduction to the Talmud and Midrash.* 2d ed. Edinburgh: T. & T. Clark.

Stendahl, K.
1968 *The School of St. Matthew and Its Use of the Old Testament.* 2d ed. Philadelphia: Fortress Press.

Stenger, W.
1974 "Timotheus und Titus als literarische Gestalten (Beobachtungen zur Form und Funktion der Pastoralbriefe)." *Kairos* 16:252–67.

Stephens, S.
1996 "Fragments of Lost Novels." In Schmeling (ed.) 1996, 655–83.

Stephens, S., and J. Winkler (eds.)
1995 *Ancient Greek Novels: The Fragments.* Princeton: Princeton University Press.

Sterling, G.
1992 *Historiography and Self-Definition: Josephos, Luke–Acts, and Apologetic Historiography.* NovTSup 64. Leiden: Brill.

Sternberg, M.
1985 *Poetics of Biblical Narrative: Ideological Literature and the Drama of Reading.* Bloomington: Indiana University Press.

Stettler, C.
2000 *Der Kolosserhymnus: Untersuchungen zu Form, traditionsgeschichtlichem Hintergrund und Aussage von Kol 1.15–20.* WUNT 2.131. Tübingen: Mohr-Siebeck.

Steudel, A.
1992 "4QMidrEschat: 'A Midrash on Eschatology." In Trebolle Barrera and Vegas Montaner 1992, 531–41.
1993 "אחרית הימים in the Texts from Qumran." *RevQ* 16:225–45.
1994 *Der Midrasch zur Eschatologie aus der Qumrangemeinde (4QMidrEschat*^{a,b}*).* STDJ 13. Leiden: Brill.

Stibbe, M. W. G. (ed.)
1992 *John as Storyteller: Narrative Criticism and the Fourth Gospel.* SNTSMS 73. Cambridge: Cambridge University Press.
1993 *The Gospel of John as Literature: An Anthology of Twentieth-Century Perspectives.* NTTS 17. Leiden: Brill.

Stierlin, H.
1972 *La vérité sur l'Apocalypse: Essai de reconstitution des textes originels.* Paris: Buchet-Chastel.

Stirewalt, M. L., Jr.
1991 "The Form and Function of the Greek Letter-Essay." In Donfried (ed.) 1991, 141–71.
1993 *Studies in Ancient Greek Epistolography.* SBLRBS 27. Atlanta: Scholars Press.
2002 *Paul the Letter Writer.* Grand Rapids: Eerdmans.

Stock, A.
1984 "Chiastic Awareness and Education in Antiquity." *BTB* 17:70–74.

Stone, M. E.
1976 "Lists of Revealed Things in the Apocalyptic Literature." In *Magnalia Dei: The Mighty Acts of God.* Edited by F. M. Cross, W. E. Lemke, and P. D. Miller Jr. Garden City, N.Y.; Doubleday.
1984a "Apocalyptic Literature." In Stone (ed.) 1984, 383–441.
1990 *Fourth Ezra: A Commentary on the Book of Fourth Ezra.* Minneapolis: Fortress Press.
1991 *Selected Studies in Pseudepigrapha and Apocrypha with Special Reference to the Armenian Tradition.* Leiden: Brill.
1992 *A History of the Literature of Adam and Eve.* Early Judaism and Its Literature 3. Atlanta: Scholars Press.

Stone, M. E. (ed.)
1984 *Jewish Writings of the Second Temple Period: Apocrypha, Pseudepigrapha, Qumran Sectarian Writings, Philo, Josephus.* CRINT 2, 2. Philadelphia: Fortress Press; Assen: Van Gorcum.

Stone, M., and E. Chazon (eds.)
1998 *Biblical Perspectives: Early Use and Interpretation of the Bible in Light of the Dead Sea Scrolls: Proceedings of the First International Symposium of the Orion Center for the Study of the Dead Sea Scrolls and Associated Literature, 12–14 May 1966.* STDJ 28. Leiden: Brill.

Stoops, R. F. (ed.)
1997 *The Apocryphal Acts of the Apostles in Intertextual Perspectives. Semeia* 80. Atlanta: Scholars Press.

Stowers, S. K.
1981 *The Diatribe and Paul's Letter to the*

Romans. SBLDS 57. Chico, Calif.: Scholars Press.

1984a "Social Status, Public Speaking, and Private Teaching: The Circumstances of Paul's Preaching Activity." *NovT* 26:59–82.

1984b "Paul's Dialogue with a Fellow Jew in Romans 3:1–9." *CBQ* 46:707–22.

1986 *Letter Writing in Greco-Roman Antiquity.* Philadelphia: Westminster Press.

1987 "Text as Interpretation: Paul and Ancient Readings of Paul." In Neusner and Frerichs (ed.) 1987, 17–27.

1988 "The Diatribe." In Aune (ed.) 1988, 71–84.

1990 "*Peri men gar* and the Integrity of 2 Cor. 8 and 9." *NovT* 32:340–48.

1994 *A Rereading of Romans: Justice, Jews, and Gentiles.* New Haven, Conn.: Yale University Press.

1995 "Romans 7.7–25 as a Speech-in-Character (προσωποποιΐα)." In Engberg-Pedersen (ed.) 1995, 180–202.

Strandhartinger, A.

1999 *Studien zur Entstehungsgeschichte und Intention des Kolosserbriefs.* NovTSup 94. Leiden: Brill.

Strecker, G.

1995 "Die Anfänge der johanneische Schule." *NTS* 32:31–47.

1996 *The Johannine Letters.* Translated by L. M. Maloney. Hermeneia. Minneapolis: Fortress Press.

1997 *History of New Testament Literature.* Translated by C. Katter. Harrisburg, Pa.: Trinity Press International.

Streeter, B. H.

1930 *The Four Gospels: A Study of Origins.* Rev. ed. London: Macmillan.

Strenger, W.

1974 "Timotheus und Titus als literarische Gestalten." *Kairos* 16:252–67.

Strobel, A.

1969 "Schreiben des Lukas? Zum sprachlichen Problem der Pastoralbriefe." *ZNW* 15:191–210.

Stroker, W. D.

1981 "Examples of Pronouncement Stories in Early Christian Apocryphal Literature." *Semeia* 20:133–41.

1988 "Extracanonical Parables and the Historical Jesus." *Semeia* 44:95–120.

1989 *Extracanonical Sayings of Jesus.* SBLRBS, 18. Atlanta: Scholars Press.

Strycker, É. de

1977 "Notes sur l'abréviation des *nomina sacra* dans des manuscrits hagiographiques grecs." In Treu (ed.) 1977, 461–68.

Stuhlmacher, P.

1977 *Historical Criticism and Theological Interpretation of Scripture: Toward a Hermeneutics of Consent.* Philadelphia: Fortress Press.

Stuhlmacher, P. (ed.)

1983 *Das Evangelium und die Evangelien.* Tübingen: Mohr-Siebeck.

1991 *The Gospel and the Gospels.* Grand Rapids: Eerdmans.

Stylianopoulos, T.

1975 *Justin Martyr and the Mosaic Law.* Missoula, Mont.: Scholars Press.

Suggs, M. J.

1972 "The Christian Two-Ways Tradition: Its Antiquity, Form, and Function." In Aune (ed.), 1972, 60–74.

Suhl, Alfred

1965 *Die Funktion der alttestamenltichen Zitate und Anspielungen im Markusevangelium.* Gütersloh: Gerd Mohn.

Sullivan, J. P.

1985 *Literature and Politics in the Age of Nero.* Ithaca and London: Cornell University Press.

Sumney, J. L.

1990 "The Bearing of a Pauline Rhetorical Pattern on the Integrity of 2 Thessalonians." *ZNW* 81:192–204.

2001 "Paul's Use of Πάθος in His Argument against the Opponents of 2 Corinthians." Olbricht and Sumney (eds.) 2001:147–60.

Sundberg, A. C.

1959 "On Testimonies." *NovT* 3:268–81.

1964 *The Old Testament in the Early Church.* HTS 20. Cambridge: Harvard University Press.

Süss, W.

1910 *Ethos: Studien zur älteren griechischen Rhetoric.* Leipzig and Berlin: B. G. Teubner.

Sussman, L.

1987 *The Major Declamations Ascribed to Quintilian: A Translation.* Frankfurt am Main.

1994 *The Declamations of Calpurnius Flaccus: Text, Translation, and Commentary.* Leiden: Brill.

Suter, D. W.

1979 *Tradition and Composition in the Parables of Enoch.* SBLDS 47. Missoula, Mont.: Scholars Press.

1981 "Mashal in the Similitudes of Enoch." *JBL* 100:193–212.

Swain, S.

1996 *Hellenism and Empire: Language, Classicism, and Power in the Greek World, A.D. 50–250.* Oxford: Oxford University Press.

1999a "Defending Hellenism: Philostratus, *In Honour of Apollonius.*" In Edwards, Goodman, Price, and Rowland (eds.) 1999, 157–96.

1999b *Oxford Readings in the Greek Novel.* New York and Oxford: Oxford University Press.

Swete, H. B.

1892 *The Apocryphal Gospel of Peter: The Greek Text of the Newly Discovered Fragment.* London: Macmillan.

Swetnam, J.

1969 "On the Literary Genre of the 'Epistle' to the Hebrews." *NovT* 11:261–69.

Swift, R. C.

1984 "The Theme and Structure of Philippians." *BSac* 141:234–54.

Sykes, A. S.

1999 *The Lamb's High Feast.* VCSup 42. Leiden: Brill.

Sykutris, J.

1924 "Epistolographie." Cols. 185–220 in *Realencyclopädie der classischen Altertumswissenschaft.* Supplement 5. Stuttgart: J. B. Metzler.

Syme, R.

1959 "Proconsuls d'Afrique sous Antonin le Pieux." *REA* 61:310–19.

Synge, F. C.

1959 *Hebrews and the Scriptures.* London: SPCK.

Tabor, J. D.

1986 *Things Unutterable: Paul's Ascent to Paradise in its Graeco-Roman, Judaic, and Early Christian Contexts.* Lanham, Md., and New York: University Press of America.

Taeger, F.

1957 *Charisma: Studien zur Geschichte des antiken Herrscherkultes.* Stuttgart: W. Kohlhammer.

Talbert, C. H.

1966 *Luke and the Gnostics.* Nashville: Abingdon Press.

1974 *Literary Patterns, Theological Themes, and the Genre of Luke–Acts.* Missoula, Mont.: Scholars Press.

1977 *What Is a Gospel? The Genre of the Canonical Gospels.* Philadelphia: Fortress Press.

1980 "Prophecies of Future Greatness: The Contributions of Greco-Roman Biographies to an Understanding of Luke 1:5–4:15." Pp. 129–42 in *The Divine Helmsman: Studies of God's Control of Human Events, Presented to Lou H. Silberman.* Edited by J. L. Crenshaw and S. Sandmel. New York: KTAV.

1982 *Reading Luke: A Literary and Theological Commentary on the Third Gospel.* New York: Crossroad.

1996 "The Acts of the Apostles: Monograph or Bios?" In Witherington (ed.) 1996, 58–72.

Talbert, C. H. (ed.)

1978 *Perspectives on Luke–Acts.* Edinburgh: T. & T. Clark.

Talmon, S.

1966 "The 'Desert Motif' in the Bible and in Qumran Literature." Pp. 31–63 in *Biblical Motifs: Origins and Transformations.* Edited by A. Altmann. Cambridge: Harvard University Press.

Tannehill, R.

1981a "Introduction: The Pronouncement Story and Its Types." *Semeia* 20:1–13.

1981b "Varieties of Synoptic Pronouncement Stories." *Semeia* 20:101–19.

1986–90 *The Narrative Unity of Luke–Acts.* 2 vols. Philadelphia: Fortress Press.

Taylor, A.

1976 *The Literary Riddle before 1600.* Originally printed in 1948. Westport: Greenwood.

Taylor, C.

1901 "Hermas and Cebes." *Journal of Philology* 27:276–319.

1903a "Hermas and Cebes." *JP* 28:24–38.

1903b "Note on Hermas and Cebes—A Reply," *JP* 28:94–98.

Taylor, J.

1992 "Ancient Texts and Modern Critics: Acts 15:1–34." *RB* 99:373–83.

Taylor, L. R.

1931 *The Divinity of the Roman Emperor.* Philological Monographs 2. Middletown: American Philological Association.

Taylor, V.

1926 *Behind the Third Gospel: A Study of the Proto-Luke Hypothesis.* Oxford: Clarendon Press.

1935 *The Formation of the Gospel Tradition.* 2d ed. London: Macmillan.

1966 *The Gospel according to St. Mark.* 2d ed. London: Macmillan.

1972 *The Passion Narrative of St. Luke.* Edited by O. E. Evans. SNTSMS 19.

Cambridge: Cambridge University Press.

Tcherikover, V. A.
1956 "Jewish Apologetic Literature Reconsidered." *Eos* 48:169–93.

Teeple, H. M.
1962 "Methodology in Source Analysis of the Fourth Gospel." *JBL* 81:279–86.
1974 *The Literary Origin of the Gospel of John.* Evanston: Religion and Ethics Institute.

Telford, W. R.
1992 "The Pre-Markan Tradition in Recent Research (1980–1990)." In Van Segbroeck et al. (eds.) 1992, 2:693–723.

Tenney, M. C.
1960 "The Footnotes of John's Gospel." *BSac* 117:350–64.

Terry, R. B.
1992 "Some Aspects of the Discourse Structure of the Book of James." *Journal of Translation and Textlinguistics* 5:106–25.

Testuz, M.
1959 *Papyrus Bodmer X-XII.* Cologny-Geneva: Bibliothèque Bodmer.
1960a "La correspondance apocryphe de saint Paul et des Corinthiens." Pp. 217–23 in *Littérature et théologie pauliniennes.* Leuven: Desclée de Brouwer.
1960b *Papyrus Bodmer XIII Meliton de Sardes Homilie sur la Paque.* Geneva: Bibliotheca Bodmeriana.

Thatcher, T.
1993 "A New Look at Asides in the Fourth Gospel." *BSac* 151:428–38.
1999 "The Sabbath Trick: Unstable Irony in the Fourth Gospel." *JSNT* 76:53–77.
2000 *The Riddles of Jesus in John: A Study in Tradition and Folklore.* SBLMS 53. Atlanta: Society of Biblical Literature.

Theissen, G.
1974 *Urchristliche Wundergeschichten: Ein Beitrag zur formgeschichtlichen Erforschung der synoptischen Evangelien.* SNT 8. Gütersloh: Gerd Mohn.

Theron, D. J.
1958 *The Evidence of Tradition.* Grand Rapids: Baker Book House.

Thiel, H. van
1992 "Zenodot, Aristarch, und Andere." *ZPE* 90:1–32.
1997 "Der Homertext in Alexandria." *ZPE* 115:13–36.

Thiselton, A. C.
2000 *The First Epistle to the Corinthians.* NIGTC. Grand Rapids: Eerdmans.

Thomas, R.
1989 *Oral Tradition and Written Record in Classical Athens.* Cambridge: Cambridge University Press.
1992 *Literacy and Orality in Ancient Greece.* Cambridge: Cambridge University Press.
1993 "Performance and Written Publication in Herodotus and the Sophistic Generation." In Kullmann and Althoff (eds.) 1993, 225–44.

Thomas, R. F.
1999 *Reading Virgil and His Texts: Studies in Intertextuality.* Ann Arbor: University of Michigan.

Thompson, A. L.
1977 *Responsibility for Evil in the Theodicy of 4 Ezra.* Missoula, Mont.: Scholars Press.

Thompson, E. M.
1901 *A Handbook of Greek and Latin Palaeography.* Oxford: Clarendon.

Thompson, J. W.
2001 "Paul's Argumentation from *Pathos* in 2 Corinthians." In Olbricht and Sumney (eds.) 2001, 127–45.

Thompson, L. S.
1952 "A Cursory Survey of Maledictions." *Bulletin of the New York Public Library* 56:55–74.

Thompson, M.
1991 *Clothed with Christ: The Example and Teaching of Jesus in Romans 12.1–15.13.* JSNTSup 59. Sheffield: JSOT.

Thompson, Steven
1985 *The Apocalypse and Semitic Syntax.* SNTSMS 52. Cambridge: Cambridge University Press.

Thompson, Stith
1955 *Motif Index of Folk Literature.* 6 vols. Rev. ed. Bloomington: Indiana University Press.

Thompson, W. N.
1974 "*Stasis* in Aristotle's *Rhetoric.*" In Erickson (ed.) 1974, 267–77.

Thomson, I. H.
1995 *Chiasmus in the Pauline Letters.* JSNTS 111. Sheffield: Sheffield Academic.

Thornton, C.-J.
1993 "Justin und das Markusevangelium." *ZNW* 84:93–110.

Thraede, K.
1970 *Grundzüge griechisch-römischer Brieftopik.* Zetemata 48. Munich: Verlag C. H. Beck.
1980 "Zum historischen Hintergrund der 'Haustafeln' des NT." Pp. 359–68 in E. Dassmann and K. S. Frank (eds.).

Pietas: Festschrift für B. Kotting. Münster: Aschendorff.

Thrall, M.
1977 "The Problem of II Cor vi.14–vii.1 in Some Recent Discussion." *NTS* 24:132–48.
1994 *A Critical and Exegetical Commentary on 2 Corinthians.* ICC. Edinburgh: T. & T. Clark.

Thurén, L.
1990 *The Rhetorical Strategy of 1 Peter: With Special Regard to Ambiguous Expressions.* Åbo: Åbo Akademis Förlag.
1995 *Argument and Theology in 1 Peter: The Origins of Christian Paraenesis.* JSNTSup 114. Sheffield: Sheffield Academic.
1996 "Style Never Goes Out of Fashion: 2 Peter Re-Evaluated." In Porter and Olbricht (eds.) 1996, 329–47.
1999 "Was Paul Angry? Derhetorizing Galatians." Porter and Stamps (eds.) 1999:302–320.

Thyen, H.
1955 *Der Stil der jüdisch-hellenistischen Homilie.* FRLANT, n.F. 47. Göttingen: Vandenhoeck & Ruprecht.

Tidball, D.
1984 *The Social Context of the New Testament: A Sociological Analysis.* Grand Rapids: Zondervan.

Tigchelaar, E. J. C.
1996 *Prophets of Old and the Day of the End: Zechariah, the Book of Watchers and Apocalyptic.* Oudtestamentische Studien 35. Leiden: Brill.

Tilborg, S. van
1996 *Reading John in Ephesus.* NovTSup 83. Leiden: Brill.

Tiller, P. A.
1993 *A Commentary on the Animal Apocalypse of 1 Enoch.* Atlanta: Scholars Press.

Tischendorf, K. von (ed.)
1852 *Codex Claromontanus sive Epistulae Pauli Omnes Graece et Latine.* Leipzig: Brockhaus.
1966 *Apocalypses Apocryphae.* 1866; reprint, Leipzig: Georg Olms, Hildesheim.

Titus, E. L.
1959 "Did Paul Write 1 Corinthians 13?" *JBR* 27:299–302.

Tobin, T.
1990 "4Q185 and Jewish Wisdom Literature." In Attridge, Collins, and Tobin (eds.) 1990, 145–52.

Todorov, T.
1978 *Symbolism and Interpretation.* Ithaca, N.Y.: Cornell University Press.

Tolbert, M. A.
1989 *Sowing the Gospel: Mark's World in Literary-Historical Perspective.* Minneapolis: Fortress Press.

Tolmie, D. F.
1999 *Narratology and Biblical Narratives: A Practical Guide.* San Francisco, London, and Bethesda: International Scholars Publications.

Tompkins, J. P.
1980 *Reader-Response Criticism.* Baltimore and London: Johns Hopkins University Press.

Too, Y. L.
1998 *The Idea of Ancient Literary Criticism.* Oxford: Clarendon Press.

Torijano, P. A.
2002 *Solomon the Esoteric King: From King to Magus, Development of a Tradition.* JSJSupp 73. Leiden: Brill.

Torm, F.
1932 "Die Psychologie der Pseudonymität im Hinblick auf die Literatur des Urchristentums." In *Pseudepigraphie in der heidnischen und jüdisch-christlichen Antike.* Gütersloh: Bertelsmann.

Torrey, C. C.
1911 "The Authorship and Character of the So-called 'Epistle to the Hebrews.'" *JBL* 30:137–56.

Tov, E.
1986 "Recensional Differences between the MT and LXX of Ezekiel." *ETL* 52:89–101.
1995 "Excerpted and Abbreviated Biblical Texts from Qumran." *RevQ* 16:581–600.
1997 *The Text-Critical Use of the Septuagint in Biblical Research.* 2d ed. Jerusalem: Simor.

Tovey, D.
1997 *Narrative Art and Act in the Fourth Gospel.* JSNTSup 151. Sheffield: Sheffield Academic.

Towner, W. S.
1973 *The Rabbinic 'Enumeration of Scriptural Examples.'* SPB 22. Leiden: Brill.

Traill, D. A.
1981 "Ring Composition in Catullus 64." *CJ* 76:232–42.

Traube, L.
1907 *Nomina Sacra: Versuch einer Geschichte der christlichen Kürzung.* Munich: Beck.

Travis, S. H.
1973 "Paul's Boasting in 2 Corinthians 10–12," *Studia Evangelica* 6:527–32.

Trebolle Barrera, J., and L. Vegas Montaner (eds.)
1992 *The Madrid Qumran Congress: Proceedings of the International Congress on the Dead Sea Scrolls, Madrid 18–21 March 1991.* STDJ 12. Leiden: Brill.

Trenker, S.
1958 *The Greek Novella in the Classical Period.* Cambridge: Cambridge University Press.

Trevett, C.
1984 "Anomaly and Consistency: Josep Rius-Camps on Ignatius and Matthew." *VC* 38:165–71.

Trites, A. A.
1974 "The Importance of Legal Scenes and Language in the Book of Acts." *NovT* 16:278–84.

Trobisch, D.
1989 *Die Entstehung der Paulusbrief Sammlung.* Göttingen: Vandenhoeck & Ruprecht.
1994 *Paul's Letter Collection: Tracing the Origins.* Minneapolis: Fortress Press.
1996 *Die Endredaktion des Neuen Testaments: Eine Untersuchung zur Entstehung der christlichen Bibel.* NTOA 31. Freiburg: Universitätsverlag; Göttingen: Vandenhoeck & Ruprecht.

Trocmé, E.
1975 *The Formation of the Gospel according to Mark.* Philadelphia: Westminster Press.
1984 *The Passion as Liturgy: A Study in the Origin of the Passion Narratives in the Four Gospels.* London: SCM.

Tsuji, M.
1997 *Glaube zwischen Vollkommenheit und Verweltlichung: Eine Untersuchung zur literarischen Gestalt und zur inhaltlichen Kohärenz des Jakobusbriefes.* WUNT 2.93. Tübingen: Mohr-Siebeck.

Tuckett, C.
1984 *Synoptic Studies: The Ampleforth Conferences of 1982 and 1983.* JSNTSup 7. Sheffield: JSOT.
1988 "Thomas and the Synoptics." *NovT* 30:132–57.
1995 *Luke's Literary Achievement: Collected Essays.* JSNTSup 116. Sheffield: Sheffield Academic.
1996a *Q and the History of Earliest Christianity: Studies on Q.* Peabody, Mass.: Hendrickson.
1996b "Synoptic Tradition in the Didache." In Draper (ed.) 1996, 92–128.

Tugwell, S.
1990 *The Apostolic Fathers.* Harrisburg, Pa.: Morehouse.

Turner, E. G.
1977 *The Typology of the Early Codex.* Philadelphia: University of Pennsylvania Press.
1980 *Greek Papyri: An Introduction.* 2d ed. Oxford: Clarendon Press.

Turner, H. E. W.
1954 *The Pattern of Christian Truth: A Study in the Relations between Orthodoxy and Heresy in the Early Church.* London: Mowbray.

Turner, J. D., and A. McGuire (eds.)
1997 *The Nag Hammadi Library after Fifty Years: Proceedings of the 1995 Society of Biblical Literature Commemoration.* NHMS 44. Leiden: Brill.

Turner, N.
1976 *Style.* Vol. 4 of *A Grammar of New Testament Greek.* Edinburgh: T. & T. Clark.

Übelacker, W. G.
1989 *Der Hebräerbrief als Appell.* I. *Untersuchungen zu* exordium, narratio *und* postscriptum *(Hebr. 1–2 und 13,22–25).* Lund: Almqvist & Wiksell.
1994 "Hebr. 7:1–10—dess struktur och funktion i foerfattarens retoriska argumentation." *Mellom tid och evighet, Religio* 42:217–20.

Ueding, G.
2000 *Klassische Rhetorik.* 3. Aufl. Munich: C. H. Beck.

Uhlig, S.
1984 *Das äthopische Henochbuch.* Gütersloh: Gütersloher Verlagshaus Gerd Mohn.

Ulmer, R.
1997 "The Advancement of Arguments in Exegetical Midrash Compared to that of the Greek Diatribe." *JSJ* 28:48–91.

Ulrich, E.
1999 *The Dead Sea Scrolls and the Origins of the Bible.* Grand Rapids: Eerdmans.

Ulrich, E., and J. C. VanderKam (eds.)
1993 *The Community of the Renewed Covenant.* Notre Dame: University of Notre Dame Press.

Ulrichsen, J. H.
1991 *Die Grundschrift der Testamente der zwölf Patriarchen: Eine Untersuchung zu Umfang, Inhalt und Eigenart der*

ursprünglichen Schrift. Stockholm: Almqvist & Wiksell.

Unger, D. J., and J. J. Dillon (trans.)
1992 *Irenaeus, Against the Heresies.* Book 1. ACW 55. Westminster: Newman; London: Longmans, Green.

Ungern-Sternberg, A. F. von
1913 *Der traditionelle alttestamentliche Schriftbeweis "de Christo" und "de Evangelio" in der alten Kirche bis zur Zeit Eusebs von Caesaria.* Halle an der Saale: Niemeyer.

Usener, H.
1887 *Epicurea.* Leipzig: Teubner.

Valantasis, R.
1997 *The Gospel of Thomas.* New York and London: Routledge.

Valette, P.
1960 *Apulée, Apologie—Florides.* Paris: Société d'Édition "Les Belles Lettres."

Valk, M. van der
1949 *Textual Criticism of Homer.* Leiden: A. W. Sijthoff.

Vallée, G.
1980 "Theological and Non-theological Motives in Irenaeus's Refutation of the Gnostics." Pp. 174–85 in *Jewish and Christian Self-Definition. Vol. 1. The Shaping of Christianity in the Second and Third Centuries.* Edited by E. P. Sanders. Philadelphia: Fortress Press.
1981 *A Study in Anti-Gnostic Polemics: Irenaeus, Hippolytus, and Epiphanes.* Studies in Christianity and Judaism 1. Waterloo, Ont.: Wilfrid Laurier University Press.

van Belle, G.
1975 *De Semeia-Bron in het Vierde Evangelie.* Leuven: Peeters.
1985 *Les Parenthéses dan L'évangile de Jean: Aperçu historique et classification.* Leuven: Peeters.
1992 "Les parentheses johanniques." In Segbroeck and Tuckett 1992, 1901–33.
2001 "Prolepsis in the Gospel of John." *NovT* 43:334–47.

van Cangh, J.-M.
1972a "La Galilée dans l'évangile de Marc: un lieu théologique?" *Rivista Biblica* 79:59–75.
1972b "Les sources de l'Évangile: les collections pré-marciennes de miracles." *Revue Théologique de Louvain* 3:76–85.

van der Horst, P. W.
1990 "Chariton and the New Testament." In van der Horst and Mussies, *Studies on the Hellenistic Background of the New Testament.* Den Haag: CIP-Gegenens Koninklijke Bibliotheek.
1991 *Ancient Jewish Epitaphs: An Introductory Survey of a Millennium of Jewish Funerary Epigraphy (300 B.C.E.–700 C.E.).* Kampen: Kok Pharos Publishing House.
1992 "Ezekiel the Tragedian." *ADB* 2:709.
1994 "Silent Prayer in Antiquity." *Numen* 41:1–25.

VanderKam, J. C.
1973 "The Theophany of Enoch 3b-7, 9." *VT* 23:129–50.
1977 *Textual and Historical Studies in the Book of Jubilees.* HSM 14. Missoula, Mont.: Scholars Press.
1981 "Intertestamental Pronouncement Stories." *Semeia* 20:65–72.
1983 "1 Enoch 77, 3 and a Babylonian Map of the World." *RevQ* 11:271–78.
1984 *Enoch and the Growth of an Apocalyptic Tradition.* CBQMS 16. Washington, D.C.: Catholic Biblical Association of America.
1992 "Righteous One, Messiah, Chosen One, and Son of Man in 1 Enoch 37–71." In Charlesworth (ed.) 1992, 169–91.
1993 "Biblical Interpretation in *1 Enoch* and *Jubilees.*" In Charlesworth and Evans (eds.) 1993, 96–125.
1994 *The Dead Sea Scrolls Today.* Grand Rapids: Eerdmans.
1995 *Enoch: A Man for All Generations.* Columbia: University of South Carolina Press.
1996 "1 Enoch, Enochic Motifs, and Enoch in Early Christian Literature." In VanderKam and Adler (eds.) 1996, 33–101.

VanderKam, J., and W. Adler (eds.)
1996 *The Jewish Apocalyptic Heritage in Early Christianity.* CRINT 3/4. Minneapolis: Fortress Press.

Van der Valk, M. H. A.
1957 "On the Edition of Books in Antiquity." *VC* 11:1ff.

Van Dyke Parunak, H.
1983 "Transitional Techniques in the Bible." *JBL* 102:525–48.

Van Groningen, B. A.
1963 "ΕΚΔΟΣΙΣ," *Mnemosyne* 16:1–17.
1965 "General Literary Tendencies in the Second Century A.D." *Mnemosyne* 18:41ff.

Vanhoye, A.
1962 "L'utilisation du livre d'Ezéchiel dans l'Apocalypse." *Biblica* 43:436–76.
1976 *La structure littéraire de l'Épitre aux*

Hébreux. 2d ed. Paris: Desclée de Brouwer.
1986 *L'Apôtre Paul: Personnalité, style et conception du ministère.* BETL 73. Leuven: Leuven University Press.

Van Noppen, J.-P., and E. Hols
1990 *Metaphor II: A Classified Bibliography of Publications 1985–1990.* Philadelphia: John Benjamin.

Van Noppen, J.-P., S. De Knop, and R. Jongen
1985 *Metaphor: A Bibliography of Post-1970 Publications.* Philadelphia: John Benjamins.

Van Ophuijsen, J. M.
2001 *Alexander of Aphrodisias On Aristotle's "Topics 1".* Ithaca: Cornell University Press.

Van Otterlo, W. A. A.
1944 "Untersuchungen über Begriff, Anwendung und Entstehung der griechischen Ringkomposition." *Mededeelingen der Kon. Nederlandse Akademie van Wetenschappen,* Afd. Letterkunde, nieuwe Reeks, Deel 7, No. 3. Amsterdam.

Van Oyen, Geert
1992 "Intercalation and Irony in the Gospel of Mark." In Van Segbroeck et al. (eds.) 1992, 2:949–74.

Van Segbroeck, F., C. M. Tuckett, G. Van Belle, and J. Verheyden (eds.)
1992 *The Four Gospels 1992: Festschrift Frans Neirynck.* 3 vols. Leuven: University Press.

Van Sickle, J.
1980 "The Book-Roll and Some Conventions of the Poetic Book," *Arethusa* 13:10–12.

Vansina, J.
1985 *Oral Tradition as History.* Madison: University of Wisconsin Press.

Van Unnik, W. C.
1961 "ἡ καινὴ διαθήκη: A Problem in the Early History of the Canon." *Studia Patristica* 4 = TU 79:212–27.
1970 "Studies over de zogenaande eerste brief van Clemens. I. Het Litteraire Genre." *Mededelingen der koninklijke Nederlandse akademie van wetenschappen, afd. letterkunde* 33:149–204.

Vatz, R.
1973 "The Myth of the Rhetorical Situation." *PR* 6:154–61.

Verbrugghe, G. P.
1989 "On the Meaning of *Annales,* on the Meaning of Annalist." *Philologus* 133:192–230.

Verdenius, W. J.
1983 "The Principles of Greek Literary Criticism." *Mnemosyne* 36:14–59.

Verheyden, J. (ed.)
1999a *The Unity of Luke-Acts.* BETL 142. Leuven: University Press; Peters.
1999b "The Unity of Luke-Acts: What Are We Up To?" In Verheyden (ed.) 1999a, 3–56.

Vermes, G.
1975 "The Qumran Interpretation of Scripture in Its Historical Setting." *Post-Biblical Jewish Studies.* SJLA 8. Leiden: Brill.
1993 *Scripture and Tradition in Judaism: Haggadic Studies.* Studia post-biblica 4. Leiden: Brill.
1997 *The Complete Dead Sea Scrolls in English.* New York: Penguin.

Vermeule, C. C.
1974 *The Goddess Roma in the Age of the Roman Empire.* 2d ed. London: Spink & Son.

Vernant, J. P.
2001 *The Universe, the Gods, and Men: Ancient Greek Myths.* New York: HarperCollins.

Verner, D.
1984 *The Household of God: The Social World of the Pastoral Epistles.* SBLDS 71. Chico, Calif.: Scholars Press.

Vetschera, R.
1911–12 *Zur griechischen Paränes.* Smichow and Prague: Rohlicek und Sievers.

Veyne, P.
1988 *Did the Greeks Believe Their Myths? An Essay on the Constitutive Imagination.* Chicago: University of Chicago Press.

Vicent Cernuda, A.
1997 "El testimonio Flaviano, alarde de solapada ironia." *Estudios Biblicos* 55:355–85, 479–508.

Vickers, B.
1988 *In Defence of Rhetoric.* Oxford: Clarendon Press.

Vielhauer, P.
1975 *Geschichte der urchristlichen Literatur: Einleitung in das Neue Testament, die Apokryphen und die apostolischen Väter.* Berlin and New York: Walter de Gruyter.

Vines, M. E.
2002 *The Problem of the Markan Genre: The Gospel of Mark and the Jewish Novel.* Atlanta: Society of Biblical Literature.

Vinson, R. B.
1991 "A Comparative Study of the Use of

Enthymemes in the Synoptic Gospels." In Watson 1991, 119–41.

Violet, B.
1910 *Die Ezra-Apokalypse.* GCS 18, 32. Leipzig: J. C. Hinrichs.

Vlastos, G.
1991 *Socrates: Ironist and Moral Philosopher.* Cambridge: Cambridge University Press.

Voelz, J.
1995 "Multiple Signs, Aspects of Meaning, and Self as Texts: Elements of Intertextuality." *Semeia* 69:149–64.

Vogel, F.
1923 "Die Kürzenmeidung in der griechischen Prosa des IV. Jahrhunderts." *Hermes* 58:109.

Vogt, H. J.
1999 *Origenes als Exeget.* Paderborn: Schöningh.

Vögtle, A.
1936 *Die Tugend- und Lasterkataloge exegetisch, religions- und formgeschichtlich untersucht.* Münster: Aaschendorff.

Volkmann, R.
1885 *Die Rhetorik der Griechen und Römer in systematischer Übersicht.* 2. Aufl. Leipzig: B. G. Teubner. Reprinted, Hildesheim: Georg Olms Verlag, 1987.

Vollmer, H. A.
1896 *Die alttestamentlichen Citate bei Paulus, textkritisch und biblisch-theologisch gewürdigt nebst einem Anhang über das Verhältnis des Apostles zu Philo.* Freiburg and Leipzig: Mohr-Siebeck.

Von der Goltz, E.
1897 *Ignatius von Antiochien als Christ und Theologe.* TU 12. Berlin: Akademie-Verlag.

Von Lips, H.
1990 *Weisheitliche Traditionen im Neuen Testament.* WMANT 64. Neukirchen-Vluyn: Neukirchener Verlag.

von Wahlde, U. C.
1976 "A Redactional Technique in the Fourth Gospel." *CBQ* 38:520–33.
1989 *The Earliest Version of John's Gospel: Recovering the Gospel of Signs.* Wilmington: Michael Glazier.

Vööbus, Arthur
1979 *The Didascalia Apostolorum in Syriac.* 4 vols.; CSCO 401, 402, 407, 408. Leuven: Secrétariat du Corpus SCO.

Vorster, J. N.
1994 "The Context of the Letter to the Romans: A Critique on the Present State of Research." *Neot* 28:127–45.

Vorster, W. S.
1989 "Intertextuality and Redaktionsgeschichte." *Intertextuality in Biblical Writings: Essays in Honor of Bas van Iersel.* Edited by S. Draisma. Kampen: Uitgeversmaatschappij.

Voss, B. R.
1979 *Der Dialog in der frühchristlichen Literatur.* Munich: Wilhelm Fink.

Votaw, C. W.
1915 "The Gospels and Contemporary Biographies." *American Journal of Theology* 19:45–73, 217–49.
1970 *The Gospels and Contemporary Biographies in the Greco-Roman Period.* Philadelphia: Fortress Press.

Vouaux, L.
1922 *Les Actes de Pierre.* Paris: Letouzey & Ané.

Vouga, F.
1988 "Zur rhetorischen Gattung des Galaterbriefes." *ZNW* 79:291–92.
1990 "La réception de la théologie johannique dans le épîtres." Pp. 283–302 in *La communauté johannique et son histoire: La trajectoire de l'évangile de Jean aux deux premiers siècles.* Edited by J.-D. Kaestli et al. Geneva: Labor et Fides.
1992 "Formgeschichtliche Überlegungen zu den Gleichnissen und zu den Fabeln der Jesus-Tradition auf dem Hintergund der hellenistischen Literaturgeschichte." In Van Segbroeck et al. 1992, 1.173–87.

Wachob, W. H.
2000 *The Voice of Jesus in the Social Rhetoric of James.* SNTSMS 106. Cambridge: Cambridge University Press.

Wachsmuth, C., and O. Hense
1884–1912 *Ioannis Stobei anthologium.* 5 vols. Berlin: Weidmann.

Wailes, Stephen L.
1987 *Medieval Allegories of Jesus' Parables.* Los Angeles: University of California Press.

Wainwright, G.
1980 *Doxology.* Oxford: Oxford University Press.

Wake, W. C.
1957 "Sentence Length Distributions of Greek Authors." *Journal of the Royal Statistical Society of London* 120:331–46.

Walker, J.
2000 "*Pathos* and *Katharsis* in 'Aristotelian'

Rhetoric: Some Implications." In Gross and Walzer 2000, 74–92.

Walker, W. O.
1973 *The Relationships among the Gospels: An Interdisciplinary Dialogue.* San Antonio: Trinity University Press.
1975 "1 Corinthians 11:2–16 and Paul's Views regarding Women." *JBL* 94:94–110.
1987 "The Burden of Proof in Identifying Interpolations in the Pauline Letters." *NTS* 33:610–18.
2001 *Interpolations in the Pauline Letters.* JSNTSup 213. Sheffield: Sheffield Academic Press.

Walker, W. O. (ed.)
1978 *The Relationships among the Gospels: An Interdisciplinary Dialogue.* San Antonio: Trinity University Press.

Wall, R. W.
1990 "James as Apocalyptic Paraenesis." *RQ* 32:11–22.
1997 *Community of the Wise: The Letter of James.* Valley Forge, Pa.: Trinity Press International.

Wall, R. W., and E. E. Lemcio
1992 *The New Testament as Canon: A Reader in Canonical Criticism.* JSNTSup 76. Sheffield: Sheffield Academic Press.

Walsh, P. G.
1994 *Apuleius: The Golden Ass.* Oxford: Clarendon Press.

Walton, S.
1994 "What Has Aristotle To Do with Paul? Rhetorical Criticism and 1 Thessalonians." *TynBul* 46:229–50.

Wanamaker, C. A.
1990 *Commentary on 1 and 2 Thessalonians.* NIGTC. Grand Rapids: Eerdmans.
2000 "Epistolary vs. Rhetorical Analysis: Is a Synthesis Possible?" In Donfried and Beutler (eds.) 2000, 255–86.

Wansbrough, H. (ed.).
1991 *Jesus and the Oral Gospel Tradition.* JSNTSuppl 64. Sheffield: Sheffield Academic Press.

Wardman, A.
1974 *Plutarch's Lives.* Berkeley and Los Angeles: University of California Press.

Warnick, B.
2000 "Two Systems of Invention: The Topics in the *Rhetoric* and *The New Rhetoric.*" In Gross and Walzer 2000, 107–29.

Watson, D. F.
1988a "A Rhetorical Analysis of Philippians and its Implications for the Unity Question." *NovT* 30:57–88.
1988b *Invention, Arrangement, and Style: Rhetorical Criticism of Jude and 2 Peter.* SBLDS 104. Atlanta: Scholars Press.
1989a "1 Corinthians 10:23–11:1 in the Light of Greco-Roman Rhetoric: The Role of the Rhetorical Questions." *JBL* 108:301–18.
1989b "A Rhetorical Analysis of 2 John according to Greco-Roman Convention." *NTS* 35:104–30.
1989c "A Rhetorical Analysis of 3 John: A Study in Epistolary Rhetoric." *CBQ* 51:479–501.
1989d "1 John 2.12–14 as *Distributio, Conduplicatio,* and *Expolitio:* A Rhetorical Understanding." *JSNT* 35:97–110.
1991 *Persuasive Artistry: Studies in New Testament Rhetoric in Honor of George A. Kennedy.* JSNTSup 50. Sheffield: JSOT Press.
1993a "James 2 in Light of Greco-Roman Schemes of Argumentation." *NTS* 39:94–121.
1993b "Paul's Rhetorical Strategy in 1 Corinthians 15." In Porter and Olbricht (eds.) 1993, 231–49.
1993c "The Rhetoric of James 3:1–12 and a Classical Pattern of Argumentation." *NovT* 35:48–64.
1993d "Diatribe." P. 213 in *Dictionary of Paul and His Letters.* Edited by G. W. Hawthorne and R. P. Martin. Downers Grove, Ill.: InterVarsity.
1997a "The Integration of Epistolary and Rhetorical Analysis of Philippians." In Porter and Olbricht (eds.) 1997, 398–426.
1997b "Rhetorical Criticism of Hebrews and the Catholic Epistles." *CurBS* 5:175–207.
1998 "The Letter of Jude." Pp. 473–500 in *The New Interpreter's Bible.* Edited by L. E. Keck. Vol. 12. Nashville: Abingdon Press.
2002 "Why We Need Socio-Rhetorical Commentary and What It Might Look Like." In Porter and Stamps (eds.) 2002, 129–57.

Watson, D. F., and A. J. Hauser (eds.).
1994 *Rhetorical Criticism of the Bible: A Comprehensive Bibliography with Notes on History and Method.* Leiden: Brill.

Watson, Duane.
2002 "Paul's Boasting in 2 Corinthians 10–13 as Defense of His Honor: A Socio-Rhetorical Analysis." Pp. 243–59

in *Rhetorical Argumentation in Biblical Texts: Essays form the Lund 200 Conference.* Harrisburg: Trinity Press International.

Watson, J. (ed.)
2001 *Speaking Volumes: Orality and Literacy in the Greek and Roman World.* Mnemosyne Supplements 218. Leiden: Brill.

Watson, W. G. E.
1984 *Classical Hebrew Poetry.* JSOTSup 26. Sheffield: JSOT Press.
1994 *Traditional Techniques in Hebrew Poetry.* JSOTSup 170. Sheffield: Sheffield Academic Press.

Wead, D. W.
1970 *The Literary Devices in John's Text.* Basel: Friedrich Reinhardt.

Weber, S.
1912 *Des hl. Irenaeus Schrift zum Erweis der apostolischen Verkündigung, aus dem Armenischen übersetzt von Dr. Simon Weber, o. Prof. an der Universität Freiburg, i. Br.* Bibliothek der Kirchenväter 4. Munich: Kempten.

Wedderburn, A. J. M.
1988 *The Reasons for Romans.* Edinburgh: T. & T. Clark.
1996 "Zur Frage der Gattung der Apostelgeschichte." In Cancik, Lichtenberger, and Schäfer 1996, 3:303–22.
2002 "The 'We'-Passages in Acts: On the Horns of a Dilemma." *ZNW* 93:78–98.

Weeden, T. J.
1971 *Mark: Traditions in Conflict.* Philadelphia: Fortress Press.

Wehnert, J.
1989 *Die Wir-Passagen der Apostelgeschichte: Ein lukanisches Stilmittel aus jüdischer Tradition.* GTA 40. Göttingen: Vandenhoeck & Ruprecht.

Wehrli, Fritz
1973 "Gnome, Anekdote und Biographie." *Museum Helveticum* 30:194–208.

Weidinger, K.
1928 *Die Haustafeln: Ein Stück urchristlicher Paraenese.* Leipzig: J. C. Heinrich.

Weima, J. A. D.
1994 *Neglected Endings: The Significance of the Pauline Letter Closings.* JSNTS 101. Sheffield: Sheffield Academic Press.
2000 "The Function of 1 Thessalonians 2:1–12 and the Use of Rhetorical Criticism: A Response to Otto Merk." In Donfried and Beutler (eds.) 2000, 114–31.

Weima, J. A. D., and S. E. Porter
1998 *An Annotated Bibliography of 1 and 2 Thessalonians.* NTTS 26. Leiden: Brill.

Weingreen, J.
1976 *From Bible to Mishna.* Manchester: Manchester University; New York: Holmes & Meier.

Weinreich, Otto
1962 *Der griechische Liebesroman.* Zurich: Artemis.

Weintraub, K. J.
1978 *The Value of the Individual: Self and Circumstance in Autobiography.* Chicago: University of Chicago.

Weiss, J.
1959 *Earliest Christianity: A History of Period A.D. 30–150.* Translated by F. C. Grant. 2 vols. New York: Harper & Bros.

Weiss, J.
1897 "Beiträge zur Paulinischen Rhetorik." Pp. 165–247 in *Theologische Studien Professor D. Bernhard Weiss zu seinem 70. Geburtstage dargebracht.* Göttingen: Vandenhoeck & Ruprecht.
1903 *Das älteste Evangelium.* Göttingen: Vandenhoeck & Ruprecht.
1910 *Der erste Korintherbrief.* 9th ed. Göttingen: Vandenhoeck & Ruprecht.

Welborn, L. L.
1987a "A Conciliatory Principle in 1 Cor. 4:6." *NovT* 29:320–46.
1987b "On the Discord in Corinth: 1 Corinthians 1–4 and Ancient Politics." *JBL* 106:83–113.
1995 "The Identification of 2 Corinthians 10–13 with the 'Letter of Tears.'" *NovT* 37:138–53.
1995 "Like Broken Pieces of a Ring: 2 Cor. 1.2–2.13; 7.5–16 and Ancient Theories of Literary Unity." *NTS* 42:559–83.
1997 *Politics and Rhetoric in the Corinthian Epistles.* Macon, Ga.: Mercer University Press.

Welch, J. W. (ed.)
1981 *Chiasmus in Antiquity: Structures, Analyses, Exegesis.* Hildesheim: Gerstenberg.

Welch, J. W., and Daniel B. McKinlay (eds.)
1999 *Chiasmus Bibliography.* Provo: Research Press.

Wellek, R.
1955 *A History of Modern Criticism: 1750–1950.* Vol. 1: *The Later Eighteenth Century.* 8 vols. Cambridge: Cambridge University Press.

Welles, C. B.
1974 *Royal Correspondence in the Hellenistic Period: A Study in Greek Epigraphy.* Chicago: Ares. Originally published in 1934.

Wellhausen, J.
1908 *Das Evangelium Johannes.* Berlin: G. Reimer.

Wendel, C.
1949 *Der griechisch-römische Buchschreibung verglichen mit der des vordern orients.* HM 3.

Wendland, P.
1895 *Philo und die kynisch-stoische Diatribe.* Berlin: Töpelmann.
1912 *Die urchristlichen Literaturformen.* HNT I,3. Tübingen: Mohr-Siebeck.

Wengst, K.
1971 *Tradition und Theologie des Barnabasbriefes.* Arbeiten zur kirchengeschichte 42. Berlin and New York: Walter de Gruyter.
1972a "Der Apostel und die Tradition. Zur theologischen Bedeutung urchristlicher Formeln bei Paulus." *ZTK* 69:145–62.
1972b *Christologische Formeln und Lieder des Urchristentums.* SUNT 7. Gütersloh: Gerd Mohn.
1984 *Didache (Apostellehre), Barnabasbrief, Zweiter Klemensbrief, Schrift an Diognet.* SUC 2. Munich: Kösel.

Wenham, D. (ed.)
1985 *The Jesus Tradition outside the Gospels.* Vol. 5 of *Gospel Perspectives.* Sheffield: JSOT Press.

Weren, W. J. C.
1997 "The Five Women in Matthew's Genealogy." *CBQ* 59:288–305.

Werner, J.
1889 *Der Paulinismus des Irenaeus: Eine kirchen- und dogmengeschichtliche Untersuchung über das Verhältnis des Irenaeus zur paulinischen Briefsammlung und Theologie.* TU 6.2. Leipzig: Hinrichs.

West, M. L.
1971–72 *Iambi et Elegi Graeci ante Alexandrum Cantati.* 2 vols. Oxford: Clarendon Press.
1973 *Textual Criticism and Editorial Technique Applicable to Greek and Latin Texts.* Stuttgart: B. G. Tuebner.
1978 *Hesiod, Works and Days: Edited with Prolegomena and Commentary.* Oxford: Clarendon Press.
1982 *Greek Metre.* Oxford: Clarendon Press.
1987 *Introduction to Greek Metre.* Oxford Clarendon Press.
1998 "Textual Criticism and the Editing of Homer." In Most (ed.) 1998, 94–110.

West, S.
1988 "The Transmission of the Text." In Heubeck, West, and Hainsworth (ed.) 1988, 33–48.

Westermann, C. (ed.)
1963 *Essays on Old Testament Hermeneutics.* Richmond: John Knox Press.

Westcott, B. F.
1889 *A General Survey of the History of the Canon of the New Testament.* 6th ed. London: Macmillan.

Whatmough, J.
1970 *The Dialects of Ancient Gaul.* Cambridge: Cambridge University Press.

Wheatley, H. B.
1968 *The Dedication of Books to Patron and Friend: A Chapter in Literary History.* London: E. Stock, 1887. Reprint, Detroit, Gale Research 1968.

Wheeldon, M. J.
1990 "'True Stories': The Reception of Historiography in Antiquity." Pp. 33–63 in Cameron (ed.) 1990.

White, J. L.
1971a "The Structural Analysis of Philemon: A Point of Departure in the Formal Analysis of the Pauline Letter." SBLSP 1, Missoula: Scholars Press, 1–47.
1971b "Introductory Formulae in the Body of the Pauline Letter." *JBL* 90:91–97.
1972a *The Form and Function of the Body of the Greek Letter.* SBLDS 2. Missoula, Mont.: Scholars Press.
1972b *The Form and Structure of the Official Petition: A Study in Greek Epistolography.* SBLDS 5. Missoula, Mont.: Scholars Press.
1986 *Light from Ancient Letters.* Philadelphia: Fortress Press.
1988 "Ancient Greek Letters." In Aune (ed.) 1988, 85–106.
1993 "Apostolic Mission and Apostolic Message: Congruence in Paul's Epistolary Rhetoric, Structure and Imagery." Pp. 145–61 in *Origins and Method: Toward a New Understanding of Judaism and Christianity: Essays in Honour of John C. Hurd.* Edited by B. H. McLean. JSNTSup 86. Sheffield: JSOT.

White, L. M.
1990 "Morality between Two Worlds: A Paradigm of Friendship in Philippians."

In Balch, Ferguson, and Meeks (eds.) 1990, 201–15.

White, P.
1978 "Amicitia and the Profession of Poetry in Early Imperial Rome." *JRS* 68:74–92.

Whitman, J. (ed.)
2000 *Interpretation and Allegory: Antiquity to the Modern Period.* Leiden: Brill.

Whittaker, M.
1956 *Der Hirt des Hermas. Die apostolischen Väter* 1. GCS. Berlin: Akademie-Verlag.
1984 "The Testament of Solomon." Pp. 733–51 in *The Apocryphal Old Testament.* Edited by H. D. F. Sparks. Oxford: Clarendon Press.

Whitters, M. F.
2001 "Some New Observations about Jewish Festal Letters." *JSJ* 32:272–88.
2002 *The Epistle of Second Baruch: Form and Message.* Sheffield: Sheffield Academic Press.

Wibbing, S.
1959 *Die Tugend- und Lasterkataloge im Neuen Testament und ihre Traditionsgeschichte unter besonderer Berücksichtigung der Qumran-Texte.* Berlin: Alfred Töpelmann.

Wick, P.
1994 *Der Philipperbrief: Der formale Aufbau des Briefs als Schlüssel zum Verständnis seines Inhalts.* Stuttgart: Kohlhammer.

Widengren, G.
1959 "Oral Tradition and Written Literature among the Hebrews in the Light of Arabic Evidence with Special 'Regard to Prose Narratives." *Acta Orientalia* 23:201–62.

Widman, M.
1957 "Irenäus und seine theologische Väter." *ZTK* 54:156–73.

Wifstrand, A.
1948 "Stylistic Problems in the Epistles of James and Peter." *Studia Theologica* 1:180–81.
1967 *Die alte Kirche und die griechische Bildung.* Bern and Munich: Francke.

Wikgren, A. P.
1942 "ΑΡΧΗ ΤΟΥ ΕΥΑΓΓΕΛΙΟΥ." *JBL* 61:11–20.
1963 "Chicago Studies in the Greek Lectionary of the New Testament." Pp. 96–121 in *Biblical and Patristic Studies in Memory of Robert Pierce Casey.* Editd by J. N. Birdsall and R. W. Thomson. Freiburg: Herder.

Wilamowitz-Moellendorff, U. von
1900 "Asianismus und Atticismus." *Hermes* 35:1–52.
1912 "Die griechischen Literatur des Altertums." Pp. 3–318 in *Die griechische und lateinische Literatur und Sprache.* 3d ed. Leipzig and Berlin: B. G. Teubner.

Wilckens, U.
1974 *Die Missionsreden der Apostelgeschichte: Form- und traditionsgeschichtliche Untersuchungen.* 3d ed. WMANT 5. Neukirchen-Vluyn: Neukirchener Verlag.

Wilcox, M.
1965 *The Semitisms of Acts.* Oxford: Clarendon Press.
1977 "On Investigating the Use of the Old Testament in the New Testament." Pp. 231–43 in *Text and Interpretation.* Edited by E. Best and R. M. Wilson. Cambridge: Cambridge University Press.
1984 "Semitisms in the New Testament." *ANRW* II, 25/2, 978–1029.
1994 "Aramaic Background of the New Testament." In Beattie and McNamara 1994, 362–78.

Wiles, M.
1967 *The Divine Apostle: The Interpretation of St. Paul's Epistles in the Early Church.* Cambridge: Cambridge University Press.

Wilhelm-Jooijbergh, A. E.
1975 "A Different View of Clemens Romanus." *The Heythrop Journal* 16:266–88.

Willert, N.
1995 "The Catalogues of Hardships in the Pauline Correspondence: Background and Function." In Borgen and Giversen (eds.) 1995, 217–43.

Willett, T. W.
1989 *Eschatology in the Theodicies of 2 Baruch and 4 Ezra.* JSPSup 4. Sheffield: Sheffield Academic Press.

Williams, A. N.
1935 *Adversus Judaeos: A Bird's-Eye View of Christian Apologiae until the Renaissance.* Cambridge: Cambridge University Press.

Williams, C. B.
1970 *Style and Vocabulary: Numerical Studies.* London: Griffin.

Williams, D. S.
1999 *The Structure of 1 Maccabees.* CBQMS

31. Washington, D.C.: Catholic Biblical Association of America.
2001 "A Literary Encircling Pattern in 1 Maccabees 1." *JBL* 120:140–42.

Williams, G.
1968 *Tradition and Originality in Roman Poetry.* Oxford: Clarendon Press.
1982 "Phases of Political Patronage of Literature in Rome." In Gold (ed.) 1982, 3–27.

Williams, H. H. D.
2001 *The Wisdom of the Wise: The Presence and Function of Scripture within 1 Cor. 1:18–3:23.* AGJU 49. Leiden: Brill.

Williams, J. G.
1981 *Those Who Ponder Proverbs: Aphoristic Thinking and Biblical Literature.* Sheffield: Almond Press.

Williams, M. A.
1996 *Rethinking "Gnosticism": An Argument for Dismantling a Dubious Category.* Princeton: Princeton University Press.

Williams, R. (ed.)
1989 *The Making of Orthodoxy: Essays in Honour of Henry Chadwick.* Cambridge: Cambridge University.

Williamson, R.
1970 *Philo and the Epistle to the Hebrews.* Leiden: Brill.

Willis, J. T.
1987 "Alternating (ABA'B') Parallelism in the Old Testament Psalms and Prophetic Literature." In Follis (ed.) 1987, 49–76.

Wills, L. M.
1984 "The Form of the Sermon in Hellenistic Judaism and Early Christianity." *HTR* 77:277–99.
1995 *The Jewish Novel in the Ancient World.* Ithaca and London: Cornell University Press.
1997 *The Quest of the Historical Gospel: Mark, John, and the Origins of the Gospel Genre.* London and New York: Routledge.

Wilson, A.
1977 "The Pragmatics of Politeness and Pauline Epistolography: A Case Study of the Letter to Philemon." In Evans and Porter (eds.) 1997, 107–19.

Wilson, N. G.
1980 "The Libraries of the Byzantine World." In Harlfinger (ed.) 1980, 276–309.

Wilson, R. M.
1960 *Studies in the Gospel of Thomas.* London: Mowbray.

Wilson, R. R.
1977 *Genealogy and History in the Biblical World.* Yale Near Eastern Research. New Haven, Conn.: Yale University Press.

Wilson, S. G.
1979 *Luke and the Pastoral Epistles.* London: SPCK.

Wilson, W. J.
1927 "The Career of the Prophet Hermas." *HTR* 20:21–62.

Wilson, W. T.
1991 *Love without Pretense: Romans 12.9–21 and Hellenistic-Jewish Wisdom Literature.* Tübingen: Mohr-Siebeck.
2001 "Urban Legends: Acts 10:1–11:18 and the Strategies of Greco-Roman Foundation Narratives." *JBL* 120:77–99.

Wimsatt, W. K., Jr., and M. C. Beardsley
1954 "The Intentional Fallacy." Pp. 3–18 in *The Verbal Icon: Studies in the Meaning of Poetry.* Lexington: University of Kentucky Press.

Winden, J. C. M. van
1971 *An Early Christian Philosopher: A Commentary to Justin Martyr, The Dialogue with Trypho, Chapters 1 to 9.* Leiden: Brill.

Windisch, H.
1920 *Die Barnabasbrief.* Vol. 3 of *Die apostolischen Väter.* Tübingen: Mohr-Siebeck.
1951 *Die katholischen Briefe.* 3d ed. Tübingen: Mohr-Siebeck.

Wingren, G.
1959 *Man and Incarnation: A Study in the Biblical Theology of Irenaeus.* Translated by Ross Mackenzie. Philadelphia: Muhlenberg Press.

Winkler, J. J.
1985 *Auctor & Actor: A Narratological Reading of Apuleius's The Golden Ass.* Berkeley: University of California Press.

Winston, D., and J. Dillon
1983 *Two Treatises of Philo of Alexandria.* BJS 25. Chico, Calif.: Scholars Press.

Winter, B. W.
1991 "The Importance of the *Captatio Benevolentiae* in the Speeches of Tertullus and Paul in Acts 24:1–21." *JTS* 42:505–31.
1993 "The Entries and Ethics of Orators and Paul (1 Thessalonians 2:1–12)." *TynBul* 44:68–70.
1996 *Philo and Paul among the Sophists: A*

Hellenistic-Jewish and a Christian Response. SNTMS 96. Cambridge: Cambridge University Press.

2001 *After Paul Left Corinth: The Influence of Secular Ethics and Social Change.* Grand Rapids: Eerdmans.

Winter, B. W., and A. C. Clarke (eds.)

1993 *Ancient Literary Setting.* Vol. 1 of *The Book of Acts in Its First Century Setting.* Grand Rapids: Eerdmans.

Winterbottom, M.

1974 *The Elder Seneca: Declamations.* 2 vols. Cambridge: Cambridge University Press.

1980 *Roman Declamation.* Bristol: Bristol Classical Press.

1984 *The Minor Declamations Ascribed to Quintilian.* Berlin and New York: Walter de Gruyter.

Wirgin, W.

1968 *Herod Agrippa I: King of the Jews.* Leeds: Leeds University Oriental Society.

Wise, M.

1990 *A Critical Study of the Temple Scroll from Qumran Cave 11.* Chicago: Oriental Institute.

Wisse, J.

1989 *Ethos and Pathos: From Aristotle to Cicero.* Amsterdam: Hakkert.

1995 "Greeks, Romans, and the Rise of Atticism." In Abenes et al. 1995, 65–82.

Witherington, B., III

1994 *Friendship and Finances in Philippi: The Letter of Paul to the Philippians.* Valley Forge, Pa.: Trinity Press International.

1995 *Conflict and Community in Corinth: A Socio-Rhetorical Commentary on 1 and 2 Corinthians.* Grand Rapids: Eerdmans.

1996 *History, Literature, and Society in the Book of Acts.* Cambridge: Cambridge University Press.

1998 *The Acts of the Apostles: A Socio-Rhetorical Commentary.* Grand Rapids: Eerdmans.

2000 *The Gospel of Mark: A Socio-Rhetorical Commentary.* Grand Rapids: Eerdmans.

Wittek, M.

1967 *Album de paléographie grecque.* Gand: E. Story-Scientia.

Wolde, E. van

1989 "Trendy Intextuality." In *Intertextuality in Biblical Writings: Essays in Honor of Bas van Iersel.* Edited by S. Draisma. Kampen: Uitgeversmaatschappij.

Wolf, E.

1997 *Le roman grec et latin.* Paris: Ellipses.

Wolfson, H. A.

1956 *The Philosophy of the Church Fathers.* Vol. 1: *Faith, Trinity, Reincarnation.* Cambridge: Harvard University Press.

Wolter, M.

1988 *Die Pastoralbriefe als Paulustradition.* FRLANT 146. Göttingen: Vandenhoeck & Ruprecht.

1993 *Der Brief an die Kolosser; Der Brief an Philemon.* Gütersloh: Verlag Gerd Mohn; Würzburg: Echter Verlag.

Woodhead, A. G.

1981 *The Study of Greek Inscriptions.* 2d ed. Cambridge: Cambridge University Press.

Woodman, A. J.

1988 *Rhetoric in Classical Historiography.* London: Croon Helm.

Wooten, Cecil

1975 "Le développement du style asiatique pendant l'époque hellénistique." *Revue des Études Grecques* 88:94–104.

1994 "The Peripatetic Tradition in the Literary Essays of Dionysius of Halicarnasus." In Fortenbaugh and Mirhady (eds.) 1994, 121–30.

Worthington, Ian

1994 "The Canon of the Ten Attic Orators." In Worthington (ed.) 1993, 244–63.

Worthington, I. (ed.)

1993 *Persuasion: Greek Rhetoric in Action.* New York and London: Routledge.

1996 *Orality and Literacy in Ancient Greece.* Leiden: Brill.

Worton, M., and J. Still (eds.)

1990 *Intertextuality: Theories and Practices.* Manchester: Manchester University Press.

Wrede, W.

1891 *Untersuchungen zum ersten Klemensbriefe.* Göttingen: Vandenhoeck & Ruprecht.

1906 *Das literarische Rätsel des Hebräerbriefs.* Göttingen: Vandenhoeck & Ruprecht.

1971 *The Messianic Secret.* Cambridge and London: James Clark & Co. Ltd. Originally published in 1901.

Wright, A. G.

1966 "The Literary Genre Midrash." *CBQ* 28:105–38, 417–57.

1967 *The Literary Genre Midrash.* Staten Island, N.Y.: Alba House.

Wright, D. F.

1985 "Apocryphal Gospels: the 'Unknown Gospel' (Pap. Egerton 2) and the *Gospel of Peter.*" In Wenham (ed.) 1985, 207–32.

Wright, M. R.

1995 *Cosmology in Antiquity.* London and New York: Routledge.

Wright, N. T.

1990 "Poetry and Theology in Colossians 1.15–20." *NTS* 36:444–68.

Wright, W.

1871 *Apocryphal Acts of the Apostles: Edited from Syriac Manuscripts in the British Museum and Other Libraries with English Translations and Notes.* London: Williams & Norgate.

Wucherpfenning, A.

2002 *Heracleon Philologus: Gnostische Johannesexegese im zweiten Jahrhundert.* WUNT 142. Tübingen: Mohr-Siebeck.

Wuellner, W.

1970 "Haggadic Homily Genre in 1 Cor. 1–3." *JBL* 89:199–204.

1976 "Paul's Rhetoric of Argumentation in Romans." *CBQ* 38:330–51.

1978 "Der Jakobusbrief im Licht der Rhetorik und Textpragmatik." *Linguistica Biblica: Interdiziplinäre Zeitschrift für Theologie und Linguistik* 43:5–66.

1979 "Greek Rhetoric and Pauline Argumentation." In Schoedel and Wilken (ed.) 1979, 177–88.

1986 "Paul as Pastor: The Function of Rhetorical Questions in First Corinthians." In Vanhoye (ed.) 1986, 49–77.

1987 "Where Is Rhetorical Criticism Taking Us?" *CBQ* 49:448–63.

1989 "Hermeneutics and Rhetorics." *Scriptura* 3:1–54.

1990 "The Argumentative Structure of 1 Thessalonians as Paradoxical Encomium." In R. F. Collins (ed.) 1990.

1991a "A Comparative Study of the Use of Enthymemes in the Synoptic Gospels." In Watson (ed.) 1991.

1991b "Paul's Rhetoric of Argumentation in Romans: An Alternative to the Donfried-Karris Debate over Romans." In Donfried (ed.) 1991, 128–46.

1991c "The Rhetorical Genre of Jesus' Sermon in Lk. 12:1–13:9." In Watson (ed.) 1991, 93–118.

1997 "Arrangement." In Porter (ed.) 1997a, 51–87.

Yamada, K.

1996 "A Rhetorical History: The Literary Genre of the Acts of the Apostles." In Porter and Olbricht (ed.) 1996, 230–50.

Yarbro Collins, A.

1976 *The Combat Myth in the Book of Revelation.* Missoula, Mont.: Scholars Press.

1979 "The Early Christian Apocalypses." In J. J. Collins (ed.) 1979, 61–121.

1984 "Numerical Symbolism in Jewish and Early Christian Apocalyptic Literature." In *ANRW* II, 21/2, 1221–87.

1990 *Is Mark's Gospel a Life of Jesus? The Question of Genre.* Milwaukee: Marquette University Press.

1992 *The Beginnings of the Gospel: Probings of Mark in Context.* Minneapolis: Fortress Press.

1993 "The Genre of the Passion Narrative." *ST* 47 (1993): 3–28.

1995 "The Seven Heavens in Jewish and Christian Apocalypses." Pp. 59–93 in *Death, Ecstasy and Other Worldly Journeys.* Edited by J. J. Collins and M. Fishbane. Albany: State University of New York.

1996 "The Apocalyptic Rhetoric of Mark 13 in Historical Context." *BR* 42:1–32.

Yarbro Collins, A. (ed.)

1998 *Ancient and Modern Perspectives on the Bible and Culture: Essays in Honor of Hans Dieter Betz.* Atlanta: Scholars Press.

Young, F.

1989 "The Rhetorical Schools and Their Influence on Patristic Exegesis." In R. Williams (ed.) 1989, 182–99.

1997 *Biblical Exegesis and the Formation of Christian Culture.* Cambridge: Cambridge University Press.

Young, G. W.

1999 *Subversive Symmetry: Exploring the Fantastic in Mark 6:45–56.* BIS 41. Leiden, Boston, and Cologne: E. J. Brill.

Zaas, P. S.

1988 "Catalogues and Context: 1 Corinthians 5 and 6." *NTS* 34:622–29.

Zahn, T.

1885–86 "Dichtung und Wahrheit in Justins Dialog mit dem Juden Tryphon." *ZKG* 8:37–66.

1900 *Forschungen zur Geschichte des neutestamentlichen Kanons und der altkirch-*

lichen Literatur. 6. Teil: I. *Apostel und Apostelschüler in der Provinz Asien,* II. *Brüder und Vettern Jesu.* Leipzig: A. Deichert.

Zanker, G.
1994 *The Heart of Achilles: Characterization of Personal Ethics in the Iliad.* Ann Arbor: University of Michigan Press.

Zeisler, J. A.
1983 "ΣΩΜΑ in the Septuagint," *NovT* 25:138–43.

Zeller, D.
1977 *Die weisheitlichen Mahnsprüche bei den Synoptikern.* Würzburg: Echter Verlag.

Zereteli, G.
1900 "Wo ist das Tetraevangelium von Porphyrius Uspenskij aus dem Jahre 835 entstanden?" *Byzantinische Zeitschrift* 9:649–53.

Zerwick, M.
1937 *Untersuchungen zum Markus-Stil: Ein Beitrag zur stilistischen Durcharbeitung des Neuen Testaments.* Rome: Pontifical Biblical Institute.

Ziegler, K.
1905 *Die precationum apud Graecos formis quaestiones selectae.* Bratislava: Gross and Barth.
1907 *Plutarchos von Chaeroneia.* 2d ed. Stuttgart: Drukenmüller.

Zilliacus, H.
1938 "Boktiteln in antik litteratur." *Eranos* 36:1–41.

Zimmerli, W.
1933 "Zur Struktur der alttestamentlichen Weisheit." *ZAW* 51:177–204.
1979 *Ezekiel 1.* Hermeneia. Translated by R. E. Clements. Philadelphia: Fortress Press.

Zimmermann, A. F.
1988 *Der urchristlichen Lehrer: Studien zum Tradentenkreis der didáskaloi im frühen Urchristentum.* 2d ed. Tübingen: Mohr-Siebeck.

Zmijewski, J.
1978 *Der Stil der paulinischen "Narrenrede."* Cologne and Bonn: Hanstein.

Zuntz, G.
1953 *The Text of the Epistles: A Disquisition upon the Corpus Paulinum.* London: Oxford University Press.

Zweck, D.
1989 "The *Exordium* of the Areopagus Speech, Acts 17.22, 23." *NTS* 35:94–103.